# College Physics

# College Physics

## Eleventh Edition



**Eugene Hecht, Ph.D.**
*Professor of Physics*
*Adelphi University*

**Schaum's Outline Series**

New York Chicago San Francisco Lisbon London
Madrid Mexico City Milan New Delhi Seoul
Singapore Sydney Toronto

*The McGraw-Hill Companies*

**EUGENE HECHT** is a full-time member of the Physics Department of Adelphi University in New York. He has authored ten books, and is working on the 5th edition of Optics, published by Addison Wesley, which has been the leading text in the field, worldwide, for more than three decades. Professor Hecht has also written *Physics: Alg/Trig, and Physics: Calculus*, both published by Brooks/Cole, and *Schaum's Outline of Optics*, and he coauthored *Schaum's Outline of Quantum Mechanics.* He has also written several books on the American ceramist George Ohr, and a number of papers on foundational issues in physics, the Special Theory of Relativity, and the history of ideas. He spends most of his time studying, writing about, and teaching physics, as well as training for a fourth-degree black belt in *Tae Kwan Do.*

Schaum's Outline of
COLLEGE PHYSICS



3 4 5 6 7 8 9 10 CUS/CUS 1 9 8 7 6 5 4 3 2

ISBN: 978-0-07-175487-3
MHID: 0-07-175487-3
e-ISBN: 978-0-07-175488-0
e-MHID: 0-07-175488-1



**Library of Congress Cataloging-in-Publication Data has been applied for.**

# Preface

The introductory noncalculus physics course at most colleges and universities is a two-semester survey of classical topics (i.e., roughly pre-20th century ideas) capped off with selected materials from what's called modern physics. *Schaum's Outline of College Physics* was designed to complement just such a course, whether given in high school or college. The requisite mathematical knowledge includes basic algebra, some trigonometry, and a bit of vector analysis, much of which will be discussed as needed, and can be learned as the reader progresses through the book. There are several appendices for those who wish to review these subjects.

The main focus of this text is to teach problem solving. Everyone who has ever taught physics has heard the all-too-common student lament, "I understand everything; I just can't do the problems." Nonetheless most professors believe that doing problems is crucial to understanding physics. Like playing the piano, one must learn the basics, the theory, and then practice, practice, practice. A single missed note in a sonata is overlookable; a single error in a calculation, however, will usually propagate throughout the entire analysis producing a totally wrong answer. A teacher, even a great teacher, can only guide the learning process. The student must, on his/her own, master the material by studying problem solving; by studying how problems of each type are analyzed. It's part of the process to make mistakes, discover those mistakes, correct them, and learn to avoid them, all at home and not in class on an exam. That's what this book is all about.

In this 11th edition, I've added new problems, diagrams, and hints, but more importantly, I've gone over every problem and rewritten most to remove possible ambiguities and make them more easily apprehended. Additionally, I've extended many of the solutions putting in guiding comments, missing mathematical steps, and providing alternative methods. All of this was field-tested on my many classes over the last half-dozen years, and fine tuned by responses to countless exams. Danielle Sofferman, a student of mine, was generous enough to work through most of the problems in the book. Her comments and critiques were invaluable, and I thank her for her kind efforts and insights.

Anyone wishing to make suggestions for this or future editions can reach me at Adelphi University, Physics Department, Garden City, New York, 11530, or at genehecht@aol.com.

Freeport, NY

EUGENE HECHT

# Contents


**CHAPTER 1 Speed, Displacement, and Velocity: An Introduction to Vectors** 1

Scalar quantity. Distance. Average speed. Instantaneous speed. Vector quantity. Displacement. Velocity. Instantaneous velocity. The addition of vectors. The tip-to-tail (or polygon) method. Parallelogram method. Subtraction of vectors. Trigonometric functions. Component of a vector. Component method for adding vectors. Unit vectors. Mathematical operations with units.

**CHAPTER 2 Uniformly Accelerated Motion** 15

Acceleration. Uniformly accelerated motion along a straight line. Direction is important. Graphical interpretations. Acceleration due to gravity. Velocity components. Projectile problems. Dimensional analysis.

**CHAPTER 3 Newton's Laws** 29

Mass. Standard kilogram. Force. Net external force. The newton. Newton's First Law. Newton's Second Law. Newton's Third Law. Law of universal gravitation. Weight. Acceleration due to gravity. Relation between mass and weight. Tensile force. Friction force. Normal force. Coefficient of kinetic friction. Coefficient of static friction.

**CHAPTER 4 Equilibrium Under the Action of Concurrent Forces** 55

Concurrent forces. An object is in equilibrium. First condition for equilibrium. Problem solution method (concurrent forces). Weight of an object. Tensile force. Friction force. Normal force. Pulleys.

**CHAPTER 5 Equilibrium of a Rigid Body Under Coplanar Forces** 65

Torque. Two conditions for equilibrium. Center of gravity. Position of the axis is arbitrary.

**CHAPTER 6 Work, Energy, and Power** 79

Work. Unit of work. Energy. Kinetic energy. Gravitational potential energy. Work-energy theorem. Forces that propel but do no work. Conservation of energy. Power. Kilowatt-hour.

**CHAPTER 7 Simple Machines** 93

A machine. Principle of work. Mechanical advantage. Efficiency.

**CHAPTER 8 Impulse and Momentum** 101

Linear momentum. Impulse. Impulse causes change in momentum. Conservation of linear momentum. Collisions and explosions. Perfectly inelastic collision. Perfectly elastic collision. Coefficient of restitution. Center of mass.

**CHAPTER 9 Angular Motion in a Plane** 115

Angular displacement. Angular speed. Angular acceleration. Equations for uniformly accelerated angular motion. Relations between angular and tangential quantities. Centripetal acceleration. Centripetal force.

**CHAPTER 10 Rigid-Body Rotation** 128

Torque. Moment of inertia. Torque and angular acceleration. Kinetic energy of rotation. Combined rotation and translation. Work. Power. Angular momentum. Angular impulse. Parallel-axis theorem. Analogous linear and angular quantities.

**CHAPTER 11 Simple Harmonic Motion And Springs** 145

Period. Frequency. Graph of a harmonic vibratory motion. Displacement. Restoring force. Hookean system. Simple harmonic motion. Elastic potential energy. Energy interchange. Speed in SHM. Acceleration in SHM. Reference circle. Period in SHM. Acceleration in terms of *T*. Simple pendulum. SHM.

**CHAPTER 12 Density; Elasticity** 158

Mass density. Specific gravity. Elasticity. Stress. Strain. Elastic limit. Young's modulus. Bulk modulus. Shear modulus.

**CHAPTER 13 Fluids at Rest** 167

Average pressure. Standard atmospheric pressure. Hydrostatic pressure. Pascal's principle. Archimedes' principle.

**CHAPTER 14 Fluids in Motion** 180

Fluid flow or discharge rate. Equation of continuity. Shear rate. Viscosity. Poiseuille's Law. Work done by a piston. Work done by a pressure. Bernoulli's equation. Torricelli's theorem. Reynolds number.

**CHAPTER 15 Thermal Expansion** 190

Temperature. Linear expansion of solids. Area expansion. Volume expansion.

**CHAPTER 16 Ideal Gases** 196

Ideal (or perfect) gas. One mole of a substance. Ideal Gas Law. Special cases. Absolute zero. Standard conditions or standard temperature and pressure (S.T.P.). Dalton's Law of partial pressures. Gas-law problems.

**CHAPTER 17 Kinetic Theory** 206

Kinetic theory. Avogadro's number. Mass of a molecule. Average translational kinetic energy. Root mean square speed. Absolute temperature. Pressure. Mean free path.

**CHAPTER 18 Heat Quantities** 213

Thermal energy. Heat. Specific heat. Heat gained (or lost). Heat of fusion. Heat of vaporization. Heat of sublimation. Calorimetry problems. Absolute humidity. Relative humidity. Dew point.

**CHAPTER 19 Transfer of Thermal Energy** 221

Energy can be transferred. Conduction. Thermal resistance. Convection. Radiation.

**CHAPTER 20 First Law of Thermodynamics** 227

Heat. Internal energy. Work done by a system. First Law of Thermodynamics. Isobaric process. Isovolumic process. Isothermal process. Adiabatic process. Specific heats of gases. Specific heat ratio. Work is related to area. Efficiency of a heat engine.

**CHAPTER 21 Entropy and The Second Law** 240

Second Law of Thermodynamics. Entropy. Entropy is a measure of disorder. Most probable state.

**CHAPTER 22 Wave Motion** 245

Propagating wave. Wave terminology. In-phase vibrations. Speed of a transverse wave. Standing waves. Conditions for resonance. Longitudinal (compression) waves.

**CHAPTER 23 Sound** 256

Sound waves. Equations for sound speed. Speed of sound in air. Intensity. Loudness. Intensity (or sound) level. Beats. Doppler effect. Interference effects.

**CHAPTER 24 Coulomb'S Law And Electric Fields** 268

Coulomb's Law. Charge quantized. Conservation of charge. Test-charge concept. Electric field. Strength of the electric field. Electric field due to a point charge. Superposition principle.

**CHAPTER 25 Electric Potential; Capacitance** 281

Potential difference. Absolute potential. Electrical potential energy. *V* related to *E*. Electron volt energy unit. Capacitor. Parallel-plate capacitor. Capacitors in parallel and series. Energy stored in a capacitor.

**CHAPTER 26 Current, Resistance, And Ohm'S Law** 297

Current. Battery. Resistance. Ohm's Law. Measurement of resistance by ammeter and voltmeter. Terminal potential difference. Resistivity. Resistance varies with temperature. Potential changes.

**CHAPTER 27 Electrical Power** 307

Electrical work. Electrical power. Power loss in a resistor. Thermal energy generated in a resistor. Convenient conversions.

**CHAPTER 28 Equivalent Resistance; Simple Circuits** 312

Resistors in series. Resistors in parallel.

**CHAPTER 29 Kirchhoff's Laws** 327

Kirchhoff's node (or junction) rule. Kirchhoff's loop (or circuit) rule. Set of equations obtained.

**CHAPTER 30 Forces in Magnetic Fields** 335

Magnetic field. Magnetic field lines. Magnet. Magnetic poles. Charge moving through a magnetic field. Direction of the force. Magnitude of the force. Magnetic field at a point. Force on a current in a magnetic field. Torque on a flat coil.

**CHAPTER 31 Sources of Magnetic Fields** 347

Magnetic fields are produced. Direction of the magnetic field. Ferromagnetic materials. Magnetic moment. Magnetic field of a current element.

**CHAPTER 32 Induced emf; Magnetic Flux** 354

Magnetic effects of matter. Magnetic field lines. Magnetic flux. Induced emf. Faraday's Law for induced emf. Lenz's Law. Motional emf.

**CHAPTER 33 Electric Generators and Motors** 365

Electric generators. Electric motors.

**CHAPTER 34 Inductance; *R-C* and *R-L* Time Constants** 372

Self-inductance. Mutual inductance. Energy stored in an inductor. *R-C* time constant. *R-L* time constant. Exponential functions.

**CHAPTER 35 Alternating Current** 381

Emf generated by a rotating coil. Meters. Thermal energy generated or power lost. Forms of Ohm's Law. Phase. Impedance. Phasors. Resonance. Power loss. Transformer.

**CHAPTER 36 Reflection of Light** 391

Nature of light. Law of reflection. Plane mirrors. Spherical mirrors. Ray tracing. Mirror equation. Size of the image.

**CHAPTER 37 Refraction of Light** 401

Speed of light. Index of refraction. Refraction. Snell's Law. Critical angle for total internal reflection. Prism.

**CHAPTER 38 Thin Lenses** 409

Type of lenses. Ray tracing. Object and image relation. Lensmaker's equation. Lens power. Lenses in contact.

**CHAPTER 39 Optical Instruments** 418

Combination of thin lenses. The eye. Angular magnification. Magnifying glass. Microscope. Telescope.

**CHAPTER 40 Interference And Diffraction Of Light** 426

Propagating wave. Coherent waves. Relative phase. Interference effects. Diffraction. Single-slit Fraunhofer diffraction. Limit of resolution. Diffraction grating equation. Diffraction of X-rays. Optical path length.

**CHAPTER 41 Relativity** 436

Reference frame. Special theory of relativity. Relativistic linear momentum. Limiting speed. Relativistic energy. Time dilation. Simultaneity. Length contraction. Velocity addition formula.

**CHAPTER 42 Quantum Physics And Wave Mechanics** 445

Quanta of radiation. Photoelectric effect. Momentum of a photon. Compton effect. De Broglie wavelength. Resonance of de Broglie waves. Quantized energies.

**CHAPTER 43 The Hydrogen Atom** 453

Hydrogen atom. Electron orbits. Energy-level diagrams. Emission of light. Spectral lines. Origin of spectral series. Absorption of light.

**CHAPTER 44 Multielectron Atoms** 459

Neutral atom. Quantum numbers. Pauli exclusion principle.

**CHAPTER 45 Nuclei And Radioactivity** 463

Nucleus. Nuclear charge and atomic number. Atomic mass unit. Mass number. Isotopes. Binding energies. Radioactivity. Nuclear equations.

**CHAPTER 46 Applied Nuclear Physics** 475

Nuclear binding energies. Fission reaction. Fusion reaction. Radiation dose. Radiation damage potential. Effective radiation dose. High-energy accelerators. Momentum of a particle.

**APPENDIX A Significant Figures** 483

**APPENDIX B Trigonometry Needed For College Physics** 485

**APPENDIX C Exponents** 489

**APPENDIX D Logarithms** 492

**APPENDIX E Prefixes for Multiples of SI Units; The Greek Alphabet** 495

**APPENDIX F Factors for Conversions to SI Units** 496

**APPENDIX G Physical Constants** 497

**APPENDIX H Table of the Elements** 498

**INDEX** 501

# College Physics

# CHAPTER 1

# Speed, Displacement, and Velocity: An Introduction to Vectors

**A Scalar Quantity,** or **scalar,** is one that has nothing to do with spatial direction. Many physical concepts such as length, time, temperature, mass, density, charge, and volume are scalars; each has a scale or size, but no associated direction. The number of students in a class, the quantity of sugar in a jar, and the cost of a house are familiar scalar quantities.

Scalars are specified by ordinary numbers and add and subtract in the usual way. Two candies in one box plus seven in another give nine candies total.

**Distance ($l$):** Get in a vehicle and travel a distance, some length in space, which we'll symbolize by the letter $l$. Suppose the tripmeter subsequently reads 100 miles (i.e., 161 kilometers); that's how far you went along whatever path you took, with no particular regard for hills or turns. Similarly, the bug in Fig. 1-1 walked a distance $l$ measured along a winding route; $l$ is also called the **path-length,** and it's a scalar quantity. (Incidentally, most people avoid using $d$ for distance because it's widely used in the representation of derivatives.)

**Average Speed ($v_{av}$)** is a measure of how fast a thing travels in space, and it too is a scalar quantity. Imagine an object that takes a time $t$ to travel a distance $l$. The ***average speed*** during that interval is defined as

$$\textit{Average speed} = \frac{\text{Total distance traveled}}{\text{Time elapsed}}$$

$$v_{av} = \frac{l}{t}$$

The everyday units of speed are miles per hour, but in scientific work we use kilometers per hour (km/h) or, better yet, meters per second (m/s). As we'll learn presently, speed is part of the more inclusive concept of velocity, and that's why we use the letter $v$. A problem may concern itself with the average speed of an object, but it can also treat the special case of a ***constant speed*** $v$, since then $v_{av} = v = l/t$ (see Problem 1.3).

You may also see this definition written as $v_{av} = \Delta l/\Delta t$, where the symbol $\Delta$ means 'the change in." That notation just underscores that we are dealing with intervals of time ($\Delta t$) and space ($\Delta l$). If we plot a curve of **distance versus time,** and look at any two points $P_i$ and $P_f$ on it, their separation in space ($\Delta l$) is the *rise,* and in time ($\Delta t$) is the *run.* Thus, $\Delta l/\Delta t$ is the *slope* of the line drawn from the initial location, $P_i$, to the final location, $P_f$. *The slope is the average speed during that particular interval* (see Problem 1.5). Keep in mind that distance traveled, as indicated, for example, by an odometer in a car, is always positive and never decreases; consequently, the graph of $l$ versus $t$ is always positive and never decreases.

**Instantaneous Speed ($v$):** Thus far we've defined "average speed," but we often want to know the speed of an object at a specific time, say, 10 s after 1:00. Similarly, we might ask for the speed of something *now*. That's a new concept called the ***instantaneous speed,*** but we can define it building on the idea of average speed. What we need is the average speed determined over a vanishingly tiny time interval centered on the desired instant. Formally, that's stated as

$$v = \lim_{\Delta t \to 0} \left[ \frac{\Delta l}{\Delta t} \right]$$

***Instantaneous speed (or just speed, for short) is the limiting value of the average speed ($\Delta l/\Delta t$) determined as the interval over which the averaging takes place ($\Delta t$) approaches zero.*** This mathematical expression becomes especially important because it leads to the calculus and the idea of the derivative. To keep the math simple, we won't worry about the details; for us it's just the general concept that should be understood. In the next chapter, we'll develop equations for the instantaneous speed of an object at any specific time.

Graphically, the slope of a line tangent to the distance versus time curve at any point (i.e., at any particular time) is the instantaneous speed at that time.

**A Vector Quantity** is a physical concept that is inherently directional and can be specified completely only if both its **magnitude** (i.e., size) and direction are provided. Many physical concepts such as displacement, velocity, acceleration, force, and momentum are vector quantities. In general, a *vector* (which stands for a specific amount of some vector quantity) is depicted as a directed line segment and is pictorially represented by an arrow (drawn to scale) whose magnitude and direction determine the vector. In printed material vectors are usually symbolically presented in boldface type (e.g., **F** for force). When written by hand it's common to distinguish a vector by just putting an arrow over the appropriate symbol (e.g., $\vec{F}$). For the sake of maximum clarity, we'll combine the two and use $\vec{\mathbf{F}}$.

**The Displacement** of an object from one location to another is a vector quantity. As shown in Fig. 1-1, the displacement of the bug in going from $P_1$ to point $P_2$ is specified by the vector $\vec{\mathbf{s}}$ (the symbol *s* comes from the century-old usage corresponding to the "space" between two points). If the straight-line distance from $P_1$ to $P_2$ is, say, 2.0 m, we simply draw $\vec{\mathbf{s}}$ to be any convenient length and label it 2.0 m. In any case, $\vec{\mathbf{s}}$ = 2.0 m—10° NORTH OF EAST.

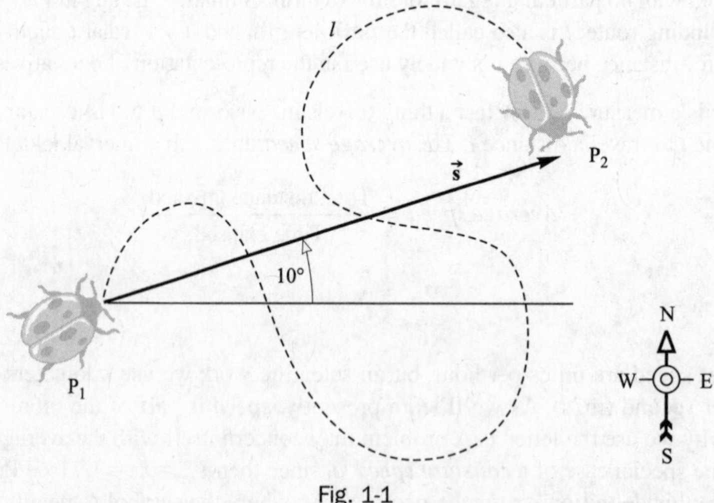


Fig. 1-1

**Velocity** is a vector quantity that embraces both the speed and the direction of motion. If an object undergoes a vector displacement $\vec{\mathbf{s}}$ in a time interval $t$, then

$$\textit{Average velocity} = \frac{\text{Vector displacement}}{\text{Time taken}}$$

$$\vec{\mathbf{v}}_{av} = \frac{\vec{\mathbf{s}}}{t}$$

The direction of the velocity vector is the same as that of the displacement vector. The units of velocity (and speed) are those of distance divided by time, such as m/s or km/h.

**Instantaneous Velocity** is the average velocity evaluated for a time interval that approaches zero. Thus, if an object undergoes a displacement $\Delta\vec{s}$ in a time $\Delta t$, then for that object the instantaneous velocity is

$$\vec{v} = \lim_{\Delta t \to 0} \frac{\Delta\vec{s}}{\Delta t}$$

where the notation means that the ratio $\Delta\vec{s}/\Delta t$ is to be evaluated for a time interval $\Delta t$ that approaches zero.

**The Addition of Vectors:** The concept of "vector" is not completely defined until we establish some rules of behavior. For example, how do several vectors (displacements, forces, whatever) add to one another? The bug in Fig. 1-2 walks from $P_1$ to $P_2$, pauses, and then goes on to $P_3$. It experiences two displacements $\vec{s}_1$ and $\vec{s}_2$, which combine to yield a net displacement $\vec{s}$. Here $\vec{s}$ is called the ***resultant*** or sum of the two constituent displacements, and it is the physical equivalent of them taken together $\vec{s} = \vec{s}_1 + \vec{s}_2$.

**The Tip-to-Tail (or Polygon) Method:** The two vectors in Fig. 1-2 show us how to graphically add two (or more) vectors. Simply place the tail of the second ($\vec{s}_2$) at the tip of the first ($\vec{s}_1$); the resultant then goes from the starting point, $P_1$ (the tail of $\vec{s}_1$), to the final point, $P_3$ (the tip of $\vec{s}_2$). Fig. 1-3(*a*) is more general; it

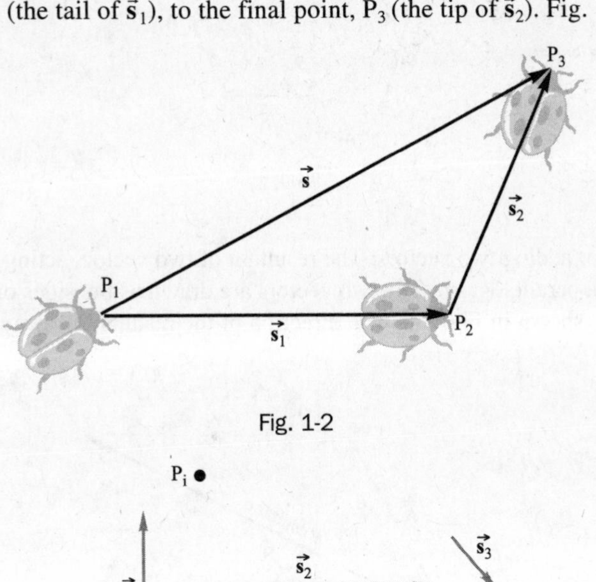


Fig. 1-2

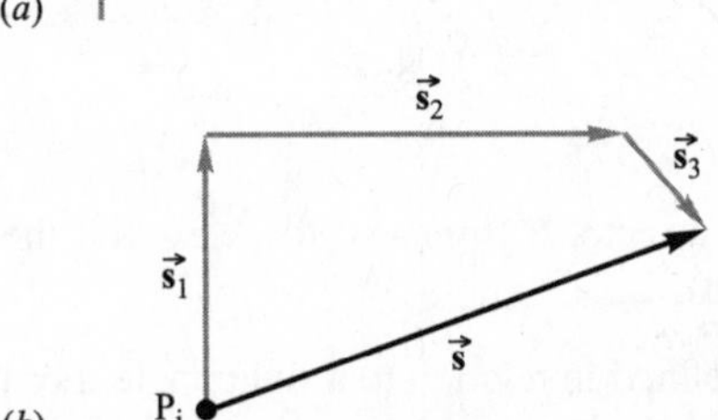




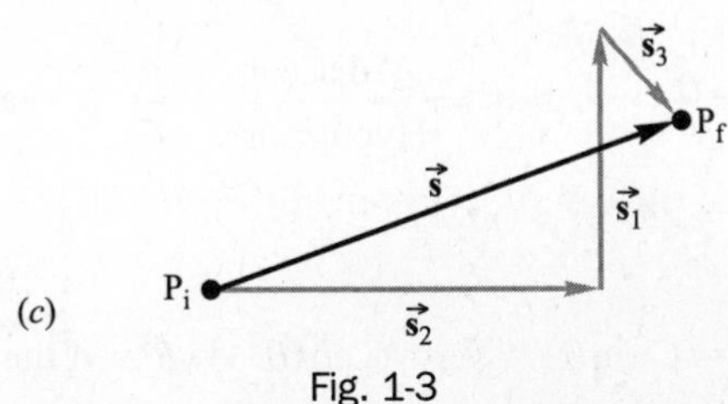


Fig. 1-3

shows an initial starting point $P_i$ and three displacement vectors. If we tip-to-tail those three displacements *in any order* [Fig. 1-3(*b*) and (*c*)] we'll arrive at the same final point $P_f$, and the same resultant $\vec{s}$. In other words:

$$\vec{s} = \vec{s}_1 + \vec{s}_2 + \vec{s}_3 = \vec{s}_2 + \vec{s}_1 + \vec{s}_3 \text{ etc.}$$

As long as the bug starts at $P_i$ and walks the three displacements, in any sequence, it will end up at $P_f$.

The same tip-to-tail procedure holds for any kind of vector, be it displacement, velocity, force, or anything else. Accordingly, the resultant ($\vec{\mathbf{R}}$) obtained by adding the generic vectors $\vec{\mathbf{A}}$, $\vec{\mathbf{B}}$, and $\vec{\mathbf{C}}$ is shown in Fig. 1-4. The size or **magnitude** of a vector, for example, $\vec{\mathbf{R}}$, is its *absolute value* indicated symbolically as $|\vec{\mathbf{R}}|$; (we'll see how to calculate it presently). It's common practice, though not always a good idea, to represent the magnitude of a vector using just a light face italic letter, for example, $R = |\vec{\mathbf{R}}|$.

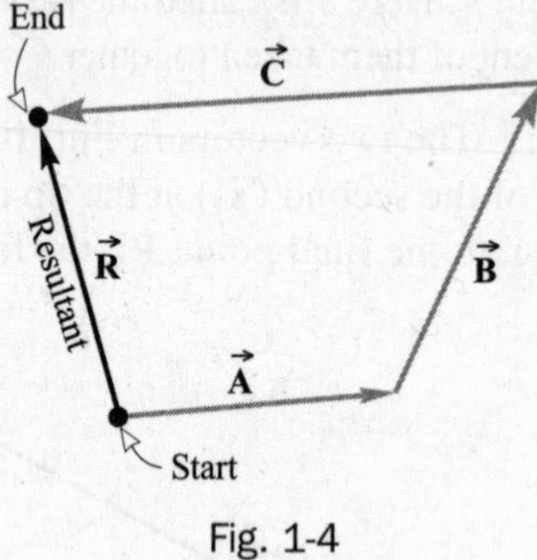


Fig. 1-4

**Parallelogram Method** for adding two vectors: The resultant of two vectors acting at any angle may be represented by the diagonal of a parallelogram. The two vectors are drawn as the sides of the parallelogram and the resultant is its diagonal, as shown in Fig. 1-5. The direction of the resultant is away from the origin of the two vectors.

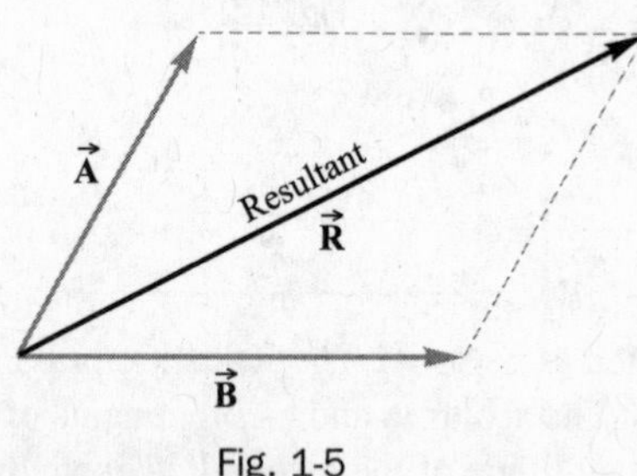


Fig. 1-5

**Subtraction of Vectors:** To subtract a vector $\vec{\mathbf{B}}$ from a vector $\vec{\mathbf{A}}$, reverse the direction of $\vec{\mathbf{B}}$ and add individually to vector $\vec{\mathbf{A}}$, that is, $\vec{\mathbf{A}} - \vec{\mathbf{B}} = \vec{\mathbf{A}} + (-\vec{\mathbf{B}})$.

**The Trigonometric Functions** are defined in relation to a right angle. For the right triangle shown in Fig. 1-6, by definition

$$\sin\theta = \frac{\text{Opposite}}{\text{Hypotenuse}} = \frac{B}{C}, \qquad \cos\theta = \frac{\text{Adjacent}}{\text{Hypotenuse}} = \frac{A}{C}, \qquad \tan\theta = \frac{\text{Opposite}}{\text{Adjacent}} = \frac{B}{A}$$

We often use these in the forms

$$B = C\sin\theta \qquad A = C\cos\theta \qquad B = A\tan\theta$$

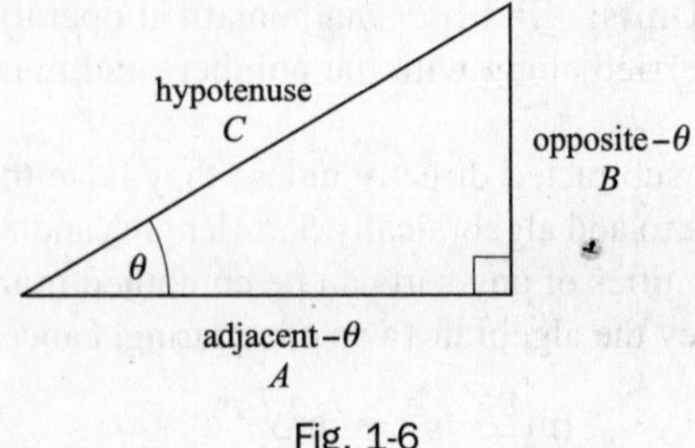


Fig. 1-6

**A Component of a Vector** is its effective value in a given direction. For example, the *x*-component of a displacement is the displacement parallel to the *x*-axis caused by the given displacement. A vector in three dimensions may be considered as the resultant of its component vectors resolved along any three *mutually perpendicular* directions. Similarly, a vector in two dimensions may be resolved into two component vectors acting along any two mutually perpendicular directions. Fig. 1-7 shows the vector $\vec{\mathbf{R}}$ and its *x* and *y* vector components, $\vec{\mathbf{R}}_x$ and $\vec{\mathbf{R}}_y$, which have magnitudes

$$|\vec{\mathbf{R}}_x| = |\vec{\mathbf{R}}| \cos\theta \qquad \text{and} \qquad |\vec{\mathbf{R}}_y| = |\vec{\mathbf{R}}| \sin\theta$$

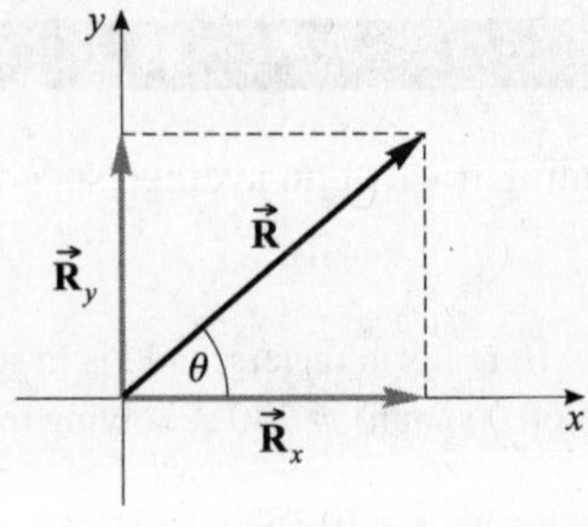


Fig. 1-7

or equivalently

$$R_x = R\cos\theta \qquad \text{and} \qquad R_y = R\sin\theta$$

**Component Method for Adding Vectors:** Each vector is resolved into its *x*-, *y*-, and *z*-components, with negatively directed components taken as negative. The scalar *x*-component $R_x$ of the resultant $\vec{\mathbf{R}}$ is the algebraic sum of all the scalar *x*-components. The scalar *y*- and *z*-components of the resultant are found in a similar way. With the components known, the magnitude of the resultant is given by

$$R = \sqrt{R_x^2 + R_y^2 + R_z^2}$$

In two dimensions, the angle of the resultant with the *x*-axis can be found from the relation

$$\tan\theta = \frac{R_y}{R_x}$$

**Unit Vectors** have a magnitude of one and are represented by a boldface symbol topped with a caret. The special unit vectors $\hat{\mathbf{i}}$, $\hat{\mathbf{j}}$, and $\hat{\mathbf{k}}$ are assigned to the *x*-, *y*-, and *z*-axes, respectively. A vector $3\hat{\mathbf{i}}$, represents a three-unit vector in the $+x$-direction, while $-5\hat{\mathbf{k}}$ represents a five-unit vector in the $-z$-direction. A vector $\vec{\mathbf{R}}$ that has scalar *x*-, *y*-, and *z*-components $R_x$, $R_y$, and $R_z$, respectively, can be written as $\vec{\mathbf{R}} = R_x\hat{\mathbf{i}} + R_y\hat{\mathbf{j}} + R_z\hat{\mathbf{k}}$.

**Mathematical Operations with Units:** In every mathematical operation, the units terms (for example, lb, cm, ft$^3$, mi/h, m/s$^2$) must be carried along with the numbers and must undergo the same mathematical operations as the numbers.

Quantities cannot be added or subtracted directly unless they have the same units (as well as the same dimensions). For example, if we are to add algebraically 5 m (length) and 8 cm (length), we must first convert m to cm or cm to m. However, quantities of any sort can be combined in multiplication or division, in which the units as well as the numbers obey the algebraic laws of squaring, cancellation, and so on. Thus:

(1) $6\,\text{m}^2 + 2\,\text{m}^2 = 8\,\text{m}^2 \qquad (\text{m}^2 + \text{m}^2 \to \text{m}^2)$

(2) $5\,\text{cm} \times 2\,\text{cm}^2 = 10\,\text{cm}^3 \qquad (\text{cm} \times \text{cm}^2 \to \text{cm}^3)$

(3) $2\,\text{m}^3 \times 1500\,\dfrac{\text{kg}}{\text{m}^3} = 3000\,\text{kg} \qquad \left(\text{m}^3 \times \dfrac{\text{kg}}{\text{m}^3} \to \text{kg}\right)$

(4) $2\,\text{s} \times 3\,\dfrac{\text{km}}{\text{s}^2} = 6\,\dfrac{\text{km}}{\text{s}} \qquad \left(\text{s} \times \dfrac{\text{km}}{\text{s}^2} \to \dfrac{\text{km}}{\text{s}}\right)$

(5) $\dfrac{15\text{g}}{3\,\text{g/cm}^3} = 5\,\text{cm}^3 \qquad \left(\dfrac{\text{g}}{\text{g/cm}^3} \to \text{g} \times \dfrac{\text{cm}^3}{\text{g}} \to \text{cm}^3\right)$

## SOLVED PROBLEMS

**1.1 [I]** A toy train moves along a winding track at an average speed of 0.25 m/s. How far will it travel in 4.00 minutes?

The defining equation is $v_{av} = l/t$. Here $l$ is in meters, and $t$ is in seconds, so the first thing to do is convert 4.00 min into seconds: (4.00 min)(60.0 s/min) = 240 s. Solving the equation for $l$,

$$l = v_{av}t = (0.25\text{ m/s})(240\text{ s})$$

Since the speed has only two significant figures, $l$ = 60 m.

**1.2 [I]** A student driving a car travels 10.0 km in 30.0 min. What was her average speed?

The defining equation is $v_{av} = l/t$. Here $l$ is in kilometers, and $t$ is in minutes, so the first thing to do is convert 10.0 km to meters and then 30.0 min into seconds: (10.0 km)(1000 m/km) = $10.0 \times 10^3$ m and (30.0 min) × (60.0 s/min) = 1800 s. We need to solve for $v_{av}$, giving the numerical answer to three significant figures:

$$v_{av} = \frac{l}{t} = \frac{10.0 \times 10^3\text{ m}}{1800\text{ s}} = 5.56\text{ m/s}$$

**1.3 [I]** Rolling along across the machine shop at a constant speed of 4.25 m/s, a robot covers a distance of 17.0 m. How long did that journey take?

Since the speed is constant the defining equation is $v = l/t$. Multiply both sides of this expression by $t$ and then divide both by $v$:

$$t = \frac{l}{v} = \frac{17.0\text{ m}}{4.25\text{ m/s}} = 4.00\text{ s}$$

**1.4 [I]** Change the speed 0.200 cm/s to units of kilometers per year.

$$0.200\,\frac{\text{cm}}{\text{s}} = \left(0.200\,\frac{\cancel{\text{cm}}}{\cancel{\text{s}}}\right)\left(10^{-5}\,\frac{\text{km}}{\cancel{\text{cm}}}\right)\left(3600\,\frac{\cancel{\text{s}}}{\cancel{\text{h}}}\right)\left(24\,\frac{\cancel{\text{h}}}{\cancel{\text{d}}}\right)\left(365\,\frac{\cancel{\text{d}}}{\text{y}}\right) = 63.1\,\frac{\text{km}}{\text{y}}$$

**1.5 [I]** A car travels along a road and its odometer readings are plotted against time in Fig. 1-8. Find the instantaneous speed of the car at points *A* and *B*. What is the car's average speed?

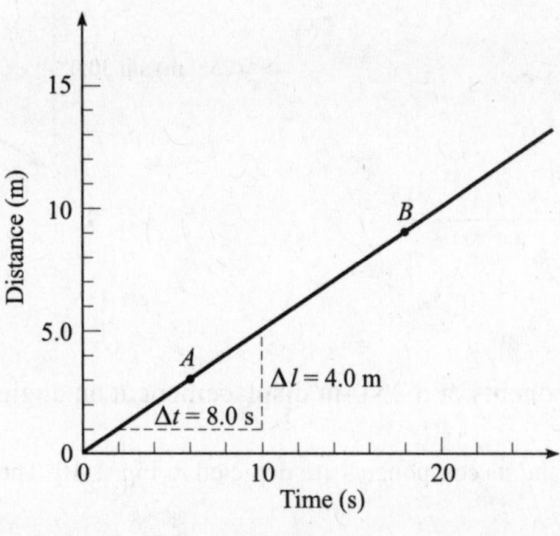


Fig. 1-8

Because the speed is given by the slope $\Delta l/\Delta t$ of the tangent line, we take a tangent to the curve at point *A*. The tangent line is the curve itself in this case, since it's a straight line. For the triangle shown near *A*, we have

$$\frac{\Delta l}{\Delta t} = \frac{4.0\,\text{m}}{8.0\,\text{s}} = 0.50\,\text{m/s}$$

This is the speed at point *A* and it's also the speed at point *B* and at every other point on the straight-line graph. It follows that $v = 0.50$ m/s $= v_{av}$.

**1.6 [I]** A kid stands 6.00 m from the base of a flagpole which is 8.00 m tall. Determine the magnitude of the displacement of the brass eagle on top of the pole with respect to the youngster's feet.

The geometry corresponds to a 3-4-5 right triangle (i.e., 3 × 2 – 4 × 2 – 5 × 2). Thus, the hypotenuse, which is the 5-side, must be 10.0 m long, and that's the magnitude of the displacement.

**1.7 [II]** A runner makes one lap around a 200-m track in a time of 25 s. What were the runner's (*a*) average speed and (*b*) average velocity?

(*a*) From the definition,

$$\text{Average speed} = \frac{\text{Distance traveled}}{\text{Time taken}} = \frac{200\text{ m}}{25\text{ s}} = 8.0\text{ m/s}$$

(*b*) Because the run ended at the starting point, the displacement vector from starting point to end point has zero length. Since $\vec{\mathbf{v}}_{av} = \vec{\mathbf{s}}/t$,

$$|\vec{\mathbf{v}}_{av}| = \frac{0\text{ m}}{25\text{ s}} = 0\text{ m/s}$$

**1.8 [I]** Using the graphical method, find the resultant of the following two displacements: 2.0 m at 40° and 4.0 m at 127°, the angles being taken relative to the $+x$-axis, as is customary. Give your answer to two significant figures. (See Appendix A on significant figures.)

Choose *x*- and *y*-axes as seen in Fig. 1-9 and lay out the displacements to scale, tip to tail from the origin. Notice that all angles are measured from the $+x$-axis. The resultant vector $\vec{\mathbf{s}}$ points from starting point to end point as shown. We measure its length on the scale diagram to find its magnitude, 4.6 m. Using a protractor, we measure its angle $\theta$ to be 101°. The resultant displacement is therefore 4.6 m at 101°.

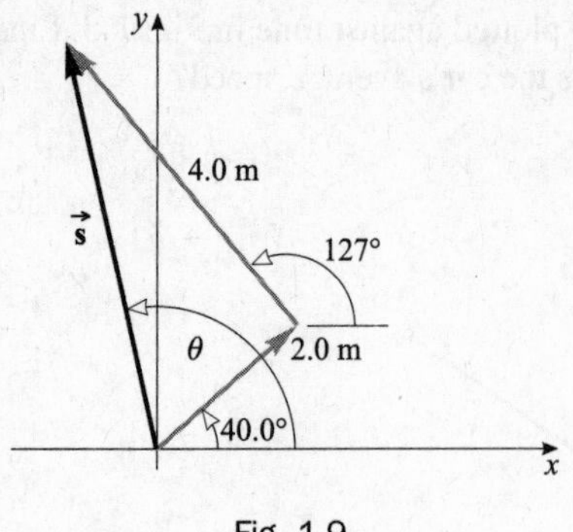

Fig. 1-9

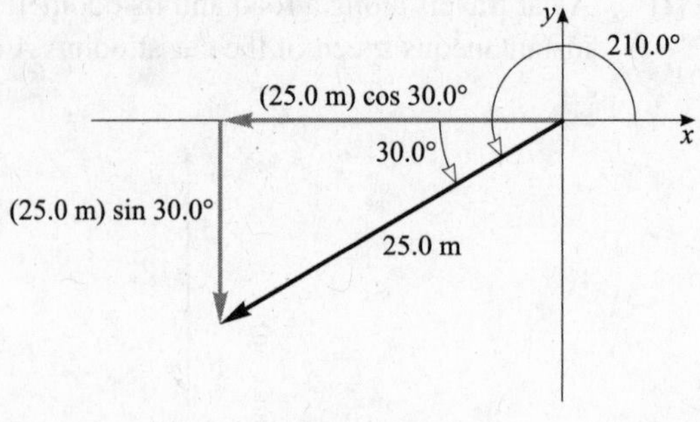

Fig. 1-10

**1.9 [I]** Find the $x$- and $y$-components of a 25.0-m displacement at an angle of 210.0°.

The vector displacement and its components are depicted in Fig. 1-10. The scalar components are

$$x\text{-component} = -(25.0 \text{ m}) \cos 30.0° = -21.7 \text{ m}$$
$$y\text{-component} = -(25.0 \text{ m}) \sin 30.0° = -12.5 \text{ m}$$

Notice in particular that each component points in the negative coordinate direction and must therefore be taken as negative.

**1.10 [II]** Solve Problem 1.8 by use of rectangular components.

We resolve each vector into rectangular components as illustrated in Fig. 1-11($a$) and ($b$). (Place a cross-hatch symbol on the original vector to show that it is replaced by its components.) The resultant has scalar components of

$$s_x = 1.53 \text{ m} - 2.41 \text{ m} = -0.88 \text{ m} \qquad s_y = 1.29 \text{ m} + 3.19 \text{ m} = 4.48 \text{ m}$$

Notice that components pointing in the negative direction must be assigned a negative value.

The resultant is shown in Fig. 1.11($c$); there,

$$s = \sqrt{(0.88 \text{ m})^2 + (4.48 \text{ m})^2} = 4.6 \text{ m} \qquad \tan \phi = \frac{4.48 \text{ m}}{0.88 \text{ m}}$$

and $\phi = 79°$, from which $\theta = 180° - \phi = 101°$. Hence, $\vec{s} = 4.6$ m $-$ 101° FROM + X-AXIS; remember, vectors must have their directions stated explicitly.

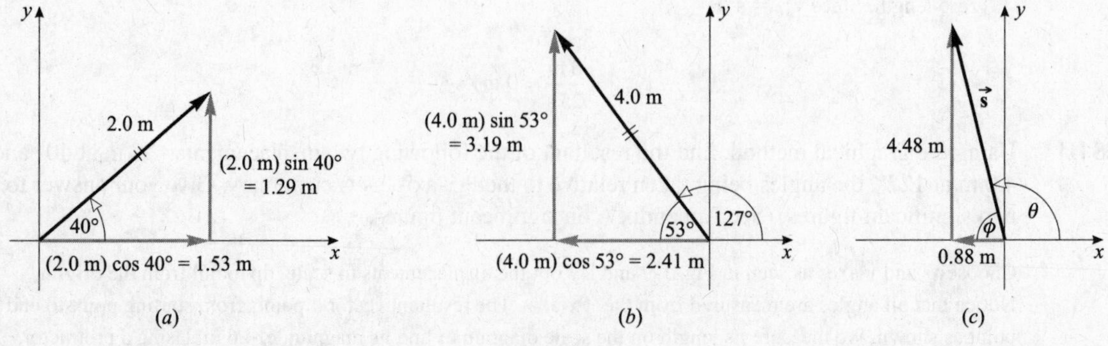

Fig. 1-11

**1.11 [II]** Add the following two displacement vectors using the parallelogram method: 30 m at 30° and 20 m at 140°. Remember that numbers like 30 m and 20 m have two significant figures.

The vectors are drawn with a common origin in Fig. 1-12(*a*). We construct a parallelogram using them as sides, as shown in Fig. 1-12(*b*). The resultant $\vec{s}$ is then represented by the diagonal. By measurement, we find that $\vec{s}$ is 30 m at 72°.

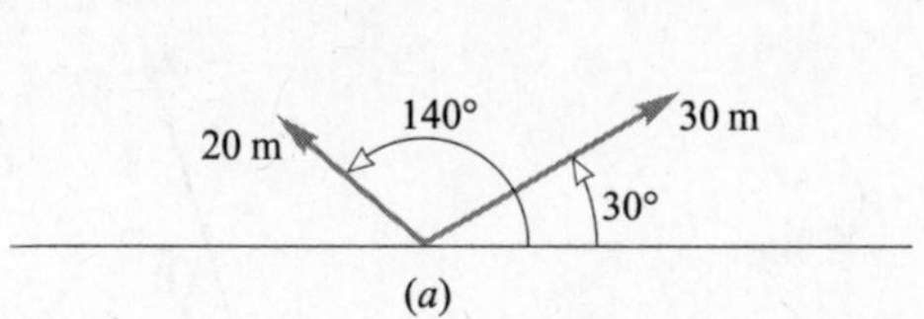


Fig. 1-12

**1.12 [II]** Express the vectors illustrated in Figs. 1-11(*c*), 1-13, 1-14, and 1-15 in the form $\vec{\mathbf{R}} = R_x\hat{\mathbf{i}} + R_y\hat{\mathbf{j}} + R_z\hat{\mathbf{k}}$ (leave out the units).

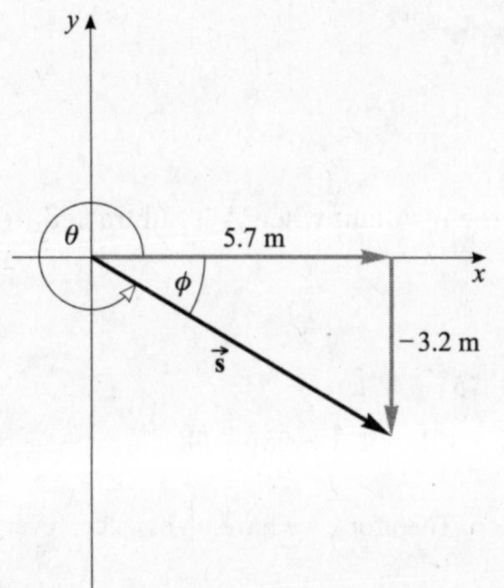


Fig. 1-13

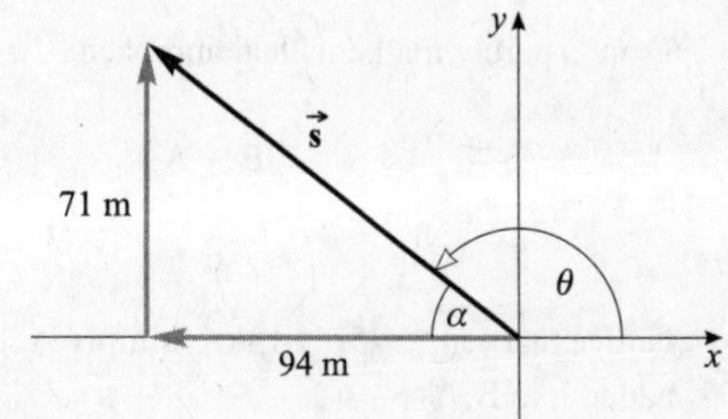


Fig. 1-14

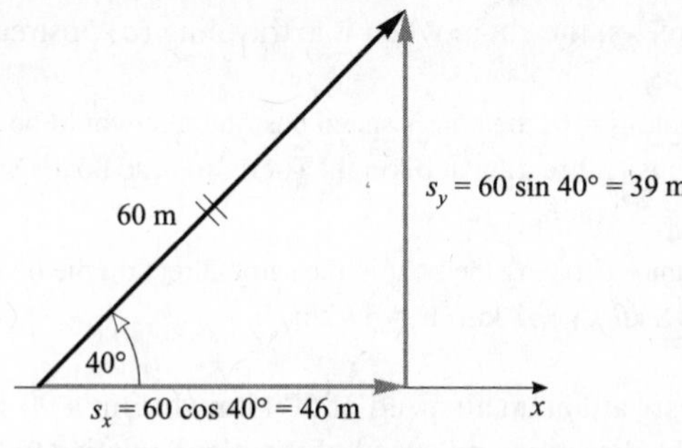


Fig. 1-15

Remembering that plus and minus signs must be used to show direction along an axis,

For Fig. 1-11(*c*): $\vec{\mathbf{R}} = -0.88\hat{\mathbf{i}} + 4.48\hat{\mathbf{j}}$

For Fig. 1-13: $\vec{\mathbf{R}} = 5.7\hat{\mathbf{i}} - 3.2\hat{\mathbf{j}}$

For Fig. 1-14: $\vec{\mathbf{R}} = -94\hat{\mathbf{i}} + 71\hat{\mathbf{j}}$

For Fig. 1-15: $\vec{\mathbf{R}} = 46\hat{\mathbf{i}} + 39\hat{\mathbf{j}}$

**1.13 [I]** Perform graphically the following vector additions and subtractions, where $\vec{\mathbf{A}}$, $\vec{\mathbf{B}}$, and $\vec{\mathbf{C}}$ are the vectors drawn in Fig. 1-16: *(a)* $\vec{\mathbf{A}}+\vec{\mathbf{B}}$; *(b)* $\vec{\mathbf{A}}+\vec{\mathbf{B}}+\vec{\mathbf{C}}$; *(c)* $\vec{\mathbf{A}}-\vec{\mathbf{B}}$; *(d)* $\vec{\mathbf{A}}+\vec{\mathbf{B}}-\vec{\mathbf{C}}$.

See Fig. 1-16(*a*) through (*d*). In (*c*), $\vec{\mathbf{A}}-\vec{\mathbf{B}}=\vec{\mathbf{A}}+(-\vec{\mathbf{B}})$; that is, to subtract $\vec{\mathbf{B}}$ from $\vec{\mathbf{A}}$, reverse the direction of $\vec{\mathbf{B}}$ and add it vectorially to $\vec{\mathbf{A}}$. Similarly, in (*d*), $\vec{\mathbf{A}}+\vec{\mathbf{B}}-\vec{\mathbf{C}}=\vec{\mathbf{A}}+\vec{\mathbf{B}}+(-\vec{\mathbf{C}})$, where $-\vec{\mathbf{C}}$ is equal in magnitude but opposite in direction to $\vec{\mathbf{C}}$.

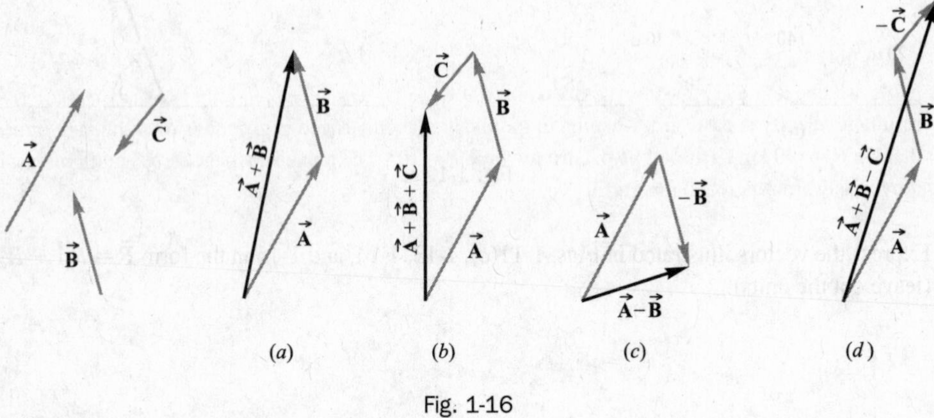


Fig. 1-16

**1.14 [II]** If $\vec{\mathbf{A}} = -12\hat{\mathbf{i}} + 25\hat{\mathbf{j}} + 13\hat{\mathbf{k}}$ and $\vec{\mathbf{B}} = -3\hat{\mathbf{j}} + 7\hat{\mathbf{k}}$, find the resultant when $\vec{\mathbf{A}}$ is subtracted from $\vec{\mathbf{B}}$.

From a purely mathematical approach,

$$\begin{aligned}\vec{\mathbf{B}}-\vec{\mathbf{A}} &= (-3\hat{\mathbf{j}} + 7\hat{\mathbf{k}}) - (-12\hat{\mathbf{i}} + 25\hat{\mathbf{j}} + 13\hat{\mathbf{k}}) \\ &= -3\hat{\mathbf{j}} + 7\hat{\mathbf{k}} + 12\hat{\mathbf{i}} - 25\hat{\mathbf{j}} - 13\hat{\mathbf{k}} = 12\hat{\mathbf{i}} - 28\hat{\mathbf{j}} - 6\hat{\mathbf{k}}\end{aligned}$$

Notice that $12\hat{\mathbf{i}} - 25\hat{\mathbf{j}} - 13\hat{\mathbf{k}}$ is simply $\vec{\mathbf{A}}$ reversed in direction. Therefore, we have, in essence, reversed $\vec{\mathbf{A}}$ and added it to $\vec{\mathbf{B}}$.

**1.15 [II]** A boat can travel at a speed of 8 km/h in still water on a lake. In the flowing water of a stream, it can move at 8 km/h relative to the water in the stream. If the stream speed is 3 km/h, how fast can the boat move past a tree on the shore when it is traveling (*a*) upstream and (*b*) downstream?

(*a*) If the water was standing still, the boat's speed past the tree would be 8 km/h. But the stream is carrying it in the opposite direction at 3 km/h. Therefore, the boat's speed relative to the tree is 8 km/h − 3 km/h = 5 km/h.

(*b*) In this case, the stream is carrying the boat in the same direction the boat is trying to move. Hence, its speed past the tree is 8 km/h + 3 km/h = 11 km/h.

**1.16 [III]** A plane is traveling eastward at an airspeed of 500 km/h. But a 90-km/h wind is blowing southward. What are the direction and speed of the plane relative to the ground?

The plane's resultant velocity with respect to the ground, $\vec{\mathbf{v}}_{PG}$, is the sum of two vectors, the velocity of the plane with respect to the air, $\vec{\mathbf{v}}_{PA}$ = 500 km/h—EAST and the velocity of the air with respect to the ground, $\vec{\mathbf{v}}_{AG}$ = 90 km/h—SOUTH. In other words, $\vec{\mathbf{v}}_{PG} = \vec{\mathbf{v}}_{PA} + \vec{\mathbf{v}}_{AG}$. These component velocities are shown in Fig. 1-17. The plane's resultant speed is

$$v_{PG} = \sqrt{(500\ \text{km/h})^2 + (90\ \text{km/h})^2} = 508\ \text{km/h}$$

The angle $\alpha$ is given by

$$\tan \alpha = \frac{90 \text{ km/h}}{500 \text{ km/h}} = 0.18$$

from which $\alpha = 10°$. The plane's velocity relative to the ground is 508 km/h at 10° south of east.

**1.17 [III]** With the same airspeed as in Problem 1.16, in what direction must the plane head in order to move due east relative to the Earth?

The sum of the plane's velocity through the air and the velocity of the wind will be the resultant velocity of the plane relative to the Earth. This is shown in the vector diagram in Fig. 1-18. Notice that, as required, the resultant velocity is eastward. Keeping in mind that the wind speed is given to two significant figures, it is seen that $\sin \theta = (90 \text{ km/h})(500 \text{ km/h})$, from which $\theta = 10°$. The plane should head 10° north of east if it is to move eastward relative to the Earth.

To find the plane's eastward speed, we note in the figure that $v_{PG} = (500 \text{ km/h}) \cos \theta = 4.9 \times 10^5 \text{ m/h}$.

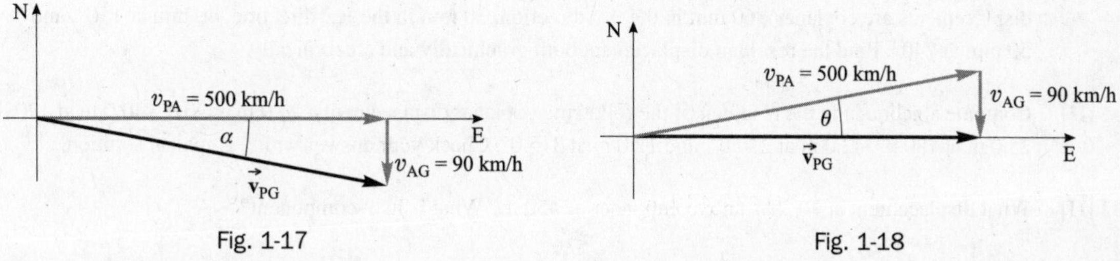


Fig. 1-17

Fig. 1-18

## SUPPLEMENTARY PROBLEMS

**1.18 [I]** Three kids in a parking lot launch a rocket that rises into the air along a 380-m long arc in 40 s. Determine its average speed.

**1.19 [I]** According to its computer, a robot that left its closet and traveled 1200 m, had an average speed of 20.0 m/s. How long did the trip take?

**1.20 [I]** A car's odometer reads 22 687 km at the start of a trip and 22 791 km at the end. The trip took 4.0 hours. What was the car's average speed in km/h and in m/s?

**1.21 [I]** An auto travels at the rate of 25 km/h for 4.0 minutes, then at 50 km/h for 8.0 minutes, and finally at 20 km/h for 2.0 minutes. Find (*a*) the total distance covered in km and (*b*) the average speed for the complete trip in m/s.

**1.22 [I]** Starting from the center of town, a car travels east for 80.0 km and then turns due south for another 192 km, at which point it runs out of gas. Determine the displacement of the stopped car from the center of town.

**1.23 [II]** A little turtle is placed at the origin of an *xy*-grid drawn on a large sheet of paper. Each grid box is 1.0 cm by 1.0 cm. The turtle walks around for a while and finally ends up at point (24, 10), that is, 24 boxes along the *x*-axis, and 10 boxes along the *y*-axis. Determine the displacement of the turtle from the origin at the point.

**1.24 [II]** A bug starts at point *A*, crawls 8.0 cm east, then 5.0 cm south, 3.0 cm west, and 4.0 cm north to point *B*. (*a*) How far south and east is *B* from *A*? (*b*) Find the displacement from *A* to *B* both graphically and algebraically.

**1.25 [II]** A runner travels 1.5 laps around a circular track in a time of 50 s. The diameter of the track is 40 m and its circumference is 126 m. Find (*a*) the average speed of the runner and (*b*) the magnitude of the runner's average velocity. Be careful here; average speed depends on the total distance traveled, whereas average velocity depends on the displacement at the end of the particular journey.

**1.26 [II]** During a race on an oval track, a car travels at an average speed of 200 km/h. (*a*) How far did it travel in 45.0 min? (*b*) Determine its average velocity at the end of its third lap.

**1.27 [II]** The following data describe the position of an object along the *x*-axis as a function of time. Plot the data, and find, as best you can, the instantaneous velocity of the object at (*a*) $t = 5.0$ s, (*b*) 16 s, and (*c*) 23 s.

| $t$(s) | 0 | 2 | 4 | 6 | 8 | 10 | 12 | 14 | 16 | 18 | 20 | 22 | 24 | 26 | 28 |
|---|---|---|---|---|---|---|---|---|---|---|---|---|---|---|---|
| $x$(cm) | 0 | 4.0 | 7.8 | 11.3 | 14.3 | 16.8 | 18.6 | 19.7 | 20.0 | 19.5 | 18.2 | 16.2 | 13.5 | 10.3 | 6.7 |

**1.28 [II]** For the object whose motion is described in Problem 1.27, as best you can, find its velocity at the following times: (*a*) 3.0 s, (*b*) 10 s, and (*c*) 24 s.

**1.29 [I]** Find the scalar *x*- and *y*-components of the following displacements in the *xy*-plane: (*a*) 300 cm at 127° and (*b*) 500 cm at 220°.

**1.30 [II]** Starting at the origin of coordinates, the following displacements are made in the *xy*-plane (that is, the displacements are coplanar): 60 mm in the $+y$-direction, 30 mm in the $-x$-direction, 40 mm at 150°, and 50 mm at 240°. Find the resultant displacement both graphically and algebraically.

**1.31 [II]** Compute algebraically the resultant of the following coplanar displacements: 20.0 m at 30.0°, 40.0 m at 120.0°, 25.0 m at 180.0°, 42.0 m at 270.0°, and 12.0 m at 315.0°. Check your answer with a graphical solution.

**1.32 [II]** What displacement at 70° has an *x*-component of 450 m? What is its *y*-component?

**1.33 [II]** What displacement must be added to a 50-cm displacement in the $+x$-direction to give a resultant displacement of 85 cm at 25°?

**1.34 [I]** Refer to Fig. 1-19. In terms of vectors $\vec{\mathbf{A}}$ and $\vec{\mathbf{B}}$, express the vectors (*a*) $\vec{\mathbf{P}}$, (*b*) $\vec{\mathbf{R}}$, (*c*) $\vec{\mathbf{S}}$, and (*d*) $\vec{\mathbf{Q}}$.

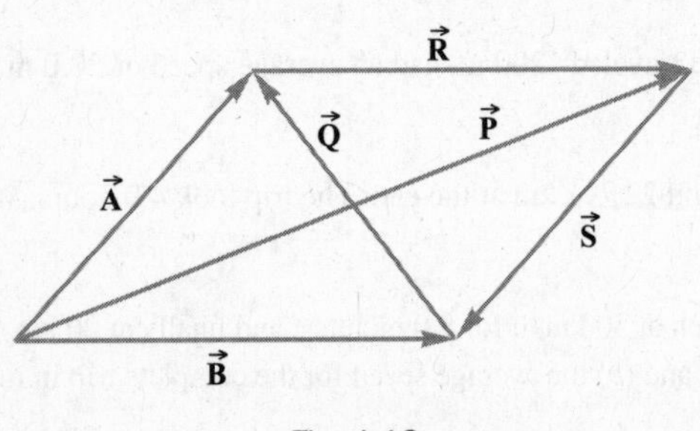

Fig. 1-19

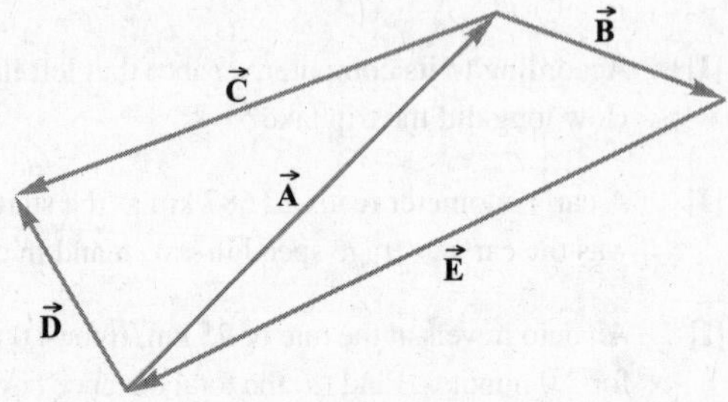

Fig. 1-20

**1.35 [I]** Refer to Fig. 1-20. In terms of vectors $\vec{\mathbf{A}}$ and $\vec{\mathbf{B}}$, express the vectors (*a*) $\vec{\mathbf{E}}$, (*b*) $\vec{\mathbf{D}} - \vec{\mathbf{C}}$, and (*c*) $\vec{\mathbf{E}} + \vec{\mathbf{D}} - \vec{\mathbf{C}}$.

**1.36 [II]** Find (*a*) $\vec{\mathbf{A}} + \vec{\mathbf{B}} + \vec{\mathbf{C}}$, (*b*) $\vec{\mathbf{A}} - \vec{\mathbf{B}}$, and (*c*) $\vec{\mathbf{A}} - \vec{\mathbf{C}}$ if $\vec{\mathbf{A}} = 7\hat{\mathbf{i}} - 6\hat{\mathbf{j}}$, $\vec{\mathbf{B}} = -3\hat{\mathbf{i}} + 12\hat{\mathbf{j}}$, and $\vec{\mathbf{C}} = 4\hat{\mathbf{i}} - 4\hat{\mathbf{j}}$.

**1.37 [II]** Find the magnitude and angle of $\vec{\mathbf{R}}$ if $\vec{\mathbf{R}} = 7.0\hat{\mathbf{i}} - 12\hat{\mathbf{j}}$.

**1.38 [II]** Determine the displacement vector that must be added to the displacement $(25\hat{\mathbf{i}} - 16\hat{\mathbf{j}})$ m to give a displacement of 7.0 m pointing in the $+x$-direction?

**1.39 [II]** A vector $(15\hat{\mathbf{i}} - 16\hat{\mathbf{j}} + 27\hat{\mathbf{k}})$ is added to a vector $(23\hat{\mathbf{j}} - 40\hat{\mathbf{k}})$. What is the magnitude of the resultant?

**1.40 [III]** A truck is moving north at a speed of 70 km/h. The exhaust pipe above the truck cab sends out a trail of smoke that makes an angle of 20° east of south behind the truck. If the wind is blowing directly toward the east, what is the wind speed at that location? [*Hint*: The smoke reveals the direction of the truck with-respect-to the air.]

**1.41 [III]** A ship is traveling due east at 10 km/h. What must be the speed of a second ship heading 30° east of north if it is always due north of the first ship?

**1.42 [III]** A boat, propelled so as to travel with a speed of 0.50 m/s in still water, moves directly across a river that is 60 m wide. The river flows with a speed of 0.30 m/s. (*a*) At what angle, relative to the straight-across direction, must the boat be pointed? (*b*) How long does it take the boat to cross the river?

**1.43 [III]** A reckless drunk is playing with a gun in an airplane that is going directly east at 500 km/h. The drunk shoots the gun straight up at the ceiling of the plane. The bullet leaves the gun at a speed of 1000 km/h. According to someone standing on the Earth, what angle does the bullet make with the vertical?

## ANSWERS TO SUPPLEMENTARY PROBLEMS

**1.18 [I]** 9.5 m/s

**1.19 [I]** 60.0 s

**1.20 [I]** 26 km/h, 7.2 m/s

**1.21 [I]** (*a*) 9.0 km; (*b*) 10.7 m/s or 11 m/s

**1.22 [I]** 208 km—67.4° SOUTH OF EAST

**1.23 [II]** 26 cm—23° ABOVE *X*-AXIS

**1.24 [II]** (*a*) 1.0 cm—SOUTH, 5.0 cm—EAST; (*b*) 5.10 cm—11.3° SOUTH OF EAST

**1.25 [II]** (*a*) 3.8 m/s; (*b*) 0.80 m/s

**1.26 [II]** (*a*) 150 km; (*b*) zero

**1.27 [II]** (*a*) 0.018 m/s in the positive *x*-direction; (*b*) 0 m/s; (*c*) 0.014 m/s in the negative *x*-direction

**1.28 [II]** (*a*) 1.9 cm/s in the positive *x*-direction; (*b*) 1.1 cm/s in the positive *x*-direction; (*c*) 1.5 cm/s in the negative *x*-direction

**1.29 [I]** (*a*) −181 cm, 240 cm; (*b*) −383 cm, −321 cm

**1.30 [II]** 97 mm at 158°

**1.31 [II]** 20.1 m at 197°

**1.32 [II]** 1.3 km, 1.2 km

**1.33 [II]** 45 cm at 53°

**1.34 [I]** (*a*) $\vec{\mathbf{A}} + \vec{\mathbf{B}}$; (*b*) $\vec{\mathbf{B}}$; (*c*) $-\vec{\mathbf{A}}$; (*d*) $\vec{\mathbf{A}} - \vec{\mathbf{B}}$

**1.35 [I]** (*a*) $-\vec{\mathbf{A}} - \vec{\mathbf{B}}$ or $-(\vec{\mathbf{A}} + \vec{\mathbf{B}})$; (*b*) $\vec{\mathbf{A}}$; (*c*) $-\vec{\mathbf{B}}$

**1.36 [II]** (*a*) $8\hat{\mathbf{i}} + 2\hat{\mathbf{j}}$; (*b*) $10\hat{\mathbf{i}} - 18\hat{\mathbf{j}}$; (*c*) $3\hat{\mathbf{i}} - 2\hat{\mathbf{j}}$

**1.37 [II]** 14 at $-60°$

**1.38 [II]** $(-18\hat{\mathbf{i}} + 16\hat{\mathbf{j}})$ m

**1.39 [II]** 21

**1.40 [III]** 25 km/h

**1.41 [III]** 20 km/h

**1.42 [III]** (*a*) 37° upstream; (*b*) $1.5 \times 10^2$ s

**1.43 [III]** 26.6°

# Uniformly Accelerated Motion

**Acceleration** measures the time rate-of-change of velocity:

$$\textit{Average acceleration} = \frac{\text{Change in velocity vector}}{\text{Time taken}}$$

$$\vec{\mathbf{a}}_{av} = \frac{\vec{\mathbf{v}}_f - \vec{\mathbf{v}}_i}{t}$$

where $\vec{\mathbf{v}}_i$ is the initial velocity, $\vec{\mathbf{v}}_f$ is the final velocity, and $t$ is the time interval over which the change occurred. The units of acceleration are those of velocity divided by time. Typical examples are (m/s)/s (or m/s$^2$) and (km/h)/s (or km/h·s). Notice that acceleration is a vector quantity. It has the direction of $\vec{\mathbf{v}}_f - \vec{\mathbf{v}}_i$, the change in velocity. It is nonetheless commonplace to speak of the magnitude of the acceleration as just the acceleration, provided there is no ambiguity.

When we concern ourselves only with accelerations tangent to the path traveled, the direction of the acceleration is known and we can write the defining equation in scalar form as

$$a_{av} = \frac{v_f - v_i}{t}$$

**Uniformly Accelerated Motion Along a Straight Line** is an important situation. In this case, the *acceleration vector is constant* and lies along the line of the displacement vector, so that the directions of $\vec{\mathbf{v}}$ and $\vec{\mathbf{a}}$ can be specified with plus and minus signs. If we represent the displacement by $s$ (positive if in the positive direction, and negative if in the negative direction), then there will be five convenient equations describing uniformly accelerated motion:

$$s = v_{av} t$$

$$v_{av} = \frac{v_f + v_i}{2}$$

$$a = \frac{v_f - v_i}{t}$$

$$v_f^2 = v_i^2 + 2as$$

$$s = v_i t + \tfrac{1}{2} a t^2$$

Often $s$ is replaced by $x$ or $y$, and sometimes $v_f$ and $v_i$ are written as $v$ and $v_0$, respectively.

**Direction Is Important,** and a positive direction must be chosen when analyzing motion along a line. Either direction may be chosen as positive. If a displacement, velocity, or acceleration is in the opposite direction, it must be taken as negative.

**Graphical Interpretations** for motion along a straight line (e.g., the $x$-axis) are as follows:

- A plot of *distance versus time* is always positive (i.e., the graph lies above the time axis). Such a curve never decreases (i.e., it can never have a negative slope or speed). Just think about the odometer and speedometer in a car.
- Because the displacement is a vector quantity, we can only graph it against time if we limit the motion to a straight line and then use plus and minus signs to specify direction. Accordingly, it's common practice to plot *displacement along a straight line versus time* using that scheme. Such a graph representing motion along, say, the $x$-axis, may be either positive (plotted above the time axis) when the object is to the right of the origin ($x = 0$), or negative (plotted below the time axis) when the object is to the left of the origin (see Fig. 2-1). The graph can be positive and get more positive, or negative and get less negative. In both cases the curve would have a positive slope, and the object a positive velocity (it would be moving in the positive $x$-direction). Furthermore, the graph can be positive and get less positive, or be negative and get more negative. In both these cases the curve would have a negative slope, and the object a negative velocity (it would be moving in the negative $x$-direction.
- The *instantaneous velocity* of an object at a certain time is the slope of the displacement versus time graph at that time. It can be positive, negative, or zero.
- The *instantaneous acceleration* of an object at a certain time is the slope of the velocity versus time graph at that time.
- For constant-velocity motion along the $x$-axis, the $x$-versus-$t$ graph is a tilted straight line. For constant-acceleration motion, the $\upsilon$-versus-$t$ graph is a straight line.

**Acceleration Due to Gravity** ($g$): The acceleration of a body moving only under the force of gravity is $g$, the gravitational (or free-fall) acceleration, which is directed vertically downward. On Earth at the surface, on average, $g = 9.81\ \text{m/s}^2$ (i.e., $32.2\ \text{ft/s}^2$); the value varies slightly from place to place. On the Moon, at the surface, the average free-fall acceleration is $1.6\ \text{m/s}^2$.

**Velocity Components:** Suppose that an object moves with a velocity $\vec{\mathbf{v}}$ at some angle $\theta$ up from the $x$-axis, as would initially be the case with a ball thrown into the air. That velocity then has $x$ and $y$ vector components (see Fig. 1-7) of $\vec{\mathbf{v}}_x$ and $\vec{\mathbf{v}}_y$. The corresponding scalar components of the velocity are

$$\upsilon_x = \upsilon\cos\theta \qquad \text{and} \qquad \upsilon_y = \upsilon\sin\theta$$

and these can turn out to be positive or negative numbers, depending on $\theta$. As a rule, if $\vec{\mathbf{v}}$ is in the first quadrant, $\upsilon_x > 0$ and $\upsilon_y > 0$; if $\vec{\mathbf{v}}$ is in the second quadrant, $\upsilon_x < 0$ and $\upsilon_y > 0$; if $\vec{\mathbf{v}}$ is in the third quadrant, $\upsilon_x < 0$ and $\upsilon_y < 0$; finally, if $\vec{\mathbf{v}}$ is in the fourth quadrant, $\upsilon_x > 0$ and $\upsilon_y < 0$. Because these quantities have signs, and therefore implied directions along known axes, it is common to refer to them as velocities. The reader will find this usage in many texts, but it is not without pedagogical drawbacks. Instead, we shall avoid applying the term "velocity" to anything but a vector quantity (written in boldface with an arrow above) whose direction is explicitly stated. Thus, for an object moving with a *velocity* $\vec{\mathbf{v}} = 100\ \text{m/s}$—WEST, the *scalar value of the velocity along the x-axis* is $\upsilon_x = -100\ \text{m/s}$; and the (always positive) *speed* is $\upsilon = 100\ \text{m/s}$.

**Projectile Problems** can be solved easily if air friction can be ignored. One simply considers the motion to consist of two independent parts: horizontal motion with $a = 0$ and $\upsilon_f = \upsilon_i = \upsilon_{av}$ (i.e., constant speed), and vertical motion with $a = g = 9.81\ \text{m/s}^2$ downward.

**Dimensional Analysis:** All mechanical quantities, such as acceleration and force, can be expressed in terms of three fundamental dimensions: length $L$, mass $M$, and time $T$. For example, acceleration is a length (a distance) divided by (time)$^2$; we say it has the *dimensions* $L/T^2$, which we write as $[LT^{-2}]$. The dimensions of volume are $[L^3]$, and those of velocity are $[LT^{-1}]$. Because force is mass multiplied by acceleration, its dimensions are

$[MLT^{-2}]$. Dimensions are helpful in checking equations, since each term of an equation must have the same dimensions. For example, the dimensions of the equation

$$s = v_i t \quad + \tfrac{1}{2} at^2$$

are

$$[L] \rightarrow [LT^{-1}][T] + [LT^{-2}][T^2]$$

so each term has the dimensions of length. *Remember, all terms in an equation must have the same dimensions.* As examples, an equation cannot have a volume $[L^3]$ added to an area $[L^2]$, or a force $[MLT^{-2}]$ subtracted from a velocity $[LT^{-1}]$; these terms do not have the same dimensions.

## SOLVED PROBLEMS

**2.1 [I]** A robot named Fred is initially moving at 2.20 m/s along a hallway in a space terminal. It subsequently speeds up to 4.80 m/s in a time of 0.20 s. Determine the size or *magnitude* of its average acceleration along the path traveled.

The defining scalar equation is $a_{av} = (v_f - v_i)/t$. Everything is in proper SI units, so we need only carry out the calculation:

$$a_{av} = \frac{4.80\text{ m/s} - 2.20\text{ m/s}}{0.20\text{ s}} = 13\text{ m/s}^2$$

Notice that the answer has two significant figures because the time has only two significant figures.

**2.2 [I]** A car is traveling at 20.0 m/s when the driver slams on the brakes and brings it to a straight-line stop in 4.2 s. What is the magnitude of its average acceleration?

The defining scalar equation is $a_{av} = (v_f - v_i)/t$. Note that the final speed is zero. Here the initial speed is greater than the final speed, so we can expect the acceleration to be negative:

$$a_{av} = \frac{0.0\text{ m/s} - 20.0\text{ m/s}}{4.2\text{ s}} = -4.76\text{ m/s}^2$$

Because the time is provided with only two significant figures, the answer is $-4.8\text{ m/s}^2$.

**2.3 [II]** An object starts from rest with a constant acceleration of 8.00 m/s² along a straight line. Find (*a*) the speed at the end of 5.00 s, (*b*) the average speed for the 5-s interval, and (*c*) the distance traveled in the 5.00 s.

We are interested in the motion for the first 5.00 s. Take the direction of motion to be the $+x$-direction (that is, $s = x$). We know that $v_i = 0$, $t = 5.00$ s, and $a = 8.00\text{ m/s}^2$. Because the motion is uniformly accelerated, the five motion equations apply.

(*a*) $v_{fx} = v_{ix} + at = 0 + (8.00\text{ m/s}^2)(5.00\text{ s}) = 40.0\text{ m/s}$

(*b*) $v_{av} = \dfrac{v_{ix} + v_{fx}}{2} = \dfrac{0 + 40.0}{2}\text{ m/s} = 20.0\text{ m/s}$

(*c*) $x = v_{ix}t + \tfrac{1}{2}at^2 = 0 + \tfrac{1}{2}(8.00\text{ m/s}^2)(5.00\text{ s})^2 = 100\text{ m}$ or $x = v_{av}t = (20.0\text{ m/s})(5.00\text{ s}) = 100\text{ m}$

**2.4 [II]** A truck's speed increases uniformly from 15 km/h to 60 km/h in 20 s. Determine (*a*) the average speed, (*b*) the acceleration, and (*c*) the distance traveled, all in units of meters and seconds.

For the 20-s trip under discussion, taking $+x$ to be in the direction of motion,

$$\upsilon_{ix} = \left(15\,\frac{\text{km}}{\text{h}}\right)\left(1000\,\frac{\text{m}}{\text{km}}\right)\left(\frac{1}{3600}\,\frac{\text{h}}{\text{s}}\right) = 4.17\ \text{m/s}$$

$$\upsilon_{fx} = 60\ \text{km/h} = 16.7\ \text{m/s}$$

(*a*) $\upsilon_{av} = \frac{1}{2}(\upsilon_{ix} + \upsilon_{fx}) = \frac{1}{2}(4.17 + 16.7)\ \text{m/s} = 10\ \text{m/s}$

(*b*) $a = \dfrac{\upsilon_{fx} - \upsilon_{ix}}{t} = \dfrac{(16.7 - 4.17)\ \text{m/s}}{20\ \text{s}} = 0.63\ \text{m/s}^2$

(*c*) $x = \upsilon_{av}\,t = (10.4\ \text{m/s})(20\ \text{s}) = 208\ \text{m} = 0.21\ \text{km}$

**2.5 [II]** An object's one-dimensional motion along the $x$-axis is graphed in Fig. 2-1. Describe its motion.

The velocity of the object at any instant is equal to the slope of the displacement–time graph at the point corresponding to that instant. Because the slope is zero from exactly $t = 0$ s to $t = 2.0$ s, the object is standing still during this time interval. At $t = 2.0$ s, the object begins to move in the $+x$-direction with constant-velocity (the slope is positive and constant). For the interval $t = 2.0$ s to $t = 4.0$ s,

$$\upsilon_{av} = \text{slope} = \frac{\text{rise}}{\text{run}} = \frac{x_f - x_i}{t_f - t_i} = \frac{3.0\ \text{m} - 0\ \text{m}}{4.0\ \text{s} - 2.0\ \text{s}} = \frac{3.0\ \text{m}}{2.0\ \text{s}} = 1.5\ \text{m/s}$$

The average velocity is then $\vec{\upsilon}_{av} = 1.5$ m/s—POSITIVE *X*-DIRECTION.

During the interval $t = 4.0$ s to $t = 6.0$ s, the object is at rest; the slope of the graph is zero and $x$ does not change for that interval.

From $t = 6.0$ s to $t = 10$ s and beyond, the object is moving in the $-x$-direction; the slope and the velocity are negative. We have

$$\upsilon_{av} = \text{slope} = \frac{x_f - x_i}{t_f - t_i} = \frac{-2.0\ \text{m} - 3.0\ \text{m}}{10.0\ \text{s} - 6.0\ \text{s}} = \frac{-5.0\ \text{m}}{4.0\ \text{s}} = -1.3\ \text{m/s}$$

The average velocity is then $\vec{\upsilon}_{av} = 1.3$ m/s—NEGATIVE *X*-DIRECTION

**2.6 [II]** The vertical motion of an object is graphed in Fig. 2-2. Describe its motion qualitatively, and find, as best you can, its instantaneous velocity at points *A*, *B*, and *C*.

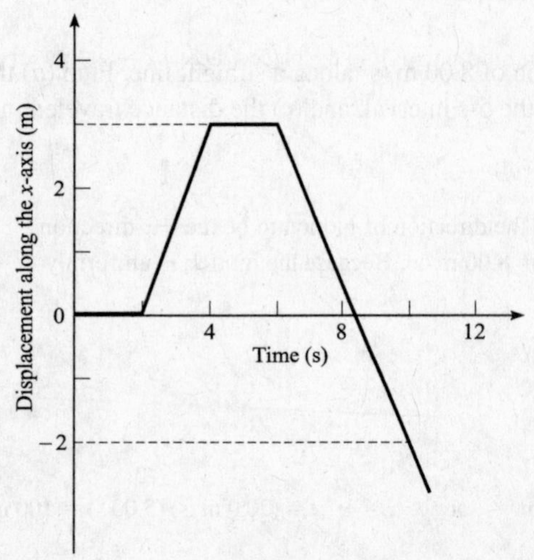

Fig. 2-1

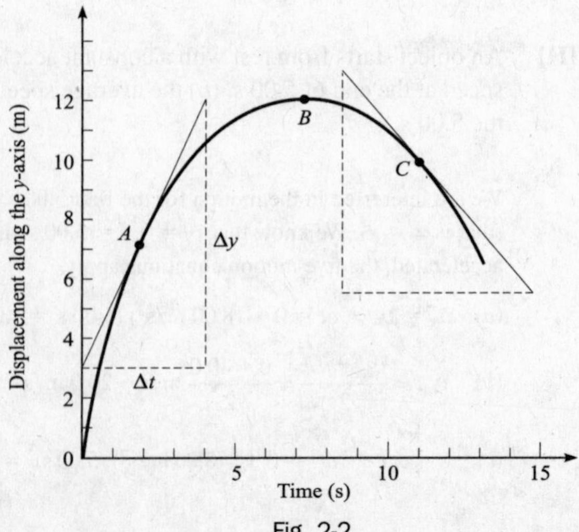

Fig. 2-2

Recalling that the instantaneous velocity is given by the slope of the graph, we see that the object is moving fastest at $t = 0$. As it rises, it slows and finally stops at $B$. (The slope there is zero.) Then it begins to fall back downward at ever-increasing speed.

At point $A$, we have

$$v_A = \text{slope} = \frac{\Delta y}{\Delta t} = \frac{12.0\text{ m} - 3.0\text{ m}}{4.0\text{ s} - 0\text{ s}} = \frac{9.0\text{ m}}{4.0\text{ s}} = 2.3\text{ m/s}$$

The velocity at $A$ is positive, so it is in the $+y$-direction: $\vec{\mathbf{v}}_A = 2.3\text{ m/s}$—UP. At points $B$ and $C$,

$$v_B = \text{slope} = 0\text{ m/s}$$

$$v_C = \text{slope} = \frac{\Delta y}{\Delta t} = \frac{5.5\text{ m} - 13.0\text{ m}}{15.0\text{ s} - 8.5\text{ s}} = \frac{-7.5\text{ m}}{6.5\text{ s}} = -1.2\text{ m/s}$$

Because it is negative, the velocity at $C$ is in the $-y$-direction: $\vec{\mathbf{v}}_C = 1.2\text{ m/s}$—DOWN. Remember that velocity is a vector quantity and direction must be specified explicitly.

**2.7 [II]** A ball is dropped from rest at a height of 50 m above the ground. (*a*) What is its speed just before it hits the ground? (*b*) How long does it take to reach the ground?

If we can ignore air friction, the ball is uniformly accelerated until it reaches the ground. Its acceleration is downward and is $9.81\text{ m/s}^2$. Taking *down* as positive, we have for the trip:

$$y = 50.0\text{ m} \qquad a = 9.81\text{ m/s}^2 \qquad v_i = 0$$

(*a*) $v_{fy}^2 = v_{iy}^2 + 2ay = 0 + 2(9.81\text{ m/s}^2)(50.0\text{m}) = 981\text{ m}^2/\text{s}^2$

and so $v_f = 31.3\text{ m/s}$.

(*b*) From $a\,(v_{fy} - v_{iy})/t$,

$$t = \frac{v_{fy} - v_{iy}}{a} = \frac{(31.3 - 0)\text{ m/s}}{9.81\text{ m/s}^2} = 3.19\text{ s}$$

(We could just as well have taken *up* as positive. How would the calculation have been changed?)

**2.8 [II]** A skier starts from rest and slides down a mountain side along a straight descending path 9.0 m long in 3.0 s. In what time after starting will the skier acquire a speed of 24 m/s? Assume that the acceleration is constant and the entire run is straight and at a fixed incline.

We must find the skier's acceleration from the data concerning the 3.0 s trip. Taking the direction of motion down the inclined path as the $+x$-direction, we have $t = 3.0$ s, $v_{ix} = 0$, and $x = 9.0$ m. Then $x = v_{ix}t + \frac{1}{2}at^2$ gives

$$a = \frac{2x}{t^2} = \frac{18\text{ m}}{(3.0\text{ s})^2} = 2.0\text{ m/s}^2$$

We can now use this value of $a$ for the longer trip, from the starting point to the place where $v_{fx} = 24\text{ m/s}$. For this trip, $v_{ix} = 0$, $v_{fx} = 24\text{ m/s}$, $a = 2.0\text{ m/s}^2$. Then, from $v_f = v_i + at$,

$$t = \frac{v_{fx} - v_{ix}}{a} = \frac{24\text{ m/s}}{2.0\text{ m/s}^2} = 12\text{ s}$$

**2.9 [II]** A bus moving in a straight line at a speed of 20 m/s begins to slow at a constant rate of 3.0 m/s each second. Find how far it goes before stopping.

Take the direction of motion to be the $+x$-direction. For the trip under consideration, $v_i = 20\text{ m/s}$, $v_f = 0\text{ m/s}$, $a = -3.0\text{ m/s}^2$. Notice that the bus is not speeding up in the positive motion direction. Instead, it is slowing in that direction and so its acceleration is negative (a deceleration). Use

$$v_{fx}^2 = v_{ix}^2 + 2ax \qquad \text{and, hence,} \qquad 0 = (20\text{ m/s})^2 + 2(-3.0\text{ m/s}^2)\,x$$

to find

$$x = \frac{-(20\text{ m/s})^2}{2(-3.0\text{ m/s}^2)} = 67\text{ m}$$

**2.10 [II]** A car moving along a straight road at 30 m/s slows uniformly to a speed of 10 m/s in a time of 5.0 s. Determine (*a*) the acceleration of the car and (*b*) the distance it moves during the third second.

Take the direction of motion to be the $+x$-direction.

(*a*) For the 5.0 s interval, we have $t = 5.0$ s, $\upsilon_{ix}$ 30 m/s, $\upsilon_f = 10$ m/s. Using $\upsilon_{fx} = \upsilon_{ix} + at$

$$a = \frac{(10 - 30)\text{ m/s}}{5.0\text{ s}} = -4.0\text{ m/s}^2$$

The distance the car moves during the third second is NOT the distance it moves in the first three seconds. Consequently:

(*b*)
$$x = (\text{Distance covered in 3.0 s}) - (\text{Distance covered in 2.0 s})$$
$$x = \left(\upsilon_{ix}t_3 + \tfrac{1}{2}at_3^2\right) - \left(\upsilon_{ix}t_2 + \tfrac{1}{2}at_2^2\right)$$
$$x = \upsilon_{ix}(t_3 - t_2) + \tfrac{1}{2}a\left(t_3^2 - t_2^2\right)$$

Using $\upsilon_{ix} = 30$ m/s, $a = -4.0$ m/s$^2$, $t_2 = 2.0$ s, and $t_3 = 3.0$ s

$$x = (30\text{ m/s})(1.0\text{ s}) - (2.0\text{ m/s}^2)(5.0\text{ s}^2) = 20\text{ m}$$

This is the distance traveled between the times $t = 20.0$ s and $t = 3.0$ s.

**2.11 [II]** The speed of a train is reduced uniformly from 15 m/s to 7.0 m/s while traveling a distance of 90 m. (*a*) Compute the acceleration. (*b*) How much farther will the train travel before coming to rest, provided the acceleration remains constant?

Take the direction of motion to be the $+x$-direction.

(*a*) We have $\upsilon_{ix} = 15$ m/s, $\upsilon_{fx} = 7.0$ m/s, $x = 90$ m. Then $\upsilon_{fx}^2 = \upsilon_{ix}^2 + 2ax$ gives

$$a = -0.98\text{ m/s}^2$$

(*b*) The new conditions $\upsilon_{ix} = 7.0$ m/s, $\upsilon_f = 0$, and $a = -0.98$ m/s$^2$ now obtain. Then

$$\upsilon_{fx}^2 = \upsilon_{ix}^2 + 2ax$$

leads to
$$x = \frac{0 - (7.0\text{ m/s})^2}{-1.96\text{ m/s}^2} = 25\text{ m}$$

**2.12 [II]** A stone is thrown straight upward and it rises to a maximum height of 20 m. With what speed was it thrown?

Take *up* as the positive *y*-direction. The stone's velocity is zero at the top of its path. Then $\upsilon_{fy} = 0$, $y = 20$ m, $a = -9.81$ m/s$^2$. (The minus sign arises because the acceleration due to gravity is always downward and we have taken *up* to be positive.) Use $\upsilon_{fy}^2 = \upsilon_{iy}^2 + 2ay$ to find

$$\upsilon_{iy} = \sqrt{-2(-9.81\text{ m/s}^2)(20\text{ m})} = 20\text{ m/s}$$

**2.13 [II]** A stone is thrown straight upward with a speed of 20 m/s. It is caught on its way down at a point 5.0 m above where it was thrown. (*a*) How fast was it going when it was caught? (*b*) How long did the trip take?

The situation is shown in Fig. 2-3. Take *up* as positive. Then, for the trip that lasts from the instant after throwing to the instant before catching, $\upsilon_{iy} = 20$ m/s, $y = +5.0$ m (since it is an upward displacement), $a = -9.81$ m/s².

(*a*) Use $\upsilon_{fy}^2 = \upsilon_{iy}^2 + 2ay$ to compute

$$\upsilon_{fy}^2 = (20\ \text{m/s})^2 + 2(-9.81\ \text{m/s}^2)(5.0\ \text{m}) = 302\ \text{m}^2/\text{s}^2$$

$$\upsilon_{fy} = \pm\sqrt{302\ \text{m}^2/\text{s}^2} = -17\ \text{m/s}$$

Take the negative sign because the stone is moving downward, in the negative direction, at the final instant.

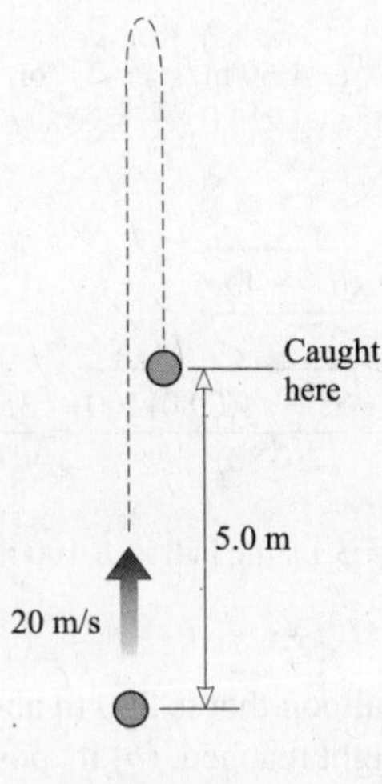


Fig. 2-3

(*b*) To find the time, use $a = (\upsilon_{fy} - \upsilon_{iy})/t$ and so

$$t = \frac{(-17.4 - 20)\ \text{m/s}}{-9.81\ \text{m/s}^2} = 3.8\ \text{s}$$

Notice that we retain the minus sign on $\upsilon_{fy}$.

**2.14 [II]** A ball that is thrown vertically upward on the Moon returns to its starting point in 4.0 s. The acceleration due to gravity there is 1.60 m/s² downward. Find the ball's original speed.

Take *up* as positive. For the trip from beginning to end, $y = 0$ (it ends at the same level it started at), $a = -1.60$ m/s², $t = 4.0$ s. Use $y = \upsilon_{iy}t + \frac{1}{2}at^2$ to find

$$0 = \upsilon_{iy}(4.0\ \text{s}) + \tfrac{1}{2}(-1.60\ \text{m/s}^2)(4.0\ \text{s})^2$$

from which $\upsilon_{iy} = 3.2$ m/s.

**2.15 [III]** A baseball is thrown straight upward on the Moon with an initial speed of 35 m/s. Compute (*a*) the maximum height reached by the ball, (*b*) the time taken to reach that height, (*c*) its velocity 30 s after it is thrown, and (*d*) when the ball's height is 100 m.

Take *up* as positive. At the highest point, the ball's velocity is zero.

(*a*) From $\upsilon_{fy}^2 = \upsilon_{iy}^2 + 2ay$, since $g = 1.60$ m/s² on the Moon,

$$0 = (35\ \text{m/s})^2 + 2(-1.60\ \text{m/s}^2)y \qquad \text{or} \qquad y = 0.38\ \text{km}$$

(*b*) From $v_{fy} = v_{iy} + at$

$$0 = 35\text{ m/s} + (-1.60\text{ m/s}^2)t \qquad \text{or} \qquad t = 22\text{ s}$$

(*c*) From $v_{fy} = v_{iy} + at$

$$v_{fy} = 35\text{ m/s} + (-1.60\text{ m/s}^2)(30\text{ s}) \qquad \text{or} \qquad v_{fy} = -13\text{ m/s}$$

Because $v_f$ is negative and we are taking *up* as positive, the velocity is directed downward. The ball is on its way down at $t = 30$ s.

(*d*) From $y = v_{iy}t + \frac{1}{2}at^2$ we have

$$100\text{ m} = (34\text{ m/s})t + \tfrac{1}{2}(-1.60\text{ m/s}^2)t^2 \qquad \text{or} \qquad 0.80t^2 - 35t + 100 = 0$$

By use of the quadratic formula,

$$x = \frac{-b \pm \sqrt{b^2 - 4ac}}{2a}$$

or

$$t = \frac{35 \pm \sqrt{35^2 - 4(0.80)\,100}}{2(0.80)} = \frac{35 \pm 30.08}{1.60}$$

we find $t = 3.1$ s and 41 s. At $t = 3.1$ s the ball is at 100 m and ascending; at $t = 41$ s it is at the same height but descending.

**2.16 [III]** A ballast bag is dropped from a balloon that is 300 m above the ground and rising at 13 m/s. For the bag, find (*a*) the maximum height reached, (*b*) its position and velocity 5.0 s after it is released, and (*c*) the time at which it hits the ground.

The initial velocity of the bag when released is the same as that of the balloon, 13 m/s upward. Choose *up* as positive and take $y = 0$ at the point of release.

(*a*) At the highest point, $v_f = 0$. From $v_{fy}^2 = v_{iy}^2 + 2ay$,

$$0 = (13\text{ m/s})^2 + 2(-9.81\text{ m/s}^2)y \qquad \text{or} \qquad y = 8.6\text{ m}$$

The maximum height is 300 + 8.6 = 308.6 m or 0.31 km.

(*b*) Take the end point to be its position at $t = 5.0$ s. Then, from $y = v_{iy}t + \frac{1}{2}at^2$,

$$y = (13\text{ m/s})(5.0\text{ s}) + \tfrac{1}{2}(-9.81\text{ m/s}^2)(5.0\text{ s})^2 = -57.6\text{ m or } -58\text{ m}$$

So its height is 300 − 58 = 242 m. Also, from $v_{fy} = v_{iy} + at$,

$$v_{fy} = 13\text{ m/s} + (-9.81\text{ m/s}^2)(5.0\text{ s}) = -36\text{ m/s}$$

It is on its way down with a velocity of 36 m/s—DOWNWARD.

(*c*) Just as it hits the ground, the bag's displacement is −300 m. Then

$$y = v_{iy}t + \tfrac{1}{2}at^2 \qquad \text{becomes} \qquad -300\text{ m} = (13\text{ m/s})t + \tfrac{1}{2}(-9.81\text{ m/s}^2)t^2$$

or $4.905t^2 - 13t - 300 = 0$. The quadratic formula gives $t = 9.3$ s and −6.6 s. Only the positive time has physical meaning, so the required answer is 9.3 s.

We could have avoided the quadratic formula by first computing $v_f$:

$$v_{fy}^2 = v_{iy}^2 + 2as \qquad \text{becomes} \qquad v_{fy}^2 = (13\text{ m/s})^2 + 2(-9.81\text{ m/s}^2)(-300\text{ m})$$

so that $v_{fy} = \pm 77.8$ m/s. Then, using the negative value for $v_{fy}$ (why?) in $v_{fy} = v_{iy} + at$ gives $t = 9.3$ s, as before.

**2.17 [II]** As depicted in Fig. 2-4, a projectile is fired horizontally with a speed of 30 m/s from the top of a cliff 80 m high. (*a*) How long will it take to strike the level ground at the base of the cliff? (*b*) How far from the foot of the cliff will it strike? (*c*) With what velocity will it strike?

(*a*) The horizontal and vertical motions are independent of each other. Consider first the vertical motion. Taking *up* as positive and $y = 0$ at the top of the cliff,

$$y = \upsilon_{iy}t + \tfrac{1}{2}a_y t^2$$

or

$$-80\ \text{m} = 0 + \tfrac{1}{2}(-9.81\ \text{m/s}^2)\,t^2$$

from which $t = 4.04$ s or 4.0 s. Notice that the initial velocity had zero vertical component and so $\upsilon_i = 0$ for the vertical motion.

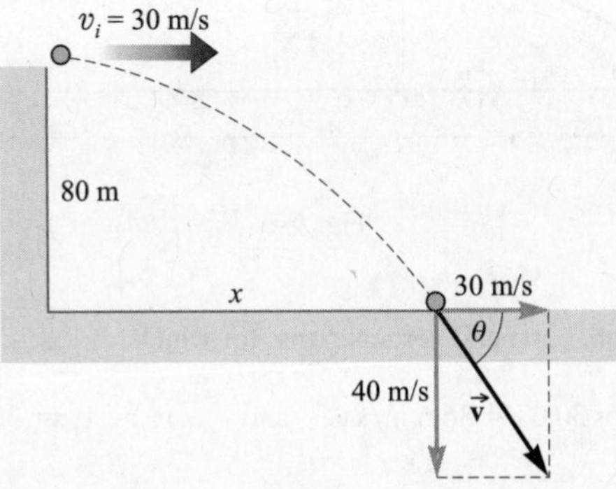


Fig. 2-4

(*b*) Now consider the horizontal motion. For it, $a = 0$ and so $\upsilon_x = \upsilon_{ix} = \upsilon_{fx} = 30$ m/s. Then, using the value of *t* found in (*a*),

$$x = \upsilon_x t = (30\ \text{m/s})\ (4.04\ \text{s}) = 121\ \text{m or } 0.12\ \text{km}$$

(*c*) The final velocity has a horizontal component of 30 m/s. But its vertical component at $t = 4.04$ s is given by $\upsilon_{fy} = \upsilon_{iy} + a_y t$ as

$$\upsilon_{fy} = 0 + (-9.81\ \text{m/s}^2)\ (4.04\ \text{s}) = -39.6\ \text{m/s or } -40\ \text{m/s}$$

The resultant of these two components is labeled $\vec{\mathbf{v}}$ in Fig. 2-4:

$$\upsilon = \sqrt{(39.6\ \text{m/s})^2 + (30\ \text{m/s})^2} = 49.68\ \text{m/s or } 50\ \text{m/s}$$

The angle $\theta$ as shown is given by $\tan\theta = 39.6/30$ and is 52.9° or 53°. Hence, $\vec{\mathbf{v}}$ = 50 m/s—53° BELOW X-AXIS.

**2.18 [I]** A stunt flier is moving at 15 m/s parallel to the flat ground 100 m below, as illustrated in Fig. 2-5. How large must the distance *x* from plane to target be if a sack of flour released from the plane is to strike the target?

Following the same procedure as in Problem 2.17, we use $y = \upsilon_{iy}t + \frac{1}{2}a_y t^2$ to get

$$-100\ \text{m} = 0 + \tfrac{1}{2}(-9.81\ \text{m/s}^2)t^2 \qquad \text{or} \qquad t = 4.52\ \text{s}$$

Now $x = \upsilon_x t = (15\ \text{m/s})\ (4.52\ \text{s}) = 67.8$ m or 68 m.

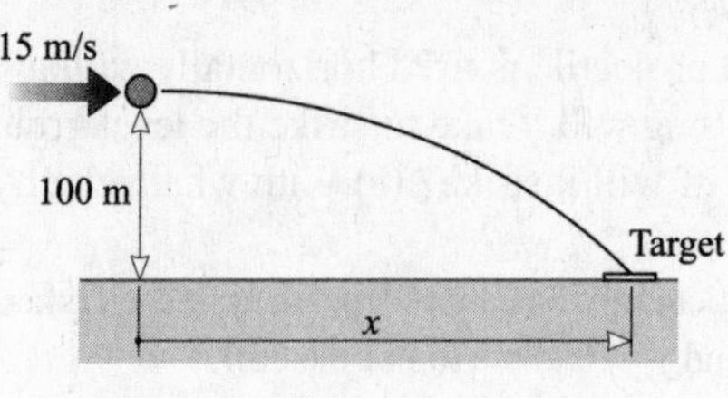


Fig. 2-5

**2.19 [II]** A baseball is thrown with an initial velocity of 100 m/s at an angle of 30.0° above the horizontal, as seen in Fig. 2-6. How far from the throwing point will the baseball attain its original level?

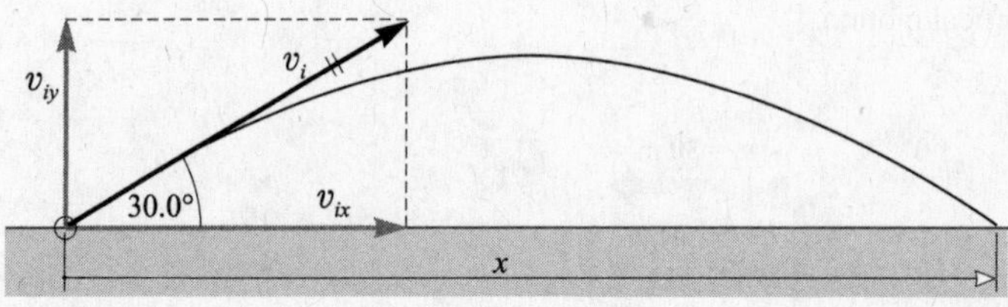


Fig. 2-6

Divide the problem into horizontal and vertical parts, for which

$$v_{ix} = v_i \cos 30.0° = 86.6\ \text{m/s} \qquad \text{and} \qquad v_{iy} = v_i \sin 30.0° = 50.0\ \text{m/s}$$

where *up* is taken as positive.

In the vertical piece of the problem, $y = 0$, since the ball returns to its original height. Then

$$y = v_{iy}t + \tfrac{1}{2}a_y t^2 \qquad \text{or} \qquad 0 = (50.0\ \text{m/s})t + \tfrac{1}{2}(-9.81\ \text{m/s}^2)t^2$$

therefore,

$$-50.0\ \text{m/s} = \tfrac{1}{2}(-9.81\ \text{m/s}^2)t$$

and $t = 10.2$ s.

In the horizontal part of the problem, $v_{ix} = v_{fx} = v_x = 86.6$ m/s. Therefore,

$$x = v_x t = (86.6\ \text{m/s})\ (10.2\ \text{s}) = 883\ \text{m}$$

**2.20 [III]** As drawn in Fig. 2-7, a ball is thrown from the top of one building toward a tall building 50 m away. The initial velocity of the ball is 20 m/s − 40° ABOVE HORIZONTAL. How far above or below its original level will the ball strike the opposite wall?

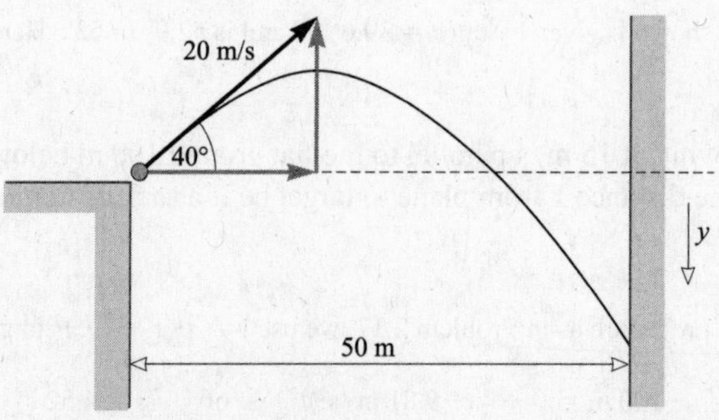


Fig. 2-7

We have

$$v_{ix} = (20 \text{ m/s}) \cos 40° = 15.3 \text{ m/s}$$
$$v_{iy} = (20 \text{ m/s}) \sin 40° = 12.9 \text{ m/s}$$

Consider first the horizontal motion. For it,

$$v_{ix} = v_{fx} = v_x \, 15.3 \text{ m/s}$$

Then $x = v_x t$ gives

$$50 \text{ m} = (15.3 \text{ m/s})t \qquad \text{or} \qquad t = 3.27 \text{ s}$$

For the vertical motion, taking *down* as positive,

$$y = v_{iy}t + \tfrac{1}{2}a_y t^2 = (-12.9 \text{ m/s})(3.27 \text{ s}) + \tfrac{1}{2}(9.81 \text{ m/s}^2)(3.27 \text{ s})^2 = 10.3 \text{ m}$$

and to two significant figures, $y = 10$ m. Since $y$ is positive, and since *down* is positive, the ball will hit at 10 m below the original level.

**2.21 [III]** **(*a*) Find the range $x$ of a gun that fires a shell with muzzle velocity $v$ at an angle of elevation $\theta$. (*b*) Find the angle of elevation $\theta$ of a gun that fires a shell with a muzzle velocity of 120 m/s and hits a target on the same level but 1300 m distant. (See Fig. 2-8.)**

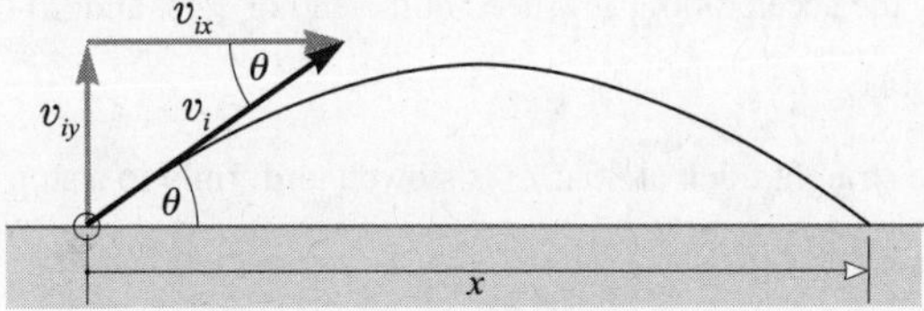


Fig. 2-8

(*a*) Let $t$ be the time it takes the shell to hit the target. Then, $x = v_{ix}t$ or $t = x/v_{ix}$. Consider the vertical motion alone, and take *up* as positive. When the shell strikes the target,

$$\text{Vertical displacement} = 0 = v_{iy}t + \tfrac{1}{2}(-g)t^2$$

Solving this equation gives $t = 2v_{iy}/g$. But $t = x/v_{ix}$, so

$$\frac{x}{v_{ix}} = \frac{2v_{iy}}{g} \qquad \text{or} \qquad x = \frac{2v_{ix}v_{iy}}{g} = \frac{2(v_i \cos\theta)(v_i \sin\theta)}{g}$$

wherein $g$ is positive. The formula $2 \sin\theta \cos\theta = \sin 2\theta$ can be used to simplify this. After substitution,

$$x = \frac{v_i^2 \sin 2\theta}{g}$$

The maximum range corresponds to $\theta = 45°$, since $\sin 2\theta$ has a maximum value of 1 when $2\theta = 90°$ or $\theta = 45°$.

(*b*) From the range equation found in (*a*),

$$\sin 2\theta = \frac{gx}{v_i^2} = \frac{(9.18 \text{ m/s}^2)(1300 \text{ m})}{(120 \text{ m/s})^2} = 0.886$$

Therefore, $2\theta = \arcsin 0.886 = 62°$ and so $\theta = 31°$.

## SUPPLEMENTARY PROBLEMS

**2.22 [I]** For the object whose motion is plotted in Fig. 2-2, find, as best you can, its instantaneous velocity at the following times: (*a*) 1.0 s, (*b*) 4.0 s, and (*c*) 10 s.

**2.23 [I]** A body with initial velocity 8.0 m/s moves along a straight line with constant positive acceleration and travels 640 m in 40 s. For the 40 s interval, find (*a*) the average velocity, (*b*) the final velocity, and (*c*) the acceleration.

**2.24 [I]** A truck starts from rest and moves with a constant acceleration of 5.0 $m/s^2$. Find its speed and the distance traveled after 4.0 s has elapsed.

**2.25 [I]** A box slides down an incline with uniform acceleration. It starts from rest and attains a speed of 2.7 m/s in 3.0 s. Find (*a*) the acceleration and (*b*) the distance moved in the first 6.0 s.

**2.26 [I]** A car is accelerating uniformly as it passes two checkpoints that are 30 m apart. The time taken between checkpoints is 4.0 s, and the car's speed at the first checkpoint is 5.0 m/s. Find the car's acceleration and its speed at the second checkpoint.

**2.27 [I]** An auto's velocity increases uniformly from 6.0 m/s to 20 m/s while covering 70 m in a straight line. Find the acceleration and the time taken.

**2.28 [I]** A plane starts from rest and accelerates uniformly in a straight line along the ground before takeoff. It moves 600 m in 12 s. Find (*a*) the acceleration, (*b*) speed at the end of 12 s, and (*c*) the distance moved during the twelfth second.

**2.29 [I]** A train running along a straight track at 30 m/s is slowed uniformly to a stop in 44 s. Find the acceleration and the stopping distance.

**2.30 [II]** An object moving at 13 m/s slows uniformly at the rate of 2.0 m/s each second for a time of 6.0 s. Determine (*a*) its final speed, (*b*) its average speed during the 6.0 s, and (*c*) the distance moved in the 6.0 s.

**2.31 [I]** A body falls freely from rest. Find (*a*) its acceleration, (*b*) the distance it falls in 3.0 s, (*c*) its speed after falling 70 m, (*d*) the time required to reach a speed of 25 m/s, and (*e*) the time taken to fall 300 m.

**2.32 [I]** A marble dropped from a bridge strikes the water in 5.0 s. Calculate (*a*) the speed with which it strikes and (*b*) the height of the bridge.

**2.33 [II]** A stone is thrown straight downward with initial speed 8.0 m/s from a height of 25 m. Find (*a*) the time it takes to reach the ground and (*b*) the speed with which it strikes.

**2.34 [II]** A baseball is thrown straight upward with a speed of 30 m/s. (*a*) How long will it rise? (*b*) How high will it rise? (*c*) How long after it leaves the hand will it return to the starting point? (*d*) When will its speed be 16 m/s?

**2.35 [II]** A bottle dropped from a balloon reaches the ground in 20 s. Determine the height of the balloon if (*a*) it was at rest in the air and (*b*) it was ascending with a speed of 50 m/s when the bottle was dropped.

**2.36 [II]** Two balls are dropped to the ground from different heights. One is dropped 1.5 s after the other, but they both strike the ground at the same time, 5.0 s after the first was dropped. (*a*) What is the difference in the heights from which they were dropped? (*b*) From what height was the first ball dropped?

**2.37 [II]** A nut comes loose from a bolt on the bottom of an elevator as the elevator is moving up the shaft at 3.00 m/s. The nut strikes the bottom of the shaft in 2.00 s. (*a*) How far from the bottom of the shaft was the elevator when the nut fell off? (*b*) How far above the bottom was the nut 0.25 s after it fell off?

**2.38 [I]** A marble, rolling with speed 20 cm/s, rolls off the edge of a table that is 80 cm high. (*a*) How long does it take to drop to the floor? (*b*) How far, horizontally, from the table edge does the marble strike the floor?

**2.39 [II]** A body projected upward from the level ground at an angle of 50° with the horizontal has an initial speed of 40 m/s. (*a*) How long will it take to hit the ground? (*b*) How far from the starting point will it strike? (*c*) At what angle with the horizontal will it strike?

**2.40 [III]** A body is projected downward at an angle of 30° with the horizontal from the top of a building 170 m high. Its initial speed is 40 m/s. (*a*) How long will it take before striking the ground? (*b*) How far from the foot of the building will it strike? (*c*) At what angle with the horizontal will it strike?

**2.41 [II]** A hose lying on the ground shoots a stream of water upward at an angle of 40° to the horizontal. The speed of the water is 20 m/s as it leaves the hose. How high up will it strike a wall that is a horizontal distance of 8.0 m away?

**2.42 [II]** A World Series batter hits a home run ball with a velocity of 40 m/s at an angle of 26° above the horizontal. A fielder who can reach 3.0 m above the ground is backed up against the bleacher wall, which is 110 m from home plate. The ball was 120 cm above the ground when hit. How high above the fielder's glove does the ball pass?

**2.43 [II]** Prove that a gun will shoot three times as high when its angle of elevation is 60° as when it is 30°, but the bullet will travel the same horizontal distance.

**2.44 [II]** A ball is thrown upward at an angle of 30° to the horizontal and lands on the top edge of a building that is 20 m away. The top edge is 5.0 m above the throwing point. How fast was the ball thrown?

**2.45 [III]** A ball is thrown straight upward with a speed $\upsilon$ from a point $h$ meters above the ground. Show that the time taken for the ball to strike the ground $(\upsilon/g)[1 + \sqrt{1 + (2hg/\upsilon^2)}]$ where $g$ is positive.

## ANSWERS TO SUPPLEMENTARY PROBLEMS

**2.22 [I]** (*a*) $\approx$3.3 m/s in the positive *y*-direction; (*b*) $\approx$1.0 m/s in the positive *y*-direction; (*c*) $\approx$0.83 m/s in the negative *y*-direction

**2.23 [I]** (*a*) 16 m/s; (*b*) 24 m/s; (*c*) 0.40 $m/s^2$

**2.24 [I]** 20 m/s, 40 m

**2.25 [I]** (*a*) 0.90 $m/s^2$; (*b*) 16 m

**2.26 [I]** 1.3 $m/s^2$, 10 m/s

**2.27 [I]** 2.6 $m/s^2$, 5.4 s

**2.28 [I]** (*a*) 8.3 $m/s^2$; (*b*) 0.10 km/s; (*c*) 96 m

**2.29 [I]** $-0.68$ $m/s^2$, 0.66 km or $6.6 \times 10^2$ m

**2.30 [II]** (*a*) 1.0 m/s; (*b*) 7.0 m/s; (*c*) 42 m

**2.31 [I]** (*a*) 9.81 $m/s^2$; (*b*) 44 m; (*c*) 37 m/s; (*d*) 2.6 s; (*e*) 7.8 s

**2.32 [I]** (*a*) 49 m/s; (*b*) 0.12 km or $1.2 \times 10^2$ m

**2.33 [II]** (*a*) 1.6 s; (*b*) 24 m/s

**2.34 [II]** (*a*) 3.1 s; (*b*) 46 m; (*c*) 6.1 s; (*d*) 1.4 s and 4.7 s

**2.35 [II]** 2.0 km; (*b*) 0.96 km

**2.36 [II]** (*a*) 63 m; (*b*) 0.12 km

**2.37 [II]** (*a*) 13.6 m; (*b*)14 m

**2.38 [I]** (*a*) 0.40 s; (*b*) 8.1 cm

**2.39 [II]** (*a*) 6.3 s; (*b*) 0.16 km; (*c*) 50°

**2.40 [III]** (*a*) 4.2 s; (*b*) 0.15 km; (*c*) 60°

**2.41 [II]** 5.4 m

**2.42 [II]** 6.0 m

**2.44 [II]** 20 m/s

# CHAPTER 3

# Newton's Laws

**The Mass** of an object is traditionally defined as a measure of the inertia of the object. **Inertia** is the tendency of a body at rest to remain at rest, and of a body in motion to continue moving with unchanged velocity. For several centuries, physicists found it useful to think of mass as a representation of the amount of or quantity-of-matter, but that idea is (as we have learned from Special Relativity) no longer tenable. The above definition of mass will serve us well, but it too is problematic.

**The Standard Kilogram** is an object whose mass is defined to be 1 kilogram. The masses of other objects are found by comparison with this mass. A *gram mass* is equivalent to exactly 0.001 kg.

**Force,** in general, is the agency of change. In mechanics it is that which changes the velocity of an object. Force is a vector quantity, having magnitude and direction. An **external force** is one whose source lies outside of the system being considered.

**The Net External Force** acting on an object causes the object to accelerate in the direction of that force. The acceleration is proportional to the force and inversely proportional to the mass of the object. (We now know from the Special Theory of Relativity that this statement is actually an excellent approximation applicable to all situations where the speed is appreciably less than the speed of light, c.)

**The Newton** is the SI unit of force. One newton (1 N) is that resultant force which will give a 1-kg mass an acceleration of 1 $\mathrm{m/s^2}$. The *pound* is 4.45 N, or alternatively a newton is about a quarter of a pound.

**Newton's First Law:** ***An object at rest will remain at rest; an object in motion will continue in motion with constant velocity, except insofar as it is acted upon by an external force.*** Force is the changer of motion.

**Newton's Second Law:** As stated by Newton, the Second Law was framed in terms of the concept of momentum. This rigorously correct statement will be treated in Chapter 8. Here we focus on a less fundamental, but highly useful, variation. If the resultant (or net), force $\vec{\mathbf{F}}$ acting on an object of mass $m$ is not zero, the object accelerates in the direction of the force. The acceleration $\vec{\mathbf{a}}$ is proportional to the force and inversely proportional to the mass of the object. With $\vec{\mathbf{F}}$ in newtons, $m$ in kilograms, and $\vec{\mathbf{a}}$ in $\mathrm{m/s^2}$, this can be written as

$$\vec{\mathbf{a}} = \frac{\vec{\mathbf{F}}}{m} \quad \text{or} \quad \vec{\mathbf{F}} = m\vec{\mathbf{a}}$$

The acceleration $\vec{\mathbf{a}}$ has the same direction as the resultant force $\vec{\mathbf{F}}$.

The vector equation $\vec{\mathbf{F}} = m\vec{\mathbf{a}}$ can be written in terms of components as

$$\sum F_x = ma_x \qquad \sum F_y = ma_y \qquad \sum F_z = ma_z$$

where the forces are the components of the net external force acting on the object.

**wton's Third Law:** Matter *interacts* with matter—forces come in pairs. ***For each force exerted on one body, there is an equal, but oppositely directed, force on some other body interacting with it.*** This is often called the *Law of Action and Reaction.* Notice that the action and reaction forces act on the two different interacting objects.

**The Law of Universal Gravitation:** When two masses $m$ and $m'$ gravitationally interact, they attract each other with forces of equal magnitude. For point masses (or spherically symmetric homogeneous bodies), the attractive force $F_G$ is given by

$$F_G = G\frac{mm'}{r^2}$$

where $r$ is the distance between mass centers, and $G = 6.672\,59 \times 10^{-11}\ \text{N}\cdot\text{m}^2/\text{kg}^2$. When $F_G$ is in newtons, $m$ and $m'$ are in kilograms, and $r$ is in meters. This is Newton's law of gravitation, and it's said to be "universal" because it applies to all objects having mass. Although it has been surpassed by Einstein's theory of gravitation, this formula will work remarkably well in all of our applications.

**The Weight** of an object ($F_W$) is the gravitational force acting downward on the object. On the Earth, it is the gravitational force exerted on the object by the planet. Its units are newtons (in the SI) and pounds (in the British system). Because the Earth is not a perfect uniform sphere, and moreover because it's spinning, the weight measured by a scale (often called the *effective weight*) will be very slightly different from that defined above.

**The Acceleration Due to Gravity:** We can distinguish two slightly different forms of the acceleration due to gravity: one symbolized by $g$ includes the effects of the Earth's spin and varies from 9.78 m/s$^2$ at the equator to 9.83 m/s$^2$ at the pole. It has an average surface-of-the-Earth value of 9.81 m/s$^2$. The other is $g_0$, the *absolute acceleration* due only to gravity. It excludes planetary spin and varies on Earth from 9.81 m/s$^2$ at the equator to 9.83 m/s$^2$ at the pole. To make things as simple as possible—because the variations are small—we will take $g = g_0 = 9.81$ m/s$^2$ everywhere at the Earth's surface.

**Relation Between Mass and Weight:** An object of mass $m$ falling freely toward the Earth is subject to only one force: the pull of gravity, which we call the weight $F_W$ of the object. The object's acceleration due to $F_W$ is the free-fall acceleration $g$. Therefore, $\vec{\mathbf{F}} = m\vec{a}$ provides us with the relation between $F = F_W$, $a = g$, and $m$; it is $F_W = mg$. Because, on average, $g = 9.81$ m/s$^2$ on Earth, a 1.00-kg object weighs 9.81 N (or 2.20 lb) at the Earth's surface.

**The Tensile Force** ($\vec{\mathbf{F}}_T$) acting on a string or chain or tendon is the applied force tending to stretch it. The magnitude of the tensile force is the **tension** ($F_T$).

**The Friction Force** ($\vec{\mathbf{F}}_f$) is a tangential force acting on an object that opposes the sliding of that object on an adjacent surface with which it is in contact. The friction force is parallel to the surface and opposite to the direction of motion or of impending motion. Only when the applied force exceeds the maximum static friction force will an object begin to slide.

**The Normal Force** ($\vec{\mathbf{F}}_N$) on an object that is being supported by a surface is the component of the supporting force that is perpendicular to the surface.

**The Coefficient of Kinetic Friction** ($\mu_k$) is defined for the case in which one surface is sliding across another at constant speed. It is

$$\mu_k = \frac{\text{Friction force}}{\text{Normal force}} = \frac{F_f}{F_N}$$

**The Coefficient of Static Friction** ($\mu_s$) is defined for the case in which one surface is just on the verge of sliding across another surface. It is

$$\mu_s = \frac{\text{Maximum friction force}}{\text{Normal force}} = \frac{F_f(\text{max})}{F_N}$$

where the maximum friction force occurs when the object is just on the verge of slipping but is nonetheless at rest. With very few exceptions (e.g., Teflon), $\mu_s > \mu_k$.

## SOLVED PROBLEMS

**3.1 [I]** As an introduction to dealing with force vectors, consider the four coplanar forces acting on a body at point $O$ as shown in Fig. 3-1($a$). Find their resultant graphically.

Starting from $O$, the four vectors are plotted in turn as drawn in Fig. 3-1($b$). Place the tail end of each vector at the tip end of the preceding one. The arrow from $O$ to the tip of the last vector represents the resultant of the vectors.

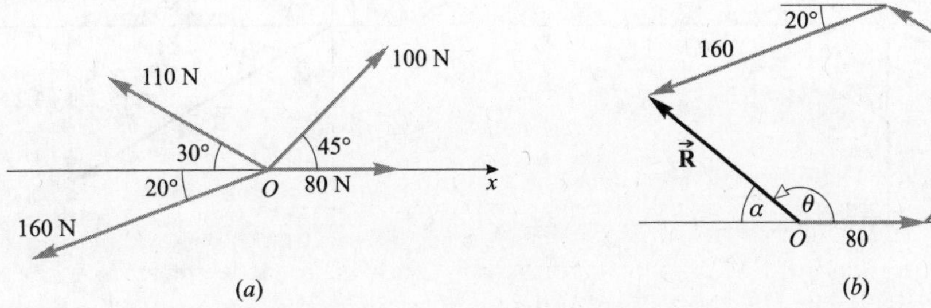


Fig. 3-1

Measure $R$ from the scale drawing in Fig. 3-1($b$) and find it to be 119 N. Angle $\alpha$ is measured by protractor and is found to be 37°. Hence, the resultant makes an angle $\theta = 180° - 37° = 143°$ with the positive $x$-axis. The resultant is 119 N at 143°.

**3.2 [II]** To gain some practice treating force vectors before we get into Newton's Laws, examine the five coplanar forces seen in Fig. 3-2($a$) acting on an object at the origin. Find their resultant analytically.

(1) First we find the $x$- and $y$-components of each force. These components are as follows:

| Force | $x$-Component | $y$-Component |
|---|---|---|
| 19.0 N | 19.0 N | 0 N |
| 15.0 N | (15.0 N) cos 60.0° = 7.50 N | (15.0 N) sin 60.0° = 13.0 N |
| 16.0 N | −(16.0 N) cos 45.0° = −11.3 N | (16.0 N) sin 45.0° = 11.3 N |
| 11.0 N | −(11.0 N) cos 30.0° = −9.53 N | −(11.0 N) sin 30.0° = −5.50 N |
| 22.0 N | 0 N | −22.0 N |

Notice the + and − signs to indicate direction.

(2) The resultant $\vec{\mathbf{R}}$ has components $R_x = \sum F_x$ and $R_y = \sum F_y$, where we read $\sum F_x$ as "the sum of all the $x$-force components." We then have

$$R_x = 19.0\text{ N} + 7.50\text{ N} - 11.3\text{ N} - 9.53\text{ N} + 0\text{ N} = +5.67\text{ N or } +5.7\text{ N}$$
$$R_y = 0\text{ N} + 13.0\text{ N} + 11.3\text{ N} - 5.50\text{ N} - 22.0\text{ N} = -3.2\text{ N}$$

(3) The magnitude of the resultant is

$$R = \sqrt{R_x^2 + R_y^2} = 6.5\text{ N}$$

(4) Finally, sketch the resultant as shown in Fig. 3-2(*b*) and find its angle. We see that

$$\tan\phi = \frac{3.2\ \text{N}}{5.7\ \text{N}} = 0.56$$

from which $\phi = 29°$. Then $\theta = 360° - 29° = 331°$. The resultant is 6.5 N at 331° (or $-29°$) or $\vec{\mathbf{R}} = 6.5$ N—331° FROM + *X*-AXIS.

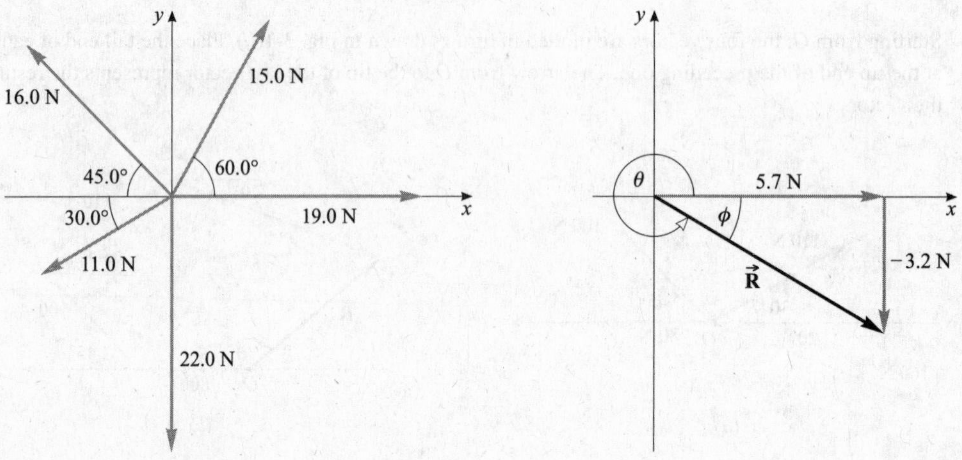


Fig. 3-2

**3.3 [II]** Solve Problem 3.1 by use of the component method. Give your answer for the magnitude to two significant figures.

The forces and their components are as follows:

| Force | *x*-Component | *y*-Component |
|---|---|---|
| 80 N | 80 N | 0 |
| 100 N | (100 N) cos 45° = 70.7 N | (100 N) sin 45° = 70.7 N |
| 110 N | −(110 N) cos 30° = −95.3 N | (110 N) sin 30° = 55.0 N |
| 160 N | −(160 N) cos 20° = −150.4 N | −(160 N) sin 20° = −54.7 N |

Notice the sign of each component. To find the resultant,

$$R_x = \sum F_x = 80\ \text{N} + 70.7\ \text{N} - 95.3\ \text{N} - 150.4\ \text{N} = -95.0\ \text{N}$$
$$R_y = \sum F_y = 0 + 70.7\ \text{N} + 55.0\ \text{N} - 54.7\ \text{N} = 71.0\ \text{N}$$

The resultant is shown in Fig. 3-3; there,

$$R = \sqrt{(95.0\ \text{N})^2 + (71.0\ \text{N})^2} = 118.6\ \text{N or } 119\ \text{N}$$

Further, $\tan\alpha = (71.0\ \text{N})/(95.0\ \text{N})$, from which $\alpha = 37°$. Therefore the resultant is 119 N at $180° - 37° = 143°$ or $\vec{\mathbf{R}} = 119$ N—143° FROM +*X*-AXIS.

**3.4 [II]** A force of 100 N makes an angle of $\theta$ with the *x*-axis and has a scalar *y*-component of 30 N. Find both the scalar *x*-component of the force and the angle $\theta$. (Remember that the number 100 N has three significant figures whereas 30 N has only two.)

Begin your analysis by drawing a diagram. Here the data are sketched roughly in Fig. 3-4. We wish to find $F_x$ and $\theta$. Since

$$\sin\theta = \frac{30\text{ N}}{100\text{ N}} = 0.30$$

$\theta = 17.46°$, and thus, to two significant figures, $\theta = 17°$. Then, using the $\cos\theta$,

$$F_x = (100\text{ N})\cos 17.46° = 95\text{ N}$$

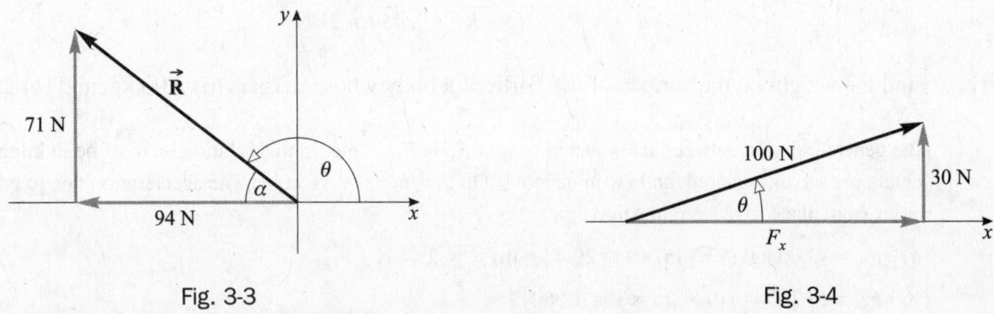


Fig. 3-3 Fig. 3-4

**3.5 [I]** A child pulls on a rope attached to a sled with a force of 60 N. The rope makes an angle of 40° to the ground. (*a*) Compute the effective value of the pull tending to move the sled along the ground. (*b*) Compute the force tending to lift the sled vertically.

As depicted in Fig. 3-5, the components of the 60 N force are 39 N and 46 N. (*a*) The pull along the ground is the horizontal component, 46 N. (*b*) The lifting force is the vertical component, 39 N.

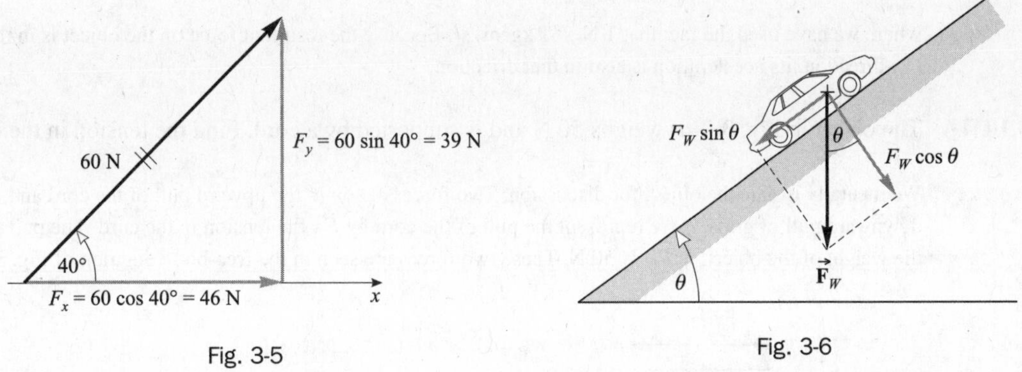


Fig. 3-5 Fig. 3-6

**3.6 [I]** A car whose weight is $F_W$ is on a ramp which makes an angle $\theta$ to the horizontal. How large a perpendicular force must the ramp withstand if it is not to break under the car's weight?

As rendered in Fig. 3-6, the car's weight is a force $\vec{\mathbf{F}}_W$ that pulls straight down on the car. We take components of $\vec{\mathbf{F}}$ along the incline and perpendicular to it. The ramp must balance the force component $F_W\cos\theta$ if the car is not to crash through the ramp. In other words, the force exerted on the car by the ramp, upwardly perpendicular to the ramp, is $F_N$ and $F_N = F_W\cos\theta$.

**3.7 [II]** Three forces that act on a particle are given by $\vec{\mathbf{F}}_1 = (20\hat{\mathbf{i}} - 36\hat{\mathbf{j}} + 73\hat{\mathbf{k}})$ N, $\vec{\mathbf{F}}_2 = (-17\hat{\mathbf{i}} + 21\hat{\mathbf{j}} - 46\hat{\mathbf{k}})$ N, and $\vec{\mathbf{F}}_3 = (-12\hat{\mathbf{k}})$ N. Find their resultant vector. Also find the magnitude of the resultant to two significant figures.

We know that

$$R_x = \sum F_x = 20\text{ N} - 17\text{ N} + 0\text{ N} = 3\text{ N}$$
$$R_y = \sum F_y = -36\text{ N} + 21\text{ N} + 0\text{ N} = -15\text{ N}$$
$$R_z = \sum F_z = 73\text{ N} - 46\text{ N} - 12\text{ N} = 15\text{ N}$$

Since $\vec{\mathbf{R}} = R_x\hat{\mathbf{i}} + R_y\hat{\mathbf{j}} + R_z\hat{\mathbf{k}}$,

$$\vec{\mathbf{R}} = 3\hat{\mathbf{i}} + 15\hat{\mathbf{j}} + 15\hat{\mathbf{k}}$$

To two significant figures, the three-dimensional Pythagorean theorem then gives

$$R = \sqrt{R_x^2 + R_y^2 + R_z^2} = \sqrt{459} = 21\text{ N}$$

**3.8 [I]** Find the weight on the surface of the Earth of a body whose mass is (*a*) 3.00 kg, and (*b*) 200 g.

The general relation between mass $m$ and weight $F_W$ is $F_W = mg$. In this relation, $m$ must be in kilograms, $g$ in meters per second squared, and $F_W$ in newtons. On Earth, $g = 9.81\text{ m/s}^2$. The acceleration due to gravity varies from place to place in the universe.

(*a*) $F_W = (3.00\text{ kg})\,(9.81\text{ m/s}^2) = 29.4\text{ kg·m/s}^2 = 29.4\text{ N}$

(*b*) $F_W = (0.200\text{ kg})\,(9.81\text{ m/s}^2) = 1.96\text{ N}$

**3.9 [I]** A 20.0 kg object that can move freely is subjected to a resultant force of 45.0 N in the $-x$-direction. Find the acceleration of the object.

We make use of the second law in component form, $\sum F_x = ma_x$, with $\sum F_x = -45.0\text{ N}$ and $m = 20.0\text{ kg}$. Then

$$a_x = \frac{\sum F_x}{m} = \frac{-45.0\text{ N}}{20.0\text{ kg}} = -2.25\text{ N/kg} = -2.25\text{ m/s}^2$$

where we have used the fact that $1\text{ N} = 1\text{ kg·m/s}^2$. Because the resultant force on the object is in the $-x$-direction, its acceleration is also in that direction.

**3.10 [I]** The object in Fig. 3-7(*a*) weighs 50 N and is supported by a cord. Find the tension in the cord.

We mentally isolate the object for discussion. Two forces act on it, the upward pull of the cord and the downward pull of gravity. We represent the pull of the cord by $F_T$, the tension in the cord. The pull of gravity, the weight of the object, is $F_W = 50\text{ N}$. These two forces are seen in the free-body diagram of Fig. 3-7(*b*).

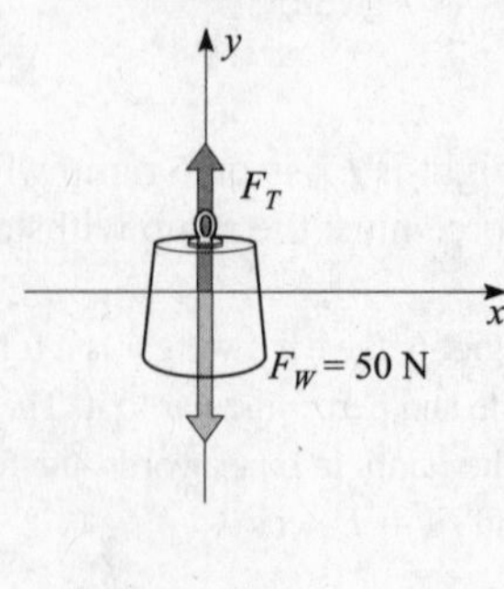


Fig. 3-7

The forces are already in component form and so we can write the first condition for equilibrium at once, taking *up* and to the *right* as positive directions:

$$\overset{+}{\rightarrow}\sum F_x = 0 \qquad \text{becomes} \qquad 0 = 0$$
$$+\uparrow\sum F_y = 0 \qquad \text{becomes} \qquad F_T - 50\text{ N} = 0$$

from which $F_T = 50$ N. Thus, when a single vertical cord (called a *hanger*) supports a body at equilibrium, the tension in the cord equals the weight of the body.

**3.11 [I]** A 5.0-kg object is to be given an upward acceleration of 0.30 m/s² by a rope pulling straight upward on it. What must be the tension in the rope?

The free-body diagram for the object is shown in Fig. 3-8(*b*). The tension in the rope is $F_T$, and the weight of the object is $F_W = mg = (5.0\text{ kg})\,(9.81\text{ m/s}^2) = 49.1$ N. Using $\sum F_y = ma_y$ with *up* taken as positive,

$$+\uparrow\sum F_y = F_T - mg = ma_y \qquad \text{or} \qquad F_T - 49.1\text{ N} = (5.0\text{ kg})(0.30\text{ m/s}^2)$$

from which $F_T = 50.6\text{ N} = 51$ N. As a check, we notice that $F_T$ is larger than $F_W$, as it must be if the object is to accelerate upward.

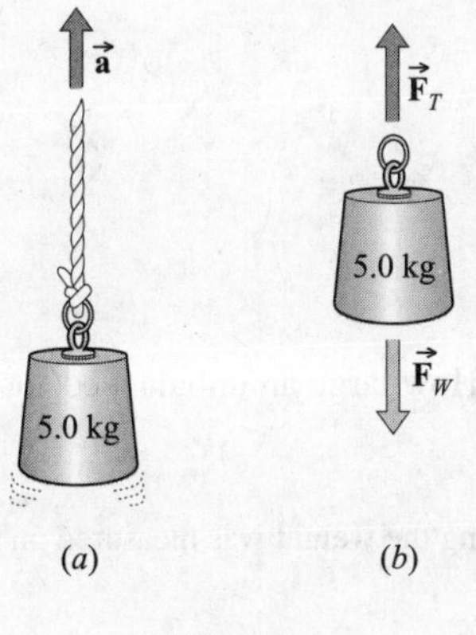


Fig. 3-8

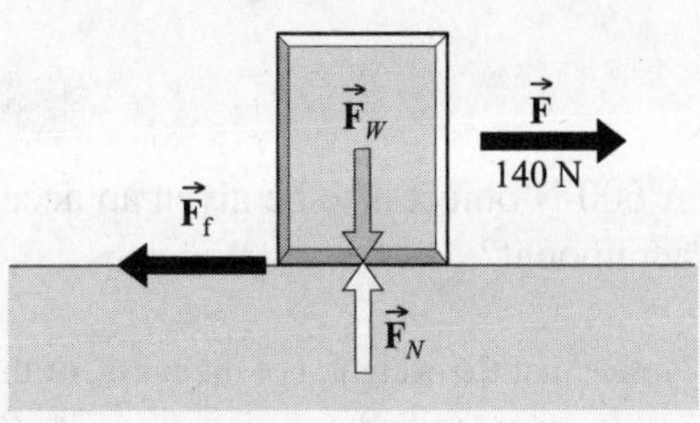


Fig. 3-9

**3.12 [II]** A horizontal force of 140 N is needed to pull a 60.0-kg box across a horizontal floor at constant speed. What is the coefficient of friction between floor and box? Determine it to three significant figures even though that's quite unrealistic.

The free-body diagram for the box is rendered in Fig. 3-9. Because the box does not move up or down, $a_y = 0$. Therefore,

$$+\uparrow\sum F_y = ma_y \qquad \text{yields} \qquad F_N - mg = (m)(0\text{ m/s}^2)$$

from which we find that $F_N = mg = (60.0\text{ kg})\,(9.81\text{ m/s}^2) = 588.6$ N. Further, because the box is moving horizontally at constant speed, $a_x = 0$ and so

$$\overset{+}{\rightarrow}\sum F_x = ma_x \qquad \text{leads to} \qquad 140\text{ N} - F_f = 0$$

from which the friction force is $F_f = 140$ N. Then

$$\mu_k = \frac{F_f}{F_N} = \frac{140\text{ N}}{588.6\text{ N}} = 0.238$$

**3.13 [II]** The only force acting on a 5.0-kg object has components $F_x = 20$ N and $F_y = 30$ N. Find the acceleration of the object.

Use $\sum F_x = ma_x$ and $\sum F_y = ma_y$ to obtain

$$a_x = \frac{\sum F_x}{m} = \frac{20\ \text{N}}{5.0\ \text{kg}} = 4.0\ \text{m/s}^2$$

$$a_y = \frac{\sum F_y}{m} = \frac{30\ \text{N}}{5.0\ \text{kg}} = 6.0\ \text{m/s}^2$$

These components of the acceleration are shown in Fig. 3-10. From the figure,

$$a = \sqrt{(4.0)^2 + (6.0)^2}\ \text{m/s}^2 = 7.2\ \text{m/s}^2$$

and $\theta = \arctan(6.0/4.0) = 56°$.

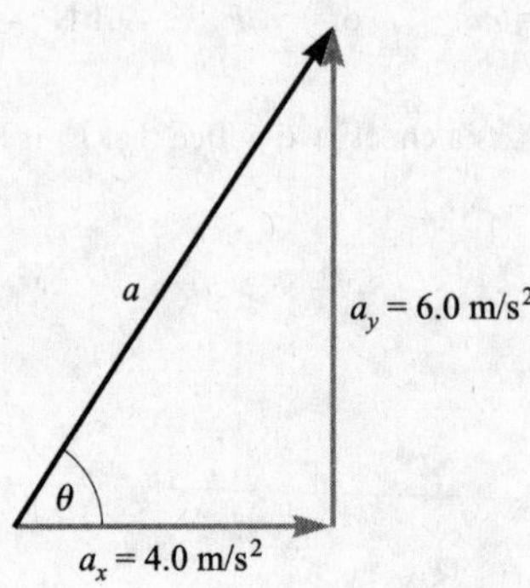


Fig. 3-10

**3.14 [II]** A 600-N object is to be given an acceleration of 0.70 m/s². How large an unbalanced force must act upon it?

Notice that the weight, not the mass, of the object is given. Assuming the weight was measured on the Earth, use $F_W = mg$ to find

$$m = \frac{F_W}{g} = \frac{600\ \text{N}}{9.81\ \text{m/s}^2} = 61.2\ \text{kg}$$

Now that we know the mass of the object (61.2 kg) and the desired acceleration (0.70 m/s²), the force is

$$F = ma = (61.2\ \text{kg})\,(0.70\ \text{m/s}^2) = 42.8\ \text{N or } 43\ \text{N}$$

**3.15 [III]** A constant force acts on a 5.0 kg object and reduces its velocity from 7.0 m/s to 3.0 m/s in a time of 3.0 s. Determine the force.

We must first find the acceleration of the object, which is constant because the force is constant. Taking the direction of motion as positive, from Chapter 2

$$a = \frac{v_f - v_i}{t} = \frac{-4.0\ \text{m/s}}{3.0\ \text{s}} = -1.33\ \text{m/s}^2$$

Use $F = ma$ with $m = 5.0$ kg:

$$F = (5.0\ \text{kg})\,(-1.33\ \text{m/s}^2) = -6.7\ \text{N}$$

The minus sign indicates that the force is a retarding force, directed opposite to the motion.

**3.16 [II]** A 400-g block with an initial speed of 80 cm/s slides along a horizontal tabletop against a friction force of 0.70 N. (*a*) How far will it slide before stopping? (*b*) What is the coefficient of friction between the block and the tabletop?

(*a*) Take the direction of motion as positive. The only unbalanced force acting on the block is the friction force, −0.70 N. Therefore,

$$\sum F = ma \qquad \text{becomes} \qquad -0.70\text{ N} = (0.400\text{ kg})\,(a)$$

from which $a = -1.75\text{ m/s}^2$. (Notice that $m$ is always in kilograms.) To find the distance the block slides, make use of $v_{ix} = 0.80\text{ m/s}$, $v_{fx} = 0$, and $a = -1.75\text{ m/s}^2$. Then $v_{fx}^2 - v_{ix}^2 = 2ax$ yields

$$x = \frac{v_{fx}^2 - v_{ix}^2}{2a} = \frac{(0 - 0.64)\text{ m}^2/\text{s}^2}{(2)\,(-1.75\text{ m/s}^2)} = 0.18\text{ m}$$

(*b*) Because the vertical forces on the block must cancel, the upward push of the table $F_N$ must equal the weight $mg$ of the block. Then

$$\mu_k = \frac{\text{Friction force}}{F_N} = \frac{0.70\text{ N}}{(0.40\text{ kg})\,(9.81\text{ m/s}^2)} = 0.178 \text{ or } 0.18$$

**3.17 [II]** A 600-kg car is coasting along a level road at 30 m/s. (*a*) How large a retarding force (assumed constant) is required to stop it in a distance of 70 m? (*b*) What is the minimum coefficient of friction between tires and roadway if this is to be possible? Assume the wheels are not locked, in which case we are dealing with static friction—there's no sliding.

(*a*) First find the car's acceleration from a constant-$a$ equation. It is known that $v_{ix} = 30\text{ m/s}$, $v_{fx} = 0$, and $x = 70\text{ m}$. Use $v_{fx}^2 = v_{ix}^2 + 2ax$ to find

$$a = \frac{v_{fx}^2 - v_{ix}^2}{2x} = \frac{0 - 900\text{ m}^2/\text{s}^2}{140\text{ m}} = -6.43\text{ m/s}^2$$

Now write

$$F = ma = (600\text{ kg})\,(-6.43\text{ m/s}^2)\; -3858\text{ N or } -3.9\text{ kN}$$

(*b*) Assume the force found in (*a*) is supplied as the friction force between the tires and roadway. Therefore, the magnitude of the friction force on the tires is $F_f = 3858$ N. The coefficient of friction is given by $\mu_s = F_f/F_N$, where $F_N$ is the normal force. In the present case, the roadway pushes up on the car with a force equal to the car's weight. Therefore,

$$F_N = F_W = mg = (600\text{ kg})\,(9.81\text{ m/s}^2) = 5886\text{ N}$$

so that

$$\mu_s = \frac{F_f}{F_N} = \frac{3858}{5886} = 0.66$$

The coefficient of friction must be at least 0.66 if the car is to stop within 70 m.

**3.18 [I]** An 8000-kg engine pulls a 40 000-kg train along a level track and gives it an acceleration $a_1 = 1.20\text{ m/s}^2$. What acceleration ($a_2$) would the engine give to a 16 000-kg train?

For a given engine force, the acceleration is inversely proportional to the total mass. Thus,

$$a_2 = \frac{m_1}{m_2}a_1 = \frac{8000\text{ kg} + 40\,000\text{ kg}}{8000\text{ kg} + 16\,000\text{ kg}}(1.20\text{ m/s}^2) = 2.40\text{ m/s}^2$$

**3.19 [I]** As shown in Fig. 3-11(*a*), an object of mass $m$ is supported by a cord. Find the tension in the cord if the object is (*a*) at rest, (*b*) moving at constant velocity, (*c*) accelerating upward with acceleration $a = 3g/2$, and (*d*) accelerating downward at $a = 0.75g$.

Two forces act on the object: the tension $F_T$ upward and the downward pull of gravity $mg$. They are shown in the free-body diagram in Fig. 3-11(*b*). As a rule begin your analysis with a diagram. Take *up* as the positive direction and write $+\uparrow\sum F_y = ma_y$ in each case.

(*a*) $a_y = 0$: $\quad F_T - mg = ma_y = 0 \quad$ or $\quad F_T = mg$

(*b*) $a_y = 0$: $\quad F_T - mg = ma_y = 0 \quad$ or $\quad F_T = mg$

(*c*) $a_y = 3g/2$: $\quad F_T - mg = m(3g/2) \quad$ or $\quad F_T = 2.5mg$

(*d*) $a_y = -3g/4$: $\quad F_T - mg = m(-3g/4) \quad$ or $\quad F_T = 0.25mg$

Notice that the tension in the cord is less than $mg$ in part (*d*); only then can the object have a downward acceleration. Can you explain why $F_T = 0$ if $a_y = -g$?

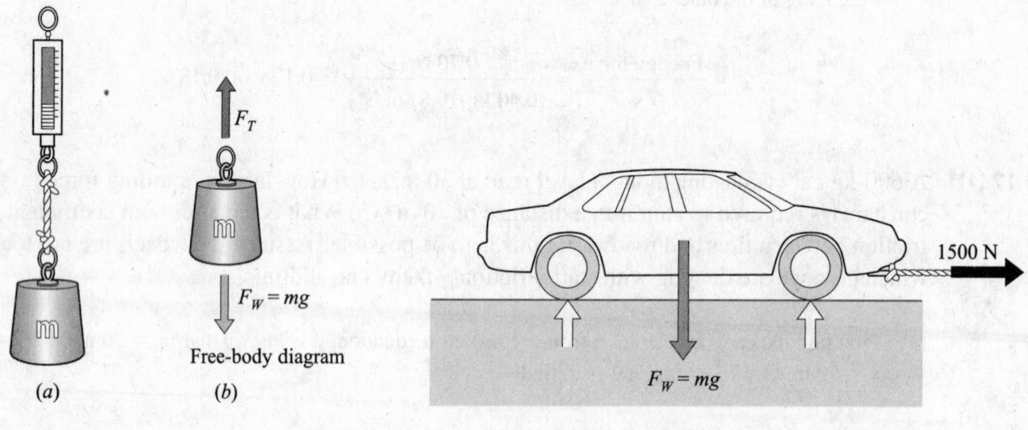


Fig. 3-11

Fig. 3-12

**3.20 [I]** A tow rope will break if the tension in it exceeds 1500 N. It is used to tow a 700-kg car along level ground. What is the largest acceleration the rope can give to the car? (Remember that 1500 has four significant figures; see Appendix A.)

The forces acting on the car are shown in Fig. 3-12. Only the $x$-directed force is of importance, because the $y$-directed forces balance each other. Indicating the positive direction with a + sign and a little arrow, we write,

$$\overset{+}{\rightarrow}\sum F_x = ma_x \quad \text{becomes} \quad 1500\text{ N} = (700\text{ kg})(a)$$

from which $a = 2.14\text{ m/s}^2$.

**3.21 [I]** Compute the least acceleration with which a 45-kg woman can slide down a rope if the rope can withstand a tension of only 300 N.

The weight of the woman is $mg = (45\text{ kg})(9.81\text{ m/s}^2) = 441\text{ N}$. Because the rope can support only 300 N, the unbalanced downward force $F$ on the woman (i.e., the accelerating force) must be at least $441\text{ N} - 300\text{ N} = 141\text{ N}$. Her minimum downward acceleration is then

$$a = \frac{F}{m} = \frac{141\text{ N}}{45\text{ kg}} = 3.1\text{ m/s}^2$$

**3.22 [II]** A 70-kg box is slid along the floor by a 400-N force as shown in Fig. 3-13. The coefficient of friction between the box and the floor is 0.50 when the box is sliding. Find the acceleration of the box.

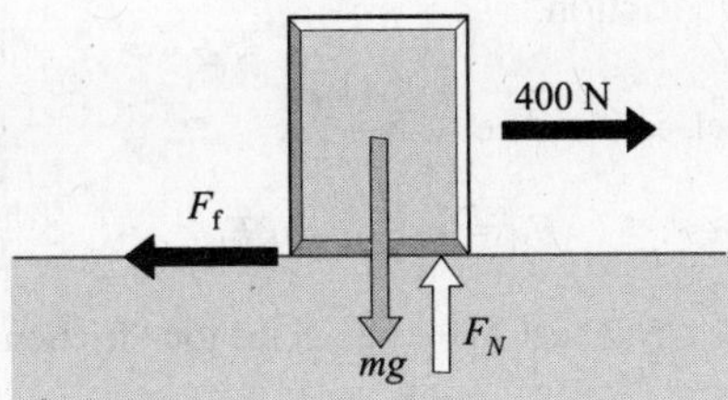


Fig. 3-13

Since the $y$-directed forces must balance,

$$F_N = mg = (70\text{ kg})\,(9.81\text{ m/s}^2) = 686.7\text{ N}$$

But the friction force $F_f$ is given by

$$F_f = \mu_k F_N = (0.50)(687\text{ N}) = 343.4\text{ N}$$

Now write $\sum F_x = ma_x$ for the box, taking the direction of motion as positive:

$$\overset{+}{\rightarrow}\sum F_x = 400\text{ N} - 343.4\text{ N} = (70\text{ kg})\,(a) \qquad \text{or} \qquad a = 0.81\text{ m/s}^2$$

**3.23 [II]** Suppose, as depicted in Fig. 3-14, that a 70-kg box is pulled by a 400-N force at an angle of 30° to the horizontal. The coefficient of kinetic friction is 0.50. Find the acceleration of the box.

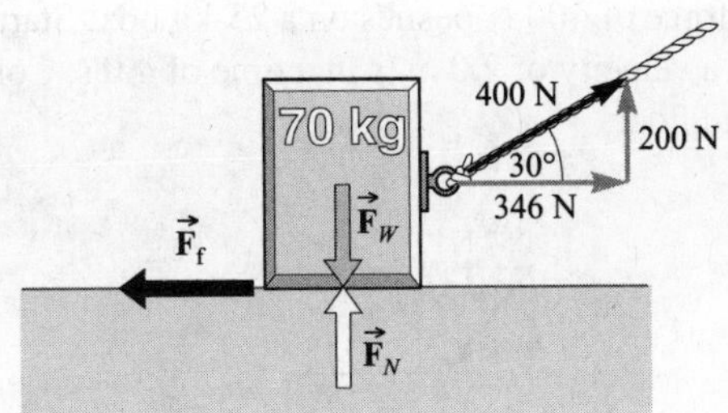


Fig. 3-14

Because the box does not move up or down, we have $\sum F_y = ma_y = 0$. From Fig. 3-14, this equation is

$$+\uparrow\sum F_y = F_N + 200\text{ N} - mg = 0$$

But $mg = (70\text{ kg})\,(9.81\text{ m/s}^2) = 686.7\text{ N}$, and it follows that $F_N = 486.7\text{ N}$.

Next find the friction force acting on the box:

$$F_f = \mu_k F_N = (0.50)(486.7\text{ N}) = 243.4\text{ N}$$

Now write $\sum F_x = ma_x$ for the box. It is

$$(346 - 243.4)\text{ N} = (70\text{ kg})\,(a_x)$$

from which $a_x = 1.466\text{ m/s}^2$ or $1.5\text{ m/s}^2$.

**3.24 [III]** A car coasting at 20 m/s along a horizontal road has its brakes suddenly applied and eventually comes to rest. What is the shortest distance in which it can be stopped if the friction coefficient between tires and road is 0.90? Assume that all four wheels brake identically. If the brakes don't lock, the car stops via static friction.

The friction force at one wheel, call it wheel 1, is

$$F_{f1} = \mu_s F_{N1} = \mu_s F_{W1}$$

where $F_{W1}$ is the weight carried by wheel 1. We obtain the total friction force $F_f$ by adding such terms for all four wheels:

$$F_f = \mu_s F_{W1} + \mu_s F_{W2} + \mu_s F_{W3} + \mu_s F_{W4} = \mu_s(F_{W1} + F_{W2} + F_{W3} + F_{W4}) = \mu_s F_W$$

where $F_W$ is the total weight of the car. (Notice that we are assuming optimal braking at each wheel.) This friction force is the only unbalanced force on the car (we neglect air friction). Writing $F = ma$ for the car with $F$ replaced by $-\mu_s F_W$ gives $-\mu_s F_W = ma$, where $m$ is the car's mass and the positive direction is taken as the direction of motion. However, $F_W = mg$; so the car's acceleration is

$$a = -\frac{\mu_s F_W}{m} = -\frac{\mu_s mg}{m} = -\mu_s g = (-0.90)(9.81\text{ m/s}^2) = -8.829\text{ m/s}^2$$

We can determine how far the car went before stopping by solving the constant-$a$ motion problem. Knowing that $v_i = 20$ m/s, $v_f = 0$, and $a = -8.829$ m/s$^2$, we find from $v_f^2 - v_i^2 = 2ax$ that

$$x = \frac{(0-400)\text{ m}^2/\text{s}^2}{-17.66\text{ m/s}^2} = 22.65\text{ m} \quad \text{or} \quad 23\text{ m}$$

If the four wheels had not all been braking optimally, the stopping distance would have been longer.

**3.25 [II]** As seen in Fig. 3-15, a force of 400 N pushes on a 25-kg box. Starting from rest, the box uniformly speeds up and achieves a velocity of 2.0 m/s in a time of 4.0 s. Compute the coefficient of kinetic friction between box and floor.

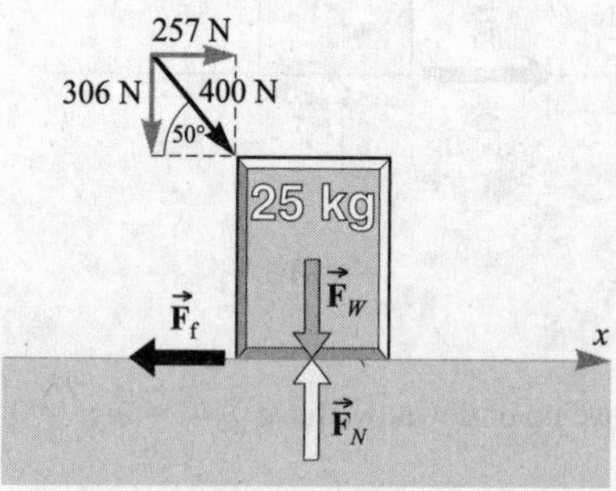


Fig. 3-15

The box experiences an unbalanced horizontal force which is the $x$-component of the applied force minus the friction force. This resultant force, $\pm\sum F_x$, accelerates the box horizontally in the $+x$-direction. We can find $a$ from the uniformly accelerated motion and, with that and Newton's Second Law, determine $\sum F_x$.

To determine $a$, make use of the fact that $v_i = 0$, $v_f = 2.0$ m/s, $t = 4.0$ s, and $v_f = v_i + at$. From which it follows that

$$a = \frac{v_f - v_i}{t} = \frac{2.0\text{ m/s}}{4.0\text{ s}} = 0.50\text{ m/s}^2$$

and so $a_x = a = 0.50\ \text{m/s}^2$. From Fig. 3-15,

$$\overset{+}{\rightarrow}\sum F_x = 257\ \text{N} - F_f = (25\ \text{kg})(0.50\ \text{m/s}^2) \qquad \text{or} \qquad F_f = 245\ \text{N}$$

To find the coefficient of friction, recall that $\mu_k = F_f/F_N$. We need $F_N$, which can be obtained from $+\uparrow\sum F_y = ma_y = 0$, since no vertical motion occurs. From Fig. 3-15,

$$+\uparrow\sum F_y = F_N - 306\ \text{N} - (25)(9.81)\ \text{N} = 0 \qquad \text{or} \qquad F_N = 551\ \text{N}$$

Finally,

$$\mu_k = \frac{F_f}{F_N} = \frac{245}{551} = 0.44$$

**3.26 [I]** A 200-N wagon is to be pulled up a 30° incline at constant speed. How large a force parallel to the incline is needed if friction effects are negligible?

The situation is shown in Fig. 3-16(*a*). Because the wagon moves at a constant speed along a straight line, its velocity vector is constant. Therefore, the wagon is in translational equilibrium, and the first condition for equilibrium applies to it.

We isolate the wagon as the object. Three non-negligible forces act on it: (1) the pull of gravity $F_W$ (its weight), directed straight down; (2) the applied force $F$ exerted on the wagon parallel to the incline to pull it up the incline; (3) the push $F_N$ of the incline that supports the wagon. These three forces are shown in the free-body diagram in Fig. 3-16.

For situations involving inclines, it is convenient to take the *x*-axis parallel to the incline and the *y*-axis perpendicular to it. After taking components along these axes, we can write the first condition for equilibrium:

$$\overset{+}{\nearrow}\sum F_x = 0 \quad \text{becomes} \quad F - 0.50\ F_W = 0$$

$$\overset{\nwarrow}{+}\sum F_y = 0 \quad \text{becomes} \quad F_N - 0.866\ F_W = 0$$

Solving the first equation and recalling that $F_W = 200$ N, we find that $F = 0.50\ F_W$. The required pulling force to two significant figures is 0.10 kN.

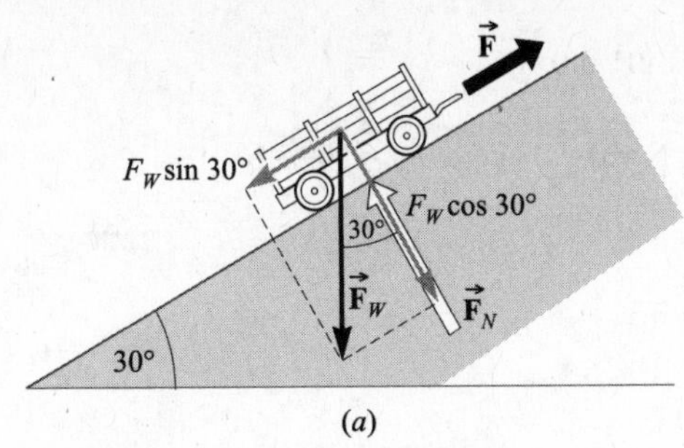


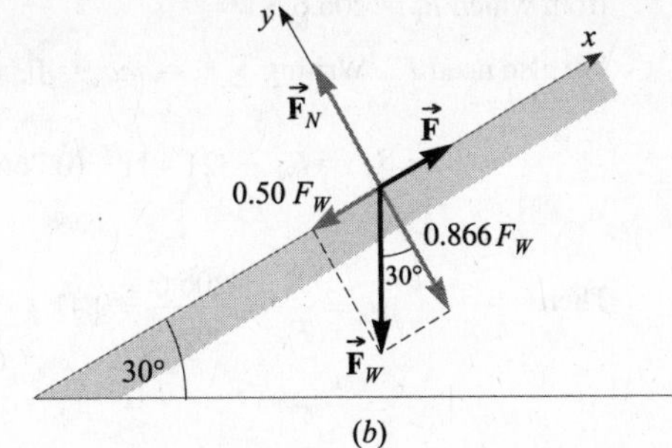


Fig. 3-16

**3.27 [II]** A 20-kg box sits on an incline as illustrated in Fig. 3-17. The coefficient of kinetic friction between box and incline is 0.30. Find the acceleration of the box down the incline.

In solving inclined-plane problems, take the *x*- and *y*-axes as shown in the figure, parallel and perpendicular to the incline. We find the acceleration by writing $\sum F_x = ma_x$. But first determine the friction force $F_f$. Using the fact that $\cos 30° = 0.866$,

$$\overset{\nwarrow}{+}\sum F_y = ma_y = 0 \quad \text{gives} \quad F_N - 0.866\ mg = 0$$

from which $F_N = (0.866)\,(20\text{ kg})\,(9.81\text{ m/s}^2) = 169.9\text{ N}$. Now find $F_f$ from

$$F_f = \mu_k F_N = (0.30)\,(169.9\text{ N}) = 50.97\text{ N}$$

Writing $+\nearrow \sum F_x = ma_x$,

$$F_f - 0.50mg = ma_x \qquad \text{or} \qquad 50.97\text{ N} - (0.50)\,(20)\,(9.81)\text{ N} = (20\text{ kg})\,(a_x)$$

from which $a_x = -2.36\text{ m/s}^2$. The box accelerates down the incline at $2.4\text{ m/s}^2$.

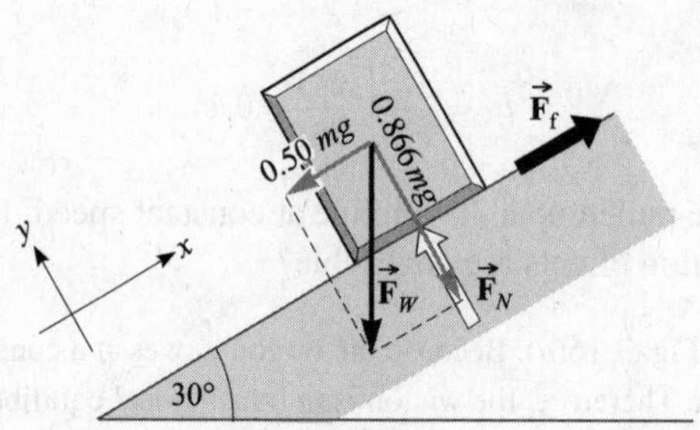


Fig. 3-17

**3.28 [III]** When a force of 500 N pushes on a 25-kg box as shown in Fig. 3-18, the resulting acceleration of the box up the incline is $0.75\text{ m/s}^2$. Compute the coefficient of kinetic friction between the box and the incline.

The acting forces and their components are shown in Fig. 3-18. Notice how the $x$- and $y$-axes are taken. Since the box moves up the incline, the friction force (which always acts to retard the motion) is directed down the incline.

First find $F_f$ by writing $\sum F_x = ma_x$. From Fig. 3-18, using $\sin 40° = 0.643$,

$$+\nearrow \sum F_x = 383\text{ N} - F_f - (0.643)\,(25)\,(9.81)\text{ N} = (25\text{ kg})\,(0.75\text{ m/s}^2)$$

from which $F_f = 206.6$ N.

We also need $F_N$. Writing $\sum F_y = ma_y = 0$, and using $\cos 40° = 0.766$,

$$+\nwarrow \sum F_y = F_N - 321.4\text{ N} - (0.766)\,(25)\,(9.81)\text{ N} = 0 \qquad \text{or} \qquad F_N = 509.3\text{ N}$$

Then $$\mu_k = \frac{F_f}{F_N} = \frac{206.6}{509.3} = 0.41$$

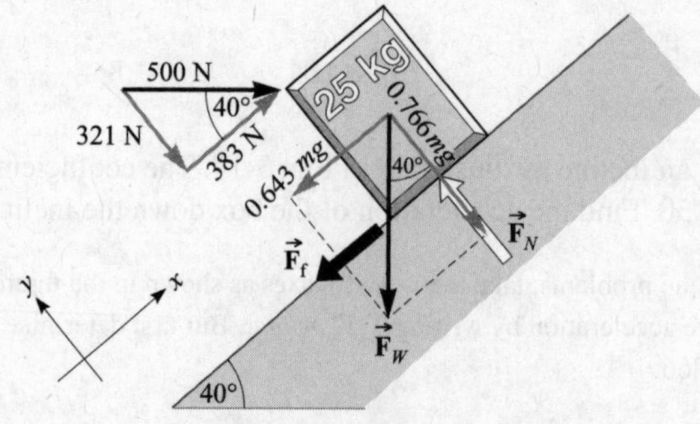


Fig. 3-18

**3.29 [III]** Two blocks, of masses $m_1$ and $m_2$, moving in the $x$-direction are pushed by a force $F$ as shown in Fig. 3-19. The coefficient of friction between each block and the table is 0.40. (*a*) What must be the value of $F$ if the blocks are to have an acceleration of 200 cm/s²? How large a force does $m_1$ then exert on $m_2$? Use $m_1 = 300$ g and $m_2 = 500$ g. Remember to work in SI units.

The friction forces on the blocks are $F_{f1} = 0.40 m_1 g$ and $F_{f2} = 0.40 m_2 g$. Take the two blocks in combination as the object for discussion; the horizontal forces on the object from outside (i.e., the *external* forces on it) are $F$, $F_{f1}$, and $F_{f2}$. Although the two blocks do push on each other, those pushes are *internal* forces; they are not part of the unbalanced external force on the two-mass object. For that object,

$$\overset{+}{\rightarrow}\sum F_x = ma_x \text{ becomes } F - F_{f1} - F_{f2} = (m_1 + m_2)a_x$$

(*a*) Solving for $F$ and substituting known values

$$F = 0.40\, g(m_1 + m_2) + (m_1 + m_2)a_x = 3.14 \text{ N} + 1.60 \text{ N} = 4.7 \text{ N}$$

(*b*) Now consider block $m_2$ alone. The forces acting on it in the $x$-direction are the push of block $m_1$ on it (which we represent by $F_b$) and the retarding friction force $F_{f2} = 0.40 m_2 g$. Then, for it,

$$\overset{+}{\rightarrow}\sum F_x = ma_x \qquad \text{becomes} \qquad F_b - F_{f2} = m_2 a_x$$

We know that $a_x = 2.0$ m/s² and so

$$F_b = F_{f2} + m_2 a_x = 1.96 \text{ N} + 1.00 \text{ N} = 2.96 \text{ N} = 3.0 \text{ N}$$

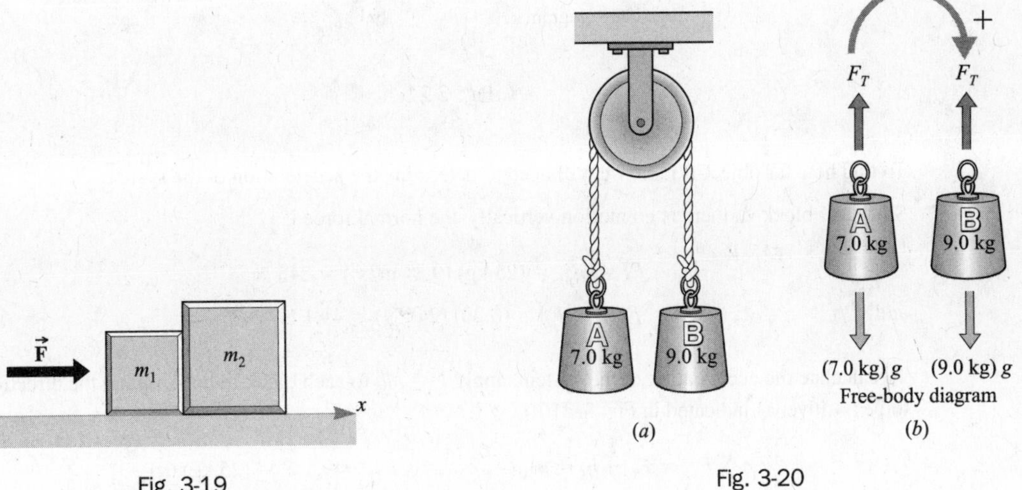

Fig. 3-19

Fig. 3-20

**3.30 [II]** A cord passing over a light frictionless pulley has a 7.0-kg mass hanging from one end and a 9.0-kg mass hanging from the other, as seen in Fig. 3-20. (This arrangement is called *Atwood's machine*.) Find the acceleration of the masses and the tension in the cord.

Because the pulley is easily turned, the tension in the cord will be the same on each side. The forces acting on each of the two masses are drawn in Fig. 3-20. Recall that the weight of an object is $mg$.

It is convenient in situations involving objects connected by cords to take the overall direction of motion of the system as the positive direction. That's often indicated by the direction of motion of the pulley when the system is let free to move. In the present case, the pulley would turn clockwise, and so we take *up* positive for the 7.0-kg mass, and *down* positive for the 9.0-kg mass. (If we do this, the acceleration will be positive for each mass. Because the cord doesn't stretch, the accelerations are numerically equal.) Writing $\sum F_y = ma_y$ for each mass in turn,

$$+\uparrow\sum F_{yA} = F_T - (7.0)(9.81)\text{ N} = (7.0\text{ kg})(a) \quad \text{and} \quad +\downarrow\sum F_{yB} = (9.0)(9.81)\text{ N} - F_T = (9.0\text{ kg})(a)$$

Add these two equations and the unknown $F_T$ drops out, giving

$$(9.0 - 7.0)\,(9.81)\text{ N} = (16\text{ kg})\,(a)$$

for which $a = 1.23\text{ m/s}^2$ or $1.2\text{ m/s}^2$. Now substitute $1.23\text{ m/s}^2$ for $a$ in either equation and obtain $F_T = 77$ N.

**3.31 [III]** In Fig. 3-21, the coefficient of kinetic friction between block-$A$ and the table is 0.20. Also, $m_A = 25$ kg, and $m_B = 15$ kg. How far will object-$B$ drop in the first 3.0 s after the system is released?

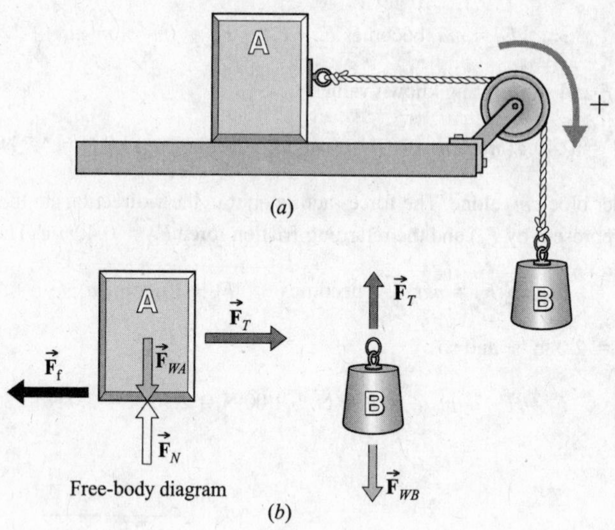


Fig. 3-21

To find how far object-$B$ falls, we will need to determine the acceleration of the system.

Since, for block-$A$, there is no motion vertically, the normal force is

$$F_N = m_A g = (25\text{ kg})\,(9.81\text{ m/s}^2) = 245\text{ N}$$

and

$$F_f = \mu_k F_N = (0.20)\,(245\text{ N}) = 49.1\text{ N}$$

To calculate the acceleration of the system, apply $F = ma$ to each block in turn. Taking the direction of motion to be positive, as indicated in Fig. 3-21($a$),

$$\overset{+}{\rightarrow}\sum F_{xA} = F_T - F_f = m_A a \qquad \text{or} \qquad F_T - 49.1\text{ N} = (25\text{ kg})\,(a)$$

and

$$+\!\downarrow\sum F_{yB} = m_B g - F_T = m_B a \qquad \text{or} \qquad -F_T + (15)\,(9.81)\text{ N} = (15\text{ kg})\,(a)$$

Eliminate $F_T$ by adding the two equations. Then, solving for $a$, we find $a = 2.45\text{ m/s}^2$. We now have to deal with a constant-acceleration motion problem where $a = 2.45\text{ m/s}^2$, $v_i = 0$, and $t = 3.0$ s. Hence,

$$y = v_{iy}t + \frac{1}{2}at^2,\text{ which leads to } y = 0 + \frac{1}{2}(2.45\text{ m/s}^2)\,(3.0\text{ s})^2 = 11\text{ m}$$

This is the distance $B$ falls in the first 3.0 s.

**3.32 [II]** How large a horizontal force in addition to $F_T$ must pull on block-$A$ in Fig. 3-21 to give it an acceleration of $0.75\text{ m/s}^2$ *toward the left*? Assume, as in Problem 3.31, that $\mu_k = 0.20$, $m_A = 25$ kg, and $m_B = 15$ kg.

Redraw Fig 3-21 for this case, including a force $F$ pulling toward the left on $A$. In addition, the retarding friction force $F_f$ must be reversed in direction. As in Problem 3.31, $F_f = 49.1$ N.

Write $F = ma$ for each block in turn, taking the direction of motion (to the left and up) to be positive. We have

$$\pm\sum F_{xA} = F - F_T - 49.1\ \text{N} = (25\ \text{kg})\ (0.75\ \text{m/s}^2) \text{ and } +\uparrow\sum F_{yB} = F_T - (15)\ (9.81)\ \text{N}$$
$$= (15\ \text{kg})\ (0.75\ \text{m/s}^2)$$

Solve the last equation for $F_T$ and substitute in the previous equation. Then solve for the single unknown $F$, and find it to be 226 N or 0.23 kN.

**3.33 [II]** **The coefficient of static friction between a box and the flat bed of a truck is 0.60. What is the maximum acceleration the truck can have along level ground if the box is not to slide?**

The box experiences only one $x$-directed force, the friction force. When the box is on the verge of slipping, $F_f = \mu_s F_W$, where $F_W$ is the weight of the box.

As the truck accelerates, the friction force must cause the box to have the same acceleration as the truck; otherwise, the box will slip. When the box is not slipping, $\sum F_x = ma_x$ applied to the box gives $F_f = ma_x$. However, if the box is on the verge of slipping, $F_f = \mu_s F_W$ so that $\mu_s F_W = ma_x$. Because $F_W = mg$,

$$a_x = \frac{\mu_s mg}{m} = \mu_s g = (0.60)\ (9.81\ \text{m/s}^2) = 5.9\ \text{m/s}^2$$

as the maximum acceleration without slipping.

**3.34 [III]** **In Fig. 3-22, the two boxes have identical masses of 40 kg. Both experience a sliding friction force with $\mu_k = 0.15$. Find the acceleration of the boxes and the tension in the tie cord.**

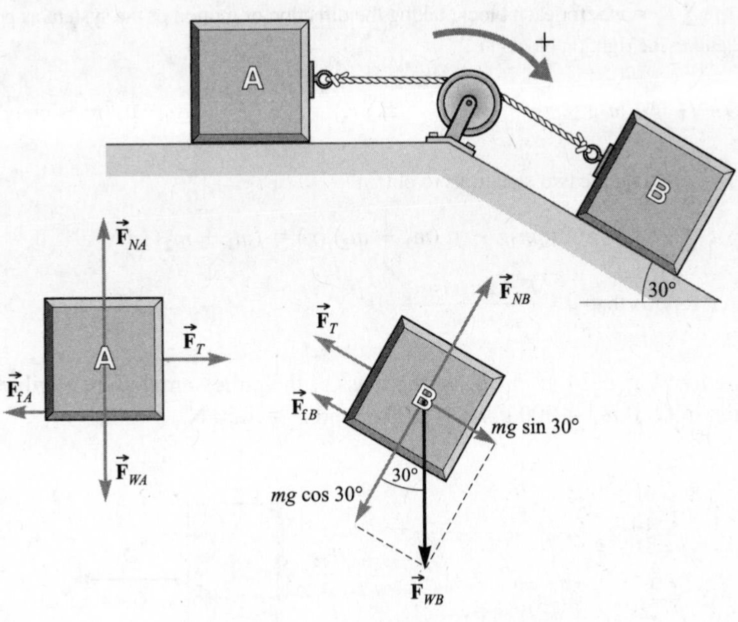


Fig. 3-22

Using $F_f = \mu_k F_N$, the friction forces on the two boxes are

$$F_{fA} = (0.15)\ (mg) \qquad \text{and} \qquad F_{fB} = (0.15)\ (0.866\ mg)$$

But $m = 40$ kg, so $F_{fA} = 58.9$ N and $F_{fB} = 51.0$ N.

Now apply $\sum F_x = ma_x$ to each block in turn, taking the direction of motion of the system as positive. We want to sum the forces parallel to each surface, and that's often indicated using a subscript $\parallel$ symbol. Accordingly

$$\pm\sum F_{\parallel A} = F_T - 58.9\text{ N} = (40\text{ kg})(a) \quad \text{and} \quad \pm\sum F_{\parallel B} = 0.5mg - F_T - 51\text{ N} = (40\text{ kg})(a)$$

Solving these two equations for $a$ and $F_T$ gives $a = 1.1\text{ m/s}^2$ and $F_T = 0.10\text{ kN}$.

**3.35 [III]** In the system shown in Fig. 3-23(*a*), force $F$ accelerates block-1 of mass $m_1$ to the right. Write an expression for its acceleration in terms of $F$ and the coefficient of friction $\mu_k$ at the contact surfaces.

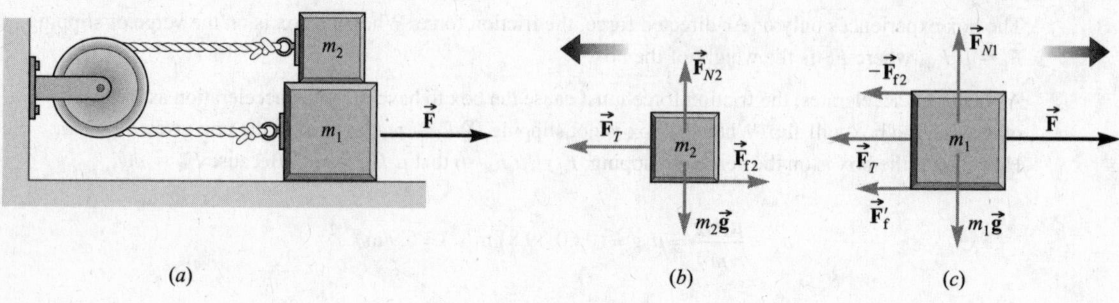


Fig. 3-23

The horizontal forces on the blocks are shown in Fig. 3-23(*b*) and (*c*). Block-2 of mass $m_2$ is pressed against block-1 by its weight $m_2g$. This is the normal force where $m_1$ and $m_2$ are in contact, so the friction force there is $F_{f2} = \mu_k m_2 g$. At the bottom surface of $m_1$, however, the normal force is $(m_1 + m_2)g$. Hence, $F'_f = \mu_k(m_1 + m_2)g$. We now write $\sum F_x = ma_x$ for each block, taking the direction of motion of the system as positive (i.e., to the left on block-2 and to the right on block-1):

$$\pm\sum F_{x2} = F_T - \mu_k m_2 g = m_2 a \quad \text{and} \quad \pm\sum F_{x1} = F - F_T - \mu m_2 g - \mu_k(m_1 + m_2)g = m_1 a$$

Eliminate $F_T$ by adding the two equations to obtain

$$F - 2\mu_k m_2 g - \mu_k(m_1 + m_2)(g) = (m_1 + m_2)(a)$$

from which it follows that $a = \dfrac{F - 2\mu_k m_2 g}{m_1 + m_2} - \mu_k g$

**3.36 [II]** In the system of Fig. 3-24, friction and the mass of the pulley are both negligible. Find the acceleration of $m_2$ if $m_1 = 300\text{ g}$, $m_2 = 500\text{ g}$, and $F = 1.50\text{ N}$.

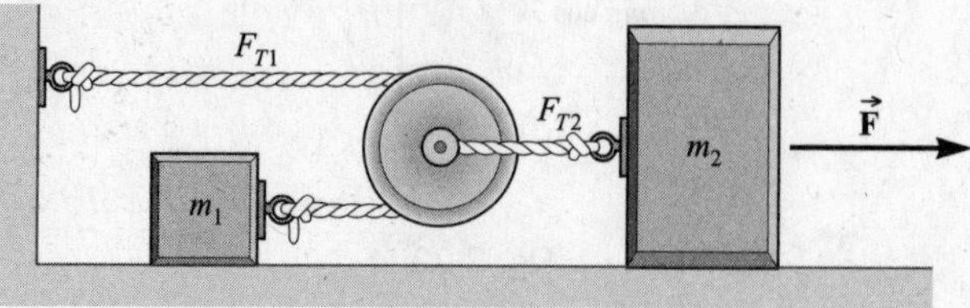


Fig. 3-24

Notice that $m_1$ has twice as large an acceleration as $m_2$. (When the pulley moves a distance $d$, $m_1$ moves a distance $2d$.) Also notice that the tension $F_{T1}$ in the cord pulling $m_1$ is half $F_{T2}$, that in the cord pulling the pulley, because the total force on the pulley must be zero. ($F = ma$ tells us that this is so because the mass of the pulley is zero.) Writing $\sum F_x = ma_x$ for each mass,

$$\overset{+}{\rightarrow}\sum F_{x1} = F_{T1} = (m_1)(2a) \text{ and } \overset{+}{\rightarrow}\sum F_{x2} = F - F_{T2} = m_2 a$$

However, we know that $F_{T1} = \frac{1}{2}F_{T2}$ and so the first equation gives $F_{T2} = 4m_1 a$. Substitution in the second equation yields

$$F = (4m_1 + m_2)(a) \quad \text{or} \quad a = \frac{F}{4m_1 + m_2} = \frac{1.50\text{ N}}{1.20\text{ kg} + 0.50\text{ kg}} = 0.882\text{ m/s}^2$$

**3.37 [III]** **In Fig. 3-25, the weights of the objects are 200 N and 300 N. The pulleys are essentially frictionless and massless. Pulley $P_1$ has a stationary axle, but pulley $P_2$ is free to move up and down. Find the tensions $F_{T1}$ and $F_{T2}$ and the acceleration of each body. Only do this problem if you are already familiar with the action of pulleys.**

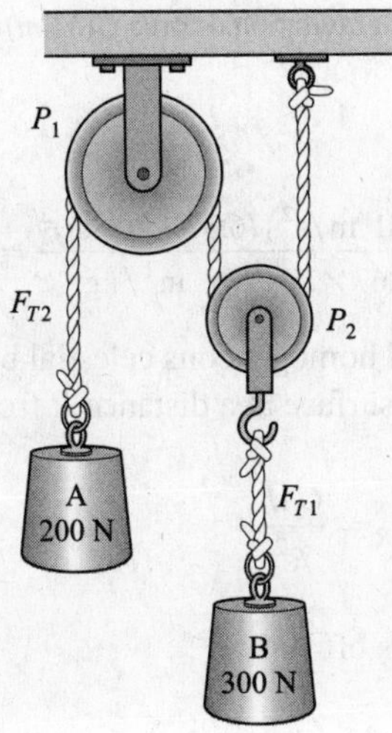


Fig. 3-25

Mass $B$ will rise and mass $A$ will fall. You can see this by noticing that the forces acting on pulley $P_2$ are $2F_{T2}$ up and $F_{T1}$ down. Since the pulley has no mass, it can have no acceleration, and so $F_{T1} = 2F_{T2}$ (the inertialess object transmits the tension). Twice as large a force is pulling upward on $B$ as on $A$.

Let $a$ be the downward acceleration of $A$. Then $a/2$ is the upward acceleration of $B$. (Why?) Now write $\sum F_y = ma_y$ for each mass in turn, taking the direction of motion as positive in each case. We have

$$+\uparrow\sum F_B = F_{T1} - 300\text{ N} = (m_B)(\tfrac{1}{2}a) \quad \text{and} \quad +\downarrow\sum F_A = 200\text{ N} - F_{T2} = m_A a$$

But $m = F_W/g$ and so $m_A = (200/9.81)$ kg and $m_B = (300/9.81)$ kg. Further $F_{T1} = 2F_{T2}$. Substitution of these values in the two equations allows us to compute $F_{T2}$ and then $F_{T1}$ and $a$. The results are

$$F_{T1} = 327\text{ N} \qquad F_{T2} = 164\text{ N} \qquad a = 1.78\text{ m/s}^2$$

**3.38.[II]** The Moon, whose mass is $7.35 \times 10^{22}$ kg, orbits the Earth, whose mass is $5.98 \times 10^{24}$ kg, at a mean distance of $3.85 \times 10^8$ m. It is held in a nearly circular orbit by the Earth-Moon gravitational interaction. Determine the force of gravity due to the planet acting on the Moon.

From the univesal law of gravitation

$$F_G = G\frac{m\,M}{R^2}$$

we get

$$F_G = 6.673 \times 10^{-11}\ \mathrm{N \cdot m^2/kg^2} \frac{(7.35 \times 10^{22}\ \mathrm{kg})(5.98 \times 10^{24})}{(3.85 \times 10^{8}\ \mathrm{m})^2}$$

which yields

$$F_G = 1.98 \times 10^{20}\ \mathrm{N}$$

This is also the force on the Earth due to the Moon.

**3.39 [II]** Compute the mass of the Earth, assuming it to be a sphere of radius 6370 km. Use the fact that $g = 9.81\ \mathrm{m/s^2}$ and give your answer to three significant figures.

Let $M_E$ be the mass of the Earth, and $m$ the mass of an object. The weight of the object on the planet's surface is equal to $mg$. It is also equal to the gravitational force $G(M_E m)R_E^2$, where $R_E$ is the Earth's radius. Hence,

$$mg = G\frac{M_E m}{R_E^2}$$

from which $$M_E = \frac{gR_E^2}{G} = \frac{(9.81\ \mathrm{m/s^2})(6.37 \times 10^6\ \mathrm{m})^2}{6.67 \times 10^{-11}\ \mathrm{N \cdot m^2/kg^2}} = 5.97 \times 10^{24}\ \mathrm{kg}$$

**3.40 [II]** Consider an essentially spherical homogeneous celestial body of mass $M$. The acceleration due to gravity in its vicinity beyond its surface at a distance $R$ from its center is $g_R$. Show that

$$g_R = \frac{GM}{R^2}$$

Notice that the acceleration drops off as $1/R^2$.

Imagine an object of mass $m$ at a distance $R$ from the center of our celestial body. Its weight is $F_W = mg_R$, but that's also the gravitation force on it due to the mass $M$, that is, $F_W = F_G$. Hence,

$$mg_R = G\frac{mM}{R^2}$$

**3.41 [II]** The mythical planet Mongo has twice the mass and twice the radius of Earth. Compute the acceleration due to gravity at its surface.

We know from Problem 3.40 that in general

$$g_R = \frac{GM}{R^2}$$

Then for the Earth at its surface

$$g_E = \frac{GM_E}{R_E^2} = g = 9.81\ \mathrm{m/s^2}$$

where $R_E$ is the Earth's radius and $M_E$ is its mass. For Mongo

$$g_M = \frac{GM_M}{R_M^2} = \frac{G(2M_E)}{(2R_E)^2}$$

and

$$g_M = \frac{1}{2}\frac{GM_E}{R_E^2} = \frac{1}{2}(9.81\ \mathrm{m/s^2})$$

or $$g_M = 4.91\ \mathrm{m/s^2}$$

## SUPPLEMENTARY PROBLEMS

**3.42 [I]** Two forces act on a point object as follows: 100 N at 170.0° and 100 N at 50.0°. Find their resultant.

**3.43 [I]** Compute algebraically the resultant of the following coplanar forces: 100 N at 30°, 141.4 N at 45°, and 100 N at 240°. Check your result graphically.

**3.44 [I]** Two forces, 80 N and 100 N, acting at an angle of 60° with each other, pull on an object. (*a*) What single force would replace the two forces? (*b*) What single force (called the *equilibrant*) would balance the two forces? Solve algebraically.

**3.45 [I]** Find algebraically the (*a*) resultant and (*b*) equilibrant (see Problem 3.44) of the following coplanar forces: 300 N at exactly 0°, 400 N at 30°, and 400 N at 150°.

**3.46 [I]** Having hauled it to the top of a tilted driveway, a child is holding a wagon from rolling back down. The driveway is inclined at 20° to the horizontal. If the wagon weighs 150 N, with what force must the child pull on the handle if the handle is parallel to and pointing up the incline?

**3.47 [II]** Repeat Problem 3.46 if the handle is now raised at an angle of 30° above the incline.

**3.48 [I]** Once ignited, a small rocket motor on a spacecraft exerts a constant force of 10 N for 7.80 s. During the burn, the rocket causes the 100-kg craft to accelerate uniformly. Determine that acceleration.

**3.49 [II]** Typically, a bullet leaves a standard 45-caliber pistol (5.0-in. barrel) at a speed of 262 m/s. If it takes 1 ms to traverse the barrel, determine the average acceleration experienced by the 16.2-g bullet within the gun, and then compute the average force exerted on it.

**3.50 [I]** A force acts on a 2-kg mass and gives it an acceleration of 3 $m/s^2$. What acceleration is produced by the same force when acting on a mass of (*a*) 1 kg? (*b*) 4 kg? (*c*) How large is the force?

**3.51 [I]** An object has a mass of 300 g. (*a*) What is its weight on Earth? (*b*) What is its mass on the Moon? (*c*) What will be its acceleration on the Moon under the action of a 0.500-N resultant force?

**3.52 [I]** A horizontal cable pulls a 200-kg cart along a horizontal track. The tension in the cable is 500 N. Starting from rest, (*a*) How long will it take the cart to reach a speed of 8.0 m/s? (*b*) How far will it have gone?

**3.53 [II]** A 900-kg car is going 20 m/s along a level road. How large a constant retarding force is required to stop it in a distance of 30 m? [*Hint:* First find its deceleration.]

**3.54 [II]** A 12.0-g bullet is accelerated from rest to a speed of 700 m/s as it travels 20.0 cm in a gun barrel. Assuming the acceleration to be constant, how large was the accelerating force? [*Hint:* Be careful of units.]

**3.55 [II]** A 20-kg crate hangs at the end of a long rope. Find its acceleration (magnitude and direction) when the tension in the rope is (*a*) 250 N, (*b*) 150 N, (*c*) zero, (*d*) 196 N.

**3.56 [II]** A 5.0-kg mass hangs at the end of a cord. Find the tension in the cord if the acceleration of the mass is (*a*) 1.5 $m/s^2$ up, (*b*) 1.5 $m/s^2$ down, (*c*) 9.81 $m/s^2$ down. Don't forget gravity.

**3.57 [II]** A 700-N man stands on a scale on the floor of an elevator. The scale records the force it exerts on whatever is on it. What is the scale reading if the elevator has an acceleration of (*a*) 1.8 m/s² up? (*b*) 1.8 m/s² down? (*c*) 9.8 m/s² down?

**3.58 [II]** Using the scale described in Problem 3.57, a 65.0-kg astronaut weighs himself on the Moon, where $g = 1.60$ m/s². What does the scale read?

**3.59 [II]** A cord passing over a frictionless, massless pulley has a 4.0-kg object tied to one end and a 12-kg object tied to the other. Compute the acceleration and the tension in the cord.

**3.60 [II]** An elevator starts from rest with a constant upward acceleration. It moves 2.0 m in the first 0.60 s. A passenger in the elevator is holding a 3.0-kg package by a vertical string. What is the tension in the string during the accelerating process?

**3.61 [II]** Just as her parachute opens, a 60-kg parachutist is falling at a speed of 50 m/s. After 0.80 s has passed, the chute is fully open and her speed has dropped to 12.0 m/s. Find the average retarding force exerted upon the chutist during this time if the deceleration is uniform.

**3.62 [II]** A 300-g mass hangs at the end of a string. A second string hangs from the bottom of that mass and supports a 900-g mass. (*a*) Find the tension in each string when the masses are accelerating upward at 0.700 m/s². Don't forget gravity. (*b*) Find the tension in each string when the acceleration is 0.700 m/s² downward.

**3.63 [II]** A 20-kg wagon is pulled along the level ground by a rope inclined at 30° above the horizontal. A friction force of 30 N opposes the motion. How large is the pulling force if the wagon is moving with (*a*) constant speed and (*b*) an acceleration of 0.40 m/s²?

**3.64 [II]** A 12-kg box is released from the top of an incline that is 5.0 m long and makes an angle of 40° to the horizontal. A 60-N friction force impedes the motion of the box. (*a*) What will be the acceleration of the box, and (*b*) how long will it take to reach the bottom of the incline?

**3.65 [II]** For the situation outlined in Problem 3.64, what is the coefficient of friction between the box and the incline?

**3.66 [II]** An inclined plane makes an angle of 30° with the horizontal. Find the constant force, applied parallel to the plane, required to cause a 15-kg box to slide (*a*) up the plane with acceleration 1.2 m/s² and (*b*) down the incline with acceleration 1.2 m/s². Neglect friction forces.

**3.67 [II]** A horizontal force $F$ is exerted on a 20-kg box to slide it up a 30° incline. The friction force retarding the motion is 80 N. How large must $F$ be if the acceleration of the moving box is to be (*a*) zero and (*b*) 0.75 m/s²? The situation resembles that of Fig. 3-18.

**3.68 [II]** An inclined plane making an angle of 25° with the horizontal has a pulley at its top. A 30-kg block on the plane is connected to a freely hanging 20-kg block by means of a cord passing over the pulley. Compute the distance the 20-kg block will fall in 2.0 s starting from rest. Neglect friction.

**3.69 [III]** Repeat Problem 3.68 if the coefficient of friction between block and plane is 0.20.

**3.70 [III]** A horizontal force of 200 N is required to cause a 15-kg block to slide up a 20° incline with an acceleration of 25 cm/s². Find (*a*) the friction force on the block and (*b*) the coefficient of friction.

**3.71 [II]** Find the acceleration of the blocks in Fig. 3-26 if friction forces are negligible. What is the tension in the cord connecting them?

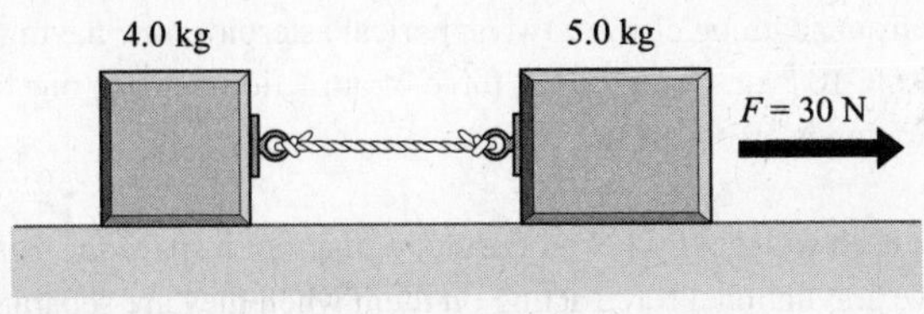


Fig. 3-26

**3.72 [III]** Repeat Problem 3.71 if the coefficient of kinetic friction between the blocks and the table is 0.30.

**3.73 [III]** How large a force $F$ is needed in Fig. 3-27 to pull out the 6.0-kg block with an acceleration of 1.50 $\mathrm{m/s^2}$ if the coefficient of friction at its surfaces is 0.40?

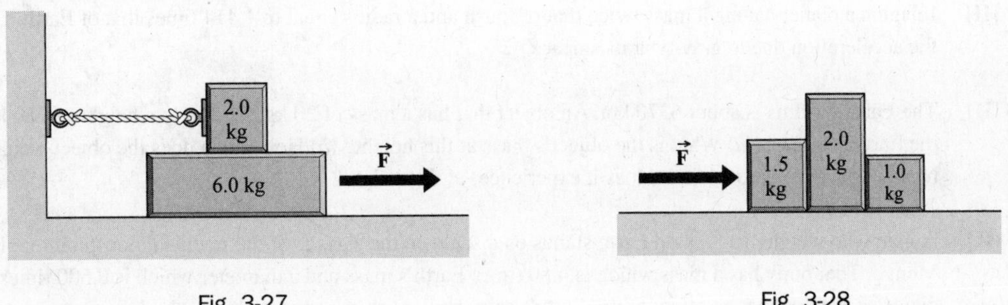


Fig. 3-27

Fig. 3-28

**3.74 [III]** In Fig. 3-28, how large a force $F$ is needed to give the blocks an acceleration of 3.0 $\mathrm{m/s^2}$ if the coefficient of kinetic friction between blocks and table is 0.20? How large a force does the 1.50-kg block then exert on the 2.0-kg block?

**3.75 [III]** (*a*) What is the smallest force parallel to a 37° incline needed to keep a 100-N weight from sliding down the incline if the coefficients of static and kinetic friction are both 0.30? (*b*) What parallel force is required to keep the weight moving up the incline at constant speed? (*c*) If the parallel pushing force is 94 N, what will be the acceleration of the object? (*d*) If the object in (*c*) starts from rest, how far will it move in 10 s?

**3.76 [III]** A 5.0-kg block rests on a 30° incline. The coefficient of static friction between the block and the incline is 0.20. How large a horizontal force must push on the block if the block is to be on the verge of sliding (*a*) up the incline and (*b*) down the incline?

**3.77 [III]** Three blocks with masses 6.0 kg, 9.0 kg, and 10 kg are connected as shown in Fig. 3-29. The coefficient of friction between the table and the 10-kg block is 0.20. Find (*a*) the acceleration of the system and (*b*) the tension in the cord on the left and in the cord on the right.

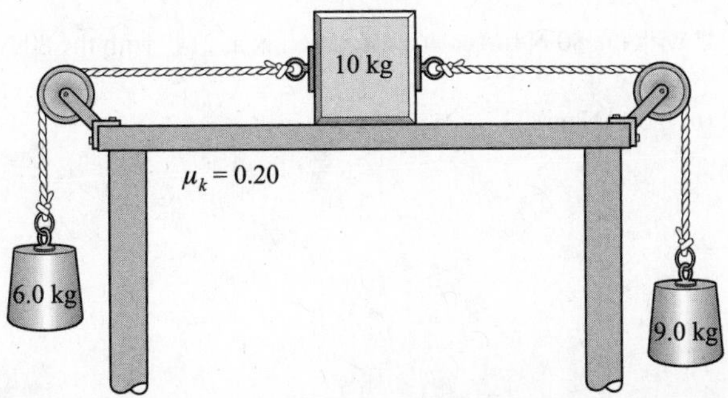


Fig. 3-29

**3.78 [I]** Floating in space far from anything else are two spherical asteroids, one having a mass of $20 \times 10^{10}$ kg and the other a mass of $40 \times 10^{10}$ kg. Compute the force of attraction on each one due to gravity when their center-to-center separation is $10 \times 10^6$ m.

**3.79 [I]** Two cannonballs that each weigh 4.00 kN on Earth are floating in space far from any other objects. Determine the mutually attractive gravitational force acting on them when they are separated, center-to-center, by 10.0 m.

**3.80 [II]** A space station that weighs 10.0 MN on Earth is positioned at a distance of ten Earth radii from the center of the planet. What would it weigh out there in space—that is, what is the value of the gravity force pulling it toward Earth?

**3.81 [II]** An object that weighs 2700 N on the surface of the Earth is raised to a height (i.e., altitude) of two Earth radii above the surface. What will it weigh up there?

**3.82 [II]** Imagine a planet having a mass twice that of Earth and a radius equal to 1.414 times that of Earth. Determine the acceleration due to gravity at its surface.

**3.83 [II]** The Earth's radius is about 6370 km. An object that has a mass of 20 kg is taken to a height of 160 km above the Earth's surface. (*a*) What is the object's mass at this height? (*b*) How much does the object weigh (i.e., how large a gravitational force does it experience) at this height?

**3.84 [II]** A man who weighs 1000 N on Earth stands on a scale on the surface of the mythical nonspinning planet Mongo. That body has a mass which is 4.80 times Earth's mass and a diameter which is 0.500 times Earth's diameter. Neglecting the effect of the Earth's spin, how much does the scale read?

**3.85 [II]** The radius of the Earth is about 6370 km, while that of Mars is about 3440 km. If an object weighs 200 N on Earth, what would it weigh, and what would be the acceleration due to gravity, on Mars? The mass of Mars is 0.11 that of Earth. Neglect planetary rotations and local mass variations.

**3.86 [II]** The fabled planet Dune has a diameter eight times that of Earth and a mass twice as large. If a robot weighs 1800 N on the surface of (nonspinning) Dune, what will it weigh at the poles on Earth? Take our planet to be a sphere.

**3.87 [III]** An astronaut weighs 480 N on Earth. She visits the planet Krypton, which has a mass and diameter each ten times that of Earth. Determine her weight at a distance of two Kryptonian radii above that fictional planet.

## ANSWERS TO SUPPLEMENTARY PROBLEMS

**3.42 [I]** 100 N at 110°

**3.43 [I]** 0.15 kN at 25°

**3.44 [I]** (*a*) $\vec{\mathbf{R}}$: 0.16 kN at 34° with the 80 N force; (*b*) $-\vec{\mathbf{R}}$: 0.16 kN at 214° with the 80 N force

**3.45 [I]** (*a*) 0.50 kN at 53°; (*b*) 0.50 kN at 233°

**3.46 [I]** 51 N

**3.47 [II]** 59 N

**3.48 [I]** 0.10 m/s$^2$

**3.49 [II]** $3 \times 10^5$ m/s$^2$; $0.4 \times 10^2$ N

**3.50 [I]** (*a*) 6 m/s$^2$; (*b*) 2 m/s$^2$; (*c*) 6 N

**3.51 [I]** (*a*) 2.94 N; (*b*) 0.300 kg; (*c*) 1.67 m/s$^2$

**3.52 [I]** (*a*) 3.2 s; (*b*) 13 m

**3.53 [II]** 6.0 kN

**3.54 [II]** 14.7 kN

**3.55 [II]** (*a*) 2.7 m/s$^2$ up; (*b*) 2.3 m/s$^2$ down; (*c*) 9.8 m/s$^2$ down; (*d*) zero

**3.56 [II]** (*a*) 57 N; (*b*) 42 N; (*c*) zero

**3.57 [II]** (*a*) 0.83 kN; (*b*) 0.57 kN; (*c*) zero

**3.58 [II]** 104 N

**3.59 [II]** 4.9 m/s$^2$, 59 N

**3.60 [II]** 63 N

**3.61 [II]** 2850 N + 588 N = 3438 N = 3.4 kN

**3.62 [II]** (*a*) 12.6 N and 9.46 N; (*b*) 10.9 N and 8.20 N

**3.63 [II]** (*a*) 35 N; (*b*) 44 N

**3.64 [II]** (*a*) 1.3 m/s$^2$; (*b*) 2.8 s

**3.65 [II]** 0.67

**3.66 [II]** (*a*) 92 N; (*b*) 56 N

**3.67 [II]** (*a*) 0.21 kN; (*b*) 0.22 kN

**3.68 [II]** 2.9 m

**3.69 [III]** 0.74 m

**3.70 [III]** (*a*) 0.13 kN; (*b*) 0.65

**3.71 [II]** 3.3 m/s$^2$, 13 N

**3.72 [III]** 0.39 m/s$^2$, 13 N

**3.73 [III]** 48 N

**3.74 [III]** 22 N, 15 N

**3.75 [III]** (*a*) 36 N; (*b*) 84 N; (*c*) 0.98 m/s$^2$ up the plane; (*d*) 49 m

**3.76 [III]** (*a*) 43 N; (*b*) 16.6 N

**3.77 [III]** (*a*) 0.39 $m/s^2$; (*b*) 61 N, 85 N

**3.78 [I]** 0.053 N on each

**3.79 [I]** $1.11 \times 10^{-7}$ N

**3.80 [II]** $10.0 \times 10^4$ N

**3.81 [II]** 300 N

**3.82 [II]** 9.81 $m/s^2$

**3.83 [II]** (*a*) 20 kg; (*b*) 0.19 kN

**3.84 [II]** 19.2 kN

**3.85 [II]** 75 N, 3.7 $m/s^2$

**3.86 [II]** 57.6 kN

**3.87 [III]** 5.3 N

# Equilibrium Under the Action of Concurrent Forces

**Concurrent Forces** are forces whose lines of action all pass through a common point. The forces acting on a point object are obviously concurrent because they are all applied at that same point.

**An Object Is in Equilibrium** under the action of concurrent forces provided it is not accelerating. It may be traveling at a constant speed, and yet as long as $a = 0$, the object is in equilibrium.

**The First Condition for Equilibrium** is the requirement that $\sum \vec{\mathbf{F}} = 0$ or, in component form,

$$\sum F_x = \sum F_y = \sum F_z = 0$$

That is, the resultant of all external forces acting on the object must be zero. This condition is sufficient for equilibrium when the external forces are concurrent. A second condition must also be satisfied if an object is to be in equilibrium under nonconcurrent forces; it is discussed in Chapter 5.

**Problem Solution Method (Concurrent Forces):**

(1) Isolate the object for discussion.
(2) Show the forces acting on the isolated object in a diagram (the *free-body diagram*).
(3) Find the rectangular components of each force.
(4) Write the first condition for equilibrium in equation form.
(5) Solve for the required quantities.

**The Weight of an Object** ($\vec{\mathbf{F}}_W$) is essentially the force with which gravity pulls downward upon it. Recall from the previous chapter that $F_W = mg$.

**The Tensile Force** ($\vec{\mathbf{F}}_T$) acting on a string or cable or chain (or, indeed, on any structural member) is the applied force tending to stretch it. The scalar magnitude of the tensile force is the *tension* ($F_T$). When an object is in tension, the forces acting *on* it point outward away from its center, and the forces it exerts point inward toward its center. Remember that ropes, cables, and chains can only function in tension.

**The Friction Force** ($\vec{\mathbf{F}}_f$) is a tangential force acting on an object that opposes the sliding of that object across an adjacent surface with which it is in contact. The friction force is parallel to the surface and opposite to the direction of motion or of impending motion.

**The Normal Force** ($\vec{\mathbf{F}}_N$) on an object that is interacting with a surface is the component of the force exerted by the surface that is perpendicular to the surface.

**Pulleys:** When a system of several frictionless light-weight pulleys in equilibrium has a single continuous rope wound around it, the tension *in each length of the rope* is the same and it equals the force applied to the end of the rope ($F$) by some external agency (usually a person). Thus, when a load is supported by $N$ lengths of a continuous rope, the net force delivered to the load, the output force, is $NF$. Often the pulley attached to the load moves with the load and we need only count up the number of lengths of rope ($N$) acting on that pulley to determine the output force. There's more material on pulleys in Chapter 7; see, for example, Problems 7.5 and 7.12.

## SOLVED PROBLEMS

**4.1 [II]** In Fig. 4-1($a$), the tension in the horizontal cord is 30 N as shown. Find the weight of the hanging body.

The tension in cord-1 is equal to the weight of the body hanging from it. Therefore, $F_{T1} = F_W$, and we wish to find $F_{T1}$ or $F_W$.

Notice that the unknown force $F_{T1}$ and the known force of 30 N both pull on the knot at point $P$. It therefore makes sense to isolate the knot at $P$ as our point object for which we will write the two sum-of-the-forces-equals-zero equations. The free-body diagram showing the forces on the knot is drawn as in Fig. 4-1 ($b$). The force components are also shown there.

We next write the first condition for equilibrium for the knot. From the free-body diagram,

$$\overset{+}{\rightarrow}\sum F_x = 0 \quad \text{becomes} \quad 30\text{ N} - F_{T2}\cos 40° = 0$$

$$+\uparrow\sum F_y = 0 \quad \text{becomes} \quad F_{T2}\sin 0° - F_w = 0$$

Solving the first equation for $F_{T2}$ gives $F_{T2} = 39.2$ N. Substituting this value in the second equation yields $F_W = 25$ N as the weight of the hanging body.

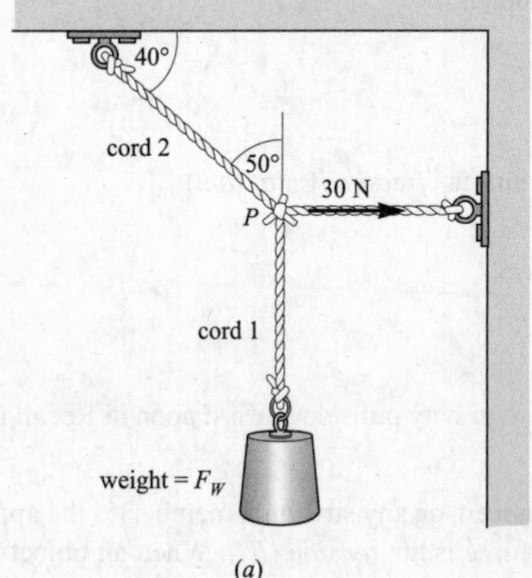


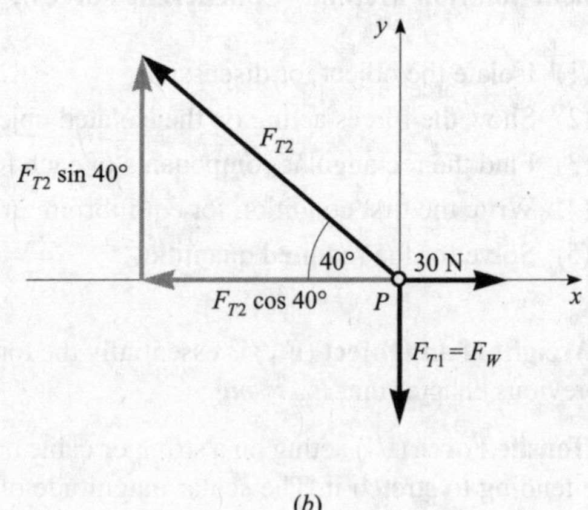


Fig. 4-1

**4.2 [II]** A rope extends between two poles. A 90-N boy hangs from it as shown in Fig. 4-2($a$). Find the tensions in the two parts of the rope.

Label the two tensions $F_{T1}$ and $F_{T2}$, and isolate the piece of rope at the boy's hands as the point object. That's the place where the three forces of interest act. And doing the analysis at that location will therefore allow $F_{T1}$, $F_{T2}$, and $F_W$, the boy's weight, to enter the equations. The free-body diagram for the object is found in Fig. 4-2($b$).

After resolving the forces into their components as shown, write the first condition for equilibrium:

$$\overset{+}{\rightarrow}\sum F_x = 0 \quad \text{becomes} \quad F_{T2}\cos 5.0° - F_{T1}\cos 10° = 0$$

$$+\uparrow\sum F_y = 0 \quad \text{becomes} \quad F_{T2}\sin 5.0° + F_{T1}\sin 10° - 90\text{ N} = 0$$

Evaluating the sines and cosines, these equations become

$$0.996F_{T2} - 0.985F_{T1} = 0 \quad \text{and} \quad 0.087F_{T2} + 0.174F_{T1} - 90 = 0$$

Solving the first for $F_{T2}$ gives $F_{T2} = 0.990F_{T1}$. Substituting this in the second equation yields

$$0.086F_{T1} + 0.174F_{T1} - 90 = 0$$

from which $F_{T1} = 0.35$ kN. Then, because $F_{T2} = 0.990F_{T1}$, it follows that $F_{T2} = 0.34$kN.

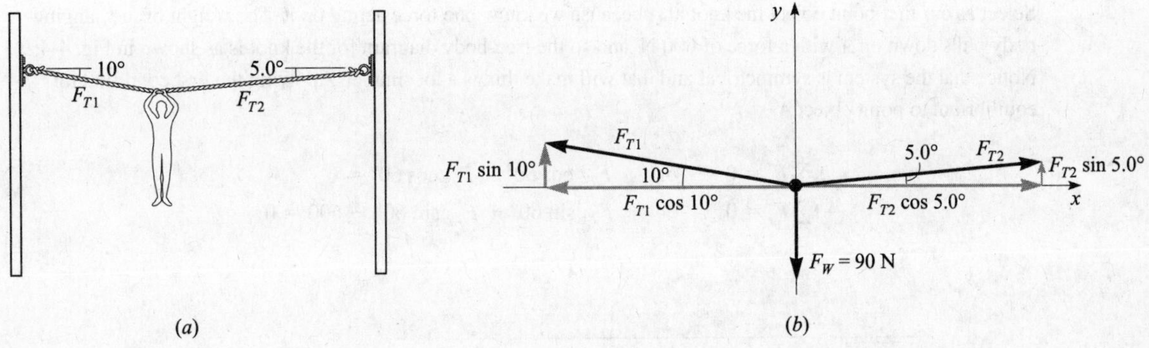


Fig. 4-2

**4.3 [II]** A 50-N box is slid straight across the floor at constant speed by a force of 25 N, as depicted in Fig. 4-3(*a*). How large a friction force impedes the motion of the box? (*b*) How large is the normal force? (*c*) Find $\mu_k$ between the box and the floor.

The forces acting on the box are shown in Fig. 4-3(*a*). The friction force is $F_f$, and the normal force, the supporting force exerted by the floor, is $F_N$. The free-body diagram and components are drawn in Fig. 4-3(*b*). Because the box is moving with constant velocity, it is in equilibrium. The first condition for equilibrium, taking to the right as positive,

$$\overset{+}{\rightarrow}\sum F_x = 0 \quad \text{or} \quad 25\cos 40° - F_f = 0$$

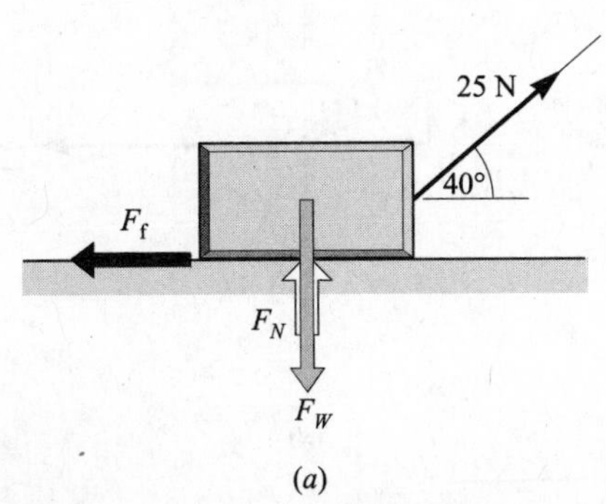


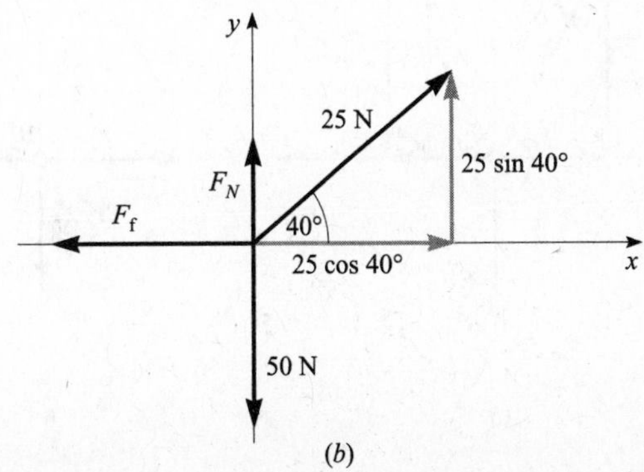


Fig. 4-3

(*a*) We can solve for the friction force $F_f$ at once to find that $F_f = 19.2$ N, or to two significant figures, $F_f = 19$ N.

(*b*) To find $F_N$, use the fact that

$$+\uparrow \sum F_y = 0 \qquad \text{or} \qquad F_N + 25 \sin 40° - 50 = 0$$

Solving gives the normal force as $F_N = 33.9$ N or, to two significant figures, $F_N = 34$ N.

(*c*) From the definition of $\mu_k$,

$$\mu_k = \frac{F_f}{F_N} = \frac{19.2\text{ N}}{33.9\text{ N}} = 0.57$$

**4.4 [II]** Find the tensions in the ropes illustrated in Fig. 4-4(*a*) if the supported body weighs 600 N.

Select as our first point object the knot at *A* because we know one force acting on it. The weight of the hanging body pulls down on *A* with a force of 600 N, and so the free-body diagram for the knot is as shown in Fig. 4-4(*b*). Notice that the system is symmetrical and that will make things a lot simpler. Applying the first condition for equilibrium to point object *A*,

$$\stackrel{+}{\rightarrow} \sum F_x = 0 \qquad \text{or} \qquad F_{T2} \cos 60° - F_{T1} \cos 60° = 0$$
$$+\uparrow \sum F_y = 0 \qquad \text{or} \qquad F_{T1} \sin 60° + F_{T2} \sin 60° - 600 = 0$$

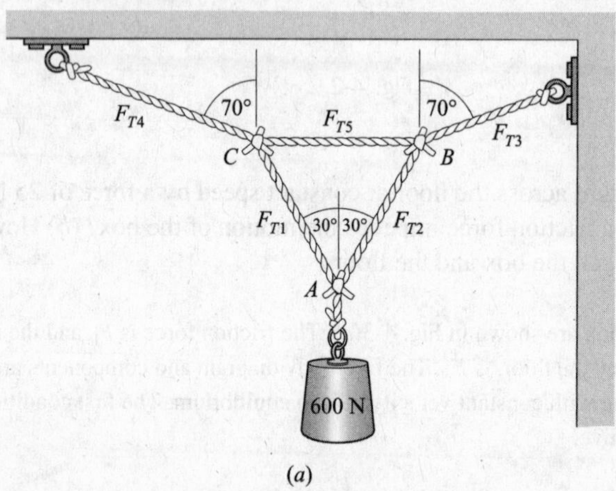

(*a*)

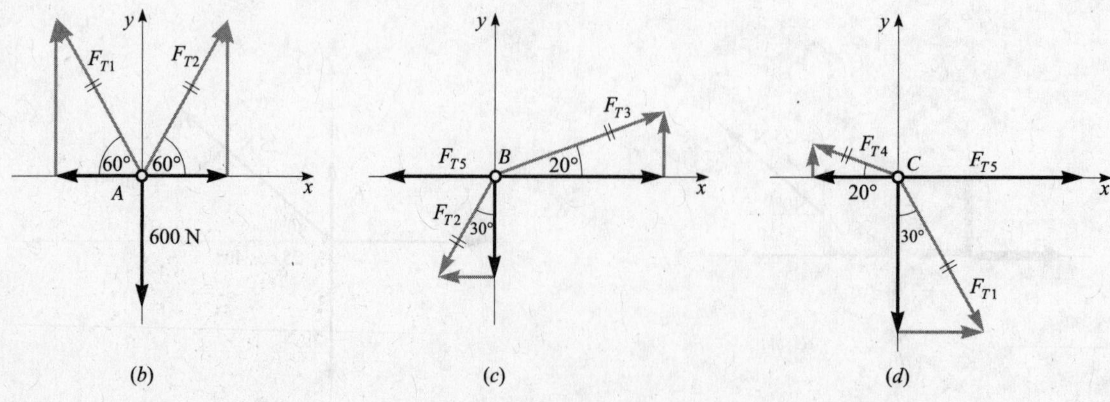

(*b*) (*c*) (*d*)

Fig. 4-4

The first equation yields $F_{T1} = F_{T2}$. (We could have inferred this from the symmetry of the system. Also from symmetry, $F_{T3} = F_{T4}$.) Substitution of $F_{T1}$ for $F_{T2}$ in the second equation gives $F_{T1} = 346$ N or 0.35 kN and so $F_{T2} = 346$ N or 0.35 kN.

Now isolate knot-*B* as our point object. Its free-body diagram is shown in Fig. 4-4(*c*). We have already found that $F_{T2} = 346$ N and so the equilibrium equations are

$$\overset{+}{\rightarrow}\sum F_x = 0 \quad \text{or} \quad F_{T3}\cos 20° - F_{T5} - 346 \sin 30° = 0$$
$$+\uparrow\sum F_y = 0 \quad \text{or} \quad F_{T3}\sin 20° - 346 \cos 30° = 0$$

The last equation yields $F_{T3} = 876$ N or 0.88 kN. Substituting this in the prior equation leads to $F_{T5} = 650$ N or 0.65 kN. As stated previously, from symmetry, $F_{T4} = F_{T3} = 876$ N or 0.88 kN. How could you have found $F_{T4}$ without recourse to symmetry? [*Hint*: See Fig. 4-4 (*d*).]

**4.5 [I]** Each of the objects in Fig. 4-5 is in equilibrium. Find the normal force $F_N$ in each case.

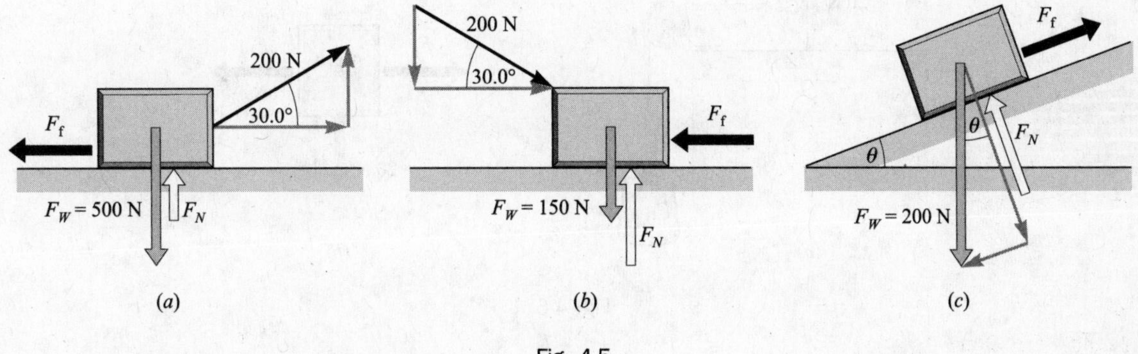


Fig. 4-5

Apply $+\uparrow\sum F_y = 0$ in each case.

(*a*) $F_N + (200\text{ N})\sin 30.0° - 500 = 0$ from which $F_N = 400$ N

(*b*) $F_N - (200\text{ N})\sin 30.0° - 150 = 0$ from which $F_N = 250$ N

(*c*) $F_N - (200\text{ N})\cos\theta = 0$ from which $F_N = (200\cos\theta)$ N

**4.6 [I]** For the situations of Problem 4.5, find the coefficient of kinetic friction if the object is moving with constant speed. Round off your answers to two significant figures.

We have already found $F_N$ for each case in Problem 4.5. To determine $F_f$, the sliding-friction force, use $\overset{+}{\rightarrow}\sum F_x = 0$. Then employ the definition of $\mu_k$.

(*a*) $200\cos 30.0° - F_f = 0$ so that $F_f = 173$ N and $\mu_k = F_f/F_N = 173/400 = 0.43$.

(*b*) $200\cos 30.0° - F_f = 0$ so that $F_f = 173$ N and $\mu_k = F_f/F_N = 173/250 = 0.69$.

(*c*) $-200\sin\theta + F_f = 0$ so that $F_f = (200\sin\theta)$ N and $\mu_k = F_f/F_N = (200\sin\theta)/(200\cos\theta) = \tan\theta$.

**4.7 [II]** Suppose that in Fig. 4-5(*c*) the block is at rest. The angle of the incline is slowly increased. At an angle $\theta = 42°$, the block begins to slide. What is the coefficient of static friction between the block and the incline? (The block and surface are not the same as in Problems 4.5 and 4.6.)

At the instant the block begins to slide, the friction force has its critical value. Therefore, $\mu_s = F_f/F_N$ at that instant. Following the method of Problems 4.5 and 4.6,

$$F_N = F_W\cos\theta \qquad \text{and} \qquad F_f = F_W\sin\theta$$

Therefore, when sliding just starts,

$$\mu_s = \frac{F_f}{F_N} = \frac{F_W \sin\theta}{F_W \cos\theta} = \tan\theta$$

But $\theta$ was found by experiment to be 42°. Therefore, $\mu_s = \tan 42° = 0.90$.

**4.8 [II]** Pulled by the 8.0-N block shown in Fig. 4-6(*a*), the 20-N block slides to the right at a constant velocity. Find $\mu_k$ between the block and the table. Assume the pulley to be both light and frictionless.

Because it is moving at a constant velocity, the 20-N block is in equilibrium. Since the pulley is frictionless, the tension in the continuous rope is the same on both sides of the pulley. Thus, $F_{T1} = F_{T2} = 8.0$ N.

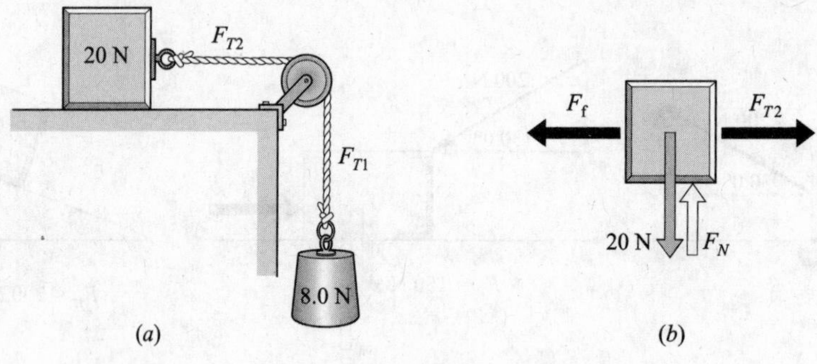


Fig. 4-6

Looking at the free-body diagram in Fig. 4-6(*b*) and recalling that the block is in equilibrium,

$$\overset{+}{\rightarrow}\sum F_x = 0 \quad \text{or} \quad F_f = F_{T2} = 8.0\text{ N}$$
$$+\uparrow\sum F_y = 0 \quad \text{or} \quad F_N = 20\text{ N}$$

Then, from the definition of $\mu_k$,

$$\mu_k = \frac{F_f}{F_N} = \frac{8.0\text{ N}}{20\text{ N}} = 0.40$$

## SUPPLEMENTARY PROBLEMS

**4.9 [I]** The load in Fig. 4-7 is hanging at rest. Take the ropes to all be vertical and the pulleys to be weightless and frictionless. (*a*) How many segments of rope support the combination of the lower pulley and load? (*b*) What is the downward force on the lowest pulley (the "floating" one)? (*c*) What must be the total upward force exerted on the floating pulley by the two lengths of rope? (*d*) What is the upward force exerted on the floating pulley by each length of rope supporting it? (*e*) What is the tension in the rope wound around the two pulleys? (*f*) How much force is the man exerting? (*g*) What is the net downward force acting on the uppermost pulley? (*h*) How much force acts downward on the hook in the ceiling?

**4.10 [I]** (*a*) A 600-N load hangs motionlessly in Fig. 4-8. Assume the ropes to all be vertical and the pulleys to be weightless and frictionless. (*a*) What is the tension in the bottom hook attached, via a ring, to the load? (*b*) How many lengths of rope support the movable pulley? (*c*) What is the tension in the long rope? (*d*) How much force does the man apply? (*e*) How much force acts downward on the ceiling?

**4.11 [I]** For the situation shown in Fig. 4-9, find the values of $F_{T1}$ and $F_{T2}$ if the hanging object's weight is 600 N.

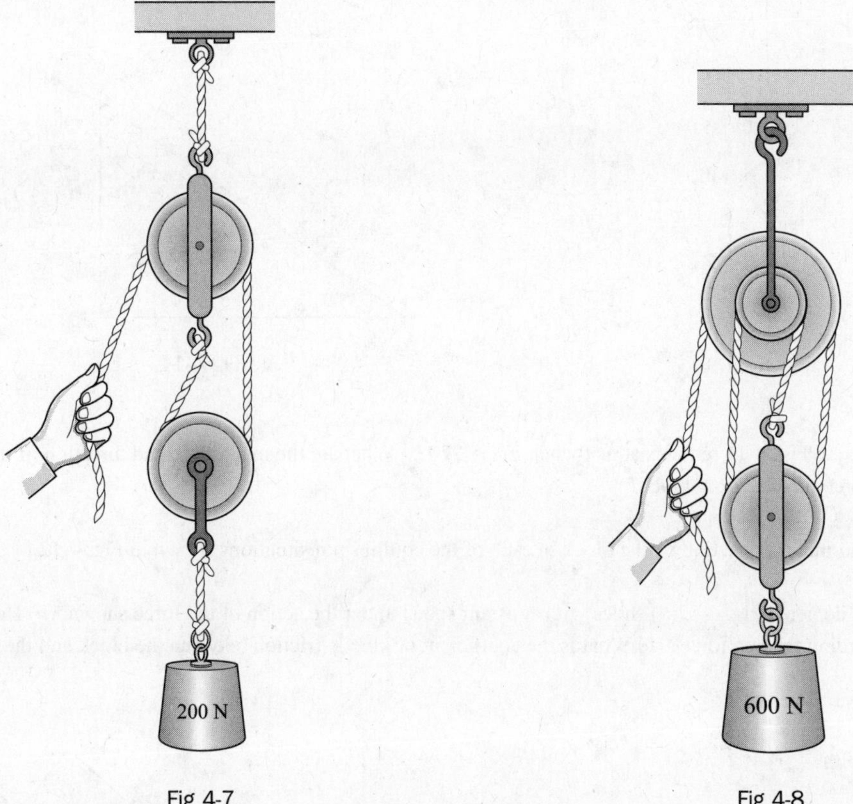


Fig 4-7

Fig 4-8

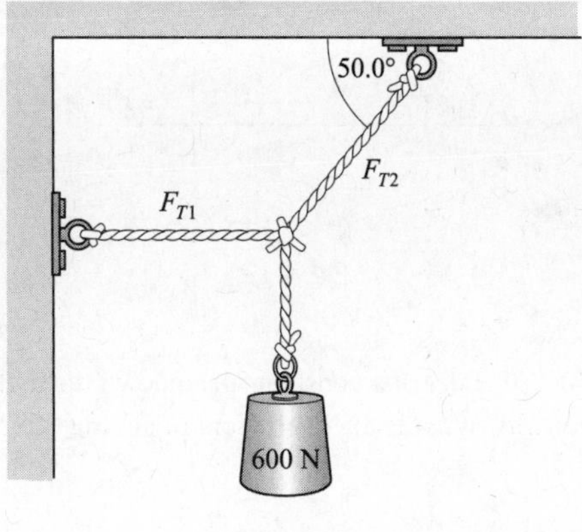


Fig 4-9

**4.12 [I]** The following coplanar forces pull on a ring: 200 N at 30.0°, 500 N at 80.0°, 300 N at 240°, and an unknown force. Find the magnitude and direction of the unknown force if the ring is in equilibrium.

**4.13 [II]** In Fig. 4-10, the pulleys are frictionless and weightless and the system hangs in equilibrium. If $F_{W3}$, the weight of the hanging object on the right, is 200 N, what are the values of $F_{W1}$ and $F_{W2}$?

**4.14 [II]** Suppose $F_{W1}$ in Fig. 4-10 is 500 N. Find the values of $F_{W2}$ and $F_{W3}$ if the system is to hang in equilibrium as shown.

**4.15 [I]** If in Fig. 4-11 the friction between the block and the incline is negligible, how much must the object on the right weigh if the 200-N block is to remain at rest?

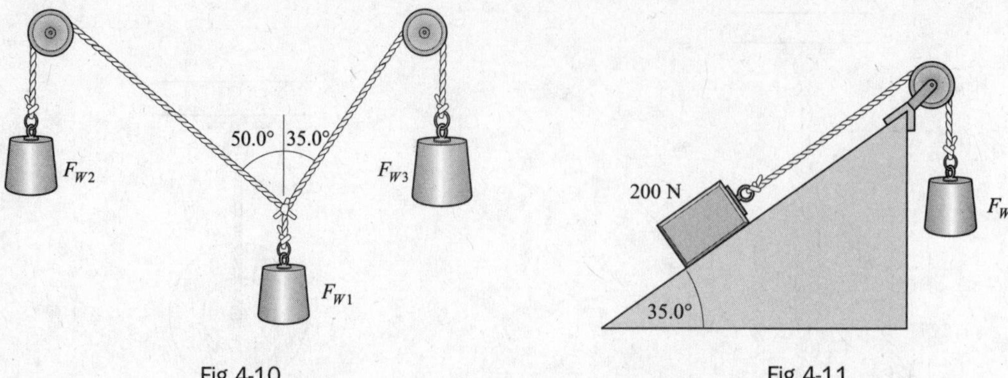


Fig 4-10

Fig 4-11

**4.16 [II]** The system in Fig. 4-11 remains at rest when $F_W = 220$ N. What are the magnitude and direction of the friction force on the 200-N block?

**4.17 [II]** Find the normal force acting on the block in each of the equilibrium situations shown in Fig. 4-12.

**4.18 [II]** The block depicted Fig. 4-12(*a*) slides with constant speed under the action of the force shown. (*a*) How large is the retarding friction force? (*b*) What is the coefficient of kinetic friction between the block and the floor?

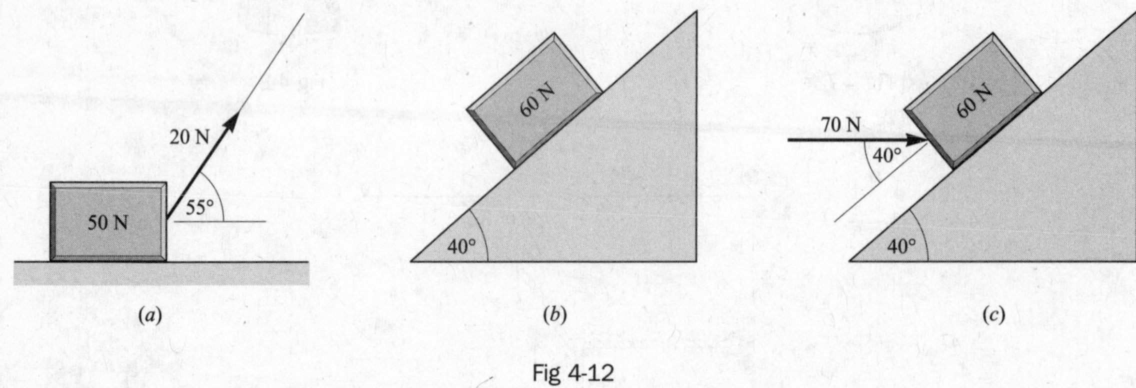


Fig 4-12

**4.19 [II]** The block shown in Fig. 4-12(*b*) slides at a constant speed down the incline. (*a*) How large is the friction force that opposes its motion? (*b*) What is the coefficient of sliding (kinetic) friction between the block and the plane?

**4.20 [II]** The block in Fig. 4-12(*c*) just begins to slide up the incline when the pushing force shown is increased to 70 N. (*a*) What is the maximum static friction force on it? (*b*) What is the value of the coefficient of static friction

**4.21 [II]** If $F_W = 40$ N in the equilibrium situation shown in Fig. 4-13, find $F_{T1}$ and $F_{T2}$.

**4.22 [III]** Refer to the equilibrium situation shown in Fig. 4-13. The cords are strong enough to withstand a maximum tension of 80 N. What is the largest value of $F_W$ that they can support as shown?

**4.23 [III]** The hanging object in Fig. 4-14 is in equilibrium and has a weight $F_W = 80$ N. Find $F_{T1}$, $F_{T2}$, $F_{T3}$, and $F_{T4}$. Give all answers to two significant figures.

**4.24 [III]** The pulleys shown in Fig. 4-15 have negligible weight and friction. The long rope has one section that is at 40°; assume its other segments are vertical. What is the value of $F_W$ if the system is at equilibrium?

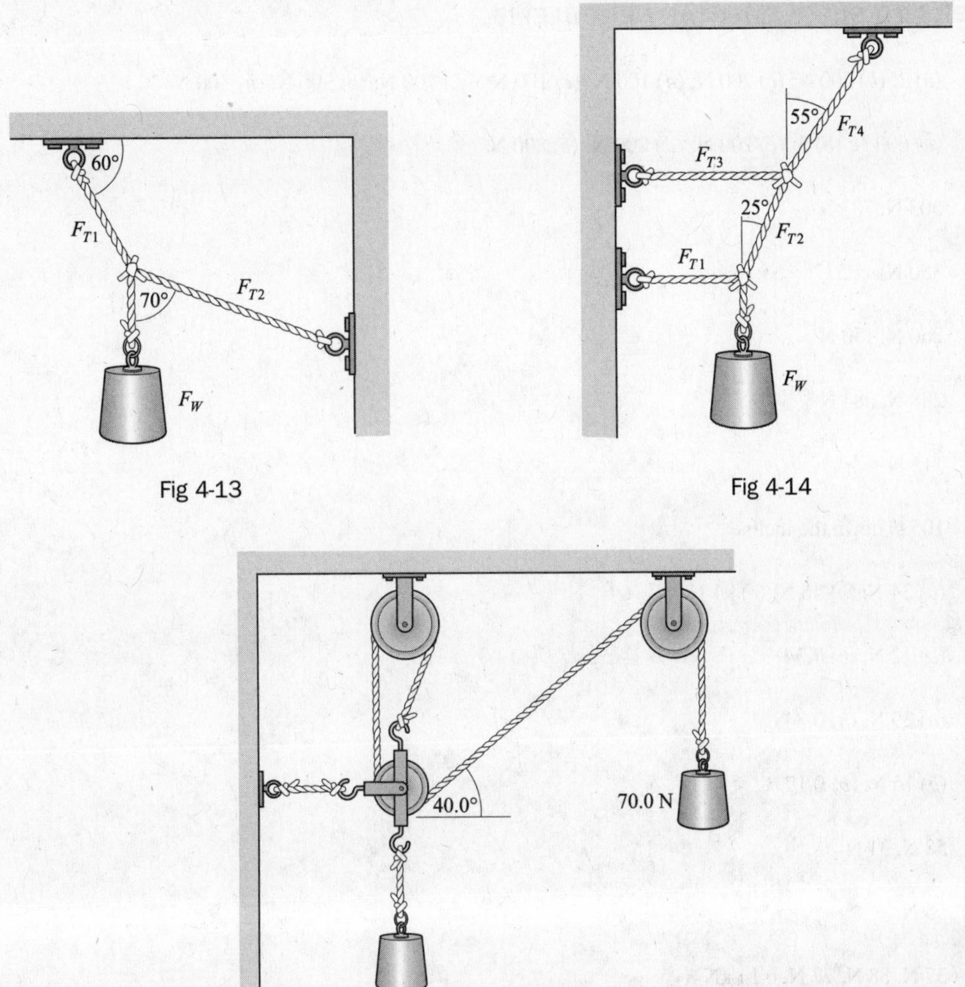


Fig 4-13

Fig 4-14

Fig 4-15

**4.25 [III]** In Fig. 4-16, the system is at rest. (*a*) What is the maximum value that $F_W$ can have if the friction force on the 40-N block cannot exceed 12.0 N? (*b*) What is the coefficient of static friction between the block and the tabletop?

**4.26 [III]** The block in Fig. 4-16 is just on the verge of slipping. If $F_W = 8.0$ N, what is the coefficient of static friction between the block and tabletop?

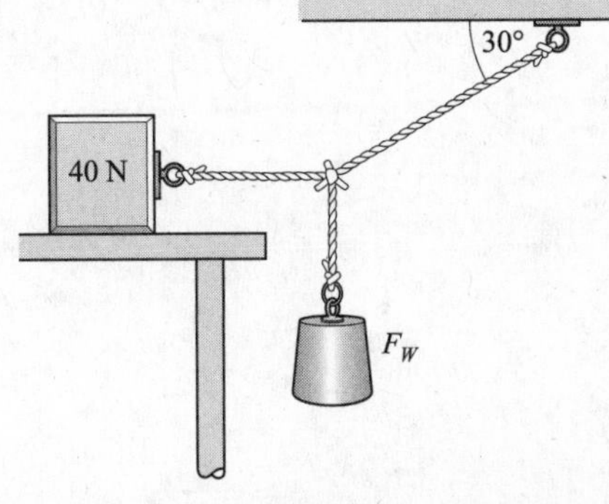


Fig 4-16

## ANSWERS TO SUPPLEMENTARY PROBLEMS

**4.9 [I]** (*a*) 2; (*b*) 200 N; (*c*) 200 N; (*d*) 100 N; (*e*) 100 N; (*f*) 100 N; (*g*) 300 N; (*h*) 300 N

**4.10 [I]** (*a*) 600 N; (*b*) 3; (*c*) 200 N; (*d*) 200 N; (*e*) 800 N

**4.11 [I]** 503 N, 783 N

**4.12 [I]** 350 N at 252°

**4.13 [II]** 260 N, 150 N

**4.14 [II]** 288 N, 384 N

**4.15 [I]** 115 N

**4.16 [II]** 105 N down the incline

**4.17 [II]** (*a*) 34 N; (*b*) 46 N; (*c*) 91 N

**4.18 [II]** (*a*) 12 N; (*b*) 0.34

**4.19 [II]** (*a*) 39 N; (*b*) 0.84

**4.20 [II]** (*a*) 15 N; (*b*) 0.17

**4.21 [II]** 58 N, 31 N

**4.22 [III]** 55 N

**4.23 [III]** 37 N, 88 N, 77 N, 0.14 kN

**4.24 [III]** 185 N

**4.25 [III]** (*a*) 6.9 N; (*b*) 0.30

**4.26 [III]** 0.35

# Equilibrium of a Rigid Body Under Coplanar Forces

**The Torque** ($\tau$) about an axis, due to a force, is a measure of the effectiveness of the force in producing rotation about that axis. The word comes from the French for "twist." It is defined in the following way:

$$\text{Torque} = \tau = rF \sin\theta$$

where $r$ is the radial distance from the axis of rotation to the point of application of the force, and $\theta$ is the acute angle between the lines-of-action of and $\vec{\mathbf{r}}$ and $\vec{\mathbf{F}}$, as shown in Fig. 5-1(*a*). Often this definition is written in terms of the *lever arm* of the force, which is the perpendicular distance from the axis of rotation to the line-of-action of the force, as shown in Fig. 5-1(*b*). Because the lever arm is simply $r \sin\theta$, the torque becomes

$$\tau = (F)\,(\text{lever arm})$$

The units of torque are newton-meters (N·m). Plus and minus signs will be assigned to torques; for example, a torque that tends to cause counterclockwise rotation about the axis might be positive, whereas one causing clockwise rotation would then be negative. This will allow us to sum the influences of several torques acting simultaneously.

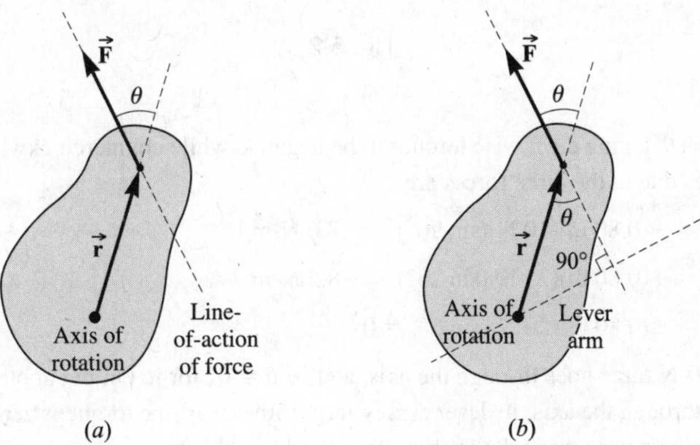


Fig. 5-1

**The Two Conditions for Equilibrium** of a rigid object under the action of *coplanar forces* are

(1) The *first* or *force condition*: The vector sum of all forces acting on the body must be zero:

$$\sum F_x = 0 \qquad \sum F_y = 0$$

where the plane of the coplanar forces is taken to be the *xy*-plane.

(2) The *second* or *torque condition*: Take any axis perpendicular to the plane of the coplanar forces. Call the torques that tend to cause clockwise rotation about that axis negative, and counterclockwise torques positive; then the sum of all the torques acting on the object must be zero:

$$\circlearrowleft\!(+)\ \sum \tau = 0$$

**The Center of Gravity** of an object is the point at which the entire weight of the object may be considered concentrated—that is, the line-of-action of the weight passes through the center of gravity. A single vertical upwardly directed force, equal in magnitude to the weight of the object, applied through its center of gravity, will keep the object in equilibrium.

**The Position of the Axis Is Arbitrary:** If the sum of the torques is zero about one axis for a body that obeys the force condition, it is zero about all other axes parallel to the first. To make the math a little simpler, we can often choose the axis in such a way that the line-of-action of an unknown force passes through the intersection of the axis and the plane of the forces. The angle $\theta$ between $\vec{\mathbf{r}}$ and $\vec{\mathbf{F}}$ is then zero; hence, that particular unknown force exerts zero torque and therefore does not appear in the torque equation.

## SOLVED PROBLEMS

**5.1 [I]** Imagine a bar of steel 80 cm long pivoted horizontally at its left end, as depicted in Fig. 5-2. Find the torque about axis-*A* (which is perpendicular to the page) due to each of the forces shown acting at its right end.

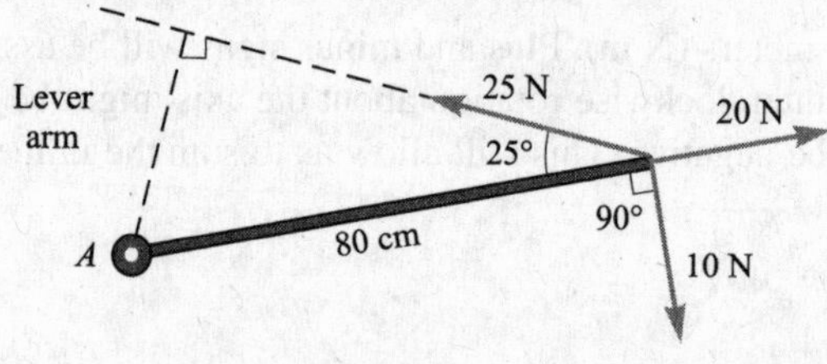


Fig. 5-2

We use $\tau = rF \sin\theta$, taking clockwise torques to be negative while counterclockwise torques are positive. The individual torques due to the three forces are

For 10 N: $\tau = -(0.80\text{ m})(10\text{ N})(\sin 90°) = -8.0\text{ N}\cdot\text{m}$

For 25 N: $\tau = +(0.80\text{ m})(25\text{ N})(\sin 25°) = +8.5\text{ N}\cdot\text{m}$

For 20 N: $\tau = \pm(0.80\text{ m})(20\text{ N})(\sin 0°) = 0$

The line of the 20-N force goes through the axis, and so $\theta = 0°$ for it. Or, put another way, because the line of the force passes through the axis, its lever arm is zero. Either way, the torque is zero for this (and any) force whose line-of-action passes through the axis. If you had trouble seeing which way the torques act, redraw the diagram on a piece of paper and imagine a pin stuck downward at A. Then put your finger at the right end of the rod and push the paper in the direction of the 10-N force. The paper will rotate clockwise around the pin. That's the angular direction of the torque due to that force.

**5.2 [II]** A uniform metal beam of length $L$ weighs 200 N and holds a 450-N object as shown in Fig. 5-3. Find the magnitudes of the forces exerted on the beam by the two supports at its ends. Assume the lengths are exact.

Rather than draw a separate free-body diagram, we show the forces on the object being considered (the beam) in Fig. 5-3. Because the beam is uniform, its center of gravity is at its geometric center. Thus, the weight of the beam (200 N) is shown acting downward at the beam's center. The forces $F_1$ and $F_2$ are exerted on the beam by the supports. Because there are no $x$-directed forces acting on the beam, we have only two equations to write for this equilibrium situation: $\sum F_y = 0$ and $\sum \tau = 0$.

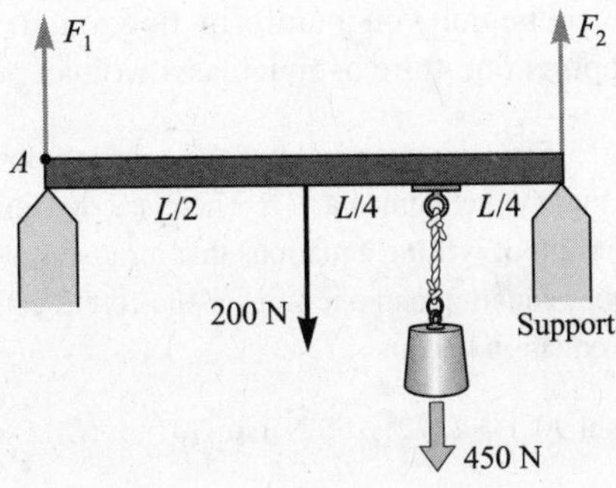


Fig. 5-3

$$+\uparrow\sum F_y = 0 \qquad \text{becomes} \qquad F_1 + F_2 - 200\text{ N} - 450\text{ N} = 0$$

Before the torque equation is written, an axis must be chosen. We choose it at $A$, so that the unknown force $F_1$ will pass through it and exert no torque. The torque equation is then

$$\circlearrowleft\!+\sum \tau_A = -(L/2)(200\text{ N})(\sin 90°) - (3L/4)(450\text{ N})(\sin 90°) + LF_2 \sin 90° = 0$$

Dividing through the equation by $L$ and solving for $F_2$, we find that $F_2 = 438$ N.

To determine $F_1$, substitute the value of $F_2$ in the force equation, thereby obtaining $F_1 = 212$ N.

**5.3 [II]** A uniform, horizontal, 100-N pipe is used as a lever, as shown in Fig. 5-4. Where must the fulcrum (the support point) be placed if a 500-N weight at one end is to balance a 200-N weight at the other end? What is the upward reaction force exerted by the support on the pipe?

The forces in question are shown in Fig. 5-4, where $F_R$ is the reaction force of the support on the pipe. The weight of the pipe acts downward at its center. We assume that the support point is at a distance $x$ from one end. Take the axis of rotation to be at the support point. Then the torque equation, $\circlearrowleft\!+\sum \tau = 0$, about that point becomes

$$+(x)(200\text{ N})(\sin 90°) + (x - L/2)(100\text{ N})(\sin 90°) - (L - x)(500\text{ N})(\sin 90°) = 0$$

This simplifies to

$$(800\text{ N})(x) = (550\text{ N})(L)$$

and so $x = 0.69L$. The support should be placed 0.69 of the way from the lighter-loaded end.

To find $F_R$ use $+\uparrow\sum F_y = 0$,

$$F_R - 200\text{ N} - 100\text{ N} - 500\text{ N} = 0$$

from which $F_R = 800$ N.

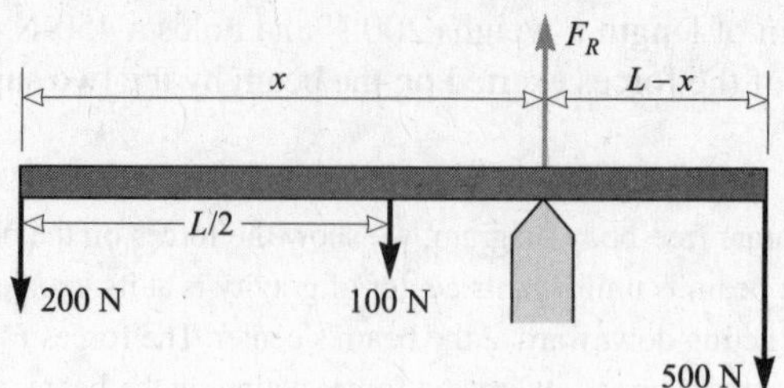

Fig. 5-4

**5.4 [II]** Where must a 0.80-kN object be hung on a uniform, horizontal, rigid 100-N pole so that a girl pushing up at one end supports one-third as much as a woman pushing up at the other end?

The situation is shown in Fig. 5-5, where the weight of the pole acts down at its center. We represent the force exerted by the girl as $F$, and that by the woman as $3F$. There are two unknowns, $F$ and $x$, and we will need two equations. To avoid the possibility of writing equations that turn out not to be independent, it's a good practice to write one sum-of-the-torques equation and one sum-of-the-forces equation. Take the rotational axis point at the left end. Then the torque equation becomes

$$-(x)(800\text{ N})(\sin 90°) - (L/2)(100\text{ N})(\sin 90°) + (L)(F)(\sin 90°) = 0$$

For the second equation write

$$+\uparrow\sum F_y = 3F - 800\text{ N} - 100\text{ N} + F = 0$$

from which $F = 225$ N. Substitution of this value in the torque equation yields

$$(800\text{ N})(x) = (225\text{ N})(L) - (100\text{ N})(L/2)$$

and so $x = 0.22L$. The load should be hung 0.22 of the way from the woman to the girl.

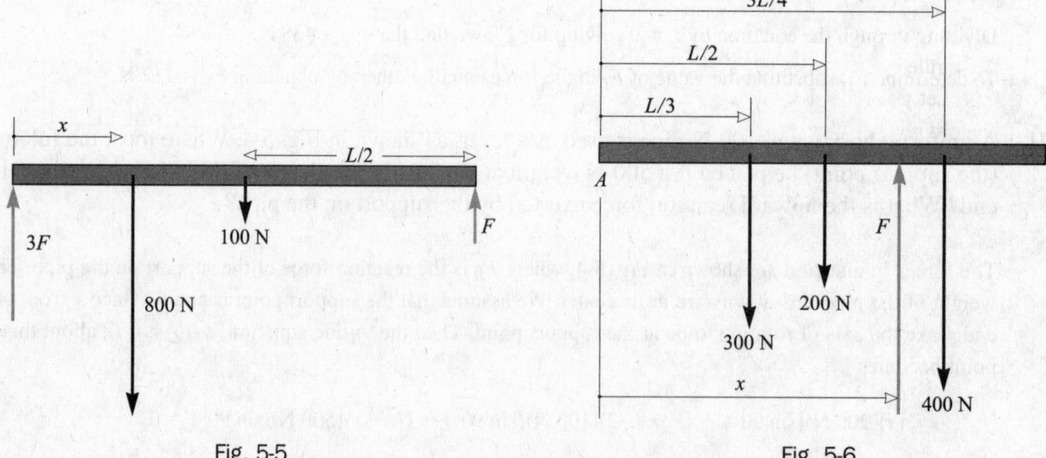

Fig. 5-5 Fig. 5-6

**5.5 [II]** A uniform, horizontal, 0.20-kN board of length $L$ has two objects hanging from it with weights of 300 N at exactly $L/3$ from one end and 400 N at exactly $3L/4$ from the same end. What single additional force acting on the board will cause the board to be in equilibrium?

The situation is drawn in Fig. 5-6, where $F$ is the force we wish to find. For equilibrium, $\sum F_y = 0$ and so

$$F = 400\text{ N} + 200\text{ N} + 300\text{ N} = 900\text{ N}$$

Because the board is to be in equilibrium, we are free to locate the axis of rotation anywhere. Choose it at point-$A$ at the left end of the board, since all the forces are measured (as to location) from that end in the diagram. Then $\sum\tau = 0$, and taking counterclockwise as positive,

$$+(x)(F)(\sin 90°) - (3L/4)(400\text{ N})(\sin 90°) - (L/2)(200\text{ N})(\sin 90°) - (L/3)(300\text{ N})(\sin 90°) = 0$$

Using $F = 900$ N, we find that $x = 0.56L$. The required force is 0.90 kN upward at $0.56L$ from the left end.

**5.6 [III]** The right-angle rule (or square) depicted in Fig. 5-7 hangs at rest from a peg as shown. It is made of a uniform metal sheet. One arm is $L$ cm long, while the other is $2L$ cm long. Find (to two significant figures) the angle $\theta$ at which it will hang.

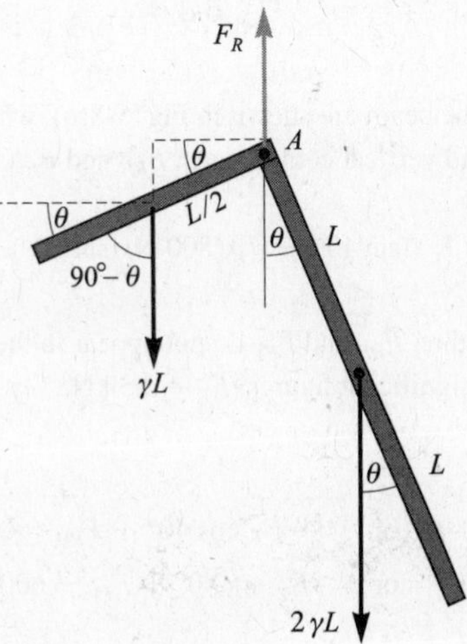


Fig. 5-7

If the rule is not too wide, we can approximate it as two thin rods of lengths $L$ and $2L$ joined perpendicularly at $A$. Let $\gamma$ be the weight of each centimeter of rule. The forces acting are indicated in Fig. 5-7, where $F_R$ is the upward reaction force of the peg.

Write the torque equation using point-$A$ as the axis of rotation. Because $\tau = rF\sin\theta$ and because the torque about $A$ due to $F_R$ is zero, the torque equation becomes

$$(+)\sum \tau_A = +(L/2)(\gamma L)[\sin(90° - \theta)] - (L)(2\gamma L)(\sin\theta) = 0$$

where the moment arm of the counterclockwise torque (due to $\gamma L$) is $(L/2)\sin(90° - \theta)$ and that of the clockwise torque (due to $2\gamma L$) is $L\sin\theta$. Recall that $\sin(90° - \theta) = \cos\theta$. After making this substitution and dividing by $2\gamma L^2\cos\theta$,

$$\frac{\sin\theta}{\cos\theta} = \tan\theta = \frac{1}{4}$$

which yields $\theta = 14°$.

**5.7 [II]** Consider the situation illustrated in Fig. 5-8($a$). The uniform 0.60-kN beam is hinged at $P$. Find the tension in the tie rope and the components of the reaction force exerted by the hinge on the beam. Give your answers to two significant figures.

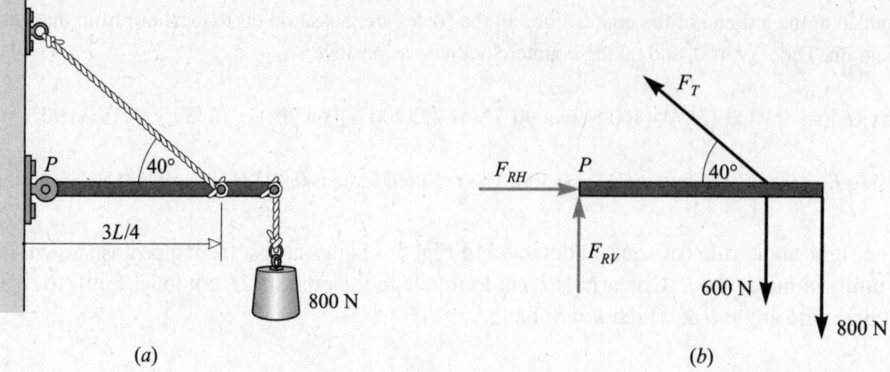


Fig. 5-8

The reaction forces acting on the beam are shown in Fig. 5-8($b$), where the force exerted by the hinge is represented by its horizontal and vertical components, $F_{RH}$ and $F_{RV}$. The torque equation about $P$ is

$$(+)\sum \tau_P = +(3L/4)(F_T)(\sin 40°) - (L)(800\text{ N})(\sin 90°) - (L/2)(600\text{ N})(\sin 90°) = 0$$

(We take the axis at $P$ because then $F_{RH}$ and $F_{RV}$ do not appear in the torque equation.) Solving this equation yields $F_T = 2280$ N or, to two significant figures, $F_T = 2.3$ kN.

To find $F_{RH}$ and $F_{RV}$, write

$$\overset{+}{\rightarrow}\sum F_x = 0 \quad \text{or} \quad -F_T \cos 40° + F_{RH} = 0$$
$$+\uparrow\sum F_y = 0 \quad \text{or} \quad F_T \sin 40° + F_{RV} - 600 - 800 = 0$$

Since we know $F_T$, these equations lead to $F_{RH} = 1750$ N or 1.8 kN and $F_{RV} = 65.6$ N or 66 N.

**5.8 [II]** A uniform, 0.40-kN boom is supported as shown in Fig. 5-9($a$). Find the tension in the tie rope and the force exerted on the boom by the pin at $P$.

The forces acting on the boom are shown in Fig. 5-9($b$). Take the pin as the axis of rotation. The torque equation is then

$$(+)\sum \tau_P = +(3L/4)(F_T)(\sin 50°) - (L/2)(400\text{ N})(\sin 40°) - (L)(2000\text{ N})(\sin 40°) = 0$$

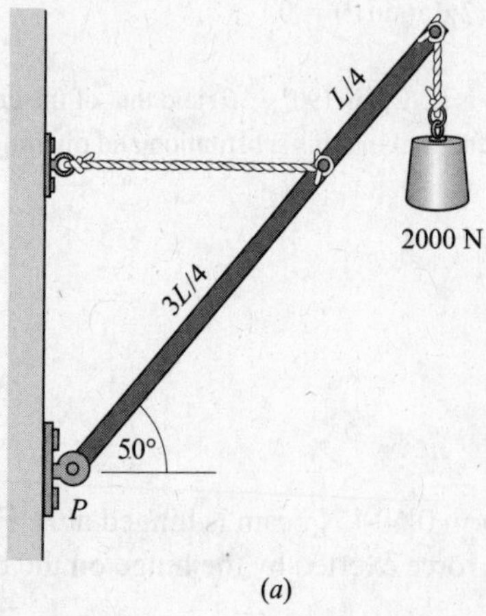


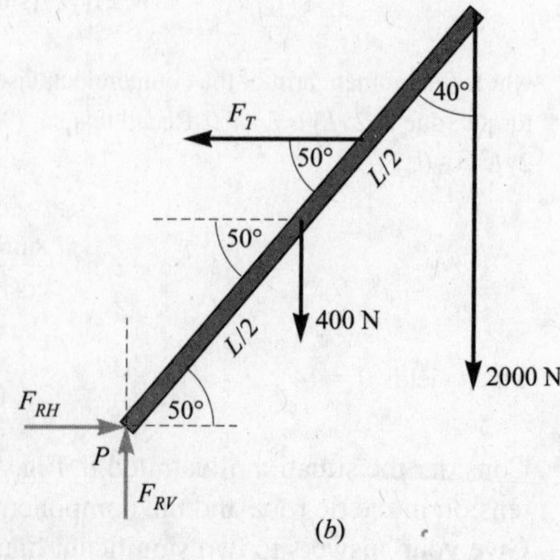


Fig. 5-9

from which it follows that $F_T = 2460$ N or 2.5 kN. Now write

$$\overset{+}{\rightarrow}\sum F_x = 0 \qquad \text{or} \qquad F_{RH} - F_T = 0$$

and so $F_{RH} = 2.5$ kN. Also,

$$+\uparrow\sum F_y = 0 \qquad \text{or} \qquad F_{RV} - 2000\text{ N} - 400\text{ N} = 0$$

and so $F_{RV} = 2.4$ kN. $F_{RV}$ and $F_{RH}$ are the components of the reaction force at the pin. The magnitude of this force is

$$\sqrt{(2400)^2 + (2460)^2} = 3.4\text{ kN}$$

The tangent of the angle it makes with the horizontal is $\tan\theta = 2400/2460$, and so $\theta = 44°$.

**5.9 [II]** As indicated in Fig. 5-10, hinges $A$ and $B$ hold a uniform, 400-N door in place. If the upper hinge happens to support the entire weight of the door, find the forces exerted on the door at both hinges. The width of the door is exactly $h/2$, where $h$ is the distance between the hinges.

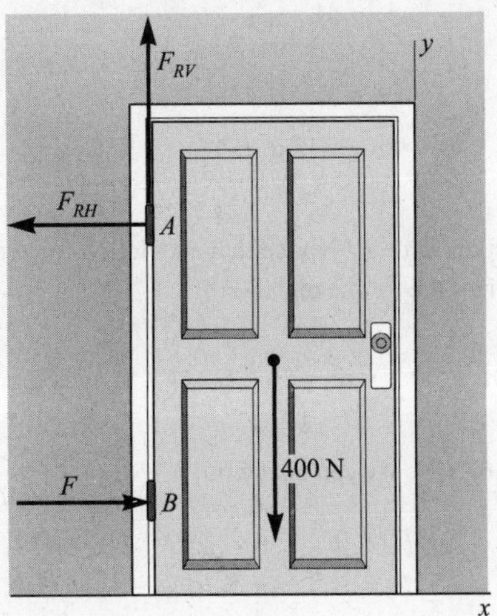


Fig. 5-10

The forces acting on the door are shown in Fig. 5-10. Only a horizontal force acts at $B$, because the upper hinge is assumed to support the door's weight. Take torques about point-$A$ as the axis of rotation:

$$(+)\sum\tau_A = 0 \qquad \text{becomes} \qquad +(h)(F)(\sin 90.0°) - (h/4)(400\text{ N})(\sin 90.0°) = 0$$

from which $F = 100$ N. We also have

$$\overset{+}{\rightarrow}\sum F_x = 0 \qquad \text{or} \qquad F - F_{RH} = 0$$
$$+\uparrow\sum F_y = 0 \qquad \text{or} \qquad F_{RV} - 400\text{ N} - 0$$

We find from these that $F_{RH} = 100$ N and $F_{RV} = 400$ N.

For the resultant reaction force $F_R$ on the hinge at $A$, we have

$$F_R = \sqrt{(400)^2 + (100)^2} = 412\text{ N}$$

The tangent of the angle that $\vec{\mathbf{F}}_R$ makes with the negative $x$-direction is $F_{RV}/F_{RH}$, and so the angle is arctan $4.00 = 76.0°$.

**5.10 [II]** A ladder leans against a smooth wall, as can be seen in Fig. 5-11. (By a "smooth" wall, we mean that the wall exerts on the ladder only a force that is perpendicular to the wall. There is no friction force.) The ladder weighs 200 N, and its center of gravity is $0.40L$ from the base, where $L$ is the ladder's length. (*a*) How large a friction force must exist at the base of the ladder if it is not to slip? (*b*) What is the necessary coefficient of static friction?

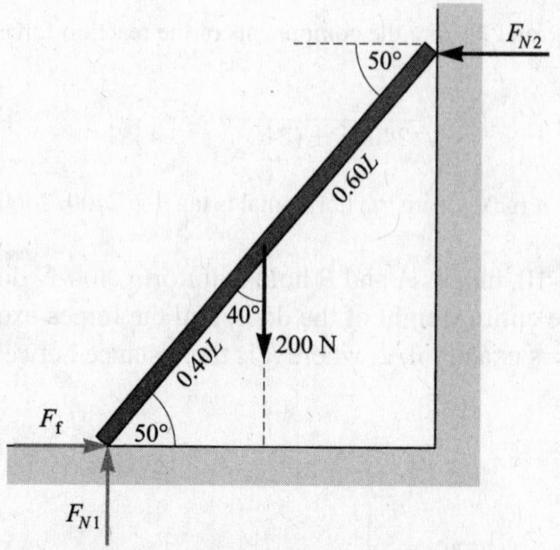


Fig. 5-11

(*a*) We wish to find the friction force $F_f$. Notice that no friction force exists at the top of the ladder. Taking torques about point $A$ gives the torque equation

$$\circlearrowleft + \sum \tau_A = -(0.40L)(200\text{ N})(\sin 40°) + (L)(F_{N2})(\sin 50°) = 0$$

Solving leads to $F_{N2} = 67.1$ N. We can also write

$$\overset{+}{\rightarrow}\sum F_x = 0 \quad \text{or} \quad F_f - F_{N2} = 0$$
$$+\uparrow\sum F_y = 0 \quad \text{or} \quad F_{N1} - 200 = 0$$

and so $F_f = 67$ N and $F_{N1} = 0.20$ kN.

(*b*)
$$\mu_s = \frac{F_f}{F_{N1}} = \frac{67.1}{200} = 0.34$$

**5.11 [III]** For the situation drawn in Fig. 5-12(*a*), find $F_{T1}$, $F_{T2}$, and $F_{T3}$. The boom is uniform and weighs 800 N.

First apply the force condition to point-$A$. The appropriate free-body diagram is shown in Fig. 5-12(*b*). We then have

$$F_{T2}\cos 50.0° - 2000\text{ N} = 0 \qquad \text{and} \qquad F_{T1} - F_{T2}\sin 50.0° = 0$$

From the first of these we find $F_{T2} = 3.11$ kN; then the second equation gives $F_{T1} = 2.38$ kN.

Let us now isolate the boom and apply the equilibrium conditions to it. The appropriate free-body diagram is found in Fig. 5-12(*c*). The torque equation, for torques taken about point $C$, is

$$\circlearrowleft + \sum \tau_C = +(L)(F_{T3})(\sin 20.0°) - (L)(3110\text{ N})(\sin 90.0°) - (L/2)(800\text{ N})(\sin 40.0°) = 0$$

Solving for $F_{T3}$, we compute it to be 9.84 kN. If it were required, we could find $F_{RH}$ and $F_{RV}$ by using the $x$- and $y$-force equations.

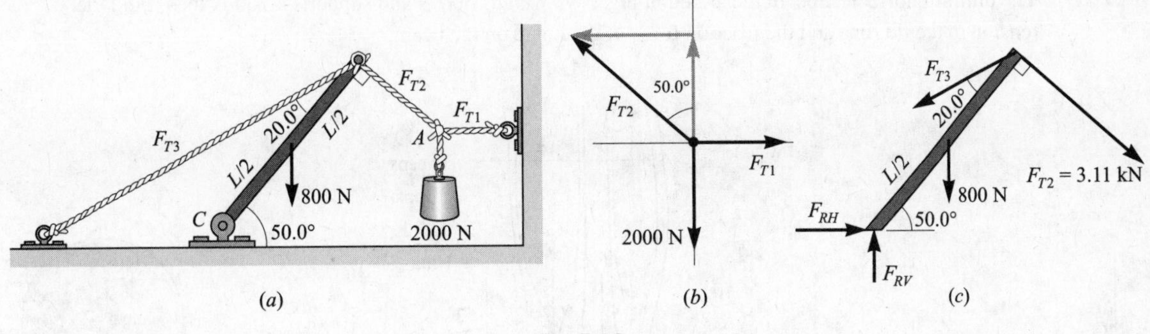


Fig. 5-12

## SUPPLEMENTARY PROBLEMS

**5.12 [II]** As depicted in Fig. 5-13, two people sit in a car that weighs 8000 N. The person in front weighs 700 N, while the one in the back weighs 900 N. Call $L$ the distance between the front and back wheels. The car's center of gravity is a distance 0.400 $L$ behind the front wheels. How much force does each front wheel and each back wheel support if the people are seated along the centerline of the car?

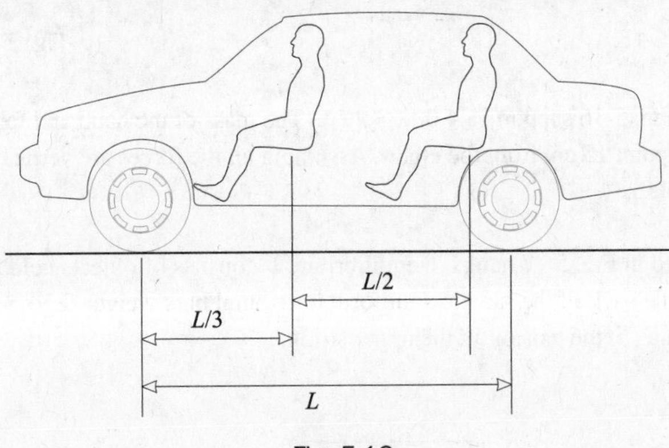


Fig. 5-13

**5.13 [I]** Two people, one at each end of a uniform beam that weighs 400 N, hold the beam at an angle of 25.0° to the horizontal. How large a vertical force must each person exert on the beam?

**5.14 [II]** Repeat Problem 5.13 if a 140-N child sits on the beam at a point one-fourth of the way along the beam from its lower end.

**5.15 [II]** Shown in Fig. 5-14 is a uniform, 1600-N beam hinged at one end and held by a horizontal tie rope at the other. Determine the tension $F_T$ in the rope and the force components at the hinge.

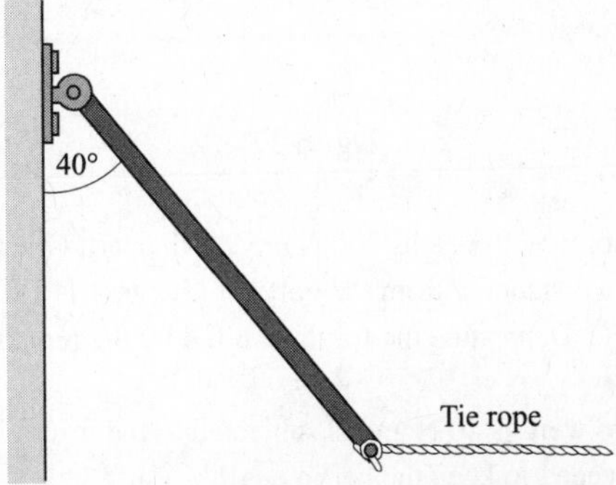


Fig. 5-14

**5.16 [II]** The uniform horizontal beam illustrated in Fig. 5-15 weighs 500 N and supports a 700-N load. Find the tension in the tie rope and the reaction force of the hinge on the beam.

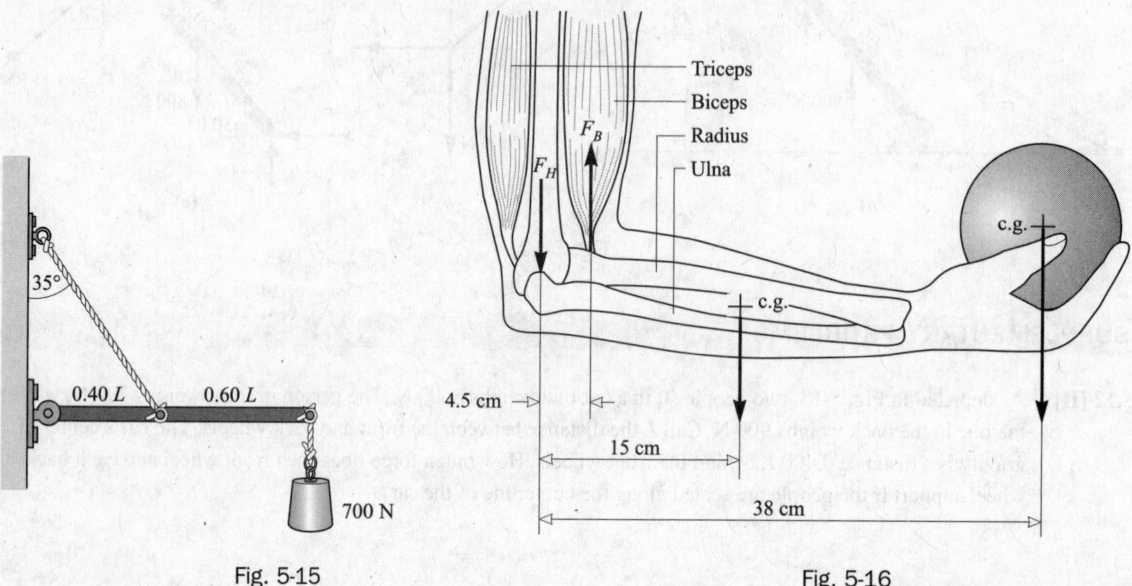


Fig. 5-15 Fig. 5-16

**5.17 [II]** The arm drawn in Fig. 5-16 supports a 4.0-kg sphere. The mass of the hand and forearm together is 3.0 kg and its weight acts at a point 15 cm from the elbow. Assuming all the forces are vertical, determine the force exerted by the biceps muscle.

**5.18 [II]** The mobile depicted in Fig. 5-17 hangs in equilibrium. It consists of objects held by vertical strings. Object-3 weighs 1.40 N, while each of the identical uniform horizontal bars weighs 0.50 N. Find *(a)* the weights of objects-1 and -2, and *(b)* the tension in the upper string.

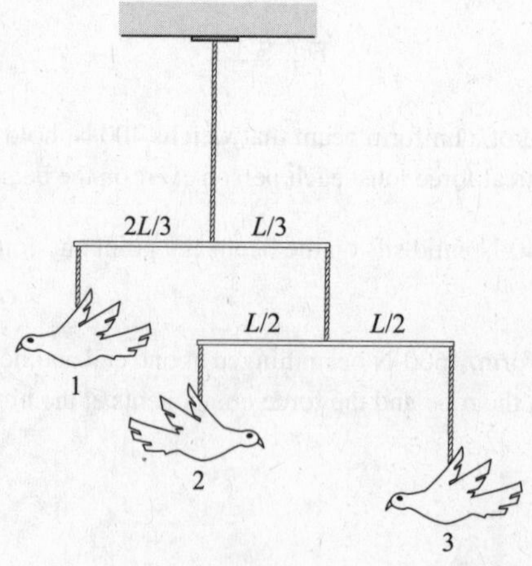


Fig. 5-17

**5.19 [II]** The hinges of a uniform door which weighs 200 N are 2.5 m apart. One hinge is a distance *d* from the top of the door, while the other is a distance *d* from the bottom. The door is 1.0 m wide. The weight of the door is supported by the lower hinge. Determine the forces exerted by the hinges on the door.

**5.20 [III]** The uniform bar in Fig. 5-18 weighs 40 N and is subjected to the forces shown. Find the magnitude, location, and direction of the force needed to keep the bar in equilibrium.

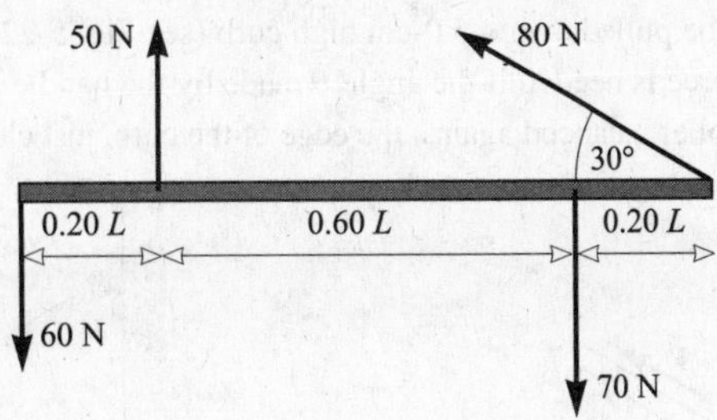


Fig. 5-18

**5.21 [III]** The horizontal, uniform, 120-N board drawn in Fig. 5-19 is supported by two ropes as shown. A 0.40-kN weight is suspended one-quarter of the way from the left end. Find $F_{T1}$, $F_{T2}$, and the angle $\theta$ made by the rope on the left.

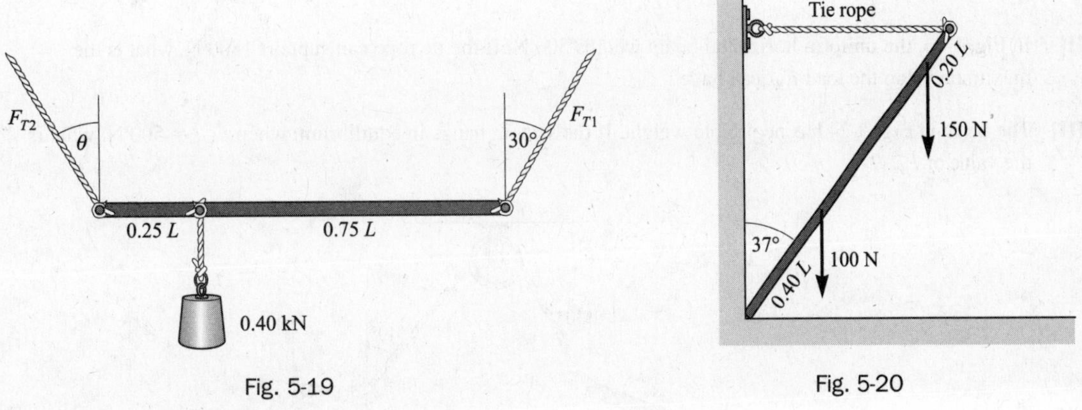


Fig. 5-19 Fig. 5-20

**5.22 [III]** The foot of a ladder rests against a wall, and its top is held by a horizontal tie rope, as indicated in Fig. 5-20. The ladder weighs 100 N, and its center of gravity is 0.40 of its length from the foot. A 150-N child hangs from a rung that is 0.20 of the length from the top. Determine the tension in the tie rope and the components of the force on the foot of the ladder.

**5.23 [III]** A truss is made by hinging two uniform, 150-N rafters as depicted in Fig. 5-21. They rest on an essentially frictionless floor and are held together by a horizontal tie rope. A 500-N load is held at their apex. Find the tension in the tie rope.

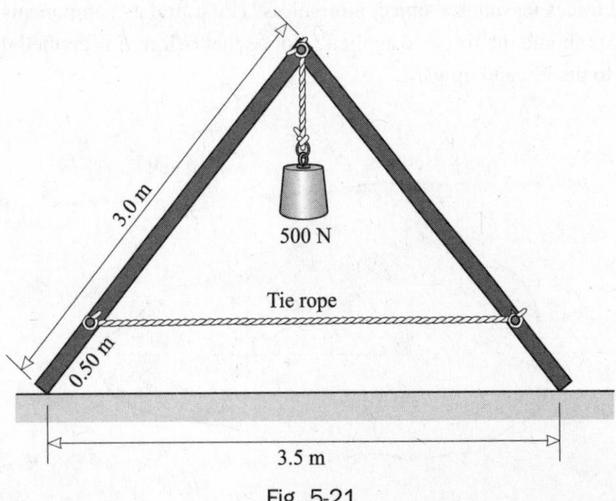


Fig. 5-21

**5.24 [III]** A 900-N lawn roller is to be pulled over a 5.0-cm high curb (see Fig. 5-22). The radius of the roller is 25 cm. What minimum pulling force is needed if the angle $\theta$ made by the handle is (*a*) 0° and (*b*) 30°? [*Hint:* Find the force needed to keep the roller balanced against the edge of the curb, just clear of the ground.]

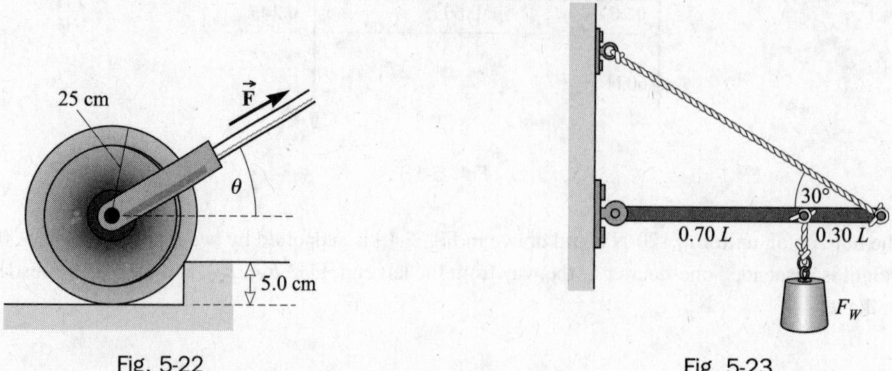

Fig. 5-22

Fig. 5-23

**5.25 [II]** In Fig. 5-23, the uniform horizontal beam weighs 500 N. If the tie rope can support 1800 N, what is the maximum value the load $F_W$ can have?

**5.26 [III]** The beam in Fig. 5-24 has negligible weight. If the system hangs in equilibrium when $F_{W1} = 500$ N, what is the value of $F_{W2}$?

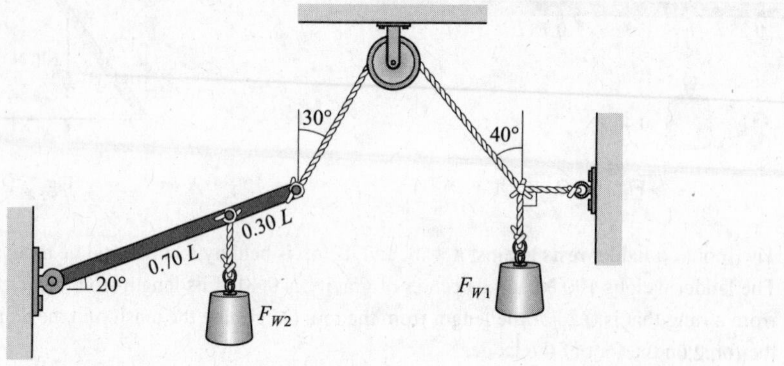

Fig. 5-24

**5.27 [III]** Repeat Problem 5.26, but now find $F_{W1}$ if $F_{W2}$ is 500 N. Here the beam weighs 300 N and is uniform.

**5.28 [III]** An object is subjected to the forces shown in Fig. 5-25. What single force $F$ applied at a point on the *x*-axis will balance these forces leaving the object motionless? (First find its components, and then find the force.) Where on the *x*-axis should the force be applied? Notice that before $F$ is applied there is an unbalanced force with components to the left and upward.

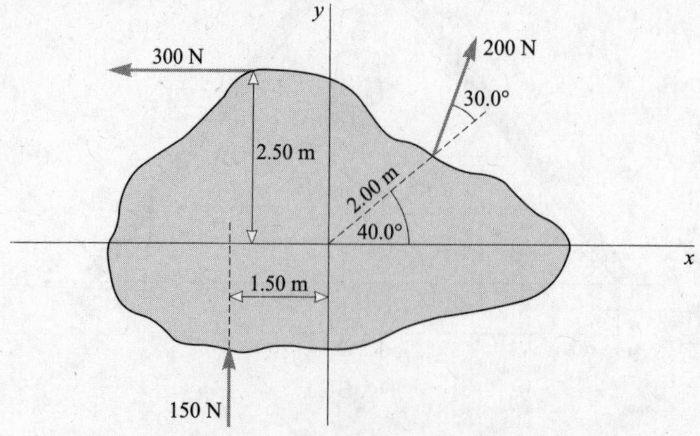

Fig. 5-25

**5.29 [III]** The solid uniform disk of radius $b$ illustrated in Fig. 5-26 can turn freely on an axle through its center. A hole of diameter $D$ is drilled through the disk; its center is a distance $r$ from the axle. The weight of the material drilled out is $F_{Wh}$. (*a*) Find the weight $F_W$ of an object hung from a string wound on the disk that will hold the disk in equilibrium in the position shown. (*b*) What would happen if the load $F_W$ vanished? Explain your answer.

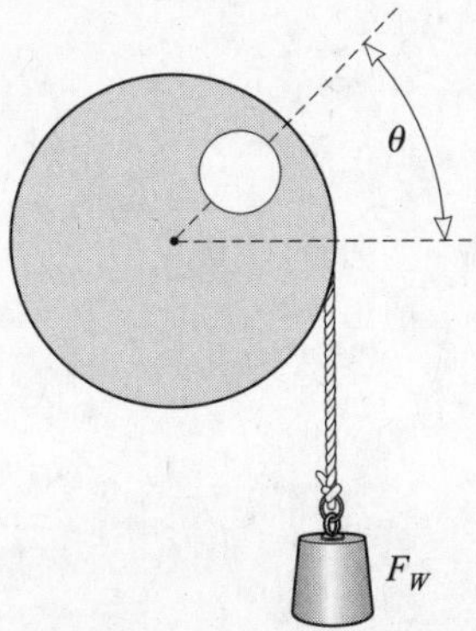


Fig. 5-26

## ANSWERS TO SUPPLEMENTARY PROBLEMS

**5.12 [II]** 2.09 kN, 2.71 kN

**5.13 [I]** 200 N

**5.14 [II]** 235 N, 305 N

**5.15 [II]** $F_T = 0.67$ kN, $F_{RH} = 0.67$ kN, $F_{RV} = 1.6$ kN

**5.16 [II]** 2.9 kN, 2.0 kN at 35° below the horizontal

**5.17 [II]** 0.43 kN

**5.18 [II]** (*a*) 1.5 N, 1.4 N; (*b*) 5.3 N

**5.19 [II]** The horizontal force at the upper hinge is 40 N. The force at the lower hinge is 0.20 kN at 79° above the horizontal.

**5.20 [III]** 0.11 kN, 0.68$L$ from right end, at 49°

**5.21 [III]** 0.19 kN, 0.37 kN, 14°

**5.22 [III]** $F_T = 0.12$ kN, $F_{RH} = 0.12$ kN, $F_{RV} = 0.25$ kN

**5.23 [III]** 0.28 kN

**5.24 [III]** (*a*) 0.68 kN; (*b*) 0.55 kN

**5.25 [II]** 0.93 kN

**5.26 [III]** 0.64 kN

**5.27 [III]** 0.56 kN

**5.28 [III]** $F_x = 232$ N, $F_y = -338$ N; $F = 410$ N at $-55.5°$; at $x = 2.14$ m

**5.29 [III]** (*a*) $F_W = F_{Wh}\,(r/b)\cos\theta$; (*b*) Imagine the disk divided into four quadrants, and notice that the second quadrant is heavier than the first. Without $F_W$, there would be an unbalanced torque about the axle and the disk would rotate counterclockwise until the hole was at the top and $\theta = 90°$. In that configuration the torque would disappear.

# CHAPTER 6

# Work, Energy, and Power

**The Work** ($W$) done by a force is expressed as the product of that force times the parallel distance over which it acts. Consider the simple case of straight-line motion shown in Fig. 6-1, where a force $\vec{\mathbf{F}}$ acts on a body that simultaneously undergoes a vector displacement $\vec{\mathbf{s}}$. The component of $\vec{\mathbf{F}}$ in the direction of $\vec{\mathbf{s}}$ is $F \cos\theta$. The work $W$ done by the force $\vec{\mathbf{F}}$ is defined to be the component of $\vec{\mathbf{F}}$ in the direction of the displacement, multiplied by the displacement:

$$W = (F \cos\theta)(s) = Fs \cos\theta$$

Notice that $\theta$ is the angle between the force and displacement vectors. Work is a scalar quantity.

If $\vec{\mathbf{F}}$ and $\vec{\mathbf{s}}$ are in the same direction, $\cos\theta = \cos 0° = 1$ and $W = Fs$. But if $\vec{\mathbf{F}}$ and $\vec{\mathbf{s}}$ are in opposite directions, then $\cos\theta = \cos 180° = -1$ and $W = -Fs$; the work is negative.

To be completely rigorous while analyzing motion along curved paths, if work is to be formulated in terms of displacements, we should write the above equation using differentials and then integrate over the arbitrary path taken. We can use the simple expression given above, provided we limit things to straight-line motion, whereupon the path traveled equals the magnitude of the displacement vector.

Forces such as friction often slow the motion of an object and are then opposite in direction to the displacement. Such forces usually do negative work. Inasmuch as the friction force opposes the motion of an object, the work done in overcoming friction (along any path, curved or straight) equals the product of $F_f$ and the path length traveled. Thus, if an object is dragged against friction, back to the point where the journey started, work is done even if the net displacement is zero.

***Work is the transfer of energy from one entity to another by way of the action of a force applied over a distance****. The point of application of the force must move if work is to be done.*

**The Unit of Work** in the SI is the *newton-meter*, called the *joule* (J). One joule is the work done by a force of 1 N when it displaces an object 1 m in the direction of the force. Other units sometimes used for work are the *erg*, where 1 erg $= 10^{-7}$ J, and the *foot-pound* (ft·lb), where 1 ft·lb = 1.355 J.

**Energy** (E) ***is a measure of the change imparted to or by a system through the action of forces***. It can be mechanically transferred to an object when a force does work on that object. The amount of energy given to an object via the action of a force over a distance equals the work done. When an object does work, it gives up an amount of energy equal to the work it does. Because change can be effectuated in many different ways, there are a variety of forms of energy. All forms of energy (including work), have the same units, joules. Energy is a scalar quantity. An object that is capable of doing work possesses energy.

**Kinetic Energy** (KE) ***is the energy possessed by an object because it is in motion***. If an object of mass $m$ is moving with a speed $v$, it has translational KE given by

$$\text{KE} = \frac{1}{2} m v^2$$

When $m$ is in kg and $\theta$ is in m/s, the units of KE are joules.

**Gravitational Potential Energy** ($PE_G$) is the energy possessed by an object because of the gravitational interaction. In falling through a vertical distance $h$, a mass $m$ can do work in the amount $mgh$. We define the $PE_G$ of an object relative to an arbitrary zero level, often the Earth's surface. If the object is at a height $h$ above the zero (or reference) level,

$$PE_G = mgh$$

where $g$ is the acceleration due to gravity. Notice that $mg$ is the weight of the object. The units of $PE_G$ are joules when $m$ is in kg, $g$ is in $m/s^2$, and $h$ is in m.

**The Work-Energy Theorem:** When work is done on a point mass or a rigid body, and there is no change in PE, the energy imparted can only appear as KE. Insofar as a body is not totally rigid, however, energy can be transferred to its parts and the work done on it will not precisely equal its change in KE.

**Forces that Propel But Do No Work:** An applied force can propel a non-rigid body and do little or no work on it because the point of application of the force does not move appreciably. For example, when a person jumps straight up off a floor, the normal force essentially does no work on the person, although it accelerates the person upward. Accordingly, one must be careful when considering the mechanics of self-propelled bodies like cars, people, and airplanes.

**Conservation of Energy:** Energy can neither be created nor destroyed, but only transformed from one kind to another. That old saying is only true if we regard mass as a form of energy. Ordinarily, the conversion of mass into energy, and vice versa, predicted by the Special Theory of Relativity can be ignored. (This subject is treated in Chapter 41; refer to Chapter 7 for additional applications of energy conservation.)

For a system that is isolated in the sense that it neither gains nor loses energy, its initial energy $E_i$ must equal its final energy $E_f$.

**Power** (P) is the time rate of doing work:

$$\text{Average power} = \frac{\text{Work done by a force}}{\text{Time taken to do this work}} = \text{Force} \times \text{speed}$$

where the speed is measured in the direction of the force applied to the object. In the SI, the unit of power is the *watt* (W), and 1 W = 1 J/s.

Another unit of power often used is *horsepower*: 1 hp = 746 W. Generally speaking, ***power is the rate at which energy is transferred.***

**The Kilowatt-Hour** is a unit of energy. If a force is doing work at a rate of 1 kilowatt (which is 1000 J/s), then in 1 hour it will do 1 kW·h of work:

$$1\,\text{kW}\cdot\text{h} = 3.6 \times 10^6\ \text{J} = 3.6\ \text{MJ}$$

## SOLVED PROBLEMS

**6.1 [I]** In Fig. 6-1, assume that the object is being pulled in a straight line along the ground by a 75-N force directed 28° above the horizontal. How much work does the force do in pulling the object 8.0 m?

The work done is equal to the product of the displacement, 8.0 m, and the component of the force that is parallel to the displacement, (75 N)(cos 28°). Thus,

$$W = (75\ \text{N})(\cos 28°)(8.0\ \text{m}) = 0.53\ \text{kJ}$$

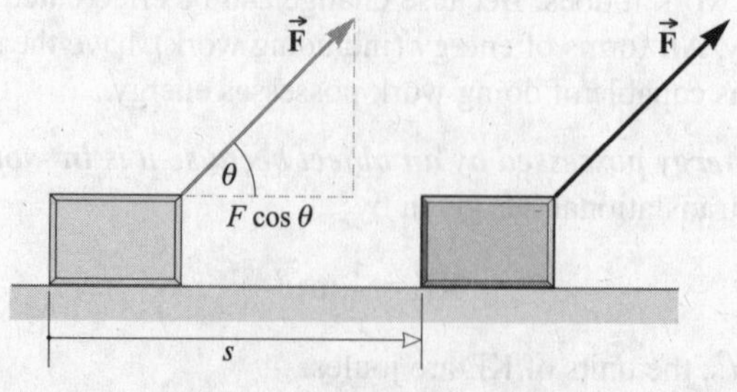


Fig. 6-1

**6.2 [I]** A block moves up a 30° incline under the action of applied forces, three of which are shown in Fig. 6-2. $\vec{\mathbf{F}}_1$ is horizontal and of magnitude 40 N. $\vec{\mathbf{F}}_2$ is normal to the plane and of magnitude 20 N. $\vec{\mathbf{F}}_3$ is parallel to the plane and of magnitude 30 N. Determine the work done by each force as the block (and point of application of each force) moves 80 cm up the incline.

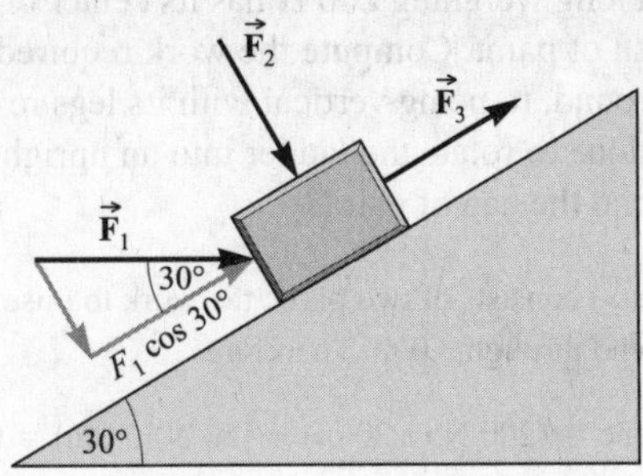


Fig. 6-2

The component of $\vec{\mathbf{F}}_1$ along the direction of the displacement is

$$F_1 \cos 30° = (40\text{ N})(0.866) = 34.6\text{ N}$$

Hence, the work done by $\vec{\mathbf{F}}_1$ is (34.6 N)(0.80 m) = 28 J. (Notice that the distance must be expressed in meters.)

Because it has no component in the direction of the displacement, $\vec{\mathbf{F}}_2$ does no work.

The component of $\vec{\mathbf{F}}_3$ in the direction of the displacement is 30 N. Hence, the work done by $\vec{\mathbf{F}}_3$ is (30 N) (0.80 m) = 24 J.

**6.3 [II]** A 300-g object slides 80 cm in a straight line along a horizontal tabletop. How much work is done in overcoming friction between the object and the table if the coefficient of kinetic friction is 0.20?

First find the friction force. Since the normal force equals the weight of the object,

$$F_f = \mu_k F_N = (0.20)(0.300\text{ kg})(9.81\text{ m/s}^2) = 0.588\text{ N}$$

The work done overcoming friction is $F_f s \cos\theta$. Because the friction force is opposite in direction to the displacement, $\theta = 180°$. Therefore,

$$\text{Work} = F_f s \cos 180° = (0.588\text{ N})(0.80\text{ m})(-1) = -0.47\text{ J}$$

The work is negative because the friction force is oppositely directed to the displacement; it slows the object and it decreases the object's kinetic energy, or more to the point, it opposes the motion.

**6.4 [I]** How much work is done against gravity in lifting a 3.0-kg object through a vertical distance of 40 cm?

An external force is needed to lift an object. If the object is raised at constant speed, the lifting force must equal the weight of the object. The work done by the lifting force is referred to as *work done against gravity*. Because the lifting force is *mg*, where *m* is the mass of the object,

$$\text{Work} = (mg)(h)(\cos\theta) = (3.0\text{ kg} \times 9.81\text{ N})(0.40\text{ m})(1) = 12\text{ J}$$

In general, the work done against gravity in lifting an object of mass *m* through a vertical distance *h* is *mgh*.

**6.5 [I]** How much work is done on an object by the force that supports it as the object is lowered at a constant speed through a vertical distance *h*? How much work does the gravitational force on the object do in this same process?

The supporting force is *mg*, where *m* is the mass of the object. It is directed upward while the displacement is downward. Hence, the work it does is negative:

$$Fs \cos\theta = (mg)(h)(\cos 180°) = -mgh$$

The force of gravity acting on the object is also $mg$, but it is directed downward in the same direction as the displacement. The work done on the object by the force of gravity is therefore positive:

$$Fs\cos\theta = (mg)(h)(\cos 0°) = mgh$$

**6.6 [II]** A narrowing ladder 3.0 m long weighing 200 N has its center of gravity 120 cm from the bottom. At its top end is a 50-N can of paint. Compute the work required to raise the ladder from being horizontal, lying on the ground, to being vertical with its legs resting on the ground. In other words, how much work must be done to rotate the ladder into an upright vertical position, thereby raising both its center of gravity and the can of paint?

The work done (against gravity) consists of two parts: the work to raise the center of gravity 1.20 m and the work to raise the load at the end through 3.0 m. Therefore,

$$\text{Work done} = (200\text{ N})(1.20\text{ m}) + (50\text{ N})(3.0\text{m}) = 0.39\text{ kJ}$$

**6.7 [II]** Compute the work done against gravity by a pump that discharges 600 liters of fuel oil into a tank 20 m above the pump's intake. One cubic centimeter of fuel oil has a mass of 0.82 g. One liter is 1000 cm$^3$.

The mass lifted is

$$(600\text{ liters})\left(1000\,\frac{\text{cm}^3}{\text{liter}}\right)\left(0.82\,\frac{\text{g}}{\text{cm}^3}\right) = 492\,000\text{ g} = 492\text{ kg}$$

The lifting work is then

$$\text{Work} = (mg)(h) = (492\text{ kg} \times 9.81\text{ m/s}^2)(20\text{ m}) = 96\text{ kJ}$$

**6.8 [I]** A 2.0-kg mass falls 400 cm. (*a*) How much work was done on it by the gravitational force? (*b*) How much $PE_G$ did it lose? (*c*) Given that work is the transfer of energy, where does that energy end up?

(*a*) Gravity pulls with a force $mg$ on the object, and the displacement is 4 m in the direction of the force. The positive work done by gravity is therefore

$$(mg)(4.00\text{ m}) = (2.0\text{ kg} \times 9.81\text{ N})(4.00\text{ m}) = 78\text{ J}$$

(*b*) The change in $PE_G$ of the object is $mgh_f - mgh_i$, where $h_i$ and $h_f$ are the initial and final heights of the object above the reference level. We then have

$$\text{Change in PE}_G = mgh_f - mgh_i = mg(h_f - h_i) - (2.0\text{ kg} \times 9.81\text{ N})(-4.0\text{ m}) = -78\text{ J}$$

The loss in $PE_G$ is 78 J.

(*c*) Gravity provides the force that accelerates the 2.0-kg mass and increases its kinetic energy by 78 J.

**6.9 [II]** A force of 1.50 N acts on a 0.20-kg cart so as to uniformly accelerate it along a straight air track. The track and force are horizontal and in line. How fast is the cart going after acceleration from rest through 30 cm, if friction is negligible?

The work done by the force causes, and is equal to, the increase in KE of the cart. Therefore,

$$\text{Work done} = (\text{KE})_{\text{end}} - (\text{KE})_{\text{start}} \quad \text{or} \quad Fs\cos 0° = \tfrac{1}{2}mv_f^2 - 0$$

Substituting gives

$$(1.50\text{ N})(0.30\text{ m}) = \tfrac{1}{2}(0.20\text{ kg})v_f^2$$

from which $v_f = 2.1\text{ m/s}$.

**6.10 [II]** A 0.50-kg block slides across a tabletop with an initial velocity of 20 cm/s and comes to rest in a distance of 70 cm. Find the average friction force that retarded its motion.

The KE of the block is decreased because of the slowing action of the friction force. That is,

$$\text{Change in KE of block} = \text{Work done on block by friction force}$$

$$\tfrac{1}{2}mv_f^2 - \tfrac{1}{2}mv_i^2 = F_f s\cos\theta$$

Because the friction force on the block is opposite in direction to the displacement, $\cos\theta = -1$. Using $v_f = 0$, $v_i = 0.20$ m/s, and $s = 0.70$ m, the above equation becomes

$$0 - \tfrac{1}{2}(0.50\text{ kg})(0.20\text{ m/s})^2 = (F_f)(0.70\text{ m})(-1)$$

from which $F_f = 0.014$ N.

**6.11 [II]** A car going 15 m/s is brought to rest in a distance of 2.0 m as it strikes a pile of dirt. How large an average force is exerted by seatbelts on a 90-kg passenger as the car is stopped?

We assume the seatbelts stop the passenger in 2.0 m. The force $F$ they apply acts through a distance of 2.0 m and decreases the passenger's KE to zero. So

$$\text{Change in KE of passenger} = \text{Work done by } F$$

$$0 - \tfrac{1}{2}(90\text{ kg})(15\text{ m/s})^2 = (F)(2.0\text{ m})(-1)$$

where $\cos\theta = -1$ because the restraining force on the passenger is opposite in direction to the displacement. Solving, we find $F = 5.1$ kN.

**6.12 [II]** A projectile is shot straight upward from the Earth with a speed of 20 m/s. Using energy considerations, how high is the projectile when its speed is 8.0 m/s? Ignore air friction.

Because the projectile's energy is conserved,

$$\text{Change in KE} + \text{change in PE}_G = 0$$
$$\tfrac{1}{2}mv_f^2 - \tfrac{1}{2}mv_i^2 + (mg)(h_f - h_i) = 0$$

We wish to find $h_f - h_i$. After a little algebra,

$$h_f - h_i = -\frac{v_f^2 - v_i^2}{2g} = -\frac{(8.0\text{ m/s})^2 - (20\text{ m/s})^2}{2(9.81\text{ m/s})^2} = 17\text{ m}$$

**Alternative Method**

Since energy, E, is conserved

$$\text{E}_i = \text{E}_f$$
$$\text{KE}_i + \text{PE}_{Gi} = \text{KE}_f + \text{PE}_{Gf}$$

and

$$\tfrac{1}{2}mv_i^2 + 0 = \tfrac{1}{2}mv_f^2 + mgh_f$$
$$\tfrac{1}{2}m(v_i^2 - v_f^2) = mgh_f$$
$$\tfrac{1}{2}(v_i^2 - v_f^2) = gh_f$$

**6.13 [II]** In an Atwood machine (see Problem 3.30), the two masses are 800 g and 700 g. The system is released from rest. How fast is the 800-g mass moving after it has fallen 120 cm?

The 700-g mass rises 120 cm while the 800-g mass falls 120 cm, so the net change in $PE_G$ is

$$\text{Change in PE}_G = (0.70\text{ kg})(9.81\text{ m/s}^2)(1.20\text{ m}) - (0.80\text{ kg})(9.81\text{ m/s}^2)(1.20\text{ m}) = -1.18\text{ J}$$

which is a loss in $PE_G$. Because energy is conserved, the KE of the masses must increase by 1.18 J. Therefore,

$$\text{Change in KE } = 1.18\text{ J} = \tfrac{1}{2}(0.70\text{ kg})(v_f^2 - v_i^2) + \tfrac{1}{2}(0.80\text{ kg})(v_f^2 - v_i^2)$$

The system started from rest, so $v_i = 0$. We solve the above equation for $v_f$ and find $v_f = 1.25$ m/s.

**6.14 [II]** Figure 6-3 shows a bead sliding on a wire. If friction forces are negligible and the bead has a speed of 200 cm/s at *A*, what will be its speed (*a*) at point *B*? (*b*) At point *C*?

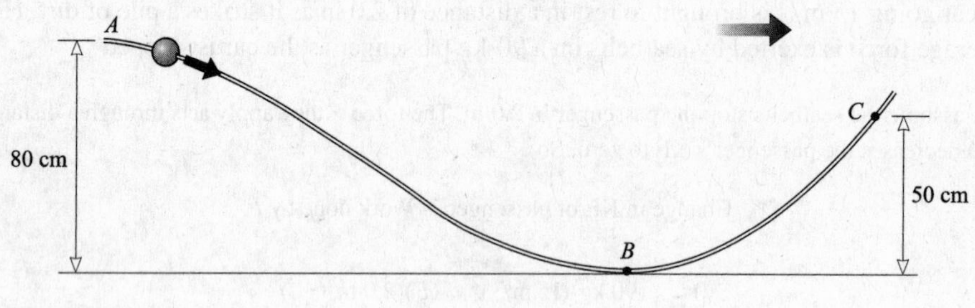


Fig. 6-3

The energy of the bead is conserved, so we can write

$$\text{Change in KE} + \text{change in PE}_G = 0$$

$$\tfrac{1}{2}mv_f^2 - \tfrac{1}{2}mv_i^2 + mg(h_f - h_i) = 0$$

(*a*) Here, $v_i = 2.0$ m/s, $h_i = 0.80$ m, and $h_f = 0$. Using these values, while noticing that *m* cancels out, gives $v_f = 4.4$ m/s.

(*b*) Here, $v_i = 2.0$ m/s, $h_i = 0.80$ m, and $h_f = 0.50$ m. Using these values leads to $v_f = 3.1$ m/s.

**Alternative Method**

Since energy, E, is conserved,

$$E_i = E_f$$

$$KE_i + PE_{Gi} = KE_f + PE_{Gf}$$

$$\tfrac{1}{2}mv_i^2 + mgh_i = \tfrac{1}{2}mv_f^2 + mgh_f$$

$$\tfrac{1}{2}v_i^2 + gh_i = \tfrac{1}{2}v_f^2 + gh_f$$

$$(2.00\text{ m/s})^2 + 2(9.81\text{ m/s}^2)(0.80\text{ m} - h_f) = v_f^2$$

**6.15 [II]** Suppose the bead in Fig. 6-3 has a mass of 15 g and a speed of 2.0 m/s at *A*, and it stops as it reaches point *C*. The length of the wire from *A* to *C* is 250 cm. How large an average friction force opposed the motion of the bead?

When the bead moves from $A$ to $C$, it experiences a change in its total energy: it loses both KE and $PE_G$. This total energy change is equal to the work done on the bead by the friction force. Therefore,

$$\text{Change in PE}_G + \text{change in KE} = \text{work done against friction force}$$

$$mg(h_A - h_C) + \tfrac{1}{2}m(v_A^2 - v_C^2) = F_f s$$

Here $v_A = 2.0$ m/s, $v_C = 0$, $h_A - h_C = 0.30$ m, $s = 2.50$ m, and $m = 0.015$ kg. Using these values, we find that $F_f = 0.030$ N.

**Alternative Method**

Since energy, E, is conserved

$$E_i = E_f$$

There is energy lost to friction, hence,

$$KE_i + PE_{Gi} = KE_f + PE_{Gf} + W_f$$

where the work done overcoming friction is $W_f = F_f s$. Hence,

$$\tfrac{1}{2}mv_i^2 + mgh_i = \tfrac{1}{2}mv_f^2 + mgh_f + F_f s$$

and

$$\tfrac{1}{2}m(v_i^2 - v_f^2) + mg(h_i - h_f) = F_f s$$

**6.16 [II]** A 1200-kg car is coasting down a 30° hill as shown in Fig. 6-4. At a time when the car's speed is 12 m/s, the driver applies the brakes. What constant force $F$ (parallel to the road) must result if the car is to stop after traveling 100 m?

The change in total energy of the car (KE + $PE_G$) is equal to the work done on it by the braking force $F$. This work is $Fs \cos 180°$ because $F$ retards the car's motion. We have

$$\tfrac{1}{2}m(v_f^2 - v_i^2) + mg(h_f - h_i) = Fs(-1)$$

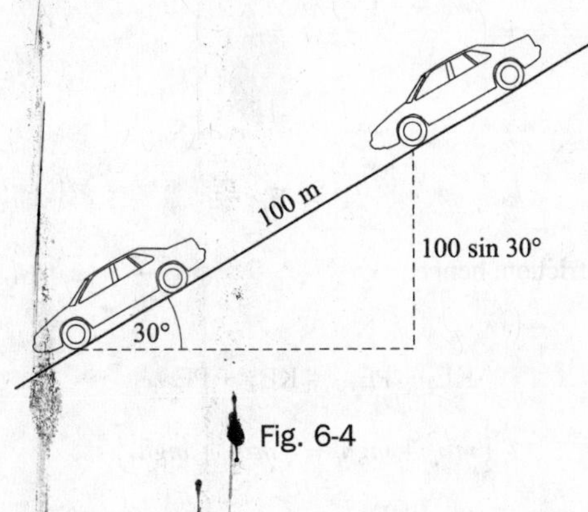


Fig. 6-4

where $m = 1200$ kg, $v_f = 0$, $v_i = 12$ m/s, $h_f - h_i = (100 \text{ m}) \sin 30°$ and $s = 100$ m

With these values, the equation yields $F = 6.7$ kN.

**Alternative Method**

Since energy, E, is conserved

$$E_i = E_f$$

There is energy removed, hence,

$$\tfrac{1}{2}mv_i^2 + mgh_i = \tfrac{1}{2}mv_f^2 + mgh_f + W_B$$

where $W_B = Fs$ is the work done (i.e., energy removed) by the brakes (i.e., by the car). Thus, since $v_f = 0$ and $h_f = 0$,

$$\tfrac{1}{2}mv_i^2 + mgh_i = Fs$$

All of the initial energy is converted to thermal energy ($W_B = Fs$) by the brakes.

**6.17 [II]** A ball at the end of a 180-cm-long string swings as a pendulum as shown in Fig. 6-5. The ball's speed is 400 cm/s as it passes through its lowest position. (*a*) To what height $h$ above this position will it rise before stopping? (*b*) What angle does the pendulum then make to the vertical? Neglect all forms of friction.

(*a*) The pull of the string on the ball is always perpendicular to the ball's motion and therefore does no work on the ball. Consequently, the ball's total energy remains constant; it loses KE but gains an equal amount of $PE_G$. That is,

$$\text{Change in KE} + \text{change in PE}_G = 0$$
$$\tfrac{1}{2}mv_f^2 - \tfrac{1}{2}mv_i^2 + mgh = 0$$

Since $v_f = 0$ and $v_i = 4.00$ m/s, we find $h = 0.8155$ m as the height to which the ball rises.

(*b*) From Fig. 6-5,

$$\cos\theta = \frac{L-h}{L} = 1 - \frac{0.8155}{1.80}$$

which gives $\theta = 56.8°$.

**Alternative Method**

Since energy, E, is conserved

$$E_i = E_f$$

There is no energy lost to friction, hence,

$$KE_i + PE_{Gi} = KE_f + PE_{Gf}$$
$$\tfrac{1}{2}mv_i^2 + mgh_i = \tfrac{1}{2}mv_f^2 + mgh_f$$
$$\tfrac{1}{2}mv_i^2 + 0 = 0 + mgh_f$$
$$h_f = \frac{v_i^2}{2g}$$

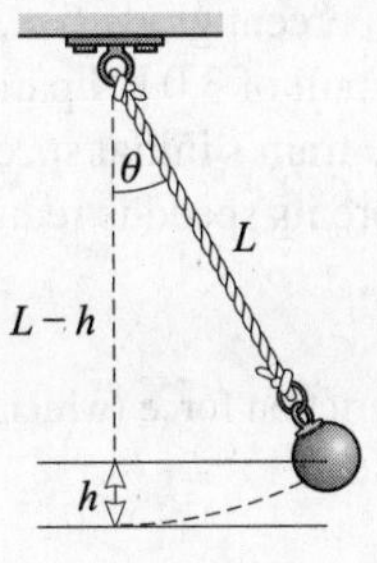


Fig. 6-5

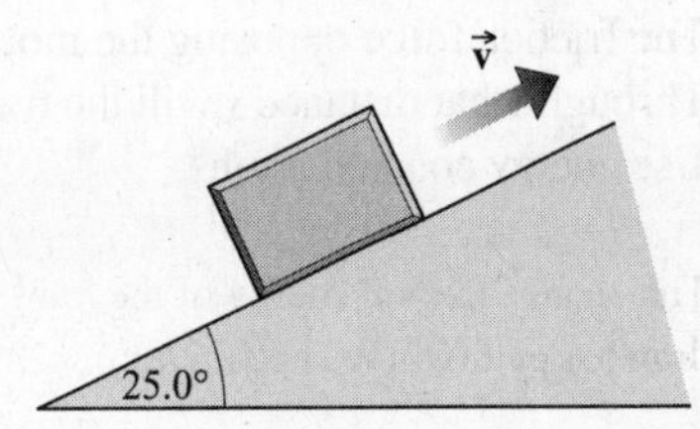


Fig. 6-6

**6.18 [II]** A 500-g block is shot up the incline in Fig. 6-6 with an initial speed of 200 cm/s. How far will it go if the coefficient of kinetic friction between it and the incline is 0.150? Use energy considerations to solve the problem.

We will need to know the energy expended in overcoming friction. To determine that, find the friction force on the block using

$$F_f = \mu F_N = \mu\,(mg\cos 25.0°)$$
$$F_f = 0.667\text{ N}$$

As the block slides up the incline a distance $D$, it rises a distance $D\sin 25.0°$. Because the change in energy of the block equals the work done on it by the friction force, we have

$$\text{Change in KE } + \text{change in PE}_G = F_f D\cos 180°$$
$$\tfrac{1}{2}m(v_f^2 - v_i^2) + mg(D\sin 25.0°) = -F_f D$$

Notice that as the KE decreases the PE increases. In other words, the KE provides the energy to overcome both gravity and friction.

The friction force opposes the motion, it's down the incline, while the displacement is up the incline; hence, the work it does is negative.

We know $v_i = 2.00$ m/s and $v_f = 0$. Notice that the mass of the block could be canceled out in this case (but only because $F_f$ is given in terms of it). Substitution yields $D = 0.365$ m.

**Alternative Method**

Since energy is conserved,

$$\text{E}_i = \text{E}_f$$

Here some of the initial energy goes into overcoming friction—call it $W_f$ and so

$$\text{KE}_i + \text{PE}_{Gi} = \text{KE}_f + \text{PE}_{Gf} + W_f$$
$$\tfrac{1}{2}mv_i^2 + 0 = 0 + mgh_f + W_f$$

Given that $D$ is the distance traveled along the incline

$$h_f = D\sin 25.0°$$

and

$$\tfrac{1}{2}mv_i^2 = mgD\sin 25.0° + F_f D$$

**6.19 [II]** A 60 000-kg train is being dragged along a straight line up a 1.0 percent grade (i.e., the road rises 1.0 m for each 100 m traveled horizontally) by a steady drawbar pull of 3.0 kN parallel to the incline. The friction force opposing the motion of the train is 4.0 kN. The train's initial speed is 12 m/s. Through what distance *s* will the train move along its tracks before its speed is reduced to 9.0 m/s? Use energy considerations.

The change in total energy of the train is due to the work done by the friction force (which is negative) and the drawbar pull (which is positive):

$$\text{Change in KE} + \text{change in PE}_G = W_{\text{drawbar}} + W_{\text{friction}}$$

The train loses KE and gains $PE_G$. It rises a height $h = s \sin\theta$, where $\theta$ is the incline angle and $\tan\theta = 1/100$. Hence, $\theta = 0.573°$, and $h = 0.010\,s$ (at small angles $\tan\theta \approx \sin\theta$). Therefore,

$$\tfrac{1}{2}m(v_f^2 - v_i^2) + mg(0.010\,s) = (3000\text{ N})(s)(1) + (4000\text{ N})(s)(-1)$$
$$-1.89 \times 10^6\text{ J} + (5.89 \times 10^3\text{ N})\,s = (-1000\text{ N})\,s$$

from which we obtain $s = 274\text{ m} = 0.27\text{ km}$.

**6.20 [III]** An advertisement claims that a certain 1200-kg car can accelerate from rest to a speed of 25 m/s in a time of 8.0 s. What average power must the motor develop to produce this acceleration? Give your answer in both watts and horsepower. Ignore friction losses.

The work done in accelerating the car is

$$\text{Work done} = \text{Change in KE} = \tfrac{1}{2}m(v_f^2 - v_i^2) = \tfrac{1}{2}mv_f^2$$

The time taken for this work to be performed is 8.0 s. Therefore, to two significant figures,

$$\text{Power} = \frac{\text{Work}}{\text{Time}} = \frac{\frac{1}{2}(1200\text{ kg})(25\text{ m/s})^2}{8.0\text{ s}} = 46\,875\text{ W} = 47\text{ kW}$$

Converting from watts to horsepower, we have

$$\text{Power} = (46875\text{ W})\left(\frac{1\text{ hp}}{746\text{ W}}\right) = 63\text{ hp}$$

**6.21 [III]** A 0.25-hp motor is used to lift a load at the rate of 5.0 cm/s. How great a load can it raise at this constant speed?

Assume the power *output* of the motor to be 0.25 hp = 186.5 W. In 1.0 s, the load $mg$ is lifted a distance of 0.050 m. Therefore,

$$\text{Work done in 1.0 s} = (\text{weight})(\text{height change in 1.0 s}) = (mg)(0.050\text{ m})$$

By definition, Power = Work / Time, and so

$$186.5\text{ W} = \frac{(mg)(0.050\text{ m})}{1.0\text{ s}}$$

Using $g = 9.81\text{ m/s}^2$, we find that $m = 381$ kg. The motor can lift a load of about $0.38 \times 10^3$ kg at this speed.

**6.22 [III]** Repeat Problem 6.20 but this time the data apply to a car going up a 20° incline.

Work must be done to lift the car as well as to accelerate it:

$$\text{Work done} = \text{change in KE} + \text{change in PE}_G$$
$$= \tfrac{1}{2}m(v_f^2 - v_i^2) + mg(h_f - h_i)$$

where $h_f - h_i = s \sin 20°$ and $s$ is the total distance the car travels along the incline in the 8.0 s under consideration. Knowing $v_i = 0$, $v_f = 25$ m/s, and $t = 8.0$ s, we have

$$s = v_{av}t = \tfrac{1}{2}(v_i + v_f)t = 100 \text{ m}$$

Then $$\text{Work done} = \frac{1}{2}(1200 \text{ kg})(625 \text{ m}^2/\text{s}^2) + (1200 \text{ kg})(9.81 \text{ m/s}^2)(100 \text{ m})(\sin 20°) = 777.6 \text{ kJ}$$

from which $$\text{Power} = \frac{778 \text{ kJ}}{8.0 \text{ s}} = 97 \text{ kW} = 0.13 \times 10^3 \text{ hp}$$

**6.23 [III]** In unloading grain from the hold of a ship, an elevator lifts the grain through a distance of 12 m. Grain is discharged at the top of the elevator at a rate of 2.0 kg each second, and the discharge speed of each grain particle is 3.0 m/s. Find the minimum power rating for a motor that can elevate grain in this way.

The power output of the motor is

$$\text{Power} = \frac{\text{Change in KE} + \text{change in PE}_G}{\text{Time taken}} = \frac{\tfrac{1}{2}m(v_f^2 - v_i^2) + mgh}{t}$$
$$= \frac{m}{t}\left[\tfrac{1}{2}(9.0 \text{ m}^2/\text{s}^2) + (9.81 \text{ m/s}^2)(12 \text{ m})\right]$$

The mass transported per second, $m/t$, is 2.0 kg/s. Using this value yields a power requirement of 0.24 kW.

## SUPPLEMENTARY PROBLEMS

**6.24 [I]** A force of 3.0 N acts through a distance of 12 m in the direction of the force. Find the work done.

**6.25 [I]** A 4.0-kg object is lifted 1.5 m. (*a*) How much work is done against the Earth's gravity? (*b*) Repeat if the object is lowered instead of lifted.

**6.26 [I]** A uniform rectangular marble slab is 3.4 m long and 2.0 m wide. It has a mass of 180 kg. It is originally lying on the flat ground with its 3.4-m × 2.0-m surface facing up. How much work is needed to stand it on its short end? [*Hint:* Think about its center of gravity.]

**6.27 [I]** How large a force is required to accelerate a 1300-kg car from rest to a speed of 20 m/s in a horizontal distance of 80 m?

**6.28 [I]** A 1200-kg car going 30 m/s applies its brakes and skids to rest. If the friction force between the sliding tires and the pavement is 6000 N, how far does the car skid before coming to rest?

**6.29 [I]** A proton ($m = 1.67 \times 10^{-27}$ kg) that has a speed of $5.0 \times 10^6$ m/s passes through a metal film of thickness 0.010 mm and emerges with a speed of $2.0 \times 10^6$ m/s. How large an average force opposed its motion through the film?

**6.30 [I]** A 200-kg cart is pushed slowly at a constant speed up an incline. How much work does the pushing force, which is parallel to the incline, do in moving the cart up to a platform 1.5 m above the starting point if friction is negligible?

**6.31 [II]** Repeat Problem 6.30 if the distance along the incline to the platform is 7.0 m and a friction force of 150 N opposes the motion.

**6.32 [II]** A 50 000-kg freight car is pulled 800 m up along a 1.20 percent grade at constant speed. (*a*) Find the work done against gravity by the drawbar pull. (*b*) If the friction force retarding the motion is 1500 N, find the total work done.

**6.33 [II]** A 60-kg woman walks up a flight of stairs that connects two floors 3.0 m apart. (*a*) How much lifting work is done by the woman? (*b*) By how much does the woman's $PE_G$ change?

**6.34 [II]** A pump lifts water from a lake to a large tank 20 m above the lake. How much work against gravity does the pump do as it transfers 5.0 $m^3$ of water to the tank? One cubic meter of water has a mass of 1000 kg.

**6.35 II]** Just before striking the ground, a 2.00-kg mass has 400 J of KE. If friction can be ignored, from what height was it dropped?

**6.36 [II]** A 0.50-kg ball falls past a window that is 1.50 m in vertical length. (*a*) How much did the KE of the ball increase as it fell past the window? (*b*) If its speed was 3.0 m/s at the top of the window, what was its speed at the bottom?

**6.37 [II]** At sea level a nitrogen molecule in the air has an average translational KE of $6.2 \times 10^{-21}$ J. Its mass is $4.7 \times 10^{-26}$ kg. (*a*) If such a molecule could shoot straight up without striking other air molecules, how high would it rise? (*b*) What is that molecule's initial upward speed?

**6.38 [II]** The coefficient of sliding friction between a 900-kg car and the pavement is 0.80. If the car is moving at 25 m/s along level pavement when it begins to skid to a stop, how far will it go before coming to rest?

**6.39 [II]** Consider the simple pendulum shown in Fig. 6-7. (*a*) If it is released from point-*A*, what will be the speed of the ball as it passes through point-*C*? (*b*) What is the ball's speed at point-*B*? [*Hint:* How far has it fallen upon arriving at point-*B*?]

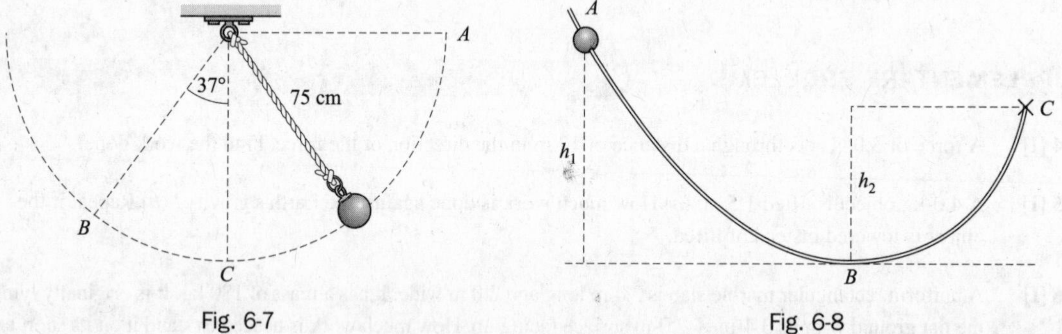


Fig. 6-7 Fig. 6-8

**6.40 [II]** A 1200-kg car coasts from rest down a driveway that is inclined 20° to the horizontal and is 15 m long. How fast is the car going at the end of the driveway if (*a*) friction is negligible and (*b*) a friction force of 3000 N opposes the motion?

**6.41 [II]** The driver of a 1200-kg car notices that the car slows from 20 m/s to 15 m/s as it coasts a distance of 130 m along level ground. How large a force opposes the motion?

**6.42 [II]** A 2000-kg elevator rises from rest in the basement to the fourth floor, a distance of 25 m. As it passes the fourth floor, its speed is 3.0 m/s. There is a constant frictional force of 500 N. Calculate the work done by the lifting mechanism.

**6.43 [II]** Figure 6-8 shows a bead sliding on a wire. How large must height $h_1$ be if the bead, starting at rest at *A*, is to have a speed of 200 cm/s at point *B*? Ignore friction.

**6.44 [II]** In Fig. 6-8, $h_1 = 50.0$ cm, $h_2 = 30.0$ cm, and the length along the wire from *A* to *C* is 400 cm. A 3.00-g bead released at *A* coasts to point *C* and stops. How large an average friction force opposed its motion?

**6.45 [III]** In Fig. 6-8, $h_1 = 200$ cm, $h_2 = 150$ cm, and at *A* the 3.00-g bead has a downward speed along the wire of 800 cm/s. (*a*) How fast is the bead moving as it passes point-*B* if friction is negligible? (*b*) How much energy did the bead lose to friction work if it rises to a height of 20.0 cm above *C* after it leaves the wire?

**6.46 [II]** A 10.0-kg block is launched up a 30.0° inclined plane at a speed of 20.0 m/s. As it slides it loses 200 J to friction. How far along the incline will it travel before coming to rest?

**6.47 [I]** Calculate the average power required to raise a 150-kg drum to a height of 20 m in a time of 1.0 minute. Give your answer in both kilowatts and horsepower.

**6.48 [I]** Compute the power output of a machine that lifts a 500-kg crate through a height of 20.0 m in a time of 60.0 s

**6.49 [I]** An engine expends 40.0 hp in propelling a car along a level track at a constant speed of 15.0 m/s. How large is the total retarding force acting on the car? Remember that 1 hp = 745.7 W.

**6.50 [II]** A 1000-kg auto travels up a 3.0 percent grade at 20 m/s. Find the cruising power required, neglecting friction.

**6.51 [II]** A 900-kg car whose motor delivers a maximum power of 40.0 hp to its wheels can maintain a steady speed of 130 km/h on a horizontal roadway. How large is the friction force that impedes its motion at this speed?

**6.52 [II]** Water flows from a reservoir at the rate of 3000 kg/min, to a turbine 120 m below. If the efficiency of the turbine is 80 percent, compute the power output of the turbine. Neglect friction in the pipe and the small KE of the water leaving the turbine. Don't forget that it's only 80 percent efficient.

**6.53 [II]** Find the mass of the largest box that a 40-hp engine can pull along a level road at 15 m/s if the friction coefficient between road and box is 0.15.

**6.54 [II]** A 1300-kg car is to accelerate from rest to a speed of 30.0 m/s in a time of 12.0 s as it climbs a 15.0° hill. Assuming uniform acceleration, what minimum power is needed to accelerate the car in this way?

## ANSWERS TO SUPPLEMENTARY PROBLEMS

**6.24 [I]** 36 J

**6.25 [I]** (*a*) 59 J; (*b*) − 59 J

**6.26 [I]** 3.0 kJ

**6.27 [I]** 3.3 kN

**6.28 [I]** 90 m

**6.29 [I]** $1.8 \times 10^{-9}$ N

**6.30 [I]** 2.9 kJ

**6.31 [II]** 4.0 kJ

**6.32 [II]** (*a*) 4.70 MJ; (*b*) 5.91 MJ

**6.33 [II]** (*a*) 1.8 kJ; (*b*) 1.8 kJ

**6.34 [II]** $9.8 \times 10^5$ J

**6.35 II]** 20.0 m

**6.36 [II]** (*a*) 7.4 J; (*b*) 6.2 m/s

**6.37 [II]** 14 km; (*b*) 0.51 km/s

**6.38 [II]** 40 m

**6.39 [II]** (*a*) 3.8 m/s; (*b*) 3.4 m/s

**6.40 [II]** (*a*) 10 m/s; (*b*) 5.1 m/s

**6.41 [II]** 0.81 kN

**6.42 [II]** 0.51 MJ

**6.43 [II]** 20.4 cm

**6.44 [II]** 1.47 mN

**6.45 [III]** (*a*) 10.2 m/s; (*b*) 105 mJ

**6.46 [II]** 36.7 m

**6.47 [I]** 0.49 kW or 0.66 hp

**6.48 [I]** 1.63 kW

**6.49 [I]** 1.99 kN

**6.50 [II]** 5.9 kW or 7.9 hp

**6.51 [II]** 826 N

**6.52 [II]** 47 kW or 63 hp

**6.53 [II]** $1.4 \times 10^3$ kg

**6.54 [II]** 98.3 kW or 132 hp

# CHAPTER 7

# Simple Machines

**A Machine** is any device by which the magnitude, direction, or method of application of a force is changed so as to achieve some advantage. Examples of simple machines are the lever, inclined plane, pulley, crank and axle, and jackscrew.

**The Principle of Work** that applies to a continuously operating machine is

$$\text{Work input} = \text{Useful work output} + \text{Work to overcome friction}$$

This is, of course, an application of conservation of energy.

In machines that operate for only a short time, some of the input work may be used to store energy within the machine. An internal spring might be stretched, or a movable pulley might be raised, for example.

**Mechanical Advantage:** The **actual mechanical advantage** (AMA) of a machine is

$$\text{AMA} = \text{Force ration} = \frac{\text{Force exerted by machine on load}}{\text{Force used to operate machine}}$$

The **ideal mechanical advantage** (IMA) of a machine is

$$\text{IMA} = \text{Distance ration} = \frac{\text{Distance moved by input force}}{\text{Distance moved by load}}$$

Because friction is always present, the AMA is always less than the IMA. In general, both the AMA and IMA are greater than one.

**The Efficiency** of a machine is

$$\text{Efficiency} = \frac{\text{Work output}}{\text{Work input}} = \frac{\text{Power output}}{\text{Power input}}$$

The efficiency is also equal to the ratio AMA/IMA.

## SOLVED PROBLEMS

**7.1 [I]** In a particular hoist system, the load is lifted 10 cm for each 70 cm of movement of the rope that operates the device. What is the smallest input force that could possibly lift a 5.0-kN load?

The most advantageous situation possible is that in which all the input work is used to lift the load—that is, in which friction and other loss mechanisms are negligible. In that case,

$$\text{Work input} = \text{Lifting work}$$

If the load is lifted a distance $l$, the lifting work is (5.0 kN)($l$). The input force $F$, however, must work through a distance $7.0l$. The above equation then becomes

$$(F)(7.0l) = (5.0\text{kN})(l)$$

which gives $F = 0.71$ kN as the smallest possible force required.

**7.2 [III]** A hoisting machine lifts a 3000-kg load a height of 8.00 m in a time of 20.0 s. The power supplied to the engine is 18.0 hp. Compute (*a*) the work output, (*b*) the power output and power input, and (*c*) the efficiency of the engine and hoist system.

(*a*) $$\text{Work output} = (\text{Lifting force})\,(\text{Height}) = (3000 \times 9.81\text{ N})\,(8.00\text{ m}) = 235\text{ kJ}$$

(*b*) $$\text{Power output} = \frac{\text{Work output}}{\text{Time taken}} = \frac{235\text{ kJ}}{20.0\text{ s}} = 11.8\text{ kW}$$

$$\text{Power input} = (18.0\text{ hp})\left(\frac{0.746\text{ kW}}{1\text{ hp}}\right) = 13.4\text{ kW}$$

(*c*) $$\text{Efficiency} = \frac{\text{Power output}}{\text{Power input}} = \frac{11.8\text{ kW}}{13.4\text{ kW}} = 0.881 = 88.1\%$$

or $$\text{Efficiency} = \frac{\text{Work output}}{\text{Work input}} = \frac{235\text{ kJ}}{(13.4\text{ kJ/s})\,(20.0\text{ s})} = 0.877 = 87.7\%$$

The efficiency is 88%; the differences arise from the rounding off process.

**7.3 [II]** What power in kW is supplied to a 12.0-hp motor having an efficiency of 90.0 percent when it is delivering its full rated output?

From the definition of efficiency,

$$\text{Power input} = \frac{\text{Power output}}{\text{Efficiency}} = \frac{(12.0\text{ hp})\,(0.746\text{ kW/hp})}{0.900} = 9.95\text{ kW}$$

**7.4 [II]** For the three levers shown in Fig. 7-1, determine the vertical forces $F_1$, $F_2$, and $F_3$ required to support the load $F_W = 90$ N. Neglect the weights of the levers. Also find the IMA, AMA, and efficiency for each system.

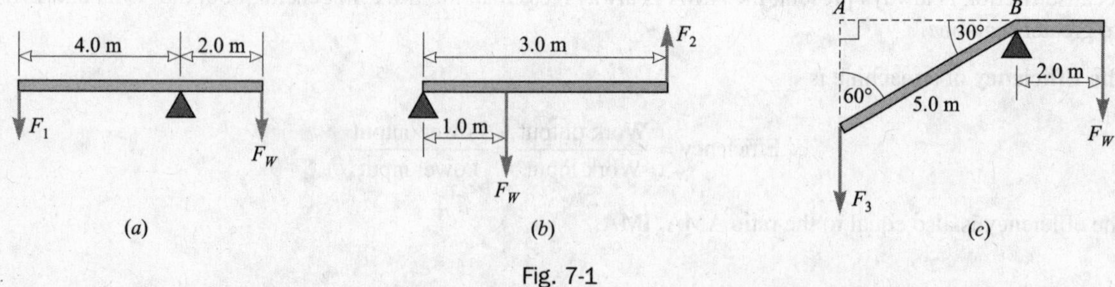


Fig. 7-1

In each case, we take torques about the fulcrum point as axis. If we assume that the lifting is occurring slowly at constant speed, then the systems are in equilibrium; the clockwise torques balance the counterclockwise torques. (Recall that torque = $r_F \sin\theta$.)

Clockwise torque = Counterclockwise torque

(*a*) (2.0 m)(90 N)(1) = (4.0 m)($F_1$)(1) from which $F_1 = 45$ N

(*b*) (1.0 m)(90 N)(1) = (3.0 m)($F_2$)(1) from which $F_2 = 30$ N

(*c*) (2.0 m)(90 N)(1) = (5.0 m)($F_3$) sin 60° from which $F_3 = 42$ N

To find the IMA of the system in Fig. 7-1($a$), we notice that the load moves only half as far as the input force, and so

$$\text{IMA} = \text{Distance ratio} = 2.0$$

Similarly, in Fig. 7-1($b$). IMA $= 3/1 = 3$. In Fig. 7-1($c$), however, the lever arm is (5.0m) sin 60° = 4.33 m and so the distance ratio is $4.33/2 = 2.16$. To summarize:

| | Lever ($a$) | Lever ($b$) | Lever ($c$) |
|---|---|---|---|
| IMA | 2.0 | 3.0 | 2.2 |
| AMA | $\frac{90\text{ N}}{45\text{ N}} = 2.0$ | $\frac{90\text{ N}}{30\text{ N}} = 3.0$ | $\frac{90\text{ N}}{41.6\text{ N}} = 2.2$ |
| Eff. | 1.0 | 1.0 | 1.0 |

The efficiencies are 1.0 because we have neglected friction at the fulcrums.

**7.5 [II]** Determine the force $F$ required to lift a 100-N load $F_W$ with each of the pulley systems shown in Fig. 7-2. Neglect friction and the weights of the pulleys.

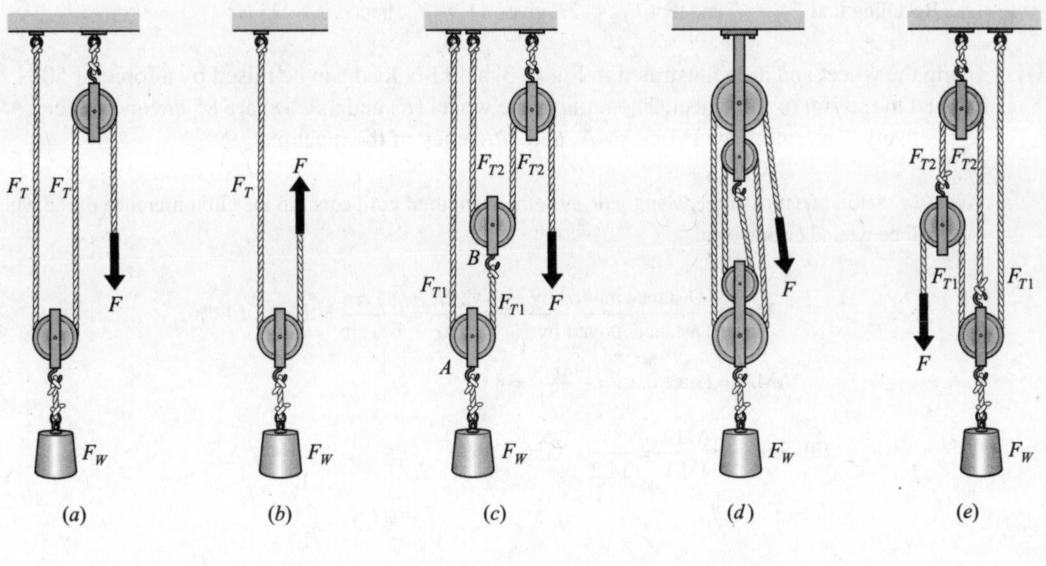


Fig. 7-2

($a$) Load $F_W$ is supported by two ropes; each rope exerts an upward pull of $F_T = \frac{1}{2} F_W$. Because the rope is continuous and the pulleys are frictionless, $F_T = F$. Then

$$F = F_T = \tfrac{1}{2} F_W = \tfrac{1}{2}(100\text{ N}) = 50\text{ N}$$

($b$) Here, too, the load is supported by the tensions in two ropes, $F_T$ and $F$, where $F_T = F$. Then

$$F_T + F = F_W \qquad \text{or} \qquad F = \tfrac{1}{2} F_W = 50\text{ N}$$

(*c*) Let $F_{T1}$ and $F_{T2}$ be tensions around pulleys-*A* and -*B*, respectively. Pulley-*A* is in equilibrium, and

$$F_{T1} + F_{T1} - F_W = 0 \qquad \text{or} \qquad F_{T1} = \tfrac{1}{2} F_W$$

Pulley-*B*, too, is in equilibrium, and

$$F_{T2} + F_{T2} - F_{T1} = 0 \qquad \text{or} \qquad F_{T2} = \tfrac{1}{2} F_{T1} = \tfrac{1}{4} F_W$$

But $F = F_{T2}$ and so $F = \frac{1}{4} F_W = 25$ N.

(*d*) Four ropes, each with the same tension $F_T$, support the load $F_W$. Therefore,

$$4F_{T1} = F_W \qquad \text{and} \qquad F = F_{T1} = \tfrac{1}{4} F_W = 25\ \text{N}$$

(*e*) We see at once $F = F_{T1}$. Because the pulley on the left is in equilibrium,

$$F_{T2} - F_{T1} - F = 0$$

But $F_{T1} = F$ and so $F_{T2} = 2F$. The pulley on the right is also in equilibrium, and therefore,

$$F_{T1} + F_{T2} + F_{T1} - F_W = 0$$

Recalling that $F_{T1} = F$ and that $F_{T2} = 2F$ gives $4F = F_W$; hence, $F = 25$ N.

**7.6 [II]** Using the wheel and axle illustrated in Fig. 7-3, a 400-N load can be raised by a force of 50 N applied to the rim of the wheel. The radii of the wheel (*R*) and axle (*r*) are 85 cm and 6.0 cm, respectively. Determine the IMA, AMA, and efficiency of the machine.

We know that in one turn of the wheel-axle system, a length of cord equal to the circumference of the wheel or axle will be wound or unwound.

$$\text{IMA} = \frac{\text{Distance moved by } F}{\text{Distance moved by } F_W} = \frac{2\pi R}{2\pi r} = \frac{85\ \text{cm}}{6.0\ \text{cm}} = 14.2 = 14$$

$$\text{AMA} = \text{Force ratio} = \frac{400\ \text{N}}{50\ \text{N}} = 8.0$$

$$\text{Efficiency} = \frac{\text{AMA}}{\text{IMA}} = \frac{8.0}{14.2} = 0.56 = 56\%$$

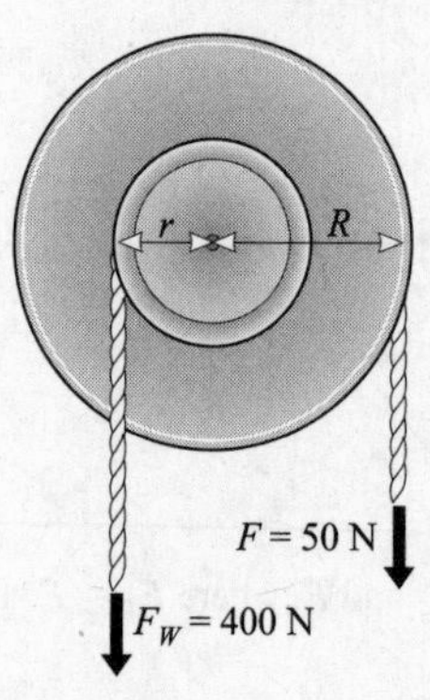


Fig. 7-3

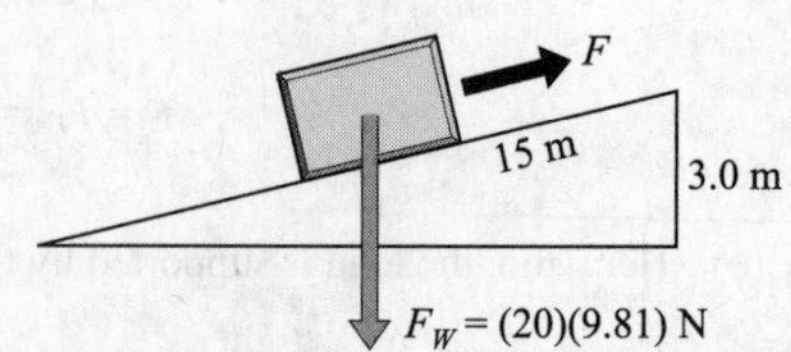


Fig. 7-4

**7.7 [II]** The inclined plane depicted in Fig. 7-4 is 15 m long and rises 3.0 m. (*a*) What minimum force $F$ parallel to the plane is required to slide a 20-kg box up the plane if friction is neglected? (*b*) What is the IMA of the plane? (*c*) Find the AMA and efficiency if a 64-N force is actually required.

(*a*) There are several ways to approach this. Let's consider energy. Since there is no friction, the work done by the pushing force, $(F)(15\text{m})$, must equal the lifting work done, $(20\text{ kg})(9.81\text{ m/s}^2)(3.0\text{ m})$. Equating these two expressions and solving for $F$ gives $F = 39$ N.

(*b*)
$$\text{IMA} = \frac{\text{Distance moved by } F}{\text{Distance } F_W \text{ is lifted}} = \frac{15\text{ m}}{3.0\text{ m}} = 5.0$$

(*c*)
$$\text{AMA} = \text{Force ratio} = \frac{F_W}{F} = \frac{196\text{ N}}{64\text{ N}} = 3.06 = 3.1$$

$$\text{Efficiency} = \frac{\text{AMA}}{\text{IMA}} = \frac{3.06}{5.0} = 0.61 = 61\%$$

Or, as a check,

$$\text{Efficiency} = \frac{\text{Work output}}{\text{Work input}} = \frac{(F_W)(3.0\text{ m})}{(F)(15\text{ m})} = 0.61 = 61\%$$

**7.8 [III]** As seen in Fig. 7-5, a jackscrew has a lever arm of 40 cm and a pitch of 5.0 mm. If the efficiency is 30 percent, what horizontal force $F$ applied perpendicularly at the end of the lever arm is required to lift a load $F_W$ of 270 kg?

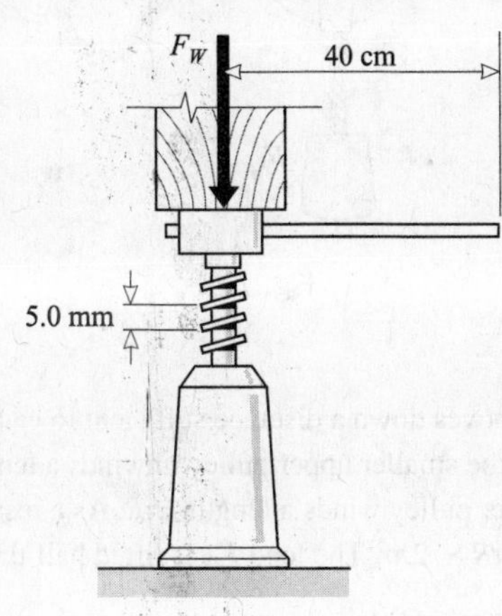


Fig. 7-5

When the jack handle is moved around one complete circle, the input force moves a distance

$$2\pi r = 2\pi(0.40\text{ m})$$

while the load is lifted a distance of 0.005 0 m. The IMA is therefore

$$\text{IMA} = \text{Distance ratio} = \frac{2\pi(0.40\text{ m})}{0.005\,0\text{ m}} = 0.50 \times 10^3$$

Since efficiency = AMA/IMA, we have

$$\text{AMA} = (\text{Efficiency})(\text{IMA}) = (0.30)(502) = 0.15 \times 10^3$$

But AMA = (Load lifted)/(Input force) and therefore

$$F = \frac{\text{Load lifted}}{\text{AMA}} = \frac{(270\text{ kg})(9.81\text{ m/s}^2)}{151} = 18\text{ N}$$

**7.9 [III]** A differential pulley (chain hoist) is drawn in Fig. 7-6. Two toothed pulleys of radii $r = 10$ cm and $R = 11$ cm are fastened together and turn on the same axle. A continuous chain passes over the smaller (10 cm) pulley, then around the movable pulley at the bottom, and finally around the 11-cm pulley. The operator exerts a downward force $F$ on the chain to lift the load $F_W$. (*a*) Determine the IMA. (*b*) What is the efficiency of the machine if an applied force of 50 N is required to lift a load of 700 N?

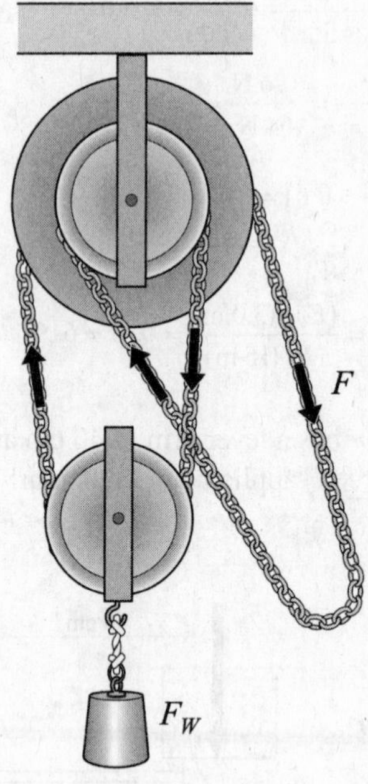


Fig. 7-6

(*a*) Suppose that the force $F$ moves down a distance sufficient to cause the upper rigid system of pulleys to turn one revolution. Then the smaller upper pulley unwinds a length of chain equal to its circumference, $27\pi r$, while the larger upper pulley winds a length $2\pi R$. As a result, the chain supporting the lower pulley is shortened by a length $2\pi R - 2\pi r$. The load $F_W$ is lifted half this distance, or

$$\tfrac{1}{2}(2\pi R - 2\pi r) = \pi(R - r)$$

when the input force moves a distance $2\pi R$. Therefore,

$$\text{IMA} = \frac{\text{Distance moved by } F}{\text{Distance moved by } F_W} = \frac{2\pi R}{\pi(R-r)} = \frac{2R}{R-r} = \frac{22 \text{ cm}}{1.0 \text{ cm}} = 22$$

(*b*) From the data,

$$\text{AMA} = \frac{\text{Load lifted}}{\text{Input force}} = \frac{700 \text{ N}}{50 \text{ N}} = 14$$

and

$$\text{Efficiency} = \frac{\text{AMA}}{\text{IMA}} = \frac{14}{22} = 0.64 = 64\%$$

## SUPPLEMENTARY PROBLEMS

**7.10 [I]** A motor furnishes 120 hp to a device that lifts a 5000-kg load to a height of 13.0 m in a time of 20 s. Find the efficiency of the machine.

**7.11 [I]** Refer back to Fig. 7-2(*d*). If a force of 200 N is required to lift a 50-kg load, find the IMA, AMA, and efficiency for the system.

**7.12 [II]** In Fig. 7-7, the 300-N load is balanced by a force $F$ in both systems. Assuming efficiencies of 100 percent, how large is $F$ in each system? Assume all ropes to be vertical.

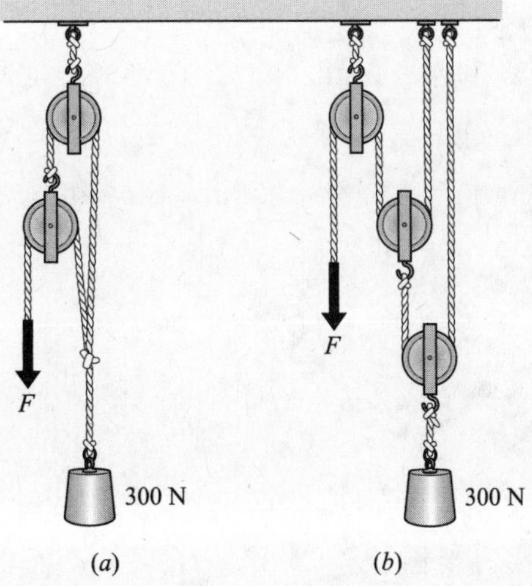


Fig. 7-7

**7.13 [II]** Consider a machine for which an applied force moves 3.3 m to raise a load 8.0 cm. Find the (*a*) IMA and (*b*) AMA if the efficiency is 60 percent. What load can be lifted by an applied force of 50 N if the efficiency is (*c*) 100 percent and (*d*) 60 percent?

**7.14 [II]** With a wheel and axle, a force of 80 N applied to the rim of the wheel can lift a load of 640 N. The diameters of the wheel and axle are 36 cm and 4.0 cm, respectively. Determine the AMA, IMA, and efficiency of the machine.

**7.15 [II]** A hydraulic jack in a gas station lifts a 900-kg car a distance of 0.25 cm when a force of 150 N pushes a piston through a distance of 20 cm. Find the IMA, AMA, and efficiency.

**7.16 [II]** The screw of a mechanical press has a pitch of 0.20 cm. The diameter of the wheel to which a tangential turning force $F$ is applied is 55 cm. If the efficiency is 40 percent, how large must $F$ be to produce a force of 12 kN in the press?

**7.17 [II]** The diameters of the two upper pulleys of a chain hoist (Fig. 7-6) are 18 cm and 16 cm. If the efficiency of the hoist is 45 percent, what force is required to lift a 400-kg crate?

## ANSWERS TO SUPPLEMENTARY PROBLEMS

**7.10 [I]** 36%

**7.11 [I]** 4, 2.5, 61%

**7.12 [II]** (*a*) 100 N; (*b*) 75.0 N

**7.13 [II]** (*a*) 41; (*b*) 25; (*c*) 2.1 kN; (*d*) 1.2 kN

**7.14 [II]** 8.0, 9.0, 89%

**7.15 [II]** 80, 59, 74%

**7.16 [II]** 35 N

**7.17 [II]** 0.48 kN

# Impulse and Momentum

**The Linear Momentum** ($\vec{\mathbf{p}}$) of a body is the product of its mass ($m$) and velocity ($\vec{\mathbf{v}}$):

$$\text{Linear momentum} = (\text{Mass of body})\ (\text{Velocity of body})$$

$$\vec{\mathbf{p}} = m\vec{\mathbf{v}}$$

Momentum is a vector quantity whose direction is that of the velocity. The units of momentum are kg·m/s in the SI.

**An Impulse** is the product of a force ($\vec{\mathbf{F}}$)and the time interval ($\Delta t$) over which the force acts:

$$\text{Impulse} = (\text{Force})\ (\text{Length of time the force acts})$$

Impulse is a vector quantity whose direction is that of the force. Its units are N·s in the SI.

**An Impulse Causes a Change in Momentum:** The change of momentum produced by an impulse is equal to the impulse in both magnitude and direction. Thus, if a constant force $\vec{\mathbf{F}}$ acting for a time $\Delta t$ on a body of mass $m$ changes its velocity from an initial value $\vec{\mathbf{v}}_i$ to a final value $\vec{\mathbf{v}}_f$, then

$$\text{Impulse} = \text{Change in momentum}$$

$$\vec{\mathbf{F}}\,\Delta t = m(\vec{\mathbf{v}}_f - \vec{\mathbf{v}}_i)$$

This is the so-called impulse equation.

Newton's Second Law, as he gave it, is $\vec{\mathbf{F}} = \Delta\vec{\mathbf{p}}/\Delta t$ from which it follows that $\vec{\mathbf{F}}\,\Delta t = \Delta\vec{\mathbf{p}}$. Moreover, $\vec{\mathbf{F}}\,\Delta t = \Delta(m\vec{\mathbf{v}})$ and if $m$ is constant, $\vec{\mathbf{F}}\,\Delta t = m(\vec{\mathbf{v}}_f - \vec{\mathbf{v}}_i)$.

**Conservation of Linear Momentum:** ***If the net external force acting on a system of objects is zero, the vector sum of the momenta of the objects will remain constant.***

**In Collisions and Explosions,** the vector sum of the momenta just before the event equals the vector sum of the momenta just after the event. The vector sum of the momenta of the objects involved does not change during the collision or explosion. Provided there are no external forces acting on the system, linear momentum is always conserved.

Thus, when two bodies of masses $m_1$ and $m_2$ collide,

$$\text{Total momentum before impact} = \text{Total momentum after impact}$$

$$m_1\vec{\mathbf{u}}_1 + m_2\vec{\mathbf{u}}_2 = m_1\vec{\mathbf{v}}_1 + m_2\vec{\mathbf{v}}_2$$

where $\vec{\mathbf{u}}_1$ and $\vec{\mathbf{u}}_2$ are the velocities before impact, and $\vec{\mathbf{v}}_1$ and $\vec{\mathbf{v}}_2$ are the velocities after. In one dimension, in component form,

$$m_1u_{1x} + m_2u_{2x} = m_1v_{1x} + m_2v_{2x}$$

and similarly for the $y$- and $z$-components when the collision takes place in three dimensions. Remember that vector quantities are always boldfaced and velocity is a vector. On the other hand, $u_{1x}$, $u_{2x}$, $v_{1x}$, and $v_{2x}$ are the scalar values of the velocities (they can be positive or negative). A positive direction is initially selected and vectors pointing opposite to this have negative numerical scalar values.

All collisions lie between (and include) the two extremes of being completely or **perfectly elastic** (or just *elastic*) and completely or **perfectly inelastic.** Macroscopic objects can never collide elastically; there will always be some energy of motion transferred into internal energy when the bodies distort upon impact. A collision is said to be completely inelastic when the colliding objects stick together. The two extremes are the easiest to deal with mathematically.

**A Perfectly Inelastic Collision** is one where the two colliding objects stick together after impact. Conservation of momentum supplies the one essential equation and allows us to solve for one unknown. Energy is always conserved, but since some is imparted internally, the KE before impact will not equal the KE after impact.

**A Perfectly Elastic Collision** is one in which linear momentum is conserved and moreover the sum of the translational KEs of the objects is not changed during the collision. In the case of two bodies,

$$\tfrac{1}{2}m_1u_1^2 + \tfrac{1}{2}m_2u_2^2 = \tfrac{1}{2}m_1v_1^2 + \tfrac{1}{2}m_2v_2^2$$

with two independent conservation equations we can solve for two unknowns.

**Coefficient of Restitution:** For any collision between two bodies in which the bodies move only along a single straight line (e.g., the $x$-axis), a **coefficient of restitution** $e$ is defined. It is a pure number given by

$$e = \frac{v_{2x} - v_{1x}}{u_{1x} - u_{2x}}$$

where $u_{1x}$ and $u_{2x}$ are the speeds before impact, and $v_{1x}$ and $v_{2x}$ are the speeds after impact. Notice that $|u_{1x} - u_{2x}|$ is the relative speed of approach and $|v_{2x} - v_{1x}|$ is the relative speed of recession.

For a perfectly elastic collision, $e = 1$. For inelastic collisions, $e < 1$. For a perfectly inelastic collision, the bodies stick together and, $e = 0$.

**The Center of Mass** of an object (of mass $m$) is the single point that moves in the same way as a point mass (of mass $m$) would move when subjected to the same external forces that act on the object. That is, if the resultant force acting on an object of mass $m$ is $\vec{\mathbf{F}}$, the acceleration of the center of mass of the object is given by $\vec{\mathbf{a}}_{cm} = \vec{\mathbf{F}}/m$.

If the object is considered to be composed of tiny masses $m_1$, $m_2$, $m_3$, and so on, at coordinates $(x_1, y_1, z_1)$, $(x_2, y_2, z_2)$, and so on, then the coordinates of the center of mass are given by

$$x_{cm} = \frac{\sum x_i m_i}{\sum m_i} \qquad y_{cm} = \frac{\sum y_i m_i}{\sum m_i} \qquad z_{cm} = \frac{\sum z_i m_i}{\sum m_i}$$

where the sums extend over all masses composing the object. In a uniform gravitational field, the center of mass and the center of gravity coincide.

## SOLVED PROBLEMS

**8.1 [II]** An 8.0-g bullet is fired horizontally into a 9.00-kg cube of wood, which is at rest on a frictionless air table. The bullet lodges in the wood. The cube is free to move and has a speed of 40 cm/s after impact. Find the initial velocity of the bullet.

This is an example of a completely inelastic collision for which momentum is conserved, although KE is not. Consider the system (cube + bullet). The velocity, and hence the momentum, of the cube before impact is zero. Take the bullet's initial motion to be positive in the positive $x$-direction. The momentum conservation law tells us that

Momentum of system before impact = Momentum of system after impact

(Momentum of bullet) + (Momentum of cube) = (Momentum of bullet + Cube)

$$m_B v_{Bx} + m_C v_{Cx} = (m_B + m_C)v_x$$

$$(0.008\,0\text{ kg})v_{Bx} + 0 = (9.008\text{ kg})\,(0.40\text{ m/s})$$

Solving yields $v_{Bx} = 0.45$ km/s and so $\vec{v}_B = 0.45$ km/s—POSITIVE *X*-DIRECTION.

**8.2 [II]** A 16-g mass is moving in the $+x$-direction at 30 cm/s, while a 4.0-g mass is moving in the $-x$-direction at 50 cm/s. They collide head on and stick together. Find their velocity after the collision. Assume negligible friction.

This is a completely inelastic collision for which KE is not conserved, although momentum is. Let the 16-g mass be $m_1$ and the 4.0-g mass be $m_2$. Take the $+x$-direction to be positive. That means that the velocity of the 4.0-g mass has a scalar value of $v_{2x} = -50$ cm/s. We apply the law of conservation of momentum to the system consisting of the two masses:

Momentum before impact = Momentum after impact

$$m_1 v_{1x} + m_2 v_{2x} = (m_1 + m_2)v_x$$

$$(0.016\text{ kg})(0.30\text{ m/s}) + (0.004\,0\text{ kg})\,(-0.50\text{ m/s}) = (0.020\text{ kg})v_x$$

$$v_x = +0.14\text{ m/s}$$

(Notice that the 4.0-g mass has negative momentum.) Hence, $\vec{v} = 0.14$ m/s—POSITIVE *X*-DIRECTION

**8.3 [I]** A 2.0-kg brick is moving at a speed of 6.0 m/s. How large a force $F$ is needed to stop the brick in a time of $7.0 \times 10^{-4}$ s?

Since we have a force and the time over which it acts, that suggests using the impulse equation (i.e., Newton's Second Law):

Impulse on brick = Change in momentum of brick

$$F\,\Delta t = mv_f - mv_i$$

$$F(7.0 \times 10^{-4}\text{ s}) = 0 - (2.0\text{ kg})(6.0\text{ m/s})$$

from which $F = -1.7 \times 10^4$ N. The minus sign indicates that the force opposes the motion.

**8.4 [II]** A 15-g bullet moving at 300 m/s passes through a 2.0-cm-thick sheet of foam plastic and emerges with a speed of 90 m/s. Assuming that the speed change takes place uniformly, what average force impeded the bullet's motion through the plastic?

We can determine the change in momentum, and that suggests using the impulse equation to find the force $F$ on the bullet as it takes a time $\Delta t$ to pass through the plastic. Taking the initial direction of motion to be positive,

$$F\,\Delta t = mv_f - mv_i$$

We can find $\Delta t$ by assuming uniform deceleration and using $x = v_{av}t$, where $x = 0.020$ m and $v_{av} = \frac{1}{2}(v_i + v_f) =$ 195 m/s. This gives $\Delta t = 1.026 \times 10^{-4}$ s. Then

$$(F)(1.026 \times 10^{-4}\text{ s}) = (0.015\text{ kg})(90\text{ m/s}) - (0.015\text{ kg})(300\text{ m/s})$$

which yields $F = -3.1 \times 10^4$ N as the average retarding force. How could this problem have been solved using $F = ma$ instead of the impulse equation? By using energy methods?

**8.5 [II]** The nucleus of an atom has a mass of $3.80 \times 10^{-25}$ kg and is at rest. The nucleus is radioactive and suddenly ejects a particle of mass $6.6 \times 10^{-27}$ kg and speed $1.5 \times 10^7$ m/s. Find the recoil speed of the nucleus that is left behind.

The particle flies off in one direction, the nucleus recoils away in the opposite direction, and momentum is conserved. Take the direction of the ejected particle as positive. We are given, $m_{ni} = 3.80 \times 10^{-25}$ kg, $m_p = 6.6 \times 10^{-27}$ kg, $m_{nf} = m_{ni} - m_p = 3.73 \times 10^{-25}$ kg, and $v_{pf} = 1.5 \times 10^7$ m/s; find the final speed of the nucleus, $v_{nf}$.

$$\text{Momentum before} = \text{Momentum after}$$

$$0 = m_{nf}v_{nf} + m_p v_{pf}$$

$$0 = (3.73 \times 10^{-25}\ \text{kg})(v_{nf}) + (6.6 \times 10^{-27}\ \text{kg})(1.5 \times 10^7\ \text{m/s})$$

Solving leads to

$$-v_{nf} = \frac{(6.6\times10^{-27}\ \text{kg})\,(1.5\times10^{7}\ \text{m/s})}{3.73\times10^{-25}\ \text{kg}} = \frac{10.0\times10^{-20}}{3.73\times10^{-25}} = 2.7\times10^{5}\ \text{m/s}$$

The fact that this is negative tells us that the velocity vector of the nucleus points in the negative direction, opposite to the velocity of the particle, which we took to be positive.

**8.6 [II]** A 0.25-kg ball moving in the $+x$-direction at 13 m/s is hit by a bat. Its final velocity leaving the bat is 19 m/s in the $x$-direction. The bat acts on the ball for 0.010 s. Find the average force $F$ exerted on the ball by the bat.

The problem provides the time over which a required force acts, as well as enough information to compute the change in momentum. That suggests the impulse equation (i.e., Newton's Second Law). We have $v_i = 13$ m/s and $v_f = -19$ m/s. Taking the initial direction of motion as positive, the impulse equation is

$$F\,\Delta t = mv_f - mv_i$$

$$F(0.010\ \text{s}) = (0.25\ \text{kg})(-19\ \text{m/s}) - (0.25\ \text{kg})(13\ \text{m/s})$$

from which $F = -0.80$ kN.

**8.7 [II]** Two girls (masses $m_1$ and $m_2$) are on roller skates and stand at rest, close to each other and face to face. Girl-1 pushes squarely against girl-2 and sends her moving backward. Assuming the girls move freely on their skates, write an expression for the speed with which girl-1 moves.

We take the two girls to comprise the system under consideration. The problem states that girl-2 moves "backward," so let that be the negative direction; therefore, the "forward" direction is positive. There is no resultant external force on the system (the push of one girl on the other is an internal force), and so momentum is conserved:

$$\text{Momentum before} = \text{Momentum after}$$

$$0 = m_1 v_1 + m_2 v_2$$

from which

$$v_1 = -\frac{m_2}{m_1} v_2$$

Girl-1 recoils with this speed. Notice that if $m_2/m_1$ is very large, $v_1$ is much larger than $v_2$. The velocity of girl-1, $\vec{\mathbf{v}}_1$, points in the positive forward direction. The velocity of girl-2, $\vec{\mathbf{v}}_2$, points in the negative backward direction. If we put numbers into the equation, $v_2$ would have to be negative and $v_1$ would come out positive.

**8.8 [II]** As shown in Fig. 8-1, a 15-g bullet is fired horizontally into a 3.000-kg block of wood suspended by a long cord. The bullet lodges in the block. Compute the speed of the bullet if the impact causes the block (and bullet) to swing 10 cm above its initial level.

Consider first the collision of block and bullet. During the collision, momentum is conserved, so

$$\text{Momentum just before} = \text{Momentum just after}$$
$$(0.015\ \text{kg})v + 0 = (3.015\ \text{kg})V$$

where $v$ is the speed of the bullet just prior to impact, and $V$ is the speed of block and bullet just after impact. We have two unknowns in this equation. To find another equation, we can use the fact that the block swings 10 cm high. If we let $PE_G = 0$ at the initial level of the block, energy conservation tells us that

$$\text{KE just after collision} = \text{Final PE}_G$$
$$\tfrac{1}{2}(3.015\ \text{kg})V^2 = (3.015\ \text{kg})(9.81\ \text{m/s}^2)(0.10\ \text{m})$$

From this $V = 1.40\ \text{m/s}$. Substituting this combined speed into the previous equation leads to $v = 0.28\ \text{km/s}$ for the speed of the bullet.

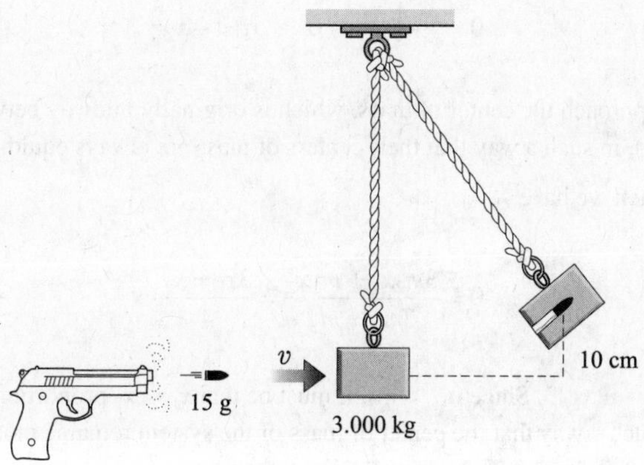


Fig. 8-1

Notice that we cannot write the conservation of energy equation $\frac{1}{2}mv^2 = (m + M)gh$, where $m = 0.015$ kg and $M = 3.000$ kg because energy is lost (through friction) in the collision process.

**8.9 [I]** Three point masses are placed on the $x$-axis: 200 g at $x = 0$, 500 g at $x = 30$ cm, and 400 g at $x = 70$ cm. Find their center of mass.

We can make the calculation with respect to any point, but since all the data is measured from the $x = 0$ origin, that point will do nicely.

$$x_{cm} = \frac{\sum x_i m_i}{\sum m_i} = \frac{(0)(0.20\ \text{kg}) + (0.30\ \text{m})(0.50\ \text{kg}) + (0.70\ \text{m})(0.40\ \text{kg})}{(0.20 + 0.50 + 0.40)\ \text{kg}} = 0.39\ \text{m}$$

The center of mass is located at a distance of 0.39 m, in the positive $x$-direction, from the origin.

The $y$- and $z$-coordinates of the center of mass are zero.

**8.10 [II]** A system consists of the following masses in the $xy$-plane: 4.0 kg at coordinates ($x = 0$, $y = 5.0$ m), 7.0 kg at (3.0 m, 8.0 m), and 5.0 kg at (−3.0 m, −6.0 m). Find the position of its center of mass.

$$x_{cm} = \frac{\sum x_i m_i}{\sum m_i} = \frac{(0)(4.0\ \text{kg}) + (3.0\ \text{m})(7.0\ \text{kg}) + (-3.0\ \text{m})(5.0\ \text{kg})}{(4.0 + 7.0 + 5.0)\ \text{kg}} = 0.38\ \text{m}$$

$$y_{cm} = \frac{\sum y_i m_i}{\sum m_i} = \frac{(5.0\ \text{m})(4.0\ \text{kg}) + (8.0\ \text{m})(7.0\ \text{kg}) + (-6.0\ \text{m})(5.0\ \text{kg})}{16\ \text{kg}} = 2.9\ \text{m}$$

and $z_{cm} = 0$. These distances are, of course, measured from the origin (0, 0, 0,).

**8.11 [III]** Two identical railroad cars sit on a horizontal track, with a distance $D$ between their two centers of mass. By means of a cable between them, a winch on one is used to pull the two together. (*a*) Describe their relative motion. (*b*) Repeat the analysis if the mass of one car is now three times that of the other.

Keep in mind that the velocity of the center of mass of a system can only be changed by an external force. Here the forces due to the cable acting on the two cars are internal to the two-car system. The net external force on the system is zero, and so its center of mass does not move, even though each car travels toward the other. Taking the origin of coordinates at the center of mass,

$$x_{cm} = 0 = \frac{\sum m_i x_i}{\sum m_i} = \frac{m_1 x_1 + m_2 x_2}{m_1 + m_2}$$

where $x_1$ and $x_2$ are the positions of the centers of mass of the two cars.

(*a*) If $m_1 = m_2$, this equation becomes

$$0 = \frac{x_1 + x_2}{2} \quad \text{or} \quad x_1 = -x_2$$

The two cars approach the center of mass, which is originally midway between the two cars (that is, $D/2$ from each), in such a way that their centers of mass are always equidistant from it.

(*b*) If $m_1 = 3m_2$, then we have

$$0 = \frac{3m_2 x_1 + m_2 x_2}{3m_2 + m_2} = \frac{3x_1 + x_2}{4}$$

from which $x_1 = -x_2/3$. Since $m_1 > m_2$, it must be that $x_1 < x_2$ proportionately. The two cars approach each other in such a way that the center of mass of the system remains motionless and the heavier car is always one-third as far away from it as the lighter car.

Originally, because $|x_1| + |x_2| = D$, we had $x_2/3 + x_2 = D$. So $m_2$ was originally a distance $x_2 = 3D/4$ from the center of mass, and $m_1$ was a distance $D/4$ from it.

**8.12 [III]** A pendulum consisting of a ball of mass $m$ is released from the position shown in Fig. 8-2 and strikes a block of mass $M$. The block slides a distance $D$ before stopping under the action of a steady friction force of $0.20Mg$. Find $D$ if the ball rebounds to an angle of 20°.

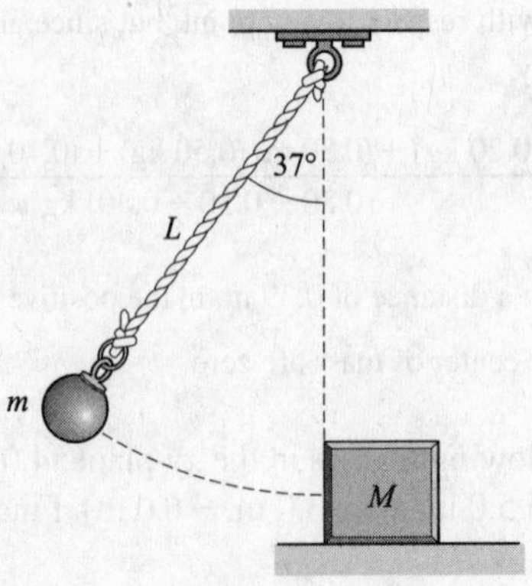


Fig. 8-2

The pendulum ball falls through a height $(L - L\cos 37°) = 0.201L$ and rebounds to a height $(L - L\cos 20°) = 0.060\,3L$. Because $(mgh)_{top} = (\frac{1}{2}mv^2)_{bottom}$ for the ball, its speed at the bottom is $v = \sqrt{2gh}$. Thus, just before it hits the block, the ball has a speed equal to $\sqrt{2g(0.201L)}$. Since the ball rises up to a height of $0.0603L$ after the collision, it must have rebounded with an initial speed of $\sqrt{2g(0.0603L)}$.

Although KE is not conserved in the collision, momentum is. Therefore, for the collision,

$$\text{Momentum just before} = \text{Momentum just after}$$
$$m\sqrt{2g(0.201L)} + 0 = -m\sqrt{2g(0.0603L)} + MV$$

where $V$ is the velocity of the block just after the collision. (Notice the minus sign on the momentum of the rebounding ball.) Solving this equation, we find

$$V = \frac{m}{M}0.981\sqrt{gL}$$

The block uses up its translational KE doing work against friction as it slides a distance $D$. Therefore,

$$\tfrac{1}{2}MV^2 = F_f D \qquad \text{or} \qquad \tfrac{1}{2}M(0.963gL)\left(\frac{m}{M}\right)^2 = (0.2Mg)(D)$$

from which $D = 2.4(m/M)^2L$.

**8.13 [II]** Two balls of equal mass approach the coordinate origin, one moving downward along the $y$-axis at 2.00 m/s and the other moving to the right along the $-x$-axis at 3.00 m/s. After they collide, one ball moves out to the right along the $+x$-axis at 1.20 m/s. Find the scalar $x$ and $y$ velocity components of the other ball.

This is a two-dimensional collision and momentum must be conserved independently in each perpendicular direction, $x$ and $y$. Take *up* and to the *right* as positive. Accordingly, keeping in mind that before impact only one ball had an $x$-component of velocity,

$$(\text{Momentum before})_x = (\text{Momentum after})_x$$

or

$$m(3.00\text{ m/s}) + 0 = m(1.20\text{ m/s}) + mv_x$$

Here $v_x$ is the unknown $x$-component of velocity of the second ball acquired on impact. Since we know that the first ball lost some of its $x$-momentum, the second ball must have gained it. Moreover,

$$(\text{Momentum before})_y = (\text{Momentum after})_y$$

or

$$0 + m(-2.00\text{ m/s}) = 0 + mv_y$$

Here $v_y$ is the $y$-component of velocity of the second ball. (Why the minus sign?) Solving each equation, after cancelling the mass we find that $v_x = 1.80$ m/s and $v_y = -2.00$ m/s.

**8.14 [III]** A 7500-kg truck traveling at 5.0 m/s east collides with a 1500-kg car moving at 20 m/s in a direction 30° south of west. After collision, the two vehicles remain tangled together. With what speed and in what direction does the wreckage begin to move?

The original momenta are shown in Fig. 8-3(*a*), while the final momentum $M\vec{\mathbf{v}}$ is shown in Fig. 8-3(*b*). Momentum must be conserved in both the north and east directions independently. Therefore,

$$(\text{Momentum before})_{\text{East}} = (\text{Momentum after})_{\text{East}}$$
$$(7500\text{ kg})(5.0\text{ m/s}) - (1500\text{ kg})\,[(20\text{ m/s})\cos 30°] = Mv_E$$

where $M = 7500\text{ kg} + 1500\text{ kg} = 9000$ kg, and $v_E$ is the scalar eastward component of the velocity of the wreckage [see Fig. 8-3(*b*)].

$$(\text{Momentum before})_{\text{North}} = (\text{Momentum after})_{\text{North}}$$
$$(7500\text{ kg})(0) - (1500\text{ kg})[(20\text{ m/s})\sin 30°] = Mv_N$$

The first equation yields $v_E = 1.28$ m/s, and the second $v_N = -1.67$ m/s. The resultant is

$$v = \sqrt{(1.67\ \text{m/s})^2 + (1.28\ \text{m/s})^2} = 2.1\ \text{m/s}$$

The angle $\theta$ in Fig. 8-3(*b*) is

$$\theta = \arctan\left(\frac{1.67}{1.28}\right) = 53°$$

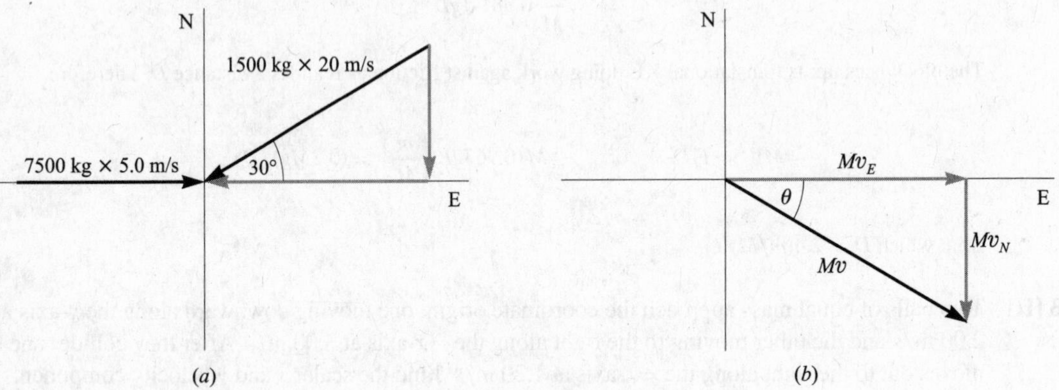


Fig. 8-3

**8.15 [III] Two identical balls collide head-on. The initial velocity of one is 0.75 m/s—EAST, while that of the other is 0.43 m/s—WEST. If the collision is perfectly elastic, what is the final velocity of each ball?**

Because the collision is perfectly elastic, both momentum and KE are conserved. Since the collision is head-on, all motion takes place along a straight line. Take east as positive and call the mass of each ball $m$. Momentum is conserved in a collision, so we can write

$$\text{Momentum before} = \text{Momentum after}$$

$$m(0.75\ \text{m/s}) + m(-0.43\ \text{m/s}) = mv_1 + mv_2$$

where $v_1$ and $v_2$ are the final values. This equation simplifies to

$$0.32\ \text{m/s} = v_1 + v_2 \qquad (1)$$

Because the collision is assumed to be perfectly elastic, KE is also conserved. Thus,

$$\text{KE before} = \text{KE after}$$

$$\tfrac{1}{2}m(0.75\ \text{m/s})^2 + \tfrac{1}{2}m(-0.43\ \text{m/s})^2 = \tfrac{1}{2}mv_1^2 + \tfrac{1}{2}mv_2^2$$

This equation can be simplified to

$$0.747 = v_1^2 + v_2^2 \qquad (2)$$

We can solve for $v_2$ in Eq. (*1*) to get $v_2 = 0.32 - v_1$ and substitute that into Eq. (*2*). This yields

$$0.747 = (0.32 - v_1)^2 + v_1^2$$

from which

$$2v_1^2 - 0.64v_1 - 0.645 = 0$$

Using the quadratic formula,

$$v_1 = \frac{0.64 \pm \sqrt{(0.64)^2 + 5.16}}{4} = 0.16 \pm 0.59 \text{ m/s}$$

from which $v_1 = 0.75$ m/s or $-0.43$ m/s. Substitution back into Eq. (*1*) gives $v_2 = -0.43$ m/s or 0.75 m/s.

Two choices for answers are available:

$$(v_1 = 0.75 \text{ m/s},\ v_2 = -0.43 \text{ m/s}) \qquad \text{and} \qquad (v_1 = -0.43 \text{ m/s},\ v_2 = 0.75 \text{ m/s})$$

We must discard the first choice because it implies that the balls continue on unchanged; that is to say, no collision occurred. The correct answer is therefore $v_1 = -0.43$ m/s and $v_2 = 0.75$ m/s, which tells us that in a perfectly elastic, head-on collision between equal masses, the two bodies simply exchange velocities. Hence, $\vec{\mathbf{v}}_1 = 0.43$ m/s—WEST and $\vec{\mathbf{v}}_2 = 0.75$ m/s—EAST.

**Alternative Method**

If we recall that $e = 1$ for a perfectly elastic head-on collision, then

$$e = \frac{v_2 - v_1}{u_1 - u_2} \qquad \text{becomes} \qquad 1 = \frac{v_2 - v_1}{(0.75 \text{ m/s}) - (-0.43 \text{ m/s})}$$

which gives

$$v_2 - v_1 = 1.18 \text{ m/s} \tag{3}$$

Equations (*1*) and (*3*) determine $v_1$ and $v_2$ uniquely.

**8.16 [III]** A 1.0-kg ball moving at 12 m/s collides head-on with a 2.0-kg ball moving in the opposite direction at 24 m/s. Determine the motion of each after impact if (*a*) $e = 2/3$, (*b*) the balls stick together, and (*c*) the collision is perfectly elastic.

In all three cases the collision occurs along a straight line, and momentum is conserved. Hence,

$$\text{Momentum before} = \text{Momentum after}$$
$$(1.0 \text{ kg})(12 \text{ m/s}) + (2.0 \text{ kg})(-24 \text{ m/s}) = (1.0 \text{ kg})v_1 + (2.0 \text{ kg})v_2$$

which becomes

$$-36 \text{ m/s} = v_1 + 2v_2$$

(*a*) When $e = 2/3$,

$$e = \frac{v_2 - v_1}{u_1 - u_2} \qquad \text{becomes} \qquad \frac{2}{3} = \frac{v_2 - v_1}{(12 \text{ m/s}) - (-24 \text{ m/s})}$$

from which $24 \text{ m/s} = v_2 - v_1$. Combining this with the momentum equation found above gives $v_2 = -4.0$ m/s and $v_1 = -28$ m/s.

(*b*) In this case $v_1 = v_2 = v$, and so the momentum equation becomes

$$3v = -36 \text{ m/s} \qquad \text{or} \qquad v = -12 \text{ m/s}$$

(*c*) Here $e = 1$, and

$$e = \frac{v_2 - v_1}{u_1 - u_2} \qquad \text{becomes} \qquad 1 = \frac{v_2 - v_1}{(12 \text{ m/s}) - (-24 \text{ m/s})}$$

from which $v_2 - v_1 = 36$ m/s. Adding this to the momentum equation yields $v_2 = 0$. Using this value for $v_2$ then leads to $v_1 = -36$ m/s.

**8.17 [III]** A ball is dropped from a height $h$ above a tile floor and rebounds to a height of $0.65h$. Find the coefficient of restitution between ball and floor.

Assign floor quantities the subscript 1, and ball quantities the subscript 2. The initial and final velocities of the floor, $u_1$ and $\upsilon_1$, are zero. Therefore,

$$e = \frac{\upsilon_2 - \upsilon_1}{u_1 - u_2} = -\frac{\upsilon_2}{u_2}$$

Since we know both the drop and rebound heights ($h$ and $0.65h$), we can write equations for the interchange of $PE_G$ and KE before and after the impact

$$mgh = \tfrac{1}{2}mu_2^2 \qquad \text{and} \qquad mg(0.65h) = \tfrac{1}{2}m\upsilon_2^2$$

Therefore, taking *down* as positive, $u_2 = \sqrt{2gh}$ and $\upsilon_2 = -\sqrt{1.30gh}$. Substitution leads to

$$e = \frac{\sqrt{1.30gh}}{\sqrt{2gh}} = \sqrt{0.65} = 0.81$$

Notice that the coefficient of restitution equals the square root of the final rebound height over the initial drop height.

**8.18 [III]** The two balls depicted in Fig. 8-4 collide off center and bounce away as shown. (*a*) What is the final velocity of the 500-g ball if the 800-g ball has a speed of 15 cm/s after the collision? (*b*) Is the collision perfectly elastic?

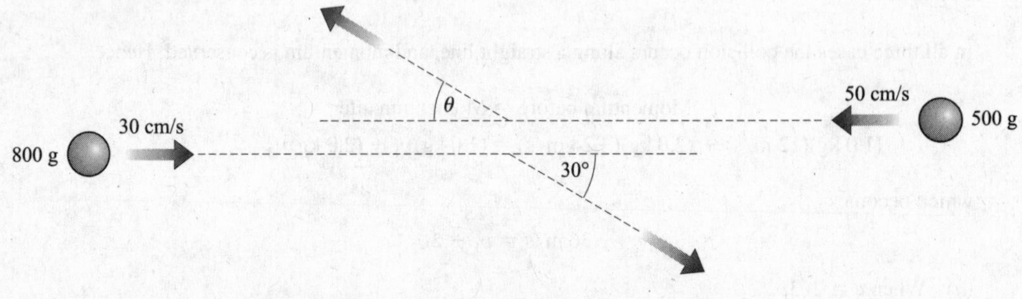


Fig. 8-4

(*a*) Take motion to the right as positive. From the law of conservation of momentum,

$$(\text{Momentum before})_x = (\text{Momentum after})_x$$

$$(0.80\text{ kg})(0.30\text{ m/s}) + (0.50\text{ kg})(-0.5\text{m/s}) = (0.80\text{ kg})[(0.15\text{ m/s})\cos 30^\circ] + (0.50\text{ kg})\upsilon_x$$

from which $\upsilon_x = -0.228$ m/s. Taking motion upward as positive,

$$(\text{Momentum before})_y = (\text{Momentum after})_y$$

$$0 = (0.80\text{ kg})[-(0.15\text{ m/s})\sin 30^\circ] + (0.50\text{ kg})\upsilon_y$$

from which $\upsilon_y = 0.120$ m/s. Then

$$\upsilon = \sqrt{\upsilon_x^2 + \upsilon_y^2} = \sqrt{(-0.228\text{ m/s})^2 + (0.120\text{ m/s})^2} = 0.26\text{ m/s}$$

and $\vec{\mathbf{v}} = 0.26$ m/s—RIGHT.

Furthermore, for the angle $\theta$ shown in Fig. 8-4,

$$\theta = \arctan\left(\frac{0.120}{0.228}\right) = 28^\circ$$

(*b*) $\text{Total KE before} = \frac{1}{2}(0.80\text{ kg})(0.30\text{ m/s})^2 + \frac{1}{2}(0.50\text{ kg})(0.50\text{ m/s})^2 = 0.099\text{ J}$

$$\text{Total KE after} = \frac{1}{2}(0.80\text{ kg})(0.15\text{ m/s})^2 + \frac{1}{2}(0.50\text{ kg})(0.26\text{ m/s})^2 = 0.026\text{ J}$$

Because KE is lost in the collision, it is not perfectly elastic.

**8.19 [II]** What force is exerted on a stationary flat plate held perpendicular to a jet of water as shown in Fig. 8-5? The horizontal speed of the water is 80 cm/s, and 30 mL of the water hit the plate each second. Assume the water moves parallel to the plate after striking it. One milliliter (mL) of water has a mass of 1.00 g.

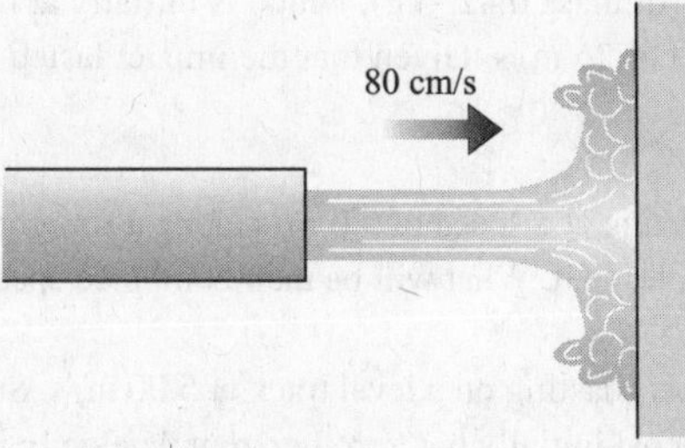


Fig. 8-5

This question deals with speed, mass, time, and force, and that suggests impulse-momentum and Newton's Second Law. The plate exerts an impulse on the water and changes its horizontal momentum. The water exerts a counterforce on the plate. Taking the direction to the right as positive,

$$(\text{Impulse})_x = \text{Change in } x\text{-directed momentum}$$

$$F_x\,\Delta t = (mv_x)_{\text{final}} - (mv_x)_{\text{initial}}$$

Let $t$ be 1.00 s so that $m$ will be the mass that strikes in 1.00 s, namely 30 g. Then the above equation becomes

$$F_x\,(1.00\text{ s}) = (0.030\text{ kg})(0\text{ m/s}) - (0.030\text{ kg})(0.80\text{ m/s})$$

from which $F_x = -0.024$ N. This is the force exerted by the plate on the water. The law of action and reaction tells us that the jet exerts an equal but opposite force on the plate.

**8.20 [III]** A rocket standing on its launch platform points straight upward. Its engines are activated and eject gas at a rate of 1500 kg/s. The molecules are expelled with an average speed of 50 km/s. How much mass can the rocket initially have if it is slowly to rise because of the thrust of the engines?

The problem provides mass flow and speed, the product of which is equivalent to the time rate-of-change of momentum. That should bring to mind the impulse-momentum relationship, which, of course, is Newton's Second Law. Since the initial motion of the rocket itself is negligible in comparison to the speed of the expelled gas, we can assume the gas is accelerated from rest to a speed of 50 km/s. The impulse required to provide this acceleration to a mass $m$ of gas is

$$F\,\Delta t = mv_f - mv_i = m(50\,000\text{ m/s}) - 0$$

from which

$$F = (50\,000\text{ m/s})\frac{m}{\Delta t}$$

But we are told that the mass ejected per second ($m/\Delta t$) is 1500 kg/s, and so the force exerted on the expelled gas is

$$F = (50\,000 \text{ m/s})(1500 \text{ kg/s}) = 75 \text{ MN}$$

An equal but opposite reaction force acts on the rocket, and this is the upward thrust on the rocket. The engines can therefore support a weight of 75 MN, so the maximum mass the rocket could have is

$$M_{\text{rocket}} = \frac{\text{weight}}{g} = \frac{75 \times 10^6 \text{ N}}{9.81 \text{ m/s}^2} = 7.7 \times 10^6 \text{ kg}$$

## SUPPLEMENTARY PROBLEMS

**8.21 [I]** Typically, a tennis ball hit during a serve travels away at about 51 m/s. If the ball is at rest mid-air when struck, and it has a mass of 0.058 kg, what is the change in its momentum on leaving the racket?

**8.22 [I]** During a soccer game a ball (of mass 0.425 kg), which is initially at rest, is kicked by one of the players. The ball moves off at a speed of 26 m/s. Given that the impact lasted for 8.0 ms, what was the average force exerted on the ball?

**8.23 [II]** A 40 000-kg freight car is coasting at a speed of 5.0 m/s along a straight level track when it strikes a 30 000-kg stationary freight car and couples to it. What will be their combined speed after impact?

**8.24 [I]** An empty 15 000-kg coal car is coasting on a level track at 5.00 m/s. Suddenly 5000 kg of coal is dumped into it from directly above it. The coal initially has zero horizontal velocity with respect to the ground. Find the final speed of the car.

**8.25 [II]** Sand drops at a rate of 2000 kg/min from the bottom of a stationary hopper onto a belt conveyer moving horizontally at 250 m/min. Determine the force needed to drive the conveyer, neglecting friction. [*Hint*: How much momentum must be imparted to the sand each second?]

**8.26 [II]** Two bodies of masses 8 kg and 4 kg move along the $x$-axis in opposite directions with velocities of 11 m/s—POSITIVE $X$-DIRECTION and 7 m/s—NEGATIVE $X$-DIRECTION, respectively. They collide and stick together. Find their combined velocity just after collision.

**8.27 [II]** A 1200-kg gun mounted on wheels shoots an 8.00-kg projectile with a muzzle velocity of 600 m/s at an angle of 30 0° above the horizontal. Find the horizontal recoil speed of the gun.

**8.28 [I]** Three masses are placed on the $y$-axis: 2 kg at $y = 300$ cm, 6 kg at $y = 150$ cm, and 4 kg at $y = -75$ cm. Find their center of mass.

**8.29 [II]** Four masses are positioned in the $xy$-plane as follows: 300 g at ($x = 0$, $y = 2.0$ m), 500 g at ($-2$ 0 m, $-3.0$ m), 700 g at (50 cm, 30 cm), and 900 g at ($-80$ cm, 150 cm). Find their center of mass.

**8.30 [II]** A ball of mass $m$ sits at the coordinate origin when it explodes into two pieces that shoot along the $x$-axis in opposite directions. When one of the pieces (which has mass $0.270m$) is at $x = 70$ cm, where is the other piece? [*Hint*: What happens to the mass center?]

**8.31 [II]** A ball of mass $m$ at rest at the coordinate origin explodes into three equal pieces. At some instant, one piece is on the $x$-axis at $x = 40$ cm and another is at $x = 20$ cm, $y = -60$ cm. Where is the third piece at that instant?

**8.32 [II]** A 2.0-kg block of wood rests on a long tabletop. A 5.0-g bullet moving horizontally with a speed of 150 m/s is shot into the block and lodges in it. The block then slides 270 cm along the table and stops. (*a*) Find the speed of the block just after impact. (*b*) Find the friction force between block and table assuming it to be constant.

**8.33 [II]** A 2.0-kg block of wood rests on a tabletop. A 7.0-g bullet is shot straight up through a hole in the table beneath the block. The bullet lodges in the block, and the block flies 25 cm above the tabletop. How fast was the bullet going initially?

**8.34 [III]** A 6000-kg truck traveling north at 5.0 m/s collides with a 4000-kg truck moving west at 15 m/s. If the two trucks remain locked together after impact, with what speed and in what direction do they move immediately after the collision?

**8.35 [I]** What average resisting force must act on a 3.0-kg mass to reduce its speed from 65 cm/s to 15 cm/s in 0.20 s?

**8.36 [II]** A 7.00-g bullet moving horizontally at 200 m/s strikes and passes through a 150-g tin can sitting on a post. Just after impact, the can has a horizontal speed of 180 cm/s. What was the bullet's speed after leaving the can?

**8.37 [III]** Two balls of equal mass, moving with speeds of 3 m/s, collide head-on. Find the speed of each after impact if (*a*) they stick together, (*b*) the collision is perfectly elastic, (*c*) the coefficient of restitution is 1/3.

**8.38 [III]** A 90-g ball moving at 100 cm/s collides head-on with a stationary 10-g ball. Determine the speed of each after impact if (*a*) they stick together, (*b*) the collision is perfectly elastic, (*c*) the coefficient of restitution is 0.90.

**8.39 [III]** A ball is dropped onto a horizontal floor. It reaches a height of 144 cm on the first bounce, and 81 cm on the second bounce. Find (*a*) the coefficient of restitution between the ball and floor and (*b*) the height it attains on the third bounce. [*Hint*: Study Problem 8.17.]

**8.40 [II]** Two identical balls undergo a collision at the origin of coordinates. Before collision their scalar velocity components are ($u_x$ = 40 cm/s, $u_y$ = 0) and ($u_x$ = −30 cm/s, $u_y$ = 20 cm/s). After collision, the first ball (the one moving along the *x*-axis) is standing still. Find the scalar velocity components of the second ball. [*Hint*: After the collision, the moving ball must have all of the momentum of the system.]

**8.41 [II]** Two identical balls traveling parallel to the *x*-axis have speeds of 30 cm/s and are oppositely directed. They collide off center perfectly elastically. After the collision, one ball is moving at an angle of 30° above the +*x*-axis. Find its speed and the velocity of the other ball.

**8.42 [II]** (*a*) What minimum thrust must the engines of a $2.0 \times 10^5$ kg rocket have if the rocket is to be able to slowly rise from the Earth when aimed straight upward? (*b*) If the engines eject gas at the rate of 20 kg/s, how fast must the gaseous exhaust be moving as it leaves the engines? Neglect the small change in the mass of the rocket due to the ejected fuel. [*Hint*: Study Problem 8.20.]

## ANSWERS TO SUPPLEMENTARY PROBLEMS

**8.21 [I]** 3.0 kg·m/s

**8.22 [I]** 1.4 kN

**8.23 [II]** 2.9 m/s

**8.24 [I]** 3.75 m/s

**8.25 [II]** 139 N

**8.26 [II]** 5 m/s—POSITIVE *X*-DIRECTION

**8.27 [II]** 3.46 m/s

**8.28 [I]** $y = 1$ m, measured from the $y = 0$ origin

**8.29 [II]** $x = -0.57$ m, and $y = 0.28$ m, both measured from the (0, 0) origin

**8.30 [II]** at $x = -26$ cm

**8.31 [II]** at $x = -60$ cm, $y = 60$ cm

**8.32 [II]** (*a*) 0.37 m/s; (*b*) 0.052 N

**8.33 [II]** 0.64 km/s

**8.34 [III]** 6.7 m/s at 27° north of west

**8.35 [I]** 7.5 N

**8.36 [II]** 161 m/s

**8.37 [III]** (*a*) 0 m/s; (*b*) each rebounds at 3 m/s; (*c*) each rebounds at 1 m/s

**8.38 [III]** (*a*) 90 cm/s; (*b*) 80 cm/s, 1.8 m/s; (*c*) 81 cm/s, 1.7 m/s

**8.39 [III]** (*a*) 0.75; (*b*) 46 cm

**8.40 [II]** $v_x = 10$ cm/s, $v_y = 20$ cm/s

**8.41 [II]** 30 cm/s, 30 cm/s at 30° below the $-x$-axis (opposite to the first ball)

**8.42 [II]** (*a*) $20 \times 10^5$ N; (*b*) 98 km/s

# Angular Motion in a Plane

**Angular Displacement** ($\theta$) is usually expressed in **radians**, in degrees, or in revolutions:

$$1 \text{ rev} = 360° = 2\pi \text{ rad} \qquad \text{or} \qquad 1 \text{ rad} = 57.3°$$

One radian is the angle subtended at the center of a circle by an arc equal in length to the radius of the circle (see Fig. 9-1). Thus, an angle $\theta$ in radians is given in terms of the arc length $l$ it subtends on a circle of radius $r$ by

$$\theta = \frac{l}{r}$$

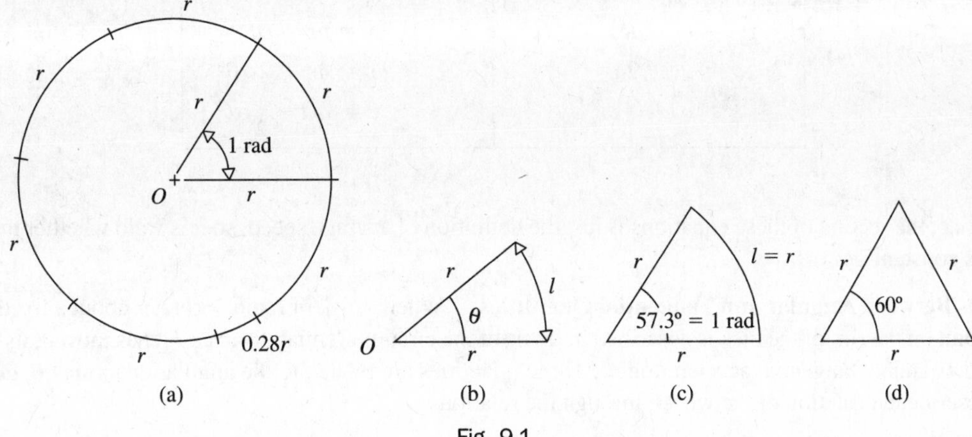


Fig. 9-1

The radian measure of an angle is a dimensionless number. Radians, like degrees, are not a physical unit—the radian is not expressible in meters, kilograms, or seconds. Nonetheless, we will use the abbreviation rad to remind us that we are working with radians. As we'll soon see, "rad" does not always carry through the equations in a consistent fashion. We will have to remove it or insert it as needed.

**The Angular Speed** ($\omega$) of an object whose axis of rotation is fixed is the rate at which its angular coordinate, the angular displacement $\theta$, changes with time. If $\theta$ changes from $\theta_i$ to $\theta_f$ in a time $t$, then the **average angular speed** is

$$\omega_{av} = \frac{\theta_f - \theta_i}{t}$$

The units of $\omega_{av}$ are exclusively rad/s. Since each complete turn or cycle of a revolving system carries it through $2\pi$ rad,

$$\omega = 2\pi f$$

where $f$ is the **frequency** often stated in revolutions per second, rotations per second, or cycles per second. Today the standard unit of frequency is the *hertz*, abbreviated Hz, where 1 cycle/second = 1 Hz. The quantity $\omega$ is also called the **angular frequency**. We can associate a direction with $\omega$ and thereby create a vector quantity $\vec{\boldsymbol{\omega}}$. Thus, if the fingers of the right hand curve around in the direction of rotation, the thumb points along the axis of rotation in the direction of $\vec{\boldsymbol{\omega}}$, the **angular velocity** vector.

**The Angular Acceleration** ($\alpha$) of an object whose axis of rotation is fixed is the rate at which its angular speed changes with time. If the angular speed changes uniformly from $\omega_i$ to $\omega_f$ in a time $t$, then the **angular acceleration** is constant and

$$\alpha = \frac{\omega_f - \omega_i}{t}$$

The units of $\alpha$ are typically rad/s$^2$, rev/min$^2$, and so forth. It is possible to associate a direction with $\Delta\omega$, and therefore with $\alpha$, thereby specifying the angular acceleration vector $\vec{\boldsymbol{\alpha}}$, but we will have no need to do so here.

**Equations for Uniformly Accelerated Angular Motion** are exactly analogous to those for uniformly accelerated linear motion. In the usual notation we have:

| LINEAR | ANGULAR |
|---|---|
| $v_{av} = \frac{1}{2}(v_i + v_f)$ | $\omega_{a\omega} = \frac{1}{2}(\omega_i + \omega_f)$ |
| $s = v_{av}t$ | $\theta = \omega_{av}t$ |
| $v_f = v_i + at$ | $\omega_f = \omega_i + \alpha t$ |
| $v_f^2 = v_i^2 + 2as$ | $\omega_f^2 = \omega_i^2 + 2\alpha\theta$ |
| $s = v_i t + \frac{1}{2}at^2$ | $\theta = \omega_i t + \frac{1}{2}\alpha t^2$ |

Taken alone, the second of these equations is just the definition of average speed, so it is valid whether the acceleration is constant or not.

**Relations Between Angular and Tangential Quantities:** When a disk of radius $r$ rotates about a fixed central axis, a point on the rim of the disk is described in terms of the circumferential distance $l$ it has moved, its tangential speed $v$, and its tangential acceleration $a_T$. These quantities are related to the angular quantities $\theta$, $\omega$, and $\alpha$, which describe the rotation of the wheel, through the relations

$$l = r\theta \qquad v = r\omega \qquad a_T = r\alpha$$

*provided* radian measure is used for $\theta$, $\omega$, and $\alpha$.

By simple reasoning, $l$ can be shown to be the distance traveled by a point on a belt wound around a portion of a rotating wheel, or the distance a wheel would roll (without slipping) if free to do so. In such cases, $v$ and $a_T$ refer to the tangential speed and acceleration of a point on the belt, or of the center of the wheel, where $r$ is the radius of the wheel. This can be seen in Fig. 9-2 which depicts a rolling wheel uniformly accelerating at an angular rate $\alpha$ (without slipping). The motion of the wheel can be thought of as composed of a simultaneous rotation about its center $O$, and a translation of $O$ to $O''$. The point initially touching the ground ($A$), is in effect rotated into $A'$ through an angle $\theta$, and translated into $A''$ over a distance $l_O = r\theta$, which is also the distance $O$ translates. Seen by someone standing still, $A$ moves along a cycloid (the dotted curve) to its position at $A''$. The speed at which $O$ translates at any instant is $v_O = r\omega$, where $\omega$ is the angular speed at that instant. The linear (or tangential) acceleration of $O$, which is constant since $\alpha$ is constant, is $a_{TO} = r\alpha$.

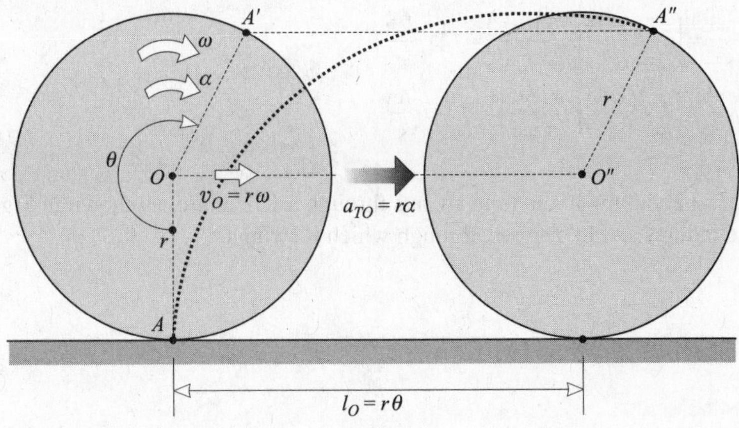


Fig. 9-2

**Centripetal Acceleration** ($a_C$): A point mass $m$ moving with constant speed $v$ around a circle of radius $r$ is undergoing acceleration. Although the magnitude of its linear velocity is not changing, the direction of the velocity is continually changing. This change in velocity gives rise to an acceleration $a_C$ of the mass which is directed toward the center of the circle. We call this acceleration the **centripetal acceleration**; its magnitude is given by

$$a_C = \frac{(\text{Tangential speed})^2}{\text{Radius of circular path}} = \frac{v^2}{r}$$

where $v$ is the speed of the mass around the perimeter of the circle.

Because $v = r\omega$, we also have $a_C = r\omega^2$, where $\omega$ must be in rad/s. Notice that the word "acceleration" is commonly used in physics as either a scalar or a vector quantity. Fortunately, there's usually no ambiguity.

**The Centripetal Force** ($\vec{\mathbf{F}}_C$) is the force that must act on a mass $m$ moving in a circular path of radius $r$ to give it the required centripetal acceleration $v^2/r$. In other words, if a body is to move along a circular arc, it must experience an inwardly directed "center seeking" force $\vec{\mathbf{F}}_C$ pushing it off its force-free straight-line inertial path. From $F = ma$, we have

$$F_C = \frac{mv^2}{r} = mr\omega^2$$

where $\vec{\mathbf{F}}_C$ is directed toward the center of the circular path. Centripetal force is not a new kind of force; it's just the name given to whatever force (be it gravity, the tension in a string, magnetism, friction, etc.) that causes an object to move (off it's straight-line inertial path) along an arc.

## SOLVED PROBLEMS

**9.1 [I]** Express each of the following in terms of other angular measures: (*a*) 28°, (*b*) $\frac{1}{4}$ rev/s, (*c*) 2.18 rad/s².

(*a*) $$28° = (28\text{ deg})\left(\frac{1\text{ rev}}{360\text{ deg}}\right) = 0.078\text{ rev}$$

$$= (28\text{ deg})\left(\frac{2\pi\text{ rad}}{360\text{ deg}}\right) = 0.49\text{ rad}$$

(*b*) $$\frac{1}{4}\frac{\text{rev}}{\text{s}} = \left(0.25\frac{\text{rev}}{\text{s}}\right)\left(\frac{360\text{ deg}}{1\text{ rev}}\right) = 90\frac{\text{deg}}{\text{s}}$$

$$= \left(0.25\frac{\text{rev}}{\text{s}}\right)\left(\frac{2\pi\text{ rad}}{1\text{ rev}}\right) = \frac{\pi}{2}\frac{\text{rad}}{\text{s}}$$

(c) $$2.18\ \frac{\text{rad}}{\text{s}^2} = \left(2.18\ \frac{\text{rad}}{\text{s}^2}\right)\left(\frac{360\ \text{deg}}{2\pi\ \text{rad}}\right) = 125\ \frac{\text{deg}}{\text{s}^2}$$
$$= \left(2.18\ \frac{\text{rad}}{\text{s}^2}\right)\left(\frac{1\ \text{rev}}{2\pi\ \text{rad}}\right) = 0.347\ \frac{\text{rev}}{\text{s}^2}$$

**9.2 [I]** The bob of a pendulum 90 cm long swings through a 15-cm arc, as shown in Fig. 9-3. Find the angle $\theta$, in radians and in degrees, through which it swings.

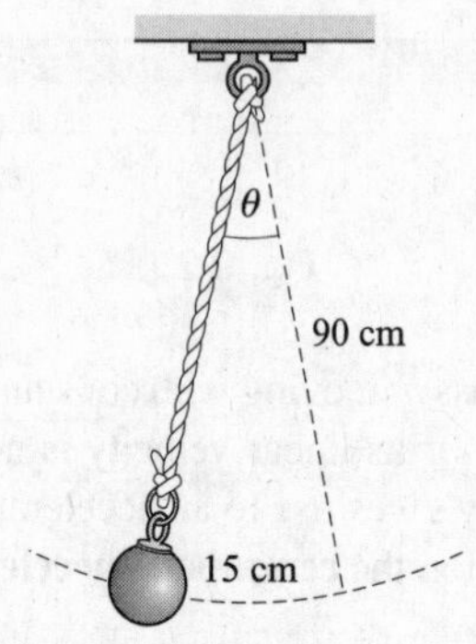


Fig. 9-3

Recall that $l = r\theta$ applies only to angles in radian measure. Therefore, in radians

$$\theta = \frac{l}{r} = \frac{0.15\ \text{m}}{0.90\ \text{m}} = 0.167\ \text{rad} = 0.17\ \text{rad}$$

Then in degrees $$\theta = (0.167\ \text{rad})\left(\frac{360\ \text{deg}}{2\pi\ \text{rad}}\right) = 9.6°$$

**9.3 [I]** A fan turns at a rate of 900 rpm (i.e., rev/min). (*a*) Find the angular speed of any point on one of the fan blades. (*b*) Find the tangential speed of the tip of a blade if the distance from the center to the tip is 20.0 cm.

(*a*) $$f = 900\ \frac{\text{rev}}{\text{min}} = 15.0\ \frac{\text{rev}}{\text{s}} = 15.0\ \text{Hz}$$

Since $\omega = 2\pi f$

$$\omega = 2\pi\ (15.0\ \text{Hz})$$

and so $$\omega = 94.2\ \frac{\text{rad}}{\text{s}}$$

for all points on the fan blade.

(*b*) The tangential speed is $r\omega$, where $\omega$ must be in rad/s. Therefore,

$$v = r\omega = (0.200\ \text{m})(94.2\ \text{rad/s}) = 18.8\ \text{m/s}$$

Notice that the rad does not carry through the equations properly—we insert it or delete it as needed.

**9.4 [I]** A belt passes over a wheel of radius 25 cm, as shown in Fig. 9-4. If a point on the belt has a speed of 5.0 m/s, how fast is the wheel turning?

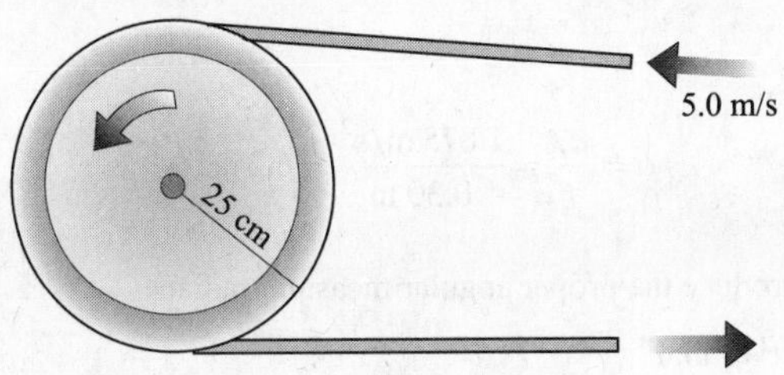


Fig. 9-4

A point on the wheel's circumference (i.e., on the belt) is moving at a linear speed $v = r\omega$. Hence,

$$\omega = \frac{v}{r} = \frac{5.0\text{ m/s}}{0.25\text{ m}} = 20\ \frac{\text{rad}}{\text{s}}$$

As a rule, $\omega$ comes out in units of $s^{-1}$ and the rad must be inserted ad hoc.

**9.5 [I]** A wheel of 40-cm radius rotates on a stationary central axle. It is uniformly sped up from rest to 900 rpm in a time of 20 s. Find (*a*) the constant angular acceleration of the wheel and (*b*) the tangential acceleration of a point on its rim.

(*a*) Because the acceleration is constant, we can use the definition $\alpha = (\omega_f - \omega_i)/t$ to get

$$\alpha = \frac{\left(2\pi\frac{\text{rad}}{\text{rev}}\right)\left(\frac{900\text{ rev}}{60\text{ s}}\right) - \left(2\pi\frac{\text{rad}}{\text{rev}}\right)\left(0\frac{\text{rev}}{\text{s}}\right)}{20\text{ s}} = 4.7\ \frac{\text{rad}}{\text{s}^2}$$

(*b*) Then $$a_T = r\alpha = (0.40\text{ m})\left(4.7\ \frac{\text{rad}}{\text{s}^2}\right) = 1.88\ \frac{\text{m}}{\text{s}^2} = 1.9\text{ m/s}^2$$

**9.6 [II]** A pulley having a 5.0-cm radius is turning at 30 rev/s about a central axis. It is slowed down uniformly to 20 rev/s in 2.0 s. Calculate (*a*) the angular acceleration of the pulley, (*b*) the angle through which it turns in this time, and (*c*) the length of belt it winds in that same time.

Because the pulley is decelerating, we can anticipate that $\alpha$ will be negative:

(*a*) $\alpha = \dfrac{\omega_f - \omega_i}{t} = 2\pi\dfrac{(20-30)\text{ rad/s}}{2.0\text{ s}} = -10\pi\text{ rad/s}^2$

And to two significant figures,

(*b*) $\theta = \omega_{av}t = \frac{1}{2}(\omega_f + \omega_i)t = \frac{1}{2}(100\pi\text{ rad/s})(2.0\text{ s}) = 100\pi\text{ rad} = 1.0\times10^2\pi\text{ rad}$

(*c*) With $\theta = 314$ rad

$$l = r\theta = (0.050\text{ m})(314\text{ rad}) = 16\text{ m}$$

**9.7 [II]** A car has wheels each with a radius of 30 cm. It starts from rest and (without slipping) accelerates uniformly to a speed of 15 m/s in a time of 8.0 s. Find the angular acceleration of its wheels and the number of rotations one wheel makes in this time.

Remember that the center of the rolling wheel accelerates tangentially at the same rate as does a point on its circumference. We know that $a_T = (v_f - v_i)/t$, and so

$$a_T = \frac{15\text{ m/s}}{8.0\text{ s}} = 1.875\text{ m/s}^2$$

Then $a_T = r\alpha$ yields

$$\alpha = \frac{a_T}{r} = \frac{1.875\ \text{m/s}^2}{0.30\ \text{m}} = 6.2\ \text{rad/s}^2$$

Notice that we must introduce the proper angular measure, radians.

Now use $\theta = \omega_i t + \frac{1}{2}\alpha t^2$ to find

$$\theta = 0 + \tfrac{1}{2}(6.2\ \text{rad/s}^2)(8.0\ \text{s})^2 = 200\ \text{rad}$$

and to get the corresponding number of turns divide by $2\pi$,

$$(200\ \text{rad})\left(\frac{1\ \text{rev}}{2\pi\ \text{rad}}\right) = 32\ \text{rev}$$

**9.8 [II]** **A spin-drier revolving at 900 rpm slows down uniformly to 300 rpm while making 50 revolutions. Find (*a*) the angular acceleration and (*b*) the time required to turn through these 50 revolutions.**

The initial angular speed ($\omega_i$) is 900 rev/min = 15.0 rev/s = $30.0\pi$ rad/s and the final angular speed ($\omega_f$) is 300 rev/min = 5.00 rev/s = $10.0\pi$ rad/s.

(*a*) Thus using $\omega_f^2 = \omega_i^2 + 2\alpha\theta$,

$$\alpha = \frac{\omega_f^2 - \omega_i^2}{2\theta} = \frac{(10.0\pi\ \text{rad/s})^2 - (30.0\pi\ \text{rad/s})^2}{2(100\pi\ \text{rad})} = -4.0\pi\ \text{rad/s}^2$$

(*b*) Because $\omega_{av} = \frac{1}{2}(\omega_i + \omega_f) = 20.0\pi$ rad/s, $\theta = \omega_{av} t$ yields

$$t = \frac{\theta}{\omega_{av}} = \frac{100\pi\ \text{rad}}{20.0\pi\ \text{rad/s}} = 5.0\ \text{s}$$

**9.9 [II]** **A 200-g object is tied to the end of a cord and whirled in a horizontal circle of radius 1.20 m at a constant 3.0 rev/s. Assume that the cord is horizontal—that is, that gravity can be neglected. Determine (*a*) the centripetal acceleration of the object and (*b*) the tension in the cord.**

(*a*) The object is not accelerating tangentially to the circle but is undergoing a radial, or centripetal, acceleration given by

$$a_C = \frac{v^2}{r} = r\omega^2$$

where $\omega$ must be in rad/s. Since 3.0 rev/s = $6.0\pi$ rad/s,

$$a_C = (1.20\ \text{m})(6.0\pi\ \text{rad/s})^2 = 426\ \text{m/s}^2 = 0.43\ \text{km/s}^2$$

(*b*) To cause the acceleration found in (*a*), the cord must pull on the 0.200-kg mass with a centripetal force given by

$$F_C = ma_C = (0.200\ \text{kg})(426\ \text{m/s}^2) = 85\ \text{N}$$

This is the tension in the cord.

**9.10 [II]** What is the maximum speed at which a car can round a curve of 25-m radius on a level road if the coefficient of static friction between the tires and road is 0.80?

The radial force required to keep the car in the curved path (the centripetal force) is supplied by friction between the tires and the road. If the mass of the car is $m$, the maximum friction force (which is the centripetal force) equals $\mu_s F_N$ or 0.80 $mg$; this arises when the car is on the verge of skidding sideways. Therefore, the maximum speed is given by

$$\frac{mv^2}{r} = 0.80mg \qquad \text{or} \qquad v = \sqrt{0.80gr} = \sqrt{(0.80)(9.81\ \text{m/s}^2)(25\ \text{m})} = 14\ \text{m/s}$$

**9.11 [II]** A spaceship orbits the Moon at a height of 20 000 m. Assuming it to be subject only to the gravitational pull of the Moon, find its speed and the time it takes for one orbit. For the Moon, $m_m = 7.34 \times 10^{22}$ kg and $r = 1.738 \times 10^6$ m.

The gravitational force of the Moon on the ship supplies the required centripetal force:

$$G = \frac{m_s m_m}{R^2} = \frac{m_s v^2}{R}$$

where $R$ is the radius of the orbit. Letting $h$ be the altitude (20 000 m), $R = h + r$. Solving for $v$:

$$v = \sqrt{\frac{Gm_m}{R}} = \sqrt{\frac{(6.67 \times 10^{-11}\ \text{N}\cdot\text{m}^2/\text{kg}^2)(7.34 \times 10^{22}\ \text{kg})}{(1.738 + 0.0200) \times 10^6\ \text{m}}} = 1.67\ \text{km/s}$$

from which it follows that

$$\text{Time for one orbit} = \frac{2\pi R}{v} = 6.62 \times 10^3\ \text{s} = 110\ \text{min}$$

**9.12 [II]** As depicted in Fig. 9-5, a ball $B$ is fastened to one end of a 24-cm string, and the other end is held fixed at point $O$. The ball whirls in the horizontal circle shown. Find the speed of the ball in its circular path if the string makes an angle of 30° to the vertical.

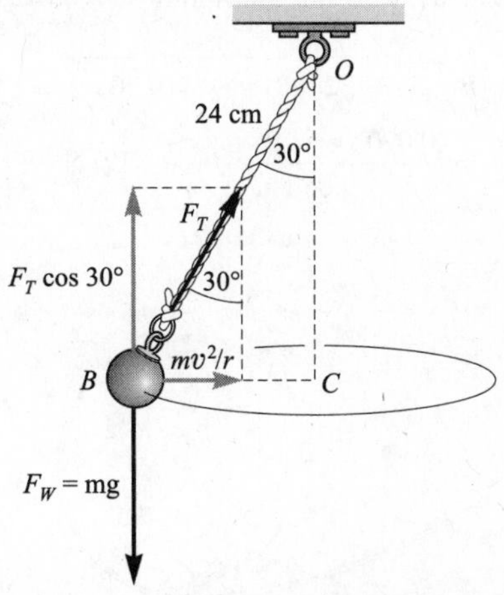


Fig. 9-5

The only forces acting on the ball are the ball's weight $mg$ and the tension $F_T$ in the cord. The tension must do two things: (1) balance the weight of the ball by means of its vertical component, $F_T \cos 30°$; (2) supply the required centripetal force by means of its horizontal component, $F_T \sin 30°$. Therefore, we can write

$$F_T \cos 30° = mg \quad \text{and} \quad F_T \sin 30° = \frac{mv^2}{r}$$

Solving for $F_T$ in the first equation and substituting it in the second gives

$$\frac{mg \sin 30°}{\cos 30°} = \frac{mv^2}{r} \quad \text{or} \quad v = \sqrt{rg(0.577)}$$

However, $r = \overline{BC} = (0.24 \text{ m}) \sin 30° = 0.12 \text{ m}$ and $g = 9.81 \text{ m/s}^2$, from which $v = 0.82 \text{ m/s}$.

**9.13 [III]** As drawn in Fig. 9-6, a 20-g bead slides from rest at $A$ along a frictionless wire. If $h$ is 25 cm and $R$ is 5.0 cm, how large a force must the wire exert on the bead when it is at (*a*) point-$B$ and (*b*) point-$D$?

(*a*) As a general rule, remember to keep a few more numerical figures in the intermediate steps of the calculation than are to be found in the answer. This will avoid round-off errors. Let us first find the speed of the bead at point-$B$. It has fallen through a distance $h - 2R$ and so its loss in $\text{PE}_G$ is $mg(h - 2R)$. This must equal its KE at point-$B$:

$$\frac{1}{2}mv^2 = mg(h - 2R)$$

where $v$ is the speed of the bead at point-$B$. Hence,

$$v = \sqrt{2g(h - 2R)} = \sqrt{2(9.81 \text{ m/s}^2)(0.15 \text{ m})} = 1.716 \text{ m/s}$$

As shown in Fig. 9-6(*b*), two forces act on the bead when it is at $B$: (1) the weight of the bead $mg$ and (2) the (assumed downward) force $F$ of the wire on the bead. Together, these two forces must supply the required centripetal force, $mv^2/R$, if the bead is to follow the circular path. Therefore, write

$$mg + F = \frac{mv^2}{R}$$

or

$$F = \frac{mv^2}{R} - mg = (0.020 \text{ kg})\left[\left(\frac{1.716^2}{0.050} - 9.81\right)\text{m/s}^2\right] = 0.98 \text{ N}$$

The wire must exert a 0.98 N downward force on the bead to hold it in a circular path.

(*b*) The situation is similar at point-$D$, but now the weight is perpendicular to the direction of the required centripetal force. Therefore, the wire alone must furnish it. Proceeding as before,

$$v = \sqrt{2g(h - R)} = \sqrt{2(9.81 \text{ m/s}^2)(0.20 \text{ m})} = 1.98 \text{ m/s}$$

and

$$F = \frac{mv^2}{R} = \frac{(0.020 \text{ kg})(1.98 \text{ m/s}^2)}{0.050 \text{ m}} = 1.6 \text{ N}$$

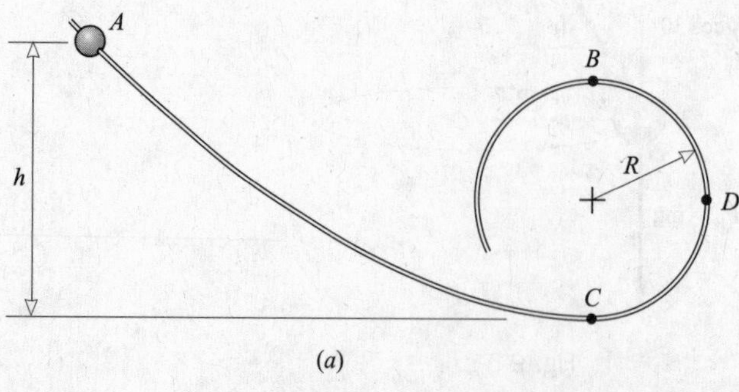

Fig. 9-6

**9.14 [III]** As illustrated in Fig. 9-7, a 0.90-kg body attached to a cord is whirled in a vertical circle of radius 2.50 m. (*a*) What minimum speed $v_t$ must the body have at the top of the circle so as not to depart from the circular path? (*b*) Under condition (*a*), what speed $v_b$ will the object have after it "falls" to the bottom of the circle? (*c*) Find the tension $F_{Tb}$ in the cord when the body is at the bottom of the circle and moving with the critical speed $v_b$.

The object is moving at its slowest speed at the very top and increases its speed as it revolves downward because of gravity ($v_b > v_t$).

(*a*) As Fig. 9-7 shows, two radial forces act on the object at the top: (1) its weight *mg* and (2) the tension $F_{Tt}$. The resultant of these two forces must supply the required centripetal force.

$$\frac{mv_t^2}{r} = mg + F_{Tt}$$

For a given *r*, *v* will be smallest when $F_{Tt} = 0$. In that case,

$$\frac{mv_t^2}{r} = mg \qquad \text{or} \qquad v_t = \sqrt{rg}$$

Using $r = 2.50$ m and $g = 9.81$ m/s$^2$ gives $v_t = 4.95$ m/s as the speed at the top.

(*b*) In traveling from top to bottom, the body falls a distance $2r$. Therefore, with $v_t = 4.95$ m/s as the speed at the top and with $v_b$ as the speed at the bottom, conservation of energy provides

$$\text{KE at bottom} = \text{KE at top} + \text{PE}_\text{G} \text{ at top}$$

$$\tfrac{1}{2}mv_b^2 = \tfrac{1}{2}mv_t^2 + mg\,(2r)$$

where we have chosen the bottom of the circle as the zero level for $\text{PE}_\text{G}$. Notice that *m* cancels. Using $v_t = 4.95$ m/s, $r = 2.50$ m, and $g = 9.81$ m/s$^2$ yields $v_b = 11.1$ m/s.

(*c*) When the object is at the bottom of its path, we see from Fig. 9-7 that the unbalanced upward radial force on it is $F_{Tb} - mg$. This force supplies the required centripetal force:

$$F_{Tb} - mg = \frac{mv_b^2}{r}$$

Using $m = 0.90$ kg, $g = 9.81$ m/s$^2$, $v_b = 11.1$ m/s, and $r = 2.50$ m leads to

$$F_{Tb} = m\left(g + \frac{v_b^2}{r}\right) = 53 \text{ N}$$

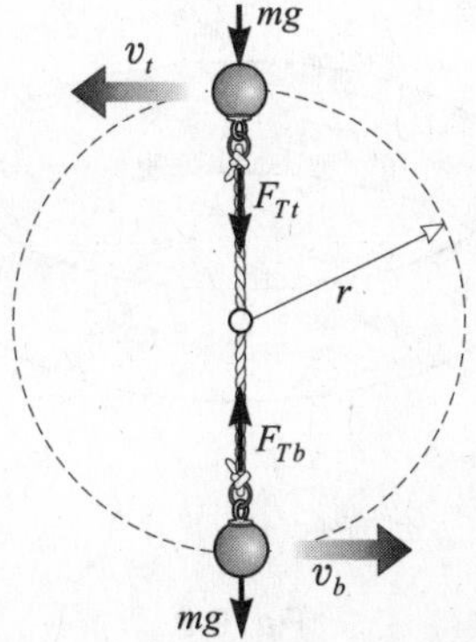


Fig. 9-7

**9.15 [III]** A curve of radius 30 m is to be banked so that a car may make the turn at a speed of 13 m/s without depending on friction. What must be the slope of the roadway (the banking angle)?

The situation is diagramed in Fig. 9-8 if friction is absent. Only two forces act upon the car: (1) the weight $mg$ of the car (which is straight downward) and (2) the normal force $F_N$ (which is perpendicular to the road) exerted by the pavement on the car.

The force $F_N$ must do two things: (1) its vertical component, $F_N \cos\theta$, must balance the car's weight; (2) its horizontal component, $F_N \sin\theta$, must supply the required centripetal force. In other words, the road pushes horizontally on the car keeping it moving in a circle. We can therefore write

$$F_N \cos\theta = mg \qquad \text{and} \qquad F_N \sin\theta = \frac{mv^2}{r}$$

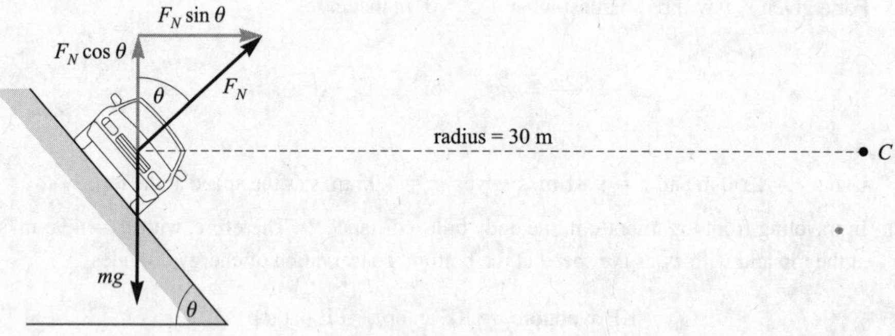


Fig. 9-8

Dividing the second equation by the first causes $F_N$ and $m$ to cancel and results in

$$\tan\theta = \frac{v^2}{gr} = \frac{(13\ \text{m/s})^2}{(9.81\ \text{m/s}^2)(30\ \text{m})} = 0.575$$

From this $\theta$, the banking angle, must be 30°.

**9.16 [III]** As illustrated in Fig. 9-9, a thin cylindrical shell of inner radius $r$ rotates horizontally, about a vertical axis, at an angular speed $\omega$. A wooden block rests against the inner surface and rotates with it. If the coefficient of static friction between block and surface is $\mu_s$, how fast must the shell be rotating if the block is not to slip and fall? Assume $r = 150$ cm and $\mu_s = 0.30$.

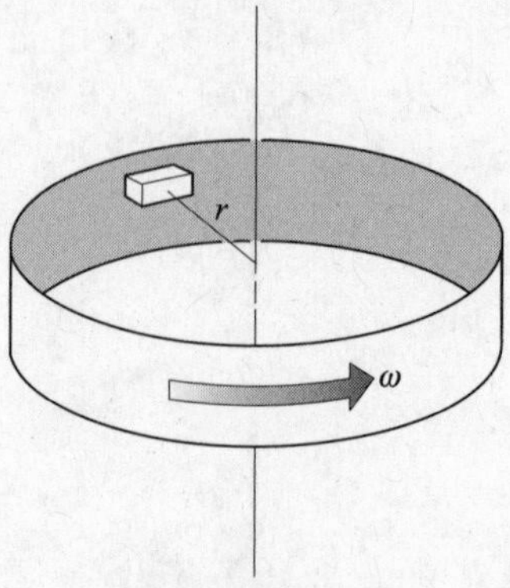


Fig. 9-9

The surface holds the block in place by pushing on it with a centripetal force $mr\omega^2$. This force is perpendicular to the surface; it is the normal force that determines the friction on the block, which in turn keeps it from sliding downward. Because $F_f = \mu_s F_N$ and $F_N = mr\omega^2$, we have

$$F_f = \mu_s F_N = \mu_s mr\omega^2$$

This friction force must balance the weight $mg$ of the block if the block is not to slip. Therefore,

$$mg = \mu_s mr\omega^2 \qquad \text{or} \qquad \omega = \sqrt{\frac{g}{\mu_s r}}$$

Inserting the given values,

$$\omega = \sqrt{\frac{9.81\ \text{m/s}^2}{(0.30)\,(1.50\ \text{m})}} = 4.7\ \text{rad/s} = 0.74\ \text{rev/s}$$

## SUPPLEMENTARY PROBLEMS

**9.17 [I]** Convert (*a*) 50.0 rev to radians, (*b*) $48\pi$ rad to revolutions, (*c*) 72.0 rps to rad/s, (*d*) $1.50 \times 10^3$ rpm to rad/s, (*e*) 22.0 rad/s to rpm, (*f*) 2.000 rad/s to deg/s.

**9.18 [I]** Express 40.0 deg/s in (*a*) rev/s, (*b*) rev/min, and (*c*) rad/s.

**9.19 [I]** A flywheel turns at 480 rpm. Compute the angular speed at any point on the wheel and the tangential speed 30.0 cm from the center.

**9.20 [I]** It is desired that the outer edge of a grinding wheel 9.0 cm in radius move at a constant rate of 6.0 m/s. (*a*) Determine the angular speed of the wheel. (*b*) What length of thin thread could be wound on the rim of the wheel in 3.0 s when it is turning at this rate?

**9.21 [I]** Through how many radians does a point fixed on the Earth's surface (anywhere off the poles) move in 6.00 h as a result of the Earth's rotation? What is the linear speed of a point on the equator? Take the radius of the Earth to be 6370 km.

**9.22 [II]** A wheel 25.0 cm in radius turning at 120 rpm uniformly increases its frequency to 660 rpm in 9.00 s. Find (*a*) the constant angular acceleration in rad/s$^2$, and (*b*) the tangential acceleration of a point on its rim.

**9.23 [II]** The angular speed of a disk decreases uniformly from 12.00 to 4.00 rad/s in 16.0 s. Compute the angular acceleration and the number of revolutions made in this time.

**9.24 [II]** A car wheel 30 cm in radius is turning at a rate of 8.0 rev/s when the car begins to slow uniformly to rest in a time of 14 s. Find the number of revolutions made by the wheel and the distance the car goes in the 14 s.

**9.25 [II]** A wheel revolving at 6.00 rev/s has an angular acceleration of 4.00 rad/s$^2$. Find the number of turns the wheel must make to reach 26.0 rev/s, and the time required.

**9.26 [II]** A thin string wound on the rim of a wheel 20 cm in diameter is pulled out at a rate of 75 cm/s causing the wheel to rotate about its central axis. Through how many revolutions will the wheel have turned by the time that 9.0 m of string have been unwound? How long will it take?

**9.27 [II]** A mass of 1.5 kg out in space moves in a circle of radius 25 cm at a constant 2.0 rev/s. Calculate (*a*) the tangential speed, (*b*) the acceleration, and (*c*) the required centripetal force for the motion.

**9.28 [II]** (*a*) Compute the radial acceleration of a point at the equator of the Earth. (*b*) Repeat for the North Pole of the Earth. Take the radius of the Earth to be $6.37 \times 10^6$ m.

**9.29 [II]** A car moving at 5.0 m/s tries to round a corner in a circular arc of 8.0 m radius. The roadway is flat. How large must the coefficient of friction be between wheels and roadway if the car is not to skid?

**9.30 [II]** A box rests at a point 2.0 m from the central vertical axis of a horizontal circular platform that is capable of revolving in the horizontal plane. The coefficient of static friction between box and platform is 0.25. As the rate of rotation of the platform is slowly increased from zero, at what angular speed will the box begin to slide?

**9.31 [II]** A stone rests in a pail which is tied to a rope and whirled in a vertical circle of radius 60 cm. What is the least speed the stone must have as it rounds the top of the circle (where the pail is inverted) if it is to remain in contact with the bottom of the pail?

**9.32 [II]** A pendulum 80.0 cm long is pulled to the side, so that its bob is raised 20.0 cm from its lowest position, and is then released. As the 50.0 g bob moves through its lowest position, (*a*) what is its speed and (*b*) what is the tension in the pendulum cord?

**9.33 [II]** Refer back to Fig. 9-6. How large must $h$ be (in terms of $R$) if the frictionless wire is to exert no force on the bead as it passes through point-$B$? Assume the bead is released from rest at $A$.

**9.34 [II]** If, in Fig. 9-6 and in Problem 9.33, $h = 2.5R$, how large a force will the 50-g bead exert on the wire as it passes through point-$C$?

**9.35 [II]** A satellite orbits the Earth at a height of 200 km in a circle of radius 6570 km. Find the linear speed of the satellite and the time taken to complete one revolution. Assume the Earth's mass is $6.0 \times 10^{24}$ kg. [*Hint*: The gravitational force provides the centripetal force.]

**9.36 [III]** A roller coaster is just barely moving as it goes over the top of the hill. It rolls nearly without friction down the hill and then up over a lower hill that has a radius of curvature of 15 m. How much higher must the first hill be than the second if the passengers are to exert no forces on their seats as they pass over the top of the lower hill?

**9.37 [III]** The human body can safely tolerate a vertical acceleration 9.00 times that due to gravity. With what minimum radius of curvature may a pilot safely turn the plane upward at the end of a dive if the plane's speed is 770 km/h?

**9.38 [III]** A 60.0-kg pilot in a glider traveling at 40.0 m/s wishes to turn an inside vertical loop such that his body exerts a force of 350 N on the seat when the glider is at the top of the loop. What must be the radius of the loop under these conditions? [*Hint*: Gravity and the seat exert forces on the pilot.]

**9.39 [III]** Suppose the Earth is a perfect sphere with $R = 6370$ km. If a person weighs exactly 600.0 N at the North Pole, how much will the person weigh at the equator? [*Hint*: The upward push of the scale on the person is what the scale will read and is what we are calling the weight in this case.]

**9.40 [III]** A mass $m$ hangs at the end of a pendulum of length $L$ which is released at an angle of 40.0° to the vertical. Find the tension in the pendulum cord when it makes an angle of 20.0° to the vertical. [*Hint*: Resolve the weight along and perpendicular to the cord.]

## ANSWERS TO SUPPLEMENTARY PROBLEMS

**9.17 [I]** (*a*) 314 rad; (*b*) 24 rev; (*c*) 452 rad/s; (*d*) 157 rad/s; (*e*) 210 rev/min; (*f*) 114.6 deg/s

**9.18 [I]** (*a*) 0.111 rev/s; (*b*) 6.67 rev/min; (*c*) 0.698 rad/s

**9.19 [I]** 50.3 rad/s, 15.1 m/s

**9.20 [I]** (*a*) 67 rad/s; (*b*) 18 m

**9.21 [I]** 1.57 rad, 463 m/s

**9.22 [II]** (*a*) 6.28 rad/s$^2$; (*b*) 157 cm/s$^2$

**9.23 [II]** −0.500 rad/s$^2$, 20.4 rev

**9.24 [II]** 56 rev, 0.11 km

**9.25 [II]** 502 rev, 31.4 s

**9.26 [II]** 14 rev, 12 s

**9.27 [II]** (*a*) 3.1 m/s; (*b*) 39 m/s$^2$ radially inward; (*c*) 59 N

**9.28 [II]** (*a*) 0.033 7 m/s$^2$; (*b*) zero

**9.29 [II]** 0.32

**9.30 [II]** 1.1 rad/s

**9.31 [II]** 2.4 m/s

**9.32 [II]** (*a*) 1.98 m/s; (*b*) 0.735 N

**9.33 [II]** 2.5 $R$

**9.34 [II]** 2.9 N

**9.35 [II]** 7.8 km/s, 88 min

**9.36 [III]** 7.5 m

**9.37 [III]** 519 m

**9.38 [III]** 102 m

**9.39 [III]** 597.9 N

**9.40 [III]** 1.29 mg

# CHAPTER 10

# Rigid-Body Rotation

**The Torque** ($\tau$) due to a force about an axis was defined in Chapter 5. It's also sometimes called the moment of the force.

$$\text{Torque} = \tau = rF \sin\theta$$

**The Moment of Inertia** ($I$) of a body is a measure of the rotational inertia of the body. If an object that is free to rotate about an axis is difficult to set into rotation, its moment of inertia about that axis is large. An object with a small $I$ has little rotational inertia.

The moment of inertia of a point mass $m_{\bullet}$ with respect to an axis which is a perpendicular distance $r$ away is given by $I_{\bullet} = m_{\bullet} r^2$

If a body is considered to be made up of point masses $m_1$, $m_2$, $m_3$ ..., at respective perpendicular distances $r_1$, $r_2$, $r_3$, ..., from an axis, its moment of inertia about that axis is

$$I = m_1 r_1^2 + m_2 r_2^2 + m_3 r_3^2 + \cdots = \sum m_i r_i^2$$

The units of $I$ are $\text{kg}\cdot\text{m}^2$.

It is convenient to define a **radius of gyration** ($k$) for an object about an axis by the relation

$$I = Mk^2$$

where $M$ is the total mass of the object. Hence, $k$ is the distance a point mass $M$ must be from the axis if the point mass is to have the same $I$ as the object.

**Torque and Angular Acceleration:** A torque $\tau$, acting on a body having a ***moment of inertia*** $I$, produces in it an angular acceleration $\alpha$ given by

$$\tau = I\alpha$$

Here $\tau$, $I$, and $\alpha$ are all computed with respect to the same axis. As for units, $\tau$ is in $\text{N}\cdot\text{m}$, $I$ is in $\text{kg}\cdot\text{m}^2$, and $\alpha$ must be in $\text{rad/s}^2$. (Recall the translational equivalent, $F = ma$.)

**The Kinetic Energy of Rotation** ($\text{KE}_r$) of a mass whose moment of inertia about an axis is $I$, and which is rotating about that axis with an angular velocity $\omega$, is

$$\text{KE}_r = \tfrac{1}{2} I\omega^2$$

where the energy is in joules and $\omega$ must be in rad/s. (Recall the translational equivalent, $\text{KE} = \frac{1}{2}mv^2$.)

**Combined Rotation and Translation:** The KE of a rolling ball or other rolling object of mass $M$ is the sum of (1) its rotational KE *about an axis through its center of mass* (i.e., c.m.; see Chapter 8) and (2) the translational KE of an equivalent point mass moving with the center of mass. In other words, putting it loosely, the total KE equals the KE around the *c.m.* plus the KE of the *c.m.* In symbols,

$$\text{KE}_{\text{total}} = \frac{1}{2}I\omega^2 + \frac{1}{2}Mv^2$$

Note that $I$ is the moment of inertia of the object about an axis through its mass center.

**The Work** ($W$) done on a rotating body during an angular displacement $\theta$ by a constant torque $\tau$ is given by

$$W = \tau\theta$$

where W is in joules and $\theta$ must be in radians. (Recall the translational equivalent, $W = Fs$.)

**The Power** (P) transmitted to a body by a torque is given by

$$\text{P} = \tau\omega$$

where $\tau$ is the applied torque about the axis of rotation, and $\omega$ is the angular speed, about that same axis. Radian measure must be used for $\omega$. (Recall the translational equivalent, $\text{P} = Fv$.)

**Angular Momentum** ($\vec{\mathbf{L}}$) is a vector quantity that has magnitude $I\omega$ and is directed along the axis of rotation. When the fingers of the right hand curl in the direction of the rotation, the thumb then points in the direction of $\vec{\boldsymbol{\omega}}$. That's also the direction of $\vec{\mathbf{L}}$ where

$$\vec{\mathbf{L}} = I\vec{\boldsymbol{\omega}}$$

(Recall the translational equivalent $\vec{\mathbf{p}} = m\vec{\mathbf{v}}$.) If the net torque on a body is zero, its angular momentum will remain unchanged in both magnitude and direction. This is the **Law of Conservation of Angular Momentum**.

**Angular Impulse** has magnitude $\tau t$, where $t$ is the time during which the constant torque $\tau$ acts on the object. In analogy to the linear case, an angular impulse $\tau t$ on a body causes a change in angular momentum of the body given by

$$\tau t = I\omega_f - I\omega_i$$

**Parallel-Axis Theorem:** The moment of inertia $I$ of a body about any axis parallel to the axis passing through the center of mass is

$$I = I_{\text{cm}} + Mh^2$$

where $I_{\text{cm}}$ = Moment of inertia about an axis through the center of mass
$M$ = Total mass of the body
$h$ = Perpendicular distance between the two parallel axes

The moments of inertia (about an axis through the center of mass) of several uniform objects, each of mass $M$, are shown in Fig. 10-1.

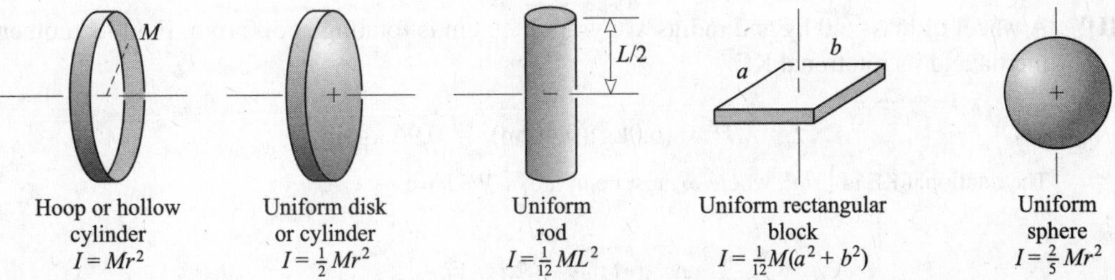


Fig. 10-1

**Analogous Linear and Angular Quantities:**

| | | | | |
|---|---|---|---|---|
| Linear displacement | $s$ | $\leftrightarrow$ | Angular displacement | $\theta$ |
| Linear speed | $v$ | $\leftrightarrow$ | Angular speed | $\omega$ |
| Linear acceleration | $a_T$ | $\leftrightarrow$ | Angular acceleration | $\alpha$ |
| Mass (inertia) | $m$ | $\leftrightarrow$ | Moment of inertia | $I$ |
| Force | $F$ | $\leftrightarrow$ | Torque | $\tau$ |
| Linear momentum | $mv$ | $\leftrightarrow$ | Angular momentum | $I\omega$ |
| Linear impulse | $Ft$ | $\leftrightarrow$ | Angular impulse | $\tau t$ |

If, in the equations for linear motion, we replace linear quantities by the corresponding angular quantities, we get the corresponding equations for angular motion. Thus,

$$\textit{Linear}: \quad F = ma \quad \text{KE} = \tfrac{1}{2}mv^2 \quad W = Fs \quad \text{P} = Fv$$

$$\textit{Angular}: \quad \tau = I\alpha \quad \text{KE}_r = \tfrac{1}{2}I\omega^2 \quad W = \tau\theta \quad \text{P} = \tau\omega$$

In these equations, $\theta$, $\omega$, and $\alpha$ must be expressed in radian measure.

## SOLVED PROBLEMS

**10.1 [I]** A small sphere of mass 2.0 kg revolves at the end of a 1.2-m-long string in a horizontal plane around a vertical axis. Determine its moment of inertia with respect to that axis.

A small sphere at the end of a long string resembles a point mass revolving about an axis at a radial distance $r$. Consequently its moment of inertia is given by

$$I_{\bullet} = m_{\bullet}r^2 = (2.0\ \text{kg})(1.2\ \text{m})^2 = 2.9\ \text{kg}\cdot\text{m}^2$$

**10.2 [I]** What is the moment of inertia of a homogeneous solid sphere of mass 10 kg and radius 20 cm about an axis passing through its center?

It follows from the last part of Fig. 10-1 that for a sphere

$$I = \tfrac{2}{5}MR^2 = \tfrac{2}{5}(10\ \text{kg})\,(0.20\ \text{m})^2 = 0.16\ \text{kg}\cdot\text{m}^2$$

**10.3 [I]** A thin cylindrical hoop having a diameter of 1.0 m and a mass of 400 g, rolls down the street. What is the hoop's moment of inertia about its central axis of rotation?

It follows from the first part of Fig. 10-1 that for a hoop

$$I = MR^2 = (0.400\ \text{kg})(0.50\ \text{m})^2 = 0.10\ \text{kg}\cdot\text{m}^2$$

**10.4 [II]** A wheel of mass 6.0 kg and radius of gyration 40 cm is rotating at 300 rpm. Find its moment of inertia and its rotational KE.

$$I = Mk^2 = (6.0\text{kg})(0.40\ \text{m})^2 = 0.96\ \text{kg}\cdot\text{m}^2$$

The rotational KE is $\frac{1}{2}I\omega^2$, where $\omega$ must be in rad/s. We have

$$\omega = \left(300\ \frac{\text{rev}}{\text{min}}\right)\left(\frac{1\ \text{min}}{60.0\ \text{s}}\right)\left(\frac{2\pi\ \text{rad}}{1\ \text{rev}}\right) = 31.4\ \text{rad/s}$$

so
$$\text{KE}_r = \tfrac{1}{2}I\omega^2 = \tfrac{1}{2}(0.96\ \text{kg}\cdot\text{m}^2)\,(31.4\ \text{rad/s})^2 = 0.47\ \text{kJ}$$

**10.5 [II]** A 500-g uniform sphere of 7.0-cm radius spins frictionlessly at 30 rev/s on an axis through its center. Find its (*a*) $KE_r$, (*b*) angular momentum, and (*c*) radius of gyration.

We need the moment of inertia of a uniform sphere about an axis through its center. From Fig. 10-1,

$$I = \tfrac{2}{5}Mr^2 = (0.40)(0.50\ \text{kg})(0.070\ \text{m})^2 = 0.000\,98\ \text{kg}\cdot\text{m}^2$$

(*a*) Knowing that $\omega = 30$ rev/s = 188 rad/s, we have

$$KE_r = \tfrac{1}{2}I\omega^2 = \tfrac{1}{2}(0.000\,98\ \text{kg}\cdot\text{m}^2)(188\ \text{rad/s})^2 = 0.017\ \text{kJ}$$

Notice that $\omega$ must be in rad/s.

(*b*) Its angular momentum is

$$L = I\omega = (0.000\,98\ \text{kg}\cdot\text{m}^2)(188\ \text{rad/s}) = 0.18\ \text{kg}\cdot\text{m}^2/\text{s}$$

(*c*) For any object, $I = Mk^2$, where $k$ is the radius of gyration. Therefore,

$$k = \sqrt{\frac{I}{M}} = \sqrt{\frac{0.000\,98\ \text{kg}\cdot\text{m}^2}{0.50\ \text{kg}}} = 0.044\ \text{m} = 4.4\ \text{cm}$$

Notice that this is a reasonable value in view of the fact that the radius of the sphere is 7.0 cm.

**10.6 [II]** An airplane propeller has a mass of 70 kg and a radius of gyration of 75 cm. Find its moment of inertia. How large a torque is needed to give it an angular acceleration of 4.0 rev/s$^2$?

$$I = Mk^2 = (70\ \text{kg})(0.75\ \text{m})^2 = 39\ \text{kg}\cdot\text{m}^2$$

To be able to use $\tau = I\alpha$, we must have $\alpha$ in rad/s$^2$:

$$\alpha = \left(4.0\ \frac{\text{rev}}{\text{s}^2}\right)\left(2\pi\ \frac{\text{rad}}{\text{rev}}\right) = 8.0\pi\ \text{rad/s}^2$$

Then $$\tau = I\alpha = (39\ \text{kg}\cdot\text{m}^2)(8.0\pi\ \text{rad/s}^2) = 0.99\ \text{kN}\cdot\text{m}$$

**10.7 [III]** As shown in Fig. 10-2, a constant force of 40 N is applied tangentially to the rim of a wheel having a 20-cm radius. The wheel, which can rotate frictionlessly, has a moment of inertia of 30 kg·m$^2$. Find (*a*) the resulting angular acceleration, (*b*) the angular speed after 4.0 s from rest, and (*c*) the number of revolutions made in that 4.0 s. (*d*) Show that the work done on the wheel in those 4.0 s is equal to the $KE_r$ of the wheel after 4.0 s.

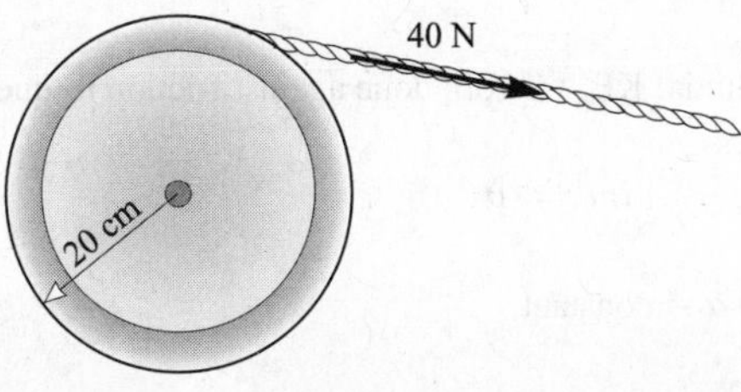


Fig. 10-2

(*a*) The torque on the wheel can be computed, and we know the moment of inertia. Therefore, to determine the angular acceleration, use $\tau = I\alpha$,

$$(40\ \text{N})(0.20\ \text{m}) = (30\ \text{kg}\cdot\text{m}^2)\alpha$$

from which it follows that $\alpha = 0.267\ \text{rad/s}^2$ or $0.27\ \text{rad/s}^2$.

(*b*) Use $\omega_f = \omega_i + \alpha t$ to find the final angular speed,

$$\omega_f = 0 + (0.267\ \text{rad/s}^2)(4.0\ \text{s}) = 1.07\ \text{rad/s} = 1.1\ \text{rad/s}$$

(*c*) Because $\theta = \omega_{av} t = \frac{1}{2}(\omega_f + \omega_i)t$,

$$\theta = \tfrac{1}{2}(1.07\ \text{rad/s})\,(4.0\ \text{s}) = 2.14\ \text{rad}$$

which is equivalent to 0.34 rev.

(*d*) We know that work = torque $\times\ \theta$, and therefore

$$\text{Work} = (40\ \text{N} \times 0.20\ \text{m})(2.14\ \text{rad}) = 17\ \text{J}$$

Notice that radian measure must be used. The final $\text{KE}_r$ is $\frac{1}{2}I\omega_f^2$, and so

$$\text{KE}_r = \tfrac{1}{2}(30\ \text{kg}\cdot\text{m}^2)\,(1.07\ \text{rad/s})^2 = 17\ \text{J}$$

The work done equals the $\text{KE}_r$.

**10.8 [II]** The wheel on a grinder is a homogeneous 0.90-kg disk with a 8.0-cm radius. It coasts uniformly to rest from 1400 rpm in a time of 35 s. How large a frictional torque slows its motion?

Let's first find $\alpha$ from the change in $\omega$; then we can use $\tau = I\alpha$ to find $\tau$. We know that $f = 1400$ rev/min $= 23.3$ rev/s, and since $\omega = 2\pi f$, $\omega_i = 146$ rad/s and $\omega_f = 0$. Therefore,

$$\alpha = \frac{\omega_f - \omega_i}{t} = \frac{-146\ \text{rad/s}}{35\ \text{s}} = -4.2\ \text{rad/s}^2$$

We also need $I$. For a uniform disk,

$$I = \tfrac{1}{2}Mr^2 = \tfrac{1}{2}(0.90\ \text{kg})\,(0.080\ \text{m})^2 = 2.9\times10^{-3}\ \text{kg}\cdot\text{m}^2$$

Then $$\tau = I\alpha = (0.0029\ \text{kg}\cdot\text{m}^2)(-4.2\ \text{rad/s}^2) = -1.2\times10^{-2}\ \text{N}\cdot\text{m}$$

**10.9 [II]** Rework Problem 10.8 using the relation between work and energy.

The wheel originally had $\text{KE}_r$, but as the wheel slowed, this energy was lost doing frictional work. We therefore write

$$\text{Initial KE}_r = \text{Work done against friction torque}$$

$$\tfrac{1}{2}I\omega_i^2 = \tau\theta$$

To find $\theta$, note that since $\alpha$ = constant,

$$\theta = \omega_{av}t = \tfrac{1}{2}(\omega_i + \omega_f)\,t = \tfrac{1}{2}(146\ \text{rad/s})\,(35\ \text{s}) = 2550\ \text{rad}$$

From Problem 10.8, $I = 0.0029\ \text{kg}\cdot\text{m}^2$ and so the work-energy equation is

$$\tfrac{1}{2}(0.0029\ \text{kg}\cdot\text{m}^2)(146\ \text{rad/s}^2) = \tau(2550\ \text{rad})$$

from which $\tau = 0.012\ \text{N}\cdot\text{m}$ or $1.2 \times 10^{-2}\ \text{N}\cdot\text{m}$.

**10.10 [II]** **A flywheel (i.e., a massive disk capable of rotating about its central axis) has a moment of inertia of 3.8 kg·m². What constant torque is required to increase the wheel's frequency from 2.0 rev/s to 5.0 rev/s in 6.0 revolutions? Neglect friction.**

Given

$$\theta = 12\pi\ \text{rad} \qquad \omega_i = 4.0\pi\ \text{rad/s} \qquad \text{and} \qquad \omega_f = 10\pi\ \text{rad/s}$$

we can write

$$\text{Work done on wheel} = \text{Change in KE}_r \text{ of wheel}$$

$$\tau\theta = \tfrac{1}{2}I\omega_f^2 - \tfrac{1}{2}I\omega_i^2$$

$$(\tau)(12\pi\ \text{rad}) = \tfrac{1}{2}(3.8\ \text{kg}\cdot\text{m}^2)[(100\pi^2 - 16\pi^2)(\text{rad/s})^2]$$

which leads to $\tau = 42\ \text{N}\cdot\text{m}$. Notice in all of these problems that radians and seconds must be used.

**10.11 [III]** **As shown in Fig. 10-3, a mass $m$ = 400 g hangs from the rim of a frictionless pulley of radius $r$ = 15 cm. When released from rest, the mass falls 2.0 m in 6.5 s. Find the moment of inertia of the wheel.**

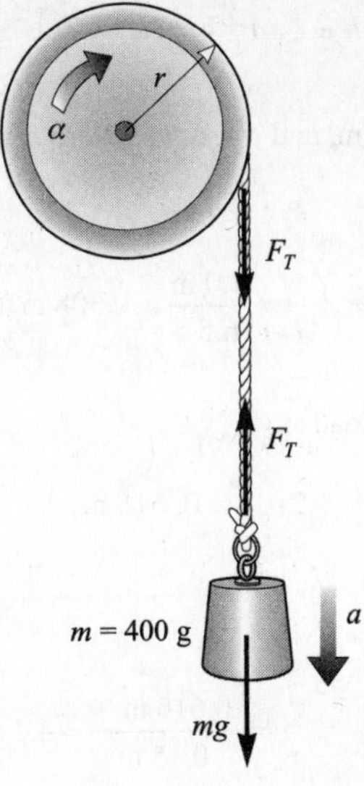


Fig. 10-3

The hanging mass linearly accelerates downward due to its weight, and the pulley angularly accelerates clockwise due to the torque produced by the rope). The two motions are linked by the fact that $a_T = r\alpha$. Consequently we will need to determine $a_T$, and then $\alpha$, and then $F_T$, and then $\tau$, and then $I$. Remember that

Newton's Second Law is central here (i.e., $\tau = I\alpha$ for the wheel and $F = ma$ for the mass). First we find $a$ using $y = v_i t + \frac{1}{2}at^2$, since the mass accelerates down uniformly:

$$2.0\text{ m} = 0 + \tfrac{1}{2}a(6.5\text{ s})^2$$

which yields $a = 0.095\text{ m/s}^2$, and that equals the tangential acceleration ($a_T$) of a point on the rim of the pulley, which equals the acceleration $a$ of the rope. Then, from $a_T = \alpha r$,

$$\alpha = \frac{a_T}{r} = \frac{0.095\text{ m/s}^2}{0.15\text{ m}} = 0.63\text{ rad/s}^2$$

The net force on the mass $m$ is $mg - F_T$ and so $F = ma$ becomes

$$mg - F_T = ma_T$$
$$(0.40\text{ kg})(9.81\text{ m/s}^2) - F_T = (0.40\text{ kg})(0.095\text{ m/s}^2)$$

from which it follows that $F_T = 3.88$ N.

Now $\tau = I\alpha$ for the wheel:

$$(F_T)(r) = I\alpha \qquad \text{or} \qquad (3.88\text{ N})(0.15\text{ m}) = I(0.63\text{ rad/s}^2)$$

from which we get $I = 0.92\text{ kg}\cdot\text{m}^2$.

**10.12 [III]** Repeat Problem 10.11 using energy considerations.

Originally the mass $m$ had $\text{PE}_G = mgh$, where $h = 2.0$ m. It loses all this $\text{PE}_G$, and an equal amount of KE results. Part of this KE is translational KE of the mass, and the rest is KE$r$ of the wheel:

$$\text{Original PE}_G = \text{Final KE of } m + \text{Final KE}_r \text{ of wheel}$$

$$mgh = \tfrac{1}{2}mv_f^2 + \tfrac{1}{2}I\omega_f^2$$

To find $v_f$, note that $v_i = 0$, $y = 2$ m, and $t = 6.5$ s. (Here $a \neq g$ for the descending mass, because it does not fall freely.) Then

$$v_{av} = \frac{y}{t} = \frac{2.0\text{ m}}{6.5\text{ s}} = 0.308\text{ m/s}$$

and $v_{av} = \frac{1}{2}(v_i + v_f)$ with $v_i = 0$ leads to

$$v_f = 2v_{av} = 0.616\text{ m/s}$$

Moreover, $v = \omega r$ and so

$$\omega_f = \frac{v_f}{r} = \frac{0.616\text{ m/s}}{0.15\text{ m}} = 4.1\text{ rad/s}$$

The above conservation of energy equation numerically becomes

$$(0.40\text{ kg})(9.81\text{ m/s}^2)(2.0\text{ m}) = \tfrac{1}{2}(0.40\text{ kg})(0.62\text{ m/s})^2 + \tfrac{1}{2}I(4.1\text{ rad/s})^2$$

from which we obtain $I = 0.92\text{ kg}\cdot\text{m}^2$.

**10.13 [III]** The moment of inertia of the frictionless pulley system illustrated in Fig. 10-4 is $I = 1.70\ \text{kg}\cdot\text{m}^2$, where $r_1 = 50$ cm and $r_2 = 20$ cm. Find the angular acceleration of the pulley system and the tensions $F_{T1}$ and $F_{T2}$.

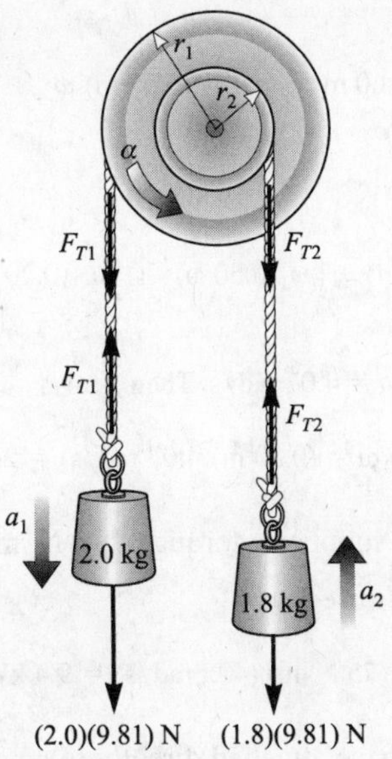

Fig. 10-4

Note at the beginning that $a = \alpha r$ leads to $a_1 = (0.50\ \text{m})\alpha$ and $a_2 = (0.20\ \text{m})\alpha$. We shall write $F = ma$ for both masses and $\tau = I\alpha$ for the wheel. Taking the direction of motion (which we guess is counterclockwise because the 2.0-kg mass generates the larger torque) to be the positive direction:

$$(2.0)(9.81)\ \text{N} - F_{T1} = 2a_1 \qquad \text{or} \qquad 19.6\text{N} - F_{T1} = (1.0\ \text{m})\alpha$$
$$F_{T2} - (1.8)\,(9.81)\ \text{N} = 1.8a_2 \qquad \text{or} \qquad F_{T2} - 17.6\ \text{N} = (0.36\ \text{m})\alpha$$
$$(F_{T1})\,(r_1) - (F_{T2})(r_2) = I\alpha \qquad \text{or} \qquad (0.50\ \text{m})F_{T1} - (0.20\ \text{m})F_{T2} = (1.70\ \text{kg}\cdot\text{m}^2)\alpha$$

These three equations have three unknowns. Solve for $F_{T1}$ in the first equation and substitute it in the third to obtain

$$(9.81\ \text{N}\cdot\text{m}) - (0.50\ \text{m})\alpha - (0.20\ \text{m})F_{T2} = (1.70\ \text{kg}\cdot\text{m}^2)\alpha$$

Solve this equation for $F_{T2}$ and substitute it in the second equation to obtain

$$-11\alpha + 49 - 17.6 = 0.36\alpha$$

from which it follows that $\alpha = 2.8\ \text{rad/s}^2$.

Now go back to the first equation to find $F_{T1} = 17$ N, and to the second to find $F_{T2} = 19$ N.

**10.14 [II]** Use energy methods to find how fast the 2.0-kg mass in Fig. 10-4 is descending after it has fallen 1.5 m from rest. Use the same values for $I$, $r_1$, and $r_2$ as in Problem 10.13.

As the 2.0-kg mass descends, its $\text{PE}_\text{G}$ decreases. Meanwhile, the 1.8-kg mass rises and its $\text{PE}_\text{G}$ increases. The energy difference ($\Delta\text{PE}_{\text{G}1} - \Delta\text{PE}_{\text{G}2}$) must go into the linear KE of the two masses and the rotational KE of the pulleys. If the angular speed of the wheel is $\omega$, then $v_1 = r_1\omega$ and $v_2 = r_2\omega$. As the wheel turns through an angle $\theta$, the 2.0-kg mass falls through a distance $s_1$ and the 1.8-kg mass rises a distance $s_2$. The angle $\theta$ links $s_1$ and $s_2$ together and allows use to determine $s_2$ from $s_1$:

$$\theta = \frac{s_1}{r_1} = \frac{s_2}{r_2} \qquad \text{from which} \qquad s_2 = s_1\frac{r_2}{r_1}$$

From energy conservation, because $PE_G$ is lost and KE is gained,

$$m_1 g s_1 - m_2 g s_2 = \tfrac{1}{2}m_1 v_1^2 + \tfrac{1}{2}m_2 v_2^2 + \tfrac{1}{2}I\omega^2$$

Since

$$s_2 = (20/50)(1.5\text{ m}) = 0.60\text{ m} \qquad v_1 = (0.50\text{ m})\,\omega \qquad \text{and} \qquad v_2 = (0.20\text{ m})\,\omega$$

the energy equation becomes

$$m_1 g(1.5\text{ m}) - m_2 g(0.60\text{ m}) = \tfrac{1}{2}m_1(0.50\,\omega)^2 + \tfrac{1}{2}m_2(0.20\,\omega)^2 + \tfrac{1}{2}(1.70\text{ kg}\cdot\text{m}^2)\omega^2$$

Solve this equation to find that $\omega = 4.07$ rad/s. Then

$$v_1 = r_1\omega = (0.50\text{ m})(4.07\text{ rad/s}) = 2.0\text{ m/s}$$

**10.15 [I]** A motor runs at 20 rev/s and supplies a torque of 75 N·m. What horsepower is it delivering?

Using $\omega = 20$ rev/s $= 40\pi$ rad/s, we have

$$P = \tau\omega = (75\text{ N}\cdot\text{m})\,(40\pi\text{ rad/s}) = 9.4\text{ kW} = 13\text{ hp}$$

**10.16 [I]** The driving wheel of a belt drive attached directly to an electric motor (as depicted in Fig. 10-5) has a diameter of 38 cm and operates at 1200 rpm. The motor turns the wheel, which moves the continuous looping belt, whose other end goes around a pulley, turning it and the shaft of some machine attached to it. The tension in the belt is 130 N on the slack side and 600 N on the tight side. Find the horsepower transmitted by the wheel to the belt and hence to the machine. Assume friction is negligible and there are no energy losses.

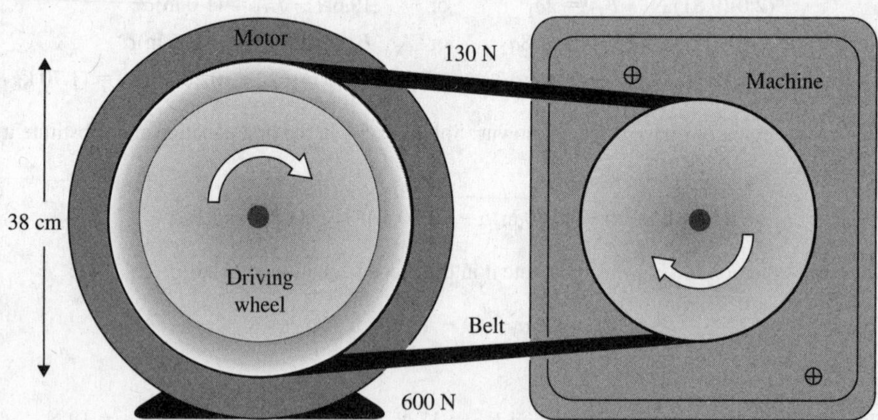


Fig. 10-5

The problem calls to mind the power equation $P = \tau\omega$. In this case, two opposing torques, due to the two parts of the belt, act on the wheel. We will have to evaluate the expression,

$$P = (\tau_t - \tau_s)\omega$$

where $\tau_t$ and $\tau_s$ are the torques due to the tight and slack belt forces. First determine $\omega$:

$$f = 1200\text{ rev/min} = 20\text{ rev/s}$$

and $$\omega = 40\pi\text{ rad/s}$$

Therefore, $$P = [(600 - 130)(0.19)\text{ N}\cdot\text{m}](40\pi\text{ rad/s}) = 11\text{ kW} = 15\text{ hp}$$

**10.17 [I]** A 0.75-hp motor acts for 8.0 s on an initially nonrotating wheel having a moment of inertia 2.0 kg·m$^2$. Find the angular speed developed in the wheel, assuming no losses.

$$\text{Work done by motor in 8.0 s} = \text{KE of wheel after 8.0 s}$$

$$(\text{Power})\,(\text{Time}) = \tfrac{1}{2}I\omega^2$$

$$(0.75\ \text{hp})\,(746\ \text{W/hp})\,(8.0\ \text{s}) = \tfrac{1}{2}(2.0\ \text{kg}\cdot\text{m}^2)\omega^2$$

from which $\omega = 67\ \text{rad/s}$.

**10.18 [II]** As illustrated in Fig. 10-6, a uniform solid sphere rolls on a horizontal surface at 20 m/s and then rolls up the incline. If friction losses are negligible, what will be the value of $h$ where the ball stops?

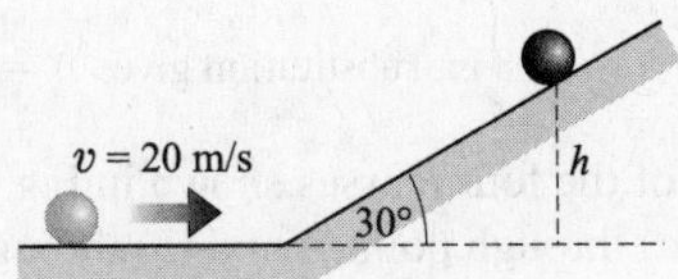


Fig. 10-6

The rotational and translational KE of the sphere at the bottom will be changed to PE$_G$ when it stops. Accordingly,

$$\left(\tfrac{1}{2}Mv^2 + \tfrac{1}{2}I\omega^2\right)_{\text{start}} = (Mgh)_{\text{end}}$$

For a solid sphere, $I = \frac{2}{5}Mr^2$. Also, $\omega = v/r$. Using these formulas the above equation becomes

$$\frac{1}{2}Mv^2 + \frac{1}{2}\left(\frac{2}{5}\right)(Mr^2)\left(\frac{v}{r}\right)^2 = Mgh \qquad \text{or} \qquad \frac{1}{2}v^2 + \frac{1}{5}v^2 = (9.81\ \text{m/s}^2)h$$

With an incoming speed of $v = 20\ \text{m/s}$, the resulting height is $h = 29$ m. Notice that the answer does not depend upon the mass of the ball or the angle of the incline.

**10.19 [II]** Starting from rest, a hoop with a 20-cm radius rolls down a hill to a place 5.0 m below its starting point. How fast is it rotating as it rolls through that point? The hoop descends 5.0 m, whereupon an amount of gravitational PE is converted into KE:

$$\text{PE}_G \text{ at start} = (\text{KE}_r + \text{KE}_t) \text{ at end}$$

$$Mgh = \tfrac{1}{2}I\omega^2 + \tfrac{1}{2}Mv^2$$

Here $I = Mr^2$ for a hoop and $v = \omega r$. The above equation becomes

$$Mgh = \tfrac{1}{2}M\omega^2 r^2 + \tfrac{1}{2}M\omega^2 r^2$$

from which

$$\omega = \sqrt{\frac{gh}{r^2}} = \sqrt{\frac{(9.81\ \text{m/s}^2)\,(5.0\ \text{m})}{(0.20\ \text{m})^2}} = 35\ \text{rad/s}$$

**10.20 [II]** As a solid disk rolls up and over the top of a hill on a track, its speed slows to 80 cm/s. It subsequently descends down the other side of the hill. If friction losses are negligible, how fast is the disk moving when it is 18 cm below the top?

At the top, the disk has translational and rotational KE, plus its $PE_G$ relative to the point 18 cm below. At that final point, $PE_G$ has been transformed to more KE of rotation and translation. Conservation of energy can be expressed as

$$(KE_t + KE_r)_{start} + Mgh = (KE_t + KE_r)_{end}$$

$$\tfrac{1}{2}Mv_i^2 + \tfrac{1}{2}I\omega_i^2 + Mgh = \tfrac{1}{2}Mv_f^2 + \tfrac{1}{2}I\omega_f^2$$

For a solid disk, $I = \frac{1}{2}Mr^2$. Also, $\omega = v/r$. Substituting these values and simplifying yields

$$\tfrac{1}{2}v_i^2 + \tfrac{1}{4}v_i^2 + gh = \tfrac{1}{2}v_f^2 + \tfrac{1}{4}v_f^2$$

Employing $v_i = 0.80$ m/s and $h = 0.18$ m, substitution gives $v_f = 1.7$ m/s.

**10.21 [II]** Find the moment of inertia of the four masses shown in Fig. 10-7 relative to an axis perpendicular to the page and extending (*a*) through point-*A* and (*b*) through point-*B*.

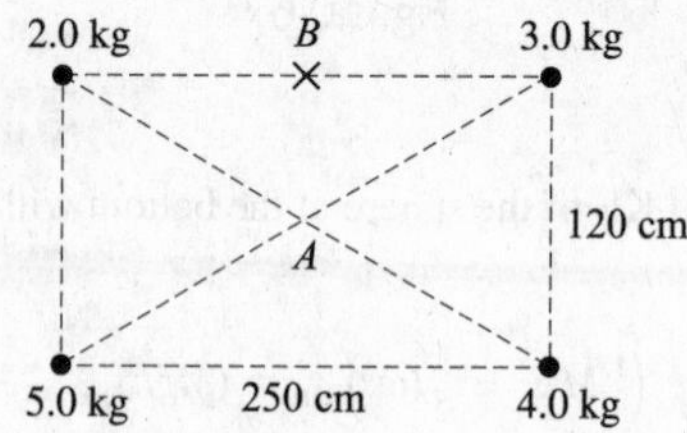


Fig. 10-7

(*a*) From the definition of moment of inertia,

$$I_A = m_1r_1^2 + m_2r_2^2 + \ldots + m_Nr_N^2 = (2.0 \text{ kg} + 3.0 \text{ kg} + 4.0 \text{ kg} + 5.0 \text{ kg})(r^2)$$

where $r$ is half the length of the diagonal:

$$r = \tfrac{1}{2}\sqrt{(1.20 \text{ m})^2 + (2.50 \text{ m})^2} = 1.39 \text{ m}$$

Thus, $I_A = 27 \text{ kg}\cdot\text{m}^2$.

(*b*) We cannot use the parallel-axis theorem here because neither *A* nor *B* is at the center of mass. Hence, we proceed as before. Because $r = 1.25$ m for the 2.0- and 3.0-kg masses, while $r = \sqrt{(1.20)^2 + (1.25)^2} =$ 1.733 for the other two masses,

$$I_B = (2.0 \text{ kg} + 3.0 \text{ kg})(1.25 \text{ m})^2 + (5.0 \text{ kg} + 4.0 \text{ kg})(1.733 \text{ m})^2 = 33 \text{ kg}\cdot\text{m}^2$$

**10.22 [II]** The uniform circular disk in Fig. 10-8 has a mass of 6.5 kg and a diameter of 80 cm. Compute its moment of inertia about an axis perpendicular to the page (*a*) through *G* and (*b*) through *A*.

(*a*) $I_G = \frac{1}{2}Mr^2 = \frac{1}{2}(6.5 \text{ kg})(0.40 \text{ m})^2 = 0.52 \text{ kg}\cdot\text{m}^2$

(*b*) By the result of (*a*) and the parallel-axis theorem,

$$I_A = I_G + Mh^2 = 0.52 \text{ kg}\cdot\text{m}^2 + (6.5\text{kg})(0.22 \text{ m})^2 = 0.83 \text{ kg}\cdot\text{m}^2$$

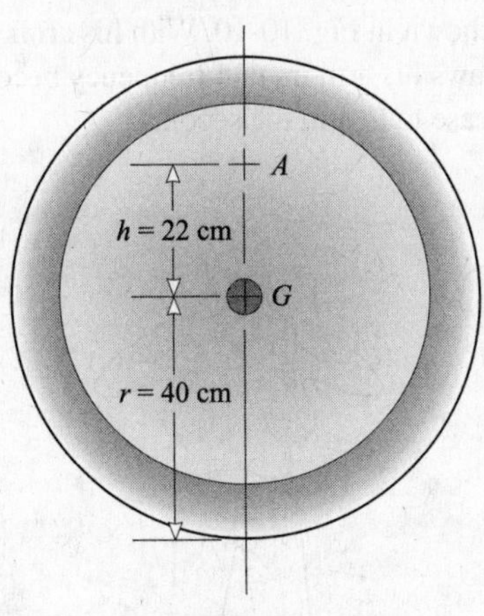

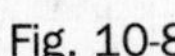
Fig. 10-8

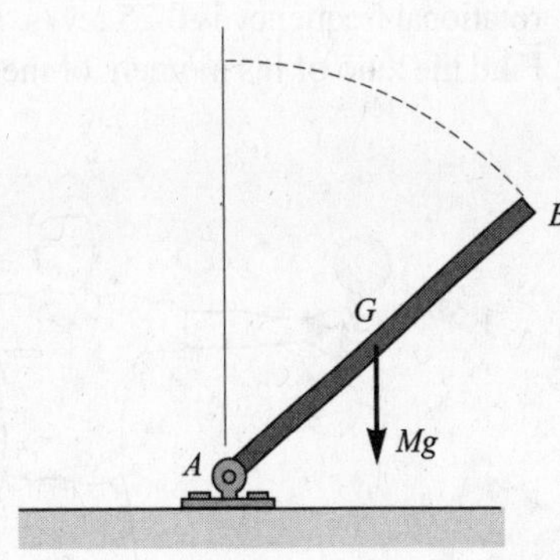

Fig. 10-9

**10.23 [III]** A large roller in the form of a uniform cylinder is pulled by a tractor to compact earth; it has a 1.80-m diameter and weighs 10 kN. If frictional losses can be ignored, what average horsepower must the tractor provide to accelerate the cylinder from rest to a speed of 4.0 m/s in a horizontal distance of 3.0 m?

The power required is equal to the work done by the tractor divided by the time it takes. The tractor does the following work:

$$\text{Work} = (\Delta\text{KE})_r + (\Delta\text{KE})_t = \tfrac{1}{2}I\omega_f^2 + \tfrac{1}{2}mv_f^2$$

We have $v_f = 4.0\ \text{m/s}$, $\omega_f = v_f/r = 4.44\ \text{rad/s}$, and $m = 10\,000/9.81 = 1019\ \text{kg}$. The moment of inertia of the cylinder is

$$I = \tfrac{1}{2}mr^2 = \tfrac{1}{2}(1019\ \text{kg})\,(0.90\ \text{m})^2 = 413\ \text{kg}\cdot\text{m}^2$$

Substituting these values, the work required turns out to be 12.23 kJ.

We still need the time taken to do this work. Because the roller went 3.0 m with an average velocity $v_{av} = \tfrac{1}{2}(4 + 0) = 2.0\ \text{m/s}$,

$$t = \frac{s}{v_{av}} = \frac{3.0\ \text{m}}{2.0\ \text{m/s}} = 1.5\ \text{s}$$

Then $$\text{Power} = \frac{\text{Work}}{\text{Time}} = \frac{12\,230\ \text{J}}{1.5\ \text{s}} = (8150\ \text{W})\left(\frac{1\ \text{hp}}{746\ \text{W}}\right) = 11\ \text{hp}$$

**10.24 [III]** As illustrated in Fig. 10-9, a thin uniform rod $AB$ of mass $M$ and length $L$ is hinged at end $A$ to the level floor. It originally stood vertically. If allowed to fall to the floor as shown, with what angular speed will it strike the floor?

Inasmuch as the rod's center of mass is at point-$G$, using Fig. 10-1 and the parallel-axis theorem, the moment of inertia about a transverse axis through end $A$ is

$$I_A = I_G + Mh^2 = \frac{1}{12}ML^2 + M\left(\frac{L}{2}\right)^2 = \frac{ML^2}{3}$$

As the rod falls to the floor, the center of mass falls a distance $L/2$. Then

$$\text{PE}_G \text{ lost by rod} = \text{KE}_r \text{ gained by rod}$$

$$Mg\left(\frac{L}{2}\right) = \frac{1}{2}\left(\frac{ML^2}{3}\right)\omega^2$$

from which we are lead to $\omega = \sqrt{3g/L}$.

**10.25 [I]** A student stands on a freely rotating platform, as shown in Fig. 10-10. With his arms extended, his rotational frequency is 0.25 rev/s. But when he draws his arm in, that frequency becomes 0.80 rev/s. Find the ratio of his moment of inertia in the first case to that in the second.

Fig. 10-10

Because there is no external torque on the system (why?), the law of conservation of angular momentum tells us that

Angular momentum before = Angular momentum after

$$I_i\omega_i = I_f\omega_f$$

Or, since we require $I_i/I_f$,

$$\frac{I_i}{I_f} = \frac{\omega_f}{\omega_i} = \frac{0.80\text{ rev/s}}{0.25\text{ rev/s}} = 3.2$$

**10.26 [II]** A horizontal disk with a moment of inertia $I_1$ is rotating freely at an angular speed of $\omega_1$ when a second, nonrotating disk with a moment of inertia $I_2$ is dropped on it (Fig. 10-11). The two then rotate as a unit. Find the final angular speed. Ignore the central rod.

From the law of conservation of angular momentum,

Angular momentum before = Angular momentum after

$$I_1\omega_1 + I_2(0) = I_1\omega + I_2\omega$$

Solving this equation leads to $$\omega = \frac{I_1\omega_1}{I_1 + I_2}$$

**10.27 [II]** A disk like the lower one in Fig. 10-11 has a moment of inertia $I_1$ about the vertical axis shown. What will be its new moment of inertia if a tiny mass $M$ is placed on it at a distance $R$ from its center?

The definition of moment of inertia tells us that, for the disk plus an added point mass $M$,

$$I = \sum_{\text{disk}} m_i r_i^2 + MR^2$$

where the sum extends over all the point masses composing the original disk. With the value of that sum given as $I_1$, the new moment of inertia is $I = I_1 + MR^2$.

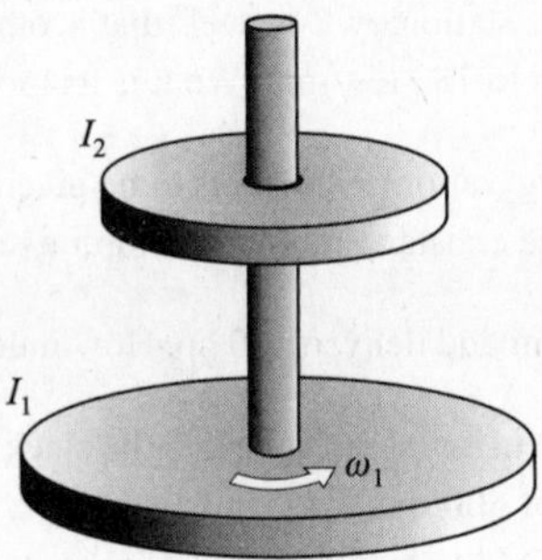


Fig. 10-11

**10.28 [III]** A disk like the lower one in Fig. 10-11 has a moment of inertia $I = 0.015\,0\ \mathrm{kg\cdot m^2}$, and is turning at 3.0 rev/s. A trickle of sand falls onto the revolving disk at a distance of 20 cm from the axis and builds a 20-cm radius narrow ring of sand on it. How much sand must fall on the disk for it to slow to 2.0 rev/s?

When a mass $\Delta m$ of sand falls onto the disk, the moment of inertia of the disk is increased by an amount $r^2\,\Delta m$, as shown in the preceding problem. After a mass $m$ has fallen on the disk, the system's moment of inertia has increased to $I + mr^2$. (Note how this agrees with the hoop in Fig.10-1.) Because the sand originally had no angular momentum, the law of conservation of momentum gives

$$(\text{Momentum before}) = (\text{Momentum after}) \qquad \text{or} \qquad I\omega_i = (I + mr^2)\omega_f$$

from which

$$m = \frac{I(\omega_i - \omega_f)}{r^2\omega_f} = \frac{(0.015\,0\ \mathrm{kg\cdot m^2})(6.0\pi - 4.0\pi)\ \mathrm{rad/s}}{(0.040\ \mathrm{m^2})(4.0\pi\ \mathrm{rad/s})} = 0.19\ \mathrm{kg}$$

## SUPPLEMENTARY PROBLEMS

**10.29 [I]** An force of 200 N acts tangentially on the rim of a wheel 25 cm in radius. (*a*) Find the torque. (*b*) Repeat if the force makes an angle of 40° to a spoke of the wheel.

**10.30 [I]** An 8.0-kg wheel has a radius of gyration of 25 cm. (*a*) What is its moment of inertia? (*b*) How large a torque is required to give it an angular acceleration of 3.0 $\mathrm{rad/s^2}$?

**10.31 [II]** Determine the constant torque that must be applied to a 50-kg flywheel, with radius of gyration 40 cm, to give it a frequency of 300 rpm in 10 s if it's initially at rest.

**10.32 [II]** A 4.0-kg wheel of 20-cm radius of gyration is rotating at 360 rpm. The retarding frictional torque is 0.12 N · m. Compute the time it will take the wheel to coast to rest.

**10.33 [II]** Compute the rotational KE of a 25-kg wheel rotating at 6.0 rev/s if the radius of gyration of the wheel is 22 cm.

**10.34 [II]** A cord 3.0 m long is wrapped around the axle of a wheel. The cord is pulled with a constant force of 40 N, and the wheel revolves as a result. When the cord leaves the axle, the wheel is rotating at 2.0 rev/s. Determine the moment of inertia of the wheel and axle. Neglect friction. [*Hint*: The easiest solution is obtained via the energy method.]

**10.35 [II]** A 500-g wheel that has a moment of inertia of 0.015 kg · m² is initially turning at 30 rev/s. It coasts uniformly to rest after 163 rev. How large is the torque that slowed it?

**10.36 [II]** When 100 J of work is done on a stationary flywheel (that is otherwise free to rotate in place), its angular speed increases from 60 rev/min to 180 rev/min. What is its moment of inertia?

**10.37 [II]** A 5.0-kg wheel with a radius of gyration of 20 cm is to be given an angular frequency of 10 rev/s in 25 revolutions from rest. Find the constant unbalanced torque required.

**10.38 [II]** An electric motor runs at 900 rpm and delivers 2.0 hp. How much torque does it deliver?

**10.39 [III]** The driving side of a belt has a tension of 1600 N, and the slack side has 500-N tension. The belt turns a pulley 40 cm in radius at a rate of 300 rpm. This pulley drives a dynamo having 90 percent efficiency. How many kilowatts are being delivered by the dynamo?

**10.40 [III]** A 25-kg wheel has a radius of 40 cm and turns freely on a horizontal axis. The radius of gyration of the wheel is 30 cm. A 1.2-kg mass hangs at the end of a thin cord that is wound around the rim of the wheel. This mass falls and causes the wheel to rotate. Find the acceleration of the falling mass and the tension in the cord, whose mass can be ignored.

**10.41 [III]** A wheel and axle having a total moment of inertia of 0.002 0 kg·m$^2$ is caused to rotate about a horizontal axis by means of an 800-g mass attached to a weightless cord wrapped around the axle. The radius of the axle is 2.0 cm. Starting from rest, how far must the mass fall to give the wheel a rotational rate of 3.0 rev/s?

**10.42 [II]** A 20-kg solid disk ($I = \frac{1}{2}Mr^2$) rolls on a horizontal surface at the rate of 4.0 m/s. Compute its total KE. [*Hint*: Do you really need $r$?]

**10.43 [II]** A 6.0-kg bowling ball ($I = 2Mr^2/5$) starts from rest and rolls, without sliding, down a gradual slope until it reaches a point 80 cm lower than its starting point. How fast is it then moving? Ignore friction losses. Do you actually need the mass? [*Hint*: Why were you not given $r$?]

**10.44 [II]** A tiny solid ball ($I = 2Mr^2/5$) rolls without slipping on the inside surface of a hemisphere as shown in Fig. 10-12. (The ball is much smaller than shown.) If the ball is released at $A$, how fast is it moving as it passes ($a$) point-$B$, and ($b$) point-$C$? Ignore friction losses. [*Hint*: Study the two previous questions. When it comes to the ball's descent, its own radius is negligible.]

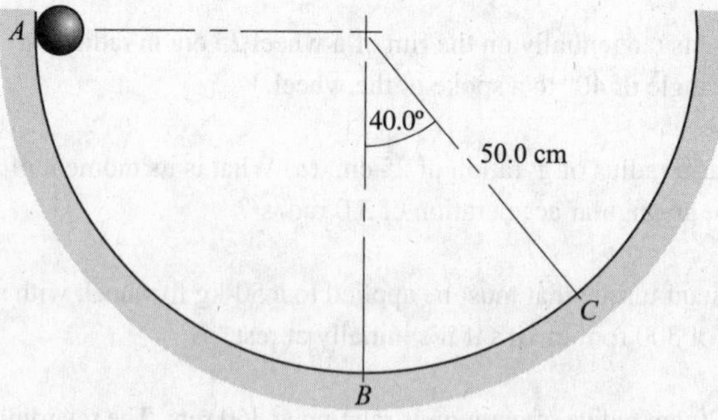


Fig. 10-12

**10.45 [I]** Compute the radius of gyration of a solid disk of diameter 24 cm about an axis through its center of mass and perpendicular to its face.

**10.46 [I]** Figure 10-13 shows four masses that are held at the corners of a square by a very light frame. What is the moment of inertia of the system about an axis perpendicular to the page ($a$) through $A$ and ($b$) through $B$?

**10.47 [I]** Determine the moment of inertia ($a$) of a vertical thin hoop of mass 2 kg and radius 9 cm about a horizontal, parallel axis at its rim; ($b$) of a solid sphere of mass 2 kg and radius 5 cm about an axis tangent to the sphere.

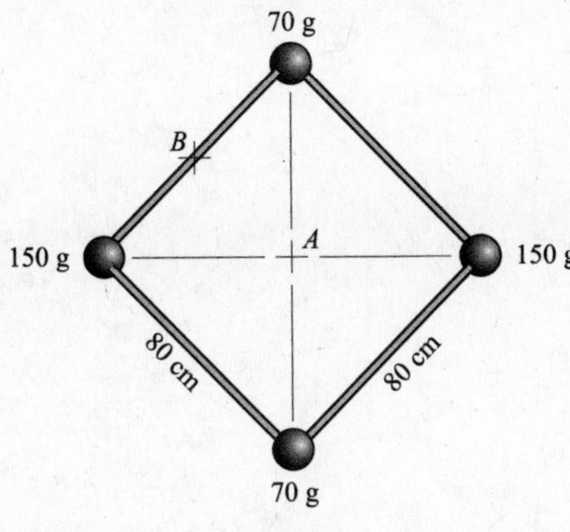


Fig. 10-13

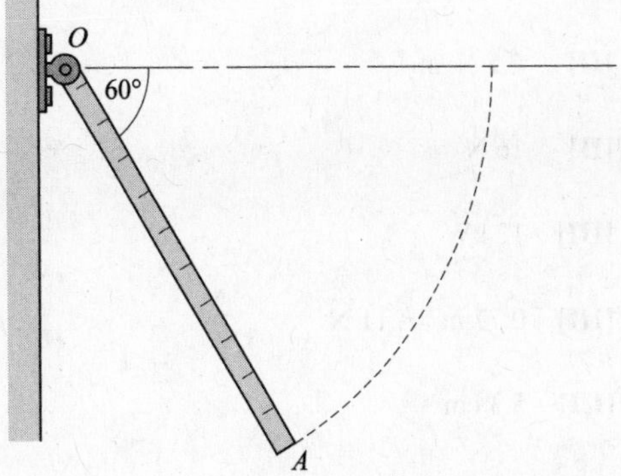

Fig. 10-14

**10.48 [II]** Rod *OA* in Fig. 10-14 is a meterstick. It is hinged at *O* so that it can turn in a vertical plane. It is held horizontally and then released. Compute the angular speed of the rod and the linear speed of its free end as it passes through the position shown in the figure. [*Hint*: Show that $I = mL^2/3$.]

**10.49 [II]** Suppose that a satellite goes around the Moon in an elliptical orbit. At its closest approach it has a speed $v_c$ and a radius $r_c$ from the center of the Moon. At its farthest distance, it has a speed $v_f$ and a radius $r_f$. Find the ratio $v_c/v_f$. [*Hint*: Angular momentum is conserved, and, moreover, the satellite can be treated as a point mass.]

**10.50 [II]** A large horizontal disk is rotating on a vertical axis through its center. Its moment of inertia is $I = 4000\ \text{kg}\cdot\text{m}^2$. The disk is revolving freely at a rate of 0.150 rev/s when a 90.0-kg person drops straight down onto it from an overhanging tree limb. The person lands and remains at a distance of 3.00 m from the axis of rotation. What will be the rate of rotation after the person has landed?

**10.51 [II]** Suppose a uniform spherical star of mass *M* and radius *R* collapses to a uniform sphere of radius $10^{-5}\,R$. If the original star had a rotation rate of 1 rev each 25 days (as does the Sun), what will be the rotation rate of the resulting object?

**10.52 [II]** A 90-kg person stands at the edge of a stationary children's merry-go-round (essentially a disk) at a distance of 5.0 m from its center. The person starts to walk around the perimeter of the disk at a speed of 0.80 m/s relative to the ground. What rotation rate does this motion impart to the disk if $I_{\text{disk}} = 20\,000\ \text{kg}\cdot\text{m}^2$? [*Hint*: For the person, $I = mr^2$.]

## ANSWERS TO SUPPLEMENTARY PROBLEMS

**10.29 [I]** (*a*) 50 N·m; (*b*) 32 N·m

**10.30 [I]** (*a*) 0.50 kg·m$^2$; (*b*) 1.5 N·m

**10.31 [II]** 25 N·m

**10.32 [II]** 50 s

**10.33 [II]** 0.86 kJ

**10.34 [II]** 1.5 kg·m$^2$

**10.35 [II]** 0.26 N·m

**10.36 [II]** $0.63\ \text{kg}\cdot\text{m}^2$

**10.37 [II]** $2.5\ \text{N}\cdot\text{m}$

**10.38 [II]** $16\ \text{N}\cdot\text{m}$

**10.39 [III]** 12 kW

**10.40 [III]** $0.77\ \text{m/s}^2$, 11 N

**10.41 [III]** 5.3 cm

**10.42 [II]** 0.24 kJ

**10.43 [II]** 3.3 m/s

**10.44 [II]** (*a*) 2.65 m/s; (*b*) 2.32 m/s

**10.45 [I]** 8.5 cm

**10.46 [I]** (*a*) $1.4\ \text{kg}\cdot\text{m}^2$; (*b*) $2.1\ \text{kg}\cdot\text{m}^2$

**10.47 [I]** (*a*) $I = Mr^2 + Mr^2 = 0.03\ \text{kg}\cdot\text{m}^2$; (*b*) $I = \frac{2}{5}Mr^2 + Mr^2 = 7 \times 10^{-3}\ \text{kg}\cdot\text{m}^2$

**10.48 [II]** 5.0 rad/s, 5.0 m/s

**10.49 [II]** $r_f/r_c$

**10.50 [II]** 0.125 rev/s

**10.51 [II]** $5 \times 10^3$ rev/s

**10.52 [II]** 0.018 rad/s

# Simple Harmonic Motion and Springs

**The Period** ($T$) of a cyclic motion of a system, one that is vibrating or rotating in a repetitive fashion, is the time required for the system to complete one full cycle. In the case of vibration, it is the total time for the combined back-and-forth motion of the system. The **period** is *the number of seconds per cycle.*

**The Frequency** ($f$) is the number of vibrations made per unit time or *the number of cycles per second.* Because ($T$) is the time for one cycle, the **frequency** is $f = 1/T$. The unit of frequency is the *hertz,* where one cycle/s is 1 hertz (Hz).

**The Graph of a Harmonic Vibratory Motion** shown in Fig. 11-1 depicts the up-and-down oscillation of a mass at the end of a spring. One complete cycle is from *a* to *b*, or from *c* to *d*, or from *e* to *f*. The time taken for one cycle is $T$, the period. The oscillation depicted here has a single frequency and is sinusoidal or *harmonic.* All real vibrations are more complicated, containing a range of frequencies.

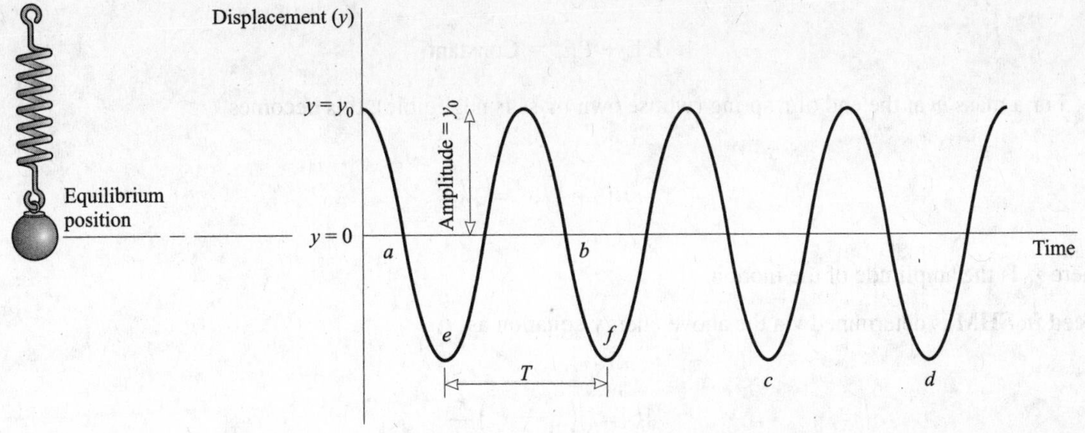


Fig. 11-1

**The Displacement** ($x$ or $y$) is the distance of the vibrating object from its equilibrium position (normal rest position)—that is, from the center of its vibration path. The maximum displacement is called the **amplitude** (see Fig. 11-1).

**A Restoring Force** is one that opposes the displacement of the system; it is necessary if vibration is to occur. In other words, a restoring force is always directed so as to push or pull the system back to its equilibrium (normal rest) position. For a mass at the end of a spring, the stretched spring pulls the mass back toward the equilibrium position, while the compressed spring pushes the mass back toward the equilibrium position.

**A Hookean System** also called an **elastic system** (a spring, wire, rod, etc.) is one that returns to its original configuration after being distorted and then released. Moreover, when such a system is stretched a distance $x$ (for compression, $x$ is negative), the ***restoring force*** exerted by the spring is given by **Hooke's Law**

$$F = -kx$$

The minus sign indicates that the restoring force is always opposite in direction to the displacement. The ***spring (or elastic) constant*** $k$ has units of N/m and is a measure of the stiffness of the spring. Most springs obey Hooke's Law for small distortions. This equation applies to any elastic system, from a steel rod to a tree limb.

It is sometimes useful to express Hooke's Law in terms of $F_{\text{ext}}$, the external force needed to stretch the spring a given amount $x$. This force is the negative of the restoring force, and so

$$F_{\text{ext}} = kx$$

An object that is stretched beyond its so-called **elastic limit** will not return to its original configuration and will no longer obey Hooke's Law.

**Simple Harmonic Motion** (SHM) is the idealized vibratory motion which a system that obeys Hooke's Law undergoes. The motion illustrated in Fig. 11-1 is SHM. Because of the resemblance of its graph to a sine or cosine curve, SHM is frequently called *sinusoidal or* ***harmonic motion***. A central feature of SHM is that the system oscillates at a single constant frequency. That's what makes it "simple" harmonic.

**The Elastic Potential Energy** ($\text{PE}_e$) stored in a Hookean spring (or wire, tendon, diving board, etc.) that is distorted a distance $x$ is $\frac{1}{2}kx^2$. If the amplitude of motion is $x_0$ for a mass at the end of a spring, then the energy of the vibrating system is $\frac{1}{2}kx_0^2$, at all times. However, this energy is stored exclusively in the spring only when $x = \pm x_0$, that is, when the mass has its maximum displacement. Otherwise, some of that energy appears as the KE of the oscillating mass.

**Energy Interchange** between kinetic and potential energy occurs constantly in a vibrating system. When the system passes through its equilibrium position, KE = Maximum and $\text{PE}_e = 0$. When the system has its maximum displacement, then KE = 0 and $\text{PE}_e$ = Maximum. From the law of conservation of energy, in the absence of friction-type losses,

$$\text{KE} + \text{PE}_e = \text{Constant}$$

For a mass $m$ at the end of a spring (whose own mass is negligible), this becomes

$$\tfrac{1}{2}mv^2 + \tfrac{1}{2}kx^2 = \tfrac{1}{2}kx_0^2$$

where $x_0$ is the amplitude of the motion.

**Speed in SHM** is determined via the above energy equation as

$$|v| = \sqrt{\left(x_0^2 - x^2\right)\frac{k}{m}}$$

Remember that speed is always a positive quantity.

**Acceleration in SHM** is determined via Hooke's Law, $F = -kx$, and $F = ma$; once displaced and released, the restoring force drives the system. Equating these two expressions for $F$ leads to

$$a = -\frac{k}{m}x$$

The minus sign indicates that in SHM the direction of $\vec{\mathbf{a}}$ (and $\vec{\mathbf{F}}$) is always opposite to the direction of the displacement $\vec{\mathbf{x}}$. Keep in mind that neither $\vec{\mathbf{F}}$ nor $\vec{\mathbf{a}}$ are constant.

**Reference Circle:** Suppose that a point-*P* moves with constant speed $|v_0|$ around a circle, as shown in Fig. 11-2. This circle is called the *reference circle* for SHM. Point-*A* is the projection of point-*P* on the *x*-axis, which coincides with the horizontal diameter of the circle. The motion of point-*A* back and forth about point *O* as center is SHM. The amplitude of the motion is $x_0$, the radius of the circle. The time taken for *P* to go around the circle once is the period *T* of the motion. For *P* located at the position shown in Fig. 11-2, the velocity, $\vec{\mathbf{v}}_0$, of point-*A* has a scalar *x*-component of

$$v_x = -|v_0| \sin\theta$$

When this quantity is positive (i.e., when $\theta$ is between 180° and 360°), $\vec{\mathbf{v}}_x$ points in the positive *x*-direction, when it's negative (i.e., when $\theta$ is between 0° and 180°), points in the negative *x*-direction.

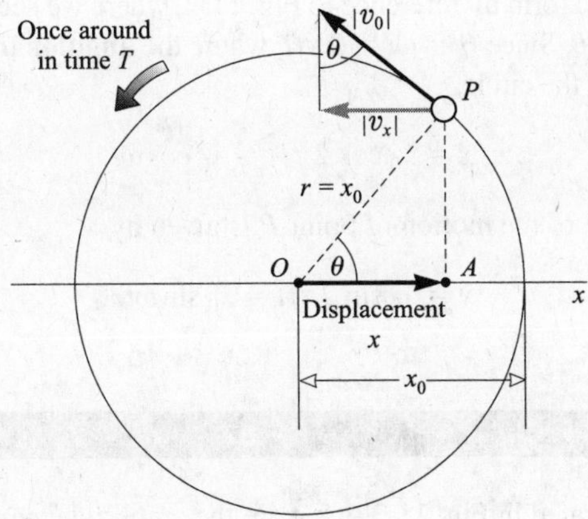


Fig. 11-2

**Period in SHM:** The period *T* of a SHM is the time taken for point-*P* to go once around the reference circle in Fig. 11-2 (i.e., the time required by the system to go through one complete cycle). Therefore,

$$T = \frac{2\pi r}{|v_0|} = \frac{2\pi x_0}{|v_0|}$$

But $|v_0|$ is the maximum speed of point-*A* in Fig. 11-2, that is, $|v_0|$ is the value of $|v_x|$ in SHM when $x = 0$:

$$|v_x| = \sqrt{\left(x_0^2 - x^2\right)\frac{k}{m}} \quad \text{leads to} \quad |v_0| = x_0\sqrt{\frac{k}{m}}$$

This calls to mind the equation $v = r\omega$, and that suggests that the *angular frequency* $\omega$ of the oscillator is expressible as

$$\omega = \sqrt{k/m}$$

This provides the period of SHM:

$$T = \frac{1}{f} = \frac{2\pi}{\omega} = 2\pi\sqrt{\frac{m}{k}}$$

for a Hookean system.

**Acceleration in Terms of $T$:** By eliminating the quantity $k/m$ between the two equations $a = -(k/m)x$ and $T = 2\pi\sqrt{m/k}$, we find

$$a = -\frac{4\pi^2}{T^2}x$$

Again, *for SHM the acceleration is proportional to the negative of the displacement.*

**The Simple Pendulum:** A pendulum very nearly undergoes SHM if its angle of swing is not large. The period of vibration for a pendulum of length $L$ at a location where the gravitational acceleration is $g$ is given by

$$T = 2\pi\sqrt{\frac{L}{g}}$$

**SHM** can be expressed in analytic form by reference to Fig. 11-2, where we see that the horizontal displacement of point-$P$ is given by $x = x_0 \cos\theta$. Since $\theta = \omega t = 2\pi f t$, where the **angular frequency** $\omega = 2\pi f$ is the angular velocity of the reference point on the circle,

$$x = x_0 \cos 2\pi f t = x_0 \cos \omega t$$

Similarly, the vertical component of the motion of point-$P$ is given by

$$y = x_0 \sin 2\pi f t = x_0 \sin \omega t$$

## SOLVED PROBLEMS

**11.1 [I]** For the motion illustrated in Fig. 11-3, what are the amplitude, period, and frequency?

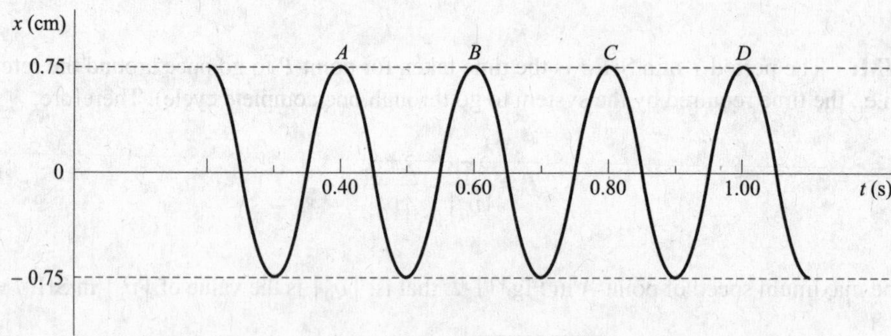


Fig. 11-3

The amplitude is the maximum displacement from the equilibrium position and so is 0.75 cm. The period is the time for one complete cycle, the time from $A$ to $B$, for example. Therefore, the period is 0.20 s. The frequency is

$$f = \frac{1}{T} = \frac{1}{0.20\text{ s}} = 5.0\text{ cycles/s} = 5.0\text{ Hz}$$

**11.2 [I]** A spring undergoes 12 vibrations in 40 s. Find the period and frequency of the oscillation.

$$T = \frac{\text{Elapsed time}}{\text{Vibrations made}} = \frac{40\text{ s}}{12} = 3.3\text{ s} \qquad f = \frac{\text{Vibrations made}}{\text{Elapsed time}} = \frac{12}{40\text{ s}} = 0.30\text{ Hz}$$

**11.3 [I]** When a 400-g mass is hung at the end of a vertical spring, the spring stretches 35 cm. Determine the elastic constant of the spring. How much farther will it stretch if an additional 400-g mass is hung from it?

Use $F_{ext} = ky$, where that force is the weight of the hanging mass:

$$F_{ext} = mg = (0.400 \text{ kg})(9.81 \text{ m/s}^2) = 3.92 \text{ N}$$

Therefore,
$$k = \frac{F_{ext}}{y} = \frac{3.92 \text{ N}}{0.35 \text{ m}} = 11.2 \text{ N/m} \qquad \text{or} \qquad 11 \text{ N/m}$$

Once the elastic constant is known, we can determine how the spring will behave. With an additional 400-g load, the total force stretching the spring is 7.84 N. Then

$$y = \frac{F}{k} = \frac{7.84 \text{ N}}{11.2 \text{ N/m}} = 0.70 \text{ m} = 2 \times 35 \text{ cm}$$

Provided it's Hookean, each 400-g load stretches the spring by the same amount, whether or not the spring is already loaded.

**11.4 [II]** A 200-g mass vibrates horizontally without friction at the end of a horizontal spring for which $k = 7.0$ N/m. The mass is displaced 5.0 cm from equilibrium and released. Find (*a*) its maximum speed and (*b*) its speed when it is 3.0 cm from equilibrium. (*c*) What is its acceleration in each of these cases?

From the conservation of energy,

$$\tfrac{1}{2}kx_0^2 = \tfrac{1}{2}mv^2 + \tfrac{1}{2}kx^2$$

where $k = 7.0$ N/m, $x_0 = 0.050$ m, and $m = 0.200$ kg. Solving for $|v|$ gives

$$|v| = \sqrt{(x_0^2 - x^2)\frac{k}{m}}$$

(*a*) The speed is a maximum when $x = 0$; that is, when the mass is passing through the equilibrium position:

$$|v| = x_0\sqrt{\frac{k}{m}} = (0.050 \text{ m})\sqrt{\frac{7.0 \text{ N/m}}{0.200 \text{ kg}}} = 0.30 \text{ m/s}$$

(*b*) When $x = 0.030$ m,

$$|v| = \sqrt{\frac{7.0 \text{ N/m}}{0.200 \text{ kg}}[(0.050)^2 - (0.030)^2] \text{ m}^2} = 0.24 \text{ m/s}$$

(*c*) Using $F = ma$ and $F = kx$,

$$a = \frac{k}{m}x = (35 \text{ s}^{-2})(x)$$

which yields $a = 0$ when the mass is at $x = 0$, and $a = 1.1 \text{ m/s}^2$ when $x = 0.030$ m.

**11.5 [II]** A 50-g mass vibrates in SHM at the end of a spring. The amplitude of the motion is 12 cm, and the period is 1.70 s. Find: (*a*) the frequency, (*b*) the spring constant, (*c*) the maximum speed of the mass, (*d*) the maximum acceleration of the mass, (*e*) the speed when the displacement is 6.0 cm, and (*f*) the acceleration when $x = 6.0$ cm.

(*a*) $f = \dfrac{1}{T} = \dfrac{1}{1.70\ \text{s}} = 0.588\ \text{Hz}$

(*b*) Since $T = 2\pi\sqrt{m/k}$,

$$k = \frac{4\pi^2 m}{T^2} = \frac{4\pi^2(0.050\ \text{kg})}{(1.70\ \text{s})^2} = 0.68\ \text{N/m}$$

(*c*) $|v_0| = x_0\sqrt{\dfrac{k}{m}} = (0.12\ \text{m})\sqrt{\dfrac{0.68\ \text{N/m}}{0.050\ \text{kg}}} = 0.44\ \text{m/s}$

(*d*) From $a = -(k/m)\,x$ it is seen that $a$ has maximum magnitude when $x$ has maximum magnitude, that is, at the endpoints $x = \pm x_0$. Thus,

$$a_0 = \frac{k}{m}x_0 = \frac{0.68\ \text{N/m}}{0.050\ \text{kg}}(0.12\ \text{m}) = 1.6\ \text{m/s}^2$$

(*e*) From $|v| = \sqrt{(x_0^2 - x^2)(k/m)}$,

$$|v| = \sqrt{\frac{[(0.12\ \text{m})^2 - (0.06\ \text{m})^2](0.68\ \text{N/m})}{(0.050\ \text{kg})}} = 0.38\ \text{m/s}$$

(*f*) $a = -\dfrac{k}{m}x = -\dfrac{0.68\ \text{N/m}}{0.050\ \text{kg}}(0.060\ \text{m}) = -0.82\ \text{m/s}^2$

**11.6 [II]** A 50-g mass hangs at the end of a Hookean spring. When 20 g more are added to the end of the spring, it stretches 7.0 cm more. (*a*) Find the spring constant. (*b*) If the 20-g mass is now removed, what will be the period of the motion?

(*a*) Under the weight of the 50-g mass, $F_{\text{ext}\,1} = kx_1$, where $x_1$ is the original stretching of the spring. When 20 g more are added, the force becomes $F_{\text{ext}\,1} + F_{\text{ext}\,2} = k(x_1 + x_2)$, where $F_{\text{ext}\,2}$ is the weight of 20 g and $x_2$ is the stretching it causes. Subtracting the two force equations leads to

$$F_{\text{ext}\,2} = kx_2$$

(Note that this is the same as $F_{\text{ext}} = kx$, where $F_{\text{ext}}$ is the additional stretching force and $x$ is the amount of stretch due to it. Hence, we could have ignored the fact that the spring had the 50-g mass at its end to begin with.) Solving for $k$,

$$k = \frac{F_{\text{ext}\,2}}{x_2} = \frac{(0.020\ \text{kg})(9.81\ \text{m/s}^2)}{0.070\ \text{m}} = 2.8\ \text{N/m}$$

(*b*) $T = 2\pi\sqrt{\dfrac{m}{k}} = 2\pi\sqrt{\dfrac{0.050\ \text{kg}}{2.8\ \text{N/m}}} = 0.84\ \text{s}$

**11.7 [II]** As depicted in Fig. 11-4, a long, light piece of spring steel is clamped at its lower end and a 2.0-kg ball is fastened to its top end. A horizontal force of 8.0 N is required to displace the ball 20 cm to one side as shown. Assume the system to undergo SHM when the ball is released. Find (*a*) the force constant of the spring and (*b*) the period with which the ball will vibrate back and forth.

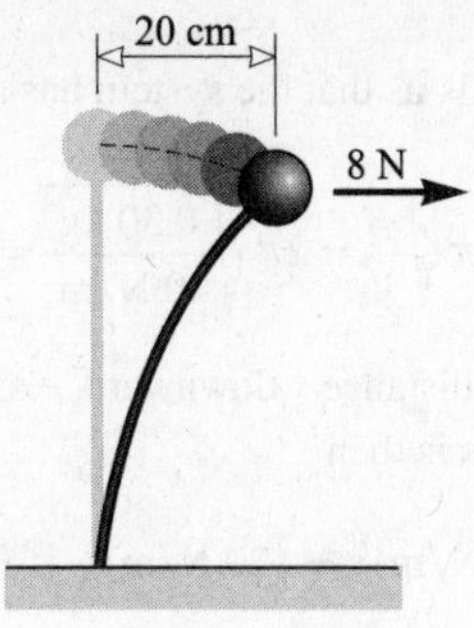


Fig. 11-4

(*a*) $k = \dfrac{\text{External force } F_{ext}}{\text{Displacement } x} = \dfrac{8.0\text{ N}}{0.20\text{ m}} = 40\text{ N/m}$

(*b*) $T = 2\pi\sqrt{\dfrac{m}{k}} = 2\pi\sqrt{\dfrac{2.0\text{ kg}}{40\text{ N/m}}} = 1.4\text{ s}$

**11.8 [II]** When a mass *m* is hung on a spring, the spring stretches 6.0 cm and comes to rest. Determine the system's period of vibration if the mass is pulled down a little more and then released.

Since the elastic constant is

$$k = \frac{F_{ext}}{x} = \frac{mg}{0.060\text{ m}}$$

the oscillatory period is
$$T = 2\pi\sqrt{\frac{m}{k}} = 2\pi\sqrt{\frac{0.060\text{ m}}{g}} = 0.49\text{ s}$$

Notice how the mass *m* cancels out of the equation.

**11.9 [II]** Two identical springs have elastic constants $k = 20$ N/m. A 0.30-kg mass is connected to them as shown in Fig. 11-5(*a*) and (*b*). Find the period of oscillation for each system. Ignore friction forces.

(*a*)

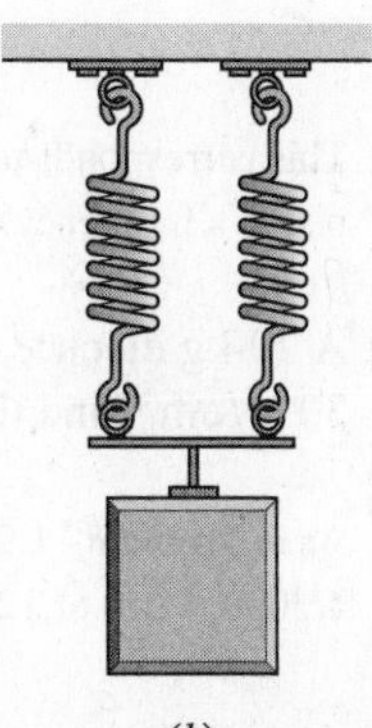

(*b*)

Fig. 11-5

(*a*) Consider what happens when the mass is given a displacement $x > 0$. One spring will be stretched an amount $x$, and the other will be compressed an amount $x$. They will each exert a force of magnitude (20 N/m)$x$ on the mass in the direction opposite to the displacement. Hence, the total restoring force will be

$$F = -(20\text{ N/m})\,x - (20\text{ N/m})\,x = -(40\text{ N/m})\,x$$

Comparison with $F = -kx$ tells us that the system has a spring constant of $k = 40$ N/m. Consequently,

$$T = 2\pi\sqrt{\frac{m}{k}} = 2\pi\sqrt{\frac{0.30\text{ kg}}{40\text{ N/m}}} = 0.54\text{ s}$$

(*b*) When the mass is displaced a distance $y$ downward, each spring is stretched the same distance $y$. The net restoring force on the mass is then

$$F = -(20\text{ N/m})y - (20\text{ N/m})y = -(40\text{ N/m})y$$

Comparison with $F = -ky$ shows $k$ to be 40 N/m, the same as in (*a*). The period in this case is also 0.54 s.

**11.10 [III]** In an old gasoline engine, a piston undergoes vertical SHM with an amplitude of 7.0 cm. A washer rests on top of the piston. As the motor speed is slowly increased, at what frequency will the washer no longer stay in contact with the piston?

The situation we are looking for is when the maximum downward acceleration of the washer equals that of free fall, namely, $g$. If the piston accelerates down faster than that, the washer will lose contact.

In SHM, the acceleration is given in terms of the displacement and the period as

$$a = -\frac{4\pi^2}{T^2}x$$

(To see this, notice that $a = -F/m = -kx/m$. But from $T = 2\pi\sqrt{m/k}$, we have $k = 4\pi^2 m/T^2$, which then gives the above expression for $a$.) With the upward direction chosen as positive, the largest downward (most negative) acceleration occurs for $x = +x_0 = 0.070$ m; it is

$$a_0 = \frac{4\pi^2}{T^2}(0.070\text{ m})$$

The washer will separate from the piston when $a_0$ first becomes equal to $g$. Therefore, the critical period for the SHM, $T_c$, is given by

$$\frac{4\pi^2}{T_c^2}(0.070\text{ m}) = g \qquad \text{or} \qquad T_c = 2\pi\sqrt{\frac{0.070\text{ m}}{g}} = 0.53\text{ s}$$

This corresponds to the frequency $f_c = 1/T_c = 1.9$ Hz. The washer will separate from the piston if the piston's frequency exceeds 1.9 cycles/s.

**11.11 [III]** A 20-kg electric motor is mounted on four vertical springs, each having an elastic constant of 30 N/cm. Find the period with which the motor vibrates vertically.

As in Problem 11.9, we may replace the springs by an equivalent single spring. Its force constant will be 4(3000 N/m) or 12 000 N/m. Then

$$T = 2\pi\sqrt{\frac{m}{k}} = 2\pi\sqrt{\frac{20\text{ kg}}{12\,000\text{ N/m}}} = 0.26\text{ s}$$

**11.12 [III]** Mercury is poured into a glass U-tube. Normally, the mercury stands at equal heights in the two columns, but when disturbed, it oscillates back and forth from arm to arm. (See Fig. 11-6.) One centimeter of the mercury column has a mass of 15.0 g. Suppose the column is displaced as shown and released, and it vibrates back and forth without friction. Compute (*a*) the effective spring constant of the motion and (*b*) its period of oscillation.

(*a*) When the mercury is displaced $x$ m from equilibrium as shown, the restoring force is the weight of the unbalanced column of length $2x$. The mercury has a mass of 1.50 kilograms per meter. The mass of the column is therefore $(2x)(1.50 \text{ kg})$, and so its weight is $mg = (29.4 \text{ kg}\cdot\text{m/s}^2)(x)$. Therefore, the restoring force is

$$F = (29.4 \text{ N/m})(x)$$

which is of the form $F = kx$ with $k = 29.4$ N/m. This is the effective elastic constant of the system.

(*b*) The period of vibration is then

$$T = 2\pi\sqrt{\frac{M}{k}} = 1.16\sqrt{M} \text{ s}$$

where $M$ is the total mass of mercury in the U-tube—that is, the total mass being moved by the restoring force.

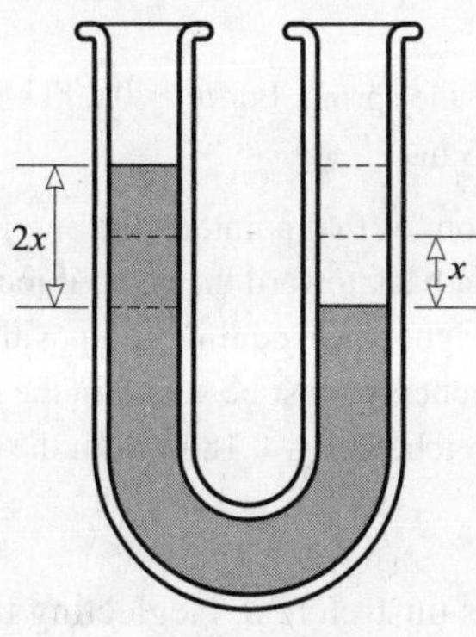


Fig. 11-6

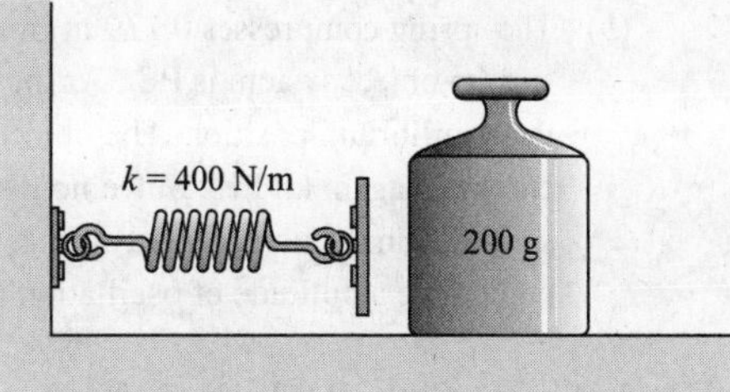


Fig. 11-7

**11.13 [II]** Compute the acceleration due to gravity at a place where a simple pendulum 150.3 cm long swings through 100.0 cycles in 246.7 s.

We have

$$T = \frac{246.7 \text{ s}}{100.0} = 2.467 \text{ s}$$

Squaring $T = 2\pi\sqrt{L/g}$ and solving for $g$ yields

$$g = \frac{4\pi^2}{T^2}L = 9.749 \text{ m/s}^2$$

**11.14 [II]** The 200-g object in Fig. 11-7 is pushed to the left, compressing the spring 15 cm from its equilibrium position. The system is then released, and the object shoots to the right. How fast will the object be moving as it sails away? Assume the mass of the spring to be very small and friction to be negligible.

When the spring is compressed, energy is stored in it. That energy is $\frac{1}{2}kx_0^2$, where $x_0 = 0.15$ m. After release, this energy will be transferred to the object as KE. When the spring passes through its equilibrium position, all the $PE_e$ will be changed to KE. (Since the mass of the spring is small, its KE can be ignored.) Therefore,

$$\text{Original } PE_e = \text{Final KE of object}$$

$$\tfrac{1}{2}kx_0^2 = \tfrac{1}{2}mv^2$$

$$\tfrac{1}{2}(400\ \text{N/m})(0.15\ \text{m})^2 = \tfrac{1}{2}(0.200\ \text{kg})\,v^2$$

from which it follows that $v = 6.7\ \text{m/s}$.

**11.15 [II]** Suppose that, in Fig. 11-7, the 200-g object initially moves to the left at a speed of 8.0 m/s. It strikes the spring and becomes attached to it. (*a*) How far does it compress the spring? (*b*) The system then oscillates back and forth; what is the amplitude of that oscillation? Ignore friction and the small mass of the spring.

(*a*) Because the spring can be considered massless, all the KE of the object will go into compressing the spring. We can therefore write

$$\text{Original KE of mass} = \text{Final } PE_e$$

$$\tfrac{1}{2}mv_0^2 = \tfrac{1}{2}kx_0^2$$

where $v_0 = 8.0\ \text{m/s}$ and $x_0$ is the maximum compression of the spring. For $m = 0.200\ \text{kg}$ and $k = 400\ \text{N/m}$, the above relation gives $x_0 = 0.179\ \text{m} = 0.18\ \text{m}$.

(*b*) The spring compresses 0.179 m from its equilibrium position. At that point, all the energy of the spring–object system is $PE_e$. As the spring pushes the object back toward the right, it moves through the equilibrium position. The object stops at a point to the right of the equilibrium position where the energy is again all $PE_e$. Since no losses occurred, the same energy must be stored in the stretched spring as in the compressed spring. Therefore, it will be stretched $x_0 = 0.18\ \text{m}$ from the equilibrium point. The amplitude of oscillation is therefore 0.18 m.

**11.16 [II]** In Fig. 11-8, the 2.0-kg body is released when the spring is unstretched. Neglecting the inertia and friction of the pulley and the mass of the spring and string, find (*a*) the amplitude of the resulting oscillation and (*b*) its center or equilibrium point.

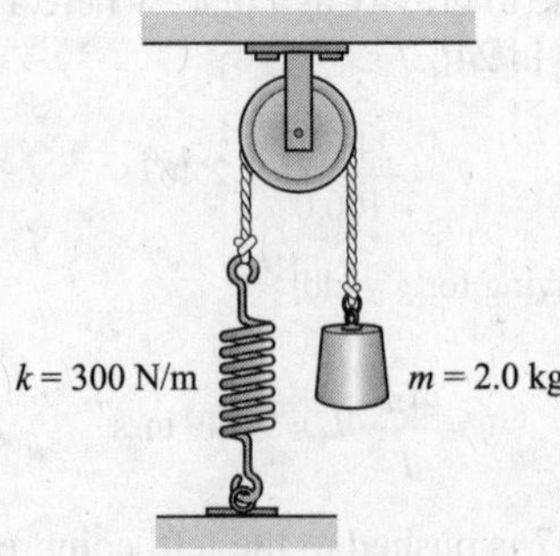


Fig. 11-8

(*a*) Suppose the 2.0-kg body falls a distance *h* before stopping. At that time, the $PE_G$ it lost (*mgh*) will be stored in the spring, so that

$$mgh = \tfrac{1}{2}kh^2 \qquad \text{or} \qquad h = 2\frac{mg}{k} = 0.13\ \text{m}$$

The body will stop in its upward motion when the energy of the system is all recovered as $PE_G$. Therefore, it will rise 0.13 m above its lowest position. The amplitude is thus $0.13/2 = 0.065$ m.

(*b*) The center point of the motion is a distance of 0.065 m below the point from which the body was released—that is, a distance equal to half the total travel below the highest point.

**11.17 [II]** A 3.0-g particle at the end of a spring moves according to the equation $y = 0.75 \sin 63t$, where $y$ is in centimeters and $t$ is in seconds. Find the amplitude and frequency of its motion, its position at $t = 0.020$ s, and the spring constant.

The equation of motion is $y = y_0 \sin 2\pi ft$. By comparison, we see that the amplitude is $y_0 = 0.75$ cm. Also,

$$2\pi f = 63\ \mathrm{s}^{-1} \qquad \text{from which} \qquad f = 10\ \mathrm{Hz}$$

(Note that the argument of the sine must be dimensionless; because $t$ is in seconds, $2\pi f$ must have the unit 1/s.) When $t = 0.020$ s, we have

$$y = 0.75 \sin (1.26\ \mathrm{rad}) = (0.75)(0.952) = 0.71\ \mathrm{cm}$$

Notice that the argument of the sine is in radians, not degrees.

To find the spring constant, use $f = (1/2\pi)\sqrt{k/m}$ to get

$$k = 4\pi^2 f^2 m = 11.9\ \mathrm{N/m} = 12\ \mathrm{N/m}$$

## SUPPLEMENTARY PROBLEMS

**11.18 [I]** A small metal sphere weighing 10.0 N is hung from a vertical spring, which comes to rest after stretching 2.0 cm. Determine the spring constant.

**11.19 [I]** How much energy is stored in a spring with an elastic constant of 1000 N/m when it is compressed 10 cm?

**11.20 [I]** A pendulum is timed as it swings back and forth. The clock is started when the bob is at the left end of its swing. When the bob returns to the left end for the 90th return, the clock reads 60.0 s. What is the period of vibration? The frequency?

**11.21 [II]** A 300-g mass at the end of a Hookean spring vibrates up and down in such a way that it is 2.0 cm above the tabletop at its lowest point and 16 cm above at its highest point. Its period is 4.0 s. Determine (*a*) the amplitude of vibration, (*b*) the spring constant, (*c*) the speed and acceleration of the mass when it is 9 cm above the tabletop, (*d*) the speed and acceleration of the mass when it is 12 cm above the tabletop.

**11.22 [II]** A coiled Hookean spring is stretched 10 cm when a 1.5-kg body is hung from it. Suppose instead that a 4.0-kg mass hangs from the spring and is set into vibration with an amplitude of 12 cm. Find (*a*) the force constant of the spring, (*b*) the maximum restoring force acting on the vibrating body, (*c*) the period of vibration, (*d*) the maximum speed and the maximum acceleration of the vibrating object, and (*e*) the speed and acceleration when the displacement is 9 cm.

**11.23 [II]** A 2.5-kg body undergoes SHM and makes exactly 3 vibrations each second. Compute the acceleration and the restoring force acting on the body when its displacement from the equilibrium position is 5.0 cm.

**11.24 [II]** A 300-g object attached to the end of a spring oscillates with an amplitude of 7.0 cm and a frequency of 1.80 Hz. (*a*) Find its maximum speed and maximum acceleration. (*b*) What is its speed when it is 3.0 cm from its equilibrium position?

**11.25 [II]** A Hookean spring is stretched 20 cm when a massive object is hung from it. What is the frequency of vibration of the object if pulled down a little and released?

**11.26 [II]** A 300-g body fixed at the end of a spring executes SHM with a period of 2.4 s. Find the period of oscillation when the body is replaced by a 133-g mass on the same spring.

**11.27 [II]** With a 50-g mass at its end, a spring undergoes SHM with a frequency of 0.70 Hz. How much work is done in stretching the spring 15 cm from its unstretched length? How much energy is then stored in the spring?

**11.28 [II]** In a situation similar to that shown in Fig. 11-7, a mass is pressed back against a light spring for which $k = 400$ N/m. The mass compresses the spring 8.0 cm and is then released. After sliding 55 cm along the flat table from the point of release, the mass uniformly comes to rest. How large a friction force opposed its motion?

**11.29 [II]** A 500-g object is attached to the end of an initially unstretched vertical spring for which $k = 30$ N/m. The object is then released, so that it falls and stretches the spring. How far will it fall before stopping? [*Hint:* The $\text{PE}_G$ lost by the falling object must appear as $\text{PE}_e$.]

**11.30 [II]** A popgun uses a spring for which $k = 20$ N/cm. When cocked, the spring is compressed 3.0 cm. How high can the gun shoot a 5.0-g projectile?

**11.31 [II]** A cubical block on an air table vibrates horizontally in SHM with an amplitude of 8.0 cm and a frequency of 1.50 Hz. If a smaller block sitting on it is not to slide, what is the minimum value that the coefficient of static friction between the two blocks can have?

**11.32 [II]** Find the frequency of vibration on Mars for a simple pendulum that is 50 cm long. Objects weigh 0.40 as much on Mars as on the Earth.

**11.33 [II]** A "seconds pendulum" beats seconds; that is, it takes 1 s for half a cycle. (*a*) What is the length of a simple "seconds pendulum" at a place where $g = 9.80$ m/s$^2$? (*b*) What is the length there of a pendulum for which $T = 1.00$ s?

**11.34 [II]** Show that the natural period of vertical oscillation of a mass hung on a Hookean spring is the same as the period of a simple pendulum whose length is equal to the elongation the mass causes when hung on the spring.

**11.35 [II]** A particle that is at the origin of coordinates at exactly $t = 0$ vibrates about the origin along the *y*-axis with a frequency of 20 Hz and an amplitude of 3.0 cm. Write out its equation of motion in centimeters.

**11.36 [II]** A particle vibrates according to the equation $x = 20 \cos 16t$, where $x$ is in centimeters. Find its amplitude, frequency, and position at exactly $t = 0$ s.

**11.37 [II]** A particle oscillates according to the equation $y = 5.0 \cos 23t$, where $y$ is in centimeters. Find its frequency of oscillation and its position at $t = 0.15$ s.

## ANSWERS TO SUPPLEMENTARY PROBLEMS

**11.18 [I]** $5.0 \times 10^2$ N/m

**11.19 [I]** 5.0 J

**11.20 [I]** 0.667 s, 1.50 Hz

**11.21 [II]** (*a*) 7.0 cm; (*b*) 0.74 N/m; (*c*) 0.11 m/s; zero; (*d*) 0.099 m/s, 0.074 $m/s^2$

**11.22 [II]** (*a*) 0.15 kN/m; (*b*)18 N; (*c*) 1.0 s; (*d*) 0.73 m/s, 4.4 $m/s^2$; (*e*) 0.48 m/s, 3.3 $m/s^2$

**11.23 [II]** 18 $m/s^2$, 44 N

**11.24 [II]** (*a*) 0.79 m/s, 8.9 $m/s^2$; (*b*) 0.72 m/s

**11.25 [II]** 1.1 Hz

**11.26 [II]** 1.6 s

**11.27 [II]** 0.011 J, 0.011 J

**11.28 [II]** 2.3 N

**11.29 [II]** 33 cm

**11.30 [II]** 18 m

**11.31 [II]** 0.72

**11.32 [II]** 0.45 Hz

**11.33 [II]** (*a*) 99.3 cm; (*b*) 24.8 cm

**11.35 [II]** $y = 3.0 \sin 125.6t$

**11.36 [II]** 20 cm, 2.6 Hz, $x = 20$ cm

**11.37 [II]** 3.7 Hz, −4.8 cm

# CHAPTER 12

# Density; Elasticity

**The Mass Density** ($\rho$) of a body is its mass per unit volume:

$$\rho = \frac{\text{Mass of body}}{\text{Volume of body}} = \frac{m}{V}$$

The SI unit for mass density is $\text{kg/m}^3$, although $\text{g/cm}^3$ is also used: $1000\ \text{kg/m}^3 = 1\ \text{g/cm}^3$. The density of water is close to $1000\ \text{kg/m}^3$. Be careful here; using 1 for the density of water in a problem involving SI units is a common error.

**The Specific Gravity** (sp gr) of a substance is the ratio of the density of the substance to the density of some standard substance. The standard is usually water (at 4°C) for liquids and solids, while for gases, it is usually air.

$$\text{sp gr} = \frac{\rho}{\rho_{\text{standard}}}$$

Since sp gr is a dimensionless ratio, it has the same value for all systems of units, which is why it was introduced centuries ago.

**Elasticity** is the property by which a body returns to its original size and shape when the forces that deformed it are removed. An elastic body is said to be Hookean in that it obeys Hooke's Law.

**The Stress** ($\sigma$) experienced within a solid is the magnitude of the force acting ($F$), divided by the area ($A$) over which it acts:

$$\text{Stress} = \frac{\text{Force}}{\text{Area of surface on which force acts}}$$

$$\sigma = \frac{F}{A}$$

The SI unit of stress is the **pascal** (Pa), where $1\ \text{Pa} = 1\ \text{N/m}^2$. Thus, if a cane supports a load, the stress at any point within the cane is the load divided by the cross-sectional area at that point; the narrowest regions experience the greatest stress.

**Strain** ($\varepsilon$) is the fractional deformation resulting from a stress. It is measured as the ratio of the change in some dimension of a body (often its length) to the original dimension in which the change occurred.

$$\text{Strain} = \frac{\text{Change in dimension}}{\text{Original dimension}}$$

Thus, the normal strain under an axial load is the change in length ($\Delta L$) over the original length $L_0$:

$$\varepsilon = \frac{\Delta L}{L_0}$$

Strain has no units because it is a ratio of like quantities.

**The Elastic Limit** of a body is the smallest stress that will produce a permanent distortion in the body. When a stress in excess of this limit is applied, the body will not return exactly to its original state after the stress is removed.

**Young's Modulus** ($Y$), or the **modulus of elasticity**, is defined as

$$\text{Modulus of elasticity} = \frac{\text{Stress}}{\text{Strain}}$$

The modulus has the same units as stress, which are $\text{N/m}^2$ or Pa. A large modulus means that a large stress is required to produce a given strain—the object is rigid.

Accordingly,

$$Y = \frac{F/A}{\Delta L/L_0} = \frac{FL_0}{A\Delta L}$$

Unlike the constant $k$ in Hooke's Law, the value of $Y$ depends only on the material of the wire or rod, and not on its dimensions or configuration. Consequently, Young's modulus is an important basic measure of the mechanical behavior of materials.

**The Bulk Modulus** ($B$) describes the volume elasticity of a material. Suppose that a uniformly distributed compressive force acts on the surface of an object and is directed perpendicular to the surface at all points. Then if $F_\perp$ is the magnitude of the force acting on and perpendicular to an area $A$, the pressure $P$ on $A$ is defined as

$$P = \frac{F_\perp}{A}$$

The SI unit for pressure is Pa. Note that pressure is a scalar quantity.

Suppose that the pressure on an object of original volume $V_0$ is increased by an amount $\Delta P$. That pressure increase causes a volume change $\Delta V$, where $\Delta V$ will be negative. We then define

$$\text{Volume stress} = \Delta P \qquad \text{Volume strain} = -\frac{\Delta V}{V_0}$$

Then

$$\text{Bulk modulus} = \frac{\text{Stress}}{\text{Strain}}$$

$$B = -\frac{\Delta P}{\Delta V/V_0} = -\frac{V_0 \Delta P}{\Delta V}$$

The minus sign is used so as to cancel the negative numerical value of $\Delta V$ and thereby make $B$ a positive number. The bulk modulus has the units of pressure.

The reciprocal of the bulk modulus is called the *compressibility* $K$ of the substance.

**The Shear Modulus** ($S$) describes the shape elasticity of a material. Suppose, as shown in Fig. 12-1, that equal and opposite tangential forces $F$ act on a rectangular block. These *shearing forces* distort the block as indicated, but its volume remains unchanged. We define

$$\text{Shearing stress} = \frac{\text{Tangential force acting}}{\text{Area of surface being sheared}}$$

$$\sigma_s = \frac{F}{A}$$

$$\text{Shearing strain} = \frac{\text{Distance sheared}}{\text{Distance between surfaces}}$$

$$\varepsilon_s = \frac{\Delta L}{L_0}$$

$$\text{Shear modulus} = \frac{\text{Stress}}{\text{Strain}}$$

$$S = \frac{F/A}{\Delta L/L_0} = \frac{FL_0}{A\,\Delta L}$$

Since $\Delta L$ is usually very small, the ratio $\Delta L/L_0$ is equal approximately to the shear angle $\gamma$ in radians. In that case,

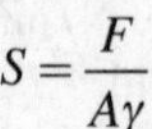

$$S = \frac{F}{A\gamma}$$

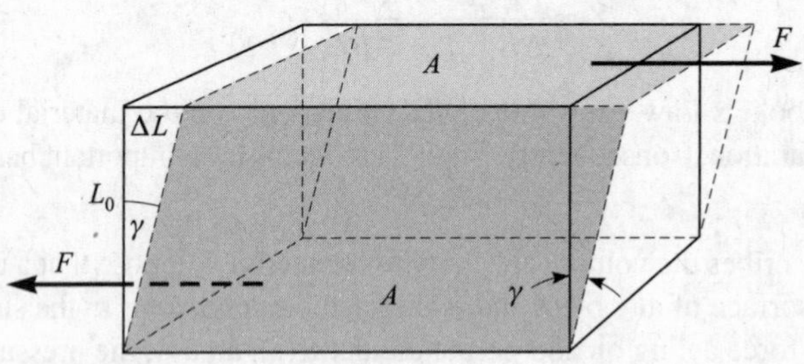


Fig. 12-1

## SOLVED PROBLEMS

**12.1 [I]** Find the density and specific gravity of gasoline if 51 g occupies 75 cm³. Make sure you know how to convert cubic centimeters to cubic meters: $1.0\ \text{m}^3 = 1.0 \times 10^6\ \text{cm}^3$.

$$\text{Density} = \frac{\text{Mass}}{\text{Volume}} = \frac{0.051\ \text{kg}}{75 \times 10^{-6}\ \text{m}^3} = 6.8 \times 10^2\ \text{kg/m}^3$$

$$\text{sp gr} = \frac{\text{Density of gasoline}}{\text{Density of water}} = \frac{6.8 \times 10^2\ \text{kg/m}^3}{1000\ \text{kg/m}^3} = 0.68$$

or

$$\text{sp gr} = \frac{\text{Mass of 75 cm}^3\ \text{gasoline}}{\text{Mass of 75 cm}^3\ \text{water}} = \frac{51\ \text{g}}{75\ \text{g}} = 0.68$$

**12.2 [I]** What volume does 300 g of mercury occupy? The density of mercury is 13 600 kg/m³.

From $\rho = m/V$,

$$V = \frac{m}{\rho} = \frac{0.300\ \text{kg}}{13\ 600\ \text{kg/m}^3} = 2.21 \times 10^{-5}\ \text{m}^3 = 22.1\ \text{cm}^3$$

**12.3 [I]** The specific gravity of cast iron is 7.20. Find its density and the mass of 60.0 cm³ of it.

Make use of

$$\text{sp gr} = \frac{\text{Density of substance}}{\text{Density of water}} \qquad \text{and} \qquad \rho = \frac{m}{V}$$

From the first equation,

$$\text{Density of iron} = (\text{sp gr})(\text{Density of water}) = (7.20)(1000\ \text{kg/m}^3) = 7200\ \text{kg/m}^3$$

and so

$$\text{Mass of } 60.0\ \text{cm}^3 = \rho V = (7200\ \text{kg/m}^3)(60.0 \times 10^{-6}\ \text{m}_3) = 0.432\ \text{kg}$$

**12.4 [I]** **The mass of a calibrated flask is 25.0 g when empty, 75.0 g when filled with water, and 88.0 g when filled with glycerin. Find the specific gravity of glycerin.**

From the data, the mass of the glycerin in the flask is 63.0 g, while an equal volume of water has a mass of 50.0 g. Then

$$\text{sp gr} = \frac{\text{Mass of glycerin}}{\text{Mass of water}} = \frac{63.0\ \text{g}}{50.0\ \text{g}} = 1.26$$

**12.5 [I]** **A calibrated flask has a mass of 30.0 g when empty, 81.0 g when filled with water, and 68.0 g when filled with an oil. Find the density of the oil.**

First find the volume of the flask from $\rho = m/V$, using the water data:

$$V = \frac{m}{\rho} = \frac{(81.0 - 30.0) \times 10^{-3}\ \text{kg}}{1000\ \text{kg/m}^3} = 51.0 \times 10^{-6}\ \text{m}^3$$

Then, for the oil,

$$\rho_{\text{oil}} = \frac{m_{\text{oil}}}{V} = \frac{(68.0 - 30.0) \times 10^{-3}\ \text{kg}}{51.0 \times 10^{-6}\ \text{m}^3} = 745\ \text{kg/m}^3$$

**12.6 [I]** **A solid cube of aluminum is 2.00 cm on each edge. The density of aluminum is 2700 kg/m³. Find the mass of the cube.**

$$\text{Mass of cube} = \rho V = (2700\ \text{kg/m}^3)(0.0200\ \text{m})^3 = 0.0216\ \text{kg} = 21.6\ \text{g}$$

**12.7 [I]** **What is the mass of 1 liter (1000 cm³) of cottonseed oil of density 926 kg/m³? How much does it weigh?**

$$m = \rho V = (926\ \text{kg/m}^3)(1000 \times 10^{-6}\ \text{m}^3) = 0.926\ \text{kg}$$
$$\text{Weight} = mg = (0.926\ \text{kg})(9.81\ \text{m/s}^2) = 9.08\ \text{N}$$

**12.8 [I]** **An electrolytic tin-plating process gives a tin coating that is $7.50 \times 10^{-5}$ cm thick. How large an area can be coated with 0.500 kg of tin? The density of tin is 7300 kg/m³.**

The volume of 0.500 kg of tin is given by $\rho = m/V$ to be

$$V = \frac{m}{\rho} = \frac{0.500\ \text{kg}}{7300\ \text{kg/m}^3} = 6.85 \times 10^{-5}\ \text{m}^3$$

The volume of a film with area $A$ and thickness $d$ is $V = Ad$. Solving for $A$, we find

$$A = \frac{V}{d} = \frac{6.85 \times 10^{-5}\ \text{m}^3}{7.50 \times 10^{-7}\ \text{m}} = 91.3\ \text{m}^2$$

as the area that can be covered.

**12.9 [I]** A thin sheet of gold foil has an area of 3.12 cm² and a mass of 6.50 mg. How thick is the sheet? The density of gold is 19 300 kg/m³.

One milligram is $10^{-6}$ kg, so the mass of the sheet is $6.50 \times 10^{-6}$ kg. Its volume is

$$V = (\text{area}) \times (\text{thickness}) = (3.12 \times 10^{-4}\ \text{m}^2(d)$$

where $d$ is the thickness of the sheet. We equate this expression for the volume to $m/\rho$ to get

$$(3.12\times 10^{-4}\ \text{m}^2)(d) = \frac{6.50\times 10^{-6}\ \text{kg}}{19300\ \text{kg/m}^3}$$

from which $d = 1.08 \times 10^{-6}$ m = 1.08 μm.

**12.10 [I]** The mass of a liter of milk is 1.032 kg. The butterfat that it contains has a density of 865 kg/m³ when pure, and it constitutes exactly 4 percent of the milk by volume. What is the density of the fat-free skimmed milk?

Volume of fat in 1000 cm³ of milk = 4% × 1000 cm³ = 40.0 cm³

$$\text{Mass of 40.0 cm}^3 \text{ fat} = V\rho = (40.0 \times 10^{-6}\ \text{m}^3)(865\ \text{kg/m}^3) = 0.0346\ \text{kg}$$

$$\text{Density of skimmed milk} = \frac{\text{Mass}}{\text{Volume}} = \frac{(1.032 - 0.0346)\ \text{kg}}{(1000 - 40.0)\times 10^{-6}\ \text{m}^3} = 1.04\times 10^3\ \text{kg/m}^3$$

**12.11 [II]** A metal wire 75.0 cm long and 0.130 cm in diameter stretches 0.035 0 cm when a load of 8.00 kg is hung on its end. Find the stress, the strain, and the Young's modulus for the material of the wire.

$$\sigma = \frac{F}{A} = \frac{(8.00\ \text{kg})(9.81\ \text{m/s}^2)}{\pi(6.50\times 10^{-4}\ \text{m})^2} = 5.91\times 10^7\ \text{N/m}^2 = 5.91\times 10^7\ \text{Pa}$$

$$\varepsilon = \frac{\Delta L}{L_0} = \frac{0.0350\ \text{cm}}{75.0\ \text{cm}} = 4.67\times 10^{-4}$$

$$Y = \frac{\sigma}{\varepsilon} = \frac{5.91\times 10^7\ \text{Pa}}{4.67\times 10^{-4}} = 1.27\times 10^{11}\ \text{Pa} = 127\ \text{GPa}$$

**12.12 [II]** A solid cylindrical steel column is 4.0 m long and 9.0 cm in diameter. What will be its decrease in length when carrying a load of 80 000 kg? $Y = 1.9 \times 10^{11}$ Pa.

First find the

$$\text{Cross-sectional area of column} = \pi r^2 = \pi(0.045\ \text{m})^2 = 6.36 \times 10^{-3}\ \text{m}^2$$

Then, from $Y = (F/A)/(\Delta L/L_0)$,

$$\Delta L = \frac{FL_0}{AY} = \frac{[(8.00\times 10^4)(9.81)\ \text{N}](4.0\ \text{m})}{(6.36\times 10^{-3}\ \text{m}^2)(1.9\times 10^{11}\ \text{Pa})} = 2.6\times 10^{-3}\text{m} = 2.6\ \text{mm}$$

**12.13 [I]** Atmospheric pressure is about $1.01 \times 10^5$ Pa. How large a force does the atmosphere exert on a 2.0-cm² area on the top of your head?

Because $P = F/A$, where $F$ is perpendicular to $A$, we have $F = PA$. Assuming that 2.0 cm² of your head is flat (nearly correct) and that the force due to the atmosphere is perpendicular to the surface (as it is),

$$F = PA = (1.01 \times 10^5\ \text{N/m}^2)(2.0 \times 10^{-4}\ \text{m}^2) = 20\ \text{N}$$

**12.14 [I]** A 60-kg woman stands on a light, cubical box that is 5.0 cm on each edge. The box sits on the floor. What pressure does the box exert on the floor?

$$P = \frac{F}{A} = \frac{(60)(9.81)\ \text{N}}{(5.0 \times 10^{-2}\ \text{m})^2} = 2.4 \times 10^5\ \text{N/m}^2$$

**12.15 [I]** The bulk modulus of water is 2.1 GPa. Compute the volume contraction of 100 mL of water when subjected to a pressure of 1.5 MPa.

From $B = -\Delta P/(\Delta V/V_0)$,

$$\Delta V = -\frac{V_0\,\Delta P}{B} = -\frac{(100\ \text{mL})(1.5 \times 10^6\ \text{Pa})}{2.1 \times 10^9\ \text{Pa}} = -0.071\ \text{mL}$$

**12.16 [II]** A box-shaped piece of gelatin dessert has a top area of 15 cm² and a height of 3.0 cm. When a shearing force of 0.50 N is applied to the upper surface, the upper surface displaces 4.0 mm relative to the bottom surface. What are the shearing stress, the shearing strain, and the shear modulus for the gelatin?

$$\sigma_s = \frac{\text{Tangential force}}{\text{Area of face}} = \frac{0.50\ \text{N}}{15 \times 10^{-4}\ \text{m}^2} = 0.33\ \text{kPa}$$

$$\varepsilon_s = \frac{\text{Displacement}}{\text{Height}} = \frac{0.40\ \text{cm}}{3.0\ \text{cm}} = 0.13$$

$$S = \frac{0.33\ \text{kPa}}{0.13} = 2.5\ \text{kPa}$$

**12.17 [III]** A 15-kg ball of radius 4.0 cm is suspended from a point 2.94 m above the floor by an iron wire of unstretched length 2.85 m. The diameter of the wire is 0.090 cm, and its Young's modulus is 180 GPa. If the ball is set swinging so that its center passes through the lowest point at 5.0 m/s, by how much does the bottom of the ball clear the floor? Discuss any approximations that you make.

Call the tension in the wire $F_T$ when the ball is swinging through the lowest point. Since $F_T$ must supply the centripetal force as well as balance the weight,

$$F_T = mg + \frac{mv^2}{r} = m\left(9.81 + \frac{25}{r}\right)$$

all in proper SI units. This is complicated, because $r$ is the distance from the pivot to the center of the ball when the wire is stretched, and so it is $r_0 + \Delta r$, where $r_0$, the unstretched length of the pendulum, is

$$r_0 = 2.85\ \text{m} + 0.040\ \text{m} = 2.89\ \text{m}$$

and where $\Delta r$ is as yet unknown. However, the unstretched distance from the pivot to the bottom of the ball is 2.85 m + 0.080 m = 2.93 m, and so the maximum possible value for $\Delta r$ is

$$2.94\ \text{m} - 2.93\ \text{m} = 0.01\ \text{m}$$

We will therefore incur no more than a 1/3 percent error in $r$ by using $r = r_0 = 2.89$ m. This gives $F_T = 277$ N. Under this tension, the wire stretches by

$$\Delta L = \frac{FL_0}{AY} = \frac{(277\ \text{N})(2.85\ \text{m})}{\pi(4.5 \times 10^{-4}\ \text{m})^2\,(1.80 \times 10^{11}\ \text{Pa})} = 6.9 \times 10^{-3}\ \text{m}$$

Hence, the ball misses by

$$2.94 \text{ m} - (2.85 + 0.006\,9 + 0.080) \text{ m} = 0.0031 \text{ m} = 3.1 \text{ mm}$$

To check the approximation we have made, we could use $r = 2.90$ m, its maximum possible value. Then $\Delta L = 6.9$ mm, showing that the approximation has caused a negligible error.

**12.18 [III]** A vertical wire 5.0 m long and of 0.008 8 cm² cross-sectional area has a modulus $Y = 200$ GPa. A 2.0-kg object is fastened to its end and stretches the wire elastically. If the object is now pulled down a little and released, the object undergoes vertical SHM. Find the period of its vibration.

The force constant of the wire acting as a vertical spring is given by $k = F/\Delta L$, where $\Delta L$ is the deformation produced by the force (weight) $F$. But, from $F/A = Y(\Delta L/L_0)$,

$$k = \frac{F}{\Delta L} = \frac{AY}{L_0} = \frac{(8.8\times10^{-7}\ \text{m}^2)(2.00\times10^{11}\ \text{Pa})}{5.0\ \text{m}} = 35\ \text{kN/m}$$

Then for the period we have

$$T = 2\pi\sqrt{\frac{m}{k}} = 2\pi\sqrt{\frac{2.0\ \text{kg}}{35\times10^{3}\ \text{N/m}}} = 0.047\ \text{s}$$

## SUPPLEMENTARY PROBLEMS

**12.19 [I]** Find the density and specific gravity of ethyl alcohol if 63.3 g occupies 80.0 mL.

**12.20 [I]** Determine the volume of 200 g of carbon tetrachloride, for which sp gr = 1.60.

**12.21 [I]** The density of aluminum is 2.70 g/cm³. What volume does 2.00 kg occupy?

**12.22 [I]** Determine the mass of an aluminum cube that is 5.00 cm on each edge. The density of aluminum is 2700 kg/m².

**12.23 [I]** A drum holds 200 kg of water or 132 kg of gasoline. Determine for the gasoline (*a*) its specific gravity and (*b*) $\rho$ in kg/m³.

**12.24 [I]** Air has a density of 1.29 kg/m³ under standard conditions. What is the mass of air in a room with dimensions 10.0 m × 8.00 m × 3.00 m?

**12.25 [I]** What is the density of the material in the nucleus of the hydrogen atom? The nucleus can be considered to be a sphere of radius $1.2 \times 10^{-15}$ m, and its mass is $1.67 \times 10^{-27}$ kg. The volume of a sphere is $(4/3)\pi r^3$.

**12.26 [I]** To determine the inner radius of a uniform capillary tube, the tube is filled with mercury. A column of mercury 2.375 cm long is found to have a mass of 0.24 g. What is the inner radius $r$ of the tube? The density of mercury is 13 600 kg/m³, and the volume of a right circular cylinder is $\pi r^2 h$.

**12.27 [I]** Battery acid has a specific gravity of 1.285 and is 38.0 percent sulfuric acid by weight. What mass of sulfuric acid is contained in a liter of battery acid?

**12.28 [II]** A thin, semitransparent film of gold ($\rho = 19\,300\ \text{kg/m}^3$) has an area of 14.5 $\text{cm}^2$ and a mass of 1.93 mg. (*a*) What is the volume of 1.93 mg of gold? (*b*) What is the thickness of the film in angstroms, where $1\ \text{Å} = 10^{-10}$ m? (*c*) Gold atoms have a diameter of about 5 Å. How many atoms thick is the film?

**12.29 [II]** In an unhealthy, dusty cement mill, there were $2.6 \times 10^9$ dust particles (sp gr = 3.0) per cubic meter of air. Assuming the particles to be spheres of 2.0 $\mu$m diameter, calculate the mass of dust (*a*) in a 20 m $\times$ 15 m $\times$ 8.0 m room and (*b*) inhaled in each average breath of 400-$\text{cm}^3$ volume.

**12.30 [II]** An iron rod 4.00 m long and 0.500 $\text{cm}^2$ in cross section mounted vertically stretches 1.00 mm when a mass of 225 kg is hung from its lower end. Compute Young's modulus for the iron.

**12.31 [II]** A load of 50 kg is applied to the lower end of a vertical steel rod 80 cm long and 0.60 cm in diameter. How much will the rod stretch? $Y = 190$ GPa for steel.

**12.32 [II]** A horizontal rectangular platform is suspended by four identical wires, one at each of its corners. The wires are 3.0 m long and have a diameter of 2.0 mm. Young's modulus for the material of the wires is 180 GPa. How far will the platform drop (due to elongation of the wires) if a 50-kg load is placed at the center of the platform?

**12.33 [II]** Determine the fractional change in volume as the pressure of the atmosphere ($1 \times 10^5$ Pa) around a metal block is reduced to zero by placing the block in vacuum. The bulk modulus for the metal is 125 GPa.

**12.34 [II]** Compute the volume change of a solid copper cube, 40 mm on each edge, when subjected to a pressure of 20 MPa. The bulk modulus for copper is 125 GPa.

**12.35 [II]** The compressibility of water is $5.0 \times 10^{-10}\ \text{m}^2/\text{N}$. Find the decrease in volume of 100 mL of water when subjected to a pressure of 15 MPa.

**12.36 [II]** Two parallel oppositely directed forces, each 4000 N, are applied tangentially to the upper and lower faces of a cubical metal block 25 cm on a side. Find the angle of shear and the displacement of the upper surface relative to the lower surface. The shear modulus for the metal is 80 GPa.

**12.37 [II]** A 60-kg motor sits on four cylindrical rubber blocks. Each cylinder has a height of 3.0 cm and a cross-sectional area of 15 $\text{cm}^2$. The shear modulus for this rubber is 2.0 MPa. (*a*) If a sideways force of 300 N is applied to the motor, how far will it move sideways? (*b*) With what frequency will the motor vibrate back and forth sideways if disturbed?

## ANSWERS TO SUPPLEMENTARY PROBLEMS

**12.19 [I]** 791 $\text{kg/m}^3$, 0.791

**12.20 [I]** 125 mL

**12.21 [I]** 740 $\text{cm}^3$

**12.22 [I]** 0.338 kg

**12.23 [I]** (*a*) 0.660; (*b*) 660 $\text{kg/m}^3$

**12.24 [I]** 310 kg

**12.25 [I]** $2.3 \times 10^{17}$ kg/m$^3$

**12.26 [I]** 0.49 mm

**12.27 [I]** 488 g

**12.28 [II]** (*a*) $1.00 \times 10^{-10}$ m$^3$; (*b*) 690 Å; (*c*) 138 atoms thick

**12.29 [II]** (*a*) 78 g; (*b*) 13 $\mu$g

**12.30 [II]** 176 GPa

**12.31 [II]** 73 $\mu$m

**12.32 [II]** 0.65 mm

**12.33 [II]** $8 \times 10^{-7}$

**12.34 [II]** $-10$ mm$^3$

**12.35 [II]** 0.75 mL

**12.36 [II]** $8.0 \times 10^{-7}$ rad, $2.0 \times 10^{-7}$ m

**12.37 [II]** (*a*) 0.075 cm; (*b*) 13 Hz

# Fluids at Rest

**The Average Pressure** on a surface of area $A$ is defined as the force acting on the area divided by the area, where it is stipulated that the force must be perpendicular (normal) to the area:

$$\text{Average pressure} = \frac{\text{Force acting normal to an area}}{\text{Area over which the force is distributed}}$$

$$P = \frac{F_{\perp}}{A}$$

Recall that the SI unit for pressure is the ***pascal*** (Pa), and 1 Pa = 1 N/m$^2$.

**Standard Atmospheric Pressure** ($P_A$) is $1.01 \times 10^5$ Pa, and this is equivalent to 14.7 lb/in.$^2$. Other units of pressure are

$$1 \text{ atmosphere (atm)} = 1.013 \times 10^5 \text{ Pa}$$

$$1 \text{ torr} = 1 \text{ mm of mercury (mmHg)} = 133.32 \text{ Pa}$$

$$1 \text{ lb/in.}^2 = 6.895 \text{ kPa}$$

**The Hydrostatic Pressure** ($P$) due to a column of fluid of height $h$ and mass density $\rho$ is

$$P = \rho g h$$

Hydrostatic pressure arises from the weight of the column (see Fig. 13-1 which shows a postage stamp submerged a distance $h$ beneath the surface.)

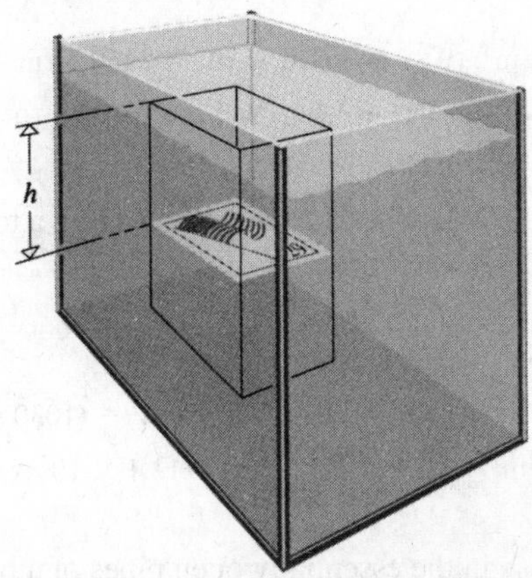


Fig. 13-1

**Pascal's Principle:** When the pressure on any part of a confined fluid (liquid or gas) is changed, the pressure on every other part of the fluid is also changed by the same amount.

**Archimedes' Principle:** A body wholly or partly immersed in a fluid is buoyed up by a force equal to the weight of the fluid it displaces. The buoyant force can be considered to act vertically upward through the center of gravity of the displaced fluid.

$$F_B = \text{Buoyant force} = \text{Weight of displaced fluid}$$

The buoyant force on an object of volume $V$ that is *totally* immersed in a fluid of density $\rho_f$ is $\rho_f Vg$, and the weight of the object is $\rho_0 Vg$, where $\rho_0$ is the density of the object. Therefore, the net force on the submerged object is

$$F_{\text{net}} = \text{Weight} - \text{Buoyant force} = Vg(\rho_0 - \rho_f)$$

## SOLVED PROBLEMS

**13.1 [I]** An 80-kg metal cylinder, 2.0 m long and with each end of area 25 cm$^2$, stands vertically on one end. What pressure does the cylinder exert on the floor?

$$P = \frac{\text{Normal force}}{\text{Area}} = \frac{(80\text{ kg})(9.81\text{ m/s}^2)}{25\times10^{-4}\text{ m}^2} = 3.1\times10^5\text{ Pa}$$

**13.2 [I]** Atmospheric pressure is about $1.0 \times 10^5$ Pa. How large a force does the still air in a room exert on the inside of a window pane that is 40 cm × 80 cm?

The atmosphere exerts a force normal to any surface placed in it. Consequently, the force on the window pane is perpendicular to the pane and is given by

$$F = PA = (1.0 \times 10^5\text{ N/m}^2)(0.40 \times 0.80\text{ m}^2) = 3.2 \times 10^4\text{ N}$$

Of course, a nearly equal force due to the atmosphere on the outside keeps the window from breaking.

**13.3 [I]** Find the pressure due to the fluid at a depth of 76 cm in still (*a*) water ($\rho_w = 1.00\text{ g/cm}^3$) and (*b*) mercury ($\rho = 13.6\text{ g/cm}^3$).

(*a*) $P = \rho_w gh = (1000\text{ kg/m}^3)(9.81\text{ m/s}^2)(0.76\text{ m}) = 7450\text{ N/m}^2 = 7.5\text{ kPa}$

(*b*) $P = \rho gh = (13\,600\text{ kg/m}^3)(9.81\text{ m/s}^2)(0.76\text{ m}) = 1.01 \times 10^5\text{ N/m}^2 \approx 1.0\text{ atm}$

**13.4 [I]** When a submarine dives to a depth of 120 m, to how large a total pressure is its exterior surface subjected? The density of seawater is about $1.03\text{ g/cm}^3$.

$$\begin{aligned} P &= \text{Atmospheric pressure} + \text{Pressure of water} \\ &= 1.01 \times 10^5\text{ N/m}^2 + \rho gh = 1.01 \times 10^5\text{ N/m}^2 + (1030\text{ kg/m}^3)(9.81\text{ m/s}^2)(120\text{ m}) \\ &= 1.01 \times 10^5\text{ N/m}^2 + 12.1 \times 10^5\text{ N/m}^2 = 13.1 \times 10^5\text{ N/m}^2 = 1.31\text{ MPa} \end{aligned}$$

**13.5 [I]** How high would water rise in the essentially open pipes of a building if the water pressure gauge shows the pressure at the ground floor to be 270 kPa (about 40 lb/in.$^2$)?

Water pressure gauges read the excess pressure just due to the water, that is, the difference between the absolute pressure in the water and the pressure of the atmosphere. The water pressure at the bottom of the highest column that can be supported is 270 kPa. Therefore, $P = \rho_w gh$ gives

$$h = \frac{P}{\rho_w g} = \frac{2.70 \times 10^5 \text{ N/m}^2}{(1000 \text{ kg/m}^3)(9.81 \text{ m/s}^2)} = 27.5 \text{ m}$$

**13.6 [I]** A reservoir dam holds an 8.00-km$^2$ lake behind it. Just behind the dam, the lake is 12.0 m deep. What is the water pressure (*a*) at the base of the dam and (*b*) at a point 3.0 m down from the lake's surface?

The area of the lake behind the dam has no effect on the pressure against the dam. At any point, $P = \rho_w gh$.

(*a*) $P = (1000 \text{ kg/m}^3)(9.81 \text{ m/s}^2)(12.0 \text{ m}) = 118 \text{ kPa}$

(*b*) $P = (1000 \text{ kg/m}^3)(9.81 \text{ m/s}^2)(3.0 \text{ m}) = 29 \text{ kPa}$

**13.7 [II]** A mass (or load) acting downward on a piston confines a fluid of density $\rho$ in a closed container, as shown in Fig. 13-2. The combined weight of the piston and load on the right is 200 N, and the cross-sectional area of the piston is $A = 8.0 \text{ cm}^2$. Find the total pressure at point-*B* if the fluid is mercury and $h = 25$ cm ($\rho_{Hg} = 13\,600 \text{ kg/m}^3$). What would an ordinary pressure gauge read at *B*?

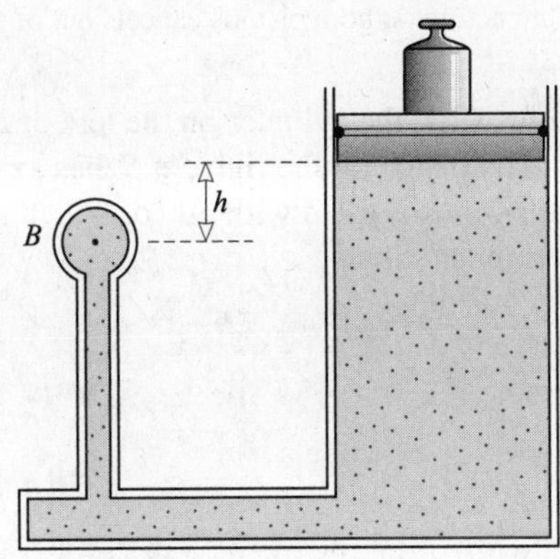


Fig. 13-2

Recall what Pascal's principle tells us about the pressure applied to the fluid by the piston and atmosphere: This added pressure is applied at all points within the fluid. Therefore, the total pressure at *B* is composed of three parts:

$$\text{Pressure of the atmosphere} = 1.0 \times 10^5 \text{ Pa}$$

$$\text{Pressure due to the piston and load} = \frac{F_W}{A} = \frac{200 \text{ N}}{8.0 \times 10^{-4} \text{ m}^2} = 2.5 \times 10^5 \text{ Pa}$$

$$\text{Pressure due to the height } h \text{ of fluid} = h\rho g = 0.33 \times 10^5 \text{ Pa}$$

In this case, the pressure of the fluid itself is relatively small. We have

$$\text{Total pressure at } B = 3.8 \times 10^5 \text{ Pa}$$

The gauge pressure does not include atmospheric pressure. Therefore,

$$\text{Gauge pressure at } B = 2.8 \times 10^5 \text{ Pa}$$

**13.8 [I]** In a hydraulic press such as the one shown in Fig. 13-3, the large piston has cross-sectional area $A_1 = 200\ \text{cm}^2$ and the small piston has cross-sectional area $A_2 = 5.0\ \text{cm}^2$. If a force of 250 N is applied to the small piston, find the force $F_1$ on the large piston.

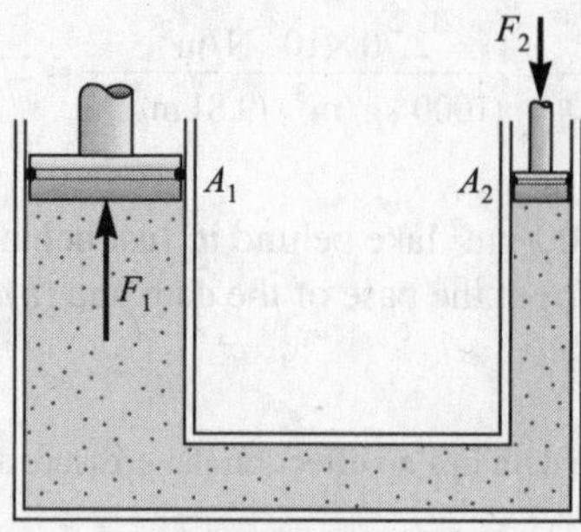


Fig. 13-3

By Pascal's principle,

$$\text{Pressure under large piston} = \text{Pressure under small piston} \quad \text{or} \quad \frac{F_1}{A_1} = \frac{F_2}{A_2}$$

so that

$$F_1 = \frac{A_1}{A_2} F_2 = \frac{200}{5.0}\, 250\ \text{N} = 10\ \text{kN}$$

Note that atmospheric pressure acting on both pistons cancels out of the calculation.

**13.9 [II]** For the system shown in Fig. 13-4, the cylinder on the left, at $L$, has a mass of 600 kg and a cross-sectional area of 800 cm². The piston on the right, at $S$, has a cross-sectional area of 25 cm² and a negligible weight. If the apparatus is filled with oil ($\rho = 0.78\ \text{g/cm}^3$), find the force $F$ required to hold the system in equilibrium as shown.

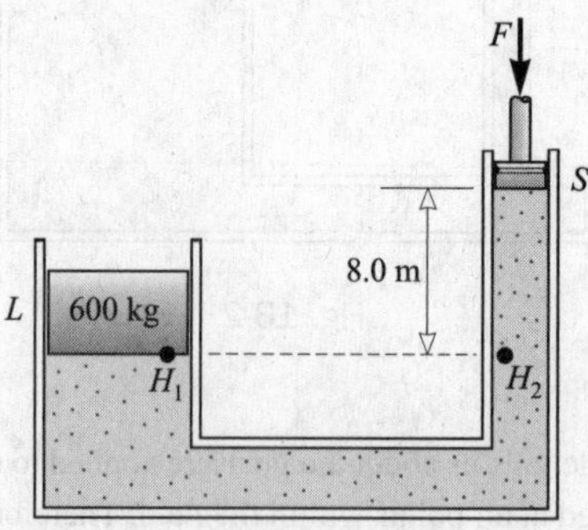


Fig. 13-4

The pressures at points $H_1$ and $H_2$ are equal because they are at the same level in a single connected fluid. Therefore,

$$\text{Pressure at } H_1 = \text{Pressure at } H_2$$

$$\begin{pmatrix}\text{Pressure due to}\\ \text{left piston}\end{pmatrix} = \begin{pmatrix}\text{Pressure due to } F\\ \text{and right piston}\end{pmatrix} + (\text{Pressure due to 8.0 m of oil})$$

$$\frac{(600)(9.81)\ \text{N}}{0.080\,0\ \text{m}^2} = \frac{F}{25 \times 10^{-4}\ \text{m}^2} + (8.0\ \text{m})(780\ \text{kg/m}^3)(9.81\ \text{m/s}^2)$$

from which $F = 31$ N.

**13.10 [I]** A barrel will rupture when the gauge pressure within it reaches 350 kPa. It is attached to the lower end of a vertical pipe, with the pipe and barrel filled with oil ($\rho = 890 \text{ kg/m}^3$). How long can the pipe be if the barrel is not to rupture?

From $P = \rho gh$ we have

$$h = \frac{P}{\rho g} = \frac{350 \times 10^3 \text{ N/m}^2}{(9.81 \text{ m/s}^2)(890 \text{ kg/m}^3)} = 40.1 \text{ m}$$

**13.11 [II]** A vertical test tube has 2.0 cm of oil ($\rho = 0.80 \text{ g/cm}^3$) floating on 8.0 cm of water. What is the pressure at the bottom of the tube due to the liquid in it?

$$P = \rho_1 g h_1 + \rho_2 g h_2 = (800 \text{ kg/m}^3)(9.81 \text{ m/s}^2)(0.020 \text{ m}) + (1000 \text{ kg/m}^3)(9.81 \text{ m/s}^2)(0.080 \text{ m})$$
$$= 0.94 \text{ kPa}$$

**13.12 [II]** As shown in Fig. 13-5, a column of water 40 cm high supports a 31-cm column of an unknown liquid. What is the density of that liquid?

The pressures at point-$A$ due to the two fluids must be equal (or the one with the higher pressure would push the lower-pressure fluid away). Therefore,

$$\text{Pressure due to water} \times \text{Pressure due to unknown liquid}$$
$$\rho_1 g h_1 = \rho_2 g h_2$$

from which $$\rho_2 = \frac{h_1}{h_2}\rho_1 = \frac{40}{31}(1000 \text{ kg/m}^3) = 1290 \text{ kg/m}^3 = 1.3 \times 10^3 \text{ kg/m}^3$$

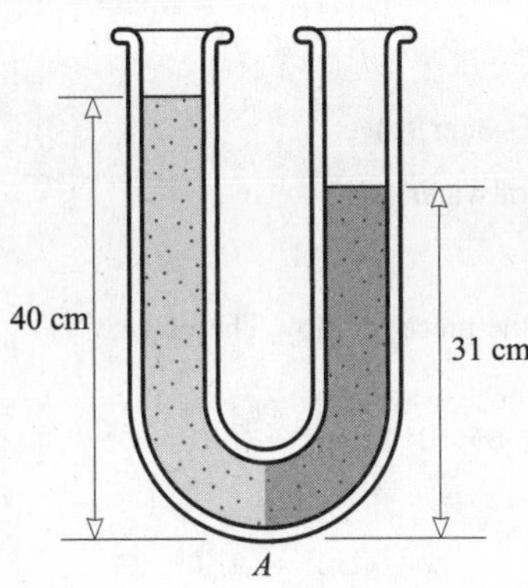


Fig. 13-5

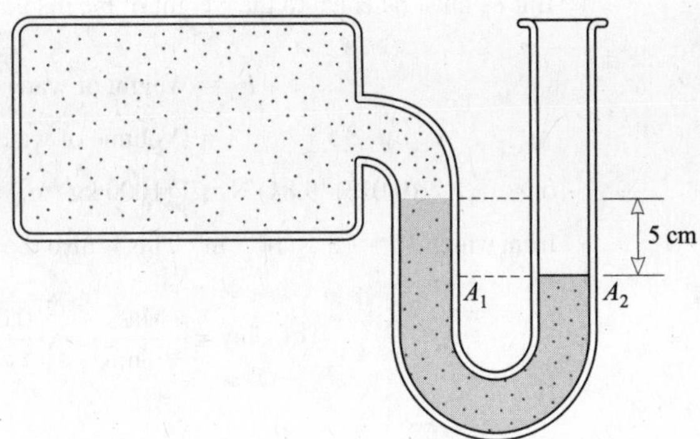


Fig. 13-6

**13.13 [II]** The U-tube device connected to the tank in Fig. 13-6 is called a *manometer*. As you can see, the mercury in the tube stands higher in one side than the other. What is the pressure in the tank if atmospheric pressure is 76 cm of mercury? The density of mercury is 13.6 g/cm³.

$$\text{Pressure at } A_1 = \text{Pressure at } A_2$$
$$(P \text{ in tank}) + (P \text{ due to 5 cm mercury}) = (P \text{ due to atmosphere})$$
$$P + (0.05 \text{ m})(13\,600 \text{ kg/m}^3)(9.81 \text{ m/s}^2) = (0.76 \text{ m})(13\,600 \text{ kg/m}^3)(9.81 \text{ m/s}^2)$$

from which $P = 95$ kPa.

Or, more simply perhaps, we could note that the pressure in the tank is 5.0 cm of mercury *lower* than atmospheric. So the pressure is 71 cm of mercury, which is 94.6 kPa.

**13.14 [II]** The mass of a block of aluminum is 25.0 g. (*a*) What is its volume? (*b*) What will be the tension in a string that suspends the block when the block is totally submerged in water? The density of aluminum is 2700 kg/m³.

This problem is basically about buoyant force. (*a*) Because $\rho = m/V$, we have

$$V = \frac{m}{\rho} = \frac{0.025\,0 \text{ kg}}{2700 \text{ kg/m}^3} = 9.26 \times 10^{-6} \text{ m}^3 = 9.26 \text{ cm}^3$$

(*b*) The block displaces $9.26 \times 10^{-6}$ m³ of water when submerged, so the buoyant force on it is

$$F_B = \text{Weight of displaced water} = (\text{Volume})(\rho \text{ of water})(g)$$
$$= (9.26 \times 10^{-6} \text{ m}^3)(1000 \text{ kg/m}^3)(9.81 \text{ m/s}^2) = 0.090\,8 \text{ N}$$

The tension in the supporting cord plus the buoyant force must equal the weight of the block if it is to be in equilibrium (see Fig. 13-7). That is, $F_T + F_B = mg$, from which

$$F_T = mg - F_B = (0.025\,0 \text{ kg})(9.81 \text{ m/s}^2) - 0.090\,8 \text{ N} = 0.154 \text{ N}$$

**13.15 [II]** Using a scale, a piece of alloy has a measured mass of 86 g in air and 73 g when immersed in water. Find its volume and its density.

The apparent change in measured mass is due to the buoyant force of the water. Figure 13-7 shows the situation when the object is in water. From the figure, $F_B + F_T = mg$, so

$$F_B = (0.086)(9.81) \text{ N} - (0.073)(9.81) \text{ N} = (0.013)(9.81) \text{ N}$$

But $F_B$ must be equal to the weight of the displaced water.

$$F_B = \text{Weight of water} = (\text{Mass of water})(g)$$
$$= (\text{Volume of water})(\text{Density of water})(g)$$

or $$(0.013)\,(9.81) \text{ N} = V(1000 \text{ kg/m}^3)\,(9.81 \text{ m/s}^2)$$

from which $V = 1.3 \times 10^{-5}$ m³. This is also the volume of the piece of alloy. Therefore,

$$\rho \text{ of alloy} = \frac{\text{Mass}}{\text{Volume}} = \frac{0.086 \text{ kg}}{1.3 \times 10^{-5} \text{m}^3} = 6.6 \times 10^3 \text{ kg/m}^3$$

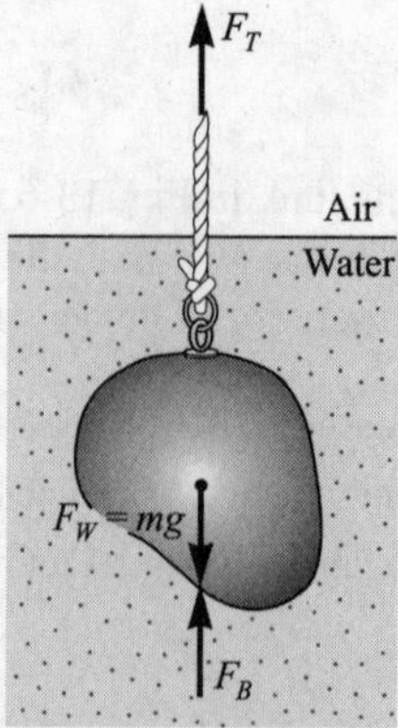


Fig. 13.7

**13.16 [II]** A solid aluminum cylinder with $\rho = 2700\ \text{kg/m}^3$ has a measured mass of 67 g in air and 45 g when immersed in turpentine. Determine the density of turpentine.

The $F_B$ acting on the immersed cylinder is

$$F_B = (0.067 - 0.045)(9.81)\ \text{N} = (0.022)(9.81)\ \text{N}$$

This is also the weight of the displaced turpentine.

The volume of the cylinder is, from $\rho = m/V$,

$$V \text{ of cylinder} = \frac{m}{\rho} = \frac{0.067\ \text{kg}}{2700\ \text{kg/m}^3} = 2.5\times10^{-5}\ \text{m}^3$$

This is also the volume of the displaced turpentine. We therefore have, for the turpentine,

$$\rho = \frac{\text{Mass}}{\text{Volume}} = \frac{(\text{Weight})/g}{\text{Volume}} = \frac{(0.022)\,(9.81)/(9.81)}{2.48\times10^{-5}}\frac{\text{kg}}{\text{m}^3} = 8.9\times10^2\ \text{kg/m}^3$$

**13.17 [II]** A glass stopper has a mass of 2.50 g when measured in air, 1.50 g in water, and 0.70 g in sulfuric acid. What is the density of the acid? What is its specific gravity?

The $F_B$ on the stopper in water is (0.002 50 − 0.001 50)(9.81) N. This is the weight of the displaced water. Since $\rho = m/V$, or $\rho g = F_W/V$,

$$\text{Volume of stopper} = \text{Volume of displaced water} = \frac{\text{weight}}{\rho g}$$

$$V = \frac{(0.001\,00)\,(9.81)\ \text{N}}{(1000\ \text{kg/m}^3)\,(9.81\ \text{m/s}^2)} = 1.00\times10^{-6}\ \text{m}^3$$

The buoyant force in acid is

$$[(2.50 - 0.70) \times 10^{-3}]\,(9.81)\ \text{N} = (0.001\,80)\,(9.81)\ \text{N}$$

But this is equal to the weight of displaced acid, $mg$. Since $\rho = m/V$, and since $m = 0.001\,80$ kg and $V = 1.00 \times 10^{-6}\ \text{m}^3$,

$$\rho \text{ of acid} = \frac{0.001\,80\ \text{kg}}{1.00\times10^{-6}\ \text{m}^3} = 1.8\times10^3\ \text{kg/m}^3$$

Then, for the acid,

$$\text{sp gr} = \frac{\rho \text{ of acid}}{\rho \text{ of water}} = \frac{1800}{1000} = 1.8$$

**Alternative Method**

$$\text{Weight of displaced water} = [(2.50 - 1.50) \times 10^{-3}](9.81)\ \text{N}$$
$$\text{Weight of displaced acid} = [(2.50 - 0.70) \times 10^{-3}](9.81)\ \text{N}$$

so
$$\text{sp gr of acid} = \frac{\text{Weight of displaced acid}}{\text{Weight of equal volume of displaced water}} = \frac{1.80}{1.00} = 1.8$$

Then, since sp gr of acid = ($\rho$ of acid)/($\rho$ of water),

$$\rho \text{ of acid} = (\text{sp gr of acid})(\rho \text{ of water}) = (1.8)(1000\ \text{kg/m}^3) = 1.8 \times 10^3\ \text{kg/m}^3$$

**13.18 [II]** The density of ice is 917 kg/m$^3$. What fraction of the volume of a piece of ice will be above the liquid when floating in fresh water?

The piece of ice will float in the water, since its density is less than 1000 kg/m$^3$, the density of water. As it does,

$$F_B = \text{Weight of displaced water} = \text{Weight of piece of ice}$$

But the weight of the ice is $\rho_{\text{ice}} g V$, where $V$ is the volume of the piece. In addition, the weight of the displaced water is $\rho_w g V'$, where $V'$ is the volume of the displaced water. Substituting into the above equation

$$\rho_{\text{ice}} g V = \rho_w g V'$$

$$V' = \frac{\rho_{\text{ice}}}{\rho_w} V = \frac{917}{1000} V = 0.917\,V$$

The fraction of the volume that is above water is then

$$\frac{V - V'}{V} = \frac{V - 0.917\,V}{V} = 1 - 0.917 = 0.083 \quad \text{or} \quad 8.3\%$$

**13.19 [II]** A 60-kg rectangular box, open at the top, has base dimensions of 1.0 m by 0.80 m and a depth of 0.50 m. (*a*) How deep will it sink in fresh water? (*b*) What weight $F_{Wb}$ of ballast will cause it to sink to a depth of 30 cm?

(*a*) Assuming that the box floats,

$$F_B = \text{Weight of displaced water} = \text{Weight of box}$$

$$(1000\ \text{kg/m}^3)\,(9.81\ \text{m/s}^2)\,(1.0\ \text{m} \times 0.80\ \text{m} \times y) = (60\ \text{kg})\,(9.81\ \text{m/s}^2)$$

where $y$ is the depth the box sinks. Solving yields $y = 0.075$ m. Because this is smaller than 0.50 m, our assumption is shown to be correct.

(*b*) $F_B$ = weight of box + weight of ballast

But the $F_B$ is equal to the weight of the displaced water. Therefore, the above equation becomes

$$(1000\ \text{kg/m}^3)(9.81\ \text{m/s}^2)(1.0\ \text{m} \times 0.80\ \text{m} \times 0.30\ \text{m}) = (60)(9.81)\ \text{N} + F_{Wb}$$

from which $F_{Wb} = 1760\ \text{N} = 1.8\ \text{kN}$. The ballast must have a mass of $(1760/9.81)\ \text{kg} = 180\ \text{kg}$.

**13.20 [III]** A foam plastic ($\rho_p = 0.58\ \text{g/cm}^3$) is to be used as a life preserver. What volume of plastic must be used if it is to keep 20 percent (by volume) of an 80-kg man above water in a lake? The average density of the man is 1.04 g/cm$^3$.

Keep in mind that a density of 1 g/cm$^3$ equals 1000 kg/m$^3$. At equilibrium

$$F_B \text{ on man} + FB \text{ on plastic} = \text{Weight of man} + \text{Weight of plastic}$$

$$(\rho_w)(0.80\,V_m)g + \rho_w V_p g = \rho_m V_m g + \rho_p V_p g$$

or

$$(\rho_w - \rho_p)V_p = (\rho_m - 0.80\rho_w)V_m$$

where subscripts $m$, $w$, and $p$ refer to man, water, and plastic, respectively.

But $\rho_m V_m = 80$ kg and so $V_m = (80/1040)\ \text{m}^3$. Substitution gives

$$[(1000 - 580)\ \text{kg/m}^3]V_p = [(1040 - 800)\ \text{kg/m}^3][(80/1040)\ \text{m}^3]$$

from which $V_p = 0.044\ \text{m}^3$.

**13.21 [III]** A partly filled beaker of water sits on a scale, and its weight is 2.30 N. When a piece of metal suspended from a thread is totally immersed in the beaker (but not touching bottom), the scale reads 2.75 N. What is the volume of the metal?

The water exerts an upward buoyant force on the metal. According to Newton's Third Law of action and reaction, the metal exerts an equal downward force on the water. It is this force that increases the scale reading from 2.30 N to 2.75 N. Hence the buoyant force is $2.75 - 2.30 = 0.45$ N. Then, because

$$F_B = \text{weight of displaced water} = \rho_w g V = (1000\ \text{kg/m}^3)(9.81\ \text{m/s}^2)(V)$$

we have the volume of the displaced water, and of the piece of metal, namely,

$$V = \frac{0.45\ \text{N}}{9810\ \text{kg/m}^2\cdot\text{s}^2} = 46\times10^{-6}\ \text{m}^3 = 46\ \text{cm}^3$$

**13.22 [II]** A piece of pure gold ($\rho = 19.3\ \text{g/cm}^3$) is suspected to have a hollow center. It has a mass of 38.25 g when measured in air and 36.22 g in water. What is the volume of the central hole in the gold?

Remember that you go from a density in $\text{g/cm}^3$ to $\text{kg/m}^3$ by multiplying by 1000. From $\rho = m/V$,

$$\text{Actual volume of 38.25 g of gold} = \frac{0.038\ 25\ \text{kg}}{19\ 300\ \text{kg/m}^3} = 1.982\times10^{-6}\ \text{m}^3$$

$$\text{Volume of displaced water} = \frac{(38.25 - 36.22)\times10^{-3}\ \text{kg}}{1000\ \text{kg/m}^3} = 2.030\times10^{-6}\ \text{m}^3$$

$$\text{Volume of hole} = (2.030 - 1.982)\ \text{cm}^3 = 0.048\ \text{cm}^3$$

**13.23 [III]** A wooden cylinder has a mass $m$ and a base area $A$. It floats in water with its axis vertical. Show that the cylinder undergoes SHM if given a small vertical displacement. Find the frequency of its motion.

When the cylinder is pushed down a distance $y$, it displaces an additional volume $Ay$ of water. Because this additional displaced volume has mass $Ay\rho_w$, an additional buoyant force $Ay\rho_w g$ acts on the cylinder, where $\rho_w$ is the density of water. This is an unbalanced force on the cylinder and is a restoring force. In addition, the force is proportional to the displacement and so is a Hooke's Law force. Therefore, the cylinder will undergo SHM, as described in Chapter 11.

Comparing $F_B = A\rho_w g y$ with Hooke's Law in the form $F = ky$, we see that the elastic constant for the motion is $k = A\rho_w g$. This, acting on the cylinder of mass $m$, causes it to have a vibrational frequency of

$$f = \frac{1}{2\pi}\sqrt{\frac{k}{m}} = \frac{1}{2\pi}\sqrt{\frac{A\rho_w g}{m}}$$

**13.24 [II]** What must be the volume $V$ of a 5.0-kg balloon filled with helium ($\rho_{He} = 0.178\ kg/m^3$) if it is to lift a 30-kg load? Use $\rho_{air} = 1.29\ kg/m^3$.

The buoyant force, $V\rho_{air}g$, must lift the weight of the balloon, its load, and the helium within it:

$$V\rho_{air}g = (35\ kg)(g) + V\rho_{He}g$$

which gives
$$V = \frac{35\ kg}{\rho_{air} - \rho_{He}} = \frac{35\ kg}{1.11\ kg/m^3} = 32\ m^3$$

**13.25 [III]** Find the density $\rho$ of a fluid at a depth $h$ in terms of its density $\rho_0$ at the surface.

If a mass $m$ of fluid has volume $V_0$ at the surface, then it will have volume $V_0 - \Delta V$ at a depth $h$. The density at depth $h$ is then

$$\rho = \frac{m}{V_0 - \Delta V} \qquad \text{while} \qquad \rho_0 = \frac{m}{V_0}$$

which gives
$$\frac{\rho}{\rho_0} = \frac{V_0}{V_0 - \Delta V} = \frac{1}{1 - (\Delta V/V_0)}$$

However, from Chapter 12, the bulk modulus is $B = P/(\Delta V/V_0)$ and so $\Delta V/V_0 = P/B$. Making this substitution, we obtain

$$\frac{\rho}{\rho_0} = \frac{1}{1 - P/B}$$

If we assume that $\rho$ is close to $\rho_0$, then the pressure at depth $h$ is approximately $\rho_0 gh$, and so

$$\frac{\rho}{\rho_0} = \frac{1}{1 - (\rho_0 gh/B)}$$

## SUPPLEMENTARY PROBLEMS

**13.26 [I]** A 60-kg performer balances on a cane. The end of the cane in contact with the floor has an area of $0.92\ cm^2$. Find the pressure exerted on the floor by the cane. (Neglect the weight of the cane.)

**13.27 [I]** A certain town receives its water directly from a water tower. If the top of the water in the tower is 26.0 m above the water faucet in a house, what should be the water pressure at the faucet? (Neglect the effects of other water users.)

**13.28 [II]** At a height of 10 km (33 000 ft) above sea level, atmospheric pressure is about 210 mm of mercury. What is the net resultant normal force on a $600\ cm^2$ window of an airplane flying at this height? Assume the pressure inside the plane is 760 mm of mercury. The density of mercury is $13\ 600\ kg/m^3$.

**13.29 [II]** A narrow tube is sealed onto a tank as shown in Fig. 13-8. The base of the tank has an area of $80\ cm^2$. (*a*) Remembering that pressure is determined by the height of the column of liquid, find the force on the bottom of the tank due to oil when the tank and capillary are filled with oil ($\rho = 0.72\ g/cm^3$) to the height $h_1$. (*b*) Repeat for an oil height of $h_2$.

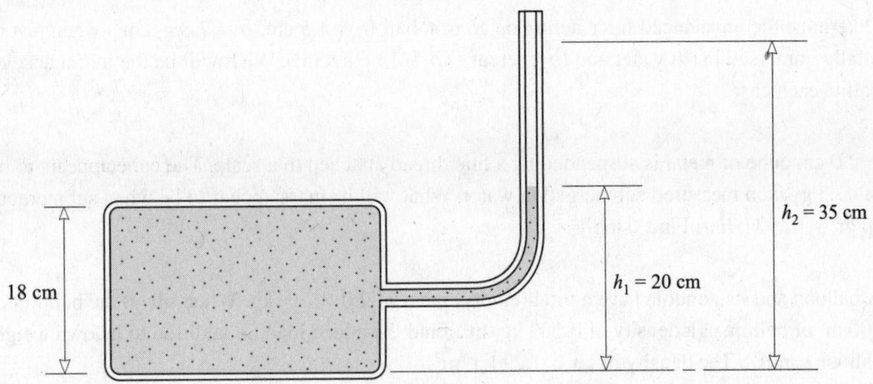


Fig. 13.8

**13.30 [II]** Repeat Problem 13.29, but now find the force on the top wall of the tank due to the oil.

**13.31 [II]** Compute the pressure required for a water supply system that will raise water 50.0 m vertically.

**13.32 [II]** The area of a piston of a force pump is 8.0 cm$^2$. What force must be applied to the piston to raise oil ($\rho = 0.78 \text{ g/cm}^2$) to a height of 6.0 m? Assume the upper end of the oil is open to the atmosphere.

**13.33 [II]** The diameter of the large piston of a hydraulic press is 20 cm, and the area of the small piston is 0.50 cm$^2$. If a force of 400 N is applied to the small piston, (*a*) what is the resulting force exerted on the large piston? (*b*) What is the increase in pressure underneath the small piston? (*c*) Underneath the large piston?

**13.34 [II]** A metal cube, 2.00 cm on each side, has a density of 6600 kg/m$^3$. Find its apparent mass when it is totally submerged in water.

**13.35 [II]** A solid wooden cube, 30.0 cm on each edge, can be totally submerged in water if it is pushed downward with a force of 54.0 N. What is the density of the wood?

**13.36 [II]** A metal object "weighs" 26.0 g in air and 21.48 g when totally immersed in water. What is the volume of the object? Its mass density?

**13.37 [II]** A solid piece of aluminum ($\rho = 2.70 \text{ g/cm}^3$) has a mass of 8.35 g when measured in air. If it is hung from a thread and submerged in a vat of oil ($\rho = 0.75 \text{ g/cm}^3$), what will be the tension in the thread?

**13.38 [II]** A beaker contains oil of density 0.80 g/cm$^3$. A 1.6-cm cube of aluminum ($\rho = 2.70 \text{ g/cm}^3$) hanging vertically on a thread is submerged in the oil. Find the tension in the thread.

**13.39 [II]** A tank containing oil of sp gr = 0.80 rests on a scale and weighs 78.6 N. By means of a very fine wire, a 6.0 cm cube of aluminum, sp gr = 2.70, is submerged in the oil. Find (*a*) the tension in the wire and (*b*) the scale reading if none of the oil overflows.

**13.40 [II]** Downward forces of 45.0 N and 15.0 N, respectively, are required to keep a plastic block totally immersed in water and in oil, respectively. If the volume of the block is 8000 cm$^3$, find the density of the oil.

**13.41 [III]** Determine the unbalanced force acting on an iron ball ($r = 1.5$ cm, $\rho = 7.8\ \text{g/cm}^3$) when just released while totally immersed in (*a*) water and (*b*) mercury ($\rho = 13.6\ \text{g/cm}^3$). What will be the initial acceleration of the ball in each case?

**13.42 [II]** A 2.0-cm cube of metal is suspended by a fine thread attached to a scale. The cube appears to have a mass of 47.3 g when measured submerged in water. What will its mass appear to be when submerged in glycerin, sp gr = 1.26? [*Hint:* Find $\rho$ too.]

**13.43 [II]** A balloon and its gondola have a total (empty) mass of $2.0 \times 10^2$ kg. When filled, the balloon contains 900 $\text{m}^3$ of helium at a density of $0.183\ \text{kg/m}^3$. Find the added load, in addition to its own weight, that the balloon can lift. The density of air is $1.29\ \text{kg/m}^3$.

**13.44 [I]** A piece of metal has a measured mass of 5.00 g in air, 3.00 g in water, and 3.24 g in benzene. Determine the mass density of the metal and of the benzene.

**13.45 [II]** A spring whose composition is not completely known might be either bronze (sp gr 8.8) or brass (sp gr 8.4). It has a mass of 1.26 g when measured in air and 1.11 g in water. Which is it made of?

**13.46 [II]** What fraction of the volume of a piece of quartz ($\rho = 2.65\ \text{g/cm}^3$) will be submerged when it is floating in a container of mercury ($\rho = 13.6\ \text{g/cm}^3$)?

**13.47 [II]** A cube of wood floating in water supports a 200-g mass resting on the center of its top face. When the mass is removed, the cube rises 2.00 cm. Determine the volume of the cube.

**13.48 [III]** A cork has a measured mass of 5.0 g in air. A sinker has a measured mass of 86 g in water. The cork is attached to the sinker and both together have a measured mass of 71 g when under water. What is the density of the cork?

**13.49 [II]** A glass of water has a 10-$\text{cm}^3$ ice cube floating in it. The glass is filled to the brim with cold water. By the time the ice cube has completely melted, how much water will have flowed out of the glass? The sp gr of ice is 0.92.

**13.50 [II]** A glass tube is bent into the form of a U. A 50.0-cm height of olive oil in one arm is found to balance 46.0 cm of water in the other. What is the density of the olive oil?

**13.51 [II]** On a day when the pressure of the atmosphere is $1.000 \times 10^5$ Pa, a chemist distills a liquid under slightly reduced pressure. The pressure within the distillation chamber is read by an oil-filled manometer (density of oil $= 0.78\ \text{g/cm}^3$). The difference in heights on the two sides of the manometer is 27 cm. What is the pressure in the distillation chamber?

## ANSWERS TO SUPPLEMENTARY PROBLEMS

**13.26 [I]** 6.4 MPa

**13.27 [I]** 255 kPa

**13.28 [II]** 4.4 kN

**13.29 [II]** (*a*) 11 N downward; (*b*) 20 N downward

**13.30 [II]** (*a*) 1.1 N upward; (*b*) 9.6 N upward

**13.31 [II]** 490 kPa

**13.32 [II]** 37 N

**13.33 [II]** (*a*) $2.5 \times 10^5$ N; (*b*) 8.0 MPa; (*c*) 8.0 MPa

**13.34 [II]** 44.8 g

**13.35 [II]** 800 kg/m$^3$

**13.36 [II]** 4.55 cm$^3$, $5.72 \times 10^3$ kg/m$^3$

**13.37 [II]** 0.059 N

**13.38 [II]** 0.076 N

**13.39 [II]** (*a*) 4.0 N; (*b*) 80 N

**13.40 [II]** 620 kg/m$^3$

**13.41 [III]** (*a*) 0.94 N down, 8.6 m/s$^2$ down; (*b*) 0.80 N up, 7.3 m/s$^2$ up

**13.42 [II]** 45 g

**13.43 [II]** 7.8 kN

**13.44 [I]** $2.50 \times 10^3$ kg/m$^3$, 880 kg/m$^3$

**13.45 [II]** brass

**13.46 [II]** 0.195

**13.47 [II]** $1.00 \times 10^3$ cm$^3$

**13.48 [III]** $2.5 \times 10^2$ kg/m$^3$

**13.49 [II]** none

**13.50 [II]** 920 kg/m$^3$

**13.51 [II]** 98 kPa

# Fluids in Motion

**Fluid Flow or Discharge Rate** ($J$): When a fluid that fills a pipe flows through the pipe with an average speed $v$, the *flow rate* $J$ is

$$J = Av$$

where $A$ is the cross-sectional area of the pipe. The units of $J$ are $m^3/s$ in the SI and $ft^3/s$ in U.S. customary units. Sometimes $J$ is called the *rate of flow* or the **discharge rate.**

**Equation of Continuity:** Suppose an *incompressible* (constant-density) fluid fills a pipe and flows through it. Suppose further that the cross-sectional area of the pipe is $A_1$ at one point and $A_2$ at another. Since the flow through $A_1$ must equal the flow through $A_2$, one has

$$J = A_1 v_1 = A_2 v_2 = \text{constant}$$

where $v_1$ and $v_2$ are the average fluid speeds across $A_1$ and $A_2$, respectively.

**The Shear Rate** of a fluid is the rate at which the shear strain within the fluid is changing. Because strain has no units, the SI unit for shear rate is $s^{-1}$.

**The Viscosity** ($\eta$) of a fluid is a measure of how large a shear stress is required to produce a shear rate of one. Its unit is that of stress per unit shear rate, or $Pa \cdot s$ in the SI. Another SI unit is the $N \cdot s/m^2$ (or $kg/m \cdot s$), called the *poiseuille* (Pl): 1 Pl = 1 $kg/m \cdot s$ = 1 $Pa \cdot s$. Other units used are the *poise* (P), where 1 P = 0.1, and the *centipoise* (cP), where 1 cP = $10^{-3}$ Pl. A viscous fluid, such as tar, has a large $\eta$.

**Poiseuille's Law:** The fluid flow through a cylindrical pipe of length $L$ and cross-sectional radius $r$ is given by

$$J = \frac{\pi r^4 (P_i - P_o)}{8\eta L}$$

where $P_i - P_o$ is the pressure difference between the two ends of the pipe (input minus output).

**The Work Done by a Piston** in forcing a volume $V$ of fluid into a cylinder against an opposing pressure $P$ is given by $PV$.

**The Work Done by a Pressure** $P$ acting on a surface of area $A$ as the surface moves through a distance $\Delta x$ normal to the surface (thereby displacing a volume $A\Delta x = \Delta V$) is

$$\text{Work} = PA\,\Delta x = P\,\Delta V$$

**Bernoulli's Equation** for the steady flow of a continuous stream of fluid: Consider two different points along the stream path. Let point-1 be at a height $h_1$ and let $v_1$, $\rho_1$, and $P_1$ be the fluid-speed, density, and absolute pressure at that point. Similarly define $h_2$, $v_2$, $\rho_2$, and $P_2$ for point-2. Then, provided the fluid is incompressible and has negligible viscosity,

$$P_1 + \tfrac{1}{2}\rho v_1^2 + h_1\rho g = P_2 + \tfrac{1}{2}\rho v_2^2 + h_2\rho g$$

where $\rho_1 = \rho_2 = \rho$ and $g$ is the acceleration due to gravity.

**Torricelli's Theorem:** Suppose that a tank contains liquid and is open to the atmosphere at its top. If an orifice (opening) exists in the tank at a distance $h$ below the top of the liquid, then the speed of *outflow* from the orifice is $\sqrt{2gh}$, provided the liquid obeys Bernoulli's Equation and the tank is big enough so that the top of the liquid may be regarded as essentially motionless.

**The Reynolds Number** ($N_R$) is a dimensionless number that applies to a fluid of viscosity $\eta$ and density $\rho$ flowing with speed $v$ through a pipe (or past an obstacle) with diameter $D$:

$$N_R = \frac{\rho v D}{\eta}$$

For systems of the same geometry, flows will usually be similar provided their Reynolds numbers are close. *Turbulent flow* occurs if $N_R$ for the flow exceeds about 2000 for pipes or about 10 for obstacles.

## SOLVED PROBLEMS

**14.1 [I]** Oil flows through a pipe 8.0 cm in diameter, at an average speed of 4.0 m/s. What is the flow rate, $J$, in $\mathrm{m^3/s}$ and $\mathrm{m^3/h}$?

$$J = Av = \pi(0.040\ \mathrm{m})^2\,(4.0\ \mathrm{m/s}) = 0.020\ \mathrm{m^3/s}$$
$$= (0.020\ \mathrm{m^3/s})\,(3600\ \mathrm{s/h}) = 72\ \mathrm{m^3/h}$$

**14.2 [I]** Exactly 250 mL of fluid flows out of a tube whose inner diameter is 7.0 mm in a time of 41 s. What is the average speed of the fluid in the tube?

From $J = Av$, since $1\ \mathrm{mL} = 10^{-6}\ \mathrm{m^3}$,

$$v = \frac{J}{A} = \frac{(250\times10^{-6}\ \mathrm{m^3})/(41\ \mathrm{s})}{\pi(0.003\,5\ \mathrm{m})^2} = 0.16\ \mathrm{m/s}$$

**14.3 [I]** A 14-cm inner diameter (i.d.) water main furnishes water to a 1.00 cm i.d. (i.e., inner diameter) faucet pipe. If the average speed in the faucet pipe is 3.0 cm/s, what will be the average speed it causes in the water main?

The two flows are equal. From the Continuity Equation,

$$J = A_1v_1 = A_2v_2$$

Letting 1 be the faucet and 2 be the water main, we have

$$v_2 = v_1\frac{A_1}{A_2} = v_1\frac{\pi r_1^2}{\pi r_2^2} = (3.0\ \mathrm{cm/s})\left(\frac{1}{14}\right)^2 = 0.015\ \mathrm{cm/s}$$

**14.4 [II]** How much water will flow in 30.0 s through 200 mm of capillary tube of 1.50 mm i.d., if the pressure differential across the tube is 5.00 cm of mercury? The viscosity of water is 0.801 cP and $\rho$ for mercury is 13 600 kg/m³.

We shall make use of Poiseuille's Law, $J = \pi r^4 (P_i - P_o)/8\eta L$, and therefore,

$$P_i - P_o = (\rho gh = (13\,600 \text{ kg}/m^3)(9.81 \text{ m/s}^2)(0.050\,0 \text{ m}) = 6660 \text{ N/m}^2$$

The viscosity expressed in kg/m·s is

$$\eta = (0.801 \text{ cP})\left(10^{-3} \frac{\text{kg/m}\cdot\text{s}}{\text{cP}}\right) = 8.01 \times 10^{-4} \text{ kg/m}\cdot\text{s}$$

Thus,

$$J = \frac{\pi r^4 (P_i - P_o)}{8\eta L} = \frac{\pi (7.5 \times 10^{-4} \text{ m})^4 (6660 \text{ N/m}^2)}{8(8.01 \times 10^{-4} \text{ kg/m}\cdot\text{s})(0.200 \text{ m})} = 5.2 \times 10^{-6} \text{ m}^3/\text{s} = 5.2 \text{ mL/s}$$

In 30.0 s, the quantity that would flow out of the tube is $(5.2 \text{ mL/s})(30 \text{ s}) = 1.6 \times 10^2$ mL.

**14.5 [II]** An artery in a person has been reduced to half its original inside diameter by deposits on the inner artery wall. By what factor will the blood flow through the artery be reduced if the pressure differential across the artery has remained unchanged?

The relationship governing flow rate, pressure differential, and opening radius is Poiseuille's Law, wherein $J \propto r^4$. Therefore,

$$\frac{J_{\text{final}}}{J_{\text{original}}} = \left(\frac{r_{\text{final}}}{r_{\text{original}}}\right)^4 = \left(\frac{1}{2}\right)^4 = 0.0625$$

**14.6 [II]** Under the same pressure differential, compare the flow of water through a pipe to the flow of SAE No. 10 oil. $\eta$ for water is 0.801 cP; $\eta$ for the oil is 200 cP.

From Poiseuille's Law, $J \propto 1/\eta$. Therefore, since everything else cancels,

$$\frac{J_{\text{water}}}{J_{\text{oil}}} = \frac{200 \text{ cP}}{0.801 \text{ cP}} = 250$$

The flow of water is 250 times as large as that of the oil under the same pressure differential.

**14.7 [II]** Calculate the power output of the heart if, in each heartbeat, it pumps 75 mL of blood at an average pressure of 100 mmHg. Assume 65 heartbeats per minute.

The work done by the heart is $P\Delta V$. In one minute, $\Delta V = (65)(75 \times 10^{-6} \text{ m}^3)$. Also

$$P = (100 \text{ mmHg}) \frac{1.01 \times 10^5 \text{ Pa}}{760 \text{ mmHg}} = 1.33 \times 10^4 \text{ Pa}$$

consequently $$\text{Power} = \frac{\text{Work}}{\text{Time}} = \frac{(1.33 \times 10^4 \text{ Pa})[(65)(75 \times 10^{-6} \text{ m}^3)]}{60 \text{ s}} = 1.1 \text{ W}$$

**14.8 [II]** What volume of water will escape per minute from an open-top tank through an opening 3.0 cm in diameter that is 5.0 m below the water level in the tank? (See Fig. 14-1.)

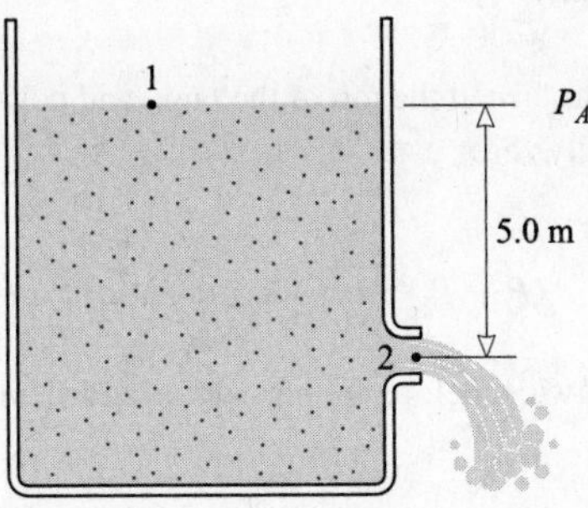


Fig. 14-1

There is a steady flow of fluid, and therefore we can use Bernoulli's Equation, with 1 representing the top level and 2 the orifice. The pressure at the outlet inside the free jet is atmospheric. Then $P_1 = P_2$ and $h_1 = 5.0$ m, $h_2 = 0$.

$$P_1 + \tfrac{1}{2}\rho v_1^2 + h_1\rho g = P_2 + \tfrac{1}{2}\rho v_2^2 + h_2\rho g$$

$$\tfrac{1}{2}\rho v_1^2 + h_1\rho g = \tfrac{1}{2}\rho v_2^2 + h_2\rho g$$

If the tank is large, $v_1$ can be approximated as zero. Then, solving for $v_2$, we obtain Torricelli's Equation:

$$v_2 = \sqrt{2g(h_1 - h_2)} = \sqrt{2(9.81\text{ m/s}^2)(5.0\text{ m})} = 9.9\text{ m/s}$$

and the flow is given by

$$J = v_2 A_2 = (9.9\text{ m/s})\pi(1.5 \times 10^{-2}\text{ m})^2 = 7.0 \times 10^{-3}\text{ m}^3\text{/s} = 0.42\text{ m}^3\text{/min}$$

**14.9 [II]** An open water tank in air springs a leak at position-2 in Fig. 14-2, where the pressure due to the water at position-1 is 500 kPa. What is the velocity of escape of the water through the hole?

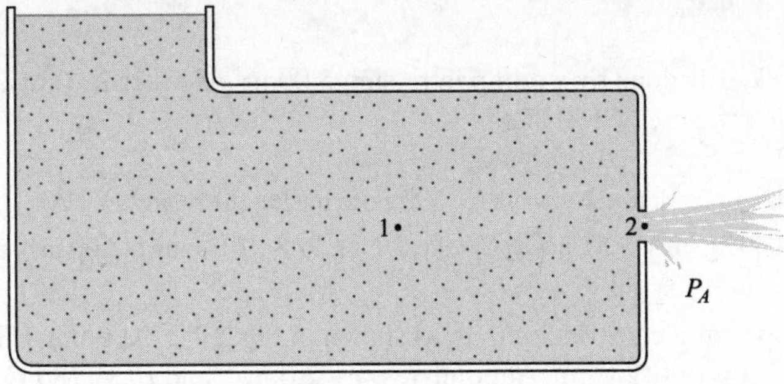


Fig. 14-2

The pressure at position-2 in the free jet is atmospheric. We use Bernoulli's Equation with $P_1 - P_2 = 5.00 \times 10^5$ N/m$^2$, $h_1 = h_2$, and the approximation $v_1 = 0$. Then

$$(P_1 - P_2) + (h_1 - h_2)\rho g = \tfrac{1}{2}\rho v_2^2$$

whence $$v_2 = \sqrt{\frac{2(P_1 - P_2)}{\rho}} = \sqrt{\frac{2(5.00 \times 10^5\text{ N/m}^2)}{1000\text{ kg/m}^3}} = 31.6\text{ m/s}$$

**14.10 [III]** Water flows at the rate of 30 mL/s through an opening at the bottom of a large tank in which the water is 4.0 m deep. Calculate the rate of escape of the water if an added pressure of 50 kPa is applied to the top of the water.

Take position-1 at the liquid surface at the top of the tank, and position-2 at the opening. From Bernoulli's Equation where $v_1$ is essentially zero,

$$(P_1 - P_2) + (h_1 - h_2)\rho g = \tfrac{1}{2}\rho v_2^2$$

We can apply this expression twice, before the pressure is added and after.

$$(P_1 - P_2)_{\text{before}} + (h_1 - h_2)\rho g = \tfrac{1}{2}\rho (v_2^2)_{\text{before}}$$

$$(P_1 - P_2)_{\text{before}} + 5\times 10^4\ \text{N/m}^2 + (h_1 - h_2)\rho g = \tfrac{1}{2}\rho (v_2^2)_{\text{after}}$$

If the opening and the top of the tank are originally at atmospheric pressure, then

$$(P_1 - P_2)_{\text{before}} = 0$$

and division of the second equation by the first gives

$$\frac{(v_2^2)_{\text{after}}}{(v_2^2)_{\text{before}}} = \frac{5\times 10^4\ \text{N/m}^2 + (h_1 - h_2)\rho g}{(h_1 - h_2)\rho g}$$

But $$(h_1 - h_2)\rho g = (4.0\ \text{m})(1000\ \text{kg/m}^3)(9.81\ \text{m/s}^2) = 3.9\times 10^4\ \text{N/m}^2$$

Therefore, $$\frac{(v_2)_{\text{after}}}{(v_2)_{\text{before}}} = \sqrt{\frac{8.9\times 10^4\ \text{N/m}^2}{3.9\times 10^4\ \text{N/m}^2}} = 1.51$$

Since $J = Av$, this can be written as

$$\frac{J_{\text{after}}}{J_{\text{before}}} = 1.51 \qquad \text{or} \qquad J_{\text{after}} = (30\ \text{mL/s})\,(1.51) = 45\ \text{mL/s}$$

**14.11 [II]** How much work $W$ is done by a pump in raising 5.00 m$^3$ of water 20.0 m and forcing it into a main at a gauge pressure of 150 kPa?

$$W = (\text{Work to raise water}) + (\text{Work to push it in}) = mgh + P\Delta V$$

$$W = (5.00\ \text{m}^3)\,(1000\ \text{kg/m}^3)\,(9.81\ \text{m/s}^2)\,(20.0\ \text{m}) + (1.50\times 10^5\ \text{N/m}^2)\,(5.00\ \text{m}^3) = 1.73\times 10^6\ \text{J}$$

**14.12 [II]** A horizontal pipe has a constriction in it, as shown in Fig. 14-3. At point-1 the diameter is 6.0 cm, while at point-2 it is only 2.0 cm. At point-1, $v_1 = 2.0$ m/s and $P_1 = 180$ kPa. Calculate $v_2$ and $P_2$.

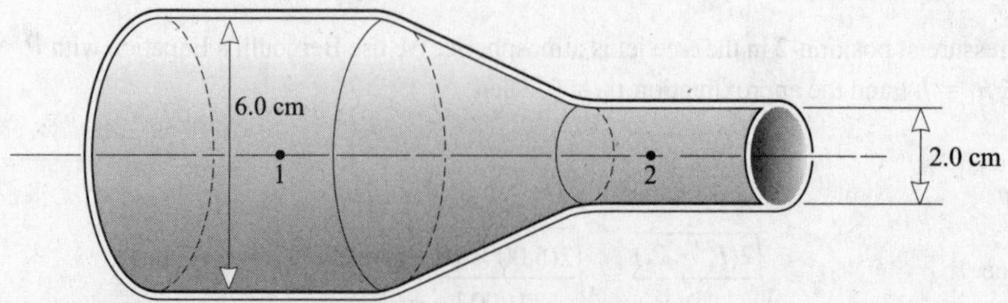


Fig. 14-3

We have two unknowns and will need two equations. Using Bernoulli's Equation with $h_1 = h_2$, we have

$$P_1 + \tfrac{1}{2}\rho v_1^2 = P_2 + \tfrac{1}{2}\rho v_2^2 \quad \text{or} \quad P_1 + \tfrac{1}{2}\rho(v_1^2 - v_2^2) = P_2$$

Furthermore, $v_1 = 2.0$ m/s, and the equation of continuity tells us that

$$v_2 = v_1 \frac{A_1}{A_2} = (2.0\text{ m/s})\left(\frac{r_1}{r_2}\right)^2 = (2.0\text{ m/s})\,(9.0) = 18\text{ m/s}$$

Substituting then gives

$$1.80 \times 10^5\text{ N/m}^2 + \tfrac{1}{2}(1000\text{ kg/m}^3)\,[(2.0\text{ m/s})^2 - (18\text{ m/s}^2)] = P_2$$

from which $P_2 = 0.20 \times 10^5\text{ N/m}^2 = 20$ kPa.

**14.13 [III]** What must be the gauge pressure in a large-diameter hose if the nozzle is to shoot water straight upward to a height of 30.0 m?

To rise to a height $h$, a projectile must have an initial speed $\sqrt{2gh}$. (We obtain this by equating to $\frac{1}{2}mv_0^2$ to $mgh$.) We can find this speed in terms of the difference between the pressures inside and outside the hose by writing Bernoulli's Equation for points just inside and outside the nozzle in terms of absolute pressure:

$$P_{\text{in}} + \tfrac{1}{2}\rho v_{\text{in}}^2 + h_{\text{in}}\rho g = P_{\text{out}} + \tfrac{1}{2}\rho v_{\text{out}}^2 + h_{\text{out}}\rho g$$

Here $h_{\text{out}} \approx h_{\text{in}}$, and because the hose is large, $v_{\text{in}} \approx 0$; therefore,

$$P_{\text{in}} - P_{\text{out}} = \tfrac{1}{2}\rho v_{\text{out}}^2$$

Substitution of $\sqrt{2gh}$ for $v_{\text{out}}$ yields

$$P_{\text{in}} - P_{\text{out}} = \rho g h = (1000\text{ kg/m}^3)(9.81\text{ m/s}^2)(30.0\text{ m}) = 294\text{ kPa}$$

Since $P_{\text{out}} = P_A$, this is the gauge pressure inside the hose. How could you obtain this latter equation directly from Torricelli's Theorem?

**14.14 [III]** At what rate does water flow from a 0.80 cm i.d. faucet if the water (or gauge) pressure is 200 kPa?

We apply Bernoulli's Equation for points just inside and outside the faucet (using absolute pressure):

$$P_{\text{in}} + \tfrac{1}{2}\rho v_{\text{in}}^2 + h_{\text{in}}\rho g = P_{\text{out}} + \tfrac{1}{2}\rho v_{\text{out}}^2 + h_{\text{out}}\rho g$$

Note that the pressure inside due only to the water is 200 kPa, and therefore $P_{\text{in}} = P_{\text{out}} = 200$ kPa since $P_{\text{out}} = P_A$. Taking $h_{\text{out}} = h_{\text{in}}$,

$$v_{\text{out}}^2 - v_{\text{in}}^2 = (200 \times 10^3\text{ Pa})\frac{2}{\rho}$$

Assuming $v_{\text{in}}^2 \ll v_{\text{out}}^2$, we solve to obtain $v_{\text{out}} = 20$ m/s. The flow rate is then

$$J = vA = (20\text{ m/s})\,(\pi r^2) = (20\text{ m/s})\,(\pi)\,(0.16 \times 10^{-4}\text{ m}^2) = 1.0 \times 10^{-3}\text{ m}^3/\text{s}$$

**14.15 [II]** The pipe shown in Fig. 14-4 has a diameter of 16 cm at section-1 and 10 cm at section-2. At section-1 the pressure is 200 kPa. Point-2 is 6.0 m higher than point-1. When oil of density 800 kg/m$^3$ flows at a rate of 0.030 m$^3$/s, find the pressure at point-2 if viscous effects are negligible.

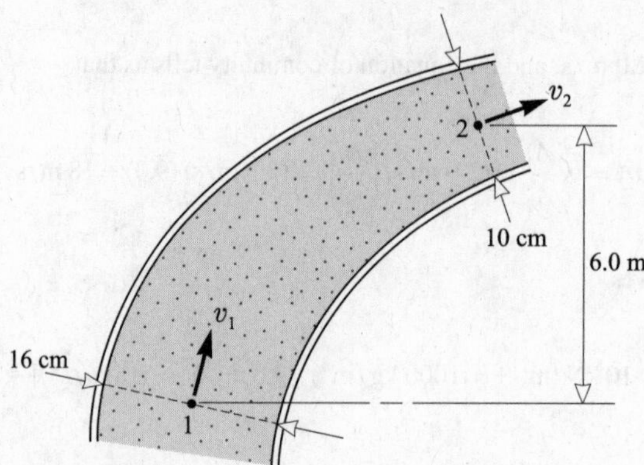


Fig. 14-4

From $J = v_1 A_1 = v_2 A_2$

$$v_1 = \frac{J}{A_1} = \frac{0.030 \text{ m}^3/\text{s}}{\pi(8.0 \times 10^{-2} \text{ m})^2} = 1.49 \text{ m/s}$$

$$v_2 = \frac{J}{A_2} = \frac{0.030 \text{ m}^3/\text{s}}{\pi(5.0 \times 10^{-2} \text{ m})^2} = 3.82 \text{ m/s}$$

We can now use Bernoulli's Equation:

$$P_1 + \tfrac{1}{2}\rho v_1^2 + \rho g(h_1 - h_2) = P_2 + \tfrac{1}{2}\rho v_2^2$$

Setting $P_1 = 2.00 \times 10^5$ N/m$^2$, $h_2 - h_1 = 6$ m and $\rho = 800$ kg/m$^3$ result in

$$P_2 = 2.00 \times 10^5 \text{ N/m}^3 + \tfrac{1}{2}(800 \text{ kg/m}^3)[(1.49 \text{ m/s})^2 - (3.82 \text{ m/s})^2] - (800 \text{ kg/m}^3)(9.81 \text{ m/s}^2)(6.0 \text{ m})$$
$$= 1.48 \times 10^5 \text{ N/m}^2 = 1.5 \times 10^5 \text{ kPa.}$$

**14.16 [III]** A venturi meter equipped with a differential mercury manometer is shown in Fig. 14-5. At the inlet, point-1, the diameter is 12 cm, while at the throat, point-2, the diameter is 6.0 cm. What is the flow $J$ of water through the meter if the mercury manometer reading is 22 cm? The density of mercury is 13.6 g/cm$^3$.

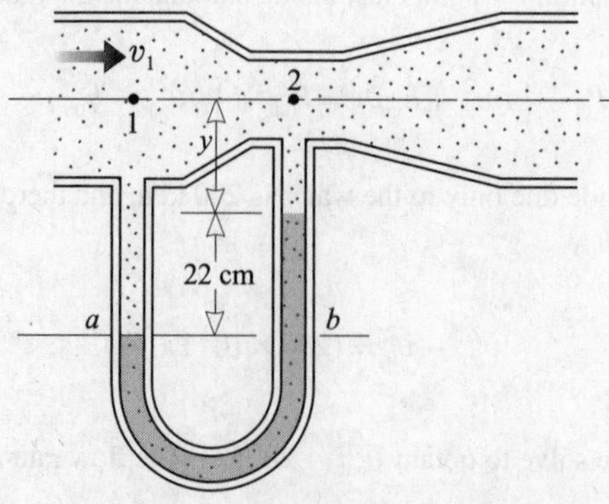


Fig. 14-5

From the manometer reading (remembering that 1 $g/cm^3 = 1000\ kg/m^3$):

$$P_1 - P_2 = \rho g h = (13\,600\ kg/m^3)(9.81\ m/s^2)(0.22\ m) = 2.93 \times 10^4\ N/m^2$$

Since $J = v_1 A_1 = v_2 A_2$, we have $v_1 = J/A_1$ and $v_2 = J/A_2$. Using Bernoulli's Equation with $h_1 - h_2 = 0$ gives

$$(P_1 - P_2) + \tfrac{1}{2}\rho(v_1^2 - v_2^2) = 0$$

$$2.93 \times 10^4\ N/m^2 + \tfrac{1}{2}(1000\ kg/m^3)\left(\frac{1}{A_1^2} - \frac{1}{A_2^2}\right)J^2 = 0$$

where

$$A_1 = \pi r_1^2 = \pi(0.060)^2\ m^2 = 0.011\,31\ m^2 \qquad \text{and} \qquad A_2 = \pi r_2^2 = \pi(0.030)^2\ m^2 = 0.002\,8\ m^2$$

Substitution then gives $J = 0.022\ m^3/s$.

**14.17 [III] A wind tunnel is to be used with a 20-cm-high model car to approximately reproduce the situation in which a 550-cm-high car is moving at 15 m/s. What should be the wind speed in the tunnel? Is the flow likely to be turbulent?**

We want the Reynolds number $N_R$ to be the same in both cases, so that the situations will be similar. That is,

$$N_R = \left(\frac{\rho v D}{\eta}\right)_{\text{tunnel}} = \left(\frac{\rho v D}{\eta}\right)_{\text{air}}$$

Both $\rho$ and $\eta$ are the same in the two cases, hence,

$$v_t D_t = v_a D_a \qquad \text{from which} \qquad v_t = v_a \frac{D_a}{D_t} = (15\ m/s)(550/20) = 0.41\ km/s$$

To investigate turbulence, evaluate $N_R$ using $\rho = 1.29\ kg/m^3$ and $\eta = 1.8 \times 10^{-5}$ Pa·s for air. Consequently $N_R = 5.9 \times 10^6$, a value far in excess of that required for turbulent flow. The flow will certainly be turbulent.

## SUPPLEMENTARY PROBLEMS

**14.18 [I]** Oil flows through a 4.0-cm-i.d. pipe at an average speed of 2.5 m/s. Find the flow in $m^3/s$ and $cm^3/s$.

**14.19 [I]** Compute the average speed of water in a pipe having an i.d. of 5.0 cm and delivering 2.5 $m^3$ of water per hour.

**14.20 [II]** The speed of glycerin flowing in a 5.0-cm-i.d. pipe is 0.54 m/s. Find the fluid's speed in a 3.0-cm-i.d. pipe that connects with it, both pipes flowing full.

**14.21 [II]** How long will it take for 500 mL of water to flow through a 15-cm-long, 3.0-mm-i.d. pipe, if the pressure differential across the pipe is 4.0 kPa? The viscosity of water is 0.80 cP.

**14.22 [II]** A molten plastic flows out of a tube that is 8.0 cm long at a rate of 13 $cm^3$/min when the pressure differential between the two ends of the tube is 18 cm of mercury. Find the viscosity of the plastic. The i.d. of the tube is 1.30 mm. The density of mercury is 13.6 $g/cm^3$.

**14.23 [II]** In a horizontal pipe system, a pipe (i.d. 4.0 mm) that is 20 cm long connects in line to a pipe (i.d. 5.0 mm) that is 30 cm long. When a viscous fluid is being pushed through the pipes at a steady rate, what is the ratio of the pressure difference across the 20-cm pipe to that across the 30-cm pipe?

**14.24 [II]** A hypodermic needle of length 3.0 cm and i.d. 0.45 mm is used to draw blood ($\eta = 4.0$ mPl). Assuming the pressure differential across the needle is 80 cmHg, how long does it take to draw 15 mL?

**14.25 [II]** In a blood transfusion, blood flows from a bottle at atmospheric pressure into a patient's vein in which the pressure is 20 mmHg higher than atmospheric. The bottle is 95 cm higher than the vein, and the needle into the vein has a length of 3.0 cm and an i.d. of 0.45 mm. How much blood flows into the vein each minute? For blood, $\eta = 0.004\,0$ Pa·s and $\rho = 1005$ kg/m$^3$

**14.26 [I]** How much work does the piston in a hydraulic system do during one 2.0-cm stroke if the end area of the piston is 0.75 cm$^2$ and the pressure in the hydraulic fluid is 50 kPa?

**14.27 [II]** A large tank of nonviscous liquid, which is open to the surrounding air, springs a leak 4.5 m below the top of the liquid. What is the theoretical velocity of outflow from the hole? If the area of the hole is 0.25 cm$^2$, how much liquid will escape in exactly 1 minute?

**14.28 [II]** Find the flow in liters/s of a nonviscous liquid through an opening 0.50 cm$^2$ in area and 2.5 m below the level of the liquid in an open tank surrounded by air.

**14.29 [II]** Calculate the theoretical velocity of efflux of water, into the surrounding air, from an aperture that is 8.0 m below the surface of water in a large tank, if an added pressure of 140 kPa is applied to the surface of the water.

**14.30 [II]** What horsepower is required to force 8.0 m$^3$ of water per minute into a water main at a pressure of 220 kPa?

**14.31 [II]** A pump lifts water at the rate of 9.0 liters/s from a lake through a 5.0-cm-i.d. pipe and discharges it into the air at a point 16 m above the level of the water in the lake. What are the theoretical (*a*) velocity of the water at the point of discharge and (*b*) power delivered by the pump.

**14.32 [II]** Water flows steadily through a horizontal pipe of varying cross section. At one place the pressure is 130 kPa and the speed is 0.60 m/s. Determine the pressure at another place in the same pipe where the speed is 9.0 m/s.

**14.33 [II]** A pipe of varying inner diameter carries water. At point-1 the diameter is 20 cm and the pressure is 130 kPa. At point-2, which is 4.0 m higher than point-1, the diameter is 30 cm. If the flow is 0.080 m$^3$/s, what is the pressure at the second point?

**14.34 [II]** Fuel oil of density 820 kg/m$^3$ flows through a venturi meter having a throat diameter of 4.0 cm and an entrance diameter of 8.0 cm. The pressure drop between entrance and throat is 16 cm of mercury. Find the flow. The density of mercury is 13 600 kg/m$^3$.

**14.35 [II]** Find the maximum amount of water that can flow through a 3.0-cm-i.d. pipe per minute without turbulence. Take the maximum Reynolds number for nonturbulent flow to be 2000. For water at 20 °C, $\eta = 1.0 \times 10^{-3}$ Pa·s.

**14.36 [I]** How fast can a raindrop ($r = 1.5$ mm) fall through air if the flow around it is to be close to turbulent—that is, for $N_R$ close to 10? For air, $\eta = 1.8 \times 10^{-5}$ Pa·s and $\rho = 1.29$ kg/m$^3$.

## ANSWERS TO SUPPLEMENTARY PROBLEMS

**14.18 [I]** $3.1 \times 10^{-3}\ m^3/s = 3.1 \times 10^3\ cm^3/s$

**14.19 [I]** 0.35 m/s

**14.20 [II]** 1.5 m/s

**14.21 [II]** 7.5 s

**14.22 [II]** $0.097\ kg/m \cdot s = 97\ cP$

**14.23 [II]** 1.6

**14.24 [II]** 17 s

**14.25 [II]** $3.4\ cm^3$

**14.26 [I]** 75 mJ

**14.27 [II]** 9.4 m/s, $0.0141\ m^3$

**14.28 [II]** 0.35 liter/s

**14.29 [II]** 21 m/s

**14.30 [II]** 39 hp

**14.31 [II]** (*a*) 4.6 m/s; (*b*) 2.0 hp

**14.32 [II]** 90 kPa

**14.33 [II]** 93 kPa

**14.34 [II]** $9.3 \times 10^{-3}\ m^3/s$

**14.35 [II]** $0.002\,8\ m^3$

**14.36 [I]** 4.6 cm/s

# Thermal Expansion

**Temperature** ($T$) may be measured on the *Celsius* scale, on which the freezing point of water is at 0 °C, and the boiling point (under standard conditions) is at 100 °C. The *Kelvin* (or *absolute*) scale is displaced 273.15 Celsius-size degrees from the Celsius or centigrade scale, so that the freezing point of water is 273.15 K and the boiling point is 373.15 K. Absolute zero, a temperature discussed further in Chapter 16, is at 0 K (−273.15 °C). The still-used *Fahrenheit* scale is related to the Celsius scale by

$$\text{Fahrenheit temperature} = \tfrac{9}{5}\,(\text{Celsius temperature}) + 32$$

Note that one does not say 0 °K or zero degrees kelvin. Kelvins are treated like any other unit; thus it's 1K, 1m, and 1N. **As a rule temperatures will be designated in kelvins.**

Because of the way the scale is constructed, a *temperature change* $\Delta T$ will be numerically, by the same in both the Celsius (centigrade) and Kelvin scales.

**Linear Expansion of Solids:** When a solid is subjected to a rise in temperature $\Delta T$, its increase in length $\Delta L$ is very nearly proportional to its initial length $L_0$ multiplied by $\Delta T$. That is,

$$\Delta L = \alpha L_0\, \Delta T$$

where the proportionality constant $\alpha$ is called the **coefficient of linear expansion**. The value of $\alpha$ depends on the nature of the substance. For our purposes, we can take $\alpha$ to be constant independent of $T$, although that's rarely, if ever, exactly true.

From the above equation, $\alpha$ is the change in length, per unit initial length, per degree change in temperature. For example, if a 1.000 000 cm length of brass becomes 1.000 019 cm long when the temperature is raised 1.0 °C, the linear expansion coefficient for brass is

$$\alpha = \frac{\Delta L}{L_0 \Delta T} = \frac{0.000\,019\ \text{cm}}{(1.0\ \text{cm})\,(1.0\ ^\circ\text{C})} = 1.9 \times 10^{-5}\ ^\circ\text{C}^{-1}$$

**Area Expansion:** If an area $A_0$ expands to $A_0 + \Delta A$ when subjected to a temperature rise $\Delta T$, then

$$\Delta A = \gamma A_0\, \Delta T$$

where $\gamma$ is the **coefficient of area expansion**. For *isotropic* solids (those that expand in the same way in all directions), $\gamma \approx 2\alpha$.

**Volume Expansion:** If a volume $V_0$ changes by an amount $\Delta V$ when subjected to a temperature change of $\Delta T$, then

$$\Delta V = \beta V_0 \, \Delta T$$

where $\beta$ is the **coefficient of volume expansion.** This can be either an increase or decrease in volume. For isotropic solids, $\beta \approx 3\alpha$.

## SOLVED PROBLEMS

**15.1 [I]** A copper bar is 80 cm long at 15 °C. What is the increase in length when it is heated to 35 °C? The linear expansion coefficient for copper is $1.7 \times 10^{-5}$ °C$^{-1}$.

$$\Delta L = \alpha L_0 \, \Delta T = (1.7 \times 10^{-5}\ °\text{C}^{-1})(0.80\ \text{m})[(35 - 15)\ °\text{C}] = 2.7 \times 10^{-4}\ \text{m}$$

**15.2 [II]** A cylinder of diameter 1.000 00 cm at 30 °C is to be slid into a hole in a steel plate. The hole has a diameter of 0.999 70 cm at 30 °C. To what temperature must the plate be heated? For steel, $\alpha = 1.1 \times 10^{-5}$ °C$^{-1}$.

The plate will expand in the same way whether or not there is a hole in it. Hence, the hole expands in the same way a circle of steel filling it would expand. We want the diameter of the hole to change by

$$\Delta L = (1.000\,00 - 0.999\,70)\ \text{cm} = 0.000\,30\ \text{cm}$$

Using $\Delta L = \alpha L_0 \, \Delta T$,

$$\Delta T = \frac{\Delta L}{\alpha L_0} = \frac{0.000\,30\ \text{cm}}{(1.1\times 10^{-5}\ °\text{C}^{-1})(0.999\,70\ \text{cm})} = 27\ °\text{C}$$

The temperature of the plate must be 30 + 27 = 57 °C

**15.3 [I]** A steel tape is calibrated at 20 °C. On a cold day when the temperature is −15 °C, what will be the percent error in the tape? $\alpha_{\text{steel}} = 1.1 \times 10^{-5}$ °C$^{-1}$.

For a temperature change from 20 °C to −15 °C, we have $\Delta T = -35$ °C. Then,

$$\frac{\Delta L}{L_0} = \alpha \, \Delta T = (1.1\times 10^{-5}\ °\text{C}^{-1})(-35\ °\text{C}) = -3.9\times 10^{-4} = -0.039\%$$

**15.4 [II]** A copper rod ($\alpha = 1.70 \times 10^{-5}$ °C$^{-1}$) is 20 cm longer than an aluminum rod ($\alpha = 2.20 \times 10^{-5}$ °C$^{-1}$). How long should the copper rod be if the difference in their lengths is to be independent of temperature?

For their difference in lengths not to change with temperature, $\Delta L$ must be the same for both rods under the same temperature change. That is,

$$(\alpha L_0 \, \Delta T)_{\text{copper}} = (\alpha L_0 \, \Delta T)_{\text{aluminum}}$$

or

$$(1.70 \times 10^{-5}\ °\text{C}^{-1}) L_0 \, \Delta T = (2.20 \times 10^{-5}\ °\text{C}^{-1})(L_0 - 0.20\ \text{m}) \, \Delta T$$

where $L_0$ is the length of the copper rod, and $\Delta T$ is the same for both rods. Solving for the original length yields $L_0 = 0.88$ m.

**15.5 [II]** At 20.0 °C a steel ball ($\alpha = 1.10 \times 10^{-5}$ °C$^{-1}$) has a diameter of 0.9000 cm, while the diameter of a hole in an aluminum plate ($\alpha = 2.20 \times 10^{-5}$ °C$^{-1}$) is 0.8990 cm. At what temperature (the same for both) will the ball just pass through the hole?

At a temperature $\Delta T$ higher than 20 0 °C, the diameters of the hole and of the ball should be equal:

$$0.900\,0 \text{ cm} + (0.900\,0 \text{ cm})(1.10 \times 10^{-5}\,°\text{C}^{-1})\,\Delta T = 0.899\,0 \text{ cm} + (0.899\,0 \text{ cm})(2.20 \times 10^{-5}\,°\text{C}^{-1})\,\Delta T$$

Solving for $\Delta T$, we find $\Delta T = 101$ °C. Because the original temperature was 20.0 °C, the final temperature must be 121 °C.

**15.6 [II]** A steel tape measures the length of a copper rod as 90.00 cm when both are at 10 °C, the calibration temperature for the tape. What would the tape read for the length of the rod when both are at 30 °C? $\alpha_{\text{steel}} = 1.1 \times 10^{-5}$ °C$^{-1}$; $\alpha_{\text{copper}} = 1.7 \times 10^{-5}$ °C$^{-1}$.

At 30 °C, the copper rod will be of length

$$L_0(1 + \alpha_c\,\Delta T)$$

while adjacent "centimeter" marks on the steel tape will be separated by a distance of

$$(1.000 \text{ cm})\,(1 + \alpha_s\,\Delta T)$$

Therefore, the number of "centimeters" read on the tape will be

$$\frac{L_0(1+\alpha_c\Delta T)}{(1 \text{ cm})\,(1+\alpha_s\Delta T)} = \frac{(90.00 \text{ cm})[1+(1.7\times10^{-5}\,°\text{C}^{-1})\,(20\,°\text{C})]}{(1.000 \text{ cm})[1+(1.1\times10^{-5}\,°\text{C}^{-1})\,(20\,°\text{C})]} = 90.00\frac{1+3.4\times10^{-4}}{1+2.2\times10^{-4}}$$

Using the approximation

$$\frac{1}{1+x} \approx 1-x$$

for $x$ small compared to 1, we have

$$90.00\frac{1+3.4\times10^{-4}}{1+2.2\times10^{-4}} \approx 90.00(1+3.4\times10^{-4})\,(1-2.2\times10^{-4}) \approx 90\,00(1+3.4\times10^{-4}-2.2\times10^{-4})$$
$$= 90.00 + 0.010\,8$$

The tape will read 90.01 cm.

**15.7 [II]** A glass flask is filled 'to the mark" with 50.00 cm³ of mercury at 18 °C. If the flask and its contents are heated to 38 °C, how much mercury will be above the mark? $\alpha_{\text{glass}} = 9.0 \times 10^{-6}$ °C$^{-1}$ and $\beta_{\text{mercury}} = 182 \times 10^{-6}$ °C$^{-1}$.

We shall take $\beta_{\text{glass}} = 3\alpha_{\text{glass}}$ as a good approximation. The flask interior will expand just as though it were a solid piece of glass. Thus,

$$\begin{aligned}\text{Volume of mercury above mark} &= (\Delta V \text{ for mercury}) - (\Delta V \text{ for glass})\\ &= \beta_m V_0\,\Delta T - \beta_g V_0\,\Delta T = (\beta_m - \beta_g)\,V_0\,\Delta T\\ &= [(182 - 27) \times 10^{-6}\,°\text{C}^{-1}]\,(50.00 \text{ cm}^3)[(38 - 18)\,°\text{C}]\\ &= 0.15 \text{ cm}^3\end{aligned}$$

**15.8 [II]** The density of mercury at exactly 0 °C is 13 600 kg/m$^3$, and its volume expansion coefficient is $1.82 \times 10^{-4}$ °C$^{-1}$. Calculate the density of mercury at 50.0 °C.

Let

$$\rho_0 = \text{Density of mercury at 0 °C}$$
$$\rho_1 = \text{Density of mercury at 50 °C}$$
$$V_0 = \text{Volume of } m \text{ kg of mercury at 0 °C}$$
$$V_1 = \text{Volume of } m \text{ kg of mercury at 50 °C}$$

Since the mass does not change, $m = \rho_0 V_0 = \rho_1 V_1$, from which it follows that

$$\rho_1 = \rho_0 \frac{V_0}{V_1} = \rho_0 \frac{V_0}{V_0 + \Delta V} = \rho_0 \frac{1}{1 + (\Delta V / V_0)}$$

But
$$\frac{\Delta V}{V_0} = \beta \Delta T = (1.82 \times 10^{-4}\ °\text{C}^{-1})(50.0\ °\text{C}) = 0.00910$$

Substitution into the first equation yields

$$\rho_1 = (13600\ \text{kg/m}^3)\frac{1}{1 + 0.00910} = 13.5 \times 10^3\ \text{kg/m}^3$$

**15.9 [II]** Show that the density of a liquid or solid changes in the following way with temperature: $\Delta\rho = -\rho\beta\,\Delta T \approx -\rho_0\beta\Delta T$.

Consider a mass $m$ of liquid having a volume $V_0$, for which $\rho_0 = m/V_0$. After a temperature change $\Delta T$, the volume will be

$$V = V_0 + V_0\beta\,\Delta T$$

and the density will be

$$\rho = \frac{m}{V} = \frac{m}{V_0(1 + \beta\Delta T)}$$

But $m/V_0 = \rho_0$, and so this can be written as

$$\rho(1 + \beta\Delta T) = \rho_0$$

Thus,

$$\Delta\rho = \rho - \rho_0 = -\rho\beta\,\Delta T.$$

In practice, $\rho$ is close enough to $\rho_0$ so that we can say $\Delta\rho \approx -\rho_0\beta\,\Delta T$.

**15.10 [II]** Solve Problem 15.8 using the result of Problem 15.9.

We have

$$\Delta\rho \approx -\rho_0\beta\,\Delta T$$

Hence
$$\Delta\rho \approx -(13\ 600\ \text{kg/m}^3)(182 \times 10^{-6}\ °\text{C}^{-1})(50.0\ °\text{C}) = -124\ \text{kg/m}^3$$

and
$$\rho_{50\ °\text{C}} = \rho_{0\ °\text{C}} - 124\ \text{kg/m}^3 = 13.5 \times 10^3\ \text{kg/m}^3$$

**15.11 [III]** A steel wire of 2.0 mm² cross section at 30 °C is held straight (but under no tension) by attaching its ends firmly to two points a distance 1.50 m apart. (Of course this will have to be done out in space so the wire is weightless, but don't worry about that.) If the temperature now decreases to −10 °C, and if the two tie points remain fixed, what will be the tension in the wire? For steel, $\alpha = 1.1 \times 10^{-5}\,°\text{C}^{-1}$ and $Y = 2.0 \times 10^{11}\ \text{N/m}^2$.

If it were free to do so, the wire would contract a distance $\Delta L$ as it cooled, where

$$\Delta L = \alpha L_0\,\Delta T = (1.1 \times 10^{-5}\,°\text{C}^{-1})\,(1.5\text{m})(40\,°\text{C}) = 6.6 \times 10^{-4}\ \text{m}$$

But the ends are fixed. As a result, forces at the ends must, in effect, stretch the wire this same length $\Delta L$. Therefore, from $Y = (F/A)\,(\Delta L/L_0)$, and

$$\text{Tension} = F = \frac{YA\,\Delta L}{L_0} = \frac{(2.0\times10^{11}\ \text{N/m}^2)(2.0\times10^{-6}\ \text{m}^2)(6.6\times10^{-4}\ \text{m})}{1.50\ \text{m}} = 176\ \text{N} = 0.18\ \text{kN}$$

Strictly, we should have substituted $(1.5 - 6.6 \times 10^{-4})$ m for $L$ in the expression for the tension. However, the error incurred in not doing so is negligible.

**15.12 [III]** When a building is constructed at −10 °C, a steel beam (cross-sectional area 45 cm²) is put in place with its ends cemented in pillars. If the sealed ends cannot move, what will be the compressional force on the beam when the temperature is 25 °C? For this kind of steel, $\alpha = 1.1 \times 10^{-5}\,°\text{C}^{-1}$ and $Y = 2.0 \times 10^{11}\ \text{N/m}^2$.

Proceed much as in Problem 15.11:

$$\frac{\Delta L}{L_0} = \alpha\Delta T = (1.1\times10^{-5}\,°\text{C}^{-1})\,(35\,°\text{C}) = 3.85\times10^{-4}$$

so $$F = YA\frac{\Delta L}{L_0} = (2.0\times10^{11}\ \text{N/m}^2)\,(45\times10^{-4}\ \text{m}^2)\,(3.85\times10^{-4}) = 3.5\times10^{5}\ \text{N}$$

## SUPPLEMENTARY PROBLEMS

**15.13 [I]** Compute the increase in length of 50 m of copper wire when its temperature changes from 12 °C to 32 °C. For copper, $\alpha = 1.7 \times 10^{-5}\,°\text{C}^{-1}$.

**15.14 [I]** A rod 3.0 m long is found to have expanded 0.091 cm in length after a temperature rise of 60 °C. What is $\alpha$ for the material of the rod?

**15.15 [I]** At 15.0 °C, a bare wheel has a diameter of 30.000 cm, and the inside diameter of its steel rim is 29.930 cm. To what temperature must the rim be heated so as to slip over the wheel? For this type of steel, $\alpha = 1.10 \times 10^{-5}\,°\text{C}^{-1}$

**15.16 [II]** An iron ball has a diameter of 6 cm and is 0.010 mm too large to pass through a hole in a brass plate when the ball and plate are at a temperature of 30 °C. At what temperature (the same for ball and plate) will the ball just pass through the hole? $\alpha = 1.2 \times 10^{-5}\,°\text{C}^{-1}$ and $1.9 \times 10^{-5}\,°\text{C}^{-1}$ for iron and brass, respectively.

**15.17 [II]** (*a*) An aluminum measuring rod, which is correct at 5.0 °C, measures a certain distance as 88.42 cm at 35.0 °C. Determine the error in measuring the distance due to the expansion of the rod. (*b*) If this aluminum rod measures a length of steel as 88.42 cm at 35.0 °C, what is the correct length of the steel at 35 °C? The coefficient of linear expansion of aluminum is $22 \times 10^{-6}\,°\text{C}^{-1}$.

**15.18 [II]** A solid sphere of mass $m$ and radius $b$ is spinning freely on its axis with angular velocity $\omega_0$. When heated by an amount $\Delta T$, its angular velocity changes to $\omega$. Find $\omega_0/\omega$ if the linear expansion coefficient for the material of the sphere is $\alpha$.

**15.19 [I]** Calculate the increase in volume of 100 cm³ of mercury when its temperature changes from 10 °C to 35 °C. The volume coefficient of expansion of mercury is 0.00018 °C$^{-1}$.

**15.20 [II]** The coefficient of linear expansion of glass is $9.0 \times 10^{-6}$ °C$^{-1}$. If a specific gravity bottle holds 50.000 mL at 15 °C, find its capacity at 25 °C.

**15.21 [II]** Determine the change in volume of a block of cast iron 5.0 cm × 10 cm × 6.0 cm, when the temperature of the block is made to change from 15 °C to 47 °C. The coefficient of linear expansion of cast iron is 0.000 010 °C$^{-1}$.

**15.22 [II]** A glass vessel is filled with exactly 1 liter of turpentine at 20 °C. What volume of the liquid will overflow if the temperature is raised to 86 °C? The coefficient of linear expansion of the glass is $9.0 \times 10^{-6}$ °C$^{-1}$; the coefficient of volume expansion of turpentine is $97 \times 10^{-5}$ °C$^{-1}$.

**15.23 [II]** The density of gold is 19.30 g/cm³ at 20.0 °C, and the coefficient of linear expansion is $14.3 \times 10^{-6}$ °C$^{-1}$. Compute the density of gold at 90.0 °C. [*Hint*: Take a look at Problem 15.9.]

## ANSWERS TO SUPPLEMENTARY PROBLEMS

**15.13 [I]** 1.7 cm

**15.14 [I]** $5.1 \times 10^{-6}$ °C$^{-1}$

**15.15 [I]** 227 °C

**15.16 [II]** 54 °C

**15.17 [II]** (*a*) 0.058 cm; (*b*) 88 cm

**15.18 [II]** $1 + 2\alpha\,\Delta T + (\alpha\,\Delta T)^2$

**15.19 [I]** 0.45 cm³

**15.20 [II]** 50.014 mL

**15.21 [II]** 0.29 cm³

**15.22 [II]** 62 mL

**15.23 [II]** 19.2 g/cm³

# Ideal Gases

**An Ideal (or Perfect) Gas** is a theoretical construct composed of tiny, moving, *noninteracting particles*. It obeys the ***Ideal Gas Law***, given below. At low to moderate pressures, and at temperatures not too low, the following common gases can be considered ideal: air, nitrogen, oxygen, helium, hydrogen, and neon. Almost any chemically stable gas behaves "ideally" if it is far removed from conditions under which it will liquefy or solidify. In other words, a real gas behaves like an ideal gas when its atoms or molecules are so far apart that they do not appreciably interact with one another.

**One Mole of a Substance** is the amount of the substance that contains as many particles as there are atoms in exactly 12 grams (0.012 kg) of the isotope carbon-12. It follows that one **kilomole** (kmol) of a substance is the mass (in kg) that is numerically equal to the molecular (or atomic) mass of the substance. For example, the molecular mass of hydrogen gas, $H_2$, is 2 kg/kmol; hence, there are 2 kg of molecular hydrogen in 1 kmol of $H_2$. Similarly, there are 32 kg of molecular oxygen in 1 kmol of $O_2$, and 28 kg of molecular nitrogen in 1 kmol of $N_2$. We shall always use *kilo*moles and *kilo*grams in our calculations. Sometimes the term molecular (or atomic) *weight* is used, rather than molecular *mass*, but the latter is correct.

**Ideal Gas Law:** The ***absolute pressure*** $P$ of $n$ kilomoles of gas contained in a volume $V$ is related to the ***absolute temperature*** $T$ by

$$PV = nRT$$

where $R = 8314.472\ \mathrm{J/kmol \cdot K}$ is called the **universal gas constant** or the **molar gas constant**. If the volume contains $m$ kilograms of gas that has a molecular (or atomic) mass $M$, then $n = m/M$. The units of $M$ are kg/kmol.

In this chapter both temperature and pressure are *absolute*; forgetting that is the most common cause of calculational error.

**Special Cases** of the Ideal Gas Law, obtained by holding all but two of its parameters constant, are

$$\textbf{Boyle's Law}\ (n, T\ \text{constant}):\quad PV = \text{constant}$$

$$\textbf{Charles' Law}\ (n, P\ \text{constant}):\quad \frac{V}{T} = \text{constant}$$

$$\textbf{Gay-Lussac's Law}\ (n, V\ \text{constant}):\quad \frac{P}{T} = \text{constant}$$

**Absolute Zero:** With $n$ and $P$ constant (Charles' Law), the volume of an ideal gas decreases linearly with $T$ and (if the gas remained ideal) would reach zero at $T = 0$ K. Similarly, with $n$ and $V$ constant (Gay-Lussac's Law), the pressure would decrease to zero with the temperature. This unique temperature, at which $P$ and $V$ would reach zero, is called **absolute zero.** It's the same 0 K introduced in the previous chapter.

**Standard Conditions or Standard Temperature and Pressure (S.T.P.)** are defined to be

$$T = 273.15\text{ K} = 0\ ^\circ\text{C} \qquad P = 1.013 \times 10^5\text{ Pa} = 1\text{ atm} = 760.1\text{ mmHg}$$

Under standard conditions, 1 kmol of *ideal gas* occupies a volume of 22.4 $m^3$. Therefore, at S.T.P., 2 kg of $H_2$ occupies the same volume as 32 kg of $O_2$ or 28 kg of $N_2$, namely 22.4 $m^3$.

**Dalton's Law of Partial Pressures:** Define the **partial pressure** of one component of a gas mixture to be the pressure that component gas would exert if it alone occupied the entire volume. Then, the total pressure of a mixture of ideal, nonreactive gases is the sum of the partial pressures of the component gases. Which makes sense, since each gas is effectively "unaware" of the presence of any of the other gases.

**Gas-Law Problems** involving a change of conditions from ($P_1$, $V_1$, $T_1$) to ($P_2$, $V_2$, $T_2$) are usually easily solved by writing the gas law as

$$\frac{P_1V_1}{T_1} = \frac{P_2V_2}{T_2} \qquad \text{(at constant } n\text{)}$$

*Remember that's absolute temperature and absolute pressure*. Notice that pressure, because it appears on both sides of the equation, can be expressed in any units you like.

## SOLVED PROBLEMS

**16.1 [II]** A mass of oxygen occupies 0.0200 $m^3$ at atmospheric pressure, 101 kPa, and 5.0 °C. Determine its volume if its pressure is increased to 108 kPa while its temperature is changed to 30 °C.

From

$$\frac{P_1V_1}{T_1} = \frac{P_2V_2}{T_2} \qquad \text{we have} \qquad V_2 = V_1\left(\frac{P_1}{P_2}\right)\left(\frac{T_2}{T_1}\right)$$

But $T_1 = 5 + 273 = 278$ K and $T_2 = 30 + 273 = 303$ K; consequently,

$$V_2 = (0.0200\text{ m}^3)\left(\frac{101}{108}\right)\left(\frac{303}{278}\right) = 0.0204\text{ m}^3$$

**16.2 [II]** On a day when atmospheric pressure is 76 cmHg, the pressure gauge on a tank reads the pressure inside to be 400 cmHg. The gas in the tank has a temperature of 9 °C. If the tank is heated to 31 °C by the Sun, and if no gas exits from it, what will the pressure gauge read?

$$\frac{P_1V_1}{T_1} = \frac{P_2V_2}{T_2} \qquad \text{and} \qquad P_2 = P_1\left(\frac{T_2}{T_1}\right)\left(\frac{V_1}{V_2}\right)$$

But gauges on tanks usually read the difference in pressure between inside and outside; this is called the *gauge pressure*. Therefore,

$$P_1 = 76\text{ cmHg} + 400\text{ cmHg} = 476\text{ cmHg}$$

Also, $V_1 = V_2$. We then have

$$P_2 = (476\text{ cmHg})\left(\frac{273+31}{273+9}\right)(1.00) = 513\text{ cmHg}$$

The gauge will read 513 cmHg − 76 cmHg = 437 cmHg.

**16.3 [II]** The gauge pressure in a car tire is 305 kPa when its temperature is 15 °C. After running at high speed, the tire has heated up and its gauge pressure is 360 kPa. What is then the temperature of the gas in the tire? Assume atmospheric pressure to be 101 kPa.

Being careful to use only absolute temperature and absolute pressures:

$$\frac{P_1V_1}{T_1} = \frac{P_2V_2}{T_2} \quad \text{or} \quad T_2 = T_1\left(\frac{P_2}{P_1}\right)\left(\frac{V_2}{V_1}\right)$$

with $P_1 = 305\ \text{kPa} + 101\ \text{kPa} = 406\ \text{kPa}$ and $P_2 = 360\ \text{kPa} + 101\ \text{kPa} = 461\ \text{kPa}$

Then $$T_2 = (273+15)\left(\frac{461}{406}\right)(1.00) = 327\ \text{K}$$

The final temperature of the tire is 327 − 273 = 54 °C.

**16.4 [II]** Gas at room temperature and pressure is confined to a cylinder by a piston. The piston is now pushed in so as to reduce the volume to one-eighth of its original value. After the gas temperature has returned to room temperature, what is the gauge pressure of the gas in kPa? Local atmospheric pressure is 740 mm of mercury.

$$\frac{P_1V_1}{T_1} = \frac{P_2V_2}{T_2} \quad \text{or} \quad P_2 = P_1\left(\frac{V_1}{V_2}\right)\left(\frac{T_2}{T_1}\right)$$

Remember that you can work in any pressure units you like. Here $T_1 = T_2$, $P_1 = 740$ mmHg, and $V_2 = V_1/8$. Substitution provides

$$P_2 = (740\ \text{mmHg})(8)(1) = 5920\ \text{mmHg}$$

Gauge pressure is the difference between actual and atmospheric pressure. Therefore,

$$\text{Gauge pressure} = 5920\ \text{mmHg} - 740\ \text{mmHg} = 5180\ \text{mmHg}$$

Since 760 mmHg = 101 kPa, the gauge reading in kPa is

$$(5180\ \text{mmHg})\left(\frac{101\ \text{kPa}}{760\ \text{mmHg}}\right) = 690\ \text{kPa}$$

**16.5 [II]** An ideal gas has a volume of exactly 1 liter at 1.00 atm and −20 °C. To how many atmospheres of pressure must it be subjected in order to be compressed to 0.500 liter when the temperature is 40 °C?

$$\frac{P_1V_1}{T_1} = \frac{P_2V_2}{T_2} \quad \text{or} \quad P_2 = P_1\left(\frac{V_1}{V_2}\right)\left(\frac{T_2}{T_1}\right)$$

from which $$P_2 = (1.00\ \text{atm})\left(\frac{1.00\ \text{L}}{0.500\ \text{L}}\right)\left(\frac{273\ \text{K}+40\ \text{K}}{273\ \text{K}-20\ \text{K}}\right) = 2.47\ \text{atm}$$

**16.6 [II]** A certain mass of hydrogen gas occupies 370 mL at 16 °C and 150 kPa. Find its volume at −21 °C and 420 kPa.

$$\frac{P_1V_1}{T_1}=\frac{P_2V_2}{T_2} \quad \text{leads to} \quad V_2=V_1\left(\frac{P_1}{P_2}\right)\left(\frac{T_2}{T_1}\right)$$

$$V_2=(370\text{ mL})\left(\frac{150\text{ kPa}}{420\text{ kPa}}\right)\left(\frac{273\text{ K}-21\text{ K}}{273\text{ K}+16\text{ K}}\right)=115\text{ mL}$$

**16.7 [II]** The density of nitrogen is 1.25 kg/m³ at S.T.P. Determine the density of nitrogen at 42 °C and 730 mm of mercury.

Since $\rho = m/V$, we have $V_1 = m/\rho_1$ and $V_2 = m/\rho_2$ for a given mass of gas under two sets of conditions. Then

$$\frac{P_1V_1}{T_1}=\frac{P_2V_2}{T_2} \quad \text{leads to} \quad \frac{P_1}{\rho_1T_1}=\frac{P_2}{\rho_2T_2}$$

Since S.T.P. are 760 mmHg and 273 K,

$$\rho_2=\rho_1\left(\frac{P_2}{P_1}\right)\left(\frac{T_1}{T_2}\right)=(1.25\text{ kg/m}^3)\left(\frac{730\text{ mmHg}}{760\text{ mmHg}}\right)\left(\frac{273\text{ K}}{273\text{ K}+42\text{ K}}\right)=1.04\text{ kg/m}^3$$

Notice that pressures in mmHg can be used here because the units cancel in the ratio $P_2/P_1$.

**16.8 [II]** A 3.0-liter tank contains oxygen gas at 20 °C and a gauge pressure of 25 × 10⁵ Pa. What mass of oxygen is in the tank? The molecular mass of oxygen gas is 32 kg/kmol. Assume atmospheric pressure to be 1 × 10⁵ Pa.

The absolute pressure of the gas is

$$P = (\text{Gauge pressure}) + (\text{Atmospheric pressure}) = (25 + 1) \times 10^5\text{ N/m}^2 = 26 \times 10^5\text{ N/m}^2$$

From the Ideal Gas Law, with $M$ = 32 kg/kmol,

$$PV=\left(\frac{m}{M}\right)RT$$

$$(26\times10^5\text{ N/m}^2)(3.0\times10^{-3}\text{m}^3)=\left(\frac{m}{32\text{ kg/kmol}}\right)\left(8314\frac{\text{J}}{\text{kmol}\cdot\text{K}}\right)(293\text{ K})$$

Solving this equation gives $m$, the mass of gas in the tank, as 0.10 kg.

**16.9 [II]** Determine the volume occupied by 4.0 g of oxygen ($M$ = 32 kg/kmol) at S.T.P.

**Method 1**

Use the Ideal Gas Law directly:

$$PV=\left(\frac{m}{M}\right)RT$$

$$V=\left(\frac{1}{P}\right)\left(\frac{m}{M}\right)RT=\frac{(4.0\times10^{-3}\text{ kg})(8314\text{ J/kmol}\cdot\text{K})(273\text{ K})}{(1.01\times10^5\text{ N/m}^2)(32\text{ kg/kmol})}=2.8\times10^{-3}\text{ m}^3$$

**Method 2**

Under S.T.P., 1 kmol occupies 22.4 m³. Therefore, 32 kg occupies 22.4 m³, and so 4 g occupies

$$\left(\frac{4.0\ \text{g}}{32\,000\ \text{g}}\right)(22.4\ \text{m}^3) = 2.8\times10^{-3}\ \text{m}^3$$

**16.10 [II]** A 2.0-mg droplet of liquid nitrogen is present in a 30 mL tube as it is sealed off at very low temperature. What will be the nitrogen pressure in the tube when it is warmed to 20 °C? Express your answer in atmospheres. ($M$ for nitrogen is 28 kg/kmol.)

Use $PV = (m/M)RT$ to find

$$P = \frac{mRT}{MV} = \frac{(2.0\times10^{-6}\ \text{kg})(8314\ \text{J/kmol}\cdot\text{K})(293\ \text{K})}{(28\ \text{kg/kmol})(30\times10^{-6}\text{m}^3)} = 5800\ \text{N/m}^2$$

$$= (5800\ \text{N/m}^2)\left(\frac{1.0\ \text{atm}}{1.01\times10^5\ \text{N/m}^2}\right) = 0.057\ \text{atm}$$

**16.11 [II]** A tank of volume 590 liters contains oxygen at 20 °C and 5.0 atm pressure. Calculate the mass of oxygen in the tank. $M = 32$ kg/kmol for oxygen.

Use $PV = (m/M)RT$ to get

$$m = \frac{PVM}{RT} = \frac{(5\times1.01\times10^5\ \text{N/m}^2)(0.59\ \text{m}^3)(32\ \text{kg/kmol})}{(8314\ \text{J/kmol}\cdot\text{K})(293\ \text{K})} = 3.9\ \text{kg}$$

**16.12 [II]** At 18 °C and 765 mmHg, 1.29 liters of an ideal gas has a mass of 2.71 g. Compute the molecular mass of the gas.

Use $PV = (m/M)RT$ and the fact that 760 mmHg = 1.00 atm to obtain

$$M = \frac{mRT}{PV} = \frac{(0.00271\ \text{kg})(8314\ \text{J/kmol}\cdot\text{K})(291\ \text{K})}{[(765/760)(1.01\times10^5\ \text{N/m}^2)](0.001\,29\ \text{m}^3)} = 50.0\ \text{kg/kmol}$$

**16.13 [II]** Compute the volume of 8.0 g of helium ($M = 4.0$ kg/kmol) at 15 °C and 480 mmHg.

Use $PV = (m/M)RT$ to obtain

$$V = \frac{mRT}{MP} = \frac{(0.0080\ \text{kg})(8314\ \text{J/kmol}\cdot\text{K})(288\ \text{K})}{(4.0\ \text{kg/kmol})[(480/760)(1.01\times10^5\ \text{N/m}^2)]} = 0.075\ \text{m}^3 = 75\ \text{liters}$$

**16.14 [II]** Find the density of methane ($M = 16$ kg/kmol) at 20 °C and 5.0 atm.

Use $PV = (m/M)RT$ and $\rho = m/V$ to get

$$\rho = \frac{PM}{RT} = \frac{(5.0\times1.01\times10^5\ \text{N/m}^2)(16\ \text{kg/kmol})}{(8314\ \text{J/kmol}\cdot\text{K})(293\ \text{K})} = 3.3\ \text{kg/m}^3$$

**16.15 [II]** A fish emits a 2.0-mm³ bubble at a depth of 15 m in a lake. Find the volume of the bubble as it reaches the surface. Assume its temperature does not change.

The absolute pressure in the bubble at a depth $h$ is

$$P = \rho gh + \text{Atmospheric pressure}$$

where $\rho = 1000\ \text{kg/m}^3$ and atmospheric pressure is about 100 kPa. At 15 m,

$$P_1 = (1000\ \text{kg/m}^3)\,(9.8\ \text{m/s}^2)\,(15\ \text{m}) + 100\ \text{kPa} = 247\ \text{kPa}$$

and at the surface, $P_2 = 100$ kPa. Following the usual procedure,

$$V_2 = V_1\left(\frac{P_1}{P_2}\right)\left(\frac{T_2}{T_1}\right) = (2.0\ \text{mm}^3)\left(\frac{247}{100}\right)(1.0) = 4.9\ \text{mm}^3$$

**16.16 [II]** A 15-cm-long test tube of uniform bore is lowered, open-end down, into a fresh-water lake. How far below the surface of the lake must the water level be in the tube if one-third of the tube is to be filled with water?

Let $h$ be the depth of the water in the tube below the lake's surface. The air pressure $P_2$ in the tube at depth $h$ must equal atmospheric pressure $P_a$ plus the pressure of water at that depth:

$$P_2 = P_a + \rho g h$$

The Ideal Gas Law gives us the value of $P_2$ as

$$P_2 = (P_1)\left(\frac{V_1}{V_2}\right)\left(\frac{T_2}{T_1}\right) = (1.01\times10^5\ \text{Pa})\left(\frac{3}{2}\right)(1.00) = 1.50\times10^5\ \text{Pa}$$

Then, from the relation between $P_2$ and $h$,

$$h = \frac{P_2 - P_a}{\rho g} = \frac{0.50\times10^5\ \text{Pa}}{(1000\ \text{kg/m}^3)\,(9.81\ \text{m/s}^2)} = 5.1\ \text{m}$$

where atmospheric pressure has been taken as 100 kPa.

**16.17 [II]** A tank contains 18 kg of $N_2$ gas ($M = 28$ kg/kmol) at a pressure of 4.50 atm. How much $H_2$ gas ($M = 2.0$ kg/kmol) at 3.50 atm would the same tank contain?

Write the Ideal Gas Law twice, once for each gas:

$$P_N V = n_N RT \qquad \text{and} \qquad P_H V = n_H RT$$

Division of one equation by the other eliminates $V$, $R$, and $T$:

$$\frac{n_H}{n_N} = \frac{P_H}{P_N} = \frac{3.50\ \text{atm}}{4.50\ \text{atm}} = 0.778$$

But
$$n_N = \frac{m}{M} = \frac{18\ \text{kg}}{28\ \text{kg/kmol}} = 0.643\ \text{kmol}$$

and so
$$n_H = (n_N)(0.778) = (0.643\ \text{kmol})\,(0.778) = 0.500\ \text{kmol}$$

Then, from $n = m/M$,

$$m_H = (0.500\ \text{kmol})\,(2.0\ \text{kg/kmol}) = 1.0\ \text{kg}$$

**16.18 [II]** In a gaseous mixture at 20 °C the partial pressures of the components are as follows: hydrogen, 200 mmHg; carbon dioxide, 150 mmHg; methane, 320 mmHg; ethylene, 105 mmHg. What are (*a*) the total pressure of the mixture and (*b*) the mass fraction of hydrogen? ($M_H = 2.0$ kg/kmol, $M_{CO_2} = 44$ kg/kmol, $M_{methane} = 16$ kg/kmol, $M_{ethylene} = 30$ kg/kmol.)

(*a*) According to Dalton's Law,

$$\text{Total pressure} = \text{Sum of partial pressures} = 200 \text{ mmHg} + 150 \text{ mmHg} + 320 \text{ mmHg} + 105 \text{ mmHg}$$
$$= 775 \text{ mmHg}$$

(*b*) From the Ideal Gas Law, $m = M(PV/RT)$. The mass of hydrogen gas present is

$$m_H = M_H P_H \left(\frac{V}{RT}\right)$$

The total mass of gas present, $m_t$, is the sum of similar terms:

$$m_t = (M_H P_H + M_{CO_2} P_{CO_2} + M_{methane} P_{methane} + M_{ethylene} P_{ethylene})\left(\frac{V}{RT}\right)$$

The required fraction is then

$$\frac{m_H}{m_t} = \frac{M_H P_H}{M_H P_H + M_{CO_2} P_{CO_2} + M_{methane} P_{methane} + M_{ethylene} P_{ethylene}}$$

$$\frac{m_H}{m_t} = \frac{(2.0 \text{ kg/kmol})(200 \text{ mmHg})}{(2.0 \text{ kg/kmol})(200 \text{ mmHg}) + (44 \text{ kg/kmol})(150 \text{ mmHg}) + (16 \text{ kg/kmol})(320 \text{ mmHg}) + (30 \text{ kg/kmol})(105 \text{ mmHg})} = 0.026$$

## SUPPLEMENTARY PROBLEMS

**16.19 [I]** A given mass of an ideal gas occupies a volume of 4.00 m³ at 758 mmHg. Compute its volume at 635 mmHg if the temperature remains unchanged.

**16.20 [I]** A mass of ideal gas occupies 38 mL at 20 °C. If its pressure is held constant, what volume does it occupy at a temperature of 45 °C?

**16.21 [I]** On a day when atmospheric pressure is 75.83 cmHg, a pressure gauge on a tank of gas reads a pressure of 258.5 cmHg. What is the absolute pressure (in atmospheres and kPa) of the gas in the tank?

**16.22 [II]** A tank of ideal gas is sealed off at 20 °C and 1.00 atm pressure. What will be the pressure (in kPa and mmHg) in the tank if the gas temperature is decreased to −35 °C?

**16.23 [II]** Given 1000 mL of helium at 15 °C and 763 mmHg, determine its volume at −6 °C and 420 mmHg.

**16.24 [II]** One kilomole of ideal gas occupies 22.4 m³ at 0 °C and 1 atm. (*a*) What pressure is required to compress 1.00 kmol into a 5.00 m³ container at 100 °C? (*b*) If 1.00 kmol was to be sealed in a 5.00 m³ tank that could withstand a gauge pressure of only 3.00 atm, what would be the maximum temperature of the gas if the tank was not to burst?

**16.25 [II]** Air is trapped in the sealed lower end of a capillary tube by a mercury column as shown in Fig. 16-1. The top of the tube is open. The temperature is 14 °C, and atmospheric pressure is 740 mmHg. What length would the trapped air column have if the temperature were 30 °C and atmospheric pressure were 760 mmHg?

**16.26 [II]** Air is trapped in the sealed lower part of the vertical capillary tube shown in Fig. 16-1 by an 8.0-cm-long mercury column. The top is open, and the system is at equilibrium. What will be the length of the trapped air column if the tube is now tilted so it makes an angle of 65° to the vertical? Take $P_a = 76$ cmHg.

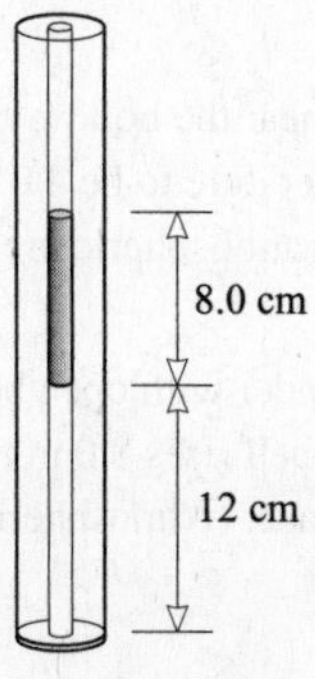


Fig. 16-1

**16.27 [II]** On a day when the barometer reads 75.23 cm, a reaction vessel holds 250 mL of ideal gas at 20.0 °C. An oil manometer ($\rho = 810$ kg/m$^3$) reads the pressure in the vessel to be 41.0 cm of oil and below atmospheric pressure. What volume will the gas occupy under S.T.P.?

**16.28 [II]** A 5000-cm$^3$ tank contains an ideal gas ($M = 40$ kg/kmol) at a gauge pressure of 530 kPa and a temperature of 25 °C. Assuming atmospheric pressure to be 100 kPa, what mass of gas is in the tank?

**16.29 [II]** The pressure of air in a reasonably good vacuum might be $2.0 \times 10^{-5}$ mmHg. What mass of air exists in a 250 mL volume at this pressure and 25 °C? Take $M = 28$ kg/kmol for air.

**16.30 [II]** What volume will 1.216 g of $SO_2$ gas ($M = 64.1$ kg/kmol) occupy at 18.0 °C and 755 mmHg if it acts like an ideal gas?

**16.31 [II]** Compute the density of $H_2S$ gas ($M = 34.1$ kg/kmol) at 27 °C and 2.00 atm, assuming it to be ideal.

**16.32 [II]** A 30-mL tube contains 0.25 g of water vapor ($M = 18$ kg/kmol) at a temperature of 340 °C. Assuming the gas to be ideal, what is its pressure?

**16.33 [II]** One method for estimating the temperature at the center of the Sun is based on the Ideal Gas Law. If the center is assumed to consist of gases whose average $M$ is 0.70 kg/kmol, and if the density and pressure are $90 \times 10^3$ kg/m$^3$ and $1.4 \times 10^{11}$ atm, respectively, calculate the temperature

**16.34 [II]** A 500-mL sealed flask contains nitrogen at a pressure of 76.00 cmHg. A tiny glass tube lies at the bottom of the flask. Its volume is 0.50 mL and it contains hydrogen gas at a pressure of 4.5 atm. Suppose the glass tube is now broken so that the hydrogen fills the flask. What is the new pressure in the flask?

**16.35 [II]** As shown in Fig. 16-2, two flasks are connected by an initially closed stopcock. One flask contains krypton gas at 500 mmHg, while the other contains helium at 950 mmHg. The stopcock is now opened so that the gases mix. What is the final pressure in the system? Assume constant temperature.

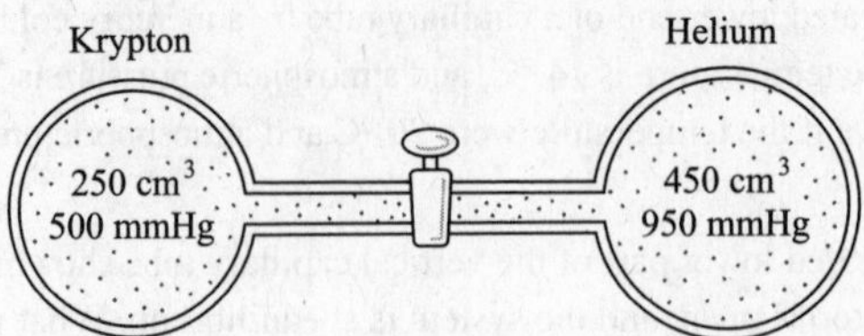


Fig. 16-2

**16.36 [II]** An air bubble of volume $V_0$ is released near the bottom of a lake at a depth of 11.0 m. What will be its new volume at the surface? Assume its temperature to be 4.0 °C at the release point and 12 °C at the surface. The water has a density of 1000 kg/m$^3$, and atmospheric pressure is 75 cmHg.

**16.37 [II]** A cylindrical diving bell (a vertical cylinder with open bottom end and closed top end) 12.0 m high is lowered in a lake until water within the bell rises 8.0 m from the bottom end. Determine the distance from the top of the bell to the surface of the lake. (Atmospheric pressure = 1.00 atm.)

## ANSWERS TO SUPPLEMENTARY PROBLEMS

**16.19 [I]** 4.77 m$^3$

**16.20 [I]** 41 mL

**16.21 [I]** 334.3 cmHg = 4.398 atm = 445.6 kPa

**16.22 [II]** 82 kPa = $6.2 \times 10^2$ mmHg

**16.23 [II]]** $1.68 \times 10^3$ mL

**16.24 [II]** (*a*) 6.12 atm; (*b*) −30 °C

**16.25 [II]** 12.4 cm

**16.26 [II]** 0.13 m

**16.27 [II]** 233 mL

**16.28 [II]** 0.051 kg

**16.29 [II]** $7.5 \times 10^{-12}$ kg

**16.30 [II]** 457 mL

**16.31 [II]** 2.76 kg/m$^3$

**16.32 [II]** 2.4 MPa

**16.33 [II]** $1.3 \times 10^7$ K

**16.34 [II]** 76.34 cmHg

**16.35 [II]** 789 mmHg

**16.36 [II]** $2.1V_0$

**16.37 [II]** 20.6 m − 4.0 m = 16.6 m

# CHAPTER 17

# Kinetic Theory

**The Kinetic Theory** considers matter to be composed of discrete tiny particles (atoms and/or molecules) moving continuously. In a gas, the molecules are in random motion with a wide distribution of speeds ranging from zero to very large values.

**Avogadro's Number** ($N_A$) is the number of particles (molecules or atoms) in 1 kmol of any substance. For all substances,

$$N_A = 6.022\,141\,79 \times 10^{26}\ \text{particles/kmol} = 6.022\,141\,79 \times 10^{23}\ \text{particles/mol}$$

As examples, $M = 2$ kg/kmol for $H_2$ and $M = 32$ kg/kmol for $O_2$. Therefore, 2 kg of $H_2$ and 32 kg of $O_2$ each contain $6.02 \times 10^{26}$ molecules.

**The Mass of a Molecule** (or atom) can be found from the molecular (or atomic) mass $M$ of the substance and Avogadro's number $N_A$. Since $M$ kg of a substance contains $N_A$ particles, the mass $m_0$ of one particle is given by

$$m_0 = \frac{M}{N_A}$$

**The Average Translational Kinetic Energy** of a gas molecule is $3k_BT/2$, where $T$ is the *absolute temperature* of the gas and $k_B = R/N_A = 1.380\,650\,4 \times 10^{-23}$ J/K is **Boltzmann's constant.** In other words, for a molecule of mass $m_0$,

$$(\text{Average of } \tfrac{1}{2}m_0v^2) = \tfrac{3}{2}k_BT$$

Note that Boltzmann's constant is also represented as $k$ (with no subscript) in the literature. It is one of a handful of what are known as *fundamental constants*.

**The Root Mean Square Speed** ($v_{\text{rms}}$) of a gas molecule is the square root of the average of $v^2$ for a molecule over a prolonged time. Equivalently, the average may be taken over all molecules of the gas at a given instant. From the expression for the average kinetic energy, the rms speed is

$$v_{\text{rms}} = \sqrt{\frac{3k_BT}{m_0}}$$

**The Absolute Temperature** ($T$) of an ideal gas has a meaning that is found by solving $\frac{1}{2}m_0 v_{rms}^2 = \frac{3}{2}k_B T$. That equation leads to

$$T = \left(\frac{2}{3k_B}\right)\left(\frac{1}{2}m_0 v_{rms}^2\right)$$

The absolute temperature of an ideal gas is a measure of its average translational kinetic energy (KE) per molecule.

**The Pressure** ($P$) of an ideal gas was given in Chapter 16 in the form $PV = (m/M)RT$. Noticing that $m = Nm_0$, where $N$ is the number of molecules in the volume $V$, and replacing $T$ by the value determined above, leads to

$$PV = \tfrac{1}{3}Nm_0 v_{rms}^2$$

Further, since $Nm_0/V = \rho$, the density of the gas,

$$P = \tfrac{1}{3}\rho v_{rms}^2$$

**The Mean Free Path (m.f.p.)** of a gas molecule is the average distance such a molecule moves between collisions. For an ideal gas of spherical molecules each with a radius $b$,

$$\text{m.f.p.} = \frac{1}{4\pi\sqrt{2}b^2\,(N/V)}$$

where $N/V$ is the number of molecules per unit volume.

## SOLVED PROBLEMS

**17.1 [I]** Ordinary nitrogen gas consists of molecules of $N_2$. Find the mass of one such molecule. The molecular mass is 28 kg/kmol.

$$m_0 = \frac{M}{N_A} = \frac{28\ \text{kg/kmol}}{6.02\times 10^{26}\ \text{kmol}^{-1}} = 4.7\times 10^{-26}\ \text{kg}$$

**17.2 [I]** Helium gas consists of separate He atoms rather than molecules. How many helium atoms, He, are there in 2.0 g of helium? $M = 4.0$ kg/kmol for He.

**Method 1**

One kilomole of He is 4.0 kg, and it contains $N_A$ atoms. But 2.0 g is equivalent to

$$\frac{0.0020\ \text{kg}}{4.0\ \text{kg/kmol}} = 0.00050\ \text{kmol}$$

of helium. Therefore,

$$\begin{aligned}\text{Number of atoms in 2.0 g} &= (0.00050\ \text{kmol})\,N_A\\ &= (0.00050\ \text{kmol})\,(6.02\times 10^{26}\ \text{kmol}^{-1}) = 3.0\times 10^{23}\end{aligned}$$

**Method 2**

The mass of a helium atom is

$$m_0 = \frac{M}{N_A} = \frac{4.0 \text{ kg/kmol}}{6.02 \times 10^{26} \text{ kmol}^{-1}} = 6.64 \times 10^{-27} \text{ kg}$$

hence, $$\text{Number in 2.0 g} = \frac{0.0020 \text{ kg}}{6.64 \times 10^{-27} \text{ kg}} = 3.0 \times 10^{23}$$

**17.3 [II]** A droplet of mercury has a radius of 0.50 mm. How many mercury atoms are in the droplet? For Hg, $M = 202$ kg/kmol and $\rho = 13600$ kg/m$^3$.

The volume of the droplet is

$$V = \frac{4\pi r^3}{3} = \left(\frac{4\pi}{3}\right)(5.0 \times 10^{-4} \text{ m})^3 = 5.24 \times 10^{-10} \text{ m}^3$$

The mass of the droplet is

$$m = \rho V = (13600 \text{ kg/m}^3)(5.24 \times 10^{-10} \text{ m}^3) = 7.1 \times 10^{-6} \text{ kg}$$

The mass of a mercury atom is

$$m_0 = \frac{M}{N_A} = \frac{202 \text{ kg/kmol}}{6.02 \times 10^{26} \text{ kmol}^{-1}} = 3.36 \times 10^{-25} \text{ kg}$$

The number of atoms in the droplet is then

$$\text{Number} = \frac{m}{m_0} = \frac{7.1 \times 10^{-6} \text{ kg}}{3.36 \times 10^{-25} \text{ kg}} = 2.1 \times 10^{19}$$

**17.4 [II]** How many molecules are there in 70 mL of benzene? For benzene, $\rho = 0.88$ g/cm$^3$ and $M = 78$ kg/kmol.

Remember that 1 g/cm$^3$ = 1000 kg/m$^3$ and so here $\rho = 880$ kg/m$^3$.

$$\text{Mass of 70 cm}^3 = m = \rho V = (880 \text{ kg/m}^3)(70 \times 10^{-6} \text{ m}^3) = 0.0616 \text{ kg}$$

$$m_0 = \frac{M}{N_A} = \frac{78 \text{ kg/kmol}}{6.02 \times 10^{26} \text{ kmol}^{-1}} = 1.30 \times 10^{-25} \text{ kg}$$

$$\text{Number in 70 cm}^3 = \frac{m}{m_0} = \frac{0.0616 \text{ kg}}{1.30 \times 10^{-25} \text{ kg}} = 4.8 \times 10^{23}$$

**17.5 [I]** Find the rms speed of a nitrogen molecule ($M = 28$ kg/kmol) in air at 0 °C.

We know that $\frac{1}{2} m_0 v^2_{\text{rms}} = \frac{3}{2} k_B T$

and so $$v_{\text{rms}} = \sqrt{\frac{3k_B T}{m_0}}$$

But $$m_0 = \frac{M}{N_A} = \frac{28 \text{ kg/kmol}}{6.02 \times 10^{26} \text{ kmol}^{-1}} = 4.65 \times 10^{-26} \text{ kg}$$

Therefore, $$v_{\text{rms}} = \sqrt{\frac{3(1.38 \times 10^{-23} \text{ J/K})(273 \text{ K})}{4.65 \times 10^{-26} \text{ kg}}} = 0.49 \text{ km/s}$$

**17.6 [II]** Suppose a particular gas molecule at the surface of the Earth happens to have the rms speed for that gas at exactly 0 °C. If it were to go straight up without colliding with other molecules, how high would it rise? Assume $g$ is constant over the trajectory.

The molecule's KE is initially

$$\text{KE} = \tfrac{1}{2} m_0 \upsilon_{\text{rms}}^2 = \tfrac{3}{2} k_B T$$

The molecule will rise until its KE has been changed to $\text{PE}_G$. Therefore, calling the height to which it rises $h$,

$$\tfrac{3}{2} k_B T = m_0 g h$$

Solving for $h$ yields

$$h = \left(\frac{1}{m_0}\right)\left(\frac{3k_B T}{2g}\right) = \left(\frac{1}{m_0}\right)\left[\frac{(3)(1.38 \times 10^{-23}\ \text{J/K})(273\ \text{K})}{2(9.81\ \text{m/s}^2)}\right]$$
$$= \frac{5.76 \times 10^{-22}\ \text{kg} \cdot \text{m}}{m_0}$$

where $m_0$ is in kg. The height varies inversely with the mass of the molecule. For an $N_2$ molecule, $m_0 = 4.65 \times 10^{-26}$ kg (Problem 17.5), and in this case $h$ turns out to be 12.4 km.

**17.7 [I]** Air at room temperature has a density of about 1.29 kg/m³. Assuming it to be entirely one gas, find $\upsilon_{\text{rms}}$ for its molecules.

Because $P = \frac{1}{3}\rho \upsilon_{\text{rms}}^2$,

$$\upsilon_{\text{rms}} = \sqrt{\frac{3P}{\rho}} = \sqrt{\frac{3(100 \times 10^3\ \text{Pa})}{1.29\ \text{kg/m}^3}} \approx 480\ \text{m/s}$$

where atmospheric pressure was assumed to be 100 kPa.

**17.8 [I]** Find the translational kinetic energy of one gram mole of any ideal gas at 0 °C.

For an ideal gas, $\frac{3}{2} k_B T = \frac{1}{2} m_0 \upsilon_{\text{rms}}^2$, which is the KE of each molecule. One gram mole contains $N_A \times 10^{-3}$ molecules. Hence, the total KE per mole is

$$\text{KE}_{\text{total}} = (N_A \times 10^{-3})\left(\frac{3}{2} k_B T\right) = 3 \times 10^{-3}\, \frac{RT}{2} = 3.4\ \text{kJ}$$

where $T$ was taken as 273 K and use was made of the fact that $k_B N_A = R$.

**17.9 [II]** There is about one hydrogen atom per cm³ in outer space, where the temperature (in the shade) is about 3.5 K. Find the rms speed of these atoms and the pressure they exert.

Keeping in mind that $k_B N_A = R$ and that $m_0 = M/N_A$,

$$\upsilon_{\text{rms}} = \sqrt{\frac{3k_B T}{m_0}} = \sqrt{\frac{3k_B T}{M/N_A}} = \sqrt{\frac{3RT}{M}} \approx 295\ \text{m/s or } 0.30\ \text{km/s}$$

where $M$ for hydrogen is 1.0 kg/kmol and $T$ = 3.5 K. We can now use $P = \rho v_{rms}^2/3$ to find the pressure. The mass $m_0$ of a hydrogen atom is (1.0 kg/kmol)/$N_A$. Since 1 m³ = 10⁶ cm³ there are $N = 10^6$ atoms/m³ and

$$\rho = \frac{Nm_0}{V} = \left(\frac{N}{V}\right)m_0 = 10^6\left(\frac{1}{N_A}\right)\ \text{kg/m}^3$$

and
$$P = \tfrac{1}{3}\rho v_{rms}^2 = \frac{1}{3}\left(\frac{10^6}{6.02\times10^{26}}\right)(295)^2 = 5\times10^{-17}\ \text{Pa}$$

**17.10 [I]** Find the following ratios for hydrogen ($M$ = 2.0 kg/kmol) and nitrogen ($M$ = 28 kg/kmol) gases at the same temperature: (*a*) $(\text{KE})_\text{H}/(\text{KE})_\text{N}$ and (*b*) (rms speed)$_\text{H}$/(rms speed)$_\text{N}$.

(*a*) The average translational KE of a molecule, $\frac{3}{2}k_BT$, depends only on temperature. Therefore, the ratio $(\text{KE})_\text{H}/(\text{KE})_\text{N} = 1$.

(*b*) $$\frac{(v_{rms})_\text{H}}{(v_{rms})_\text{N}} = \sqrt{\frac{3k_BT/m_{0\text{H}}}{3k_BT/m_{0\text{N}}}} = \sqrt{\frac{m_{0\text{N}}}{m_{0\text{H}}}}$$

But $m_0 = M/N_A$, and so

$$\frac{(v_{rms})_\text{H}}{(v_{rms})_\text{N}} = \sqrt{\frac{M_\text{N}}{M_\text{H}}} = \sqrt{\frac{28}{2.0}} = 3.7$$

**17.11 [II]** Certain ideal gas molecules behave like spheres of radius 3.0 × 10⁻¹⁰ m. Find the mean free path of these molecules under S.T.P.

**Method 1**

We know that at S.T.P. 1.00 kmol of substance occupies 22.4 m³. The number of molecules per unit volume, $N/V$, can be found from the fact that in 22.4 m³ there are $N_A = 6.02 \times 10^{26}$ molecules. The mean free path is given by

$$\text{m.f.p.} = \frac{1}{4\pi\sqrt{2}b^2(N/V)} = \frac{1}{4\pi\sqrt{2}(3.0\times10^{-10}\ \text{m})^2}\left(\frac{22.4\ \text{m}^3}{6.02\times10^{26}}\right) = 2.4\times10^{-8}\ \text{m}$$

**Method 2**

Because $M = m_0N_A = m_0\,(R/k_B)$ and $m = Nm_0$,

$$PV = \left(\frac{m}{M}\right)RT \quad \text{becomes} \quad PV = Nk_BT$$

and so
$$\frac{N}{V} = \frac{P}{k_BT} = \frac{1.01\times10^5\ \text{N/m}^2}{(1.38\times10^{-23}\ \text{J/K})\,(273\ \text{K})} = 2.68\times10^{25}\ \text{m}^{-3}$$

We then use the mean free path equation as in method 1.

**17.12 [II]** At what pressure will the mean free path be 50 cm for spherical molecules of radius 3.0 × 10⁻¹⁰ m? Assume an ideal gas at 20 °C.

From the expression for the mean free path,

$$\frac{N}{V} = \frac{1}{4\pi\sqrt{2}b^2(\text{m.f.p.})}$$

Combining this with the Ideal Gas Law in the form $PV = Nk_B T$ (see Problem 17.11) yields

$$P = \frac{k_B T}{4\pi\sqrt{2}b^2(\text{m.f.p.})} = \frac{(1.38\times10^{-23}\ \text{J/K})(293\ \text{K})}{4\pi\sqrt{2}\,(3.0\times10^{-10}\ \text{m})^2\,(0.50\ \text{m})} = 5.1\ \text{mPa}$$

## SUPPLEMENTARY PROBLEMS

**17.13 [I]** Find the mass of a neon atom. The atomic mass of neon is 20.2 kg/kmol.

**17.14 [II]** A typical polymer molecule in polyethylene might have a molecular mass of $15 \times 10^3$. (*a*) What is the mass in kilograms of such a molecule? (*b*) How many such molecules would make up 2 g of polymer?

**17.15 [II]** A certain strain of tobacco mosaic virus has $M = 4.0 \times 10^7$ kg/kmol. How many molecules of the virus are present in 1.0 mL of a solution that contains 0.10 mg of virus per mL?

**17.16 [II]** An old electronic vacuum tube was sealed off during manufacture at a pressure of $1.2 \times 10^{-7}$ mmHg at 27 °C. Its volume was 100 cm$^3$. (*a*) What was the pressure in the tube (in Pa)? (*b*) How many gas molecules remained in the tube?

**17.17 [II]** The pressure of helium gas in a tube is 0.200 mmHg. If the temperature of the gas is 20 °C, what is the density of the gas? (Use $M_{\text{He}} = 4.0$ kg/kmol.)

**17.18 [II]** At what temperature will the molecules of an ideal gas have twice the rms speed they have at 20 °C?

**17.19 [II]** An object must have a speed of at least 11.2 km/s to escape from the Earth's gravitational field. At what temperature will $v_{\text{rms}}$ for $H_2$ molecules equal the escape speed? Repeat for $N_2$ molecules. ($M_{H2} = 2.0$ kg/kmol and $M_{N2} = 28$ kg/kmol.)

**17.20 [II]** In a certain region of outer space there are an average of only five molecules per cm$^3$. The temperature there is about 3 K. What is the average pressure of this very dilute gas?

**17.21 [II]** A cube of aluminum has a volume of 1.0 cm$^3$ and a mass of 2.7 g. (*a*) How many aluminum atoms are there in the cube? (*b*) How large a volume is associated with each atom? (*c*) If each atom were a cube, what would be its edge length? $M = 108$ kg/kmol for aluminum.

**17.22 [II]** The rms speed of nitrogen molecules in the air at S.T.P. is about 490 m/s. Find their mean free path and the average time between collisions. The radius of a nitrogen molecule can be taken to be $2.0 \times 10^{-10}$ m.

**17.23 [II]** What is the mean free path of a gas molecule (radius $2.5 \times 10^{-10}$ m) in an ideal gas at 500 °C when the pressure is $7.0 \times 10^{-6}$ mmHg?

## ANSWERS TO SUPPLEMENTARY PROBLEMS

**17.13 [I]** $3.36 \times 10^{-26}$ kg

**17.14 [II]** (*a*) $2.5 \times 10^{-23}$ kg; (*b*) $8 \times 10^{19}$

**17.15 [II]** $1.5 \times 10^{12}$

**17.16 [II]** (*a*) $1.6 \times 10^{-5}$ Pa; (*b*) $3.8 \times 10^{11}$

**17.17 [II]** $4.4 \times 10^{-5}$ kg/m$^3$

**17.18 [II]** 1170 K $\approx$ 900 °C

**17.19 [II]** $1.0 \times 10^4$ K; $1.4 \times 10^5$ K

**17.20 [II]** $2 \times 10^{-16}$ Pa

**17.21 [II]** (*a*) $1.5 \times 10^{22}$; (*b*) $6.6 \times 10^{-29}$ m$^3$; (*c*) $4.0 \times 10^{-10}$ m

**17.22 [II]** $5.2 \times 10^{-8}$ m, $1.1 \times 10^{-10}$ s

**17.23 [II]** 10 m

# CHAPTER 18

# Heat Quantities

**Thermal Energy** is the random kinetic energy of the particles (usually electrons, ions, atoms, and molecules) composing a system.

**Heat** ($Q$) is thermal energy in transit from a system (or aggregate of electrons, ions, and atoms) at one temperature to a system that is in contact with it but is at a lower temperature. Its SI unit is the joule. Other units used for heat are the ***calorie*** (1 cal = 4.1858 J) and the British thermal unit (1 Btu = 1054 J). The "Calorie" used by nutritionists is called the "large calorie" and is actually a kilocalorie (1 Cal = 1 kcal = $10^3$ cal = 4185.8 J where 1 J = 0.2389 cal).

**The Specific Heat** (or ***specific heat capacity***, $c$) of a substance is the quantity of heat required to change the temperature of a unit mass of the substance by one degree Celsius or equivalently by one kelvin.

If a quantity of heat $\Delta Q$ is required to produce a temperature change $\Delta T$ in a mass $m$ of substance, then the specific heat is

$$c = \frac{\Delta Q}{m \Delta T} \quad \text{or} \quad \Delta Q = cm\,\Delta T$$

In the SI, $c$ has the unit J/kg·K, which is equivalent to J/kg·°C. Specific heats are often tabulated in kJ/kg·K; be careful with these units. Also widely used is the unit cal/g·°C, where 1 cal/g·°C = 4.186 J/kg·°C = 4.186 kJ/kg·K = 1 kcal/kg·K.

Each substance has a characteristic value of specific heat, which varies slightly with temperature. For water, $c$ = 4180 J/kg·°C = 1.00 cal/g·°C.

**The Heat Gained (or Lost)** by a body (whose phase does not change) as it undergoes a temperature change $\Delta T$, is given by

$$\Delta Q = mc\,\Delta T$$

**The Heat of Fusion** ($L_f$) of a crystalline solid is the quantity of heat required to melt a unit mass of the solid at constant temperature. It is also equal to the quantity of heat given off by a unit mass of the molten solid as it crystallizes at this same temperature. The heat of fusion of water at 0 °C is about 335 kJ/kg or 80 cal/g.

**The Heat of Vaporization** ($L_v$) of a liquid is the quantity of heat required to vaporize a unit mass of the liquid at constant temperature. For water at 100 °C, $L_v$ is about 2.26 MJ/kg or 540 cal/g.

**The Heat of Sublimation** of a solid substance is the quantity of heat required to convert a unit mass of the substance from the solid to the gaseous state at constant temperature.

**Calorimetry Problems** involve the sharing of thermal energy among initially hot objects and cold objects. Since energy must be conserved, one can write the following equation:

$$\text{Sum of heat changes for all object} = 0$$

Here the heat flowing out of the high temperature system ($\Delta Q_{out} < 0$) numerically equals the heat flowing into the low temperature system ($\Delta Q_{in} > 0$) and so the sum is zero. This, of course, assumes that no thermal energy is otherwise lost from the system.

**Absolute Humidity** is the mass of water vapor present per unit volume of gas (usually the atmosphere). Typical units are $kg/m^3$ and $g/cm^3$.

**Relative Humidity** (R.H.) is the ratio obtained by dividing the mass of water vapor per unit volume *present in the air* by the mass of water vapor per unit volume *present in saturated air at the same temperature.* When it is expressed in percent, the ratio is multiplied by 100.

**Dew Point:** Cooler air at saturation contains less water than warmer air does at saturation. When air is cooled, it eventually reaches a temperature at which it is saturated. This temperature is called the *dew point.* At temperatures lower than this, water condenses out of the air.

## SOLVED PROBLEMS

**18.1 [I]** (*a*) How much heat is required to raise the temperature of 250 mL of water from 20.0 °C to 35.0 °C? (*b*) How much heat is lost by the water as it cools back down to 20.0 °C?

Since 250 mL of water has a mass of 250 g, and since $c = 1.00\ \text{cal/g}\cdot{}^\circ\text{C}$ for water, we have

(*a*) $\Delta Q = mc\,\Delta T = (250\ \text{g})(1.00\ \text{cal/g}\cdot{}^\circ\text{C})(15.0\ {}^\circ\text{C}) = 3.75 \times 10^3\ \text{cal} = 15.7\ \text{kJ}$

(*b*) $\Delta Q = mc\,\Delta T = (250\ \text{g})(1.00\ \text{cal/g}\cdot{}^\circ\text{C})(-15.0\ {}^\circ\text{C}) = -3.75 \times 10^3\ \text{cal} = -15.7\ \text{kJ}$

Notice that heat-in (i.e., the heat that enters an object) is taken to be positive, whereas heat-out (i.e., the heat that leaves an object) is taken to be negative.

**18.2 [I]** How much heat does 25 g of aluminum give off as it cools from 100 °C to 20 °C? For aluminum, $c = 880\ \text{J/kg}\cdot{}^\circ\text{C}$.

$$\Delta Q = mc\,\Delta T = (0.025\ \text{kg})(880\ \text{J/kg}\cdot{}^\circ\text{C})(-80\ {}^\circ\text{C}) = -1.76\ \text{kJ}$$

or to two significant figures, −1.8 kJ.

**18.3 [I]** A certain amount of heat is added to a mass of aluminum ($c = 0.21\ \text{cal/g}\cdot{}^\circ\text{C}$), and its temperature is raised 57 °C. Suppose that the same amount of heat is added to the same mass of copper ($c = 0.093\ \text{cal/g}\cdot{}^\circ\text{C}$). How much does the temperature of the copper rise?

Because $\Delta Q$ is the same for both, we have

$$mc_{\text{Al}}\,\Delta T_{\text{Al}} = mc_{\text{Cu}}\,\Delta T_{\text{Cu}}$$

or
$$\Delta T_{\text{Cu}} = \left(\frac{c_{\text{Al}}}{c_{\text{Cu}}}\right)(\Delta T_{\text{Al}}) = \left(\frac{0.21}{0.093}\right)(57\ {}^\circ\text{C}) = 1.3\times 10^2\ {}^\circ\text{C}$$

**18.4 [I]** Two identical metal plates (mass = $m$, specific heat = $c$) have different temperatures; one is at 20 °C, and the other is at 90 °C. They are placed in good thermal contact. What is their final temperature?

Because the plates are identical, we would guess the final temperature to be midway between 20 °C and 90 °C, namely 55 °C. This is correct, but let us show it mathematically. From the law of conservation of energy, the *heat lost by one plate must equal the heat gained by the other*. Thus, *the total heat change of the system is zero*. In equation form,

$$(\text{Heat change of hot plate}) + (\text{Heat change of cold plate}) = 0$$
$$mc(\Delta T)_{\text{hot}} + mc(\Delta T)_{\text{cold}} = 0$$

which is short-hand for $m_{\text{hot}}\, c_{\text{hot}}\, \Delta T_{\text{hot}} + m_{\text{cold}}\, c_{\text{cold}}\, \Delta T_{\text{cold}} = 0$.

Be careful about $\Delta T$: It is the final temperature (which we denote by $T_f$ in this case) minus the initial temperature. The above equation thus becomes

$$mc(T_f - 90\ °\text{C}) + mc(T_f - 20\ °\text{C}) = 0$$

After canceling $mc$ from each term, solve the equation and find $T_f = 55$ °C, the expected answer.

**18.5 [II]** A thermos bottle contains 250 g of coffee at 90 °C. To this is added 20 g of milk at 5 °C. After equilibrium is established, what is the temperature of the liquid? Assume no heat loss to the thermos bottle.

Water, coffee, and milk all have the same value of $c$, 1.00 cal/g · °C. The law of energy conservation allows us to write

$$(\text{Heat change of coffee}) + (\text{Heat change of milk}) = 0$$
$$(cm\, \Delta T)_{\text{coffee}} + (cm\, \Delta T)_{\text{milk}} = 0$$

In other words, the heat lost by the coffee equals the heat gained by the milk. If the final temperature of the liquid is $T_f$, then

$$\Delta T_{\text{coffee}} = T_f = 90\ °\text{C} \qquad \Delta T_{\text{milk}} = T_f - 5\ °\text{C}$$

Substituting and canceling $c$ yields

$$(250\ \text{g})(T_f - 90\ °\text{C}) + (20\ \text{g})(T_f - 5\ °\text{C}) = 0$$

Solving this equation leads to $T_f = 84$ °C.

**18.6 [II]** A thermos bottle contains 150 g of water at 4 °C. Into this is placed 90 g of metal at 100 °C. After equilibrium is established, the temperature of the water and metal is 21 °C. What is the specific heat of the metal? Assume no heat loss to the thermos bottle.

$$(\text{Heat change of metal}) + (\text{Heat change of water}) = 0$$
$$(cm\, \Delta T)_{\text{metal}} + (cm\, \Delta T)_{\text{water}} = 0$$
$$c_{\text{metal}}(90\ \text{g})(-79\ °\text{C}) + (1.00\ \text{cal/g}\cdot°\text{C})(150\ \text{g})(17\ °\text{C}) = 0$$

Solving yields $c_{\text{metal}} = 0.36$ cal/g·°C. Notice that $\Delta T_{\text{metal}} = 21 - 90 = -79$ °C.

**18.7 [II]** A 200-g copper calorimeter can contains 150 g of oil at 20 °C. To the oil is added 80 g of aluminum at 300 °C. What will be the temperature of the system after equilibrium is established? $c_{\text{Cu}} = 0.093$ cal/g·°C, $c_{\text{Al}} = 0.21$ cal/g·°C, $c_{\text{oil}} = 0.37$ cal/g·°C.

$$(\text{Heat change of aluminum}) + (\text{Heat change of can and oil}) = 0$$
$$(cm\, \Delta T)_{\text{Al}} + (cm\, \Delta T)_{\text{cu}} + (cm\, \Delta T)_{\text{oil}} = 0$$

With given values substituted, this becomes

$$\left(0.21\frac{\text{cal}}{\text{g}\cdot{}^\circ\text{C}}\right)(80\text{ g})(T_f-300\,^\circ\text{C})+\left(0.093\frac{\text{cal}}{\text{g}\cdot{}^\circ\text{C}}\right)(200\text{ g})(T_f-20\,^\circ\text{C})$$

$$+\left(0.37\frac{\text{cal}}{\text{g}\cdot{}^\circ\text{C}}\right)(150\text{ g})(T_f-20\,^\circ\text{C})=0$$

Solving this equation yields $T_f = 72\,^\circ\text{C}$.

**18.8 [II]** Exactly 3.0 g of carbon was burned to $CO_2$ in a copper calorimeter. The mass of the calorimeter is 1500 g, and there is 2000 g of water in the calorimeter. The initial temperature was 20 °C, and the final temperature is 31 °C. Calculate the heat given off per gram of carbon. $c_{\text{Cu}} = 0.093\text{ cal/g}\cdot{}^\circ\text{C}$. Neglect the small heat capacity of the carbon and carbon dioxide.

Conservation of energy tells us that

$$\text{(Heat change of carbon)} + \text{(Heat change of calorimeter)} + \text{(Heat change of water)} = 0$$

$$\text{(Heat change of carbon)} + (0.093\text{ cal/g}\cdot{}^\circ\text{C})(1500\text{ g})(11\,^\circ\text{C}) + (1\text{ cal/g}\cdot{}^\circ\text{C})(2000\text{ g})(11\,^\circ\text{C}) = 0$$

$$\text{(Heat change of carbon)} = -23\,500\text{ cal}$$

Therefore, the heat given off by one gram of carbon as it burns is

$$\frac{23\,500\text{ cal}}{3.0\text{ g}} = 7.8\text{ kcal/g} = 33\text{ kJ/g}$$

**18.9 [II]** Determine the temperature $T_f$ that results when 150 g of ice at 0 °C is mixed with 300 g of water at 50 °C.

From energy conservation,

$$\text{(Heat change of ice)} + \text{(Heat change of water)} = 0$$

$$\text{(Heat to melt ice)} + \text{(Heat to warm ice water)} + \text{(Heat change of water)} = 0$$

$$(mL_f)_{\text{ice}} + (cm\,\Delta T)_{\text{ice water}} + (cm\,\Delta T)_{\text{water}} = 0$$

$$(150\text{ g})(80\text{ cal/g}) + (1.00\text{ cal/g}\cdot{}^\circ\text{C})(150\text{ g})(T_f - 0\,^\circ\text{C}) + (1.00\text{ cal/g}\cdot{}^\circ\text{C})(300\text{ g})(T_f - 50\,^\circ\text{C}) = 0$$

from which $T_f = 6.7\,^\circ\text{C}$.

**18.10 [II]** How much heat is given up when 20 g of steam at 100 °C is condensed and cooled to 20 °C?

$$\begin{aligned}\text{Heat change} &= \text{(Condensation heat change)} + \text{(Heat change of water during cooling)}\\ &= mL_v + cm\,\Delta T\\ &= (20\text{ g})(-540\text{ cal/g}) + (1.00\text{ cal/g}\cdot{}^\circ\text{C})(20\text{ g})(20\,^\circ\text{C} - 100\,^\circ\text{C})\\ &= -12\,400\text{ cal} = -12\text{ kcal} = -50\text{ kJ}\end{aligned}$$

**18.11 [II]** A 20-g piece of aluminum ($c = 0.21\text{ cal/g}\cdot{}^\circ\text{C}$) at 90 °C is dropped into a cavity in a large block of ice at 0 °C. How much ice does the aluminum melt?

$$\text{(Heat change of Al as it cools to 0 °C)} + \text{(Heat change of mass } m \text{ of ice melted)} = 0$$

$$(mc\,\Delta T)_{\text{Al}} + (L_f m)_{\text{ice}} = 0$$

$$(20\text{ g})(0.21\text{ cal/g}\cdot{}^\circ\text{C})(0\,^\circ\text{C} - 90\,^\circ\text{C}) + (80\text{ cal/g})m = 0$$

from which $m = 4.7$ g is the quantity of ice melted.

**18.12 [II]** In a calorimeter can (which behaves thermally as if it were equivalent to 40 g of water) are 200 g of water and 50 g of ice, all at exactly 0 °C. Into this is poured 30 g of water at 90 °C. What will be the final condition of the system?

Let us start by assuming (perhaps incorrectly) that the final temperature is $T_f > 0$ °C. Then

$$\begin{pmatrix}\text{Heat change of}\\ \text{hot water}\end{pmatrix}+\begin{pmatrix}\text{Heat to}\\ \text{melt ice}\end{pmatrix}+\begin{pmatrix}\text{Heat to warm}\\ \text{250 g of water}\end{pmatrix}+\begin{pmatrix}\text{Heat to warm}\\ \text{calorimeter}\end{pmatrix}=0$$

$$(30\text{ g})(1.00\text{ cal/g}\cdot{}^\circ\text{C})(T_f - 90\,^\circ\text{C}) + (50\text{ g})(80\text{ cal/g}) + (250\text{ g})(1\text{ cal/g}\cdot{}^\circ\text{C})(T_f - 0\,^\circ\text{C})$$
$$+(40\text{ g})(1.00\text{ cal/g}\cdot{}^\circ\text{C})(T_f - 0\,^\circ\text{C}) = 0$$

Solving gives $T_f = -4.1$ °C, contrary to our assumption that the final temperature is above 0 °C. Apparently, not all the ice melts. Therefore, $T_f = 0$ °C.

To find how much ice melts, we write

$$\text{Heat lost by hot water} = \text{Heat gained by melting ice}$$
$$(30\text{ g})(1.00\text{ cal/g}\cdot{}^\circ\text{C})(90\,^\circ\text{C}) = (80\text{ cal/g})m$$

where $m$ is the mass of ice that melts. Solving this equation yields $m = 34$ g. The final system has 50 g − 34 g = 16 g of ice not melted.

**18.13 [I]** An electric heater that produces 900 W of power is used to vaporize water. How much water at 100 °C can be changed to steam at 100 °C in 3.00 min by the heater? (For water at 100 °C, $L_v = 2.26 \times 10^6$ J/kg.)

The heater produces 900 J of heat energy per second. So the heat produced in 3.00 min is

$$\Delta Q = (900\text{ J/s})(180\text{ s}) = 162\text{ kJ}$$

The heat required to vaporize a mass $m$ of water is

$$\Delta Q = mL_v = m(2.26 \times 10^6\text{ J/kg})$$

Equating these two expressions for $\Delta Q$ and solving for $m$ gives $m = 0.0717$ kg = 71.7 g as the mass of water vaporized.

**18.14 [I]** A 3.00-g bullet ($c = 0.030\,5$ cal/g·°C = 128 J/kg·°C) moving at 180 m/s enters a bag of sand and stops. By what amount does the temperature of the bullet change if all its KE becomes thermal energy that is added to the bullet?

The bullet loses KE in the amount

$$\text{KE} = \tfrac{1}{2}mv^2 = \tfrac{1}{2}(3.00 \times 10^{-3}\text{ kg})\,(180\text{ m/s})^2 = 48.6\text{ J}$$

This results in the addition of $\Delta Q = 48.6$ J of thermal energy to the bullet. Then, since $\Delta Q = mc\,\Delta T$, we can find $\Delta T$ for the bullet:

$$\Delta T = \frac{\Delta Q}{mc} = \frac{48.6\text{ J}}{(3.00\times 10^{-3}\text{ kg})\,(128\text{ J/kg}\cdot{}^\circ\text{C})} = 127\,^\circ\text{C}$$

Notice that we had to use $c$ in J/kg·°C, and not in cal/g·°C.

**18.15 [I]** Suppose a 60-kg person consumes 2500 Cal of food in one day. If the entire heat equivalent of this food were retained by the person's body, how large a temperature change would it cause? (For the body, $c = 0.83$ cal/g·°C.) Remember that 1 Cal = 1 kcal = 1000 cal.

The equivalent amount of heat added to the body in one day is

$$\Delta Q = (2500 \text{ Cal})(1000 \text{ cal/Cal}) = 2.5 \times 10^6 \text{ cal}$$

Then, by use of $\Delta Q = mc\,\Delta T$,

$$\Delta T = \frac{\Delta Q}{mc} = \frac{2.5 \times 10^6 \text{ cal}}{(60 \times 10^3 \text{ g})(0.83 \text{ cal/g}\cdot°\text{C})} = 50°\text{C}$$

**18.16 [II]** A thermometer in a 10 m × 8.0 m × 4.0 m room reads 22 °C and a humidistat reads the R.H. to be 35 percent. What mass of water vapor is in the room? Saturated air at 22 °C contains 19.33 g $H_2O/m^3$.

$$\%\text{R.H.} = \frac{\text{Mass of water/m}^3}{\text{Mass of water/m}^3 \text{of saturated air}} \times 100$$

$$35 = \frac{\text{Mass/m}^3}{0.019\,33 \text{ kg/m}^3} \times 100$$

from which mass/m$^3$ = $6.77 \times 10^{-3}$ kg/m$^3$. But the room in question has a volume of 10m × 8.0m × 4.0 m = 320 m$^3$. Therefore, the total mass of water in it is

$$(320 \text{ m}^3)(6.77 \times 10^{-3} \text{ kg/m}^3) = 2.2 \text{ kg}$$

**18.17 [II]** On a day when the temperature is 28 °C, moisture forms on the outside of a glass of cold drink if the glass is at a temperature of 16 °C or lower. What is the R.H. on that day? Saturated air at 28 °C contains 26.93 g/m$^3$ of water, while, at 16 °C, it contains 13.50 g/m$^3$.

Dew forms at a temperature of 16 °C or lower, so the dew point is 16 °C. The air is saturated at that temperature and therefore contains 13.50 g/m$^3$. Then

$$\text{R.H.} = \frac{\text{Mass present/m}^3}{\text{Mass/m}^3 \text{ in saturated air}} = \frac{13.50}{26.93} = 0.50 = 50\%$$

**18.18 [II]** Outside air at 5 °C and 20 percent relative humidity is introduced into a heating and air-conditioning plant where it is heated to 20 °C and its relative humidity is increased to a comfortable 50 percent. How many grams of water must be evaporated into a cubic meter of outside air to accomplish this? Saturated air at 5 °C contains 6.8 g/m$^3$ of water, and at 20 °C it contains 17.3 g/m$^3$.

$$\text{Mass/m}^3 \text{ of water vapor in air at 5 °C} = 0.20 \times 6.8 \text{ g/m}^3 = 1.36 \text{ g/m}^3$$
$$\text{Comfortable mass/m}^3 \text{ at 20 °C} = 0.50 \times 17.3\text{g/m}^3 = 8.65 \text{ g/m}^3$$
$$1 \text{ m}^3 \text{ of air at 5 °C expands to } (293/278) \text{ m}^3 = 1.054 \text{ m}^3 \text{ at 20 °C}$$
$$\text{Mass of water vapor in 1.054 m}^3 \text{ at 20 °C} = 1.054 \text{ m}^3 \times 8.65 \text{ g/m}^3 = 9.12 \text{ g}$$
$$\text{Mass of water to be added to each m}^3 \text{ of air at 5 °C} = (9.12 - 1.36) \text{ g} = 7.8 \text{ g}$$

## SUPPLEMENTARY PROBLEMS

**18.19 [I]** How many calories are required to heat each of the following from 15 °C to 65 °C? (*a*) 3.0 g of aluminum, (*b*) 5.0 g of Pyrex glass, (*c*) 20 g of platinum. The specific heats, in cal/g·°C, for aluminum, Pyrex, and platinum are 0.21, 0.20, and 0.032, respectively.

**18.20 [I]** When 5.0 g of a certain type of coal is burned, it raises the temperature of 1000 mL of water from 10 °C to 47 °C. Calculate the thermal energy produced per gram of coal. Neglect the small heat capacity of the coal.

**18.21 [II]** Furnace oil has a heat of combustion of 44 MJ/kg. Assuming that 70 percent of the heat is useful, how many kilograms of oil are required to raise the temperature of 2000 kg of water from 20 °C to 99 °C?

**18.22 [II]** What will be the final temperature if 50 g of water at exactly 0 °C is added to 250 g of water at 90 °C?

**18.23 [II]** A 50-g piece of metal at 95 °C is dropped into 250 g of water at 17.0 °C and warms it to 19.4 °C. What is the specific heat of the metal?

**18.24 [II]** How long does it take a 2.50-W heater to boil away 400 g of liquid helium at the temperature of its boiling point (4.2 K)? For helium, $L_v = 5.0$ cal/g.

**18.25 [II]** A 55-g copper calorimeter ($c = 0.093$ cal/g·°C) contains 250 g of water at 18.0 °C. When 75 g of an alloy at 100 °C is dropped into the calorimeter, the final resulting temperature is 20.4 °C. What is the specific heat of the alloy?

**18.26 [II]** Determine the temperature that results when 1.0 kg of ice at exactly 0 °C is mixed with 9.0 kg of water at 50 °C and no heat is lost.

**18.27 [II]** How much heat is required to change 10 g of ice at exactly 0° C to steam at 100° C?

**18.28 [II]** Ten kilograms of steam at 100 °C is condensed by passing it into 500 kg of water at 40.0 °C. What is the resulting temperature?

**18.29 [II]** The heat of combustion of ethane gas is 373 kcal/mole. Assuming that 60.0 percent of the heat is useful, how many liters of ethane, measured at standard temperature and pressure, must be burned to convert 50.0 kg of water at 10.0° C to steam at 100.0 °C? One mole of a gas occupies 22.4 liters at precisely 0 °C and 1 atm.

**18.30 [II]** Calculate the heat of fusion of ice from the following data for ice at 0 °C added to water:

| | |
|---|---|
| Mass of calorimeter | 60 g |
| Mass of calorimeter plus water | 460 g |
| Mass of calorimeter plus water and ice | 618 g |
| Initial temperature of water | 38.0 °C |
| Final temperature of mixture | 5.0 °C |
| Specific heat of calorimeter | 0.10 cal/g·°C |

**18.31 [II]** Determine the result when 100 g of steam at 100° C is passed into a mixture of 200 g of water and 20 g of ice at exactly 0 °C in a calorimeter which behaves thermally as if it were equivalent to 30 g of water.

**18.32 [II]** Determine the result when 10 g of steam at 100 °C is passed into a mixture of 400 g of water and 100 g of ice at exactly 0 °C in a calorimeter which behaves thermally as if it were equivalent to 50 g of water.

**18.33 [II]** Suppose a person who eats 2500 Cal of food each day loses the heat equivalent of the food through evaporation of water from the body. How much water must evaporate each day? At body temperature, $L_v$ for water is about 600 cal/g.

**18.34 [II]** How long will it take a 500-W heater to raise the temperature of 400 g of water from 15.0 °C to 98.0 °C.

**18.35 [II]** A 0.250-hp drill causes a dull 50.0-g steel bit to heat up rather than to deepen a hole in a block of hard wood. Assuming that 75.0 percent of the friction-loss energy causes heating of the bit, by what amount will its temperature change in 20.0 s? For steel, $c = 450$ J/kg·°C.

**18.36 [II]** On a certain day the temperature is 20 °C and the dew point is 5.0 °C. What is the relative humidity? Saturated air at 20 °C and 5.0 °C contains 17.12 and 6.80 $g/m^3$ of water, respectively.

**18.37 [II]** How much water vapor exists in a 105-$m^3$ room on a day when the relative humidity in the room is 32 percent and the room temperature is 20 °C? Saturated air at 20 °C contains 17.12 $g/m^3$ of water.

**18.38 [II]** Air at 30 °C and 90 percent relative humidity is drawn into an air conditioning unit and cooled to 20 °C. The relative humidity is simultaneously reduced to 50 percent. How many grams of water are removed from a cubic meter of air at 30 °C by the air conditioner? Saturated air contains 30.4 $g/m^3$ and 17.1 $g/m^3$ of water at 30 °C and 20 °C, respectively.

## ANSWERS TO SUPPLEMENTARY PROBLEMS

**18.19 [I]** (*a*) 32 cal; (*b*) 50 cal; (*c*) 32 cal

**18.20 [I]** 7.4 kcal/g or $7.4 \times 10^3$ kcal/kg or $31 \times 10^3$ kJ/kg

**18.21 [II]** 22 kg

**18.22 [II]** 75 °C

**18.23 [II]** 0.16 cal/g·°C or 0.67 kJ/kg·K

**18.24 [II]** 56 min

**18.25 [II]** 0.10 cal/g·°C or 0.42 kJ/kg·K

**18.26 [II]** 37 °C

**18.27 [II]** 7.2 kcal

**18.28 [II]** 51.8 °C

**18.29 [II]** $3.15 \times 10^3$ liters

**18.30 [II]** 80 cal/g or 335 kJ/kg

**18.31 [II]** 49 g of steam condensed, final temperature 100 °C

**18.32 [II]** 80 g of ice melted, final temperature 0 °C

**18.33 [II]** 4.17 kg

**18.34 [II]** 278 s

**18.35 [II]** 124 °C

**18.36 [II]** 40%

**18.37 [II]** 0.58 kg

**18.38 [II]** 19 g

# Transfer of Thermal Energy

**Thermal Energy Can Be Transferred** into or out of a system via the mechanisms of **conduction, convection**, and **radiation**. Remember that heat is the thermal energy transferred from a system at a higher temperature to a system at a lower temperature (with which it is in contact) via the collisions of their constituent particles.

**Conduction** occurs when thermal energy moves through a material as a result of collisions between the free electrons, ions, atoms, and/or molecules of the material. The hotter a substance, the higher the average KE of its atoms. When a temperature difference exists between materials in contact, the higher-energy atoms in the warmer substance transfer energy to the lower-energy atoms in the cooler substance when atomic collisions occur between the two. Heat thus flows from hot to cold.

Consider the slab of material shown in Fig. 19-1. Its thickness is $L$, and its cross-sectional area is $A$. The temperatures of its two faces are $T_1$ and $T_2$, so the temperature difference across the slab is $\Delta T = T_1 - T_2$. The quantity $\Delta T/L$ is called the **temperature gradient**. It is the rate-of-change of temperature with distance.

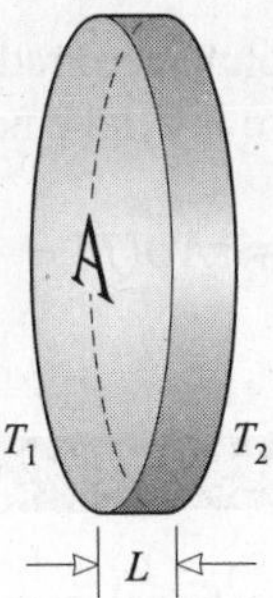


Fig. 19-1

The quantity of heat $\Delta Q$ transmitted from face 1 to face 2 in time $\Delta t$ is given by

$$\frac{\Delta Q}{\Delta t} = k_T A \frac{\Delta T}{L}$$

where $k_T$ depends on the material of the slab and is called the **thermal conductivity** of the material. In the SI, $k_T$ has the unit W/m·K, and $\Delta Q/\Delta t$ is in J/s (i.e., W). Other units sometimes used to express $k_T$ are related to W/m·K as follows:

$$1\ \text{cal/s}\cdot\text{cm}\cdot{}^\circ\text{C} = 418.4\ \text{W/m}\cdot\text{K} \qquad \text{and} \qquad 1\ \text{Btu}\cdot\text{in./h}\cdot\text{ft}^2\cdot{}^\circ\text{F} = 0.144\ \text{W/m}\cdot\text{K}$$

**The Thermal Resistance** (or *R value*) of a slab is defined by the heat-flow equation in the form

$$\frac{\Delta Q}{\Delta t} = \frac{A\,\Delta T}{R} \qquad \text{where} \qquad R = \frac{L}{k_T}$$

Its SI unit is $m^2 \cdot K/W$. Its customary unit is $ft^2 \cdot h \cdot °F/Btu$, where $1\ ft^2 \cdot h \cdot °F/Btu = 0.176\ m^2 \cdot K/W$. (It is unlikely that you will have occasion to confuse this symbol $R$ with the symbol for the universal gas constant.)

For several slabs of the same surface area in series, the combined $R$ value is

$$R = R_1 + R_2 + \dots + R_N$$

where $R_1$, ..., are the $R$ values of the individual slabs.

**Convection** of thermal energy occurs in a fluid when warm material flows so as to displace cooler material. Typical examples are the flow of warm air from a register in a heating system and the flow of warm water in the Gulf Stream.

**Radiation** is the mode of transport of radiant electromagnetic energy through vacuum (e.g., the space between atoms). Radiant energy is distinct from heat, though both correspond to energy in transit. Heat is heat; electromagnetic radiation is electromagnetic radiation—don't confuse the two.

A **blackbody** is a body that absorbs all the radiant energy falling on it. At thermal equilibrium, a body emits as much energy as it absorbs. Hence, a good absorber of radiation is also a good emitter of radiation.

Suppose a surface of area $A$ has absolute temperature $T$ and radiates only a fraction $\epsilon$ as much energy as would a blackbody surface. Then $\epsilon$ is called the **emissivity** of the surface, and the energy per second (i.e., the power) radiated by the surface is given by the **Stefan-Boltzmann Law**:

$$P = \epsilon A \sigma T^4$$

where $\sigma = 5.67 \times 10^{-8}\ W/m^2 \cdot K^4$ is the *Stefan-Boltzmann constant*, and $T$ is the absolute temperature. The emissivity of a blackbody is unity.

All objects whose temperature is above absolute zero radiate energy. When an object at absolute temperature $T$ is in an environment where the temperature is $T_e$, the net energy radiated per second by the object is

$$P = \varepsilon A \sigma (T^4 - T_e^4)$$

## SOLVED PROBLEMS

**19.1 [I]** An iron plate 2 cm thick has a cross-sectional area of 5000 cm². One face is at 150 °C, and the other is at 140 °C. How much heat passes through the plate each second? For iron, $k_T = 80\ W/m \cdot K$.

$$\frac{\Delta Q}{\Delta t} = k_T A \frac{\Delta T}{L} = (80\ W/m \cdot K)\ (0.50\ m^2)\left(\frac{10\ °C}{0.02\ m}\right) = 20\ kJ/s$$

**19.2 [I]** A metal plate 4.00 mm thick has a temperature difference of 32.0 °C between its faces. It transmits 200 kcal/h through an area of 5.00 cm². Calculate the thermal conductivity of this metal in W/m·K.

$$k_T = \frac{\Delta Q}{\Delta t}\frac{L}{A(T_1 - T_2)} = \frac{(2.00 \times 10^5\ cal)\ (4.184\ J/cal)}{(1.00\ h)\ (3600\ s/h)} \frac{4.00 \times 10^{-3}\ m}{(5.00 \times 10^{-4}\ m^2)\ (32.0\ K)}$$

$$= 58.5\ W/m \cdot K$$

**19.3 [II]** Two metal plates are soldered together as shown in Fig. 19-2. It is known that $A = 80\ \text{cm}^2$, $L_1 = L_2 = 3.0$ mm, $T_1 = 100$ °C, $T_2 = 0$ °C. For the plate on the left, $k_{T1} = 48.1$ W/m·K; for the plate on the right $k_{T2} = 68.2$ W/m·K. Find the heat flow rate through the plates and the temperature $T$ of the soldered junction.

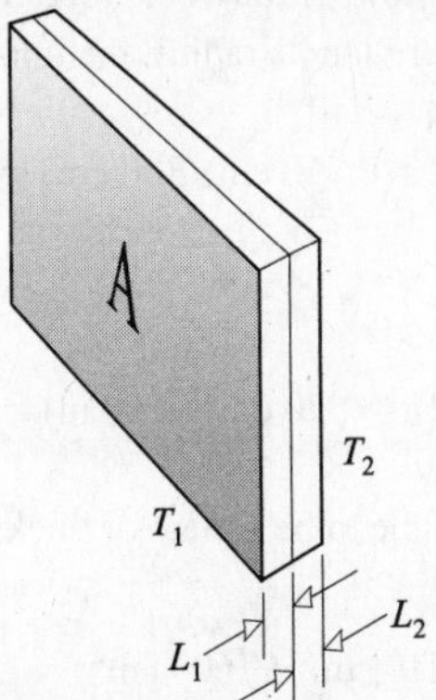


Fig. 19-2

We assume equilibrium conditions so that the heat flowing through plate-1 equals that through plate-2. Then

$$k_{T1}\,A\,\frac{T_1 - T}{L_1} = k_{T2}\,A\,\frac{T - T_2}{L_2}$$

But $L_1 = L_2$, so this becomes

$$k_{T1}(100\ ^\circ\text{C} - T) = k_{T2}(T - 0\ ^\circ\text{C})$$

from which $$T = (100\ ^\circ\text{C})\left(\frac{k_{T1}}{k_{T1} + k_{T2}}\right) = (100\ ^\circ\text{C})\left(\frac{48.1}{48.1 + 68.2}\right) = 41.4\ ^\circ\text{C}$$

The heat flow rate is then

$$\frac{\Delta Q}{\Delta t} = k_{T1}A\,\frac{T_1 - T}{L_1} = \left(48.1\,\frac{\text{W}}{\text{m}\cdot\text{K}}\right)(0.008\,0\ \text{m}^2)\,\frac{(100 - 41.4)\text{K}}{0.003\,0\ \text{m}} = 7.5\ \text{kJ/s}$$

**19.4 [II]** A beverage cooler is in the shape of a cube, 42 cm on each inside edge. Its 3.0-cm-thick walls are made of plastic ($k_T = 0.050$ W/m·K). When the outside temperature is 20 °C, how much ice will melt inside the cooler each hour?

We have to determine the amount of heat conducted into the box. The cubical box has six sides, each with an area of about $(0.42\ \text{m})^2$. From $\Delta Q/\Delta t = k_T A\, \Delta T/L$, we have, with the ice inside at 0 °C,

$$\frac{\Delta Q}{\Delta t} = (0.050\ \text{W/m}\cdot\text{K})\,(0.42\ \text{m})^2\ (6)\left(\frac{20\ ^\circ\text{C}}{0.030\ \text{m}}\right) = 35.3\ \text{J/s} = 8.43\ \text{cal/s}$$

In one hour, $\Delta Q = (60)^2\,(8.43) = 30\,350$ cal. To melt 1.0 g of ice requires 80 cal, so the mass of ice melted in one hour is

$$m = \frac{30\,350\ \text{cal}}{80\ \text{cal/g}} = 0.38\ \text{kg}$$

**19.5 [III]** A copper tube (length, 3.0 m; inner diameter, 1.500 cm; outer diameter, 1.700 cm) extends across a 3.0-m-long vat of rapidly circulating water maintained at 20 °C. Live steam at 100 °C passes through the tube. (*a*) What is the heat flow rate from the steam into the vat? (*b*) How much steam is condensed each minute? For copper, $k_T = 1.0\ \text{cal/s}\cdot\text{cm}\cdot{}^\circ\text{C}$.

To determine the rate at which heat flows through the tube wall, approximate it as a flat sheet. Because the thickness of the tube is much smaller than its radius, the inner surface area of the tube,

$$2\pi r_i L = 2\pi(0.750\ \text{cm})(300\ \text{cm}) = 1410\ \text{cm}^2$$

nearly equals its outer surface area,

$$2\pi r_O L = 2\pi(0.850\ \text{cm})(300\ \text{cm}) = 1600\ \text{cm}^2$$

As an approximation, consider the tube to be a plate of thickness 0.100 cm and area given by

$$A = \tfrac{1}{2}(1410\ \text{cm}^2 + 1600\ \text{cm}^2) = 1500\ \text{cm}^2$$

(*a*) $$\frac{\Delta Q}{\Delta t} = k_T A \frac{\Delta T}{L} = \left(1.0\ \frac{\text{cal}}{\text{s}\cdot\text{cm}\cdot{}^\circ\text{C}}\right)\frac{(1500\ \text{cm}^2)(80\ {}^\circ\text{C})}{(0.100\ \text{cm})} = 1.2\times10^6\ \text{cals/s}$$

(*b*) In one minute, the heat conducted from the tube is

$$\Delta Q = (1.2\times10^6\ \text{cal/s})(60\ \text{s}) = 72\times10^6\ \text{cal}$$

It takes 540 cal to condense 1.0 g of steam at 100 °C. Therefore,

$$\text{Steam condensed per min} = \frac{72\times10^6\ \text{cal}}{540\ \text{cal/g}} = 13.3\times10^4\ \text{g} = 1.3\times10^2\ \text{kg}$$

In practice, various factors would greatly reduce this theoretical value.

**19.6 [I]** (*a*) Calculate the $R$ value for a wall consisting of the following layers: concrete block ($R = 1.93$), 1.0 inch of insulating board ($R = 4.3$), and 0.50 inch of drywall ($R = 0.45$), all in U.S. Customary Units. (*b*) If the wall has an area of 15 m², find the heat flow per hour through it when the temperature just outside is 20 °C lower than inside.

(*a*) $R = R_1 + R_2 + \ldots + R_N = 1.93 + 4.3 + 0.45 = 6.7$ in U.S. Customary Units. Using the fact that 1 U.S. Customary Unit of $R = 0.176\ \text{m}^2\cdot\text{K/W}$, we get $R = 1.18\ \text{m}^2\cdot\text{K/W}$.

(*b*) $$\Delta Q = \frac{A\,\Delta T}{R}(\Delta t) = \frac{(15\ \text{m}^2)(20\ {}^\circ\text{C})}{1.18\ \text{m}^2\cdot\text{K/W}}(3600\ \text{s}) = 0.915\ \text{MJ} = 2.2\times10^2\ \text{kcal}$$

**19.7 [I]** A spherical body of 2.0 cm diameter is maintained at 600 °C. Assuming that it radiates as if it were a blackbody, at what rate (in watts) is energy radiated from the sphere?

$$A = \text{Surface area} = 4\pi r^2 = 4\pi(0.01\ \text{m})^2 = 1.26\times10^{-3}\ \text{m}^2$$
$$\text{P} = A\sigma T^4 = (1.26\times10^{-3}\ \text{m}^2)(5.67\times10^{-8}\ \text{W/m}^2\cdot\text{K}^4)(873\ \text{K})^4 = 41\ \text{W}$$

**19.8 [I]** An unclothed person whose body has a surface area of 1.40 m² with an emissivity of 0.85 has a skin temperature of 37 °C and stands in a 20 °C room. How much energy does the person lose through radiation per minute?

Energy is power (P) multiplied by time ($\Delta t$). From $P = \epsilon A\sigma(T^4 - T_e^4)$, the energy loss is

$$\epsilon A\sigma(T^4 - T_e^4)\,\Delta t = (0.85)(1.40\ \text{m}^2)(\sigma)(T^4 - T_e^4)(60\ \text{s})$$

Using $\sigma = 5.67 \times 10^{-8}\ \text{W/m}^2\cdot\text{K}^4$, $T = 273 + 37 = 310$ K, and $T_e = 273 + 20 = 293$ K results in an energy loss of

$$7.6\ \text{kJ} = 1.8\ \text{kcal}$$

## SUPPLEMENTARY PROBLEMS

**19.9 [I]** What temperature gradient must exist in an aluminum rod for it to transmit 8.0 cal per second per cm$^2$ of cross section down the rod? $k_T$ for aluminum is 210 W/K·m.

**19.10 [I]** A single-thickness glass window on a house actually has layers of stagnant air on its two surfaces. But if it did not, how much heat would flow out of an 80-cm × 40-cm × 3.0-mm window each hour on a day when the outside temperature was precisely 0 °C and the inside temperature was 18 °C? For glass, $k_T$ is 0.84 W/K·m.

**19.11 [I]** How many grams of water at 100 °C can be evaporated per hour per cm$^2$ by the heat transmitted through a steel plate 0.20 cm thick, if the temperature difference between the plate faces is 100 °C? For steel, $k_T$ is 42 W/K·m.

**19.12 [II]** A certain double-pane window consists of two glass sheets, each 80 cm × 80 cm × 0.30 cm, separated by a 0.30-cm stagnant air space. The indoor surface temperature is 20 °C, while the outdoor surface temperature is exactly 0 °C. How much heat passes through the window each second? $k_T = 0.84$ W/K·m for glass and about 0.080 W/K·m for air.

**19.13 [II]** A small hole in a furnace acts like a blackbody. Its area is 1.00 cm$^2$, and its temperature is the same as that of the interior of the furnace, 1727 °C. How many calories are radiated out of the hole each second?

**19.14 [I]** An incandescent lamp filament has an area of 50 mm$^2$ and operates at a temperature of 2127 °C. Assume that all the energy furnished to the bulb is radiated from it. If the filament's emissivity is 0.83, how much power must be furnished to the bulb when it is operating?

**19.15 [I]** A sphere of 3.0 cm radius acts like a blackbody. It is in equilibrium with its surroundings and absorbs 30 kW of power radiated to it from the surroundings. What is the temperature of the sphere?

**19.16 [II]** A 2.0-cm-thick brass plate ($k_T = 105$ W/K·m) is sealed face-to-face to a glass sheet ($k_T = 0.80$ W/K·m), and both have the same area. The exposed face of the brass plate is at 80 °C, while the exposed face of the glass is at 20 °C. How thick is the glass if the glass-brass interface is at 65 °C?

## ANSWERS TO SUPPLEMENTARY PROBLEMS

**19.9 [I]** 16 °C/cm

**19.10 [I]** $1.4 \times 10^3$ kcal/h

**19.11 [I]** 0.33 kg/h·cm$^2$

**19.12 [II]** 69 cal/s

**19.13 [II]** 21.7 cal/s

**19.14 [I]** 78 W

**19.15 [I]** $2\,6 \times 10^3$ K

**19.16 [II]** 0.46 mm

CHAPTER 20

# First Law of Thermodynamics

**Heat** ($\Delta Q$) is the thermal energy that flows from one body or system to another, which is in contact with it, because of their temperature difference. Heat always flows from hot to cold (i.e., from the higher temperature to the lower temperature). For two objects in contact to be in thermal equilibrium with each other (i.e., for no net heat transfer from one to the other), their temperatures must be the same. If each of two objects is in thermal equilibrium with a third body, then the two are in thermal equilibrium with each other. (This fact is often referred to as the **Zeroth Law of Thermodynamics.**)

By convention we will take heat flowing into a system (i.e., heat-in) as positive and heat flowing out of a system (i.e., heat-out) as negative.

**The Internal Energy** ($U$) of a system is the total energy content of the system. It is the sum of all forms of energy possessed by the atoms and molecules of the system.

**The Work Done by a System** ($\Delta W$) is positive if the system thereby loses energy to its surroundings. In other words, work-out is positive. When the surroundings do work *on* the system so as to give it energy, $\Delta W$ is a negative quantity. In other words, work-in is negative. In a small expansion $\Delta V$, a fluid at constant pressure $P$ does work given by

$$\Delta W = P\,\Delta V$$

**The First Law of Thermodynamics** is a statement of the law of conservation of energy. It maintains that if an amount of heat $\Delta Q$ flows into a system, then this energy must appear as either increased internal energy $\Delta U$ for the system and/or work $\Delta W$ done *by* the system on its surroundings. As an equation, the First Law can be stated as

$$\Delta Q = \Delta U + \Delta W$$

Remember that we are using the convention that $\Delta W_{\text{out}} > 0$ and $\Delta Q_{\text{in}} > 0$.

**An Isobaric Process** is a process carried out at *constant pressure*.

**An Isovolumic Process** is a process carried out at *constant volume*. When a gas undergoes such a process,

$$\Delta W = P\,\Delta V = 0$$

and so the First Law of Thermodynamics becomes

$$\Delta Q = \Delta U$$

Any heat that flows into the system appears as increased internal energy of the system.

**An Isothermal Process** is a *constant-temperature* process. In the case of an ideal gas where the constituent atoms or molecules do not interact, $\Delta U = 0$ in an isothermal process. However, this is not true for many other systems. For example, $\Delta U \neq 0$ as ice melts to water at 0 °C, even though the process is isothermal.

For an ideal gas, $\Delta U = 0$ in an isothermal change and so the First Law becomes

$$\Delta Q = \Delta W \qquad \text{(Ideal gas)}$$

Thus for an ideal gas changing isothermally from $(P_1, V_1)$ to $(P_2, V_2)$, where $P_1V_1 = P_2V_2$,

$$\Delta Q = \Delta W = P_1 V_1 \ln\left(\frac{V_2}{V_1}\right)$$

Here, ln is the logarithm to the base $e$.

**An Adiabatic Process** is one in which no heat is transferred to or from the system. For such a process, $\Delta Q = 0$. Hence, in an adiabatic process, the first law becomes

$$0 = \Delta U + \Delta W$$

Any work done by the system is done at the expense of the internal energy. Any work done on the system serves to increase the internal energy.

For an ideal gas changing from conditions $(P_1, V_1, T_1)$ to $(P_2, V_2, T_2)$ in an adiabatic process,

$$P_1 V_1^{\gamma} = P_2 V_2^{\gamma} \qquad \text{and} \qquad T_1 V_1^{\gamma-1} = T_2 V_2^{\gamma-1}$$

where $\gamma = c_p/c_v$ is discussed below.

**Specific Heats of Gases:** When a gas is heated *at constant volume*, the heat supplied goes to increase the internal energy of the gas molecules. But when a gas is heated *at constant pressure*, the heat supplied not only increases the internal energy of the molecules but also does mechanical work in expanding the gas against the opposing constant pressure. Hence, the specific heat of a gas at constant pressure $c_p$, is greater than its specific heat at constant volume, $c_v$. It can be shown that for an ideal gas of molecular mass $M$,

$$c_p - c_v = \frac{R}{M} \qquad \text{(Idea gas)}$$

where $R$ is the universal gas constant. In the SI, $R = 8314$ J/kmol·K and $M$ is in kg/kmol; then $c_p$ and $c_v$ must be in J/kg·K = J/kg·°C. Some people use $R = 1.98$ cal/mol·°C and $M$ in g/mol, in which case $c_p$ and $c_v$ are in cal/g·°C.

**Specific Heat Ratio ($\gamma = c_p/c_v$):** As discussed above, this ratio is greater than unity for a gas. The kinetic theory of gases indicates that for monatomic gases (such as He, Ne, and Ar), $\gamma = 1.67$. For most diatomic gases (the ones that are rigidly bonded such as $O_2$, and $N_2$), $\gamma = 1.40$ at ordinary temperatures.

**Work Is Related to Area** in a *P–V* diagram. The work done by a fluid in an expansion is equal to the area beneath the expansion curve on a *P–V* diagram. Figure 20-1 shows several different processes that carry the system from state-A to state-C. In each case the work done, the shaded area, is different.

In a cyclic process, the work output per cycle done by a fluid is equal to the area enclosed by the *P–V* diagram representing the cycle.

**The Efficiency of a Heat Engine** is defined as

$$\text{eff} = \frac{\text{Work output}}{\text{Heat input}}$$

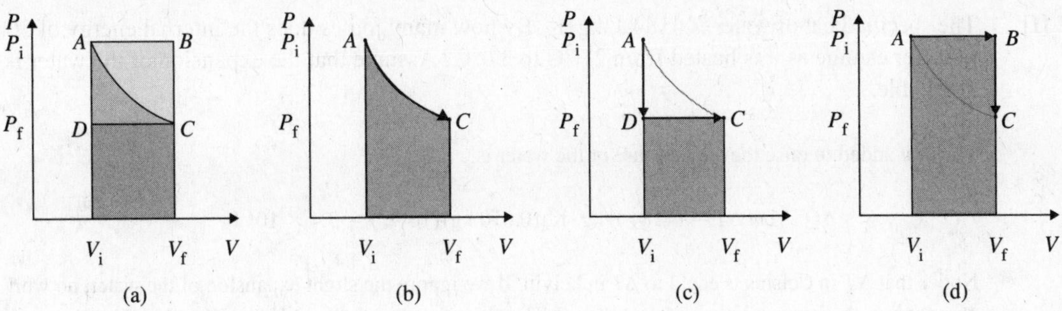


Fig. 20-1

The **Carnot cycle** is the most efficient cycle possible for a heat engine. That special sequence of processes (depicted in Fig. 20-2) is formed by an isothermal expansion from $A$ to $B$, followed by an adiabatic expansion from $B$ to $C$, followed by an isothermal contraction from $C$ to $D$, and finally an adiabatic contraction back to $A$. In the process an amount of heat $Q_H$ enters the system from a high-temperature reservoir, and an amount $Q_L$ is expelled to a low-temperature reservoir. The gray-shaded area corresponds to the work done by the system. An engine that operates in accordance with this cycle between a hot reservoir ($T_H$) and a cold reservoir ($T_L$) has an efficiency

$$\text{eff}_{\text{max}} = 1 - \frac{T_L}{T_H}$$

Kelvin temperatures must be used in this equation.

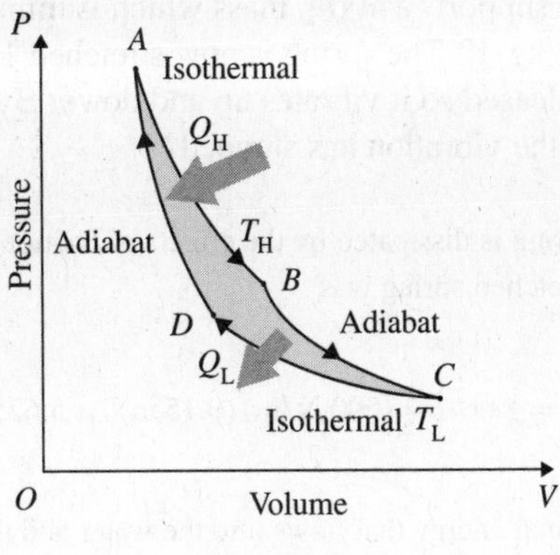


Fig. 20-2

## SOLVED PROBLEMS

**20.1 [I]** In a certain process, 8.00 kcal of heat is furnished to the system while the system does 6.00 kJ of work. By how much does the internal energy of the system change during the process?

Here 8.00 kcal is heat-in and 6.00 kJ is work-out, both of which are positive. Consequently,

$$\Delta Q = (8000\ \text{cal})(4.184\ \text{J/cal}) = 33.5\ \text{kJ} \quad \text{and} \quad \Delta W = 6.00\ \text{kJ}$$

Therefore, from the First Law $\Delta Q = \Delta U + \Delta W$,

$$\Delta U = \Delta Q - \Delta W = 33.5\ \text{kJ} - 6.00\ \text{kJ} = 27.5\ \text{kJ}$$

**20.2 [I]** The specific heat of water is 4184 J/kg·K. By how many joules does the internal energy of 50 g of water change as it is heated from 21 °C to 37 °C? Assume that the expansion of the water is negligible.

The heat added to raise the temperature of the water is

$$\Delta Q = cm\,\Delta T = (4184\ \text{J/kg}\cdot\text{K})(0.050\ \text{kg})(16\ ^\circ\text{C}) = 3.4 \times 10^3\ \text{J}$$

Notice that $\Delta T$ in Celsius is equal to $\Delta T$ in kelvin. If we ignore the slight expansion of the water, no work was done on the surroundings and so $\Delta W = 0$. Then, the first law, $\Delta Q = \Delta U + \Delta W$, tells us that

$$\Delta U = \Delta Q = 3.4\ \text{kJ}$$

**20.3 [I]** How much does the internal energy of 5.0 g of ice at precisely 0 °C increase as it is changed to water at 0 °C? Neglect the change in volume.

The heat needed to melt the ice is

$$\Delta Q = mL_f = (5.0\ \text{g})(80\ \text{cal/g}) = 400\ \text{cal}$$

No external work is done by the ice as it melts and so $\Delta W = 0$. Therefore, the First Law, $\Delta Q = \Delta U + \Delta W$, tells us that

$$\Delta U = \Delta Q = (400\ \text{cal})(4.184\ \text{J/cal}) = 1.7\ \text{kJ}$$

**20.4 [II]** A spring ($k = 500$ N/m) supports a 400-g mass which is immersed in 900 g of water. The specific heat of the mass is 450 J/kg·K. The spring is now stretched 15 cm, and after thermal equilibrium is reached, the mass is released so it vibrates up and down. By how much has the temperature of the water changed when the vibration has stopped?

The energy stored in the spring is dissipated by the effects of friction and goes to heat the water and mass. The energy stored in the stretched spring was

$$\text{PE}_e = \tfrac{1}{2}kx^2 = \tfrac{1}{2}(500\ \text{N/m})\,(0.15\ \text{m})^2 = 5.625\ \text{J}$$

This energy appears as thermal energy that flows into the water and the mass. Using $\Delta Q = cm\,\Delta T$,

$$5.625\ \text{J} = (4184\ \text{J/kg}\cdot\text{K})(0.900\ \text{kg})\,\Delta T + (450\ \text{J/kg}\cdot\text{K})(0.40\ \text{kg})\,\Delta T$$

which leads to $$\Delta T = \frac{5.625\ \text{J}}{3950\ \text{J/K}} = 0.0014\ \text{K}$$

**20.5 [II]** Find $\Delta W$ and $\Delta U$ for a 6.0-cm cube of iron as it is heated from 20 °C to 300 °C at atmospheric pressure. For iron, $c = 0.11$ cal/g·°C and the volume coefficient of thermal expansion is $3.6 \times 10^{-5}\ ^\circ\text{C}^{-1}$. The mass of the cube is 1700 g.

Given that $\Delta T = 300\ ^\circ\text{C} - 20\ ^\circ\text{C} = 280\ ^\circ\text{C}$,

$$\Delta Q = cm\,\Delta T = (0.11\ \text{cal/g}\cdot{}^\circ\text{C})(1700\ \text{g})(280\ ^\circ\text{C}) = 52\ \text{kcal}$$

To find that the work done by the expansion of the cube, we need to determine $\Delta V$.

The volume of the cube is $V = (6.0\ \text{cm})^3 = 216\ \text{cm}^3$. Using $(\Delta V)/V = \beta \Delta T$,

$$\Delta V = V\beta\,\Delta T = (216 \times 10^{-6}\ \text{m}^3)(3.6 \times 10^{-5}\ {}^\circ\text{C}^{-1})(280\ {}^\circ\text{C}) = 2.18 \times 10^{-6}\ \text{m}^3$$

Then, assuming atmospheric pressure to be $1.0 \times 10^5$ Pa,

$$\Delta W = P\,\Delta V = (1.0 \times 10^5\ \text{N/m}^2)(2.18 \times 10^{-6}\ \text{m}^3) = 0.22\ \text{J}$$

But the First Law tells us that

$$\Delta U = \Delta Q - \Delta W = (52\,000\ \text{cal})(4.184\ \text{J/cal}) - 0.22\ \text{J}$$
$$= 218\,000\ \text{J} - 0.22\ \text{J} \approx 2.2 \times 10^5\ \text{J}$$

Notice how very small the work of expansion against the atmosphere is in comparison to $\Delta U$ and $\Delta Q$. Often $\Delta W$ can be neglected when dealing with liquids and solids.

**20.6 [II]** A motor supplies 0.4 hp to stir 5 kg of water. Assuming that all the work goes into heating the water by friction losses, how long will it take to increase the temperature of the water 6 °C?

The heat required to heat the water is

$$\Delta Q = mc\,\Delta T = (5000\ \text{g})(1\ \text{cal/g}\cdot{}^\circ\text{C})(6\ {}^\circ\text{C}) = 30\ \text{kcal}$$

This is actually supplied by friction work, so

$$\text{Friction work done} = \Delta Q = (30\ \text{kcal})(4.184\ \text{J/cal}) = 126\ \text{kJ}$$

and this equals the work done by the motor. But

$$\text{Work done by motor in time } t = (\text{Power})(t) = (0.4\ \text{hp} \times 746\ \text{W/hp})(t)$$

Equating this to our previous value for the work done yields

$$t = \frac{1.26 \times 10^5\ \text{J}}{(0.4 \times 746)\ \text{W}} = 420\ \text{s} = 7\ \text{min}$$

**20.7 [I]** In each of the following situations, find the change in internal energy of the system. (*a*) A system absorbs 500 cal of heat and at the same time does 400 J of work. (*b*) A system absorbs 300 cal and at the same time 420 J of work is done on it. (*c*) Twelve hundred calories are removed from a gas held at constant volume. Give your answers in kilojoules.

(*a*) $\Delta U = \Delta Q - \Delta W = (500\ \text{cal})(4.184\ \text{J/cal}) - 400\ \text{J} = 1.69\ \text{kJ}$

(*b*) $\Delta U = \Delta Q - \Delta W = (300\ \text{cal})(4.184\ \text{J/cal}) - (-420\ \text{J}) = 1.68\ \text{kJ}$

(*c*) $\Delta U = \Delta Q - \Delta W = (-1200\ \text{cal})(4.184\ \text{J/cal}) - 0 = -5.02\ \text{kJ}$

Notice that $\Delta Q$ is positive when heat is added to the system and $\Delta W$ is positive when the system does work. In the reverse cases, $\Delta Q$ and $\Delta W$ must be taken negative.

**20.8 [I]** For each of the following adiabatic processes, find the change in internal energy. (*a*) A gas does 5 J of work while expanding adiabatically. (*b*) During an adiabatic compression, 80 J of work is done on a gas.

During an adiabatic process, no heat is transferred to or from the system.

(*a*) $\Delta U = \Delta Q - \Delta W = 0 - 5\ \text{J} = -5\ \text{J}$

(*b*) $\Delta U = \Delta Q - \Delta W = 0 - (-80\ \text{J}) = +80\ \text{J}$

**20.9 [III]** The temperature of 5.00 kg of $N_2$ gas is raised from 10.0 °C to 130.0 °C. If this is done at constant volume, find the increase in internal energy $\Delta U$. Alternatively, if the same temperature change now occurs at constant pressure determine both $\Delta V$ and the external work $\Delta W$ done by the gas. For $N_2$ gas, $c_v = 0.177$ cal/g·°C and $c_p = 0.248$ cal/g·°C.

If the gas is heated at constant volume, then no work is done during the process. In that case $\Delta W = 0$, and the first law tells us that $(\Delta Q)_v = \Delta U$. Because $(\Delta Q)_v = c_v m \Delta T$,

$$\Delta U = (\Delta Q)_v = (0.177 \text{ cal/g}\cdot{}^\circ\text{C})(5000 \text{ g})(120\ {}^\circ\text{C}) = 106 \text{ kcal} = 443 \text{ kJ}$$

The temperature change is a manifestation of the internal energy change.

When the gas is heated 120 °C at constant pressure, the same change in internal energy occurs. In addition, however, work is done. The first law then becomes

$$(\Delta Q)_p = \Delta U + \Delta W = 443 \text{ kJ} + \Delta W$$

But $$(\Delta Q)_p = c_p m \Delta T = (0.248 \text{ cal/g}\cdot{}^\circ\text{C})(5000 \text{ g})(120\ {}^\circ\text{C})$$
$$= 149 \text{ kcal} = 623 \text{ kJ}$$

Hence $$\Delta W = (\Delta Q)_p - \Delta U = 623 \text{ kJ} - 443 \text{ kJ} = 180 \text{ kJ}$$

**20.10 [II]** One kilogram of steam at 100 °C and 101 kPa occupies 1.68 $m^3$. (*a*) What fraction of the observed heat of vaporization of water is accounted for by the expansion of water into steam? (*b*) Determine the increase in internal energy of 1.00 kg of water as it is vaporized at 100 °C.

(*a*) One kilogram of water expands from 1000 $cm^3$ to 1.68 $m^3$, so $\Delta V = 1.68 - 0.001 \approx 1.68 \text{ m}^3$. Therefore, the work done in the expansion is

$$\Delta W = P\Delta V = (101 \times 10^3 \text{ N/m}^2)(1.68 \text{ m}^3) = 169 \text{ kJ}$$

The heat of vaporization of water is 540 cal/g, which is 2.26 MJ/kg. The required fraction is therefore

$$\frac{\Delta W}{mL_v} = \frac{169 \text{ kJ}}{(1.00 \text{ kg})(2260 \text{ kJ/kg})} = 0.074\,8$$

(*b*) From the First Law, $\Delta U = \Delta Q - \Delta W$, and so

$$\Delta U = 2.26 \times 10^6 \text{ J} - 0.169 \times 10^6 \text{ J} = 2.07 \text{ MJ}$$

**20.11 [I]** For nitrogen gas, $c_v = 740$ J/kg·K. Assuming it to behave like an ideal gas, find its specific heat at constant pressure. (The molecular mass of nitrogen gas is 28.0 kg/kmol.)

**Method 1**

$$c_p = c_v + \frac{R}{M} = \frac{740 \text{ J}}{\text{kg}\cdot\text{K}} + \frac{8314 \text{ J/kmol}\cdot\text{K}}{28.0 \text{ kg/kmol}} = 1.04 \text{ kJ/kg}\cdot\text{K}$$

**Method 2**

Since $N_2$ is a diatomic gas, and since $\gamma = c_p/c_v = 1.40$ for such a gas,

$$c_p = 1.40 c_v = 1.40(740 \text{ J/kg}\cdot\text{K}) = 1.04 \text{ kJ/kg}\cdot\text{K}$$

**20.12 [I]** How much work is done by an ideal gas in expanding isothermally from an initial volume of 3.00 liters at 20.0 atm to a final volume of 24.0 liters?

For an isothermal expansion by an ideal gas,

$$\Delta W = P_1 V_1 \ln\left(\frac{V_2}{V_1}\right)$$

$$= (20.0 \times 1.01 \times 10^5 \text{ N/m}^2)(3.00 \times 10^{-3} \text{ m}^3) \ln\left(\frac{24.0}{3.00}\right) = 12.6 \text{ kJ}$$

**20.13 [I]** The *P-V* diagram in Fig. 20-3 applies to a gas undergoing a cyclic change in a piston-cylinder arrangement. What is the work done by the gas (*a*) During portion *AB* of the cycle? (*b*) During portion *BC*? (*c*) During portion *CD*? (*d*) During portion *DA*?

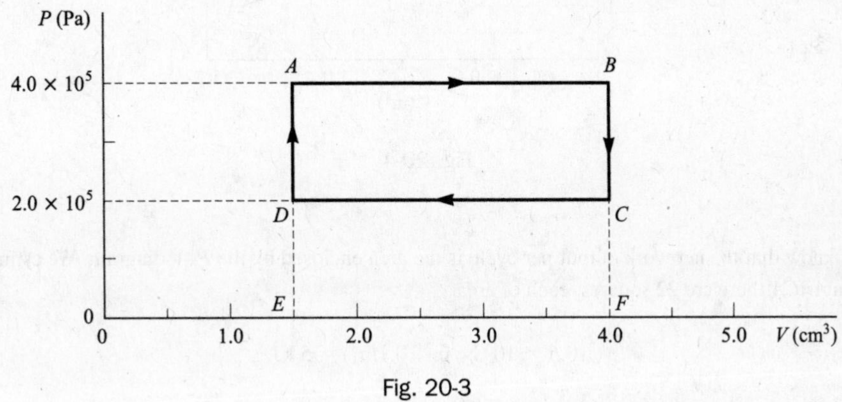


Fig. 20-3

In expansion, the work done is equal to the area under the pertinent portion of the *P-V* curve. In contraction, the work is numerically equal to the area but is negative.

(*a*) Work = Area *ABFEA* = $[(4.0 - 1.5) \times 10^{-6} \text{ m}^3](4.0 \times 10^5 \text{ N/m}^2) = 1.0 \text{ J}$

(*b*) Work = Area under *BC* = 0

In portion *BC*, the volume does not change; therefore, $P\Delta V = 0$.

(*c*) This is a contraction, $\Delta V$ is negative, and so the work is negative:

$$W = -(\text{Area } CDEFC) = -(2.5 \times 10^{-6} \text{ m}^3)(2.0 \times 10^5 \text{ N/m}^2) = -0.50 \text{ J}$$

(*d*) $W = 0$

**20.14 [I]** For the thermodynamic cycle shown in Fig. 20-3, find (*a*) the net work output of the gas during the cycle and (*b*) the net heat flow into the gas per cycle.

**Method 1**

(*a*) From Problem 20.13, the net work done is 1.0J − 0.50 J = 0.5 J.

**Method 2**

The net work done is equal to the area enclosed by the *P–V* diagram:

$$\text{Work} = \text{Area } ABCDA = (2.0 \times 10^5 \text{ N/m}^2)(2.5 \times 10^{-6} \text{ m}^3) = 0.50 \text{ J}$$

(*b*) Suppose the cycle starts at point-*A*. The gas returns to this point at the end of the cycle, so there is no difference in the gas at its start and end points. For one complete cycle, $\Delta U$ is therefore zero. We have then, if the first law is applied to a complete cycle,

$$\Delta Q = \Delta U + \Delta W = 0 + 0.50 \text{ J} = 0.50 \text{ J} = 0.12 \text{ cal}$$

**20.15 [I]** What is the net work output per cycle for the thermodynamic cycle in Fig. 20-4?

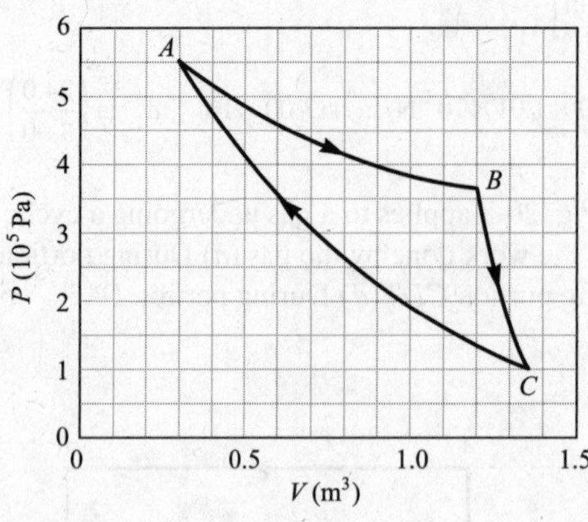


Fig. 20-4

We know that the net work output per cycle is the area enclosed by the *P–V* diagram. We estimate that in area *ABCA* there are 22 squares, each of area

$$(0.5 \times 10^5\ \text{N/m}^2)(0.1\text{m}^3) = 5\ \text{kJ}$$

Therefore,

$$\text{Area enclosed by cycle} \approx (22)(5\text{kJ}) = 1 \times 10^2\ \text{kJ}$$

The net work output per cycle is $1 \times 10^2$ kJ.

**20.16 [II]** Twenty cubic centimeters of monatomic gas at 12 °C and 100 kPa is suddenly (and adiabatically) compressed to 0.50 cm³. Assume that we are dealing with an ideal gas. What are its new pressure and temperature?

For an adiabatic change involving an ideal gas, $P_1 V_1^\gamma = P_2 V_2^\gamma$ where $\gamma = 1.67$ for a monatomic gas. Hence,

$$P_2 = P_1\left(\frac{V_1}{V_2}\right)^\gamma = (1.00\times 10^5\ \text{N/m}^2)\left(\frac{20}{0.50}\right)^{1.67} = 4.74\times 10^7\ \text{N/m}^2 = 47\ \text{MPa}$$

To find the final temperature, we could use $P_1 V_1/T_1 = P_2 V_2/T_2$. Instead, let us use

$$T_1 V_1^{\gamma-1} = T_2 V_2^{\gamma-1}$$

or

$$T_2 = T_1\left(\frac{V_1}{V_2}\right)^{\gamma-1} = (285\ \text{K})\left(\frac{20}{0.50}\right)^{0.67} = (285\ \text{K})\,(11.8) = 3.4\times 10^3\ \text{K}$$

As a check,

$$\frac{P_1 V_1}{T_1} = \frac{P_2 V_2}{T_2}$$

$$\frac{(1\times 10^5\ \text{N/m}^2)\,(20\ \text{cm}^3)}{285\ \text{K}} = \frac{(4.74\times 10^7\ \text{N/m}^2)\,(0.50\ \text{cm}^3)}{3370\ \text{K}}$$

$$7000 = 7000 \checkmark$$

**20.17 [I]** Compute the maximum possible efficiency of a heat engine operating between the temperature limits of 100 °C and 400 °C.

Remember that our thermodynamic equations are expressed in terms of absolute temperature. The most efficient engine is the Carnot engine, for which

$$\text{Efficiency} = 1 - \frac{T_L}{T_H} = 1 - \frac{373\text{ K}}{673\text{ K}} = 0.446 = 44.6\%$$

**20.18 [II]** A steam engine operating between a boiler temperature of 220 °C and a condenser temperature of 35.0 °C delivers 8.00 hp. If its efficiency is 30.0 percent of that for a Carnot engine operating between these temperature limits, how many calories are absorbed each second by the boiler? How many calories are exhausted to the condenser each second?

$$\text{Actual efficiency} = (0.30)\,(\text{Carnot efficiency}) = (0.300)\left(1 - \frac{308\text{ K}}{493\text{ K}}\right) = 0.113$$

We can determine the input heat from the relation for the efficiency

$$\text{Efficiency} = \frac{\text{Output work}}{\text{Input heat}}$$

and so every second

$$\text{Input heat/s} = \frac{\text{Output work/s}}{\text{Efficiency}} = \frac{(8.00\text{ hp})\,(746\text{ W/hp})\left(\dfrac{1.00\text{ cal/s}}{4.184\text{ W}}\right)}{0.113} = 12.7\text{ kcal/s}$$

To find the energy rejected to the condenser, we use the law of conservation of energy:

$$\text{Input energy} = (\text{Output work}) + (\text{Rejected energy})$$

$$\text{Rejected energy/s} = (\text{Input energy/s}) - (\text{Output work/s})$$

Thus,

$$= (\text{Input energy/s}) - (\text{Input energy/s})(\text{Efficiency})$$
$$= (\text{Input energy/s})[1 - (\text{Efficiency})]$$
$$= (12.7\text{ kcal/s})(1 - 0.113) = 11.3\text{ kcal/s}$$

**20.19 [II]** Three kilomoles (6.00 kg) of hydrogen gas at S.T.P. expands isobarically to precisely twice its volume. (*a*) What is the final temperature of the gas? (*b*) What is the expansion work done by the gas? (*c*) By how much does the internal energy of the gas change? (*d*) How much heat enters the gas during the expansion? For $H_2$, $c_v = 10.0\text{ kJ/kg}\cdot\text{K}$. Assume the hydrogen will behave as an ideal gas.

(*a*) From $P_1 V_1/T_1 = P_2 V_2/T_2$ with $P_1 = P_2$,

$$T_2 = T_1\left(\frac{V_2}{V_1}\right) = (273\text{ K})\,(2.00) = 546\text{ K}$$

(*b*) Because 1 kmol at S.T.P. occupies 22.4 m³, we have $V_1 = 67.2\text{ m}^3$. Then

$$\Delta W = P\,\Delta V = P(V_2 - V_1) = (1.01 \times 10^5\text{ N/m}^2)(67.2\text{ m}^3) = 6.8\text{ MJ}$$

(*c*) To raise the temperature of this ideal gas by 273 K at constant volume requires

$$\Delta Q = c_v m \Delta T = (10.0\text{ kJ/kg}\cdot\text{K})(6.00\text{ kg})(273\text{ K}) = 16.4\text{ MJ}$$

Because the volume is constant here, no work is done and $\Delta Q$ equals the internal energy that must be added to the 6.00 kg of $H_2$ to change its temperature from 273 K to 546 K. Therefore, $\Delta U = 16.4$ MJ.

(*d*) The system obeys the First Law during the process and so

$$\Delta Q = \Delta U + \Delta W = 16.4\text{ MJ} + 6.8\text{ MJ} = 23.2\text{ MJ}$$

**20.20 [II]** A cylinder of ideal gas is closed by an 8.00 kg movable piston (area = 60.0 cm$^2$) as illustrated in Fig. 20-5. Atmospheric pressure is 100 kPa. When the gas is heated from 30.0 °C to 100.0 °C, the piston rises 20.0 cm. The piston is then fastened in place, and the gas is cooled back to 30.0 °C. Calling $\Delta Q_1$ the heat added to the gas in the heating process, and $\Delta Q_2$ the heat lost during cooling, find the difference between $\Delta Q_1$ and $\Delta Q_2$.

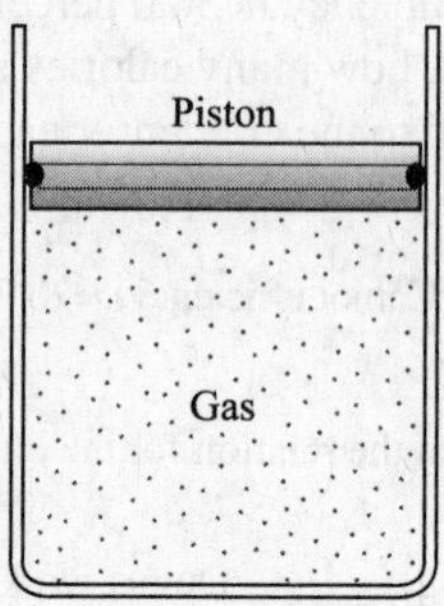


Fig. 20-5

During the heating process, the internal energy changed by $\Delta U_1$, and an amount of work $\Delta W_1$ was done. The absolute pressure of the gas was

$$P = \frac{mg}{A} + P_A$$

$$P = \frac{(8.00)\,(9.81)\text{ N}}{60.0 \times 10^{-4}\text{ m}^2} + 1.00 \times 10^5\text{ N/m}^2 = 1.13 \times 10^5\text{ N/m}^2$$

Therefore, $$\Delta Q_1 = \Delta U_1 + \Delta W_1 = \Delta U_1 + P\,\Delta V$$
$$= \Delta U_1 + (1.13 \times 10^5\text{ N/m}^2)(0.200 \times 60.0 \times 10^{-4}\text{ m}^3) = \Delta U_1 + 136\text{ J}$$

During the cooling process, $\Delta W = 0$ and so (since $\Delta Q_2$ is heat *lost*)

$$-\Delta Q_2 = \Delta U_2$$

But the ideal gas returns to its original temperature, and so its internal energy is the same as at the start. Therefore $\Delta U_2 = -\Delta U_1$, or $\Delta Q_2 = \Delta U_1$. It follows that $\Delta Q_1$ exceeds $\Delta Q_2$ by 136 J = 32.5 cal.

## SUPPLEMENTARY PROBLEMS

**20.21 [I]** A 2.0 kg metal block ($c = 0.137$ cal/g·°C) is heated from 15 °C to 90 °C. By how much does its internal energy change?

**20.22 [I]** By how much does the internal energy of 50 g of oil ($c = 0.32$ cal/g·°C) change as the oil is cooled from 100 °C to 25 °C.

**20.23 [II]** A 70-g metal block moving at 200 cm/s slides across a tabletop a distance of 83 cm before it comes to rest. Assuming 75 percent of the thermal energy developed by friction goes into the block, how much does the temperature of the block rise? For the metal, $c = 0.106$ cal/g·°C.

**20.24 [II]** If a certain mass of water falls a distance of 854 m and all the energy is effective in heating the water, what will be the temperature rise of the water?

**20.25 [II]** How many joules of heat per hour are produced in a motor that is 75.0 percent efficient and requires 0.250 hp to run it?

**20.26 [II]** A 100-g bullet ($c = 0.030$ cal/g·°C) is initially at 20 °C. It is fired straight upward with a speed of 420 m/s, and on returning to the starting point strikes a cake of ice at exactly 0 °C. How much ice is melted? Neglect air friction.

**20.27 [II]** To determine the specific heat of an oil, an electrical heating coil is placed in a calorimeter with 380 g of the oil at 10 °C. The coil consumes energy (and gives off heat) at the rate of 84 W. After 3.0 min, the oil temperature is 40 °C. If the water equivalent of the calorimeter and coil is 20 g, What is the specific heat of the oil?

**20.28 [I]** How much external work is done by an ideal gas in expanding from a volume of 3.0 liters to a volume of 30.0 liters against a constant pressure of 2.0 atm?

**20.29 [I]** As 3.0 liters of ideal gas at 27 °C is heated, it expands at a constant pressure of 2.0 atm. How much work is done by the gas as its temperature is changed from 27 °C to 227 °C?

**20.30 [I]** An ideal gas expands adiabatically to three times its original volume. In doing so, the gas does 720 J of work. (*a*) How much heat flows from the gas? (*b*) What is the change in internal energy of the gas? (*c*) Does its temperature rise or fall?

**20.31 [I]** An ideal gas expands at a constant pressure of 240 cmHg from 250 cm$^3$ to 780 cm$^3$. It is then allowed to cool at constant volume to its original temperature. What is the net amount of heat that flows into the gas during the entire process?

**20.32 [I]** As an ideal gas is compressed isothermally, the compressing agent does 36 J of work on the gas. How much heat flows from the gas during the compression process?

**20.33 [II]** The specific heat of air at constant volume is 0.175 cal/g·°C. (*a*) By how much does the internal energy of 5.0 g of air change as it is heated from 20 °C to 400 °C? (*b*) Suppose that 5.0 g of air is adiabatically compressed so as to rise its temperature from 20 °C to 400 °C. How much work must be done on the air to compress it?

**20.34 [II]** Water is boiled at 100 °C and 1.0 atm. Under these conditions, 1.0 g of water occupies 1.0 cm$^3$, 1.0 g of steam occupies 1670 cm$^3$, and $L_v = 540$ cal/g. Find (*a*) the external work done when 1.0 g of steam is formed at 100 °C and (*b*) the increase in internal energy.

**20.35 [II]** The temperature of 3.0 kg of krypton gas is raised from −20 °C to 80 °C. (*a*) If this is done at constant volume, compute the heat added, the work done, and the change in internal energy. (*b*) Repeat if the heating process is at constant pressure. For the monatomic gas Kr, $c_v = 0.0357$ cal/g·°C and $c_p = 0.0595$ cal/g·°C.

**20.36 [I]** (*a*) Compute $c_v$ for the monatomic gas argon, given $c_p = 0.125$ cal/g·°C and $\gamma = 1.67$. (*b*) Compute $c_p$ for the diatomic gas nitric oxide (NO), given $c_v = 0.166$ cal/g·°C and $\gamma = 1.40$.

**20.37 [I]** Compute the work done in an isothermal compression of 30 liters of ideal gas at 1.0 atm to a volume of 3.0 liters.

**20.38 [II]** Five moles of neon gas at 2.00 atm and 27.0 °C is adiabatically compressed to one-third its initial volume. Find the final pressure, final temperature, and external work done on the gas. For neon, $\gamma = 1.67$, $c_v = 0.148$ cal/g·°C, and $M = 20.18$ kg/kmol.

**20.39 [II]** Determine the work done by the gas in going from *A* to *B* in the thermodynamic cycle shown in Fig. 20-2. Repeat for portion *CA*. Give answers to one significant figure.

**20.40 [II]** Find the net work output per cycle for the thermodynamic cycle in Fig. 20-6. Give your answer to two significant figures.

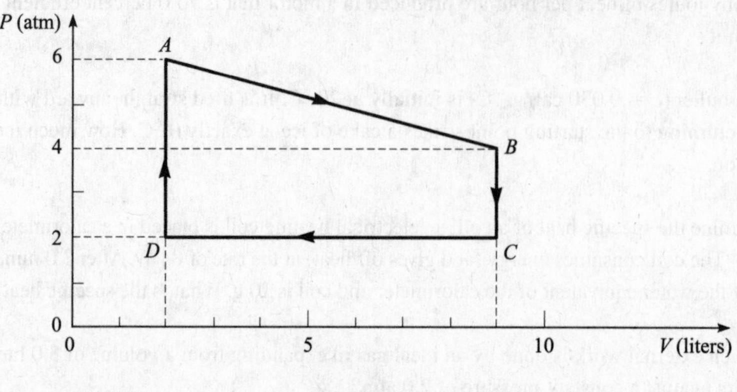


Fig. 20-6

**20.41 [II]** Four grams of gas, confined to a cylinder, is carried through the cycle shown in Fig. 20-6. At *A* the temperature of the gas is 400 °C. (*a*) What is its temperature at *B*? (*b*) If, in the portion from *A* to *B*, 2.20 kcal flows into the gas, what is $c_v$ for the gas? Give your answers to two significant figures.

**20.42 [II]** Figure 20-6 is the *P-V* diagram for 25.0 g of an enclosed ideal gas. At *A* the gas temperature is 200 °C. The value of $c_v$ for the gas is 0.150 cal/g·°C. (*a*) What is the temperature of the gas at *B*? (*b*) Find $\Delta U$ for the portion of the cycle from *A* to *B*. (*c*) Find $\Delta W$ for this same portion. (*d*) Find $\Delta Q$ for this same portion.

## ANSWERS TO SUPPLEMENTARY PROBLEMS

**20.21 [I]** 86 kJ

**20.22 [I]** −1.2 kcal

**20.23 [II]** $3.4 \times 10^{-3}$ °C

**20.24 [II]** 2.00 °C

**20.25 [II]** 168 kJ

**20.26 [II]** 26 g

**20.27 [II]** 0.26 cal/g·°C

**20.28 [I]** 5.5 kJ

**20.29 [I]** 0.40 kJ

**20.30 [I]** (*a*) none; (*b*) −720 J; (*c*) it falls

**20.31 [I]** 40.5 cal

**20.32 [I]** 8.6 cal

**20.33 [II]** (*a*) 0.33 kcal; (*b*) 1.4 kJ or since work done on the system is negative, −1.4 kJ

**20.34 [II]** (*a*) 0.17 kJ; (*b*) 0.50 kcal

**20.35 [II]** (*a*) 11 kcal, 0, 45 kJ; (*b*) 18 kcal, 30 kJ, 45 kJ

**20.36 [I]** (*a*) 0.0749 cal/g·°C; (*b*) 0.232 cal/g·°C

**20.37 [I]** 7.0 kJ

**20.38 [II]** 1.27 MPa, 626 K, 20.4 kJ

**20.39 [II]** 0.4 MJ, −0.3 MJ

**20.40 [II]** 2.1 kJ

**20.41 [II]** (*a*) $2.0 \times 10^3$ K; (*b*) 0.25 cal/g·°C

**20.42 [II]** (*a*) $1.42 \times 10^3$ K; (*b*) 3.55 kcal = 14.9 kJ; (*c*) 3.54 kJ; (*d*) 18.4 kJ

# Entropy and the Second Law

**The Second Law of Thermodynamics** can be stated in three equivalent ways:

(1) Heat flows spontaneously from a hotter to a colder object, but not vice versa.
(2) No heat engine that cycles continuously can change all its heat-in to useful work-out.
(3) If a system undergoes spontaneous change, it will change in such a way that its entropy will increase or, at best, remain constant.

The Second Law tells us the manner in which a spontaneous change will occur, while the First Law tells us whether or not the change is possible. The First Law deals with the conservation of energy; the Second Law deals with the dispersal of energy.

**Entropy** ($S$) is a *state variable* for a system in equilibrium. By this is meant that $S$ is always the same for the system when it is in a given equilibrium state. Like $P$, $V$, and $U$, the entropy is a characteristic of the system at equilibrium.

When heat $\Delta Q$ enters a system at an absolute temperature $T$, the resulting change in entropy of the system is

$$\Delta S = \frac{\Delta Q}{T}$$

provided the system changes in a reversible way. The SI unit for entropy is J/K.

A **reversible change** (or process) is one in which the values of $P$, $V$, $T$, and $U$ are well-defined during the change. If the process is reversed, then $P$, $V$, $T$, and $U$ will take on their original values when the system is returned to where it started. To be reversible, a process must usually be slow, and the system must be close to equilibrium during the entire change.

Another fully equivalent definition of entropy can be given from a detailed molecular analysis of the system. If a system can achieve a particular state (i.e., particular values of $P$, $V$, $T$, and $U$) in $\Omega$ (omega) different ways (different arrangements of the molecules, for example), then the entropy of the state is

$$S = k_B \ln \Omega$$

where ln is the logarithm to base $e$, and $k_B$ is Boltzmann's constant, $1.38 \times 10^{-23}$ J/K.

**Entropy Is a Measure of Disorder:** A state that can occur in only one way (one arrangement of its molecules, for example) is a state of high order. But a state that can occur in many ways is a more disordered state. One way to associate a number with disorder is to take the disorder of a state as being proportional to $\Omega$, the number of ways the state can occur. Because $S = k_B \ln \Omega$, entropy is a measure of disorder.

Spontaneous processes in systems that contain many molecules always occur in a direction from a

$$\begin{pmatrix}\text{State that can exist}\\ \text{in only a few ways}\end{pmatrix} \rightarrow \begin{pmatrix}\text{State that can exist}\\ \text{in many ways}\end{pmatrix}$$

Hence, when left to themselves, systems either retain their original state of order or else increase their disorder.

**The Most Probable State** of a system is the state with the largest entropy. It is also the state with the most disorder and the state that can occur in the largest number of ways.

## SOLVED PROBLEMS

**21.1 [I]** Twenty grams of ice at precisely 0 °C melts into water with no change in temperature. By how much does the entropy of the 20-g mass change in this process?

By slowly adding heat to the ice, we can melt it in a reversible way. The heat needed is

$$\Delta Q = mL_f = (20\ \text{g})\,(80\ \text{cal/g}) = 1600\ \text{cal}$$

and so

$$\Delta S = \frac{\Delta Q}{T} = \frac{1600\ \text{cal}}{273\ \text{K}} = 5.86\ \text{cal/K} = 25\ \text{J/K}$$

Notice that melting increases the entropy (and disorder); ice is more ordered than water.

**21.2 [I]** As depicted in Fig. 21-1, an ideal gas is confined to a cylinder by a piston. The piston is pushed down slowly so that the gas temperature remains at 20.0 °C. During the compression, 730 J of work is done on the gas. Find the entropy change of the gas.

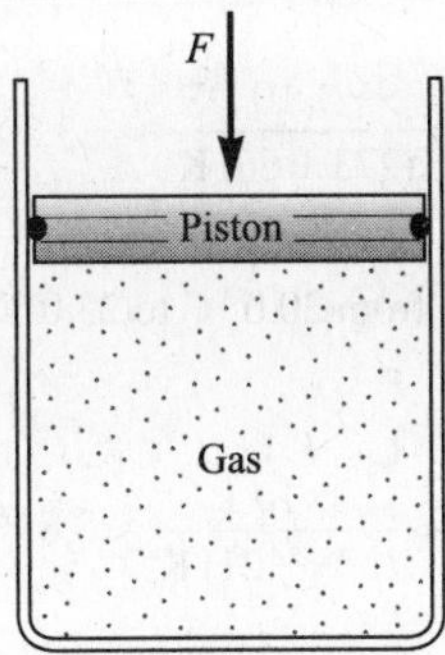


Fig. 21-1

The First Law tells us that

$$\Delta Q = \Delta U + \Delta W$$

Because the process was isothermal, the internal energy of the ideal gas did not change. Therefore, $\Delta U = 0$ and

$$\Delta Q = \Delta W = -730\ \text{J}$$

(Because the gas was compressed, the gas did negative work, hence the minus sign. In other words, the work done on the gas is negative.) Now we can write

$$\Delta S = \frac{\Delta Q}{T} = \frac{-730\ \text{J}}{293\ \text{K}} = -2.49\ \text{J/K}$$

Notice that the entropy change is negative. The disorder of the gas decreased as it was pushed into a smaller volume.

**21.3 [II]** As shown in Fig. 21-2, a container is separated into two equal-volume compartments. The two compartments contain equal masses of the same gas, 0.740 g in each, and $c_v$ for the gas is 745 J/kg·K. At the start, the hot gas is at 67.0 °C, while the cold gas is at 20.0 °C. No heat can leave or enter the compartments except slowly through the partition *AB*. Find the entropy change of each compartment as the hot gas cools from 67.0 °C to 65.0 °C.

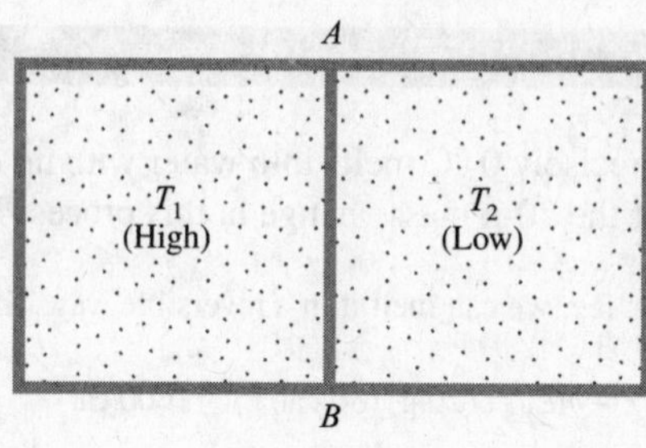


Fig. 21-2

The heat lost by the hot gas in the process is

$$\Delta Q = mc_v\,\Delta T = (0.000\,740\text{ kg})(745\text{ J/kg}\cdot\text{K})(-2.0\text{ °C}) = -1.10\text{ J}$$

The entropy change is for a constant-temperature process, so we will have to approximate what's going on. For the hot gas (taking the temperature to be a constant 66 °C),

$$\Delta S_{\text{H}} = \frac{\Delta Q}{T_{\text{H}}} \approx \frac{-1.10\text{ J}}{(273+66)\text{ K}} \approx -3.2\times10^{-3}\text{ J/K}$$

The cold gas will gain 1.10 J, and go from 20.0 °C to 22.0 °C. Take its temperature to be a constant 21.0 °C, whereupon

$$\Delta S_{\text{L}} = \frac{\Delta Q}{T_{\text{L}}} \approx \frac{1.10\text{ J}}{(273+21)\text{ K}} \approx 3.8\times10^{-3}\text{ J/K}$$

As you can see, the entropy changes were different for the two compartments; more was gained than was lost. The total entropy of the universe increased as a result of this process.

**21.4 [II]** The ideal gas in the cylinder in Fig. 21-1 is initially at conditions $P_1$, $V_1$, $T_1$. It is slowly expanded at constant temperature by allowing the piston to rise. Its final conditions are $P_2$, $V_2$, $T_1$, where $V_2 = 3V_1$. Find the change in entropy of the gas during this expansion. The mass of gas is 1.5 g, and $M = 28$ kg/kmol for it.

Recall from Chapter 20 that, for an isothermal expansion of an ideal gas (where $\Delta U = 0$),

$$\Delta W = \Delta Q = P_1V_1 \ln\left(\frac{V_2}{V_1}\right)$$

Consequently,
$$\Delta S = \frac{\Delta Q}{T} = \frac{P_1V_1}{T_1} \ln = \left(\frac{V_2}{V_1}\right) = \frac{m}{M} R \ln\left(\frac{V_2}{V_1}\right)$$

where we have used the Ideal Gas Law. Substituting the data leads to

$$\Delta S = \left(\frac{1.5\times10^{-3}\ \text{kg}}{28\ \text{kg/kmol}}\right)\left(8314\frac{\text{J}}{\text{kmol}\cdot\text{K}}\right)(\ln 3) = 0.49\ \text{J/K}$$

**21.5 [I]** Two vats of water, one at 87 °C and the other at 14 °C, are separated by a metal plate. If heat flows through the plate at 35 cal/s, what is the change in entropy of the system that occurs in a time of one second?

The higher-temperature vat loses entropy, while the cooler one gains entropy:

$$\Delta S_{\text{H}} = \frac{\Delta Q}{T_{\text{H}}} = \frac{(-35\ \text{cal})\,(4.186\ \text{J/cal})}{360\ \text{K}} = -0.41\ \text{J/K}$$

$$\Delta S_{\text{L}} = \frac{\Delta Q}{T_{\text{L}}} = \frac{(35\ \text{cal})\,(4.186\ \text{J/cal})}{287\ \text{K}} = 0.51\ \text{J/K}$$

Therefore, 0.51 J/K − 0.41 J/K = 0.10 J/K.

**21.6 [I]** A system consists of 3 coins that can come up either heads or tails. In how many different ways can the system have (*a*) all heads up? (*b*) All tails up? (*c*) One tail and two heads up? (*d*) Two tails and one head up?

(*a*) There is only one way all the coins can be heads-up: Each coin must be heads up.

(*b*) Here, too, there is only one way.

(*c*) There are three ways, corresponding to the three choices for the coin showing the tail.

(*d*) By symmetry with (*c*), there are three ways.

**21.7 [I]** Find the entropy of the three-coin system described in Problem 21.6 if (*a*) all coins are heads up, (*b*) two coins are heads up.

We use the Boltzmann relation $S = k_B \ln \Omega$, where $\Omega$ is the number of ways the state can occur, and $k_B = 1.38 \times 10^{-23}$ J/K.

(*a*) Since this state can occur in only one way,

$$S = k_B \ln 1 = (1.38 \times 10^{-23}\ \text{J/K})(0) = 0$$

(*b*) Since this state can occur in three ways,

$$S = (1.38 \times 10^{-23}\ \text{J/K}) \ln 3 = 1.52 \times 10^{-23}\ \text{J/K}$$

## SUPPLEMENTARY PROBLEMS

**21.8 [I]** Compute the entropy change of 5.00 g of water at 100 °C as it changes to steam at 100 °C under standard pressure.

**21.9 [I]** By how much does the entropy of 300 g of a metal ($c$ = 0.093 cal/g · °C) change as it is cooled from 90 °C to 70 °C? You may approximate $T = \frac{1}{2}(T_1 + T_2)$

**21.10 [II]** An ideal gas was slowly expanded from 2.00 m$^3$ to 3.00 m$^3$ at a constant temperature of 30 °C. The entropy change of the gas was +47 J/K during the process. (*a*) How much heat was added to the gas during the process? (*b*) How much work did the gas do during the process?

**21.11 [II]** Starting at standard conditions, 3.0 kg of an ideal gas ($M$ = 28 kg/kmol) is isothermally compressed to one-fifth of its original volume. Find the change in entropy of the gas.

**21.12 [I]** Four poker chips are red on one side and white on the other. In how many different ways can (*a*) only 3 reds come up? (*b*) Only two reds come up?

**21.13 [II]** When 100 coins are tossed, there is one way in which all can come up heads. There are 100 ways in which only one tail comes up. There are about $1 \times 10^{29}$ ways that 50 heads can come up. One hundred coins are placed in a box with only one head up. They are shaken and then there are 50 heads up. What was the change in entropy of the coins caused by the shaking?

## ANSWERS TO SUPPLEMENTARY PROBLEMS

**21.8 [I]** 7.24 cal/K = 30.3 J/K

**21.9 [I]** −6.6 J/K

**21.10 [II]** (*a*) 3.4 kcal; (*b*) 14 kJ

**21.11 [II]** −1.4 kJ/K

**21.12 [I]** (*a*) 4; (*b*) 6

**21.13 [II]** $9 \times 10^{-22}$ J/K

# Wave Motion

**A Propagating Wave** is a self-sustaining disturbance of a medium that travels from one point to another, carrying energy and momentum. Mechanical waves are aggregate phenomena arising from the motion of constituent particles. The wave advances, but the particles of the medium only oscillate in place. A wave has been generated on the string in Fig. 22-1 by the sinusoidal vibration of the hand at its end. Energy is carried by the wave from the source to the right, along the string. This direction, the direction of energy transport, is called the *direction of propagation* of the wave.

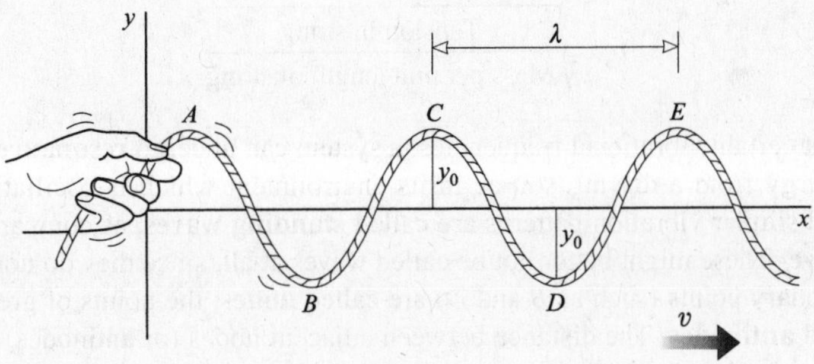


Fig. 22-1

Each particle of the string (such as the one at point-*C*) vibrates up and down, perpendicular to the direction of propagation. Any wave in which the vibration direction is perpendicular to the direction of propagation is called a **transverse wave.** Typical transverse waves, besides those on a string, are electromagnetic waves (e.g., light and radio waves). By contrast, in sound waves the vibration direction is parallel to the direction of propagation, as you will see in Chapter 23. Such a wave is called a **longitudinal** (or *compressional*) **wave**.

**Wave Terminology:** The **period** ($T$) of a wave is the time it takes the wave to go through one complete cycle. It is the time taken for a particle, such as the one at $A$, to move through one complete vibration or cycle, down from point-$A$ and then back to $A$. The period is the number of seconds per cycle. The **frequency** ($f$) of a wave is the number of cycles per second: Thus,

$$f = \frac{1}{T}$$

If $T$ is in seconds, then $f$ is in hertz (Hz), where 1 Hz = 1 $s^{-1}$. The period and frequency of the wave are the same as the period and frequency of the vibration.

The top points on the wave, such as $A$ and $C$, are called wave *crests*. The bottom points, such as $B$ and $D$, are called *troughs*. As time goes on, the crests and troughs move to the right with speed $v$, the speed of the wave.

The **amplitude** of a wave is the maximum disturbance undergone during a vibration cycle, distance $y_0$ in Fig. 22-1.

The wavelength ($\lambda$) is the distance along the direction of propagation between corresponding points on the wave, distance $AC$, for example. In a time $T$, a crest moving with speed $v$ will move a distance $\lambda$ to the right. Therefore, $s = vt$ and

$$\lambda = vT = \frac{v}{f}$$

whereupon

$$v = f\lambda$$

This relation holds for all waves, not just for waves on a string.

**In-Phase Vibrations** exist at two points on a wave if those points undergo vibrations that are in the same direction, in step. For example, the particles of the string at points-$A$ and -$C$ in Fig. 22-1 vibrate ***in-phase***, since they move up together and down together. Vibrations are in-phase if the points are a whole number of wavelengths apart. The pieces of the string at $A$ and $B$ vibrate opposite to each other; the vibrations there are said to be 180°, or half a cycle, ***out-of-phase***.

**The Speed of a Transverse Wave** on a stretched string or wire is

$$v = \sqrt{\frac{\text{Tension in string}}{\text{Mass per unit length of string}}}$$

**Standing Waves:** At certain vibrational frequencies, a system can undergo **resonance**. That is to say, it can efficiently absorb energy from a driving source in its environment which is oscillating at that frequency (Fig. 22-2). These and similar vibration patterns are called **standing waves,** as compared to the propagating waves considered above. These might better not be called waves at all, since they do not transport energy and momentum. The stationary points (such as $B$ and $D$) are called **nodes**; the points of greatest motion (such as $A$, $C$, and $E$) are called **antinodes**. The distance between adjacent nodes (or antinodes) is $\frac{1}{2}\lambda$. We sometimes call the portion of the string between adjacent nodes a *segment*, and the length of a segment is also $\frac{1}{2}\lambda$.

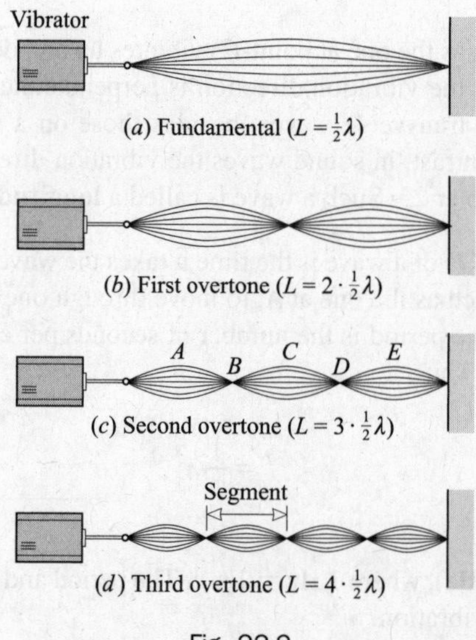


Fig. 22-2

**Conditions for Resonance:** A string will resonate only if the vibration wavelength has certain special values: the wavelength must be such that a whole number of wave segments (each $\frac{1}{2}\lambda$ long) exactly fit on the string. A proper fit occurs when nodes and antinodes exist at positions demanded by the constraints on the string. In particular, the fixed ends of the string must be nodes. Thus, as shown in Fig. 22-2, the relation between the wavelength $\lambda$ and the length $L$ of the resonating string is $L = n(\frac{1}{2}\lambda)$, where $n$ is any integer. Because $\lambda = vT = v/f$, the shorter the wave segments at resonance, the higher will be the resonant frequency. If we call the fundamental resonant frequency $f_1$, then Fig. 22-2 shows that the higher resonant frequencies are given by $f_n = nf_1$.

When driven at its *natural* or *resonant frequency* a mechanical system (e.g., a wine glass, or a loose window on a bus) will absorb energy and vibrate vigorously.

**Longitudinal (Compression) Waves** occur as lengthwise vibrations of air columns, solid bars, and the like. At resonance, nodes exist at fixed points, such as the closed end of an air column in a tube, or the location of a clamp on a bar. Diagrams such as Fig. 22-2 are used to display the resonance of longitudinal waves as well as transverse waves. However, for longitudinal waves, the diagrams are mainly schematic and are used to indicate the locations of nodes and antinodes. In analyzing such diagrams, we use the fact that the distance between node and adjacent antinode is $\frac{1}{4}\lambda$.

## SOLVED PROBLEMS

**22.1 [I]** Suppose that Fig. 22-1 represents a 50-Hz wave on a string. Take distance $y_0$ to be 3.0 mm, and distance $AE$ to be 40 cm. Find the following for the wave: its (*a*) amplitude, (*b*) wavelength, and (*c*) speed

(*a*) By definition, the amplitude is distance $y_0$ and is 3.0 mm.

(*b*) The distance between adjacent crests is the wavelength, and so $\lambda = 20$ cm.

(*c*) $v = \lambda f = (0.20\text{ m})(50\text{ s}^{-1}) = 10\text{ m/s}$

**22.2 [I]** Measurements show that the wavelength of a sound wave in a certain material is 18.0 cm. The frequency of the wave is 1900 Hz. What is the speed of the sound wave?

From $\lambda = vT = v/f$, which applies to all waves,

$$v = \lambda f = (0.180\text{ m})(1900\text{ s}^{-1}) = 342\text{ m/s}$$

**22.3 [I]** A horizontal cord 5.00 m long has a mass of 1.45 g. What must be the tension in the cord if the wavelength of a 120-Hz wave on it is to be 60.0 cm? How large a mass must be hung from its end (say, over a pulley) to give it this tension?

We know that the speed of a wave on a rope depends on both the tension and the mass per unit length. Moreover,

$$v = \lambda f = (0.600\text{ m})(120\text{ s}^{-1}) = 72.0\text{ m/s}$$

Further, since $v = \sqrt{(\text{Tension})/(\text{Mass per unit length})}$

$$\text{Tension} = (\text{Mass per unit length})(v^2) = \left(\frac{1.45\times10^{-3}\text{ kg}}{5.00\text{ m}}\right)(72.0\text{ m/s})^2 = 1.50\text{ N}$$

The tension in the cord balances the weight of the mass hung at its end. Therefore,

$$F_T = mg \quad \text{or} \quad m = \frac{F_T}{g} = \frac{1.50\text{ N}}{9.81\text{ m/s}^2} = 0.153\text{ kg}$$

**22.4 [II]** A uniform flexible cable is 20 m long and has a mass of 5.0 kg. It hangs vertically under its own weight and is vibrated (perpendicularly) from its upper end with a frequency of 7.0 Hz. (*a*) Find the speed of a transverse wave on the cable at its midpoint. (*b*) What are the frequency and wavelength at the midpoint?

(*a*) We shall use $v = \sqrt{\text{(Tension/(Mass per unit length)}}$. The midpoint of the cable supports half its weight, so the tension there is

$$F_T = \tfrac{1}{2}(5.0\text{ kg})(9.81\text{ m/s}^2) = 24.5\text{ N}$$

Further
$$\text{Mass per unit length} = \frac{5.0\text{ kg}}{20\text{ m}} = 0.25\text{ kg/m}$$

so that
$$v = \sqrt{\frac{24.5\text{ N}}{0.25\text{ kg/m}}} = 9.9\text{ m/s}$$

(*b*) Because wave crests do not pile up along a string or cable, the number passing one point must be the same as that for any other point. Therefore, the frequency, 7.0 Hz, is the same at all points.

To find the wavelength at the midpoint, we must use the speed we found for that point, 9.9 m/s. That gives us

$$\lambda = \frac{v}{f} = \frac{9.9\text{ m/s}}{7.0\text{ Hz}} = 1.4\text{ m}$$

**22.5 [II]** Suppose that Fig. 22-2 depicts standing waves on a metal string under a tension of 88.2 N. Its length is 50.0 cm and its mass is 0.500 g. (*a*) Compute $v$ for transverse waves on the string. (*b*) Determine the frequencies of its fundamental, first overtone, and second overtone.

(*a*) $$v = \sqrt{\frac{\text{Tension}}{\text{Mass per unit length}}} = \sqrt{\frac{88.2\text{ N}}{(5.00\times10^{-4}\text{ kg})/(0.500\text{ m})}} = 297\text{ m/s}$$

(*b*) We recall that the length of the segment is $\lambda/2$ and we use $\lambda = v/f$. For the fundamental:

$$\lambda = 1.00\text{ m} \quad\text{and}\quad f = \frac{297\text{ m/s}}{1.00\text{ m}} = 297\text{ Hz}$$

For the first overtone:

$$\lambda = 0.500\text{ m} \quad\text{and}\quad f = \frac{297\text{ m/s}}{0.500\text{ m}} = 594\text{ Hz}$$

For the second overtone:

$$\lambda = 0.333\text{ m} \quad\text{and}\quad f = \frac{297\text{ m/s}}{0.333\text{ m}} = 891\text{ Hz}$$

**22.6 [II]** A string 2.0 m long is driven by a 240-Hz vibrator at its end. The string resonates in four segments forming a standing wave pattern. What would be the speed of a transverse wave on such a string?

Let's first determine the wavelength of the wave from part (d) of Fig. 22-2. Since each segment is $\lambda/2$ long,

$$4\left(\frac{\lambda}{2}\right) = L \quad\text{or}\quad \lambda = \frac{L}{2} = \frac{2.0\text{ m}}{2} = 1.0\text{ m}$$

Then, using $\lambda = vT = v/f$,

$$v = f\lambda = (240\ \mathrm{s}^{-1})(1.0\ \mathrm{m}) = 0.24\ \mathrm{km/s}$$

**22.7 [II]** A banjo string 30 cm long oscillates in a standing-wave pattern. It resonates in its fundamental mode at a frequency of 256 Hz. What is the tension in the string if 80 cm of the string have a mass of 0.75 g?

First we'll find $v$ and then the tension. The string vibrates in one segment when $f = 256$ Hz. Therefore, from Fig. 22-2 (a):

$$\frac{\lambda}{2} = L \quad \text{or} \quad \lambda = (0.30\ \mathrm{m})(2) = 0.60\ \mathrm{m}$$

and $$v = f\lambda = (256\ \mathrm{s}^{-1})(0.60\ \mathrm{m}) = 154\ \mathrm{m/s}$$

The mass per unit length of the string is

$$\frac{0.75 \times 10^{-3}\ \mathrm{kg}}{0.80\ \mathrm{m}} = 9.4 \times 10^{-4}\ \mathrm{kg/m}$$

Then, from, $v = \sqrt{(\text{Tension})/(\text{Mass per unit length})}$,

$$F_T = (154\ \mathrm{m/s})^2 (9.4 \times 10^{-4}\ \mathrm{kg/m}) = 22\ \mathrm{N}$$

**22.8 [II]** A string vibrates in five segments at a frequency of 460 Hz. (*a*) What is its fundamental frequency? (*b*) What frequency will cause it to vibrate in three segments?

**Detailed Method**

If the string is $n$ segments long, then from Fig. 22-2 we have $n\left(\frac{1}{2}\lambda\right) = L$. But $\lambda = v/f_n$, so $L = n(v/2f_n)$. Solving for $f_n$ provides

$$f_n = n\left(\frac{v}{2L}\right)$$

We are told that $f_5 = 460$ Hz, and so

$$460\ \mathrm{Hz} = 5\left(\frac{v}{2L}\right) \quad \text{or} \quad \frac{v}{2L} = 92.0\ \mathrm{Hz}$$

Substituting this in the above relation gives

$$f_n = (n)(92.0\ \mathrm{Hz})$$

(*a*) $f_1 = 92.0$ Hz.

(*b*) $f_3 = (3)(92\ \mathrm{Hz}) = 276$ Hz

**Alternative Method**

Recall that for a string held at both ends, $f_n = nf_1$. Knowing that $f_5 = 460$ Hz, it follows that $f_1 = 92.0$ Hz and $f_3 = 276$ Hz.

**22.9 [II]** A string fastened at both ends resonates at 420 Hz and 490 Hz with no resonant frequencies in between. Find its fundamental resonant frequency.

In general, $f_n = nf_1$. We are told that $f_n = 420$ Hz and $f_{n+1} = 490$ Hz. Therefore,

$$420 \text{ Hz} = nf_1 \quad \text{and} \quad 490 \text{ Hz} = (n+1)f_1$$

Subtract the first equation from the second to obtain $f_1 = 70.0$ Hz.

**22.10 [II]** A violin string resonates at its fundamental frequency of 196 Hz. Where along the string must you place your finger so its fundamental becomes 440 Hz?

For the fundamental, $L = \frac{1}{2}\lambda$. Since $\lambda = v/f$, it follows that $f_1 = v/2L$. Originally, the string of length $L_1$ resonated at a frequency of 196 Hz, and therefore

$$196 \text{ Hz} = \frac{v}{2L_1}$$

with a resonance at 440 Hz,

$$440 \text{ Hz} = \frac{v}{2L_2}$$

Eliminate $v$ from these two simultaneous equations and find

$$\frac{L_2}{L_1} = \frac{196 \text{ Hz}}{440 \text{ Hz}} = 0.445$$

To obtain the desired resonance, the finger must shorten the string to 0.445 of its original length.

**22.11 [II]** A 60-cm-long bar, clamped at its middle, is vibrated lengthwise by an alternating force at its end. (See Fig. 22-3.) Its fundamental resonance frequency is found to be 3.0 kHz. What is the speed of longitudinal waves in the bar?

Because its ends are free, the bar must have antinodes there. The clamp point at its center must be a node. Therefore, the fundamental resonance is as shown in Fig. 22-3. Because the distance from node to antinode is always $\frac{1}{4}\lambda$, we see that $L = 2\left(\frac{1}{4}\lambda\right)$. Since $L = 0.60$ m, we find $\lambda = 1.20$ m.
Then, from the basic relation (p. 246) $\lambda = v/f$, we have

$$v = \lambda f = (1.20 \text{ m})(3.0 \text{ kHz}) = 3.6 \text{ km/s}$$

**22.12 [II]** Compression waves (sound waves) are sent down an air-filled tube 90 cm long and closed at one end. The tube resonates at several frequencies, the lowest of which is 95 Hz. Find the speed of sound waves in air.

The tube and several of its resonance forms are shown in Fig. 22-4. Recall that the distance between a node and an adjacent antinode is $\lambda/4$. In our case, the top resonance form applies, since the segments are longest for it and its frequency is therefore lowest. For that form, $L = \lambda/4$, so

$$\lambda = 4L = 4(0.90 \text{ m}) = 3.6 \text{ m}$$

Using $\lambda = vT = v/f$ gives

$$v = \lambda f = (3.6 \text{ m})(95 \text{ s}^{-1}) = 0.34 \text{ km/s}$$

**22.13 [II]** At what other frequencies will the tube described in Problem 22.12 resonate?

The first few resonances are shown in Fig. 22-4. We see that, at resonance,

$$L = n\left(\tfrac{1}{4}\lambda_n\right)$$

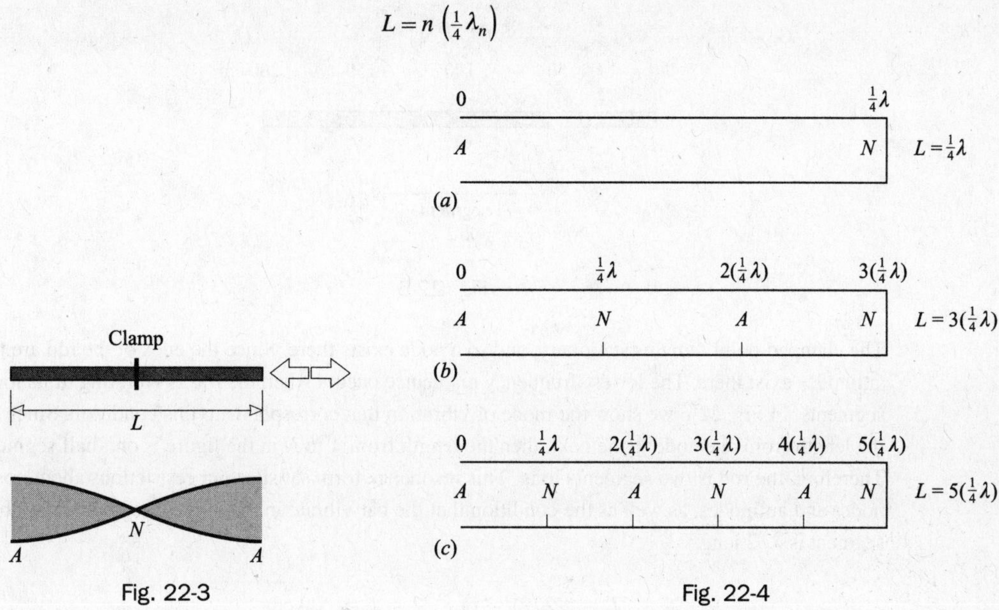


Fig. 22-3 Fig. 22-4

where $n = 1, 3, 5, 7, \ldots$, is an odd integer, and $\lambda_n$ is the resonant wavelength. But $\lambda_n = \upsilon/f_n$, and so

$$L = n\frac{\upsilon}{4f_n} \quad \text{or} \quad f_n = n\frac{\upsilon}{4L} = nf_1$$

where, from Problem 22.12, $f_1 = 95$ Hz. The first few resonant frequencies are thus 95 Hz, 0.29 kHz, 0.48 kHz, … .

**22.14 [II]** A metal rod 40 cm long is dropped, end first, onto a wooden floor and rebounds into the air. Compression waves of many frequencies are thereby set up in the bar. If the speed of compression waves in the bar is 5500 m/s, to what lowest-frequency compression wave will the bar resonate as it rebounds?

Both ends of the bar will be free, and so antinodes will exist there. In the lowest resonance form (i.e., the one with the longest segments), only one node will exist on the bar, at its center, as illustrated in Fig. 22-5. We will then have

$$L = 2\left(\frac{\lambda}{4}\right) \quad \text{or} \quad \lambda = 2L = 2(0.40\ \text{m}) = 0.80\ \text{m}$$

Then, from $\lambda = \upsilon T = \upsilon/f$,

$$f = \frac{\upsilon}{\lambda} = \frac{5500\ \text{m/s}}{0.80\ \text{m}} = 6875\ \text{Hz} = 6.9\ \text{kHz}$$

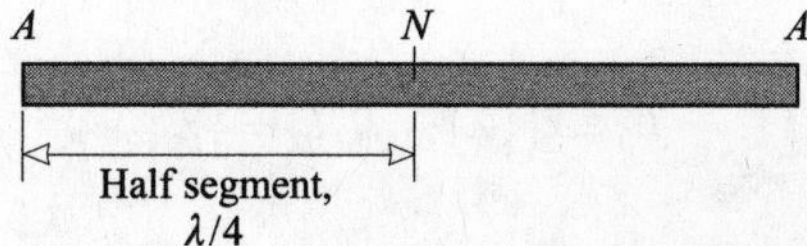


Fig. 22-5

**22.15 [II]** A rod 200 cm long is clamped 50 cm from one end, as shown in Fig. 22-6. It is set into longitudinal vibration by an electrical driving mechanism at one end. As the frequency of the driver is slowly increased from a very low value, the rod is first found to resonate at 3 kHz. What is the speed of sound (compression waves) in the rod?

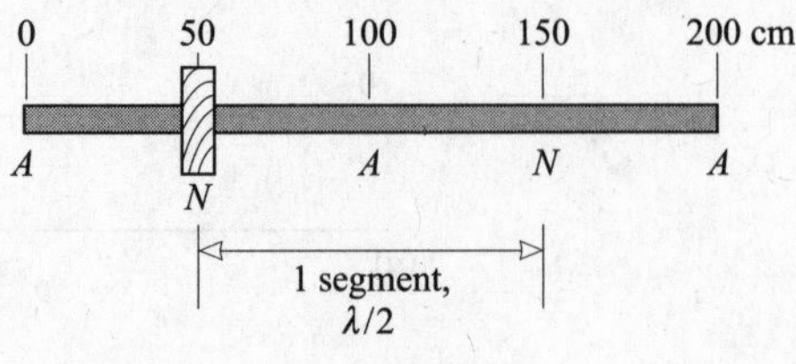


Fig. 22-6

The clamped point remains stationary, and so a node exists there. Since the ends of the rod are free, antinodes exist there. The lowest-frequency resonance occurs when the rod is vibrating in its longest possible segments. In Fig. 22-6 we show the mode of vibration that corresponds to this condition. Since a segment is the length from one node to the next, then the length from $A$ to $N$ in the figure is one-half segment. Therefore, the rod is two segments long. This resonance form satisfies our restrictions about positions of nodes and antinodes, as well as the condition that the bar vibrate in the longest segments possible. Since one segment is $\lambda/2$ long,

$$L = 2(\lambda/2) \quad \text{or} \quad \lambda = L = 200 \text{ cm}$$

Then, from $\lambda = vT = v/f$,

$$v = \lambda f = (2.00 \text{ m})(3 \times 10^3 \text{ s}^{-1}) = 6 \text{ km/s}$$

**22.16 [II]** (*a*) Determine the shortest length of pipe closed at one end that will resonate in air when driven by a sound source of frequency 160 Hz. Take the speed of sound in air to be 340 m/s. (*b*) Repeat the analysis for a pipe open at both ends.

(*a*) Figure 22-4(*a*) applies in this case. The shortest pipe will be $\lambda/4$ long. Therefore,

$$L = \tfrac{1}{4}\lambda = \tfrac{1}{4}\left(\frac{v}{f}\right) = \frac{340 \text{ m/s}}{4(160 \text{ s}^{-1})} = 0.531 \text{ m}$$

(*b*) In this case the pipe will have antinodes at both ends and a node at its center. Then,

$$L = 2\left(\tfrac{1}{4}\lambda\right) = \tfrac{1}{2}\left(\frac{v}{f}\right) = \frac{340 \text{ m/s}}{2(160 \text{ s}^{-1})} = 1.06 \text{ m}$$

**22.17 [II]** A pipe 90 cm long is open at both ends. How long must a second pipe, closed at one end, be if it is to have the same fundamental resonance frequency as the open pipe?

The two pipes and their fundamental resonances are shown in Fig. 22-7. As can be seen in the diagram,

$$L_o = 2\left(\tfrac{1}{4}\lambda\right) \qquad L_c = \tfrac{1}{4}\lambda$$

from which $L_c = \tfrac{1}{2}L_o = 45$ cm.

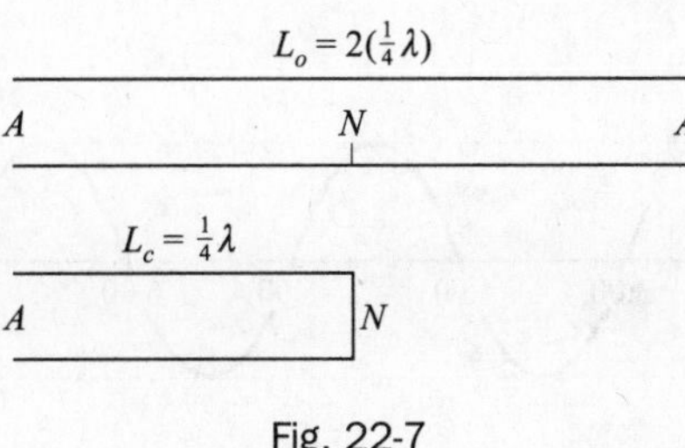


Fig. 22-7

**22.18 [II]** A glass tube that is 70.0 cm long is open at both ends. Find the frequencies at which it will resonate when driven by sound waves that have a speed of 340 m/s.

A pipe that is open at both ends must have an antinode at each end. It will therefore resonate as in Fig. 22-8. From the diagram it can be seen that the resonance wavelengths $\lambda_n$ are given by

$$L = n\left(\frac{\lambda_n}{2}\right) \quad \text{or} \quad \lambda_n = \frac{2L}{n}$$

where $n$ is an integer. But $\lambda_n = v/f_n$, therefore

$$f_n = \left(\frac{n}{2L}\right)(v) = (n)\left(\frac{340\text{ m/s}}{2 \times 0.700\text{ m}}\right) = 243n\text{ Hz}$$

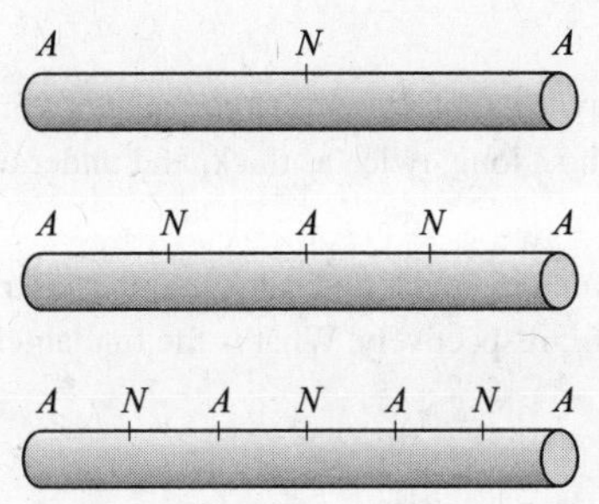


Fig. 22-8

## SUPPLEMENTARY PROBLEMS

**22.19 [I]** The average person can hear sound waves ranging in frequency from about 20 Hz to 20 kHz. Determine the wavelengths at these limits, taking the speed of sound to be 340 m/s.

**22.20 [I]** Radio station WJR broadcasts at 760 kHz. The speed of radio waves is $3.00 \times 10^8$ m/s. What is the wavelength of WJR's waves?

**22.21 [I]** Radar waves with 3.4 cm wavelength are sent out from a transmitter. Their speed is $3.00 \times 10^8$ m/s. What is their frequency?

**22.22 [I]** When driven by a 120-Hz vibrator, a string has transverse waves of 31 cm wavelength traveling along it. (*a*) What is the speed of the waves on the string? (*b*) If the tension in the string is 1.20 N, what is the mass of 50 cm of the string?

**22.23 [I]** The wave shown in Fig. 22-9 is being sent out by a 60-cycle/s vibrator. Find the following for the wave: (*a*) amplitude, (*b*) frequency, (*c*) wavelength, (*d*) speed, (*e*) period.

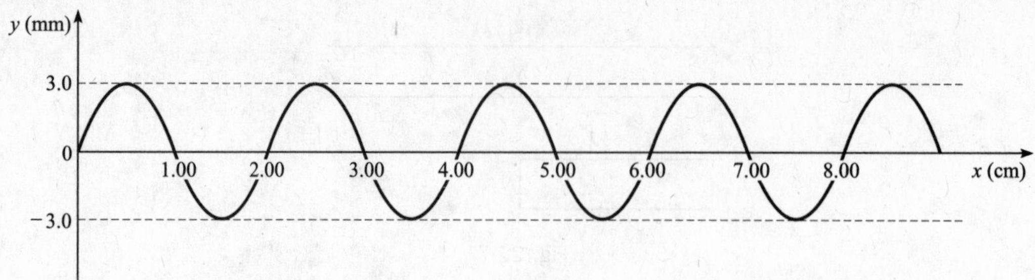


Fig. 22-9

**22.24 [II]** A copper wire 2.4 mm in diameter is 3.0 m long and is used to suspend a 2.0-kg mass from a beam. If a transverse disturbance is sent along the wire by striking it lightly with a pencil, how fast will the disturbance travel? The density of copper is 8920 kg/m$^3$.

**22.25 [II]** A string 180-cm-long resonates in a standing wave that has three segments when driven by a 270-Hz vibrator. What is the speed of the waves on the string?

**22.26 [II]** A string resonates in three segments at a frequency of 165 Hz. What frequency must be used if it is to resonate in four segments?

**22.27 [II]** A flexible cable, 30 m long and weighing 70 N, is stretched by a force of 2.0 kN. If the cable is struck sideways at one end, how long will it take the transverse wave to travel to the other end and return?

**22.28 [II]** A wire under tension vibrates with a fundamental frequency of 256 Hz. What would be the fundamental frequency if the wire were half as long, twice as thick, and under one-fourth the tension?

**22.29 [II]** Steel and silver wires of the same diameter and same length are stretched with equal tension. Their densities are 7.80 g/cm$^3$ and 10.6 g/cm$^3$, respectively. What is the fundamental frequency of the silver wire if that of the steel is 200 Hz?

**22.30 [II]** A string has a mass of 3.0 gram and a length of 60 cm. What must be the tension so that when vibrating transversely its first overtone has frequency 200 Hz?

**22.31 [II]** (*a*) At what point should a stretched string be plucked to make its fundamental tone most prominent? At what point should it be plucked and then at what point touched (*b*) to make its first overtone most prominent and (*c*) to make its second overtone most prominent?

**22.32 [II]** What must be the length of an iron rod that has the fundamental frequency 320 Hz when clamped at its center? Assume longitudinal vibration at a speed of 5.00 km/s.

**22.33 [II]** A rod 120 cm long is clamped at the center and is stroked in such a way as to give its first overtone. Make a drawing showing the location of the nodes and antinodes, and determine at what other points the rod might be clamped and still emit the same tone.

**22.34 [II]** A metal bar 6.0 m long, clamped at its center and vibrating longitudinally in such a manner that it gives its first overtone, vibrates in unison with a tuning fork marked 1200 vibration/s. Compute the speed of sound in the metal.

**22.35 [II]** Determine the length of the shortest air column in a cylindrical jar that will strongly reinforce the sound of a tuning fork having a vibration rate of 512 Hz. Use $v$ = 340 m/s for the speed of sound in air.

**22.36 [II]** A long, narrow pipe closed at one end does not resonate to a tuning fork having a frequency of 300 Hz until the length of the air column reaches 28 cm. (*a*) What is the speed of sound in air at the existing room temperature? (*b*) What is the next length of column that will resonate to the fork?

**22.37 [II]** An organ pipe closed at one end is 61.0 cm long. What are the frequencies of the first three overtones if $v$ for sound is 342 m/s?

## ANSWERS TO SUPPLEMENTARY PROBLEMS

**22.19 [I]** 17 m, 1.7 cm

**22.20 [I]** 395 m

**22.21 [I]** $8.8 \times 10^9$ Hz = 8.8 GHz

**22.22 [I]** (*a*) 37 m/s; (*b*) 0.43 g

**22.23 [I]** (*a*) 3.0 mm; (*b*) 60 Hz; (*c*) 2.00 cm; (*d*) 1.2 m/s; (*e*) 0.017 s

**22.24 [II]** 22 m/s

**22.25 [II]** 324 m/s

**22.26 [II]** 220 Hz

**22.27 [II]** 0.65 s

**22.28 [II]** 128 Hz

**22.29 [II]** 172 Hz

**22.30 [II]** 72 N

**22.31 [II]** (*a*) center; (*b*) plucked at 1/4 of its length from one end, then touched at center; (*c*) plucked at 1/6 of its length from one end, then touched at 1/3 of its length from that end

**22.32 [II]** 7.81 m

**22.33 [II]** 20.0 cm from either end

**22.34 [II]** 4.8 km/s

**22.35 [II]** 16.6 cm

**22.36 [II]** (*a*) 0.34 km/s; (*b*) 84 cm

**22.37 [II]** 420 Hz, 700 Hz, 980 Hz

# CHAPTER 23

# Sound

**Sound Waves** are ***longitudinal compression waves*** in a material medium such as air, water, or steel. When the compressions and rarefactions of the waves strike the eardrum, they result in the sensation of sound, provided the frequency of the waves is between about 20 Hz and 20 000 Hz. Waves with frequencies above 20 kHz are called *ultrasonic* waves. Those with frequencies below 20 Hz are called *infrasonic* waves.

**Equations for Sound Speed:** In an ideal gas of molecular mass $M$ and absolute temperature $T$, the speed of sound $\upsilon$ is given by

$$\upsilon = \sqrt{\frac{\gamma RT}{M}} \qquad \text{(Ideal gas)}$$

where $R$ is the gas constant and $\gamma$ is the ratio of specific heats $c_p/c_\upsilon$. $\gamma$ is about 1.67 for monatomic gases (He, Ne, Ar) and about 1.40 for diatomic gases ($N_2$, $O_2$, $H_2$).

The speed of compression waves in other materials is given by

$$\upsilon = \sqrt{\frac{\text{Modulus}}{\text{Density}}}$$

If the material is in the form of a solid bar, Young's modulus $Y$ is used. For liquids, one must use the bulk modulus.

**The Speed of Sound in Air** at 0 °C is 331 m/s. The speed increases with temperature by about 0.61 m/s for each 1 °C rise. More precisely, sound speeds $\upsilon_1$ and $\upsilon_2$ at absolute temperatures $T_1$ and $T_2$ are related by

$$\frac{\upsilon_1}{\upsilon_2} = \sqrt{\frac{T_1}{T_2}}$$

The speed of sound is essentially independent of pressure, frequency, and wavelength.

**The Intensity** ($I$) of any wave is the energy per unit area, per unit time; in practice, it is the average power ($P_{av}$) carried by the wave through a unit area erected perpendicular to the direction of propagation of the wave. Suppose that in a time $\Delta t$ an amount of energy $\Delta E$ is carried through an area $\Delta A$ that is perpendicular to the propagation direction of the wave. Then

$$I = \frac{\Delta E}{\Delta A\, \Delta t} = \frac{P_{av}}{\Delta A}$$

It can be shown that for a sound wave with amplitude $a_0$ and frequency $f$, traveling with speed $v$ in a material of density $\rho$, the intensity is

$$I = 2\pi^2 f^2 \rho v a_0^2$$

If $f$ is in Hz, $\rho$ is in $kg/m^3$, $v$ is in m/s, and $a_0$ (the maximum displacement of the atoms or molecules of the medium) is in m, then $I$ is in $W/m^2$. Note that $I \propto a_0^2$, and that sort of relationship is true for all kinds of waves.

**Loudness** is a measure of the human perception of sound. Although a sound wave of high intensity is perceived as louder than a wave of lower intensity, the relation is far from linear. The sensation of sound is roughly proportional to the logarithm of the sound intensity. But the exact relation between loudness and intensity is complicated and not the same for all individuals.

**Intensity (or Sound) Level** ($\beta$) is defined by an arbitrary scale that corresponds roughly to the sensation of loudness. The zero on this scale occurs when $I_0 = 1.00 \times 10^{-12}\ W/m^2$, which corresponds roughly to the weakest audible sound. The intensity level, in decibels, is then defined by

$$\beta = 10 \log_{10}\left(\frac{I}{I_0}\right)$$

Notice that when $I = I_0$ the sound level equals zero, since $\log_{10} 1 = 0$. The **decibel** (dB) is a dimensionless unit. The normal ear can distinguish between intensities that differ by an amount down to about 1 dB.

**Beats:** The alternations of maximum and minimum intensity produced by the superposition of two waves of slightly different frequencies are called **beats**. The number of beats per second is equal to the difference between the frequencies of the two waves that are combined.

**Doppler Effect:** Suppose that a moving sound source emits a sound of frequency $f_s$. Let $v$ be the speed of sound, and let the source approach the listener or observer at speed $v_s$, measured relative to the medium conducting the sound. Suppose further that the observer is moving toward the source at speed $v_o$, also measured relative to the medium. Then the observer will hear a sound of frequency $f_o$ given by $f_o = f_s[(v + v_o)/(v - v_s)]$. In general

$$f_o = f_s \frac{v \pm v_o}{v \mp v_s}$$

*Draw an arrow from the observer to the source—that's the positive direction.* When the velocity of the source is in that direction, we use the plus sign in front of $v_s$. And the same is true for $v_o$ and the observer; when the velocity of the observer is in the direction of the observer-to-source arrow, $v_o$ is preceded by a + sign in the equation.

When the source and observer are approaching each other, more wave crests strike the ear each second than when both are at rest. This causes the ear to perceive a higher frequency than that emitted by the source. When the two are receding, the opposite effect occurs; the frequency appears to be lowered.

Of course, when either the observer or the source is at rest, the corresponding speed (either $v_o$ or $v_s$) must be zero.

**Interference Effects:** Two sound waves of the same frequency and amplitude may give rise to easily observed interference effects at a point through which they both pass. If the crests of one wave fall on the crests of the other, the two waves are said to be *in-phase*. In that case, they reinforce each other and give rise to a high intensity at that point.

However, if the crests of one wave fall on the troughs of the other, the two waves will exactly cancel each other. No sound will then be heard at the point. We say that the two waves are then 180° (or a half wavelength) *out-of-phase*.

Intermediate effects are observed if the two waves are neither in-phase nor 180° out-of-phase, but have a fixed phase relationship somewhere in between.

## SOLVED PROBLEMS

**23.1 [I]** An explosion occurs at a distance of 6.00 km from a person. How long after the explosion does the person hear it? Assume the temperature is 14.0 °C.

We need to determine the speed of sound at 14.0 °C, knowing its value at 0 °C. Because the speed of sound increases by 0.61 m/s for each 1.0 °C, the sought-after speed is

$$v = 331 \text{ m/s} + (0.61)(14) \text{ m/s} = 340 \text{ m/s}$$

Using $s = vt$, the time taken is

$$t = \frac{s}{v} = \frac{600 \text{ m}}{340 \text{ m/s}} = 17.6 \text{ s}$$

**23.2 [I]** To find how far away a lightning flash is, a rough rule is the following: "Divide the time in seconds between the flash and the sound, by three. The result equals the distance in km to the flash." Justify this.

The speed of sound is $v \approx 333 \text{ m/s} \approx \frac{1}{3} \text{ km/s}$, and so the distance to the flash is approximately

$$s = vt \approx \frac{t}{3}$$

where $t$, the travel time of the sound, is in seconds and $s$ is in kilometers. The light from the flash travels so fast, $3 \times 10^8$ m/s, that it reaches the observer almost instantaneously. Hence, $t$ is essentially equal to the time between *seeing* the flash and hearing the thunder. The rule works.

**23.3 [I]** Compute the speed of sound in neon gas at 27.0 °C. For neon, $M = 20.18$ kg/kmol.

Neon, being monatomic, has $\gamma \approx 1.67$. Therefore, remembering that $T$ is the absolute temperature,

$$v = \sqrt{\frac{\gamma RT}{M}} = \sqrt{\frac{(1.67)(8314 \text{ J/kmol}\cdot\text{K})(300 \text{ K})}{20.18 \text{ kg/kmol}}} = 454 \text{ m/s}$$

**23.4 [II]** Find the speed of sound in a diatomic ideal gas that has a density of 3.50 kg/m³ and a pressure of 215 kPa.

We know that $v = \sqrt{\gamma RT/M}$ and can find the temperature from the pressure. Using the gas law $PV = (m/M)RT$,

$$\frac{RT}{M} = P\frac{V}{m}$$

Moreover, $\rho = m/V$, and so the expression for the speed becomes

$$v = \sqrt{\frac{\gamma P}{\rho}} = \sqrt{\frac{(1.40)(215 \times 10^3 \text{ Pa})}{3.50 \text{ kg/m}^3}} = 293 \text{ m/s}$$

We used the fact that $\gamma \approx 1.40$ for a diatomic ideal gas, as discussed in Chapter 20.

**23.5 [II]** A metal rod 60 cm long is clamped at its center. It resonates in its fundamental mode when driven by longitudinal waves of 3.00 kHz. What is Young's modulus for the material of the rod? The density of the metal is 8700 kg/m$^3$.

This same rod was discussed in Problem 22.11. It was shown there that the speed of longitudinal waves in it is 3.6 km/s. We know that $\upsilon = \sqrt{Y/\rho}$, and so

$$Y = \rho\upsilon^2 = (8700\text{ kg/m}^3)(3600\text{ m/s})^2 = 1.1 \times 10^{11}\text{ N/m}^2$$

**23.6 [I]** What is the speed of compression waves (sound waves) in water? The bulk modulus for water is $2.2 \times 10^9$ N/m$^2$.

$$\upsilon = \sqrt{\frac{\text{Bulk modulus}}{\text{Density}}} = \sqrt{\frac{2.2\times 10^9\text{ N/m}^2}{1000\text{ kg/m}^3}} = 1.5\text{ km/s}$$

**23.7 [I]** A tuning fork oscillates at 284 Hz in air. Compute the wavelength of the tone emitted at 25 °C.

Remembering that the speed of sound increases by 0.61 m/s for each 1 °C increase in temperature, at 25 °C,

$$\upsilon = 331\text{ m/s} + (0.61)(25)\text{ m/s} = 346\text{ m/s}$$

Using $\lambda = \upsilon T = \upsilon/f$,

$$\lambda = \frac{\upsilon}{f} = \frac{346\text{ m/s}}{284\text{ s}^{-1}} = 1.22\text{ m}$$

**23.8 [II]** An organ pipe whose length is held constant resonates at a frequency of 224.0 Hz when the air temperature is 15 °C. What will be its resonant frequency when the air temperature is 24 °C?

The resonant wavelength must have the same value at each temperature because it depends only on the length of the pipe. (Its nodes and antinodes must fit properly within the pipe.) But $\lambda = \upsilon/f$, and so $\upsilon/f$ must be the same at the two temperatures. Consequently,

$$\frac{\upsilon_1}{224\text{ Hz}} = \frac{\upsilon_2}{f_2} \qquad \text{or} \qquad f_2 = (224\text{ Hz})\left(\frac{\upsilon_2}{\upsilon_1}\right)$$

At temperatures near room temperature, $\upsilon = (331 + 0.61T_c)$ m/s, where $T_c$ is the Celsius temperature. Then

$$f_2 = (224.0\text{ Hz})\left[\frac{331 + (0.61)(24)}{331 + (0.61)(15)}\right] = 0.228\text{ kHz}$$

**23.9 [I]** An uncomfortably loud sound might have an intensity of 0.54 W/m$^2$. Find the maximum displacement of the molecules of air in a sound wave if its frequency is 800 Hz. Take the density of air to be 1.29 kg/m$^3$ and the speed of sound to be 340 m/s.

We are given $I$, $f$, $\rho$, and $\upsilon$, and have to find $a_0$. From $I = 2\pi^2 f^2 \rho\upsilon a_0^2$,

$$a_0 = \frac{1}{\pi f}\sqrt{\frac{I}{2\rho\upsilon}} = \frac{1}{(800\text{ s}^{-1}\pi)}\sqrt{\frac{0.54\text{ W/m}^2}{(2)(1.29\text{ kg/m}^3)(340\text{ m/s})}} = 9.9\times 10^{-6}\text{ m} = 9.9\ \mu\text{m}$$

**23.10 [I]** A sound has an intensity of $3.00 \times 10^{-8}$ W/m$^2$. What is the sound level in dB?

Sound level is $\beta$ where $I_0 = 1.00 \times 10^{-12}$ W/m$^2$ and

$$\beta = 10 \log_{10}\left(\frac{I}{1.00 \times 10^{-12}\,\text{W/m}^2}\right)$$

$$= 10 \log_{10}\left(\frac{3.00 \times 10^{-8}}{1.00 \times 10^{-12}}\right) = 10 \log_{10} (3.00 \times 10^4) = 10(4 + \log_{10} 3.00)$$

$$= 10(4 + 0.477) = 44.8 \text{ dB}$$

**23.11 [II]** A noise-level meter reads the sound level in a room to be 85.0 dB. What is the sound intensity in the room?

Sound level ($\beta$), in dB, is given by $\beta = 10 \log_{10} (I/I_0)$ and here it equals 85.0 dB. Accordingly,

$$\beta = 10 \log_{10}\left(\frac{I}{1.00 \times 10^{-12}\,\text{W/m}^2}\right) = 85.0 \text{ dB}$$

$$\log_{10}\left(\frac{I}{1.00 \times 10^{-12}\,\text{W/m}^2}\right) = \frac{85.0}{10} = 8.50$$

$$\frac{I}{1.00 \times 10^{-12}\,\text{W/m}^2} = \text{antilog}_{10}\, 8.50 = 3.16 \times 10^8$$

and $$I = (1.00 \times 10^{-12}\,\text{W/m}^2)(3.16 \times 10^8) = 3.16 \times 10^{-4}\,\text{W/m}^2$$

**23.12 [II]** Two sound waves have intensities of 10 $\mu$W/cm$^2$ and 500 $\mu$W/cm$^2$. What is the difference in their intensity levels?

Call the 10 $\mu$W/cm$^2$ sound $A$, and the other $B$. Then

$$\beta_A = 10 \log_{10}\left(\frac{I_A}{I_0}\right) = 10(\log_{10} I_A - \log_{10} I_0)$$

$$\beta_B = 10 \log_{10}\left(\frac{I_B}{I_0}\right) = 10(\log_{10} I_B - \log_{10} I_0)$$

Subtracting $\beta_A$ from $\beta_B$,

$$\beta_B - \beta_A = 10 (\log_{10} I_B - \log_{10} I_A) = 10 \log_{10}\left(\frac{I_B}{I_A}\right)$$

$$= 10 \log_{10}\left(\frac{500}{10}\right) = 10 \log_{10} 50 = (10)(1.70)$$

$$= 17 \text{ dB}$$

**23.13 [II]** Find the ratio of the intensities of two sounds if one is 8.0 dB louder than the other. We saw in Problem 23.12 that

$$\beta_B - \beta_A = 10 \log_{10}\left(\frac{I_B}{I_A}\right)$$

In the present case this becomes

$$8.0 = 10\log_{10}\left(\frac{I_B}{I_A}\right) \quad \text{or} \quad \frac{I_B}{I_A} = \text{antilog}_{10}\, 0.80 = 6.3$$

**23.14 [II]** **A tiny sound source emits sound uniformly in all directions. The intensity level at a distance of 2.0 m is 100 dB. How much sound power is the source emitting?**

The energy emitted by a point source can be considered to flow out through a spherical surface which has the source at its center. Hence, if we find the rate of flow through such a surface, it will equal the flow from the source. Take a concentric sphere of radius 2.0 m. We know that the sound level on its surface is 100 dB. You can show that this corresponds to $I = 0.010\ \text{W/m}^2$. Thus, the energy flowing each second through each $\text{m}^2$ of surface is 0.010 W. The total energy flow through the spherical surface is then $I(4\pi r^2)$, where $I = 0.010\ \text{W/m}^2$ and $r = 2.0$ m:

$$\text{Power from source} = (0.010\ \text{W/m}^2)\,(4\pi)(2\ \text{m})^2 = 0.50\ \text{W}$$

Notice how little power issues as sound from even such an intense source.

**23.15 [III]** **Back in the days before computers, a single typist typing furiously could generate an average sound level nearby of 60.0 dB. What would be the decibel level in the vicinity if three equally noisy typists were working close to one another?**

If each typist emits the same amount of sound energy, then the final sound intensity $I_f$ should be three times the initial intensity $I_i$. We have

$$\beta_f = \log_{10}\left(\frac{I_f}{I_0}\right) = \log_{10} I_f - \log_{10} I_0$$

and $$\beta_i = \log_{10} I_i - \log_{10} I_0$$

Subtracting these yields the change in sound level in going from $I_i$ to $I_f = 3I_i$,

$$\beta_f - \beta_i = \log_{10} I_f - \log_{10} I_i$$

from which $$\beta_f = \beta_i + \log_{10}\left(\frac{I_f}{I_i}\right) = 60.0\ \text{dB} + \log_{10} 3 = 60.5\ \text{dB}$$

The sound level, being a logarithmic measure, rises very slowly with the number of sources.

**23.16 [I]** **An automobile moving at 30.0 m/s is approaching a factory whistle that has a frequency of 500 Hz. (*a*) If the speed of sound in air is 340 m/s, what is the apparent frequency of the whistle as heard by the driver? (*b*) Repeat for the case of the car leaving the factory at the same speed.**

This is a Doppler shift problem. Draw an arrow from observer to source; this is the positive direction. Here in part (*a*) the observer is moving in the positive direction, and $v_s = 0$. Hence, use $+v_o$ and so

$$(a) \quad f_o = f_s\frac{v \pm v_o}{v \mp v_s} = (500\ \text{Hz})\frac{340\ \text{m/s} + 30.0\ \text{m/s}}{340\ \text{m/s} - 0} = 544\ \text{Hz}$$

With the car leaving in the negative direction use $-v_o$ and

$$(b)\quad f_o = f_s \frac{v \pm v_o}{v \mp v_s} = (500\text{ Hz})\frac{340\text{ m/s} - 30.0\text{ m/s}}{340\text{ m/s} - 0} = 456\text{ Hz}$$

**23.17 [I]** A car moving at 20 m/s with its horn blowing ($f = 1200$ Hz) is chasing another car going at 15 m/s in the same direction. What is the apparent frequency of the horn as heard by the driver being chased? Take the speed of sound to be 340 m/s.

This is a Doppler problem. Draw the observer-to-source arrow; that's the positive direction (see Fig. 23-1). Both the source and the observer are moving in the negative direction. Hence, we use $-v_o$ and $-v_s$.

$$f_o = f_s \frac{v \pm v_o}{v \mp v_s} = (1200\text{ Hz})\frac{340 - 15}{340 - 20} = 1.22\text{ kHz}$$

Because the source is approaching the observer, the latter will measure an increase in frequency.

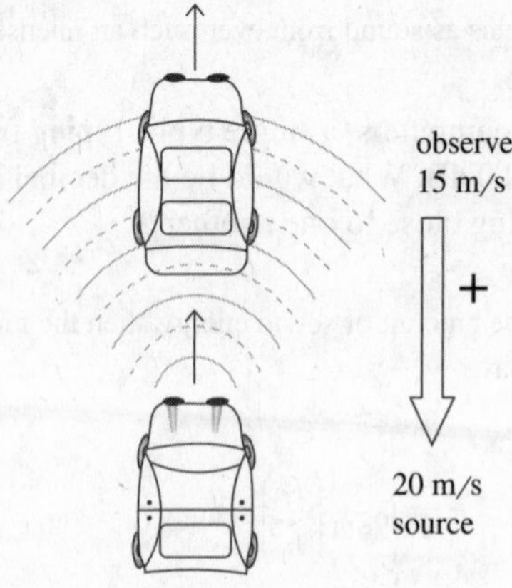


Fig. 23-1

**23.18 [I]** When two tuning forks are sounded simultaneously, they produce one beat every 0.30 s. (*a*) By how much do their frequencies differ? (*b*) A tiny piece of chewing gum is placed on a prong of one fork. Now there is one beat every 0.40 s. Was this tuning fork the lower- or the higher-frequency fork?

The number of beats per second equals the frequency difference.

$$(a)\quad \text{Frequency difference} = \frac{1}{0.30\text{ s}} = 3.3\text{ Hz}$$

$$(b)\quad \text{Frequency difference} = \frac{1}{0.40\text{ s}} = 2.5\text{ Hz}$$

Adding gum to the prong increases its mass and thereby decreases its vibrational frequency. This lowering of frequency caused it to come closer to the frequency of the other fork. Hence, the fork in question had the higher frequency.

**23.19 [II]** A tuning fork having a frequency of 400 Hz (shown in Fig. 23-2) is moved away from an observer and toward a flat wall with a speed of 2.0 m/s. What is the apparent frequency (*a*) of the unreflected sound waves coming directly to the observer, and (*b*) of the sound waves coming to the observer after reflection? (*c*) How many beats per second are heard? Assume the speed of sound in air to be 340 m/s.

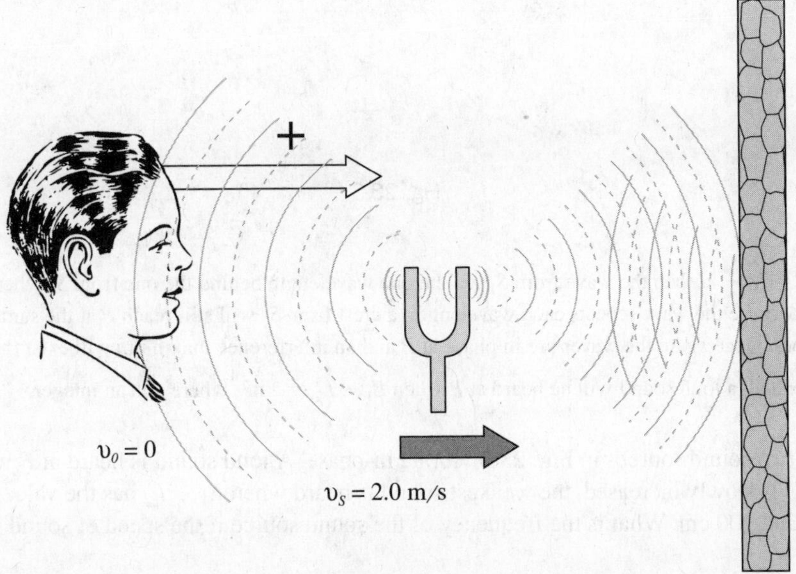


Fig. 23-2

(*a*) The fork, the source, is receding from the observer in the positive direction and so we use $+\upsilon_s$. It doesn't matter what the sign associated with $\upsilon_o$ is since $\upsilon_o = 0$.

$$f_o = f_s \frac{\upsilon \pm \upsilon_o}{\upsilon \mp \upsilon_s} = (400 \text{ Hz}) \frac{340 \text{ m/s} + 0}{340 \text{ m/s} + 2.0 \text{ m/s}} = 397.7 \text{ Hz} = 398 \text{ Hz}$$

The source is moving away from the observer and the frequency is properly shifted down from 400 Hz to 398 Hz.

(*b*) Think of the wall as a source that reflects sound of the same frequency as that which impinges upon it. The wave crests reaching the wall are closer together than normally because the fork is moving toward the wall. Therefore, the wall will appear as a stationary source emitting sound of a higher frequency than 400 Hz. due to the 2.0-m/s motion of the fork. Alternatively we can think of the reflected wave as if it came from a source (the wall) moving at 2.0 m/s toward the observer. Hence, we enter $-\upsilon_s$:

$$f_o = f_s \frac{\upsilon \pm \upsilon_o}{\upsilon \mp \upsilon_s} = (400 \text{ Hz}) \frac{340 \text{ m/s} + 0}{340 \text{ m/s} - 2.0 \text{ m/s}} = 402.4 \text{ Hz} = 402 \text{ Hz}$$

and the frequency is properly shifted up.

(*c*) Beats per second = Difference between frequencies = (402.4 − 397.7) Hz = 4.7 beats per second

**23.20 [I]** In Fig. 23-3, $S_1$ and $S_2$ are identical sound sources. They send out their wave crests simultaneously (the sources are in phase). For what values of $L_1 - L_2$ will constructive interference obtain and a loud sound be heard at point $P$?

If $L_1 = L_2$, the waves from the two sources will take equal times to reach $P$. Crests from one will arrive there at the same times as crests from the other. The waves will therefore be in phase at $P$ and an interference maximum will result.

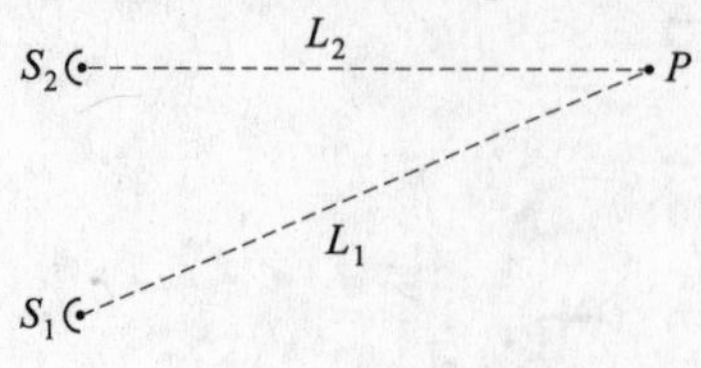


Fig. 23-3

If $L_1 = L_2 + \lambda$, then the wave from $S_1$ will be one wavelength behind the one from $S_2$ when they reach $P$. But because the wave repeats each wavelength, a crest from $S_1$ will still reach $P$ at the same time a crest from $S_2$ does. Once again the waves are in phase at $P$ and an interference maximum will exist there.

In general, a loud sound will be heard at $P$ when $L_1 - L_2 = \pm n\lambda$, where $n$ is an integer.

**23.21 [II]** The two sound sources in Fig. 23-3 vibrate in-phase. A loud sound is heard at $P$ when $L_1 = L_2$. As $L_1$ is slowly increased, the weakest sound is heard when $L_1 - L_2$ has the values 20.0 cm, 60.0 cm, and 100 cm. What is the frequency of the sound source if the speed of sound is 340 m/s?

The waves coming down directly from the fork toward the guy must be a little longer (more spaced) than the waves going up from the fork and back down from the wall which have same spacings.

The weakest sound will be heard at $P$ when a crest from $S_1$ and a trough from $S_2$ reach there at the same time. This will happen if $L_1 - L_2$ is $\frac{1}{2}\lambda$, or $\lambda + \frac{1}{2}\lambda$, or $2\lambda + \frac{1}{2}\lambda$, and so on. Hence, the increase in $L_1$ between weakest sounds is $\lambda$, and from the data we see that $\lambda = 0.400$ m. Then, from $\lambda = v/f$,

$$f = \frac{v}{\lambda} = \frac{340 \text{ m/s}}{0.400 \text{ m}} = 850 \text{ Hz}$$

## SUPPLEMENTARY PROBLEMS

**23.22 [I]** Three seconds after a gun is fired, the person who fired the gun hears an echo. How far away was the surface that reflected the sound of the shot? Use 340 m/s for the speed of sound.

**23.23 [I]** What is the speed of sound in air when the air temperature is 31 °C?

**23.24 [II]** A shell fired at a target 800 m away was heard by someone standing near the gun to strike the target 5.0 s after leaving the gun. Compute the average horizontal velocity of the shell. The air temperature is 20 °C.

**23.25 [II]** In an experiment to determine the speed of sound, two observers, A and B, were stationed 5.00 km apart. Each was equipped with a gun and a stopwatch. Observer-A heard the report of B's gun 15.5 s after seeing its flash. Later, A fired his gun and B heard the report 14.5 s after seeing the flash. Determine the speed of sound and the component of the speed of the wind along the line joining A to B.

**23.26 [II]** A disk has 40 holes around its circumference and is rotating at 1200 rpm. Determine the frequency and wavelength of the tone produced by the disk when a jet of air is blown against it. The temperature is 15 °C.

**23.27 [II]** Determine the speed of sound in carbon dioxide ($M = 44$ kg/kmol, $\gamma = 1.30$) at a pressure of 0.50 atm and a temperature of 400 °C.

**23.28 [II]** Compute the molecular mass $M$ of a gas for which $\gamma = 1.40$ and in which the speed of sound is 1260 m/s at precisely 0 °C.

**23.29 [II]** At S.T.P., the speed of sound in air is 331 m/s. Determine the speed of sound in hydrogen at S.T.P. if the specific gravity of hydrogen relative to air is 0.069 0 and if $\gamma = 1.40$ for both gases.

**23.30 [II]** Helium is a monatomic gas that has a density of 0.179 kg/m$^3$ at a pressure of 76.0 cm of mercury and a temperature of precisely 0 °C. Find the speed of compression waves (sound) in helium at this temperature and pressure.

**23.31 [II]** A bar of dimensions 1.00 cm$^2$ × 200 cm and mass 2.00 kg is clamped at its center. When vibrating longitudinally, it emits its fundamental tone in unison with a tuning fork making 1000 vibration/s. How much will the bar be elongated if, when clamped at one end, a stretching force of 980 N is applied at the other end? [*Hint*: Look at Problem 22.11 and Chapter 12.]

**23.32 [I]** Find the speed of compression waves in a metal rod if the material of the rod has a Young's modulus of $1.20 \times 10^{10}$ N/m$^2$ and a density of 8920 kg/m$^3$.

**23.33 [II]** An increase in pressure of 100 kPa causes a certain volume of water to decrease by $5 \times 10^{-3}$ percent of its original volume. (*a*) What is the bulk modulus of water? (*b*) What is the speed of sound (compression waves) in water?

**23.34 [I]** A sound has an intensity of $5.0 \times 10^{-7}$ W/m$^2$. What is its intensity level?

**23.35 [I]** A person riding a power mower may be subjected to a sound of intensity $2.00 \times 10^{-2}$ W/m$^2$. What is the intensity level to which the person is subjected?

**23.36 [II]** A rock band might easily produce a sound level of 107 dB in a room. To two significant figures, what is the sound intensity at 107 dB?

**23.37 [II]** A whisper has an intensity level of about 15 dB. What is the corresponding intensity of the sound?

**23.38 [II]** What sound intensity is 3.0 dB louder than a sound of intensity of 10 $\mu$W/cm$^2$?

**23.39 [II]** Calculate the intensity of a sound wave in air at precisely 0 °C and 1.00 atm if its amplitude is 0.002 0 mm and its wavelength is 66.2 cm. The density of air at S.T.P. is 1.293 kg/m$^3$.

**23.40 [II]** What is the amplitude of vibration in a 8000 Hz sound beam if its intensity level is 62 dB? Assume that the air is at 15 °C and its density is 1.29 kg/m$^3$.

**23.41 [II]** One sound has an intensity level of 75.0 dB, while a second has an intensity level of 72.0 dB. What is the intensity level when the two sounds are combined?

**23.42 [II]** An organ pipe is tuned to emit a frequency of 196.00 Hz. When it and the G string of a violin are sounded together, ten beats are heard in a time of exactly 8 s. The beats become slower as the violin string is slowly tightened. What was the original frequency of the violin string?

**23.43 [I]** A locomotive moving at 30.0 m/s approaches and passes a person standing beside the track. Its whistle is emitting a note of frequency 2.00 kHz. What frequency will the person hear (*a*) as the train approaches and (*b*) as it recedes? The speed of sound is 340 m/s.

**23.44 [II]** Two cars are heading straight at each other with the same speed. The horn of one ($f$ = 3.0 kHz) is blowing, and is heard to have a frequency of 3.4 kHz by the people in the other car. Find the speed at which each car is moving if the speed of sound is 340 m/s.

**23.45 [II]** To determine the speed of a harmonic oscillator, a beam of sound is sent along the line of the oscillator's motion. The sound, which is emitted at a frequency of 8000.0 Hz, is reflected straight back by the oscillator to a detector system. The detector observes that the reflected beam varies in frequency between the limits of 8003.1 Hz and 7996.9 Hz. What is the maximum speed of the oscillator? Take the speed of sound to be 340 m/s.

**23.46 [II]** In Fig. 23-1 are shown two identical sound sources sending waves to point *P*. They send out wave crests simultaneously (they are in-phase), and the wavelength of the wave is 60 cm. If $L_2 = 200$ cm, give the values of $L_1$ for which (*a*) maximum sound is heard at *P* and (*b*) minimum sound is heard at *P*.

**23.47 [II]** The two sources shown in Fig. 23-4 emit identical beams of sound ($\lambda = 80$ cm) toward one another. Each sends out a crest at the same time as the other (the sources are in-phase). Point *P* is a position of

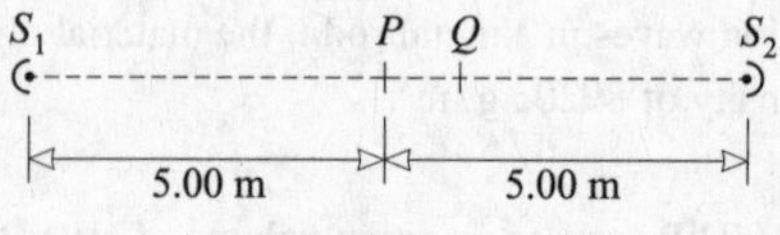


Fig. 23-4

maximum intensity, that is, loud sound. As one moves from *P* toward *Q*, the sound decreases in intensity. (*a*) How far from *P* will a sound minimum first be heard? (*b*) How far from *P* will a loud sound be heard once again?

## ANSWERS TO SUPPLEMENTARY PROBLEMS

**23.22 [I]** 510 m

**23.23 [I]** 0.35 km/s

**23.24 [II]** 0.30 km/s

**23.25 [II]** 334 m/s, 11.1 m/s

**23.26 [II]** 0.80 kHz, 0.43 m

**23.27 [II]** 0.41 km/s

**23.28 [II]** 2.00 kg/kmol (hydrogen)

**23.29 [II]** 1.26 km/s

**23.30 [II]** 970 m/s

**23.31 [II]** 0.123 mm

**23.32 [I]** 1.16 km/s

**23.33 [II]** (*a*) $2 \times 10^9$ N/m$^2$; (*b*) 1 km/s

**23.34 [I]** 57 dB

**23.35 [I]** 103 dB

**23.36 [II]** 0.050 $W/m^2$

**23.37 [II]** $3.2 \times 10^{-11}$ $W/m^2$

**23.38 [II]** 20 $\mu W/cm^2$

**23.39 [II]** $8.4 \times 10^{-3}$ $W/m^2$

**23.40 [II]** $1.7 \times 10^{-9}$ m

**23.41 [II]** 76.8 dB

**23.42 [II]** 194.75 Hz

**23.43 [I]** (*a*) 2.19 kHz; (*b*) 1.84 kHz

**23.44 [II]** 21 m/s

**23.45 [II]** 0.132 m/s

**23.46 [II]** (*a*) $(200 \pm 60n)$ cm, where $n = 0, 1, 2, \ldots$; (*b*) $(230 \pm 60n)$ cm, where $n = 0, 1, 2, \ldots$ .

**23.47 [II]** (*a*) 20 cm; (*b*) 40 cm

# Coulomb's Law and Electric Fields

**Coulomb's Law:** Suppose that two point charges, $q$ and $q'$, are a distance $r$ apart in vacuum. If $q$ and $q'$ have the same sign, the two charges repel each other; if they have opposite signs, they attract each other. The force experienced by either charge due to the other is called a **Coulomb** or **electric force** and it is given by **Coulomb's Law**

$$F_E = k_0 \frac{qq'}{r^2} \qquad \text{(in vacuum)}$$

As always in the SI, distances are measured in meters, and forces in newtons. The SI unit for charge is the *coulomb* (C). The constant $k_0$ (corresponding to vacuum) in Coulomb's Law has the value

$$k_0 = 8.988 \times 10^9 \text{ N}\cdot\text{m}^2/\text{C}^2$$

which we shall usually approximate as $9.0 \times 10^9 \text{ N}\cdot\text{m}^2/\text{C}^2$. Often, $k_0$ is replaced by $1/4\pi\epsilon_0$, where $\epsilon_0 = 8.85 \times 10^{-12} \text{ C}^2/\text{N}\cdot\text{m}^2$ is called the **permittivity of free space.** Then Coulomb's Law becomes

$$F_E = \frac{1}{4\pi\epsilon_0}\frac{qq'}{r^2} \qquad \text{(in vacuum)}$$

When the surrounding medium is not a vacuum, forces caused by induced charges in the material reduce the force between point charges. If the material has a **dielectric constant** $K$, then $\epsilon_0$ in Coulomb's Law must be replaced by $K\epsilon_0 = \epsilon$, where $\epsilon$ is called the *permittivity of the material.* Then

$$F_E = \frac{1}{4\pi\epsilon}\frac{qq'}{r^2} = \frac{k_0}{K}\frac{qq'}{r^2}$$

For vacuum, $K = 1$; for air, $K = 1.0006$.

Coulomb's Law also applies to charged conducting spheres and spherical shells, as well as to uniform spheres of charge. This is true provided that these are all small enough, in comparison to their separations, so that the charge distribution on each doesn't become asymmetrical when two or more of them interact. In that case, $r$, the distance between the centers of the spheres, must be much larger than the sum of the radii of the two spheres.

**Charge Is Quantized:** The magnitude of the smallest charge ever measured is denoted by $e$ (called the **quantum of charge**), where $e = 1.60218 \times 10^{-19}$ C. All free charges, ones that can be isolated and measured, are integer multiples of $e$. The electron has a charge of $-e$, while the proton's charge is $+e$. Although there is good reason to believe that quarks carry charges of magnitude $e/3$ and $2e/3$, they only exist in bound systems that have a net charge equal to an integer multiple of $e$.

**Conservation of Charge:** The algebraic sum of the charges in the universe is constant. When a particle with charge $+e$ is created, a particle with charge $-e$ is simultaneously created in the immediate vicinity. When a particle with charge $+e$ disappears, a particle with charge $-e$ also disappears in the immediate vicinity. Hence, the net charge of the universe remains constant.

**The Test-Charge Concept:** A **test-charge** is a very small charge that can be used in making measurements on an electric system. It is assumed that such a charge, which is tiny both in magnitude and physical size, has a negligible effect on its environment.

**An Electric Field** is said to exist at any point in space when a test charge, placed at that point, experiences an electrical force. The direction of the electric field at a point is the same as the direction of the force experienced by a *positive* test charge placed at the point.

Electric field lines can be used to sketch electric fields. The line through a point has the same direction at that point as the electric field. Where the field lines are closest together, the electric field is largest. Field lines come out of positive charges (because a positive charge repels a positive test charge) and come into negative charges (because they attract the positive test charge).

**The Strength of the Electric Field ($\vec{\mathbf{E}}$)** at a point is equal to the force experienced by a unit positive test charge placed at that point. Because the electric field strength is a force per unit charge, it is a vector quantity. The units of $\vec{\mathbf{E}}$ are N/C or (see Chapter 25) V/m.

If a charge $q$ is placed at a point where the electric field due to other charges is $\vec{\mathbf{E}}$, the charge will experience a force $\vec{\mathbf{F}}_E$ given by

$$\vec{\mathbf{F}}_E = q\vec{\mathbf{E}}$$

If $q$ is negative, $\vec{\mathbf{F}}_E$ will be opposite in direction to $\vec{\mathbf{E}}$.

**Electric Field Due to a Point Charge:** To find $E$ (the signed magnitude of $\vec{\mathbf{E}}$) due to a point charge $q_{\bullet}$, we make use of Coulomb's Law. If a point charge $q'_{\bullet}$ is placed at a distance $r$ from the charge $q_{\bullet}$, it will experience a force

$$F_E = \frac{1}{4\pi\epsilon}\frac{q_{\bullet}q'_{\bullet}}{r^2} = q'_{\bullet}\left(\frac{1}{4\pi\epsilon}\frac{q_{\bullet}}{r^2}\right)$$

But if a point charge $q'_{\bullet}$ is placed at a position where the electric field is $E$, then the force on $q'_{\bullet}$ is

$$F_E = q'_{\bullet}E$$

Comparing these two expressions for $F_E$, we see that the ***electric field of a point charge*** $q_{\bullet}$ is

$$E_{\bullet} = \frac{1}{4\pi\epsilon}\frac{q_{\bullet}}{r^2}$$

The same relation applies at points outside of a small spherical charge $q$. For $q$ positive, $E$ is positive and $\vec{\mathbf{E}}$ is directed radially outward from $q$; for $q$ negative, $E$ is negative and $\vec{\mathbf{E}}$ is directed radially inward.

**Superposition Principle:** The force experienced by a charge due to other charges is the vector sum of the Coulomb forces acting on it due to these other charges. Similarly, the electric intensity $\vec{\mathbf{E}}$ at a point due to several charges is the vector sum of the intensities due to the individual charges.

## SOLVED PROBLEMS

**24.1 [I]** **Two small spheres in vacuum are 1.5 m apart center-to-center. They carry identical charges. Approximately how large is the charge on each if each sphere experiences a force of 2 N?**

The diameters of the spheres are small compared to the 1.5 m separation. We may therefore approximate them as point charges. Coulomb's Law, $F_E = k_0\, q_{\bullet 1} q_{\bullet 2}/r^2$, leads to

$$q_{\bullet 1} q_{\bullet 2} = q^2 = \frac{F_E r^2}{k_0} = \frac{(2\text{ N})(1.5\text{ m})^2}{9\times10^9\text{ N}\cdot\text{m}^2/\text{C}^2} = 5\times10^{-10}\text{ C}^2$$

from which $q = 2 \times 10^{-5}$ C.

**24.2 [I]** **Repeat Problem 24.1 if the spheres are separated by a center-to-center distance of 1.5 m in a large vat of water. The dielectric constant of water is about 80.**

From Coulomb's Law,

$$F_E = \frac{k_0}{K}\frac{q^2}{r^2}$$

where $K$, the dielectric constant, is now 80. Then

$$q = \sqrt{\frac{F_E r^2 K}{k_0}} = \sqrt{\frac{(2\text{ N})(1.5\text{ m})^2(80)}{9\times10^9\text{ N}\cdot\text{m}^2/\text{C}^2}} = 2\times10^{-4}\text{C}$$

**24.3 [I]** **A helium nucleus has a charge of $+2e$, and a neon nucleus has a charge of $+10e$, where $e$ is the quantum of charge, $1.60 \times 10^{-19}$ C. Find the repulsive force exerted on one by the other when they are separated by a distance of 3.0 nanometers (1 nm = $10^{-9}$ m). Assume the system to be in vacuum.**

Nuclei have radii of order $10^{-15}$ m. We can assume them to be point charges in this case. Then

$$F_E = k_0\frac{q_{\bullet} q'_{\bullet}}{r^2} = (9.0\times10^9\text{ N}\cdot\text{m}^2/\text{C}^2)\frac{(2)(10)(1.6\times10^{-19}\text{ C})^2}{(3.0\times10^{-9}\text{ m})^2} = 5.1\times10^{-10}\text{ N} = 0.51\text{ nN}$$

**24.4 [II]** **In the Bohr model of the hydrogen atom, an electron ($q = -e$) circles a proton ($q' = e$) in an orbit of radius $5.3 \times 10^{-11}$ m. The attraction between the proton and electron furnishes the centripetal force needed to hold the electron in orbit. Find (*a*) the force of electrical attraction between the particles and (*b*) the electron's speed. The electron mass is $9.1 \times 10^{-31}$ kg.**

The electron and proton are essentially point charges. Accordingly,

(*a*) $$F_E = k_0\frac{q_{\bullet} q'_{\bullet}}{r^2} = (9.0\times10^9\text{ N}\cdot\text{m}^2/\text{C}^2)\frac{(1.6\times10^{-19}\text{C})^2}{(5.3\times10^{-11}\text{ m})^2} = 8.2\times10^{-8}\text{ N} = 82\text{ nN}$$

(*b*) The force found in (*a*) is the centripetal force, $mv^2/r$. Therefore,

$$8.2\times10^{-8}\text{ N} = \frac{mv^2}{r}$$

from which it follows that

$$v = \sqrt{\frac{(8.2\times10^{-8}\text{ N})(r)}{m}} = \sqrt{\frac{(8.2\times10^{-8}\text{ N})(5.3\times10^{-11}\text{ m})}{9.1\times10^{-31}\text{ kg}}} = 2.2\times10^6\text{ m/s}$$

**24.5 [II]** Three point charges in vacuum are placed on the *x*-axis in Fig. 24-1. Find the net force on the $-5\mu C$ charge due to the two other charges.

Because unlike charges attract, the forces on the $-5\mu C$ charge are as shown. The *magnitudes* of $\vec{\mathbf{F}}_{E3}$ and $\vec{\mathbf{F}}_{E8}$ are given by Coulomb's Law:

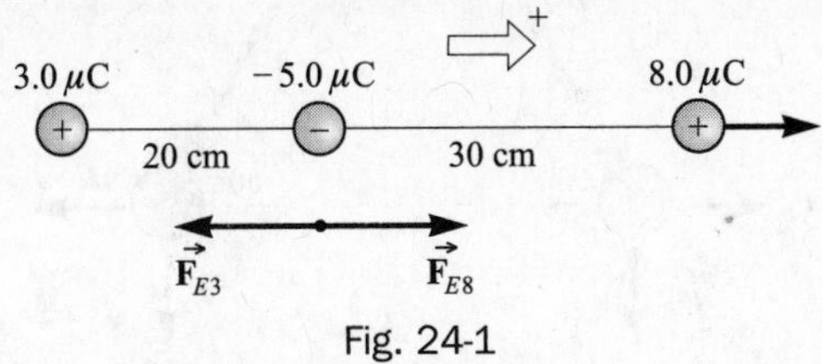


Fig. 24-1

$$F_{E3} = (9.0\times10^9\ \text{N}\cdot\text{m}^2/\text{C}^2)\frac{(3.0\times10^{-6}\ \text{C})(5.0\times10^{-6}\ \text{C})}{(0.20\ \text{m})^2} = 3.4\ \text{N}$$

$$F_{E8} = (9.0\times10^9\ \text{N}\cdot\text{m}^2/\text{C}^2)\frac{(8.0\times10^{-6}\ \text{C})(5.0\times10^{-6}\ \text{C})}{(0.30\ \text{m})^2} = 4.0\ \text{N}$$

Keep in mind the following: (1) Proper units (coulombs and meters) must be used. (2) Because we want only the magnitudes of the forces, *we do not carry along the signs of the charges*. That is, we use their absolute values. Determine if the forces are attractive or repulsive and then draw them in your diagram. Pick a direction to be positive and sum the forces.

From the diagram, the resultant force on the center charge is

$$F_E = F_{E8} - F_{E3} = 4.0\ \text{N} - 3.4\ \text{N} = 0.6\ \text{N}$$

and it is in the $+x$-direction, to the right.

**24.6 [II]** Find the ratio of the Coulomb electric force $F_E$ to the gravitational force $F_G$ between two electrons in vacuum.

From Coulomb's Law and Newton's Law of gravitation,

The electric force is much stronger than the gravitational force.

$$F_E = k\frac{q_\bullet^2}{r^2} \quad \text{and} \quad F_G = G\frac{m^2}{r^2}$$

Therefore, $$\frac{F_E}{F_G} = \frac{kq_\bullet^2/r^2}{Gm^2/r^2} = \frac{kq_\bullet^2}{Gm^2}$$

$$= \frac{(9.0\times10^9\ \text{N}\cdot\text{m}^2/\text{C}^2)(1.6\times10^{-19}\text{C})^2}{(6.67\times10^{-11}\ \text{N}\cdot\text{m}^2/\text{kg}^2)(9.1\times10^{-31}\ \text{kg})^2} = 4.2\times10^{42}$$

**24.7 [II]** Illustrated in Fig. 24-2, are two identical balls in vaccuum, each of mass 0.10 g. They carry identical charges and are suspended by two threads of equal length. At equilibrium they position themselves as indicated. Find the charge on either ball.

Consider the ball on the left. It is in equilibrium under three forces: (1) the tension $F_T$ in the thread; (2) the force of gravity,

$$mg = (1.0\times10^{-4}\ \text{kg})(9.81\ \text{m/s}^2) = 9.8\times10^{-4}\ \text{N}$$

and (3) the Coulomb repulsion $F_E$.

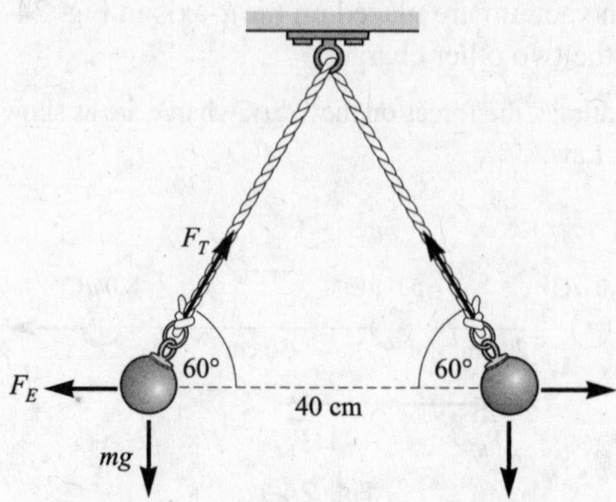


Fig. 24-2

Writing $\sum F_x = 0$ and $\sum F_y = 0$ for the ball on the left,

$$F_T \cos 60° - F_E = 0 \qquad \text{and} \qquad F_T \sin 60° - mg = 0$$

From the second equation,

$$F_T = \frac{mg}{\sin 60°} = \frac{9.8 \times 10^{-4}\ \text{N}}{0.866} = 1.13 \times 10^{-3}\ \text{N}$$

Substituting into the first equation gives

$$F_E = F_T \cos 60° = (1.13 \times 10^{-3}\ \text{N})(0.50) = 5.7 \times 10^{-4}\ \text{N}$$

But this is the Coulomb force, $kqq'/r^2$. Therefore,

$$qq' = q^2 = \frac{F_E r^2}{k} = \frac{(5.7 \times 10^{-4}\ \text{N})\,(0.40\ \text{m})^2}{9.0 \times 10^9\ \text{N}\cdot\text{m}^2/\text{C}^2}$$

from which $q = 0.10\ \mu$C.

**24.8 [II]** The charges represented in Fig. 24-3 are held stationary in vaccum. Find the force on the 4.0 $\mu$C charge due to the other two.

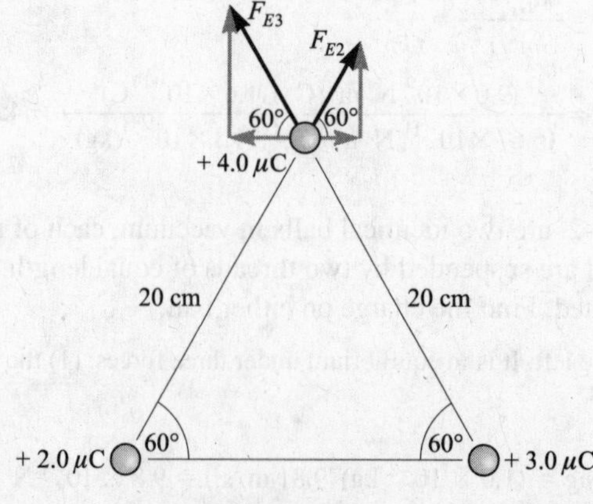


Fig. 24-3

From Coulomb's Law

$$F_{E2} = k_0 \frac{qq'}{r^2} = (9.0\times10^9\ \text{N}\cdot\text{m}^2/\text{C}^2)\frac{(2.0\times10^{-6}\,\text{C})(4.0\times10^{-6}\,\text{C})}{(0.20\ \text{m})^2} = 1.8\ \text{N}$$

$$F_{E3} = k_0 \frac{qq'}{r^2} = (9.0\times10^9\ \text{N}\cdot\text{m}^2/\text{C}^2)\frac{(3.0\times10^{-6}\,\text{C})(4.0\times10^{-6}\,\text{C})}{(0.20\ \text{m})^2} = 2.7\ \text{N}$$

The resultant force on the 4 $\mu$C charge has components

$$F_{Ex} = F_{E2}\cos 60° - F_{E3}\cos 60° = (1.8 - 2.7)(0.50)\ \text{N} = -0.45\ \text{N}$$

$$F_{Ey} = F_{E2}\sin 60° + F_{E3}\sin 60° = (1.8 + 2.7)(0.866)\ \text{N} = 3.9\ \text{N}$$

and so $$F_E = \sqrt{F_{Ex}^2 + F_{Ey}^2} = \sqrt{(0.45)^2 + (3.9)^2}\ \text{N}$$

The resultant makes an angle of $\tan^{-1}(0.45/3.9) = 7°$ with the positive $y$-axis, that is, $\theta = 97°$.

**24.9 [II]** Two small charged spheres are placed in vacuum on the $x$-axis: $+3.0\ \mu$C at $x = 0$ and $-5.0\ \mu$C at $x = 40$ cm. Where must a third charge $q$ be placed if the force it experiences is to be zero?

The situation is represented in Fig. 24-4. We know that $q$ must be placed somewhere on the $x$-axis. (Why?) Suppose that $q$ is positive. When it is placed in interval $BC$, the two forces on it are in the same direction and cannot cancel. When it is placed to the right of $C$, the attractive force from the $-5\ \mu$C charge is always larger than the repulsion of the $+3.0\ \mu$C charge. Therefore, the force on $q$ cannot be zero in this region. Only in the region to the left of $B$ can cancellation occur. (Can you show that this is also true if $q$ is negative?)

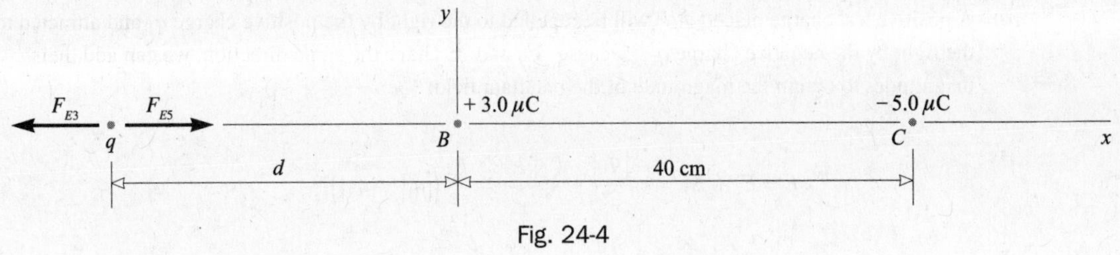


Fig. 24-4

For $q$ placed as shown, when the net force on it is zero, we have $F_{E3} = F_{E5}$ and so, for distances in meters,

$$k_0 \frac{q(3.0\times10^{-6}\ \text{C})}{d^2} = k_0 \frac{q(5.0\times10^{-6}\ \text{C})}{(0.40\ \text{m} + d)^2}$$

After canceling $q$, $k_0$, and $10^{-6}$ C from each side, cross-multiply to obtain

$$5d^2 = 3.0(0.40 + d)^2 \qquad \text{or} \qquad d^2 - 1.2d - 0.24 = 0$$

Using the quadratic formula,

$$d = \frac{-b \pm \sqrt{b^2 - 4ac}}{2a} = \frac{1.2 \pm \sqrt{1.44 + 0.96}}{2} = 0.60 \pm 0.775\ \text{m}$$

Two values, 1.4 m and $-0.18$ m, are therefore found for $d$. The first is the correct one; the second gives the point in $BC$ where the two forces have the same magnitude but do not cancel.

**24.10 [II]** Compute (*a*) the electric field $E$ in air at a distance of 30 cm from a point charge $q_{\bullet 1} = 5.0 \times 10^{-9}$ C, (*b*) the force on a charge $q_{\bullet 2} = 4.0 \times 10^{-10}$ C placed 30 cm from $q_{\bullet 1}$, and (*c*) the force on a charge $q_{\bullet 3} = -4.0 \times 10^{-10}$ C placed 30 cm from $q_{\bullet 1}$ (in the absence of $q_{\bullet 2}$).

(*a*) $$E = k_0 \frac{q_{\bullet 1}}{r^2} = (9.0 \times 10^9 \text{ N}\cdot\text{m}^2/\text{C}^2)\frac{5.0 \times 10^{-9}\text{ C}}{(0.30\text{ m})^2} = 0.50 \text{ kN/C}$$

directed away from $q_{\bullet 1}$.

(*b*) $F_E = Eq_{\bullet 2} = (500 \text{ N/C})(-4.0 \times 10^{-10}\text{ C}) = 2.0 \times 10^{-7}\text{ N} = 0.20\ \mu\text{N}$

directed away from $q_{\bullet 1}$.

(*c*) $F_E = Eq_{\bullet 3} = (500 \text{ N/C})(-4.0 \times 10^{-10}\text{ C}) = -0.20\ \mu\text{N}$

This force is directed toward $q_{\bullet 1}$.

**24.11 [III]** The situation depicted in Fig. 24-5 is that of two tiny charged spheres separated by 10.0 cm in air. Find (*a*) the electric field $E$ at point $P$,(*b*) the force on a $-4.0 \times 10^{-8}$ C charge placed at $P$, and (*c*) where in the region the electric field would be zero (in the absence of the $-4.0 \times 10^{-8}$ C charge).

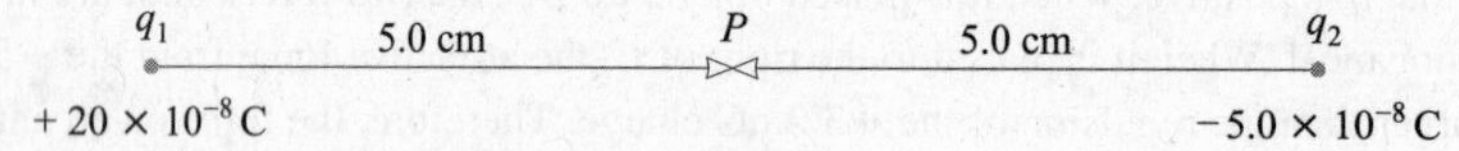

$q_1$ 5.0 cm $P$ 5.0 cm $q_2$

$+20 \times 10^{-8}$ C $-5.0 \times 10^{-8}$ C

Fig. 24-5

(*a*) A positive test charge placed at $P$ will be repelled to the right by the positive charge $q_1$ and attracted to the right by the negative charge $q_2$. Because $\vec{\mathbf{E}}_1$ and $\vec{\mathbf{E}}_2$ have the same direction, we can add their magnitudes to obtain the magnitude of the resultant field:

$$E = E_1 + E_2 = k_0\frac{|q_1|}{r_1^2} + k_0\frac{|q_2|}{r_2^2} = \frac{k_0}{r_1^2}\left(|q_1| + |q_2|\right)$$

where $r_1 = r_2 = 0.05$ m, and $|q_1|$ and $|q_2|$ are the absolute values of $q_1$ and $q_2$. Hence,

$$E = \frac{9.0 \times 10^9 \text{ N}\cdot\text{m}^2/\text{C}^2}{(0.050\text{ m})^2}(25 \times 10^{-8}\text{ C}) = 9.0 \times 10^5 \text{ N/C}$$

directed toward the right.

(*b*) A charge $q$ placed at $P$ will experience a force $Eq$. Therefore,

$$F_E = Eq = (9.0 \times 10^5 \text{ N/C})(-4.0 \times 10^{-8}\text{ C}) = -0.036 \text{ N}$$

The negative sign tells us the force is directed toward the left. This is correct because the electric field represents the force on a positive charge. The force on a negative charge is opposite in direction to the field.

(*c*) Reasoning as in Problem 24.9, we conclude that the field will be zero somewhere to the right of the $-5.0 \times 10^{-8}$ C charge. Represent the distance to that point from the $-5.0 \times 10^{-8}$ C charge by $d$. At that point,

$$E_1 - E_2 = 0$$

because the field due to the positive charge is to the right, while the field due to the negative charge is to the left. Thus,

$$k_0\left(\frac{|q_1|}{r_1^2} - \frac{|q_2|}{r_2^2}\right) = (9.0 \times 10^9\,\mathrm{N \cdot m^2/C^2})\left[\frac{20 \times 10^{-8}\,\mathrm{C}}{(d + 0.10\,\mathrm{m})^2} - \frac{5.0 \times 10^{-8}\,\mathrm{C}}{d^2}\right] = 0$$

Simplifying, we obtain

$$3d^2 - 0.2d - 0.01 = 0$$

The quadratic formula yields $d = 0.10$ m and $-0.03$ m. Only the plus sign has meaning here, and therefore $d = 0.10$ m. The point in question is 10 cm to the right of the negative charge.

**24.12 [II]** Three charges are placed on three corners of a square, as shown in Fig. 24-6. Each side of the square is 30.0 cm and the arrangement is in air. Compute $\vec{\mathbf{E}}$ at the fourth corner. What would be the force on a 6.00 $\mu$C charge placed at the vacant corner?

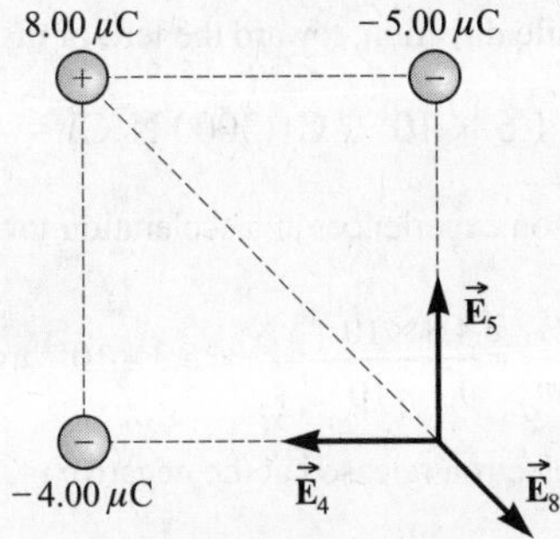


Fig. 24-6

The contributions of the three charges to the field at the vacant corner are as indicated. Notice in particular their directions which correspond to the directions of the forces that would exist on a positive test charge if it was at that location. Their magnitudes are given by $E = k_0 q/r^2$ to be

$$E_4 = 4.00 \times 10^5\ \mathrm{N/C} \qquad E_8 = 4.00 \times 10^5\ \mathrm{N/C} \qquad E_5 = 5.00 \times 10^5\ \mathrm{N/C}$$

Because the $E_8$ vector makes an angle of 45.0° to the horizontal,

$$E_x = E_8 \cos 45.0° - E_4 = -1.17 \times 10^5\ \mathrm{N/C}$$

$$E_y = E_5 - E_8 \cos 45.0° = 2.17 \times 10^5\ \mathrm{N/C}$$

Using $E = \sqrt{E_x^2 + E_y^2}$ and $\tan\theta = E_y/E_x$, we find $E = 2.47 \times 10^5$ N at 118°.

The force on a charge placed at the vacant corner would be simply $F_E = Eq$. Since $q = 6.00 \times 10^{-6}$ C, we have $F_E = 1.48$ N at an angle of 118°.

**24.13 [III]** Two charged metal plates in vacuum are 15 cm apart as drawn in Fig. 24-7. The electric field between the plates is uniform and has a strength of $E = 3000$ N/C. An electron ($q = -e$, $m_e = 9.1 \times 10^{-31}$ kg) is released from rest at point $P$ just outside the negative plate. ($a$) How long will it take to reach the other plate? ($b$) How fast will it be going just before it hits?

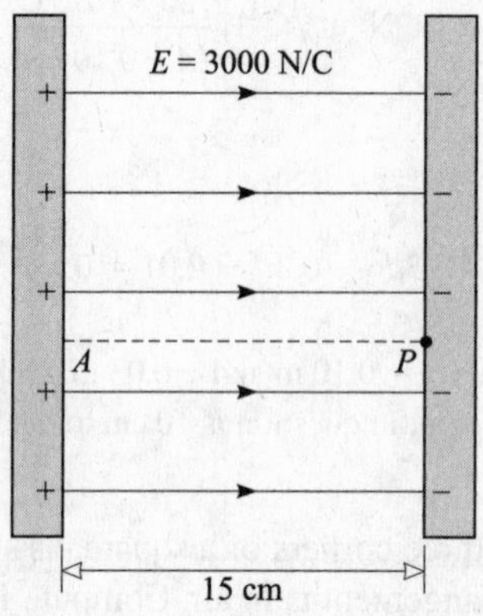


Fig. 24-7

The electric field lines show the force on a positive charge. (A positive charge would be repelled to the right by the positive plate and attracted to the right by the negative plate.) An electron, being negative, will experience a force in the opposite direction, toward the left, of magnitude

$$F_E = |q|E = (1.6 \times 10^{-19}\ \text{C})(3000\ \text{N/C}) = 4.8 \times 10^{-16}\ \text{N}$$

Because of this force, the electron experiences an acceleration toward the left given by

$$a = \frac{F_E}{m} = \frac{4.8\times10^{-16}\ \text{N}}{9.1\times10^{-31}\ \text{kg}} = 5.3\times10^{14}\ \text{m/s}^2$$

In the motion problem for the electron released at the negative plate and traveling to the positive plate,

$$v_i = 0 \qquad x = 0.15\ \text{m} \qquad a = 5.3 \times 10^{14}\ \text{m/s}^2$$

($a$) From $x = v_i t + \frac{1}{2}at^2$ we have

$$t = \sqrt{\frac{2x}{a}} = \sqrt{\frac{(2)(0.15\ \text{m})}{5.3\times10^{14}\ \text{m/s}^2}} = 2.4\times10^{-8}\ \text{s}$$

($b$) $v = v_i + at = 0 + (5.3 \times 10^{14}\ \text{m/s}^2)(2.4 \times 10^{-8}\ \text{s}) = 1.30 \times 10^7$ m/s

As you will see in Chapter 41, relativistic effects begin to become important at speeds above this. Therefore, this approach must be modified for very fast particles.

**24.14 [I]** Suppose in Fig. 24-7 an electron is shot straight upward from point-$P$ with a speed of $5.0 \times 10^6$ m/s. How far above $A$ will it strike the positive plate?

This is a projectile problem. (Since the gravitational force is so small compared to the electrical force, we can ignore gravity.) The only force acting on the electron after its release is the horizontal electric force. We found in Problem 24.13($a$) that under the action of this force the electron has a time-of-flight of $2.4 \times 10^{-8}$ s. The vertical displacement in this time is

$$(5.0 \times 10^6\ \text{m/s})\,(2.4 \times 10^{-8}\ \text{s}) = 0.12\ \text{m}$$

The electron travels along an arc and strikes the positive plate 12 cm above point-$A$.

**24.15 [II]** In Fig. 24-7 a proton ($q_e = +e$, $m = 1.67 \times 10^{-27}$ kg) is shot with a speed of $2.00 \times 10^5$ m/s toward $P$ from $A$. What will be its speed just before hitting the plate at $P$?

Let's first calculate the acceleration knowing the electric field, and from it the force:

$$a = \frac{F_E}{m} = \frac{qE}{m} = \frac{(1.60 \times 10^{-19}\ \text{C})\,(3000\ \text{N/C})}{1.67 \times 10^{-27}\ \text{kg}} = 2.88 \times 10^{11}\ \text{m/s}^2$$

For the problem involving horizontal motion,

$$v_i = 2.00 \times 10^5\ \text{m/s} \qquad x = 0.15\ m \qquad a = 2.88 \times 10^{11}\ \text{m/s}^2$$

Use $v_f^2 = v_i^2 + 2ax$ to find

$$v_f = \sqrt{v_i^2 + 2ax} = \sqrt{(2.00 \times 10^5\ \text{m/s})^2 + (2)\,(2.88 \times 10^{11}\ \text{m/s}^2)\,(0.15\ \text{m})} = 356\ \text{km/s}$$

**24.16 [II]** Two identical tiny metal balls in air have charges $q_1$ and $q_2$. The repulsive force one exerts on the other when they are 20 cm apart is $1.35 \times 10^{-4}$ N. After the balls are touched together and then separated once again to 20 cm, the repulsive force is found to be $1.406 \times 10^{-4}$ N. Find $q_1$ and $q_2$.

Because the force is one of repulsion, $q_1$ and $q_2$ have the same sign. After the balls are touched, they share charge equally, so each has a charge $\frac{1}{2}(q_1 + q_2)$. Writing Coulomb's Law for the two situations described, we have

$$0.000\,135\ \text{N} = k_0 \frac{q_1 q_2}{0.040\ \text{m}^2}$$

and
$$0.000\,140\,6\ \text{N} = k_0 \frac{\left[\frac{1}{2}(q_1 + q_2)\right]^2}{0.040\ \text{m}^2}$$

After substitution for $k_0$, these equations reduce to

$$q_1 q_2 = 6.00 \times 10^{-16}\ \text{C}^2 \qquad \text{and} \qquad q_1 + q_2 = 5.00 \times 10^{-8}\ \text{C}$$

Solving these equations simultaneously leads to $q_1 = 20$ nC and $q_2 = 30$ nC (or vice versa). Alternatively, both charges could have been negative.

## SUPPLEMENTARY PROBLEMS

**24.17 [I]** How many electrons are contained in 1.0 C of charge? What is the mass of the electrons in 1.0 C of charge?

**24.18 [I]** If two equal point charges, each of 1 C, were separated in air by a distance of 1 km, what would be the force between them?

**24.19 [I]** Determine the force between two free electrons spaced 1.0 angstrom ($10^{-10}$ m) apart in vacuum.

**24.20 [I]** What is the force of repulsion between two argon nuclei that are separated in vacuum by 1.0 nm ($10^{-9}$ m)? The charge on an argon nucleus is $+18e$.

**24.21 [I]** Two equally charged small balls are 3 cm apart in air and repel each other with a force of 40 $\mu$N. Compute the charge on each ball.

**24.22 [II]** Three point charges are placed at the following locations on the $x$-axis: $+2.0\ \mu$C at $x = 0$, $-3.0\ \mu$C at $x = 40$ cm, $-5.0\ \mu$C at $x = 120$ cm. Find the force (*a*) on the $-3.0\ \mu$C charge, (*b*) on the $-5.0\ \mu$C charge.

**24.23 [II]** Four equal point charges of $+3.0\ \mu$C are placed in air at the four corners of a square that is 40 cm on a side. Find the force on any one of the charges.

**24.24 [II]** Four equal-magnitude point charges (3.0 $\mu$C) are placed in air at the corners of a square that is 40 cm on a side. Two, diagonally opposite each other, are positive, and the other two are negative. Find the force on either negative charge.

**24.25 [II]** Charges of +2.0, +3.0, and $-8.0\ \mu$C are placed in air at the vertices of an equilateral triangle of side 10 cm. Calculate the magnitude of the force acting on the $-8.0\ \mu$C charge due to the other two charges.

**24.26 [II]** One charge of ($+5.0\ \mu$C) is placed in air at exactly $x = 0$, and a second charge ($+7.0\ \mu$C) at $x = 100$ cm. Where can a third be placed so as to experience zero net force due to the other two?

**24.27 [II]** Two identical tiny metal balls carry charges of +3 nC and $-12$ nC. They are 3 m apart in vacuum. (*a*) Compute the force of attraction. (*b*) The balls are now touched together and then separated to 3 cm. Describe the forces on them now.

**24.28 [II]** A charge of $+6.0\ \mu$C experiences a force of 2.0 mN in the $+x$-direction at a certain point in space. (*a*) What was the electric field at that point before the charge was placed there? (*b*) Describe the force a $-2.0\ \mu$C charge would experience if it were used instead of the $+6.0\ \mu$C charge.

**24.29 [I]** A point charge of $-3.0 \times 10^{-5}$ C is placed at the origin of coordinates in vacuum. Find the electric field at the point $x = 5.0$ m on the $x$-axis.

**24.30 [III]** Four equal-magnitude (4.0 $\mu$C) charges in vacuum are placed at the four corners of a square that is 20 cm on each side. Find the electric field at the center of the square (*a*) if the charges are all positive, (*b*) if the charges alternate in sign around the perimeter of the square, (*c*) if the charges have the following sequence around the square: plus, plus, minus, minus.

**24.31 [II]** A 0.200-g ball in air hangs from a thread in a uniform vertical electric field of 3.00 kN/C directed upward. What is the charge on the ball if the tension in the thread is (*a*) zero and (*b*) 4.00 mN?

**24.32 [II]** Determine the acceleration of a proton ($q = +e$, $m = 1.67 \times 10^{-27}$ kg) immersed in an electric field of strength 0.50 kN/C in vacuum. How many times is this acceleration greater than that due to gravity?

**24.33 [II]** A small, 0.60-g ball in air carries a charge of magnitude 8.0 $\mu$C. It is suspended by a vertical thread in a downward 300 N/C electric field. What is the tension in the thread if the charge on the ball is (*a*) positive, (*b*) negative?

**24.34 [III]** The tiny sphere at the end of the weightless thread illustrated in Fig. 24-8 has a mass of 0.60 g. It is immersed in air and exposed to a horizontal electric field of strength 700 N/C. The ball is in equilibrium in the position shown. What are the magnitude and sign of the charge on the ball?

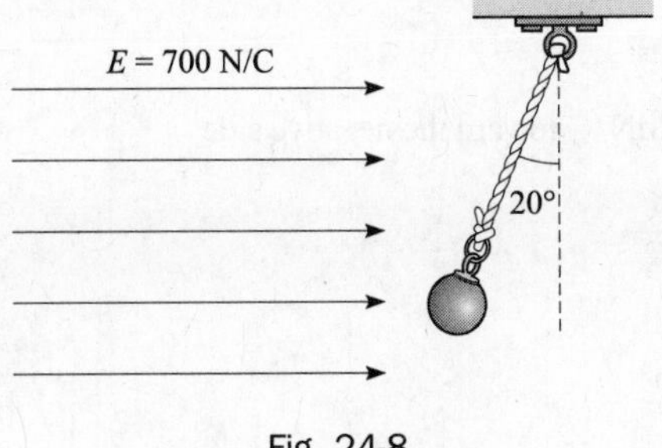


Fig. 24-8

**24.35 [III]** An electron ($q = -e$, $m_e = 9.1 \times 10^{-31}$ kg) is projected out along the $+x$-axis in vacuum with an initial speed of $3.0 \times 10^6$ m/s. It goes 45 cm and stops due to a uniform electric field in the region. Find the magnitude and direction of the field.

**24.36 [III]** A particle of mass $m$ and charge $-e$ while in a region of vacuum is projected with horizontal speed $v$ into an electric field ($E$) directed downward. Find (*a*) the horizontal and vertical components of its acceleration, $a_x$ and $a_y$; (*b*) its horizontal and vertical displacements, $x$ and $y$, after time $t$; (*c*) the equation of its trajectory.

## ANSWERS TO SUPPLEMENTARY PROBLEMS

**24.17 [I]** $6.2 \times 10^{18}$ electrons, $5.7 \times 10^{-12}$ kg

**24.18 [I]** 9 kN repulsion

**24.19 [I]** 23 nN repulsion

**24.20 [I]** 75 nN

**24.21 [I]** 2 nC

**24.22 [II]** (*a*) $-0.55$ N; (*b*) 0.15 N

**24.23 [II]** 0.97 N outward along the diagonal

**24.24 [II]** 0.46 N inward along the diagonal

**24.25 [II]** 31 N

**24.26 [II]** at $x = 46$ cm

**24.27 [II]** (*a*) $4 \times 10^{-4}$ N attraction; (*b*) $2 \times 10^{-4}$ N repulsion

**24.28 [II]** (*a*) 0.33 kN/C in $+x$-direction; (*b*) 0.67 mN in $-x$-direction

**24.29 [I]** 11 kN/C in $-x$-direction

**24.30 [III]** (*a*) zero; (*b*) zero; (*c*) 5.1 MN/C toward the negative side

**24.31 [II]** (*a*) +653 nC; (*b*) −680 nC

**24.32 [II]** $4.8 \times 10^{10}$ m/s$^2$, $4.9 \times 10^9$

**24.33 [II]** (*a*) 8.3 mN; (*b*) 3.5 mN

**24.34 [III]** −3.1 μC

**24.35 [III]** 57 N/C in $+x$-direction

**24.36 [III]** (*a*) $a_x = 0$, $a_y = Ee/m$; (*b*) $x = vt$, $y = \frac{1}{2}a_y t^2 = \frac{1}{2}(Ee/m)t^2$; (*c*) $y = \frac{1}{2}(Ee/mv^2)x^2$ (a parabola)

# Electric Potential; Capacitance

**The Potential Difference** between point-*A* and point-*B* is the work done against electrical forces in carrying a *unit* positive test-charge from *A* to *B*. We represent the potential difference between *A* and *B* by $V_B - V_A$ or just by $V$ when there is no ambiguity. Its units are those of work per charge (joules/coulomb) and are designated as **volts** (V):

$$1\text{ V} = 1\text{ J/C}$$

Because work is a scalar quantity, so too is potential difference. Like work, potential difference may be positive or negative. The work $W$ done in transporting a charge $q$ from one point-*A* to a second point-*B* is

$$W = q(V_B - V_A) = qV$$

where the appropriate sign (+ or −) must be given to the charge. If both $(V_B - V_A)$ and $q$ are positive (or negative), the work done is positive. If $(V_B - V_A)$ and $q$ have opposite signs, the work done is negative.

**Absolute Potential:** The absolute potential at a point is the work done against electric forces in carrying a unit positive test-charge from infinity to that point. Hence, the absolute potential at point-*B* is the difference in potential from *A* at ∞ to *B*.

Consider a point charge $q_{\bullet}$ in vacuum and a point-*P* at a distance $r$ from the point charge. The absolute potential at *P* due to the charge $q$ is

$$V = k_0 \frac{q_{\bullet}}{r}$$

where $k_0 = 8.99 \times 10^9\text{ N·m}^2/\text{C}^2$ is the Coulomb constant for vacuum. The absolute potential at infinity (at $r = \infty$) is zero.

Because of the superposition principle and the scalar nature of potential difference, the absolute potential at a point due to a number of point charges is

$$V = k_0 \sum \frac{q_{\bullet i}}{r_i}$$

where the $r_i$ are the distances of the charges $q_{\bullet i}$ from the point in question. Negative $q_{\bullet}$'s contribute negative terms to the potential, while positive $q_{\bullet}$'s contribute positive terms.

The absolute potential due to a uniformly charged sphere, at points *outside* the sphere or *on* its surface, is $V = k_0 q/r$, where $q$ is the charge on the sphere. This potential is the same as that due to a point charge $q_{\bullet}$ placed at the position of the sphere's center.

**Electrical Potential Energy** ($\text{PE}_E$): To carry a charge $q$ from infinity to a point where the absolute potential is $V$, work in the amount $qV$ must be done on the charge. This work appears as electrical potential energy ($\text{PE}_E$).

Similarly, when a charge $q$ is carried through a **potential difference** $V$, work in the amount $qV$ must be done on the charge. This work results in a change $qV$ in the $\text{PE}_E$ of the charge. For a potential *rise*, $V$ will be positive and the $\text{PE}_E$ will increase if $q$ is positive. But for a potential *drop*, $V$ will be negative and the $\text{PE}_E$ of the charge will decrease if $q$ is positive.

***V* Related to *E*:** Suppose that in a certain region the electric field is uniform and is in the $x$-direction. Call its magnitude $E_x$. Because $E_x$ is the force on a unit positive test-charge, the work done in moving the test-charge through a distance $x$ is (from $W = F_x x$)

$$V = E_x x$$

The field between two large, parallel, oppositely charged, closely spaced metal plates is uniform. We can therefore use this equation to relate the electric field $E$ between the plates to the plate separation $d$ and their potential difference $V$. For parallel plates,

$$V = Ed$$

**Electron Volt Energy Unit:** The work done in carrying a charge $+e$ (coulombs) through a potential rise of exactly 1 volt is defined to be 1 **electron volt** (eV). Therefore,

$$1\ \text{eV} = (1.602 \times 10^{-19}\ \text{C})(1\ \text{V}) = 1.602 \times 10^{-19}\ \text{J}$$

Equivalently,

$$\text{Work or energy (in eV)} = \frac{\text{work (in joules)}}{e}$$

**A Capacitor** is a device that stores charge. The human body could be a capacitor, albeit a poor one. Often, although certainly not always, it consists of two conductors separated by an insulator or dielectric (and that includes vacuum). The **capacitance** ($C$) of a capacitor is defined as

$$\text{Capacitance} = \frac{\text{Magnitude of charge on either conductor}}{\text{Magnitude of potential difference between conductors}}$$

For $q$ in coulombs and $V$ in volts, $C$ is in **farads** (F).

**Parallel-Plate Capacitor:** The capacitance of a parallel-plate capacitor whose opposing plate faces, each of area $A$, are separated by a small distance $d$ is given by

$$C = K\epsilon_0 \frac{A}{d} = \epsilon \frac{A}{d}$$

where $K = \epsilon/\epsilon_0$ is the dimensionless dielectric constant (see Chapter 24) of the nonconducting material (the *dielectric*) between the plates, and

$$\epsilon_0 = 8.85 \times 10^{-12}\ \text{C}^2/\text{N}\cdot\text{m}^2 = 8.85 \times 10^{-12}\ \text{F/m}$$

For vacuum, $K = 1$, so that a dielectric-filled parallel-plate capacitor has a capacitance $K$ times larger than the same capacitor with vacuum between its plates. This result holds for a capacitor of arbitrary shape.

**Capacitors in Parallel and Series:** As shown in Fig. 25-1, capacitances add for capacitors in parallel, whereas reciprocal capacitances add for capacitors in series. When you are dealing with capacitors in series, it's convenient

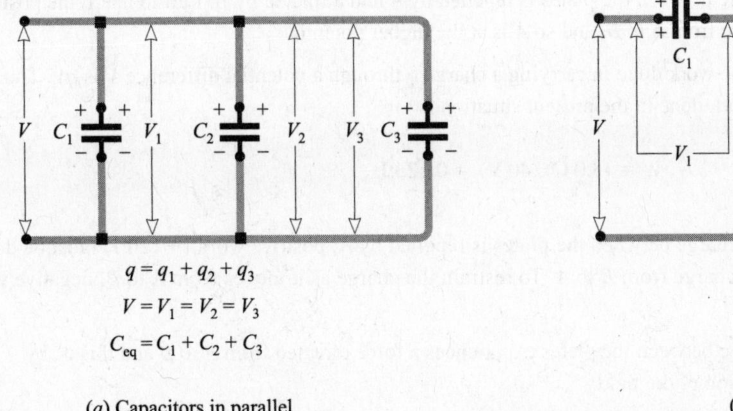

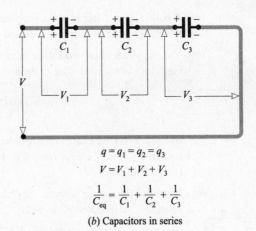

(*a*) Capacitors in parallel (*b*) Capacitors in series

Fig. 25-1

to use the $1/x$ key on your calculator. It is also helpful when you have two or more capacitors in series to keep in mind that for any two, $C_1$ and $C_2$,

$$C_{eq} = \frac{C_1 C_2}{C_1 + C_2}$$

and so you can add them all two at a time.

**Energy Stored in a Capacitor:** The energy ($PE_E$) stored in a capacitor of capacitance $C$ that has a charge $q$ and a potential difference $V$ is

$$PE_E = \tfrac{1}{2}qV = \tfrac{1}{2}CV^2 = \tfrac{1}{2}\frac{q^2}{C}$$

## SOLVED PROBLEMS

**25.1 [I]** In Fig. 25-2, the potential difference between the metal plates in air is 40 V. (*a*) Which plate is at the higher potential? (*b*) How much work must be done to carry a +3.0 C charge from $B$ to $A$? From $A$ to $B$? (*c*) How do we know that the electric field is in the direction indicated? (*d*) If the plate separation is 5.0 mm, what is the magnitude of $\vec{\mathbf{E}}$?

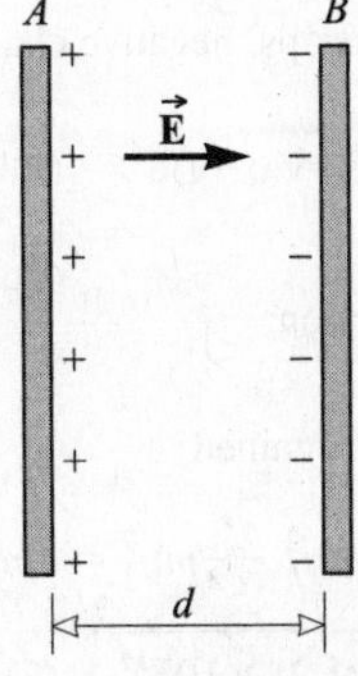


Fig. 25-2

(*a*) A positive test charge between the plates is repelled by *A* and attracted by *B*. Left to itself, the positive test charge will move from *A* to *B*, and so *A* is at the higher potential.

(*b*) The magnitude of the work done in carrying a charge $q$ through a potential difference $V$ is $qV$. Thus the magnitude of the work done in the present situation is

$$W = (3.0\ \text{C})\,(40\ \text{V}) = 0.12\ \text{kJ}$$

Because a positive charge between the plates is repelled by *A*, positive work (+120 J) must be done to drag the +3.0 C charge from *B* to *A*. To restrain the charge as it moves from *A* to *B*, negative work (−120 J) is done.

(*c*) A positive test-charge between the plates experiences a force directed from *A* to *B* and this is, by definition, the direction of the field.

(*d*) For closely spaced parallel plates, $V = Ed$. Therefore,

$$E = \frac{V}{d} = \frac{40\ \text{V}}{0.0050\ \text{m}} = 8.0\ \text{kV/m}$$

Notice that the SI units for electric field, V/m and N/C, are identical.

**25.2 [I]** How much work is required to carry an electron from the positive terminal of a 12-V battery to the negative terminal?

Going from the positive to the negative terminal, one passes through a potential drop. In this case it is $V = -12$ V. Then

$$W = qV = (-1.6 \times 10^{-19}\ \text{C})\,(-12\ \text{V}) = 1.9 \times 10^{-18}\ \text{J}$$

As a check, notice that an electron, if left to itself, will move from negative to positive because it is a negative charge. Hence, positive work must be done to carry it in the reverse direction as required here.

**25.3 [I]** How much electrical potential energy does a proton lose as it falls through a potential drop of 5 kV?

The proton carries a positive charge. It will therefore move from regions of high potential to regions of low potential if left free to do so. Its change in potential energy as it moves through a potential difference $V$ is $Vq$. In our case, $V = -5$ kV. Therefore,

$$\text{Change in PE}_E = Vq = (-5 \times 10^3\ \text{V})(1.6 \times 10^{-19}\ \text{C}) = -8 \times 10^{-16}\ \text{J}$$

**25.4 [II]** An electron starts from rest and falls through a potential rise of 80 V. What is its final speed?

Positive charges fall through potential drops; negative charges, such as electrons, fall through potential rises.

$$\text{Change in PE}_E = Vq = (80\ \text{V})(-1.6 \times 10^{-19}\ \text{C}) = -1.28 \times 10^{-17}\ \text{J}$$

This lost $\text{PE}_E$ appears as KE of the electron:

$$\text{PE}_E \text{ lost} = \text{KE gained}$$

$$1.28 \times 10^{-17}\ \text{J} = \tfrac{1}{2}mv_f^2 - \tfrac{1}{2}mv_i^2 = \tfrac{1}{2}mv_f^2 - 0$$

and

$$v_f = \sqrt{\frac{(1.28 \times 10^{-17}\ \text{J})\,(2)}{9.1 \times 10^{-31}\ \text{kg}}} = 5.3 \times 10^6\ \text{m/s}$$

**25.5 [I]** (*a*) What is the absolute potential at each of the following distances from a charge of $+2.0\ \mu$C in air: $r = 10$ cm and $r = 50$ cm? (*b*) How much work is required to carry a 0.05-$\mu$C charge from the point at $r = 50$ cm to that at $r = 10$ cm?

(*a*) $$V_{10} = k_0\frac{q}{r} = (9.0\times10^9\ \text{N}\cdot\text{m}^2/\text{C}^2)\frac{2.0\times10^{-6}\ \text{C}}{0.10\text{m}} = 1.8\times10^5\ \text{V}$$

$$V_{50} = \frac{10}{50}V_{10} = 36\ \text{kV}$$

(*b*) Work $= q(V_{10} - V_{50}) = (5\times10^{-8}\ \text{C})(1.44\times10^5\ \text{V}) = 7.2$ mJ

**25.6 [II]** Suppose [in Problem 25.5(*a*) where there is a $+2.0\ \mu$C charge] that a proton is released at $r = 10$ cm. How fast will it be moving as it passes a point at $r = 50$ cm?

This is a situation where $\text{PE}_E$ goes into KE. As the proton moves from one point to the other, there is a potential drop of

$$\text{Potential drop} = 1.80\times10^5\ \text{V} - 0.36\times10^5\ \text{V} = 1.44\times10^5\ \text{V}$$

The proton acquires KE as it falls through this potential drop:

$$\text{KE gained} = \text{PE}_E\ \text{lost}$$

$$\tfrac{1}{2}mv_f^2 - \tfrac{1}{2}mv_i^2 = qV$$

$$\tfrac{1}{2}(1.67\times10^{-27}\ \text{kg})v_f^2 - 0 = (1.6\times10^{-19}\ \text{C})(1.44\times10^5\ \text{V})$$

from which $v_f = 5.3\times10^6$ m/s.

**25.7 [II]** In Fig. 25-2, which depicts two closely spaced charged parallel plates in vacuum, let $E = 2.0$ kV/m and $d = 5.0$ mm. A proton is shot from plate-*B* toward plate-*A* with an initial speed of 100 km/s. What will be its speed just before it strikes plate-*A*?

The proton, being positive, is repelled by plate-*A* and will therefore be slowed down. We need the potential difference between the plates, which is

$$V = Ed = (2.0\ \text{kV/m})(0.0050\ \text{m}) = 10\ \text{V}$$

Now, from the conservation of energy, for the proton,

$$\text{KE lost} = \text{PE}_E\ \text{gained}$$

$$\tfrac{1}{2}mv_B^2 - \tfrac{1}{2}mv_A^2 = qV$$

Substituting $m = 1.67\times10^{-27}$ kg, $v_B = 1.00\times10^5$ m/s, $q = 1.60\times10^{-19}$ C, and $V = 10$ V results in $v_A = 90$ km/s. The proton is indeed slowed.

**25.8 [III]** The nucleus of a tin atom in vacuum has a charge of $+50e$. (*a*) Find the absolute potential $V$ at a radial distance of $1.0\times10^{-12}$ m from the nucleus. (*b*) If a proton is released from this point, how fast will it be moving when it is 1.0 m from the nucleus?

(*a*) $$V = k_0\frac{q}{r} = (9.0\times10^9\ \text{N}\cdot\text{m}^2/\text{C}^2)\frac{(50)(1.6\times10^{-19}\text{C})}{10^{-12}\ \text{m}} = 72\ \text{kV}$$

(*b*) The proton is repelled by the nucleus and flies out to infinity. The absolute potential at a point is the potential difference between the point in question and infinity. Hence, there is a potential drop of 72 kV as the proton flies to infinity.

Usually we would simply assume that 1.0 m is far enough from the nucleus to consider it to be at infinity. But, as a check, compute $V$ at $r$ = 1.0 m:

$$V_{1\text{m}} = k_0\frac{q}{r} = (9.0\times10^9\ \text{N}\cdot\text{m}^2/\text{C}^2)\,\frac{(50)\,(1.6\times10^{-19}\ \text{C})}{1.0\ \text{m}} = 7.2\times10^{-8}\ \text{V}$$

which is essentially zero in comparison with 72 kV.

As the proton falls through 72 kV,

$$\text{KE gained} = \text{PE}_E \text{ lost}$$

$$\tfrac{1}{2}mv_f^2 - \tfrac{1}{2}mv_i^2 = qV$$

$$\tfrac{1}{2}(1.67\times10^{-27}\ \text{kg})\,v_f^2 - 0 = (1.6\times10^{-19}\ \text{C})\,(72\,000\ \text{V})$$

from which $v_f = 3.7 \times 10^6$ m/s.

**25.9 [II]** The following point charges are placed on the $x$-axis in air: +2.0 $\mu$C at $x$ = 20 cm, −3.0 $\mu$C at $x$ = 30 cm, −4.0 $\mu$C at $x$ = 40 cm. Find the absolute potential on the axis at $x$ = 0.

Potential is a scalar, and so

$$V = k_0\sum\frac{q_i}{r_i} = (9.0\times10^9\ \text{N}\cdot\text{m}^2/\text{C}^2)\left(\frac{2.0\times10^{-6}\ \text{C}}{0.20\ \text{m}} + \frac{-3.0\times10^{-6}\ \text{C}}{0.30\ \text{m}} + \frac{-4.0\times10^{-6}\ \text{C}}{0.40\ \text{m}}\right)$$

$$= (9.0\times10^9\ \text{N}\cdot\text{m}^2/\text{C}^2)\,(10\times10^{-6}\ \text{C/m} - 10\times10^{-6}\ \text{C/m} - 10\times10^{-6}\ \text{C/m}) = -90\ \text{kV}$$

**25.10 [I]** Two point charges, $+q$ and $-q$, are separated by a distance $d$ in air. Where, besides at infinity, is the absolute potential zero?

At the point (or points) in question,

$$0 = k_0\frac{q}{r_1} + k_0\frac{-q}{r_2} \qquad \text{or} \qquad r_1 = r_2$$

This condition holds everywhere on a plane which is the perpendicular bisector of the line joining the two charges. Therefore, the absolute potential is zero everywhere on that plane.

**25.11 [II]** Four point charges in air are placed at the four corners of a square that is 30 cm on each side. Find the potential at the center of the square if (*a*) the four charges are each +2.0 $\mu$C and (*b*) two of the four charges are +2.0 $\mu$C and two are −2.0 $\mu$C.

(*a*) $$V = k_0\sum\frac{q_i}{r_i} = k_0\frac{\Sigma q_i}{r} = (9.0\times10^9\ \text{N}\cdot\text{m}^2/\text{C}^2)\,\frac{(4)\,(2.0\times10^{-6}\ \text{C})}{(0.30\ \text{m})\,(\cos 45°)} = 3.4\times10^5\ \text{V}$$

(*b*) $$V = (9.0\times10^9\ \text{N}\cdot\text{m}^2/\text{C}^2)\,\frac{(2.0+2.0-2.0-2.0)\times10^{-6}\ \text{C})}{(0.30\ \text{m})\,(\cos 45°)} = 0$$

**25.12 [III]** In Fig. 25-3, the medium is vacuum. Charge at $A$ is $+200$ pC, while the charge at $B$ is $-100$ pC. (*a*) Find the absolute potentials at points-$C$ and -$D$. (*b*) How much work must be done to transfer a charge of $+500\ \mu$C from point-$C$ to point-$D$?

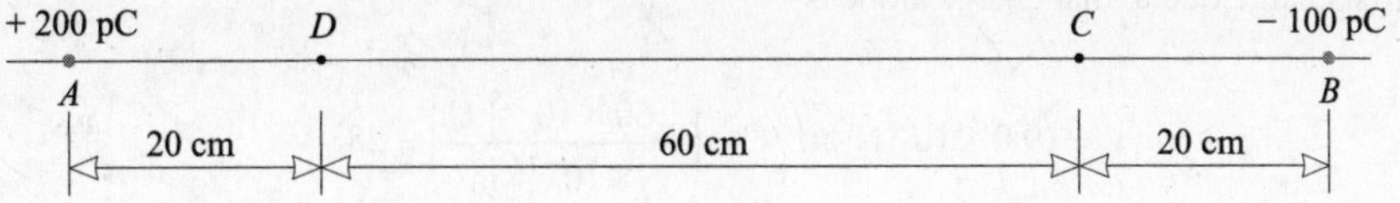


Fig. 25-3

$$(a)\quad V_C = k_0 \sum \frac{q_i}{r_i} = (9.0\times10^9\ \text{N}\cdot\text{m}^2/\text{C}^2)\left(\frac{2.00\times10^{-10}\ \text{C}}{0.80\ \text{m}} - \frac{1.00\times10^{-10}\ \text{C}}{0.20\ \text{m}}\right) = -2.25\ \text{V} = -2.3\ \text{V}$$

$$V_D = (9.0\times10^9\ \text{N}\cdot\text{m}^2/\text{C}^2)\left(\frac{2.00\times10^{-10}\ \text{C}}{0.20\ \text{m}} - \frac{1.00\times10^{-10}\ \text{C}}{0.80\ \text{m}}\right) = +7.88\ \text{V} = +7.9\ \text{V}$$

(*b*) There is a potential rise from $C$ to $D$ of $V = V_D - V_C = 7.88\ \text{V} - (-2.25\ \text{V}) = 10.13$ V. So

$$W = Vq = (10.13\ \text{V})(5.00 \times 10^{-4}\ \text{C}) = 5.1\ \text{mJ}$$

**25.13 [III]** Find the electrical potential energy of three point charges placed in vacuum as follows on the $x$-axis: $+2.0\ \mu$C at $x = 0$, $+3.0\ \mu$C at $x = 20$ cm, and $+6.0\ \mu$C at $x = 50$ cm. Take the $\text{PE}_E$ to be zero when the charges are separated far apart.

Compute how much work must be done to bring the charges from infinity to their places on the axis. Bring in the 2.0 $\mu$C charge first; this requires no work because there are no other charges in the vicinity.

Next bring in the 3.0 $\mu$C charge, which is repelled by the $+2.0\ \mu$C charge. The potential difference between infinity and the position to which we bring it is due to the $+2.0\ \mu$C charge and is

$$V_{x=0.2} = k_0 \frac{2.0\ \mu\text{C}}{0.20\ \text{m}} = (9.0\times10^9\ \text{N}\cdot\text{m}^2/\text{C}^2)\left(\frac{2\times10^{-6}\ \text{C}}{0.20\ \text{m}}\right) = 9.0\times10^4\ \text{V}$$

Therefore the work required to bring in the 3 $\mu$C charge is

$$W_{3\mu\text{C}} = qV_{x=0.2} = (3.0 \times 10^{-6}\ \text{C})(9.0 \times 10^4\ \text{V}) = 0.270\ \text{J}$$

Finally bring the 6.0 $\mu$C charge in to $x = 0$ 50 m. The potential there due to the two charges already present is

$$V_{x=0.5} = k_0\left(\frac{2.0\times10^{-6}\ \text{C}}{0.50\ \text{m}} + \frac{3.0\times10^{-6}\ \text{C}}{0.30\ \text{m}}\right) = 12.6\times10^4\ \text{V}$$

Therefore the work required to bring in the 6.0 $\mu$C charge is

$$W_{6\mu\text{C}} = qV_{x=0.5} = (6.0 \times 10^{-6}\ \text{C})(12.6 \times 10^4\ \text{V}) = 0.756\ \text{J}$$

Adding the amounts of work required to assemble the charges gives the energy stored in the system:

$$\text{PE}_E = 0.270\ \text{J} + 0.756\ \text{J} = 1.0\ \text{J}$$

Can you show that the order in which the charges are brought in from infinity does not affect this result?

**25.14 [III]** Two protons are held at rest in vacuum, $5.0 \times 10^{-12}$ m apart. When released, they fly apart. How fast will each be moving when they are far from each other?

Their original $\mathrm{PE}_E$ will be changed to KE. Proceed as in Problem 25.13. The potential at $5.0 \times 10^{-12}$ m from the first charge due to that charge alone is

$$V = (9.0\times10^{9}\ \mathrm{N\cdot m^2/C^2})\left(\frac{1.60\times10^{-19}\ \mathrm{C}}{5\times10^{-12}\ \mathrm{m}}\right) = 288\ \mathrm{V}$$

The work needed to bring in the second proton is then

$$W = qV = (1.60 \times 10^{-19}\ \mathrm{C})(288\ \mathrm{V}) = 4.61 \times 10^{-17}\ \mathrm{J}$$

and this is the $\mathrm{PE}_E$ of the original system. From the conservation of energy,

$$\text{Original PE}_E = \text{final KE}$$

$$4.61 \times 10^{-17}\ \mathrm{J} = \tfrac{1}{2}\, m_1 v_1^2 = \tfrac{1}{2}\, m_2 v_2^2$$

Since the particles are identical, $v_1 = v_2 = v$. Solving, we find that $v = 1.7 \times 10^5$ m/s when the particles are far apart.

**25.15 [III]** Figure 25-4 depicts two large, closely spaced metal plates (perpendicular to the page) connected to a 120-V battery. Assume the plates to be in vacuum and to be much larger than shown. Find (*a*) $E$ between the plates, (*b*) the force experienced by an electron between the plates, (*c*) the $\mathrm{PE}_E$ lost by an electron as it moves from plate-*B* to plate-*A*, and (*d*) the speed of the electron released from plate-*B* just before striking plate-*A*.

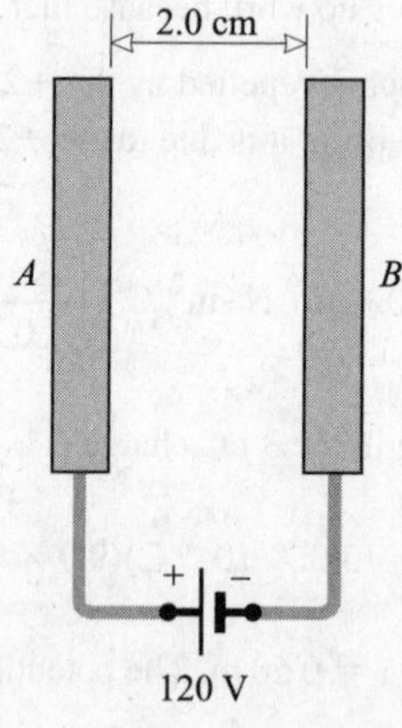


Fig. 25-4

(*a*) $E$ is directed from the positive plate-*A* to the negative plate-*B*. It is uniform between large parallel plates and is given by

$$E = \frac{V}{d} = \frac{120\ \mathrm{V}}{0.020\ \mathrm{m}} = 6000\ \mathrm{V/m} = 6.0\ \mathrm{kV/m}$$

directed from left to right.

(*b*) $F_E = qE = (-1.6 \times 10^{-19}\ \mathrm{C})(6000\ \mathrm{V/m}) = -9.6 \times 10^{-16}\ \mathrm{N}$

The minus sign tells us that $\vec{\mathbf{F}}_E$ is directed oppositely to $\vec{\mathbf{E}}$. Since plate-*A* is positive, the electron is attracted by it. The force on the electron is toward the left.

(c) Change in $PE_E = Vq = (120\text{ V})(-1.6\times10^{-19}\text{ C}) = -1.92\times10^{-17}\text{ J} = 1.9\times10^{-17}\text{ J}$

Notice that $V$ is a potential rise from $B$ to $A$

(d) $PE_E$ lost = KE gained

$$1.92\times10^{-17}\text{ J} = \tfrac{1}{2}mv_f^2 - \tfrac{1}{2}mv_i^2$$

$$1.92\times10^{-17}\text{ J} = \tfrac{1}{2}(9.1\times10^{-31}\text{ kg})v_f^2 - 0$$

from which $v_f = 6.5\times10^6$ m/s.

**25.16 [II]** As shown in Fig. 25-5, a charged particle in vacuum remains stationary between the two large horizontal charged plates. The plate separation is 2.0 cm, and $m = 4.0\times10^{-13}$ kg and $q = 2.4\times10^{-18}$ C for the particle. Find the potential difference between the plates.

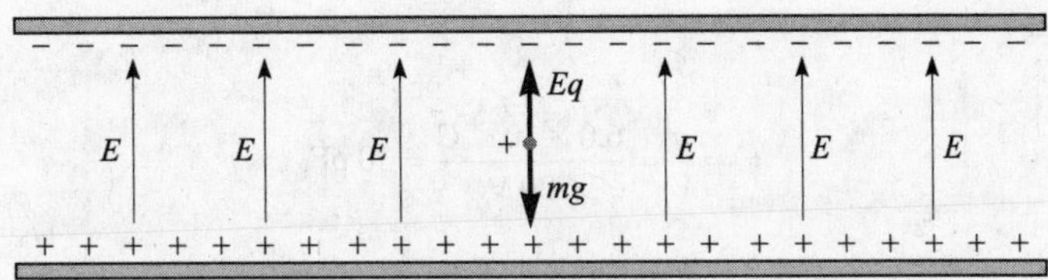


Fig. 25-5

Since the particle is in equilibrium, the weight of the particle is equal to the upward electrical force. That is,

$$mg = qE$$

or

$$E = \frac{mg}{q} = \frac{(4.0\times10^{-13}\text{ kg})(9.81\text{ m/s}^2)}{2.4\times10^{-18}\text{ C}} = 1.63\times10^6\text{ V/m}$$

But for a parallel-plate system,

$$V = Ed = (1.63\times10^6\text{ V/m})(0.020\text{ m}) = 33\text{ kV}$$

**25.17 [II]** An alpha particle ($q = 2e$, $m = 6.7\times10^{-27}$ kg) falls in vacuum from rest through a potential drop of $3.0\times10^6$ V (i.e., 3.0 MV). (a) What is its KE in electron volts? (b) What is its speed?

(a) $$\text{Energy in eV} = \frac{qV}{e} = \frac{(2e)(3.0\times10^6)}{e} = 6.0\times10^6\text{ eV} = 6.0\text{ MeV}$$

(b) $PE_E$ lost = KE gained

$$qV = \tfrac{1}{2}mv_f^2 - \tfrac{1}{2}mv_i^2$$

$$(2)(1.6\times10^{-19}\text{ C})(3.0\times10^6\text{ V}) = \tfrac{1}{2}(6.7\times10^{-27}\text{ kg})v_f^2 - 0$$

from which $v_f = 1.7\times10^7$ m/s.

**25.18 [II]** What is the speed of a 400 eV (a) electron, (b) proton, and (c) alpha particle?

In each case we know that the particle's kinetic energy is

$$\tfrac{1}{2}mv^2 = (400\text{ eV})\left(\frac{1.60\times10^{-19}\text{ J}}{1.00\text{ eV}}\right) = 6.40\times10^{-17}\text{ J}$$

Substituting $m_e = 9.1 \times 10^{-31}$ kg for the electron, $m_p = 1.67 \times 10^{-27}$ kg for the proton, and $m_\alpha = 4$ $(1.67 \times 10^{-27}$ kg) for the alpha particle gives their speeds as (*a*) $1.186 \times 10^7$ m/s, (*b*) $2.77 \times 10^5$ m/s, and (*c*) $1.38 \times 10^5$ m/s.

**25.19 [I]** A parallel-plate capacitor has a capacitance of 8.0 $\mu$F with air between its plates. Determine its capacitance when a dielectric with dielectric constant 6.0 is placed between its plates.

$$C \text{ with dielectric} = K(C \text{ with air}) = (6.0)(8.0\ \mu\text{F}) = 48\ \mu\text{F}$$

**25.20 [I]** What is the charge on a 300-pF capacitor when it is charged to a voltage of 1.0 kV?

$$q = CV = (300 \times 10^{-12}\ \text{F})(1000\ \text{V}) = 3.0 \times 10^{-7}\ \text{C} = 0.30\ \mu\text{C}$$

**25.21 [I]** A metal sphere mounted on an insulating rod carries a charge of 6.0 nC when its potential is 200 V higher than its surroundings. What is the capacitance of the capacitor formed by the sphere and its surroundings?

$$C = \frac{q}{V} = \frac{6.0 \times 10^{-9}\ \text{C}}{200\ \text{V}} = 30\ \text{pF}$$

**25.22 [I]** A 1.2-$\mu$F capacitor is charged to 3.0 kV. Compute the energy stored in the capacitor.

$$\text{Energy} = \tfrac{1}{2}qV = \tfrac{1}{2}CV^2 = \tfrac{1}{2}(1.2 \times 10^{-6}\ \text{F})(3000\ \text{V})^2 = 5.4\ \text{J}$$

**25.23 [II]** The series combination of two capacitors shown in Fig. 25-6 is connected across 1000 V. Compute (*a*) the equivalent capacitance $C_{eq}$ of the combination, (*b*) the magnitudes of the charges on the capacitors, (*c*) the potential differences across the capacitors, and (*d*) the energy stored in the capacitors.

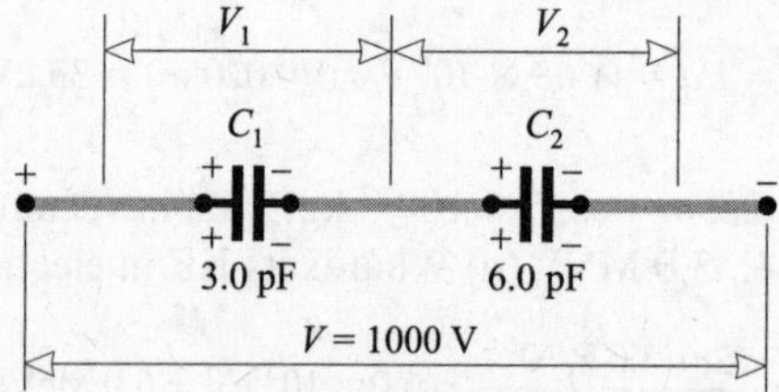


Fig. 25-6

(*a*) $$\frac{1}{C_{eq}} = \frac{1}{C_1} + \frac{1}{C_2} = \frac{1}{3.0\ \text{pF}} + \frac{1}{6.0\ \text{pF}} = \frac{1}{2.0\ \text{pF}}$$

from which C = 2.0 pF.

(*b*) *In a series combination, each capacitor carries the same charge* [see Fig. 25-1(*b*)], which is the charge on the combination. Thus, using the result of (*a*), we have

$$q_1 = q_2 = q = C_{eq}V = (2.0 \times 10^{-12}\ \text{F})(1000\ \text{V}) = 2.0\ \text{nC}$$

(*c*) $$V_1 = \frac{q_1}{C_1} = \frac{2.0 \times 10^{-9}\ \text{C}}{3.0 \times 10^{-12}\ \text{F}} = 667\ \text{V} = 0.67\ \text{kV}$$

$$V_2 = \frac{q_2}{C_2} = \frac{2.0 \times 10^{-9}\ \text{C}}{6.0 \times 10^{-12}\ \text{F}} = 333\ \text{V} = 0.33\ \text{kV}$$

(*d*) Energy in $C_1 = \frac{1}{2}q_1V_1 = \frac{1}{2}(2.0 \times 10^{-9}\text{ C})(667\text{ V}) = 6.7 \times 1^{-7}\text{ J} = 0.67\ \mu\text{J}$

Energy in $C_2 = \frac{1}{2}q_2V_2 = \frac{1}{2}(2.0 \times 10^{-9}\text{ C})(333\text{ V}) = 3.3 \times 10^{-7}\text{ J} = 0.33\ \mu\text{J}$

Energy in combination $= (6.7 + 3.3) \times 10^{-7}\text{ J} = 10 \times 10^{-7}\text{ J} = 1.0\ \mu\text{J}$

The last result is also directly given by $\frac{1}{2}qV$ or $\frac{1}{2}C_{eq}V^2$.

**25.24 [II]** The parallel capacitor combination shown in Fig. 25-7 is connected across a 120-V source. Determine the equivalent capacitance $C_{eq}$, the charge on each capacitor, and the charge on the combination.

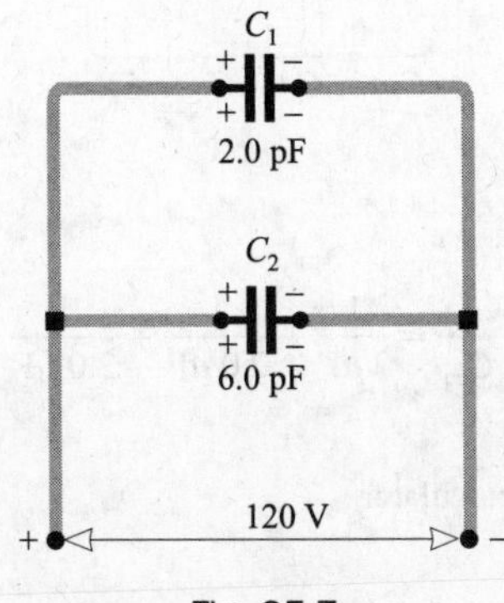


Fig. 25-7

For a parallel combination,

$$C_{eq} = C_1 + C_2 = 2.0\text{ pF} + 6.0\text{ pF} = 8.0\text{ pF}$$

Each capacitor has a 120-V potential difference impressed on it. Therefore,

$$q_1 = C_1V_1 = (2.0 \times 10^{-12}\text{ F})(120\text{ V}) = 0.24\text{ nC}$$

$$q_2 = C_2V_2 = (6.0 \times 10^{-12}\text{ F})(120\text{ V}) = 0.72\text{ nC}$$

The charge on the combination is $q_1 + q_2 = 960$ pC. Or, we could write

$$q = C_{eq}V = (8.0 \times 10^{-12}\text{ F})(120\text{ V}) = 0.96\text{ nC}$$

**25.25 [II]** Examine the circuit drawn in Fig. 25-8(*a*). Determine the equivalent capacitance (*a*) between terminals A and B (*b*) between terminals B and C.

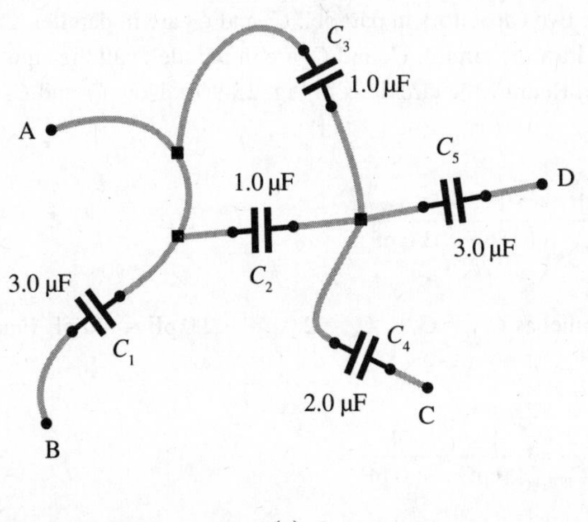


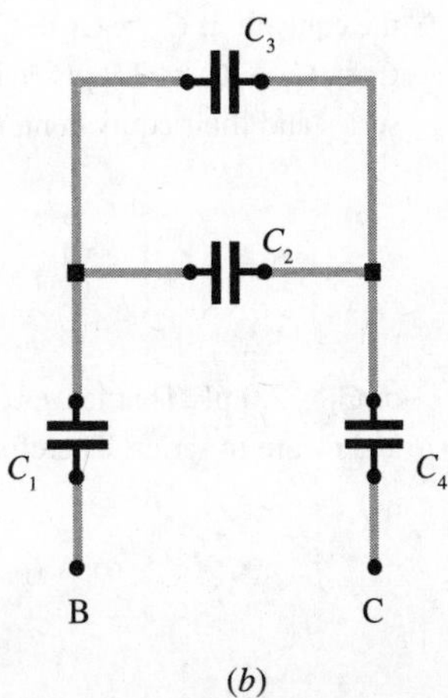


Fig. 25-8

(*a*) We can go directly from A to B by only one path and it's through $C_1$. The rest of the circuit is shorted out and does not contribute to the equivalent capacitance. Hence, the capacitance measured across A-B is just 3.0 μF. In other words, a voltage source placed A-B would only charge $C_1$.

(*b*) By contrast, we can go from B to C along two paths, and if a voltage were put across B-C, all the capacitors in those two paths ($C_1$, $C_2$, $C_3$, and $C_4$) would become charged. As for $C_5$ it's not in either path from B to C and can be ignored. Now redraw the circuit as in Fig. 25-8(*b*). Capacitors $C_2$ and $C_3$ are in parallel, and their equivalent, call it $C_6$, is given by $C_6 = C_2 + C_3 = 1.0\ \mu\text{F} + 1.0\ \mu\text{F} = 2.0\ \mu\text{F}$. Capacitors $C_1$, $C_6$, and $C_4$ are then in series between terminals B and C. Hence,

$$\frac{1}{C_{eq}} = \frac{1}{C_1} + \frac{1}{C_6} + \frac{1}{C_4}$$

and

$$\frac{1}{C_{eq}} = \frac{1}{3\ \mu\text{F}} + \frac{1}{2.0\ \mu\text{F}} + \frac{1}{2.0\ \mu\text{F}}$$

Using the $1/x$ key on your calculator

$$\frac{1}{C_{eq}} = 1.333\ \mu\text{F}^{-1} \quad \text{and} \quad C_{eq} = 0.75\ \mu\text{F}$$

Alternatively, combining series capacitors two at a time and calling $C_7$ the equivalent of $C_6$ and $C_4$,

$$C_7 = \frac{C_6\, C_4}{C_6 + C_4} = \left(\frac{2.0 \times 2.0}{2.0 + 2.0}\right)\mu\text{F} = 1.0\ \mu\text{F}$$

Thus for the whole circuit,

$$C_{eq} = \frac{C_7\, C_1}{C_7 + C_1} = \left(\frac{1.0 \times 3.0}{1.0 + 4.0}\right)\mu\text{F} = \tfrac{3}{4}\ \mu\text{F}$$

and that's the same result we got above.

**25.26 [III]** For the circuit pictured in Fig. 25-9(*a*) find the equivalent capacitance between terminals A and B.

Start the analysis someplace where you see two capacitors in parallel. $C_1$ and $C_2$ are in parallel. Call the equivalent $C_7 = C_1 + C_2 = 6.0$ pF. Redraw the circuit. $C_5$ and $C_6$ are in parallel; call the equivalent $C_8 = C_5 + C_6 = 2.0\ \text{pF} + 2.0\ \text{pF} = 4.0$ pF. Redraw the circuit as in Fig. 25-9(*b*). Now $C_7$ and $C_3$ are in series and their equivalent, $C_9$, is given by

$$\frac{1}{C_9} = \frac{1}{C_7} + \frac{1}{C_3} = \frac{1}{6.0\ \text{pF}} + \frac{1}{3.0\ \text{pF}}$$

or $C_9 = 2.0$ pF. That leaves $C_9$ and $C_4$ in parallel as $C_{10} = C_9 + C_4 = 2.0\ \text{pF} + 2.0\ \text{pF} = 4.0$ pF. Finally, $C_{10}$ and $C_8$ are in series. Therefore,

$$\frac{1}{C_{eq}} = \frac{1}{C_{10}} + \frac{1}{C_8} = \frac{1}{4.0\ \text{pF}} + \frac{1}{4.0\ \text{pF}}$$

and $C_{eq} = 2.0$ pF.

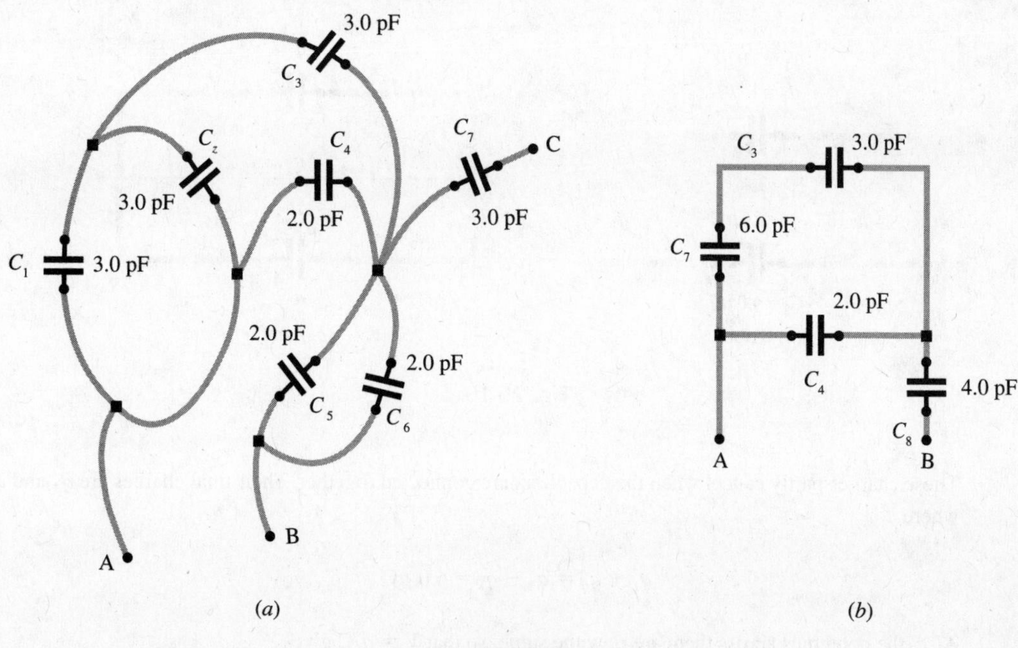


Fig. 25-9

**25.27 [III]** A laboratory capacitor consists of two parallel conducting plates, each with area 200 cm$^2$, separated by a 0.40-cm air gap. (*a*) Compute its capacitance. (*b*) If the capacitor is connected across a 500-V source, find the charge on it, the energy stored in it, and the value of $E$ between the plates. (*c*) If a liquid with $K$ = 2.60 is poured between the plates so as to fill the air gap, how much additional charge will flow onto the capacitor from the 500-V source?

(*a*) For a parallel-plate capacitor with air gap,

$$C = K\epsilon_0 \frac{A}{d} = (1)\,(8.85\times10^{-12}\ \text{F/m})\,\frac{200\times10^{-4}\ \text{m}^2}{4.0\times10^{-3}\ \text{m}} = 4.4\times10^{-11}\ \text{F} = 44\ \text{pF}$$

(*b*) $q = CV = (4.4\times10^{-11}\ \text{F})\,(500\ \text{V}) = 2.2\times10^{-8}\ \text{C} = 22\ \text{nC}$

$$\text{Energy} = \tfrac{1}{2}qV = \tfrac{1}{2}(2.2\times10^{-8}\ \text{C})\,(500\ \text{V}) = 5.5\times10^{-6}\ \text{J} = 5.5\ \mu\text{J}$$

$$E = \frac{V}{d} = \frac{500\ \text{V}}{4.0\times10^{-3}\ \text{m}} = 1.3\times10^{5}\ \text{V/m}$$

(*c*) The capacitor will now have a capacitance $K$ = 2.60 times larger than before. Therefore,

$$q = CV = (2.60 \times 4.4 \times 10^{-11}\ \text{F})\,(500\ \text{V}) = 5.7 \times 10^{-8}\ \text{C} = 57\ \text{nC}$$

The capacitor already had a charge of 22 nC, and so 57 nC − 22 nC or 35 nC must have been added to it.

**25.28 [II]** Two capacitors, 3.0 $\mu$F and 4.0 $\mu$F, are individually charged across a 6.0-V battery. After being disconnected from the battery, they are connected together with a negative plate of one attached to the positive plate of the other. What is the final charge on each capacitor?

Let 3.0 $\mu$F = $C_1$ and 4.0 $\mu$F = $C_2$. The situation is shown in Fig. 25-10. Before being connected, their charges are

$$q_1 = C_1V = (3.0 \times 10^{-6}\ \text{F})(6.0\text{V}) = 18\ \mu\text{C}$$
$$q_2 = C_2V = (4.0 \times 10^{-6}\ \text{F})(6.0\text{V}) = 24\ \mu\text{C}$$

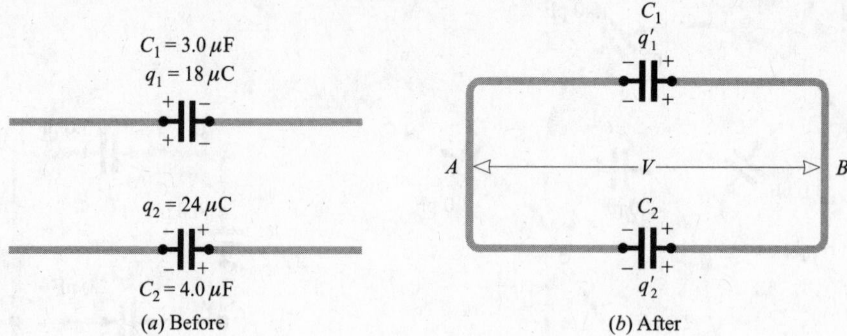


Fig. 25-10

These charges partly cancel when the capacitors are connected together. Their final charges are $q_1'$ and $q_2'$, where

$$q_1' + q_2' = q_2 - q_1 = 6.0\ \mu\text{C}$$

Also, the potentials across them are now the same, so that $V = q/C$ gives

$$\frac{q_1'}{3.0 \times 10^{-6}\ \text{F}} = \frac{q_2'}{4.0 \times 10^{-6}\ \text{F}} \quad \text{or} \quad q_1' = 0.75 q_2'$$

Substitution in the previous equation gives

$$0.75 q_2' + q_2' = 6.0\ \mu\text{C} \quad \text{or} \quad q_2' = 3.4\ \mu\text{C}$$

Then $q_1' = 0.75 q_2' = 2.6\ \mu$C.

## SUPPLEMENTARY PROBLEMS

**25.29 [I]** Two metal plates are attached to the two terminals of a 1.50-V battery. How much work is required to carry a + 5.0-$\mu$C charge across the gap (a) from the negative to the positive plate, (b) from the positive to the negative plate?

**25.30 [II]** The plates described in Problem 25.29 are in vacuum. An electron ($q = -e$, $m_e = 9.1 \times 10^{-31}$ kg) is released at the negative plate and falls freely to the positive plate. How fast is it going just before it strikes the plate?

**25.31 [II]** A proton ($q = e$, $m_p = 1.67 \times 10^{-27}$ kg) is accelerated from rest through a potential difference of 1.0 MV. What is its final speed?

**25.32 [II]** An electron gun shoots electrons ($q = -e$, $m_e = 9.1 \times 10^{-31}$ kg) at a metal plate that is 4.0 mm away in vacuum. The plate is 5.0 V lower in potential than the gun. How fast must the electrons be moving as they leave the gun if they are to reach the plate?

**25.33 [I]** The potential difference between two large parallel metal plates is 120 V. The plate separation is 3.0 mm. Find the electric field between the plates.

**25.34 [II]** An electron ($q = -e$, $m_e = 9.1 \times 10^{-31}$ kg) is shot with speed $5.0 \times 10^6$ m/s parallel to a uniform electric field of strength 3.0 kV/m. How far will the electron go before it stops?

**25.35 [II]** A potential difference of 24 kV maintains a downward-directed electric field between two horizontal parallel plates separated by 1.8 cm in vacuum. Find the charge on an oil droplet of mass $2.2 \times 10^{-13}$ kg that remains stationary in the field between the plates.

**25.36 [I]** Determine the absolute potential in air at a distance of 3.0 cm from a point charge of 500 $\mu$C.

**25.37 [II]** Compute the magnitude of the electric field and the absolute potential at a distance of 1.0 nm from a helium nucleus of charge $+2e$. What is the potential energy (relative to infinity) of a proton at this position?

**25.38 [II]** A charge of 0.20 $\mu$C is 30 cm from a point charge of 3.0 $\mu$C in vacuum. What work is required to bring the 0.20-$\mu$C charge 18 cm closer to the 3.0-$\mu$C charge?

**25.39 [II]** A point charge of $+2.0$ $\mu$C is placed at the origin of coordinates. A second, of $-3.0$ $\mu$C, is placed on the $x$-axis at $x = 100$ cm. At what point (or points) on the $x$-axis will the absolute potential be zero?

**25.40 [II]** In Problem 25.39, what is the difference in potential between the following two points on the $x$-axis: point-$A$ at $x = 0.1$ m and point-$B$ at $x = 0.9$ m? Which point is at the higher potential?

**25.41 [II]** An electron is moving in the $+x$-direction with a speed of $5.0 \times 10^6$ m/s. There is an electric field of 3.0 kV/m in the $+x$-direction. What will be the electron's speed after it has moved 1.00 cm along the field?

**25.42 [II]** An electron has a speed of $6.0 \times 10^5$ m/s as it passes point-$A$ on its way to point-$B$. Its speed at $B$ is $12 \times 10^5$ m/s. What is the potential difference between $A$ and $B$, and which is at the higher potential?

**25.43 [I]** A capacitor with air between its plates has capacitance 3.0 $\mu$F. What is its capacitance when wax of dielectric constant 2.8 is placed between the plates?

**25.44 [I]** Determine the charge on each plate of a 0.050-$\mu$F parallel-plate capacitor when the potential difference between the plates is 200 V.

**25.45 [I]** A capacitor is charged with 9.6 nC and has a 120 V potential difference between its terminals. Compute its capacitance and the energy stored in it.

**25.46 [I]** Compute the energy stored in a 60-pF capacitor (*a*) when it is charged to a potential difference of 2.0 kV and (*b*) when the charge on each plate is 30 nC.

**25.47 [II]** Three capacitors, each of capacitance 120 pF, are each charged to 0.50 kV and then connected in series. Determine (*a*) the potential difference between the end plates, (*b*) the charge on each capacitor, and (*c*) the energy stored in the system.

**25.48 [I]** Three capacitors (2.00 $\mu$F, 5.00 $\mu$F, and 7.00 $\mu$F) are connected in series. What is their equivalent capacitance?

**25.49 [I]** Three capacitors (2.00 $\mu$F, 5.00 $\mu$F, and 7.00 $\mu$F) are connected in parallel. What is their equivalent capacitance?

**25.50 [I]** The capacitor combination in Problem 25.48 is connected in series with the combination in Problem 25.49. What is the capacitance of this new combination?

**25.51 [II]** Two capacitors (0.30 and 0.50 $\mu$F) are connected in parallel. (*a*) What is their equivalent capacitance? A charge of 200 $\mu$C is now placed on the parallel combination. (*b*) What is the potential difference across it? (*c*) What are the charges on the capacitors?

**25.52 [II]** A2.0-$\mu$F capacitor is charged to 50 V and then connected in parallel (positive plate to positive plate) with a 4.0-$\mu$F capacitor charged to 100 V. (*a*) What are the final charges on the capacitors? (*b*) What is the potential difference across each?

**25.53 [II]** Repeat Problem 25.52 if the positive plate of one capacitor is connected to the negative plate of the other.

**25.54 [II]** (*a*) Calculate the capacitance of a capacitor consisting of two parallel plates separated by a layer of paraffin wax 0.50 cm thick, the area of each plate being 80 $cm^2$. The dielectric constant for the wax is 2.0. (*b*) If the capacitor is connected to a 100-V source, calculate the charge on the capacitor and the energy stored in the capacitor.

## ANSWERS TO SUPPLEMENTARY PROBLEMS

**25.29 [I]** (*a*) 7.5 $\mu$J; (*b*) −7.5 $\mu$J

**25.30 [II]** $7.3 \times 10^5$ m/s

**25.31 [II]** $1.4 \times 10^7$ m/s

**25.32 [II]** $1.3 \times 10^6$ m/s

**25.33 [I]** 40 kV/m toward negative plate

**25.34 [II]** 2.4 cm

**25.35 [II]** $1.6 \times 10^{-18}$ C = 10$e$

**25.36 [I]** 15 kV

**25.37 [II]** $2.9 \times 10^9$ N/C, 2.9 V, $4.6 \times 10^{-19}$ J

**25.38 [II]** 0.027 J

**25.39 [II]** $x = 40$ cm and $x = -0.20$ m

**25.40 [II]** $4 \times 10^5$ V, point-*A*

**25.41 [II]** $3.8 \times 10^6$ m/s

**25.42 [II]** 3.1 V, *B*

**25.43 [I]** 8.4 $\mu$F

**25.44 [I]** 10 $\mu$C

**25.45 [I]** 80 pF, 0.58 $\mu$J

**25.46 [II]** (*a*) 12 mJ; (*b*) 7.5 $\mu$J

**25.47 [II]** (*a*) 1.5 kV; (*b*) 60 nC; (*c*) 45 $\mu$J

**25.48 [I]** 1.19 $\mu$F

**25.49 [I]** 14.00 $\mu$F

**25.50 [I]** 1.09 $\mu$F

**25.51 [II]** (*a*) 0.80 $\mu$F; (*b*) 0.25 kV; (*c*) 75 $\mu$C, 0.13 mC

**25.52 [II]** (*a*) 0.17 mC, 0.33 mC, (*b*) 83V

**25.53 [II]** (*a*) 0.10 mC, 0.20 mC; (*b*) 50 V

**25.54 [II]** (*a*) 28 pF; (*b*) 2.8 nC, 0.14 $\mu$J

# CHAPTER 26

# Current, Resistance, and Ohm's Law

**A Current** ($I$) of electricity exists in a region when a net electric charge is transported from one point to another in that region. Suppose the charge is moving through a wire. If a charge $q$ is transported through a given cross section of the wire in a time $t$, then the current through the wire is

$$I = \frac{q}{t}$$

Here, $q$ is in coulombs, $t$ is in seconds, and $I$ is in **amperes** (1 A = 1 C/s). By custom ***the direction of the current is taken to be in the direction of flow of positive charge***. Thus, a flow of electrons to the right corresponds to a current to the left.

**A Battery** is a source of electrical energy. If no internal energy losses occur in the battery, then the potential difference (see Chapter 25) between its terminals is called the **electromotive force** (emf) of the battery. Unless otherwise stated, it will be assumed that the terminal potential difference of a battery is equal to its emf. The unit for emf is the same as the unit for potential difference, the volt.

**The Resistance** ($R$) of a wire or other object is a measure of the potential difference ($V$) that must be impressed across the object to cause a current of one ampere to flow through it:

$$R = \frac{V}{I}$$

The unit of resistance is the **ohm**, for which the symbol Ω (Greek omega) is used: 1Ω = 1 V/A.

**Ohm's Law** originally contained two parts. Its first part was simply the defining equation for resistance, $V = IR$. We often refer to this equation as being Ohm's Law. However, Ohm also stated that $R$ is a constant independent of $V$ and $I$. This latter part of the law is only approximately correct.

The relation $V = IR$ can be applied to any resistor, where $V$ is the potential difference (p.d.) between the two ends of the resistor, $I$ is the current through the resistor, and $R$ is the resistance of the resistor under those conditions. It is common usage to refer to $V$ as the voltage across the resistor.

**Measurement of Resistance by Ammeter and Voltmeter:** Imagine a series circuit consisting of the resistance to be measured, an ammeter, and a battery. The current is measured by the (low-resistance) ammeter. The potential difference is measured by connecting the terminals of a (high-resistance) voltmeter across the resistance—that is, in parallel with it. The resistance is computed by dividing the voltmeter reading by the ammeter reading according to Ohm's Law, $R = V/I$. (If the exact value of the resistance is required, the resistances of the voltmeter and ammeter must be considered parts of the circuit.)

**The Terminal Potential Difference** (or **voltage**) of a battery or generator when it delivers a current $I$ is related to its electromotive force $\mathscr{E}$ and its **internal resistance** $r$ as follows:

(1) When delivering current (*on discharge*):

$$\text{Terminal voltage} = (\text{emf}) - (\text{Voltage drop in internal resistance})$$

$$V = \mathscr{E} - Ir$$

(2) When receiving current (*on charge*):

$$\text{Terminal voltage} = \text{emf} + (\text{Voltage drop in internal resistance})$$

$$V = \mathscr{E} + Ir$$

(3) When no current exists:

$$\text{Terminal voltage} = \text{emf of battery or generator}$$

**Resistivity:** The resistance $R$ of a wire of length $L$ and cross-sectional area $A$ is

$$R = \rho\frac{L}{A}$$

where $\rho$ is a constant called the **resistivity**. The resistivity is a characteristic of the material from which the wire is made. For $L$ in m, $A$ in m$^2$, and $R$ in $\Omega$, the units of $\rho$ are $\Omega \cdot \text{m}$.

**Resistance Varies with Temperature:** If a wire has a resistance $R_0$ at a temperature $T_0$, then its resistance $R$ at a temperature $T$ is

$$R = R_0 + \alpha R_0(T - T_0)$$

where $\alpha$ is the **temperature coefficient of resistance** of the material of the wire. Usually $\alpha$ varies with temperature, and so this relation is applicable only over a small temperature range. The units of $\alpha$ are $\text{K}^{-1}$ or $^\circ\text{C}^{-1}$.

A similar relation applies to the variation of resistivity with temperature. If $\rho_0$ and $\rho$ are the resistivities at $T_0$ and $T$, respectively, then

$$\rho = \rho_0 + \alpha\rho_0(T - T_0)$$

**Potential Changes:** The potential difference across a resistor $R$ through which a current $I$ flows is, by Ohm's Law, $IR$. The end of the resistor at which the current enters is the high-potential end of the resistor. Current always flows "downhill," from high to low potential, through a resistor.

The positive terminal of a battery is always the high-potential terminal if internal resistance of the battery is negligible or small. This is true irrespective of the direction of the current through the battery.

## SOLVED PROBLEMS

**26.1 [I]** A steady current of 0.50 A flows through a wire. How much charge passes through the wire in one minute?

Because $I = q/t$, it follows that $q = It = (0.50\text{ A})(60\text{ s}) = 30\text{ C}$. (Recall that $1\text{ A} = 1\text{ C/s}$.)

**26.2 [I]** How many electrons flow through a light bulb each second if the current through the light bulb is 0.75 A?

From $I = q/t$, the charge flowing through the bulb in 1.0 s is

$$q = It = (0.75\text{ A})(1.0\text{ s}) = 0.75\text{ C}$$

But the magnitude of the charge on each electron is $e = 1.6 \times 10^{-19}$ C. Therefore,

$$\text{Number} = \frac{\text{Charge}}{\text{Charge/electron}} = \frac{0.75\text{ C}}{1.6\times10^{-19}\text{C}} = 4.7\times10^{18}$$

**26.3 [I]** A light bulb has a resistance of 240 Ω when lit. How much current will flow through it when it is connected across 120 V, its normal operating voltage?

$$I = \frac{V}{R} = \frac{120\text{ V}}{240\ \Omega} = 0.500\text{ A}$$

**26.4 [I]** An electric heater uses 5.0 A when connected across 110 V. Determine its resistance.

$$R = \frac{V}{I} = \frac{110\text{ V}}{5.0\text{ A}} = 22\ \Omega$$

**26.5 [I]** What is the potential drop across an electric hot plate that draws 5.0 A when its hot resistance is 24 Ω?

$$V = IR = (5.0\text{A})(24\ \Omega) = 0.12\text{ kV}$$

**26.6 [II]** The current in Fig. 26-1 is 0.125 A in the direction shown. For each of the following pairs of points, what is their potential difference, and which point is at the higher potential? *(a) A, B*; *(b) B, C*; *(c) C, D*; *(d) D, E*; *(e) C, E*; *(f) E, C*.

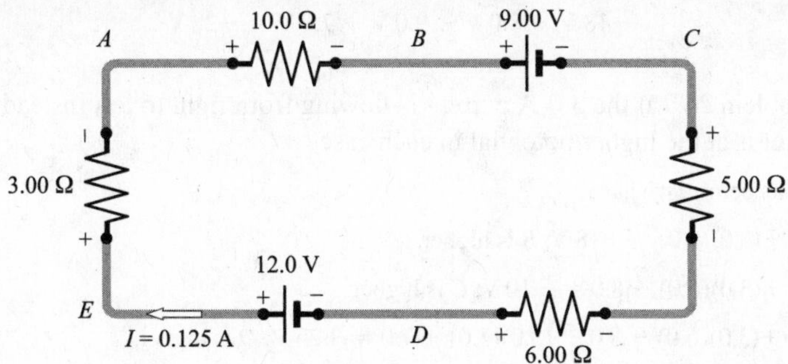


Fig. 26-1

Recall the following facts: (1) The current is the same (0.125 A) at all points in this circuit because the charge has no other place to flow. (2) Current always flows from high to low potential through a resistor. (3) The positive terminal of a pure emf (the long side of its symbol) is always the high-potential terminal. Mark the long sides of the batteries with plus signs (+) and the short sides with minus signs (−). Current streams out of the positive terminal of the 12-V battery and, in this case, flows clockwise around the circuit because the 12-V battery dominates over the 9.0-V battery. For each resistor place a + on the side where current enters and a − where it leaves. When current passes through a resistor from + to − it experiences what is called a "voltage drop." Taking potential drops as negative:

(*a*) $V_{AB} = -IR = -(0.125\ \text{A})(10.0\ \Omega) = -1.25\ \text{V}$; *A* is higher.

(*b*) $V_{BC} = -\mathscr{E} = -9.00\ \text{V}$; *B* is higher.

(*c*) $V_{CD} = -(0.125\ \text{A})(5.00\ \Omega) - (0.125\ \text{A})(6.00\ \Omega) = -1.38\ \text{V}$; *C* is higher.

(*d*) $V_{DE} = +\mathscr{E} = +12.0\ \text{V}$; *E* is higher.

(*e*) $V_{CE} = -(0.125\ \text{A})(5.00\ \Omega) - (0.125\ \text{A})(6.00\ \Omega) + 12.0\ \text{V} = +10.6\ \text{V}$; *E* is higher.

(*f*) $V_{EC} = -(0.125\ \text{A})(3.00\ \Omega) - (0.125\ \text{A})(10.0\ \Omega) - 9.00\ \text{V} = -10.6\ \text{V}$; *E* is higher.

Notice that the answers to (*e*) and (*f*) agree with each other.

**26.7 [II]** A current of 3.0 A flows through the wire shown in Fig. 26-2. What will a voltmeter read when connected from (*a*) *A* to *B*, (*b*) *A* to *C*, (*c*) *A* to *D*?

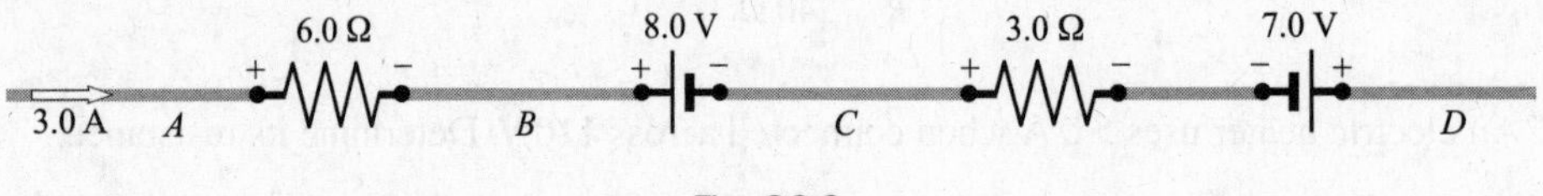


Fig. 26-2

Put plus and minus signs on all of the resistors given that the current flows from left to right. Label each battery, as ever, with the + on the long side of the symbol.

(*a*) Point-*A* is at the higher potential because current always flows "downhill" through a resistor (+ to −). There is a potential drop of $IR = (3.0\ \text{A})(6.0\ \Omega) = 18\ \text{V}$ from *A* to *B*. The voltmeter will read −18 V.

(*b*) In going from *B* to *C*, one goes from the positive to the negative side of the battery; hence, there is a potential drop of 8.0 *V* from *B* to *C*. The drop adds to the drop of 18 V from *A* to *B*, found in (*a*), to give a 26 V drop from *A* to *C*. The voltmeter will read −26 V from *A* to *C*.

(*c*) From *C* to *D*, there is first a drop of $IR = (3.0\text{A})(3.0\ \Omega) = 9.0\ \text{V}$ through the resistor. Then, because one goes from the negative to the positive terminal of the 7.0 V battery, there is a 7.0-V rise through the battery. The voltmeter connected from *A* to *D* will read

$$-18\ \text{V} - 8.0\ \text{V} - 9.0\ \text{V} + 7.0\ \text{V} = -28\ \text{V}$$

**26.8 [II]** Repeat Problem 26.7 if the 3.0-A current is flowing from right to left instead of from left to right. Which point is at the higher potential in each case?

Proceeding as before, we have

(*a*) $V_{AB} = +(3.0)(6.0) = +18\ \text{V}$; *B* is higher.

(*b*) $V_{AC} = +(3.0)(6.0) - 8.0 = +10\ \text{V}$; *C* is higher.

(*c*) $V_{AD} = +(3.0)(6.0) - 8.0 + (3.0)(3.0) + 7.0 = +26\ \text{V}$; *D* is higher.

**26.9 [I]** A dry cell has an emf of 1.52 V. Its terminal potential drops to zero when a current of 25 A passes through it. What is its internal resistance?

As is shown in Fig. 26-3, the battery acts like a pure emf $\mathscr{E}$ in series with a resistor *r*. We are told that, under the conditions shown, the potential difference from *A* to *B* is zero. Therefore,

$$0 = +\mathscr{E} - Ir \quad \text{or} \quad 0 = 1.52\ \text{V} - (25\ \text{A})r$$

from which the internal resistance is $r = 0.061\ \Omega$.

**26.10 [II]** A direct-current generator has an emf of 120 V; that is, its terminal voltage is 120 V when no current is flowing from it. At an output of 20 A, the terminal potential is 115 V. (*a*) What is the internal resistance $r$ of the generator? (*b*) What will be the terminal voltage at an output of 40 A?

The situation is much like that shown in Fig. 26-3. Now, however, $\mathscr{E} = 120$ V and $I$ is no longer 25 A.

(*a*) In this case, $I = 20$ A and the p.d. from $A$ to $B$ is 115 V. Therefore,

$$115\text{ V} = +120\text{ V} - (20\text{ A})r$$

from which $r = 0.25\ \Omega$.

(*b*) Now $I = 40$ A. So

Terminal p.d. $= \mathscr{E} - Ir = 120\text{ V} - (40\text{ A})(0.25\ \Omega) = 110\text{ V}$

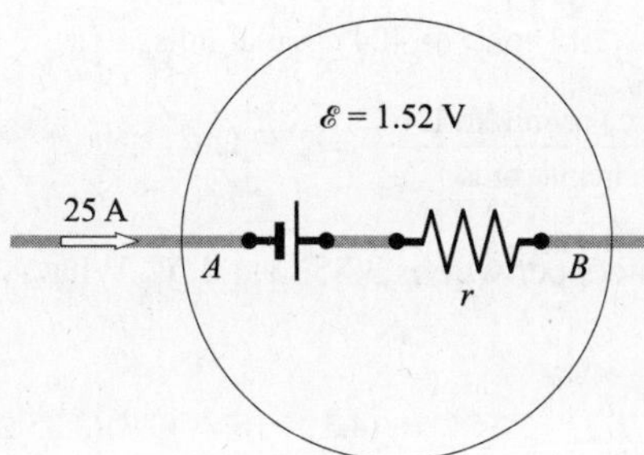


Fig. 26-3

**26.11 [I]** As shown in Fig. 26-4 the ammeter–voltmeter method is used to measure an unknown resistance $R$. The ammeter reads 0.3 A, and the voltmeter reads 1.50 V. Compute the value of $R$ if the ammeter and voltmeter are ideal.

$$R = \frac{V}{I} = \frac{1.50\text{ V}}{0.3\text{ A}} = 5\ \Omega$$

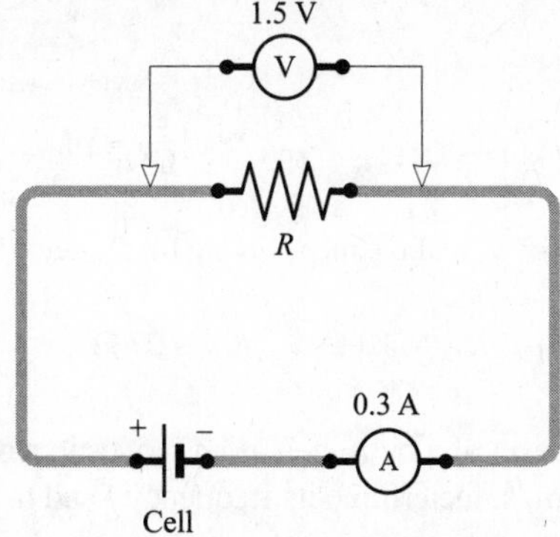


Fig. 26-4

**26.12 [I]** A metal rod is 2 m long and 8 mm in diameter. Compute its resistance if the resistivity of the metal is $1.76 \times 10^{-8}\ \Omega \cdot \text{m}$.

$$R = \rho\frac{L}{A} = (1.76\times10^{-8}\,\Omega\cdot\text{m})\frac{2\text{ m}}{\pi(4\times10^{-3}\text{ m})^2} = 7\times10^{-4}\ \Omega$$

**26.13 [I]** Number 10 wire has a diameter of 2.59 mm. How many meters of number 10 aluminum wire are needed to give a resistance of 1.0 Ω? $\rho$ for aluminum is $2.8 \times 10^{-8}\ \Omega \cdot \text{m}$.

From $R = \rho L/A$,

$$L = \frac{RA}{\rho} = \frac{(1.0\ \Omega)(\pi)(2.59 \times 10^{-3}\ \text{m})^2/4}{2.8 \times 10^{-8}\ \Omega \cdot \text{m}} = 0.19\ \text{km}$$

**26.14 [II]** (This problem introduces a unit sometimes used in the United States.) Number 24 copper wire has diameter 0.020 1 in. Compute (*a*) the cross-sectional area of the wire in circular mils and (*b*) the resistance of 100 ft of the wire. The resistivity of copper is 10.4 Ω·circular mils/ft.

The area of a circle in circular mils is defined as the square of the diameter of the circle expressed in mils, where 1 mil = 0.001 in.

(*a*) Area in circular mils = $(20.1\ \text{mil})^2$ = 404 circular mils

(*b*) $$R = \rho \frac{L}{A} = \frac{(10.4\ \Omega \cdot \text{circular mil/ft})\ 100\ \text{ft}}{404\ \text{circular mils}} = 2.57\ \Omega$$

**26.15 [I]** The resistance of a coil of copper wire is 3.35 Ω at 0 °C. What is its resistance at 50 °C? For copper, $\alpha = 4.3 \times 10^{-3}\ ^\circ\text{C}^{-1}$.

$$R = R_0 + \alpha R_0(T - T_0) = 3.35\ \Omega + (4.3 \times 10^{-3}\ ^\circ\text{C}^{-1})(3.35\ \Omega)(50\ ^\circ\text{C}) = 4.1\ \Omega$$

**26.16 [II]** A resistor is to have a constant resistance of 30.0 Ω, independent of temperature. For this, an aluminum resistor with resistance $R_{01}$ at 0 °C is used in series with a carbon resistor with resistance $R_{02}$ at 0 °C. Evaluate $R_{01}$ and $R_{02}$, given that $\alpha_1 = 3.9 \times 10^{-3}\ ^\circ\text{C}^{-1}$ for aluminum and $\alpha_2 = -0.50 \times 10^{-3}\ ^\circ\text{C}^{-1}$ for carbon.

The combined resistance at temperature $T$ will be

$$\begin{aligned} R &= [R_{01} + \alpha_1 R_{01}(T - T_0)] + [R_{02} + \alpha_2 R_{02}(T - T_0)] \\ &= (R_{01} + R_{02}) + (\alpha_1 R_{01} + \alpha_2 R_{02})(T - T_0) \end{aligned}$$

We thus have the two conditions

$$R_{01} + R_{02} = 30.0\ \Omega \qquad \text{and} \qquad \alpha_1 R_{01} + \alpha_2 R_{02} = 0$$

Substituting the given values of $\alpha_1$ and $\alpha_2$, then solving for $R_{01}$ and $R_{02}$,

$$R_{01} = 3.4\ \Omega \qquad R_{02} = 27\ \Omega$$

**26.17 [II]** In the Bohr model, the electron of a hydrogen atom moves in a circular orbit of radius $5.3 \times 10^{-11}$ m with a speed of $2.2 \times 10^6$ m/s. Determine its frequency $f$ and the current $I$ in the orbit.

$$f = \frac{v}{2\pi r} = \frac{2.2 \times 10^6\ \text{m/s}}{2\pi(5.3 \times 10^{-11}\ \text{m})} = 6.6 \times 10^{15}\ \text{rev/s}$$

Each time the electron goes around the orbit, it carries a charge $e$ around the loop. The charge passing a point on the loop each second is

$$I = ef = (1.6 \times 10^{-19}\ \text{C})(6.6 \times 10^{15}\ \text{s}^{-1}) = 1.06 \times 10^{-3}\ \text{A} = 1.1\ \text{mA}$$

**26.18 [II]** A wire that has a resistance of 5.0 Ω is passed through an extruder so as to make it into a new wire three times as long as the original. What is the new resistance?

Use $R = \rho L/A$ to find the resistance of the new wire. To find $\rho$, use the original data for the wire. Let $L_0$ and $A_0$ be the initial length and cross-sectional area, respectively. Then

$$5.0\ \Omega = \rho L_0/A_0 \qquad \text{or} \qquad \rho = (A_0/L_0)(5.0\ \Omega)$$

We were told that $L = 3L_0$. To find $A$ in terms of $A_0$, note that the volume of the wire cannot change. Hence,

$$V_0 = L_0 A_0 \qquad \text{and} \qquad V_0 = LA$$

from which

$$LA = L_0 A_0 \qquad \text{or} \qquad A = \left(\frac{L_0}{L_0}\right)(A_0) = \frac{A_0}{3}$$

Therefore,

$$R = \frac{\rho L}{A} = \frac{(A_0/L_0)(5.0\ \Omega)(3L_0)}{A_0/3} = 9(5.0\ \Omega) = 45\ \Omega$$

**26.19 [II]** It is desired to make a wire that has a resistance of 8.0 Ω from 5.0 $\text{cm}^3$ of metal that has a resistivity of $9.0 \times 10^{-8}\ \Omega \cdot \text{m}$. What should the length and cross-sectional area of the wire be?

Use $R = \rho L/A$ with $R = 8.0\ \Omega$ and $\rho = 9.0 \times 10^{-8}\ \Omega \cdot \text{m}$. We know further that the volume of the wire (which is $LA$) is $5.0 \times 10^{-6}\ \text{m}^3$. Therefore, we have two equations to solve for $L$ and $A$:

$$R = 8.0\ \Omega = (9.0 \times 10^{-8}\ \Omega \cdot \text{m})\left(\frac{L}{A}\right) \qquad \text{and} \qquad LA = 5.0 \times 10^{-6}\ \text{m}^3$$

From them, it follows that $L = 21$ m and $A = 2.4 \times 10^{-7}\ \text{m}^2$.

## SUPPLEMENTARY PROBLEMS

**26.20 [I]** How many electrons per second pass through a section of wire carrying a current of 0.70 A?

**26.21 [I]** An electron gun in a TV set shoots out a beam of electrons. The beam current is $1.0 \times 10^{-5}$ A. How many electrons strike the TV screen each second? How much charge strikes the screen in a minute?

**26.22 [I]** What is the current through an 8.0-Ω toaster when it is operating on 120 V?

**26.23 [I]** What potential difference is required to pass 3.0 A through 28 Ω?

**26.24 [I]** Determine the potential difference between the ends of a wire of resistance 5.0 Ω if 720 C passes through it per minute.

**26.25 [I]** A copper bus bar carrying 1200 A has a potential drop of 1.2 mV along 24 cm of its length. What is the resistance per meter of the bar?

**26.26 [I]** An ammeter is connected in series with an unknown resistance, and a voltmeter is connected across the terminals of the resistance. If the ammeter reads 1.2 A and the voltmeter reads 18 V, compute the value of the resistance. Assume ideal meters.

**26.27 [I]** An electric utility company runs two 100 m copper wires from the street mains up to a customer's premises. If the wire resistance is 0.10 Ω per 1000 m, calculate the line voltage drop for an estimated load current of 120 A.

**26.28 [I]** When the insulation resistance between a motor winding and the motor frame is tested, the value obtained is 1.0 megohm ($10^6$ Ω). How much current passes through the insulation of the motor if the test voltage is 1000 V?

**26.29 [I]** Compute the internal resistance of an electric generator which has an emf of 120 V and a terminal voltage of 110 V when supplying 20 A.

**26.30 [I]** A dry cell delivering 2 A has a terminal voltage of 1.41 V. What is the internal resistance of the cell if its open-circuit voltage is 1.59 V?

**26.31 [II]** A cell has an emf of 1.54 V. When it is in series with a 1.0-Ω resistance, the reading of a voltmeter connected across the cell terminals is 1.40 V. Determine the cell's internal resistance.

**26.32 [I]** The internal resistance of a 6.4-V storage battery is 4.8 mΩ. What is the theoretical maximum current on short circuit? (In practice the leads and connections have some resistance, and this theoretical value would not be attained.)

**26.33 [I]** A battery has an emf of 13.2 V and an internal resistance of 24.0 mΩ. If the load current is 20.0 A, find the terminal voltage.

**26.34 [I]** A storage battery has an emf of 25.0 V and an internal resistance of 0.200 Ω. Compute its terminal voltage (*a*) when it is delivering 8.00 A and (*b*) when it is being charged with 8.00 A.

**26.35 [II]** A battery charger supplies a current of 10 A to charge a storage battery which has an open-circuit voltage of 5.6 V. If the voltmeter connected across the charger reads 6.8 V, what is the internal resistance of the battery at this time?

**26.36 [II]** Find the potential difference between points-*A* and -*B* in Fig. 26-5 if *R* is 0.70 Ω. Which point is at the higher potential?

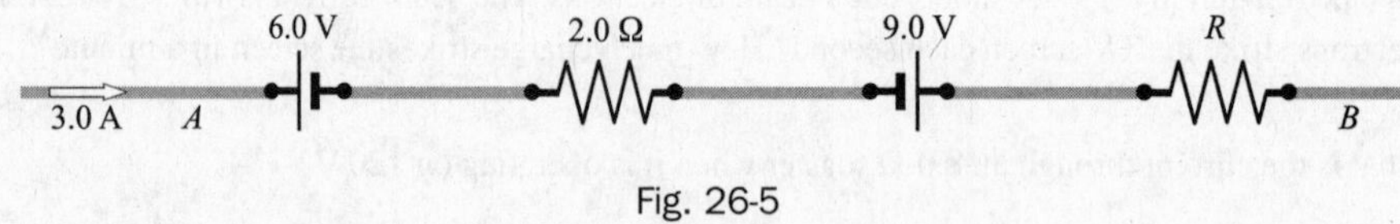


Fig. 26-5

**26.37 [II]** Repeat Problem 26.36 if the current flows in the opposite direction and $R = 0.70$ Ω.

**26.38 [II]** In Fig. 26-5, how large must *R* be if the potential drop from *A* to *B* is 12 V?

**26.39 [II]** For the circuit of Fig. 26-6, find the potential difference from (*a*) *A* to *B*, (*b*) *B* to *C*, and (*c*) *C* to *A*. Notice that the current is given as 2.0 A.

**26.40 [I]** Compute the resistance of 180 m of silver wire having a cross section of 0.30 mm$^2$. The resistivity of silver is $1.6 \times 10^{-8}$ Ω·m.

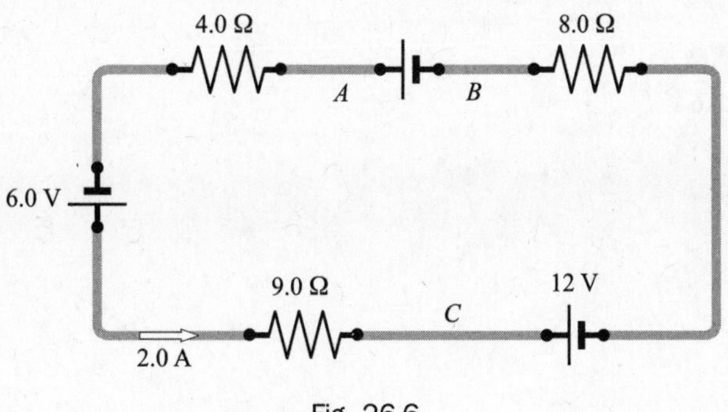


Fig. 26-6

**26.41 [I]** The resistivity of aluminum is $2.8 \times 10^{-8}\ \Omega \cdot \text{m}$. How long a piece of aluminum wire 1.0 mm in diameter is needed to give a resistance of 4.0 Ω?

**26.42 [II]** Number 6 copper wire has a diameter of 0.162 in. (*a*) Calculate its area in circular mils. (*b*) If $\rho = 10.4\ \Omega \cdot \text{circular mils/ft}$, find the resistance of $1.0 \times 10^3$ ft of the wire. (Refer to Problem 26.14.)

**26.43 [II]** A coil of wire has a resistance of 25.00 Ω at 20 °C and a resistance of 25.17 Ω at 35 °C. What is its temperature coefficient of resistance?

## ANSWERS TO SUPPLEMENTARY PROBLEMS

**26.20 [I]** $4.4 \times 10^{18}$ electrons/s

**26.21 [I]** $6.3 \times 10^{13}$ electrons/s, $-6.0 \times 10^{-4}$ C/min

**26.22 [I]** 15 A

**26.23 [I]** 84 V

**26.24 [I]** 60 V

**26.25 [I]** 4.2 $\mu\Omega$/m

**26.26 [I]** 15 Ω

**26.27 [I]** 2.4 V

**26.28 [I]** 1.0 mA

**26.29 [I]** 0.50 Ω

**26.30 [I]** 0.09 Ω

**26.31 [II]** 0.10 Ω

**26.32 [I]** 1.3 kA

**26.33 [I]** 12.7 V

**26.34 [I]** (*a*) 23.4 V; (*b*) 26.6 V

**26.35 [II]** 0.12 Ω

**26.36 [II]** −5.1 V, point-*A*

**26.37 [II]** 11.1 V, point-*B*

**26.38 [II]** 3.0 Ω

**26.39 [II]** (*a*) −48 V; (*b*) +28 V; (*c*) +20 V

**26.40 [I]** 9.6 Ω

**26.41 [I]** 0.11 km

**26.42 [II]** (*a*) $26.0 \times 10^3$ circular mils; (*b*) 0.40 Ω

**26.43 [II]** $4.5 \times 10^{-4}$ °C$^{-1}$

# CHAPTER 27

# Electrical Power

**The Electrical Work** (in joules) required to transfer a charge $q$ (in coulombs) through a potential difference $V$ (in volts) is given by

$$W = qV$$

When $q$ and $V$ are given their proper signs (i.e., voltage rises are positive, and drops negative), the work will have its proper sign. Thus, to carry a positive charge through a potential rise, a positive amount of work must be done on the charge.

**The Electrical Power** (P), in watts, delivered by an energy source as it carries a charge $q$ (in coulombs) through a potential rise $V$ (in volts) in a time $t$ (in seconds) is

$$\text{Power finished} = \frac{\text{Work}}{\text{Time}}$$

$$\text{P} = \frac{Vq}{t}$$

Because $q/t = I$, this can be rewritten as

$$\text{P} = VI$$

where $I$ is in amperes.

**The Power Loss in a Resistor** is found by replacing $V$ in $VI$ by $IR$, or by replacing $I$ in $VI$ by $V/R$, to obtain

$$\text{P} = VI = I^2R = \frac{V^2}{R}$$

**The Thermal Energy Generated in a Resistor** per second is equal to the power loss in the resistor:

$$\text{P} = VI = I^2R$$

**Convenient Conversions:**

$$1\text{ W} = 1\text{ J/s} = 0.239\text{ cal/s} = 0.738\text{ ft}\cdot\text{lb/s}$$

$$1\text{ kW} = 1.341\text{ hp} = 56.9\text{ Btu/min}$$

$$1\text{ hp} = 746\text{ W} = 33\,000\text{ ft}\cdot\text{lb/min} = 42.4\text{ Btu/min}$$

$$1\text{ kW}\cdot\text{h} = 3.6 \times 10^6\text{ J} = 3.6\text{ MJ}$$

## SOLVED PROBLEMS

**27.1 [I]** Compute the work and the average power required to transfer 96 kC of charge in one hour (1.0 h) through a potential rise of 50 V.

The work done equals the change in potential energy:

$$W = qV = (96\,000 \text{ C})(50 \text{ V}) = 4.8 \times 10^6 \text{ J} = 4.8 \text{ MJ}$$

Power is the rate of transferring energy:

$$\text{P} = \frac{W}{t} = \frac{4.8 \times 10^6 \text{ J}}{3600 \text{ s}} = 1.3 \text{ kW}$$

**27.2 [I]** How much current does a 60-W light bulb draw when connected to its proper voltage of 120 V?

From $\text{P} = VI$,

$$I = \frac{\text{P}}{V} = \frac{60 \text{ W}}{120 \text{ V}} = 0.50 \text{ A}$$

**27.3 [I]** An electric motor takes 5.0 A from a 110 V line. Determine the power input and the energy, in J and kW·h, supplied to the motor in 2.0 h.

$$\begin{aligned}\text{Power} &= \text{P} = VI = (110 \text{ V})(5.0 \text{ A}) = 0.55 \text{ kW}\\ \text{Energy} &= \text{P}t = (550 \text{ W})(7200 \text{ s}) = 4.0 \text{ MJ}\\ &= (0.55 \text{ kW})(2.0 \text{ h}) = 1.1 \text{ kW}\cdot\text{h}\end{aligned}$$

**27.4 [I]** An electric iron of resistance 20 Ω takes a current of 5.0 A. Calculate the thermal energy, in joules, developed in 30 s.

$$\begin{aligned}\text{Energy} &= \text{P}t\\ \text{Energy} &= I^2Rt = (5 \text{ A})^2(20\ \Omega)(30 \text{ s}) = 15\text{kJ}\end{aligned}$$

**27.5 [II]** An electric heater of resistance 8.0 Ω draws 15 A from the service mains. At what rate is thermal energy developed, in W? What is the cost of operating the heater for a period of 4.0 h at 10 ¢/kW·h?

$$W = I^2R = (15 \text{ A})^2(8.0\ \Omega) = 1800 \text{ W} = 1.8 \text{ kW}$$

$$\text{Cost} = (1.8 \text{ kW})(4.0 \text{ h})(10\ \text{¢}/\text{kW}\cdot\text{h}) = 72\ \text{¢}$$

**27.6 [II]** A coil develops 800 cal/s when 20 V is supplied across its ends. Compute its resistance.

$$\text{P} = (800 \text{ cal/s})(4.184 \text{ J/cal}) = 3347 \text{ J/s}$$

Then, because $\text{P} = V^2/R$,

$$R = \frac{(20 \text{ V})^2}{3347 \text{ J/s}} = 0.12\ \Omega$$

**27.7 [II]** A line having a total resistance of 0.20 Ω delivers 10.00 kW at 250 V to a small factory. What is the efficiency of the transmission?

The line dissipates power due to its resistance. Consequently we'll need to find the current in the line. Use P = $VI$ to find $I$ = P/$V$. Then

$$\text{Power lost in line} = I^2R = \left(\frac{P}{V}\right)^2 R = \left(\frac{10\,000\ \text{W}}{250\ \text{V}}\right)^2 (0.20\ \Omega) = 0.32\ \text{kW}$$

$$\text{Efficiency} = \frac{\text{Power delivered by line}}{\text{Power supplied to line}} = \frac{10.00\ \text{kW}}{(10.00 + 0.32)\ \text{kW}} = 0.970 = 97.0\%$$

**27.8 [II]** A hoist motor supplied by a 240-V source requires 12.0 A to lift an 800-kg load at a rate of 9.00 m/min. Determine the power input to the motor and the power output, both in horsepower, and the overall efficiency of the system.

$$\text{Power input} = IV = (12.0\ \text{A})\,(240\ \text{V}) = 2880\ \text{W} = (2.88\ \text{kW})\,(1.34\ \text{hp/kW}) = 3.86\ \text{hp}$$

$$\text{Power output} = Fv = (800 \times 9.81\ \text{N})\left(\frac{9.00\ \text{m}}{\text{min}}\right)\left(\frac{1.00\ \text{min}}{60.0\ \text{s}}\right)\left(\frac{1.00\ \text{hp}}{746\ \text{J/s}}\right) = 1.58\ \text{hp}$$

$$\text{Efficiency} = \frac{1.58\ \text{hp output}}{3.86\ \text{hp input}} = 0.408 = 40.8\%$$

**27.9 [II]** The lights on a car are inadvertently left on. They dissipate 95.0 W. About how long will it take for the fully charged 12.0-V car battery to run down if the battery is rated at 150 ampere-hours (A·h)?

As an approximation, assume the battery maintains 12.0 V until it goes dead. Its 150-A·h rating means it can supply the energy equivalent of a 150-A current that flows for 1.00 h (3600 s). Therefore, the total energy the battery can supply is

Total output energy = (Power)(Time) = $(VI)t$ = (12.0 V × 150 A)(3600 s) = 6.48 × $10^6$ J

The energy consumed by the lights in a time $t$ is

$$\text{Energy dissipated} = (95\ \text{W})(t)$$

Equating these two energies and solving for $t$, we find $t$ = 6.82 × $10^4$ s = 18.9 h.

**27.10 [II]** What is the cost of electrically heating 50 liters of water from 40 °C to 100 °C at 8.0 ¢/kW·h?

$$\text{Heat gained by water} = (\text{Mass}) \times (\text{Specific heat}) \times (\text{Temperature rise})$$

$$= (50\ \text{kg}) \times (1000\ \text{cal/kg} \cdot {}^\circ\text{C}) \times (60\ {}^\circ\text{C}) = 3.0 \times 10^6\ \text{cal}$$

$$\text{Cost} = (3.0 \times 10^6\ \text{cal})\left(\frac{4.184\ \text{J}}{1\ \text{cal}}\right)\left(\frac{1\ \text{kW}\cdot\text{h}}{3.6 \times 10^6\ \text{J}}\right)\left(\frac{8.0\ ¢}{1\ \text{kW}\cdot\text{h}}\right) = 28\ ¢$$

## SUPPLEMENTARY PROBLEMS

**27.11 [I]** A resistive heater is labeled 1600 W/120 V. How much current does the heater draw from a 120-V source?

**27.12 [I]** A bulb is stamped 40 W/120 V. What is its resistance when lighted by a 120-V source?

**27.13 [II]** A spark of artificial 10.0-MV lightning had an energy output of 0.125 MW·s. How many coulombs of charge flowed?

**27.14 [II]** A current of 1.5 A exists in a conductor whose terminals are connected across a potential difference of 100 V. Compute the total charge transferred in one minute, the work done in transferring this charge, and the power expended in heating the conductor if all the electrical energy is converted into heat.

**27.15 [II]** An electric motor takes 15.0 A at 110 V. Determine (*a*) the power input and (*b*) the cost of operating the motor for 8.00 h at 10.0 ¢/kW·h.

**27.16 [I]** A current of 10 A exists in a line of 0.15 Ω resistance. Compute the rate of production of thermal energy in watts.

**27.17 [II]** An electric broiler develops 400 cal/s when the current through it is 8.0 A. Determine the resistance of the broiler.

**27.18 [II]** A 25.0-W, 120-V bulb has a cold resistance of 45.0 Ω. When the voltage is switched on, what is the instantaneous current? What is the current under normal operation?

**27.19 [II]** While carrying a current of 400 A, a defective switch becomes overheated due to faulty surface contact. A millivoltmeter connected across the switch shows a 100-mV drop. What is the power loss due to the contact resistance?

**27.20 [II]** How much power does a 60-W/120-V incandescent light bulb dissipate when operated at a voltage of 115 V? Neglect the bulb's decrease in resistance with lowered voltage.

**27.21 [II]** A house wire is to carry a current of 30 A while dissipating no more than 1.40 W of heat per meter of its length. What is the minimum diameter of the wire if its resistivity is $1.68 \times 10^{-8}\,\Omega\cdot\text{m}$?

**27.22 [II]** A 10.0-Ω electric heater operates on a 110-V line. Compute the rate at which it develops thermal energy in W and in cal/s.

**27.23 [III]** An electric motor, which has 95 percent efficiency, uses 20 A at 110 V. What is the horsepower output of the motor? How many watts are lost in thermal energy? How many calories of thermal energy are developed per second? If the motor operates for 3.0 h, what energy, in MJ and in kW·h, is dissipated?

**27.24 [II]** An electric crane uses 8.0 A at 150 V to raise a 450-kg load at the rate of 7.0 m/min. Determine the efficiency of the system.

**27.25 [III]** What should be the resistance of a heating coil which will be used to raise the temperature of 500 g of water from 28 °C to the boiling point in 2.0 minutes, assuming that 25 percent of the heat is lost? The heater operates on a 110-V line.

**27.26 [II]** Compute the cost per hour at 8.0 ¢/kW·h of electrically heating a room, if it requires 1.0 kg/h of anthracite coal having a heat of combustion of 8000 kcal/kg.

**27.27 [II]** Power is transmitted at 80 kV between two stations. If the voltage can be increased to 160 kV without a change in cable size, how much additional power can be transmitted for the same current? What effect does the power increase have on the line heating loss?

**27.28 [II]** A storage battery, of emf 6.4 V and internal resistance 0.080 Ω, is being charged by a current of 15 A. Calculate (*a*) the power loss in internal heating of the battery, (*b*) the rate at which energy is stored in the battery, and (*c*) its terminal voltage.

**27.29 [II]** A tank containing 200 kg of water was used as a constant-temperature bath. How long would it take to heat the bath from 20 °C to 25 °C with a 250-W immersion heater? Neglect the heat capacity of the tank frame and any heat losses to the air.

## ANSWERS TO SUPPLEMENTARY PROBLEMS

**27.11 [I]** 13.3 A

**27.12 [I]** 0.36 kΩ

**27.13 [II]** 0.012 5 C

**27.14 [II]** 90 C, 9.0 kJ, 0.15 kW

**27.15 [II]** (*a*) 1.65 kW; (*b*) $1.32

**27.16 [I]** 15 W

**27.17 [II]** 26 Ω

**27.18 [II]** 2.67 A, 0.208 A

**27.19 [II]** 40.0 W

**27.20 [II]** 55 W

**27.21 [II]** 3.7 mm

**27.22 [II]** 1.21 kW = 290 cal/s

**27.23 [III]** 2.8 hp, 0.11 kW, 26 cal/s, 24 MJ = 6.6 kW·h

**27.24 [II]** 43%

**27.25 [III]** 7.2 Ω

**27.26 [II]** 74 ¢/h

**27.27 [II]** Additional power = Original power, no effect

**27.28 [II]** (*a*) 18 W; (*b*) 96 W; (*c*) 7.6 V

**27.29 [II]** 4.6 h

# Equivalent Resistance; Simple Circuits

**Resistors in Series:** When current can follow only one path as it flows through two or more resistors connected in line, the resistors are in **series**. In other words, when one and only one terminal of a resistor is connected directly to one and only one terminal of another resistor, the two are in series and the same current passes through both. A **node** is a point where three or more current-carrying wires or branches meet. There are no nodes between circuit elements (such as capacitors, resistors, and batteries) that are connected in series. A typical case is shown in Fig. 28-1(*a*). For several resistors in series, their equivalent resistance $R_{eq}$ is given by

$$R_{eq} = R_1 + R_2 + R_3 + \dots \qquad \text{(series combination)}$$

where $R_1, R_2, R_3, \dots,$ are the resistances of the several resistors and each is in series with all of the others. Observe that resistances in series combine like capacitances in parallel (see Chapter 25). It is assumed that all connection wire is effectively resistanceless.

In a series combination, the current through each resistance is the same as that through all the others. The potential drop (p.d.) across the combination is equal to the sum of the individual potential drops. *The equivalent resistance in series is always greater than the largest of the individual resistances.*

**Resistors in Parallel:** Several resistors are connected in **parallel** between two nodes if one end of each resistor is connected to one node and the other end of each is connected to the other node. A typical case is shown in Fig. 28-1(*b*), where points *a* and *b* are nodes. Their equivalent resistance $R_{eq}$ is given by

$$\frac{1}{R_{eq}} = \frac{1}{R_1} + \frac{1}{R_2} + \frac{1}{R_3} + \cdots \qquad \text{(parallel combination)}$$

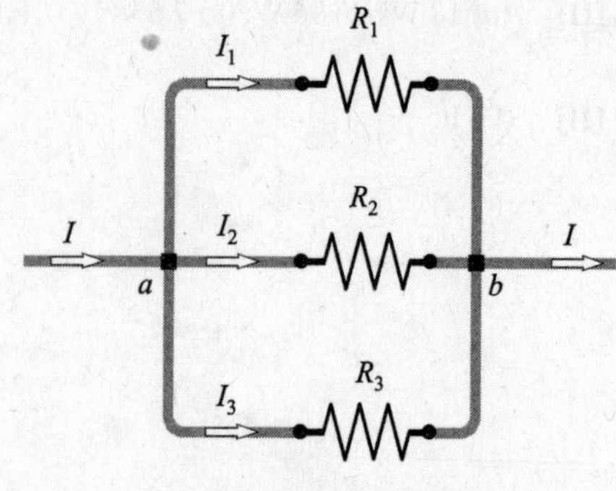


(*a*) Resistors in series

(*b*) Resistors in parallel

Fig. 28-1

*The equivalent resistance in parallel is always less than the smallest of the individual resistances.* Connecting additional resistances in parallel decreases $R_{eq}$ for the combination. Observe that resistances in parallel combine like capacitances in series (see Chapter 25).

The potential drop $V$ across any one resistor in a parallel combination is the same as the potential drop across each of the others. The current through the $n$th resistor is $I_n = V/R_n$ and the total current entering the combination is equal to the sum of the individual branch currents [see Fig. 28-1(*b*)].

## SOLVED PROBLEMS

**28.1 [II]** Derive the formula for the equivalent resistance $R_{eq}$ of resistors $R_1$, $R_2$, and $R_3$ (*a*) in series and (*b*) in parallel, as shown in Fig. 28-1(*a*) and (*b*).

(*a*) For the series network,

$$V_{ad} = V_{ab} + V_{bc} + V_{cd} = IR_1 + IR_2 + IR_3$$

since the current $I$ is the same in all three resistors. Dividing by $I$ gives

$$\frac{V_{ad}}{I} = R_1 + R_2 + R_3 \qquad \text{or} \qquad R_{eq} = R_1 + R_2 + R_3$$

since $V_{ad}/I$ is by definition the equivalent resistance $R_{eq}$ of the network.

(*b*) The p.d. is the same for all three resistors, whence

$$I_1 = \frac{V_{ab}}{R_1} \qquad I_2 = \frac{V_{ab}}{R_2} \qquad I_3 = \frac{V_{ab}}{R_3}$$

Since the line current $I$ is the sum of the branch currents,

$$I = I_1 + I_2 + I_3 = \frac{V_{ab}}{R_1} + \frac{V_{ab}}{R_2} + \frac{V_{ab}}{R_3}$$

Dividing by $V_{ab}$ gives

$$\frac{I}{V_{ab}} = \frac{1}{R_1} + \frac{1}{R_2} + \frac{1}{R_3} \qquad \text{or} \qquad \frac{1}{R_{eq}} = \frac{1}{R_1} + \frac{1}{R_2} + \frac{1}{R_3}$$

since $V_{ab}/I$ is by definition the equivalent resistance $R_{eq}$ of the network.

**28.2 [II]** As shown in Fig. 28-2(*a*), a battery (internal resistance 1 Ω) is connected in series with two resistors. Compute (*a*) the current in the circuit, (*b*) the p.d. across each resistor, and (*c*) the terminal p.d. of the battery.

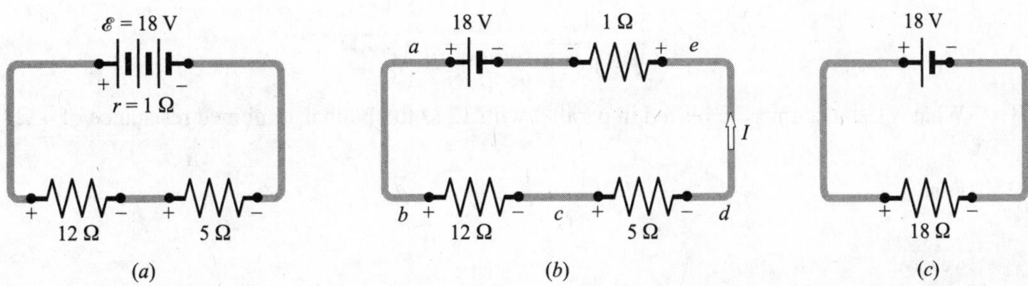


Fig. 28-2

The circuit is redrawn in Fig. 28-2(*b*) so as to show the battery resistance. The resistors are in series,

$$R_{eq} = 5\ \Omega + 12\ \Omega + 1\ \Omega = 18\ \Omega$$

Hence, the circuit is equivalent to the one shown in Fig. 28-2(*c*). Applying $V = IR$,

(*a*)
$$I = \frac{V}{R} = \frac{18\text{ V}}{18\ \Omega} = 1.0\text{ A}$$

(*b*) Since $I = 1.0$ A, we can find the p.d. from point-*b* to point-*c* as

$$V_{bc} = IR_{bc} = (1.0\text{ A})(12\ \Omega) = 12\text{ V}$$

and that from *c* to *d* as

$$V_{cd} = IR_{cd} = (1.0\text{ A})(5\ \Omega) = 5\text{ V}$$

Notice that $I$ is the same at all points in a series circuit.

(*c*) The terminal p.d. of the battery is the p.d. from *a* to *e*. Therefore,

$$\text{Terminal p.d.} = V_{bc} + V_{cd} = 12 + 5 = 17\text{ V}$$

Or, we could start at *e* and keep track of the voltage changes as we go through the battery from *e* to *a*. Taking voltage drops as negative,

$$\text{Terminal p.d.} = -Ir + \mathscr{E} = -(1.0\text{ A})(1\ \Omega) + 18\text{ V} = 17\text{ V}$$

**28.3 [II]** A 120-V house circuit has the following light bulbs turned on: 40.0 W, 60.0 W, and 175.0 W. Find the equivalent resistance of these lights.

House circuits are so constructed that each device is connected in parallel with the others. From $P = VI = V^2/R$, for the first bulb

$$R_1 = \frac{V^2}{P_1} = \frac{(120\text{ V})^2}{40.0\text{ W}} = 360\ \Omega$$

Similarly, $R_2 = 240\ \Omega$ and $R_3 = 192\ \Omega$. Because devices in a house circuit are in parallel,

$$\frac{1}{R_{eq}} = \frac{1}{360\ \Omega} + \frac{1}{240\ \Omega} + \frac{1}{192\ \Omega} \quad \text{or} \quad R_{eq} = 82.3\ \Omega$$

As a check, note that the total power drawn from the line is 40.0 W + 60.0 W + 75.0 W = 75.0 W. Then, using $P = V^2/R$,

$$R_{eq} = \frac{V^2}{\text{total power}} = \frac{(120\text{ V})^2}{175.0\text{ W}} = 82.3\ \Omega$$

**28.4 [I]** What resistance must be placed in parallel with 12 Ω to obtain a combined resistance of 4 Ω?

From
$$\frac{1}{R_{eq}} = \frac{1}{R_1} + \frac{1}{R_2}$$

we have
$$\frac{1}{4\ \Omega} = \frac{1}{12\ \Omega} + \frac{1}{R_2}$$

and so
$$R_2 = 6\ \Omega$$

**28.5 [II]** Several 40-Ω resistors are to be connected so that 15 A flows from a 120-V source. How can this be done?

The equivalent resistance must be such that 15 A flows from 120 V. Thus,

$$R_{eq} = \frac{V}{I} = \frac{120\text{ V}}{15\text{ A}} = 8\ \Omega$$

The resistors must be in parallel, since the combined resistance is to be smaller than any of them. If the required number of 40-Ω resistors is $n$, then

$$\frac{1}{80\ \Omega} = n\left(\frac{1}{40\ \Omega}\right) \qquad \text{or} \qquad n = 5$$

**28.6 [II]** For each circuit shown in Fig. 28-3, determine the current $I$ through the battery.

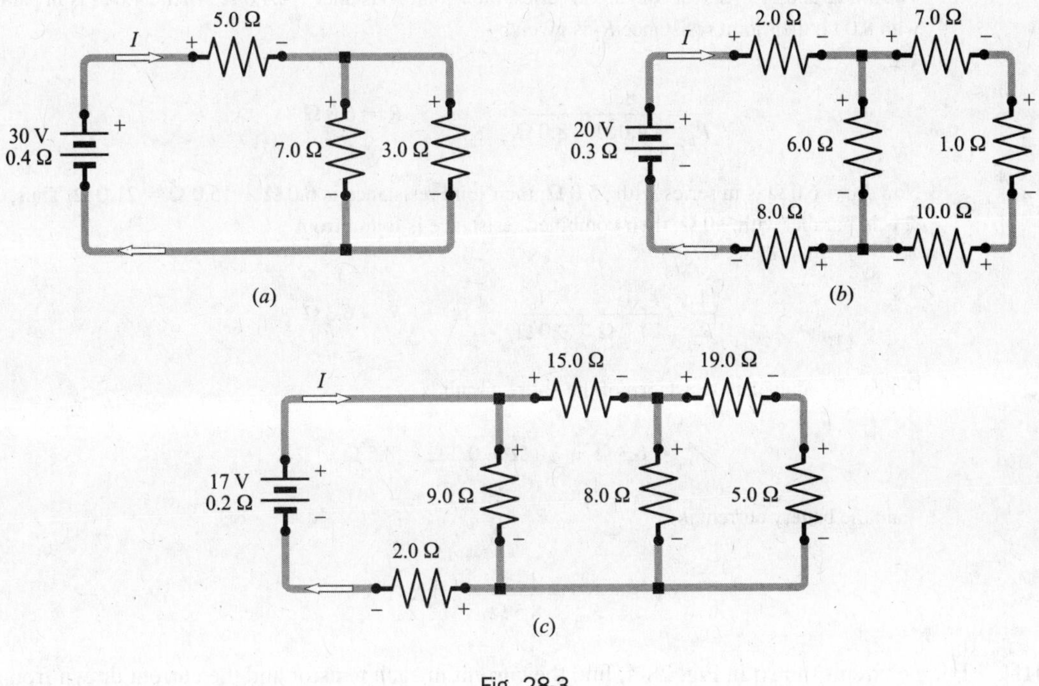


Fig. 28-3

(*a*) The 3.0-Ω and 7.0-Ω resistors are in parallel; their joint resistance $R_1$ is found from

$$\frac{1}{R_1} = \frac{1}{3.0\ \Omega} + \frac{1}{7.0\ \Omega} = \frac{10}{21\ \Omega} \qquad \text{or} \qquad R_1 = 2.1\ \Omega$$

Then the equivalent resistance of the entire circuit is

$$R_{eq} = 2.1\ \Omega + 5.0\ \Omega + 0.4\ \Omega = 7.5\ \Omega$$

and the battery current is

$$I = \frac{\mathscr{E}}{R_{eq}} = \frac{30\text{ V}}{7.5\ \Omega} = 4.0\text{ A}$$

(*b*) The 7.0-Ω, 1.0-Ω, and 10.0-Ω resistors are in series; their joint resistance is 18.0 Ω. Then 18.0 Ω is in parallel with 6.0 Ω; their combined resistance $R_1$ is given by

$$\frac{1}{R_1} = \frac{1}{18.0\ \Omega} + \frac{1}{6.0\ \Omega} \qquad \text{or} \qquad R_1 = 4.5\ \Omega$$

Hence, the equivalent resistance of the entire circuit is

$$R_{eq} = 4.5\ \Omega + 2.0\ \Omega + 8.0\ \Omega + 0.3\ \Omega = 14.8\ \Omega$$

and the battery current is

$$I = \frac{\mathscr{E}}{R_{eq}} = \frac{20\ \text{V}}{14.8\ \Omega} = 1.4\ \text{A}$$

(*c*) The 5.0-Ω and 19.0-Ω resistors are in series; their joint resistance is 24.0 Ω. Then 24.0 Ω is in parallel with 8.0 Ω; their joint resistance $R_1$ is given by

$$\frac{1}{R_1} = \frac{1}{24.0\ \Omega} + \frac{1}{8.0\ \Omega} \qquad \text{or} \qquad R_1 = 6.0\ \Omega$$

Now $R_1$ = 6.0 Ω is in series with 15.0 Ω; their joint resistance is 6.0 Ω + 15.0 Ω = 21.0 Ω. Thus, 21.0 Ω is in parallel with 9.0 Ω; their combined resistance is found from

$$\frac{1}{R_2} = \frac{1}{21.0\ \Omega} + \frac{1}{9.0\ \Omega} \qquad \text{or} \qquad R_2 = 6.3\ \Omega$$

Hence, the equivalent resistance of the entire circuit is

$$R_{eq} = 6.3\ \Omega + 2.0\ \Omega + 0.2\ \Omega = 8.5\ \Omega$$

and the battery current is

$$I = \frac{\mathscr{E}}{R_{eq}} = \frac{17\ \text{V}}{8.5\ \Omega} = 2.0\ \text{A}$$

**28.7 [II]** For the circuit shown in Fig. 28-4, find the current in each resistor and the current drawn from the 40-V source.

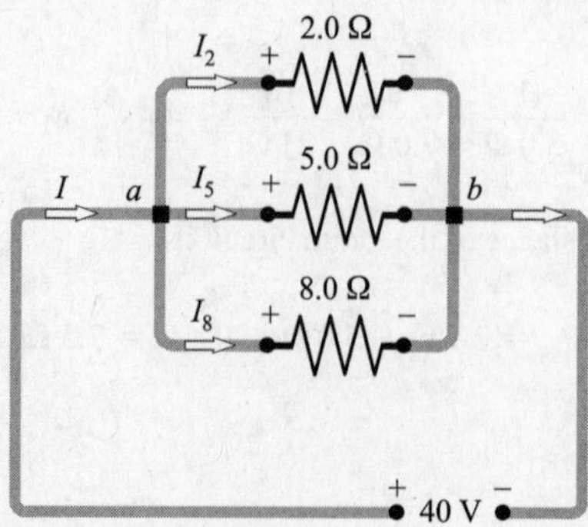


Fig. 28-4

Notice that the p.d. from $a$ to $b$ is 40 V. Therefore, the p.d. across each resistor is 40 V. Then,

$$I_2 = \frac{40\text{ V}}{2.0\,\Omega} = 20\text{ A} \qquad I_5 = \frac{40\text{ V}}{5.0\,\Omega} = 8.0\text{ A} \qquad I_8 = \frac{40\text{ V}}{8.0\,\Omega} = 5.0\text{ A}$$

Because $I$ splits into three currents:

$$I = I_2 + I_5 + I_8 = 20\text{ A} + 8.0\text{ A} + 5.0\text{ A} = 33\text{ A}$$

**28.8 [II]** In Fig. 28-5, the battery has an internal resistance of 0.7 Ω. Find (*a*) the current drawn from the battery, (*b*) the current in each 5-Ω resistor, and (*c*) the terminal voltage of the battery.

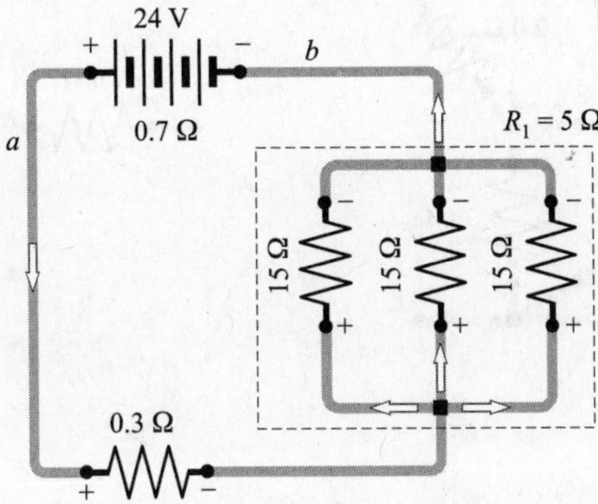


Fig. 28-5

(*a*) First we'll have to find the equivalent resistance of the entire circuit, and with that and Ohm's Law, determine the current. For parallel group resistance $R_1$ we have

$$\frac{1}{R_1} = \frac{1}{15\,\Omega} + \frac{1}{15\,\Omega} + \frac{1}{15\,\Omega} = \frac{3}{15\,\Omega} \qquad \text{or} \qquad R_1 = 5.0\,\Omega$$

Then
$$R_{eq} = 5.0\,\Omega + 0.3\,\Omega + 0.7\,\Omega = 6.0\,\Omega$$

and
$$I = \frac{\mathscr{E}}{R_{eq}} = \frac{24\text{ V}}{6.0\,\Omega} = 4.0\text{ A}$$

(*b*) **Method 1**

The three-resistor combination is equivalent to $R_1 = 5.0\ \Omega$. A current of 4.0 A flows through it. Hence, the p.d. across the combination is

$$IR_1 = (4.0\text{ A})(5.0\,\Omega) = 20\text{ V}$$

This is also the p.d. across each 15-Ω resistor. Therefore, the current through each 15-Ω resistor is

$$I_{15} = \frac{V}{R} = \frac{20\text{ V}}{15\,\Omega} = 1.3\text{ A}$$

**Method 2**

In this special case, we know that one-third of the current will go through each 15-Ω resistor. Hence,

$$I_{15} = \frac{4.0\text{ A}}{3} = 1.3\text{ A}$$

(*c*) Start at *a* and go to *b* outside the battery:

$$V \text{ from } a \text{ to } b = -(4.0\text{ A})(0.3\ \Omega) - (4.0\text{ A})(5.0\ \Omega) = -21.2\text{ V}$$

The terminal p.d. of the battery is 21.2 V. Or, we could write for this case of a discharging battery,

$$\text{Terminal p.d.} = \mathscr{E} - Ir = 24\text{ V} - (4.0\text{ A})(0.7\ \Omega) = 21.2\text{ V}$$

**28.9 [II]** Find the equivalent resistance between points-*a* and -*b* for the combination shown in Fig. 28-6(*a*).

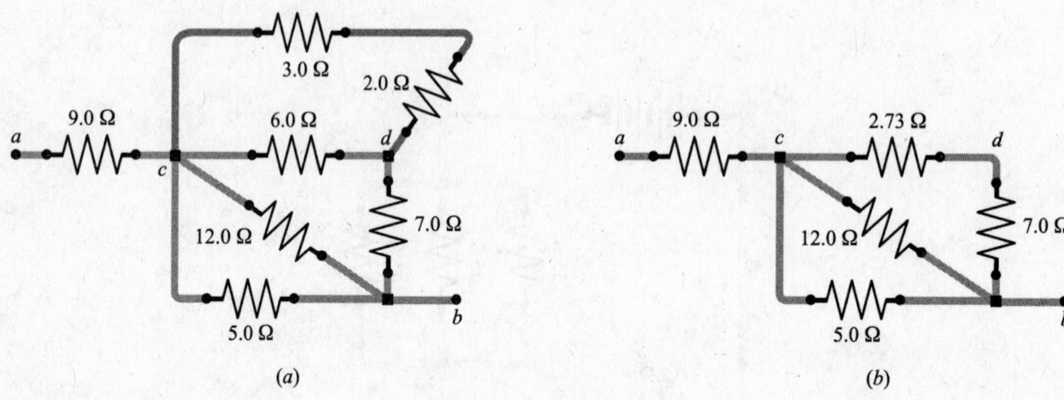


Fig. 28-6

The 3.0-Ω and 2.0-Ω resistors are in series and are equivalent to a 5.0-Ω resistor. The equivalent 5.0 Ω is in parallel with the 6.0 Ω, and their equivalent, $R_1$, is

$$\frac{1}{R_1} = \frac{1}{5.0\ \Omega} + \frac{1}{6.0\ \Omega} = 0.20 + 0.167 = 0.367\ \Omega^{-1} \qquad \text{or} \qquad R_1 = 2.73\ \Omega$$

The circuit thus far reduced is shown in Fig. 28-6(*b*).

The 7.0 Ω and 2.73 Ω are equivalent to 9.73 Ω. Now the 5.0 Ω, 12.0 Ω, and 9.73 Ω are in parallel, and their equivalent, $R_2$, is

$$\frac{1}{R_2} = \frac{1}{5.0\ \Omega} + \frac{1}{12.0\ \Omega} + \frac{1}{9.73\ \Omega} = 0.386\ \Omega^{-1} \qquad \text{or} \qquad R_2 = 2.6\ \Omega$$

This 2.6 Ω is in series with the 9.0-Ω resistor. Therefore, the equivalent resistance of the combination is 9.0 Ω + 2.6 Ω = 11.6 Ω.

**28.10 [II]** A current of 5.0 A flows into the circuit in Fig. 28-6 (*a*) at point-*a* and out at point-*b*. (*a*) What is the potential difference from *a* to *b*? (*b*) How much current flows through the 12.0-Ω resistor?

In Problem 28.9, we found that the equivalent resistance for this combination is 11.6 Ω, and we are told the current through it is 5.0 A.

(*a*) Voltage drop from *a* to *b* = $IR_{eq}$ = (5.0 A)(11.6 Ω) = 58 V

(*b*) The voltage drop from *a* to *c* is (5.0 A)(9.0 Ω) 45 V. Hence, from part (*a*), the voltage drop from *c* to *b* is

$$58\text{ V} - 45\text{ V} = 13\text{ V}$$

and the current in the 12.0-Ω resistor is

$$I_{12} = \frac{V}{R} = \frac{13\text{ V}}{12\ \Omega} = 1.1\text{ A}$$

**28.11 [II]** As shown in Fig. 28-7, the current $I$ divides into $I_1$ and $I_2$. Find $I_1$ and $I_2$ in terms of $I$, $R_1$, and $R_2$.

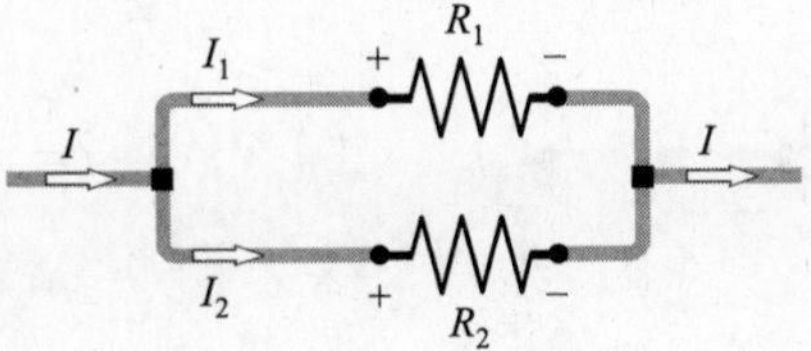


Fig. 28-7

The potential drops across $R_1$ and $R_2$ are the same because the resistors are in parallel, so

$$I_1R_1 = I_2R_2$$

But $I = I_1 + I_2$ and so $I_2 = I - I_1$. Substituting in the first equation gives

$$I_1R_1 = (I - I_1)R_2 = IR_2 - I_1R_2 \qquad \text{or} \qquad I_1 = \frac{R_2}{R_1 + R_2} I$$

Using this result together with the first equation gives

$$I_2 = \frac{R_1}{R_2} I_1 = \frac{R_1}{R_1 + R_2} I$$

**28.12 [II]** Find the potential difference between points-$P$ and -$Q$ in Fig. 28-8. Which point is at the higher potential?

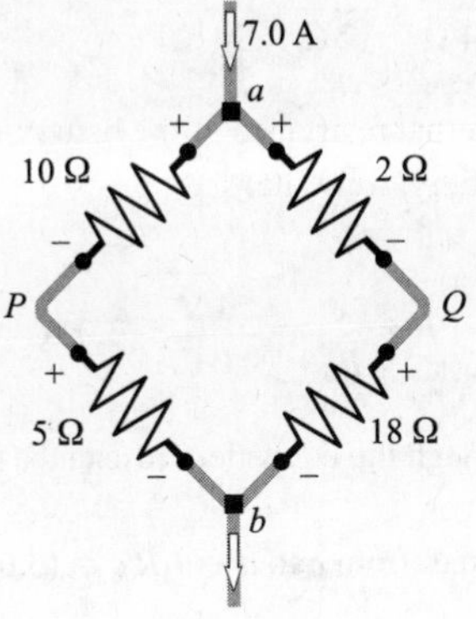


Fig. 28-8

From the result of Problem 28.11, the currents through $P$ and $Q$ are

$$I_P = \frac{2\,\Omega + 18\,\Omega}{10\,\Omega + 5\,\Omega + 2\,\Omega + 18\,\Omega}(7.0\text{ A}) = 4.0\text{ A}$$

$$I_Q = \frac{10\,\Omega + 5\,\Omega}{10\,\Omega + 5\,\Omega + 2\,\Omega + 18\,\Omega}(7.0\text{ A}) = 3.0\text{ A}$$

Now we start at point-$P$ and go through point-$a$ to point-$Q$, to find

$$\text{Voltage change from } P \text{ to } Q = +(4.0\text{ A})(10\,\Omega) - (3.0\text{ A})(2\,\Omega) = +34\text{ V}$$

(Notice that we go through a potential rise from $P$ to $a$ because we are going against the current. From $a$ to $Q$ there is a drop.) Therefore, the voltage difference between $P$ and $Q$ is 34 V, with $Q$ being at the higher potential.

**28.13 [II]** For the circuit of Fig. 28-9(*a*), find (*a*) $I_1$ $I_2$, and $I_3$; (*b*) the current in the 12-Ω resistor.

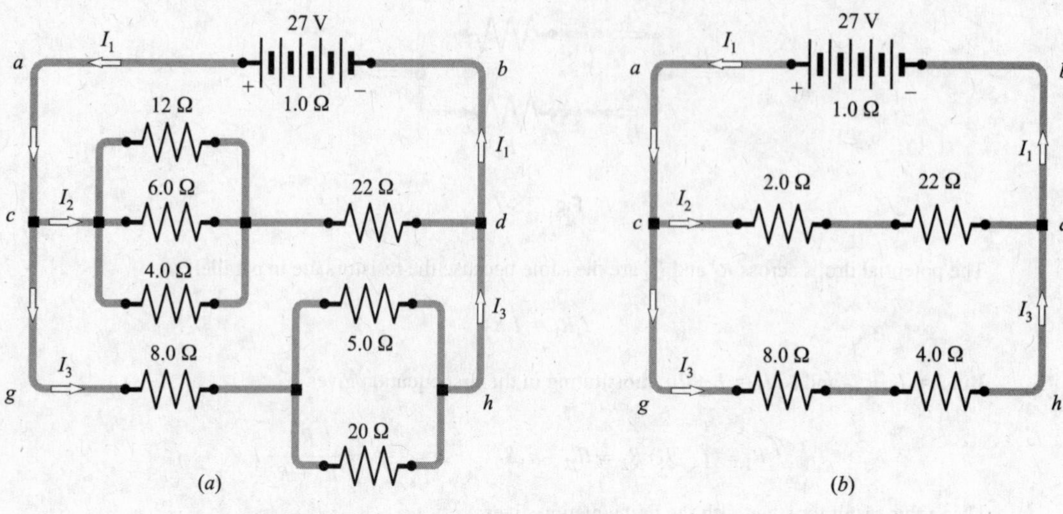


Fig. 28-9

*a*) The circuit reduces at once to that shown in Fig. 28-9(*b*). There we have 24 Ω in parallel with 12 Ω, so the equivalent resistance below points-*a* and -*b* is

$$\frac{1}{R_{ab}} = \frac{1}{24\ \Omega} + \frac{1}{12\ \Omega} = \frac{3}{24\ \Omega} \qquad \text{or} \qquad R_{ab} = 8.0\ \Omega$$

Adding to this the 1.0-Ω internal resistance of the battery gives a total equivalent resistance of 9.0 Ω. To find the current from the battery, we write

$$I_1 = \frac{\mathscr{E}}{R_{\text{eq}}} = \frac{24\ \text{V}}{9.0\ \Omega} = 3.0\ \text{A}$$

This same current flows through the equivalent resistance below *a* and *b*, and so

$$\text{p.d. from } a \text{ to } b = \text{p.d. from } c \text{ to } d = I_1 R_{ab} = (3.0\ \text{A})(8.0\ \Omega) = 24\ \text{V}$$

Applying $V = IR$ to branch *cd* gives

$$I_2 = \frac{V_{cd}}{R_{cd}} = \frac{24\ \text{V}}{24\ \Omega} = 1.0\ \text{A}$$

Similarly, $$I_3 = \frac{V_{gh}}{R_{gh}} = \frac{24\ \text{V}}{12\ \Omega} = 2.0\ \text{A}$$

As a check, note that $I_2 + I_3 = 3.0\ \text{A} = I_1$, as it should be.

(*b*) Because $I_2 = 1.0$ A, the p.d. across the 2.0-Ω resistor in Fig. 28-9(*b*) is (1.0 A)(2.0 Ω) = 2.0 V. But this is also the p.d. across the 12-Ω resistor in Fig. 28-9(*a*). Applying $V = IR$ to the 12 Ω gives

$$I_{12} = \frac{V_{12}}{R} = \frac{2.0\ \text{V}}{12\ \Omega} = 0.17\ \text{A}$$

**28.14 [II]** A galvanometer has a resistance of 400 Ω and deflects full scale for a current of 0.20 mA through it. How large a shunt resistor is required to change it to a 3.0-A ammeter?

In Fig. 28-10 we label the galvanometer G and the shunt resistance $R_s$. At full-scale deflection, the currents are as shown:

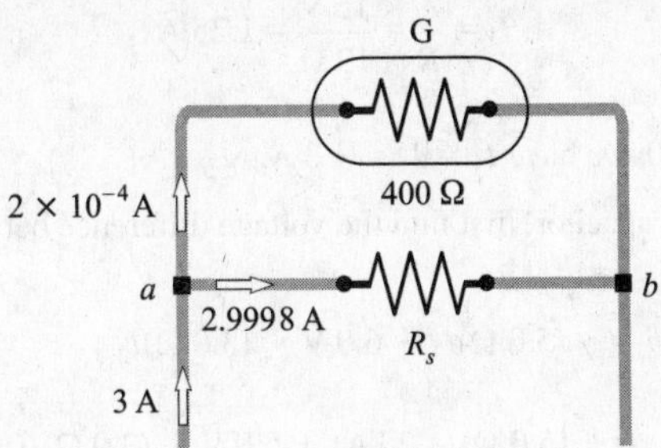


Fig. 28-10

The voltage drop from *a* to *b* across G is the same as that across *Rs*. Therefore,

$$(2.9998\ \text{A})R_s = (2.0 \times 10^{-4}\ \text{A})(400\ \Omega)$$

from which $R_s = 0.027\ \Omega$.

**28.15 [II]** A voltmeter is to deflect full scale for a potential difference of 5.000 V across it and is to be made by connecting a resistor $R_x$ in series with a galvanometer. The 80.00-Ω galvanometer deflects full scale for a potential of 20.00 mV across it. Find $R_x$.

When the galvanometer is deflecting full scale, the current through it is

$$I = \frac{V}{R} = \frac{20.00 \times 10^{-3}\ \text{V}}{80.00\ \Omega} = 2.500 \times 10^{-4}\ \text{A}$$

When $R_x$ is connected in series with the galvanometer, we wish $I$ to be $2.500 \times 10^{-4}$ A for a potential difference of 5.000 V across the combination. Hence, $V = IR$ becomes

$$5.000\ \text{V} = (2.500 \times 10^{-4}\ \text{A})\ (80.00\ \Omega + R_x)$$

from which $R_x = 19.92\ \text{k}\Omega$.

**28.16 [III]** The currents in the circuit in Fig. 28-11 are steady. Find $I_1$, $I_2$, $I_3$, and the charge on the capacitor.

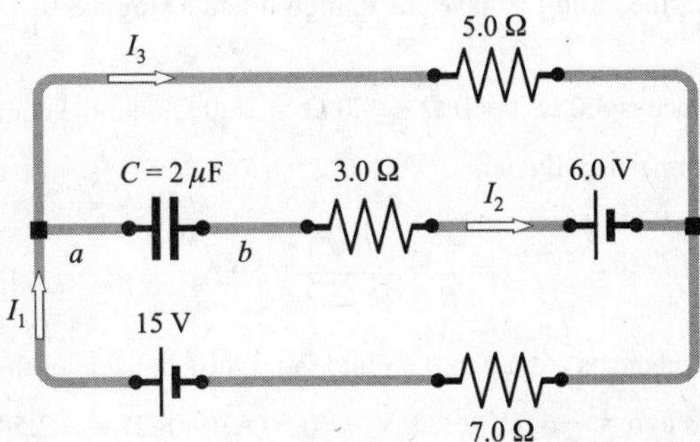


Fig. 28-11

When a capacitor has a constant charge, as it does here, the current flowing to it is zero. Therefore, $I_2 = 0$, and the circuit behaves just as though the center wire were missing.

With the center wire missing, the remaining circuit is simply 12 Ω connected across a 15-V battery. Therefore,

$$I_1 = \frac{\mathscr{E}}{R} = \frac{15\ \text{V}}{12\ \Omega} = 1.25\ \text{A}$$

In addition, because $I_2 = 0$, we have $I_3 = I_1 = 1.3$ A.

To find the charge on the capacitor, first find the voltage difference between points-$a$ and -$b$. Start at $a$ and go around the upper path.

Voltage change from $a$ to $b = -(5.0\ \Omega)I_3 + 6.0\ \text{V} + (3.0\ \Omega)I_2$

$$= -(5.0\ \Omega)(1.25\ \text{A}) + 6.0\ \text{V} + (3.0\ \Omega)(0) = -0.25\ \text{V}$$

Therefore, $b$ is at the lower potential and the capacitor plate at $b$ is negative. To find the charge on the capacitor,

$$Q = CV_{ab} = (2 \times 10^{-6}\ \text{F})(0.25\ \text{V}) = 0.5\ \mu\text{C}$$

**28.17 [II]** Find the ammeter reading and the voltmeter reading in the circuit in Fig. 28-12. Assume both meters to be ideal.

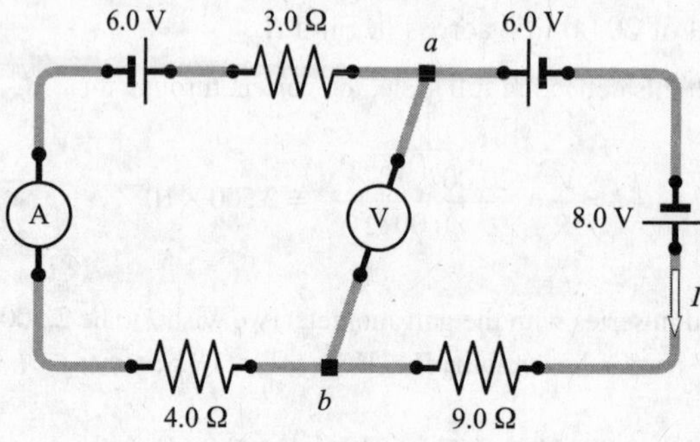


Fig. 28-12

The ideal voltmeter has infinite resistance, and so its wire can be removed without altering the circuit. The ideal ammeter has zero resistance. It can be shown (see Chapter 29) that batteries in series simply add or subtract. The two 6.0-V batteries cancel each other because they tend to push current in opposite directions. As a result, the circuit behaves as though it had a single 8.0-V battery that causes a clockwise current.

The equivalent resistance is 3.0 Ω + 4.0 Ω + 9.0 Ω = 16.0 Ω, and the equivalent battery is 8.0 V. Therefore, and this is what the ammeter will read.

$$I = \frac{\mathscr{E}}{R} = \frac{8.0\ \text{V}}{16\ \Omega} = 0.50\ \text{A}$$

Adding up the voltage changes from $a$ to $b$ around the right-hand side of the circuit gives

Voltage change from $a$ to $b = -6.0\ \text{V} + 8.0\ \text{V} - (0.50\ \text{A})(9.0\ \Omega) = -2.5\ \text{V}$

Therefore, a voltmeter connected from $a$ to $b$ will read 2.5 V, with $b$ being at the lower potential.

## SUPPLEMENTARY PROBLEMS

**28.18 [I]** Compute the equivalent resistance of 4.0 Ω and 8.0 Ω (*a*) in series and (*b*) in parallel.

**28.19 [I]** Compute the equivalent resistance of (*a*) 3.0 Ω, 6.0 Ω, and 9.0 Ω in parallel; (*b*) 3.0 Ω, 4.0 Ω, 7.0 Ω, 10.0 Ω, and 12.0 Ω in parallel; (*c*) three 33-Ω heating elements in parallel; (*d*) twenty 100-Ω lamps in parallel.

**28.20 [I]** What resistance must be placed in parallel with 20 Ω to make the combined resistance 15 Ω?

**28.21 [II]** How many 160-Ω resistors (in parallel) are required to carry a total of 5.0 A on a 100-V line?

**28.22 [II]** Three resistors, of 8.0 Ω, 12 Ω, and 24 Ω, are in parallel, and a current of 20 A is drawn by the combination. Determine (*a*) the potential difference across the combination and (*b*) the current through each resistance.

**28.23 [II]** By use of one or more of the three resistors 3.0 Ω, 5.0 Ω, and 6.0 Ω, a total of 18 resistances can be obtained. What are they?

**28.24 [II]** Two resistors, of 4.00 Ω and 12.0 Ω, are connected in parallel across a 22-V battery having internal resistance 1.00 Ω. Compute (*a*) the battery current, (*b*) the current in the 4.00-Ω resistor, (*c*) the terminal voltage of the battery, (*d*) the current in the 12.0-Ω resistor.

**28.25 [II]** Three resistors, of 40 Ω, 60 Ω, and 120 Ω, are connected in parallel, and this parallel group is connected in series with 15 Ω in series with 25 Ω. The whole system is then connected to a 120-V source. Determine (*a*) the current in the 25 Ω, (*b*) the potential drop across the parallel group, (*c*) the potential drop across the 25 Ω, (*d*) the current in the 60 Ω, (*e*) the current in the 40 Ω.

**28.26 [II]** What shunt resistance should be connected in parallel with an ammeter having a resistance of 0.040 Ω so that 25 percent of the total current will pass through the ammeter?

**28.27 [II]** A 36-Ω galvanometer is shunted by a resistor of 4.0 Ω. What part of the total current will pass through the instrument?

**28.28 [II]** A relay having a resistance of 6.0 Ω operates with a minimum current of 0.030 A. It is required that the relay operate when the current in the line reaches 0.240 A. What resistance should be used to shunt the relay?

**28.29 [II]** Show that if two resistors are connected in parallel, the rates at which they produce thermal energy vary inversely as their resistances.

**28.30 [II]** For the circuit shown in Fig. 28-13, find the current through each resistor and the potential drop across each resistor.

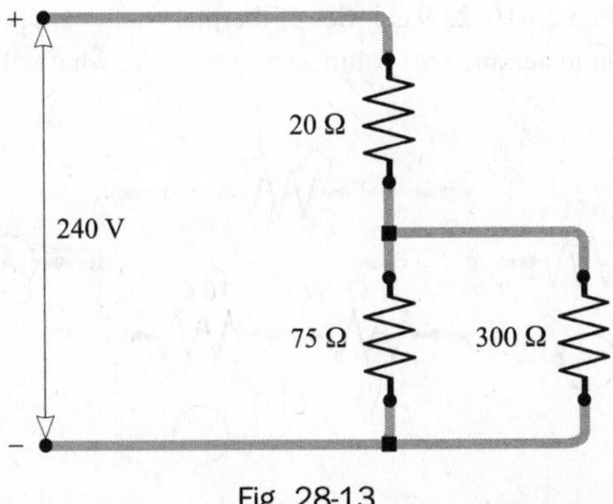


Fig. 28-13

**28.31 [II]** For the circuit shown in Fig. 28-14, find (*a*) its equivalent resistance; (*b*) the current drawn from the power source; (*c*) the potential differences across *ab*, *cd*, and *de*; (*d*) the current in each resistor.

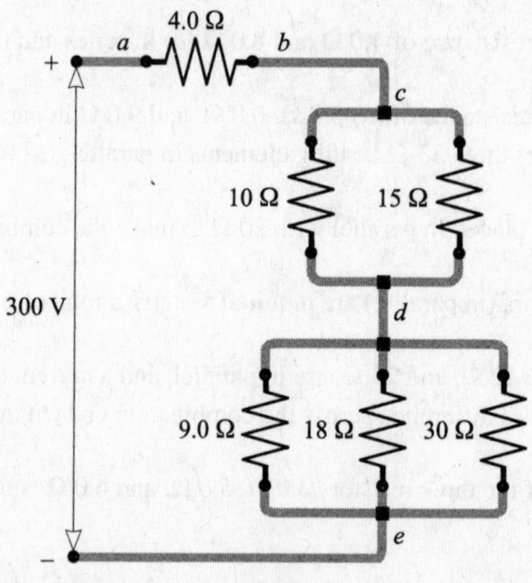


Fig. 28-14

**28.32 [II]** It is known that the potential difference across the 6.0-Ω resistance in Fig. 28-15 is 48 V. Determine (*a*) the entering current *I*, (*b*) the potential difference across the 8.0-Ω resistance, (*c*) the potential difference across the 10-Ω resistance, (*d*) the potential difference from *a* to *b*. [*Hint:* The wire connecting *c* and *d* can be shrunk to zero length without altering the currents or potentials.]

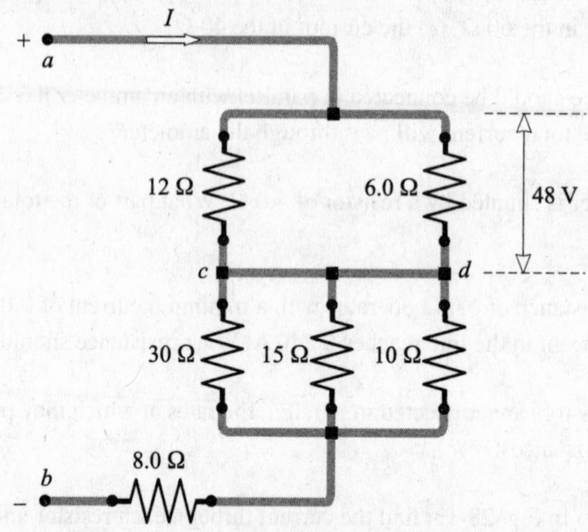


Fig. 28-15

**28.33 [II]** In the circuit shown in Fig. 28-16, 23.9 calories of thermal energy are produced each second in the 4.0-Ω resistor. Assuming the ammeter and two voltmeters to be ideal, what will be their readings?

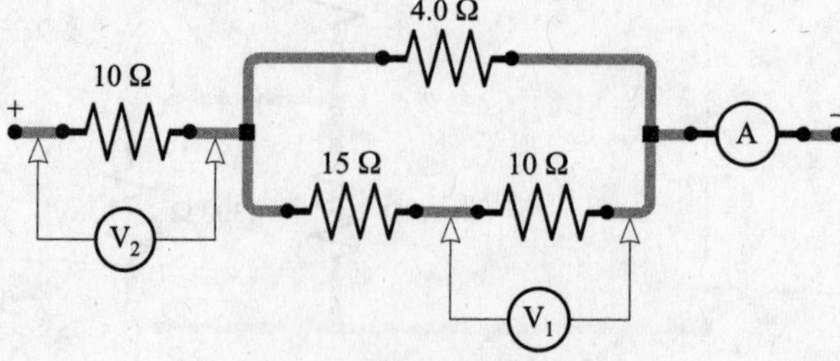


Fig. 28-16

**28.34 [II]** For the circuit shown in Fig. 28-17, find (*a*) the equivalent resistance; (*b*) the currents through the 5.0-Ω, 7.0-Ω, and 3.0-Ω resistors; (*c*) the total power delivered by the battery to the circuit.

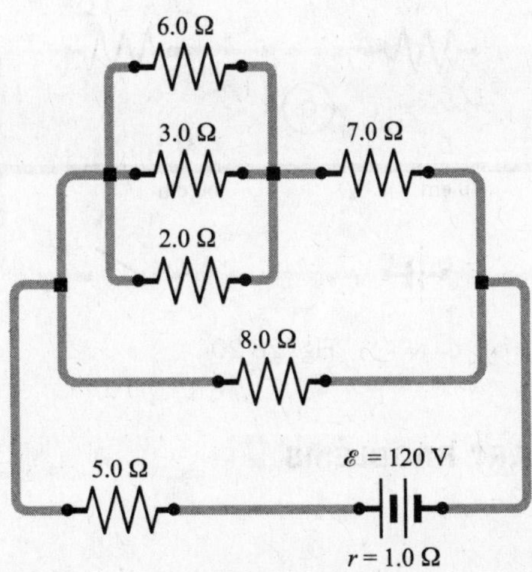


Fig. 28-17

**28.35 [II]** In the circuit shown in Fig. 28-18, the ideal ammeter registers 2.0 A. (*a*) Assuming *XY* to be a resistance, find its value. (*b*) Assuming *XY* to be a battery (with 2.0-Ω internal resistance) that is being charged, find its emf. (*c*) Under the conditions of part (*b*), what is the potential change from point-*Y* to point-*X*?

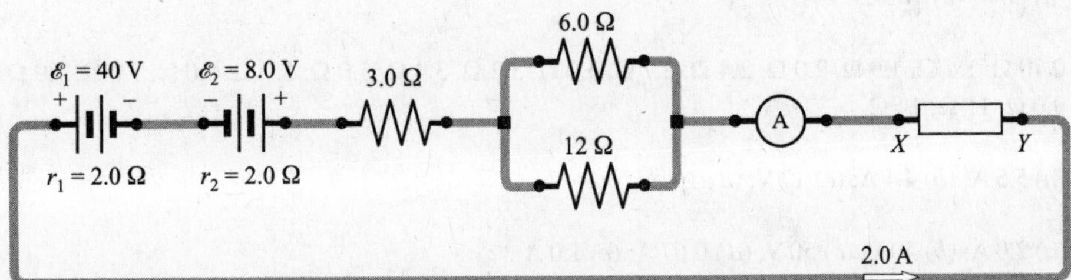


Fig. 28-18

**28.36 II]** The *Wheatstone bridge* shown in Fig. 28-19 is being used to measure resistance *X*. At balance, the current through the galvanometer G is zero and resistances *L, M*, and *N* are 3.0 Ω, 2.0 Ω, and 10 Ω, respectively. Find the value of *X*.

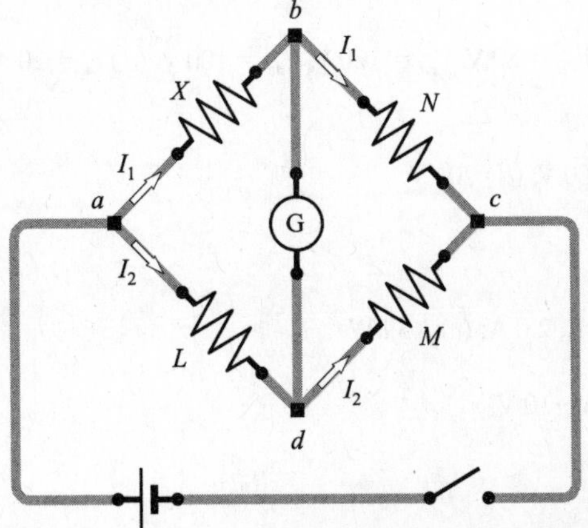


Fig. 28-19

**28.37 [II]** The slidewire Wheatstone bridge shown in Fig. 28-20 is balanced (refer back to Problem 28.36) when the uniform resistive slide wire $AB$ is divided as shown. Find the value of the resistance $X$.

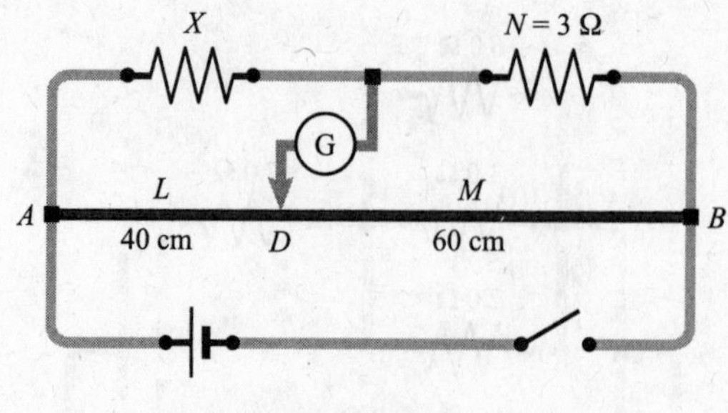


Fig. 28-20

## ANSWERS TO SUPPLEMENTARY PROBLEMS

**28.18 [I]** (*a*) 12 Ω; (*b*) 2.7 Ω

**28.19 [I]** (*a*) 1.6 Ω; (*b*) 1.1 Ω; (*c*) 11 Ω; (*d*) 5.0 Ω

**28.20 [I]** 60 Ω

**28.21 [II]** 8

**28.22 [II]** (*a*) 80 V; (*b*) 10 A, 6.7 A, 3.3 A

**28.23 [II]** 0.70 Ω, 1.4 Ω, 1.9 Ω, 2.0 Ω, 2.4 Ω, 2.7 Ω, 3.0 Ω, 3.2 Ω, 3.4 Ω, 5.0 Ω, 5.7 Ω, 6.0 Ω, 7.0 Ω, 7.9 Ω, 8.0 Ω, 9.0 Ω, 11 Ω, 14 Ω

**28.24 [II]** (*a*) 5.5 A; (*b*) 4.1 A; (*c*) 17 V; (*d*) 1.4 A

**28.25 [II]** (*a*) 2.0 A; (*b*) 40 V; (*c*) 50 V; (*d*) 0.67 A; (*e*) 1.0 A

**28.26 [II]** 0.013 Ω

**28.27 [II]** 1/10

**28.28 [II]** 0.86 Ω

**28.30 [II]** for 20 Ω, 3.0 A and 60 V; for 75 Ω, 2.4 A and 180 V; for 300 Ω, 0.6 A and 180 V

**28.31 [II]** (*a*) 15 Ω; (*b*) 20 A; (*c*) $V_{ab} = 80$ V, $V_{cd} = 120$ V, $V_{de} = 100$ V; (*d*) $I_4 = 20$ A, $I_{10} = 12$ A, $I_{15} = 8$ A, $I_9 = 11.1$ A, $I_{18} = 5.6$ A, $I_{30} = 3.3$ A

**28.32 [II]** (*a*) 12 A; (*b*) 96 V; (*c*) 60 V; (*d*) 204 V

**28.33 [II]** 5.8 A, 8.0 V, 58 V

**28.34 [II]** (*a*) 10 Ω; (*b*) 12 A, 6.0 A, 2.0 A; (*c*) 1.3 kW

**28.35 [II]** (*a*) 5.0 Ω; (*b*) 6.0 V; (*c*) −10 V

**28.36 [II]** 15 Ω

**28.37 [II]** 2 Ω

# Kirchhoff's Laws

**Kirchhoff's Node (or Junction) Rule:** The sum of all the currents coming into a ***node*** (i.e., a junction where three or more current-carrying leads or ***branches*** attach) must equal the sum of all the currents leaving that node. If we designate the currents-in as positive and the currents-out as negative, then *the sum of the currents equals zero* is a common alternative statement of the rule.

**Kirchhoff's Loop (or Circuit) Rule:** As one traces around any closed path (or ***loop***) in a circuit, the algebraic sum of the potential changes encountered is zero. In this sum, a potential (i.e., voltage) rise is positive and a potential drop is negative.

Current always flows from high to low potential through a resistor. As one traces through a resistor in the direction of the current, the potential change is negative because it is a potential drop. Once you either know or assume the direction of current, label the resistors with a + sign on the side at which current enters and a – sign on the side at which current emerges.

The positive terminal of a pure emf source is always the high-potential terminal, independent of the direction of the current through the emf source. Label all voltage sources with a + sign on the high side and a – sign on the low side. When dealing with the symbol for a battery the longer line is the high side.

**The Set of Equations Obtained** by use of Kirchhoff's loop rule will be independent provided that each new loop equation contains at least one voltage change not included in a previous equation.

## SOLVED PROBLEMS

**29.1 [II]** Find the currents in the circuit shown in Fig. 29-1.

Notice that the signs of the voltage drops have been provided in the circuit diagram. You will not need them in this solution, but it's a good habit to put them in as a first step.

This circuit cannot be reduced further because it contains no resistors in simple series or parallel combinations. We therefore revert to Kirchhoff's rules. If the currents had not been labeled and shown by arrows, we would do that first. In general, special care is needed in assigning the current directions, since those chosen incorrectly will simply give negative numerical values. In this problem there are three branches connecting nodes-*a* and -*b*, and therefore three currents.

Apply the node rule to node-*b* in Fig. 29-1:

$$\text{Current into } b = \text{Current out of } b$$

$$I_1 + I_2 + I_3 = 0 \qquad (1)$$

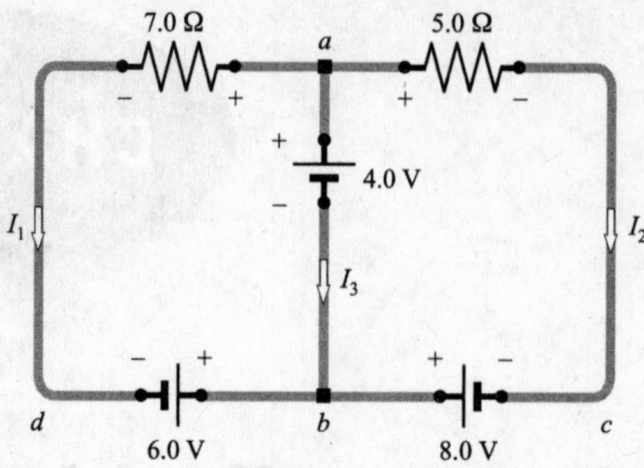


Fig. 29-1

Next apply the loop rule to loop *adba*. In volts,

$$-7.0I_1 + 6.0 + 4.0 = 0 \quad \text{or} \quad I_1 = \frac{10.0}{7.0}\ \text{A}$$

(Why must the term $7.0I_1$ have a negative sign?) Then apply the loop rule to loop *abca*. In volts,

$$-4.0 - 8.0 + 5.0\,I_2 = 0 \quad \text{or} \quad I_2 = \frac{12.0}{5.0}\ \text{A}$$

(Why must the signs be as written?)

Now return to Eq. (*1*) to find

$$I_3 = -I_1 - I_2 = -\frac{10.0}{7.0} - \frac{12.0}{5.0} = \frac{-50 - 84}{35} = -3.8\ \text{A}$$

The minus sign tells us that $I_3$ is opposite in direction to that shown in the figure.

**29.2 [II]** For the circuit shown in Fig. 29-2, find $I_1$, $I_2$, and $I_3$ if switch $S$ is (*a*) open and (*b*) closed.

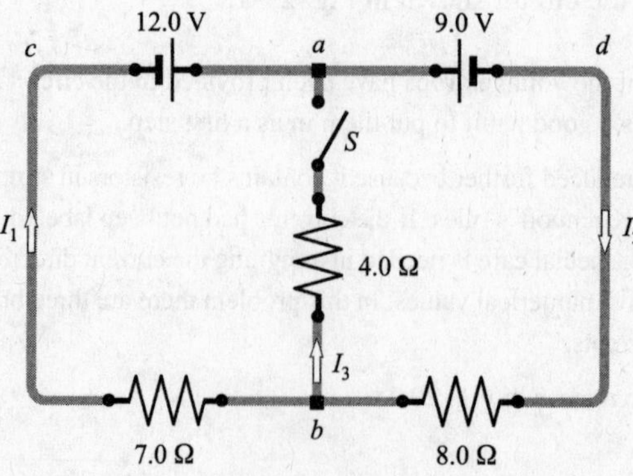


Fig. 29-2

(*a*) When $S$ is open, $I_3 = 0$, because no current can flow through the middle branch. Applying the node rule to point-*a*,

$$I_1 + I_3 = I_2 \qquad \text{or} \qquad I_2 = I_1 + 0 = I_1$$

Applying the loop rule to the outer loop *acbda* yields

$$-12.0 + 7.0\,I_1 + 8.0\,I_2 + 9.0 = 0 \tag{1}$$

To understand the use of signs, remember that current always flows from high to low potential through a resistor.

Because $I_2 = I_1$, Eq. (*1*) becomes

$$15.0\,I_1 = 3.0 \qquad \text{or} \qquad I_1 = 0.20\ \text{A}$$

Also, $I_2 = I_1 = 0.20$ A. Notice that this is the same result that one would obtain by replacing the two batteries by a single 3.0-V battery.

(*b*) With $S$ closed, $I_3$ is no longer necessarily zero. Applying the node rule to point-*a* gives

$$I_1 + I_3 = I_2 \tag{2}$$

Applying the loop rule to loop *acba*

$$-12.0 + 7.01\,I_1 - 4.0\,I_3 = 0 \tag{3}$$

and to loop *adba* gives

$$-9.0 - 8.0\,I_2 - 4.0\,I_3 = 0 \tag{4}$$

Applying the loop rule to the remaining loop, *acbda*, would yield a redundant equation, because it would contain no new voltage change.

Now solve Eqs. (*2*), (*3*), and (*4*) for $I_1$, $I_2$, and $I_3$. From Eq. (*4*),

$$I_3 = -2.0\,I_2 - 2.25$$

Substituting this in Eq. (*3*) yields

$$-\,12.0 + 7.0\,I_1 + 9.0 + 8.0\,I_2 = 0 \qquad \text{or} \qquad 7.0\,I_1 + 8.0\,I_2 = 3.0$$

Substituting for $I_3$ in Eq. (*2*) also gives

$$I_1 - 2.0\,I_2 - 2.25 - I_2 \qquad \text{or} \qquad I_1 = 3.0\,I_2 + 2.25$$

Substituting this value in the previous equation finally leads to

$$21.0\,I_2 + 15.75 + 8.0\,I_2 = 3.0 \qquad \text{or} \qquad I_2 = -0.44\ \text{A}$$

Using this in the equation for $I_1$,

$$I_1 = 3.0(-0.44) + 2.25 = -1.32 + 2.25 = 0.93\ \text{A}$$

Notice that the minus sign is a part of the value we have found for $I_2$. It must be carried along with its numerical value. Now use (*2*) to find

$$I_3 = I_2 - I_1 = (-0.44) - 0.93 = -1.37\ \text{A}$$

**29.3 [II]** Each of the cells shown in Fig. 29-3 has an emf of 1.50 V and a 0.0750-Ω internal resistance. Find $I_1$, $I_2$, and $I_3$.

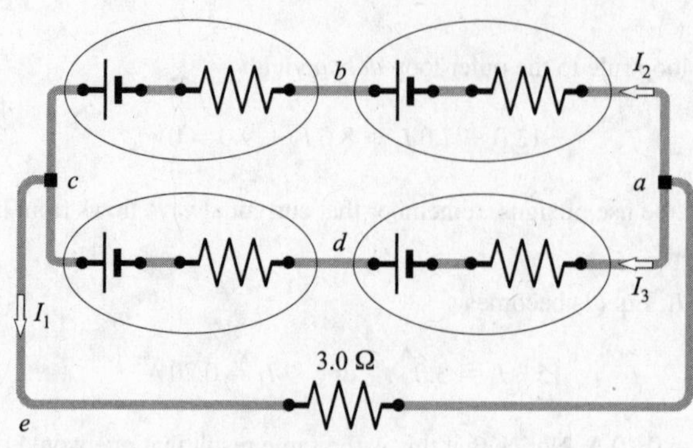


Fig. 29-3

Applying the node rule to point-*a* gives

$$I_1 = I_2 + I_3 \qquad (1)$$

Applying the loop rule to loop *abcea* yields, in volts,

$$-(0.0750)I_2 + 1.50 - (0.0750)\,I_2 + 1.50 - 3.00\,I_1 = 0$$

or

$$3.00\,I_1 + 0.150\,I_2 = 3.00 \qquad (2)$$

Also, for loop *adcea*,

$$-(0.0750)\,I_3 + 1.50 - (0.0750)\,I_3 + 1.50 - 3.00\,I_1 = 0$$

or

$$3.00\,I_1 + 0.150\,I_3 = 3.00 \qquad (3)$$

Solve Eq. (*2*) for $3.00\,I_1$ and substitute in Eq. (*3*) to get

$$3.00 - 0.150\,I_3 + 0.150\,I_2 = 3.00 \qquad \text{or} \qquad I_2 = I_3$$

as we might have guessed from the symmetry of the problem. Then Eq. (*1*) yields

$$I_1 = 2I_2$$

and substituting this in Eq. (*2*),

$$6.00\,I_2 + 0.150\,I_2 = 3.00 \qquad \text{or} \qquad I_2 = 0.488\text{ A}$$

Then, $I_3 = I_2 = 0.488$ A and $I_1 = 2I_2 = 0.976$ A.

**29.4 [III]** The currents are steady in the circuit of Fig. 29-4. Find $I_1$, $I_2$, $I_3$, $I_4$, $I_5$, and the charge on the capacitor.

The capacitor passes no current when charged, and so $I_5 = 0$. Consider loop *acba*. The loop rule leads to

$$-8.0 + 4.0\,I_2 = 0 \qquad \text{or} \qquad I_2 = 2.0\text{ A}$$

Using loop *adeca* gives

$$-3.0\,I_1 - 9.0 + 8.0 = 0 \qquad \text{or} \qquad I_1 = -0.33\text{ A}$$

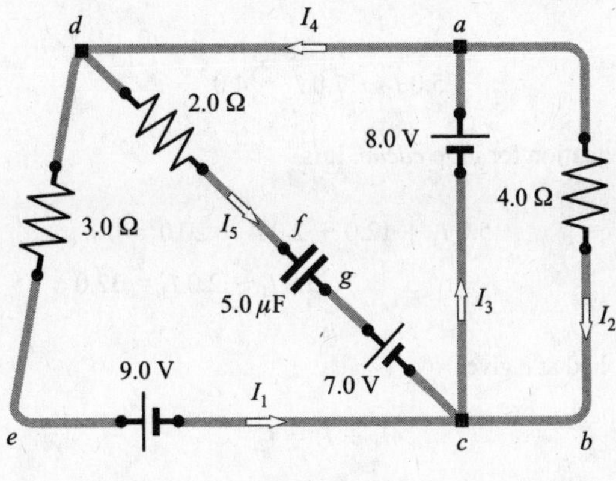


Fig. 29-4

Applying the node rule at point-$c$ results in

$$I_1 + I_5 + I_2 = I_3 \qquad \text{or} \qquad I_3 = 1.67 \text{ A} = 1.7 \text{ A}$$

and at point-$a$, it yields

$$I_3 = I_4 + I_2 \qquad \text{or} \qquad I_4 = -0.33 \text{ A}$$

(We should have realized this at once, because $I_5 = 0$ and so $I_4 = I_1$.)

To find the charge on the capacitor, we need the voltage $V_{fg}$ across it. Put in all the signs on the resistors, batteries, and capacitor. Applying the loop rule to loop *dfgced* gives

$$-2.0\,I_5 + V_{fg} - 7.0 + 9.0 + 3.0\,I_1 = 0 \qquad \text{or} \qquad 0 + V_{fg} - 7.0 + 9.0 - 1.0 = 0$$

from which $V_{fg} = -1.0$ V. The minus sign tells us that plate $g$ is negative. The capacitor's charge is

$$Q = CV = (5.0\ \mu\text{F})(1.0\text{ V}) = 5.0\ \mu\text{C}$$

**29.5 [III]** For the circuit shown in Fig. 29-5, the resistance $R$ is 5.0 Ω and $\mathscr{E} = 20$ V. Find the readings of the ammeter and the voltmeter. Assume the meters to be ideal.

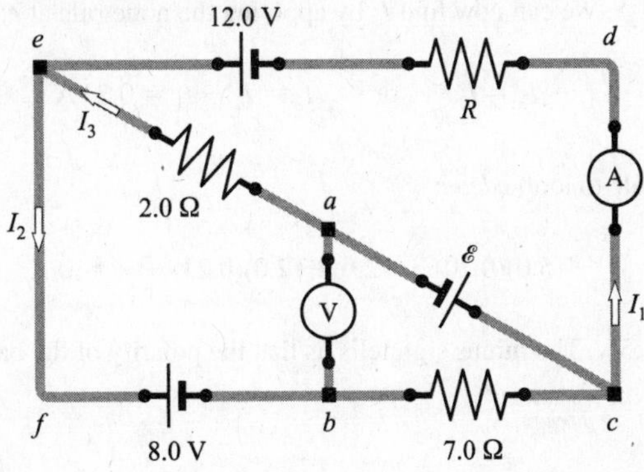


Fig. 29-5

The ideal voltmeter has infinite resistance (no current passes through it), and so it can be removed from the circuit with no effect. Write the loop equation for loop *cdefc*:

$$-RI_1 + 12.0 - 8.0 - 7.0\,I_2 = 0$$

which becomes

$$5.0\,I_1 + 7.0\,I_2 = 4.0 \tag{1}$$

Next write the loop equation for loop *cdeac*. It is

$$-5.0\,I_1 + 12.0 + 2.0\,I_3 + 20.0 = 0$$

$$5.0\,I_1 - 2.0\,I_3 = 32.0 \tag{2}$$

But the node rule applied at *e* gives

$$I_1 + I_3 = I_2 \tag{3}$$

Substituting Eq. (*3*) in Eq. (*1*) yields

$$5.0\,I_1 + 7.0\,I_1 + 7.0\,I_3 = 4.0$$

Solve this for $I_3$ and substitute in (*2*) to get

$$5.0\,I_1 - 2.0\left(\frac{4.0 - 12.0\,I_1}{7.0}\right) = 32.0$$

which yields $I_1 = 3.9$ A, which is the ammeter reading. Then Eq. (*1*) gives $I_2 = -2.2$ A.

To find the voltmeter reading $V_{ab}$, write the loop equation for loop *abca*:

$$V_{ab} - 7.0\,I_2 - \mathscr{E} = 0$$

Substituting the known values of $I_2$ and $\mathscr{E}$, then solving, we obtain $V_{ab} = 4.3$ V. Since this is the potential difference between *a* to *b*, point *b* must be at the higher potential.

**29.6 [III]** In the circuit in Fig. 29-5, $I_1 = 0.20$ A and $R = 5.0\ \Omega$. Find $\mathscr{E}$.

We write the loop equation for loop *cdefc*:

$$-RI_1 + 12.0 - 8.0 - 7.0\,I_2 = 0 \qquad \text{or} \qquad -(5.0)(0.20) + 12.0 - 8.0 - 7.0\,I_2 = 0$$

from which $I_2 = 0.43$ A. We can now find $I_3$ by applying the node rule at *e*:

$$I_1 + I_3 = I_2 \qquad \text{or} \qquad I_3 = I_2 - I_1 = 0.23\ \text{A}$$

Now apply the loop rule to loop *cdeac*:

$$-\,(5.0)(0.20) + 12.0 + (2.0)(0.23) + \mathscr{E} = 0$$

from which $\mathscr{E} = -11.5$ V. The minus sign tells us that the polarity of the battery is actually the reverse of that shown.

## SUPPLEMENTARY PROBLEMS

**29.7 [II]** For the circuit shown in Fig. 29-6, find the current in the 0.96-Ω resistor and the terminal voltages of the batteries.

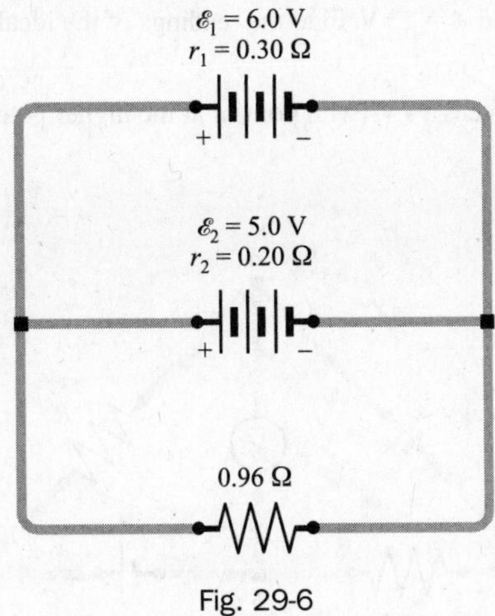

Fig. 29-6

**29.8 [III]** For the network shown in Fig. 29-7, determine (*a*) the three currents $I_1$, $I_2$, and $I_3$, and (*b*) the terminal voltages of the three batteries.

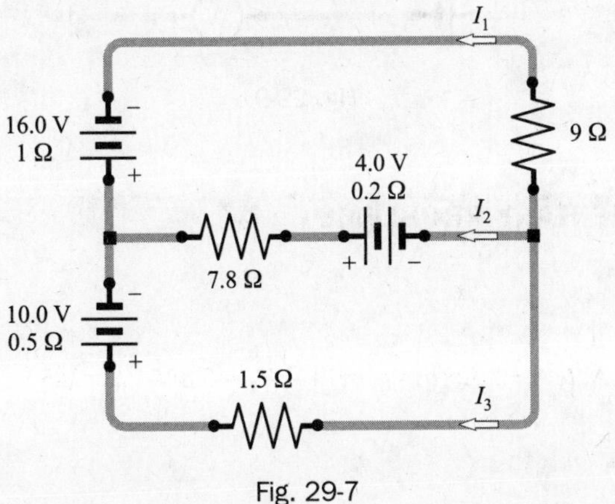

Fig. 29-7

**29.9 [II]** Refer back to Fig. 29-5. If the voltmeter reads 16.0 V (with point-*b* at the higher potential) and $I_2 = 0.20$ A, find $\mathscr{E}$, *R*, and the ammeter reading.

**29.10 [III]** Find $I_1$, $I_2$, $I_3$, and the potential difference between point-*b* to point-*e* in Fig. 29-8.

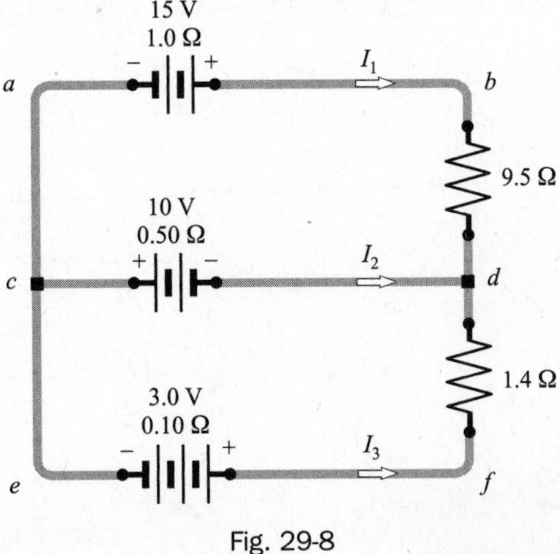

Fig. 29-8

**29.11 [II]** In Fig. 29-9, $R = 10.0\ \Omega$ and $\mathscr{E} = 13$ V. Find the readings of the ideal ammeter and voltmeter.

**29.12 [II]** In Fig. 29-9, the voltmeter reads 14 V (with point-*a* at the higher potential) and the ammeter reads 4.5 A. Find $\mathscr{E}$ and $R$.

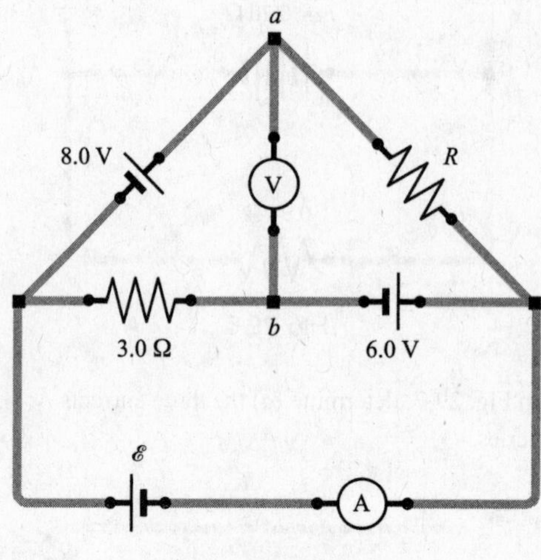


Fig. 29-9

## ANSWERS TO SUPPLEMENTARY PROBLEMS

**29.7 [II]** 5.0 A, 4.8 V, 4.8 V

**29.8 [III]** (*a*) $I_1 = 2$ A, $I_2 = 1$ A, $I_3 = -3$ A; (*b*) $V_{16} = 14$ V, $V_4 = 3.8$ V, $V_{10} = 8.5$ V

**29.9 [II]** 14.6 V, 0.21 Ω, 12 A

**29.10 [III]** 2.0 A, −8.0 A, 6.0 A, −13.0 V

**29.11 [II]** 8.4 A, 27 V with point-*a* positive

**29.12 [II]** $\mathscr{E} = 0$, $R = 3.2\ \Omega$

# Forces in Magnetic Fields

**A Magnetic Field ($\vec{B}$)** exists in an otherwise empty region of space if a charge moving through that region can experience a force due to its motion (as shown in Fig. 30-1). Frequently, a magnetic field is detected by its effect on a compass needle (a tiny *bar magnet*). The compass needle lines up in the direction of the magnetic field.

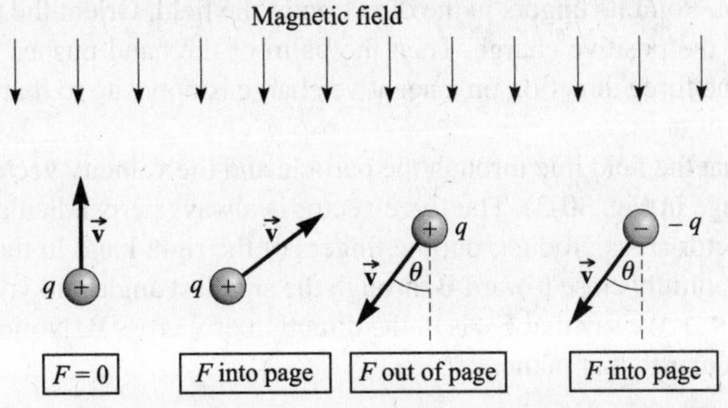


Fig. 30-1

**Magnetic Field Lines** drawn in a region correspond to the direction in which a compass needle placed in that region will point. A method for determining the field lines near a bar magnet is shown in Fig. 30-2. By tradition, we take the direction of the compass needle to be the direction of the field.

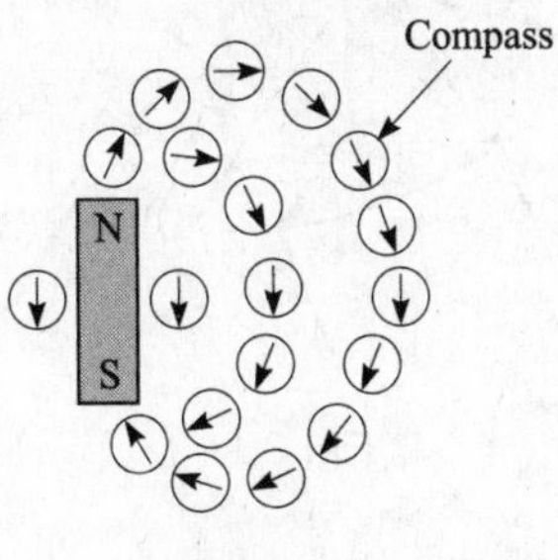


Fig. 30-2

**A Magnet** may have two or more poles, although it must have at least one *north pole* and one *south pole*. Because a compass needle points away from a north pole (N in Fig. 30-2) and toward a south pole (S), ***magnetic field lines exit north poles and enter south poles***.

**Magnetic Poles** of the same type (north or south) repel each other, while unlike poles attract each other.

**A Charge Moving Through a Magnetic Field** experiences a force due to the field, provided its velocity vector is not along a magnetic field line. In Fig. 30-1, charge ($q$) is moving with velocity $\vec{\mathbf{v}}$ in a magnetic field directed as shown. The direction of the force $\vec{\mathbf{F}}$ on each charge is indicated. Notice that ***the direction of the force on a negative charge is opposite to that on a positive charge*** with the same velocity.

**The Direction of the Force** acting on a charge $+q$ moving in a magnetic field can be found from a **right-hand rule** (Fig. 30-3):

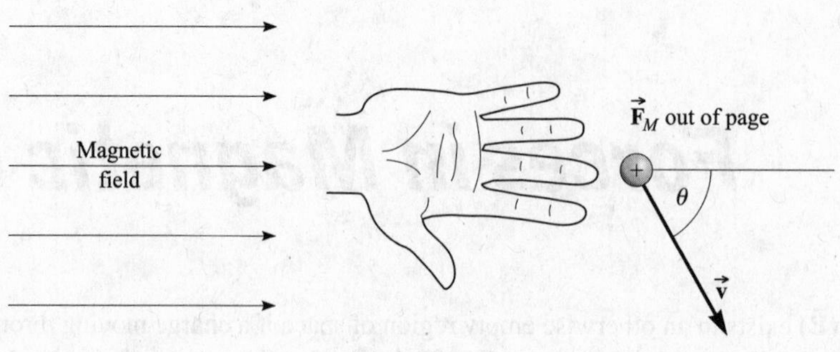


Fig. 30-3

> Hold the right hand flat. Point its fingers in the direction of the field. Orient the thumb along the direction of the velocity of the positive charge. Then the palm of the hand pushes in the direction of the force on the charge. The force direction on a negative charge is opposite to that on a positive charge.

It is often helpful to note that the field line through the particle and the velocity vector of the particle determine a plane (the plane of the page in Fig. 30-3). The force vector is always perpendicular to this plane. An alternative rule is based on the vector cross product: put the fingers of the right hand in the direction of $\vec{\mathbf{v}}$ rotate your hand until the fingers can naturally close toward $\vec{\mathbf{B}}$ through the smallest angle and your thumb then points in the direction $\vec{\mathbf{F}}_M$ of (see Fig. 30-4). We say that $\vec{\mathbf{F}}_M$ is in the direction of $\vec{\mathbf{v}}$ cross $\vec{\mathbf{B}}$. Notice that again $\vec{\mathbf{v}}$ and $\vec{\mathbf{B}}$ define a plane and $\vec{\mathbf{F}}_M$ is perpendicular to that plane.

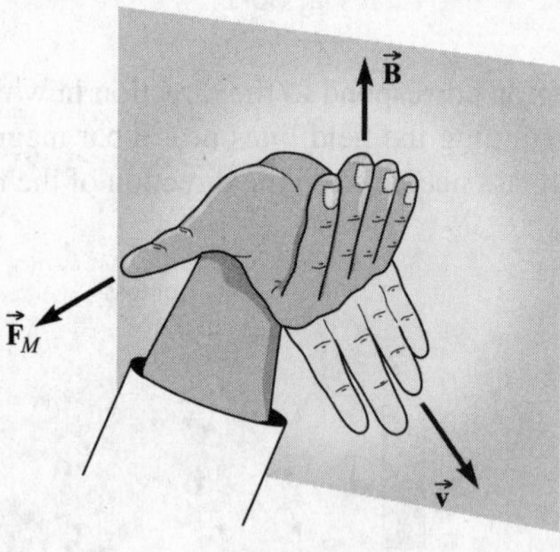


Fig. 30-4

**The Magnitude of the Force** ($F_M$) on a charge moving in a magnetic field depends upon the product of four factors:

(1) $q$, the charge (in C)
(2) $v$, the magnitude of the velocity of the charge (in m/s)
(3) $B$, the strength of the magnetic field
(4) $\sin\theta$, where $\theta$ is the angle between the field lines and the velocity $\vec{\mathbf{v}}$.

**The Magnetic Field at a Point** is represented by a vector $\vec{\mathbf{B}}$ that was once called the *magnetic induction*, or the *magnetic flux density*, and is now simply known as the **magnetic field**.

Define the magnitude of $\vec{\mathbf{B}}$ and its units by way of the equation

$$F_M = qvB \sin\theta$$

where $F_M$ is in newtons, $q$ is in coulombs, $v$ is in m/s, and $B$ is the magnetic field in a unit called the *tesla* (T). For reasons we will see later, a tesla can also be expressed as a **weber per square meter**: 1 T = 1 Wb/m$^2$ (see Chapter 32). Still encountered is the cgs unit for $B$, the **gauss** (G), where

$$1\text{ G} = 10^{-4}\text{ T}$$

The Earth's magnetic field is a few tenths of a gauss. Also note that

$$1\text{ T} = 1\text{ Wb/m}^2 = 1\frac{\text{N}}{\text{C}\cdot(\text{m/s})} = 1\frac{\text{N}}{\text{A}\cdot\text{m}}$$

**Force on a Current in a Magnetic Field:** Since a current is simply a stream of positive charges, a current experiences a force due to a magnetic field. The direction of the force is found by the right-hand rule shown in Figure 30-3 or 30-4, with the direction of the current used in place of the velocity vector.

The magnitude $\Delta F_M$ of the force on a small length $\Delta L$ of wire carrying current $I$ is given by

$$\Delta F_M = I(\Delta L)B \sin\theta$$

where $\theta$ is the angle between the direction of the current $I$ and the direction of the field. For a straight wire of length $L$ completely immersed in a uniform magnetic field, this becomes

$$F_M = ILB \sin\theta$$

Notice that the force is zero if the wire is in line with the field lines. The force is maximum if the field lines are perpendicular to the wire. In analogy to the case of a moving charge, the force is perpendicular to the plane defined by the wire and the field lines.

**Torque on a Flat Coil** in a uniform magnetic field: The torque $\tau$ on a flat coil of $N$ loops, each carrying a current $I$, in an external magnetic field $B$ is

$$\tau = NIAB \sin\theta$$

where $A$ is the area of the coil, and $\theta$ is the angle between the field lines and a perpendicular to the plane of the coil. For the direction of rotation of the coil, we have the following right-hand rule:

> Orient the right thumb perpendicular to the plane of the coil, such that the fingers run in the direction of the current flow. Then the torque acts to rotate the thumb into alignment with the external field (at which orientation the torque will be zero).

Fig. 30-5 illustrates the rule. It depicts a coil of four turns perpendicular to the page, immersed in a uniform $\vec{\mathbf{B}}$-field. In part (*a*) we see how the current, $I$, causes the coil to produce its own dipole field as if it were a small bar magnet. That imaginary bar magnet "wants" to swing into alignment with the $\vec{\mathbf{B}}$-field just as a compass needle would.

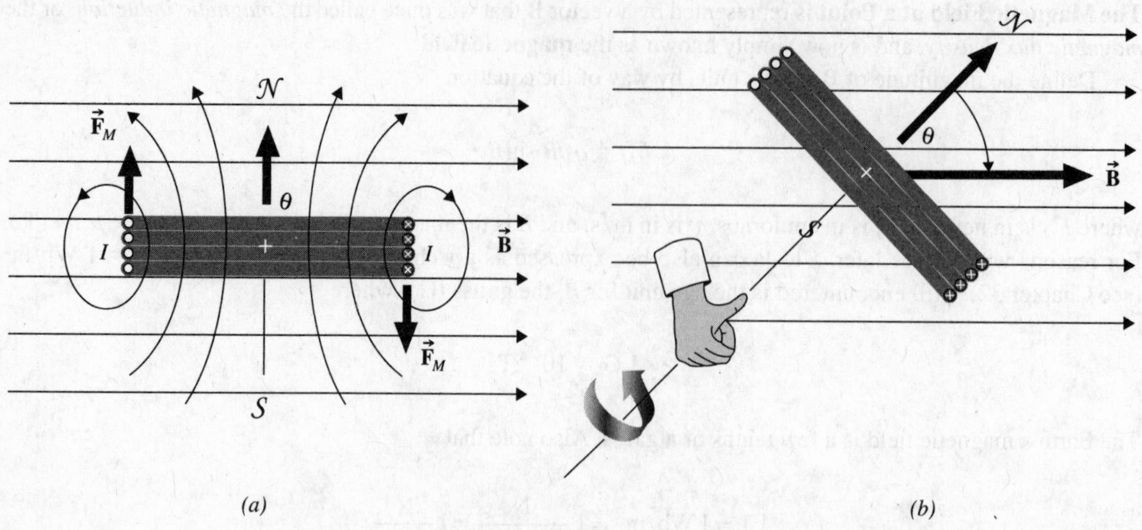


Fig. 30-5

## SOLVED PROBLEMS

**30.1 [I]** A uniform magnetic field, $B = 3.0$ G, exists in the $+x$-direction. A proton ($q = +e$) shoots through the field in the $+y$-direction with a speed of $5.0 \times 10^6$ m/s. (*a*) Find the magnitude and direction of the force on the proton. (*b*) Repeat with the proton replaced by an electron.

(*a*) The situation is shown in Fig. 30-6. We have, after changing 3.0 G to $3.0 \times 10^{-4}$ T,

$$F_M = qvB \sin\theta = (1.6 \times 10^{-19}\text{ C})(5.0 \times 10^6\text{ m/s})(3.0 \times 10^{-4}\text{ T}) \sin 90^\circ = 2.4 \times 10^{-16}\text{ N}$$

The force is perpendicular to the *xy*-plane, the plane defined by the field lines and $\vec{v}$ The right-hand rule tells us that the force is in the $-z$-direction.

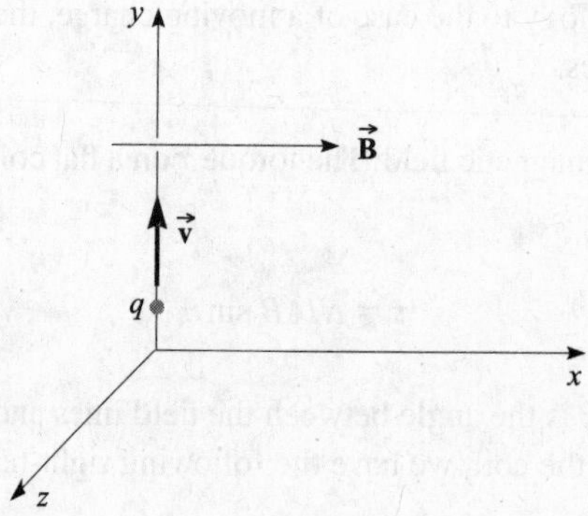


Fig. 30-6

(*b*) The magnitude of the force is the same as in (*a*), $2.4 \times 10^{-16}$ N. But, because the electron is negative, the force direction is reversed. The force is in the $+z$-direction.

**30.2 [II]** The charge shown in Fig. 30-7 is a proton ($q = +e$, $m_p = 1.67 \times 10^{-27}$ kg) with speed $5.0 \times 10^6$ m/s. It is passing through a uniform magnetic field directed up out of the page; $B$ is 30 G. Describe the path followed by the proton.

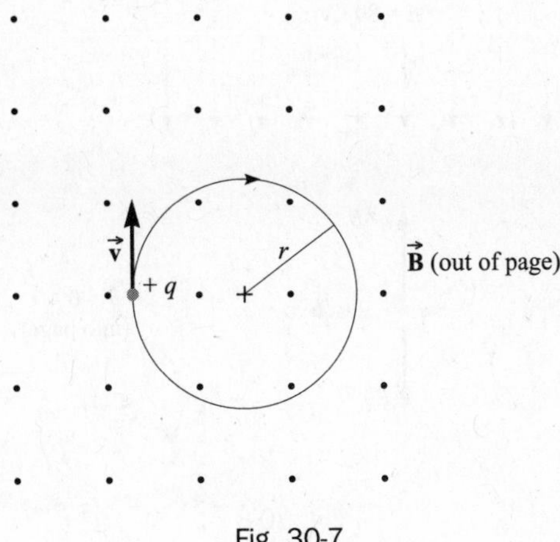


Fig. 30-7

Because the proton's velocity is perpendicular to $\vec{B}$, the force on the proton is

$$qvB \sin 90° = qvB$$

This force is perpendicular to $\vec{v}$, and so it does no work on the proton. It simply deflects the proton and causes it to follow the circular path shown, as you can verify using the right-hand rule. The force $qvB$ is radially inward and supplies the centripetal force for the circular motion: $F_M = qvB = ma = mv^2/r$ and

$$r = \frac{mv}{qB} \qquad (1)$$

For the given data,

$$r = \frac{(1.67 \times 10^{-27}\ \text{kg})\,(5.0 \times 10^{6}\ \text{m/s})}{(1.6 \times 10^{-19}\ \text{C})\,(30 \times 10^{-4}\ \text{T})} = 17\ \text{m}$$

Observe from Eq. (*1*) that the momentum of the charged particle is directly proportional to the radius of its circular orbit.

**30.3 [I]** A proton enters a magnetic field of flux density 1.5 Wb/m² with a velocity of $2.0 \times 10^7$ m/s at an angle of 30° with the field. Compute the magnitude of the force on the proton.

$$F_M = qvB \sin\theta = (1.6 \times 10^{-19}\ \text{C})(2.0 \times 10^7 \text{m/s})(1.5\ \text{Wb/m}^2) \sin 30° = 2.4 \times 10^{-12}\ \text{N}$$

**30.4 [I]** A cathode ray beam (i.e., an electron beam; $m_e = 9.1 \times 10^{-31}$ kg, $q = -e$) is bent in a circle of radius 2.0 cm by a uniform field with $B = 4.5 \times 10^{-3}$ T. What is the speed of the electrons?

To describe a circle like this, the particles must be moving perpendicular to $\vec{B}$ From Eq. (*1*) of Problem 30.2,

$$v = \frac{rqB}{m} = \frac{(0.020\ \text{m})\,(1.6 \times 10^{-19}\ \text{C})\,(4.5 \times 10^{-3}\ \text{T})}{9.1 \times 10^{-31}\ \text{kg}} = 1.58 \times 10^{7}\ \text{m/s} = 1.6 \times 10^{4}\ \text{km/s}$$

**30.5 [II]** As shown in Fig. 30-8, a particle of charge $q$ enters a region where an electric field is uniform and directed downward. Its value $E$ is 80 kV/m. Perpendicular to $\vec{E}$ and directed into the page is a magnetic field $B = 0.4$ T. If the speed of the particle is properly chosen, the particle will not be deflected by these crossed electric and magnetic fields. What speed should be selected in this case? (This device is called a velocity selector.)

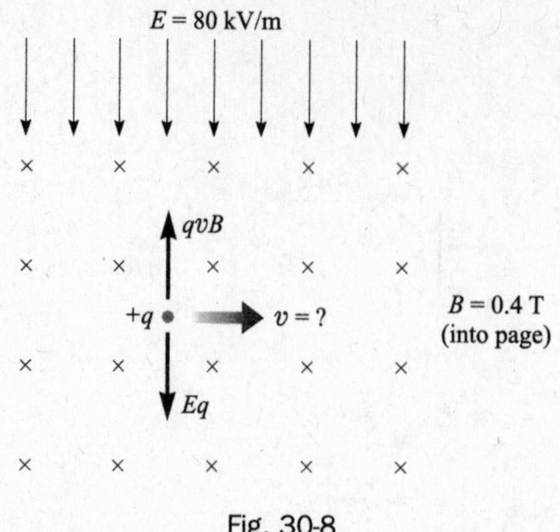


Fig. 30-8

The electric field causes a downward force $Eq$ on the charge if it is positive. The right-hand rule tells us that the magnetic force, $qvB \sin 90°$, is upward if $q$ is positive. If these two forces are to balance so that the particle does not deflect, then

$$Eq = qvB \sin 90° \qquad \text{or} \qquad v = \frac{E}{B} = \frac{80 \times 10^3 \text{ V/m}}{0.4 \text{ T}} = 2 \times 10^5 \text{ m/s}$$

When $q$ is negative, both forces are reversed, so the result $v = E/B$ still holds.

**30.6 [III]** In Fig. 30-9($a$), a proton ($q = +e$, $m_p = 1.67 \times 10^{-27}$ kg) is shot with a speed of $8.0 \times 10^6$ m/s at an angle of 30.0° to an $x$-directed field $B = 0.15$ T. Describe the path followed by the proton.

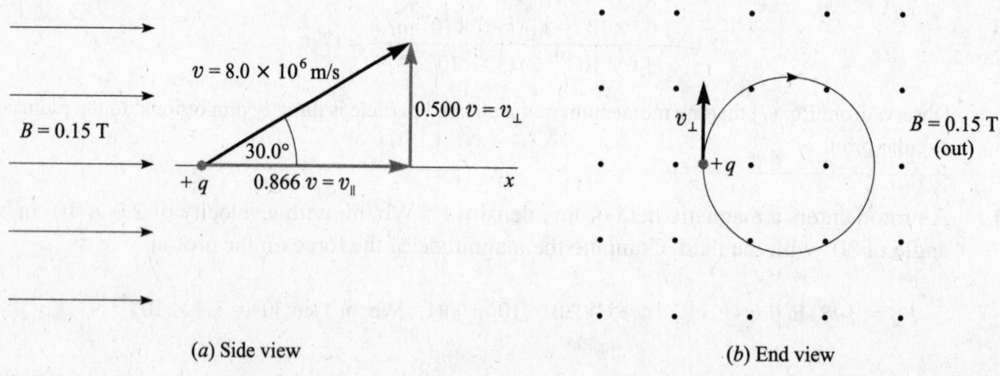


Fig. 30-9

Resolve the particle velocity into components parallel to and perpendicular to the magnetic field. The magnetic force in the direction of $v_\parallel$ is zero ($\sin \theta = 0$); the magnetic force in the direction of $v_\perp$ has no $x$-component. Therefore, the motion in the $x$-direction is uniform, at speed

$$v_\parallel = (0.866)(8.0 \times 10^6 \text{ m/s}) = 6.93 \times 10^6 \text{ m/s}$$

while the transverse motion is circular (see Problem 30.2), with radius

$$r = \frac{mv_\perp}{qB} = \frac{(1.67 \times 10^{-27} \text{ kg})\,(0.500 \times 8.0 \times 10^6 \text{ m/s})}{(1.6 \times 10^{-19} \text{ C})\,(0.15 \text{ T})} = 0.28 \text{ m}$$

The proton will spiral along the $x$-axis; the radius of the spiral (or helix) will be 28 cm.

To find the **pitch** of the helix (the $x$-distance traveled during one revolution), note that the time taken to complete one circle is

$$\text{Period} = \frac{2\pi r}{v_\perp} = \frac{2\pi(0.28\text{ m})}{(0.500)(8.0\times10^6\text{ m/s})} = 4.4\times10^{-7}\text{ s}$$

During that time, the proton will travel an $x$-distance of

$$\text{Pitch} = (v_\parallel)(\text{period}) = (6.93\times10^6\text{ m/s})(4.4\times10^{-7}\text{ s}) = 3.0\text{ m}$$

**30.7 [II]** Alpha particles ($m_\alpha = 6.68\times10^{-27}$ kg, $q = +2e$) are accelerated from rest through a p.d. of 1.0 kV. They then enter a magnetic field $B = 0.20$ T perpendicular to their direction of motion. Calculate the radius of their path.

Their final KE is equal to the electric potential energy they lose during acceleration, $Vq$:

$$\tfrac{1}{2}mv^2 = Vq \qquad \text{or} \qquad v = \sqrt{\frac{2Vq}{m}}$$

From Problem 30.2, they follow a circular path in which

$$r = \frac{mv}{qB} = \frac{m}{qB}\sqrt{\frac{2Vq}{m}} = \frac{1}{B}\sqrt{\frac{2Vm}{q}}$$

$$= \frac{1}{0.20\text{ T}}\sqrt{\frac{2(1000\text{ V})(6.68\times10^{-27}\text{ kg})}{3.2\times10^{-19}\text{ C}}} = 0.032\text{ m}$$

**30.8 [I]** In Fig. 30-10, the magnetic field is up out of the page and $B = 0.80$ T. The wire shown carries a current of 30 A. Find the magnitude and direction of the force on a 5.0 cm length of the wire.

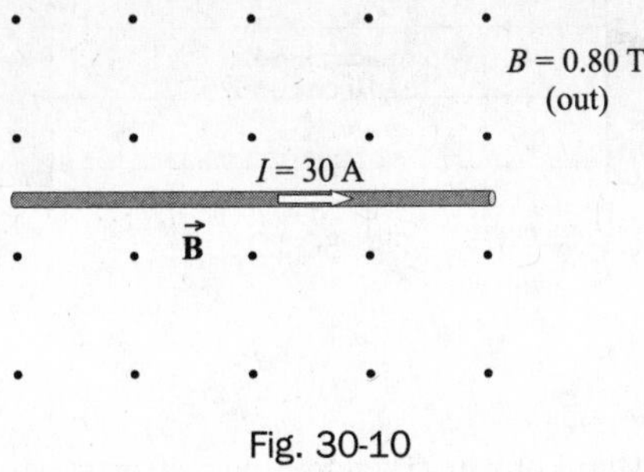


Fig. 30-10

We know that

$$\Delta F_M = I(\Delta L)B\sin\theta = (30\text{ A})(0.050\text{ m})(0.80\text{ T})(1) = 1.2\text{ N}$$

By the right-hand rule, the force is perpendicular to both the wire and the field and is directed toward the bottom of the page.

**30.9 [I]** As shown in Fig. 30-11, a loop of wire carries a current $I$ and its plane is perpendicular to a uniform magnetic field $\vec{\mathbf{B}}$. What are the resultant force and torque on the loop?

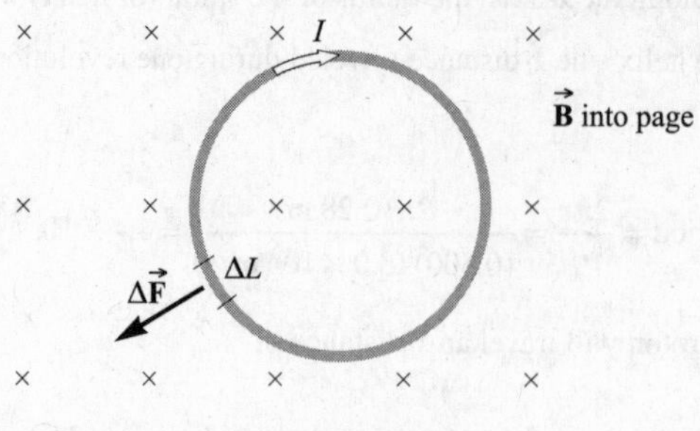


Fig. 30-11

Consider the length $\Delta L$ shown. The force $\Delta \vec{F}$ on it has the direction indicated. A point directly opposite this on the loop has an equal, but opposite, force acting on it. Hence, the forces on the loop cancel and the resultant force on it is zero.

We see from the figure that the $\Delta \vec{F}$'s acting on the loop are trying to expand it, not rotate it. Therefore, the torque ($\tau$) on the loop is zero. Or, making use of the torque equation,

$$\tau = NIAB \sin \theta$$

where $\theta$ is the angle between the field lines and the perpendicular to the plane of the loop. That angle is zero. Therefore, $\sin 0 = 0$ and the torque is zero.

**30.10 [I]** The 40-loop coil shown in Fig. 30-12 carries a current of 2.0 A in a magnetic field $B = 0.25$ T. Find the torque on it. How will it rotate?

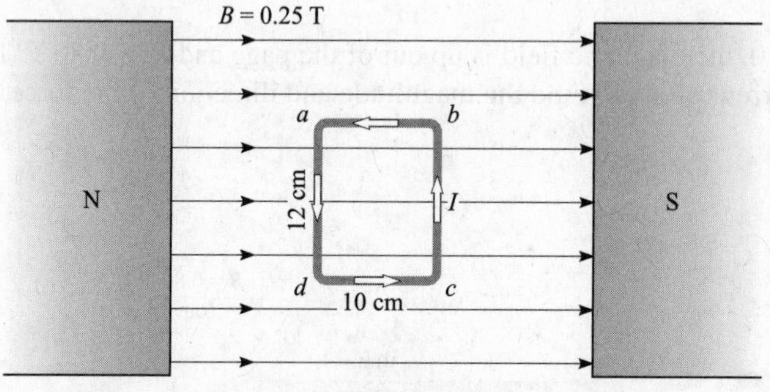


Fig. 30-12

**Method 1**

The coil is composed of 40 turns of wire. Therefore, $N = 40$ and

$$\tau = NIAB \sin \theta = (40)(2.0\text{ A})(0.10\text{ m} \times 0.12\text{ m})(0.25\text{ T})(\sin 90°) = 0.24\text{ N}\cdot\text{m}$$

(Remember that $\theta$ is the angle between the field lines and the perpendicular to the loop.) By the right-hand rule, the coil will turn about a vertical axis in such a way that side *ad* moves up out of the page and side *bc* moves down into the page.

**Method 2**

Because sides *dc* and *ab* are in line with the field, the force on each of them is zero, while the force on each vertical wire is

$$F_M = ILB = (2.0\text{ A})(0.12\text{ m})(0.25\text{ T}) = 0.060\text{ N}$$

out of the page on side *ad* and into the page on side *bc*. If we take torques about side *bc* as axis, only the force on side *ad* gives a nonzero torque. It is

$$\tau = (40 \times 0.060 \text{ N})(0.10 \text{ m}) = 0.24 \text{ N}\cdot\text{m}$$

and it tends to rotate side *ad* up out of the page.

**30.11 [I]** **In Fig. 30-13 is shown only one-quarter of a single complete circular loop of wire that carries a current of 14 A. Its radius is $a = 5.0$ cm. A uniform magnetic field, $B = 300$ G, is directed in the $+x$-direction. Find the torque on the loop and the direction in which it will rotate.**

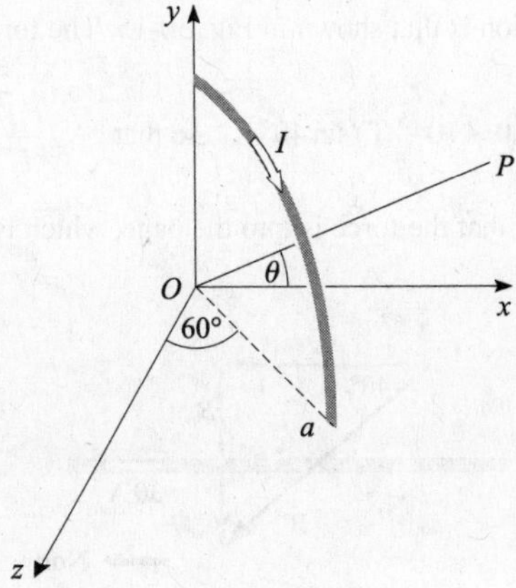

Fig. 30-13

The normal to the loop, $\overline{OP}$, makes an angle $\theta = 60°$ with the $+x$-direction, the field direction. Hence,

$$\tau = NIAB \sin\theta = (1)(14 \text{ A})(\pi \times 25 \times 10^{-4} \text{ m}^2)(0.030\,0 \text{ T}) \sin 60° = 2.9 \times 10^{-3} \text{ N}\cdot\text{m}$$

The right-hand rule shows that the loop will rotate about the *y*-axis so as to decrease the angle labeled 60°.

**30.12 [II]** **Two electrons, both with speed $5.0 \times 10^6$ m/s, are shot into a uniform magnetic field $\vec{\mathbf{B}}$. The first is shot from the origin out along the $+x$-axis, and it moves in a circle that intersects the $+z$-axis at $z = 16$ cm. The second is shot out along the $+y$-axis, and it moves in a straight line. Find the magnitude and direction of $\vec{\mathbf{B}}$.**

The situation is shown in Fig. 30-14. Because a charge experiences no force when moving along a field line, the field must be in either the $+y$- or $-y$-direction. Use of the right-hand rule for the motion shown in the diagram for the *negative* electron charge leads us to conclude that the field is in the $-y$-direction.

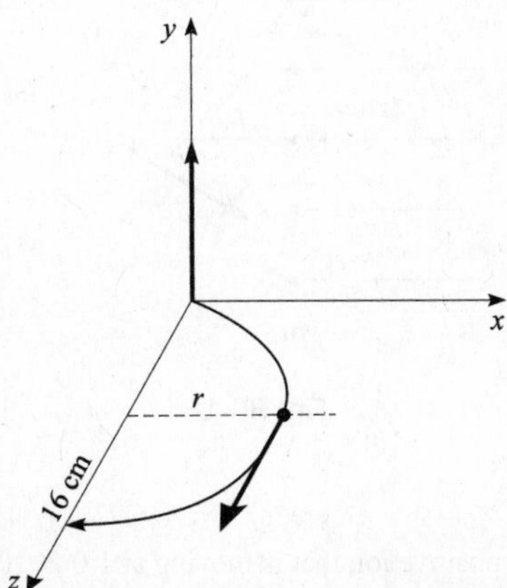

Fig. 30-14

To find the magnitude of $\vec{\mathbf{B}}$, we notice that $r = 8$ cm. The magnetic force $Bqv$ provides the needed centripetal force $mv^2/r$, and so

$$B = \frac{mv}{qr} = \frac{(9.1\times10^{-31}\ \text{kg})\,(5.0\times10^{6}\ \text{m/s})}{(1.6\times10^{-19}\ \text{C})\,(0.080\ \text{m})} = 3.6\times10^{-4}\ \text{T}$$

**30.13 [I]** **At a certain place on the planet, the Earth's magnetic field is $5.0 \times 10^{-5}$ T, directed 40° below the horizontal. Find the force per meter of length on a horizontal wire that carries a current of 30 A northward.**

Nearly everywhere, the Earth's field is directed northward. (That is the direction in which a compass needle points.) Therefore, the situation is that shown in Fig. 30-15. The force on the wire is

$$F_M = (30\ \text{A})\,(L)\,(5.0\times10^{-5}\ \text{T})\sin 40° \qquad \text{so that} \qquad \frac{F_M}{L} = 9.6\times10^{-4}\ \text{N/m}$$

The right-hand rule indicates that the force is into the page, which is west.

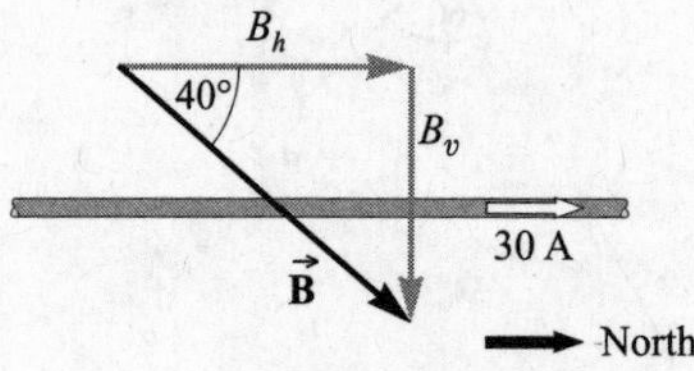


Fig. 30-15

## SUPPLEMENTARY PROBLEMS

**30.14 [I]** An ion ($q = +2e$) enters a magnetic field of 1.2 Wb/m$^2$ at a speed of $2.5 \times 10^5$ m/s perpendicular to the field. Determine the force on the ion.

**30.15 [II]** Calculate the speed of ions that pass undeflected through crossed $E$ and $B$ fields for which $E = 7.7$ kV/m and $B = 0.14$ T.

**30.16 [I]** The particle shown in Fig. 30-16 is positively charged in all three cases. What is the direction of the force on it due to the magnetic field? Give its magnitude in terms of $B$, $q$, and $v$.

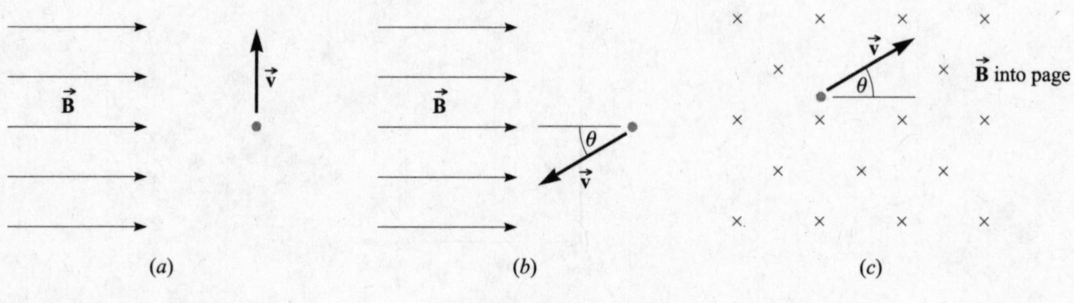


Fig. 30-16

**30.17 [II]** What might be the mass of a positive ion that is moving at $1.0 \times 10^7$ m/s and is bent into a circular path of radius 1.55 m by a magnetic field of 0.134 Wb/m$^2$? (There are several possible answers.)

**30.18 [II]** An electron is accelerated from rest through a potential difference of 3750 V. It enters a region where $B = 4.0 \times 10^{-3}$ T perpendicular to its velocity. Calculate the radius of the path it will follow.

**30.19 [II]** An electron is shot with speed $5.0 \times 10^6$ m/s out from the origin of coordinates. Its initial velocity makes an angle of 20° to the $+x$-axis. Describe its motion if a magnetic field $B = 2.0$ mT exists in the $+x$-direction.

**30.20 [II]** A beam of electrons passes undeflected through two mutually perpendicular electric and magnetic fields. If the electric field is cut off and the same magnetic field maintained, the electrons move in the magnetic field in a circular path of radius 1.14 cm. Determine the ratio of the electronic charge to the electron mass if $E = 8.00$ kV/m and the magnetic field has flux density 2.00 mT.

**30.21 [I]** A straight wire 15 cm long, carrying a current of 6.0 A, is in a uniform field of 0.40 T. What is the force on the wire when it is (*a*) at right angles to the field and (*b*) at 30° to the field?

**30.22 [I]** What is the direction of the force, due to the Earth's magnetic field, on a wire carrying current vertically downward?

**30.23 [I]** Find the force on each segment of the wire shown in Fig. 30-17 if $B = 0.15$ T. Assume the current in the wire to be 5.0 A.

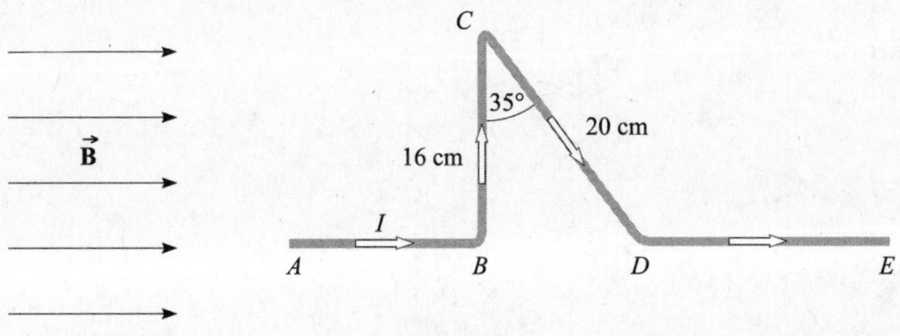


Fig. 30-17

**30.24 [II]** A flat rectangular coil of 25 loops is suspended in a uniform magnetic field of 0.20 Wb/m². The plane of the coil is parallel to the direction of the field. The dimensions of the coil are 15 cm perpendicular to the field lines and 12 cm parallel to them. What is the current in the coil if there is a torque of 5.4 N·m acting on it?

**30.25 [II]** An electron is accelerated from rest through a potential difference of 800 V. It then moves perpendicularly to a magnetic field of 30 G. Find the radius of its orbit and its orbital frequency.

**30.26 [II]** A proton and a deuteron ($m_d \approx 2m_p$, $q_d = e$) are both accelerated through the same potential difference and enter a magnetic field along the same line. If the proton follows a path of radius $R_p$, what will be the radius of the deuteron's path?

## ANSWERS TO SUPPLEMENTARY PROBLEMS

**30.14 [I]** $9.6 \times 10^{-14}$ N

**30.15 [II]** 55 km/s

**30.16 [I]** (*a*) into the page, $qvB$; (*b*) out of the page, $qvB \sin\theta$; (*c*) in the plane of the page at angle $\theta + 90°$, $qvB$

**30.17 [II]** $n(3.3 \times 10^{-27}$ kg), where $ne$ is the ion's charge

**30.18 [II]** 5.2 cm

**30.19 [II]** helix, $r = 0.49$ cm, pitch $= 8.5$ cm

**30.20 [II]** $e/m_e = 175$ GC/kg where that G is not gauss

**30.21 [I]** (*a*) 0.36 N; (*b*) 0.18 N

**30.22 [I]** horizontally toward east

**30.23 [I]** In sections *AB* and *DE*, the force is zero; in section *BC*, 0.12 N into page; in section *CD*, 0.12 N out of page

**30.24 [II]** 60 A

**30.25 [II]** 3.2 cm, 84 MHz

**30.26 [II]** $R_d = R_p\sqrt{2}$

# Sources of Magnetic Fields

**Magnetic Fields Are Produced** by moving charges, and of course that includes electric currents. Figure 31-1 shows the nature of the magnetic fields produced by several current configurations. Below each is given the value of B at the indicated point-$P$. The constant $\mu_0 = 4\pi \times 10^{-7}\ \text{T}\cdot\text{m/A}$ is called the *permeability of free space*. It is assumed that the surrounding material is either vacuum or air.

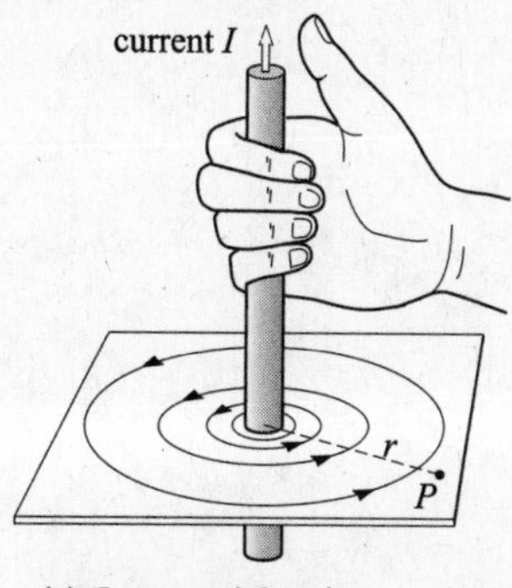


(*a*) Long straight wire:

$$B = \frac{\mu_0 I}{2\pi r}$$

where $r$ is distance to $P$ from the axis of the wire

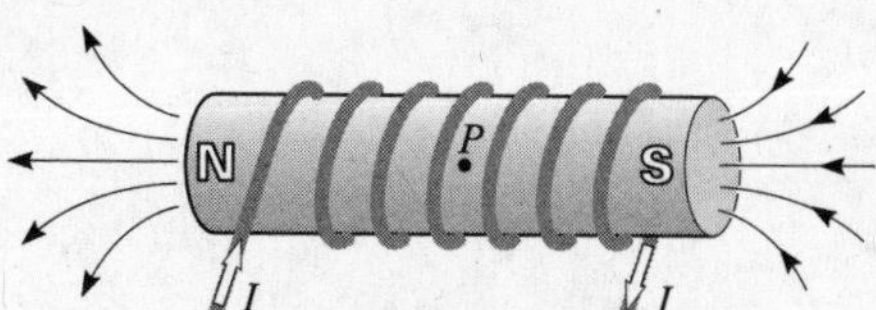


(*c*) Interior point of long solenoid with $n$ loops per meter:

$$B = \mu_0 nI$$

It is constant in the interior

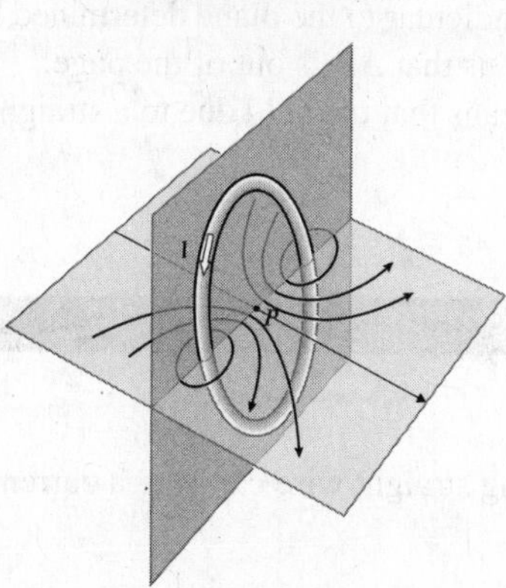


(*b*) Center of a circular coil with radius $r$ and $N$ loops:

$$B = \frac{\mu_0 NI}{2r}$$

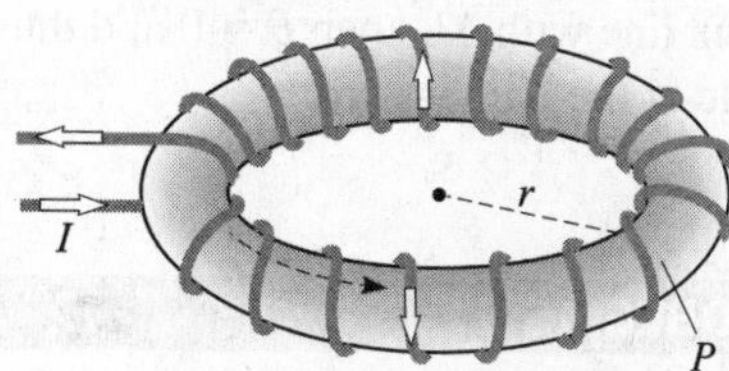


(*d*) Interior point of toroid having $N$ loops:

$$B = \frac{\mu_0 NI}{2\pi r}$$

where $r$ is the radius of the circle on which $P$ lies

Fig. 31-1

**The Direction of the Magnetic Field** of a current-carrying wire can be found by using a right-hand rule, as illustrated in Fig. 31-1(*a*):

> Grasp the wire in the right hand, with the thumb pointing in the direction of the current. The fingers then circle the wire in the same direction as the magnetic field does.
>
> This same rule can be used to find the direction of the field for a current loop such as that shown in Fig. 31-1(*b*).

**Ferromagnetic Materials**, primarily iron and the other transition elements, greatly enhance magnetic fields. Other materials influence *B*-fields only slightly. The ferromagnetic materials contain *domains,* or regions of aligned atoms, that act as tiny bar magnets. When the domains within an object are aligned with each other, the object becomes a magnet. The alignment of domains in permanent magnets is not easily disrupted.

**The Magnetic Moment** of a flat current-carrying loop (current = $I$, area = $A$) is $IA$. The magnetic moment is a vector quantity that points along the field line perpendicular to the plane of the loop. In terms of the magnetic moment, the torque on a flat coil with $N$ loops in a magnetic field $B$ is $\tau = N(IA)B\sin\theta$, where $\theta$ is the angle between the field and the magnetic moment vector.

**Magnetic Field of a Current Element:** The current element of length $\Delta L$ shown in Fig. 31-2 contributes $\Delta\vec{\mathbf{B}}$ to the field at $P$. The magnitude of $\Delta\vec{\mathbf{B}}$ is given by the *Biot-Savart Law*:

$$\Delta B = \frac{\mu_0 I\,\Delta L}{4\pi r^2}\sin\theta$$

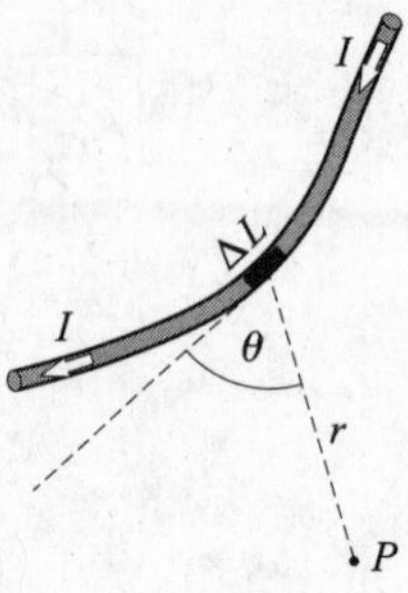

Fig. 31-2

where $r$ and $\theta$ are defined in the figure. The direction of $\Delta\vec{\mathbf{B}}$ is perpendicular to the plane determined by $\Delta L$ and $r$ (the plane of the page). In the case shown, the right-hand rule tells us that $\Delta\vec{\mathbf{B}}$ is out of the page.

When $r$ is in line with $\Delta L$, then $\theta = 0$ and thus $\Delta B = 0$. This means that the field due to a straight wire at a point on the line of the wire is zero.

## SOLVED PROBLEMS

**31.1 [I]** Compute the value of $B$ in air at a point 5 cm from a long straight wire carrying a current of 15 A.

From Fig. 31-1(*a*),

$$B = \frac{\mu_0 I}{2\pi r} = \frac{(4\pi\times10^{-7}\ \text{T}\cdot\text{m/A})(15\ \text{A})}{2\pi(0.05\ \text{m})} = 6\times10^{-5}\ \text{T}$$

**31.2 [I]** A flat circular coil with 40 loops of wire has a diameter of 32 cm. What current must flow in its wires to produce a field in air of $3.0\times10^{-4}$ Wb/m$^2$ at its center?

From Fig. 31-1(*b*),

$$B = \frac{\mu_0 NI}{2r} \qquad \text{or} \qquad 3.0 \times 10^{-4}\ \text{T} = \frac{(4\pi \times 10^{-7}\ \text{T}\cdot\text{m/A})(40)(I)}{2(0.16\ \text{m})}$$

Which gives $I = 1.9$ A.

**31.3 [I]** **An air-core solenoid with 2000 loops is 60 cm long and has a diameter of 2.0 cm. If a current of 5.0 A is sent through it, what will be the flux density within it?**

From Fig. 31-3(*c*),

$$B = \mu_0 nI = (4\pi \times 10^{-7}\ \text{T}\cdot\text{m/A})\left(\frac{2000}{0.60\ \text{m}}\right)(5.0\ \text{A}) = 0.021\ \text{T}$$

**31.4 [I]** **In Bohr's model of the hydrogen atom, the electron travels with speed $2.2 \times 10^6$ m/s in a circle ($r = 5.3 \times 10^{-11}$ m) about the nucleus. Find the value of $B$ at the nucleus due to the electron's motion. Assume vacuum.**

In Problem 26.17 we found that the orbiting electron corresponds to a current loop with $I = 1.06$ mA. The field at the center of the current loop is

$$B = \frac{\mu_0 I}{2r} = \frac{(4\pi \times 10^{-7}\ \text{T}\cdot\text{m/A})(1.06 \times 10^{-3}\ \text{A})}{2(5.3 \times 10^{-11}\ \text{m})} = 13\ \text{T}$$

**31.5 [II]** **A long straight wire coincides with the $x$-axis, and another coincides with the $y$-axis. Each carries a current of 5 A in the positive coordinate direction. (See Fig. 31-3.) Where is their combined field equal to zero?**

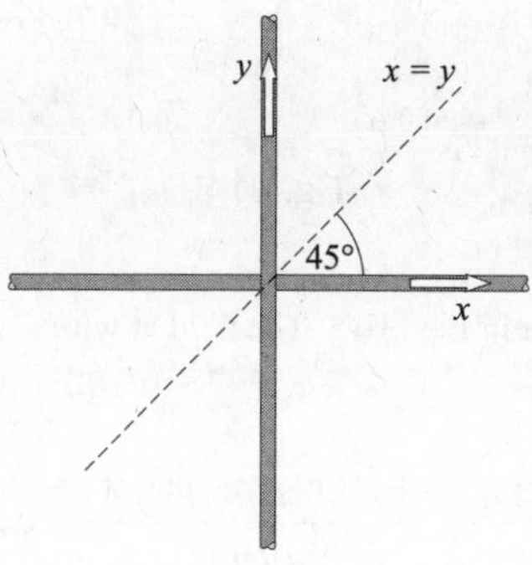


Fig. 31-3

Use of the right-hand rule should convince you that their fields tend to cancel in the first and third quadrants. A line at $\theta = 45°$ passing through the origin is equidistant from the two wires in these quadrants. Hence, the fields exactly cancel along the line $x = y$, the 45° line.

**31.6 [II]** **A long wire carries a current of 20 A along the axis of a long solenoid in air. The field due to the solenoid is 4.0 mT. Find the resultant field at a point 3.0 mm from the solenoid axis.**

The situation is shown in Fig. 31-4. The field of the solenoid, $\vec{\mathbf{B}}_s$, is directed parallel to the wire. The field of the long straight wire, $\vec{\mathbf{B}}_w$, circles the wire and is perpendicular to $\vec{\mathbf{B}}_s$ We have $B_s = 4.0$ mT and

$$B_w = \frac{\mu_0 I}{2\pi r} = \frac{(4\pi \times 10^{-7}\ \text{T}\cdot\text{m/A})(20\ \text{A})}{2\pi(3.0 \times 10^{-3}\ \text{m})} = 1.33\ \text{mT}$$

Since $\vec{\mathbf{B}}_s$ and $\vec{\mathbf{B}}_w$ are perpendicular, their resultant $\vec{\mathbf{B}}$ has magnitude

$$B = \sqrt{(4.0\ \text{mT})^2 + (1.33\ \text{mT})^2} = 4.2\ \text{mT}$$

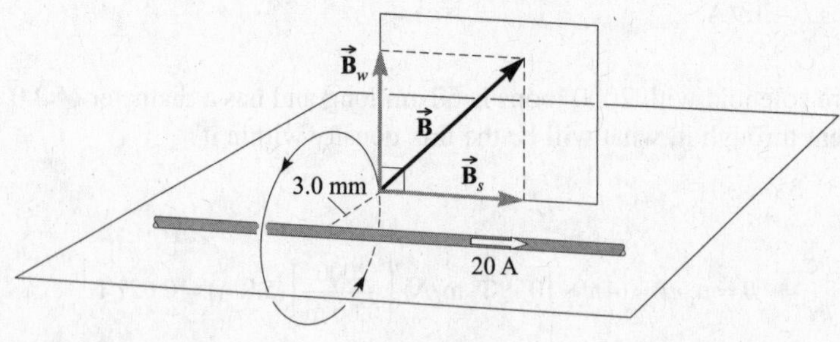


Fig. 31-4

**31.7 [II]** As shown in Fig. 31-5, two long parallel wires are 10 cm apart in air and carry currents of 6.0 A and 4.0 A. Find the force on a 1.0-m length of wire *D* if the currents are (*a*) parallel and (*b*) antiparallel.

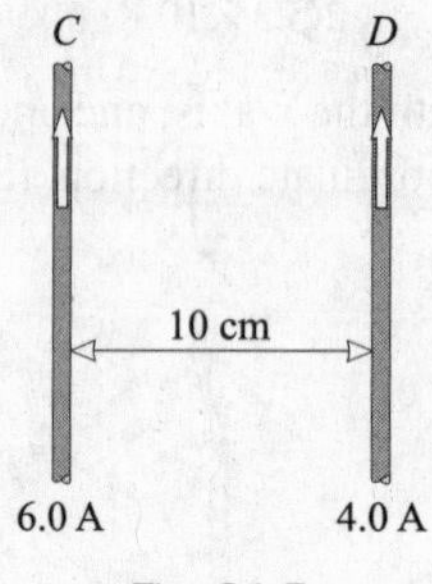


Fig. 31-5

(*a*) This is the situation shown in Fig. 31-5. The field at wire *D* due to wire *C* is directed into the page and has the value

$$B = \frac{\mu_0 I}{2\pi r} = \frac{(4\pi \times 10^{-7}\ \text{T}\cdot\text{m/A})\ (6.0\ \text{A})}{2\pi(0.10\ \text{m})} = 1.2 \times 10^{-5}\ \text{T}$$

The force on 1 m of wire *D* due to this field is

$$F_M = ILB \sin\theta = (4.0\ \text{A})\ (1.0\ \text{m})\ (1.2 \times 10^{-5}\ \text{T})\ (\sin 90°) = 48\ \mu\text{N}$$

The right-hand rule applied to wire *D* tells us the force on *D* is toward the left. The wires attract each other.

(*b*) If the current in *D* flows in the reverse direction, the force direction will be reversed. The wires will repel each other. The force per meter of length is still 48 $\mu$N.

**31.8 [III]** Consider the three long, straight, parallel wires in air shown in Fig. 31-6. Find the force experienced by a 25-cm length of wire *C*.

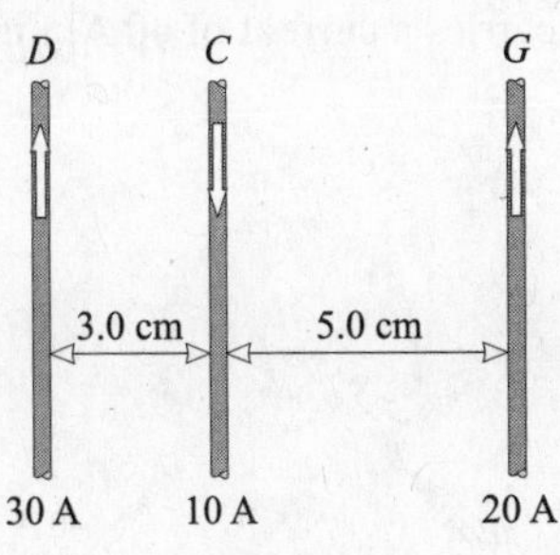


Fig. 31-6

The fields due to wires $D$ and $G$ at wire $C$ are

$$B_D = \frac{\mu_0 I}{2\pi r} = \frac{(4\pi \times 10^{-7}\ \mathrm{T\cdot m/A})\,(30\ \mathrm{A})}{2\pi(0.030\ \mathrm{m})} = 2.0 \times 10^{-4}\ \mathrm{T}$$

into the page, and

$$B_G = \frac{(4\pi \times 10^{-7}\ \mathrm{T\cdot m/A})\,(20\ \mathrm{A})}{2\pi(0.050\ \mathrm{m})} = 0.80 \times 10^{-4}\ \mathrm{T}$$

out of the page. Therefore, the field at the position of wire $C$ is

$$B = 2.0 \times 10^{-4} - 0.80 \times 10^{-4} = 1.2 \times 10^{-4}\ \mathrm{T}$$

into the page. The force on a 25-cm length of $C$ is

$$F_M = ILB \sin\theta = (10\ \mathrm{A})(0.25\mathrm{m})(1.2 \times 10^{-4}\ \mathrm{T})\,(\sin 90°) = 0.30\ \mathrm{mN}$$

Using the right-hand rule at wire $C$ tells us that the force on wire $C$ is toward the right.

**31.9 [III]** A flat circular coil having 10 loops of wire has a diameter of 2.0 cm and carries a current of 0.50 A. It is mounted inside a long solenoid immersed in air, that has 200 loops on its 25-cm length. The current in the solenoid is 2.4 A. Compute the torque required to hold the coil with its central axis perpendicular to that of the solenoid.

Let the subscripts $s$ and $c$ refer to the solenoid and coil, respectively. Then

$$\tau = N_c I_c A_c B_s \sin 90°$$

But $B_s = \mu_0 n I_s = \mu_0 (N_s/L_s) I_s$, which gives

$$\tau = \frac{\mu_0 N_c N_s I_c I_s\,(\pi r_c^2)}{L_s}$$

$$= \frac{(4\pi \times 10^{-7}\mathrm{T\cdot m/A})\,(10)\,(200)\,(0.50\ \mathrm{A})\,(2.4\ \mathrm{A})\,\pi\,(0.010\ \mathrm{m})^2}{0.25\ \mathrm{m}}$$

$$= 3.8 \times 10^{-6}\ \mathrm{N\cdot m}$$

**31.10 [III]** The wire shown in Fig. 31-7 carries a current of 40 A. Find the field at point-*P*.

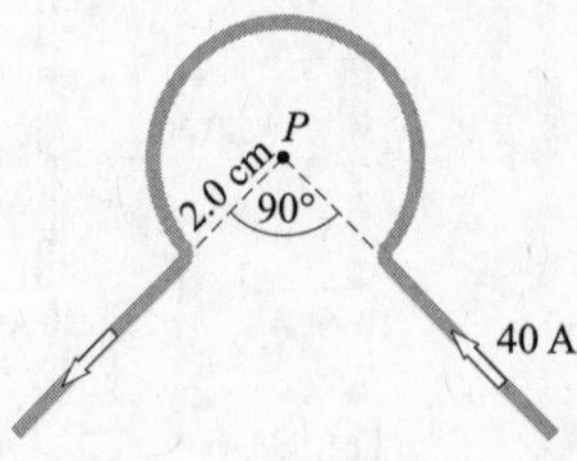


Fig. 31-7

Since *P* lies on the lines of the straight wires, those wires contribute no field at *P*. A circular loop of radius *r* gives a field of $B = \mu_0 I/2r$ at its center point. Here we have only three-fourths of a loop, and so we can assume that

$$B \text{ at point-}P = \left(\frac{3}{4}\right)\left(\frac{\mu_0 I}{2r}\right) = \frac{(3)\,(4\pi\times10^{-7}\ \text{T}\cdot\text{m/A})(40\ \text{A})}{(4)\,(2)\,(0.020\ \text{m})}$$

$$= 9.4\times10^{-4}\ \text{T} = 0.94\ \text{mT}$$

The field is out of the page.

## SUPPLEMENTARY PROBLEMS

**31.11 [I]** Compute the magnitude of the magnetic field in air at a point 6.0 cm from a long straight wire carrying a current of 9.0 A.

**31.12 [I]** A closely wound, flat, circular coil of 25 turns of wire has a diameter of 10 cm and carries a current of 4.0 A. Determine the value of *B* at its center when immersed in air.

**31.13 [I]** An air-core solenoid 50 cm long has 4000 turns of wire wound on it. Compute *B* in its interior when a current of 0.25 A exists in the winding.

**31.14 [I]** A uniformly wound air-core toroid has 750 loops on it. The radius of the circle through the center of its windings is 5 cm. What current in the winding will produce a field of 1.8 mT on this central circle?

**31.15 [II]** Two long parallel wires in vacuum are 4 cm apart and carry currents of 2 A and 6 A in the same direction. Compute the force between the wires per meter of wire length.

**31.16 [II]** Two long fixed parallel wires, *A* and *B*, are 10 cm apart in air and carry 40 A and 20 A, respectively, in opposite directions. Determine the resultant field (*a*) on a line midway between the wires and parallel to them and (*b*) on a line 8.0 cm from wire *A* and 18 cm from wire *B*. (*c*) What is the force per meter on a third long wire, midway between *A* and *B* and in their plane, when it carries a current of 5.0 A in the same direction as the current in *A*?

**31.17 [II]** The long straight wires in Fig. 31-3 both carry a current of 12 A, in the directions shown. Find *B* at the points (*a*) $x = -5.0$ cm, $y = 5.0$ cm, and (*b*) $x = -7.0$ cm, $y = -6.0$ cm in air.

**31.18 [II]** A certain electromagnet consists of a solenoid (5.0 cm long with 200 turns of wire) wound on a soft-iron core that intensifies the field 130 times. (We say that the *relative permeability* of the iron is 130.) Find *B* within the iron when the current in the solenoid is 0.30 A.

**31.19 [III]** A particular solenoid (50 cm long with 2000 turns of wire) carries a current of 0.70 A and is in vacuum. An electron is shot at an angle of 10° to the solenoid axis from a point on the axis. (*a*) What must be the speed of the electron if it is to just miss hitting the inside of the 1.6-cm-diameter solenoid? (*b*) What is then the pitch of the electron's helical path?

## ANSWERS TO SUPPLEMENTARY PROBLEMS

**31.11 [I]** 30 $\mu$T

**31.12 [I]** $1.3 \times 10^{-3}$ Wb/m$^2$

**31.13 [I]** 2.5 mT

**31.14 [I]** 0.6 A

**31.15 [II]** $6 \times 10^{-5}$ N/m, attraction

**31.16 [II]** (*a*) $2.4 \times 10^{-4}$ T; (*b*) $7.8 \times 10^{-5}$ T; (*c*) $1.2 \times 10^{-3}$ N/m, toward *A*

**31.17 [II]** (*a*) 96 $\mu$T, out; (*b*) 5.7 $\mu$T, in

**31.18 [II]** 0.20 T

**31.19 [III]** (*a*) $1.4 \times 10^{7}$ m/s; (*b*) 14 cm

# CHAPTER 32

# Induced EMF; Magnetic Flux

**Magnetic Effects of Matter:** Most materials have only a slight effect on a steady magnetic field. To explore that phenomenon further, suppose that a very long solenoid is located in vacuum. Suppose that with a fixed current in the coil, the magnetic field at a point inside the solenoid is $B_0$, where the subscript $_0$ stands for vacuum. If now the solenoid core is filled with a material, the field at that point will be changed to a new value $B$. We define:

$$\textit{Relative permeability} \text{ of the material} = k_M = \frac{B}{B_0}$$

$$\textit{Permeability} \text{ of the material} = \mu = k_M \mu_0$$

Recall that $\mu_0$ is the permeability of free space, $4\pi \times 10^{-7}\ \text{T}\cdot\text{m/A}$.

**Diamagnetic materials** have values of $k_M$ slightly below unity (e.g., 0.999984 for solid lead). They slightly decrease the value of $B$ in the solenoid.

**Paramagnetic materials** have values for $k_M$ slightly larger than unity (e.g., 1.000021 for solid aluminum). They slightly increase the value of $B$ in the solenoid.

**Ferromagnetic materials**, such as iron and its alloys, have $k_M$ values of about 50 or larger. They greatly increase the value of $B$ in the solenoid.

**Magnetic Field Lines:** A magnetic field may be represented pictorially using lines, to which $\vec{\mathbf{B}}$ is everywhere tangential. These magnetic field lines are constructed in such a way that the number of lines piercing a unit area perpendicular to them is proportional to the local value of $B$.

**The Magnetic Flux** ($\Phi_M$) through an area $A$ is defined to be the product of $B_\perp$ and $A$ where $B_\perp$ is the component of $\vec{\mathbf{B}}$ perpendicular to the surface of area $A$:

$$\Phi_M = B_\perp A = BA\cos\theta$$

Here $\theta$ is the angle between the direction of the magnetic field and the perpendicular to the area. The flux is expressed in **webers** (Wb).

**An Induced Emf** exists in a loop of wire whenever there is a change in the magnetic flux passing through the area surrounded by the loop. The induced emf exists only during the time that the flux through the area is changing, either increasing or decreasing.

**Faraday's Law for Induced Emf:** Suppose that a coil with $N$ loops or turns is subject to a changing magnetic flux passing through the coil. If a change in flux $\Delta\Phi_M$ occurs in a time $\Delta t$, then the average emf induced between the two terminals of the coil is given by

$$\mathscr{E} = -N\frac{\Delta\Phi_M}{\Delta t}$$

The emf $\mathscr{E}$ is measured in volts if $\Delta\Phi_M/\Delta t$ is in Wb/s. The minus sign indicates that the induced emf opposes the change which produces it, as stated generally in **Lenz's Law.**

**Lenz's Law:** An induced emf always has such a direction as to oppose the change in magnetic flux that produced it. For example, if the flux is increasing through a coil, the current produced by the induced emf will generate a flux that tends to cancel the increasing flux (though it generally does not succeed at doing it completely). Or, if the flux is decreasing through the coil, that current will produce a flux that tends to restore the decreasing flux (though it generally does not succeed at doing it completely). Lenz's Law is a consequence of Conservation of Energy. If this were not the case, the induced currents would enhance the flux change that caused them to begin with and the process would build endlessly.

**Motional Emf:** When a conductor moves through a magnetic field so as to cut field lines, an induced emf will exist in it, in accordance with Faraday's Law. In this case,

$$|\mathscr{E}| = \frac{\Delta\Phi_M}{\Delta t}$$

The symbol $|\mathscr{E}|$ means that we are concerned here only with the magnitude of the average induced emf; its direction will be considered below.

The induced emf in a straight conductor of length $L$ moving with velocity $\vec{\mathbf{v}}$ perpendicular to a field $\vec{\mathbf{B}}$ is given by

$$|\mathscr{E}| = BLv$$

where $\vec{\mathbf{B}}$, $\vec{\mathbf{v}}$, and the wire must be mutually perpendicular.

In this case, Lenz's Law still tells us that the induced emf opposes that which causes it. But now the opposition is produced by way of the force exerted by the magnetic field on the induced current in the conductor. The current direction must be such that the force opposes the motion of the conductor (though it generally does not completely cancel it). Knowing the current direction, we also know the direction of $\mathscr{E}$.

## SOLVED PROBLEMS

**32.1 [II]** A solenoid is 40 cm long, has a cross-sectional area of 8.0 cm$^2$, and is wound with 300 turns of wire that carry a current of 1.2 A. The relative permeability of its iron core is 600. Compute (*a*) $B$ for an interior point and (*b*) the flux through the solenoid.

(*a*) From Fig. 31-1(*c*), in air

$$B_0 = \frac{\mu_0 NI}{L} = \frac{(4\pi \times 10^{-7}\ \text{T}\cdot\text{m/A})(300)(1.2\ \text{A})}{0.40\ \text{m}} = 1.13\ \text{mT}$$

and so $$B = k_M B_0 = (600)(1.13 \times 10^{-3}\ \text{T}) = 0.68\ \text{T}$$

(*b*) Because the field lines are perpendicular to the cross section of the solenoid,

$$\Phi_M = B_\perp A = BA = (0.68\ \text{T})(8.0 \times 10^{-4}\ \text{m}^2) = 54\ \mu\text{Wb}$$

**32.2 [I]** The flux through a current-carrying toroidal coil changes from 0.65 mWb to 0.91 mWb when the air core is replaced by another material. What are the relative permeability and the permeability of the material?

The air core is essentially the same as a vacuum core. Since $k_M = B/B_0$ and $\Phi_M = B_\perp A$,

$$k_M = \frac{0.91\text{ mWb}}{0.65\text{ mWb}} = 1.40$$

This is the relative permeability. The magnetic permeability is

$$\mu = k_M\mu_0 = (1.40)(4\pi \times 10^{-7}\text{ T}\cdot\text{m/A}) = 5.6\pi \times 10^{-7}\text{ T}\cdot\text{m/A}$$

**32.3 [I]** The quarter-circle loop shown in Fig. 32-1 has an area of 15 cm². A constant magnetic field, $B = 0.16$ T, pointing in the $+x$-direction, fills the space independent of the loop. Find the flux through the loop in each orientation shown.

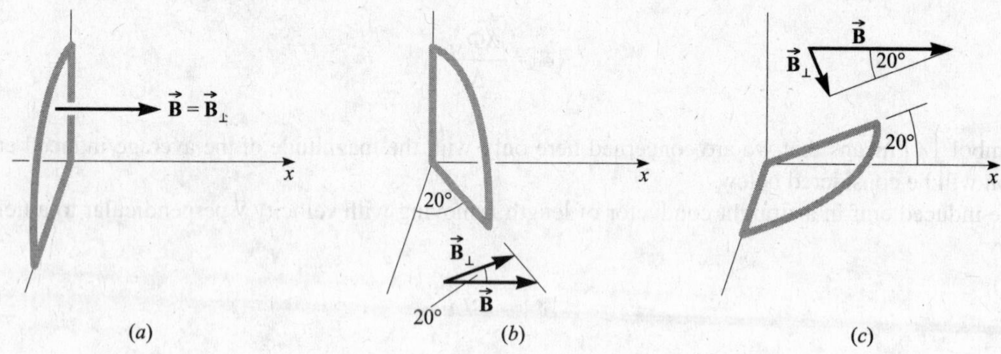


Fig. 32-1

The magnetic flux is determined by the amount of $\vec{B}$-field passing perpendicularly through the particular area, times that area. That is, $\Phi_M = B_\perp A$.

(*a*) $\Phi_M = B_\perp A = BA = (0.16\text{ T})(15 \times 10^{-4}\text{ m}^2) = 2.4 \times 10^{-4}\text{ Wb}$

(*b*) $\Phi_M = (B \cos 20°)A = (2.4 \times 10^{-4}\text{ Wb})(\cos 20°) = 2.3 \times 10^{-4}\text{ Wb}$

(*c*) $\Phi_M = (B \sin 20°)A = (2.4 \times 10^{-4}\text{ Wb})(\sin 20°) = 8.2 \times 10^{-5}\text{ Wb}$

**32.4 [II]** A hemispherical surface of radius $R$ is placed in a uniform magnetic field $\vec{B}$ as shown in Fig. 32-2. What is the magnetic flux through the hemispherical surface?

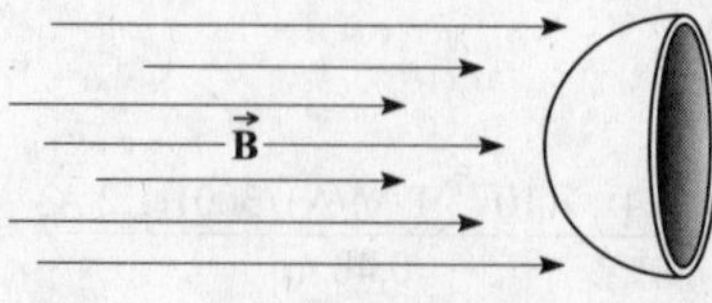


Fig. 32-2

The same number of field lines pass through the curved surface as through the shaded flat circular cross-section. Therefore,

$$\text{Flux through curved surface} = \text{Flux through flat surface} = B_\perp A$$

where in this case $B_\perp = B$ and $A = \pi R^2$. Then $\Phi_M = \pi BR^2$.

**32.5 [I]** A 50-loop circular coil has a radius of 3.0 cm. It is oriented so that the field lines of a magnetic field are normal to the area of the coil. Suppose that the magnetic field is varied so that $B$ increases from 0.10 T to 0.35 T in a time of 2.0 milliseconds. Find the average induced emf in the coil. (Study Problem 32.11 after this one.)

$$\Delta\Phi_M = B_{\text{final}}A - B_{\text{initial}}A = (0.25\text{ T})(\pi r^2) = (0.25\text{ T})\pi(0.030\text{ m})^2 = 7.1\times10^{-4}\text{ Wb}$$

$$|\mathscr{E}| = N\left|\frac{\Delta\Phi_M}{\Delta t}\right| = (50)\left(\frac{7.1\times10^{-4}\text{ Wb}}{2\times10^{-3}\text{ s}}\right) = 18\text{ V}$$

**32.6 [II]** The cylindrical permanent magnet in the center of Fig. 32-3 induces an emf in the coils as the magnet moves toward the right or the left. Find the directions of the induced currents through both resistors when the magnet is moving (*a*) toward the right and (*b*) toward the left. In each case discuss the voltage across the resistor:

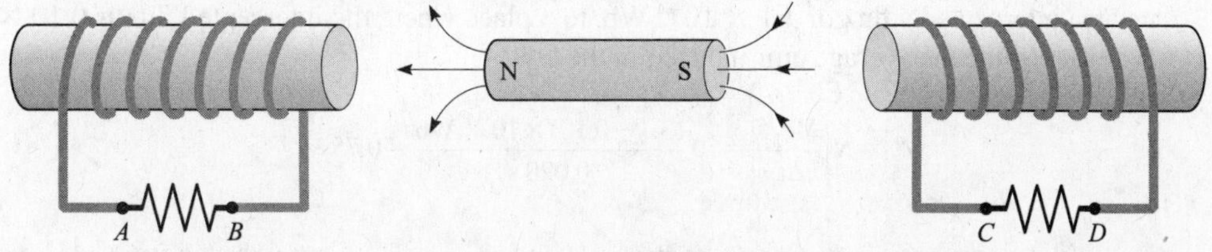


Fig. 32-3

(*a*) Consider first the coil on the left. As the magnet moves to the right, the flux through that coil, which is directed more or less to the left, decreases. To compensate for this, the induced current in the coil on the left will flow so as to produce a flux toward the left through itself. Apply the right-hand rule to the loop on the left end. For it to produce flux inside the coil toward the left, the current must flow directly through the resistor from $B$ to $A$. The voltage at $B$ is higher than at $A$.

Now consider the coil on the right. As the magnet moves toward the right, the flux inside that coil on the right, which is more or less directed to the left, increases. The induced current in the coil will produce a flux toward the right to cancel this increased flux. Applying the right-hand rule to the loop on the right end, we find that the loop generates flux to the right inside itself if the current flows from $D$ to $C$ directly through the resistor. The voltage at $D$ is higher than at $C$.

(*b*) In this case the flux change caused by the magnet's motion toward the left is opposite to what it was in (*a*). Using the same type of reasoning, we find that the induced currents flow through the resistors directly from $A$ to $B$ and from $C$ to $D$. The voltage at $A$ is higher than at $B$, and it's higher at $C$ than at $D$.

**32.7 [III]** In Fig. 32-4(*a*) there is a uniform magnetic field in the $+x$-direction, with a value of $B = 0.20$ T. The circular loop of wire is in the $yz$-plane. The loop has an area of 5.0 cm$^2$ and rotates about line $CD$ as axis. Point-$A$ rotates toward positive $x$-values from the position shown. If the loop rotates through 50° from its indicated position, as shown in Fig. 32-4(*b*), in a time of 0.20 s, (*a*) what is the change in flux through the coil, (*b*) what is the average induced emf in it, and (*c*) does the induced current flow directly from $A$ to $C$ or $C$ to $A$ in the upper part of the coil?

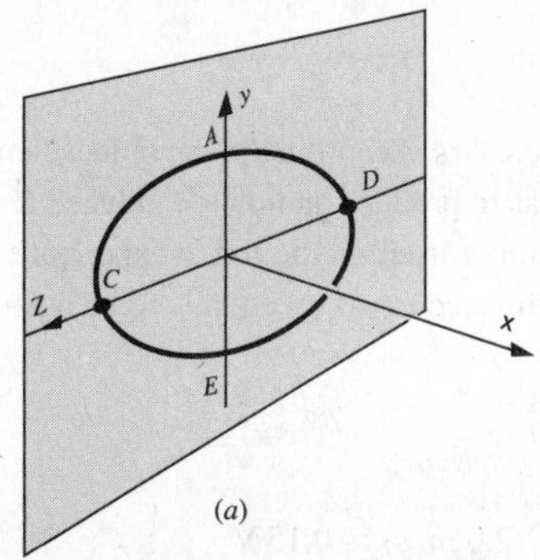


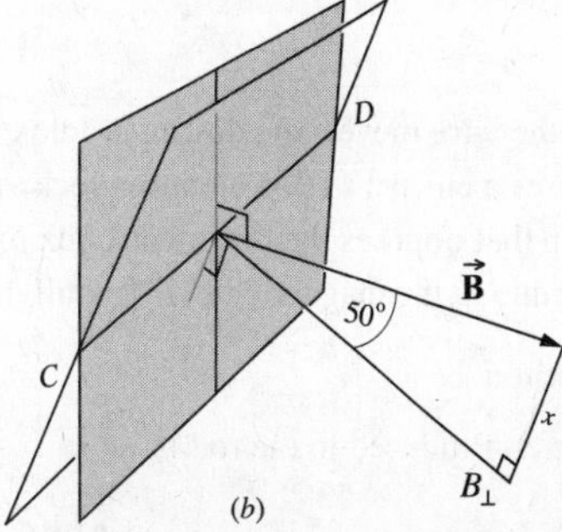


Fig. 32-4

(*a*) Initial flux = $B_{\perp}A = BA = (0.20\text{ T})(5.0 \times 10^{-4}\text{ m}^2) = 1.0 \times 10^{-4}\text{ Wb}$
Final flux = $(B\cos 50°)A = (1.0 \times 10^{-4}\text{ Wb})(\cos 50°) = 0.64 \times 10^{-4}\text{ Wb}$

$$\Delta\Phi_M = 0.64 \times 10^{-4}\text{ Wb} - 1.0 \times 10^{-4}\text{ Wb} = -0.36 \times 10^{-4}\text{ Wb} = -36\ \mu\text{Wb}$$

(*b*) $$|\mathscr{E}| = N\left|\frac{\Delta\Phi_M}{\Delta t}\right| = (1)\left(\frac{0.36\times 10^{-4}\text{ Wb}}{0.20\text{ s}}\right) = 1.8\times 10^{-4}\text{ V} = 0.18\text{ mV}$$

(*c*) The flux through the loop from left to right decreased. The induced current will tend to set up flux from left to right through the loop. By the right-hand rule, the current flows directly from *A* to *C*. Alternatively, a torque must be set up that tends to rotate the loop back into its original position. The appropriate right-hand rule from Chapter 30 again gives a current flow directly from *A* to *C*.

**32.8 [I]** A coil having 50 turns of wire is removed in 0.020 s from between the poles of a magnet, where its area intercepted a flux of $3.1 \times 10^{-4}$ Wb, to a place where the intercepted flux is $0.10 \times 10^{-4}$ Wb. Determine the average emf induced in the coil.

$$|\mathscr{E}| = N\left|\frac{\Delta\Phi_M}{\Delta t}\right| = 50\,\frac{(3.1-0.10)\times 10^{-4}\text{ Wb}}{0.020\text{ s}} = 0.75\text{ V}$$

**32.9 [I]** A copper bar 30 cm long is perpendicular to a uniform magnetic field of 0.80 Wb/m² and moves at right angles to the field with a speed of 0.50 m/s. Determine the emf induced in the bar.

$$|\mathscr{E}| = BLv = (0.80\text{ Wb/m}^2)(0.30\text{ m})(0.50\text{ m/s}) = 0.12\text{ V}$$

**32.10 [II]** As shown in Fig. 32-5, a metal rod makes contact with two parallel wires and completes the circuit. The circuit is perpendicular to a magnetic field with $B = 0.15$ T. If the resistance is 3.0 Ω, how large a force is needed to move the rod to the right with a constant speed of 2.0 m/s? At what rate is energy dissipated in the resistor?

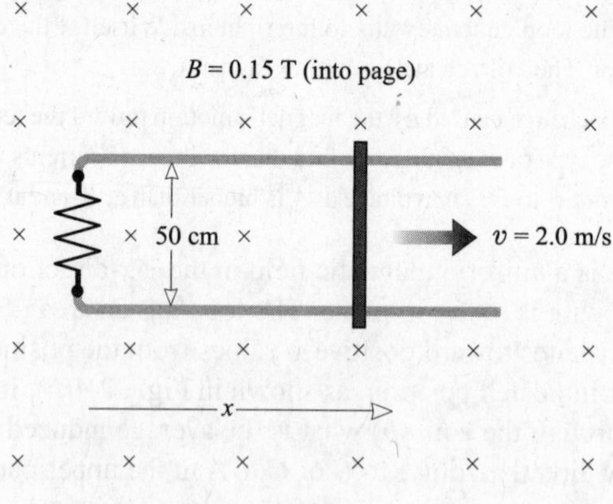


Fig. 32-5

As the wire moves, the downward flux through the loop increases. Accordingly, the induced emf in the rod causes a current to flow counterclockwise in the circuit so as to produce an upward induced $\vec{\mathbf{B}}$-field in the loop that opposes the downward flux increase. Because of this current in the rod, it experiences a force to the left due to the magnetic field. To pull the rod to the right with a constant speed, this force must be balanced.

**Method 1**

The emf induced in the rod is

$$|\mathscr{E}|\, BLv = (0.15\text{ T})(0.50\text{ m})(2.0\text{ m/s}) = 0.15\text{ V}$$

and $$I = \frac{|\mathscr{E}|}{R} = \frac{0.15\text{ V}}{3.0\ \Omega} = 0.050\text{ A}$$

from which $$F_M = ILB \sin 90° = (0.050\text{ A})(0.50\text{ m})(0.15\text{ T})(1) = 3.8\text{ mN}$$

**Method 2**

The emf induced in the loop is

$$|\mathscr{E}| = N\left|\frac{\Delta\Phi_M}{\Delta t}\right| = (1)\frac{B\Delta A}{\Delta t} = \frac{B(L\Delta x)}{\Delta t} = BL\upsilon$$

as before. Now proceed as in Method 1.

To find the power loss in the resistor, we can use

$$P = I^2R = (0.050\text{ A})^2(3.0\ \Omega) = 7.5\text{ mW}$$

Alternatively, $$P = F\upsilon = (3.75 \times 10^{-3}\text{ N})(2.0\text{ m/s}) = 7.5\text{ mW}$$

**32.11 [II]** A horizontal circular flat coil having three turns and an area of 2.4 m$^2$ is illustrated in Fig. 32-6. It is in a uniform vertical increasing magnetic field that goes from 1.0 T to 2.4 T in 20 milliseconds. (a) What voltage will appear across terminals A and B? (b) From the perspective of looking down on the coil, the wire winds clockwise from B to A. What is the direction of the induced *B*-field? (c) What is the direction of the induced current? (d) Which has the higher potential, A or B?

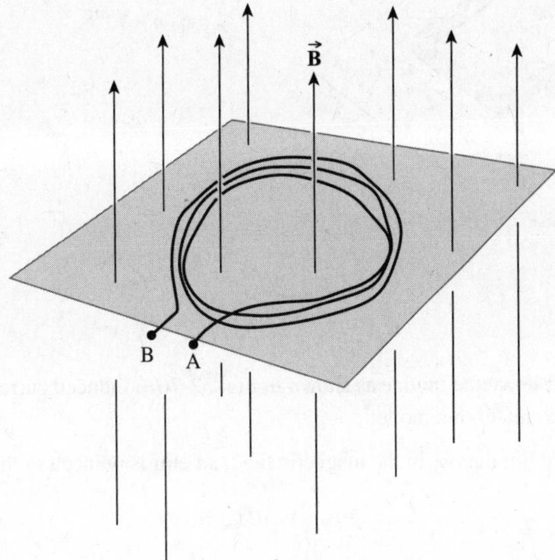


Fig. 32-6

(a) The emf is given by Faraday's Law,

$$|\mathscr{E}| = N\left|\frac{\Delta\Phi_M}{\Delta t}\right|$$

where $\Phi_M = B_\perp A$. Here $\Delta B_\perp = (2.4\text{ T} - 1.0\text{ T})$ and $\Delta\Phi_M = \Delta B_\perp A = (1.4\text{ T})(2.4\text{ m}^2) = 3.36\text{ T}\cdot\text{m}^2$. Hence

$$\frac{\Delta\Phi_M}{\Delta t} = \frac{3.36\text{ T}\cdot\text{m}^2}{0.020\text{ s}} = 168\text{ V}$$

That's the induced voltage in each turn, and so the total emf is

$$|\mathscr{E}| = 3(168\text{V}) = 504\text{V} = 0.50\text{ kV}$$

(*b*) The induced *B*-field must oppose an upwardly increasing field and therefore must be downward.

(*c*) To produce a downward induced *B*-field inside the coil, current must flow clockwise looking down; that is, from terminal-B to terminal-A.

(*d*) To determine which terminal is at a higher potential, imagine a resistor across A and B, and label the side where current enters + and leaves −. In that external circuit, current flows from A to B, and hence, $V_A > V_B$.

**32.12 [III]** The metal bar of length *L*, mass *m*, and resistance *R* depicted in Fig. 32-7(*a*) slides without friction on a rectangular circuit composed of resistanceless wire resting on an inclined plane. There is a vertical uniform magnetic field $\vec{\mathbf{B}}$. Find the terminal speed of the bar (that is, the constant speed it attains).

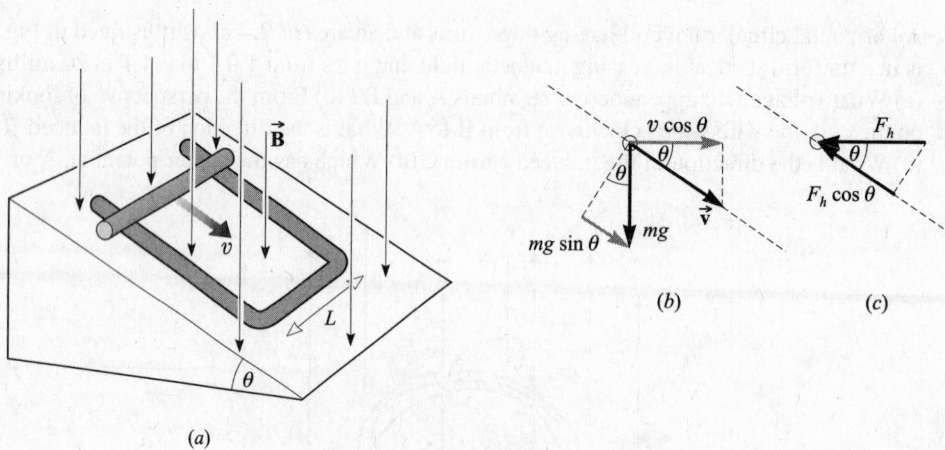


Fig. 32-7

Gravity pulls the bar down the incline as shown in Fig. 32-7(*b*). Induced current flowing in the bar interacts with the field so as to retard this motion.

Because of the motion of the bar in the magnetic field, an emf is induced in the bar:

$$\mathscr{E} = (Blv)_{\perp} = BL(v\cos\theta)$$

This causes a current

$$I = \frac{\text{emf}}{R} = \left(\frac{BLv}{R}\right)\cos\theta$$

in the loop. A wire carrying a current in a magnetic field experiences a force that is perpendicular to the plane defined by the wire and the magnetic field lines. The bar thus experiences a horizontal force $\vec{\mathbf{F}}_h$ (perpendicular to the plane of $\vec{\mathbf{B}}$ and the bar) given by

$$F_h = BIL = \left(\frac{B^2L^2v}{R}\right)\cos\theta$$

and shown in Fig. 32-7(*c*). However, we want the force component along the plane, which is

$$F_{\text{up plane}} = F_h \cos\theta = \left(\frac{B^2L^2v}{R}\right)\cos^2\theta$$

When the bar reaches its terminal velocity, this force equals the gravitational force down the plane. Therefore,

$$\left(\frac{B^2L^2v}{R}\right)\cos^2\theta = mg\sin\theta$$

from which the terminal speed is

$$v = \left(\frac{Rmg}{B^2L^2}\right)\left(\frac{\sin\theta}{\cos^2\theta}\right)$$

Can you show that this answer is reasonable in the limiting cases $\theta = 0$, $B = 0$, and $\theta = 90°$, and for $R$ very large or very small?

**32.13 [III]** The rod shown in Fig. 32-8 rotates about point-$C$ as pivot with a constant frequency of 5.0 rev/s. Find the potential difference between its two ends, which are 80 cm apart, due to the magnetic field $B = 0.30$ T directed into the page.

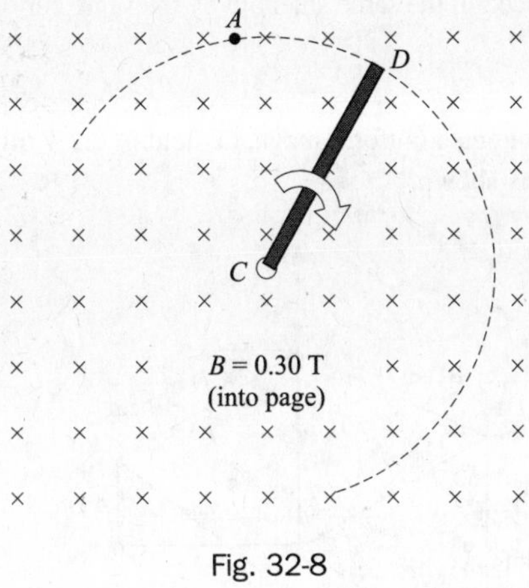


Fig. 32-8

Consider an imaginary loop *CADC*. As time goes on, its area and the flux through it will both increase. The induced emf in this loop will equal the potential difference we seek.

$$|\mathscr{E}| = N\left|\frac{\Delta\Phi_M}{\Delta t}\right| = (1)\left(\frac{B\Delta A}{\Delta t}\right)$$

It takes one-fifth second for the area to change from zero to that of a full circle, $\pi r^2$. Therefore,

$$|\mathscr{E}| = B\frac{\Delta A}{\Delta t} = B\frac{\pi r^2}{0.20\text{ s}} = (0.30\text{ T})\frac{\pi(0.80\text{ m})^2}{0.20\text{ s}} = 3.0\text{ V}$$

**32.14 [III]** A 5.0-Ω coil, of 100 turns and diameter 6.0 cm, is placed between the poles of a magnet so that the magnetic flux is maximum through the coil's cross-sectional area. When the coil is suddenly removed from the field of the magnet, a charge of $1.0 \times 10^{-4}$ C flows through a 595-Ω galvanometer connected to the coil. Compute $B$ between the poles of the magnet.

As the coil is removed, the flux changes from $BA$, where $A$ is the coil's cross-sectional area, to zero. Therefore,

$$|\mathscr{E}| = N\left|\frac{\Delta\Phi_M}{\Delta t}\right| = N\frac{BA}{\Delta t}$$

We are told that $\Delta q = 1.0 \times 10^{-4}$ C. But, by Ohm's Law,

$$|\mathscr{E}| = IR = \frac{\Delta q}{\Delta t}R$$

where $R = 600\ \Omega$ is the total resistance. If we now equate these two expressions for $|\mathscr{E}|$ and solve for $B$, we find

$$B = \frac{R\,\Delta q}{NA} = \frac{(600\ \Omega)(1.0\times10^{-4}\ \text{C})}{(100)(\pi\times9.0\times10^{-4}\ \text{m}^2)} = 0.21\ \text{T}$$

## SUPPLEMENTARY PROBLEMS

**32.15 [II]** A flux of $9.0 \times 10^{-4}$ Wb is produced in the iron core of a solenoid. When the core is removed, a flux (in air) of $5.0 \times 10^{-7}$ Wb is produced in the same solenoid by the same current. What is the relative permeability of the iron?

**32.16 [I]** In Fig. 32-9 there is a $+x$-directed uniform magnetic field of 0.2 T filling the space. Find the magnetic flux through each face of the box shown.

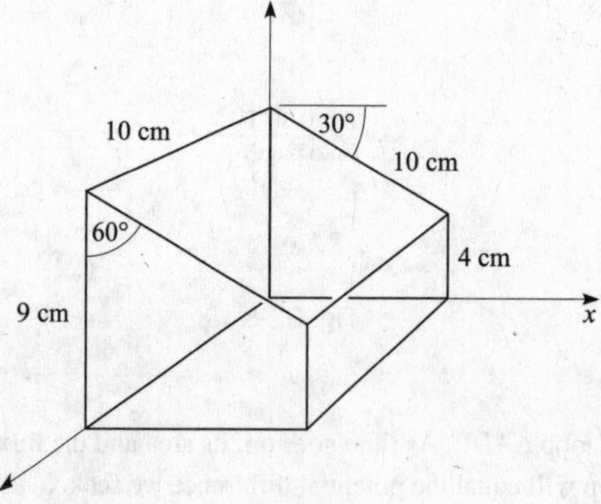


Fig. 32-9

**32.17 [II]** A solenoid 60 cm long has 5000 turns of wire and is wound on an iron rod having a 0.75 cm radius. Find the flux inside the solenoid when the current through the wire is 3.0 A. The relative permeability of the iron is 300.

**32.18 [II]** A room has its walls aligned accurately with respect to north, south, east, and west. The north wall has an area of 15 m², the east wall has an area of 12 m², and the floor's area is 35 m². At the site the Earth's magnetic field has a value of 0.60 G and is directed 50° below the horizontal and 7.0° east of north. Find the magnetic flux through the north wall, the east wall, and the floor.

**32.19 [I]** The flux through the solenoid of Problem 32.17 is reduced to a value of 1.0 mWb in a time of 0.050 s. Find the induced emf in the solenoid.

**32.20 [II]** A flat coil with a radius of 8.0 mm has 50 turns of wire. It is placed in a magnetic field $B = 0.30$ T in such a way that the maximum flux goes through it. Later, it is rotated in 0.020 s to a position such that no flux goes through it. Find the average emf induced between the terminals of the coil.

**32.21 [II]** The square coil shown in Fig. 32-10 is 20 cm on a side and has 15 turns of wire. It is moving to the right at 3.0 m/s. Find the induced emf (magnitude and direction) in it (*a*) at the instant shown and (*b*) when the entire coil is in the field region. The uniform magnetic field is 0.40 T into the page.

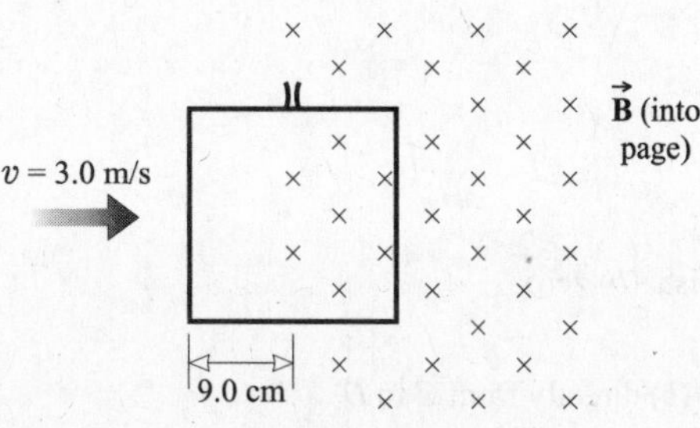


Fig. 32-10

**32.22 [I]** The cylindrical magnet at the center of Fig. 32-11 rotates as shown on a pivot through its center. At the instant shown, in what direction is the induced current flowing (*a*) in resistor *AB*? (*b*) in resistor *CD*?

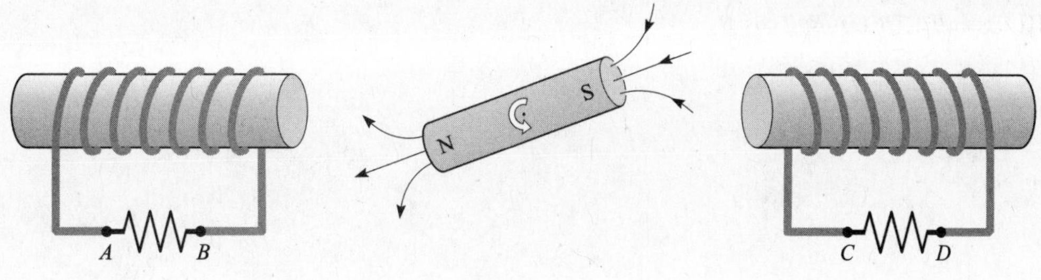


Fig. 32-11

**32.23 [II]** A train is moving directly south at a constant speed of 10 m/s. If the downward vertical component of the Earth's magnetic field is 0.54 G, compute the magnitude and direction of the emf induced in a rail car axle 1.2 m long.

**32.24 [III]** A copper disk of 10-cm radius is rotating at 20 rev/s about its central symmetry axis. The plane of the disk is perpendicular to a uniform magnetic field $B = 0.60$ T. What is the potential difference between the center and rim of the disk? [*Hint*: There is some similarity with Problem 32.13.]

**32.25 [II]** How much charge will flow through a 200-Ω galvanometer connected to a 400-Ω circular coil of 1000 turns wound on a wooden stick 2.0 cm in diameter, if a uniform magnetic field $B = 0.0113$ T parallel to the axis of the stick is decreased suddenly to zero?

**32.26 [III]** In Fig. 32-7, described in Problem 32.12, what is the acceleration of the rod when its speed down the incline is $v$?

## ANSWERS TO SUPPLEMENTARY PROBLEMS

**32.15 [II]** $1.8 \times 10^3$

**32.16 [I]** Zero through bottom and rear and front sides; through top, 1 mWb; through left side, 2 mWb; through right side, 0.8 mWb.

**32.17 [II]** 1.7 mWb

**32.18 [II]** 0.57 mWb, 56 $\mu$Wb, 1.6 mWb

**32.19 [I]** 67 V

**32.20 [II]** 0.15 V

**32.21 [II]** (*a*) 3.6 V counterclockwise; (*b*) zero

**32.22 [I]** (*a*) directly from *B* to *A*; (*b*) directly from *C* to *D*

**32.23 [II]** 0.65 mV from west to east

**32.24 [III]** 0.38 V

**32.25 [II]** 5.9 $\mu$C

**32.26 [III]** $g \sin\theta - (B^2L^2v/Rm)\cos^2\theta$

# CHAPTER 33

# Electric Generators and Motors

**Electric Generators** are machines that convert mechanical energy into electrical energy. A simple generator that produces an ac voltage is shown in Fig. 33-1(*a*). An external energy source (such as a diesel motor or a steam turbine) turns the armature coil in a magnetic field $\vec{\mathbf{B}}$. The wires of the coil cut the field lines, and an emf

$$\mathscr{E} = 2\pi NABf \cos 2\pi ft$$

is induced between the terminals of the coil. In this relation, $N$ is the number of loops (each of area $A$) on the coil, and $f$ is the frequency of its rotation. Figure 33-1(*b*) shows the emf in graphical form.

As current is drawn from the generator, the wires of its coil experience a retarding force because of the interaction between current and field. Thus, the work required to rotate the coil is the source of the electrical energy supplied by the generator. For any generator,

(Input mechanical energy) = (Output electrical energy) + (Friction and heat losses)

Usually the losses are only a very small fraction of the input energy.

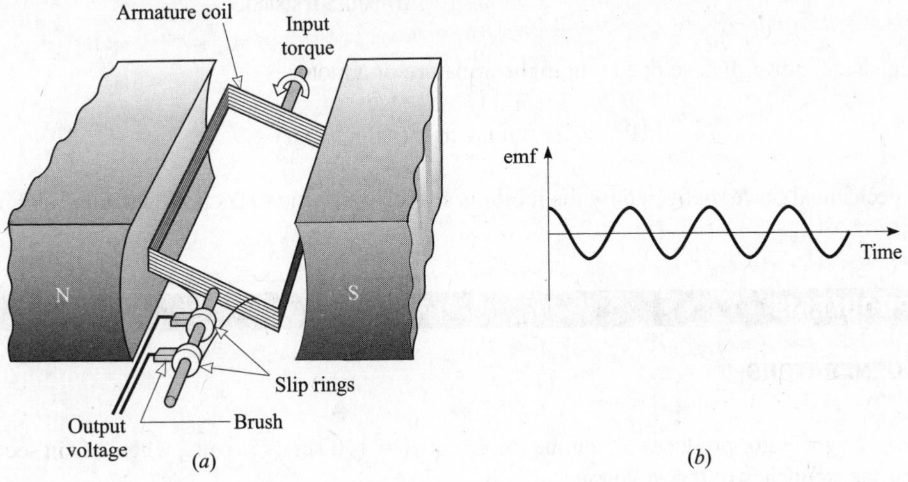


Fig. 33-1

**Electric Motors** convert electrical energy into mechanical energy. A simple dc motor (i.e., one that runs on a constant voltage) is shown in Fig. 33-2. The current through the armature coil interacts with the magnetic field to cause a torque

$$\tau = NIAB \sin\theta$$

on the coil (see Chapter 30), which rotates the coil and shaft. Here, $\theta$ is the angle between the field lines and the perpendicular to the plane of the coil. The split-ring commutator reverses $I$ each time $\sin\theta$ changes sign, thereby ensuring that the torque always rotates the coil in the same sense. For such a motor,

$$\text{Average torque} = (\text{Constant})\ |\text{NIAB}|$$

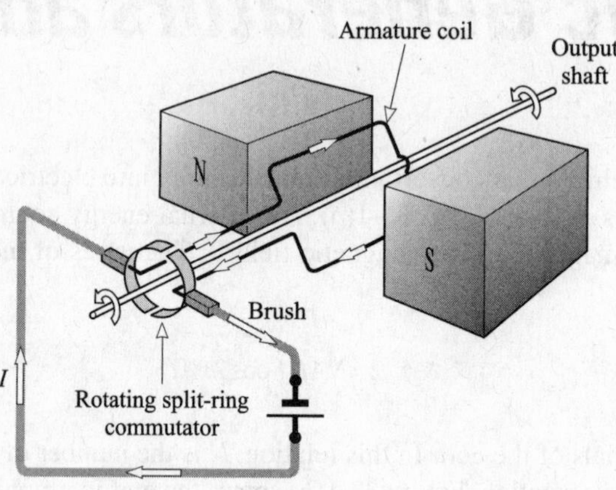


Fig. 33-2

Because the rotating armature coil of the motor acts as a generator, a **back** (or **counter**) **emf** is induced in the coil. The back emf opposes the voltage source that drives the motor. Hence, the net potential difference that causes current through the armature is

$$\text{Net p.d. across armature} = (\text{Line voltage}) - (\text{Back emf})$$

and

$$\text{Armature current} = \frac{(\text{Line voltage}) - (\text{Back emf})}{\text{Armature resistance}}$$

The mechanical power P developed within the armature of a motor is

$$\text{P} = (\text{Armature current})(\text{Back emf})$$

The useful mechanical power delivered by the motor is slightly less, due to friction, windage, and iron losses.

## SOLVED PROBLEMS

### ELECTRIC GENERATORS

**33.1 [I]** An ac generator produces an output voltage of $\mathscr{E} = 170 \sin 377t$ volts, where $t$ is in seconds. What is the frequency of the ac voltage?

A sine curve plotted as a function of time is no different from a cosine curve, except for the location of $t = 0$. Since $\mathscr{E} = 2\pi NABf \cos 2\pi ft$, we have $377t = 2\pi ft$, from which we find that the frequency $f = 60$ Hz.

**33.2 [II]** How fast must a 1000-turn coil (each with a 20 cm$^2$ area) turn in the Earth's magnetic field of 0.70 G to generate a voltage that has a maximum value (i.e., an amplitude) of 0.50 V?

We assume the coil's axis to be oriented in the field so as to give maximum flux change when rotated. Then $B = 7.0 \times 10^{-5}$ T in the expression

$$\mathscr{E} = 2\pi NABf \cos 2\pi ft$$

Because $\cos 2\pi ft$ has a maximum value of unity, the amplitude of the voltage is $2\pi NABf$. Therefore,

$$f = \frac{0.50 \text{ V}}{2\pi NAB} = \frac{0.50 \text{ V}}{(2\pi)(1000)(20\times10^{-4}\text{ m}^2)(7.0\times10^{-5}\text{ T})} = 0.57 \text{ kHz}$$

**33.3** When turning at 1500 rev/min, a certain generator produces 100.0 V. What must be its frequency in rev/min if it is to produce 120.0 V?

Because the amplitude of the emf is proportional to the frequency, we have, for two frequencies $f_1$ and $f_2$,

$$\frac{\mathscr{E}_1}{\mathscr{E}_2} = \frac{f_1}{f_2} \quad \text{or} \quad f_2 = f_1\frac{\mathscr{E}_2}{\mathscr{E}_1} = (1500 \text{ rev/min})\left(\frac{120.0 \text{ V}}{100.0 \text{ V}}\right) = 1800 \text{ rev/min}$$

**33.4 [II]** A certain generator has armature resistance 0.080 Ω and develops an induced emf of 120 V when driven at its rated speed. What is its terminal voltage when 50.0 A is being drawn from it?

The generator acts like a battery with emf = 120 V and internal resistance $r = 0.080\ \Omega$. As with a battery,

$$\text{Terminal p.d.} = (\text{emf}) - Ir = 120 \text{ V} - (50.0 \text{ A})(0.080\ \Omega) = 116 \text{ V}$$

**33.5 [III]** Some generators, called *shunt generators,* use electromagnets in place of permanent magnets, with the field coils for the electromagnets activated by the induced voltage. The magnet coil is in parallel with the armature coil (it shunts the armature). As shown in Fig. 33-3, a certain shunt generator has an armature resistance of 0.060 Ω and a shunt resistance of 100 Ω. What power is developed in the armature when it delivers 40 kW at 250 V to an external circuit?

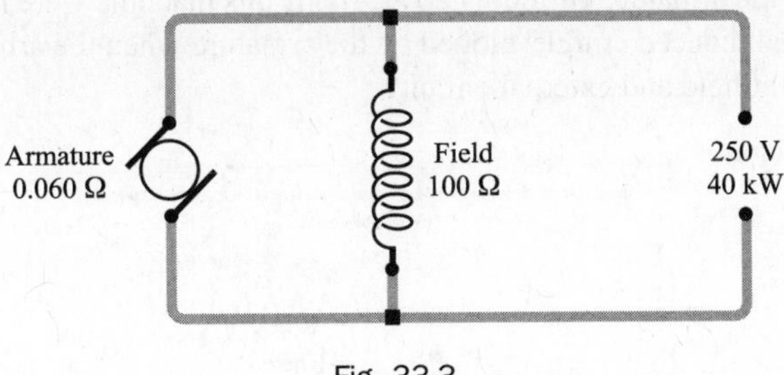


Fig. 33-3

From P = *VI*,

$$\text{Current to the external circuit} = I_x = \frac{\text{P}}{V} = \frac{40\,000 \text{ W}}{250 \text{ V}} = 160 \text{ A}$$

$$\text{Field current} = I_f = \frac{V_f}{r_f} = \frac{250 \text{ V}}{100\ \Omega} = 2.5 \text{ A}$$

$$\text{Armature current} = I_a = I_x + I_f = 162.5 \text{ A}$$

$$\text{Total induced emf} = |\mathscr{E}| = (250 \text{ V} + I_a r_a \text{ drop in armature}$$

$$= 250 \text{ V} + (162.5 \text{ A})(0.06\ \Omega) = 260 \text{ V}$$

$$\text{Armature power} = I_a|\mathscr{E}| = (162.5 \text{ A})(260 \text{ V}) = 42 \text{ kW}$$

**Alternative Method**

Power loss in the armature $= I_a^2 r_a = (162.5\ \text{A})^2(0.06\ \Omega) = 1.6\ \text{kW}$

Power loss in the field $= I_f^2 r_f = (2.5\ \text{A})^2(100\ \Omega) = 0.6\ \text{kW}$

Power developed = (Power delivered) + (Power loss in armature) + (Power loss in field)

$= 40\ \text{kW} + 1.6\ \text{kW} + 0.6\ \text{kW} = 42\ \text{kW}$

## ELECTRIC MOTORS

**33.6 [II]** The resistance of the armature in the motor shown in Fig. 33-2 is 2.30 Ω. It draws a current of 1.60 A when operating on 120 V. What is its back emf under these circumstances?

The motor acts like a back emf in series with an *IR* drop through its internal resistance. Therefore,

$$\text{Line voltage} = \text{back emf} + Ir$$

or

$$\text{Back emf} = 120\ \text{V} - (1.60\ \text{A})(2.30\ \Omega) = 116\ \text{V}$$

**33.7 [II]** A 0.250-hp motor (like that in Fig. 33-2) has a resistance of 0.500 Ω. (*a*) How much current does it draw on 110 V when its output is 0.250 hp? (*b*) What is its back emf?

(*a*) Assume the motor to be 100 percent efficient so that the input power *VI* equals its output power (0.250 hp). Then

$$(110\ \text{V})(I) = (0.250\ \text{hp})(746\ \text{W/hp}) \qquad \text{or} \qquad I = 1.695\ \text{A}$$

(*b*) Back emf = (line voltage) $- Ir = 110\ \text{V} - (1.695\ \text{A})(0.500\ \Omega) = 109\ \text{V}$

**33.8 [III]** In a *shunt motor,* the permanent magnet is replaced by an electromagnet activated by a field coil that shunts the armature. The shunt motor shown in Fig. 33-4 has an armature resistance of 0.050? and is connected to a 120 V line. (*a*) What is the armature current at the starting instant, i.e., before the armature develops any back emf? (*b*) What starting rheostat resistance *R*, in series with the armature, will limit the starting current to 60 A? (*c*) With no starting resistance, what back emf is generated when the armature current is 20 A? (*d*) If this machine were running as a generator, what would be the total induced emf developed by the armature when the armature is delivering 20 A at 120 V to the shunt field and external circuit?

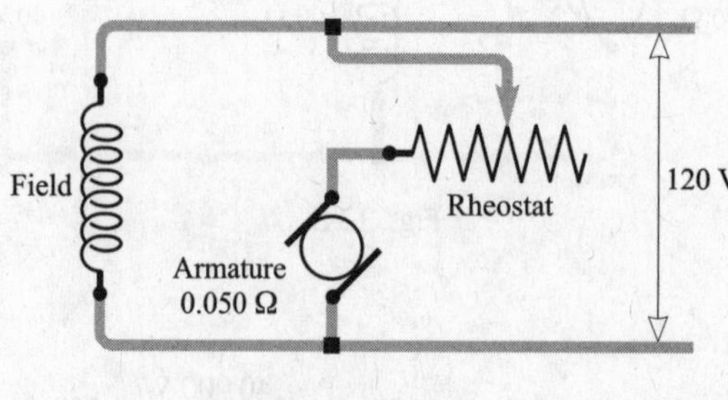


Fig. 33-4

(*a*) $$\text{Armature current} = \frac{\text{Impressed voltage}}{\text{Armature resistance}} = \frac{120\ \text{V}}{0.050\ \Omega} = 2.4\ \text{kA}$$

(*b*) $$\text{Armature current} = \frac{\text{Impressed voltage}}{0.050\ \Omega + R} \qquad \text{or} \qquad 60\ \text{A} = \frac{120\ \text{V}}{0.050\ \Omega + R}$$

from which $R = 2.0\ \Omega$.

(*c*) Back emf = (Impressed voltage) − (Voltage drop in armature resistance)

$$= 120\text{ V} - (20\text{ A})(0.050\ \Omega) = 119\text{ V} = 0.12\text{ kV}$$

(*d*) Induced emf = (Terminal voltage) + (Voltage drop in armature resistance)

$$= 120\text{ V} + (20\text{ A})(0.050\ \Omega) = 121\text{ V} = 0.12\text{ kV}$$

**33.9 [III]** The shunt motor shown in Fig. 33-5 has an armature resistance of 0.25 Ω and a field resistance of 150 Ω. It is connected across 120-V mains and is generating a back emf of 115 V. Compute: (*a*) the armature current $I_a$, the field current $I_f$, and the total current $I_t$ taken by the motor; (*b*) the total power taken by the motor; (*c*) the power lost in heat in the armature and field circuits; (*d*) the electrical efficiency of this machine (when only heat losses in the armature and field are considered).

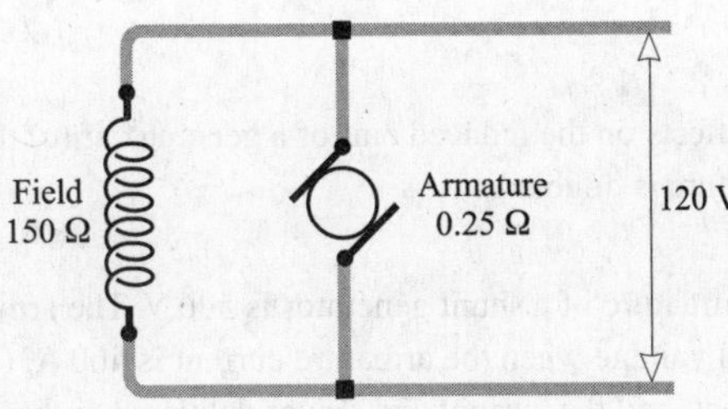


Fig. 33-5

(*a*)
$$I_a = \frac{\text{(Impressed voltage)} - \text{(Back emf)}}{\text{Armature resistance}} = \frac{(120-115)}{0.25\ \Omega} = 20\text{ A}$$

$$I_f = \frac{\text{Impressed voltage}}{\text{Field resistance}} = \frac{120\text{ V}}{150\ \Omega} = 0.80\text{ A}$$

$$I_t = I_a + I_f = 20.80\text{ A} = 21\text{ A}$$

(*b*) Power input = (120 V) (20.80 A) = 2.5 kW

(*c*) $I_a^2 r_a$ loss in armature = $(20\text{ A})^2\ (0.25\ \Omega) = 0.10\text{ kW}$

$I_f^2 r_f$ loss in field = $(0.80\text{ A})^2\ (150\ \Omega = 96\text{ W}$

(*d*) Power output = (Power input) − (Power losses) = 2496 − (100 + 96) = 2.3 kW

Alternatively.

Power output = (Armature current)(Back emf) = (20 A)(115 V) = 2.3 kW

Then
$$\text{Efficiency} = \frac{\text{Power output}}{\text{Power input}} = \frac{2300\text{ W}}{2496\text{ W}} = 0.921 = 92\%$$

**33.10 [II]** A motor has a back emf of 110 V and an armature current of 90 A when running at 1500 rpm. Determine the power and the torque developed within the armature.

Power = (Armature current) (Back emf) = (90 A)(110 V) = 9.9 kW

From Chapter 10, power = $\tau\omega$ where $\omega = 2\pi f = 2\pi(1500 \times 1/60)$ rad/s

$$\text{Torque} = \frac{\text{Power}}{\text{Angular speed}} = \frac{9900\text{ W}}{(2\pi \times 25)\text{ rad/s}} = 63\text{ N}\cdot\text{m}$$

**33.11 [III]** A motor armature develops a torque of 100 N·m when it draws 40 A from the line. Determine the torque developed if the armature current is increased to 70 A and the magnetic field strength is reduced to 80 percent of its initial value.

The torque developed by the armature of a given motor is proportional to the armature current and to the field strength (see Chapter 30). In other words, the ratio of the torques equals the ratio of the two sets of values of $|NIAB|$. Using subscripts *i* and *f* for *initial* and *final* values, $\tau_f/\tau_i = I_f B_f / I_i B_i$, hence,

$$\tau_f = (100 \text{ N}\cdot\text{m})\left(\frac{70}{40}\right)(0.80) = 0.14 \text{ kN}\cdot\text{m}$$

## SUPPLEMENTARY PROBLEMS

### ELECTRIC GENERATORS

**33.12 [I]** Determine the separate effects on the induced emf of a generator if (*a*) the flux per pole is doubled, and (*b*) the speed of the armature is doubled.

**33.13 [II]** The emf induced in the armature of a shunt generator is 596 V. The armature resistance is 0.100 Ω. (*a*) Compute the terminal voltage when the armature current is 460 A. (*b*) The field resistance is 110 Ω. Determine the field current, and the current and power delivered to the external circuit.

**33.14 [II]** A dynamo (generator) delivers 30.0 A at 120 V to an external circuit when operating at 1200 rpm. What torque is required to drive the generator at this speed if the total power losses are 400 W?

**33.15 [II]** A 75.0-kW, 230-V shunt generator has a generated emf of 243.5 V. If the field current is 12.5 A at rated output, what is the armature resistance?

**33.16 [III]** A 120-V generator is run by a windmill that has blades 2.0 m long. The wind, moving at 12 m/s, is slowed to 7.0 m/s after passing the windmill. The density of air is 1.29 kg/m$^3$. If the system has no losses, what is the largest current the generator can produce? [*Hint:* How much energy does the wind lose per second?]

### ELECTRIC MOTORS

**33.17 [II]** A generator has an armature with 500 turns, which cut a flux of 8.00 mWb during each rotation. Compute the back emf it develops when run as a motor at 1500 rpm.

**33.18 [I]** The active length of each armature conductor of a motor is 30 cm, and the conductors are in a field of 0.40 Wb/m$^2$. A current of 15 A flows in each conductor. Determine the force acting on each conductor.

**33.19 [II]** A shunt motor with armature resistance 0.080 Ω is connected to 120 V mains. With 50 A in the armature, what are the back emf and the mechanical power developed within the armature?

**33.20 [II]** A shunt motor is connected to a 110-V line. When the armature generates a back emf of 104 V, the armature current is 15 A. Compute the armature resistance.

**33.21 [II]** A shunt dynamo has an armature resistance of 0.120 Ω. (*a*) If it is connected across 220-V mains and is running as a motor, what is the induced (back) emf when the armature current is 50.0 A? (*b*) If this machine is running as a generator, what is the induced emf when the armature is delivering 50.0 A at 220 V to the shunt field and external circuit?

**33.22 [II]** A shunt motor has a frequency of 900 rpm when it is connected to 120-V mains and delivering 12 hp. The total losses are 1048 W. Compute the power input, the line current, and the motor torque.

**33.23 [II]** A shunt motor has armature resistance 0.20 Ω and field resistance 150 Ω, and draws 30 A when connected to a 120-V supply line. Determine the field current, the armature current, the back emf, the mechanical power developed within the armature, and the electrical efficiency of the machine.

**33.24 [II]** A shunt motor develops 80 N·m of torque when the flux density in the air gap is 1.0 $Wb/m^2$ and the armature current is 15 A. What is the torque when the flux density is 1.3 $Wb/m^2$ and the armature current is 18 A?

**33.25 [II]** A shunt motor has a field resistance of 200 Ω and an armature resistance of 0.50 Ω and is connected to 120-V mains. The motor draws a current of 4.6 A when running at full speed. What current will be drawn by the motor if the speed is reduced to 90 percent of full speed by application of a load?

## ANSWERS TO SUPPLEMENTARY PROBLEMS

**33.12 [I]** (*a*) doubled; (*b*) doubled

**33.13 [II]** (*a*) 550 V; (*b*) 5 A, 455 A, 250 kW

**33.14 [II]** 31.8 N·m

**33.15 [II]** 0.0399 Ω

**33.16 [III]** 77 A

**33.17 [II]** 100 V

**33.18 [I]** 1.8 N

**33.19 [II]** 0.12 kV, 5.8 kW

**33.20 [II]** 0.40 Ω

**33.21 [II]** (*a*) 214 V; (*b*) 226 V

**33.22 [II]** 10 kW, 83 A, 93 N·m

**33.23 [II]** 0.80 A, 29 A, 0.11 kV, 3.3 kW, 93%

**33.24 [II]** 0.13 kN·m

**33.25 [II]** 28 A

# Inductance; R-C and R-L Time Constants

**Self-Inductance** ($L$): A coil can induce an emf in itself. If the current in a coil changes, the flux through the coil due to the current also changes. As a result, the changing current in a coil induces an emf in that same coil.

Because an induced emf $\mathcal{E}$ is proportional to $\Delta\Phi_M/\Delta t$ and because $\Delta\Phi_M$ is proportional to $\Delta i$, where $i$ is the current that causes the flux,

$$\mathcal{E} = -(\text{constant})\frac{\Delta i}{\Delta t}$$

Here $i$ is the current through the same coil in which $\mathcal{E}$ is induced. (We shall denote a time-varying current by $i$ instead of $I$.) The minus sign indicates that the self-induced emf $\mathcal{E}$ is a back emf and opposes the change in current.

The proportionality constant depends upon the geometry of the coil. We represent it by $L$ and call it the **self-inductance** of the coil. Then

$$\mathcal{E} = -L\frac{\Delta i}{\Delta t}$$

For $\mathcal{E}$ in units of V, $i$ in units of A, and $t$ in units of s, $L$ is in **henries** (H).

**Mutual Inductance** ($M$): When the flux from one coil threads through another coil, an emf can be induced in either one by the other. The coil that contains the power source is called the *primary coil.* The other coil, in which an emf is induced by the changing current in the primary, is called the *secondary coil.* The induced secondary emf $\mathcal{E}_s$ is proportional to the time rate of change of the primary current, $\Delta i_p/\Delta t$:

$$\mathcal{E}_s = M\frac{\Delta i_p}{\Delta t}$$

where $M$ is a constant called the **mutual inductance** of the two-coil system.

**Energy Stored in An Inductor:** Because of its self-induced back emf, work must be done to increase the current through an inductor from zero to $I$. The energy furnished to the coil in the process is stored in the coil and can be recovered as the coil's current is decreased once again to zero. If a current $I$ is flowing in an inductor of self-inductance $L$, then the energy stored in the inductor is

$$\text{Stored energy} = \tfrac{1}{2}LI^2$$

For $L$ in units of H and $I$ in units of A, the energy is in J.

**R-C Time Constant:** Consider the *R-C* circuit shown in Fig. 34-1(*a*). The capacitor is initially uncharged. If the switch is now closed, the current *i* in the circuit and the charge *q* on the capacitor vary as shown in Fig. 34-1(*b*). If we call the p.d. across the capacitor $\upsilon_c$, writing the loop rule for this circuit gives

$$-iR - \upsilon_c + \mathcal{E} = 0 \quad \text{or} \quad i = \frac{\mathcal{E} - \upsilon_c}{R}$$

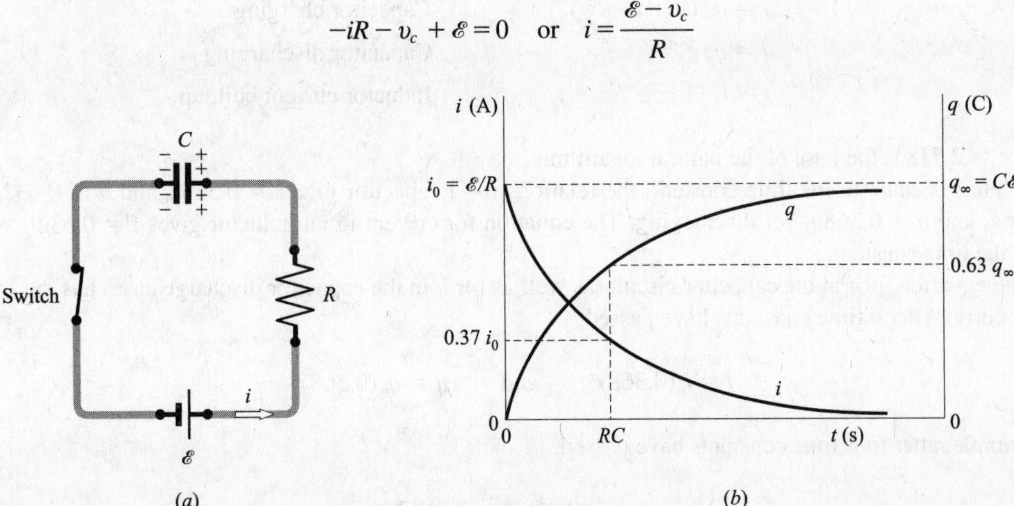


Fig. 34-1

At the first instant after the switch is closed, $\upsilon_c = 0$ and $i = \mathcal{E}/R$. As time goes on, $\upsilon_c$ increases and *i* decreases. The time, in seconds, taken for the current to drop to 1/2.718 or 0.368 of its initial value is *RC*, which is called the **time constant** of the *R-C* circuit.

Also shown in Fig. 34-1(*b*) is the variation of *q*, the charge on the capacitor, with time. At $t = RC$, *q* has attained 0.632 of its final value.

When a charged capacitor *C* with initial charge $q_0$ is discharged through a resistor *R*, its discharge current follows the same curve as for charging. The charge *q* on the capacitor follows a curve similar to that for the discharge current. At time *RC*, $i = 0.368 i_0$ and $q = 0.368 q_0$ during discharge.

**R-L Time Constant:** Consider the circuit in Fig. 34-2(*a*). The symbol ⅿⅿ represents a coil having a self-inductance of *L* henries. When the switch in the circuit is first closed, the current in the circuit rises as shown in Fig. 34-2(*b*). The current does not jump to its final value because the changing flux through the coil induces a back emf in the coil, which opposes the rising current. After $L/R$ seconds, the current has risen to 0.632 of its final value $i_\infty$. This time, $t = L/R$, is called the **time constant** of the *R-L* circuit. After a long time, the current is changing so slowly that the back emf in the inductor, $L(\Delta i/\Delta t)$, is negligible. Then $i = i_\infty = \mathcal{E}/R$.

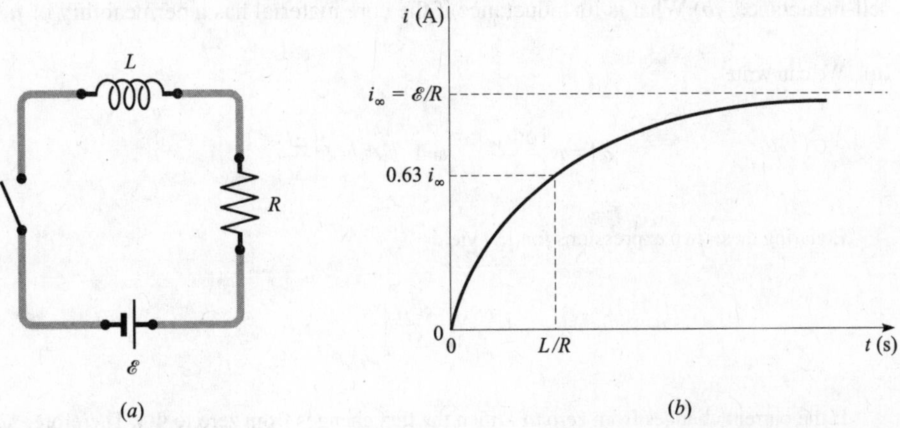


Fig. 34-2

**Exponential Functions** are used as follows to describe the curves of Figs 34-1 and 34-2:

| | |
|---|---|
| $i = i_0\, e^{-t/RC}$ | Capacitor charging and discharging |
| $q = q_\infty\,(1 - e^{-t/RC})$ | Capacitor charging |
| $q = q_\infty\, e^{-t/RC}$ | Capacitor discharging |
| $i = i_\infty\,(1 - e^{-t/(L/R)})$ | Inductor current buildup |

where $e = 2.718$ is the base of the natural logarithms.

When $t$ is equal to the time constant, the relations for a capacitor give $i = 0.368 i_0$ and $q = 0.632 q_\infty$ for charging, and $q = 0.368 q_\infty$ for discharging. The equation for current in an inductor gives $i = 0.632 i_\infty$ when $t$ equals the time constant.

The equation for $i$ in the capacitor circuit (as well as for $q$ in the capacitor discharge case) has the following property: After $n$ time constants have passed,

$$i = i_0(0.368)^n \quad \text{and} \quad q = q_\infty(0.368)^n$$

For example, after four time constants have passed,

$$i = i_0(0.368)^4 = 0.0183 i_0$$

## SOLVED PROBLEMS

**34.1 [II]** A steady current of 2 A in a coil of 400 turns causes a flux of $10^{-4}$ Wb to link (pass through) the loops of the coil. Compute (*a*) the average back emf induced in the coil if the current is stopped in 0.08 s, (*b*) the inductance of the coil, and (*c*) the energy stored in the coil.

(*a*) $|\mathscr{E}| = N\left|\frac{\Delta\Phi_M}{\Delta t}\right| = 400\frac{(10^{-4} - 0)\text{ Wb}}{0.08\text{ s}} = 0.5\text{ V}$

(*b*) $|\mathscr{E}| = N\left|\frac{\Delta i}{\Delta t}\right|$ or $L = \left|\frac{\mathscr{E}\Delta t}{\Delta i}\right| = \frac{(0.5\text{V})(0.08\text{ s})}{(2-0)\text{ A}} = 0.02\text{ H}$

(*c*) $\text{Energy} = \frac{1}{2}LI^2 = \frac{1}{2}(0.02\text{ H})(2\text{ A})^2 = 0.04\text{ J}$

**34.2 [III]** A long air-core solenoid has cross-sectional area $A$ and $N$ loops of wire on its length $d$. (*a*) Find its self-inductance. (*b*) What is its inductance if the core material has a permeability of $\mu$?

(*a*) We can write

$$|\mathscr{E}| = N\left|\frac{\Delta\Phi_M}{\Delta t}\right| \quad \text{and} \quad |\mathscr{E}| = L\left|\frac{\Delta i}{\Delta t}\right|$$

Equating these two expressions for $|\mathscr{E}|$ yields

$$L = N\left|\frac{\Delta\Phi_M}{\Delta i}\right|$$

If the current changes from zero to $I$, then the flux changes from zero to $\Phi_M$. Therefore, $\Delta i = I$ and $\Delta\Phi_M = \Phi_M$ in this case. The self-inductance, assumed constant for all cases, is then

$$L = N\frac{\Phi_M}{I} = N\frac{BA}{I}$$

But for an air-core solenoid, $B = \mu_0 nI = \mu_0(N/d)I$. Substitution gives $L = \mu_0 N^2 A/d$.

(*b*) If the material of the core has permeability $\mu$ instead of $\mu_0$, then $B$, and therefore $L$, will be increased by the factor $\mu/\mu_0$. In that case, $L = \mu N^2 A/d$. An iron-core solenoid has a much higher self-inductance than an air-core solenoid has.

**34.3 [II]** A solenoid 30 cm long is made by winding 2000 turns of wire on an iron rod whose cross-sectional area is 1.5 cm$^2$. If the relative permeability of the iron is 600, what is the self-inductance of the solenoid? What average emf is induced in the solenoid as the current in it is decreased from 0.60 A to 0.10 A in a time of 0.030 s? Refer back to Problem 34.2.

From Problem 34.2(*b*) with $k_M = \mu/\mu_0$,

$$L = \frac{k_m \mu_0 N^2 A}{d} = \frac{(600)\,(4\pi\times 10^{-7}\ \text{T}\cdot\text{m/A})(2000)^2\,(1.5\times 10^{-4}\ \text{m}^2)}{0.30\ \text{m}} = 1.51\ \text{H}$$

and

$$|\mathscr{E}| = L\left|\frac{\Delta i}{\Delta t}\right| = (1.51\ \text{H})\frac{0.50\ \text{A}}{0.030\ \text{s}} = 25\ \text{V}$$

**34.4 [II]** At a certain instant, a coil with a resistance of 0.40 Ω and a self-inductance of 200 mH carries a current of 0.30 A that is increasing at the rate of 0.50 A/s. (*a*) What is the potential difference across the coil at that instant? (*b*) Repeat if the current is decreasing at 0.50 A/s.

We can represent the coil by a resistance in series with an emf (the induced emf), as shown in Fig. 34.3.

(*a*) Because the current is increasing, $\mathscr{E}$ will oppose the current and therefore have the polarity shown. We write the loop equation for the circuit:

$$V_{ba} - iR - \mathscr{E} = 0$$

Since $V_{ba}$ is the voltage across the coil, and since $\mathscr{E} = L|\Delta i/\Delta t|$, we have

$$V_{\text{coil}} = iR + \mathscr{E} = (0.30\ \text{A})(0.40\ \Omega) + (0.200\ \text{H})(0.50\ \text{A/s}) = 0.22\ \text{V}$$

(*b*) With $i$ decreasing, the induced emf must be reversed in Fig. 34-3. This gives $V_{\text{coil}} = iR - \mathscr{E} = 0.020$ V.

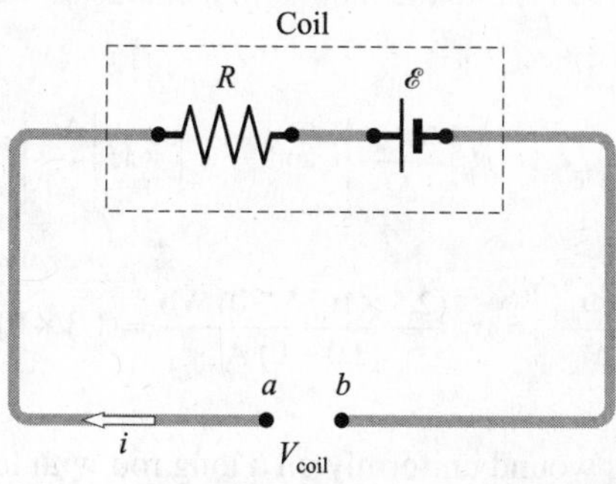


Fig. 34-3

**34.5 [II]** A coil of resistance 15 Ω and inductance 0.60 H is connected to a steady 120-V power source. At what rate will the current in the coil rise (*a*) at the instant the coil is connected to the power source, and (*b*) at the instant the current reaches 80 percent of its maximum value?

The effective driving voltage in the circuit is the 120 V power supply minus the induced back emf, $L(\Delta i/\Delta t)$. This equals the p.d. in the resistance of the coil:

$$120\text{ V} - L\frac{\Delta i}{\Delta t} = iR$$

[This same equation can be obtained by writing the loop equation for the circuit of Fig. 34-2(*a*). In doing so, remember that the inductance acts as a back emf of value $L\,\Delta i/\Delta t$.]

(*a*) At the first instant, *i* is essentially zero. Then

$$\frac{\Delta i}{\Delta t} = \frac{120\text{ V}}{L} = \frac{120\text{ V}}{0.60\text{ H}} = 0.20\text{ mA/s}$$

(*b*) The current reaches a maximum value of $(120\text{ V})/R$ when the current finally stops changing (i.e., when $\Delta i/\Delta t = 0$). We are interested in the case when

$$i = (0.80)\left(\frac{120\text{ V}}{R}\right)$$

Substitution of this value for *i* in the loop equation gives

$$120\text{ V} - L\frac{\Delta i}{\Delta t} = (0.80)\left(\frac{120\text{ V}}{R}\right)R$$

from which $$\frac{\Delta i}{\Delta t} = \frac{(0.20)(120\text{ V})}{L} = \frac{(0.20)(120\text{ V})}{0.60\text{ H}} = 40\text{ A/s}$$

**34.6 [II]** When the current in a certain coil is changing at a rate of 3.0 A/s, it is found that an emf of 7.0 mV is induced in a nearby coil. What is the mutual inductance of the combination?

$$\mathscr{E}_s = M\frac{\Delta i_p}{\Delta t} \quad\text{or}\quad M = \mathscr{E}_s\frac{\Delta t}{\Delta i_p} = (7.0\times10^{-3}\text{ V})\frac{1.0\text{ s}}{3.0\text{ A}} = 2.3\text{ mH}$$

**34.7 [II]** Two coils are wound on the same iron rod so that the flux generated by one passes through the other also. The primary coil has $N_p$ loops and, when a current of 2.0 A flows through it, the flux in it is $2.5 \times 10^{-4}$ Wb. Determine the mutual inductance of the two coils if the secondary coil has $N_s$ loops.

$$|\mathscr{E}_s| = N_s\left|\frac{\Delta\Phi_{Ms}}{\Delta t}\right| \quad\text{and}\quad |\mathscr{E}_s| = M\left|\frac{\Delta i_p}{\Delta t}\right|$$

give $$M = N_s\left|\frac{\Delta\Phi_{Ms}}{\Delta i_p}\right| = N_s\frac{(2.5\times10^{-4} - 0)\text{ Wb}}{(2.0 - 0)\text{ A}} = (1.3\times10^{-4}\,N_s)\text{ H}$$

**34.8 [II]** A 2000-loop solenoid is wound uniformly on a long rod with length *d* and cross-section *A*. The relative permeability of the iron is $k_m$. On top of this is wound a 50-loop coil which is used as a secondary. Find the mutual inductance of the system.

The flux through the solenoid is

$$\Phi_M = BA = (k_M \mu_0 n I_p)A = (k_M \mu_0 n I_p A)\left(\frac{2000}{d}\right)$$

This same flux goes through the secondary. We have, then,

$$|\mathscr{E}_s| = N_s\left|\frac{\Delta\Phi_M}{\Delta t}\right| \quad \text{and} \quad |\mathscr{E}_s| = M\left|\frac{\Delta i_p}{\Delta t}\right|$$

from which

$$M = N_s\left|\frac{\Delta\Phi_M}{\Delta i_p}\right| = N_s\frac{\Phi_M - 0}{I_p - 0} = 50\,\frac{k_M \mu_0 I_p A(2000/d)}{I_p} = \frac{10\times10^4\ k_M \mu_0 A}{d}$$

**34.9 [II]** A certain series circuit consists of a 12-V battery, a switch, a 1.0-MΩ resistor, and a 2.0-μF capacitor, initially uncharged. If the switch is now closed, find (*a*) the initial current in the circuit, (*b*) the time for the current to drop to 0.37 of its initial value, (*c*) the charge on the capacitor then, and (*d*) the final charge on the capacitor.

(*a*) The loop rule applied to the circuit of Fig. 34-1(*a*) at any instant gives

$$12\text{ V} - iR - v_c = 0$$

where $v_c$ is the p.d. across the capacitor. At the first instant, $q$ is essentially zero and so $v_c = 0$. Then

$$12\text{ V} - iR - 0 = 0 \quad \text{or} \quad i = \frac{12\text{ V}}{1.0\times10^6\ \Omega} = 12\ \mu\text{A}$$

(*b*) The current drops to 0.37 of its initial value when

$$t = RC = (1.0\times10^6\ \Omega)(2.0\times10^{-6}\text{ F}) = 2.0\text{ s}$$

(*c*) At $t = 2.0$ s the charge on the capacitor has increased to 0.63 of its final value. [See part (*d*) below.]

(*d*) The charge ceases to increase when $i = 0$ and $v_c = 12$ V. Therefore,

$$q_{\text{final}} = Cv_c = (2.0\times10^{-6}\text{ F})(12\text{ V}) = 24\ \mu\text{C}$$

**34.10 [II]** A 5.0-μF capacitor is charged to a potential difference of 20 kV across its plates. After being disconnected from the power source, it is connected across a 7.0-MΩ resistor to discharge. What is the initial discharge current, and how long will it take for the capacitor voltage to decrease to 37 percent of the 20 kV?

The loop equation for the discharging capacitor is

$$v_c - iR = 0$$

where $v_c$ is the p.d. across the capacitor. At the first instant, $v_c = 20$ kV, so

$$i = \frac{v_c}{R} = \frac{20\times10^3\text{ V}}{7.0\times10^6\ \Omega} = 2.9\text{ mA}$$

The potential across the capacitor, as well as the charge on it, will decrease to 0.37 of its original value in one time constant. The required time is

$$RC = (7.0 \times 10^6\ \Omega)\ (5.0 \times 10^{-6}\ \text{F}) = 35\ \text{s}$$

**34.11 [II]** A coil has an inductance of 1.5 H and a resistance of 0.60 Ω. If the coil is suddenly connected across a 12-V battery, find the time required for the current to rise to 0.63 of its final value. What will be the final current through the coil?

The time required is the time constant of the circuit:

$$\text{Time constant} = \frac{L}{R} = \frac{1.5\ \text{H}}{0.60\ \Omega} = 2.5\ \text{s}$$

After a long time, the current will be steady, and so no back emf will exist in the coil. Under those conditions,

$$I = \frac{\mathscr{E}}{R} = \frac{12\ \text{V}}{0.60\ \Omega} = 20\ \text{A}$$

**34.12 [I]** A capacitor that has been charged to $2.0 \times 10^5$ V is allowed to discharge through a resistor. What will be the voltage across the capacitor after five time constants have elapsed?

We know (p. 374) that after $n$ time constants, $q = q_\infty(0.368)^n$. Because $v$ is proportional to $q$ (that is, $v = q/C$), we may write

$$v_{n=5} = (2.0 \times 10^5\ \text{V})\ (0.368)^5 = 1.4\ \text{kV}$$

**34.13 [II]** A 2.0-μF capacitor is charged through a 30-MΩ resistor by a 45-V battery. Find (*a*) the charge on the capacitor and (*b*) the current through the resistor, both determined 83 s after the charging process starts.

The time constant of the circuit is $RC = 60$ s. Also,

$$q_\infty = V_\infty C = (45\ \text{V})\ (2.0 \times 10^{-6}\ \text{F}) = 9.0 \times 10^{-5}\ \text{C}$$

(*a*) $q = q_\infty\ (1 - e^{-t/RC}) = (9.0 \times 10^{-5}\ \text{C})\ (1 - e^{-83/60})$

But $e^{-83/60} = e^{-1.383} = 0.25$

Then substitution gives

$$q = (9.0 \times 10^{-5}\ \text{C})(1 - 0.25) = 67\ \mu\text{C}$$

(*b*) $i = i_0 e^{-t/RC} = \left(\dfrac{45\ \text{V}}{30 \times 10^6\ \Omega}\right)(e^{-1.383}) = 0.38\ \mu\text{A}$

**34.14 [II]** If, in Fig. 34-2, $R = 20\ \Omega$, $L = 0.30$ H, and $\mathscr{E} = 90$ V, what will be the current in the circuit 0.050 s after the switch is closed?

We are going to use the exponential equation for $i$ given on p. 374.
The time constant for this circuit is $L/R = 0.015$ s, and $i_\infty = \mathscr{E}/R = 4.5$ A. Then

$$i = i_\infty\ (1 - e^{-t/(L/R)}) = (4.5\ \text{A})(1 - e^{-3.33}) = (4.5\ \text{A})(1 - 0.0357) = 4.3\ \text{A}$$

## SUPPLEMENTARY PROBLEMS

**34.15 [I]** An emf of 8.0 V is induced in a coil when the current in it changes at the rate of 32 A/s. Compute the inductance of the coil.

**34.16 [I]** A steady current of 2.5 A creates a flux of $1.4 \times 10^{-4}$ Wb in a coil of 500 turns. What is the inductance of the coil?

**34.17 [I]** The mutual inductance between the primary and secondary of a transformer is 0.30 H. Compute the induced emf in the secondary when the primary current changes at the rate of 4.0 A/s.

**34.18 [II]** A coil of inductance 0.20 H and 1.0-Ω resistance is connected to a constant 90-V source. At what rate will the current in the coil grow (*a*) at the instant the coil is connected to the source, and (*b*) at the instant the current reaches two-thirds of its maximum value?

**34.19 [II]** Two neighboring coils, *A* and *B*, have 300 and 600 turns, respectively. A current of 1.5 A in *A* causes $1.2 \times 10^{-4}$ Wb to pass through *A* and $0.90 \times 10^{-4}$ Wb to pass through *B*. Determine (*a*) the self-inductance of *A*, (*b*) the mutual inductance of *A* and *B*, and (*c*) the average induced emf in *B* when the current in *A* is interrupted in 0.20 s.

**34.20 [I]** A coil of 0.48 H carries a current of 5 A. Compute the energy stored in it.

**34.21 [I]** The iron core of a solenoid has a length of 40 cm and a cross section of 5.0 cm², and is wound with 10 turns of wire per cm of length. Compute the inductance of the solenoid, assuming the relative permeability of the iron to be constant at 500.

**34.22 [I]** Show that (*a*) $1\ \text{N/A}^2 = 1\ \text{T}\cdot\text{m/A} = 1\ \text{Wb/A}\cdot\text{m} = 1\ \text{H/m}$, and (*b*) $1\ \text{C}^2/\text{N}\cdot\text{m}^2 = 1\ \text{F/m}$.

**34.23 [II]** A series circuit consisting of an uncharged 2.0-$\mu$F capacitor and a 10-MΩ resistor is connected across a 100-V power source. What are the current in the circuit and the charge on the capacitor (*a*) after one time constant, and (*b*) when the capacitor has acquired 90 percent of its final charge?

**34.24 [II]** A charged capacitor is connected across a 10-kΩ resistor and allowed to discharge. The potential difference across the capacitor drops to 0.37 of its original value after a time of 7.0 s. What is the capacitance of the capacitor?

**34.25 [II]** When a long iron-core solenoid is connected across a 6-V battery, the current rises to 0.63 of its maximum value after a time of 0.75 s. The experiment is then repeated with the iron core removed. Now the time required to reach 0.63 of the maximum is 0.0025 s. Calculate (*a*) the relative permeability of the iron and (*b*) *L* for the air-core solenoid if the maximum current is 0.5 A.

**34.26 [I]** What fraction of the initial current still flows in the circuit of Fig. 34-1 seven time constants after the switch has been closed?

**34.27 [II]** By what fraction does the current in Fig. 34-2 differ from $i_\infty$ three time constants after the switch is first closed?

**34.28 [II]** In Fig. 34-2, $R = 5.0\ \Omega$, $L = 0.40$ H, and $\mathscr{E} = 20$ V. Find the current in the circuit 0.20 s after the switch is first closed.

**34.29 [II]** The capacitor in Fig. 34-1 is initially uncharged when the switch is closed. Find the current in the circuit and the charge on the capacitor five seconds later. Use $R = 7.00$ MΩ, C = 0.300 $\mu$F, and $\mathscr{E} = 12.0$ V.

## ANSWERS TO SUPPLEMENTARY PROBLEMS

**34.15 [I]** 0.25 H

**34.16 [I]** 28 mH

**34.17 [I]** 1.2 V

**34.18 [II]** (*a*) 0.45 kA/s; (*b*) 0.15 kA/s

**34.19 [II]** (*a*) 24 mH; (*b*) 36 mH; (*c*) 0.27 V

**34.20 [I]** 6 J

**34.21 [I]** 0.13 H

**34.23 [II]** (*a*) 3.7 $\mu$A, 0.13 mC; (*b*) 1.0 $\mu$A, 0.18 mC

**34.24 [II]** 0.70 mF

**34.25 [II]** (*a*) $0.3 \times 10^3$; (*b*) 0.03 H

**34.26 [I]** 0.000 91

**34.27 [II]** $(i_\infty - i)/i_\infty = 0.050$

**34.28 [II]** 3.7 A

**34.29 [II]** 159 nA, 3.27 $\mu$C

# CHAPTER 35

# Alternating Current

**The Emf Generated by a Rotating Coil** in a magnetic field has a graph similar to the one shown in Fig. 35-1. It is called an *ac voltage* because there is a reversal of polarity (i.e., the voltage changes sign); ac voltages need not be sinusoidal. If the coil rotates with a frequency of $f$ revolutions per second, then the emf has a frequency of $f$ in hertz (cycles per second). The instantaneous voltage $v$ that is generated has the form

$$v = v_0 \sin \omega t = v_0 \sin 2\pi f t$$

where $v_0$ is the amplitude (maximum value) of the voltage in volts, and $\omega = 2\pi f$ is the angular velocity in rad/s. The frequency $f$ of the voltage is related to its period $T$ by

$$T = \frac{1}{f}$$

where $T$ is in seconds.

Rotating coils are not the only source of ac voltages; electronic devices for generating ac voltages are very common. Alternating voltages produce alternating currents.

An alternating current produced by a typical generator has a graph much like that for the voltage shown in Fig. 35-1. Its instantaneous value is $i$, and its amplitude is $i_0$. Often the current and voltage do not reach a maximum at the same time, even though they both have the same frequency.

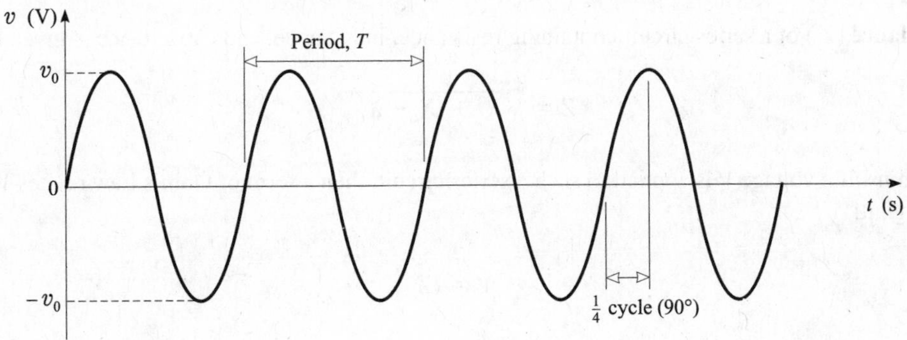


Fig. 35-1

**Meters** (i.e., measuring devices) for use in ac circuits read the **effective**, or **root mean square** (rms), values of the current and voltage. These values are always positive and are related to the amplitudes of the instantaneous sinusoidal values through

$$V = V_{\text{rms}} = \frac{\upsilon_0}{\sqrt{2}} = 0.707\upsilon_0$$

$$I = I_{\text{rms}} = \frac{i_0}{\sqrt{2}} = 0.707 i_0$$

It is customary to represent meter readings by capital letters ($V$, $I$), while instantaneous values are represented by small letters ($\upsilon$, $i$).

**The Thermal Energy Generated or Power Lost** by an rms current $I$ in a resistor $R$ is given by $I^2R$.

**Forms of Ohm's Law:** Suppose that a sinusoidal current of frequency $f$ with rms value $I$ flows through a pure resistor $R$, or a pure inductor $L$, or a pure capacitor $C$. Then an ac voltmeter placed across the element in question will read an rms voltage $V$ as follows:

$$\text{Pure resistor:} \quad V = IR$$

$$\text{Pure inductor:} \quad V = IX_L$$

where $X_L = 2\pi fL$ is called the **inductive reactance**. Its unit is ohms when $L$ is in henries and $f$ is in hertz.

$$\text{Pure capacitor:} \quad V = IX_C$$

where $X_C = 1/2\pi fC$ is called the **capacitive reactance**. Its unit is ohms when $C$ is in farads.

**Phase:** When an ac voltage is applied to a pure resistance, the voltage across the resistance and the current through it attain their maximum values at the same instant and their zero values at the same instant; the voltage and current are said to be *in-phase*.

When an ac voltage is applied to a pure inductance, the voltage across the inductance reaches its maximum value one-quarter cycle ahead of the current—that is, when the current is zero. The back emf of the inductance causes the current through the inductance to lag behind the voltage by one-quarter cycle (or 90°), and the two are 90° *out-of-phase*.

When an ac voltage is applied to a pure capacitor, the voltage across it lags 90° behind the current flowing through it. Current must flow before the voltage across (and charge on) the capacitor can build up.

In more complicated situations involving combinations of $R$, $L$, and $C$, the voltage and current are usually (but not always) out-of-phase. The angle by which the voltage lags or leads the current is called the **phase angle**.

**The Impedance** ($Z$) of a series circuit containing resistance, inductance, and capacitance is given by

$$Z = \sqrt{R^2 + (X_L - X_C)^2}$$

with $Z$ in ohms. If a voltage $V$ is applied to such a series circuit, then a form of Ohm's Law relates $V$ to the current $I$ through it:

$$V = IZ$$

The phase angle $\phi$ between $V$ and $I$ is given by

$$\tan\phi = \frac{X_L - X_C}{R} \quad \text{or} \quad \cos\phi = \frac{R}{Z}$$

**Phasors:** A **phasor** is a quantity that behaves, in many regards, like a vector. Phasors are used to describe series *R-L-C* circuits because the above expression for the impedance can be associated with the Pythagorean theorem for a right triangle. As shown in Fig. 35-2(*a*), $Z$ is the hypotenuse of the right triangle, while $R$ and $(X_L - X_C)$ are its two legs. The angle labeled $\phi$ is the phase angle between the current and the voltage.

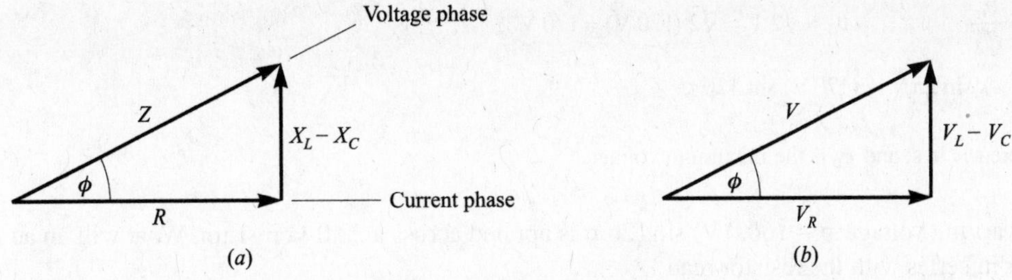


Fig. 35-2

A similar relation applies to the voltages across the elements in the series circuit. As illustrated in Fig. 35-2(*b*), it is

$$V^2 = V_R^2 + (V_L - V_C)^2$$

Because of the phase differences a measurement of the voltage across a series circuit is not equal to the algebraic sum of the individual voltage readings across its elements. Instead, the above relation must be used.

**Resonance** occurs in a series *R-L-C* circuit when $X_L = X_C$. Under this condition $Z = R$ is minimum, so that $I$ is maximum for a given value of $V$. Equating $X_L$ to $X_C$, we find for the **resonant** (or **natural**) **frequency** of the circuit

$$f_0 = \frac{1}{2\pi\sqrt{LC}}$$

**Power Loss:** Suppose that an ac voltage $V$ is impressed across an impedance of any type. It gives rise to a current $I$ through the impedance, and the phase angle between $V$ and $I$ is $\phi$. The power loss in the impedance is given by

$$\text{Power loss} = VI\cos\phi$$

The quantity $\cos\phi$ is called the **power factor**. It is unity for a pure resistor; but it is zero for a pure inductor or capacitor (no power loss occurs in a pure inductor or capacitor).

**A Transformer** is a device used to raise or lower the voltage in an ac circuit. It consists of a primary and a secondary coil wound on the same iron core. An alternating current in one coil creates a continuously changing magnetic flux through the core. This change of flux induces an alternating emf in the other coil.

The efficiency of a transformer is usually very high. Thus, we may often *neglect losses* and write

$$\text{Power in primary} = \text{Power in secondary}$$
$$V_1 I_1 = V_2 I_2$$

The voltage ratio equals the ratio of the numbers of turns on the two coils; the current ratio equals the inverse ratio of the numbers of turns:

$$\frac{V_1}{V_2} = \frac{N_1}{N_2} \quad \text{and} \quad \frac{I_1}{I_2} = \frac{N_2}{N_1}$$

## SOLVED PROBLEMS

**35.1 [I]** A sinusoidal, 60.0-Hz, ac voltage is read to be 120 V by an ordinary ac voltmeter. (*a*) What is the maximum value the voltage takes on during a cycle? (*b*) What is the equation for the voltage?

(*a*) $V = \dfrac{\upsilon_0}{\sqrt{2}}$ or $\upsilon_0 = \sqrt{2}\,V = \sqrt{2}\,(120\text{ V}) = 170\text{ V}$

(*b*) $\upsilon = \upsilon_0 \sin 2\pi f t = (170\text{ V}) \sin 120\pi t$

where $t$ is in s, and $\upsilon_0$ is the maximum voltage.

**35.2 [I]** A time-varying voltage $\upsilon = (60.0\text{ V}) \sin 120\pi t$ is applied across a 20.0-Ω resistor. What will an ac ammeter in series with the resistor read?

The rms voltage across the resistor is

$$V = 0.707\upsilon_0 = (0.707)(60.0\text{ V}) = 42.4\text{ V}$$

Then $$I = \frac{V}{R} = \frac{42.4\text{ V}}{20.0\ \Omega} = 2.12\text{ A}$$

**35.3 [II]** A 120-V ac voltage source is connected across a 2.0-$\mu$F capacitor. Find the current to the capacitor if the frequency of the source is (*a*) 60 Hz and (*b*) 60 kHz. (*c*) What is the power loss in the capacitor?

(*a*) $$X_C = \frac{1}{2\pi f C} = \frac{1}{2\pi\left(60\text{ s}^{-1}\right)\left(2.0\times10^{-6}\text{F}\right)} = 1.33\text{ k}\Omega$$

Then $$I = \frac{V}{X_C} = \frac{120\text{ V}}{1330\ \Omega} = 0.090\text{ A}$$

(*b*) Now $X_C = 1.33\ \Omega$, so $I = 90$ A. Notice that the impedance of a capacitor varies inversely with the frequency.

(*c*) Inasmuch as $\cos\phi = R/Z$ and $R = 0$;

$$\text{Power loss} = VI\cos\phi = VI\cos 90^\circ = 0$$

**35.4 [II]** A 120-V ac voltage source is connected across a pure 0.700-H inductor. Find the current through the inductor if the frequency of the source is (*a*) 60.0 Hz and (*b*) 60.0 kHz. (*c*) What is the power loss in the inductor?

(*a*) $X_L = 2\pi f L = 2\pi(60.0\text{ s}^{-1})(0.700\text{ H}) = 264\ \Omega$

Then $$I = \frac{V}{X_L} = \frac{120\text{ V}}{264\ \Omega} = 0.455\text{ A}$$

(*b*) Now $X_L = 264 \times 10^3\ \Omega$, so $I = 0.455 \times 10^{-3}$ A. Notice that the impedance of an inductor varies directly with the frequency.

(*c*) Inasmuch as $\cos\phi = R/Z$ and $R = 0$;

$$\text{Power loss} = VI\cos\phi = VI\cos 90^\circ = 0$$

**35.5 [II]** A coil having inductance 0.14 H and resistance of 12 Ω is connected across a 110-V, 25-Hz line. Compute (*a*) the current in the coil, (*b*) the phase angle between the current and the supply voltage, (*c*) the power factor, and (*d*) the power loss in the coil.

(*a*) $X_L = 2\pi fL = 2\pi(25)(0.14) = 22.0\ \Omega$

and $$Z = \sqrt{R^2 + (X_L - X_C)^2} = \sqrt{(12)^2 + (22-0)^2} = 25.1\ \Omega$$

so $$I = \frac{V}{Z} = \frac{110\text{ V}}{25.1\ \Omega} = 4.4\text{ A}$$

(*b*) $\tan\phi = \dfrac{X_L - X_C}{R} = \dfrac{22-0}{12} = 1.83$ or $\phi = 61.3°$

The voltage leads the current by 61°.

(*c*) Power factor = $\cos\phi = \cos 61.3° = 0.48$

(*d*) Power loss = $VI\cos\phi = (110\text{ V})(4.4\text{ A})(0.48) = 0.23\text{ kW}$

Or, since power loss occurs only because of the resistance of the coil,

$$\text{Power loss} = I^2R = (4.4\text{ A})^2(12\ \Omega) = 0.23\text{ kW}$$

**35.6 [II]** A capacitor is in series with a resistance of 30 Ω and is connected to a 220-V ac line. The reactance of the capacitor is 40 Ω. Determine (*a*) the current in the circuit, (*b*) the phase angle between the current and the supply voltage, and (*c*) the power loss in the circuit.

(*a*) $$Z = \sqrt{R^2 + (X_L - X_C)^2} = \sqrt{(30)^2 + (0-40)^2} = 50\ \Omega$$

so $$I = \frac{V}{Z} = \frac{220\text{ V}}{50\ \Omega} = 4.4\text{ A}$$

(*b*) $\tan\phi = \dfrac{X_L - X_C}{R} = \dfrac{0-40}{30} = -1.33$ or $\phi = -53°$

The minus sign tells us that the voltage *lags* the current by 53°. The angle $\phi$ in Fig. 35-2 would lie below the horizontal axis.

(*c*) **Method 1**

$$\text{Power loss} = VI\cos\phi = (220)(4.4)\cos(-53°) = (220)(4.4)\cos 53° = 0.58\text{ kW}$$

**Method 2**

Because the power loss occurs only in the resistor, and not in the pure capacitor,

$$\text{Power loss} = I^2R = (4.4\text{ A})^2(30\ \Omega) = 0.58\text{ kW}$$

**35.7 [III]** A series circuit consisting of a 100-Ω noninductive resistor, a coil with a 0.10-H inductance and negligible resistance, and a 20-$\mu$F capacitor is connected across a 110-V, 60-Hz power source. Find (*a*) the current, (*b*) the power loss, (*c*) the phase angle between the current and the source voltage, and (*d*) the voltmeter readings across the three elements.

(*a*) For the entire circuit, $Z = \sqrt{R^2 + (X_L - X_C)^2}$, with

$$R = 100\ \Omega$$

$$X_L = 2\pi fL = 2\pi(60\text{ s}^{-1})(0.10\text{ H}) = 37.7\ \Omega$$

$$X_C = \frac{1}{2\pi fC} = \frac{1}{2\pi(60\text{ s}^{-1})(20\times10^{-6}\text{ F})} = 132.7\ \Omega$$

from which

$$Z = \sqrt{(100)^2 + (38-133)^2} = 138\ \Omega \quad\text{and}\quad I = \frac{V}{Z} = \frac{110\text{ V}}{138\ \Omega} = 0.79\text{ A}$$

(*b*) The power loss all occurs in the resistor, so

$$\text{Power loss} = I^2R = (0.79\text{ A})^2(100\ \Omega) = 63\text{ W}$$

(*c*) $\tan\phi = \dfrac{X_L - X_C}{R} = \dfrac{-95\ \Omega}{100\ \Omega} = -0.95$ or $\phi = -44°$

The voltage lags the current.

(*d*) $V_R = IR = (0.79\text{ A})(100\ \Omega) = 79\text{ V}$

$V_C = IX_C = (0.79\text{ A})(132.7\ \Omega) = 0.11\text{ kV}$

$V_L = IX_L = (0.79\text{ A})(37.7\ \Omega) = 30\text{ V}$

Notice that $V_C + V_L + V_R$ does not equal the source voltage. From Fig. 35-2(*b*), the correct relationship is

$$V = \sqrt{V_R^2 + (V_L - V_C)^2} = \sqrt{(79)^2 + (-75)^2} = 109\text{ V}$$

which checks within the limits of rounding-off errors.

**35.8 [III]** A 5.00-Ω resistance is in a series circuit with a 0.200-H pure inductance and a 40.0-nF pure capacitance. The combination is placed across a 30.0-V, 1780-Hz power supply. Find (*a*) the current in the circuit, (*b*) the phase angle between source voltage and current, (*c*) the power loss in the circuit, and (*d*) the voltmeter reading across each element of the circuit.

(*a*)

$$X_L = 2\pi fL = 2\pi(1780\text{ s}^{-1})(0.200\text{ H}) = 2.24\text{ k}\Omega$$

$$X_C = \frac{1}{2\pi fC} = \frac{1}{2\pi(1780\text{ s}^{-1})(4.00\times10^{-8}\text{ F})} = 2.24\text{ k}\Omega$$

and

$$Z = \sqrt{R^2 + (X_L - X_C)^2} = R = 5.00\ \Omega$$

Then

$$I = \frac{V}{Z} = \frac{30.0\text{ V}}{5.00\ \Omega} = 6.00\text{ A}$$

(*b*)

$$\tan\phi = \frac{X_L - X_C}{R} = 0 \quad \text{or} \quad \phi = 0°$$

(*c*)

$$\text{Power loss} = VI\cos\phi = (30.0\text{ V})(6.00\text{ A})(1) = 180\text{ W}$$

or

$$\text{Power loss} = I^2R = (6.00\text{ A})^2(5.00\ \Omega) = 180\text{ W}$$

(*d*)

$$V_R = IR = (6.00\text{ A})(5.00\ \Omega) = 30.00\text{ V}$$

$$V_C = IX_C = (6.00\text{ A})(2240\ \Omega) = 13.4\text{ kV}$$

$$V_L = IX_L = (6.00\text{ A})(2240\ \Omega) = 13.4\text{ kV}$$

This circuit is in resonance because $X_C = X_L$. Notice how very large the voltages across the inductor and capacitor become, even though the source voltage is low.

**35.9 [III]** As shown in Fig. 35-3, a series circuit connected across a 200-V, 60-Hz line consists of a capacitor of capacitive reactance 30 Ω, a noninductive resistor of 44 Ω, and a coil of inductive reactance 90 Ω and resistance 36 Ω. Determine (*a*) the current in the circuit, (*b*) the potential difference across each element, (*c*) the power factor of the circuit, and (*d*) the power absorbed by the circuit.

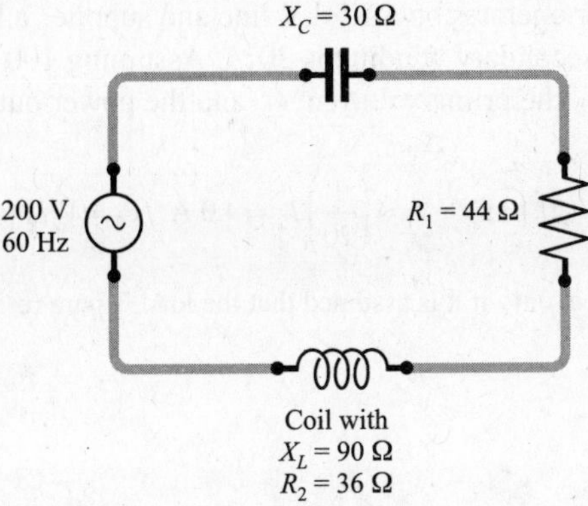


Fig. 35-3

(*a*) $$Z = \sqrt{(R_1 + R_2)^2 + (X_L - X_C)^2} = \sqrt{(44+36)^2 + (90-30)^2} = 0.10\ \text{k}\Omega$$

So $$I = \frac{V}{Z} = \frac{200\ \text{V}}{100\ \Omega} = 2.0\ \text{A}$$

(*b*) p.d. across capacitor $= IX_C = (2.0\ \text{A})(30\ \Omega) = 60\ \text{V}$

p.d. across resistor $= IR_1 = (2.0\ \text{A})(44\ \Omega) = 88\ \text{V}$

Impedance of coil $= \sqrt{R_2^2 + X_L^2} = \sqrt{(36)^2 + (90)^2} = 97\ \Omega$

p.d. across coil $= (2.0\ \text{A})(97\ \Omega) = 0.19\ \text{kV}$

(*c*) Powder factor $= \cos\phi = \dfrac{R}{Z} = \dfrac{80}{100} = 0.80$

(*d*) Power used $= VI\cos\phi = (200\ \text{V})(2\ \text{A})(0.80) = 0.32\ \text{kW}$

or Power used $= I^2R = (2\ \text{A})^2(80\ \Omega) = 0.32\ \text{kW}$

**35.10 [I]** **Calculate the resonant frequency of a circuit of negligible resistance containing an inductance of 40.0 mH and a capacitance of 600 pF.**

$$f_0 = \frac{1}{2\pi\sqrt{LC}} = \frac{1}{2\pi\sqrt{(40.0\times10^{-3}\ \text{H})(600\times10^{-12}\ \text{F})}} = 32.5\ \text{kHz}$$

**35.11 [I]** **A step-up transformer is used on a 120-V line to furnish 1800 V. The primary has 100 turns. How many turns are on the secondary?**

$$\frac{V_1}{V_2} = \frac{N_1}{N_2} \quad \text{or} \quad \frac{120\ \text{V}}{1800\ \text{V}} = \frac{100\ \text{turns}}{N_2}$$

from which $N_2 = 1.50 \times 10^3$ turns.

**35.12 [I]** **A transformer used on a 120-V line delivers 2.0 A at 900 V. What current is drawn from the line? Assume 100 percent efficiency.**

Power in primary = Power in secondary

$$I_1(120\ \text{V}) = (2.0\ \text{A})(900\ \text{V})$$

$$I_1 = 15\ \text{A}$$

**35.13 [I]** A step-down transformer operates on a 2.5-kV line and supplies a load with 80 A. The ratio of the primary winding to the secondary winding is 20 : 1. Assuming 100 percent efficiency, determine the secondary voltage $V_2$, the primary current $I_1$, and the power output $P_2$.

$$V_2 = \left(\frac{1}{20}\right)V_1 = 0.13\ \text{kV} \quad I_1 = \left(\frac{1}{20}\right)I_2 = 4.0\ \text{A} \quad P_2 = V_2 I_2 = 10\ \text{kW}$$

The last expression is correct only if it is assumed that the load is pure resistive, so that the power factor is unity.

## SUPPLEMENTARY PROBLEMS

**35.14 [I]** A voltmeter reads 80.0 V when it is connected across the terminals of a sinusoidal power source with $f = 1000$ Hz. Write the equation for the instantaneous voltage provided by the source.

**35.15 [I]** An ac current in a 10 Ω resistance produces thermal energy at the rate of 360 W. Determine the effective values of the current and voltage.

**35.16 [I]** A 40.0-Ω resistor is connected across a 15.0-V variable-frequency electronic oscillator. Find the current through the resistor when the frequency is (*a*) 100 Hz and (*b*) 100 kHz.

**35.17 [I]** Solve Problem 35.16 if the 40.0-Ω resistor is replaced by a 2.00-mH inductor.

**35.18 [I]** Solve Problem 35.16 if the 40.0-Ω resistor is replaced by 0.300-$\mu$F capacitor.

**35.19 [II]** A coil has resistance 20 Ω and inductance 0.35 H. Compute its reactance and its impedance to an alternating current of 25 cycles/s.

**35.20 [II]** A current of 30 mA is supplied to a 4.0-$\mu$F capacitor connected across an alternating current line having a frequency of 500 Hz. Compute the reactance of the capacitor and the voltage across the capacitor.

**35.21 [II]** A coil has an inductance of 0.100 H and a resistance of 12.0 Ω. It is connected to a 110-V, 60.0-Hz line. Determine (*a*) the reactance of the coil, (*b*) the impedance of the coil, (*c*) the current through the coil, (*d*) the phase angle between current and supply voltage, (*e*) the power factor of the circuit, and (*f*) the reading of a wattmeter connected in the circuit.

**35.22 [III]** A 10.0-$\mu$F capacitor is in series with a 40.0-Ω resistance, and the combination is connected to a 110-V, 60.0-Hz line. Calculate (*a*) the capacitive reactance, (*b*) the impedance of the circuit, (*c*) the current in the circuit, (*d*) the phase angle between current and supply voltage, and (*e*) the power factor for the circuit.

**35.23 [III]** A circuit having a resistance, an inductance, and a capacitance in series is connected to a 110-V ac line. For the circuit, $R = 9.0\ \Omega$, $X_L = 28\ \Omega$, and $X_C = 16\ \Omega$. Compute (*a*) the impedance of the circuit, (*b*) the current, (*c*) the phase angle between the current and the supply voltage, and (*d*) the power factor of the circuit.

**35.24 [II]** An experimenter has a coil of inductance 3.0 mH and wishes to construct a circuit whose resonant frequency is 1.0 MHz. What should be the value of the capacitor used?

**35.25 [II]** A circuit has a resistance of 11 Ω, a coil of inductive reactance 120 Ω, and a capacitor with a 120-Ω reactance, all connected in series with a 110-V, 60-Hz power source. What is the potential difference across each circuit element?

**35.26 [II]** A 120-V, 60-Hz power source is connected across an 800-Ω noninductive resistance and an unknown capacitance in series. The voltage drop across the resistor is 102 V. (*a*) What is the voltage drop across the capacitor? (*b*) What is the reactance of the capacitor?

**35.27 [II]** A coil of negligible resistance is connected in series with a 90-Ω resistor across a 120-V, 60-Hz line. A voltmeter reads 36 V across the resistance. Find the voltage across the coil and the inductance of the coil.

**35.28 [I]** A step-down transformer is used on a 2.2-kV line to deliver 110 V. How many turns are on the primary winding if the secondary has 25 turns?

**35.29 [I]** A step-down transformer is used on a 1650-V line to deliver 45 A at 110 V. What current is drawn from the line? Assume 100 percent efficiency.

**35.30 [II]** A step-up transformer operates on a 110-V line and supplies a load with 2.0 A. The ratio of the primary and secondary windings is 1:25. Determine the secondary voltage, the primary current, and the power output. Assume a resistive load and 100 percent efficiency.

## ANSWERS TO SUPPLEMENTARY PROBLEMS

**35.14 [I]** $v = (113\text{ V}) \sin 2000\pi t$ for $t$ in seconds

**35.15 [I]** 6.0 A, 60 V

**35.16 [I]** (*a*) 0.375 A; (*b*) 0.375 A

**35.17 [I]** (*a*) 11.9 A; (*b*) 11.9 mA

**35.18 [I]** (*a*) 2.83 mA; (*b*) 2.83 A

**35.19 [II]** 55 Ω, 59 Ω

**35.20 [II]** 80 Ω, 2.4 V

**35.21 [II]** (*a*) 37.7 Ω; (*b*) 39.6 Ω; (*c*) 2.78 A; (*d*) voltage leads by 72.3°; (*e*) 0.303; (*f*) 92.6 W

**35.22 [III]** (*a*) 266 Ω; (*b*) 269 Ω; (*c*) 0.409 A; (*d*) voltage lags by 81.4°; (*e*) 0.149

**35.23 [III]** (*a*) 15 Ω; (*b*) 7.3 A; (*c*) voltage leads by 53°; (*d*) 0.60

**35.24 [II]** 8.4 pF

**35.25 [II]** $V_R = 0.11$ kV, $V_L = V_C = 1.2$ kV

**35.26 [II]** (*a*) 63 V; (*b*) 0.50 kΩ

**35.27 [II]** 0.11 kV, 0.76 H

**35.28 [I]** $5.0 \times 10^2$

**35.29 [I]** 3.0 A

**35.30 [II]** 2.8 kV, 50 A, 5.5 kW

# Reflection of Light

**The Nature of Light:** Light (along with all other forms of electromagnetic radiation) is a fundamental entity and physics is still struggling to understand it. On an observable level, light manifests two seemingly contradictory behaviors, crudely pictured via wave and particle models. Usually the amount of energy present is so large that light behaves as if it were an ideal continuous wave, a wave of interdependent electric and magnetic fields. The interaction of light with lenses, mirrors, prisms, slits, and so forth, can satisfactorily be understood via the wave model (provided we don't probe too deeply into what's happening on a microscopic level). On the other hand, when light is emitted or absorbed by the atoms of a system, these processes occur as if the radiant energy is in the form of minute, localized, well-directed blasts; that is, as if light is a stream of "particles". Fortunately, without worrying about the very nature of light, we can predict its behavior in a wide range of practical situations.

**Law of Reflection:** A ray is a mathematical line drawn perpendicular to the wavefronts of a lightwave. It shows the direction of propagation of electromagnetic energy. In *specular* (or *mirror*) reflection, the angle of incidence ($\theta_i$) equals the angle of reflection ($\theta_r$), as shown in Fig. 36-1. Furthermore, the incident ray, reflected ray, and normal to the surface all lie in the same plane, called the **plane-of-incidence.**

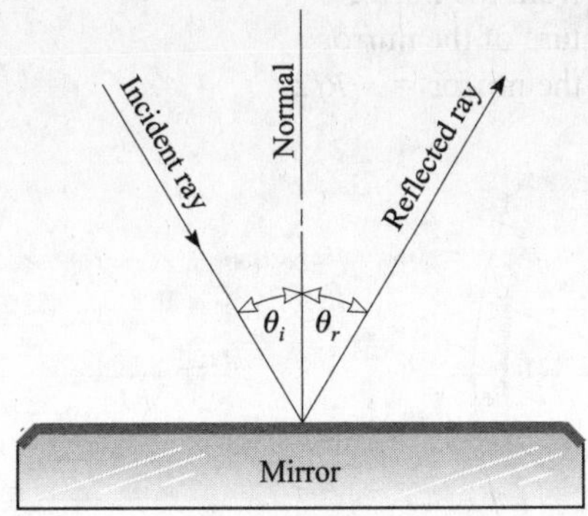


Fig. 36-1

**Plane Mirrors** form images that are erect, of the same size as the object, and as far behind the reflecting surface as the object is in front of it. Such an image is **virtual**—the image will not appear on a screen located at the position of the image because the light does not converge there. In other words, an image is virtual when it is formed by diverging rays.

**Spherical Mirrors:** The **principal focus** of a spherical mirror, such as the ones depicted in Fig. 36-2, is the point $F$ where rays parallel to and very close to the *central* or **optical axis** of the mirror are focused. This focus is real for a concave mirror and virtual for a convex mirror. It is located on the optical axis and midway between the center of curvature $C$ and the mirror.

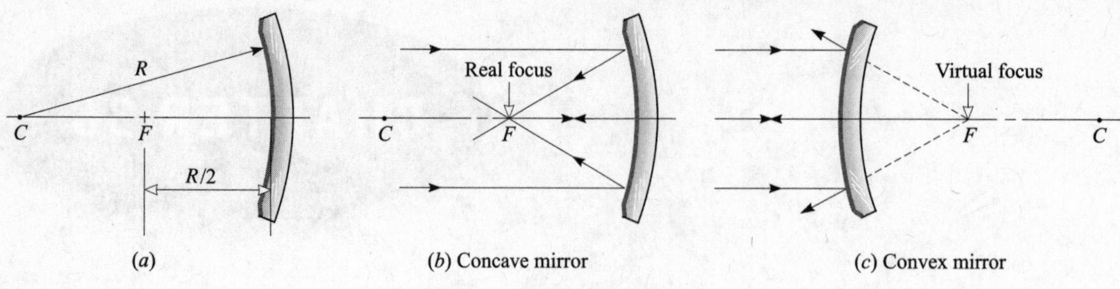


(*a*) (*b*) Concave mirror (*c*) Convex mirror

Fig. 36-2

**Concave mirrors** form inverted real images of objects placed beyond the principal focus. If the object is between the principal focus and the mirror, the image is virtual, erect, and enlarged.

**Convex mirrors** produce only erect virtual images of objects placed in front of them. The images are diminished (smaller than the object) in size. Examine a polished spoon.

**Ray Tracing:** We can locate the image of any point on an object by tracing at least two rays from that point through the optical system that forms the image—in this case the system is a mirror. There are four especially convenient rays to use because we know, without making any calculations, exactly how they will reflect from the mirror. These rays are shown for a concave spherical mirror in Fig. 36-3, and for a convex spherical mirror in Fig. 36-4. Notice that a line drawn from $C$ to the point of reflection is a radius and therefore normal to the mirror's surface. That line always bisects the angle formed by the incident and reflected rays (i.e., $\theta_i = \theta_r$).

**Mirror Equation** for both concave and convex spherical mirrors:

$$\frac{1}{s_o} + \frac{1}{s_i} = \frac{2}{R} = \frac{1}{f}$$

where $s_o$ = Object distance from the mirror
$s_i$ = Image distance from the mirror
$R$ = Radius of curvature of the mirror
$f$ = Focal length of the mirror $= -R/2$.

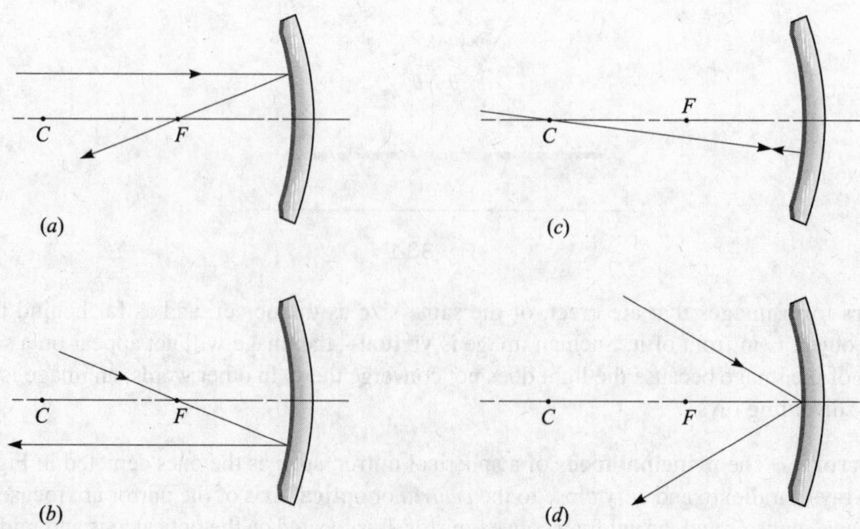


Fig. 36-3

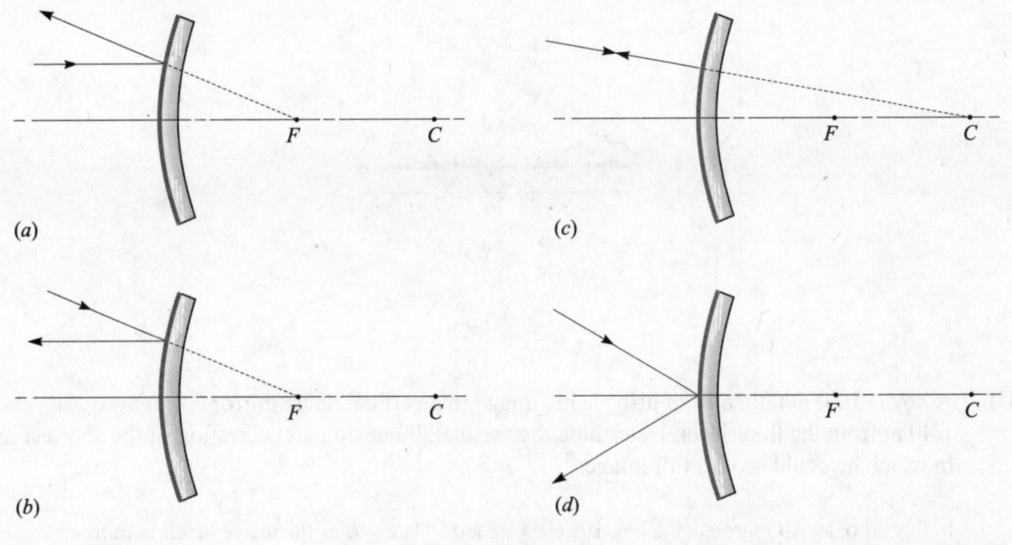


Fig. 36-4

There are several sign conventions; the following is the most widely used one. With light entering from the left:

- $s_o$ is positive when the object is in front (i.e., to the left) of the mirror.
- $s_i$ is positive when the image is real (i.e., in front or to the left of the mirror).
- $s_i$ is negative when the image is virtual (i.e., behind or to the right of the mirror).
- $f$ is positive for a concave mirror and negative for a convex mirror.
- $R$ is positive when $C$ is to the right of the mirror (i.e., when the mirror is convex).
- $R$ is negative when $C$ is to the left of the mirror (i.e, when the mirror is concave).

**The Size of the Image** formed by a spherical mirror is given by

$$\text{Transverse magnification} = \frac{\text{Length of image}}{\text{Length of object}} = -\frac{\text{Image distance from mirror}}{\text{Object distance from mirror}}$$

$$M_T = \frac{y_i}{y_o} = -\frac{s_i}{s_o}$$

A negative magnification tells us that the image is inverted. Here $y_i$ and $y_o$ are the heights of the image and object, respectively, where either one is positive when above the central axis and negative when below it.

## SOLVED PROBLEMS

**36.1 [II]** Two plane mirrors make an angle of 30° with each other. Locate graphically four images of a luminous point $A$ placed between the two mirrors. (See Fig. 36-5.)

From $A$ draw normals $AA'$ and $AB'$ to mirrors $OY$ and $OX$, respectively, making $\overline{AL} = \overline{LA'}$ and $\overline{AM} = \overline{MB'}$. Then $A'$ and $B'$ are images of $A$.

Next, from $A'$ and $B'$ draw normals to $OX$ and $OY$, making $\overline{A'N} = \overline{NA''}$ and $\overline{B'P} = \overline{PB''}$. Then $A''$ is the image of $A'$ in $OX$ and $B''$ is the image of $B'$ in $OY$.

The four images of $A$ are $A'$, $B'$, $A''$, $B''$. Additional images also exist, for example, images of $A''$ and $B''$.

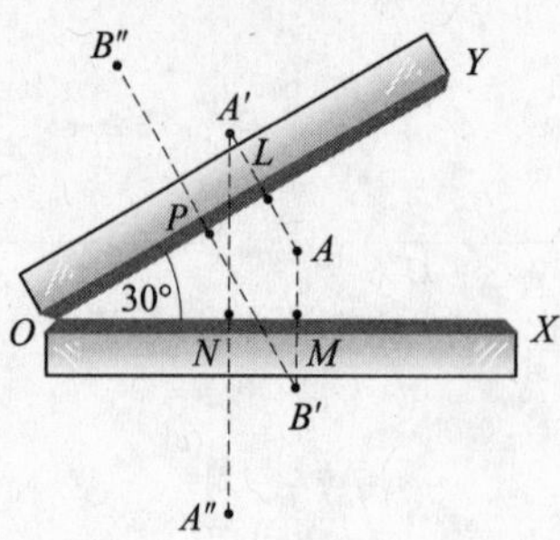


Fig. 36-5

**36.2 [II]** A boy is 1.50 m tall and can just see his image in a vertical plane mirror 3.0 m away. His eyes are 1.40 m from the floor level. Determine the vertical dimension and elevation of the shortest mirror in which he could see his full image.

In Fig. 36-6, let *AB* represent the boy. His eyes are at *E*. Then *A'B'* is the image of *AB* in mirror *MR*, and *DH* represents the shortest mirror necessary for the eye to view the image *A'B'*.

Triangles *DEC* and *DA'M* are congruent and so

$$\overline{CD} = \overline{DM} = 5.0 \text{ cm}$$

Triangles *HRB'* and *HCE* are congruent and so

$$\overline{RH} = \overline{HC} = 70 \text{ cm}$$

The dimension of the mirror is $\overline{HC} + \overline{CD} = 75$ cm and its elevation is $\overline{RH} = 70$ cm.

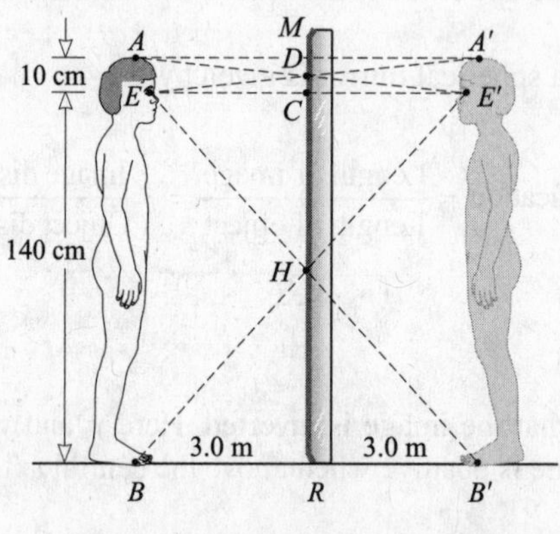


Fig. 36-6

**36.3 [II]** As shown in Fig. 36-7, a light ray *IO* is incident on a small plane mirror. The mirror reflects this ray back onto a straight ruler *SC* which is 1 m away from and parallel to the undeflected mirror *MM*. When the mirror turns through an angle of 8.0° and assumes the position *M'M'*, across what distance on the scale will the spot of light move? (This device, called an *optical lever*, is useful in measuring small deflections.)

When the mirror turns through 8.0° the normal to it also turns through 8.0°, and the incident ray makes an angle of 8.0° with the normal *NO* to the deflected mirror *M'M'*. Because the incident ray *IO* and the reflected ray *OR* make equal angles with the normal, angle *IOR* is twice the angle through which the mirror has turned, or 16°. Then

$$\overline{IR} = \overline{IO} \tan 16° = (1.0 \text{ m})(0.287) = 29 \text{ cm}$$

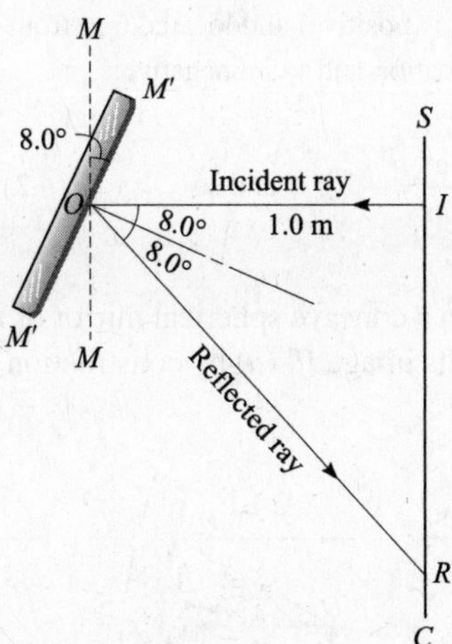


Fig. 36-7

**36.4 [II]** The concave spherical mirror shown in Fig. 36-8 has radius of curvature 4 m. An object $OO'$, 5 cm high, is placed 3 m in front of the mirror. By (*a*) construction and (*b*) computation, determine the position and height of the image $II'$.

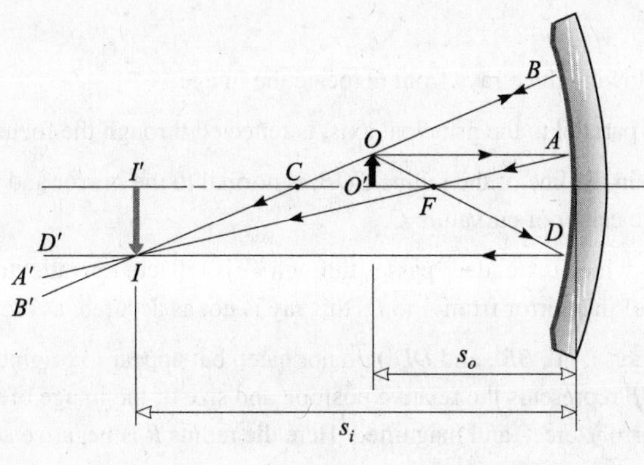


Fig. 36-8

In Fig. 36-8, $C$ is the center of curvature, 4 m from the mirror, and $F$ is the principal focus, 2 m from the mirror.

(*a*) Two of the following three convenient rays from $O$ will locate the image.

(1) The ray $OA$, parallel to the principal axis. This ray, like all parallel rays, is reflected through the principal focus $F$ in the direction $AFA'$.

(2) The ray $OB$, drawn as if it passed through the center of curvature $C$. This ray is normal to the mirror and is reflected back on itself in the direction $BCB'$.

(3) The ray $OFD$ which passes through the principal focus $F$ and, like all rays passing through $F$, is reflected parallel to the principal axis in the direction $DD'$.

The intersection $I$ of any two of these reflected rays is the image of $O$. Thus $II'$ represents the position and size of the image of $OO'$. The image is real, inverted, magnified, and at a greater distance from the mirror than the object. (*Note*: If the object were at $II'$, the image would be at $OO'$ and would be real, inverted, and smaller.)

(*b*) Using the mirror equation in which $R = -4$ m,

$$\frac{1}{s_o}+\frac{1}{s_i}=-\frac{2}{R} \quad \text{or} \quad \frac{1}{3}+\frac{1}{s_i}=-\frac{2}{-4} \quad \text{or} \quad s_i = 6\text{ m}$$

The image is real (since $s_i$ is positive) and located 6 m from the mirror. Also, since the image is inverted, both the magnification and $y_i$ are negative:

$$M_T = -\frac{s_i}{s_o} = -\frac{6\text{ m}}{3\text{ m}} = -2 \quad \text{and so} \quad y_i = (-2)(5\text{ cm}) = -0.10\text{ m}$$

**36.5 [II]** An object $OO'$ is 25 cm from a concave spherical mirror of radius 80 cm (Fig. 36-9). Determine the position and relative size of its image $II'$ (*a*) by construction and (*b*) by use of the mirror equation.

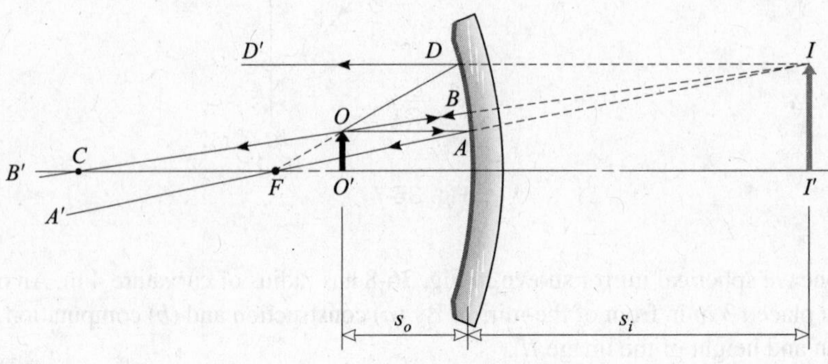


Fig. 36-9

(*a*) Two of the following three rays from $O$ locate the image.

(1) A ray $OA$, parallel to the principal axis, is reflected through the focus $F$, 40 cm from the mirror.

(2) A ray $OB$, in the line of the radius $COB$, is normal to the mirror and is reflected back on itself through the center of curvature $C$.

(3) A ray $OD$, which (extended) passes through $F$, is reflected parallel to the axis. Because of the large curvature of the mirror from $A$ to $D$, this ray is not as accurate as the other two.

The reflected rays ($AA'$, $BB'$, and $DD'$) do not meet, but appear to originate from a point $I$ behind the mirror. Thus, $II'$ represents the relative position and size of the image of $OO'$. The image is virtual (behind the mirror), erect, and magnified. Here the radius $R$ is negative and so

(*b*) $$\frac{1}{s_o} + \frac{1}{s_i} = -\frac{2}{R} \quad \text{or} \quad \frac{1}{25} + \frac{1}{s_i} = -\frac{2}{-80} \quad \text{or} \quad s_i = -67\text{ cm}$$

The image is virtual (since $s_i$ is negative) and 66.7 cm behind the mirror. Also,

$$M_T = -\frac{s_i}{s_o} = -\frac{-66.7\text{ cm}}{25\text{ cm}} = 2.7\text{ times}$$

Notice that $M_T$ is positive and so the image is right-side-up.

**36.6 [II]** As shown in Fig. 36-10, an object 6 cm high is located 30 cm in front of a convex spherical mirror of radius 40 cm. Determine the position and height of its image, (*a*) by construction and (*b*) by use of the mirror equation.

(*a*) Choose two convenient rays coming from $O$ at the top of the object:

(1) A ray $OA$, parallel to the principal axis, is reflected in the direction $AA'$ as if it passed through the principal focus $F$.

(2) A ray $OB$, directed toward the center of curvature $C$, is normal to the mirror and is reflected back on itself.

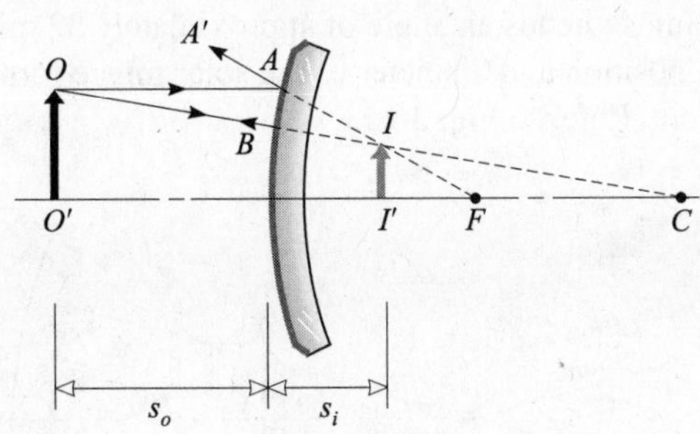


Fig. 36-10

The reflected rays, $AA'$ and $BO$, never meet but appear to originate from a point $I$ behind the mirror. Then $II'$ represents the size and position of the image of $OO'$.

All images formed by convex mirrors are virtual, erect, and reduced in size, provided the object is in front of the mirror (i.e., a real object). For a convex mirror the radius is positive; here $R = 40$ cm. And so

(b) $$\frac{1}{s_o}+\frac{1}{s_i}=-\frac{2}{R} \quad \text{or} \quad \frac{1}{30}+\frac{1}{s_i}=-\frac{2}{40} \quad \text{or} \quad s_i=-12\text{ cm}$$

The image is virtual ($s_i$ is negative) and 12 cm behind the mirror. Also,

$$M_T=-\frac{s_i}{s_o}=-\frac{-12\text{ cm}}{30\text{ cm}}=0.40$$

Moreover, $M_T = y_i/y_o$ and so $y_i = M_T y_o = (0.40)(6.0\text{ cm}) = 2.4$ cm

**36.7 [II]** Where should an object be placed, with reference to a concave spherical mirror of radius 180 cm, to form a real image that is half the size of the object?

All real images formed by the mirror are inverted and so the magnification is to be $-1/2$; hence, $s_i = s_o/2$. Then, since $R = -180$ cm,

$$\frac{1}{s_o}+\frac{1}{s_i}=-\frac{2}{R} \quad \text{or} \quad \frac{1}{s_o}+\frac{2}{s_o}=-\frac{2}{-180} \quad \text{or} \quad s_o=270\text{ cm from mirror}$$

**36.8 [II]** How far must a girl stand in front of a concave spherical mirror of radius 120 cm to see an erect image of her face four times its natural size?

The erect image must be virtual; hence, $s_i$ is negative. Since the magnification is $+4$ and $M_T = -s_i/s_o$, it follows that $s_i = -4s_o$. Then using $R = -120$ cm

$$\frac{1}{s_o}+\frac{1}{s_i}=-\frac{2}{R} \quad \text{or} \quad \frac{1}{s_o}-\frac{2}{4s_o}=\frac{2}{120} \quad \text{or} \quad s_o=45\text{ cm from mirror}$$

**36.9 [II]** What kind of spherical mirror must be used, and what must be its radius, in order to give an erect image one-fifth as large as an object placed 15 cm in front of it?

An erect image produced by a spherical mirror is virtual; hence, $s_i$ is negative. Moreover, since the magnification is $+1/5$, $s_i = -s_o/5 = -15/5 = -3$ cm. Because the virtual image is smaller than the object, a convex mirror is required. Its radius can be found using

$$\frac{1}{s_o}+\frac{1}{s_i}=-\frac{2}{R} \quad \text{or} \quad \frac{1}{15}-\frac{1}{3}=-\frac{2}{R} \quad \text{or} \quad R=+7.5\text{ cm (convex mirror)}$$

**36.10 [II]** The diameter of the Sun subtends an angle of approximately 32 minutes (32′) at any point on the Earth. Determine the position and diameter of the solar image formed by a concave spherical mirror of radius 400 cm. Refer to Fig. 36-11.

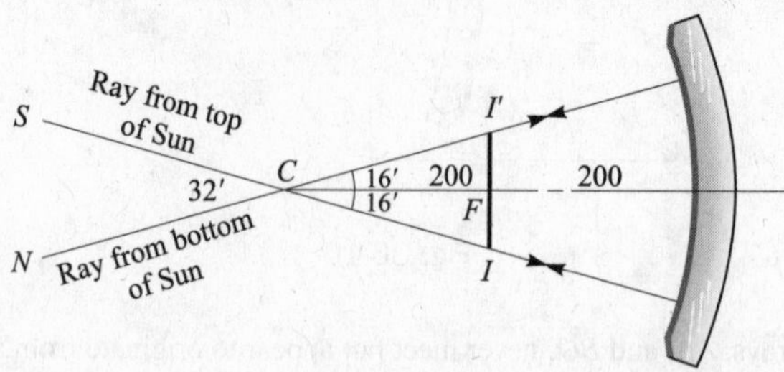


Fig. 36.11

Since the sun is very distant, $s_o$ is very large and $1/s_o$ is practically zero. So with $R = -400$ cm

$$\frac{1}{s_o} + \frac{1}{s_i} = -\frac{2}{R} \quad \text{or} \quad 0 + \frac{1}{s_i} = \frac{2}{400}$$

and $s_i = 200$ cm. The image is at the principal focus $F$, 200 cm from the mirror.

The diameter of the Sun and its image $II'$ subtend equal angles at the center of curvature $C$ of the mirror. From the figure,

$$\tan 16' = \frac{\overline{II'}/2}{\overline{CF}} \quad \text{or} \quad \overline{II'} = 2\overline{CF} \tan 16' = (2)\,(2.00 \text{ m})\,(0.004\,65) = 1.9 \text{ cm}$$

**36.11 [II]** A dental technician uses a small mirror that gives a magnification of 4.0 when it is held 0.60 cm from a tooth. What is the radius of curvature of the mirror?

In order for the mirror to produce a right-side-up magnified image it must be concave. Accordingly $R$ is negative.

Because the magnification is positive $-s_i/s_o = 4$ and with $s_o = 0.60$ cm, it follows that $s_i = -2.4$ cm. The mirror equation becomes (in cm)

$$\frac{1}{0.60} + \frac{1}{-2.4} = -\frac{2}{R} \quad \text{or} \quad 1.667 - 0.417 = -\frac{2}{R}$$

and $R = -1.6$ cm. (This agrees with the fact that the image formed by a convex mirror is diminished, not magnified.)

## SUPPLEMENTARY PROBLEMS

**36.12 [I]** If you wish to take a photo of yourself as you stand 3 m in front of a plane mirror, for what distance should you focus the camera you are holding?

**36.13 [I]** Two plane mirrors make an angle of 90° with each other. A point-like luminous object is placed between them. How many images are formed?

**36.14 [I]** Two plane mirrors are parallel to each other and spaced 20 cm apart. A luminous point is placed between them and 5.0 cm from one mirror. Determine the distance from each mirror of the three nearest images in each.

**36.15 [I]** Two plane mirrors make an angle of 90° with each other. A beam of light is directed at one of the mirrors, reflects off it and the second mirror, and leaves the mirrors. What is the angle between the incident beam and the reflected beam?

**36.16 [I]** A ray of light makes an angle of 25° with the normal to a plane mirror. If the mirror is turned through 6.0°, making the angle of incidence 31°, through what angle is the reflected ray rotated?

**36.17 [II]** Describe the image of a candle flame located 40 cm from a concave spherical mirror of radius 64 cm.

**36.18 [II]** Describe the image of an object positioned 20 cm from a concave spherical mirror of radius 60 cm.

**36.19 [II]** How far should an object be from a concave spherical mirror of radius 36 cm to form a real image one-ninth its size?

**36.20 [II]** An object 7.0 cm high is placed 15 cm from a convex spherical mirror of radius 45 cm. Describe its image.

**36.21 [II]** What is the focal length of a convex spherical mirror which produces an image one-sixth the size of an object located 12 cm from the mirror?

**36.22 [II]** It is desired to cast the image of a lamp, magnified 5 times, upon a wall 12 m distant from the lamp. What kind of spherical mirror is required, and what is its position?

**36.23 [II]** Compute the position and diameter of the image of the Moon in a polished sphere of diameter 20 cm. The diameter of the Moon is 3500 km, and its distance from the Earth is 384 000 km, approximately.

## ANSWERS TO SUPPLEMENTARY PROBLEMS

**36.12 [I]** 6 m

**36.13 [I]** 3

**36.14 [I]** 5.0, 35, 45 cm; 15, 25, 55 cm

**36.15 [I]** 180°

**36.16 [I]** 12°

**36.17 [II]** real, inverted, 0.16 m in front of mirror, magnified 4 times

**36.18 [II]** virtual, erect, 60 cm behind mirror, magnified 3 times

**36.19 [II]** 180 cm

**36.20 [II]** virtual, erect, 9.0 cm behind mirror, 4.2 cm high

**36.21 [II]** −2.4 cm

**36.22 [II]** concave, radius 5.0 m, 3.0 m from lamp

**36.23 [II]** 5.0 cm inside sphere, 0.46 mm

# Refraction of Light

**The Speed of Light** (c) as ordinarily measured varies from material to material. Light (treated macroscopically) travels fastest in vacuum, where its speed is $c = 2.998 \times 10^8$ m/s. Its speed in air is c/1.000 3. In water its speed is c/1.33, and in ordinary glass it is about c/1.5. Nonetheless, on a microscopic level light is composed of photons, and photons exist only at the speed c. The apparent slowing down in material media arises from the absorption and re-emission as the light passes from atom to atom.

**Index of Refraction** ($n$): The ***absolute index of refraction*** of a material is defined as

$$n = \frac{\text{Speed of light in vacuum}}{\text{Speed of light in the material}} = \frac{c}{v}$$

For any two materials, the *relative index of refraction* of material-1, with respect to material-2, is

$$\text{Relative index} = \frac{n_1}{n_2}$$

where $n_1$ and $n_2$ are the absolute refractive indices of the two materials.

**Refraction:** When a ray of light is transmitted obliquely through the boundary between two materials of unlike index of refraction, the ray bends. This phenomenon, called ***refraction***, is shown in Fig. 37-1. If $n_t > n_i$, the ray refracts as shown in the figure; it bends toward the normal as it enters the second material. If $n_t < n_i$, however, the ray refracts away from the normal. This would be the situation in Fig. 37-1 if the direction of the ray were

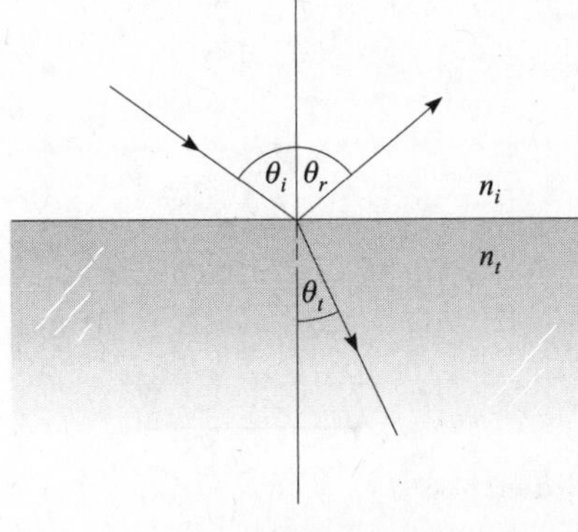


Fig. 37-1

reversed. In either case, the incident and refracted (or transmitted) rays and the normal all lie in the same plane. The angles $\theta_i$ and $\theta_t$ in Fig. 37-1 are called the ***angle of incidence*** and ***angle of transmission*** (or refraction), respectively.

**Snell's Law:** The way in which a ray refracts at an interface between materials with indices of refraction $n_i$ and $n_t$ is given by **Snell's Law:**

$$n_i \sin \theta_i = n_t \sin \theta_t$$

where $\theta_i$ and $\theta_t$ are as shown in Fig. 37-1. Because this equation applies to light moving in either direction along the ray, a ray of light follows the same path when its direction is reversed.

**Critical Angle for Total Internal Reflection:** When light reflects off an interface where $n_i < n_t$ the process is called ***external reflection***; when $n_t > n_t$ it's ***internal reflection***. Suppose that a ray of light passes from a material of higher index of refraction to one of lower index, as shown in Fig. 37-2. Part of the incident light is refracted and part is reflected at the interface. Because $\theta_t$ must be larger than $\theta_i$, it is possible to make $\theta_i$ large enough so that $\theta_t = 90°$. This value for $\theta_i$ is called the ***critical angle*** $\theta_c$. *For* $\theta_i$ larger than this, no refracted ray can exist; all the light is reflected.

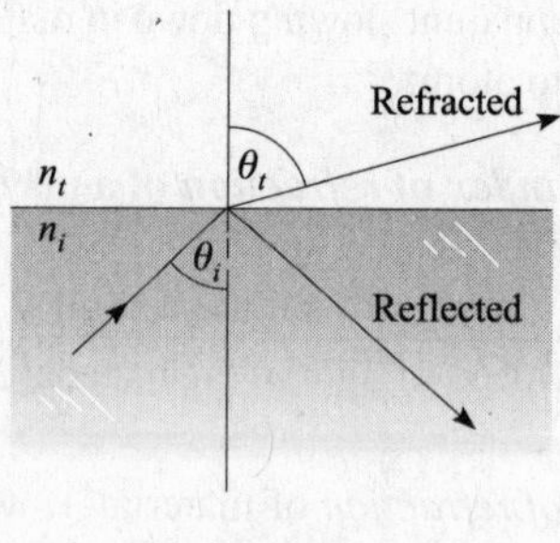


Fig. 37-2

The condition for ***total internal reflection*** is that $\theta_i$ equal or exceed the critical angle $\theta_c$ where

$$n_i \sin \theta_c = n_t \sin 90° \qquad \text{or} \qquad \sin \theta_c = \frac{n_t}{n_i}$$

Because the sine of an angle can never be larger than unity, this relation confirms that total internal reflection can occur only if $n_i > n_t$.

**A Prism** can be used to disperse light into its various colors, as shown in Fig. 37-3. Because the index of refraction of a material varies with wavelength, different colors of light refract differently. In nearly all materials, red is refracted least and blue is refracted most.

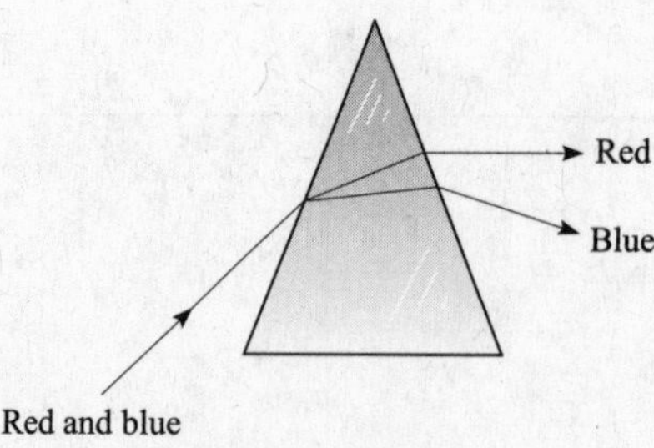


Fig. 37-3

## SOLVED PROBLEMS

**37.1 [I]** The speed of light in water is (3/4)c. What is the effect, on the frequency and wavelength of light, of passing from vacuum (or air, to good approximation) into water? Compute the refractive index of water.

The same number of wave peaks leave the air each second as enter into the water. Hence, **the frequency is the same in the two materials**. But because Wavelength = (Speed)/(Frequency), the wavelength in water is three-fourths that in air.

The (absolute) refractive index of water is

$$n = \frac{\text{Speed in vacuum}}{\text{Speed in water}} = \frac{c}{(3/4)c} = \frac{4}{3} = 1.33$$

**37.2 [I]** A glass plate is 0.60 cm thick and has a refractive index of 1.55. How long does it take for a pulse of light incident normally to pass through the plate?

$$t = \frac{x}{v} = \frac{0.006\,0\text{ m}}{(2.998 \times 10^8/1.55)\text{ m/s}} = 3.1 \times 10^{-11}\text{ s}$$

**37.3 [I]** As is drawn in Fig. 37-4, a ray of light in air strikes a glass plate ($n$ = 1.50) at an incidence angle of 50°. Determine the angles of the reflected and transmitted rays.

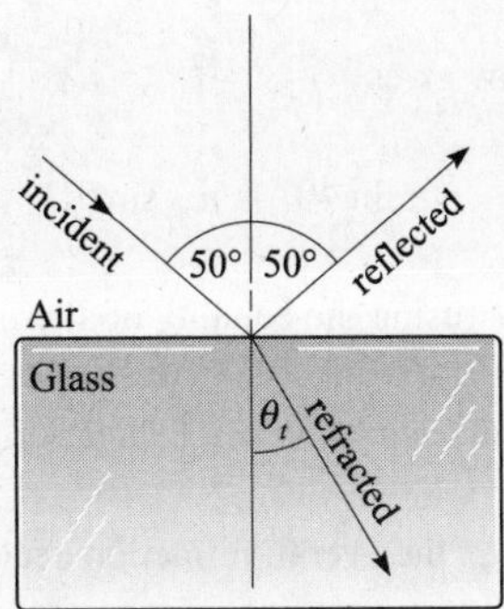


Fig. 37-4

The law of reflection applies to the reflected ray. Therefore, the angle of reflection is 50°, as shown.

For the refracted ray, $n_i \sin\theta_i = n_t \sin\theta_t$ becomes

$$\sin\theta_t = \frac{n_i}{n_t}\sin\theta_i = \frac{1.0}{1.5}\sin 50° = 0.51$$

from which it follows that $\theta_t = 31°$.

**37.4 [I]** The refractive index of diamond is 2.42. What is the critical angle for light passing from diamond to air?

We use $n_i \sin\theta_i = n_t \sin\theta_t$ to obtain

$$(2.42)\sin\theta_c = (1)\sin 90.0°$$

from which it follows that $\sin\theta_c = 0.413$ and $\theta_c = 24.4°$.

**37.5 [I]** What is the critical angle for light passing from glass ($n$ = 1.54) to water ($n$ = 1.33)?

$$n_i \sin\theta_i = n_t \sin\theta_t \quad \text{becomes} \quad n_i \sin\theta_c = n_t \sin 90°$$

from which we get

$$\sin\theta_c = \frac{n_t}{n_i} = \frac{1.33}{1.54} = 0.864 \quad \text{or} \quad \theta_c = 59.7°$$

**37.6 [II]** A layer of oil ($n$ = 1.45) floats on water ($n$ = 1.33). A ray of light shines onto the oil with an incidence angle of 40.0°. Find the angle the ray makes in the water. (See Fig. 37-5.)

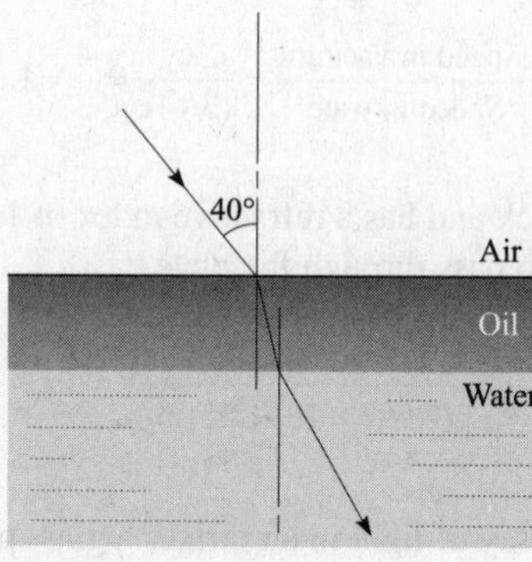


Fig. 37-5

At the air–oil interface, Snell's Law gives

$$n_{\text{air}} \sin 40° = n_{\text{oil}} \sin\theta_{\text{oil}}$$

At the oil-water interface, we have (using the equality of alternate angles)

$$n_{\text{oil}} \sin\theta_{\text{oil}} = n_{\text{water}} \sin\theta_{\text{water}}$$

Thus, $n_{\text{air}} \sin 40.0° = n_{\text{water}} \sin\theta_{\text{water}}$; the overall refraction occurs just as though the oil layer were absent. Solving gives

$$\sin\theta_{\text{water}} = \frac{n_{\text{air}} \sin 40.0°}{n_{\text{water}}} = \frac{(1)(0.643)}{1.33} \quad \text{or} \quad \theta_{\text{water}} = 28.9°$$

**37.7 [II]** As shown in Fig. 37-6, a small luminous body, at the bottom of a pool of water ($n = 4/3$) 2.00 m deep, emits rays upward in all directions. A circular area of light is formed at the surface of the water. Determine the radius $R$ of the circle of light.

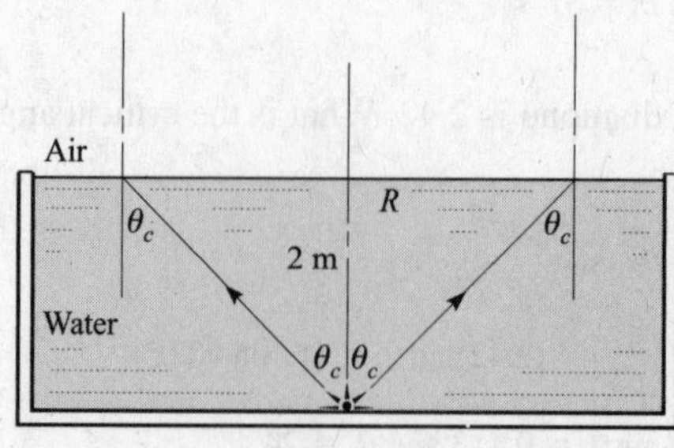


Fig. 37-6

The circular area is formed by rays refracted into the air. The angle $\theta_c$ must be the critical angle, because total internal reflection, and hence no refraction, occurs when the angle of incidence in the water is greater than the critical angle. We have, then,

$$\sin\theta_c = \frac{n_a}{n_w} = \frac{1}{4/3} \qquad \text{or} \qquad \theta_c = 48.6°$$

From the figure,

$$R = (2.00 \text{ m}) \tan\theta_c = (2.00 \text{ m})\,(1.13) = 2.26 \text{ m}$$

**37.8 [I]** What is the minimum value of the refractive index for a 45.0° prism which is used to turn a beam of light by total internal reflection through a right angle? (See Fig. 37-7.)

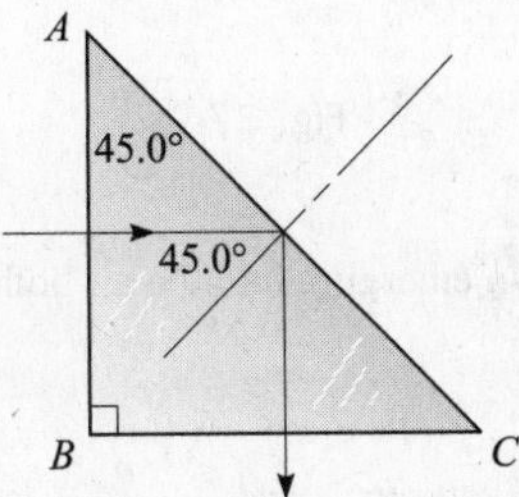


Fig. 37-7

The ray enters the prism without deviation, since it strikes side *AB* normally. It then makes an incidence angle of 45.0° with normal to side *AC*. The critical angle of the prism must be smaller than 45.0° if the ray is to be totally reflected at side *AC* and thus turned through 90°. From $n_i \sin\theta_c = n_t \sin 90°$ with $n_t = 1.00$,

$$\text{Minimum } n_i = \frac{1}{\sin 45.0°} = 1.41$$

**37.9 [II]** The glass prism shown in Fig. 37-8 has an index of refraction of 1.55. Find the angle of deviation *D* for the case shown.

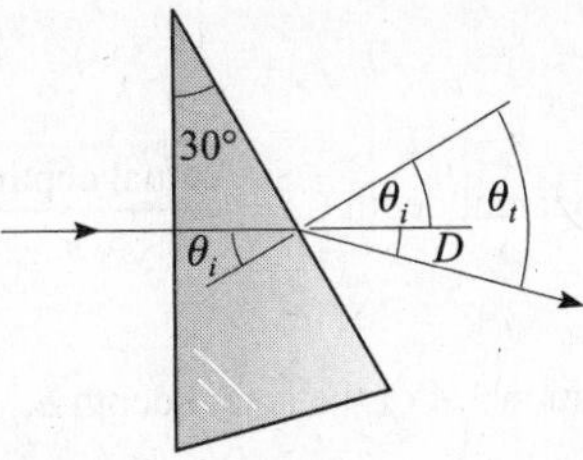


Fig. 37-8

No deflection occurs at the entering surface, because the incidence angle is zero. At the second surface, $\theta_i = 30°$ (because its sides are mutually perpendicular to the sides of the apex angle). Then, Snell's Law becomes

$$n_i \sin\theta_i = n_t \sin\theta_t \qquad \text{or} \qquad \sin\theta_t = \frac{1.55}{1} \sin 30°$$

from which $\theta_t = 50.8°$. But $D = \theta_t - \theta_i$ and so $D = 21°$.

**37.10 [III]** As shown in Fig. 37-9, an object is at a depth $d$ beneath the surface of a transparent material of refractive index $n$. As viewed from a point almost directly above, how deep does the object appear to be?

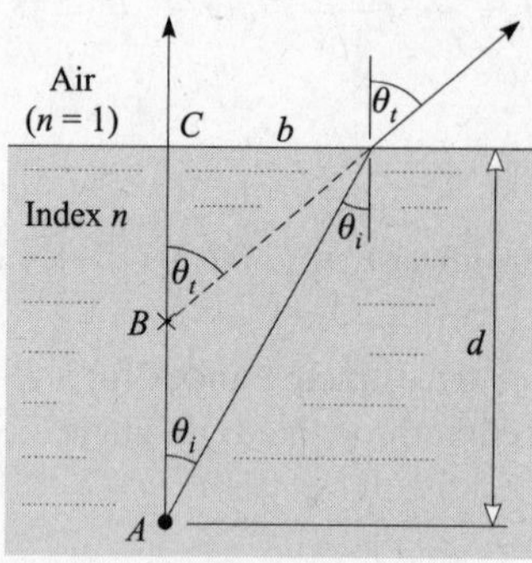


Fig. 37-9

The two rays from $A$ that are shown emerging into the air both appear to come from point-$B$. Therefore, the apparent depth is $CB$. We have

$$\frac{b}{\overline{CB}} = \tan\theta_t \quad \text{and} \quad \frac{b}{\overline{CA}} = \tan\theta_i$$

If the object is viewed from nearly straight above, then angles $\theta_t$ and $\theta_i$ will be very small. For small angles, the sine and tangent are nearly equal. Therefore,

$$\frac{\overline{CB}}{\overline{CA}} = \frac{\tan\theta_i}{\tan\theta_t} \approx \frac{\sin\theta_i}{\sin\theta_t}$$

But $n\sin\theta_i = (1)\sin\theta_t$ from which

$$\frac{\sin\theta_i}{\sin\theta_t} = \frac{1}{n}$$

Hence,

$$\text{Apparent depth } \overline{CB} = \frac{\text{actual depth } \overline{CA}}{n}$$

The apparent depth is only a fraction $1/n$ of the actual depth $d$.

**37.11 [I]** A glass plate 4.00 mm thick is viewed from above through a microscope. The microscope must be lowered 2.58 mm as the operator shifts from viewing the top surface to viewing the bottom surface through the glass. What is the index of refraction of the glass? Use the results of Problem 37.10.

We found in Problem 37.10 that the apparent depth of the plate will be $1/n$ as large as its actual depth. Hence,

$$(\text{Actual thickness})(1/n) = \text{Apparent thickness}$$

or

$$(4.00\text{ mm})\,(1/n) = 2.58\text{ mm}$$

This yields $n = 1.55$ for the glass.

**37.12 [III]** As shown in Fig. 37-10, a ray enters the flat end of a long rectangular block of glass that has a refractive index of $n_2$. Show that all entering rays can be totally internally reflected only if $n_2 > 1.414$.

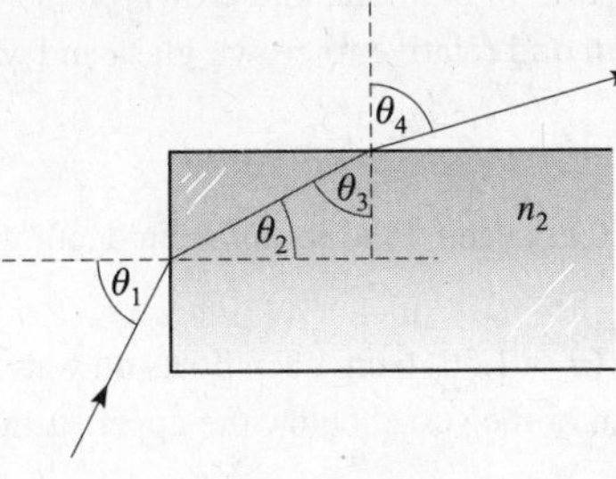


Fig. 37-10

The larger $\theta_1$ is, the larger $\theta_2$ will be, and the smaller $\theta_3$ will be. Therefore, the ray is most likely to leak out through the side of the block if $\theta_1 = 90°$. In that case,

$$n_1 \sin\theta_1 = n_2 \sin\theta_2 \quad \text{becomes} \quad (1)(1) = n_2 \sin\theta_2$$

For the ray to just escape, $\theta_4 = 90°$. Then

$$n_2 \sin\theta_3 = n_1 \sin\theta_4 \quad \text{becomes} \quad n_2 \sin\theta_3 = (1)(1)$$

We thus have two conditions to satisfy: $n_2 \sin\theta_2 = 1$ and $n_2 \sin\theta_3 = 1$. Their ratio gives

$$\frac{\sin\theta_2}{\sin\theta_3} = 1$$

But we see from the figure that $\sin\theta_3 = \cos\theta_2$, and so this becomes

$$\tan\theta_2 = 1 \quad \text{or} \quad \theta_2 = 45.00°$$

Then, because $n_2 \sin\theta_2 = 1$, we have

$$n_2 = \frac{1}{\sin 45.00°} = 1.414$$

This is the smallest possible value the index can have for total internal reflection of all rays that enter the end of the block. It is possible to obtain this answer by inspection. How?

## SUPPLEMENTARY PROBLEMS

**37.13 [I]** The speed of light in a certain glass is $1.91 \times 10^8$ m/s. What is the refractive index of the glass?

**37.14 [I]** What is the frequency of light which has a wavelength in air of 546 nm? What is its frequency in water ($n = 1.33$)? What is its speed in water? What is its wavelength in water?

**37.15 [I]** A beam of light strikes the surface of water at an incidence angle of 60°. Determine the directions of the reflected and refracted rays. For water, $n = 1.33$.

**37.16 [I]** The critical angle for light passing from rock salt into air is 40.5°. Calculate the index of refraction of rock salt.

**37.17 [I]** What is the critical angle when light passes from glass ($n = 1.50$) into air?

**37.18 [II]** The absolute indices of refraction of diamond and crown glass are 5/2 and 3/2, respectively. Compute (*a*) the refractive index of diamond relative to crown glass and (*b*) the critical angle between diamond and crown glass.

**37.19 [II]** A pool of water ($n = 4/3$) is 60 cm deep. Find its apparent depth when viewed vertically through air.

**37.20 [III]** In a vessel, a layer of benzene ($n = 1.50$) 6 cm deep floats on water ($n = 1.33$) 4 cm deep. Determine the apparent distance of the bottom of the vessel below the upper surface of the benzene when viewed vertically through air.

**37.21 [II]** A mirror is made of plate glass ($n = 3/2$) 1.0 cm thick and silvered on the back. A man is 50.0 cm from the front face of the mirror. If he looks perpendicularly into it, at what distance behind the front face of the mirror will his image appear to be?

**37.22 [II]** A straight rod is partially immersed in water ($n = 1.33$). Its submerged portion appears to be inclined 45° with the surface when viewed vertically through air. What is the actual inclination of the rod?

**37.23 [II]** The index of refraction for a certain type of glass is 1.640 for blue light and 1.605 for red light. When a beam of white light (one that contains all colors) enters a plate of this glass at an incidence angle of 40°, what is the angle in the glass between the blue and red parts of the refracted beam?

## ANSWERS OF SUPPLEMENTARY PROBLEMS

**37.13 [I]** 1.57

**37.14 [I]** 549 THz, 549 THz, $2.25 \times 10^8$ m/s, 411 nm

**37.15 [I]** 60° reflected into air, 41° refracted into water

**37.16 [I]** 1.54

**37.17 [I]** 41.8°

**37.18 [II]** (*a*) 5/3; (*b*) 37°

**37.19 [II]** 45 cm

**37.20 [III]** 7 cm

**37.21 [II]** 51.3 cm

**37.22 [II]** arctan 1.33 = 53°

**37.23 [II]** 0.53°

# Thin Lenses

**Types of Lenses:** As indicated in Fig. 38-1, **converging**, or **positive**, lenses are thicker at the center than at the rim and will converge a beam of parallel light to a real focus. **Diverging**, or **negative**, lenses are thinner at the center than at the rim and will diverge a beam of parallel light from a virtual focus. This of course assumes the lens is made of a material whose index of refraction is greater than that of the surrounding medium.

The *principal focus* (or **focal point**) of a thin lens with spherical surfaces is the point $F$ where rays parallel to and near the central or optical axis are brought to a focus; this focus is real for a converging lens and virtual for a diverging lens. The **focal length** $f$ is the axial distance of the principal focus from the lens. Because each lens in Fig. 38-1 can be reversed without altering the rays, two symmetric focal points exist for each lens.

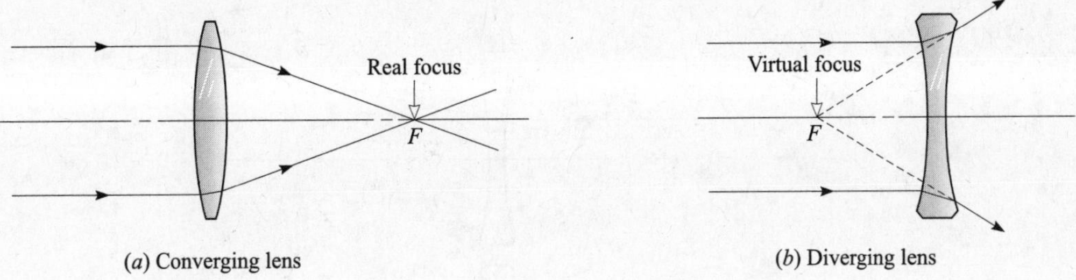


Fig. 38-1

**Ray Tracing:** When a ray passes through a lens it refracts or "bends" at each interface, as drawn in Fig. 38-1. When dealing with thin lenses all of the bending can, for simplicity, be assumed to occur along a vertical plane running down the middle of the lens (see Fig. 38-2).

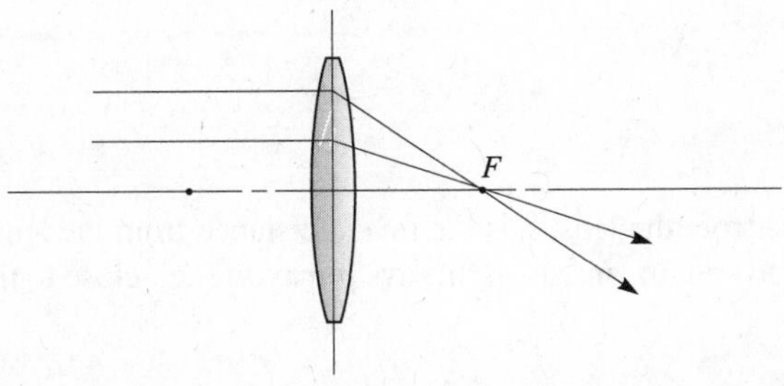


Fig. 38-2

As in our previous treatment of mirrors (Chapter 36), any two rays originating from a point on the object, drawn through the system, will locate the image of that point. There are three especially convenient rays to use because we know, without making any calculations, exactly how they will pass through a lens. These rays are shown in Fig. 38-3 propagating through both a convex and a concave lens. Notice that a ray heading for the center ($C$) of a thin lens passes straight through it unbent.

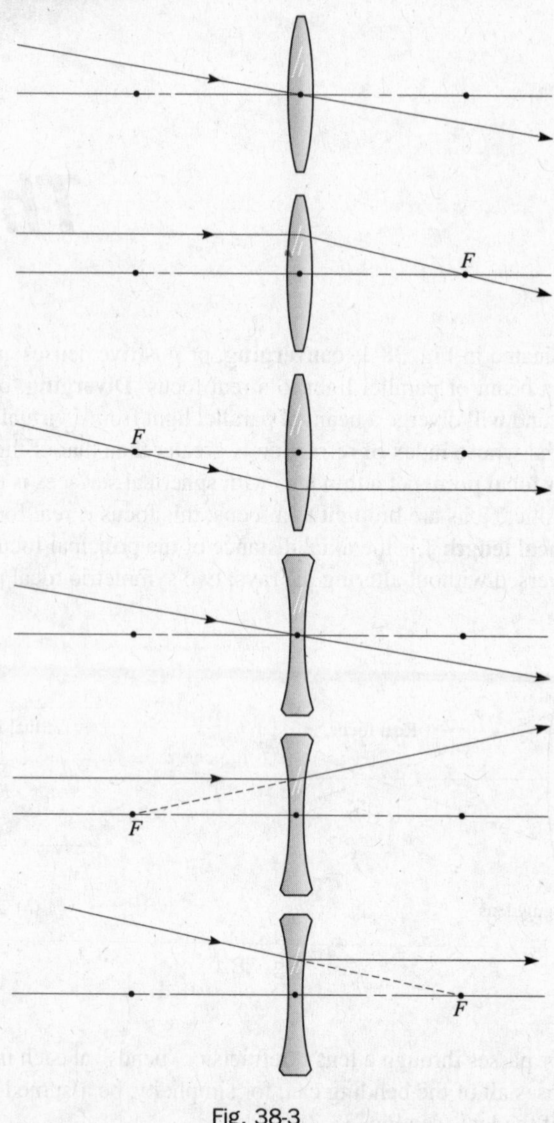


Fig. 38-3

**Object and Image Relation** for converging and diverging thin lenses:

$$\frac{1}{s_o} + \frac{1}{s_i} = \frac{1}{f}$$

where $s_o$ is the object distance from the lens, $s_i$ is the image distance from the lens, and $f$ is the focal length of the lens. The lens is assumed to be thin, and the light rays **paraxial** (i.e., close to the principal axis). Then, with light entering from the left,

- $s_o$ is positive when the object is to the left of the lens.
- $s_o$ is positive for a real object, and negative for a virtual object (see Chapter 39).

- $s_i$ is positive when the image is to the right of the lens.
- $s_i$ is positive for a real image, and negative for a virtual image.
- $f$ is positive for a converging lens, and negative for a diverging lens.
- $y_i$ is positive for a right-side-up image (i.e., one above the axis).
- $y_o$ is positive for a right-side-up object (i.e., one above the axis).

Also,
$$M_T = \frac{y_i}{y_o} = -\frac{s_i}{s_o}$$

- $M_T$ is negative when the image is inverted.

Converging lenses form inverted real images of real objects when those objects are located to the left of the focal point, in front of the lens (see Fig. 38-4). When the object is between the focal point and the lens, the resulting image is virtual (on the same side of the lens as the object), erect, and enlarged.

Diverging lenses produce only virtual, erect, and minified images of real objects.

**Lensmaker's Equation:**

$$\frac{1}{f} = (n-1)\left(\frac{1}{R_1} - \frac{1}{R_2}\right)$$

where $n$ is the refractive index of the lens material, and $R_1$ and $R_2$ are the radii of curvature of the two lens surfaces. This equation holds for all types of thin lenses. A radius of curvature, $R$, is positive when its center of curvature lies to the right of the surface, and negative when its center of curvature lies to the left of the surface.

If a lens with refractive index $n_1$ is immersed in a material with index $n_2$, then $n$ in the lensmaker's equation is to be replaced by $n_1/n_2$.

**Lens Power** in **diopters** ($m^{-1}$) is equal to $1/f$, where $f$ is the focal length expressed in meters.

**Lenses in Contact:** When two thin lenses having focal lengths $f_1$ and $f_2$ are in close contact, the focal length $f$ of the combination is given by

$$\frac{1}{f} = \frac{1}{f_1} + \frac{1}{f_2}$$

Quite generally, for lenses in close contact, the power of the combination is equal to the sum of their individual powers.

## SOLVED PROBLEMS

**38.1 [II]** An object $OO'$, 4.0 cm high, is 20 cm in front of a thin convex lens of focal length +12 cm. Determine the position and height of its image $II'$ (*a*) by construction and (*b*) by computation.

(*a*) The following two convenient rays from $O$ will locate the images (see Fig. 38-4).

(1) A ray $OP$, parallel to the optical axis, must after refraction pass through the focus $F$.

(2) A ray passing through the optical center $C$ of a thin lens is not appreciably deviated. Hence, ray $OCI$ may be drawn as a straight line.

The intersection $I$ of these two rays is the image of $O$. Thus, $II'$ represents the position and size of the image of $OO'$. The image is real, inverted, enlarged, and at a greater distance from the lens than the object. (If the object were at $II'$, the image at $OO'$, would be real, inverted, and smaller.)

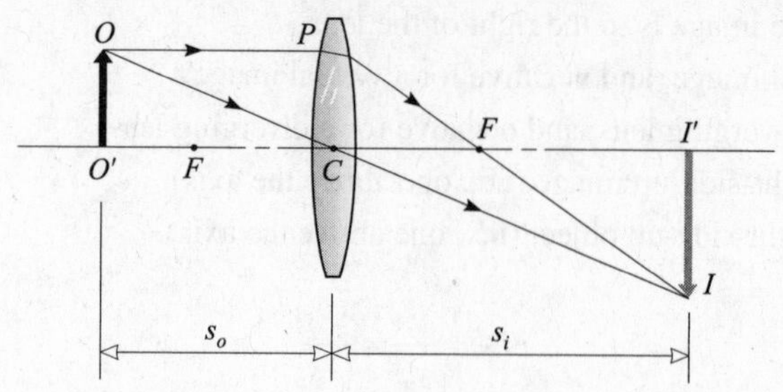


Fig. 38-4

(b) $\frac{1}{s_o}+\frac{1}{s_i}=\frac{1}{f}$ or $\frac{1}{20\text{ cm}}+\frac{1}{s_i}=\frac{1}{12\text{ cm}}$ or $s_i = 30\text{ cm}$

The image is real (since $s_i$ is positive) and 30 cm behind the lens.

$$M_T = \frac{y_i}{y_o} = -\frac{s_i}{s_o} = -\frac{30\text{ cm}}{20\text{ cm}} = -1.5 \quad \text{or} \quad y_i = M_T y_o = (-1.5)(4.0\text{ cm}) = -6.0\text{ cm}$$

The negative magnification and image height both indicate an inverted image.

**38.2 [II]** An object $OO'$ is 5.0 cm in front of a thin convex lens of focal length +7.5 cm. Determine the position and magnification of its image $II'$ (*a*) by construction and (*b*) by computation.

(*a*) Choose two convenient rays from $O$, as in Fig. 38-5.

(1) A ray $OP$, parallel to the optical axis, is refracted so as to pass through the focus $F$.

(2) A ray $OCN$, through the optical center of the lens, is drawn as a straight line.

These two rays do not meet, but appear to originate from a point $I$. Thus, $II'$ represents the position and size of the image of $OO'$.

When the object is between $F$ and $C$, the image is virtual, erect, and enlarged, as shown.

(b) $\frac{1}{s_o}+\frac{1}{s_i}=\frac{1}{f}$ or $\frac{1}{5.0\text{ cm}}+\frac{1}{s_i}=\frac{1}{7.5\text{ cm}}$ or $s_i = -15\text{ cm}$

Since $s_i$ is negative, the image is virtual (on the same side of the lens as the object), and it is 15 cm in front of the lens. Also,

$$M_T = \frac{y_i}{y_o} = -\frac{s_i}{s_o} = -\frac{-15\text{ cm}}{5.0\text{ cm}} = 3.0$$

Because the magnification is positive the image is right-side-up.

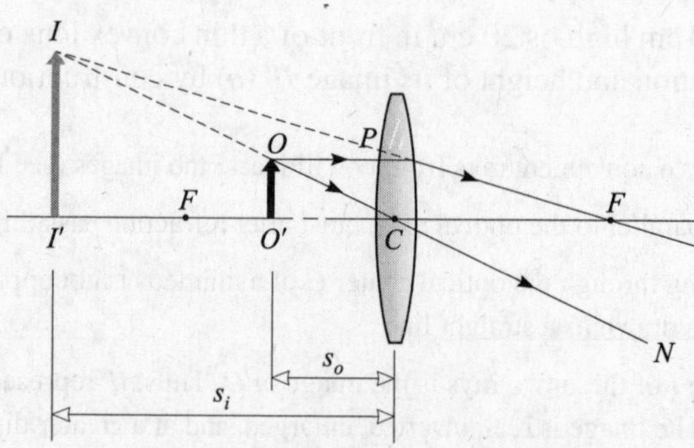


Fig. 38-5

**38.3 [II]** An object $OO'$, 9.0 cm high, is 27 cm in front of a thin concave lens of focal length −18 cm. Determine the position and height of its image $II'$ (*a*) by construction and (*b*) by computation.

(*a*) Choose the two convenient rays from $O$ shown in Fig. 38-6.

(1) A ray $OP$, parallel to the optical axis, is refracted outward in the direction $D$ as if it came from the principal focus $F$.

(2) A ray through the optical center of the lens is drawn as a straight line $OC$.

Then $II'$ is the image of $OO'$. Images formed by concave or divergent lenses are virtual, erect, and smaller.

(*b*) $\dfrac{1}{s_o}+\dfrac{1}{s_i}=\dfrac{1}{f}$ or $\dfrac{1}{27\text{ cm}}+\dfrac{1}{s_i}=-\dfrac{1}{18\text{ cm}}$ or $s_i=-10.8\text{ cm}=-11\text{ cm}$

Since $s_i$ is negative, the image is virtual, and it is 11 cm in front of the lens.

$$M_T=\frac{y_i}{y_o}=-\frac{s_i}{s_o}=-\frac{-10.8\text{ cm}}{27\text{ cm}}=0.40 \quad \text{and so} \quad y_i=y_oM_T=(0.40)\,(9.0\text{ cm})=3.6\text{ cm}$$

When $M_T>0$, the image is upright, and the same conclusion follows from the fact that $y_i>0$.

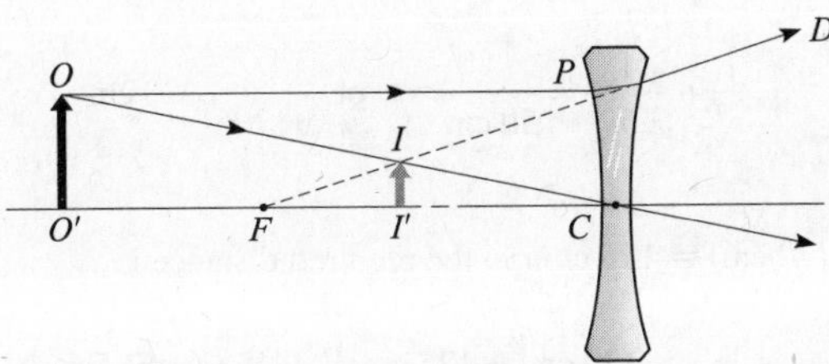


Fig. 38-6

**38.4 [I]** A converging thin lens ($f = 20$ cm) is placed 37 cm in front of a screen. Where should the object be placed if its image is to appear on the screen?

We know that $s_i = +37$ cm and $f = +20$ cm. The lens equation gives

$$\frac{1}{s_o}+\frac{1}{37\text{ cm}}=\frac{1}{20\text{ cm}} \quad \text{and} \quad \frac{1}{s_o}=0.050\text{ cm}^{-1}-0.027\text{ cm}^{-1}=0.023\text{ cm}^{-1}$$

from which $s_o = 43.5$ cm. The object should be placed 44 cm from the lens.

**38.5 [II]** Compute the position and focal length of the converging thin lens which will project the image of a lamp, magnified 4 times, upon a screen 10.0 m from the lamp.

Here $s_o + s_i = 10.0$. Moreover, $M_T = -s_i/s_o$, but all such real images are inverted, hence $M_T = -4$. And so $s_i = 4s_o$, consequently $s_o = 2.0$ m and $s_i = 8.0$ m. Then

$$\frac{1}{f}=\frac{1}{s_o}+\frac{1}{s_i}=\frac{1}{2.0\text{ m}}+\frac{1}{8.0\text{ cm}}=\frac{5}{8.0\text{ m}} \quad \text{or} \quad f=\frac{8.0\text{ m}}{5}=+1.6\text{ m}$$

**38.6 [II]** In what two positions will a converging thin lens of focal length +9.00 cm form images of a luminous object on a screen located 40.0 cm from the object?

Given $s_o + s_i = 40.0$ cm and $f = +9.00$ cm, we have

$$\frac{1}{s_o} + \frac{1}{40.0\text{ cm} - s_o} = \frac{1}{9.0\text{ cm}} \qquad \text{or} \qquad s_o^2 - 40.0s_o + 360 = 0$$

The use of the quadratic formula gives

$$s_o = \frac{40.0 \pm \sqrt{1600 - 1440}}{2}$$

from which $s_o = 13.7$ cm and $s_o = 26.3$ cm. The two lens positions are 13.7 cm and 26.3 cm from the object.

**38.7 [II]** A converging thin lens with 50-cm focal length forms a real image that is 2.5 times larger than the object. How far is the object from the image?

Real images formed by single converging lenses are all inverted. Accordingly, $M_T = -s_i/s_o = -2.5$ and so $s_i = 2.5s_o$. Therefore,

$$\frac{1}{s_o} + \frac{1}{2.5s_o} = \frac{1}{50\text{ cm}} \qquad \text{or} \qquad s_o = 70\text{ cm}$$

This gives $S_i = (2.5)\ (70\text{ cm}) = 175$ cm. So the required distance is

$$s_i + s_o = 70\text{ cm} + 175\text{ cm} = 245\text{ cm} = 2.5\text{m}$$

**38.8 [II]** A thin lens of focal length $f$ projects upon a screen the image of a luminous object magnified $N$ times. Show that the lens distance from the screen is $(N + 1)f$.

The image is real, since it can be shown on a screen, and so $s_i > 0$. We then have

$$N = \left|-\frac{s_i}{s_o}\right| = s_i\left(\frac{1}{s_o}\right) = s_i\left(\frac{1}{f} - \frac{1}{s_i}\right) = \frac{s_i}{f} - 1 \qquad \text{or} \qquad s_i = (N+1)f$$

**38.9 [II]** A thin lens has a convex surface of radius 20 cm and a concave surface of radius 40 cm and is made of glass of refractive index 1.54. Compute the focal length of the lens, and state whether it is a converging or a diverging lens.

First, notice that $R_1 > 0$ and $R_2 > 0$ because both surfaces have their centers of curvature to the right. Consequently,

$$\frac{1}{f} = (n-1)\left(\frac{1}{R_1} - \frac{1}{R_2}\right) = (1.54 - 1)\left(\frac{1}{20\text{ cm}} - \frac{1}{40\text{ cm}}\right) = \frac{0.54}{40\text{ cm}} \qquad \text{or} \qquad f = +74\text{ cm}$$

Since $f$ turns out to be positive, the lens is converging.

**38.10 [II]** A thin double convex lens has faces of radii 18 and 20 cm. When an object is 24 cm from the lens, a real image is formed 32 cm from the lens. Determine (*a*) the focal length of the lens and (*b*) the refractive index of the lens material.

Remember that a convex lens has a positive focal length.

(*a*) $\frac{1}{f}=\frac{1}{s_o}+\frac{1}{s_i}=\frac{1}{24\text{ cm}}+\frac{1}{32\text{ cm}}=\frac{7}{96\text{ cm}}$ or $f=\frac{96\text{ cm}}{7}=+13.7\text{ cm}=14\text{ cm}$

Here $R_1>0$ and $R_2<0$.

(*b*) $\frac{1}{f}=(n-1)\left(\frac{1}{R_1}-\frac{1}{R_2}\right)$ or $\frac{1}{13.7}=(n-1)\left(\frac{1}{18\text{ cm}}-\frac{1}{-20\text{ cm}}\right)$ or $n=1.7$

**38.11 [II]** A thin glass lens ($n$ = 1.50) has a focal length of +10 cm in air. Compute its focal length in water ($n$ = 1.33).

Using

$$\frac{1}{f}=\left(\frac{n_1}{n_2}-1\right)\left(\frac{1}{R_1}-\frac{1}{R_2}\right)$$

we get *For air*: $\frac{1}{10}=(1.50-1)\left(\frac{1}{R_1}-\frac{1}{R_2}\right)$

*For water*: $\frac{1}{f}=\left(\frac{1.50}{1.33}-1\right)\left(\frac{1}{R_1}-\frac{1}{R_2}\right)$

Divide one equation by the other to obtain $f$ = 5.0/0.128 = 39 cm.

**38.12 [III]** A double convex thin lens has radii of 20.0 cm. The index of refraction of the glass is 1.50. Compute the focal length of this lens (*a*) in air and (*b*) when it is immersed in carbon disulfide ($n$ = 1.63).

For a thin lens with an index of $n_1$, immersed in a surrounding medium of index $n_2$,

$$\frac{1}{f}=\left(\frac{n_1}{n_2}-1\right)\left(\frac{1}{R_1}-\frac{1}{R_2}\right)$$

Here $R_1$ = +20.0 cm and $R_2$ = −20.0 cm and so

(*a*) $\frac{1}{f}=(1.50-1)\left(\frac{1}{20\text{ cm}}-\frac{1}{-20\text{ cm}}\right)$ or $f=+20.0\text{ cm}$

(*b*) $\frac{1}{f}=\left(\frac{1.50}{1.63}-1\right)\left(\frac{1}{20\text{ cm}}-\frac{1}{-20\text{ cm}}\right)$ or $f=-125\text{ cm}$

When $n_2>n_1$ the focal length is negative and the lens is a diverging lens.

**38.13 [I]** Two thin lenses, of focal lengths +9.0 and −6.0 cm, are placed in contact. Calculate the focal length of the combination.

$$\frac{1}{f}=\frac{1}{f_1}+\frac{1}{f_2}=\frac{1}{9.0\text{ cm}}-\frac{1}{6.0\text{ cm}}=-\frac{1}{18\text{ cm}}\quad\text{or}\quad f=-18\text{ cm}$$

The combination lens is diverging.

**38.14** An achromatic lens is formed from two thin lenses in contact, having powers of +10.0 diopters and −6.0 diopters. Determine the power and focal length of the combination.

Since reciprocal focal lengths add,

$$\text{Power} = +10.0 - 6.0 = +4.0 \text{ diopters} \qquad \text{and} \qquad \text{Focal length} = \frac{1}{\text{Power}} = \frac{1}{+4.0\ \text{m}^{-1}} = +25\ \text{cm}$$

## SUPPLEMENTARY PROBLEMS

**38.15 [I]** Draw diagrams to indicate qualitatively the position, nature, and size of the image formed by a converging lens of focal length $f$ for the following object distances: (*a*) infinity, (*b*) greater than $2f$, (*c*) equal to $2f$, (*d*) between $2f$ and $f$, (*e*) equal to $f$, (*f*) less than $f$.

**38.16 [I]** Determine the nature, position, and transverse magnification of the image formed by a thin converging lens of focal length +100 cm when the object distance from the lens is (*a*) 150 cm, (*b*) 75.0 cm.

**38.17 [II]** Determine the two locations of an object such that its image will be enlarged 8.0 times by a thin lens of focal length +4.0 cm.

**38.18 [II]** What are the nature and focal length of the thin lens that will form a real image having one-third the dimensions of an object located 9.0 cm from the lens?

**38.19 [II]** Describe fully the image of an object which is 10 cm high and 28 cm from a diverging lens of focal length −7.0 cm.

**38.20 [II]** Compute the focal length of a lens which will give an erect image 10 cm from the lens when the object distance from the lens is (*a*) 200 cm, (*b*) very great.

**38.21 [II]** A luminous object and a screen are 12.5 m apart. What are the position and focal length of the lens which will throw upon the screen an image of the object magnified 24 times?

**38.22 [II]** A plano-concave lens has a spherical surface of radius 12 cm, and its focal length is −22.2 cm. Compute the refractive index of the lens material.

**38.23 [II]** A convex-concave lens has faces of radii 3.0 and 4.0 cm, respectively, and is made of glass of refractive index 1.6. Determine (*a*) its focal length and (*b*) the linear magnification of the image when the object is 28 cm from the lens.

**38.24 [II]** A double convex glass lens ($n$ = 1.50) has faces of radius 8 cm each. Compute its focal length in air and when immersed in water ($n$ = 1.33).

**38.25 [II]** Two thin lenses, of focal lengths +12 and −30 cm, are in contact. Compute the focal length and power of the combination.

**38.26 [II]** What must be the focal length of a third thin lens, placed in close contact with two thin lenses of 16 cm and −23 cm focal length, to produce a lens with −12 cm focal length?

## ANSWERS OF SUPPLEMENTARY PROBLEMS

**38.16 [I]** (*a*) real, inverted, 300 cm beyond lens, 2:1; (*b*) virtual, erect, 300 cm in front of lens, 4:1

**38.17 [II]** 4.5 cm from lens (image is real and inverted), 3.5 cm from lens (image is virtual and erect)

**38.18 [II]** converging, +2.3 cm

**38.19 [II]** virtual, erect, smaller, 5.6 cm in front of lens, 2.0 cm high

**38.20 [II]** (*a*) −11 cm; (*b*) −10 cm

**38.21 [II]** 0.50 m from object, +0.48 m

**38.22 [II]** 1.5

**38.23 [II]** (*a*) +20 cm; (*b*) 2.5:1

**38.24 [II]** +8 cm, +0.3 m

**38.25 [II]** +20 cm, +5.0 diopters

**38.26 [II]** −9.8 cm

# Optical Instruments

**Combination of Thin Lenses:** To locate the image produced by two lenses acting in combination, (1) compute the position of the intermediate image produced by the first lens alone, disregarding the second lens; (2) then consider this image as the object for the second lens, and locate its image as produced by the second lens alone. This latter image is the required image.

If the intermediate image formed by the first lens alone is computed to be behind the second lens, then that image is a virtual object for the second lens, and its distance from the second lens is considered negative.

**The Eye** uses a variable-focus lens to form an image on the retina at the rear of the eye. The **near point** of the eye, represented by $d_n$, is the closest distance to the eye from which an object can be viewed clearly. For the normal eye, $d_n$ is about 25 cm. *Farsighted* persons can see distinctly only objects that are far from the eye; *nearsighted* persons can see distinctly only objects that are close to the eye.

**Angular Magnification** ($M_A$), also sometimes called the ***magnifying power***, is the ratio of the respective angles subtended by the images on the retina with and without the instrument in place (see Fig. 39-1).

**A Magnifying Glass** is a converging lens used so that it forms an erect, enlarged, virtual image of an object placed inside its focal point (i.e., at a distance less than one focal length from the lens). The angular magnification due to a magnifier with a focal length $f$ (where the lens is close to the eye) is $(d_n/f) + 1$ if the image it casts is at the near point [Fig. 39-1(b)]. Alternatively, if the image is at infinity, for relaxed viewing, the angular magnification is $d_n/f$.

**A Microscope** that consists of two converging lenses, an objective lens (focal length $f_O$) and an eyepiece lens ($f_E$), has an angular magnification of:

$$M_A = M_{AE} M_{TO}$$

$$M_A = \left(\frac{d_n}{f_E} + 1\right)\left(\frac{s_{iO}}{f_O} - 1\right)$$

where $s_{iO}$ is the distance from the objective lens to the intermediate image it forms. This equation holds when the final image is at the near point, $d_n = 25$ cm.

**A Telescope** that has an objective lens (or mirror) with a focal length, $f_O$, and an eyepiece with focal length, $f_E$, produces a magnification $M_A = -f_O/f_E$.

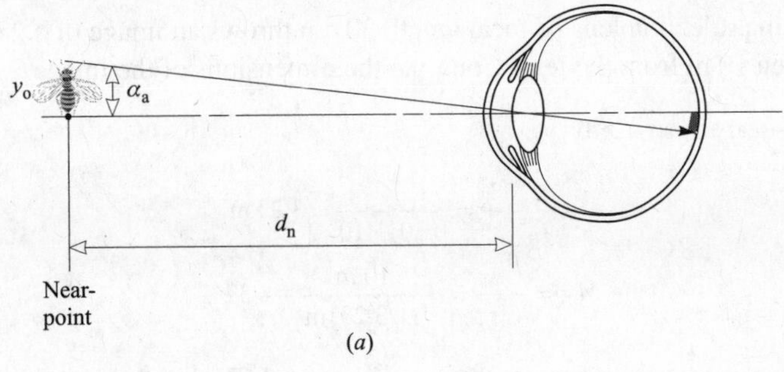


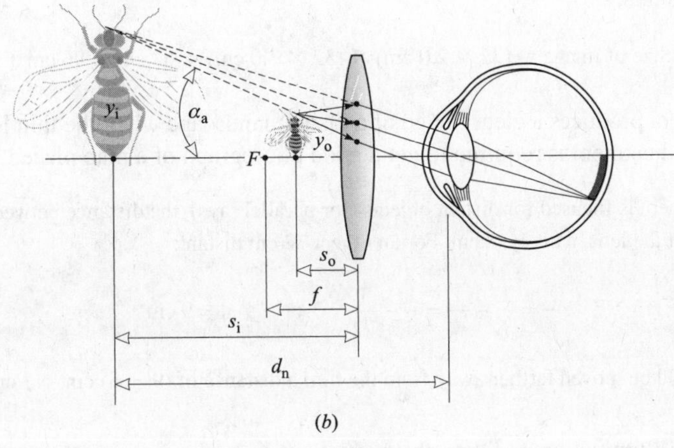


Fig.39-1

## SOLVED PROBLEMS

**39.1 [II]** A nearsighted person named George cannot see distinctly objects beyond 80 cm from the eye. What is the power in diopters of the spectacle lenses that will enable him to see distant objects clearly?

The image, which must be right-side-up, must be on the same side of the lens as the distant object (hence, the image is virtual and $s_i = -80$ cm), and nearer to the lens than the object (hence, diverging or negative lenses are indicated). Keep in mind that for virtual images formed by a concave lens $s_O > |s_i|$. As the object is at a great distance, $s_O$ is very large and $1/s_O$ is practically zero. Then

$$\frac{1}{s_o}+\frac{1}{s_i}=\frac{1}{f} \qquad \text{or} \qquad 0-\frac{1}{80}=\frac{1}{f} \qquad \text{or} \qquad f=-80 \text{ cm (diverging)}$$

and $$\text{Power in diopters} = \frac{1}{f \text{ in meters}} = \frac{1}{-0.80 \text{ m}} = -1.3 \text{ diopters}$$

**39.2 [II]** A farsighted person named Amy cannot see clearly objects closer to the eye than 75 cm. Determine the power of the spectacle lenses which will enable her to read type at a distance of 25 cm.

The image, which must be right-side-up, must be on the same side of the lens as the type (hence, the image is virtual and $s_i = -75$ cm), and farther from the lens than the type (hence, converging or positive lenses are prescribed). Keep in mind that for virtual images formed by a convex lens $|s_i| > s_O$. We have

$$\frac{1}{f}=\frac{1}{25}-\frac{1}{75} \qquad \text{or} \qquad f=+37.5 \text{ cm}$$

and $$\text{Power} = \frac{1}{0.375 \text{ m}} = 2.7 \text{ diopters}$$

**39.3 [II]** A single thin projection lens of focal length 30 cm throws an image of a 2.0 cm × 3.0 cm slide onto a screen 10 m from the lens. Compute the dimensions of the image.

The image is real and so $s_i > 0$:

$$\frac{1}{s_o} = \frac{1}{f} - \frac{1}{s_i} = \frac{1}{0.30} - \frac{1}{10} = 3.23\ \text{m}^{-1}$$

and so
$$M_T = -\frac{s_i}{s_o} = -\frac{10\ \text{m}}{(1/3.23)\,\text{m}} = -32$$

The magnification is negative because the image is inverted. The length and width of the slide are each magnified 32 times, so

$$\text{Size of image} = (32 \times 2.0\ \text{cm}) \times (32 \times 3.0\ \text{cm}) = 64\ \text{cm} \times 96\ \text{cm}$$

**39.4 [II]** An old camera produces a clear image of a distant landscape when the thin lens is 8 cm from the film. What adjustment is required to get a good photograph of a map placed 72 cm from the lens?

When the camera is focused for distant objects (for parallel rays), the distance between lens and film is the focal length of the lens, namely, 8 cm. For an object 72 cm distant:

$$\frac{1}{s_i} = \frac{1}{f} - \frac{1}{s_o} = \frac{1}{8} - \frac{1}{72} \qquad \text{or} \qquad s_i = 9\ \text{cm}$$

The lens should be moved farther away from the film a distance of $(9 - 8)$ cm = 1 cm.

**39.5 [II]** With a given illumination and film, the correct exposure for a camera lens set at $f/12$ is (1/5) s. What is the proper exposure time with the lens working at $f/4$?

A setting of $f/12$ means that the diameter of the opening, or stop, of the lens is 1/12 of the focal length; $f/4$ means that it is 1/4 of the focal length.

The amount of light passing through the opening is proportional to its area, and therefore to the square of its diameter. The diameter of the stop at $f/4$ is three times that at $f/12$, so $3^2 = 9$ times as much light will pass through the lens at $f/4$, and the correct exposure at $f/4$ is

$$(1/9)(\text{exposure time at } f/12) = (1.45)\ \text{s}$$

**39.6 [II]** An engraver who has normal eyesight uses a converging lens of focal length 8.0 cm which he holds very close to his eye. At what distance from the work should the lens be placed, and what is the magnification of the lens?

**Method 1**

When a converging lens is used as a magnifying glass, the object is between the lens and the focal point. The virtual erect, and enlarged image forms at the distance of distinct vision, 25 cm from the eye. For a virtual image $s_i < 0$. Thus,

$$\frac{1}{s_o} + \frac{1}{s_i} = \frac{1}{f} \qquad \text{or} \qquad \frac{1}{s_o} + \frac{1}{-25\ \text{cm}} = \frac{1}{8.0\ \text{cm}} \qquad \text{or} \qquad s_o = \frac{200}{33} = 6.06\ \text{cm} = 6.1\ \text{cm}$$

and
$$M_T = -\frac{s_i}{s_o} = -\frac{25\ \text{cm}}{6.06\ \text{cm}} = 4.1$$

**Method 2**

By the formula,

$$M_A = \frac{d_n}{f} + 1 = \frac{25}{8.0} + 1 = 4.1$$

Note that in this simple case $M_T = M_A$.

**39.7 [III]** Two positive lenses, having focal lengths of +2.0 cm and +5.0 cm, are 14 cm apart as shown in Fig. 39-2. An object $AB$ is placed 3.0 cm in front of the +2.0 lens. Determine the position and magnification of the final image $A''B''$ formed by this combination of lenses.

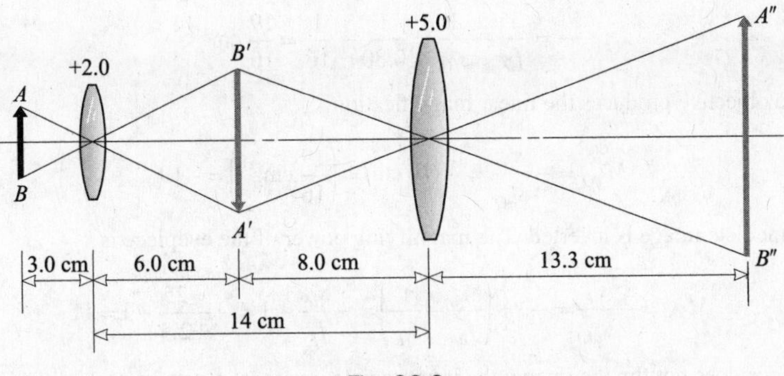


Fig. 39-2

To locate image $A'B'$ formed by the +2.0 lens alone:

$$\frac{1}{s_i} = \frac{1}{f} - \frac{1}{s_o} = \frac{1}{2.0} - \frac{1}{3.0} = \frac{1}{6.0} \qquad \text{or} \qquad s_i = 6.0 \text{ cm}$$

The image $A'B'$ is real, inverted, and 6.0 cm beyond the +2.0 lens.

To locate the final image $A''B''$: The image $A'B'$ is (14 − 6.0) cm = 8.0 cm in front of the +5.0 lens and is taken as a real object for the +5.0 lens.

$$\frac{1}{s_i} = \frac{1}{5.0} - \frac{1}{8.0} \qquad \text{or} \qquad s_i = 13.3 \text{ cm}$$

$A''B''$ is real, erect, and 13 cm from the +5 lens. Then,

$$M_T = \frac{\overline{A''B''}}{\overline{AB}} = \frac{\overline{A'B'}}{\overline{AB}} \times \frac{\overline{A''B''}}{\overline{A'B'}} = \frac{6.0}{3.0} \times \frac{13.3}{8.0} = 3.3$$

Note that the magnification produced by a combination of lenses is the product of the individual magnifications.

**39.8 [II]** In the compound microscope shown in Fig. 39-3, the objective and eyepiece have focal lengths of +0.80 and +2.5 cm, respectively. The real intermediate image $A'B'$ formed by the objective is 16 cm from the objective. Determine the total magnification if the eye is held close to the eyepiece and views the virtual image $A''B''$ at a distance of 25 cm.

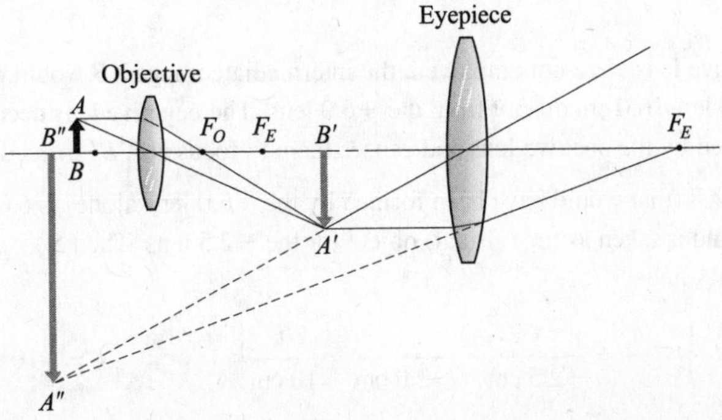


Fig. 39-3

**Method 1**

Let $s_{oO}$ = Object distance from the objective

$s_{iO}$ = Real-image distance from objective

$$\frac{1}{s_{oO}}=\frac{1}{f_O}-\frac{1}{s_{iO}}=\frac{1}{0.80}-\frac{1}{16}=\frac{19}{16}\text{ cm}^{-1}$$

and so the objective produces the linear magnification

$$M_{TO}=-\frac{s_{iO}}{s_{oO}}=-(16\text{ cm})=\left(\frac{19}{16}\text{ cm}^{-1}\right)=-19$$

The intermediate image is inverted. The magnifying power of the eyepiece is

$$M_{TE}=-\frac{s_{iE}}{s_{oE}}=-s_{iE}\left(\frac{1}{f_E}-\frac{1}{s_{iE}}\right)=-\frac{s_{iE}}{f_E}+1=-\frac{-25}{+2.5}+1=11$$

The eyepiece does not flip the image: the intermediate image is inverted and the final image is inverted. Therefore, the magnifying power of the instrument is $-19 \times 11 = -2.1 \times 10^2$.

Alternatively, under the conditions stated, the magnifying power of the eyepiece can be found as

$$\frac{25}{f_E}+1=\frac{25}{2.5}+1=11$$

**Method 2**

By the formula on p. 418, with $S_{iO} = 16$ cm,

$$\text{Magnification}=\left(\frac{d_n}{f_E}+1\right)\left(\frac{s_{iO}}{f_O}-1\right)=\left(\frac{25}{2.5}+1\right)\left(\frac{16}{0.8}-1\right)=2.1\times 10^2$$

**39.9 [III]** The telephoto lens shown in Fig. 39-4 consists of a converging lens of focal length +6.0 cm placed 4.0 cm in front of a diverging lens of focal length −2.5 cm. (*a*) Locate the image of a very distant object. (*b*) Compare the size of the image formed by this lens combination with the size of the image that could be produced by the positive lens alone.

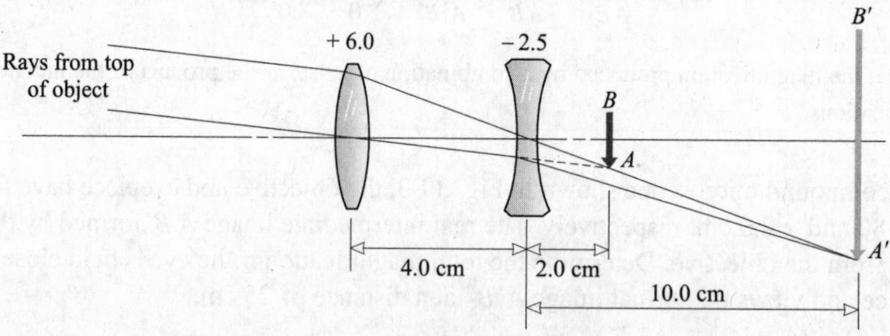


Fig. 39-4

(*a*) If the negative lens were not employed, the intermediate image *AB* would be formed at the focal point of the +6.0 lens, 6.0 cm distant from the +6.0 lens. The negative lens decreases the convergence of the rays refracted by the positive lens and causes them to focus at *A′B′* instead of *AB*.

The image *AB* (that would have been formed by the +6.0 lens alone) is 6.0 − 4.0 = 2.0 cm beyond the −2.5 lens and is taken as the (virtual) object for the −2.5 lens. Then $S_o = -2.0$ cm (negative because *AB* is virtual), and

$$\frac{1}{s_i}=\frac{1}{f}-\frac{1}{s_o}=\frac{1}{-2.5\text{ cm}}-\frac{1}{-2.0\text{ cm}}=\frac{1}{10\text{ cm}}\qquad\text{or}\qquad s_i=+10\text{ cm}$$

The final image *A′B′* is real and 10 cm beyond the negative lens.

(*b*) Magnification by negative lens $= \frac{A'B'}{AB} = -\frac{s_i}{s_o} = -\frac{10 \text{ cm}}{-2.0 \text{ cm}} = 5.0$

so the diverging lens increases the magnification by a factor of 5.0.

Notice that the magnification produced by the convex lens is negative and so the net magnification of both lenses is negative: the final image is inverted.

**39.10 [II]** A microscope has two interchangeable objective lenses (3.0 mm and 7.0 mm) and two interchangeable eyepieces (3.0 cm and 5.0 cm). What magnifications can be obtained with the microscope if it is adjusted so that the image formed by the objective is 17 cm from that lens?

Because $S_{iO} = 17$ cm the magnification formula for a microscope, with $d_n = 25$ cm, gives the following possibilities for $M_A$:

For $f_E = 3$ cm, $f_O = 0.3$ cm : $\quad M_A = (9.33)(55.6) = 518 = 5.2 \times 10^2$

For $f_E = 3$ cm, $f_O = 0.7$ cm : $\quad M_A = (9.33)(23.2) = 216 = 2.2 \times 10^2$

For $f_E = 5$ cm, $f_O = 0.3$ cm : $\quad M_A = (5)(55.6) = 278 = 2.8 \times 10^2$

For $f_E = 5$ cm, $f_O = 0.7$ cm : $\quad M_A = (5)(23.2) = 116 = 1.2 \times 10^2$

**39.11 [I]** Compute the magnifying power of a telescope, having objective and eyepiece lenses of focal lengths +60 and +3.0 cm, respectively, when it is focused for parallel rays.

$$\text{Magnifying power} = -\frac{\text{Focal length of objective}}{\text{Focal length of eyepiece}} = -\frac{60 \text{ cm}}{3.0 \text{ cm}} = -20$$

The image is inverted.

**39.12 [II]** *Reflecting telescopes* make use of a concave mirror, in place of the objective lens, to bring the distant object into focus. What is the magnifying power of a telescope that has a mirror with 250 cm radius and an eyepiece whose focal length is 5.0 cm?

As it is for a refracting telescope (i.e., one with two lenses), $M_A = -f_O/f_E$ again applies where, in this case, $f_O = -R/2 = 125$ cm and $f_E = 5.0$ cm. Thus, $M_A = -25$.

**39.13 [III]** As shown in Fig. 39-5, an object is placed 40 cm in front of a converging lens that has $f = +8.0$ cm. A plane mirror is 30 cm beyond the lens. Find the positions of all images formed by this system.

For the lens

$$\frac{1}{s_i} = \frac{1}{f} - \frac{1}{s_o} = \frac{1}{8.0} - \frac{1}{40} = \frac{4}{40} \qquad \text{or} \qquad s_i = 10 \text{ cm}$$

This is image $A'B'$ in the figure. It is real and inverted.

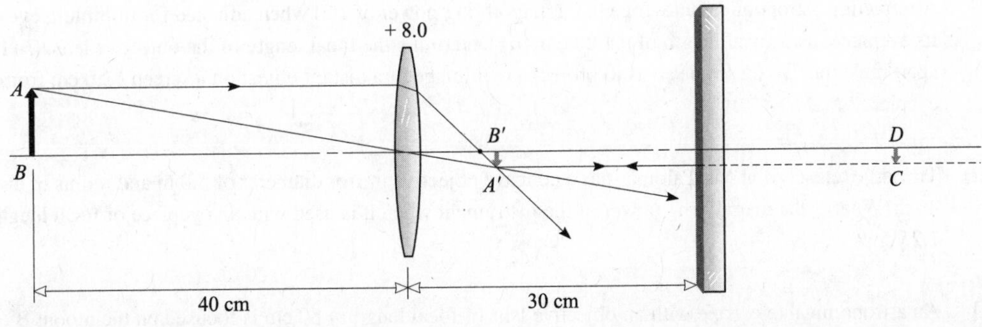


Fig. 39-5

$A'B'$ acts as an object for the plane mirror, 20 cm away. A virtual image $CD$ is formed 20 cm behind the mirror. Light reflected by the mirror appears to come from the image at $CD$. With $CD$ as object, the lens forms an image of it to the left of the lens. The distance $s_i$ from the lens to this latter image is given by

$$\frac{1}{s_i} = \frac{1}{f} - \frac{1}{s_o} = \frac{1}{8} - \frac{1}{50} = 0.105 \qquad \text{or} \qquad s_i = 9.5 \text{ cm}$$

The real images are therefore located 10 cm to the right of the lens and 9.5 cm to the left of the lens. (This latter image is upright.) A virtual inverted image is found 20 cm behind the mirror.

## SUPPLEMENTARY PROBLEMS

**39.14 [II]** A farsighted woman cannot see objects clearly that are closer to her eye than 60.0 cm. Determine the focal length and power of the spectacle lenses that will enable her to read a book at a distance of 25.0 cm.

**39.15 [II]** A nearsighted man cannot see objects clearly that are beyond 50 cm from his eye. Determine the focal length and power of the glasses that will enable him to see distant objects clearly.

**39.16 [II]** A projection lens is employed to produce 2.4 m × 3.2 m pictures from 3.0 cm × 4.0 cm slides on a screen that is 25 cm from the lens. Compute its focal length.

**39.17 [II]** A camera gives a life-size picture of a flower when the thin lens is 20 cm from the film. What should be the distance between lens and film to photograph a flock of birds high overhead?

**39.18 [II]** What is the maximum stop rating of a camera lens having a focal length of +10 cm and a diameter of 2.0 cm? If the correct exposure at $f/6$ is (1/90) s, what exposure is needed when the diaphragm setting is changed to $f/9$?

**39.19 [I]** What is the magnifying power of a lens of focal length +2.0 cm when it used as a magnifying glass (or simple microscope)? The lens is held close to the eye, and the virtual image forms at the distance of distinct vision, 25 cm from the eye.

**39.20 [II]** When the object distance from a converging lens is 5.0 cm, a real image is formed 20 cm from the lens. What magnification is produced by this lens when it is used as a magnifying glass, the distance of most distinct vision being 25 cm?

**39.21 [II]** In a compound microscope, the focal lengths of the objective and eyepiece are +0.50 cm and +2.0 cm, respectively. The instrument is focused on an object 0.52 cm from the objective lens. Compute the magnifying power of the microscope if the virtual image is viewed by the eye at a distance of 25 cm.

**39.22 [II]** A refracting astronomical telescope has a magnifying power of 150 when adjusted for minimum eyestrain. Its eyepiece has a focal length of +1.20 cm. (*a*) Determine the focal length of the objective lens. (*b*) How far apart must the two lenses be so as to project a real image of a distant object on a screen 12.0 cm from the eyepiece?

**39.23 [III]** The large telescope at Mt. Palomar has a concave objective mirror diameter of 5.0 m and radius of curvature 46 m. What is the magnifying power of the instrument when it is used with an eyepiece of focal length 1.25 cm?

**39.24 [II]** An astronomical telescope with an objective lens of focal length +80 cm is focused on the moon. By how much must the eyepiece be moved to focus the telescope on an object 40 meters distant?

**39.25 [II]** A lens combination consists of two lenses with focal lengths of +4.0 cm and +8.0 cm, which are spaced 16 cm apart. Locate and describe the image of an object placed 12 cm in front of the +4.0-cm lens.

**39.26 [II]** Two lenses, of focal lengths +6.0 cm and −10 cm, are spaced 1.5 cm apart. Locate and describe the image of an object 30 cm in front of the +6.0-cm lens.

**39.27 [II]** A telephoto lens consists of a positive lens of focal length +3.5 cm placed 2.0 cm in front of a negative lens of focal length −1.8 cm. (*a*) Locate the image of a very distant object. (*b*) Determine the focal length of the single lens that would form as large an image of a distant object as is formed by this lens combination.

**39.28 [II]** An opera glass has an objective lens of focal length +3.60 cm and a negative eyepiece of focal length −1.20 cm. How far apart must the two lenses be for the viewer to see a distant object at 25.0 cm from the eye?

**39.29 [II]** Repeat Problem 39.13 if the distance between the plane mirror and the lens is 8.0 cm.

**39.30 [II]** Solve Problem 39.13 if the plane mirror is replaced by a concave mirror with a 20 cm radius of curvature.

## ANSWERS TO SUPPLEMENTARY PROBLEMS

**39.14 [II]** +42.9 cm, +2.33 diopters

**39.15 [II]** −50 cm, −2.0 diopters

**39.16 [II]** 31 cm

**39.17 [II]** 10 cm

**39.18 [II]** $f/5$, (1/40) s

**39.19 [I]** 14

**39.20 [II]** 7.3

**39.21 [II]** $3.4 \times 10^2$

**39.22 [II]** (*a*) +180 cm; (*b*) 181 cm

**39.23 [III]** $1.8 \times 10^3$

**39.24 [II]** 1.6 cm

**39.25 [II]** 40 cm beyond +8.0 lens, real, erect

**39.26 [II]** 15 cm beyond negative lens, real, inverted, 5/8 as large as the object.

**39.27 [II]** (*a*) real image 9.0 cm in back of negative lens; (*b*) +21 cm

**39.28 [II]** 2.34 cm

**39.29 [II]** at 6.0 cm (real) and 24 cm (virtual) to the right of the lens

**39.30 [II]** at 10 cm (real, inverted), 10 cm (real, upright), −40 cm (real, inverted) to the right of the lens

# Interference and Diffraction of Light

**A Propagating Wave** is a self-sustaining disturbance of a medium that carries energy and momentum from one location to another. All such waves are ultimately associated with the motion of an underlying distribution of particles.

**Coherent Waves** (be they light, sound, or disturbances on a string) are waves that have the same form, the same frequency, and a fixed phase difference (i.e., the amount by which the peaks of one wave lead or lag those of the other wave does not change with time).

**The Relative Phase** of two coherent waves traveling along the same line specifies their relative positions on the line. If the crests of one wave fall on the crests of the other, the waves are completely **in-phase**. If the crests of one fall on the troughs of the other, the waves are 180° (or one-half wavelength) **out-of-phase**. Two waves can be out of phase by any amount greater than zero up to and including 180°.

**Interference Effects** occur when two or more coherent waves overlap. If two coherent waves of the same amplitude are superposed, **total destructive interference** (cancellation, or in the case of light, darkness) occurs when the waves are 180° out-of-phase. **Total constructive interference** (reinforcement, or in the case of light, brightness) occurs when they are in-phase.

**Diffraction** refers to the deviation from straight-line propagation that occurs when a wave passes beyond a partial obstruction. It usually corresponds to the bending or spreading of waves around the edges of apertures and obstacles. The simplest form of the diffraction of light is *far-field* or ***Fraunhofer diffraction***. It is observed on a screen that is far away from the aperture or obstacle which is obstructing an incident stream of plane waves. Diffraction places a limit on the size of details that can be observed optically.

**Single-Slit Fraunhofer Diffraction:** When parallel rays of light of wavelength $\lambda$ are incident normally upon a slit of width $D$, a diffraction pattern is observed beyond the slit. On a far-away screen complete darkness is observed at angles $\theta_{m'}$ to the straight-through beam, where

$$m'\lambda = D \sin \theta_{m'}$$

Here, $m' = \pm 1, \pm 2, \pm 3$, is the *order number* of the diffraction dark band (or minimum). The pattern consists of a broad central bright band flanked on both sides by an alternating succession of faint narrow light and dark bands ($m' = \pm 1, \pm 2$, etc.).

**Limit of Resolution** of two objects due to diffraction: If two objects are viewed through an optical instrument, the diffraction patterns caused by the aperture of the instrument limit our ability to distinguish the objects from each other. For distinguishability, the angle $\theta$ subtended at the aperture by the objects must be larger than a critical value $\theta_{cr}$, given by

$$\sin \theta_{cr} = (1.22)\frac{\lambda}{D}$$

where $D$ is the diameter of the circular aperture of the instrument (be it an eye, telescope, or camera).

**Diffraction Grating Equation:** A **diffraction grating** is a repetitive array of apertures or obstacles that alters the amplitude or phase of a wave. It usually consists of a large number of equally spaced, parallel slits or ridges; the distance between slits is the grating spacing $a$. When waves of wavelength $\lambda$ are incident normally upon a grating with spacing $a$, maxima are observed beyond the grating at angles $\theta_m$ to the normal, where

$$m\lambda = a \sin \theta_m$$

Here, $m = 0, \pm 1, \pm 2, \pm 3, \ldots$ is the *order number* of the diffracted image. Usually there will be a bright central undeviated band of colored light ($m = 0$) flanked on either side by blackness and then another band of colored light ($m = \pm 1$), and so on. These are known as the zeroth order spectrum, the first order spectrum, and so forth.

This same relation applies to the major maxima in the interference patterns of even two and three slits. In these cases, however, the maxima are not nearly so sharply defined as for a grating consisting of hundreds or thousands of slits. The pattern may become quite complex if the slits are wide enough so that the single-slit diffraction pattern from each slit shows several minima.

**The Diffraction of X-Rays** of wavelength $\lambda$ by reflection from a crystal is described by the *Bragg equation.* Strong reflections are observed at grazing angles $\phi_m$ (where $\phi$ is the angle between the face of the crystal and the reflected beam) given by

$$m\lambda = 2d \sin \phi_m$$

where $d$ is the distance between reflecting planes in the crystal, and $m = 1, 2, 3, \ldots$ is the *order* of reflection.

**Optical Path Length:** In the same time that it takes a beam of light to travel a distance $d$ in a material of index of refraction $n$, the beam would travel a distance $nd$ in a vacuum. For this reason, $nd$ is defined as the **optical path length** of the material.

## SOLVED PROBLEMS

**40.1 [II]** Figure 40-1 shows a thin film of a transparent material of thickness $d$ and index $n_f$ where $n_2 > n_f > n_1$. For what three smallest film thicknesses will reflected light rays-1 and -2 interfere totally (*a*) constructively and (*b*) destructively? Assume the monochromatic light has a wavelength in the film of 600 nm.

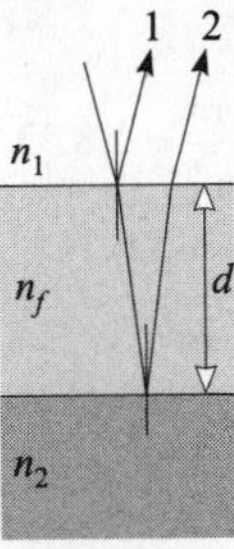


Fig. 40-1

Because $n_2 > n_f > n_1$ each reflection is at the interface with a more optically dense medium and so each is an *external reflection.* Accordingly, the two rays will not experience a relative phase shift due to the reflections.

(*a*) Ray-2 travels a distance of roughly $2d$ farther than ray-1. The rays reinforce if this distance is 0, $\lambda$, $2\lambda$, $3\lambda$, ..., $m\lambda$, where $m$ is an integer. Hence, for reinforcement,

$$m\lambda = 2d \qquad \text{or} \qquad d = \left(\tfrac{1}{2}m\right)(600\text{ nm}) = 300m\text{ nm}$$

The three smallest values for $d$ are 0, 300 nm, and 600 nm.

(*b*) The waves cancel if they are 180° out-of-phase. This occurs when $2d$ is $\frac{1}{2}\lambda$, $\left(\lambda + \frac{1}{2}\lambda\right)$, $\left(2\lambda + \frac{1}{2}\lambda\right)$, ..., $\left(m\lambda + \frac{1}{2}\right)$, ..., with $m$ an integer. Therefore, for cancellation,

$$2d = m\lambda + \tfrac{1}{2}\lambda \qquad \text{or} \qquad d = \tfrac{1}{2}\left(m + \tfrac{1}{2}\right)\lambda = \left(m + \tfrac{1}{2}\right)(300)\text{ nm}$$

The three smallest values for $d$, that is, the ones corresponding to $m = 0$, 1, and 2 are 150 nm, 450 nm, and 750 nm, respectively.

**40.2 [III]** **Two narrow, horizontal, parallel slits (a distance $a = 0.60$ mm apart) are illuminated by a beam of 500-nm light as shown in Fig. 40-2. Light that is diffracted at certain angles $\theta$ reinforces; at others, it cancels. Find the three smallest values for $\theta$ at which (*a*) reinforcement occurs and (*b*) cancellation occurs. (See Fig. 40-3.)**

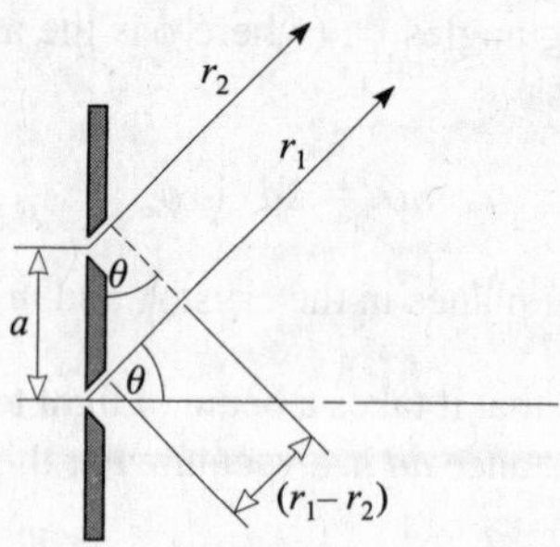


Fig. 40-2

The difference in path lengths for the two beams is $(r_1 - r_2)$. From Fig. 40-2:

$$\sin\theta = \frac{(r_1 - r_2)}{a}$$

(*a*) For reinforcement, $(r_1 - r_2) = 0, \pm\lambda, \pm 2\lambda, \ldots$, and so $\sin\theta_m = m\lambda/a$, where $m = 0, \pm 1, \pm 2, \ldots$ The corresponding three smallest values for $\theta_m$ are found using

$$m = 0 \quad \sin\theta_0 = 0 \qquad \text{or} \qquad \theta_0 = 0$$

$$m = \pm 1 \quad \sin\theta_1 = \pm\frac{500\times10^{-9}\text{ m}}{6\times10^{-4}\text{ m}} = \pm 8.33\times10^{-4} \qquad \text{or} \qquad \theta_1 = \pm 0.048°$$

$$m = \pm 2 \quad \sin\theta_2 = \pm\frac{2(500\times10^{-9}\text{ m})}{6\times10^{-4}\text{ m}} = \pm 16.7\times10^{-4} \qquad \text{or} \qquad \theta_2 = \pm 0.095°$$

(*b*) For cancellation, $(r_1 - r_2) = \pm\frac{1}{2}\lambda, \pm\left(\lambda + \frac{1}{2}\lambda\right), \pm\left(2\lambda + \frac{1}{2}\lambda\right), \ldots$ and so $\sin\theta_{m'} = \frac{1}{2}m'\lambda/a$, where $m' = \pm 1, \pm 3, \pm 5, \ldots$ The corresponding three smallest values for $\theta_{m'}$ are found using

$$m' = \pm 1 \quad \sin\theta_1 = \pm\frac{250\text{ nm}}{600\,000\text{ nm}} = \pm 4.17\times10^{-4} \qquad \text{or} \qquad \theta_1 = \pm 0.024°$$

$$m' = \pm 3 \quad \sin\theta_3 = \pm\frac{750\text{ nm}}{600\,000\text{ nm}} = \pm 0.00125 \qquad \text{or} \qquad \theta_3 = \pm 0.072°$$

$$m' = \pm 5 \quad \sin\theta_5 = \pm\frac{1250\text{ nm}}{600\,000\text{ nm}} = \pm 0.00208 \qquad \text{or} \qquad \theta_5 = \pm 0.12°$$

**40.3 [II]** Monochromatic light from a point source illuminates two narrow, horizontal, parallel slits. The centers of the two slits are $a = 0.80$ mm apart, as shown in Fig. 40-3. An interference pattern forms on the screen, 50 cm away. In the pattern, the bright and dark fringes are evenly spaced. The distance $y_1$ shown is 0.304 mm. Compute the wavelength $\lambda$ of the light.

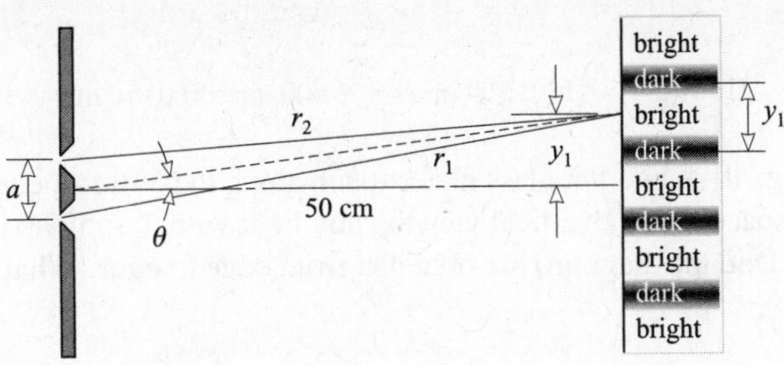


Fig. 40-3

Notice first that Fig. 40-3 is not to scale. The rays from the slits would actually be nearly parallel. We can therefore use the result of Problem 40.2 with $(r_1 - r_2) = m\lambda$ at the maxima (bright spots), where $m = 0, \pm1, \pm2, \ldots$ Then

$$\sin\theta = \frac{(r_1 - r_2)}{a} \qquad \text{becomes} \qquad m\lambda = a\sin\theta_m$$

Or, alternatively, we could use the grating equation, since a double slit is simply a grating with two lines. Both approaches result in $m\lambda = a\sin\theta_m$.

We know that the distance from the central maximum to the first maximum on either side is 0.304 mm. Therefore, from Fig. 40-3,

$$\sin\theta_1 = \frac{0.030\,4 \text{ cm}}{50 \text{ cm}} = 0.000\,608$$

Then, for $m = 1$,

$$m\lambda = a\sin\theta_m \qquad \text{becomes} \qquad (1)\lambda = (0.80 \times 10^{-3}\text{ m})(6.08 \times 10^{-4})$$

from which $\lambda = 486$ nm, or to two significant figures, $0.49 \times 10^3$ nm.

**40.4 [III]** Repeat Problem 40.1 for the case in which $n_1 < n_f > n_2$ or $n_1 > n_f < n_2$.

Experiment shows that, in this situation, cancellation occurs when $d$ is near zero. This is due to the fact that light generally undergoes a phase shift upon reflection. The process is rather complicated, but for incident angles less than about 30° it's fairly straightforward. Then there will be a net phase difference of 180° introduced between the internally and externally reflected beams. Thus, when the film is very thin compared to $\lambda$ and $d \approx 0$, there will be an apparent path difference for the two beams of $\frac{1}{2}\lambda$ and cancellation will occur. (This was not the situation in Problem 40.1, because there both beams were externally reflected.)

Destructive interference occurs for $d \approx 0$, as we have just seen. When $d = \frac{1}{2}\lambda$, cancellation again occurs. The same thing happens at $d = \frac{1}{2}\lambda + \frac{1}{2}\lambda$ Therefore, in this problem cancellation occurs at $d = 0$, 300 nm, and 600 nm.

Reinforcement occurs when $d = \frac{1}{4}\lambda$, because then beam-2 acts as though it had traveled an additional $\frac{1}{2}\lambda + (2)\left(\frac{1}{4}\lambda\right) = \lambda$. Reinforcement again occurs when $d$ is increased by $\frac{1}{2}\lambda$ and by $\lambda$. Hence, for reinforcement, $d = 150$ nm, 450 nm, and 750 nm.

**40.5 [III]** When one leg of a Michelson interferometer is lengthened slightly, 150 dark fringes sweep through the field of view. If the light used has a wavelength of $\lambda = 480$ nm, how far was the mirror in that leg moved?

Darkness is observed when the light beams from the two legs are 180° out-of-phase. As the length of one leg is increased by $\frac{1}{2}\lambda$, the path length (down and back) increases by $\lambda$ and the field of view changes from dark to bright to dark. When 150 fringes pass, the leg is lengthened by an amount

$$(150)\left(\tfrac{1}{2}\lambda\right) = (150)\,(240\text{ nm}) = 36\,000\text{ nm} = 0.0360\text{ mm}$$

**40.6 [III]** As shown in Fig. 40-4, two flat glass plates touch along the leftmost edge and are separated at the other end by a spacer. Using vertical viewing and light with $\lambda = 589.0$ nm, five dark fringes (indicated by a D in the diagram) are obtained from edge to edge. What is the thickness of the spacer?

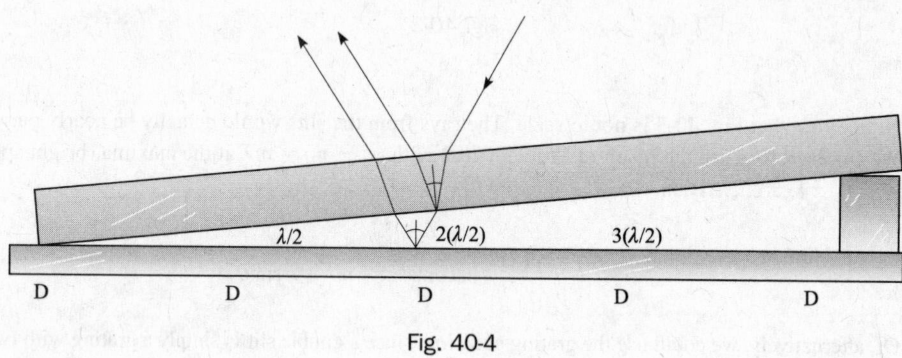


Fig. 40-4

The pattern is caused by interference between a beam reflected from the upper surface of the air wedge and a beam reflected from the lower surface of the wedge. The two reflections are of different natures in that reflection at the upper surface takes place at the boundary of a medium (air) of lower refractive index, while reflection at the lower surface occurs at the boundary of a medium (glass) of higher refractive index. In such cases, the act of reflection by itself involves a phase displacement of 180° between the two reflected beams. This explains the presence of a dark fringe at the left-hand edge.

As we move from a dark fringe to the next dark fringe, the beam that traverses the wedge must be held back by a path-length difference of $\lambda$. Because the beam travels twice through the wedge (down and back up), the wedge thickness changes by only $\frac{1}{2}\lambda$ as we move from fringe to fringe. Thus,

$$\text{Spacer thickness} = 4\left(\tfrac{1}{2}\lambda\right) = 2(589.0\text{ nm}) = 1178\text{ nm}$$

**40.7 [III]** In an experiment used to show *Newton's rings*, a plano-convex lens is placed on a flat glass plate, as in Fig. 40-5. When the lens is illuminated from directly above, a top-side viewer sees a series of bright and dark rings centered on the contact point, which is dark. Find the air-gap thickness at (*a*) the third dark ring and (*b*) the second bright ring. Assume 500-nm light is being used.

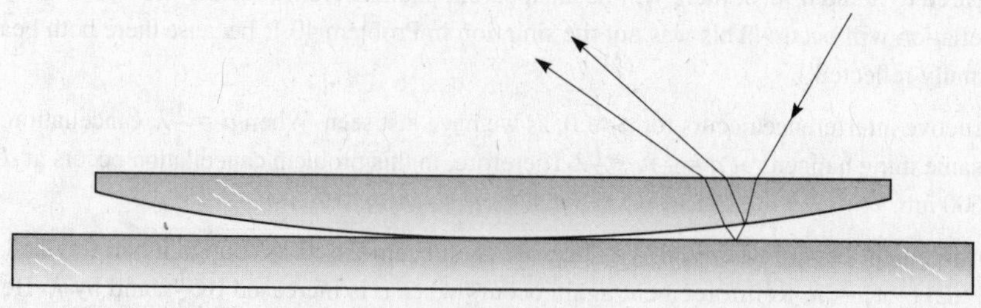

Fig. 40-5

Because one reflection is internal and the other external, there will be a relative phase shift of 180°.

(*a*) The gap thickness is zero at the central dark spot. It increases by $\frac{1}{2}\lambda$ as we move from a position of darkness to the next position of darkness. (Why $\frac{1}{2}\lambda$?) Therefore, at the third dark ring,

$$\text{Gap thickness} = 3\left(\tfrac{1}{2}\lambda\right) = 3(250\text{ nm}) = 750\text{ nm}$$

(*b*) The gap thickness at the first bright ring must be large enough to increase the path length by $\frac{1}{2}\lambda$. Since the ray traverses the gap twice, the thickness there is $\frac{1}{4}\lambda$. As we go from one bright ring to the next, the gap thickness increases by $\frac{1}{2}\lambda$. Therefore, at the second bright ring,

$$\text{Gap thickness} = \tfrac{1}{4}\lambda + \tfrac{1}{2}\lambda = (0.750)\,(500\text{ nm}) = 375\text{ nm}$$

**40.8 [II]** Discuss the thickness of a soap film in air which will appear black when viewed with sodium light ($\lambda = 589.3$ nm) reflected perpendicular to the film. The refractive index for soap solution is $n = 1.38$.

The situation is shown in Fig. 40-6. Ray-$b$ has an extra equivalent path length of $2nd = 2.76d$. In addition, there is a relative phase shift of 180°, or $\frac{1}{2}\lambda$, between the beams because of the reflection process, as described in Problems 40-4 and 40-6.

Cancellation (and darkness) occurs if the retardation between the two beams, is, $\frac{1}{2}\lambda$, or $\frac{3}{2}\lambda$, or $\frac{5}{2}\lambda$, and so on. Therefore, for darkness,

$$2.76d + \tfrac{1}{2}\lambda = m\left(\tfrac{1}{2}\lambda\right) \qquad \text{where} \qquad m = 1,3,5,\ldots$$

When $m = 1$, it follows that $d = 0$. For $m = 3$,

$$d = \frac{\lambda}{2.76} = \frac{589.3\text{ nm}}{2.76} = 214\text{ nm}$$

as the thinnest possible film other than zero. In practice, the film will become black when $d << \lambda/4$.

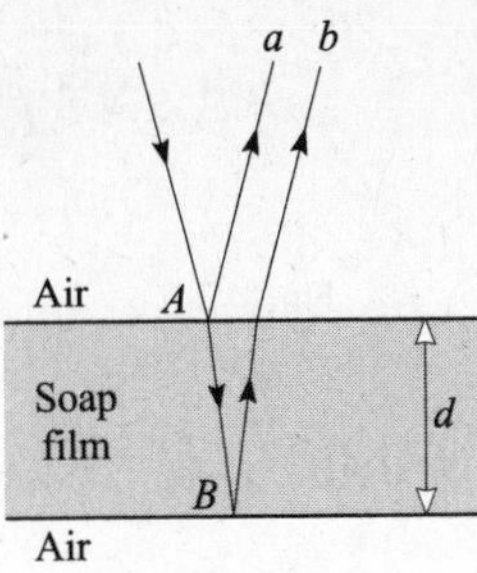


Fig. 40-6

**40.9 [II]** A single slit of width $D = 0.10$ mm is illuminated by parallel light of wavelength 600 nm, and diffraction bands are observed on a screen 40 cm from the slit. How far is the third dark band from the central bright band? (Refer to Fig. 40-7.)

For a single slit, the locations of dark bands are given by the equation $m'\lambda = D\sin\theta_{m'}$. Then

$$\sin\theta_3 = \frac{3\lambda}{D} = \frac{3(6.00\times10^{-7}\text{ m})}{0.10\times10^{-3}\text{ m}} = 0.018 \qquad \text{or} \qquad \theta_3 = 1.0°$$

From the figure, $\tan\theta_3 = y/40$ cm, and so

$$y = (40\text{ cm})(\tan\theta_3) = (40\text{ cm})(0.018) = 0.72\text{ cm}$$

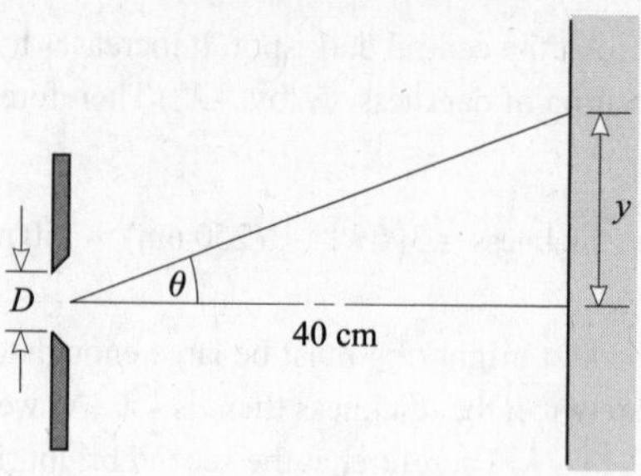


Fig. 40-7

**40.10 [I]** Red light falls normally on a diffraction grating ruled 4000 lines/cm, and the second-order image is diffracted 34.0° from the normal. Compute the wavelength of the light.

From the grating equation $m\lambda = a \sin\theta_m$

$$\lambda = \frac{a \sin\theta_2}{2} = \frac{\left(\frac{1}{4000}\text{ cm}\right)(0.559)}{2} = 6.99 \times 10^{-5}\text{ cm} = 699\text{ nm}$$

**40.11 [I]** Figure 40-8 depicts a laboratory setup for grating experiments. The diffraction grating has 5000 lines/cm and is 1.00 m from the slit, which is illuminated with sodium light. On either side of the slit, and parallel to the grating, is a meterstick. The eye, placed close to the grating, sees virtual images of the slit along the metersticks. Determine the wavelength of the light if each first-order image is 31.0 cm from the slit.

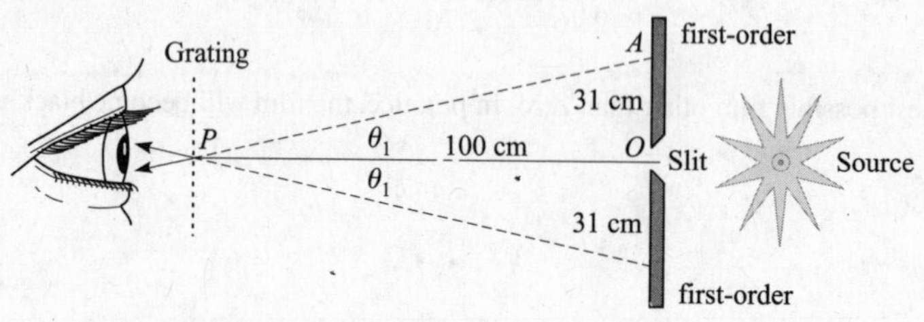


Fig. 40-8

$$\tan\theta_1 = 31.0/100 \qquad \text{or} \qquad \theta_1 = 17.2°$$

so

$$\lambda = \frac{a \sin\theta_1}{1} = \frac{(0.000\,200\text{ cm})(0.296)}{1} = 592 \times 10^{-7}\text{ cm} = 592\text{ nm}$$

**40.12 [I]** Green light of wavelength 540 nm is diffracted by a grating ruled with 2000 lines/cm. (*a*) Compute the angular deviation of the third-order image. (*b*) Is a 10th-order image possible?

(a) $$\sin\theta_3 = \frac{3\lambda}{a} = \frac{3(5.40 \times 10^{-5}\text{ cm})}{5.00 \times 10^{-4}\text{ cm}} = 0.324 \qquad \text{or} \qquad \theta = 18.9°$$

(b) $$\sin\theta_{10} = \frac{10\lambda}{a} = \frac{10(5.40 \times 10^{-5}\text{ cm})}{5.00 \times 10^{-4}\text{ cm}} = 1.08 \quad \text{(impossible)}$$

Since the value of $\sin\theta_{10}$ cannot exceed 1, a 10th-order image is impossible.

**40.13 [II]** Show that, in a spectrum of white light obtained with a grating, the red ($\lambda_r = 700$ nm) of the second order overlaps the violet ($\lambda_v = 400$ nm) of the third order.

$$\text{For the red:} \quad \sin\theta_2 = \frac{2\lambda_r}{a} = \frac{2(700)}{a} = \frac{1400}{a} \quad (a \text{ in nm})$$

$$\text{For the violet:} \quad \sin\theta_3 = \frac{3\lambda_v}{a} = \frac{3(400)}{a} = \frac{1200}{a}$$

As $\sin\theta_2 > \sin\theta_3$, $\theta_2 > \theta_3$. Thus, the angle of diffraction of red in the second order is greater than that of violet in the third order.

**40.14 [I]** A parallel beam of X-rays is diffracted by a rock salt crystal. The first-order strong reflection is obtained when the glancing angle (the angle between the crystal face and the beam) is 6°50′. The distance between reflection planes in the crystal is 2.8 Å. What is the wavelength of the X-rays? (1 angstrom = 1 Å = 0.1 nm.)

Note that the Bragg equation involves the glancing angle, not the angle of incidence.

$$\lambda = \frac{2d\sin\phi_1}{1} = \frac{(2)(2.8\text{ Å})(0.119)}{1} = 0.67\text{Å} = 0.67\times10^{-10}\text{ m}$$

**40.15 [II]** Two point sources of light are 50 cm apart, as shown in Fig. 40-9. They are viewed by the eye at a distance *L*. The entrance opening (pupil) of the viewer's eye has a diameter of 3.0 mm. If the eye were perfect, the limiting factor for resolution of the two sources would be diffraction. In that limit, how large could we make L and still have the sources seen as separate entities?

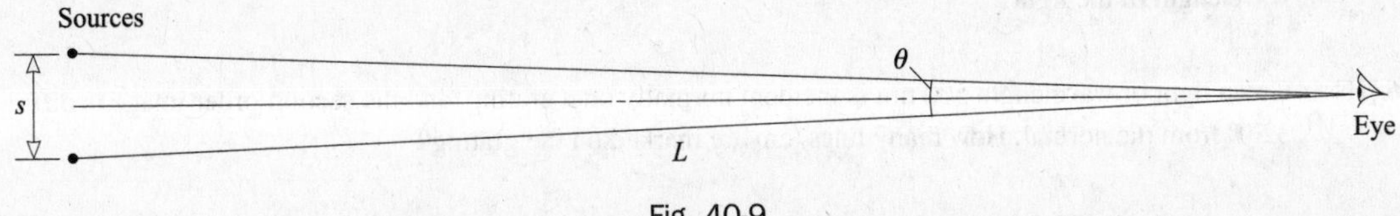


Fig. 40-9

This problem is about the *limit of resolution* as defined on p. 381. In the limiting case, $\theta = \theta_{cr}$, where $\sin\theta_{cr} = (1.22)(\lambda/D)$. But we see from the figure that $\sin\theta_{cr}$ is nearly equal to $s/L$, because $s$ is so much smaller than $L$. Substitution of this value gives

$$L \approx \frac{sD}{1.22\lambda} \approx \frac{(0.50\text{ m})(3.0\times10^{-3}\text{ m})}{(1.22)(5.0\times10^{-7}\text{ m})} = 2.5\text{ km}$$

We have taken $\lambda = 500$ nm, about the middle of the visible range.

## SUPPLEMENTARY PROBLEMS

**40.16 [II]** Two sound sources send identical waves of 20-cm wavelength out along the $+x$-axis. At what separations of the sources will a listener on the axis beyond him or her hear (*a*) the loudest sound and (*b*) the weakest sound?

**40.17 [II]** In an experiment such as that described in Problem 40.1, brightness is observed for the following film thicknesses: $2.90\times10^{-7}$ m, $5.80\times10^{-7}$ m, and $8.70\times10^{-7}$ m. (*a*) What is the wavelength of the light being used? (*b*) At what thicknesses would darkness be observed?

**40.18 [I]** A double-slit experiment is done in the usual way with 480-nm light and narrow slits that are 0.050 cm apart. At what angle to the central axis will one observe (*a*) the third-order bright spot and (*b*) the second minimum from the central maximum?

**40.19 [I]** In Problem 40.18, if the slit-to-screen distance is 200 cm, how far from the central maximum are (*a*) the third-order bright spot and (*b*) the second minimum?

**40.20 [I]** Red light of wavelength 644 nm, from a point source, passes through two parallel and narrow slits which are 1.00 mm apart. Determine the distance between the central bright fringe and the third dark interference fringe formed on a screen parallel to the plane of the slits and 1.00 m away.

**40.21 [I]** Two flat glass plates are pressed together at the top edge and separated at the bottom edge by a strip of tinfoil. The air wedge is examined in yellow sodium light (589 nm) reflected normally from its two surfaces, and 42 dark interference fringes are observed. Compute the thickness of the tinfoil.

**40.22 [I]** A mixture of yellow light of wavelength 580 nm and blue light of wavelength 450 nm is incident normally on an air film 290 nm thick. What is the color of the reflected light?

**40.23 [II]** Repeat Problem 40.1 if the film has a refractive index of 1.40 and the vacuum wavelength of the incident light is 600 nm.

**40.24 [II]** Repeat Problem 40.6 if the wedge is filled with a fluid that has a refractive index of 1.50 instead of air.

**40.25 [II]** A single slit of width 0.140 mm is illuminated by monochromatic light, and diffraction bands are observed on a screen 2.00 m away. If the second dark band is 16.0 mm from the central bright band, what is the wavelength of the light?

**40.26 [II]** Green light of wavelength 500 nm is incident normally on a grating, and the second-order image is diffracted 32.0° from the normal. How many lines/cm are marked on the grating?

**40.27 [II]** A narrow beam of yellow light of wavelength 600 nm is incident normally on a diffraction grating ruled 2000 lines/cm, and images are formed on a screen parallel to the grating and 1.00 m distant. Compute the distance along the screen from the central bright line to the first-order lines.

**40.28 [II]** Blue light of wavelength $4.7 \times 10^{-7}$ m is diffracted by a grating ruled 5000 lines/cm. (*a*) Compute the angular deviation of the second-order image. (*b*) What is the highest-order image theoretically possible with this wavelength and grating?

**40.29 [II]** Determine the ratio of the wavelengths of two spectral lines if the second-order image of one line coincides with the third-order image of the other line, both lines being examined by means of the same grating.

**40.30 [II]** A spectrum of white light is obtained with a grating ruled with 2500 lines/cm. Compute the angular separation between the violet ($\lambda_v = 400$ nm) and red ($\lambda_r = 700$ nm) in the (*a*) first order and (*b*) second order. (*c*) Does yellow ($\lambda_y = 600$ nm) in the third order overlap the violet in the fourth order?

**40.31 [II]** A spectrum of the Sun's radiation in the infrared region is produced by a grating. What is the wavelength being studied if the infrared line in the first order occurs at an angle of 25.0° with the normal and the fourth-order image of the hydrogen line of wavelength 656.3 nm occurs at 30.0°?

**40.32 [III]** How far apart are the diffracting planes in a NaCl crystal for which X-rays of wavelength 1.54 Å make a glancing angle of 15°54′ in the first order

## ANSWERS TO SUPPLEMENTARY PROBLEMS

**40.16 [II]** (*a*) $m(20\ \text{cm})$, where $m = 0, 1, 2, \ldots$; (*b*) $10\ \text{cm} + m\ (20\ \text{cm})$

**40.17 [II]** (*a*) 580 nm; (*b*) $145(1 + 2m)$ nm

**40.18 [I]** (*a*) 0.17°; (*b*) 0.083°

**40.19 [I]** (*a*) 0.58 cm; (*b*) 0.29 cm

**40.20 [I]** 1.61 mm

**40.21 [I]** 12.4 $\mu$m

**40.22 [I]** blue

**40.23 [II]** (*a*) 0, 214 nm, 429 nm; (*b*) 107 nm, 321 nm, 536 nm

**40.24 [II]** 785 nm

**40.25 [II]** 560 nm

**40.26 [II]** $5.30 \times 10^3$ lines/cm

**40.27 [II]** 12.1 cm

**40.28 [II]** (*a*) 28°; (*b*) fourth

**40.29 [II]** 3:2

**40.30 [II]** (*a*) 4°20′; (*b*) 8°57′; (*c*) yes

**40.31 [II]** $2.22 \times 10^{-6}$ m

**40.32 [III]** 2.81 Å

# CHAPTER 41

# Relativity

**A Reference Frame** is a coordinate system relative to which physical measurements are taken. An ***inertia reference frame*** is one which moves with constant velocity—that is, one which is not accelerating.

**The Special Theory of Relativity** was proposed by Albert Einstein (1905) and is concerned with bodies that are moving with constant velocity. The theory is predicated on two postulates:

(1) The laws of physics are the same in all inertial reference frames. The velocity of an object can only be given relative to some other object.
(2) The speed of light in free space, c, has the same value for all observers, independent of the motion of the source (or the motion of the observer).

These postulates lead to the following conclusions.

**The Relativistic Linear Momentum** ($\vec{\mathbf{p}}$) of a body of mass $m$ and speed $\upsilon$ is

$$\vec{\mathbf{p}} = \frac{m\vec{\mathbf{v}}}{\sqrt{1-(\upsilon/c)^2}} = \gamma m\vec{\mathbf{v}}$$

where $\gamma = 1/\sqrt{1-(\upsilon/c)^2}$ and $\gamma > 1$. Some physicists prefer to associate the $\gamma$ with the mass and introduce a relativistic mass $m_R = \gamma m$. That allows you to write the momentum as $p = m_R \upsilon$, but $m_R$ is then speed dependent. That approach was once quite popular but is now in disfavor. Here we will use only one mass, $m$, which is independent of its speed, just like the two other fundamental properties of particles of matter, charge and spin.

**Limiting Speed:** When $\upsilon = c$, the momentum of an object becomes infinite. We conclude that no object can be accelerated to the speed of light c, and so c is an upper limit for speed.

**Relativistic Energy** ($E$): The total energy of a body of mass $m$ is given by

$$E' = \gamma mc^2$$

where

$$\text{Total energy} = \text{Kinetic energy} + \text{Rest energy}$$

or

$$E = KE + E_0$$

When a body is at rest $\gamma = 1$, KE $= 0$ and the **rest energy** ($E_0$) is given by

$$E_0 = mc^2$$

The rest energy includes all forms of energy internal to the system.

The **kinetic energy** of a body of mass $m$ is

$$KE = \gamma mc^2 - mc^2$$

If the speed of the object is not too large, this reduces to the usual expression

$$KE = \tfrac{1}{2}mv^2 \qquad (v \ll c)$$

Using the expression $p = \gamma mv$, the total energy of a body can be written as

$$E^2 = m^2c^4 + p^2c^2$$

**Time Dilation:** *Time is relative*; it "flows" at different rates for differently moving observers. Suppose a spaceship and a planet are moving with respect to one another at a relative speed $v$ and each carries an identical clock. The ship's pilot will see an interval of time $\Delta t_S$ pass on her clock, with respect to which she is *stationary*. An observer on the ground will also notice a time interval $\Delta t_S$ pass on the ship's clock, which is *moving* with respect to him. He, however, will notice that interval to take a time (measured via his own clock) of $\Delta t_M$ where $\Delta t_M > \Delta t_S$. The observer on the ground will see time running more slowly on board the ship. For example, he might see 10 min (i.e., $\Delta t_S$) go by on the clock in the spaceship while his own clock shows that perhaps 20 min (i.e., $\Delta t_M$) went by. Accordingly,

$$\Delta t_M = \gamma\, \Delta t_S$$

A clock, or indeed any process, seen to be moving, progresses more slowly than when observed at rest. Remember that $\gamma > 1$. Similarly the pilot will see time running more slowly on the ground.

The time taken for an event to occur, as recorded by a stationary observer at the site of the event, is called the **proper time**, $\Delta t_S$. All observers moving past the site record a longer time for the event to occur. Hence, the proper time for the duration of an event is the smallest measured time for the event. The interval $\Delta t_M$ is in **laboratory time**, also called **coordinate time**. You may see the above *time dilation equation* written as $\Delta t = \gamma \Delta\tau$ where $\tau$ is proper time.

**Simultaneity:** Imagine that for a given observer two events occur at *different locations*, but at the same time. The events are simultaneous for this observer, but in general they are not simultaneous for a second observer moving relative to the first.

**Length Contraction:** Suppose an object is measured to have an $x$-component length $L_S$ when stationary ($L_S$ is called the **proper length**). The object is then given an $x$-directed speed $v$, so that it is moving with respect to an observer. That observer will see the object to have been shortened in the $x$-direction (but not in the $y$- and z-directions). Its $x$-length as measured by the observer with respect to whom it is moving ($L_M$) will then be

$$L_M = L_S\sqrt{1-(v/c)^2}$$

where $L_S > L_M$; the length of the object as measured by someone who is stationary with respect to it is always greater then the length measured by someone who sees the object moving by.

**Velocity Addition Formula:** Fig. 41-1 shows a coordinate system $S'$ moving at a speed $v_{O'O}$ with respect to a coordinate system $S$. Now consider an object at point $P$ moving in the $x$-direction at a speed $v_{PO'}$ relative to

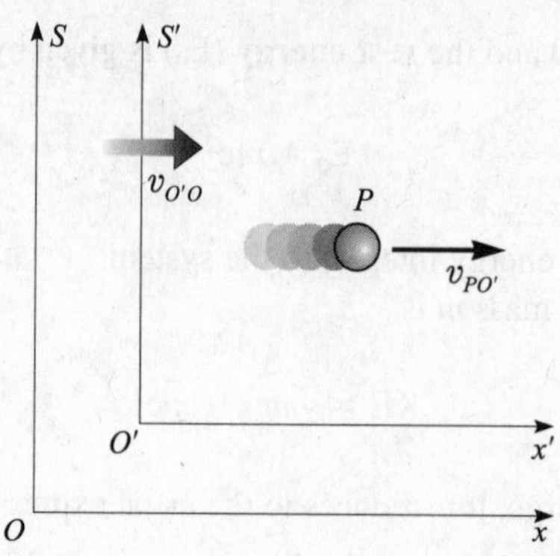


Fig 41-1

point $O'$. Special Relativity establishes that the speed of the object with respect to $O$ is not the classical value of $v_{PO'} + v_{O'O}$, but instead

$$v_{PO} = \frac{v_{PO'} + v_{O'O}}{1 + \dfrac{v_{PO'}\, v_{O'O}}{c^2}}$$

Notice that even when $v_{PO'} = v_{O'O} = c$ the value of $v_{PO} = c$.

## SOLVED PROBLEMS

**41.1 [I]** How fast must an object be moving if its corresponding value of $\gamma$ is to be 1.0 percent larger than $\gamma$ is when the object is at rest? Give your answer to two significant figures.

Use the definition $\gamma = 1/\sqrt{1-(v/c)^2}$ to find that at $v = 0$, $\gamma = 1.0$. Hence, the new value of $\gamma = 1.01(1.0)$, and so

$$1 - \left(\frac{v}{c}\right)^2 = \left(\frac{1}{1.01}\right)^2 = 0.980$$

Solving yields $v = 0.14c = 4.2 \times 10^7$ m/s.

**41.2 [I]** Compute the value of $\gamma$ for a particle traveling at half the speed of light. Give your answer to three significant figures.

$$\gamma = \frac{1}{\sqrt{1-(v/c)^2}} = \frac{1}{\sqrt{1-(0.500)^2}} = \frac{1}{\sqrt{0.750}} = \frac{1}{0.866} = 1.15$$

**41.3 [II]** If 1.00 g of matter could be converted entirely into energy, what would be the value of the energy so produced, at 10.0 cents per kW·h?

We make use of $\Delta E_0 = (\Delta m)c^2$ to find

Energy gained = (Mass lost)$c^2$ = $(1.00 \times 10^{-3}\text{ kg})(2.998 \times 10^8\text{ m/s})^2 = 8.99 \times 10^{13}$ J

$$\text{Value of energy} = (8.99 \times 10^{13}\text{ J})\left(\frac{1\text{ kW}\cdot\text{h}}{3.600 \times 10^6\text{ J}}\right)\left(\frac{\$\,0.10}{\text{kW}\cdot\text{h}}\right) = \$\,2.50 \times 10^6$$

**41.4 [II]** A 2.0-kg object is lifted from the floor to a tabletop 30 cm above the floor. By how much did the mass of the system consisting of the Earth and the object increase because of this increased $PE_G$?

We use $\Delta E_0 = (\Delta m)c^2$, with $\Delta E_0 = mgh$. Therefore,

$$\Delta m = \frac{\Delta E_0}{c^2} = \frac{mgh}{c^2} = \frac{(2.0\text{ kg})(9.81\text{ m/s}^2)(0.30\text{ m})}{(2.998\times10^8\text{ m/s})^2} = 6.5\times10^{-17}\text{ Kg}$$

**41.5 [III]** An electron is accelerated from rest through a potential difference of 1.5 MV and thereby acquires 1.5 MV of energy. Find its final speed.

Using $KE = \gamma mc^2 - mc^2$ and the fact that $KE = \Delta PE_E$, we have

$$KE = (1.5\times10^6\text{ eV})(1.6\times10^{-19}\text{ J/eV}) = 2.4\times10^{-13}\text{ J}$$

Then $$(\gamma m - m) = \frac{KE}{c^2} = \frac{2.4\times10^{-13}\text{ J}}{(2.998\times10^8\text{ m/s})^2} = 2.67\times10^{-30}\text{ kg}$$

But $m = 9.11\times10^{-31}$ kg and so $\gamma m = 3.58\times10^{-30}$ kg.

To find its speed, we use $\gamma = 1/\sqrt{1-(v/c)^2}$, which gives us

$$\frac{1}{\gamma^2} = 1 - \left(\frac{v}{c}\right)^2 = \left(\frac{m}{\gamma m}\right)^2 = \left(\frac{0.91}{3.58}\right)^2 = 0.0646$$

from which $$v = c\sqrt{1-0.0646} = 0.967c = 2.9\times10^8\text{ m/s}$$

**41.6 [II]** Determine the energy required to give an electron a speed equal to 0.90 that of light, starting from rest.

$$KE = (\gamma m - m)c^2 = \left[\frac{m}{\sqrt{1-(v/c)^2}} - m\right]c^2 = mc^2\left[\frac{1}{\sqrt{1-(v/c)^2}} - 1\right]$$

$$= (9.11\times10^{-31}\text{ kg})(2.998\times10^8\text{ m/s})^2\left[\frac{1}{\sqrt{1-(0.90)^2}} - 1\right] = 1.06\times10^{-13}\text{ J} = 0.66\text{ MeV}$$

**41.7 [III]** Show that $KE = (\gamma m - m)c^2$ reduces to $KE = \frac{1}{2}mv^2$ when $v$ is very much smaller than c.

$$KE = (\gamma m - m)c^2 = \left[\frac{m}{\sqrt{1-(v/c)^2}} - m\right]c^2 = mc^2\left[\left(1-\frac{v^2}{c^2}\right)^{-1/2} - 1\right]$$

Let $b = -v^2/c^2$ and expand $(1+b)^{-1/2}$ by the binomial theorem:

$$(1+b)^{-1/2} = 1 + (-1/2)b + \frac{(-1/2)(-3/2)}{2!}b^2 + \cdots = 1 + \frac{1}{2}\frac{v^2}{c^2} + \frac{3}{8}\frac{v^4}{c^4} + \cdots$$

Then $$KE = mc^2\left[\left(1 + \frac{1}{2}\frac{v^2}{c^2} + \frac{3}{8}\frac{v^4}{c^4} + \cdots\right) - 1\right] = \frac{1}{2}mv^2 + \frac{3}{8}mv^2\frac{v^2}{c^2} + \cdots$$

If $v$ is very much smaller than c, the terms after $\frac{1}{2}mv^2$ are negligibly small.

**41.8 [III]** An electron traveling at high (or relativistic) speed moves perpendicularly to a magnetic field of 0.20 T. Its path is circular, with a radius of 15 m. Find (*a*) the momentum, (*b*) the speed, and (*c*) the kinetic energy of the electron. Recall that, in nonrelativistic situations, the magnetic force $qvB$ furnishes the centripetal force $mv^2/r$. Thus, since $p = mv$, it follows that

$$p = qBr$$

and this relation holds even when relativistic effects are important.

First find the momentum using $p = qBr$

(*a*) $p = (1.60 \times 10^{-19}\ \text{C})(0.20\ \text{T})(15\ \text{m}) = 4.8 \times 10^{-19}\ \text{kg·m/s}$

(*b*) Because $p = mv/\sqrt{1-(v^2/c^2)}$ with $m = 9.11 \times 10^{-31}$ kg, we have

$$4.8\times10^{-19}\ \text{kg}\cdot\text{m/s} = \frac{(mc)\,(v/c)}{\sqrt{1-(v^2/c^2)}}$$

Squaring both sides and solving for $(v/c)^2$ give

$$\frac{v^2}{c^2} = \frac{1}{1+3.23\times10^{-7}} \qquad \text{or} \qquad \frac{v}{c} = \frac{1}{\sqrt{1+3.23\times10^{-7}}}$$

Most hand calculators cannot handle this. Accordingly, we make use of the fact that $1/\sqrt{1+x} \approx 1-\frac{1}{2}x$ for $x \ll 1$. Then

$$v/c \approx 1 - 1.61 \times 10^{-7} = 0.99999984$$

(*c*) $$\text{KE} = (\gamma m - m)c^2 = mc^2\left[\frac{1}{\sqrt{1-(v^2/c^2)}} - 1\right]$$

But we already found $(v/c)^2 = 1/(1 + 3.23 \times 10^{-7})$. If we use the approximation $1/(1 + x) \approx 1 - x$ for $x \ll 1$, we have $(v/c)^2 \approx 1 - 3.23 \times 10^{-7}$. Then

$$\text{KE} = mc^2\left(\frac{1}{\sqrt{3.23\times10^{-7}}} - 1\right) = (mc^2)\,(1.76\times10^3)$$

Evaluating the above expression yields

$$\text{KE} = 1.4 \times 10^{-10}\ \text{J} = 9.0 \times 10^8\ \text{eV}$$

An alternative solution method would be to use $E^2 = p^2c^2 + m^2c^4$ and recall that $\text{KE} = E - mc^2$.

**41.9 [II]** The Sun radiates energy equally in all directions. At the position of the Earth ($r = 1.50 \times 10^{11}$ m), the irradiance of the Sun's radiation is 1.4 kW/m$^2$. How much mass does the Sun lose per day because of the radiation?

The area of a spherical shell centered on the Sun and passing through the Earth is

$$\text{Area} = 4\pi r^2 = 4\pi(1.50 \times 10^{11}\ \text{m})^2 = 2.83 \times 10^{23}\ \text{m}^2$$

Through each square meter of this area, the Sun radiates an energy per second of 1.4 kW/m$^2$. Therefore, the Sun's total radiation per second is

$$\text{Energy/s} = (\text{area})(1400\ \text{W/m}^2) = 3.96 \times 10^{26}\ \text{W}$$

The energy radiated in one day (86 400 s) is

$$\text{Energy/day} = (3.96 \times 10^{26}\ \text{W})(86400\ \text{s/day}) = 3.42 \times 10^{31}\ \text{J/day}$$

Because mass and energy are related through $\Delta E_0 = \Delta mc^2$, the mass loss per day is

$$\Delta m = \frac{\Delta E_0}{c^2} = \frac{3.42 \times 10^{31}\ \text{J}}{(2.998 \times 10^8\ \text{m/s})^2} = 3.8 \times 10^{14}\ \text{kg}$$

For comparison, the Sun's mass is $2 \times 10^{30}$ kg.

**41.10 [I]** A beam of radioactive particles is measured as it shoots through the laboratory. It is found that, on the average, each particle "lives" for a time of $2.0 \times 10^{-8}$ s; after that time, the particle changes to a new form. When at rest in the laboratory, the same particles "live" $0.75 \times 10^{-8}$ s on the average. How fast are the particles in the beam moving?

Some sort of timing mechanism within the particle determines how long it "lives." This internal clock, which gives the proper lifetime, must obey the time-dilation relation. We have $\Delta t_M = \gamma \Delta t_S$ where the observer with respect to whom the particle (clock) is moving sees a time interval of $\Delta t_M = 2.0 \times 10^{-8}$ s. Hence,

$$2.0 \times 10^{-8}\ \text{s} = \gamma(0.75 \times 10^{-8}\ \text{s}) \qquad \text{or} \qquad 0.75 \times 10^{-8} = (2.0 \times 10^{-8})\sqrt{1 - (v/c)^2}$$

Squaring both sides of the equation and solving for $v$ leads to $v = 0.927c = 2.8 \times 10^8$ m/s.

**41.11 [II]** Two twins are 25.0 years old when one of them sets out on a journey through space at nearly constant speed. The twin in the spaceship measures time with an accurate watch. When he returns to Earth, he claims to be 31.0 years old, while the twin left on Earth knows that she is 43.0 years old. What was the speed of the spaceship?

The spaceship clock as seen by the space-twin reads the trip time to be $\Delta t_S$, which is 6.0 years long. The Earth-bound twin sees her brother age 6.0 years, but her clocks tell her that a time $\Delta t_M = 18.0$ years has actually passed. Hence, $\Delta t_M = \gamma \Delta t_S$ becomes $\Delta t_S = \Delta t_M \sqrt{1 - (v/c)^2}$ and so

$$6 = 18\sqrt{1 - (v/c)^2}$$

from which $\quad (v/c)^2 = 1 - 0.111 \quad$ or $\quad v = 0.943c = 2.83 \times 10^8$ m/s

**41.12 [II]** Two cells that subdivide on Earth every 10.0 s start from the Earth on a journey to the Sun ($1.50 \times 10^{11}$ m away) in a spacecraft moving at 0.850c. How many cells will exist when the spacecraft crashes into the Sun?

According to Earth observers, with respect to whom the cells are moving, the time taken for the trip to the Sun is the distance traveled ($x$) over the speed ($v$),

$$\Delta t_M = \frac{x}{v} = \frac{1.50 \times 10^{11}\ \text{m}}{(0.850)(2.998 \times 10^8\ \text{m/s})} = 588\ \text{s}$$

Because spacecraft clocks are moving with respect to the planet, they appear from Earth to run more slowly. The time these clocks read is

$$\Delta t_S = \Delta t_M/\gamma = \Delta t_M \sqrt{1 - (v/c)^2}$$

and so $\qquad \Delta t_S = 310$ s

The cells divide according to the spacecraft clock, a clock that is at rest relative to them. They therefore undergo 31 divisions in this time, since they divide each 10.0 s. Therefore, the total number of cells present on crashing is

$$(2)^{31} = 2.1 \times 10^9 \text{ cells}$$

**41.13 [I]** A person in a spaceship holds a meterstick as the ship shoots past the Earth with a speed $v$ parallel to the Earth's surface. What does the person in the ship notice as the stick is rotated from parallel to perpendicular to the ship's motion?

The stick behaves normally; it does not change its length, because it has no translational motion relative to the observer in the spaceship. However, an observer on Earth would measure the stick to be $(1 \text{ m})\sqrt{1 - (v/c)^2}$ long when it is parallel to the ship's motion, and 1 m long when it is perpendicular to the ship's motion.

**41.14 [II]** A spacecraft moving at 0.95c travels from the Earth to the star Alpha Centauri, which is 4.5 light years away. How long will the trip take according to (*a*) Earth clocks and (*b*) spacecraft clocks? (*c*) How far is it from Earth to the star according to spacecraft occupants? (*d*) What do they compute their speed to be?

A light year is the distance light travels in 1 year, namely

$$1 \text{ light year} = (2.998 \times 10^8 \text{ m/s})(3.16 \times 10^7 \text{ s}) = 9.47 \times 10^{15} \text{ m}$$

Hence the distance to the star (according to earthlings) is

$$d_e = (4.5)(9.47 \times 10^{15} \text{ m}) = 4.3 \times 10^{16} \text{ m}$$

(*a*) $$\Delta t_e = \frac{d_e}{v} = \frac{4.3 \times 10^{16} \text{ m}}{(0.95)(2.998 \times 10^8 \text{ m/s})} = 1.5 \times 10^8 \text{ s}$$

(*b*) Because clocks on the moving spacecraft run slower,

$$\Delta t_{\text{craft}} = \Delta t_e \sqrt{1 - (v/c)^2} = (1.51 \times 10^8 \text{ s})(0.312) = 4.7 \times 10^7 \text{ s}$$

(*c*) For the spacecraft occupants, the Earth-star distance is moving past them with speed 0.95c. Therefore, that distance is shortened for them; they find it to be

$$d_{\text{craft}} = (4.3 \times 10^{16} \text{ m})\sqrt{1 - (0.95)^2} = 1.3 \times 10^{16} \text{ m}$$

(*d*) For the spacecraft occupants, their relative speed is

$$v = \frac{d_{\text{craft}}}{\Delta t_{\text{craft}}} = \frac{1.34 \times 10^{16} \text{ m}}{4.71 \times 10^7 \text{ s}} = 2.8 \times 10^8 \text{ m/s}$$

which is 0.95c. Both Earth and spacecraft observers measure the same relative speed.

**41.15 [II]** As a rocket ship sweeps past the Earth with speed $v$, it sends out a pulse of light ahead of it. How fast does the light pulse move according to people on the Earth?

**Method 1**

With speed c (by the second postulate of Special Relativity).

**Method 2**

Here $v_{O'O} = v$ and $v_{PO'} = c$. According to the velocity addition formula, the observed speed will be (since $u = c$ in this case)

$$v_{PO} = \frac{v_{PO'} + v_{O'O}}{1 + \frac{v_{PO'}v_{O'O}}{c^2}} = \frac{v + c}{1 + (v/c)} = \frac{(v + c)c}{c + v} = c$$

## SUPPLEMENTARY PROBLEMS

**41.16 [I]** At what speed must a particle move for $\gamma$ to be 2.0?

**41.17 [I]** A particle is traveling at a speed $v$ such that $v/c = 0.99$. Find $\gamma$ for the particle.

**41.18 [I]** Compute the *rest energy* of an electron—that is, the energy equivalent of its mass, $9.11 \times 10^{-31}$ kg.

**41.19 [I]** Determine the speed of an electron having a kinetic energy of $1.0 \times 10^5$ eV (or equivalently $1.6 \times 10^{-14}$ J).

**41.20 [II]** A proton ($m = 1.67 \times 10^{-27}$ kg) is accelerated to a kinetic energy of 200 MeV. What is its speed at this energy?

**41.21 [II]** Starting with the definition of linear momentum and the relation between mass and energy, prove that $E^2 = p^2c^2 + m^2c^4$. Use this relation to show that the translational KE of a particle of mass $m$ is $\sqrt{m^2c^4 + p^2c^2} - mc^2$.

**41.22 [II]** A certain strain of bacteria doubles in number each 20 days. Two of these bacteria are placed on a spaceship and sent away from the Earth for 1000 Earth-days. During this time, the speed of the ship is 0.9950c. How many bacteria are aboard when the ship lands on the Earth?

**41.23 [II]** A certain light source sends out $2 \times 10^{15}$ pulses each second. As a spaceship travels parallel to the Earth's surface with a speed of 0.90c, it uses this source to send pulses to the Earth. The pulses are sent perpendicular to the path of the ship. How many pulses are recorded on Earth each second?

**41.24 [II]** The insignia painted on the side of a spaceship is a circle with a line across it at 45° to the vertical. As the ship shoots past another ship in space, with a relative speed of 0.95c, the second ship observes the insignia. What angle does the observed line make to the vertical?

**41.25 [II]** As a spacecraft moving at 0.92c travels past an observer on Earth, the Earthbound observer and the occupants of the craft each start identical alarm clocks that are set to ring after 6.0 h have passed. According to the Earthling, what does the Earth clock read when the spacecraft clock rings?

**41.26 [III]** Find the speed and momentum of a proton ($m = 1.67 \times 10^{-27}$ kg) that has been accelerated through a potential difference of 2000 MV. (We call this a 2 GeV proton.) Give your answers to three significant figures.

## ANSWERS TO SUPPLEMENTARY PROBLEMS

**41.16 [I]** $2.6 \times 10^8$ m/s

**41.17 [I]** 7.1

**41.18 [I]** 0.512 MeV = 820 pJ

**41.19 [I]** $1.6 \times 10^8$ m/s

**41.20 [II]** $1.70 \times 10^8$ m/s

**41.22 [II]** 64

**41.23 [II]** $8.7 \times 10^{14}$ pulses/s

**41.24 [II]** $\tan\theta = 0.31$ and $\theta = 17°$

**41.25 [II]** 15 h

**41.26 [III]** 0.948 c, $1.49 \times 10^{-18}$ kg·m/s

# CHAPTER 42

# Quantum Physics and Wave Mechanics

**Quanta of Radiation:** All the various forms of electromagnetic radiation, including light, have a dual nature. When traveling through space, they act like waves and give rise to interference and diffraction effects. But when electromagnetic radiation interacts with atoms and molecules, the beam acts like a stream of energy corpuscles called **photons** or *light-quanta*.

The energy (E) of each photon depends upon the frequency $f$ (or wavelength $\lambda$) of the radiation:

$$E = hf = \frac{hc}{\lambda}$$

where $h = 6.626 \times 10^{-34}$ J·s is a constant of nature called **Planck's constant**.

**Photoelectric Effect:** When electromagnetic radiation is incident on the surface of certain metals electrons may be ejected. A photon of energy $hf$ penetrates the material and is absorbed by an electron. If enough energy is available, the electron will be raised to the surface and ejected with some kinetic energy, $\frac{1}{2}mv^2$. Depending on how deep in the material they are, electrons having a range of values of KE will be emitted. Let $\phi$ be the energy required for an electron to break free of the surface, the so-called **work function**. For electrons up near the surface to begin with, an amount of energy $(hf - \phi)$ will be available and this is the maximum kinetic energy that can be imparted to any electron.

Accordingly, *Einstein's* **photoelectric equation** is

$$\frac{1}{2}mv_{\text{max}}^2 = hf - \phi$$

The energy of the ejected electron may be found by determining what potential difference must be applied to stop its motion; then $\frac{1}{2}mv^2 = V_s e$. For the most energetic electron,

$$hf - \phi = V_s e$$

where $V_s$ is called the **stopping potential**.

For any surface, the radiation must be of short enough wavelength so that the photon energy $hf$ is large enough to eject the electron. At the **threshold wavelength** (or *frequency*), the photon's energy just equals the work function. For ordinary metals the threshold wavelength lies in the visible or ultraviolet range. X-rays will eject photoelectrons readily; far-infrared photons will not.

**The Momentum of a Photon:** Because $E^2 = m^2c^4 + p^2c^2$, when $m = 0$, $E = pc$. Hence, since $E = hf$

$$E = pc = hf \qquad \text{and} \qquad p = \frac{hf}{c} = \frac{h}{\lambda}$$

The momentum of a photon is $p = h/\lambda$.

**Compton Effect:** A photon can collide with a particle having mass, such as an electron. When it does so, the scattered photon can have a new energy and momentum. If a photon of initial wavelength $\lambda_i$ collides with an essentially free, stationary electron of mass $m_e$ and is deflected through an angle $\theta$, then its scattered wavelength is increased to $\lambda_s$, where

$$\lambda_s = \lambda_i + \frac{h}{m_e c}(1 - \cos\theta)$$

The fractional change in wavelength is very small except for high-energy radiation such as X-rays or $\gamma$-rays.

**De Broglie Wavelength ($\lambda$):** A particle of mass $m$ moving nonrelativistically with momentum $p$ has associated with it a **de Broglie wavelength**

$$\lambda = \frac{h}{p} = \frac{h}{mv}$$

A beam of particles can be diffracted and can undergo interference phenomena. These wavelike properties of particles can be computed by assuming the particles to behave like waves (*de Broglie waves*) having the de Broglie wavelength.

**Resonance of de Broglie Waves:** A particle that is confined to a finite region of space is said to be a *bound* particle. Typical examples of bound-particle systems are a gas molecule in a closed container and an electron in an atom. The de Broglie wave that represents a bound particle will undergo resonance within the confinement region if the wavelength fits properly into the region. We call each possible resonance form a (stationary) *state* of the system. The particle is most likely to be found at the positions of the antinodes of the resonating wave; it is never found at the positions of the nodes.

**Quantized Energies** for bound particles arise because each resonance situation has a discrete energy associated with it. Since the particle is likely to be found only in a resonance state, its observed energies are discrete (*quantized*). Only in atomic (and smaller) particle systems are the energy differences between resonance states large enough to be easily observable.

## SOLVED PROBLEMS

**42.1 [I]** Show that the photons in a 1240-nm infrared beam have energies of 1.00 eV.

$$E = hf = \frac{hc}{\lambda} = \frac{(6.63 \times 10^{-34}\ \text{J}\cdot\text{s})(2.998 \times 10^8\ \text{m/s})}{1240 \times 10^{-9}\ \text{m}} = 1.602 \times 10^{-19}\ \text{J} = 1.00\ \text{eV}$$

**42.2 [I]** Compute the energy of a photon of blue light of wavelength 450 nm.

$$E = \frac{hc}{\lambda} = \frac{(6.63 \times 10^{-34}\ \text{J}\cdot\text{s})(2.998 \times 10^8\ \text{m/s})}{450 \times 10^{-9}\ \text{m}} = 4.42 \times 10^{-19}\ \text{J} = 2.76\ \text{eV}$$

**42.3 [I]** To break a chemical bond in the molecules of human skin and thus cause sunburn, a photon energy of about 3.50 eV is required. To what wavelength does this correspond?

$$\lambda = \frac{hc}{E} = \frac{(6.63 \times 10^{-34}\ \text{J}\cdot\text{s})(2.998 \times 10^8\ \text{m/s})}{(3.50\ \text{eV})(1.602 \times 10^{-19}\ \text{J/eV})} = 354\ \text{nm}$$

Ultraviolet radiation causes sunburn.

**42.4 [II]** The work function of sodium metal is 2.3 eV. What is the longest-wavelength light that can cause photoelectron emission from sodium?

At threshold, the photon energy just equals the energy required to tear the electron loose from the metal. In other words, the electron's KE is zero and so $hf = \phi$. Since $f = c/\lambda$,

$$\phi = \frac{hc}{\lambda}$$

$$(2.3\text{ eV})\left(\frac{1.602\times10^{-19}\text{ J}}{1.00\text{ eV}}\right) = \frac{(6.63\times10^{-34}\text{ J}\cdot\text{s})\,(2.998\times10^{8}\text{ m/s})}{\lambda}$$

$$\lambda = 5.4\times10^{-7}\text{ m}$$

**42.5 [II]** What potential difference must be applied to stop the fastest photoelectrons emitted by a nickel surface under the action of ultraviolet light of wavelength 200 nm? The work function of nickel is 5.01 eV.

$$E = \frac{hc}{\lambda} = \frac{(6.63\times10^{-34}\text{ J}\cdot\text{s})\,(2.998\times10^{8}\text{ m/s})}{2000\times10^{-10}\text{ m}} = 9.95\times10^{-19}\text{ J} = 6.21\text{ eV}$$

Then, from the photoelectric equation, the energy of the fastest emitted electron is

$$6.21\text{ eV} - 5.01\text{ eV} = 1.20\text{ eV}$$

Hence, a negative retarding potential of 1.20 V is required. This is the stopping potential.

**42.6 [II]** Will photoelectrons be emitted by a copper surface, of work function 4.4 eV, when illuminated by visible light?

As in Problem 42.4, the released-electron's KE = 0 and so

$$\text{Threshold } \lambda = \frac{hc}{\phi} = \frac{(6.63\times10^{-34}\text{ J}\cdot\text{s})\,(2.998\times10^{8}\text{ m/s})}{4.4(1.602\times10^{-19})\text{ J}} = 282\text{ nm}$$

Hence, visible light (350 nm to 700 nm) cannot eject photoelectrons from copper.

**42.7 [II]** A beam ($\lambda = 633$ nm) from a typical laser designed for student use has an intensity of 3.0 mW. How many photons pass a given point in the beam each second?

The energy that is carried past the point each second is 0.0030 J. Because the energy per photon is $hc/\lambda$, which works out to be $3.14 \times 10^{-19}$ J, the number of photons passing the point per second is

$$\text{Number/s} = \frac{0.003\,0\text{ J/s}}{3.14\times10^{-19}\text{ J/photon}} = 9.5\times10^{15}\text{ photon/s}$$

**42.8 [III]** In a process called *pair production*, a photon is transformed into an electron and a positron. A positron has the same mass ($m_e$) as the electron, but its charge is $+e$. To three significant figures, what is the minimum energy a photon can have if this process is to occur? What is the corresponding wavelength?

The electron-positron pair will come into existence moving with some minimum amount of KE. The particles will separate, and as they do they will slow down. When far apart each will have a mass of $9.11 \times 10^{-31}$ kg. In effect, KE goes into PE, which is manifested as mass.

Thus, the minimum energy photon at the start of the process must have the energy equivalent of the free-particle mass of the pair at the end of the process. Hence,

$$E = 2m_ec^2 = (2)(9.11 \times 10^{-31}\ \text{kg})(2.998 \times 10^8\ \text{m/s})^2 = 1.64 \times 10^{-13}\ \text{J} = 1.02\ \text{MeV}$$

Because this energy must equal $hc/\lambda$, the photon's energy,

$$\lambda = \frac{hc}{1.64 \times 10^{-13}\ \text{J}} = 1.21 \times 10^{-12}\ \text{m}$$

This wavelength is in the very short X-ray region, the region of $\gamma$-rays.

**42.9 [II]** What wavelength must electromagnetic radiation have if a photon in the beam is to have the same momentum as an electron moving with a speed of $2.00 \times 10^5$ m/s?

The requirement is that $(mv)_{\text{electron}} = (h/\lambda)_{\text{photon}}$. From this,

$$\lambda = \frac{h}{mv} = \frac{6.63 \times 10^{-34}\ \text{J}\cdot\text{s}}{(9.11 \times 10^{-31}\ \text{kg})\,(2.00 \times 10^5\ \text{m/s}} = 3.64\ \text{nm}$$

This wavelength is in the X-ray region.

**42.10 [II]** Suppose that a 3.64-nm photon moving in the $+x$-direction collides head-on with a $2 \times 10^5$ m/s electron moving in the $-x$-direction. If the collision is perfectly elastic, find the conditions after collision.

From the law of conservation of momentum,

$$\text{Momentum before} = \text{Momentum after}$$

$$\frac{h}{\lambda_0} - mv_0 = \frac{h}{\lambda} - mv$$

But, from Problem 42.9, $h/\lambda_0 = mv_0$ in this case. Hence, $h/\lambda = mv$. Also, for a perfectly elastic collision,

$$\text{KE before} = \text{KE after}$$

$$\frac{hc}{\lambda_0} + \tfrac{1}{2}mv_0^2 = \frac{hc}{\lambda} + \tfrac{1}{2}mv^2$$

Using the facts that $h/\lambda_0 = mv_0$ and $h/\lambda = mv$, we find

$$v_0\left(c + \tfrac{1}{2}v_0\right) = v\left(c + \tfrac{1}{2}v\right)$$

Therefore, $v = v_0$ and the electron moves in the $+x$-direction with its original speed. Because $h/\lambda = mv = mv_0$, the photon also "rebounds," and with its original wavelength.

**42.11 [I]** A photon ($\lambda = 0.400$ nm) strikes an electron at rest and rebounds at an angle of 150° to its original direction. Find the speed and wavelength of the photon after the collision.

The speed of a photon is always the speed of light in vacuum, c. To obtain the wavelength after collision, use the equation for the Compton Effect:

$$\lambda_s = \lambda_i + \frac{h}{m_e c}(1 - \cos\theta)$$

$$\lambda_s = 4.00 \times 10^{-10}\ \text{m} + \frac{6.63 \times 10^{-34}\ \text{J}\cdot\text{s}}{(9.11 \times 10^{-31}\ \text{kg})(2.998 \times 10^{8}\ \text{m/s})}(1 - \cos 150°)$$

$$\lambda_s = 4.00 \times 10^{-10}\ \text{m} + (2.43 \times 10^{-12}\ \text{m})(1 + 0.866) = 0.405\ \text{nm}$$

**42.12 [I]** What is the de Broglie wavelength for a particle moving with speed $2.0 \times 10^6$ m/s if the particle is (*a*) an electron, (*b*) a proton, and (*c*) a 0.20-kg ball?

We make use of the definition of the de Broglie wavelength:

$$\lambda = \frac{h}{mv} = \frac{6.63 \times 10^{-34}\ \text{J}\cdot\text{s}}{m(2.0 \times 10^{6}\ \text{m/s})} = \frac{3.31 \times 10^{-40}\ \text{m}\cdot\text{kg}}{m}$$

Substituting the required values for $m$, one finds that the wavelength is $3.6 \times 10^{-10}$ m for the electron, $2.0 \times 10^{-13}$ m for the proton, and $1.7 \times 10^{-39}$ m for the 0.20-kg ball.

**42.13 [II]** An electron falls from rest through a potential difference of 100 V. What is its de Broglie wavelength?

Its speed will still be far below c, so relativistic effects can be ignored. The KE gained, $\frac{1}{2}mv^2$, equals the electrical PE lost, $Vq$. Therefore,

$$v = \sqrt{\frac{2Vq}{m}} = \sqrt{\frac{2(100\ \text{V})(1.60 \times 10^{-19}\ \text{C})}{9.11 \times 10^{-31}\ \text{kg}}} = 5.927 \times 10^{6}\ \text{m/s}$$

and
$$\lambda = \frac{h}{mv} = \frac{6.626 \times 10^{-34}\ \text{J}\cdot\text{s}}{(9.11 \times 10^{-31}\ \text{kg})(5.927 \times 10^{6}\ \text{m/s})} = 0.123\ \text{nm}$$

**42.14 [II]** What potential difference is required in an electron microscope to give electrons a wavelength of 0.500 Å?

$$\text{KE of electron} = \tfrac{1}{2}mv^2 = \tfrac{1}{2}m\left(\frac{h}{m\lambda}\right)^2 = \frac{h^2}{2m\lambda^2}$$

where use has been made of the de Broglie relation, $\lambda = h/mv$. Substitution of the known values gives the KE as $9.66 \times 10^{-17}$ J. But KE $= Vq$, and so

$$V = \frac{\text{KE}}{q} = \frac{9.66 \times 10^{-17}\ \text{J}}{1.60 \times 10^{-19}\ \text{C}} = 600\ \text{V}$$

**42.15 [II]** By definition, a thermal neutron is a free neutron in a neutron gas at about 20 °C (293 K). What are the KE and wavelength of such a neutron?

From Chapter 17, the thermal energy of a gas molecule is $3kT/2$, where $k$ is Boltzmann's constant ($1.38 \times 10^{-23}$ J/K). Then

$$\text{KE} = \tfrac{3}{2}kT = 6.07 \times 10^{-21}\ \text{J}$$

This is a nonrelativistic situation for which we can write

$$\text{KE} = \tfrac{1}{2}mv^2 = \frac{m^2v^2}{2m} = \frac{p^2}{2m} \qquad \text{or} \qquad p^2 = (2m)\,(\text{KE})$$

Then $$\lambda = \frac{h}{p} = \frac{h}{\sqrt{(2m)\,(\text{KE})}} = \frac{6.63 \times 10^{-34}\ \text{J}\cdot\text{s}}{\sqrt{(2)\,(1.67 \times 10^{-27}\ \text{kg})\,(6.07 \times 10^{-21}\ \text{J})}} = 0.147\ \text{nm}$$

**42.16 [III]** Find the pressure exerted on a surface by the photon beam of Problem 42.7 if the cross-sectional area of the beam is 3.0 mm$^2$. Assume perfect reflection at normal incidence.

Each photon has a momentum

$$p = \frac{h}{\lambda} = \frac{6.63 \times 10^{-34}\ \text{J}\cdot\text{s}}{633 \times 10^{-9}\ \text{m}} = 1.05 \times 10^{-27}\ \text{kg}\cdot\text{m/s}$$

When a photon reflects, it changes momentum from $+p$ to $-p$, a total change of $2p$. Since (from Problem 42.7) $9.5 \times 10^{15}$ photons strike the surface each second,

Momentum change/s = $(9.5 \times 10^{15}/\text{s})(2)(1.05 \times 10^{-27}\ \text{kg}\cdot\text{m/s}) = 2.0 \times 10^{-11}\ \text{kg}\cdot\text{m/s}^2$

From the impulse equation (Chapter 8),

$$\text{Impulse} = Ft = \text{Change in momentum}$$

we have $$F = \text{Momentum change/s} = 1.99 \times 10^{-11}\ \text{kg}\cdot\text{m/s}^2$$

Then $$\text{Pressure} = \frac{F}{A} = \frac{1.99 \times 10^{-11}\ \text{kg}\cdot\text{m/s}^2}{3.0 \times 10^{-6}\ \text{m}^2} = 6.6 \times 10^{-6}\ \text{N/m}^2$$

**42.17 [III]** A particle of mass $m$ is confined to a narrow tube of length $L$. Find (*a*) the wavelengths of the de Broglie waves which will resonate in the tube, (*b*) the corresponding particle momenta, and (*c*) the corresponding energies. (*d*) Evaluate the energies for an electron in a tube with $L = 0.50$ nm.

(*a*) The de Broglie waves will resonate with a node at each end of the tube because the ends are impervious. A few of the possible resonance forms are shown in Fig. 42-1. They indicate that, for resonance, $L = \frac{1}{2}\lambda_1, 2\left(\frac{1}{2}\lambda_2\right), 3\left(\frac{1}{2}\lambda_3\right), \ldots, n\left(\frac{1}{2}\lambda_n\right), \ldots$ or

$$\lambda_n = \frac{2L}{n} \qquad n = 1, 2, 3, \ldots$$

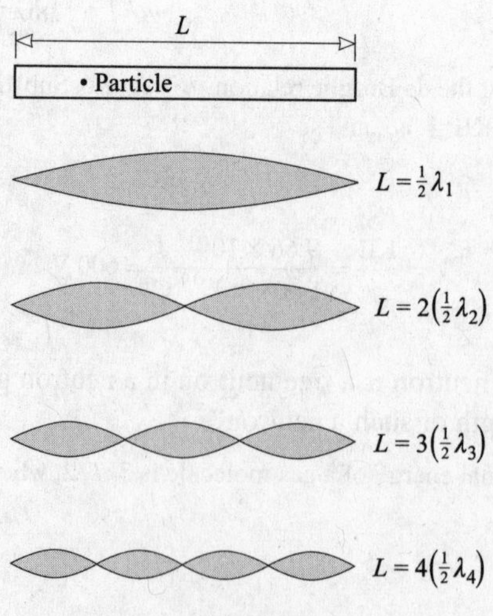


Fig. 42-1

(*b*) Because the de Broglie wavelengths are $\lambda_n = h/p_n$, the resonance momenta are

$$p_n = \frac{nh}{2L} \qquad n = 1, 2, 3, \ldots$$

(*c*) As shown in Problem 42.15, $p^2 = (2m)(\text{KE})$, and so

$$(\text{KE})_n = \frac{n^2h^2}{8L^2m} \qquad n = 1, 2, 3, \ldots$$

Notice that the particle can assume only certain discrete energies. The energies are quantized.

(*d*) With $m = 9.1 \times 10^{-31}$ kg and $L = 5.0 \times 10^{-10}$ m, substitution yields

$$(\text{KE})_n = 2.4 \times 10^{-19} n^2 \text{ J} = 1.5n^2 \text{ eV}$$

**42.18 [III]** A particle of mass $m$ is confined to a circular orbit with radius $R$. For resonance of its de Broglie wave on this orbit, what energies can the particle have? Determine the KE for an electron with $R = 0.50$ nm.

To resonate on a circular orbit, a wave must circle back on itself in such a way that crest falls upon crest and trough falls upon trough. One resonance possibility (for an orbit circumference that is four wavelengths long) is shown in Fig. 42-2. In general, resonance occurs when the circumference is $n$ wavelengths long, where $n = 1, 2, 3, \ldots$. For such a de Broglie wave

$$n\lambda_n = 2\pi R \qquad \text{and} \qquad p_n = \frac{h}{\lambda_n} = \frac{nh}{2\pi R}$$

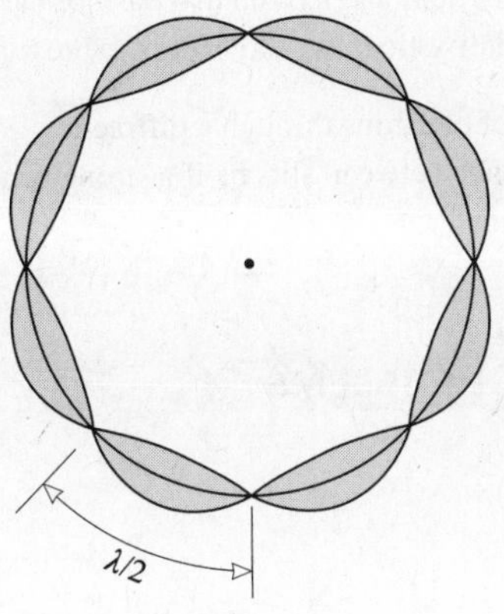


Fig. 42-2

As in Problem 42.17,

$$(\text{KE})_n = \frac{p_n^2}{2m} = \frac{n^2h^2}{8\pi^2R^2m}$$

The energies are obviously quantized. Placing in the values requested leads to

$$(\text{KE})_n = 2.4 \times 10^{-20} n^2 \text{ J} = 0.15n^2 \text{ eV}$$

## SUPPLEMENTARY PROBLEMS

**42.19 [I]** Compute the energy of a photon of blue light ($\lambda = 450$ nm), in joules and in eV.

**42.20 [I]** What is the wavelength of light in which the photons have an energy of 600 eV?

**42.21 [I]** A certain sodium lamp radiates 20 W of yellow light ($\lambda = 589$ nm). How many photons of the yellow light are emitted from the lamp each second?

**42.22 [I]** What is the work function of sodium metal if the photoelectric threshold wavelength is 680 nm?

**42.23 [II]** Determine the maximum KE of photoelectrons ejected from a potassium surface by ultraviolet radiation of wavelength 200 nm. What retarding potential difference is required to stop the emission of electrons? The photoelectric threshold wavelength for potassium is 440 nm.

**42.24 [II]** With what speed will the fastest photoelectrons be emitted from a surface whose threshold wavelength is 600 nm, when the surface is illuminated with light of wavelength $4 \times 10^{-7}$ m?

**42.25 [II]** Electrons with a maximum KE of 3.00 eV are ejected from a metal surface by ultraviolet radiation of wavelength 150 nm. Determine the work function of the metal, the threshold wavelength of the metal, and the retarding potential difference required to stop the emission of electrons.

**42.26 [I]** What are the speed and momentum of a 500-nm photon?

**42.27 [II]** An X-ray beam with a wavelength of exactly $5.00 \times 10^{-14}$ m strikes a proton that is at rest ($m = 1.67 \times 10^{-27}$ kg). If the X-rays are scattered through an angle of 110°, what is the wavelength of the scattered X-rays?

**42.28 [III]** A photon produces an electron and a positron which each have a kinetic energy of 220 keV even when they are separated by a great distance. Find the energy and wavelength of the photon.

**42.29 [II]** Show that the de Broglie wavelength of an electron accelerated from rest through a potential difference of $V$ volts is $1.228/\sqrt{V}$ nm. Ignore relativistic effects and take a look at Problem 42.13.

**42.30 [II]** Compute the de Broglie wavelength of an electron that has been accelerated through a potential difference of 9.0 kV. Ignore relativistic effects.

**42.31 [III]** What is the de Broglie wavelength of an electron that has been accelerated through a potential difference of 1.0 MV? (You must use the relativistic mass and energy expressions at this high energy.)

**42.32 [II]** It is proposed to send a beam of electrons through a diffraction grating. The electrons have a speed of 400 m/s. How large must the distance between slits be if a strong beam of electrons is to emerge at an angle of 25° to the straight-through beam?

## ANSWERS TO SUPPLEMENTARY PROBLEMS

**42.19 [I]** $4.41 \times 10^{-19}$ J = 2.76 eV

**42.20 [I]** 2.07 nm

**42.21 [I]** $5.9 \times 10^{19}$

**42.22 [I]** 1.82 eV

**42.23 [II]** 3.38 eV, 3.38 V

**42.24 [II]** $6 \times 10^5$ m/s

**42.25 [II]** 5.27 eV, 235 nm, 3.00 V

**42.26 [I]** $2.998 \times 10^8$ m/s, $133 \times 10^{-27}$ kg·m/s

**42.27 [II]** $5.18 \times 10^{-14}$ m

**42.28 [III]** 1.46 MeV, $8.49 \times 10^{-13}$ m

**42.30 [II]** $1.3 \times 10^{-11}$ m

**42.31 [III]** $8.7 \times 10^{-13}$ m

**42.32 [II]** $n(4.3 \times 10^{-6}$ m), where $n = 1, 2, 3, \ldots$.

# CHAPTER 43

# The Hydrogen Atom

**The Hydrogen Atom** has a diameter of about 0.1 nm; it consists of a proton as the nucleus (with a radius of about $10^{-15}$ m) and a single electron.

**Electron Orbits:** The first effective model of the atom was introduced by Niels Bohr in 1913. Although it has been surpassed by quantum mechanics, many of its simple results are still valid. The earliest version of the ***Bohr model*** pictured electrons in circular orbits around the nucleus. The hydrogen atom was then one electron circulating around a single proton. For the electron's de Broglie wave to resonate or "fit" (see Fig. 42-2) in an orbit of radius r, the following must be true (see Problem 42.18):

$$mv_n r_n = \frac{nh}{2\pi}$$

where $n$ is an integer. The quantity $mv_n r_n$ is the angular momentum of the electron in its $n$th orbit. The speed of the electron is $v$, its mass is $m$, and $h$ is Planck's constant, $6.63 \times 10^{-34}$ J·s.

The centripetal force that holds the electron in orbit is supplied by Coulomb attraction between the nucleus and the electron. Hence, $F = k_0 e^2/r^2 = ma = mv_n^2/r_n$ and

$$\frac{mv_n^2}{r_n} = k_0 \frac{e^2}{r^2}$$

Simultaneous solution of these equations gives the radii of stable orbits as $r_n = (0.053\text{ nm})\,n^2$. The energy of the atom when it is in the $n$th state (i.e., with its electron in the $n$th orbit configuration) is

$$E_n = -\frac{13.6}{n^2}\text{ eV}$$

As in Problems 42.17 and 42.18, the energy is quantized because a stable configuration corresponds to a resonance form of the bound system. For a nucleus with charge $Ze$ orbited by a single electron, the corresponding relations are

$$r_n = (0.053\text{ nm})\left(\frac{n^2}{Z}\right) \quad \text{and} \quad E_n = -\frac{13.6Z^2}{n^2}\text{ eV}$$

where $Z$ is called the **atomic number** of the nucleus.

**Energy-Level Diagrams** summarize the allowed energies of a system. On a vertical energy scale, the allowed energies are shown by horizontal lines. The energy-level diagram for hydrogen is shown in Fig. 43-1. Each horizontal line represents the energy of a resonance state of the atom. The zero of energy is taken to be the ionized atom—that is, the state in which the atom has an infinite orbital radius. As the electron falls closer to the nucleus, its potential energy decreases from the zero level, and thus the energy of the atom is negative as indicated. The lowest possible state, $n = 1$, corresponds to the electron in its smallest possible orbit; it is called the **ground state**.

**Emission of Light:** When an isolated atom falls from one energy level to a lower one, a photon is emitted. This photon carries away the energy lost by the atom in its transition to the lower energy state. The wavelength and frequency of the photon are given by

$$hf = \frac{hc}{\lambda} = \text{energy lost by the system}$$

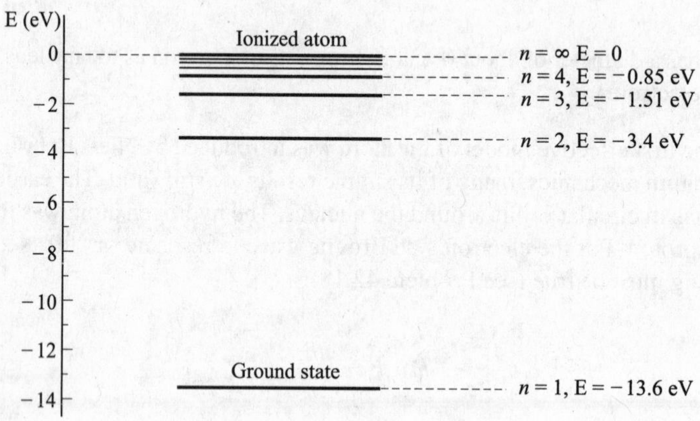


Fig. 43-1

The emitted radiation has a precise wavelength and gives rise to a single *spectral line* in the emission spectrum of the atom. It is convenient to remember that a 1240 nm photon has an energy of 1 eV. Moreover, photon energy varies *inversely* with wavelength.

**The Spectral Lines** emitted by excited isolated hydrogen atoms occur in series. Typical is the series that appears at visible wavelengths, the ***Balmer series*** shown in Fig. 43-2. Other series exist; one, in the ultraviolet, is called the ***Lyman series;*** there are others in the infrared, the one closest to the visible portion of the spectrum being the ***Paschen series***. Their wavelengths are given by simple formulas:

$$\text{Lyman:} \quad \frac{1}{\lambda} = R\left(\frac{1}{1^2} - \frac{1}{n^2}\right) \qquad n = 2, 3, \ldots$$

$$\text{Balmer:} \quad \frac{1}{\lambda} = R\left(\frac{1}{2^2} - \frac{1}{n^2}\right) \qquad n = 3, 4, \ldots$$

$$\text{Paschen:} \quad \frac{1}{\lambda} = R\left(\frac{1}{3^2} - \frac{1}{n^2}\right) \qquad n = 4, 5, \ldots$$

where $R = 1.0974 \times 10^7\ \text{m}^{-1}$ is called the **Rydberg constant**.

**Origin of Spectral Series:** The Balmer series of lines in Fig. 43-2 arises when an electron in the atom falls from higher states to the $n = 2$ state. The transition from $n = 3$ to $n = 2$ gives rise to a photon energy $\Delta E_{3,2} = 1.89$ eV, which is equivalent to a wavelength of 656 nm, the first line of the series. The second line originates in the transition from $n = 4$ to $n = 2$. The series limit line represents the transition from $n = \infty$ to $n = 2$. Similarly, transitions ending in the $n = 1$ state give rise to the Lyman series; transitions that end in the $n = 3$ state give lines in the Paschen series.

**Absorption of Light:** An atom in its ground state can absorb a photon in a process called *resonance absorption* only if that photon will raise the atom to one of its allowed energy levels.

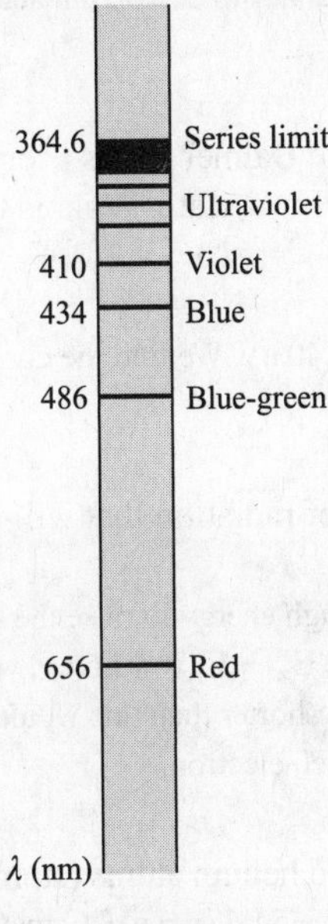


Fig. 43-2

## SOLVED PROBLEMS

**43.1 [II]** What wavelength does a hydrogen atom emit as its excited electron falls from the $n = 5$ state to the $n = 2$ state? Give your answer to three significant figures.

From the Bohr model we know that the energy levels of the hydrogen atom are given by $E_n = -13.6/n^2$ eV, and therefore

$$E_5 = -0.54 \text{ eV} \qquad \text{and} \qquad E_2 = -3.40 \text{ eV}$$

The energy difference between these states is $3.40 - 0.54 = 2.86$ eV. Because 1240 nm corresponds to 1.00 eV in an inverse proportion, we have, for the wavelength of the emitted photon,

$$\lambda = \left(\frac{1.00 \text{ eV}}{2.86 \text{ eV}}\right)(1240 \text{ nm}) = 434 \text{ nm}$$

**43.2 [II]** When a hydrogen atom is bombarded, the atom may be raised into a higher energy state. As the excited electron falls back to the lower energy levels, light is emitted. What are the three longest-wavelength spectral lines emitted by the hydrogen atom as it returns to the $n = 1$ state from higher energy states? Give your answers to three significant figures.

We are interested in the following transitions (see Fig. 43-1):

$$n = 2 \rightarrow n = 1: \qquad \Delta E_{2,1} = -3.4 - (-13.6) = 102 \text{ eV}$$

$$n = 3 \rightarrow n = 1: \qquad \Delta E_{3,1} = -1.5 - (-13.6) = 12.1 \text{ eV}$$

$$n = 4 \rightarrow n = 1: \qquad \Delta E_{4,1} = -0.85 - (-13.6) = 12.8 \text{ eV}$$

To find the corresponding wavelengths, proceed as in Problem 43.1, or use $\Delta E = hf = hc/\lambda$. For example, for the $n = 2$ to $n = 1$ transition,

$$\lambda = \frac{hc}{\Delta E_{2,1}} = \frac{(6.63 \times 10^{-34}\ \text{J}\cdot\text{s})(2.998 \times 10^{8}\ \text{m/s})}{(10.2\ \text{eV})(1.60 \times 10^{-19}\ \text{J/eV})} = 1.22\ \text{nm}$$

The other lines are found in the same way to be 102 nm and 96.9 nm. These are the first three lines of the Lyman series.

**43.3 [I]** The ***series limit*** wavelength of the Balmer series is emitted as the electron in the hydrogen atom falls from the $n = \infty$ state to the $n = 2$ state. What is the wavelength of this line (to three significant figures)?

From Fig. 43-1, $\Delta E = 3.40 - 0 = 3.40$ eV. We find the corresponding wavelength in the usual way from $\Delta E = hc/\lambda$. The result is 365 nm.

**43.4 [I]** What is the greatest wavelength of radiation that will ionize unexcited hydrogen atoms?

The incident photons must have enough energy to raise the atom from the $n = 1$ level to the $n = \infty$ level when absorbed by the atom. Because $E_\infty - E_1 = 13.6$ eV, we can use $E_\infty - E_1 = hc/\lambda$ to find the wavelength as 91.2 nm. Wavelengths shorter than this would not only remove the electron from the atom but would add KE to the removed electron.

**43.5 [I]** The energy levels for singly ionized helium atoms (atoms from which one of the two electrons has been removed) are given by $E_n = (-54.4/n^2)$ eV. Construct the energy-level diagram for this system.

See Fig. 43-3.

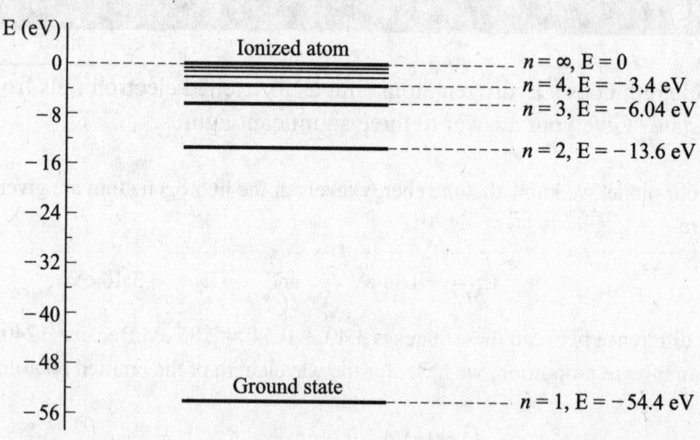


Fig. 43-3

**43.6 [I]** What are the two longest wavelengths of the Balmer series for singly ionized helium atoms?

The pertinent energy-level diagram is shown in Fig. 43-3. Recall that the Balmer series corresponds to transitions from higher states to the $n = 2$ state. From the diagram, the two smallest-energy transitions to the $n = 2$ states are

$$n = 3 \rightarrow n = 2 \qquad \Delta E_{3,2} = 13.6 - 6.04 = 7.6\ \text{eV}$$
$$n = 4 \rightarrow n = 2 \qquad \Delta E_{4,2} = 13.6 - 3.4 = 10.2\ \text{eV}$$

Using the fact that 1 eV corresponds to 1240 nm, we find the corresponding wavelengths to be 163 nm and 122 nm; both wavelengths are in the far ultraviolet or long X-ray region.

**43.7 [II]** Unexcited hydrogen atoms are bombarded with electrons that have been accelerated through 12.0 V. What wavelengths will the atoms emit?

When an atom in the ground state is given 12.0 eV of energy, the most these electrons can supply, the atom can be excited no higher than 12.0 eV above the ground state. Only one state exists in this energy region, the $n = 2$ state. Hence, the only transition possible is

$$n = 2 \rightarrow n = 1: \qquad \Delta E_{2,1} = 13.6 - 3.4 = 10.2 \text{ eV}$$

The only emitted wavelength will be

$$\lambda = (1240 \text{ nm})\left(\frac{1.00 \text{ eV}}{10.2 \text{ eV}}\right) = 122 \text{ nm}$$

which is the longest-wavelength line in the Lyman series.

**43.8 [II]** Unexcited hydrogen gas is an electrical insulator because it contains no free electrons. What maximum-wavelength photon beam incident on the gas can cause the gas to conduct electricity?

The photons in the beam must ionize the atom so as to produce free electrons. (This is called the *atomic photoelectric effect*.) To do this, the photon energy must be at least 13.6 eV, and so the maximum wavelength is

$$\lambda = (1240 \text{ nm})\left(\frac{1.00 \text{ eV}}{13.6 \text{ eV}}\right) = 91.2 \text{ nm}$$

which is the series limit for the Lyman series.

## SUPPLEMENTARY PROBLEMS

**43.9 [I]** One spectral line in the hydrogen spectrum has a wavelength of 821 nm. What is the energy difference between the two states that gives rise to this line?

**43.10 [II]** What are the energies of the two longest-wavelength lines in the Paschen series for hydrogen? What are the corresponding wavelengths? Give your answers to two significant figures.

**43.11 [I]** What is the wavelength of the series limit line for the hydrogen Paschen series? Consult Problem 43.3 for an explanation of "series limit."

**43.12 [II]** The lithium atom has a nuclear charge of $+3e$. Find the energy required to remove the third electron from a lithium atom that has already lost two of its electrons. Assume the third electron to be initially in the ground state.

**43.13 [II]** Electrons in an electron beam are accelerated through a potential difference $V$ and are incident on hydrogen atoms in their ground state. What is the maximum value for $V$ if the collisions are to be perfectly elastic?

**43.14 [II]** What are the three longest photon wavelengths that singly ionized helium atoms (in their ground state) will absorb strongly? (See Fig. 43-3.)

**43.15 [II]** How much energy is required to remove the second electron from a singly ionized helium atom? What is the maximum wavelength of an incident photon that could tear this electron from the ion?

**43.16 [II]** In the spectrum of singly ionized helium, what is the series limit for its Balmer series?

## ANSWERS TO SUPPLEMENTARY PROBLEMS

**43.9 [I]** 1.51 eV

**43.10 [II]** 0.66 eV and 0.97 eV, $1.9 \times 10^{-6}$ m and $1.3 \times 10^{-6}$ m

**43.11 [I]** 821 nm

**43.12 [II]** 122 eV

**43.13 [II]** < 10.2 V

**43.14 [II]** 30.4 nm, 25.6 nm, 24.3 nm

**43.15 [II]** 54.4 eV, 22.8 nm

**43.16 [II]** 91 nm

# CHAPTER 44

# Multielectron Atoms

**A Neutral Atom** whose nucleus carries a positive charge of *Ze* has *Z* electrons. When the electrons have the least energy possible, the atom is in its *ground state*. The state of an atom is specified by the *quantum numbers* for its individual electrons.

**The Quantum Numbers** that are used to specify the parameters of an atomic electron are as follows:

- The **principal quantum number** $n$ specifies the orbit, or shell, in which the electron is to be found. In the hydrogen atom, it specifies the electron's energy via $E_n = -13.6/n^2$ eV.
- The **orbital quantum number** $\ell$ specifies the angular momentum $L$ of the electron in its orbit:

$$L = \left(\frac{h}{2\pi}\right)\sqrt{\ell(\ell+1)}$$

  where $h$ is Planck's constant, and $\ell = 0, 1, 2, \ldots, n - 1$.
- The **magnetic quantum number** $m_\ell$ describes the orientation of the orbital angular momentum vector relative to the $z$ direction, the direction of an impressed magnetic field:

$$L_z = \left(\frac{h}{2\pi}\right)(m_\ell)$$

  where $m_\ell = 0, \pm 1, \pm 2, \ldots, \pm\ell$.
- The **spin quantum number** $m_s$ has allowed values of $\pm\frac{1}{2}$.

**The Pauli Exclusion Principle** maintains that no two electrons in the same atom can have the same set of quantum numbers. In other words, no two electrons can be in the same state.

## SOLVED PROBLEMS

**44.1 [II]** Estimate the energy required to remove an $n = 1$ (i.e., inner-shell) electron from a gold atom ($Z = 79$).

Because an electron in the innermost shell of the atom is not much influenced by distant electrons in outer shells, we can consider it to be the only electron present. Then its energy is given approximately by an appropriately modified version of the energy formula of Chapter 43 that takes into consideration the charge ($Ze$) of the nucleus. With $n = 1$, that formula—which was given on the first page of Chapter 43—is $E_n = -13.6Z^2/n^2$, whereupon

$$E_1 = -13.6(79)^2 = -84900 \text{ eV} = -84.9 \text{ keV}$$

To tear the electron loose (i.e., remove it to the $E_\infty = 0$ level), we must give it an energy of about 84.9 keV.

**44.2 [II]** What are the quantum numbers for the electrons in the lithium atom ($Z = 3$) when the atom is in its ground state?

Start with $n = 1$ and go up from there until you run out of electrons. Keeping in mind that $\ell = 0, 1, 2, \ldots, (n-1)$ and $m_\ell = 0, \pm1, \pm2, \ldots, \pm\ell$ while $m_s = \pm\frac{1}{2}$, the Pauli Exclusion Principle tells us that the lithium atom's three electrons can take on the following quantum numbers:

$$\text{Electron 1:} \quad n=1, \quad \ell=0, \quad m_\ell=0, \quad m_s=+\tfrac{1}{2}$$

$$\text{Electron 2:} \quad n=1, \quad \ell=0, \quad m_\ell=0, \quad m_s=-\tfrac{1}{2}$$

$$\text{Electron 3:} \quad n=2, \quad \ell=0, \quad m_\ell=0, \quad m_s=+\tfrac{1}{2}$$

Notice that, when $n = 1$, $\ell$ must be zero and $m_\ell$ must be zero (why?). Then there are only two $n = 1$ possibilities, and the third electron has to go into the $n = 2$ level. Since it is in the second Bohr orbit, it is more easily removed from the atom than an $n = 1$ electron. That is why lithium ionizes easily to $Li^+$.

**44.3 [II]** Why is sodium ($Z = 11$) the next univalent atom after lithium?

Sodium has a single electron in the $n = 3$ shell. To see why this is necessarily so, notice that the Pauli Exclusion Principle allows only two electrons in the $n = 1$ shell. The next eight electrons can fit in the $n = 2$ shell, as follows:

$$n=2, \quad \ell=0, \quad m_\ell=0, \quad m_s=\pm\tfrac{1}{2}$$

$$n=2, \quad \ell=1, \quad m_\ell=0, \quad m_s=\pm\tfrac{1}{2}$$

$$n=2, \quad \ell=1, \quad m_\ell=1, \quad m_s=\pm\tfrac{1}{2}$$

$$n=2, \quad \ell=1, \quad m_\ell=-1, \quad m_s=\pm\tfrac{1}{2}$$

The eleventh electron must go into the $n = 3$ shell, from which it is easily removed to yield $Na^+$.

**44.4 [II]** *(a)* Estimate the wavelength of the photon emitted as an electron falls from the $n = 2$ shell to the $n = 1$ shell in the gold atom ($Z = 79$). *(b)* About how much energy must bombarding electrons have to excite gold to radiate this emission line?

*(a)* As noted in Problem 44.1, to a first approximation the energies of the innermost electrons of a large-$Z$ atom are given by $E_n = -13.6Z^2/n^2$ eV. Thus,

$$\Delta E_{2,1} = 13.6(79)^2\left(\frac{1}{1} - \frac{1}{4}\right) = 63700 \text{ eV}$$

This corresponds to a photon with

$$\lambda = (1240 \text{ nm})\left(\frac{1 \text{ eV}}{63700 \text{ eV}}\right) = 0.0195 \text{ nm}$$

It is clear from this result that inner-shell transitions in high-$Z$ atoms give rise to the emission of X-rays.

(*b*) Before an $n = 2$ electron can fall to the $n = 1$ shell, an $n = 1$ electron must be thrown to an empty state of large $n$, which we approximate as $n = \infty$ (with $E_\infty = 0$). This requires an energy

$$\Delta E_{1,\infty} = 0 - \frac{-13.6\,Z^2}{n^2} = \frac{13.6\,(79)^2}{1} = 84.9\text{ keV}$$

The bombarding electrons must thus have an energy of about 84.9 keV.

**44.5 [II]** Suppose electrons had no spin, so that the spin quantum number did not exist. If the Exclusion Principle still applied to the remaining quantum numbers, what would be the first three univalent atoms?

The electrons would take on the following quantum numbers:

| | | | | |
|---|---|---|---|---|
| Electron 1: | $n = 1,$ | $\ell = 0,$ | $m_\ell = 0$ | (univalent) |
| Electron 2: | $n = 2,$ | $\ell = 0,$ | $m_\ell = 0$ | (univalent) |
| Electron 3: | $n = 2,$ | $\ell = 1,$ | $m_\ell = 0$ | |
| Electron 4: | $n = 2,$ | $\ell = 1,$ | $m_\ell = +1$ | |
| Electron 5: | $n = 2,$ | $\ell = 1,$ | $m_\ell = -1$ | |
| Electron 6: | $n = 3,$ | $\ell = 0,$ | $m_\ell = 0$ | (univalent) |

Each electron marked "univalent" is the first electron in a new shell. Since an electron is easily removed if it is the outermost electron in the atom, atoms with that number of electrons are univalent. They are the atoms with $Z = 1$ (hydrogen), $Z = 2$ (helium), and $Z = 6$ (carbon). Can you show that $Z = 15$ (phosphorus) would also be univalent?

**44.6 [II]** Electrons in an atom that have the same value for $\ell$ but different values for $m_\ell$ and $m_s$ are said to be in the same *subshell*. How many electrons exist in the $\ell = 3$ subshell?

Because $m_\ell$ is restricted to the values 0, $\pm 1$, $\pm 2$, $\pm 3$, and $m_s = \pm\frac{1}{2}$ only, the possibilities for $\ell = 3$ are

$$(m_\ell, m_s) = \left(0, \pm\tfrac{1}{2}\right), \left(1, \pm\tfrac{1}{2}\right), \left(-1, \pm\tfrac{1}{2}\right), \left(2, \pm\tfrac{1}{2}\right), \left(-2, \pm\tfrac{1}{2}\right), \left(3, \pm\tfrac{1}{2}\right), \left(-3, \pm\tfrac{1}{2}\right)$$

which gives 14 possibilities. Therefore, 14 electrons can exist in this subshell.

**44.7 [II]** An electron beam in an X-ray tube is accelerated through 40 kV and is incident on a tungsten target. What is the shortest wavelength emitted by the tube?

When an electron in the beam is stopped by the target, the photons emitted have an upper limit for their energy, namely, the energy of the incident electron. In this case, that energy is 40 keV. The corresponding photon has a wavelength given by

$$\lambda = (1240\text{ nm})\left(\frac{1.0\text{ eV}}{40\,000\text{ eV}}\right) = 0.031\text{ nm}$$

## SUPPLEMENTARY PROBLEMS

**44.8 [II]** If there were no $m_\ell$ quantum number, what would be the first four univalent atoms?

**44.9 [II]** Helium has a closed (completely filled) outer shell and is nonreactive because the atom does not easily lose an electron. Show why neon ($Z = 10$) is the next nonreactive element.

**44.10 [II]** It is desired to eject an electron from the $n = 1$ shell of a uranium atom ($Z = 92$) by means of the atomic photoelectric effect. Approximately what is the longest-wavelength photon capable of doing this?

**44.11 [II]** Show that the maximum number of electrons that can exist in the $\ell$th subshell is $2(2\ell + 1)$.

## ANSWERS TO SUPPLEMENTARY PROBLEMS

**44.8 [II]** H, Li, N, Al

**44.10 [II]** 0.010 8 nm

# CHAPTER 45

# Nuclei and Radioactivity

**The Nucleus** of an atom is a positively charged entity at the atom's center. Its radius is roughly $10^{-15}$ m, which is about $10^{-5}$ as large as the radius of the atom. Hydrogen is the lightest and simplest of all the atoms. Its nucleus is a single proton. All other nuclei contain both protons and neutrons. Protons and neutrons are collectively called ***nucleons***. Although the positively charged protons repel each other, the much stronger, short-range *nuclear force* (which is a manifestation of the more fundamental *strong force*) holds the nucleus together. The nuclear attractive force between nucleons decreases rapidly with particle separation and is essentially zero for nucleons more than about $5 \times 10^{-15}$ m apart.

**Nuclear Charge and Atomic Number:** Each proton within the nucleus carries a charge $+e$, whereas the neutrons carry no electromagnetic charge. If there are $Z$ protons in a nucleus, then the charge on the nucleus is $+Ze$. We call $Z$ the **atomic number** of that nucleus.

Because normal atoms are neutral electrically, the atom has $Z$ electrons outside the nucleus. These $Z$ electrons determine the chemical behavior of the atom. As a result, all atoms of the same chemical element have the same value of Z. For example, all hydrogen atoms have $Z = 1$, while all carbon atoms have $Z = 6$.

**Atomic Mass Unit** (u): A convenient mass unit used in nuclear calculations is the **atomic mass unit** (u). By definition, 1 u is exactly 1/12 of the mass of the common form of carbon atom found on the Earth. It turns out that

$$1 \text{ u} = 1.6605 \times 10^{-27} \text{ kg} = 931.494 \text{ MeV/c}^2$$

Table 45-1 lists the masses of some common particles and nuclei, as well as their charges.

**TABLE 45-1**

| Particle | Symbol | Mass, u | Charge |
|---|---|---|---|
| Proton | $p, {}_1^1\text{H}$ | 1.007 276 | $+e$ |
| Neutron | $n, {}_0^1n$ | 1.008 665 | 0 |
| Electron | $e^-, \beta^-, {}_{-1}^{0}e$ | 0.000 548 6 | $-e$ |
| Positron | $e^+, \beta^+, {}_{+1}^{0}e$ | 0.000 548 6 | $+e$ |
| Deuteron | $d, {}_1^2\text{H}$ | 2.013 55 | $+e$ |
| Alpha particle | $\alpha, {}_2^4\text{He}$ | 4.001 5 | $+2e$ |

**The Mass Number** ($A$) of an atom is equal to the number of nucleons (neutrons plus protons) in the nucleus of the atom. Because each nucleon has a mass close to 1 u, the mass number $A$ is nearly equal to the nuclear mass in atomic mass units. In addition, because the atomic electrons have such small mass, $A$ is nearly equal to the mass of the atom in atomic mass units.

**Isotopes:** The number of neutrons in the nucleus has very little effect on the chemical behavior of all but the lightest atoms. In nature, atoms of the same element (same $Z$) often exist that have unlike numbers of neutrons in their nuclei. Such atoms are called **isotopes** of each other. For example, ordinary oxygen consists of three isotopes that have mass numbers 16, 17, and 18. Each of the isotopes has $Z = 8$, or eight protons in the nucleus. Hence, these isotopes have the following numbers of neutrons in their nuclei: $16 - 8 = 8$, $17 - 8 = 9$, and $18 - 8 = 10$. It is customary to represent the isotopes in the following way: ${}^{16}_{8}\text{O}$, ${}^{17}_{8}\text{O}$, ${}^{18}_{8}\text{O}$, or simply as ${}^{16}\text{O}$, ${}^{17}\text{O}$, and ${}^{18}\text{O}$, where it is understood that oxygen always has $Z = 8$.

In keeping with this notation, we designate the nucleus having mass number $A$ and atomic number $Z$ by the symbolism

$${}^{A}_{Z}(\text{CHEMICAL SYMBOL})$$

**Binding Energies:** The mass of an atom is not equal to the sum of the masses of its component protons, neutrons, and electrons. Imagine a reaction in which free electrons, protons, and neutrons combine to form an atom; in such a reaction, you would find that the mass of the atom is *slightly less* than the combined masses of the component parts, and that a tremendous amount of energy is released when the reaction occurs. The loss in mass is exactly equal to the mass equivalent of the released energy, according to Einstein's equation $\Delta E_0 = (\Delta m)c^2$. Conversely, this same amount of energy, $\Delta E_0$ would have to be given to the atom to separate it completely into its component particles. We call $\Delta E_0$ the **binding energy** of the atom. A mass loss of $\Delta m = 1$ u is equivalent to

$$(1.66 \times 10^{-27}\ \text{kg})(2.99 \times 10^{8}\ \text{m/s})^2 = 1.49 \times 10^{-10}\ \text{J} = 931\ \text{MeV}$$

of binding energy.

The percentage "loss" of mass is different for each isotope of any element. The atomic masses of some of the lighter isotopes are given in Table 45-2. These masses are for neutral atoms and include the orbital electrons.

**TABLE 45-2**

| Neutral atom | Atomic mass, u | Neutral atom | Atomic mass, u |
|---|---|---|---|
| ${}^{1}_{1}\text{H}$ | 1.007 83 | ${}^{7}_{4}\text{Be}$ | 7.016 93 |
| ${}^{2}_{1}\text{H}$ | 2.014 10 | ${}^{9}_{4}\text{Be}$ | 9.012 19 |
| ${}^{3}_{1}\text{H}$ | 3.016 04 | ${}^{12}_{6}\text{C}$ | 12.000 00 |
| ${}^{4}_{2}\text{He}$ | 4.002 60 | ${}^{14}_{7}\text{N}$ | 14.003 07 |
| ${}^{6}_{3}\text{Li}$ | 6.015 13 | ${}^{16}_{8}\text{O}$ | 15.994 91 |
| ${}^{7}_{3}\text{Li}$ | 7.016 00 | | |

**Radioactivity:** Nuclei found in nature with $Z$ greater than that of lead, 82, are unstable or **radioactive**. Many artificially produced elements with smaller $Z$ are also radioactive. A radioactive nucleus spontaneously ejects one or more particles in the process of transforming into a different nucleus.

The stability of a radioactive nucleus against spontaneous decay is measured by its **half-life** $t_{1/2}$. The half-life is defined as the time in which half of any large sample of identical nuclei will undergo decomposition. The half-life is a fixed number for each isotope.

Radioactive decay is a random process. No matter when one begins to observe a material, only half the material will remain unchanged after a time $t_{1/2}$; after an additional time of $t_{1/2}$ only $\frac{1}{2} \times \frac{1}{2} = \frac{1}{4}$ of the material will remain unchanged. After $n$ half-lives have passed, only $\left(\frac{1}{2}\right)^n$ of the material will remain unchanged.

A simple relation exists between the number $N$ of atoms of radioactive material present and the number $\Delta N$ that will decay in a short time $\Delta t$. It is

$$\Delta N = \lambda N \Delta t$$

where $\lambda$, the **decay constant**, is related to the half-life $t_{1/2}$ through

$$\lambda t_{1/2} = 0.693$$

The decay constant has the unit of $s^{-1}$, and can be thought of as the fractional disintegration rate. The quantity $\Delta N/\Delta t$, which is the rate of disintegrations, is called the **activity** of the sample. It is equal to $\lambda N$, and therefore it steadily decreases with time. The SI unit for activity is the **becquerel (Bq)**, where 1 Bq = 1 decay/s.

**Nuclear Equations:** In a balanced equation the sum of the subscripts (atomic numbers) must be the same on the two sides of the equation. The sum of the superscripts (mass numbers) must also be the same on the two sides of the equation. Thus the equation for the primary radioactivity of radium is

$$^{226}_{88}\text{Ra} \rightarrow {}^{222}_{86}\text{Rn} + {}^{4}_{2}\text{He}$$

Many nuclear processes may be indicated by a condensed notation, in which a light bombarding particle and a light product particle are represented by symbols in parentheses between the symbols for the initial target nucleus and the final product nucleus. The symbols $n$, $p$, $d$, $\alpha$, $e^-$, and $\gamma$ are used to represent neutron, proton, deuteron ($^2_1$H), alpha, particle, electron, and gamma rays (photons), respectively. Here are three examples of corresponding long and condensed notations:

$$^{14}_{7}\text{N} + {}^{1}_{1}\text{H} \rightarrow {}^{11}_{6}\text{C} + {}^{4}_{2}\text{He} \qquad {}^{14}\text{N}(p, \alpha)^{11}\text{C}$$
$$^{27}_{13}\text{Al} + {}^{1}_{0}n \rightarrow {}^{27}_{12}\text{Mg} + {}^{1}_{1}\text{H} \qquad {}^{27}\text{Al}(n, p)^{27}\text{Mg}$$
$$^{55}_{25}\text{Mn} + {}^{2}_{1}\text{H} \rightarrow {}^{55}_{26}\text{Fe} + 2{}^{1}_{0}n \qquad {}^{55}\text{Mn}(d, 2n)^{55}\text{Fe}$$

The slow neutron is a very efficient agent in causing transmutations, since it has no positive charge and hence can approach the nucleus without being repelled. By contrast, a positively charged particle such as a proton must have a high energy to cause a transformation. Because of their small masses, even very high-energy electrons are relatively inefficient in causing nuclear transmutations.

## SOLVED PROBLEMS

**45.1 [II]** The radius of a carbon nucleus is about $3 \times 10^{-15}$ m and its mass is 12 u. Find the average density of the nuclear material. How many more times dense than water is this?

$$\rho = \frac{m}{V} = \frac{m}{4\pi r^3/3} = \frac{(12\text{ u})(1.66\times10^{-27}\text{ kg/u})}{4\pi(3\times10^{-15}\text{ m})^3/3} = 1.8\times10^{17}\text{ kg/m}^3$$

$$\frac{\rho}{\rho_{\text{water}}} = \frac{1.8\times10^{17}\text{ kg/m}^3}{1000\text{ kg/m}^3} = 2\times10^{14}$$

**45.2 [II]** In a *mass spectrograph*, the masses of ions are determined from their deflections in a magnetic field. Suppose that singly charged ions of chlorine are shot perpendicularly into a magnetic field $B = 0.15$ T with a speed of $5.0 \times 10^4$ m/s. (The speed could be measured by use of a velocity selector.) Chlorine has two major isotopes, of masses 34.97 u and 36.97 u. What would be the radii of the circular paths described by the two isotopes in the magnetic field? (See Fig. 45-1.)

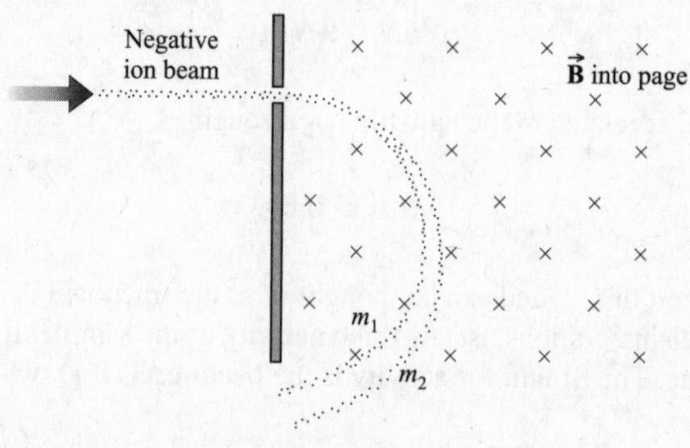


Fig. 45-1

The masses of the two isotopes are

$$m_1 = (34.97 \text{ u})(1.66 \times 10^{-27} \text{ kg/u}) = 5.81 \times 10^{-26} \text{ kg}$$
$$m_2 = (36.97 \text{ u})(1.66 \times 10^{-27} \text{ kg/u}) = 6.14 \times 10^{-26} \text{ kg}$$

Because the magnetic force $qvB$ must provide the centripetal force $mv^2/r$, we have

$$r = \frac{mv}{qB} = \frac{m(5.0 \times 10^4 \text{ m/s})}{(1.6 \times 10^{-19} \text{ C})(0.105 \text{ T})} = m(2.98 \times 10^{24} \text{ m/kg})$$

Substituting the values for $m$ found above gives the radii as 0.17 m and 0.18 m.

**45.3 [I]** How many protons, neutrons, and electrons are there in (*a*) $^3$He, (*b*) $^{12}$C, and (*c*) $^{206}$Pb?

(*a*) The atomic number of He is 2; therefore, the nucleus must contain 2 protons. Since the mass number of this isotope is 3, the sum of the protons and neutrons in the nucleus must equal 3; therefore, there is 1 neutron. The number of electrons in the atom is the same as the atomic number, 2.

(*b*) The atomic number of carbon is 6; hence, the nucleus must contain 6 protons. The number of neutrons in the nucleus is equal to $12 - 6 = 6$. The number of electrons is the same as the atomic number, 6.

(*c*) The atomic number of lead is 82; hence, there are 82 protons in the nucleus and 82 electrons in the atom. The number of neutrons is $206 - 82 = 124$.

**45.4 [II]** What is the binding energy of the atom $^{12}$C?

One atom of $^{12}$C consists of 6 protons, 6 electrons, and 6 neutrons. The mass of the uncombined protons and electrons is the same as that of six $^1$H atoms (if we ignore the very small binding energy of each proton-electron pair). The component particles may thus be considered as six $^1$H atoms and six neutrons. A mass balance may be computed as follows.

| | |
|---|---|
| Mass of six $^1$H atoms $= 6 \times 1.0078$ u | $= 6.0468$ u |
| Mass of six neutrons $= 6 \times 1.0087$ u | $= 6.0522$ u |
| Total mass of component particles | $= 12.0990$ u |
| Mass of $^{12}$C atom | $= 12.0000$ u |
| Loss in mass on forming $^{12}$C | $= 0.0990$ u |
| Binding energy $= (931 \times 0.0990)$ MeV | $= 92$ MeV |

**45.5 [II]** Cobalt-60 ($^{60}$Co) is often used as a radiation source in medicine. It has a half-life of 5.25 years. How long after a new sample is delivered will its activity have decreased (*a*) to about one-eighth its original value? (*b*) to about one-third its original value? Give your answers to two significant figures.

The activity is proportional to the number of undecayed atoms ($\Delta N/\Delta t = \lambda N$).

(*a*) In each half-life, half the remaining sample decays. Because $\frac{1}{2} \times \frac{1}{2} \times \frac{1}{2} \times \frac{1}{8}$, three half-lives, or 16 years, are required for the sample to decay to one-eighth its original strength.

(*b*) Using the fact that the material present decreased by one-half during each 5.25 years, we can plot the graph shown in Fig. 45-2. From it, we see that the sample decays to 0.33 its original value after a time of about 8.3 years.

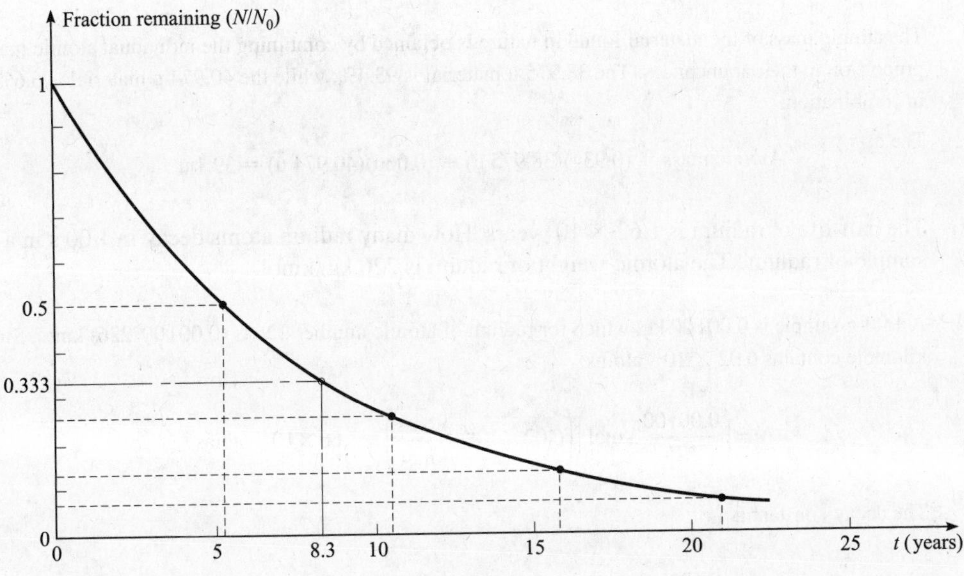


Fig. 45-2

**45.6 [II]** Solve Problem 45.5(*b*) by using the exponential function.

The curve in Fig. 45-2 is an *exponential decay curve* and it is expressed by the equation

$$\frac{N}{N_0} = e^{-\lambda t}$$

where $\lambda$ is the decay constant, and $N/N_0$ is the fraction of the original $N_0$ particles that remain undecayed after a time $t$. Inasmuch as $\lambda t_{1/2} = 0.693$, $\lambda = 0.693/t_{1/2} = 0.132/\text{year}$ and $N/N_0 = 0.333$. Thus,

$$0.333 = e^{-0.132t/\text{year}}$$

Take the natural logarithm of each side to find

$$\ln (0.333) = -0.132t/\text{year}$$

from which $t = 8.3$ years.

**45.7 [II]** For the situation described in Problems 45.5 and 45.6, what is $N/N_0$ after 20 years?

As in the previous problem, where now $\lambda = 0.132$/year

$$\frac{N}{N_0} = e^{-\lambda t} = e^{-(0.132)(20)} = e^{-2.64}$$

from which $N/N_0 = 0.071$.

In this and the previous problem, we used $t$ in years because $\lambda$ was expressed in (years)$^{-1}$. More often, $\lambda$ would be expressed in s$^{-1}$ and $t$ would be in seconds. Be careful that the same time units are used for $t$ and $\lambda$.

**45.8 [II]** Potassium found in nature contains two isotopes. One isotope constitutes 93.4 percent of the whole and has an atomic mass of 38.975 u; the other 6.6 percent has a mass of 40.974 u. Compute the atomic mass of potassium as found in nature.

The atomic mass of the material found in nature is obtained by combining the individual atomic masses in proportion to their abundances. The 38.975 u material is 93.4%, while the 40.974 u material is 6.6%. Hence, in combination:

$$\text{Atomic mass} = (0.934)(38.975\text{ u}) + (0.066)(40.974\text{ u}) = 39.1\text{ u}$$

**45.9 [III]** The half-life of radium is $1.62 \times 10^3$ years. How many radium atoms decay in 1.00 s in a 1.00 g sample of radium? The atomic weight of radium is 226 kg/kmol.

A 1.00-g sample is 0.001 00 kg, which for radium of atomic number 226 is (0.001 00/226) kmol. Since each kilomole contains $6.02 \times 10^{26}$ atoms,

$$N = \left(\frac{0.00100}{226}\text{ kmol}\right)\left(6.02 \times 10^{26}\,\frac{\text{atoms}}{\text{kmol}}\right) = 2.66 \times 10^{21}\text{ atoms}$$

The decay constant is

$$\lambda = \frac{0.693}{t_{1/2}} = \frac{0.693}{(1620\text{ y})(3.156 \times 10^7\text{ s/y})} = 1.36 \times 10^{-11}\text{ s}^{-1}$$

Then
$$\frac{\Delta N}{\Delta t} = \lambda N = (1.36 \times 10^{-11}\text{ s}^{-1})(2.66 \times 10^{21}) = 3.61 \times 10^{10}\text{ s}^{-1}$$

is the number of disintegrations per second in 1.00 g of radium.

The above result leads to the definition of the *curie* (Ci) as a unit of activity:

$$1\text{ Ci} = 3.7 \times 10^{10}\text{ disintegrations/s}$$

Because of its convenient size, we shall sometimes use the curie in subsequent problems, even though the official SI unit of activity is the becquerel.

**45.10 [III]** Technetium-99 ($^{99}_{43}$Tc) has an excited state that decays by emission of a gamma ray. The half-life of the excited state is 360 min. What is the activity, in curies, of 1.00 mg of this excited isotope?

Because we have the half-life ($t_{1/2}$) we can determine the decay constant since $\lambda t_{1/2} = 0.693$. The activity of a sample is $\lambda N$. In this case,

$$\lambda = \frac{0.693}{t_{1/2}} = \frac{0.693}{21600\ \text{s}} = 3.21 \times 10^{-5}\ \text{s}^{-1}$$

We also know that 99.0 kg of Tc contains $6.02 \times 10^{26}$ atoms. A mass $m$ will therefore contain $[m/(99.0\text{kg})](6.02 \times 10^{26})$ atoms. In our case, $m = 1.00 \times 10^{-6}$ kg, and so

$$\text{Activity} = \lambda N = (3.21 \times 10^{-5}\ \text{s}^{-1})\left(\frac{1.00 \times 10^{-6}\ \text{kg}}{99.0\ \text{kg}}\right)(6.02 \times 10^{26})$$

$$= 1.95 \times 10^{14}\ \text{s}^{-1} = 1.95 \times 10^{14}\ \text{Bq}$$

**45.11 [III]** How much energy must a bombarding proton possess to cause the reaction $^7\text{Li}(p, n)^7\text{Be}$? Give your answer to three significant figures.

The reaction is as follows:

$$^7_3\text{Li} + ^1_1\text{H} \rightarrow ^7_4\text{Be} + ^1_0n$$

where the symbols represent the *nuclei* of the atoms indicated. Because the masses listed in Table 45-2 include the masses of the atomic electrons, the appropriate number of electron masses ($m_e$) must be subtracted from the values given.

| | **Reactant mass** | | **Product mass** |
|---|---|---|---|
| $^7_3\text{Li}$ | $7.016\,00 - 3m_e$ | $^7_4\text{Be}$ | $7.016\,93 - 4m_e$ |
| $^1_1\text{H}$ | $1.007\,83 - 1m_e$ | $^1_0n$ | $1.008\,66$ |
| TOTAL | $8.023\,83 - 4m_e$ | TOTAL | $8.025\,59 - 4m_e$ |

Subtracting the total reactant mass from the total product mass gives the increase in mass as 0.001 76 u. (Notice that the electron masses cancel out. This happens frequently, but not always.)

To create this mass in the reaction, energy must have been supplied to the reactants. The energy corresponding to 0.001 76 u is $(931 \times 0.001\,76)$ MeV = 1.65 MeV. This energy is supplied as KE of the bombarding proton. The incident proton must have more than this energy because the system must possess some KE even after the reaction, so that momentum is conserved. With momentum conservation taken into account, the minimum KE that the incident particle must have can be found with the formula

$$\left(1 + \frac{m}{M}\right)(1.65)\ \text{MeV}$$

where $M$ is the mass of the target particle, and $m$ that of the incident particle. Therefore, the incident particle must have an energy of at least

$$\left(1 + \frac{1}{7}\right)(1.65)\ \text{MeV} = 1.89\ \text{MeV}$$

**45.12 [II]** Complete the following nuclear equations:

(*a*) $^{14}_7\text{N} + ^4_2\text{He} \rightarrow ^{17}_8\text{O} + ?$

(*b*) $^9_4\text{Be} + ^4_2\text{He} \rightarrow ^{12}_6\text{C} + ?$

(*c*) $^9_4\text{Be}(p, \alpha)?$

(*d*) $^{30}_{15}\text{P} \rightarrow ^{30}_{14}\text{Si} + ?$

(*e*) $^3_1\text{H} \rightarrow ^3_2\text{He} + ?$

(*f*) $^{43}_{20}\text{Ca}(\alpha,?)\,^{46}_{21}\text{Sc}$

(*a*) The sum of the subscripts on the left is $7 + 2 = 9$. The subscript of the first product on the right is 8. Hence, the second product on the right must have a subscript (net charge) of 1. Also, the sum of the superscripts on the left is $14 + 4 = 18$. The superscript of the first product is 17. Hence, the second product on the right must have a superscript (mass number) of 1. The particle with nuclear charge 1 and mass number 1 is the proton, ${}_1^1\text{H}$.

(*b*) The nuclear charge of the second product particle (its subscript) is $(4 + 2) - 6 = 0$. The mass number of the particle (its superscript) is $(9 + 4) - 12 = 1$. Hence, the particle must be the neutron, ${}_0^1n$.

(*c*) The reactants ${}_4^9\text{Be}$ and ${}_1^1\text{H}$ have a combined nuclear charge of 5 and a mass number of 10. In addition to the alpha particle, a product will be formed of charge $5 - 2 = 3$ and mass number $10 - 4 = 6$. This is ${}_3^6\text{Li}$.

(*d*) The nuclear charge of the second product particle is $15 - 14 = +1$. Its mass number is $30 - 30 = 0$. Hence, the particle must be a positron, ${}_{+1}^{0}e$.

(*e*) The nuclear charge of the second product particle is $1 - 2 = -1$. Its mass number is $3 - 3 = 0$. Hence, the particle must be a beta particle (an electron), ${}_{-1}^{0}e$.

(*f*) The reactants, ${}_{20}^{43}\text{Ca}$ and ${}_2^4\text{He}$, have a combined nuclear charge of 22 and mass number of 47. The ejected product will have charge $22 - 21 = 1$, and mass number $47 - 46 = 1$. This is a proton and should be represented in the parentheses by $p$.

*In some of these reactions a neutrino and/or a photon are emitted. We ignore them for this discussion since the charge for both are zero.* Moreover the mass of the photon is zero and the mass of each of the several neutrinos, although not zero, is negligibly small.

**45.13 [II]** Uranium-238 (${}_{92}^{238}\text{U}$) is radioactive and decays into a succession of different elements. The following particles are emitted before the nucleus reaches a stable form: $\alpha, \beta, \beta, \alpha, \alpha, \alpha, \alpha, \alpha, \beta, \beta, \alpha, \beta, \beta$, and $\alpha$ ($\beta$ stands for "beta particle," $e^-$). What is the final stable nucleus?

The original nucleus emitted 8 alpha particles and 6 beta particles. When an alpha particle is emitted, $Z$ decreases by 2, since the alpha particle carries away a charge of $+2e$. A beta particle carries away a charge of $-1e$, and so as a result the charge on the nucleus must increase to $(Z + 1)e$. We then have, for the final nucleus,

$$\text{Final } Z = 92 + 6 - (2)(8) = 82$$

$$\text{Final } A = 238 - (6)(0) - (8)(4) = 206$$

The final stable nucleus is ${}_{82}^{206}\text{Pb}$.

**45.14 [I]** The half-life of uranium-238 is about $4.5 \times 10^9$ years, and its end product is lead-206. We notice that the oldest uranium-bearing rocks on Earth contain about a 50:50 mixture of ${}^{238}\text{U}$ and ${}^{206}\text{Pb}$. Roughly, what is the age of these rocks?

Apparently about half the ${}^{238}\text{U}$ has decayed to ${}^{206}\text{Pb}$ during the existence of the rock. Hence, the rock must have been formed about 4.5 billion years ago.

**45.15 [II]** A 5.6-MeV alpha particle is shot directly at a uranium atom ($Z = 92$). About how close will it get to the center of the uranium nucleus?

At such high energies the alpha particle will easily penetrate the electron cloud and the effects of the atomic electrons can be ignored. We also assume the uranium atom to be so massive that it does not move appreciably.

Then the original KE of the alpha particle will be changed into electrostatic potential energy. This energy, for a charge $q'$ at a distance $r$ from a point charge $q$, is (Chapter 25)

$$\text{Potential energy} = q'V = k_0 \frac{qq'}{r}$$

Equating the KE of the alpha particle to this potential energy,

$$(5.6 \times 10^6 \text{ eV})(1.60 \times 10^{-19} \text{ J/eV}) = (8.99 \times 10^9) \frac{(2e)(92e)}{r}$$

where $e = 1.60 \times 10^{-19}$ C. We find from this that $r = 4.7 \times 10^{-14}$ m.

**45.16 [II]** Neon-23 beta-decays in the following way:

$$^{23}_{10}\text{Ne} \rightarrow {}^{23}_{11}\text{Na} + {}^{0}_{-1}e + {}^{0}_{0}\bar{\nu}$$

where $\bar{\nu}$ is an antineutrino, a particle with no charge and almost no mass. Depending on circumstances, the energy carried away by the antineutrino can range from zero to the maximum energy available from the reaction. Find the minimum and maximum KE that the beta particle ${}^{0}_{-1}e$ can have. Pertinent atomic masses are 22.9945 u for $^{23}$Ne, and 22.9898 u for $^{23}$Na. The mass of the beta particle is 0.00055 u.

Note that the given reaction is a *nuclear* reaction, while the masses provided are those of neutral *atoms*. To calculate the mass lost in the reaction, subtract the mass of the atomic electrons from the atomic masses given. We have the following nuclear masses:

| | Reactant mass | | Product mass |
|---|---|---|---|
| $^{23}_{10}$Ne | $22.9945 - 10m_e$ | $^{23}_{11}$Na | $22.9898 - 11m_e$ |
| | | ${}^{0}_{-1}e$ | $m_e$ |
| | | ${}^{0}_{0}\bar{\nu}$ | 0 |
| TOTAL | $22.9945 - 10m_e$ | TOTAL | $22.9898 - 10m_e$ |

which gives a mass loss of $22.9945 - 22.9898 = 0.0047$ u. Since 1.00 u corresponds to 931 MeV, this mass loss corresponds to an energy of 4.4 MeV. The beta particle and antineutrino share this energy. Hence, the energy of the beta particle can range from zero to 4.4 MeV.

**45.17 [II]** A nucleus $^{M}_{n}$P, the *parent* nucleus, decays to a *daughter* nucleus D by positron decay:

$$^{M}_{n}\text{P} \rightarrow \text{D} + {}^{0}_{+1}e + {}^{0}_{0}\nu$$

where $\nu$ is a neutrino, a particle that has nearly zero mass and zero charge. (*a*) What are the subscript and superscript for D? (*b*) Prove that the mass loss in the reaction is $M_p - M_d - 2m_e$, where $M_p$ and $M_d$ are the *atomic* masses of the parent and daughter.

(*a*) To balance the subscripts and superscripts, we must have $_{n-1}^{M}$D.

(*b*) The table of masses for the *nuclei* involved is

| | Reactant mass | | Product mass |
|---|---|---|---|
| ${}^{M}_{n}\text{P}$ | $M_p - nm_e$ | ${}^{M}_{n-1}\text{D}$ | $M_d - (n-1)m_e$ |
| | | ${}^{0}_{1}e$ | $m_e$ |
| | | ${}^{0}_{0}\nu$ | $\approx 0$ |
| TOTAL | $M_p - nm_e$ | TOTAL | $M_d - nm_e + 2m_e$ |

Subtraction gives the mass loss:

$$(M_p - nm_e) - (M_d - nm_e + 2m_e) = M_p - M_d - 2m_e$$

Notice how important it is to keep track of the electron masses in this and the previous problem.

## SUPPLEMENTARY PROBLEMS

**45.18 [I]** How many protons, neutrons, and electrons does an atom of ${}^{235}_{92}\text{U}$ possess?

**45.19 [I]** By how much does the mass of a heavy nucleus change when it emits a 4.8-MeV gamma ray?

**45.20 [II]** Find the binding energy of ${}^{107}_{47}\text{Ag}$, which has an atomic mass of 106.905 u. Give your answer to three significant figures.

**45.21 [II]** The binding energy per nucleon for elements near iron in the periodic table is about 8.90 MeV per nucleon. What is the atomic mass, including electrons, of ${}^{56}_{26}\text{Fe}$?

**45.22 [II]** What mass of ${}^{60}_{27}\text{Co}$ has an activity of 1.0 Ci? The half-life of cobalt-60 is 5.25 years.

**45.23 [II]** An experiment is done to determine the half-life of a radioactive substance that emits one beta particle for each decay process. Measurements show that an average of 8.4 beta particles are emitted each second by 2.5 mg of the substance. The atomic mass of the substance is 230. Find the half-life of the substance.

**45.24 [II]** The half-life of carbon-14 is $5.7 \times 10^3$ years. What fraction of a sample of ${}^{14}\text{C}$ will remain unchanged after a period of five half-lives?

**45.25 [II]** Cesium-124 has a half-life of 31 s. What fraction of a cesium-124 sample will remain after 0.10 h?

**45.26 [II]** A certain isotope has a half-life of 7.0 h. How many seconds does it take for 10 percent of the sample to decay?

**45.27 [II]** By natural radioactivity ${}^{238}\text{U}$ emits an $\alpha$-particle. The heavy residual nucleus is called $\text{UX}_1$. $\text{UX}_1$ in turn emits a beta particle. The resultant nucleus is called $\text{UX}_2$. Determine the atomic number and mass number for (*a*) $\text{UX}_1$ and (*b*) $\text{UX}_2$.

**45.28 [I]** Upon decaying ${}^{239}_{93}\text{Np}$ emits a beta particle. The residual heavy nucleus is also radioactive, and gives rise to ${}^{235}\text{U}$ by the radioactive process. What small particle is emitted simultaneously with the formation of uranium-235?

**45.29 [II]** Complete the following equations. (See Appendix H for a table of the elements.)

(*a*) ${}^{23}_{11}\text{Na} + {}^{4}_{2}\text{He} \rightarrow {}^{26}_{12}\text{Mg} + ?$

(*b*) ${}^{64}_{29}\text{Cu} \rightarrow {}^{0}_{+1}e + ?$

(*c*) ${}^{106}\text{Ag} \rightarrow {}^{106}\text{Cd} + ?$

(*d*) ${}^{10}_{5}\text{B} + {}^{4}_{2}\text{He} \rightarrow {}^{13}_{6}\text{N} + ?$

(*e*) ${}^{105}_{48}\text{Cd} + {}^{0}_{-1}e = \rightarrow ?$

(*f*) ${}^{238}_{92}\text{U} \rightarrow {}^{234}_{90}\text{Th} + ?$

**45.30 [II]** Complete the notations for the following processes.

(*a*) ${}^{24}\text{Mg}(d, \alpha)?$

(*b*) ${}^{26}\text{Mg}(d, p)?$

(*c*) ${}^{40}\text{Ar}(\alpha, p)?$

(*d*) ${}^{12}\text{C}(d, n)?$

(*e*) ${}^{130}\text{Te}(d, 2n)?$

(*f*) ${}^{55}\text{Mn}(n, \gamma)?$

(*g*) ${}^{59}\text{Co}(n, \alpha)?$

**45.31 [II]** How much energy is released during reactions (*a*) ${}^{1}_{1}\text{H} + {}^{7}_{3}\text{Li} \rightarrow 2{}^{4}_{2}\text{He}$ and (*b*) ${}^{3}_{1}\text{H} + {}^{2}_{1}\text{H} \rightarrow {}^{4}_{2}\text{He} + {}^{1}_{0}n$?

**45.32 [II]** In the ${}^{14}\text{N}(n, p){}^{14}\text{C}$ reaction, the proton is ejected with an energy of 0.600 MeV. Very slow neutrons are used. Calculate the mass of the ${}^{14}\text{C}$ atom.

## ANSWERS TO SUPPLEMENTARY PROBLEMS

**45.18 [I]** 92, 143, 92

**45.19 [I]** $5.2 \times 10^{-3}$ u $= 8.6 \times 10^{-30}$ kg

**45.20 [II]** 915 eV

**45.21 [II]** 55.9 u

**45.22 [II]** $8.8 \times 10^{-7}$ kg

**45.23 [II]** $1.7 \times 10^{10}$ years

**45.24 [II]** 0.031

**45.25 [II]** 0.000 32

**45.26 [II]** $3.8 \times 10^{3}$ s

**45.27 [II]** (*a*) 90, 234; (*b*) 91, 234

**45.28 [I]** alpha particle

**45.29 [II]** (*a*) ${}^{1}_{1}$H; (*b*) ${}^{64}_{28}$Ni; (*c*) ${}^{0}_{-1}e$; (*d*) ${}^{1}_{0}n$; (*e*) ${}^{105}_{47}$Ag; (*f*) ${}^{4}_{2}$He

**45.30 [I]** (*a*) $^{22}$Na; (*b*) $^{27}$Mg; (*c*) $^{43}$K; (*d*) $^{13}$N; (*e*) $^{130}$I; (*f*) $^{56}$Mn; (*g*) $^{56}$Mn

**45.31 [II]** (*a*) 17.4 MeV; (*b*) 17.6 MeV

**45.32 [II]** 14.003 u

# CHAPTER 46

# Applied Nuclear Physics

**Nuclear Binding Energies** differ from the atomic binding energies discussed in Chapter 45 by the relatively small amount of energy that binds the electrons to the nucleus. The **binding energy per nucleon** (the total energy liberated on assembling the nucleus, divided by the number of protons and neutrons) turns out to be largest for nuclei near $Z = 30$ ($A = 60$). Hence, the nuclei at the two ends of the table of elements can liberate energy if they are in some way transformed into middle-sized nuclei.

**Fission Reaction:** A very large nucleus, such as the nucleus of the uranium atom, liberates energy as it is split into two or three middle-sized nuclei. Such a **fission reaction** can be induced by striking a large nucleus with a low- or moderate-energy neutron. The fission reaction produces additional neutrons, which, in turn, can cause further fission reactions and more neutrons. If the number of neutrons remains constant or increases in time, the process is a self-perpetuating *chain reaction.*

**Fusion Reaction:** In a ***fusion reaction***, small nuclei, such as those of hydrogen or helium, are joined together to form more massive nuclei, thereby liberating energy.

This reaction is usually difficult to initiate and sustain because the nuclei must be fused together even though they repel each other with the Coulomb force. Only when the particles move toward each other with very high energies do they come close enough for the strong force to bind them together. The fusion reaction can occur in stars because of the high densities and high thermal energies of the particles in these extremely hot objects.

**Radiation Dose** ($D$) is defined as the amount of energy imparted to a unit mass of substance via the absorption of ionizing radiation. A material receives a dose of 1 **gray** (Gy) when 1 J of radiation is absorbed in each kilogram of the material:

$$D = \frac{\text{Energy absorbed in J}}{\text{Mass of absorber in kg}}$$

so a gray is 1 J/kg. Although the gray is the SI unit for radiation dose, another unit is widely used. It is the **rad** (rd), where 1 rd = 0.01 Gy.

**Radiation Damage Potential:** Each type (and energy) of radiation causes its own characteristic degree of damage to living tissue. The damage also varies among types of tissue. The potential damaging effects of a specific type of radiation are expressed as the **quality factor** $Q$ of that radiation. Arbitrarily, the damage potential is determined relative to the damage caused by 200-keV X-rays:

$$Q = \frac{\text{Biological effect of 1 Gy of the radiation}}{\text{Biological effect of 1 Gy of 200-keV X-rays}}$$

For example, if 10 Gy of a particular radiation will cause 7 times more damage than 10 Gy of 200-keV X-rays, then the $Q$ for that radiation is 7. Quite often, the unit RBE (relative biological effectiveness) is used in place of quality factor. The two are equivalent.

**Effective Radiation Dose** ($H$), also called the ***equivalent dose***, is the radiation dose modified to express radiation damage to living tissue. The SI unit of $H$ is the sievert (Sv). It is defined as the product of the dose in grays and the quality factor of the radiation:

$$H = QD$$

For example, suppose a certain type of tissue is subjected to a dose of 5 Gy of a radiation for which the quality factor is 3. Then the dose in sieverts is $3 \times 5 = 15$ Sv. Note that the units of $Q$ are Sv/Gy.

While the sievert is the SI unit, another unit, the *rem* (radiation equivalent, man), is very widely used. The two are related through 1 rem = 0.01 Sv.

**High-Energy Accelerators:** Charged particles can be accelerated to high energies by causing them to follow a circular path repeatedly. Each time a particle (of charge $q$) circles the path, it is caused to fall through a potential difference $V$. After $n$ trips around the path, its energy is $q(nV)$.

Magnetic fields are used to supply the centripetal force required to keep the particle moving in a circle. Equating magnetic force $qvB$ to centripetal force $mv^2/r$ gives

$$mv = qBr$$

In this expression, $m$ is the mass of the particle that is traveling with speed $v$ on a circle of radius $r$ perpendicular to a magnetic field $B$.

**The Momentum of A Particle** is related to its KE. From Chapter 41, since the total energy of a particle is the sum of its kinetic energy plus its rest energy, $E = KE + mc^2$, and with $E^2 = m^2c^4 + p^2c^2$, it follows that

$$KE = \sqrt{p^2c^2 + m^2c^4} - mc^2$$

## SOLVED PROBLEMS

**46.1 [I]** The binding energy per nucleon for $^{238}U$ is about 7.6 MeV, while it is about 8.6 MeV for nuclei of half that mass. If a $^{238}U$ nucleus were to split into two equal-size nuclei, about how much energy would be released in the process?

There are 238 nucleons involved. Each nucleon will release about $8.6 - 7.6 = 1.0$ MeV of energy when the nucleus undergoes fission. The total energy liberated is therefore about 238 MeV or $2.4 \times 10^2$ MeV.

**46.2 [II]** What is the binding energy per nucleon for the $^{238}_{92}U$ nucleus? The *atomic* mass of $^{238}U$ is 238.050 79 u; also $m_p = 1.007\,276$ u and $m_n = 1.008\,665$ u.

The mass of 92 free protons plus $238 - 92 = 146$ free neutrons is

$$(92)(1.007\,276 \text{ u}) + (146)(1.008\,665 \text{ u}) = 239.934\,48 \text{ u}$$

The mass of the $^{238}U$ *nucleus* is

$$238.050\,79 - 92m_e = 238.050\,79 - (92)(0.000\,549) = 238.000\,28 \text{ u}$$

The mass lost in assembling the nucleus is then

$$\Delta m = 239.934\,48 - 238.000\,28 = 1.934\,2 \text{ u}$$

Since 1.00 u corresponds to 931 MeV,

$$\text{Binding energy} = (1.934\,2 \text{ u})(931 \text{ MeV/u}) = 1800 \text{ MeV}$$

and
$$\text{Binding energy per nucleon} = \frac{1800 \text{ MeV}}{238} = 7.57 \text{ MeV}$$

**46.3 [III]** When an atom of $^{235}$U undergoes fission in a reactor, about 200 MeV of energy is liberated. Suppose that a reactor using uranium-235 has an output of 700 MW and is 20 percent efficient. (*a*) How many uranium atoms does it consume in one day? (*b*) What mass of uranium does it consume each day?

(*a*) Each fission yields

$$200 \text{ MeV} = (200 \times 10^6)(1.6 \times 10^{-19}) \text{ J}$$

of energy. Only 20 percent of this is utilized efficiently, and so

$$\text{Usable energy per fission} = (200 \times 10^6)(1.6 \times 10^{-19})(0.20) = 6.4 \times 10^{-12} \text{ J}$$

Because the reactor's usable output is $700 \times 10^6$ J/s, the number of fissions required per second is

$$\text{Fissions/s} = \frac{7 \times 10^8 \text{ J/s}}{6.4 \times 10^{-12} \text{ J}} = 1.1 \times 10^{20} \text{ s}^{-1}$$

and
$$\text{Fissions/day} = (86\,400 \text{ s/d})(1.1 \times 10^{20} \text{ s}^{-1}) = 9.5 \times 10^{24} \text{ d}^{-1}$$

(*b*) There are $6.02 \times 10^{26}$ atoms in 235 kg of uranium-235. Therefore, the mass of uranium-235 consumed in one day is

$$\text{Mass} = \left(\frac{9.5 \times 10^{24}}{6.02 \times 10^{26}}\right)(235 \text{ kg}) = 3.7 \text{ kg}$$

**46.4 [III]** Neutrons produced by fission reactions must be slowed by collisions with moderator nuclei before they are effective in causing further fissions. Suppose an 800-keV neutron loses 40 percent of its energy on each collision. How many collisions are required to decrease its energy to 0.040 eV? (This is the average thermal energy of a gas particle at 35 °C.)

After one collision, the neutron energy is down to (0.6)(800 keV). After two, it is (0.6)(0.6)(800 keV); after three, it is $(0.6)^3$(800 keV). Therefore, after $n$ collisions, the neutron energy is $(0.6)^n$(800 keV). We want $n$ large enough so that

$$(0.6)^n (8 \times 10^5 \text{ eV}) = 0.040 \text{ eV}$$

Taking the logarithms of both sides of this equation yields

$$n \log_{10} 0.6 + \log_{10}(8 \times 10^5) = \log_{10} 0.04$$
$$(n)(-0.222) + 5.903 = -1.398$$

from which we find $n$ to be 32.9. So 33 collisions are required.

**46.5 [II]** To examine the structure of a nucleus, pointlike particles with de Broglie wavelengths below about $10^{-16}$ m must be used. Through how large a potential difference must an electron fall to have this wavelength? Assume the electron is moving in a relativistic way.

The KE and momentum of the electron are related through

$$\text{KE} = \sqrt{p^2c^2 + m^2c^4} - mc^2$$

Because the de Broglie wavelength is $\lambda = h/p$, this equation becomes

$$\text{KE} = \sqrt{\left(\frac{hc}{\lambda}\right)^2 + m^2c^4} - mc^2$$

Using $\lambda = 10^{-16}$ m, $h = 6.63 \times 10^{-34}$ J · s, and $m = 9.1 \times 10^{-31}$ kg, we find that

$$\text{KE} = 1.99 \times 10^{-9}\ \text{J} = 1.24 \times 10^{10}\ \text{eV}$$

The electron must be accelerated through a potential difference of about $10^{10}$ eV.

**46.6 [III]** The following fusion reaction takes place in the Sun and furnishes much of its energy:

$$4{}^1_1\text{H} \rightarrow 4{}^4_2\text{He} + 2{}^{\ 0}_{+1}e + \text{energy}$$

where ${}^{\ 0}_{+1}e$ is a positron electron. How much energy is released as 1.00 kg of hydrogen is consumed? The masses of ${}^1$H, ${}^4$He, and ${}^{\ 0}_{+1}e$ are, respectively, 1.007825, 4.002604, and 0.000549 u, where atomic electrons are included in the first two values.

Ignoring the electron binding energy, the mass of the reactants, 4 protons, is 4 times the atomic mass of hydrogen (${}^1$H), less the mass of 4 electrons:

$$\begin{aligned}\text{Reactant Mass} &= (4)(1.007825\ \text{u}) - 4m_e \\ &= 4.031300\ \text{u} - 4m_e\end{aligned}$$

where $m_e$ is the mass of the electron (or positron). The reaction products have a combined mass

$$\begin{aligned}\text{Product mass} &= (\text{Mass of } {}^4_2\text{He nucleus}) + 2m_e \\ &= (4.002604\ \text{u} - 2m_e) + 2m_e \\ &= 4.002604\ \text{u}\end{aligned}$$

The mass loss is therefore

$$(\text{Reactant mass}) - (\text{Product mass}) = (4.0313\ \text{u} - 4m_e) - 4.0026\ \text{u}$$

Substituting $m_e = 0.000549$ u gives the mass loss as 0.0265 u.

But 1.00 kg of ${}^1$H contains $6.02 \times 10^{26}$ atoms. For each four atoms that undergo fusion, 0.0265 u is lost. The mass lost when 1.00 kg undergoes fusion is therefore

$$\begin{aligned}\text{Mass loss/kg} &= (0.0265\ \text{u})(6.02 \times 10^{26}/4) = 3.99 \times 10^{24}\ \text{u} \\ &= (3.99 \times 10^{24}\ \text{u})(1.66 \times 10^{-27}\ \text{kg/u}) = 0.00663\ \text{kg}\end{aligned}$$

Then, from the Einstein relation,

$$\Delta\text{E} = (\Delta m)c^2 = (0.00663\ \text{kg})(2.998 \times 10^8\ \text{m/s})^2 = 5.96 \times 10^{14}\ \text{J}$$

**46.7 [III]** Lithium hydride, LiH, has been proposed as a possible nuclear fuel. The nuclei to be used and the reaction involved are as follows:

$$\begin{array}{ccccc} {}^6_3\text{Li} & + & {}^2_1\text{H} & \rightarrow & 2{}^4_2\text{He} \\ 6.01513 & & 2.01410 & & 4.00260 \end{array}$$

the listed masses being those of the neutral atoms. Calculate the expected power production, in megawatts, associated with the consumption of 1.00 g of LiH per day. Assume 100 percent efficiency.

Ignoring the electron binding energies, the change in mass for the reaction must be computed first:

| | Reactant mass | | Product mass |
|---|---|---|---|
| $^{6}_{3}Li$ | $6.015\,13\text{ u} - 3m_e$ | $2\,^{4}_{2}He$ | $2(4.002\,60\text{ u} - 2m_e)$ |
| $^{2}_{1}H$ | $2.014\,10\text{ u} - 1m_e$ | | |
| TOTAL | $8.029\,23\text{ u} - 4m_e$ | TOTAL | $8.005\,20\text{ u} - 4m_e$ |

We find the loss in mass by subtracting the product mass from the reactant mass. In the process, the electron masses drop out and the mass loss is found to be 0.024 03 u.

The fractional loss in mass is $0.024\,0/8.029 = 2.99 \times 10^{-3}$. Therefore, when 1.00 g reacts, the mass loss is

$$(2.99 \times 10^{-3})(1.00 \times 10^{-3}\text{ kg}) = 2.99 \times 10^{-6}\text{ kg}$$

This corresponds to an energy of

$$\Delta E = (\Delta m)c^2 = (2.99 \times 10^{-6}\text{ kg})(2.998 \times 10^{8}\text{ m/s})^2 = 2.687 \times 10^{11}\text{ J}$$

Then $$\text{Power} = \frac{\text{Energy}}{\text{Time}} = \frac{2.687 \times 10^{11}\text{ J}}{86\,400\text{ s}} = 3.11\text{ MW}$$

**46.8 [II]** Cosmic rays bombard the $CO_2$ in the atmosphere and, by nuclear reaction, cause the formation of the radioactive carbon isotope $^{14}_{6}C$. This isotope has a half-life of 5730 years. It mixes into the atmosphere uniformly and is taken up in plants as they grow. After a plant dies, the $^{14}C$ decays over the ensuing years. How old is a piece of wood that has a $^{14}C$ content which is only 9 percent as large as the average $^{14}C$ content of new-grown wood?

During the years, the $^{14}C$ has decayed to 0.090 its original value. Hence (see Problem 45.6),

$$\frac{N}{N_0} = e^{-\lambda t} \quad \text{becomes} \quad 0.090 = e^{-0.693t/(5730\text{ years})}$$

After taking the natural logarithms of both sides,

$$\ln 0.090 = \frac{-0.693t}{5730\text{ years}}$$

from which $$t = \left(\frac{5730\text{ years}}{-0.693}\right)(-2.41) = 1.99 \times 10^{4}\text{ years}$$

The piece of wood is about 20 000 years old.

**46.9 [III]** Iodine-131 has a half-life of about 8.0 days. When consumed in food, it localizes in the thyroid. Suppose 7.0 percent of the $^{131}I$ localizes in the thyroid and that 20 percent of its disintegrations are detected by counting the emitted gamma rays. How much $^{131}I$ must be ingested to yield a thyroid count rate of 50 counts per second?

Because only 20 percent of the disintegrations are counted, there must be a total of 50/20% or 50/0.20 = 250 disintegrations per second, which is what $\Delta N/\Delta t$ is. From Chapter 45,

$$\frac{\Delta N}{\Delta t} = \lambda N = \frac{0.693N}{t_{1/2}} \quad \text{and so} \quad 250\text{ s}^{-1} = \frac{0.693N}{(8.0\text{ d})(3600\text{ s/h})(24\text{ h/d})}$$

from which $N = 2.49 \times 10^{8}$.

However, this is only 7.0 percent of the ingested $^{131}I$. Hence the number of ingested atoms is $N/0.070 = 3.56 \times 10^{9}$. And, since 1.00 kmol of $^{131}I$ is approximately 131 kg, this number of atoms represents

$$\left(\frac{3.56 \times 10^{9}\text{ atoms}}{6.02 \times 10^{26}\text{ atoms/kmol}}\right)(131\text{ kg/kmol}) = 7.8 \times 10^{-16}\text{ kg}$$

which is the mass of $^{131}I$ that must be ingested.

**46.10 [II]** A beam of gamma rays has a cross-sectional area of 2.0 cm$^2$ and carries $7.0 \times 10^8$ photons through the cross section each second. Each photon has an energy of 1.25 MeV. The beam passes through a 0.75 cm thickness of flesh ($\rho = 0.95$ g/cm$^3$) and loses 5.0 percent of its intensity in the process. What is the average dose (in Gy and in rd) applied to the flesh each second?

The dose in this case is the energy absorbed per kilogram of flesh. Since 5.0% of the intensity is absorbed,

$$\text{Number of photons absorbed/s} = (7.0 \times 10^8\ \text{s}^{-1})(0.050) = 3.5 \times 10^7\ \text{s}^{-1}$$

and each such photon carries an energy of 1.25 MeV. Hence,

$$\text{Energy absorbed/s} = (3.5 \times 10^7\ \text{s}^{-1})(1.25\ \text{MeV}) = 4.4 \times 10^7\ \text{MeV/s}$$

We need the mass of flesh in which this energy was absorbed. The beam was delivered to a region of area 2.0 cm$^2$ and thickness 0.75 cm. Thus,

$$\text{Mass} = \rho V = (0.95\ \text{g/cm}^3)\ [(2.0\ \text{cm}^2)(0.75\ \text{cm})] = 1.43\ \text{g}$$

Keeping in mind that 1rd = 0.01 Gy,

$$\text{Dose/s} = \frac{\text{Energy/s}}{\text{Mass}} = \frac{(4.4 \times 10^7\ \text{MeV/s})\ (1.6 \times 10^{-13}\ \text{J/MeV})}{1.43 \times 10^{-3}\ \text{kg}} = 4.9\ \text{mGy/s} = 0.49\ \text{rd/s}$$

**46.11 [II]** A beam of alpha particles passes through flesh and deposits 0.20 J of energy in each kilogram of flesh. The $Q$ for these particles is 12 Sv/Gy. Find the dose in Gy and rd, as well as the effective dose in Sv and rem.

Recall that $H = QD$ where

$$D = \text{Dose} = \frac{\text{Absorbed energy}}{\text{Mass}} = 0.20\ \text{J/kg} = 0.20\ \text{Gy} = 20\ \text{rd}$$

$$\text{Hence, } H = \text{Effective dose} = Q(\text{dose}) = (12\ \text{Sv/Gy})(0.20\ \text{Gy}) = 2.4\ \text{Sv} = 2.4 \times 10^2\ \text{rem}$$

**46.12 [III]** A tumor on a person's leg has a mass of 3.0 g. What is the minimum activity a radiation source can have if it is to furnish a dose of 10 Gy to the tumor in 14 min? Assume each disintegration within the source, on the average, provides an energy 0.70 MeV to the tumor.

A dose of 10 Gy corresponds to 10 J of radiation energy being deposited per kilogram. Since the tumor has a mass of 0.0030 kg, the energy required for a 10 Gy dose is (0.0030 kg)(10 J/kg) = 0.030 J.

Each disintegration provides 0.70 MeV, which in joules is

$$(0.70 \times 10^6\ \text{eV})(1.60 \times 10^{-19}\ \text{J/eV}) = 1.12 \times 10^{-13}\ \text{J}$$

A dose of 10 Gy requires that an energy of 0.030 J be delivered. That total energy divided by the energy per disintegration, yields the number of disintegrations:

$$\frac{0.030\ \text{J}}{1.12 \times 10^{-13}\ \text{J/disintegration}} = 2.68 \times 10^{11}\ \text{disintegrations}$$

They are to occur in 14 min (or 840 s), and so the disintegration rate is

$$\frac{2.68 \times 10^{11}}{840\ \text{s}}\ \text{disintegrations} = 3.2 \times 10^8\ \text{disintegrations/s.}$$

Hence, the source activity must be at least $3.2 \times 10^8$ Bq. Since 1 Ci = $3.70 \times 10^{10}$ Bq, the source activity must be at least 8.6 mCi.

**46.13 [II]** A beam of 5.0 MeV alpha particles ($q = 2e$) has a cross-sectional area of 1.50 cm². It is incident on flesh ($\rho = 950\ \mathrm{kg/m^3}$) and penetrates to a depth of 0.70 mm. (*a*) What dose (in Gy) does the beam provide to the flesh in a time of 3.0 s? (*b*) What effective dose does it provide? Assume the beam to carry a current of $2.50 \times 10^{-9}$ A and to have $Q = 14$.

Using the current, find the number of particles deposited in the flesh in 3.0 s, keeping in mind that for each particle $q = 2e$:

$$\text{Number in 3.0 s} = \frac{It}{q} = \frac{(2.50\times10^{-9}\ \mathrm{C/s})\,(3.0\ \mathrm{s})}{3.2\times10^{-19}\ \mathrm{C}} = 2.34\times10^{10}\ \text{particles}$$

Each 5.0-MeV alpha particle deposits an energy of $(5.0 \times 10^6\ \mathrm{eV})(1.60 \times 10^{-19}\ \mathrm{J/eV}) = 8.0 \times 10^{-13}$ J. In 3.0 s a total energy of $2.34 \times 10^{10}$ particles) $(8.0 \times 10^{-13}$ J/particle) is deposited. And it is delivered to a volume of area 1.50 cm² and thickness 0.70 mm. Therefore,

$$\text{Dose} = \frac{\text{Energy}}{\text{Mass}} = \frac{(2.34\times10^{10})\,(8.0\times10^{-13}\ \mathrm{J})}{(950\ \mathrm{kg/m^3})\,(0.070\times1.5\times10^{-6}\ \mathrm{m^3})} = 188\ \mathrm{Gy} = 1.9\times10^2\ \mathrm{Gy}$$

Effective dose = $Q$(dose) = (14)(188) = $2.6 \times 10^3$ Sv

## SUPPLEMENTARY PROBLEMS

**46.14 [II]** Consider the following fission reaction:

$$\underset{1.0087}{{}^{1}_{0}n} + \underset{235.0439}{{}^{235}_{92}\mathrm{U}} \rightarrow \underset{137.9050}{{}^{138}_{56}\mathrm{Ba}} + \underset{92.9060}{{}^{93}_{41}\mathrm{Nb}} + \underset{1.0087}{5\,{}^{1}_{0}n} + \underset{0.00055}{5\,{}^{0}_{-1}e}$$

where the neutral atomic masses are given. How much energy is released when (*a*) 1 atom undergoes this type of fission, and (*b*) 1.0 kg of atoms undergoes fission?

**46.15 [II]** It is proposed to use the nuclear fusion reaction

$$\underset{2.014\,102}{2\,{}^{2}_{1}\mathrm{H}} \rightarrow \underset{4.002\,604}{{}^{4}_{2}\mathrm{He}}$$

to produce industrial power (neutral atomic masses are given). If the output is to be 150 MW and the energy of the reaction will be used with 30 percent efficiency, how many grams of deuterium fuel will be needed per day?

**46.16 [II]** One of the most promising fusion reactions for power generation involves deuterium ($^2$H) and tritium ($^3$H):

$$\underset{2.01410}{{}^{2}_{1}\mathrm{H}} + \underset{3.016\,05}{{}^{3}_{1}\mathrm{H}} \rightarrow \underset{4.00260}{{}^{4}_{2}\mathrm{He}} + \underset{1.008\,67}{{}^{1}_{0}n}$$

where the atomic masses including electrons are as given. How much energy is produced when 2.0 kg of $^2$H fuses with 3.0 kg of $^3$H to form $^4$He?

**46.17 [I]** What is the average KE of a neutron at the center of the Sun, where the temperature is about $10^7$ K? Give your answer to two significant figures.

**46.18 [II]** Find the energy released when two deuterons ($^2_1$H, atomic mass = 2.014 10 u) fuse to form $^3_2$He (atomic mass = 3.016 03 u) with the release of a neutron. Give your answer to three significant figures.

**46.19 [II]** The tar in an ancient tar pit has a $^{14}$C activity that is only about 4.00 percent of that found for new wood of the same density. What is the approximate age of the tar?

**46.20 [II]** Rubidium-87 has a half-life of $4.9 \times 10^{10}$ years and decays to strontium-87, which is stable. In an ancient rock, the ratio of $^{87}$Sr to $^{87}$Rb is 0.005 0. If we assume all the strontium came from rubidium decay, about how old is the rock? Repeat if the ratio is 0.210.

**46.21 [II]** The luminous dial of an old watch gives off 130 fast electrons each minute. Assume that each electron has an energy of 0.50 MeV and deposits that energy in a volume of skin that is 2.0 cm$^2$ in area and 0.20 cm thick. Find the dose (in both Gy and rd) that the volume experiences in 1.0 day. Take the density of skin to be 900 kg/m$^3$.

**46.22 [II]** An alpha-particle beam enters a charge collector and is measured to carry $2.0 \times 10^{-14}$ C of charge into the collector each second. The beam has a cross-sectional area of 150 mm$^2$, and it penetrates human skin to a depth of 0.14 mm. Each particle has an initial energy of 4.0 MeV. The $Q$ for such particles is about 15. What effective dose, in Sv and in rem, does a person's skin receive when exposed to this beam for 20 s? Take $\rho = 900$ kg/m$^3$ for skin.

## ANSWERS TO SUPPLEMENTARY PROBLEMS

**46.14 [II]** (*a*) 182 MeV; (*b*) $7.5 \times 10^{13}$ J

**46.15 [II]** 75 g/day

**46.16 [II]** $1.7 \times 10^{15}$ J

**46.17 [I]** 1.3 keV

**46.18 [II]** 3.27 MeV

**46.19 [II]** $26.6 \times 10^3$ years

**46.20 [II]** $3.5 \times 10^8$ years, $1.35 \times 10^{10}$ years

**46.21 [II]** 42 $\mu$Gy, 4.2 mrd

**46.22 [II]** 0.63 Sv, 63 rem

# Appendix A

# Significant Figures

**Introduction:** The numerical value of every measurement is an approximation. Consider that the length of an object is recorded as 15.7 cm. By convention, this means that the length was measured to the *nearest* tenth of a centimeter and that its exact value lies between 15.65 and 15.75 cm. If this measurement were exact to the nearest hundredth of a centimeter, it would have been recorded as 15.70 cm. The value 15.7 cm represents *three significant figures* (1, 5, 7), while the value 15.70 represents *four significant figures* (1, 5, 7, 0). A significant figure is one that is known to be reasonably reliable.

Similarly, a recorded mass of 3.4062 kg means that the mass was determined to the nearest tenth of a gram and represents five significant figures (3, 4, 0, 6, 2), the last figure (2) being reasonably correct and guaranteeing the certainty of the preceding four figures.

**Zeros** may be significant or they may merely serve to locate the decimal point. We will take zeros to the left of the normal position of the decimal point (in numbers like 100, 2500, 40, etc.) to be significant. For instance, the statement that a body weighs 9800 N will be understood to mean that we know the weight to the nearest newton: there are four significant figures here. Alternatively, if it was weighed to the nearest hundred newtons, the weight contains only two significant figures (9, 8) and may be written exponentially as $9.8 \times 10^3$ N. If it was weighed to the nearest ten newtons, it should be written as $9.80 \times 10^3$ N, displaying three significant figures. If the object was weighed to the nearest newton, the weight can also be written as $9.800 \times 10^3$ N (four significant figures). Of course, if a zero stands between two significant figures, it is itself significant. Zeros to the immediate right of the decimal are significant only when there is a nonzero figure to the left of the decimal. Thus, the numbers 0.001, 0.0010, 0.00100, and 1.001 have one, two, three, and four significant figures, respectively.

**Rounding Off:** A number is rounded off to the desired number of significant figures by dropping one or more digits to the right. When the first digit dropped is less than 5, the last digit retained should remain unchanged; when it is 5 or more, 1 is added to the last digit retained.

**Addition and Subtraction:** The result of adding or subtracting should be rounded off, so as to retain digits only as far as the first column containing estimated figures. (Remember that the last significant figure is estimated.) In other words, the answer should have the same number of figures to the right of the decimal point as does the least precisely known number being added or subtracted.

**Examples:** Add the following quantities expressed in meters.

| (*a*) | (*b*) | (*c*) | (*d*) |
|---|---|---|---|
| 25.340 | 58.0 | 4.20 | 415.5 |
| 5.465 | 0.0038 | 1.6523 | 3.64 |
| 0.322 | 0.00001 | 0.015 | 0.238 |
| 31.127 m (*Ans.*) | 58.00381 | 5.8673 | 419.378 |
| | = 58.0 m (*Ans.*) | = 5.87 m (*Ans.*) | =419.4 m (*Ans.*) |

**Multiplication And Division:** Here the result should be rounded off to contain only as many significant figures as are contained in the least exact factor.

There are some exceptional cases, however. Consider the division $9.84 \div 9.3 = 1.06$, to three places. By the rule given above, the answer should be 1.1 (two significant figures). However, a difference of 1 in the last place of 9.3 ($9.3 \pm 0.1$) results in an error of about 1 percent, while a difference of 1 in the last place of 1.1 ($1.1 \pm 0.1$) yields an error of roughly 10 percent. Thus, the answer 1.1 is of much lower percentage accuracy than 9.3. Hence, in this case the answer should be 1.06, since a difference of 1 in the last place of the least exact factor used in the calculation (9.3) yields a percentage of error about the same (about 1 percent) as a difference of 1 in the last place of 1.06 ($1.06 \pm 0.01$). Similarly, $0.92 \times 1.13 = 1.04$. We shall not worry about such exceptions.

**Trigonometric Functions:** As a rule, the values of sines, cosines, tangents, and so forth should have the same number of significant figures as their arguments. For example, $\sin 35° = 0.57$, whereas $\sin 35.0° = 0.574$.

## EXERCISES

**1 [I]** How many significant figures are given in the following quantities?

| | | | | | |
|---|---|---|---|---|---|
| (*a*) | 454 g | (*e*) | 0.0353 m | (*i*) | $1.118 \times 10^{-3}$ V |
| (*b*) | 2.2 N | (*f*) | 1.0080 hr | (*j*) | 1030 kg/m$^3$ |
| (*c*) | 2.205 N | (*g*) | 14.0 A | (*k*) | 125000 N |
| (*d*) | 0.3937 s | (*h*) | $9.3 \times 10^7$ km | | |

**2 [I]** Add:

| (*a*) | (*b*) | (*c*) | (*d*) |
|---|---|---|---|
| 703 h | 18.425 cm | 0.003 5 s | 4.0 N |
| 7 h | 7.21 cm | 0.097 s | 0.632 N |
| 0.66 h | 5.0 cm | 0.225 s | 0.148 N |

**3 [I]** Subtract:

| (*a*) | (*b*) | (*c*) |
|---|---|---|
| 7.26 J | 562.4 m | 34 kg |
| 0.2 J | 16.8 m | 0.2 kg |

**4 [I]** Multiply:

(*a*) $2.21 \times 0.3$ (*d*) $107.88 \times 0.610$

(*b*) $72.4 \times 0.084$ (*e*) $12.4 \times 84.0$

(*c*) $2.02 \times 4.113$ (*f*) $72.4 \times 8.6$

**5[I]** Divide: (*a*) $\dfrac{97.52}{2.54}$ (*b*) $\dfrac{14.28}{0.714}$ (*c*) $\dfrac{0.032}{0.004}$ (*d*) $\dfrac{9.80}{9.30}$

## ANSWERS TO EXERCISES

**1 [I]**

(*a*) 3 (*e*) 3 (*i*) 4

(*b*) 2 (*f*) 5 (*j*) 4

(*c*) 4 (*g*) 3 (*k*) 6

(*d*) 4 (*h*) 2

**2 [I]** (*a*) 711 h, (*b*) 30.6 cm, (*c*) 0.326 s, (*d*) 4.8 N

**3 [I]** (*a*) 7.1 J, (*b*) 545.6 m, (*c*) 34 kg

**4 [I]**

(*a*) 0.7 (*d*) 65.8

(*b*) 6.1 (*e*) $1.04 \times 10^3$

(*c*) 8.31 (*f*) $6.2 \times 10^2$

**5 [I]** (*a*) 38.4, (*b*) 20.0, (*c*) 8, (*d*) 1.05

# Trigonometry Needed for College Physics

**Functions of An Acute Angle:** The trigonometric functions most often used are the sine, cosine, and tangent. It is convenient to put the definitions of the functions of an acute angle in terms of the sides of a right triangle.

In any right triangle: The **sine** of either acute angle is equal to the length of the side opposite that angle divided by the length of the hypotenuse. The **cosine** of either acute angle is equal to the length of the side adjacent to that angle divided by the length of the hypotenuse. The **tangent** of either acute angle is equal to the length of the side opposite that angle divided by the length of the side adjacent to that angle.

$$\sin\theta = \frac{\text{opposite}}{\text{hypotenuse}} = \frac{B}{C} \qquad \sin\phi = \frac{\text{opposite}}{\text{hypotenuse}} = \frac{A}{C}$$

$$\cos\theta = \frac{\text{adjacent}}{\text{hypotenuse}} = \frac{A}{C} \qquad \cos\phi = \frac{\text{adjacent}}{\text{hypotenuse}} = \frac{B}{C}$$

$$\tan\theta = \frac{\text{opposite}}{\text{adjacent}} = \frac{B}{A} \qquad \tan\phi = \frac{\text{opposite}}{\text{adjacent}} = \frac{A}{B}$$

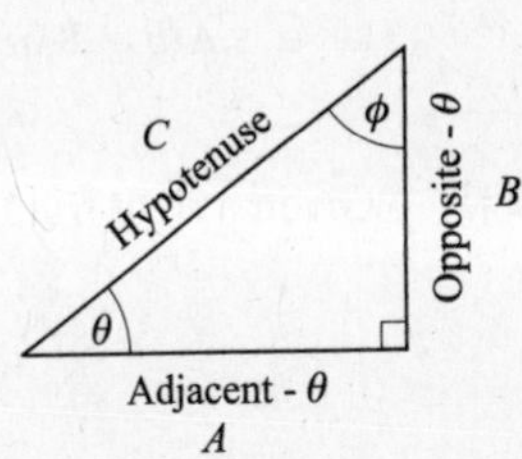


If $\theta$ and $\phi$ are the acute angles of any right triangle and $A$, $B$, and $C$ are the sides, as shown in the diagram, then Note that $\sin\theta = \cos\phi$; thus, the sine of any angle equals the cosine of its complementary angle. For example,

$$\sin 30^\circ = \cos(90^\circ - 30^\circ) = \cos 60^\circ \qquad \cos 50^\circ = \sin(90^\circ - 50^\circ) = \sin 40^\circ$$

As an angle increases from 0° to 90°, its sine increases from 0 to 1, its tangent increases from 0 to infinity, and its cosine decreases from 1 to 0.

**Law of Sines and of Cosines:** These two laws give the relations between the sides and angles of *any* plane triangle. In any plane triangle with angles $\alpha$, $\beta$, and $\gamma$ and sides opposite $A$, $B$, and $C$, respectively, the following relations apply:

**Law of Sines**

$$\frac{A}{\sin\alpha} = \frac{B}{\sin\beta} = \frac{C}{\sin\gamma}$$

or

$$\frac{A}{B} = \frac{\sin\alpha}{\sin\beta} \quad \frac{B}{C} = \frac{\sin\beta}{\sin\gamma} \quad \frac{C}{A} = \frac{\sin\gamma}{\sin\alpha}$$

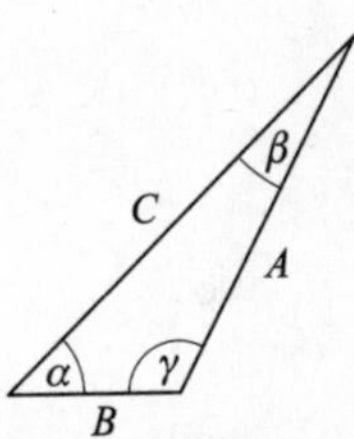

**Law of Cosines**

$$A^2 = B^2 + C^2 - 2BC\cos\alpha$$
$$B^2 = A^2 + C^2 - 2AC\cos\beta$$
$$C^2 = A^2 + B^2 - 2AB\cos\gamma$$

If the angle $\theta$ is between 90° and 180°, as in the case of angle $C$ in the above diagram, then

$$\sin\theta = \sin(180° - \theta) \qquad \text{and} \qquad \cos\theta = -\cos(180° - \theta)$$

Thus

$$\sin 120° = \sin(180° - 120°) = \sin 60° = 0.866$$
$$\cos 120° = -\cos(180° - 120°) = -\cos 60° = -0.500$$

## SOLVED PROBLEMS

**1 [I]** In right triangle $ABC$, given $A = 8$, $B = 6$, $\gamma = 90°$. Find the values of the sine, cosine, and tangent of angle $\alpha$ and of angle $\beta$.

$$C = \sqrt{8.0^2 + 6.0^2} = \sqrt{100} = 10$$

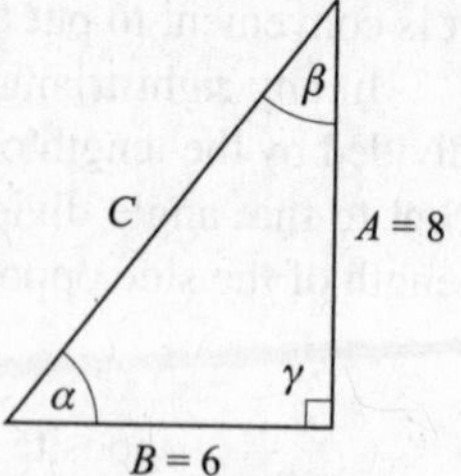


$\sin\alpha = A/C = 8.0/10 = 0.80 \qquad \sin\beta = B/C = 6.0/10 = 0.60$

$\cos\alpha = B/C = 6.0/10 = 0.60 \qquad \cos\beta = A/C = 8.0/10 = 0.80$

$\tan\alpha = A/B = 8.0/6.0 = 1.3 \qquad \tan\beta = B/A = 6.0/8.0 = 0.75$

**2 [I]** Given a right triangle with one acute angle 40.0° and hypotenuse 400, find the other sides and angles.

$$\sin 40.0° = \frac{A}{400} \qquad \text{and} \qquad \cos 40.0° = \frac{B}{400}$$

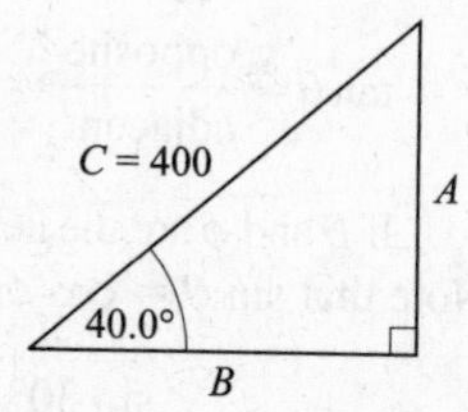


Using a calculator, we find that sin 40.0° = 0.642 8 and cos 40.0° = 0.766 0. Then

$$a = 400 \sin 40.0° = 400\,(0.642\,8) = 257$$
$$b = 400 \cos 40.0° = 400\,(0.766\,0) = 306$$
$$B = 90.0° - 40.0° = 50.0°$$

**3 [II]** Given triangle $ABC$ with $\alpha = 64.0°$, $\beta = 71.0°$, $B = 40.0°$, find $A$ and $C$.

$$\gamma = 180.0° - (\alpha + \beta) = 180.0° - (64.0° + 71.0°) = 45.0°$$

By the law of sines,

$$\frac{A}{\sin\alpha} = \frac{B}{\sin\beta} \qquad \text{and} \qquad \frac{C}{\sin\gamma} = \frac{B}{\sin\beta}$$

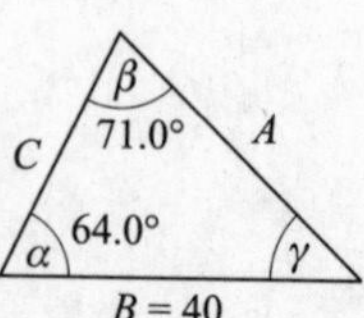


so

$$A = \frac{B\sin\alpha}{\sin\beta} = \frac{40.0\sin 64.0°}{\sin 71.0°} = \frac{40.0(0.898\,8)}{0.945\,5} = 38.0$$

and

$$C = \frac{B\sin\gamma}{\sin\beta} = \frac{40.0\sin 45.0°}{\sin 71.0°} = \frac{40.0(0.7071)}{0.945\,5} = 29.9$$

**4 [I]** (*a*) If $\cos\alpha = 0.438$, find $\alpha$ to the nearest degree. (*b*) If $\sin\beta = 0.8000$, find $\beta$ to the nearest tenth of a degree. (*c*) If $\cos\gamma = 0.7120$, find $\gamma$ to the nearest tenth of a degree.

(*a*) On your calculator use the inverse and cosine keys to get $\alpha = 64°$; or if you have a $\cos^{-1}$ key, use it.

(*b*) Enter 0.8000 on your calculator and use the inverse and sine keys to get $\beta = 53.1°$.

(*c*) Use your calculator as in (*a*) to get 44.6°.

**5 [II]** Given triangle *ABC* with $\alpha = 130.8°$, $A = 525$, $C = 421$, find $B$, $\beta$, and $\gamma$.

$$\sin 130.8° = \sin(180° - 130.8°) = \sin 49.2° = 0.757$$

Most hand calculators give sin 130.8° directly.

For $\gamma$: $\sin\gamma = \dfrac{C\sin\alpha}{A} = \dfrac{421\sin 30.8°}{525} = \dfrac{421(0.757)}{525} = 0.607$

from which $\gamma = 37.4°$

For $\beta$: $\beta = 180° - (\gamma + \alpha) = 180° - (37.4° + 130.8°) = 11.8°$

For $B$: $B = \dfrac{A\sin\beta}{\sin\alpha} = \dfrac{525\sin 11.8°}{\sin 130.8°} = \dfrac{525(0.204)}{0.757} = 142$

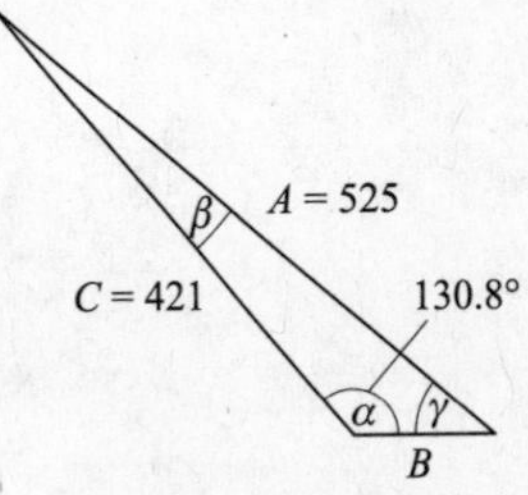


**6 [II]** Given triangle *ABC* with $A = 14$, $B = 8.0$, $\gamma = 130°$, find $C$, $\alpha$, and $\beta$.

$$\cos 130° = -\cos(180° - 130°) = -\cos 50° = -0.64$$

For $C$: By the law of cosines,

$$C^2 = A^2 + B^2 - 2AB\cos 130°$$
$$= 14^2 + 8.0^2 - 2(14)(8.0)(-0.643) = 404$$

and $C = \sqrt{404} = 20$.

For $\alpha$: By the law of sines,

$$\sin\alpha = \frac{A\sin\gamma}{C} = \frac{14(0.766)}{20.1} = 0.533$$

and $\alpha = 32°$

For $\beta$: $\beta = 180° - (\alpha + \gamma) = 180° - (32° + 130°) = 18°$

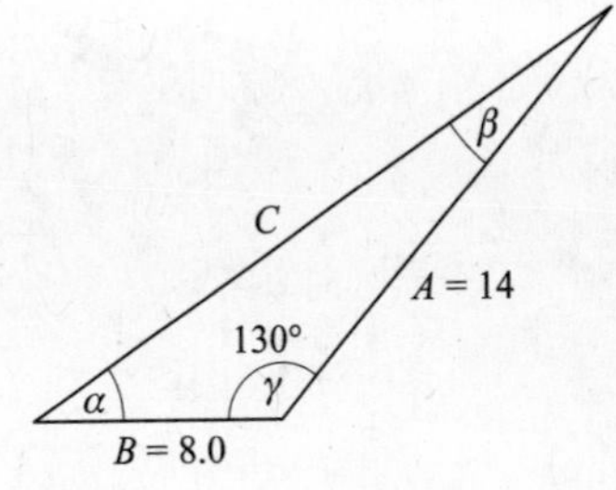


**7 [II]** Determine the unspecified sides and angles of the following right triangles *ABC*, with $\gamma = 90°$.

(*a*) $\alpha = 23.3°$, $C = 346$

(*b*) $\beta = 49.2°$, $B = 222$

(*c*) $\alpha = 66.6°$, $A = 113$

(*d*) $A = 25.4$, $B = 38.2$

(*e*) $B = 673$, $C = 888$

(*a*) $\beta = 66.7°$, $A = 137$, $B = 318$

(*b*) $\alpha = 40.8°$, $A = 192$, $C = 293$

(*c*) $\beta = 23.4°$, $B = 48.9$, $C = 123$

(*d*) $\alpha = 33.6°$, $\beta = 56.4°$, $C = 45.9$

(*e*) $\alpha = 40.7°$, $\beta = 49.3°$, $A = 579$

**8 [II]** Determine the unspecified sides and angles of the following oblique triangles *ABC*.

(*a*) $A = 125$, $\alpha = 54.6°$, $\beta = 65.2°$
(*b*) $B = 321$, $\alpha = 75.3°$, $\gamma = 38.5°$
(*c*) $B = 215$, $C = 150$, $\beta = 42.7°$
(*d*) $A = 512$, $B = 426$, $\alpha = 48.8°$
(*e*) $B = 50.4$, $C = 33.3$, $\beta = 118.5°$
(*f*) $B = 120$, $C = 270$, $\alpha = 118.7°$
(*g*) $A = 24.5$, $B = 18.6$, $C = 26.4$
(*h*) $A = 6.34$, $B = 7.30$, $C = 9.98$

(*a*) $B = 139$, $C = 133$, $\gamma = 60.2°$
(*b*) $A = 339$, $C = 218$, $\beta = 66.2°$
(*c*) $A = 300$, $\alpha = 109.1°$, $\gamma = 28.2°$
(*d*) $C = 680$, $\beta = 38.8°$, $\gamma = 92.4°$
(*e*) $A = 25.1$, $\alpha = 26.0°$, $\gamma = 35.5°$
(*f*) $A = 344$, $\beta = 17.8°$, $\gamma = 43.5°$
(*g*) $\alpha = 63.2°$, $\beta = 42.7°$, $\gamma = 74.1°$
(*h*) $\alpha = 39.3°$, $\beta = 46.9°$, $\gamma = 93.8°$

# Appendix C

# Exponents

**Powers of 10:** The following is a partial list of powers of 10. (See also Appendix E.)

$$10^0 = 1 \qquad 10^{-1} = \frac{1}{10} = 0.1$$

$$10^1 = 10$$

$$10^2 = 10 \times 10 = 100 \qquad 10^{-2} = \frac{1}{10^2} = \frac{1}{100} = 0.01$$

$$10^3 = 10 \times 10 \times 10 = 1000$$

$$10^4 = 10 \times 10 \times 10 \times 10 = 10\,000 \qquad 10^{-3} = \frac{1}{10^3} = \frac{1}{1000} = 0.001$$

$$10^5 = 10 \times 10 \times 10 \times 10 \times 10 = 100\,000$$

$$10^6 = 10 \times 10 \times 10 \times 10 \times 10 \times 10 = 1\,000\,000 \qquad 10^{-4} = \frac{1}{10^4} = \frac{1}{10\,000} = 0.0001$$

In the expression $10^5$, the *base* is 10 and the *exponent* is 5.

**Multiplication and Division:** In multiplication, exponents of like bases are added:

$$a^3 \times a^5 = a^{3+5} = a^8 \qquad 10^7 \times 10^{-3} = 10^{7-3} = 10^4$$

$$10^2 \times 10^3 = 10^{2+3} = 10^5 \qquad (4 \times 10^4)(2 \times 10^{-6}) = 8 \times 10^{4-6} = 8 \times 10^{-2}$$

$$10 \times 10 = 10^{1+1} = 10^2 \qquad (2 \times 10^5)(3 \times 10^{-2}) = 6 \times 10^{5-2} = 6 \times 10^3$$

In division, exponents of like bases are subtracted:

$$\frac{a^5}{a^3} = a^{5-3} = a^2 \qquad \frac{8 \times 10^2}{2 \times 10^{-6}} = \frac{8}{2} \times 10^{2+6} = 4 \times 10^8$$

$$\frac{10^2}{10^3} = 10^{2-5} = 10^{-3} \qquad \frac{5.6 \times 10^{-2}}{1.6 \times 10^4} = \frac{5.6}{1.6} \times 10^{-2-4} = 3.5 \times 10^{-6}$$

**Scientific Notation:** Any number may be expressed as an integral power of 10, or as the product of two numbers one of which is an integral power of 10. For example,

$$2806 = 2.806 \times 10^3 \qquad 0.0454 = 4.54 \times 10^{-2}$$

$$22\,406 = 2.2406 \times 10^4 \qquad 0.000\,06 = 6 \times 10^{-5}$$

$$454 = 4.54 \times 10^2 \qquad 0.003\,06 = 3.06 \times 10^{-3}$$

$$0.454 = 4.54 \times 10^{-1} \qquad 0.000\,000\,5 = 5 \times 10^{-7}$$

**Other Operations:** A nonzero expression with an exponent of zero is equal to 1. Thus,

$$a^0 = 1 \qquad 10^0 = 1 \qquad (3 \times 10)^0 = 1 \qquad 8.2 \times 10^0 = 8.2$$

A power may be transferred from the numerator to the denominator of a fraction, or vice versa, by changing the sign of the exponent. For example,

$$10^{-4} = \frac{1}{10^4} \qquad 5 \times 10^{-3} = \frac{5}{10^3} \qquad \frac{7}{10^{-2}} = 7 \times 10^2 \qquad -5a^{-2} = -\frac{5}{a^2}$$

The meaning of the fractional exponent is illustrated by the following:

$$10^{2/3} = \sqrt[3]{10^2} \qquad 10^{3/2} = \sqrt{10^3} \qquad 10^{1/2} = \sqrt{10} \qquad 4^{3/2} = \sqrt{4^3} = \sqrt{64} = 8$$

To take a power to a power, multiply exponents:

$$(10^3)^2 = 10^{3 \times 2} = 10^6 \qquad (10^{-2})^3 = 10^{-2 \times 3} = 10^{-6} \qquad (a^3)^{-2} = a^{-6}$$

To extract the square root, divide the exponent by 2. If the exponent is an odd number, it should first be increased or decreased by 1, and the coefficient adjusted accordingly. To extract the cube root, divide the exponent by 3. The coefficients are treated independently. Thus,

$$\sqrt{9 \times 10^4} = 3 \times 10^2 \qquad \sqrt{4.9 \times 10^{-5}} = \sqrt{49 \times 10^{-6}} = 7.0 \times 10^{-3}$$

$$\sqrt{3.6 \times 10^7} = \sqrt{36 \times 10^6} = 6.0 \times 10^3 \qquad \sqrt[3]{1.25 \times 10^8} = \sqrt[3]{125 \times 10^6} = 5.00 \times 10^2$$

Most hand calculators give square roots directly. Cube roots and other roots are easily found using the $y^x$ key.

## EXERCISES

**1 [I]** Express the following in powers of 10.

(*a*) 326 (*d*) 36 000 008 (*g*) 0.000 002 (*i*) $\sqrt{0.000\,081}$

(*b*) 32 608 (*e*) 0.831 (*h*) 0.000 706 (*j*) $\sqrt[3]{0.000\,027}$

(*c*) 1006 (*f*) 0.03

**2 [I]** Evaluate the following and express the results in powers of 10.

(*a*) $1500 \times 260$

(*b*) $220 \times 35000$

(*c*) $40 \div 20000$

(*d*) $82800 \div 0.12$

(*e*) $\dfrac{1.728 \times 17.28}{0.000\,1728}$

(*f*) $\dfrac{(16000)(0.0002)(1.2)}{(2000)(0.006)(0.00032)}$

(*g*) $\dfrac{0.004 \times 32\,000 \times 0.6}{6400 \times 3000 \times 0.08}$

(*h*) $(\sqrt{14400})(\sqrt{0.000\,025})$

(*i*) $\sqrt[3]{2.7 \times 10^7}\ \sqrt[3]{1.25 \times 10^{-4}}$

(*j*) $(1 \times 10^{-3})(2 \times 10^5)^2$

(*k*) $\dfrac{(3 \times 10^2)^3(2 \times 10^{-5})^2}{3.6 \times 10^{-8}}$

(*l*) $8(2 \times 10^{-2})^{-3}$

## ANSWERS TO EXERCISES

**1 [I]** (*a*) $3.26 \times 10^2$ (*b*) $3.2608 \times 10^4$ (*c*) $1.006 \times 10^3$ (*d*) $3.6000008 \times 10^7$ (*e*) $8.31 \times 10^{-1}$ (*f*) $3 \times 10^{-2}$ (*g*) $2 \times 10^{-6}$ (*h*) $7.06 \times 10^{-4}$ (*i*) $9.0 \times 10^{-3}$ (*j*) $3.0 \times 10^{-2}$

**2 [I]** (*a*) $3.90 \times 10^5$ (*b*) $7.70 \times 10^6$ (*c*) $2.0 \times 10^{-3}$ (*d*) $6.9 \times 10^5$ (*e*) $1.728 \times 10^5$ (*f*) $1 \times 10^3$ (*g*) $5 \times 10^{-5}$ (*h*) $6.0 \times 10^{-1}$ (*i*) $1.5 \times 10^1$ (*j*) $4 \times 10^7$ (*k*) $3 \times 10^5$ (*l*) $1 \times 10^6$

# Appendix D

# Logarithms

**The Logarithm to Base 10** of a number is the exponent or power to which 10 must be raised to yield that number. Since 1000 is $10^3$, the logarithm to base 10 of 1000 (written log 1000) is 3. Similarly, log 10 000 = 4, log 10 = 1, log 0.1 = −1, and log 0.001 = −3.

Most hand calculators have a log key. When a number is entered into the calculator, its logarithm to base 10 can be found by pressing the log key. In this way we find that log 50 = 1.698 97 and log 0.035 = −1.455 93. Also, log 1 = 0, which reflects the fact that $10^0 = 1$.

**Natural Logarithms** are taken to the base $e = 2.718$, rather than 10. They can be found on most hand calculators by pressing the ln key. Since $e^0 = 1$, we have ln 1 = 0.

**Examples:**

$$\log 971 = 2.9872 \qquad \ln 971 = 6.8783$$
$$\log 9.71 = 0.9872 \qquad \ln 9.71 = 2.2732$$
$$\log 0.097\,1 = -1.0128 \qquad \ln 0.097\,1 = -2.3320$$

**Exercises:** Find the logarithms to base 10 of the following numbers.

(*a*) 454 (*f*) 0.621
(*b*) 5280 (*g*) 0.9463
(*c*) 96 500 (*h*) 0.0353
(*d*) 30.48 (*i*) 0.0022
(*e*) 1.057 (*j*) 0.000 264 5

(*a*) 2.6571 (*f*) −0.2069
(*b*) 3.7226 (*g*) −0.023 97
(*c*) 4.9845 (*h*) −1.4522
(*d*) 1.4840 (*i*) −2.6576
(*e*) 0.0241 (*j*) −3.5776

**Antilogarithms:** Suppose we have an equation such as $3.5 = 10^{0.544}$; then we know that 0.544 is the log to base 10 of 3.5. Or, inversely, we can say that 3.5 is the *antilogarithm* (or *inverse logarithm*) of 0.544. Finding the antilogarithm of a number is simple with most hand calculators: Enter the number; then press first the inverse key and then the log key. Or, if the base is *e* rather than 10, press the inverse and ln keys.

**Exercises:** Find the numbers corresponding to the following logarithms.

(*a*) 3.1568 (*f*) 0.9142

(*b*) 1.6934 (*g*) 0.0008

(*c*) 5.6934 (*h*) −0.2493

(*d*) 2.5000 (*i*) −1.9965

(*e*) 2.0436 (*j*) −2.7994

(*a*) 1435 (*f*) 8.208

(*b*) 49.37 (*g*) 1.002

(*c*) $4.937 \times 10^5$ (*h*) 0.5632

(*d*) 316.2 (*i*) 0.01008

(*e*) 110.6 (*j*) 0.001587

**Basic Properties of Logarithms:** Since logarithms are exponents, all properties of exponents are also properties of logarithms.

(1) The logarithm of the product of two numbers is the sum of their logarithms. Thus,

$$\log ab = \log a + \log b \qquad \log(5280 \times 48) = \log 5280 + \log 48$$

(2) The logarithm of the quotient of two numbers is the logarithm of the numerator minus the logarithm of the denominator. For example,

$$\log\frac{a}{b} = \log a - \log b \qquad \log\frac{536}{24.5} = \log 536 - \log 24.5$$

(3) The logarithm of the *n*th power of a number is *n* times the logarithm of the number. Thus,

$$\log a^n = n \log a \qquad \log(4.28)^3 = 3 \log 4.28$$

(4) The logarithm of the *n*th root of a number is $1/n$ times the logarithm of the number. Thus,

$$\log\sqrt[n]{a} = \frac{1}{n}\log a \qquad \log\sqrt{32} = \frac{1}{2}\log 32 \qquad \log\sqrt[3]{792} = \frac{1}{3}\log 792$$

## SOLVED PROBLEM

**1 [I]** Use a hand calculator to evaluate (*a*) $(5.2)^{0.4}$, (*b*) $(6.138)^3$, (*c*) $\sqrt[3]{5}$, (*d*) $(7.25 \times 10^{-11})^{0.25}$.

(*a*) Enter 5.2; press $y^x$ key; enter 0.4; press = key. The displayed answer is 1.934.

(*b*) Enter 6.138; press $y^x$ key; enter 3; press = key. The displayed answer is 231.2.

(*c*) Enter 5; press $y^x$ key; enter 0.3333; press = key. The displayed answer is 1.710.

(*d*) Enter $7.25 \times 10^{-11}$; press $y^x$ key; enter 0.25; press = key. The displayed answer is $2.918 \times 10^{-3}$.

## EXERCISES

**2 [I]** Evaluate each of the following.

(1) $28.32 \times 0.08254$

(2) $573 \times 6.96 \times 0.00481$

(3) $\dfrac{79.28}{63.57}$

(4) $\dfrac{65.38}{225.2}$

(5) $\dfrac{1}{239}$

(6) $\dfrac{0.572 \times 31.8}{96.2}$

(7) $47.5 \times \dfrac{779}{760} \times \dfrac{273}{300}$

(8) $(8.642)^2$

(9) $(0.08642)^2$

(10) $(11.72)^3$

(11) $(0.0523)^3$

(12) $\sqrt{9463}$

(13) $\sqrt{946.3}$

(14) $\sqrt{0.00661}$

(15) $\sqrt[3]{1.79}$

(16) $\sqrt[4]{0.182}$

(17) $\sqrt{643 \times (1.91)^3}$

(18) $(8.73 \times 10^{-2})(7.49 \times 10^{6})$

(19) $(3.8 \times 10^{-5})(1.9 \times 10^{-5})$

(20) $\dfrac{8.5 \times 10^{-45}}{1.6 \times 10^{-22}}$

(21) $\sqrt{2.54 \times 10^{6}}$

(22) $\sqrt{9.44 \times 10^{5}}$

(23) $\sqrt{7.2 \times 10^{-13}}$

(24) $\sqrt[3]{7.3 \times 10^{-14}}$

(25) $\sqrt{\dfrac{(1.1 \times 10^{-23})(6.8 \times 10^{-2})}{1.4 \times 10^{-24}}}$

(26) $2.04 \log 97.2$

(27) $37 \log 0.0298$

(28) $6.30 \log (2.95 \times 10^{3})$

(29) $8.09 \log (5.68 \times 10^{-16})$

(30) $(2.00)^{0.714}$

## ANSWERS TO EXERCISES

**2 [I].**

| | | | | | | | |
|---|---|---|---|---|---|---|---|
| (1) | 2.337 | (9) | 0.007467 | (17) | 177 | (25) | 0.73 |
| (2) | 19.2 | (10) | 1611 | (18) | $6.54 \times 10^{5}$ | (26) | 4.05 |
| (3) | 1.247 | (11) | 0.000143 | (19) | $2.7 \times 10^{-14}$ | (27) | −56 |
| (4) | 0.2902 | (12) | 97.27 | (20) | $5.3 \times 10^{-23}$ | (28) | 21.9 |
| (5) | 0.00418 | (13) | 30.76 | (21) | $1.59 \times 10^{3}$ | (29) | −123 |
| (6) | 0.189 | (14) | 0.0813 | (22) | $9.72 \times 10^{2}$ | (30) | 1.64 |
| (7) | 44.3 | (15) | 1.21 | (23) | $8.5 \times 10^{-7}$ | | |
| (8) | 74.67 | (16) | 0.653 | (24) | $4.2 \times 10^{-5}$ | | |

# Appendix E

## Prefixes for Multiples of SI Units

| Multiplication Factor | Prefix | Symbol |
|---|---|---|
| $10^{12}$ | tera | T |
| $10^{9}$ | giga | G |
| $10^{6}$ | mega | M |
| $10^{3}$ | kilo | k |
| $10^{2}$ | hecto | h |
| 10 | deka | da |
| $10^{-1}$ | deci | d |
| $10^{-2}$ | centi | c |
| $10^{-3}$ | milli | m |
| $10^{-6}$ | micro | $\mu$ |
| $10^{-9}$ | nano | n |
| $10^{-12}$ | pico | p |
| $10^{-15}$ | femto | f |
| $10^{-18}$ | atto | a |

## The Greek Alphabet

| | | | | | | | | | | | |
|---|---|---|---|---|---|---|---|---|---|---|---|
| Α | $\alpha$ | alpha | Η | $\eta$ | eta | Ν | $\nu$ | nu | Τ | $\tau$ | tau |
| Β | $\beta$ | beta | Θ | $\theta$ | theta | Ξ | $\xi$ | xi | Υ | $\upsilon$ | upsilon |
| Γ | $\gamma$ | gamma | Ι | $\iota$ | iota | Ο | $o$ | omicron | Φ | $\phi$ | phi |
| Δ | $\delta$ | delta | Κ | $\kappa$ | kappa | Π | $\pi$ | pi | Χ | $\chi$ | chi |
| Ε | $\varepsilon$ | epsilon | Λ | $\lambda$ | lambda | Ρ | $\rho$ | rho | Ψ | $\psi$ | psi |
| Ζ | $\zeta$ | zeta | Μ | $\mu$ | mu | Σ | $\sigma$ | sigma | Ω | $\omega$ | omega |

# Factors for Conversions to SI Units

**Acceleration**
$1\ \text{ft/s}^2 = 0.3048\ \text{m/s}^2$
$g = 9.807\ \text{m/s}^2$

**Area**
$1\ \text{acre} = 4047\ \text{m}^2$
$1\ \text{ft}^2 = 9.290 \times 10^{-2}\ \text{m}^2$
$\text{in.}^2 = 6.45 \times 10^{-4}\ \text{m}^2$
$1\ \text{mi}^2 = 2.59 \times 10^6\ \text{m}^2$

**Density**
$1\ \text{g/cm}^3 = 10^3\ \text{kg/m}^3$

**Energy**
$1\ \text{Btu} = 1054\ \text{J}$
$1\ \text{calorie (cal)} = 4.184\ \text{J}$
$1\ \text{electron volt (eV)} = 1.602 \times 10^{-19}\ \text{J}$
$1\ \text{foot pound (ft} \cdot \text{lb)} = 1.356\ \text{J}$
$1\ \text{kilowatt hour (kW} \cdot \text{h)} = 3.60 \times 10^6\ \text{J}$

**Force**
$1\ \text{dyne} = 10^{-5}\ \text{N}$
$1\ \text{lb} = 4.448\ \text{N}$

**Length**
$1\ \text{angstrom (Å)} = 10^{-10}\ \text{m}$
$1\ \text{ft} = 0.3048\ \text{m}$
$1\ \text{in.} = 2.54 \times 10^{-2}\ \text{m}$
$1\ \text{light year} = 9.461 \times 10^{15}\ \text{m}$
$1\ \text{mile} = 1069\ \text{m}$

**Mass**
$1\ \text{atomic mass unit (u)} = 1.6606 \times 10^{-27}\ \text{kg}$
$1\ \text{gram} = 10^{-3}\ \text{kg}$

**Power**
$1\ \text{Btu/s} = 1054\ \text{W}$
$1\ \text{cal/s} = 4.184\ \text{W}$
$1\ \text{ft} \cdot \text{lb/s} = 1.356\ \text{W}$
$1\ \text{horsepower (hp)} = 746\ \text{W}$

**Pressure**
$1\ \text{atmosphere (atm)} = 1.013 \times 10^5\ \text{Pa}$
$1\ \text{bar} = 10^5\ \text{Pa}$
$1\ \text{cmHg} = 1333\ \text{Pa}$
$1\ \text{lb/ft}^2 = 47.88\ \text{Pa}$
$1\ \text{lb/in.}^2\ \text{(psi)} = 6895\ \text{Pa}$
$1\ \text{N/m}^2 = 1\ \text{pascal (Pa)}$
$1\ \text{torr} = 133.3\text{Pa}$

**Speed**
$1\ \text{ft/s (fps)} = 0.3048\ \text{m/s}$
$1\ \text{km/h} = 0.2778\ \text{m/s}$
$1\ \text{mi/h (mph)} = 0.44704\ \text{m/s}$

**Temperature**
$T_{\text{Kelvin}} = T_{\text{Celsius}} + 273.15$
$T_{\text{Kelvin}} = \frac{5}{9}\,(T_{\text{Fahrenheit}} + 459.67)$
$T_{\text{Celsius}} = \frac{5}{9}\,(T_{\text{Fahrenheit}} - 32)$
$T_{\text{Kelvin}} = \frac{5}{9}\,T_{\text{Rankine}}$

**Time**
$1\ \text{day} = 86400\ \text{s}$
$1\ \text{year} = 3.16 \times 10^7\ \text{s}$

**Volume**
$1\ \text{ft}^3 = 2.832 \times 10^{-2}\ \text{m}^3$
$1\ \text{gallon} = 3.785 \times 10^{-3}\ \text{m}^3$
$1\ \text{in.}^3 = 1.639 \times 10^{-5}\ \text{m}^3$
$1\ \text{liter} = 10^{-3}\ \text{m}^3$

# Physical Constants

| | | |
|---|---|---|
| Speed of light in free space | c | $= 2.997\,924\,58 \times 10^8$ m/s |
| Acceleration due to gravity (normal) | $g$ | $= 9.807$ m/s$^2$ |
| Gravitational constant | $G$ | $= 6.672\,59 \times 10^{-11}$ N·m$^2$/kg$^2$ |
| Coulomb constant | $k_0$ | $= 8.988 \times 10^9$ N·m$^2$/C$^2$ |
| Density of water (maximum) | | $= 0.999\,972 \times 10^3$ kg/m$^3$ |
| Density of mercury (S.T.P.) | | $= 13.595 \times 10^3$ kg/m$^3$ |
| Standard atmosphere | | $= 1.0132 \times 10^5$ N/m$^2$ |
| Volume of ideal gas at S.T.P. | | $= 22.4$ m$^3$/kmol |
| Avogadro's number | $N_A$ | $= 6.022 \times 10^{26}$ kmol$^{-1}$ |
| Universal gas constant | $R$ | $= 8314$ J/kmol·K |
| Ice point | | $= 273.15$ K |
| Mechanical equivalent of heat | | $= 4.184$ J/cal |
| Stefan–Boltzmann constant | $\sigma$ | $= 5.67 \times 10^{-8}$ W/m$^2$·K$^4$ |
| Planck's constant | $h$ | $= 6.626 \times 10^{-34}$ J·s |
| Faraday | F | $= 9.6485 \times 10^4$ C/mol |
| Electronic charge | $e$ | $= 1.6022 \times 10^{-19}$ C |
| Boltzmann's constant | $k_B$ | $= 1.38 \times 10^{-23}$ J/K |
| Ratio of electron charge to mass | $e/m_e$ | $= 1.7588 \times 10^{11}$ C/kg |
| Electron mass | $m_e$ | $= 9.109 \times 10^{-31}$ kg |
| Proton mass | $m_p$ | $= 1.6726 \times 10^{-27}$ kg |
| Neutron mass | $m_n$ | $= 1.6749 \times 10^{-27}$ kg |
| Alpha particle mass | | $= 6.645 \times 10^{-27}$ kg |
| Atomic mass unit (1/12 mass of $^{12}$C) | u | $= 1.6606 \times 10^{-27}$ kg |
| Rest energy of 1 u | | $= 931.5$ MeV |

# Appendix H

# Table of the Elements

The masses listed are based on ${}^{12}_{6}C$ = 12 u. A value in parentheses is the mass number of the most stable (long-lived) of the known isotopes.

| Element | Symbol | Atomic Number Z | Average Atomic Mass, u |
|---|---|---|---|
| Actinium | Ac | 89 | (227) |
| Aluminum | Al | 13 | 26.9815 |
| Americium | Am | 95 | (243) |
| Antimony | Sb | 51 | 121.75 |
| Argon | Ar | 18 | 39.948 |
| Arsenic | As | 33 | 74.9216 |
| Astatine | At | 85 | (210) |
| Barium | Ba | 56 | 137.34 |
| Berkelium | Bk | 97 | (247) |
| Beryllium | Be | 4 | 9.0122 |
| Bismuth | Bi | 83 | 208.980 |
| Boron | B | 5 | 10.811 |
| Bromine | Br | 35 | 79.904 |
| Cadmium | Cd | 48 | 112.40 |
| Calcium | Ca | 20 | 40.08 |
| Californium | Cf | 98 | (251) |
| Carbon | C | 6 | 12.0112 |
| Cerium | Ce | 58 | 140.12 |
| Cesium | Cs | 55 | 132.905 |
| Chlorine | Cl | 17 | 35.453 |
| Chromium | Cr | 24 | 51.996 |
| Cobalt | Co | 27 | 58.9332 |
| Copper | Cu | 29 | 63.546 |
| Curium | Ce | 96 | (247) |
| Dysprosium | Dy | 66 | 162.50 |
| Einsteinium | Es | 99 | (254) |
| Erbium | Er | 68 | 167.26 |
| Europium | Eu | 63 | 151.96 |

| Element | Symbol | Atomic Number Z | Average Atomic Mass, u |
|---|---|---|---|
| Fermium | Fm | 100 | (257) |
| Fluorine | F | 9 | 18.9984 |
| Francium | Fr | 87 | (223) |
| Gadolinium | Gd | 64 | 157.25 |
| Gallium | Ga | 31 | 69.72 |
| Germanium | Ge | 32 | 72.59 |
| Gold | Au | 79 | 196.967 |
| Hafnium | Hf | 72 | 178.49 |
| Helium | He | 2 | 4.0026 |
| Holmium | Ho | 67 | 164.930 |
| Hydrogen | H | 1 | 1.0080 |
| Indium | In | 49 | 114.82 |
| Iodine | I | 53 | 126.9044 |
| Iridium | Ir | 77 | 192.2 |
| Iron | Fe | 26 | 55.847 |
| Krypton | Kr | 36 | 83.80 |
| Lanthanum | La | 57 | 138.91 |
| Lawrencium | Lr | 103 | (257) |
| Lead | Pb | 82 | 207.19 |
| Lithium | Li | 3 | 6.939 |
| Lutetium | Lu | 71 | 174.97 |
| Magnesium | Mg | 12 | 24.312 |
| Manganese | Mn | 25 | 54.9380 |
| Mendelevium | Md | 101 | (256) |
| Mercury | Hg | 80 | 200.59 |
| Molybdenum | Mo | 42 | 95.94 |
| Neodymium | Nd | 60 | 144.24 |
| Neon | Ne | 10 | 20.183 |
| Neptunium | Np | 93 | (237) |
| Nickel | Ni | 28 | 58.71 |
| Niobium | Nb | 41 | 92.906 |
| Nitrogen | N | 7 | 14.0067 |
| Nobelium | No | 102 | (254) |
| Osmium | Os | 76 | 190.2 |
| Oxygen | O | 8 | 15.9994 |
| Palladium | Pd | 46 | 106.4 |
| Phosphorus | P | 15 | 30.9738 |
| Platinum | Pt | 78 | 195.09 |
| Plutonium | Pu | 94 | (244) |
| Polonium | Po | 84 | (209) |
| Potassium | K | 19 | 39.102 |
| Praseodymium | Pr | 59 | 140.907 |
| Promethium | Pm | 61 | (145) |
| Protactinium | Pa | 91 | (231) |

*(Continued)*

| Element | Symbol | Atomic Number Z | Average Atomic Mass, u |
|---|---|---|---|
| Radium | Ra | 88 | (226) |
| Radon | Rn | 86 | 222 |
| Rhenium | Re | 75 | 186.2 |
| Rhodium | Rh | 45 | 102.905 |
| Rubidium | Rb | 37 | 85.47 |
| Ruthenium | Ru | 44 | 101.07 |
| Samarium | Sm | 62 | 150.35 |
| Scandium | Sc | 21 | 44.956 |
| Selenium | Se | 34 | 78.96 |
| Silicon | Si | 14 | 28.086 |
| Silver | Ag | 47 | 107.868 |
| Sodium | Na | 11 | 22.9898 |
| Strontium | Sr | 38 | 87.62 |
| Sulfur | S | 16 | 32.064 |
| Tantalum | Ta | 73 | 180.948 |
| Technetium | Tc | 43 | (97) |
| Tellurium | Te | 52 | 127.60 |
| Terbium | Tb | 65 | 158.924 |
| Thallium | Tl | 81 | 204.37 |
| Thorium | Th | 90 | 232.0381 |
| Thulium | Tm | 69 | 168.934 |
| Tin | Sn | 50 | 118.69 |
| Titanium | Ti | 22 | 47.90 |
| Tungsten | W | 74 | 183.85 |
| Uranium | U | 92 | 238.03 |
| Vanadium | V | 23 | 50.942 |
| Xenon | Xe | 54 | 131.30 |
| Ytterbium | Yb | 70 | 173.04 |
| Yttrium | Y | 39 | 88.905 |
| Zinc | Zn | 30 | 65.37 |
| Zirconium | Zr | 40 | 91.22 |

INDEX

Absolute humidity, 214
Absolute potential, 281
Absolute temperature, 190, 207
and molecular energy, 207
Absolute zero, 196
Absorption of light, 455
ac circuits, 381
ac generator, 381
Acceleration, 15
angular, 116
centripetal, 117
due to gravity, 16
and force, 29
radial, 116
in SHM, 146
tangential, 116
Accelerator, high energy, 476
Action–Reaction Law, 30
Activity, nuclear, 465
Actual mechanical advantage, 93
Addition of vectors, 3
Adiabatic process, 228
Alpha particle, 463
Alternating voltage, 381
Ammeter, 297
Ammeter–voltmeter method, 297
Ampere (unit), 297
Amplitude of vibration, 145, 246
Analogies, linear and rotational
motion, 116, 130
Angular acceleration, 116, 128
and torque, 128
Angular displacement, 115
Angular frequency, 115, 147
Angular impulse, 129
Angular kinetic energy, 128
Angular momentum, 129
conservation of, 129
Angular motion, 115–127
equations for, 116
Angular speed, 115
Angular velocity, 116
Antinode, 246
Apparent depth in refraction, 406
Archimedes' principle, 168
Armature, 365
Astronomical telescope, 418
Atmospheric pressure, 167
Atomic mass, 464
Atomic mass unit, 463
Atomic number, 453
Atomic photoelectric effect, 457
Atomic table, 498
Atwood's machine, 43, 84
Average speed, 1
Avogadro's number, 206
Axis for torque, 66

Back emf, 366
Ballistic pendulum, 105
Balmer series, 454
Banking of curves, 124
Battery, 297
ampere-hour rating, 309
Beats, 257
Becquerel (unit), 465
Bernoulli's Equation, 181
Beta particle, 464
Binding energy, 464, 475
Biot-Savart Law, 348
Blackbody, 222
Bohr model, 270, 302, 453

Boltzmann's constant, 206
Boyle's Law, 196
Bragg equation, 427
British thermal unit, 213
Bulk modulus, 159
Buoyant force, 168

Calorie (unit), 213
  nutritionist's, 213
Calorimetry, 214
Capacitance, 281, 282
Capacitive reactance, 382
Capacitors, 281, 330, 373
  in ac circuit, 381, 383
  charging of, 373
  energy of, 283
  in parallel, 282, 283
  in series, 282, 283
Carbon dating, 479
Carnot cycle, 229
Celsius temperature, 190
Center of gravity, 66
Center of mass, 102
Centigrade temperature (*see* Celsius temperature)
Centipoise (unit), 180
Centripetal acceleration, 117
Centripetal force, 117
Chain hoist, 98
Chain reaction, 475
Charge:
  conservation of, 268
  of electron, 268
Charge motion in $\vec{\mathbf{B}}$ field, 335–339
Charge quantum, 268
Charles' Law, 196
Circuit rule, 327
Coefficient of restitution, 102
Coherent waves, 426
Collisions, 101, 102
Component method, 5
Components of a vector, 5
Compressibility, 159
Compressional waves, 247
Compton effect, 446
Concave mirror, 392
  ray diagram for, 392
Concurrent forces, 55
Conduction of heat, 221
Conductivity, thermal, 221
Conical pendulum, 121
Conservation:
  of angular momentum, 129
  of charge, 269
  of energy, 80
  of linear momentum, 101
Constants, table of, 497
Continuity equation, 180
Convection of heat, 222
Conversion factors, 496
Convex mirror, 392
  ray diagram for, 393
Coplanar forces, 65
Coulomb (unit), 268
Coulomb force, 268
Coulomb's Law, 268–280
Counter emf, 366
Crest of wave, 245
Critical angle, 402
Curie (unit), 468
Current, electric, 297–306
Current loop, torque on, 337

Dalton's Law of partial pressures, 197
Daughter nucleus, 471
de Broglie wavelength, 446
de Broglie waves, resonance, 446, 450
Decay constant, 465
Decay law, radioactivity, 464, 465
Decibel (unit), 257
Density, 158
Deuteron, 463
Dew point, 214
Diamagnetism, 354
Dielectric constant, 268
Differential pulley, 98
Diffraction, 426
  and limit of resolution, 426
  by single slit, 426
  of X-rays, 427

Diffraction grating, 427
Dimensional analysis, 16
Diopter (unit), 411
Direct current circuits, 297–306
Discharge rate, fluids, 180
Disorder, 240
Displacement, angular, 115
Displacement vector, 2
Distance, 1
Domain, magnetic, 348
Doppler effect, 257
Dose, of radiation, 475
Double-slit interference, 428

Earth
  magnetic field of, 337
Effective radiation dose, 476
Effective values of circuits, 382
Efficiency, 93, 228
Elastic collision, 102
Elastic constant, 146
Elastic limit, 159
Elasticity, 158
Electric current, 297
Electric field, 269
  of parallel plates, 282
  of point charge, 269
  related to potential, 282
Electric field strength, 269
Electric generator, 365–371
Electric motor, 365–371
Electric potential, 282
Electric potential energy, 282
Electric power, 307–311
Electromotive force (*see* emf)
Electron, 268, 453
Electron orbits, 453
Electron volt (unit), 282
emf (electromotive force), 298
  induced, 354–364
  motional, 355
Emission of light, 454
Emissivity, 222
Energy, 79
  in a capacitor, 283
  conservation of, 80
  electric potential, 282
  gravitational potential, 80
  heat, 227
  in an inductor, 372
    internal, 227
  kinetic, 79
  levels, 454
    quantization of, 446
  relativistic, 436
  rotational kinetic, 128
  in SHM, 146
  in a spring, 146
  of vibration, 146
Energy-level diagram, 454
  helium ion, 456
  hydrogen, 454
Entropy, 240–244
Equation of continuity, 180
Equations:
  uniform accelerated motion, 15
Equilibrant, 49
Equilibrium, 55–78
  under concurrent forces, 55–64
  under coplanar forces, 65–78
  first condition for, 55
  of rigid body, 65–78
  second condition for, 66
  thermal, 227
Equivalent capacitance, 283
Equivalent optical path length, 427
Equivalent resistance, 312–326
Erg (unit), 79
Exclusion principle, 459
Explosions, 101
Exponential decay, 467
Exponential functions, in *R-C*
    circuit, 374
Exponents, math review, 489
External reflection, 402
Eye, 418

$\vec{\mathbf{F}} = m\vec{\mathbf{a}}$, 29
*f* stop of lens, 420
Fahrenheit temperature, 190

Farad (unit), 282
Faraday's Law, 355
Farsightedness, 418, 419
Ferromagnetism, 348, 354
Field:
  electric, 268
  magnetic, 347
Field lines, 269
First condition for equilibrium, 55
First Law of Thermodynamics, 227–239
Fission, nuclear, 475
Five motion equations, 15
Flow and flow rate, 180
Fluid pressure, 167
Fluids:
  in motion, 180–189
  at rest, 167–179
Flux:
  magnetic, 354
Focal length:
  lens, 409, 410
  mirror, 392
Focal point:
  lens, 409
  mirror, 392
Foot-pound (unit), 76
Force, 29
  and acceleration, 29
  centripetal, 117
  friction, 30
  on current, 337
  on moving charge, 337
  normal, 30
  nuclear, 414
  restoring, 145
  tensile, 30
Fraunhofer diffraction, 426
Free-body diagram, 34, 35, 38, 57
Free fall, 16, 30
Frequency and period, 116, 145
Frequency of vibration, 145
Friction force, 30, 35
Fundamental frequency, 246
Fusion, heat of, 213
Fusion, nuclear, 475

Galvanometer, 321
Gamma ray, 465
Gas, speed of molecules in, 206
Gas constant, 196
Gas Law, 196
Gas-Law problems, 197
Gauge pressure, 197
Gauss (unit), 337
Gay-Lussac's Law, 196
Generator, electric, 365
Graphing of motion, 16
Grating equation, 427
Gravitation, Law of, 30
Gravitational potential energy, 80
Gravity:
  acceleration due to, 16
  center of, 66
  Universal Law of, 30
Gray (unit), 475
Greek alphabet, 495
Ground state, 454
Gyration radius, 128

Half-life, 415
Harmonic motion, 146
Heat, 213–220
  conduction of, 221
  convection of, 222
  of fusion, 213
  radiation of, 222
  in resistors, 307
  of sublimation, 213
  transfer of, 221–226
  of vaporization, 213
Heat capacity, 213
Heat conductivity, 221
Heat energy, 192, 227
Heat engine efficiency, 228
Helium energy levels, 456
Henry (unit), 372
Hertz (unit), 145
High-energy accelerators, 476
Hookean spring, 146

Hooke's Law, 146, 158
Horsepower (unit), 80
House circuit, 314
Humidity, 214
Hydraulic press, 170
Hydrogen atom, 453–458
  energy levels of, 453
Hydrostatic pressure, 167

Ideal gas, 196–205
  mean-free path,
  pressure of, 196
Ideal Gas Law, 196
Ideal mechanical advantage, 93
Image size, 393, 411
Imaginary image (*see* Virtualimage)
Impedance, 382
Impulse, 101
  angular, 129
Index of refraction, 401
Induced emf, 354–364
  motional, 355
Inductance, 372–380
  energy in, 372
  mutual, 372
  self, 372
  of solenoid, 374
Inductive reactance, 382
Inelastic collision, 102
Inertia, 29
  moment of, 128
Inertial reference frame, 436
Infrasonic waves, 256
In-phase vibrations, 246, 257
Instantaneous acceleration, 16
Instantaneous speed, 2
Instantaneous velocity, 3, 16
Intensity:
  of sound, 256
Intensity level, 257
Interference, 426
  double-slit, 429
  of sound waves, 257
  thin film, 427
Internal energy, 227
Internal reflection, 402
Internal resistance, 298
Isobaric process, 227
Isothermal process, 228
Isotope, 464
Isotropic material, 190
Isovolumic process, 227

Jackscrew, 97
Joule (unit), 79
Junction rule, 327

Kelvin scale, 190, 229
  and molecular energy, 207
Kilogram (unit), 30
Kilomole (unit), 196
Kilowatt-hour (unit), 80
Kinetic energy, 79, 437
  of gas molecule, 206
  rotational, 128
  translational, 79
  Kinectic friction, 30
Kinetic theory of gases, 206–212
Kirchhoff's Laws, 327

Large calorie, 213
Law:
  of cosines, 485
  of reflection, 391
  of sines, 485
  of universal gravitation, 30
Length contraction, 437
Lens(es):
  combinations of, 418
  in contact, 411
  equation for, 410, 411
  power of, 411
ray diagrams for, 409–417
Lensmaker's equation, 411
Lenz's Law, 355
Lever arm, 65
Levers, 94
Light:
  absorption of, 455
  diffraction of, 426

Light (*Cont.*)
emission of, 454
interference of, 426
reflection of, 319–400
refraction of, 401–409
speed of, 401
Light quantum, 445
Limit of resolution, 426
Limiting speed, relativity, 436
Linear momentum, 101–114
Logarithms, 492
Longitudinal waves, 247
resonance of, 247
speed of, 246
Loop rule, 327
Loudness level, 257
Loudness of sound, 257
Lyman series, 454

Machines, 93–100
Magnet, 335
Magnetic field, 335
charge motion in, 335, 336
lines of, 335
of long straight wire, 347
of magnet, 335
sources of, 335–346
torque due to, 337
Magnetic field strength, 335
Magnetic flux, 337, 354
Magnetic flux density, 337
Magnetic force:
on current, 337
on magnet, 336
on moving charge, 335
Magnetic induction, 337
Magnetic moment of coil, 348
Magnetic permeability, 348, 354
Magnetic quantum number, 459
Magnification, 393
Magnifying glass, 418
Manometer, 171
Mass, 29
of atoms and molecules, 206
relativistic, 436
and weight, 30
Mass center, 102
Mass density, 158
Mass number, 463
Mass spectrograph, 466
Mean free path, 207
Mechanical advantage, 93
Meters, ac, 382
Metric prefixes, 495
Michelson interferometer, 430
Microscope, 418, 421, 424
Mirrors, 391
equations for, 392
ray diagrams for, 392
Modulus of elasticity, 159
Mole (unit), 196
Molecular mass, 196, 199
Molecular speeds, 206
Molecular weight, 196
Moment arm (*see* Lever arm)
Moment of inertia, 128
of various objects, 129
Momentum:
angular, 129
linear, 101–114
relativistic, 436
Motion,
five equations for, 15
relative, 11
Motion, rotational, 115–144
equations for, 116
Motional emf, 355
Motor, 366
Multielectron atoms, 459–462
Mutual inductance, 372

Natural frequency (*see* Resonance frequency)
Nature of light, 391
Nearpoint of eye, 418
Nearsightedness, 418, 419
Neutrino, 471
Neutron, 463
Newton (unit), 29
Newton's Law of Gravitation, 30

Newton's Laws of Motion, 29–54
Newton's rings, 430
Node, 246
Node rule, 327
Normal force, 30, 55
Nuclear equations, 465
Nuclear fission, 475
Nuclear force, 463
Nuclear fusion, 475
Nuclear physics, 463–474
Nucleon, 463
Nucleus of atom, 463
Nutritionist's calorie, 213

Ohm (unit), 297
Ohm's Law, 297
  ac circuit forms, 382
Opera glass, 425
Optical instruments, 418–425
Optical path length, 427
Orbital quantum number, 459
Order number, 426
Out-of-phase vibrations, 246, 257
Overtones, 246

Pair production, 447
Parallel-axis theorem, 129
Parallel plates, 283
Parallelogram method, 4
Paramagnetism, 354
Parent nucleus, 471
Partial pressure, 197
Particle in a tube, 450
Pascal (unit), 158
Pascal's principle, 168
Paschen series, 454
Path length, 1
Path length, optical, 427
Pauli exclusion principle, 459
Pendulum, 148
  ballistic, 105
  conical, 121
  energy in., 86
  seconds, 156
Perfectly elastic collision, 102
Period, 145, 147, 148, 245
  and frequency, 245
  in SHM, 145, 147, 148
Permeability:
  of free space, 348,
  magnetic, 348, 354
  relative, 354
Permittivity, 268
Phase, 246, 257, 426
  in ac circuits, 382
  change upon reflection, 430
  in light waves, 426
Photoelectric effect, 445
  atomic, 457
Photoelectric equation, 445
Photon, 445, 446
Physical constants, table of, 497
Pipes, resonance of, 251
Planck's constant, 445
Plane mirror, 391, 394, 395
Point charge:
  field of, 269
  potential of, 281
Poise (unit), 180
Poiseuille (unit), 180
Poiseuille's Law, 180
Pole of magnet, 335
Polygon method, 3
Positron, 463
Postulates of relativity, 436
Potential, absolute, 281
Potential difference, 281
  related to *E*, 282
  and work, 281
Potential, electric, 281
Potential energy:
  elastic, 146
  electric, 283
  gravitational, 80
  spring, 145
Power, 80–89
  ac electrical, 383
  dc electrical, 307–311
  of lens, 411
  in rotation, 129
Power factor, 383, 385

Prefixes, SI, 495
Pressure, 167, 207
  due to a fluid, 167
  of ideal gas, 207
  standard, 167
  and work, 180
Principal focus, 391, 409
Principal quantum number, 459
Prism, 402
Probability and entropy, 240, 243
Projectile motion, 16
  and range, 20–27
Proper length, 437
Proper time, 437
Proton, 463
Pulley systems, 56, 95, 133
  differential, 98

Quality factor, radiation, 475
Quantized energies, 446
Quantum numbers, 459
Quantum physics, 445–452
Quantum of radiation, 445
*R* value, 222
Rad (unit), 475
Radial acceleration, 116
Radian measure, 115
Radiation damage, 475
Radiation dose, 475
Radiation of heat, 222
Radioactivity, 463
Radium, 468
Radius of gyration, 128
Range of projectile, 25
Ray diagrams:
  lenses, 409
  mirrors, 391, 392
RBE, 476
*R-C* circuit, 372–380
  current in, 373, 374
  time constant of, 373
Reactance, 382
Real image, 392
Recoil, 104
Reference circle, 147
Reference frame, 436
Reflection, Law of, 391
Refraction, 401–409
Refractive index, 401
Relative humidity, 214
Relative motion, 10
Relative permeability, 354
Relativistic mass, 436
Relativity, 436–444
  energy in, 436
  length in, 437
  linear momentum in, 436
  mass in, 436
  time in, 437
  velocity addition in, 438
Rem (unit), 476
Resistance, 297
  temperature variation of, 298
Resistivity, 298
Resistors:
  in parallel, 312
  power loss in, 307
  in series, 312
Resolution, limit of, 426
Resonance, 246, 247
  of de Broglie waves, 446, 450
  of *L-C* circuit, 383
Resonance frequency, 246, 247
Rest energy, 437
Restitution coefficient, 102
Restoring force, 145
Resultant, 3, 4, 5
Reversible change, 240
Reynolds number, 181
Right-hand rule:
  force on moving charge, 335
  force on wire, 337
  magnetic field of wire, 347
  torque on coil, 337, 366
Rigid-body rotation, 128–144
*R-L* circuit, 372, 373
Rocket propulsion, 111
Root mean square (rms) values, 206
Rotation of rigid bodies, 128–144

Rotational kinetic energy, 128
Rotational momentum, 129
Rotational motion:
in a plane, 115–127
of rigid bodies, 128–144
and translation, 129
Rotational power, 129
Rotational work, 129
Rydberg constant, 454

Scalar, 1
Scientific notation, 489
Screw jack, 97
Second Law of Thermodynamics, 240–244
Seconds pendulum, 156
Self-inductance, 372
Series connection, 312
Series limit, 455
Shear modulus, 159
Shear rate, 180
Shunt resistance, 321
SI prefixes, 495
Sievert (unit), 476
Significant figures, 483
Simple harmonic motion (SHM), 145–157
acceleration in, 148
energy interchange in, 146
velocity in, 146
Simple machines, 93–100
Simultaneity in relativity, 437
Single-slit diffraction, 426, 431
Sinusoidal motion, 147
Slip ring, 365
Slope, 2, 7, 18
Snell's Law, 402
Solenoid:
field of, 347, 355
self-inductance of, 372
Sound, 256–267
intensity of, 256
resonance of, 246
speed of, 256
Sources of magnetic fields, 347–353
Special Theory of Relativity, 436–444
Specific gravity, 158
Specific heat capacity, 213
of gases, 228
Spectral line, 454
Spectral series, 454
Specular reflection, 391
Speed, 2, 16
of compressional waves, 256
of gas molecules, 206
of light, 401
limiting, 436
of sound, 256,
of waves on a string, 245, 246
Spherical mirror, 392
Spin quantum number, 459
Spring:
constant of, 146
energy of, 146
Hookean, 146
period of, 147
vibration of, 145–157
Standard atmospheric pressure, 167
Standard conditions for a gas, 197
Standing waves, 246
State variables, 240
Static friction, 30
Stationary state, 446
Stefan–Boltzmann Law, 222
Stopping potential, 445
Strain, 158
Stress, 158
Sublimation, heat of, 213
Subtraction of vectors, 4
Sun, energy source of, 478
Superposition principle, 269

Tangential quantities, 116
Telephoto lens, 422
Telescope, 418, 422, 424
Temperature:
coefficient of resistance, 298
gradient of, 221
molecular basis for, 206

Temperature scales, 190, 207
Tensile force, 30, 55
Terminal potential, 298
Tesla (unit), 337
Test charge, 269
Thermal conductivity, 221
Thermal expansion, 190–195
Thermal neutron, 449
Thermal resistance, 222
Thermodynamics, 227–239
  First Law of, 227
  Second Law of, 240
  Zeroth Law of, 227
Thin lens formula, 410, 411
Thin lenses, 409, 417
  types of, 364
Threshold wavelength, 445
Time constant:
  *R-C*, 373
  *R-L*, 373
Time dilation, 437
Toroid, field of, 347
Torque, 65, 128
  and angular acceleration, 128
  axis for, 65
  on current loop, 337
  and power, 129
  work done by, 129
Torr (unit), 167
Torricelli's theorem, 181
Total internal reflection, 402
Transfer of heat, 221–226
Transformer, 383
Transverse wave, 246
Trigonometric functions, 4
  review of, 485–488
Trough of a wave, 246
Twin paradox, 441
Ultrasonic waves, 256
Uniformly accelerated motion, 15–28
Unit vectors, 5
Units, operations with, 6
Universal gas constant, 196
Uranium-235, 477
Uranium–238, 476

Vaporization, heat of, 213
Vector addition:
  component method, 5
  graphical method, 3
  parallelogram method, 4
  polygon method, 3
Vector notation, 2
Vector quantity, 2
Vector subtraction, 4
Vectors (phasors) in ac circuits, 383
Velocity, 2
  angular, 116
  components, 16
  of gas molecules, 206
  instantaneous, 3
Velocity addition, relativistic, 437
Velocity selector, 339
Venturi meter, 186
Vibratory motion, 145
Virtual image, 391, 392
Viscosity, 180
Volt (unit), 281
Voltmeter, 297

Watt (unit), 80
Wave mechanics, 445–452
Wave motion, 245–255, 426
Wave terminology, 245
Wavelength, 245
  relation to velocity and frequency, 246
Weber (unit), 354
Weight, 30, 55
  and mass, 30
Wheatstone bridge, 325
Wheel and axle, 96
Work, 79
  against gravity, 81
  electrical, 281, 307
  of expansion, 180
  in machines, 93

and *P-V* area, 228
and rotation, 129
and torque, 129
Work-energy theorem, 80
Work function, 445

X-ray diffraction, 427

Young's double slit, 429
Young's modulus, 159

Zeroth Law of Thermodynamics, 227

FIFTH EDITION



*BEARD'S MASSAGE*

# Principles and Practice *of* Soft Tissue Manipulation

**Giovanni De Domenico**
Grad Dip (Physiotherapy), Dip TP, MSc, PhD
MCSP, MAPA, MCPA
Professor and Chairman
Department of Physical Therapy
School of Allied Health Sciences
University of Texas Health Science Center at San Antonio
San Antonio, Texas

11830 Westline Industrial Drive
St. Louis, Missouri 63146

BEARD'S MASSAGE: PRINCIPLES AND PRACTICE OF SOFT TISSUE MANIPULATION, Fifth Edition ISBN 978-0-7216-0350-6



**Notice**

Knowledge and best practice in this field are constantly changing. As new research and experience broaden our knowledge, changes in practice, treatment and drug therapy may become necessary or appropriate. Readers are advised to check the most current information provided (i) on procedures featured or (ii) by the manufacturer of each product to be administered, to verify the recommended dose or formula, the method and duration of administration, and contraindications. It is the responsibility of the practitioner, relying on their own experience and knowledge of the patient, to make diagnoses, to determine dosages and the best treatment for each individual patient, and to take all appropriate safety precautions. To the fullest extent of the law, neither the Publisher nor the Author assumes any liability for any injury and/or damage to persons or property arising out or related to any use of the material contained in this book.

**Library of Congress Control Number 2007922950**



*Publishing Director:* Linda Duncan
*Senior Editor:* Kellie White
*Senior Developmental Editor:* Jennifer Watrous
*Editorial Assistant:* Elizabeth Clark
*Publishing Services Manager:* Patricia Tannian
*Project Manager:* Jonathan M. Taylor
*Designer:* Margaret Reid



Printed in the United States of America

Last digit is the print number: 9 8 7 6 5 4 3 2 1

This book is dedicated to the memory of
Gertrude Beard, RN, RPT
(1887-1971)
and to all those who seek to learn the skills of this ancient art
for the benefit of others.

# Contributors

**Patricia A. Brewer, BS, PhD**
Associate Professor, Department of Physical Therapy
Assistant Dean for Student Affairs
School of Allied Health Sciences
University of Texas Health Science Center at San Antonio
San Antonio, Texas

**Rachel Fey-Larsen, PT**
President, Forte Rehabilitation and Wellness Center
San Antonio, Texas

**Catherine Ortega, EdD, PT, ATC, OCS**
Assistant Professor, Department of Physical Therapy
School of Allied Health Sciences
University of Texas Health Science Center at San Antonio
San Antonio, Texas

**Elizabeth C. Wood, MA, MS, RPT**
Co-author of previous editions

**Colleen Liston, AUA, Grad Dip (Physiotherapy), Grad Dip Hlth Sc, MSc, PhD**
Contributor to the fourth edition

# Foreword to the First Edition

There are some things in every man's life that have a great effect upon his future success and the success of some of the people around him. One of these things happened to me when a physical therapist named Gertrude Beard came to Chicago shortly after the First World War, after she was discharged from the Army.

Miss Beard was taken onto the staff of Wesley Hospital immediately and started work on my patients, most of them workers who had been injured at the stockyards. She worked in a place called the "bath department," which consisted of one shower, one Scotch douche, a table and a couple of sinks. She and the patients had to sit on stools, and no one in the hospital took her appearance with any great degree of hope that she was going to do anything that had not been done before. At that time (1919-1920) physical therapy, in my experience, was something to do when you couldn't think of anything else to do to get rid of the patient.

Miss Beard had made a study of what was not considered a very great science at that time, and went on to develop physical therapy techniques which have brought help to many patients who would never have recovered had it not been for her efforts.

In 1927 she became the technical director of Northwestern University's new school of physical therapy. She and her teaching colleagues have taught more than five hundred physical therapists the techniques and principles of physical therapy since that date. The story of their work is worth noting—a story of devoted, dedicated persons who believe in what they know, and who continue to educate doctors and patients as well as students in the benefits of physical therapy and especially massage.

Massage has often been neglected in favor of other physical measures which can be used more easily. Massage requires skilled use of the hands and brain for its curative effects—producing or regaining elasticity of tissues, stimulating blood supply, giving the patient confidence and at the same time giving him encouragement and psychological stimulation to use the part that is disabled—and no machine can substitute. There is a psychology that goes along with any form of medical treatment, and if the physical therapist is not using his or her powers of encouragement to get the patient to do what he should do, then he or she is not doing a job in whatever is being done.

In my opinion massage is one of the things that can be neglected, misused, paid for and thrown out the window without accomplishing what it should unless it is understood and properly applied. This book presents a clear picture of techniques and the principles upon which they are based. The text is well written and illustrated and should be read and reread by the doctor and the physical therapist to the ever-lasting benefit of the patient's recovery.

**Paul B. Magnuson, MD**
Professor of Bone and Joint Surgery,
Emeritus, Northwestern University Medical School
Founder and Honorary Chairman,
Rehabilitation Institute of Chicago
Former Chief Medical Director,
Veterans Administration
May 1964

# Preface

As outlined in the previous edition, the basic principles and techniques of soft tissue manipulation (massage) have changed very little with the passage of time. Although a variety of new techniques have been introduced in recent years, together with a few new treatment concepts, in the main we continue to use and develop the time-honored principles of this most ancient healing art. Since the publication of the fourth edition in 1997, there has been a significant interest in the concepts of health and wellness and the importance of a holistic approach to the maintenance and promotion of health in all its dimensions. This has prompted a change in title for the fifth edition of this classic text.

## BACKGROUND

As a pioneer in the development of the physical therapy profession in the United States, Gertrude Beard played an important role in promoting the use of soft tissue massage. However, she did not develop a particular system of massage that could be called *Beard's Massage*. Instead, she promoted an understanding and use of many of the classical techniques of massage. For this reason, the fifth edition has been retitled, but still includes the name of Ruth Beard as a tribute to her enduring legacy in promoting the use of massage. It is evident from a study of the history of massage that there were, and still are, many different systems and schools of massage. However, all types of massage fall under the general concept of soft tissue manipulation (STM), because they are in most cases performed by the hands on a wide variety of the soft tissues of the body. The new title of this book reflects this reality while giving the founding author her rightful place of honor. In addition, the retention of the dedication to Gertrude Beard from the first edition's Foreword by Dr. Paul B. Magnuson (1884-1968) continues to honor these two pioneers in physical therapy and rehabilitation over a period of some 50 years.

The fourth edition marked a significant rearrangement of material from previous editions and the addition of several new sections. In particular, the new photographs were a major feature. The fourth edition was very successful and was translated into Spanish, Portuguese, Italian, and Japanese. The fifth edition builds on the success of its predecessor and includes an exciting new concept in the study of this most ancient of therapeutic arts.

## NEW TO THIS EDITION

The fifth edition contains many new features, including new chapters: Anatomical Landmarks for Therapeutic Massage (Chapter 2), Focal Massage Sequences (Chapter 9), Decongestive Therapy for the Treatment of Lymphedema (Chapter 12), Massage in Sport (Chapter 13), Massage for the Baby and Infant (Chapter 14), and Soft Tissue Manipulation in Complementary/Alternative Medicine (Chapter 16). Chapter 17, Eastern Systems of Soft Tissue Manipulation, has been greatly expanded. The newest and most exciting feature is a companion DVD video that complements the text and photographs, providing the necessary guide to the proper techniques for each of the strokes discussed. Although still photographs are helpful in showing hand positions, they cannot show the proper timing and flow of the techniques as well as video. Each stroke is described and demonstrated on several body areas. The text indicates the applicable chapter on the DVD by using the prefix *DVD* before the specific chapter numbers. For example, *DVD 4-12* indicates video clip number 12 from Chapter 4 of the text. These cross-references should be a tremendous help to students of massage, because they will be able to easily find a demonstration of each technique on the DVD that matches the description and information in the text. In addition to demonstrations of the basic Swedish remedial massage techniques, the DVD features an important section on surface anatomy. This section supports all of the practical chapters of the text. The DVD also demonstrates the basic techniques of passive movement to the neck and the upper and lower limbs. In addition to these innovations, the DVD contains demonstrations of the specialized decongestive massage techniques used in the management of lymphedema, which is described in Chapter 12 of the text.

Many of the photographs in the text are new, especially those in Chapter 4. They were taken as still shots from the video used to produce the DVD. In this way, readers of the text will be able to see the same photographic illustration in the text as that seen on the DVD. Once again, without the assistance of the models, the new photographs would not have turned out so well. Sincere thanks are extended to Mark DeAnder, Lauren Burns, Tim Hoover, and Robert Culp for their important contribution to this work. Likewise, I am very grateful to Eric Hanken and all of his staff at Bauhaus Media Group, especially Steve Cox, who edited the video. Sincere thanks are also extended to Rachel Fey-Larsen, who in addition to her work on the video and the chapter on the management of lymphedema, generously allowed me to use her physical therapy clinic as the venue for the filming of the DVD.

The Swedish remedial massage tradition continues to be the heart of the techniques described in the text. Each massage stroke is described in expanded detail and is complemented by the photographs and video. This will enable readers to develop their own massage sequences, properly based on knowledge of the effects of the stroke and the specific needs of each patient. As an important guide to planning sequences of massage strokes, Chapters 5 and 6 on general and local massage techniques continue to follow quite closely the methods described in the previous editions. In this regard, I wish to acknowledge the tremendous contribution of the authors of the third edition, Elizabeth Wood and Paul Becker, whose work I have continued to incorporate into the present text.

In the previous edition, several new chapters considered massage systems from a number of different traditions. These important contributions have been expanded in the fifth edition. Once again, the material in these chapters is intended to provide only an expanded outline of the subject areas, since a complete examination of each concept is well beyond the scope and intent of the present text. I am therefore deeply grateful to Dr. Patricia Brewer, Rachel Fey-Larsen, and Dr. Catherine Ortega for their outstanding commitment and dedication to providing this important information.

## NOTE TO THE STUDENT

The fifth edition of this classic text is once again intended for those pursuing a serious study of massage. The material is arranged to facilitate such study, especially with the inclusion of the DVD demonstrating each basic technique through video. Of course, effective massage cannot be learned entirely from a textbook or a video. Only close guidance from an experienced teacher will ensure that the student reaches the appropriate level of competence in what is, after all, a finely tuned motor skill on the part of the therapist.

As with previous editions, the current text does not pretend to be sufficient in itself, but I believe it does provide the background information and concepts necessary to give the theoretical framework for the subject area, along with the basic elements of the practical techniques for several types of soft tissue manipulation. Together with an experienced teacher and sufficient practice, the student should expect to be able to reach high levels of competence. A serious study of soft tissue manipulation continues to be one of the very best ways of developing sensitivity and competence in using the hands for therapeutic purposes. In my view, significant training in massage should be an essential part of the preparation of rehabilitation professionals.

**Giovanni De Domenico**
San Antonio, Texas
January 2007

# Contents


**PART ONE GENERAL PRINCIPLES**

Chapter 1 Historical Perspectives, *3*

An Overview of the History of Massage, *3*
A Review of the Historical Writings on Massage, *6*

Chapter 2 Anatomical Landmarks for Therapeutic Massage, *37*

***Patricia A. Brewer***

Head and Neck, *37*
Upper Limb, *38*
Back, *41*
Lower Limb, *42*

Chapter 3 Essential Requirements for Soft Tissue Manipulation, *49*

Ethical Issues, *49*
Knowledge of Surface Anatomy, *50*
Preparation of the Hands for Massage, *50*
Lubricants: Powders, Creams, and Oils, *52*
Treatment Tables, Chairs, and Accessories, *53*
Draping and Positioning the Patient, *55*
Body Mechanics of the Therapist, *57*
Essential Components of Massage, *61*
Indications and Contraindications for the Use of Massage, *66*

Chapter 4 Classification, Definitions, and Descriptions of the Basic Massage Strokes and Relaxed Passive Movements, *69*

Classification of Massage Strokes, *70*
Stroking Manipulations, *71*
Pressure Manipulations, *79*
Percussive Manipulations (Tapotement), *91*
Vibration and Shaking, *97*
Deep Frictions (Cyriax Frictions), *99*
Relaxed Passive Movements, *104*

Chapter 5 Mechanical, Physiological, Psychological, and Therapeutic Effects of Soft Tissue Manipulation, *117*

Mechanical Effects, *118*
Physiological Effects, *119*
Psychological Effects, *131*
Primary Therapeutic Effects of Massage, *133*
Therapeutic Uses of Massage, *133*
Indications for Therapeutic Massage, *133*
Contraindications to Massage, *133*
General Precautions, *136*

**PART TWO PRACTICE**

Chapter 6 Soft Tissue Manipulation Techniques as an Evaluation Tool, *145*

Stroking and Effleurage, *146*
Pressure Manipulations (Pétrissage), *146*
Percussion and Vibration Manipulations, *146*
Deep Friction Techniques, *146*

Chapter 7 General Massage Sequences, *149*

A Sequence and Technique for General Massage, *149*
Techniques for a General Massage Sequence, *150*
Specific Techniques for a General Massage Sequence, *152*

Chapter 8 Local Massage Sequences, *183*

The Hoffa System, *184*
Technique for a Local Massage Sequence, *188*

Chapter 9 Focal Massage Sequences, *215*

Depletive Massage, *215*
Chronic Edema, *217*
Hematoma, *217*
Cutaneous Scar Tissue, *219*
Muscle, Tendon, or Ligament Adhesion, *221*
Colon Dysfunction, *222*
Muscle Dysfunction: Facilitation of Muscle Contraction, *223*

**Chapter 10** Massage for the Patient with a Respiratory Condition, *225*

Relaxation, *225*
Airway Clearance, *226*
Postural Drainage, *226*
Percussion Techniques, *227*
Vibration and Shaking, *232*
Deep Breathing and Coughing, *233*
Passive Movements of the Lower Limbs, *233*

**Chapter 11** Connective Tissue Massage, *235*

Brief History and Theoretical Foundations, *235*
Reflex Zones (Head's Zones), *235*
Basic Diagnostic Technique for Connective Tissue Massage, *237*
Basic Treatment Technique, *239*
Effects of Connective Tissue Massage, *240*
Treatment Indications, *241*
Treatment Frequency and Duration, *241*
Contraindications, *241*

**Chapter 12** Decongestive Therapy for the Treatment of Lymphedema, *245*

***Rachel Fey-Larsen***

The Lymphatic System, *245*
Pathophysiology, *247*
Principles of Treatment, *247*
Evaluation, *249*
Skin and Wound Care, *250*
Lymph Fluid Mobilization, *250*
Strokes, *251*
Sequences and Pathways, *252*
Compression Therapy, *259*
Therapeutic Exercises, *260*
Patient Education, *260*

**Chapter 13** Massage in Sport, *266*

***Catherine Ortega***

History of Sports Massage, *267*
Therapeutic Effects of Massage for an Athlete, *267*

**Chapter 14** Massage for the Baby and Infant, *279*

Technique for Baby or Infant Massage, *280*
General Whole-Body Stroking, *280*
Head and Face, *281*
Upper Limbs, *281*
Chest and Abdomen, *283*
Lower Limbs, *283*
Back, *285*
Buttocks, *285*
Suckling, *286*

**Chapter 15** Massage in Palliative Care, *290*

Ancient versus Modern Care of the Dying, *290*
Massage Techniques for the Elderly Patient Who Is Terminally Ill, *291*
Techniques, *291*

**Chapter 16** Soft Tissue Manipulation in Complementary/Alternative Medicine, *294*

Myofascial Release Techniques, *295*
Trigger Point Therapy, *297*
Reflexology, *301*
Rolfing Structural Integration, *304*
Point Percussion Therapy, *304*
Craniosacral Therapy, *305*

**Chapter 17** Eastern Systems of Soft Tissue Manipulation, *310*

Acupressure, *310*
Shiatsu, *314*
Traditional Oriental Massage, *316*
Traditional Thai Massage, *317*
Huna Massage, *318*

**Appendix** Closed-Chest (External) Cardiac Massage, *321*

**Index**, *323*

# Part One
## General Principles

# Chapter 1

# Historical Perspectives

Massage is an ancient healing art, and there is growing scientific evidence of its effectiveness in the management of patients in a wide variety of diseased and traumatic states. As a medical art, it is practiced in many different ways among the diverse cultures around the world. This chapter concentrates primarily on the historical development of massage as it pertains to the use of Western concepts of medical practice. In particular, the chapter concentrates on the history of the place of massage in modern rehabilitation practice.

The modern French words *masser* (verb) and *massage* (noun) could have derived from any of three original roots, namely the Hebrew word *mashesh,* the Arabic word *mass,* or the Greek word *massin.* Although obviously French in origin, *masseur* (male) and *masseuse* (female) are used in the English language to denote those who practice massage. By the early 1780s, the word *massage* was used in India, and it appeared in most European cultures around 1800.

Massage is mentioned as a form of treatment in the earliest medical records, and its use has persisted throughout recorded history. Writings of physicians, philosophers, poets, and historians show that people from the most ancient of times in cultures all around the world used some form of rubbing or anointing. The history of massage is large and complex. This chapter presents a broad overview of its chronology and a more detailed review of a number of the important aspects of massage.

## AN OVERVIEW OF THE HISTORY OF MASSAGE

### Prehistoric Times

Although there is little direct evidence that massage was practiced as a healing art in prehistoric times, it seems likely that it was. There is a certain instinctive quality to the use of the hands in a rubbing and squeezing motion that is both soothing and comforting. Indeed, many animal species, especially primates, use grooming behavior, and, although it is not necessarily therapeutic, it is certainly part of the behavioral repertoire of many species. In short, touching as an activity probably has its genesis at the earliest times in the development of human culture. It seems quite likely that some type of manual techniques (e.g., massage) were in regular use then, together with the application of various medicinal compounds derived from plants, animal sources, and inorganic materials.

Although such ancient cultures had little, if any, recorded history, massage techniques almost certainly were part of their medical culture. Certainly, prehistoric humans were capable of practicing sophisticated medicine, including brain surgery. The well-known prehistoric practice of removing small circles of bone from the skull, called *trephining* (or *trepanning*), clearly shows that the practitioners of the day were capable of complex medical tasks (Broca, 1876; Prunieres, 1874). Not only were they able to make holes in the skulls of their patients, but these latter-day surgeons were able to do this more than once in a given person. In addition, the findings clearly show that many people survived the procedure, as evidenced by the presence of healed areas of bone in the skull. One cannot help but believe that a culture capable of this level of surgical practice must long before have discovered the considerable and obvious benefits of massage-like treatments.

### Ancient History

The use of manual massage techniques in many ancient cultures is well documented in extensive written and pictorial records. For example, at the time of Hwang Ti, the Yellow Emperor (d. 2599 BC), the great Chinese medical work known as the *Nei Chang* was written (ca. 2760 BC).

This work contains detailed descriptions of massage-like procedures and a great many details of their use (Veith, 1949). During the Tang dynasty (AD 619-907), four primary kinds of medical practitioners were recognized: physicians, acupuncturists, masseurs, and exorcists; however, following the Sung dynasty (AD 960-1279), the use of massage declined greatly. Massage is also described in one of ancient India's first great medical writings, the *Ayur-Veda* books of wisdom (about 1800 BC). Most of the great ancient cultures of the world have described in some detail the uses and benefits of massage, which was often combined with other kinds of traditional treatment, particularly bath treatments. The Egyptian, Persian, and Japanese cultures, in particular, placed great emphasis on the use of massage and these allied treatments.

The ancient Greeks used massage widely to maintain physical health and ensure lasting beauty. Homer described in *The Odyssey* how war-torn soldiers were massaged back to health. Hippocrates (460-360 BC) also wrote on the subject and described many of the uses of massage in medical practice. In discussing treatment following reduction of a dislocated shoulder, Hippocrates said:

> *And it is necessary to rub the shoulder gently and smoothly. The physician must be experienced in many things, but assuredly also in rubbing; for things that have the same name have not the same effects. For rubbing can bind a joint which is too loose and loosen a joint that is too hard. However, a shoulder in the condition described should be rubbed with soft hands and, above all things, gently; but the joint should be moved about, not violently, but so far as it can be done without producing pain. (Johnson, 1866)*

The ancient Greeks, perhaps more than other cultures, are responsible for giving massage such a high level of social acceptance. They established elaborate bathhouses where exercise, massage, and bathing were available, but the patrons were lovers of luxury and questionable behaviors rather than seekers of health. The bathhouses were the playgrounds of the rich and powerful. Ordinary citizens were not so fortunate.

The Romans inherited much of the tradition of massage from the Greeks, and it was widely used, especially in conjunction with hot baths. Galen (AD 131-201), the most famous physician in the Roman Empire, wrote extensively on the topic of massage and described several ways in which it could be administered. Julius Caesar (ca. 100 BC) is said to have had himself pinched all over as a cure for a complaint similar to neuralgia. The influence of Galen on all aspects of medical thinking cannot be overstated; it is probably because of him that massage and its allied treatments survived long after the fall of Rome. Galen strongly recommended that in preparation for impending combat, gladiators be rubbed all over until their skin was red. The use of massage continued, and it was not until the early part of the Middle Ages that it fell into some decline in Europe and Asia. This era was known as the Dark Ages, when many aspects of ancient culture and practice were abandoned.

## Modern History of Medical Massage (European, Mainly British)

Much of ancient culture and tradition in medicine and science was lost through the Middle Ages, and it was not until the Renaissance, especially in the sixteenth century, that some of the older methods of medical practice were again used. Advances in the study of anatomy and physiology enabled scientists of the time to understand more about the effects and uses of some of these more ancient traditions. Ambroise Paré (1518-1590), the famous French surgeon, was among the earliest writers to consider and discuss the effects of massage. Paré was particularly interested in the use of friction and general massage movements to treat patients who had dislocated a joint.

Harvey's discovery of the circulation of the blood in 1628 did much to enhance the acceptance of massage as a therapeutic measure. Despite these seemingly important advances, massage treatments did not become popular throughout Europe until the eighteenth century. At that time, two of the more notable exponents of the treatment were Germans, namely Hoffmann (1660-1742) and Guthsnuths. Another famous physician, who claimed in the 1880s that massage could be a very useful treatment, particularly to the soft tissues following fracture, was the famous French physician Just Lucas-Championnière (1843-1913). In the late 1890s, Sir William Bennett was impressed with Lucas-Championnière's work and began what was then a revolutionary treatment using massage at St. George's Hospital in London, England. Other authors also strongly advocated massage for a variety of soft tissue problems, especially writer's cramp (Robins, 1885; de Watteville, 1885a, 1885b).

The era of modern massage is usually said to have begun during the early 1800s, when a wide variety of authors were advocating massage and developing their own systems. A famous thesis by Estradere in 1886 was an important contribution to the developing science of massage (Estradere, 1863).

Arguably, the most famous and enduring influence on massage is the contribution made by Pehr Henrik Ling (1776-1839). Ling developed his own style of massage and exercises, which later gained international recognition as Swedish remedial massage and exercise (Benjamin, 1993; Ostrom, 1918). Ling was a fencing instructor, and in 1805 he was appointed gymnastics and fencing master to the University of Lund in Sweden. He designed a system of his own that consisted of four types of gymnastics: educational, military, medical, and aesthetic. In 1813 he founded the Central Institute of Gymnastics in Stockholm, and he taught there until his death in 1839. Much of Ling's work was published after his death, mainly owing to the efforts of his students and colleagues (Kellgren, 1890). He gained international recognition for the terminology that bears his name, and in many cases modifications of his basic concepts of exercise have been used throughout the world. In more recent times, however, many of Ling's original ideas faded from popularity, but his work remains an important influence in the early development of the profession of physical therapy (physiotherapy).

In Holland, Johann Mezger (1839-1909) also used massage widely and developed his own style. By 1900 modern medical massage techniques were being used in most parts of the developed world and, of course, their use continued in the more ancient cultures. In fact, "manual medicine" had become an integrated part of a modern approach to the treatment of trauma and disease (Harris & McPartland, 1996).

In England in 1894, a group of four dedicated women founded the Society of Trained Masseuses with the aim of raising the standards of massage and the status of women taking up the work. In 1900 the society was incorporated by license to the Board of Trade and became known as the Incorporated Society of Trained Masseuses. During World War I, membership rose, and by 1920 some 5000 members were practicing. In 1920 the society merged with the Institute of Massage and Remedial Exercises (Manchester). These two bodies were then granted a Royal Charter and became known as the Chartered Society of Massage and Medical Gymnastics (CSMMG). World War II saw the emergence of a young profession, as large numbers of soldiers returned from various parts of the world, and the role of physiotherapy became more important. Massage alone became less important as other means of rehabilitation were developed. For this reason, in 1943 the name of the society was changed to the Chartered Society of Physiotherapy (CSP).

From similar beginnings in many other countries, the modern profession of physical therapy as it is now known developed and branched into most parts of the world, developing differently in each region to accommodate particular needs. Medical massage is rarely used in modern rehabilitation practice as a treatment in its own right, but it is used as part of an overall treatment plan for some patients. It has largely been superseded by other, more active treatments, but it remains one of the most important means of developing hand skills in the therapist. In physical therapy practice, soft tissue massage has developed into many types of manual mobilizing techniques that take the form of a wide variety of manipulations performed on both soft tissues and joint structures. In effect, the skilled use of the hands is still the cornerstone of the profession of physical therapy and is likely to remain so for the foreseeable future. Although massage is rarely used as the sole treatment in physical therapy and many other manual techniques have become popular, it is still an important part of the range of soft tissue techniques that aspiring therapists should learn (Domenech, 1996).

In many older Asian cultures such as China, Japan, and India, massage is still used extensively as part of the traditional methods of treatment. Massage as a specific treatment in its own right plays a relatively small role in modern Western medicine; however, in recent years in many countries, specific massage professionals (massage therapists) have emerged. In this case, the treatment modality is massage itself. It is important to remember that the modern profession of physical therapy came into existence around the turn of the twentieth century and that massage techniques were established in medical practice long before that time. In fact, massage has a long tradition of use in the nursing profession (Estabrooks, 1987; Goldstone, 1999, 2000), which predates the rehabilitation professions by many centuries. In recent decades, the nursing profession has rediscovered its massage heritage and is once more employing the benefits of massage, along with other newly emerging massage professions (Huebscher, 1998; Mallios, 1996; Palmer, 1992; Wright, 1995).

Massage techniques can be used to promote a general sense of relaxation and wellness. These days, thanks to the resurgence of interest in holistic medicine and popular concepts of wellness, the general public still has great faith in the "laying on of hands"; however, such forms of massage need to be differentiated from the medical massage techniques used in other health professions, especially physical therapy. These more general massage techniques, performed on persons who are otherwise healthy, may be termed *recreational massage* and should not be confused with the term *therapeutic massage*. These terms are defined in more detail in Chapter 3.

Another technique that appears to be similar to massage is known as "therapeutic touch." This somewhat controversial technique needs to be clearly differentiated from therapeutic massage. Essentially, although the name implies that touching is involved, in its original conception therapeutic touch does not actually require the therapist to touch the patient. The therapist's hands simply move *over* the part to be treated without actually making contact. Supporters claim that the technique balances energy fields around the affected parts (Feltham, 1991; Ireland & Olson, 2000; Krieger, 1979, 1981).

Because the primary effects of therapeutic massage are mechanical, a technique that does not have a mechanical component cannot work on the same principles. Other effects must be invoked to explain its efficacy. Although therapeutic touch is a popular facet of New Age medicine, it is a long way from enjoying strong scientific acceptance. Paradoxically, this concept is not new. Traditional Chinese medicine has many techniques that are similar to so-called therapeutic touch.

This text considers only the theory and practice of therapeutic massage. In this regard, the major influence behind the techniques described is the Swedish remedial massage tradition (Benjamin, 1993; Ostrom, 1918). Before describing these techniques in detail, the history of various aspects of medical massage must be explored. This section is self-contained and may be referred to in relative isolation from the rest of the text, as many of the concepts mentioned here are expanded upon throughout the remainder of the book. The review focuses on a number of aspects of the practice of massage rather than on a chronological history. Readers interested in the history of soft tissue manipulation from these perspectives are directed to the following sources: Beard (1952), Bohm (1918), Braverman and Schulman (1999), Bucholz (1917), Cole and Stovell (1991), Despard (1932), Graham (1884, 1913), Henry (1884), Johnson (1866), Kamentz (1960, 1985), Mason (1992), Quintner (1993, 1994), and Stockton (1994).

## A REVIEW OF THE HISTORICAL WRITINGS ON MASSAGE

A review of the early literature on massage demonstrates a surprising lack of detailed descriptions of the massage strokes themselves. Even the more recent material reveals a lack of information on the actual techniques of massage. Given the great variations in massage techniques used today and the limited scientific rationale for their use, one might wonder if it is possible to draw any conclusions about their value—or lack of it—in modern rehabilitation. The remainder of this chapter considers the paucity of detailed information on techniques and confusion about the meaning of the terms currently in use. It is not a complete account of the history of massage, as only the techniques are considered and the methods compared to determine, if possible, their influence on the development of present-day methods and techniques. This account does not cover every technique that can be found in the literature, only the most common ones still in use. Some techniques that were once popular are not considered here because they are no longer used to any great degree. An excellent example is the many different types of nerve manipulation. Once quite popular, these techniques could involve direct stroking, friction, or stretching of the major peripheral nerves (Jabre, 1994; Lace, 1946). It will be interesting to see if in the future these techniques are rediscovered.

### Definitions of Massage

A comprehensive definition of massage cannot be found in the early medical literature. *Thomas's Medical Dictionary* (1886) offers the following description: "Massage, from the Greek, meaning to knead. Signifying the act of shampooing." (*Shampoo* is from the Hindi, meaning "to press.") Throughout much of the history of medicine, massage and exercises are referred to simultaneously, and early writers make little distinction between the two. Kleen (1847-1923) of Sweden, who first published a handbook of massage in 1895, claimed to be the first to show clearly that massage is not an exercise therapy (Kleen, 1906, 1921).

William Murrell (1853-1912) of Edinburgh and London, writing at about the same time, was more specific when he defined massage as "the scientific mode of treating certain forms of a disease by systematic manipulations." He limited massage to the amelioration of disease but evidently realized the need for a system for its use. He placed no limit on the means of massage. At the same time, Douglas Graham of Boston, writing from 1884 to 1918, described massage as

> *a term now generally accepted by European and American physicians to signify a group of procedures which are usually done with the hands, such as friction, kneading, manipulations, rolling, and percussion of the external tissues of the body in a variety of ways, either with a curative, palliative, or hygienic object in view.*

He went much further than Murrell (in recognizing that the term needed definition) and limited the means to the hand and the surfaces involved to the external tissues. Graham identified the objectives as being curative, palliative, or hygienic.

Kleen, one of Graham's contemporaries, limited the areas involved to the soft tissues. In addition to the hand as a means of administering massage, he included ancillary apparatuses. This seems contradictory given that he eliminated the idea that massage is exercise. In this he differed from his early compatriot, Ling.

Albert Hoffa (1859-1907) of Germany also limited the means of massage to the hand but embraced its broad application—to all the mechanical procedures that can cure illness (Hoffa, 1897). At about the same time, another German, J.B. Zabludowski (1851-1906), also limited the administration of massage to the hand but specified "skillful hand grasps, skillfully and systematically applied to the body." While limiting the movement to skillful hand grasps, he, like Murrell, recognized the use of systems (Zabludowski, 1903).

C. Herman Bucholz of the United States (Boston) and Germany was as imprecise as any of his predecessors. He did not mention the hand or any other means of administering massage in his recommendations for therapeutic manipulation of the soft tissues. Even James B. Mennell (1880-1957), whose great contributions have made the science of massage what it is today, gave no formal definition of massage.

In 1932, John S. Coulter (1885-1949) said:

> *According to the present, generally accepted meaning of the word, massage includes a great number of manipulations of the tissues and organs of the body for therapeutic purposes.*

In 1952, Gertrude Beard (1887-1971) wrote of massage as

> *the term used to designate certain manipulations of the soft tissues of the body; these manipulations are most effectively performed with the hands and are administered for the purpose of producing effects on the nervous, muscular, and respiratory systems and the local and general circulation of the blood and lymph.*

### Massage Terminology

A study of the literature in this area might easily lead to confusion over the number of different terms used to describe the various techniques of massage. Despite some similarities, there is considerable confusion, and a comparison reveals that few writers have given the same meanings to these terms. A survey of these differences seems useful if one is to interpret correctly any reading of earlier massage techniques and at the same time possess a clear idea of the meanings as they are presently accepted and used in this text. Much of the background information in this area comes from the work of Graham (1884, 1913).

The various advocates of massage among the ancient Greeks and Romans, from the time of Homer in the eighth century BC through the fourth and fifth centuries AD, used relatively consistent terminology. For example, these writers most frequently used the terms *friction, rubbing,* and *anointing.* Celsus of Rome (25 BC-AD 50) used, in addition, the term *unction* (Cellsus, 1665). Hippocrates used the terms *anatripsis* and *rubbing.* Galen adopted the term *anatripsis* from Hippocrates but added *tripsis, tripsisparaskeu lasthke,* and *apotherapeia.* Oribasius (325-403), a Roman who followed Galen a century later, described *apotherapeia* as bathing, friction, and inunction. Other terms used in this period were *pommeling, squeezing,* and *pinching.*

There is little literature on medical practice during the Dark Ages, but massage practitioners in many European cultures during the fifteenth, sixteenth, and seventeenth centuries adopted the terminology used in the earlier period. Among those who strongly advocated the use of massage were the noted French surgeon Ambroise Pare and the famous English physician Thomas Sydenham (1624-1689), who confined their terminology to *friction.* Alpinus (1553-1617) of Italy used *rubbing* but added *maxalation, manipulation,* and *pressure.* Frederick Hoffman (1660-1742) of Prussia adopted Galen's term *apotherapeia.* Hieronymus Fabricius (1537-1619), an Italian, seems to be the first to have used the term *kneading,* and he also used *rubbing.*

In the early part of the nineteenth century, there was a definite change in terminology, evidently owing to the influence of Ling. Ling, who has been credited as the originator of the Swedish system of remedial massage, traveled widely all over Europe and incorporated into his system the French terms *effleurage, pétrissage, massage à friction,* and *tapotement.* To these he added *rolling, slapping, pinching, shaking, vibration,* and *joint movement*—a specific example of a part of the present-day exercise in the classification of massage movements.

Mezger (1839-1909) of Holland used the French terminology exclusively, and William Beveridge (1774-1839) of Scotland seems to have originated the use of the term *finger rubbing.* Lucas-Championnière of France also used unique terminology: his gentle massage, which he termed *glucokinesis* and *effrayan,* influenced the massage techniques used to this day. Blundell (1864) of England used the terms *inunction, friction, pressure,* and *percussion.* In contrast, the islanders of Tonga in this same period used the terms *toogi toogi, mili,* and *fota;* Hawaiians used the term *lomi-lomi.*

In the early twentieth century, physicians in the United States contributed to the literature of massage. Graham avoided the French terms and listed "friction, kneading, manipulation, rolling, pinching, percussion, movement, pressure, squeezing" and the very early Italian term *maxalation.* In his 1919 book, J.H. Kellogg (1852-1943) describes different movements, in contrast to some of the English writers of a century earlier (e.g., John Grosvenor), who used only the term *friction.*

Murrell of Scotland and England, Kleen of Sweden, Hoffa of Germany, Bucholz of Germany and the United States, and John K. Mitchell (1859-1917) of the United States embraced the French terminology, whereas Zabludowski of Germany and Mennell of England dropped it almost entirely.

Kleen, Zabludowski, Mitchell, Bucholz, and Mennell gave a rather simple general classification of the terminology with subdivisions of the movements. Mennell's general classification identified "stroking, compression, and percussion." McMillan (1925) used "effleurage, pétrissage, friction, tapotement, and vibration." Louisa Despard (1932), Frances Tappan (1978, 1998), and Lace (1946) used a mixture of French and English terms. Elizabeth Dicke and associates (1978) used both German and English terms to describe the specialized techniques used in connective tissue massage (CTM).

The chronology described in the previous paragraphs is presented in tabular form in Table 1-1, which presents a chronology of the terminology of massage.

## Description of Massage Techniques (Strokes)

The early literature offers little description of the individual massage techniques. The present analysis has been limited to information available since the time of Ling and to those used most commonly today. To understand the meaning of the terms used by various authors, it is helpful to analyze several aspects of the techniques, including direction of the movement, amount of pressure applied, parts of the hand used to perform the technique, the actual motion performed, and the specific tissues of the body to which the massage is applied.

### Pétrissage

Several techniques come under the general heading of *pétrissage* (a French term meaning "kneading"). Essentially, these techniques involve applying pressure to the tissues in a kneading manner. They can be performed with the whole hand, the fingers, or the thumb. They may be performed with either hand or both hands at the same time. To create greater pressure to some body areas, one hand can reinforce the other.

To perform pétrissage strokes, Ling grasped the tissues between the thumb and fingers, whereas Mitchell (1904), Kellogg (1919), Bucholz (1917), and Mennell (1945) recommended chiefly using the palm in contact with the tissues.

*Text continued on p. 11.*

## Table 1-1 Terminology of Massage

| DATE | NAME | PLACE | TERMINOLOGY |
|---|---|---|---|
| **CIRCA 1000 BC to AD 500*** | | | |
| 1000 BC | Homeric Age | Greece | Anointing<br>Rubbing |
| Circa 500 BC | Herodikus | Greece | Rubbing<br>Friction |
| 484-425 BC | Herodotus | Greece | Rubbing<br>Friction |
| 460-380 BC | Hippocrates | Greece | Rubbing<br>Anatripsis |
| 128-56 BC | Asclepiades | Rome | Friction |
| 25 BC-AD 50 | Celsus; Aurelius | Rome | Friction<br>Rubbing<br>Unction |
| AD 130-200 | Galen; Claudius | Rome | Tripsis<br>Anatripsis<br>Tripsisparaskeulasthke<br>Apotherapeia |
| AD 325-403 | Oribasius | Rome | Apotherapeia<br>1. Bathing<br>2. Friction<br>3. Inunction |
| **Fifteenth, Sixteenth, and Seventeenth Centuries†** | | | |
| 1492-1541 | Paracelsus | Switzerland | Friction |
| 1510-1590 | Paré, Ambroise | France | Friction |
| 1553-1617 | Alpinus, Prospero | Italy | Rubbing<br>Maxalation<br>Manipulations<br>Pressure |
| 1537-1619 | Fabricius, Hieronymus | Italy | Rubbing<br>Kneading |
| 1624-1689 | Sydenham, Thomas | England | Friction |
| 1660-1742 | Hoffmann, Friedrich | Prussia | Apotherapeia |
| **Eighteenth and Nineteenth Centuries** | | | |
| 1731-1823 | Henry, Admiral | | Rubbing |
| 1742-1823 | Grosvenor, John | England | Friction |
| 1774-1839 | Beveridge, William | Scotland | Finger rubbing |
| 1776-1839 | Ling, Pehr Henrik | Sweden | Effleurage<br>Pétrissage<br>Massage a friction<br>Rolling<br>Slapping<br>Pinching<br>Shaking<br>Vibration<br>Tapotement<br>Joint movement |
| 1819 (date of writing) | Balfour, William | Scotland (Edinburgh) | Compression<br>Percussion<br>Friction |
| 1839-1901 | Mezger, Johann Georg | Holland (Amsterdam) | Effleurage<br>Massage à friction<br>Pétrissage<br>Tapotement<br>1. Beating<br>2. Clapping |

*Other terms used in this period were *pummeling, squeezing,* and *pinching*.

†*Sau-Tsai-Tow-Hooe,* published in Japan in the sixteenth century, shows that the Japanese used the terms *pressure, percussion,* and *vibration* (and *rubbing*) from very early periods. *Cong-Fou of the Tao-Sse* is the Chinese expression applied to physicians who use mechanical therapeutics. They rubbed the entire body with the hands and gently pressed the muscles between the fingers.

**Table 1-1 Terminology of Massage—cont'd**

| DATE | NAME | PLACE | TERMINOLOGY |
|---|---|---|---|
| **Nineteenth and Twentieth Centuries‡** | | | |
| 1843-1913 | Lucas-Championnière, Just Marie | France | Glucokinesis<br>Effrayante |
| 1847-1923 | Kleen, Emil Andreas Gabriel | Sweden | Effleurage-stroking<br>Frictions-rubbing<br>Pétrissage<br>1. Pinching<br>2. Rolling<br>3. Kneading<br>Tapotement<br>1. Slapping<br>2. Pushing<br>3. Beating<br>4. Clapping<br>5. Vibration<br>6. Shaking |
| 1848-1928 | Graham, Douglas | United States | Friction<br>Kneading<br>Manipulation<br>Rolling<br>Pinching<br>Percussion<br>Movement<br>Maxalation<br>Pressure<br>Squeezing |
| 1851-1906 | Zabludowski, J.B. | Germany | Pressure manipulations<br>1. Intermittent pounding<br>2. Slapping<br>3. Vibration<br>4. Hacking<br>5. Pinching<br>6. Shaking<br>Stroking manipulations<br>1. Rubbing<br>2. Kneading<br>3. Muscle rolling<br>4. Pressing<br>5. Stroking |
| 1852-1943 | Kellogg, J.H. | United States | Describes 37 movements including:<br>Touch<br>Stroking<br>Friction<br>Pétrissage<br>Kneading<br>1. Superficial<br>2. Deep<br>a. Palmar kneading<br>b. Fist kneading<br>c. Digital kneading<br>d. Rolling<br>e. Wringing<br>f. Chucking<br>Vibration<br>Percussion<br>Joint movement |

‡At this time, the islanders of Tonga used the terms *toogi-toogie, mili,* and *fota.* Hawaiians used the term *lomi-lomi.*

*Continued*

Table 1-1 **Terminology of Massage—cont'd**

| DATE | NAME | PLACE | TERMINOLOGY |
|---|---|---|---|
| **Nineteenth and Twentieth Centuries‡—cont'd** | | | |
| 1853-1912 | Murrell, William | Scotland and England | Effleurage<br>Pétrissage<br>Friction<br>Massage à friction<br>Tapotement |
| 1859-1907 | Hoffa, Albert | Germany | Effleurage<br>Stroking<br>Friction<br>Finger friction<br>Pétrissage<br>1. Two-hand<br>2. Two-finger<br>Vibration<br>Tapotement<br>1. Hacking<br>2. Slapping |
| 1859-1917 | Mitchell, John K. | United States (Philadelphia) | Effleurage<br>Pétrissage<br>1. Rolling<br>2. Fist kneading<br>3. Digital kneading<br>4. Wringing<br>5. Pulling<br>Friction<br>Tapotement |
| 1874 (book published in 1917) | Bucholz, C. Herman | United States | Rubbing<br>1. Simple<br>2. Effleurage<br>3. Stroking<br>Kneading<br>1. Pétrissage<br>a. Deep<br>b. Grasping<br>c. Lifting<br>d. Wringing<br>e. Pressing<br>f. Rolling<br>g. Harping<br>2. Friction<br>Clapping<br>Shaking<br>Tapotement |
| 1880-1957 | Mennell, James B. | England | Stroking<br>1. Deep<br>2. Superficial<br>Compression<br>1. Kneading<br>2. Pétrissage<br>3. Frictions<br>4. Pressure<br>Percussion<br>1. Hacking<br>2. Clapping<br>3. Beating<br>4. Vibration<br>5. Shaking |

Table 1-1 **Terminology of Massage—cont'd**

| DATE | NAME | PLACE | TERMINOLOGY |
|---|---|---|---|
| **Nineteenth and Twentieth Centuries‡—cont'd** | | | |
| Books published in 1910 and 1932 | Despard, Louisa L. | England | Effleurage<br>1. Deep<br>2. Superficial<br>Stroking<br>Massage à friction<br>Pétrissage<br>Tapotement<br>1. Clapping<br>2. Hacking<br>3. Beating<br>4. Pounding<br>Vibration<br>Shaking |
| Books published in 1944 and 1952 | Dicke, Elizabeth | Germany | Stroking<br>1. Pulling<br>2. Pull and hook-on<br>3. Widening |
| Book published in 1946 | Lace | | |
| Book published in 1959 | Cyriax, James | England | Deep massage<br>Deep friction |
| Book published in 1961 | Tappan, Frances | United States | Effleurage<br>Pétrissage<br>Tapotement<br>Friction<br>Vibration |
| Book published in 1962 | Ebner, Maria | England | Lifting<br>Pressure<br>Stroking<br>Tensile stroke<br>Lifting stroke<br>Stretching |
| Book published in 1974 | Wood, Elizabeth | United States | Stroking<br>1. Deep<br>2. Superficial<br>Kneading<br>Friction |

Hoffa and Mennell emphasized that the hand must fit the contour of the tissues. It was Hoffa (1897) who distinguished different types of pétrissage, depending on which parts of one or both hands were used to perform the movement.

According to Ling and Murrell, the motion is a rolling one and the skin moves with the fingers, but Hoffa, Mitchell, Kellogg, Despard (1932), Bucholz, and Mennell lifted the mass of tissues and used a squeezing movement. In addition to the rolling, Murrell (1886) recommended that the tissues be pressed and squeezed, similar to squeezing out a sausage. Bucholz and Mennell recommended that the hand glide over the skin instead of moving the skin along with the hand. Despard and Mennell alternately compressed the tissues between the thumb of one hand and the fingers of the other. Mezger lifted the tissues and kneaded them between the hands. In addition to lifting the tissues for pétrissage, Despard also described a type of pétrissage in which the tissues are grasped and pressed down onto the underlying structures and at the same time squeezed (compression kneading). Murrell and Hoffa stipulated firm pressure, Ling said that it varies, and Mennell prescribed that it should be gentle. Mitchell and Despard alternately increased and decreased the pressure. Kellogg stated that it must not be so great as to prevent deeper parts from gliding over still deeper structures.

Many authors mentioned that pétrissage is applied to muscle groups, individual muscles, or some part of a muscle.

Ling mentioned specifically that the skin, subcutaneous tissues, and muscles are grasped. Mitchell was not specific; he mentioned only tissues. Murrell said a portion of muscle or other tissue was manipulated. Most authors describe the direction as centripetal; Hoffa and Mennell described compression given transversely to the muscle fibers although the general movement was centripetal, and Bucholz stated that the manipulations might be either centripetal or centrifugal. Table 1-2 summarizes the various descriptions of pétrissage.

Table 1-2 **Description of Massage Movements: Pétrissage**

| NAME | DIRECTION | PRESSURE | PART OF HAND | MOTION | TISSUES |
|---|---|---|---|---|---|
| Ling | | Varying | Grasped between thumb and fingers | Kneading movements; rolled between thumb and fingers; skin moves with fingers | Skin, subcutaneous, tissue, and muscle |
| Mezger | | | | Lifting, then kneading between hands | Some part of muscle |
| Murrell | Centripetal; hands move simultaneously in opposite directions | Firm | Both hand or fingers of one hand; thumb and fingers wide apart | Pressed and rolled between fingers and subadjacent tissues; skin must move with hands; similar to squeezing out a sausage | Portion of muscle or other tissue |
| Kleen | | | | Rollings, kneadings, or pinchings | |
| Hoffa (one hand) | | Not with fingertips, but chiefly with base of thumb and index finger | Chiefly base of thumb and index finger—not tips | Lift from underlying tissues; press out like a sponge | Grasp entire bulk of muscle; begin at insertion |
| (two hands) | Transversely to muscle fibers backward and forward in opposite directions | | Both hands | Pick up and squeeze out | Crosswise before masseur; around as much of muscle as possible |
| (two fingers) | | Firm | Tip of thumb, index, and middle finger | Twisting movement of skin | Muscles that spread out and cannot be grasped by entire hand, particularly if covered by fascia |
| Mitchell | | Close—alternately tightening and loosening of the hold | Whole palm and parts of fingers nearest palm—not fingertips; fingers close together | Lifting mass a little; kneading skin to move with hands over underlying tissues | "Tissues" |

Table 1-2 **Description of Massage Movements: Pétrissage—cont'd**

| NAME | DIRECTION | PRESSURE | PART OF HAND | MOTION | TISSUES |
|---|---|---|---|---|---|
| Kellogg | Upward | Not so great as to prevent deeper parts from gliding over still deeper structures | As much of palmar surface as possible; fingers close together and opposing thenar eminence | Tissues squeezed and lifted from bone or deeper tissues, rolled, and stretched; grasp released when strain is at its maximum | Individual muscles or muscle groups |
| Despard | Centripetal | Intermittent | One or both hands | Grasped, raised from attachment (picked up, lifted from underlying tissues), then compressed alternately between fingers of one hand and thumb of other; move onward or between each compression or grasped; tissues are pressed down upon underlying structures and at same time squeezed | Muscles, singly or in groups |
| Bucholz | Follows outline of muscle; succession of single manipulations may be either centripetal or centrifugal | | One or both working simultaneously; as much of hand as possible held close to skin | Grasped, lifted as much as possible from base, and kneaded or wrung; glided 1 or 2 inches, repeated from one end of muscle to the other; if muscle cannot be lifted, rolled and pressed | Muscles or muscle groups |
| Mennell | Compression lateral | Gentle | Entire surface of hand relaxed | Entire muscle group picked up in hands and squeezed, compressing alternately between thumb of one hand and fingers of other hand; hands glided gently over surface | Muscles |

### Kneading

Only the most recent authors described kneading as a separate technique; earlier authors used the French term *pétrissage* to describe the movement, which was similar in many respects to kneading, as we now understand it.

Several authors described pétrissage as a kneading movement and made little distinction between the two. Other descriptions of kneading were similar to those of pétrissage. Mennell stated that they resemble each other very closely, the only difference being that pétrissage is a picking-up movement with lateral compression, whereas in kneading the compression is vertical. Kellogg's concept is opposite to that of Mennell: he stated that the tissues are lifted in kneading but not in pétrissage. According to Graham (1913), in kneading the fingers and hand slip on the skin, whereas Kellogg cautioned that the surface of the hand must *not* be allowed to slip across the surface of the skin.

McMillan (1925) used pétrissage, or kneading. Graham used kneading on the tissues beneath the skin, whereas Kellogg subdivided kneading as superficial for skin and underlying tissues as well as deep for muscles. Graham and Kellogg differed also on direction. Graham stated that movements should be congruent with the return circulation, and Kellogg stated that for superficial kneading the relation to the veins is not important. Mennell began kneading of the limbs at the proximal portion of an area and progressed to the more distal portion. This kneading is performed with the two hands on opposite sides of the limb, the whole palmar surface being in contact with the part. Gentle pressure is then applied, usually as the hands work in opposite directions. He stated that the pressure is gentle, alternating waves of compression and relaxation are applied to a series of points, and the pressure is greatest when the hand is engaged with the "lowest part of the circumference of the circle and least when at the opposite pole" (Mennell, 1945). Table 1-3 provides a summary of the various descriptions of kneading.

### Friction

The various descriptions of friction in the literature betray much confusion among those who used this form of massage. Kleen (1921) and Mennell, unlike the other authors, used the plural *frictions,* although they did not agree on pressure. Kleen prescribed that the pressure be quite hard, and Mennell said it should be light, slowly progressing to deep, depending on the conditions. Hoffa asserted that the pressure seeks to penetrate deeply; Mitchell and Kellogg described it as moderate.

Grosvenor (1825) and Graham stated that friction is given with long strokes, whereas most of the other authors wanted it performed with small circular motions. Graham said friction may be circular or rectilinear (the latter parallel or horizontal to the long axis of the limb). According to Kellogg, the direction is from below upward, following the large veins, and the motion is centripetal, centrifugal, circular, or spiral rotary. Kellogg also stated that the hands should slip over the skin and that the entire surface of the palms should be used. Grosvenor and Graham also shared this view. Hoffa, Bucholz, Despard, and Mennell prescribed that the movement be done with the ball of the thumb or fingers, which remain in contact with the skin and move it over the underlying tissues. Influenced by Ling, several authors used the French term *massage à friction,* which is no doubt similar to the contemporary technique of friction, or frictions.

The modern proponents of friction techniques are Cyriax (1959, 1977, 1978) and Dicke et al. (1978). Cryiax described deep transverse frictions of muscles, tendons, and ligaments; the pulling strokes of Dicke and associates use dry, forceful friction between the fingertips and the skin.

With regard to the tissues to which friction should be applied, Kleen, Mitchell, and Mennell used it on small areas, whereas Graham extended each stroke from joint to joint. There seem to be two distinct ideas about this movement. One holds that the friction occurs between the hand and the skin surface (e.g., Dicke uses a distinct pattern of short pulling strokes in specific areas). The other (which seems currently to be more acceptable) prescribes that the part of the hand being used be kept in contact with the skin and that the superficial tissues be moved over the deeper (underlying) ones. Table 1-4 summarizes the various descriptions of the technique of friction.

### Stroking and Effleurage

Stroking and effleurage are similar in many respects and can be discussed together. Like kneading and pétrissage, these French and English terms have been used almost interchangeably. Mennell did not include the term *effleurage* in his classification of massage movements. It is generally agreed that the direction of the movement is centripetal; however, Mennell and Kellogg differ. They both used the term *stroking,* and Kellogg stated that the direction is with the blood current in the arteries, though he did not mention the amount of pressure. Mennell divided stroking into superficial and deep manipulations. Superficial stroking may be either centripetal or centrifugal, but the pressure, though firm, must be only the lightest touch possible to maintain contact. Deep stroking was given in the direction of the venous and lymphatic flow.

Despard used both stroking and effleurage: the direction of both is centripetal, but the pressure in stroking is vigorous, and Despard noted that in effleurage it should vary according to the condition of the patient. Other factors in the movements were similar, and she described the motion of effleurage as stroking, as did Ling, Mezger, Kleen, and Mitchell.

Ling said the pressure of effleurage varies from the lightest touch to pressure of considerable force. Murrell and Kleen said that it varies, whereas Hoffa and Bucholz used light pressure at the beginning of the stroke, increased it over the fleshy part of the muscle, and decreased it again at the end. Mitchell varied the pressure according to the region

Table 1-3 **Description of Massage Movements: Kneading**

| NAME | DIRECTION | PRESSURE | PART OF HAND | MOTION | TISSUES |
|---|---|---|---|---|---|
| Graham | From insertion to origin of muscles, with return circulation | | As much as possible of fingers and hand; slip on skin | Kneading, rolling, squeezing, manipulatory; circulatory | Tissues beneath skin |
| Kellogg (superficial) | Relation to veins not important | | Thumb and last two phalanges of first or first and second fingers | Essentially a pinching movement; tissues underlying skin simultaneously compressed and lifted from underlying bone or muscle | Skin and loose cellular |
| (deep) | | Little on thin tissues, greater on thick, firm tissues | Surface of hand not allowed to slip along surface of skin | Grasped or compressed | Muscles |
| (digital) | | | Ends of fingers and thumbs alone | Tissues rubbed and pressed against underlying bony surface | |
| Mennell | Centripetal; begin proximal portion, advance to more distal; compression vertical | Gentle; alternating wave of compression and relaxation; applied series of points, with greatest pressure when hand is engaged with lowest part of circle; least pressure when at opposite pole | Whole of palmar surface of both hands on opposite sides of limb, alternating heel of hand and then fingers | Circular, hands working in opposite directions | Muscle mass |

being treated and used heavy pressure on the upward stroke, keeping the hand in contact for a return stroke, but with much less pressure. Bucholz also kept the hand in contact for a return stroke, touching the skin very lightly.

Most authors agreed that stroking and effleurage are to be given over large areas. Mennell emphasized that the muscles must be relaxed, and Hoffa and Bucholz said that the movement should follow the anatomical outlines of the muscles. Nearly all authors advocated using the palm of the hand for effleurage and stroking. In addition to the palm, some used the heel of the hand, its edge, the tips of the fingers, the ball of the thumb, and the knuckles for effleurage and stroking. Hoffa, Bucholz, Despard, and Mennell recommended that the palm be in good contact and conform to the contour of the area being treated. Table 1-5 summarizes the various descriptions of effleurage and stroking given by some of the best-known writers on massage.

## Components of Massage

When applying therapeutic massage techniques, the following factors must be considered: direction of the movement, amount of pressure, rate and rhythm of the movements, media (lubricants) used (including instruments other than the hand), position of the patient and therapist, and duration and frequency of the treatment. Each of these is considered from a historical perspective.

Table 1-4 **Description of Massage Movements: Friction**

| NAME | DIRECTION | PRESSURE | PART OF HAND | MOTION | TISSUE |
|---|---|---|---|---|---|
| Grosvenor | One hand ascends as other descends | | Palm of hand | Long strokes | |
| Kleen (frictions) | | Quite hard | Volar side of thumb or three middle fingers or sometimes base of hand, occasionally with entire hand flat | Rubbings | Small surface |
| Hoffa | Circular | Seeks to penetrate deeply | Tips of fingers, either thumb or middle and | Index and middle fingers seek firm point of support; ball of thumb held | Part placed on solid support |
| Graham | Circular or rectilinear; latter may be vertical or parallel to long axis of limb; or horizontal, transverse or at right angles to the long axis | Upward strokes, stronger returning lightly, graze surface for soothing influence; heavy in centripetal direction | | Both hands move at same time; one ascends as other descends | Each stroke reaching from joint to joint |
| Mitchell | | Moderate—steady | Thumb or fingertips of one or more fingers; hand to slip over surface | Rubbing in small circles | Areas where larger grasp of pétrissage is not possible |
| Kellogg | From below upward, following large veins; centripetal, centrifugal, circular, spiral rotary | Considerable, depending on area; amount never such that the hand will not slip over surface or so great as to interfere with arterial circulation | Hand | Slipping over skin | |
| Bucholz | Circular | | | Moving skin over underlying parts | |

Table 1-4 **Description of Massage Movements: Friction—cont'd**

| NAME | DIRECTION | PRESSURE | PART OF HAND | MOTION | TISSUE |
|---|---|---|---|---|---|
| Mennell (frictions) | Circular or transversely to long axis of muscle fibers | Light—slowly progressive to deep, depending on condition present | Usually tips of fingers or tip or ball thumb | | Muscles must be relaxed |
| Despard | Circular | | Palmar aspects or tips of fingers or ball of thumb, also dorsal aspect of middle phalanges of fingers | Moving tissues upon underlying ones | Tissues |

Table 1-5 **Description of Massage Movements: Effleurage and Stroking**

| NAME | DIRECTION | PRESSURE | PART OF HAND | MOTION | TISSUES |
|---|---|---|---|---|---|
| Ling | Centripetal | Varying from lightest touch to one of considerable force | | Stroking | |
| Mezger | Centripetal | Superficial and gentle | Flat | Stroking | |
| Murrell | Direction of muscle fibers, centripetally | Varying | Palm or knuckles | | |
| Kleen | Centripetal | Varying | Large portion with hand flat, its ulnar or radial side or with thumb and forefinger; one or both hands | Stroking | Large area of skin |
| Hoffa | Toward the heart | Begin lightly, then increase and diminish again toward end of stroke | Conform to part treated as broadly and closely as possible; whole of hand or part of it (according to extent of part treated) flat for broad surfaces; ball of thumb; fingertip; knuckle (when part is covered by thick fascia) | Hand conforms closely to limb; thumb and fingertips proceed along grooves between muscles | Follows strictly anatomical structures of muscles along grooves between muscles, over veins and lymph channels; begins beyond affected part, extends over affected region, finishes in well part |

*Continued*

**Table 1-5 Description of Massage Movements: Effleurage and Stroking—cont'd**

| NAME | DIRECTION | PRESSURE | PART OF HAND | MOTION | TISSUES |
|---|---|---|---|---|---|
| Mitchell | Centripetal | Depends on region; return stroke much less pressure than upward but keeping contact | Flat hand, heel of hand, edge of hand, thumb, thumb and fingers or fingertips | Stroking | |
| Bucholz | Centripetal; with lymphatic flow | Slight at distal part of muscle, increase over fleshy part, decrease toward proximal part; return stroke in centrifugal direction, touching skin lightly | Fits as closely as possible to muscle | Where possible, lift up and grasp around muscle and stroke with thumb and fingers; if not possible to lift, hand presses muscle against underlying base | Anatomical outlines of muscle |
| Despard | Centripetal | Vary according to condition of patient | Whole of one or both hands of palmar surface of fingers and thumb; hand molded to fit part | Stroking | |
| Kellogg | Blood current in arteries | | Fingers, palm, knuckles | Touch combined with motion | |
| Mennell (superficial) | Centripetal or centrifugal, but continue same once direction is established | Superficial—firm but lightest touch | Flat surface; hand supple to mold to contour with wide area | Rhythmic | Extended area of body; muscles must be relaxed |
| (deep) | Centripetal with venous and lymph flow | Deep—light | | | |
| Despard | Centripetal | Vigorous | Tips of fingers | | |

### *Direction*

The literature shows that until the time of Hippocrates, the direction of massage was centrifugal (Johnson, 1866). Hippocrates's contributions to medicine are outstanding, and he demonstrated his genius in the use of massage and in many other medical treatments. He favored the centripetal direction for massage movements. He was unusual in his emphasis on clinical observation, and it is likely that he based his choice of direction on clinical observations of the effects of treatment. (The circulation of the blood was not described until nearly 2000 years later.) Asclepiades (125-56 BC), a Roman who lived a few centuries after Hippocrates, believed that the body was composed of regularly distributed canals in which nutritive fluids moved. Sickness was thought to be a disturbance of the normal movement of these fluids. He attempted to restore free flow of the nutritive juices by rubbing but gave no direction for the movement (Johnson, 1866).

Five centuries after Hippocrates, Galen varied the direction of massage movements depending on the purpose of the massage and its relation to exercise. At the beginning of the nineteenth century, Ling advocated light stroking in a centrifugal direction and deeper pressure with centripetal movements. This concept has held to the present day. In Lucas-Championnière's superficial stroking technique, as described by Mennell, the direction may be either centrifugal or centripetal but without deviation once the direction is established (Mennell, 1945). These later writers expressed clearly what effects were expected from movements in the centripetal direction as compared with those in the centrifugal direction. Murrell (1886) asserted that the direction be from below upward and in the direction of the muscle fibers. Hoffa and Bucholz were among the first to mention that the direction should be congruent with the venous and lymphatic circulation. Mennell said all deep movements of massage should be performed centripetally to aid venous and lymphatic flow. Many authors advocated beginning the movement at the proximal (rather than the distal) portion of a segment, but with the direction of the pressure in each movement being in the direction of venous flow (centripetal) even though the succession of the movements is in the opposite (centrifugal) direction.

Some massage techniques, such as deep friction and CTM, are specific about the direction of the movement in the area where they are applied.

### *Pressure*

Consideration of pressure seems to have been important from the earliest description of massage movements, although there was no consensus among early practitioners. The Greek authors Herodikus (ca. 500 BC) and Herodotus (484-425 BC) varied the pressure during the movement: gentle at first, then greater, and toward the end gentle again (Johnson, 1866). Later, Hippocrates distinguished the types of pressure, mentioning gentle, hard, soft, and moderate. He emphasized the importance of selecting the correct pressure for a given technique to obtain the desired result, as in the frequently quoted statement, "Hard rubbing binds; soft rubbing loosens; much rubbing causes parts to waste; moderate rubbing makes them grow."

Ambroise Pare, the most renowned surgeon of the sixteenth century, recognized a difference in the amount of pressure used (Graham, 1884) and described three kinds of friction—gentle, medium, and vigorous—and the effects of each. From the fifteenth through the beginning of the eighteenth century, emphasis on heavy pressure seemed to be growing. The extremist in this regard was Admiral Henry (1731-1823) of the British Navy, who believed that "great violence" was important (Johnson, 1866). He described some of the manipulations as painful, "but they cease to be so if persevered in, and become even pleasant." (Rolfing seems to some to be a modern-day application of Henry's beliefs.) Eventually massage became a well-accepted part of medical treatment in the British Royal Navy, where it has a proud tradition (Stockton, 1994).

Beveridge emphasized the importance of touch with varying pressure and the differences in the effects produced depending on the amount of pressure. In the early part of the nineteenth century he wrote, "The finger of a good rubber will descend upon an excited and painful nerve as gently as the dew on the grass, but upon a torpid callosity as heavily as the hoof of an elephant."

Mezger varied the pressure with the type of movement. The pressure for effleurage was gentle, and that for massage à friction was "with considerable force" (Berghman & Helleday, 1873). This force must have been considerable, as Colombo, one of his contemporaries, stated that Mezger's patients frequently had blue spots on their bodies. Zabludowski, who was known as the king of German masseurs, criticized the gentle massage advocated by Lucas-Championnière for the treatment of fractures. Zabludowski said that when massage became painless it ceased to be massage and was merely treatment by suggestion; although in a book written later (1903), Zabludowski wrote that massage is not in most cases painful and that when it necessarily becomes painful the pain should subside. Bucholz, writing in 1917, did not agree with Zabludowski's early concepts. He believed all needed effects could be obtained without such abuse of force.

About the same time, Kleen and Hoffa showed they appreciated the finesse of technique together with knowledge, and they regulated the pressure according to the bulk of the tissues, increasing it when working on the belly of a muscle and lessening it at the ends of the muscle. (In this there is evident recognition of the early concepts of Herodikus and Herodotus.) They also observed that the proper amount can be judged only by practice.

Throughout the late nineteenth and early twentieth centuries, many authors gave the impression that the greater the pressure, the more effective the massage. They began the treatment, or series of treatments, with gentle pressure and worked up to the tolerance level of the patient. Kellogg stated that the patient's tolerance is established during prolonged treatment, beginning gently and increasing pressure gradually until almost the "whole strength of the operator might be employed without injuring the patient." Despard stated that the vigor and amount of pressure should vary according to the condition of the patient, being always gentle at the beginning of the course of treatment and gradually increasing as the patient improves.

Mennell was outstanding in his rationale for the use of massage. He stated that the amount of pressure depends solely on the relaxation of the muscles. When the muscles are relaxed throughout the treatment, even a light pressure must influence every structure throughout the part being treated. He believed that movement can be deep without in any sense being forced. He reasoned that if the muscles are relaxed they offer no more resistance to the movement than does so much fluid, and any pressure applied on the surface will be transmitted freely to all structures under the hand. He said that practice with a skill born only of a delicate sense of touch will show how very light may be the pressure that suffices to compress any structure to its fullest extent and, therefore, incidentally to empty the veins and lymphatic spaces. He also said, "The delusion is deep rooted—and will die hard—that 'stimulation' in massage is impossible without the expenditure of muscle energy and vigour. A delusion, nevertheless, it is."

### *Rate and Rhythm*

Some authors mentioned briefly the rate of massage movements, but few addressed rhythm. Others combined the two. Of the early writers, Herodikus and Herodotus both considered pressure and rate. They advocated gentle and slow movements in the beginning, rapid and heavy ones next, and slow and gentle movements to end a treatment (Kellogg, 1919). Hippocrates, describing the treatment of a dislocated shoulder, stated, "It is necessary to rub the shoulder gently and smoothly." None of the users of massage after Hippocrates made mention of rate or rhythm until the eighteenth century. Beveridge evidently considered great speed an advantage: he believed that flexibility of the fingers is important because it permits rapid motion. Ling varied rate according to the type of movement: effleurage should be given slowly; rolling, shaking, and tapotement (percussion) rapidly. Mezger agreed that effleurage should be given slowly.

Graham, Kellogg, and Bucholz were specific about the rate (number of strokes per minute) but not about the distance covered in each stroke; thus, the number of strokes had no specific relationship to rhythm. These authors specified different numbers of strokes. For friction, Graham specified 90 to 180 strokes per minute. Bucholz (1917) prescribed that the speed should depend on the desired effect:

> *In irritable cases a slow gentle stroke may produce a marked effect, while in treating an atrophic limb of an otherwise healthy person, considerable speed, up to 50 to 60 times a minute or more, with a good deal of pressure may be applied.*

Kellogg adjusted the speed depending on the type of movement and stated the distance to be covered with each stroke. Stroking, he thought, should not cover more than 1 or 2 inches per second; friction, 30 to 80 strokes per minute, depending on the length of the stroke; and pétrissage, a not-too-rapid 30 to 90 strokes per minute (although he specified that the pace could be more rapid in small parts).

Kleen varied the rate according to the area treated: he thought effleurage on the shoulder and back should be rapid. Lucas-Championnière emphasized that massage should be slow and uniform, with rhythmic repetitions. Zabludowski stated that the area covered to some extent determines the speed. He compared the rhythm with that of music and suggested that a metronome be used in practice but not as a regular guide. Despard varied the rate and rhythm according to the effect desired. For a soothing effect, she recommended effleurage be given slowly and rhythmically, and for a stimulating effect, she suggested that the strokes be quick and strong. She varied the rate and vigor according to the condition of the patient and performed all movements rhythmically.

In describing stroking movements, some authors distinguished between the rate of the primary stroke and that of the return stroke, making the return stroke more rapid, which creates an uneven rhythm. Mitchell advised this and asserted that a common fault of massage is making the movements too fast. Mennell identified these essentials of superficial stroking: (1) the movements must be slow, gentle, and rhythmic, and there must be no hesitancy or irregularity about it; and (2) the time between the end of the stroke and the beginning of the next should be identical with the time of stroking throughout the movement. He believed the rhythm must be even to produce an even stimulus. For the stroke from shoulder to hand, he prescribed 15 movements per minute. For deep stroking, he said that there is no need for great speed, as the flow of venous blood is slow and that of the lymph even slower. He thought that kneading too rapidly is inimical to success and that for frictions the rhythm should be slow and steady. The movements in connective tissue massage are unhurried but not of any precise rate or rhythm.

### *Media (Lubricant)*

The stories of Homer imply that as early as 1000 BC an oily medium was used for massage. According to Homer's *Odyssey,* women rubbed and anointed the war-torn heroes to rest and refresh them. Herodotus advised that a "greasy mixture" should be poured over the body before rubbing, and Plato (427-347 BC) and Socrates (470-399 BC) referred to the benefit received from anointing with oils and rubbing as an "assuager of pain" (Graham, 1913). Olive oil was the preferred medium (lubricant), and it was believed that the oil itself had some therapeutic value. Roman history records that Cicero's health was much improved by his anointer's ministrations.

Celsus made a distinction between rubbing and unction, or anointing. The rubbing in of greasy substances he called *unction.* Other authors later contended that unction could not be performed without friction of some sort. In the days of Galen, the massage following exercise used more oil than the one given before exercise. Galen recommended rubbing with a towel to produce redness, followed by rubbing with oil for the purpose of warming up and softening the body in preparation for exercise.

Henry used unique media. He also devised various instruments and tools that he said prevented nerves and tendons from falling asleep or becoming fixed. If these structures were kept in constant motion, "the blood would pass quickly through the blood vessels, leaving no fur behind it, so that ossification which so frequently terminates the human existence is prevented." The instruments were made of wood and bone. He principally used cattle ribs, as it was useful to have curved instruments. He also used a hammer with a piece of cork covered with leather as well as the rounded end of a glass vial (Johnson, 1866). Graham followed a similar method to a certain extent for percussion. He suggested that the back of a brush or the sole of a slipper could be used, but even better were India rubber balls attached to steel or whalebone handles (Graham, 1913).

In exceptional circumstances, Murrell said, a bundle of swan feathers, lightly tied together, could be used for tapotement (percussion). For reflex stroking, Kellogg used the fingernail, the end of a lead pencil, a wooden toothpick, or the head of a pin. On the island of Tonga in the early nineteenth century, Graham (1913) reported that "three or four little children tread under their feet the whole body of the patient." At about this time, the Russians and the Finns used bundles of birch twigs for flagellation before steam baths, and the Hawaiians gave massage while patients were submerged in water.

The more recent users of massage have different opinions concerning the various lubricants and equipment used. Some object to any sort of lubricant, and those who use a medium choose either an oily lubricant or a powder. Those who use no medium, in a technique called *dry massage,* assert that it is cleaner, gives a more certain feeling to the hands and steadier movements, is more stimulating, and makes it unnecessary to expose the patient's body. It seems incredible, but frequently massage has been administered through the patient's clothing. Galen records that when a gymnast asked Quintas what was the value of anointing (rubbing with oil), he replied, "It makes you take off your tunic." Some types of massage, however, do require a dry technique for effective treatment (e.g., deep friction and connective tissue massage).

Of those who use oil as a lubricant for massage, many different compounds, both liquid and solid, have been suggested. The more commonly mentioned ones are olive oil, glycerin, coconut oil, oil of sweet almonds, and neat's-foot oil. Some users prefer solid lubricants because the liquid oils are difficult to handle. The solid lubricants suggested are wool fat, petroleum jelly, lanolin, hog's lard, cold cream, and cocoa butter.

Zabludowski was quite specific in his preference for white Virginia petroleum jelly because it was odorless, tasteless, and neutral. He said that the chief basis for the use of any lubricant was personal preference. Those who recommend oily lubricants say that they make the skin soft, smooth, and slippery; prevent the pain of pulling hair; and prevent acne. Some of those who are opposed to the use of oily lubricants claim that they promote hair growth.

Others recommend powder as a lubricant, as they believe it is more pleasant for general massage, makes deep kneading possible, and improves the sense of touch. Several users recommend it particularly to absorb the moisture from the patient's skin and the therapist's hands. Grosvenor recommended the use of fine hair powder, and more recent writers have suggested talcum or boric acid powder. A few writers suggest soapsuds as a medium, especially to help remove dead skin from a limb following the removal of a plaster cast.

Mennell said the selection of a medium is a personal preference and believed the best one is the simplest, namely French chalk, which might be improved by adding oil. He, as well as other users, recommended an oily medium, especially when the skin is dry and scaly. Some suggested that it be used on children and older patients. Of the later users in this group, the reason, although it was not stated, undoubtedly was to avoid abrading sensitive skin. Although there was no credible evidence at the time to support their contention, earlier writers believed that the medium itself had curative power.

## Position of the Patient and Therapist

The early writers gave little indication of the position of the patient or of the therapist while performing massage. Nothing was written of this until about the seventeenth century. However, a bas-relief of the return of soldiers from war, as described in Homer's *Odyssey,* depicts massage being given to Odysseus. He is seated, and the masseuse is crouching in a most uncomfortable position in front of him and is massaging his leg (Figure 1-1).

Alpinus said the patient should be extended horizontally. Many of the later writers described the patient's position in detail and emphasized that the patient should be relaxed—this after the patient had been placed in such a position that relaxation would seem to be utterly impossible. Few of them gave a rationale for the positions they prescribed, and they seemed to disregard entirely any effect that gravity might have on venous or lymphatic flow. Ling emphasized that the muscles must be relaxed for many movements and yet described rolling and shaking the arm while the seated patient held the arm horizontal with the hand on a table or the back of a chair (Kellgren, 1890).

**Figure 1-1** An Early Record of Massage in Bas-Relief

In Homer's *Odyssey,* warriors on their return home from battle were rubbed and kneaded to promote recovery from their battle trauma. This image depicts the return of Odysseus.

Cleoburey described Grosvenor's position for massage of the lower extremity:

> *The female rubber [Grosvenor always employed females] is seated on a low stool, and taking the patient's limb in her lap (which position gave her command over it) so as to enable her to rub with extended hands.*

The position of the patient is not described. One would assume that he or she was seated in a position similar to the one shown in the Greek bas-relief of Odysseus (see Figure 1-1).

Graham said the patient should be in a comfortable position, with joints midway between flexion and extension, and he warned that if the "manipulator" was too close to the patient, his movements would be cramped, and if he was too far away, the movements would be indefinite, superficial, and lacking in energy (Graham, 1913).

Kleen described a bench on which the patient was to lie and which was approachable from all sides. The masseur stood or sat beside it. He gave much detail of patient positions for the treatment of various areas. For massage of the neck and throat, he had the patient sit on the bench (Kleen, 1921).

Hoffa recommended support to the entire length of the part of the body that is being treated, so that the muscles are relaxed, yet he had the patient sit on a stool for massage of the head, neck, shoulders, and upper arms. For massage of the elbow, forearm, hand, and fingers, an illustration shows the patient sitting with these parts resting on a table. To treat the leg and foot, the patient sits on the table with the foot supported in the lap of the masseur. He said that the masseur's position should be comfortable, not strained, always beside the patient's bed, and avoiding as much as possible frequent and unnecessary changes of position. For the thigh, the masseur sits beside the reclining patient (Hoffa, 1897).

Zabludowski recommended a comfortable and relaxed position for the patient. The exact position depended on the part to be treated. The patient's glasses were to be removed and the lighting and room temperature adjusted to ensure comfort. Some work might even be done with the patient standing, and small children might be held in the masseur's lap if a table was not available. He emphasized the posture of the masseur and said the standing position was preferred. The masseur should have a sure footing and coordinated movements, to ease his work and avoid too much flexing and extending in many joints. Zabludowski added some quaint rules for the masseur: he should observe his watch chain so it does not bother the patient; he should wear glasses instead of *pince-nez,* which might slide off the nose if he perspired; he should wear a jersey (knit) undershirt, heavy or light according to the season; he should not work in street clothes, should remove his rings, wear short sleeves, and even remove things from pockets that are in the way when he is sitting (Zabludowski, 1903).

Mitchell (1904) recommended that the patient be reclining and for some areas that the operator sit on the edge of the bed with the patient's foot in his lap. Bucholz said the patient should be in a relaxing position that would also allow the operator to work with sufficient comfort. Bucholz also did not favor the sitting position for massaging the legs, although he thought it might be used for the foot and calf if the patient was sitting on a table and the operator was in front of the patient on a chair (Bucholz, 1917).

Despard recommended that the patient be in a comfortable position with the muscles relaxed, yet for back stroking she said the patient might stand with the hands resting against a wall or other support (Despard, 1932).

Mennell said the most important factors in performing all stroking movements are the position of the patient and of the masseur, and the relative position of one to the other. He gave no set rules for either's position but said there should be a reason for every position of the masseur and for the position in which the part under treatment is placed. Some of the illustrations in his text show the masseur standing, and others show the masseur sitting. Stroking of the lower extremity was illustrated to point out some common faults of positioning of the patient and of the masseur (Mennell, 1945).

In discussing the effect of massage on venous flow, Mennell considered the effect of gravity to be very important. He recommended that the patient lie recumbent on the table, in a position that allows relaxation of abdominal muscles, with the thighs supported to enhance venous and lymphatic flow from the distal part of the lower extremity. To treat edema of an extremity, he recommended elevating the part while giving the massage. For patients with respiratory problems, there are specific positions for postural drainage (see Chapter 10), and the therapist accommodates his or her position and stance accordingly.

In the basic position for CTM, the patient sits with the back toward the therapist. Lighting is important when the therapist is assessing the patient's tissues. In addition to the basic back section, other parts of the body can be treated with CTM, and the patient is positioned accordingly (see Chapter 11).

### *Duration*

Galen was one of the first massage users to address the duration of a treatment, although he advocated a trial-and-error approach. He wrote:

> *What shall be the duration of the rubbing it is impossible to declare in words; but the director, being experienced in these matters, on the first day must form a conjecture, which shall not be very accurate, but the next day, having already acquired some experience in the constitution of this subject, he will reduce his conjecture continually to greater accuracy.*

Grosvenor gave specific directions for the duration of treatment. He said that friction should at first be continued for an hour, "observing always to rub by the watch" (Cleoburey, 1825; Johnson, 1866). Murrell said the entire duration of a local massage should not exceed 8 to 10 minutes and that other authorities thought 4 minutes was enough. Kleen believed the duration of a treatment was important, but that no hard and fast rule could be given. Local massage, he thought, usually should last 15 minutes, and general massage at least half an hour and sometimes longer. Hoffa suggested 10 to 20 minutes for local and 30 to 45 minutes for general massage.

Zabludowski said the duration might be 5 to 30 minutes, depending on the size of the affected area, the patient's age, the duration of the illness, and the patient's constitution and habits. With regard to the time frame over which treatments should continue, he said it depends on the condition to be treated, the prognosis, and so forth, but is usually 2 to 3 weeks. According to Graham, the patient's condition and the effect of the massage should determine the duration of the treatment. Bucholz said the duration of the treatment should depend on the desired effect. For a fresh injury, he stated that 5 to 10 minutes may be adequate, whereas a general massage should last 40 to 50 minutes. Despard prescribed a definite period of time for massaging each area of the body and said the duration of the treatment should increase as the patient's condition improves.

Mennell believed it necessary to consider the age of the patient when administering massage. If the sole aim is to secure a reflex effect, in very young and aged persons, Mennell believed that the duration of treatment should be lessened. For treatment of neurasthenia, Mennell said the maximum duration is 75 minutes, which may be attained in comparatively few cases (and never during the earlier stages of treatment). At first, 20 minutes is often sufficient and the treatments may be gradually increased in duration and, toward the end, should be decreased in a similar manner. In cases of injury, however, he emphasized the danger of prolonging the series of the massage treatments in lieu of active exercise as the patient improves.

### *Frequency*

Celsus, a noted medical author although not a physician, wrote merely as an encyclopedist in his *De Medicina* (1665), presenting ideas that appealed to him and were drawn from the available literature. It may be assumed, therefore, that his writings express some of the ideas that were popular at that time. He gave some details of massage technique and appreciated the value of correct dosage. He stated:

> *We should pay no attention to those who define numerically how often anyone is to be rubbed; for this must be gathered from the individual; and if he is very feeble, 50 times may be enough; if more robust, it may be requisite to rub 200 times, and between both limits according to the strength.*

He also believed treatments should be done less frequently for women, children, and elders than for men (Celsus, 1665; Johnson, 1866).

Grosvenor advised daily treatment (more or less as the case would permit), gradually increased to three times daily. Murrell also believed in frequent treatment (three or four times daily), but each treatment was much briefer than Grosvenor's. Kleen believed massage should be given at least once daily—and in some cases, for injury, several times daily. Hoffa recommended daily massage. Zabludowski advocated daily massage in most cases but believed that the physical and psychological reactions of the patient should determine the frequency. For quick results, he believed treatments should be given twice daily, but in cases that necessitated weaning from massage, the frequency of treatments should be lessened gradually to two or three per week.

Graham recognized the frequency of treatment as part of the dosage of massage, which should be regulated according to the patient's condition. He associated force with the frequency and duration of treatment, local massage being done frequently and general massage at least once daily. In contrast to Zabludowski's weaning from massage, Graham said the frequency could be increased after four or five treatments. Bucholz said that the frequency of treatment depends largely on the patient's social condition but advised twice-daily massage in many surgical cases. He believed it wise to begin with short sessions and to increase according to the patient's reaction. Table 1-6 compares the various components of massage treatments according to some of the best-known exponents of the technique.

## SUMMARY

Historically, many pioneers of soft tissue massage treatment seemed to have no physiological basis for their techniques, particularly in relation to pressure, rate of movements, and positioning of the patient. The heavy pressure advocated in the fifteenth through the early eighteenth centuries was supplanted by more gentle massage, as introduced by Lucas-Championnière and Mennell in the early twentieth century. Amazingly, Hippocrates, who certainly did not have access to the scientific and physiological data available today, came to the same conclusion. At the beginning of the twentieth century Bucholz and Hoffa began to show some rational application of massage technique based on knowledge of physiology, but in this respect Mennell is outstanding.

Clearly, then, opinions differ widely on most aspects of the various techniques described in the literature as medical massage. Over the centuries, some aspects of the techniques have received considerable attention at the expense of others. As a result, it is difficult to identify well-reasoned rationales for most of the techniques used in massage. In this respect, of course, massage treatments were no different from other so-called medical treatments of the same era. Medical treatments were often based on anecdotal information. Except for the fact that they appeared to help many patients and seemed worth continuing, medical understanding of the efficacy of massage owed little to science. Certainly the focus was on the art of massage rather than its scientific basis in medical practice.

*Text continued on p. 34.*

Table 1-6 **Components of Massage Techniques**

| NAME | DIRECTION | PRESSURE | RATE AND RHYTHM | MEDIUM | POSITION OF PATIENT AND PHYSICAL THERAPIST | DURATION | FREQUENCY |
|---|---|---|---|---|---|---|---|
| **Circa 500 BC to AD 200** | | | | | | | |
| Herodikus (circa 500 BC) | Centrifugal | Initial—gentle Interim—heavy End—gentle | Slow beginning; rapid interim; slow ending | Greasy mixture | | | |
| Herodotus (484-425 BC) | Centrifugal | Initial—gentle Interim—heavy End—gentle | Slow beginning; rapid interim; slow ending | | | | |
| Hippocrates (460-380 BC) | Centrifugal | Gentle—hard rubbing, soft rubbing, moderate rubbing | Smooth | | | Much—or moderate | |
| Asclepiades (128-56 BC) | | Gentle | | | | | |
| Celsus (25 BC-AD 50) | | | | Greasy substances | | Regulated entirely by strength and reaction of patient; total of 50 to 200 times | |
| Galen (AD 130-200) | Tripsis—centripetal; Anatripsis—centrifugal | | | Towel for tripsis; olive oil—greater amount for apotherapeia | | | |

| | | | | | | | |
|---|---|---|---|---|---|---|---|
| **Fifteenth, Sixteenth, and Seventeenth Centuries** | | | | | | | |
| Paracelsus (1492-1541) | | Friction—gentle, medium, vigorous | | | | | |
| Paré (1517-1590) | | Friction—gentle, medium, vigorous | | | | | |
| Alpinus (1553-1617) | | | | | Patient extended horizontally | | |
| **Nineteenth and Twentieth Centuries** | | | | | | | |
| Mezger (1853-1901 [1909]) | Effleurage—centripetal; Massage à friction—circular and centripetal | Effleurage—superficial and gentle; Massage à friction—considerable force | Effleurage—slow | Fat well rubbed into skin | | | |
| Graham (1848-1928) | In general, centripetal from extremities to trunk with return circulation from insertion to origin; Friction—circular, heavy pressure of strokes is centripetal; circular and rectilinear parallel to long axis of limbs or horizontal transverse or at right angles to long axis | | Friction—90-180 per minute | Back of brush, sole of slipper; India rubber balls attached to whalebone handle for percussion | Comfortable position with joints midway between flexion and extension; a manipulator who is too near the patient will be cramped; if too far away, the manipulator's movements will be indefinite, superficial, and lacking in energy | Local, not more than 8-10 minutes | Short sittings frequently repeated 3 or 4 times daily |

Continued

Table 1-6 **Components of Massage Techniques—cont'd**

| NAME | DIRECTION | PRESSURE | RATE AND RHYTHM | MEDIUM | POSITION OF PATIENT AND PHYSICAL THERAPIST | DURATION | FREQUENCY |
|---|---|---|---|---|---|---|---|
| **Nineteenth and Twentieth Centuries—cont'd** | | | | | | | |
| Murrell (1853-1912) | Pétrissage—hand simultaneously opposite directions from below and upward; Effleurage—follow direction muscle fibers | Pétrissage—firm pressure | Rate varies—initial and final, quick; massage à friction, quick; effleurage, varying | Dry massage; bundle of swan's feathers may be used for tapotement | | Based on effect on patient and frequency of manipulation | Regulate dosage |
| Kleen (1847-1923) | Effleurage of limbs—Centripetal; of abdomen—Circular; Throat—from top downward | Quite hard pressure—amount can be judged only by practice Pétrissage—firm over belly of muscle; new patient and painful cases, begin with little force, gradually increased Friction—quite hard pressure | Effleurage—should be rapid; stroking on back—rapid | Glycerin, petroleum jelly, lanolin, lard, cold cream, olive oil, coconut oil, talcum, and other powders; lard preferred; no lubricant if dry hands; also use instruments and apparatus for vibration | Patient undressed and in bed; bench on which patient lies 60 cm high, approachable from all sides; masseur sits or stands beside it; lower part of arm—patient and physical therapist sit on opposite sides of bench, patient's arm resting on bench; throat or neck—patient sits on bench; physical therapist stands at front, side, or back | Important; no hard and fast rule; local—15 minutes; general—½ hour | Daily in acute injuries, sometimes several times daily |

| | | | | | | | |
|---|---|---|---|---|---|---|---|
| Lucas-Championnière (1843-1913) | Usually centrifugal (no deviation in direction, once established) | Little more than a caress | Slow and uniform; rhythmic repetition | | | | |
| Hoffa (1859-1907) | Friction—circular; Pétrissage—from insertion to origin of muscle; two-hand transverse to muscle fiber | Friction—seeks to penetrate deeply; Pétrissage—hand presses firmly against belly of muscle; correct amount can be judged only by practice; grasp must be gentle, sympathetic, yet of sufficient firmness; new patients and painful cases, begin with little force and increase gradually | | Powder preferred | Entire length of part supported so that muscles are relaxed; patient sits on stool for massage of hand, neck, shoulder, and upper arm; for elbow, forearm, hand, and fingers, parts should rest on table; for leg and foot, masseur sits opposite patient, foot supported in masseur's lap; patient lies down for back, abdomen, thighs, or knee joints; thigh, masseur sits beside patient; details of change in position of patient and masseur for various muscle groups of thigh are given; illustrations in 1897 edition show both patient and masseur seated | Local—10-20 minutes; General—30-45 minutes | Daily |

Continued

Table 1-6 **Components of Massage Techniques—cont'd**

| NAME | DIRECTION | PRESSURE | RATE AND RHYTHM | MEDIUM | POSITION OF PATIENT AND PHYSICAL THERAPIST | DURATION | FREQUENCY |
|---|---|---|---|---|---|---|---|
| **Nineteenth and Twentieth Centuries—cont'd** | | | | | | | |
| | | | | | for massage of elbow, shoulders, and neck; for foot, knee, and thigh, patient seated on table and masseur seated with patient's foot in masseur's lap; height of table should be somewhat above knee of operator and the operator's position should be comfortable and not strained | | |
| Kellogg (1852-1943) | Stroking, friction, and pétrissage—centripetal | Friction—considerable pressure on thick masses, light on bony and thin tissues<br>Percussion—varying degrees of force; deep kneading varies with tissues<br>Fist kneading—greatest degree of force and pressure | Depends on type of movement<br>Stroking—not more than 1 or 2 inches per second<br>Friction—30-180 strokes per minute, varying with length of stroke<br>Pétrissage—not too rapid, 30- | For reflex stroking—fingernail, end of lead pencil, wooden toothpick, or head of a pin | | | |

| | | | | | | | |
|---|---|---|---|---|---|---|---|
| | | communicated to deepest part; rolling and wringing sufficient to keep hand from slipping on skin; tolerance of pressure established by prolonged treatment, gentle at beginning of treatment, gradually increased until almost the whole strength might be employed without injuring the patient | 90 per minute, more rapid in small parts Wringing—not to exceed 30 per minute | | | | |
| Zabludowski (1851-1906) | Centripetal (return with light stroke) | Most cases should not be painful; when necessarily painful, pain should subside shortly; criticism of Championnière's gentleness in massage: "Massage which becomes painless ceases to be massage, only | Determined by area covered; beginning usually measured, swelling to speed, ending more slowly; rhythm important, may be cultivated by practice with a metronome | Lard, powder, soapsuds, lanolin oil, creams, white Virginia petroleum jelly preferred | Relaxation of entire body is important; position of patient depends on parts treated; some work can be done in standing position; small children can be held in lap if no table is available; support given by sound side; by hand of masseur while | 5-30 minutes, varying with size of area, age of patient, duration of illness, constitution and habits of patient | Usually daily, depending on physical and psychological reactions; entire period usually 2-3 weeks |

*Continued*

Table 1-6 **Components of Massage Techniques—cont'd**

| NAME | DIRECTION | PRESSURE | RATE AND RHYTHM | MEDIUM | POSITION OF PATIENT AND PHYSICAL THERAPIST | DURATION | FREQUENCY |
|---|---|---|---|---|---|---|---|
| **Nineteenth and Twentieth Centuries—cont'd** | | | | | | | |
| | | treatment by suggestion" | | | massaging with the other hand; masseur should stand at back or side of patient for most work; masseur should have a sure footing; posture is important for masseur's own and patient's confidence; this is best in standing position; if masseur is sitting, the elbow (when arms flexed) should be above the area treated; coordinated movement recommended for masseur to avoid flexing and extending many joints | | |
| Mitchell (1859-1917) | | Light if patient is apprehensive | Slow if patient is apprehensive<br>Effleurage—return stroke faster than upward | None, except in special circumstances (promotes growth of hair); if any used, | Patient reclines; physical therapist stands at patient's side or foot of bed; in some | Depends on condition of patient<br>Local—5-15 minutes<br>General—50-60 minutes | 2-4 times daily |

| | | | | | | |
|---|---|---|---|---|---|---|
| | | | | suggests wool fat or oil of sweet almonds; but only on dry scaly skin or on emaciated and older patients | positions, physical therapist sits on table | |
| Despard (published 1910) | Friction—circular; Effleurage—centripetal; Pétrissage—centripetal; soothing Stroking—centrifugal; Colon—along course | Soothing, stroking—gentle; Stimulating effect—strong Vigor regulated by condition of patient | Soothing stroking—slow Stimulating stroking—quick Rhythm important in all movements | Dry rubbing preferred; lubricant for young children, rickety subjects, old and emaciated persons, stiff joints, limbs previously in splints, skin dry, sensitive, or hairy; suggested lubricants: coconut butter, olive oil, neat's-foot oil, white petroleum jelly, lanolin; dry hands; powder: talc or boric acid | Patient in comfortable position; for back stroking, either prone, sitting, or standing with hands resting against wall or other support; masseur's position convenient for carrying out many manipulations; should support limbs except in percussion; general massage—describes position of patient for each area and position of masseur in relation to patient when treating each area | Definite periods, varying for each area and increasing under improvement; varies 5-20 minutes |

*Continued*

Table 1-6 **Components of Massage Techniques—cont'd**

| NAME | DIRECTION | PRESSURE | RATE AND RHYTHM | MEDIUM | POSITION OF PATIENT AND PHYSICAL THERAPIST | DURATION | FREQUENCY |
|---|---|---|---|---|---|---|---|
| **Nineteenth and Twentieth Centuries—cont'd** | | | | | | | |
| Bucholz (1874- ) | Effleurage—with lymphatic flow (return lightly)<br>Pétrissage—each manipulation may be centripetal or centrifugal | Effleurage at distal part of muscle, slight; increase over fleshy part; decrease at proximal; moderate, fine, delicate touch more important than athletic hand | Shaking—quick<br>Vibration—quick;<br>Irritable cases—slow; kneading depends on desired effects; healthy persons 50-60 times per minute; important in pétrissage; shaking, and vibration quick rhythm | Use common sense; for mild effleurage or large areas of dry skin—cold cream, petrolatum; kneading and friction—no medium | Patient in comfortable position, one that will allow operator to work with sufficient comfort; muscles of patient may be either in sitting or lying position for treating arms and shoulders, but for the rest of the body the patient should be lying; does not favor sitting position for treating the legs, although it may be used for the foot and calf if the patient is sitting on a table and the operator in front of him on a chair | Dependent on desired effect; increase dependent on patient's reaction; fresh injury—5-10 minutes; general—40-50 minutes | Dependent on patient's social condition; surgical cases twice daily |

| | | | | | | |
|---|---|---|---|---|---|---|
| Mennell (1880-1957) | Friction—circular, superficial stroking direction of minor importance, but once established must be continued<br>Deep stroking—centripetal<br>Kneading—begin proximal; deep pressure, centripetal | Amount dependent solely on relaxation of musculature; when relaxed, slight pressure will reach even deeper than when not<br>Kneading—greatest pressure when hand is at lowest part of circle, least when at opposite; superficial<br>Stroking—gentle, sufficient only to ensure patient's consciousness of passage of hand throughout the movement<br>Frictions—initially light, slowly and progressively increased; gentleness essential to success | Excessive rapidity inimical to success<br>Superficial stroking—slow, 15 times per minute (shoulder to hand); slowness indispensable to rhythm and gentleness<br>Deep stroking—slow, to coordinate with normal flow of venous blood and lymph<br>Kneading—rapidity inimical to success<br>Friction—slow, unbroken rhythm essential; no time lag between end of stroke and commencement of next<br>Frictions—slow and unbroken | Personal factor; French chalk and oil, soap and water; oil on hard scaly skin | | Dependent entirely on results attained<br>Neurasthenia—initial 20 minutes; increase to 75 minutes; gradually decrease in similar manner |

This text is mindful of the heritage and rich tradition of massage treatments and continues to seek a more reasoned approach to the practice of this ancient art. To this end, a classification system is described, which pulls from several earlier traditions and uses a consistent and well-reasoned methodology. Each of the various massage strokes is carefully described, and, where appropriate, the clinical and scientific rationale for their use is considered. It is hoped that this approach will dispel much of the confusion apparent in the early writings on massage.

## REFERENCES


Beard G: History of massage technique, *Phys Ther Rev* 32:613-624, 1952.

Benjamin PJ: Massage therapy in the 1940's and the College of Swedish Massage in Chicago, *Massage Ther J* (Fall):57-62, 1993.

Berghman G, Helleday U: Anteckningar om massage, *Nord Med Arkin* 5(7), 1873.

Blundell JWF: *The muscles and their story from the earliest times,* London, 1864, Chapman & Hall.

Bohm M: *Massage: its principles and technic,* Philadelphia, 1918, Saunders.

Braverman D, Schulman R: Massage techniques in rehabilitation medicine, *Phys Med Rehabil Clin N Am* 10(3):631-649, 1999.

Broca P: Sur l'age des sujets à la trépanation chirurgicale néolithique, *Bull Soc Anthrop de Paris* xi:572, 1876.

Bucholz CH: *Therapeutic exercise and massage,* Philadelphia, 1917, Lea & Febiger.

Celsus AC: *De medicina,* 1665, Leiden, Netherlands.

Cleoburey W: *System of friction,* ed 3, London, 1825, Munday & Slatter.

Cole J, Stovell E: Exercise and massage in health care through the ages. In Winterton P, Gurry D, editors: *The impact of the past upon the present: Second National Conference of the Australian Society of the History of Medicine,* Perth, Australia, 1991, Hawthorn Press.

Cyriax J: *Treatment by massage and manipulation,* New York, 1959, Paul Hoeber.

Cyriax J: *Textbook of orthopedic medicine,* ed 7, vol 1, New York, 1978, Macmillan.

Cyriax J, Russell G: *Textbook of orthopedic medicine,* ed 9, vol 2, Baltimore, 1977, Williams & Wilkins.

Despard L: *Textbook of massage and remedial gymnastics,* ed 3, New York, 1932, Oxford University Press.

de Watteville A: The cure of writer's cramp, *Br Med J* 1:323-324, 1885a.

de Watteville A: Further observations on the cure of writer's cramp, *Lancet* i:790-792, 1885b.

Dicke E et al: *A manual of reflexive therapy of the connective tissue: Bindegewebs-massage (connective tissue massage),* Scarsdale, NY, 1978, Simon.

Domenech MA: Massage education and clinical use in the United States, *J Phys Ther Ed* 10(2):68-71, 1996.

Estabrooks CA: Touch in nursing practice: a historical perspective, *Am J Nurs* 2(2):34-48, 1987.

Estradere J: *Du massage,* Pans, France, 1863, Ecole de Medecine.

Feltham E: Therapeutic touch and massage, *Nurs Standard* 5(45):26-28, 1991.

Galen: *Hygiene,* Springfield, Ill, 1951, Charles C Thomas (Translated by RM Green).

Goldstone L: From orthodox to complementary: the fall and rise of massage, with specific reference to orthopaedic and rheumatology nursing, *J Orthopaedic Nurs* 3(3):152-159, 1999.

Goldstone LA: Massage as an orthodox medical treatment past and future, *Complement Ther Nurs Midwifery* 6(4):169-175, 2000.

Graham D: *Practical treatise on massage,* New York, 1884, Wm. Wood.

Graham D: *Massage: manual treatment and remedial movements,* Philadelphia, 1913, Lippincott.

Graham D: Writer's cramp and allied affections: their treatment by massage and kinesitherapy, *Edin Med J* 19:231-239, 1917.

Grosvenor J: *A full account of the system of friction adopted and pursued with the greatest success in cases of contracted joints and lameness from various causes,* Oxford, 1925.

Harris JD, McPartland JM: Historical perspectives of manual medicine, *Phys Med Rehabil Clin N Am* 7(4):679-692, 1996.

Henry L: Massage, *Aust Med J* 6:337-347, 1884.

Hoffa A: *Tecknik der massage,* Stuttgart, 1897, Ferdinand Ernke.

Homer: *The odyssey,* New York, 1996, Penguin (Translated by R Fagles).

Huebscher R: An overview of massage, part 1: history, types of massage, credentialing, and literature, *Nurse Practitioner Forum* 9(4):197-199, 1998.

Ireland M, Olson M: Massage therapy and therapeutic touch in children: state of the science, *Alt Ther Health Med* 6(5):54-63, 2000.

Jabre J: "Nerve rubbing" in the symptomatic treatment of ulnar nerve paresthesiae, *Nerve Muscle* October:1237, 1994.

Johnson W: *The anatriptic art,* London, 1866, Simpkin Marshall.

Kamenetz HL: History of massage. In Licht S, editor: *Massage, manipulation and traction,* New Haven, Conn, 1960, Elizabeth Licht.

Kamenetz HL: History of massage. In Basmajian JV, editor: *Manipulation, traction and massage,* ed 3, Baltimore, 1985, Williams & Wilkins.

Kellgren A: *The technic of Ling's system of manual treatment,* Edinburgh and London, 1890, Young J Pentland.

Kellogg JH: *The art of massage,* ed 12, revised, Battle Creek, Mich, 1919, Modern Medical.

Kleen EAG: *Handbook i massage och sjukgymnastik,* Stockholm, 1906, Nordin & Josephson.

Kleen EAG: *Massage and medical gymnastics,* ed 2, New York, 1921, William Wood.

Krieger D: *Therapeutic touch: how to use your hands to help or to heal,* Englewood Cliffs, NJ, 1979, Prentice Hall.

Krieger D: *Foundations of holistic health nursing practices: the renaissance nurse,* Philadelphia, 1981, Lippincott.

Lace MV: *Massage and medical gymnastics,* London, 1946, J&A Churchill.

Mallios JB: Massage: an ancient healing therapy rediscovered in the 1990s, *Home Health Care Manage Prac* 8(2):15-20, 1996.

Mason A: Rub, rub, rubbish: massage in the nineteenth century, *Physiotherapy, JCSP* 78(9):666, 1992.

McMillan M: *Massage and therapeutic exercise,* Philadelphia, 1925, Saunders.

Mennell JB: *Physical treatment,* ed 5, Philadelphia, 1945, Blakiston.

Mitchell JK: *Massage and exercise in system of physiologic therapeutics,* Philadelphia, 1904, Blakiston.

Murrell W: Massage as a therapeutic agent, *Br Med J* 1:926-927, 1886a.

Murrell W: *Massage as a mode of treatment,* London, 1886b, Lewis.

Ostrom KW: *Massage and the original Swedish movements, their application to various diseases of the body,* Philadelphia, 1918, Blakiston.

Palmer D: The next three decades of massage, *Massage Therapy J* Fall: 27-31, 1992.

Prunieres A: Sur les crânes artificiellement perforés et les rondelles crâniennes à l'époque des dolmens, *Bull Soc Anthrop de Paris* 9:185, 1874.

Quintner J: Apropos rub, rub, rubbish: massage in the nineteenth century, *Physiotherapy, JCSP* 79(1):32, 1993.

Quintner J: Aye, there's the rub, down under, *Physiotherapy, JCSP* 80(8):519-520, 1994.

Robins RP: On writer's cramp. In Braithwaite J, editor: *The retrospect of medicine,* vol 92, London, 1885, Simpkin, Marshall.

Stockton J: The history of massage and physiotherapy in the Royal Navy, *Physiotherapy, JCSP* 80(1):40-42, 1994.

Tappan FM: *Healing massage techniques: a study of eastern and western methods,* Reston, Va, 1978, Reston.

Tappan FM, Benjamin P: *Tappen's handbook of healing massage techniques: classic, holistic, and emerging methods,* ed 3, Norwalk, Conn, 1998, Appleton & Lange.

*Thomas's medical dictionary,* Philadelphia, 1886, Lippincott.

Veith I: *Huang Ti: the yellow emperor's classic of internal medicine,* Baltimore, 1949, Williams & Wilkins.

Wright CK: Massage by nurses in the United States and the People's Republic of China: a comparison, *J Transcultural Nurs* 7(1):24-27, 1995.

Zabludowski JB: *Technique of massage,* Leipzig, 1903, Thieme.

Chapter 2

# Anatomical Landmarks for Therapeutic Massage

Patricia A. Brewer

Knowledge of anatomy, especially that which is on the surface or creates superficial landmarks, is essential for performing therapeutic massage. It is important to know in which direction muscles run, where they attach to bone or cartilage, their relationships with blood vessels and nerves, and whether these structures are deep or superficial. Bony structures visible or palpable from the surface are key elements to identifying these soft tissue structures. Arteries and nerves are delicate and easily damaged, so it is vital to be aware of their position when performing soft tissue massage. Also, deep friction massage can be done to specific tendons and ligaments, so knowledge of their position is important.

When describing or defining the position of structures of the body, it is important to always maintain relationships with respect to the anatomical position. The *anatomical position* is defined as the body standing erect, head facing forward, trunk straight, and upper limbs extended with the palms upward. All structures are related to one another with the body in this position.

## HEAD AND NECK

Therapeutic massage of the head and neck region must be done carefully. Several important nerves and blood vessels travel through this area, often superficially. Knowledge of these structures is important to avoid causing damage, either temporary or permanent.

### Head

Bony prominences of the head and neck provide a frame of reference for location of important structures. The mastoid process is a prominent bony process of the temporal bone and is found posterior to the ear. It is important as the insertion for the sternocleidomastoid muscle. Another significant bony prominence is the external occipital protuberance (or inion), found on the occipital bone (Figure 2-1). Extending caudally from the external occipital protuberance and the posterior border of the foramen magnum, there is a superficial ligament of significance, the ligamentum nuche (or nuchal ligament). This structure extends from the external occipital protuberance along the spinous processes of the cervical vertebrae. This ligament helps to provide a site for muscle attachments.

Laterally, another structure of significance in the head is the transverse process (TP) of the second cervical vertebra (C2). This landmark is identified by first locating the angle of the mandible. The TP of C2 is found between the angle of the mandible and the mastoid process. An important muscle landmark in the neck, just posterior to the TP of C2, is the sternocleidomastoid muscle (Figure 2-2), best viewed with the neck extended against resistance. This muscle originates from the manubrium of the sternum and the clavicle and inserts onto the mastoid process of the temporal bone and the superior nuchal line of the occipital bone.

### Neck

Posterior to the sternocleidomastoid muscle is a large muscle of the neck, the trapezius. When the patient's shoulders are elevated, this muscle is easily visible. This muscle extends from the skull and the ligamentum nuchae, along the spinous processes of cervical and thoracic vertebrae, to insert onto the clavicle as well as both the spine and acromion of the scapula.

Deep to the trapezius muscle are the splenius muscles (cervicis and capitis). These muscles reflect the meaning of the word *splenion,* meaning *bandage,* and extend from the spinous processes of cervical and thoracic vertebrae to the transverse processes of the cervical vertebrae and the skull. In the posterior neck, this muscle is found in a space bounded

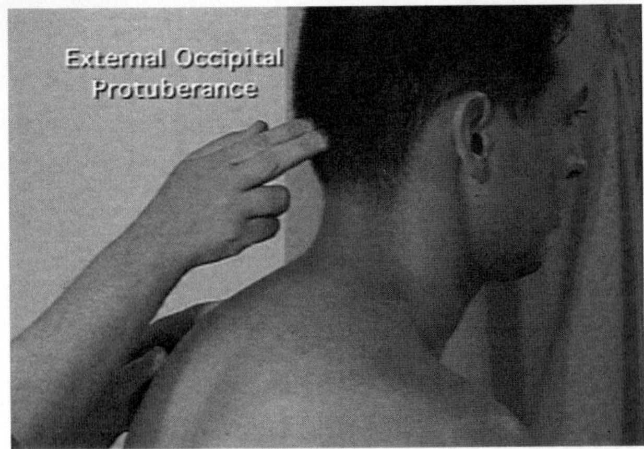


Figure 2-1 External occipital protuberance

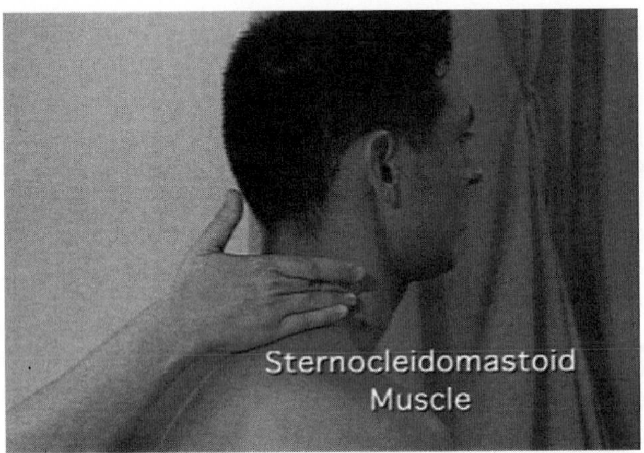


Figure 2-2 Sternocleidomastoid muscle

by the trapezius muscle posteriorly, the levator scapulae inferiorly, and the sternocleidomastoid muscle anteriorly.

Anterior to the splenius muscles are three pairs of scalene muscles: anterior, middle, and posterior. These muscles are involved in respiration and are important landmarks in the neck for locating the roots of the brachial plexus. The anterior and middle scalenes attach to the first rib, whereas the posterior scalene attaches to the second rib. All three muscles originate from the transverse processes of the fourth through sixth cervical vertebrae. At this origin, all three muscles can be palpated as one muscle mass, posterior to the sternocleidomastoid muscle. The roots of the brachial plexus are found in the neck between the anterior and middle scalenes.

## UPPER LIMB

Massage to the upper limb most often involves the superficial muscle groups present. Although nerves and vessels are present in the upper limb, most are deep to muscle compartments and thereby protected. Massage to the upper limb is commonly needed in athletes, repetitive injury rehabilitation patients, or breast cancer patients.

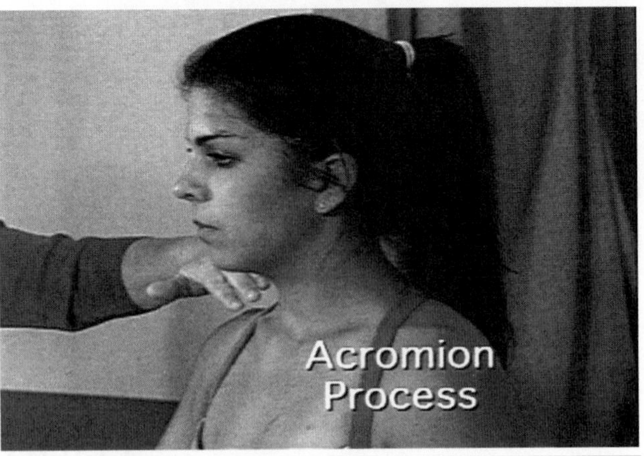


Figure 2-3 Acromion process

### Shoulder

Bony landmarks of significance in the shoulder are focused on the scapula and the clavicle. The clavicle is palpated on the anterior and superior aspect of the chest. Inferior to the clavicle is the space occupied by the subclavian artery, from which a pulse can be felt.

The scapula is a prominent flat bone on the dorsal aspect of the shoulder, between ribs 2 and 7. It articulates with the clavicle anteriorly and the humerus laterally. The medial border of the scapula can be pulled away from the back, along with the inferior border (at T8). The anterior border of the scapula is palpated best from the axilla. The most prominent posterior portion of the scapula is the spine (at T3), which provides a surface landmark to divide the posterior aspect of the scapula into supraspinous and infraspinous portions. The lateral end of the spine widens to form the acromion (Figure 2-3). At the angle of the acromion, where it changes direction, the deltoid muscle originates to form a cap over the shoulder. An additional important bony prominence on the scapula is the coracoid process. This process is medial to the head of the humerus as well as the acromion and is inferior to the clavicle. Several important muscles attach here (pectoralis minor, coracobrachialis, short head of the biceps).

The head of the humerus articulates with the scapula to form the shoulder, or glenohumeral joint. Just distal to the head of the humerus are the greater and lesser tubercles. By gripping the clavicle and the acromion and rotating the shoulder, the therapist can feel the head of the humerus as it rotates and can also feel the greater and lesser tubercles.

The deltoid muscle caps the shoulder. It has anterior, intermediate, and posterior portions. With the upper extremity in the anatomical position, the anterior portion is visible when the patient flexes the shoulder against resistance. The intermediate portion is visible when the patient abducts the arm against resistance. With the shoulder in extension, the posterior portion of the deltoid is visible at the shoulder.

## Arm

The arm, or brachium, is separated into anterior and posterior compartments. The most superficial, visible muscle of the anterior compartment is the biceps brachii muscle. It has, as the name implies, two heads of origin. The short head takes its origin from the coracoid process of the scapula, whereas the long head originates from the supraglenoid tubercle within the shoulder joint. Both heads are observed with the arm in the anatomical position. With the patient's shoulder flexed and forearm supinated, the therapist can easily see the belly of the long head along its entire length until it disappears under the anterior portion of the deltoid. The insertion of the biceps, the biceps tendon, can be palpated as it attaches to the radius. The biceps muscle also ends as an aponeurosis (Figure 2-4), or broadened flat tendon, inserting into the ulna. This bicipital aponeurosis forms the roof of the cubital fossa and protects the brachial artery and the median nerve.

The triceps muscle, with three heads of origin, is the major muscle of the posterior compartment of the arm. The lateral head is located on the lateral aspect of the arm, the long head is medial and proximal, and the short head is distal.

The olecranon process is an easily palpated proximal posterior prominence of the ulna. It can be felt with the upper limb in extension, and, even more pronounced, with the elbow in flexion. The olecranon fossa, a depression in the distal humerus, can be palpated with the elbow in flexion. It is the site where the olecranon process of the ulna rests when the elbow is extended.

The medial and lateral epicondyles are bony prominences at the distal end of the humerus. The medial epicondyle is the site of attachment for many of the flexors of the forearm (pronator teres, flexor carpi radialis, palmaris longus, flexor carpi ulnaris, and flexor digitorum superficialis), as well as the landmark for locating the ulnar nerve as it passes posterior to the medial epicondyle. The ulnar nerve is very superficial, running in a groove posterior to the medial epicondyle of the humerus. It can be palpated both proximal and distal to this point, as a tight cord. The medial epicondyle feels sharp and is more prominent than the lateral epicondyle. It provides a point of attachment for many of the forearm extensor muscles (extensor carpi radialis brevis, extensor digitorum, extensor digiti minimi, extensor carpi ulnaris, and supinator).

Medial and lateral thickenings of the fibrous capsule of the elbow are the radial collateral (lateral) and ulnar collateral (medial) ligaments. The radial collateral ligament is fan shaped and runs from the lateral epicondyle of the humerus to blend with the annular ligament of the radius. The ulnar collateral ligament extends from the medial epicondyle to the coronoid and olecranon processes of the ulna. It is composed of three bands, although these are not distinguishable on palpation.

An important anatomical space on the anterior upper limb is the cubital fossa. This space is found anteriorly at the transition from the arm to the forearm. The cubital fossa is defined superiorly by a line connecting the medial and lateral epicondyles of the humerus. The inferior medial border is the pronator teres muscle, and the inferior lateral border is the brachioradialis. The cubital fossa is an important region because of the presence of several structures. Superficially, the median cubital vein is the most common site for venipuncture. Found deep in the cubital fossa, the brachial artery and median nerve are protected by the bicipital aponeurosis.

## Forearm

The ulna is the medial bone of the forearm and serves to stabilize this area. The posterior border of the ulna can be palpated, extending from the olecranon process to the wrist. The distal end of the ulna is the styloid process (Figure 2-5).

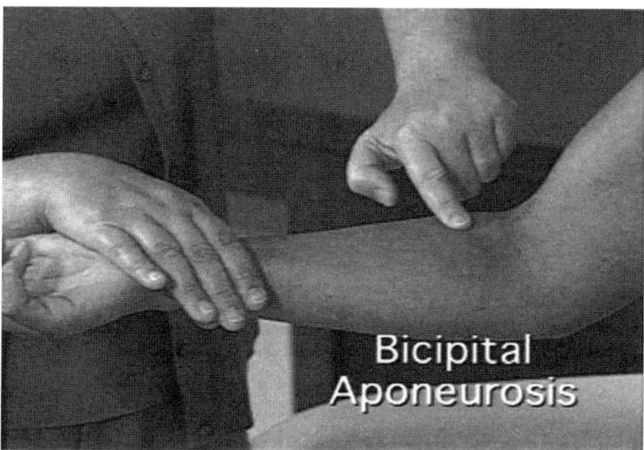


**Figure 2-4** Bicipital aponeurosis

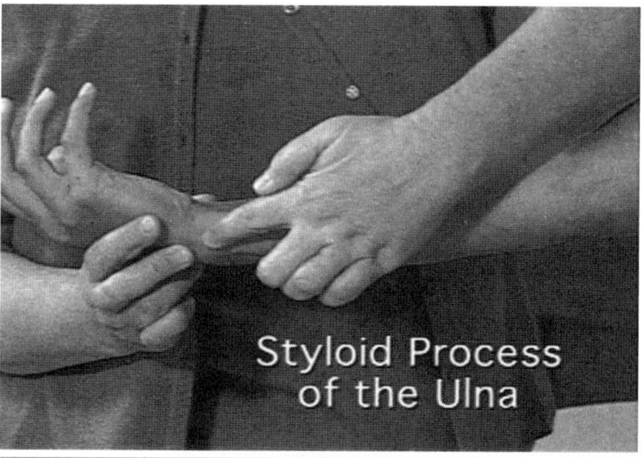


**Figure 2-5** Styloid process of the ulna

This superficial bony eminence can be seen and palpated easily with the wrist in both extension and flexion.

The radius is the lateral bone of the forearm. It is shorter than the ulna. The head of the radius is a proximal structure found just distal to the lateral epicondyle. It is best palpated with the subject's elbow flexed. Ask the subject to alternately supinate and pronate the forearm, and you will feel the radial head rotate as it articulates with the humeral capitulum. The groove felt between the radial head and the trochlea of the humerus during this rotation indicates the humero-radial joint line (HRJ). The radius ends distally as the styloid process. This process can be felt laterally, proximal to the thumb. The dorsal tubercle of the radius (Lister's tubercle) can be palpated medial and posterior to the styloid process and separates the tendons of the extensor digitorum, extensor indicis, and extensor pollicis longus muscles from those of the extensor carpi radialis longus and brevis.

The wrist extensors are found in the posterior compartment of the forearm, and most originate as the common extensor tendon from the lateral epicondyle of the humerus. One prominent posterior compartment muscle, which is not a forearm extensor, is the brachioradialis muscle. The brachioradialis muscle is most obvious when the subject flexes the forearm against resistance, keeping the forearm in the neutral position. Once the brachioradialis muscle is identified, the rest of the superficial posterior compartment muscles can be determined. The extensor carpi radialis longus and brevis, extensor digitorum, and the extensor carpi ulnaris comprise the muscles in this compartment, from lateral to medial, relating to the brachioradialis. The tendons of these muscles, found on the dorsum of the wrist, are held in place during extension by the extensor retinaculum. The tendons of the extensor digitorum muscle are clearly visible on the dorsal surface of the hand, when the wrist is hyperextended.

Most of the forearm flexors originate from the medial epicondyle as the common flexor tendon. These muscles include the pronator teres, flexor carpi radialis, palmaris longus, flexor carpi ulnaris, and flexor digitorum superficialis. Placing your hand on the medial epicondyle and asking the subject to flex and ulnar deviate the wrist will cause the muscles originating here to be felt.

## Wrist

The anatomical snuffbox is an important landmark near the wrist for localization of carpal bones, muscles, and the course of the radial artery. The boundaries of the snuffbox are tendons of the abductor pollicus longus, extensor pollicus brevis (both together at the anterior surface and often together in a sheath and therefore hard to distinguish as two separate muscles), and extensor pollicus longus (the posterior border of the snuffbox). These muscles become more visible if the subject abducts the thumb. The floor of this triangular area is the scaphoid bone proximally and the trapezium distally.

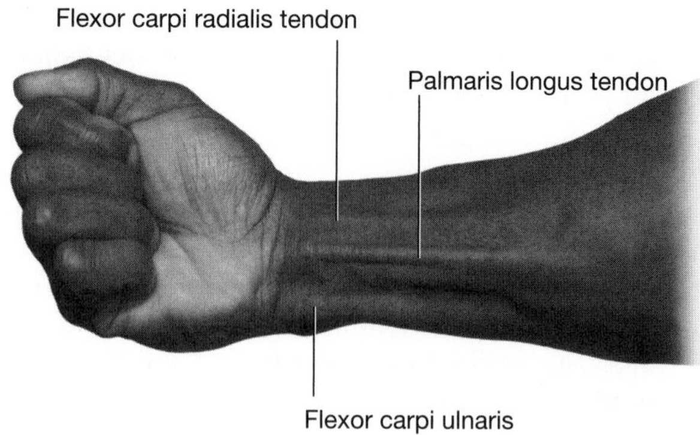


**Figure 2-6**
This figure illustrates the important relationships at the wrist of tendons, arteries, and nerves. *(Modified from Drake RL, Vogl L, Mitchel AWM:* Gray's anatomy for students, *Philadelphia, 2005, Elsevier.)*

Once the boundaries of the snuffbox have been established, the pulse of the radial artery can be easily palpated at the wrist, proximal to the snuffbox and lateral to the tendon of the flexor carpi radialis muscle.

The ulnar artery is also found superficially at the wrist, just lateral to the ulnar nerve, which can be felt close to the ulnar artery, just lateral to the tendon of the flexor carpi ulnaris muscle. The ulnar artery pulse can be taken at this location, just proximal to the pisiform bone, especially if the wrist is in extension (Figure 2-6).

The radial carpal (wrist) joint line correlates with the first crease of skin on the ventral surface of the wrist. This line is located at the base of the thenar eminence and indicates the articulation of the distal radius with the first row of carpal bones.

## Hand

The proximal, or first, row of carpal bones consists of the scaphoid, lunate, triquetrum, and pisiform, listed from lateral to medial. To palpate the scaphoid, locate the anatomical snuffbox and slide your finger to the base of this depression. The scaphoid is located here, just distal to the radial styloid process. On the anterior, palmar, surface of the hand, with the wrist extended, the scaphoid is felt as a bulge proximal to the thenar eminence. The lunate, which is medial to the scaphoid, appears as a slight bulge on the dorsal surface when the wrist is flexed. The triquetrum can be found by flexing the wrist with the forearm in supination, just distal to the styloid process of the ulna. To find the pisiform, a small round carpal bone, find the flexor carpi ulnaris. This muscle inserts onto the pisiform, which is located at the base of the hypothenar eminence. The pisiform projects as a small bump on the palmar surface of the hand.

The distal, or second, row of carpal bones consists of the trapezium, trapezoid, capitate, and hamate, listed from lateral to medial. The trapezium, the most lateral bone of the distal row, can be found between the scaphoid and the base of the first metacarpal, using the snuffbox as a guide. The trapezoid is best felt with the wrist in flexion. Palpate the proximal end of the second metacarpal to a slight depression. The trapezoid is a small prominence proximal to that depression. The capitate is the largest of all the carpal bones. It is large enough to articulate with the second, third, and fourth metacarpals. The capitate is found in a depression just proximal to the base of the third metacarpal. The final carpal bone, the hamate, is medial to the capitate, proximal to the base of the fifth metacarpal. On the palmar surface of the hand, the hamate has a hook, which can be palpated just distal to the pisiform. The hook of the hamate and the pisiform bone are important landmarks because of the close relationship they share with the ulnar nerve. This nerve can be easily trapped in the tunnel between these two bones or can be damaged if massage is too vigorous.

The five metacarpal bones articulate proximally with the carpals (at the base of the metacarpal) and distally with the phalanges (at the head of the metacarpal). The base of the first metacarpal, which articulates only with the trapezium, can be seen at the distal end of the snuffbox. The head of the first metacarpal articulates with the base of the proximal phalanx. The other four metacarpal bases can be palpated at their respective articulations with the second row of carpal bones. With the digits flexed, the heads of the second through fourth metacarpals are visible on the dorsum of the hand. The metacarpophalangeal joints (MCP joints) are the articulations of the metacarpal heads and the proximal phalanges. Ask the subject to flex and extend at these joints to appreciate the movement.

There are 14 phalanges in each hand, 3 (proximal, middle, and distal) in digits 2 through 4 and 2 (proximal and distal) in the thumb, or first digit. Ask the subject to alternately flex and extend at each of these joints to appreciate their flexion and extension.

The thenar eminence is the raised area visible on the palmar surface of the hand, at the base of the thumb. It is formed by three muscles, the abductor pollicis brevis, flexor pollicis brevis, and opponens pollicis. The hypothenar eminence is a comparable structure, at the base of the fifth digit, and it has three muscles: the abductor digiti minimi, flexor digiti minimi, and opponens digiti minimi.

The median nerve, the main innervation of the intrinsic muscles of the hand, runs deep through the cubital fossa. It becomes superficial in the distal third of the forearm. It continues its course through the forearm to pass into the palmar surface of the hand at the wrist. It can be localized at the wrist just medial to the tendon of the palmaris longus.

## BACK

The back is probably the most commonly requested area for massage. Knowledge of the bony landmarks and muscle groups of the back is essential for effective treatment.

With the subject seated and spine flexed, the spinous processes of all vertebrae become visible. The most prominent spinous process is that of the seventh cervical vertebra (C7), a significant superficial bony landmark also known as the *vertebra prominens* (Figure 2-7). With the subject seated and neck flexed, this process is readily visible in the midline of the neck as a single tubercle. When the subject's head is in the neutral position and rotated from side to side, the vertebra prominens will move slightly while the spinous process of the first thoracic vertebra (T1), below it, will not. The six cervical vertebrae above this can be counted, as can the 12 thoracic vertebrae below. The spinous process of T1 is located about a finger's breadth above the superior angle of the scapula. The spinous process of the third thoracic vertebra (T3) is at the level of the medial part of the scapular spine. The spinous process of the seventh thoracic vertebra (T7) is about a finger's breadth below the inferior angle of the scapula. The five lumbar vertebrae can be seen inferior to the twelfth thoracic vertebra (T12). With hands placed on the iliac crest and thumbs pointing toward the spine, thumbs will be at the L4/L5 disc space.

The trapezius muscle is a major superficial muscle of the posterior neck and shoulder. It connects the pectoral girdle to the trunk, extending from the skull, and the cervical and thoracic spinous processes to the clavicle, acromion, and spine of the scapula. Elevating the shoulders will allow the therapist to visualize this muscle.

The rhomboid muscles, major and minor, are found deep to the trapezius muscle, between the scapulae and the spine. They originate from the spinous processes of the vertebrae and insert on the medial border of the scapula.

Deep to the trapezius muscle at the shoulder are muscles that comprise the rotator cuff. This is a group of four muscles (supraspinatus, infraspinatus, subscapularis, and teres minor), which reinforces and stabilizes the shoulder joint. The supraspinatus muscle is found deep to the trapezius, above the spine of the scapula, nestled in the supraspinous fossa. The main function of this muscle is to initiate

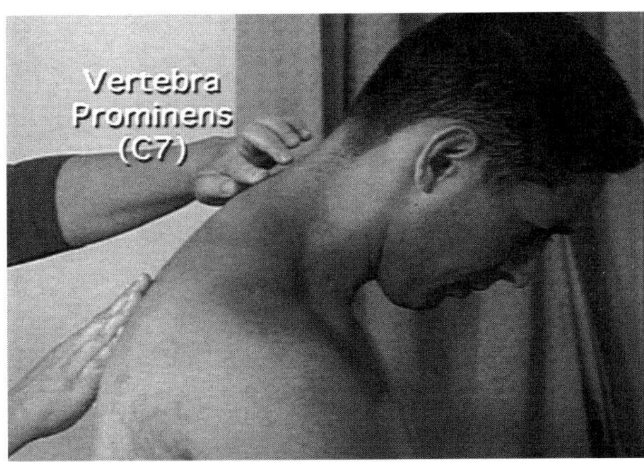


Figure 2-7 Vertebra prominens (C7)

abduction of the shoulder. Asking the subject to perform this action will isolate this muscle. The infraspinatus is found deep to the trapezius and below the spine of the scapula. These two rotator cuff muscles can be distinguished at their origin, but their insertions blend to form the rotator cuff tendon as it inserts on the greater tubercle of the humerus.

As the name implies, the serratus anterior muscle has a separated, or serrated, insertion into several ribs as it forms the lateral wall of the thorax. This can be viewed anteriorly if the upper limb is slightly extended at the shoulder.

The latissimus dorsi is the largest superficial muscle of the back (Figure 2-8). The anterolateral border of the muscle is most prominent, but this large muscle can also be seen as it originates from the thoracic and lumbar processes, sacrum, and the iliac crest.

The erector spinae are a deep group of muscles that run longitudinally alongside the spine. They extend from the cervical region to the sacrum. If the subject is prone and extends the trunk, the erector spinae will be seen as a muscular mass on either side of the spinous processes of the vertebrae.

The quadratus lumborum is a deep posterior muscle of the lower back. It is found laterally in the lumbar quadrangle between the iliac crest and the twelfth rib. It is involved in lateral bending of the back.

There are twelve pairs of ribs. Superior to the quadratus lumborum and inferior to the latissimus dorsi, the inferior border of the tenth rib can be palpated. These 10 ribs are attached, either directly or indirectly, via costal cartilages to the sternum. The last two pairs, 11 and 12, are not attached anteriorly to the sternum. For this reason, they are called "floating" ribs. It is possible to grasp rib 11 by standing behind the subject, placing both hands on the inferior border of the costal arch (formed by the cartilage connecting ribs 8 through 10 to the sternum), and moving the hands anterolaterally on the abdomen, toward the iliac crest. The eleventh rib will have a free anterior border. After locating the eleventh rib, move the hand down and back toward the iliac crest to find the shorter twelfth rib.

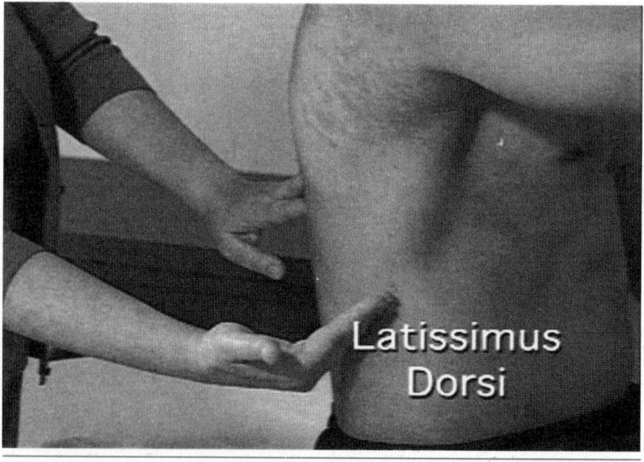


**Figure 2-8** Latissimus dorsi

## LOWER LIMB

Muscle groups and bony landmarks of the lower limb are generally larger and more prominent than those of the upper limb. It is often necessary to massage the lower limb of athletes and rehabilitation patients.

### Hip

The lower limb is attached to the trunk at the hip. The hip bone is actually composed of three bones, each distinct during embryonic development but fused in the adult. These three bones are the ilium, ishium, and pubis. The iliac crest is a major surface landmark of the ilium in the region of the hip. The anterior portion of the crest is more easily palpated than the posterior. The crest can be followed from front to back, as well as its medial and lateral borders. The most superior border of the iliac crests lies at level with the L4/L5 intervertebral disc. This is an important landmark for the site of a lumbar spinal puncture.

The anterior superior iliac spine (ASIS) and the anterior inferior iliac spine (AIIS) are prominent landmarks associated with the iliac crest. If the iliac crest is followed to its opposite posterior end, the posterior superior iliac spine (PSIS) is also visible and palpable. The PSIS can be seen on the posterior aspect of the subject, visible as a small dimple. A line connecting the PSIS lies at the level of S2, passing through the sacroiliac (SI) joints.

The second bone of the pelvis, and the most posterior, is the ischium. A prominent large oval ischial tuberosity can be palpated in the gluteal region.

A hand's width inferior to the umbilicus on the anterior abdomen are the pubic bones. The symphysis pubis is found in the midline, but it is often covered with soft tissue, making it difficult to palpate. Found a thumb's width to either side of the symphysis pubis are the pubic tubercles. These bony prominences provide a landmark for identifying the location of the superficial inguinal ring, a common site of herniation of abdominal contents into the lower limb.

#### *Anterior Structures: Thigh*

A prominent landmark separating the hip from the lower limb is the inguinal ligament (Figure 2-9). This soft tissue structure is the inferior margin of the external oblique muscle and aponeurosis. It extends between the ASIS and the pubic tubercle.

The anterior compartment of the thigh contains the quadriceps femoris muscle group. This group of muscles consists of the rectus femoris, the vastus medialis, vastus lateralis, and vastus intermedius. These muscles all flex the hip and extend the knee. All of these muscles insert by a common tendon onto the tibial tuberosity. This structure is known as the *quadriceps tendon superior to the patella* and the *patellar ligament (or tendon) inferior to the patella.* The tendon contains a sesamoid bone, the patella. With the knee in flexion, it is clearly visible anteriorly. To see this tendon/ligament, flex or extend the knee. It runs slightly obliquely and laterally, inferior to the patella.

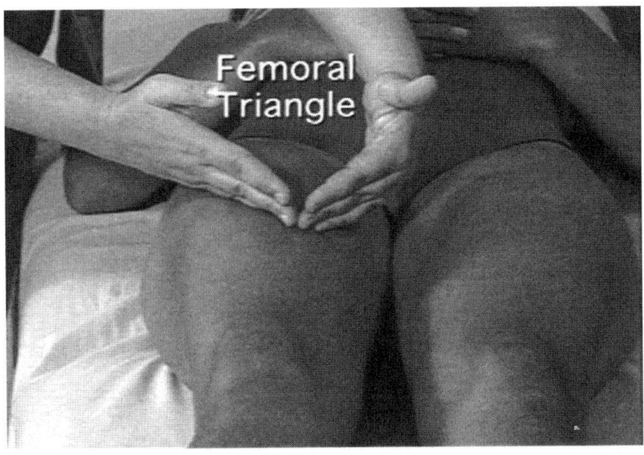


A

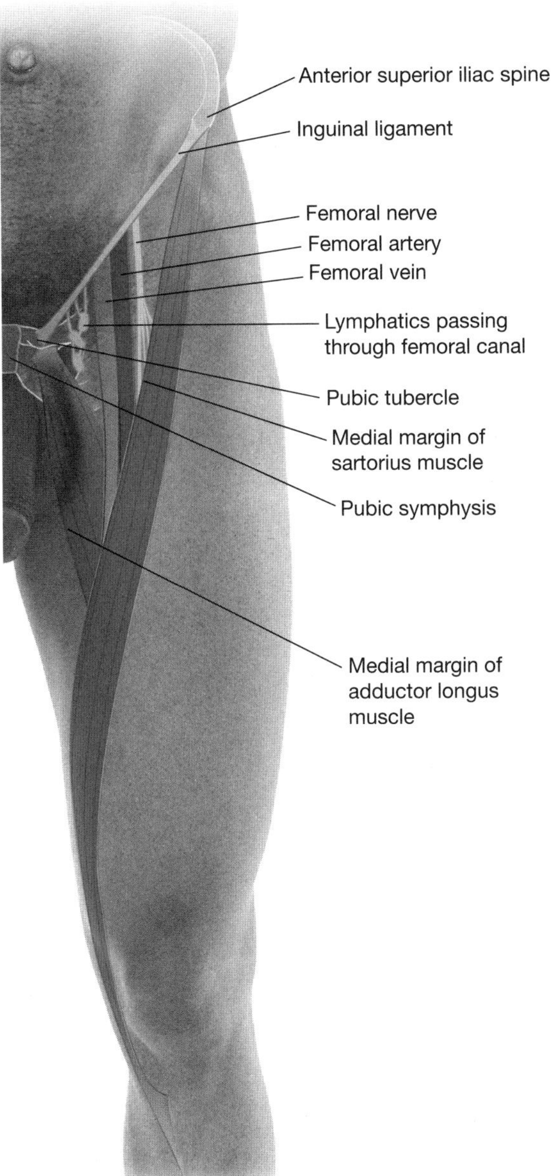


B

**Figure 2-9**

**A,** Femoral triangle. **B,** This figure illustrates the boundaries and contents of the femoral triangle in the anterior thigh. *(B, modified from Drake RL, Vogl L, Mitchel AWM:* Gray's anatomy for students, *Philadelphia, 2005, Elsevier.)*

An important area on the anterior thigh is the femoral triangle (see Figure 2-9). The superficial boundaries of the femoral triangle are visible and palpable. The most lateral boundary is the sartorius muscle. This muscle originates from the ASIS and extends distally at a 45-degree angle through the anterior thigh, where it inserts medially as part of the pes anserinus onto the tibia. The medial boundary of the femoral triangle is the adductor longus muscle. Another structure related to the femoral triangle is the superior border, defined by a line extending from the ASIS to the pubic tubercle. The pectineus muscle forms the floor of this triangle. The inferior apex of the triangle is called *Scarpa's triangle,* where the sartorius and the adductor longus muscles meet. Running perpendicular through the femoral triangle are its contents. The femoral artery is in the middle of the triangle, and one can feel the pulse of this artery if the leg is in extension. To locate the femoral nerve, move laterally in the femoral triangle from the femoral artery. The nerve will feel like a cord.

A prominent superficial bony landmark of the thigh is the greater trochanter of the femur. With the patient supine, as the hip is rotated, the greater trochanter of the femur can be palpated in the lateral hip region, inferior to the iliac crest. A line passing through the greater trochanters is at the level of the pubic tubercles and the center of the femoral heads.

The iliotibial tract or band (IT band) is a long, flat tendon running from the hip through the thigh to insert on the tibia at Gerdy's tubercle. The tensor of the fascia lata (TFL) is a small muscle found proximally in the IT band. The IT band also serves as the tendon of insertion for the gluteus maximus muscle.

### *Anterior Structures: Knee*

With the knee in full flexion, you can observe two external ligaments of the knee. The lateral collateral ligament (LCL, or peroneal/fibular collateral ligament) extends from the lateral tuberosity of the femur to the head of the fibula. This ligament feels like a thin cord. The medial collateral ligament (MCL, or tibial collateral ligament) is a broad, flat band that runs from the medial epicondyle of the femur to the medial condyle of the tibia.

The pes anserinus, or goose's foot, is the insertion of the sartorius, gracilis, and semitendinosus muscles into the medial aspect of the tibia. All three muscles are internal rotators of the leg.

The medial and lateral femoral condyles are superficial and easy to palpate when the knee is flexed. The condyles

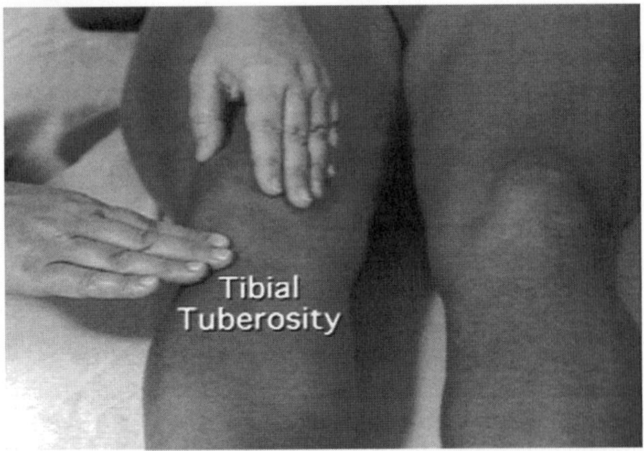


Figure **2-10** Tibial tuberosity

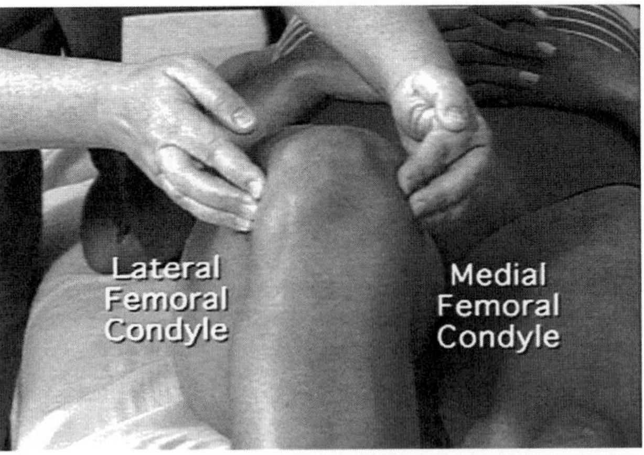


Figure **2-11** Lateral and medial femoral condyle

are the distal expansions of the femur. The flattened superior surfaces of the tibia, which articulate with the distal femur, are the tibial plateaus. With the knee flexed, these plateaus can be palpated. The horizontal groove at the level of the tibial plateaus constitutes the knee joint line. Finding this line allows palpation medially and laterally to locate the medial and lateral collateral ligaments of the knee. The adductor tubercle of the femur is a small prominence of bone on the superior aspect of the medial femoral condyle, best palpated with the knee in flexion. Slightly above each femoral condyle is an epicondyle. The medial epicondyle and the lateral epicondyle are prominent bony ridges on the femur. The lateral epicondyle is above the insertion point of the LCL (peroneal/fibular collateral ligament) of the knee.

The tibial tuberosity is an elevation on the anterior surface of the tibia (Figure 2-10). This is the point of attachment for the patellar tendon, the insertion for all of the muscles of the quadriceps femoris group. Distal to the tibial tuberosity, the anterior border of the tibia (Figure 2-11) can be palpated. This bone is superficial and directly palpable beneath the skin. When the knee is flexed, the tibial condyles can be palpated on either side of the tibial tuberosity. Gerdy's tubercle, or the tubercle of the lateral condyle of the tibia, is a structure found on the anterior aspect of the tibia.

### *Anterior Structures: Leg*

The distal termination of the tibia, the medial malleolus, is easily seen when the ankle is inverted. It serves as the point of insertion for medial ligaments of the ankle. Posterior leg muscles (posterior tibialis, flexor digitorum longus, and flexor hallucis longus) pass directly posterior to the medial malleolus. Between the flexor digitorum longus and flexor hallucis longus muscles lie the posterior tibial artery and vein, as well as the tibial nerve (Figure 2-12).

The lateral bone of the leg, the fibula, is small and thin. The head of the fibula can be palpated at the level of the tibial tuberosity, posterior and distal to Gerdy's tubercle. The neck of the fibula is found just distal to the head. The most distal prominence of the fibula is the lateral malleolus, providing a site of insertion for many ligaments of the ankle. With the foot in plantar flexion, it can be seen and palpated easily. The tendons of the fibularis longus and fibularis brevis muscles pass posterior to this landmark. The lateral malleolus extends more distally than does the medial malleolus and is sharper.

### *Anterior Structures: Ankle and Foot*

With the subject extending the great toe against resistance, the tendon of the extensor hallucis longus muscle is visible near its insertion on the base of the distal phalanx, as well as along its proximal course at the ankle as it enters the dorsum of the foot. The tendon of the tibialis anterior muscle is located medially to the proximal part of the extensor hallucis longus tendon as it passes to insert on the medial cuneiform and the first metatarsal. This tendon is the most medial of the tendons on the dorsum of the foot and lies just anterior to the medial malleolus. By resisting extension of the other toes, the tendon of the extensor digitorum longus can be found laterally to the proximal part of the extensor hallucis tendon and splits to insert on the middle and distal phalanges of the lateral four digits.

The fibularis muscles (longus, brevis, and tertius) are found laterally in the leg and foot. (These muscles were previously known as *peroneal muscles.*) With the foot everted and dorsiflexed, the tendon of the fibularis longus is visible passing posterior to the lateral malleolus as it inserts on the medial cuneiform and the first metatarsal. The fibularis brevis muscle is deep to the tendon of the fibularis longus. The fibularis brevis tendon courses laterally across the ankle into the foot to insert into the tuberosity of the fifth metatarsal. The fibularis tertius, an inconsistent muscle that comes off the extensor digitorum longus, passes

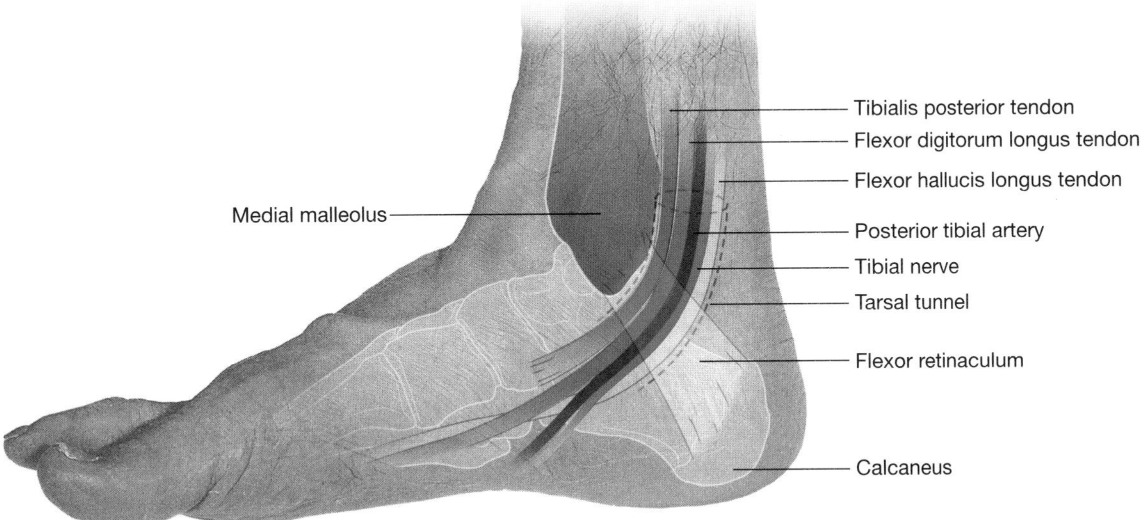


**Figure 2-12**
This figure demonstrates the relationships of the tendons, vessels, and nerves that pass posterior to the medial malleolus. *(Modified from Drake RL, Vogl L, Mitchel AWM:* Gray's anatomy for students, *Philadelphia, 2005, Elsevier.)*

anterior to the lateral malleolus to insert on the fifth metatarsal (Figure 2-13).

The lateral collateral ligament (LCL) and the medial collateral ligament (MCL or deltoid ligament) of the ankle reinforce the fibrous capsule of the ankle. The MCL is larger and stronger than the LCL. Both ligaments are found inferior to their respective malleoli.

An important superficial vascular landmark on the anterior ankle is the dorsalis pedis artery (or dorsal artery of the foot). This is the main source of blood supply to the toes and is the direct continuation of the anterior tibial artery. It is an important site for taking the pulse, especially if circulation in the upper limb is compromised. It is found midway between the lateral and medial malleoli.

The foot is composed of the tarsal bones. These tarsal bones include the talus, calcaneus, navicular, cuboid, and three cuneiforms. The talus, which forms the ankle joint with the distal tibia, has a talar head, which can be palpated distal to the malleoli. The calcaneus is the largest tarsal bone. It articulates with the talus and forms the heel of the foot. A significant structure of the calcaneus is the sustentaculum tali. This shelflike structure is located on the medial aspect of the calcaneus, a finger's breadth inferior to the medial malleolus of the tibia, and helps to support the talus. A small lateral extension of the calcaneus, the fibular (peroneal) trochlea is palpated just anterior to the lateral malleolus. The navicular bone has a prominence called the *navicular tuberosity*. This is found just distal to the talar head on the medial side of the foot. The heads of all five metatarsals can be seen if the toes are plantarflexed, together or separately. The first metatarsal is the shortest and broad-

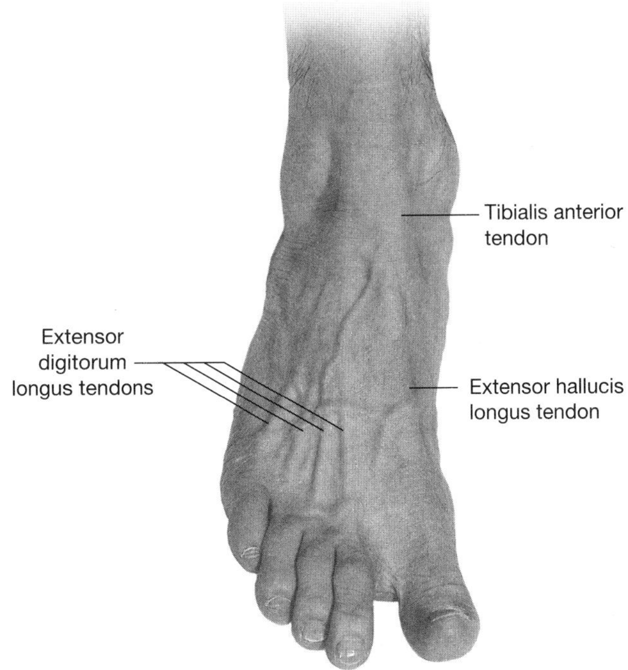


**Figure 2-13**
This figure shows the relationships between the tendons of the tibialis anterior, extensor hallucis longus, and extensor digitorum longus on the dorsum of the foot. *(Modified from Drake RL, Vogl L, Mitchel AWM:* Gray's anatomy for students, *Philadelphia, 2005, Elsevier.)*

est of the metatarsals. The second metatarsal is the longest. A plantar view of the heads of the metatarsals is possible if the toes are dorsiflexed. The tuberosity, or styloid process of the fifth metatarsal, provides for the insertion of the peroneus brevis. This bony landmark can be found by following the fifth metatarsal from its head, proximally, until it articulates with the cuboid. The cuboid, found proximally to the fifth metatarsal, can be palpated if the peroneus brevis muscle is relaxed by inverting the foot.

### *Posterior Structures: Thigh and Leg*

The gluteal group of muscles is considered to be the lateral compartment of the thigh but is found posteriorly at the region of the hip. This group of three muscles—maximus, medius, and minimus—is found in the area bounded by the iliac crest, the gluteal fold, the coccyx, the ischial tuberosity, and a lateral border extending from the ASIS to the greater trochanter. The most superficial muscle of the group is the gluteus maximus.

The large and important nerve of the lower extremity that passes through the gluteal region is the sciatic nerve (Figure 2-14). It innervates no musculature in the gluteal region but serves as the innervation for the muscles of the thigh, leg, and foot. The sciatic nerve bifurcates to form the tibial and common fibular nerves, usually at midthigh level. These nerves can be distinguished from one another at the level of the popliteal fossa. When the subject is supine, with hip and knee flexed, the tibial nerve is visible in the posterior aspect of the popliteal fossa. The popliteal artery is found just medial to this nerve. The pulse from this vessel can be taken at this location, even though the artery is deep in the popliteal fossa. This relationship renders this artery subject to injury with a posterior dislocation of the knee joint. The direct continuation of the popliteal artery into the posterior leg is the posterior tibial artery. This artery lies deep to the gastrocnemius and soleus muscles and provides the primary blood supply to the foot. It becomes more superficial at the ankle, running behind the medial malleolus. Lateral to the tibial nerve, running at a 45-degree angle, is the common fibular nerve. This nerve is superficial and vulnerable to injury as it winds around the head of the fibula.

The posterior compartment of the thigh contains the hamstring muscles. These muscles (biceps femoris, semimembranosus, semitendinosus) can all be palpated together as they arise from the ischial tuberosity. These muscles also comprise the borders of the anatomical space at the posterior aspect of the knee, known as the *popliteal fossa* (Figure 2-15).

The popliteal fossa is defined superiorly by the biceps femoris (lateral) and the semimembranosus and semitendinosus (medial). It is defined inferiorly by the medial and

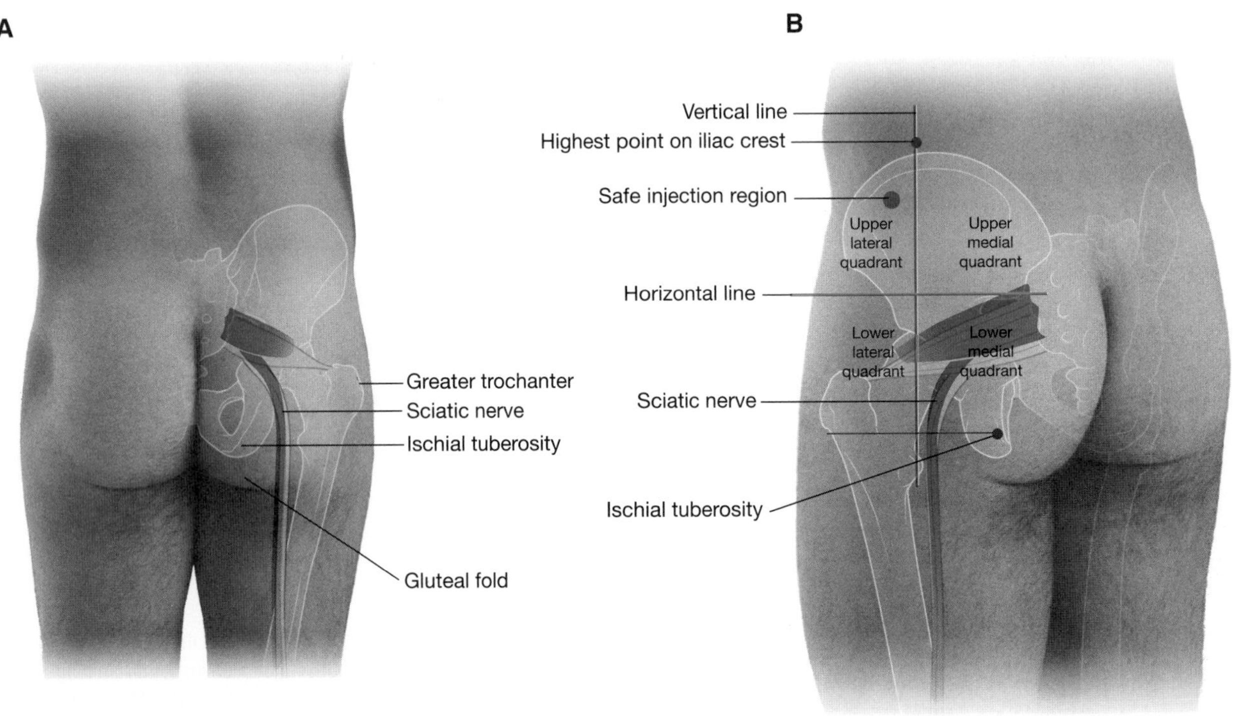


**Figure 2-14**
This figure illustrates the course of the sciatic nerve through the gluteal region. *(Modified from Drake RL, Vogl L, Mitchel AWM:* Gray's anatomy for students, *Philadelphia, 2005, Elsevier.)*

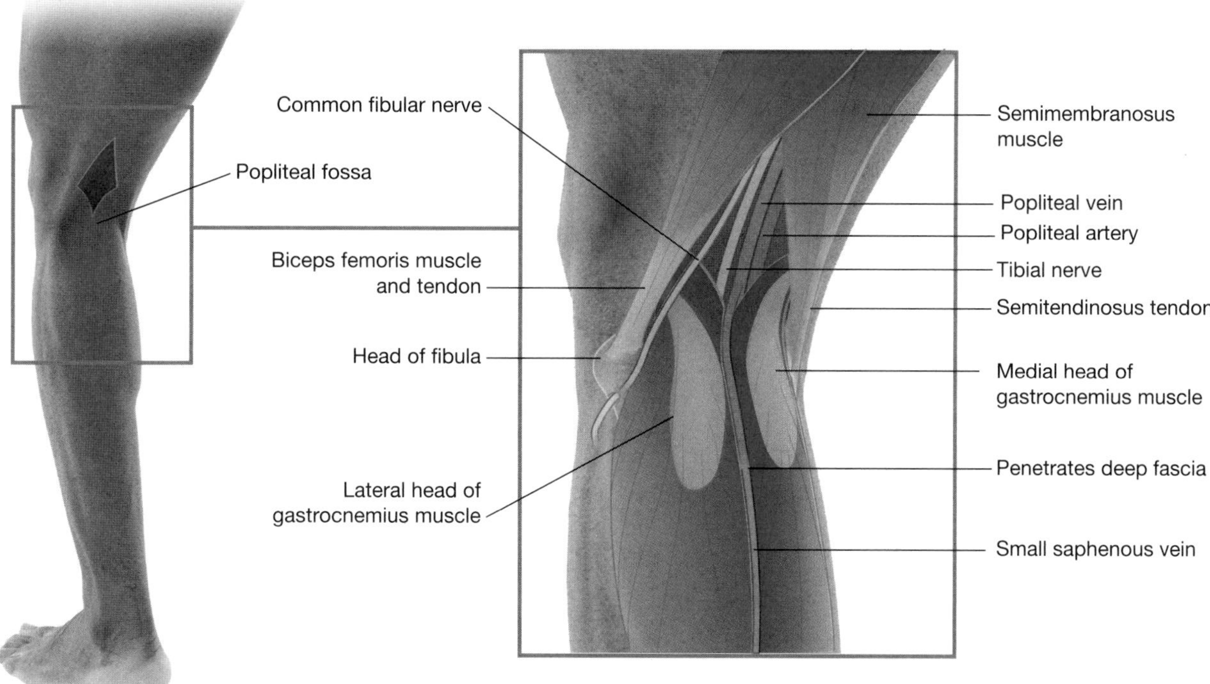


**Figure 2-15**

This figure shows the boundaries of the popliteal fossa, as well as the course of the common fibular nerve as it winds around the fibula. *(Modified from Drake RL, Vogl L, Mitchel AWM:* Gray's anatomy for students, *Philadelphia, 2005, Elsevier.)*

lateral heads of the gastrocnemius. With the subject lying prone, the belly of the gastrocnemius muscle is seen in the posterior compartment of the leg, halfway between the knee and the ankle. This muscle has two heads of origin, and the medial head is more prominent than the lateral head. The calcaneal or Achilles tendon for this muscle continues distally to insert on the calcaneus. This tendon is easily and palpated at the heel.

## REFERENCES

Drake RL, Vogl L, Mitchel AWM: *Gray's anatomy for students,* Philadelphia, 2005, Elsevier.

Moore KL, Dalley AF: *Clinically oriented anatomy,* ed 5, Baltimore, 2005, Lippincott Williams and Wilkins.

Moses KP, Banks JC, Nava PB et al: *Atlas of clinical gross anatomy,* Philadelphia, 2005, Elsevier.

Tixa F: *Atlas of palpatory anatomy of limbs and trunk,* Teterboro, NJ, 2003, Icon Learning Systems.

Chapter 3

# Essential Requirements for Soft Tissue Manipulation

The professional practice of soft tissue manipulation (including massage) requires consideration of a number of essential requirements. Important ethical considerations are clearly relevant to the practice of this medical art, and the basic issues are outlined in this chapter. The technical requirements for the administration of soft tissue manipulation include the type of equipment to be used, methods of positioning the patient, and various lubricants, to mention just a few. All of these issues are considered in this chapter, so as to separate them from the descriptions of the basic massage strokes in the following chapter. Each of the issues discussed in this chapter is relevant to the material discussed in most of the remainder of the text.

This chapter does not explore the many types of mechanical device claimed to be useful for massage treatment. A discussion of these devices has been deliberately omitted because in most cases they do not deliver a true massage treatment. These devices usually impart a simple vibration wave to the tissues, typically at a frequency from 50 to 60 Hz. Although a mechanical stimulus of this type will certainly have an effect on the tissues, it is not, nor can it be, the same kind of stimulus as that given by trained human hands.

## ETHICAL ISSUES

All health professionals involved in direct patient care are expected to, and are honor bound, to adhere to high levels of ethical practice. This is especially the case when it comes to the practice of soft tissue manipulation (including massage), because massage requires direct contact with the patient's skin and the patient will necessarily be undressed for treatment. Therefore, every therapist should conduct him- or herself with the highest standard of professionalism during massage treatments, indeed, in the same manner as they would to deliver any other treatment modality (Mykietiuch, 1991; Norton, 1995). In addition, by observing the usual high standards of personal hygiene and cleanliness, the therapist leaves the patient feeling confident of an effective and professional treatment. Because massage treatment involves the exposure of the body part to be treated and direct touching of the patient by the therapist, inappropriate touching and unnecessary exposure are to be avoided at all times. Many of these ethical issues will be addressed in the chapters that follow.

All of the major professional associations in which massage is practiced have extensive codes of ethics. These codes are excellent sources of information on the various issues related to the ethical practice of massage. Although much has been written on these issues, the various codes of practice are an excellent starting place for the reader to find more detailed information in this area. The web sites of professional associations such as the American Physical Therapy Association (APTA), the American Massage Therapy Association (AMTA), the American Nursing Association (ANA), the American Occupational Therapy Association (AOTA), the Australian Physiotherapy Association (APA), the Canadian Physiotherapy Association (CPA), and the Chartered Society of Physiotherapy (CSP) are listed at the end of the chapter for easy reference. There are, of course, many other professional associations that could be added to this list, but to include all of the appropriate associations is beyond the scope of this chapter. The intent is only to list a few examples.

The therapist should be relaxed in his or her manner and movements, which allows the therapist to concentrate on the treatment. As in all treatments, an adequate explanation to the patient is an essential prerequisite. There is considerable risk of scratching the patient if the therapist wears jewelry, such as watches and rings (with large stones and settings), on the wrists or fingers. In this respect, therapists are advised to work without such jewelry. In addition, any jewelry that the patient may be wearing should be removed from the part of the body to be treated.

It is essential for the therapist to maintain the confidentiality of each patient's health-related information. A discussion of one patient's situation with another patient is an obvious breech of confidence and an ethical violation. Indeed, in some instances this behavior may be against the applicable law.

Undressing and appropriately draping the patient are important aspects of all massage treatments. Instructing the patient on what to wear for treatment is helpful because it can greatly facilitate the treatment. It will also reduce embarrassment for both therapist and patient. Explaining the procedures and the need for undressing and draping are important steps in gaining the patient's confidence and verbal consent to treatment. In this regard, a male therapist needs to be especially diligent when treating a female patient. In this case, it may even be helpful to have a female assistant present during the draping and positioning of the patient. Examining the patient, both before and after treatment, is another essential component of modern rehabilitation practice. Obviously this involves undressing, draping, touching, and often moving the patient. All of these procedures require the same high standards of ethical practice. Unnecessary touching and exposure must be avoided.

## KNOWLEDGE OF SURFACE ANATOMY

The effective use of soft tissue manipulation techniques requires a thorough knowledge and practical application of surface anatomy. Because the therapist's hands are moving over the patient's tissues, it is essential that the therapist be able to recognize the anatomical structures involved, especially when performing techniques that are designed to affect specific structures, such as a tendon or part of a muscle. Obviously, if a technique is performed to the wrong structure, treatment is unlikely to be successful. Clearly, there can be no substitute for thorough preparation in surface and gross anatomy. Although it is not the primary intention of this text to review surface anatomy in detail, the therapist must be familiar with a number of important structures. These structures are listed in Boxes 3-1, 3-2, 3-3, and 3-4 and have been covered in Chapter 2. In addition, most of these landmarks are identified on the accompanying DVD. They are listed here as a record of the major landmarks and structures that can be regarded as essential knowledge for the effective use of soft tissue manipulation. From time to time anatomical terms change, and this can be confusing when deciding what to call a particular structure. Whenever possible, the latest and most widely accepted anatomical nomenclature has been used. Where appropriate, former names have been included in parentheses, if it seemed this would be helpful.

### BOX 3-1 Head and Neck

| Bony Landmarks | Soft Tissue Structures |
|---|---|
| Mandible | Ligamentum nuche (nuchal ligament) |
| Angle of the mandible | Splenius capitus |
| Nasal bones | Scalene muscles |
| Frontal bones | Supraclavicular lymph nodes |
| Temporal bones | Jugular veins |
| Occiput | Carotid artery and pulse |
| External occipital protuberance | External auditory canal |
| Mastoid process | Pinna of the ear |
| Supraorbital ridge | Facial muscles |
| Infraorbital ridge | Muscles of mastication |
| Zygomatic arch | |
| Transverse process of C2 | |
| Spinous process of C2, 3, 4, 5, 6, 7 | |

### BOX 3-2 Trunk and Pelvis

| Bony Landmarks | Soft Tissue Structures |
|---|---|
| Acromion | Rhomboids |
| Angle of the acromion | Supraspinatus |
| Scapular borders | Infraspinatus |
| Spine of the scapula (T3 level) | Serratus anterior |
| Inferior angle (T8 level) | Latissimus dorsi |
| Spinous processes (all levels) | Erector spinae |
| "Floating" ribs | Quadratus lumborum |
| Symphysis pubis | Gluteal muscles |
| Iliac crest | Inguinal ligament |
| Anterior superior iliac spine (ASIS) | |
| Posterior superior iliac spine (PSIS) | |
| Sacroiliac joints | |
| Sacral borders | |
| Ischial tuberosity | |

## PREPARATION OF THE HANDS FOR MASSAGE

Because soft tissue manipulation is performed with the hands, the condition of the hands is extremely important to both therapist and patient. The therapist's hands must be clean and well groomed yet strong and flexible. The nails should be kept reasonably short and the tips rounded so that they do not injure the patient during any of the strokes. The ideal hands for massage are well padded, warm, supple, and dry. They should express sensitivity and gentleness and yet have firmness and strength. Beginning massage practitioners may increase the suppleness of their hands by partaking in various hand exercises. Some individuals have naturally flexible hands and are able to move them rhythmically, and they seem to be able to learn the techniques of massage more readily than others. Nonetheless, with appropriate

## BOX 3-3 Upper Limb

| Bony Landmarks | Soft Tissue Structures |
|---|---|
| Acromion | Subacromial bursa |
| Coracoid process | Rotator cuff |
| Greater and lesser tuberosities/tubercles | Deltoid |
| Bicipital groove | Biceps |
| Olecranon | Triceps |
| Olecranon fossa | Ulnar nerve |
| Medial and lateral epicondyles | Wrist extensors |
| Radial head | Common extensor origin/tendon |
| Humero-radial joint (HRJ) line | Common flexororigin/ tendon |
| Radial styloid process | Radial collateral ligament (lateral) |
| Posterior border of the ulna | Ulnar collateral ligament (medial) |
| Ulnar styloid process | Cubital fossa |
| Radial carpal (wrist) joint line | Anatomical snuffbox |
| Dorsal tubercle of the radius (Lister's) | Radial artery |
| Carpal bones | Flexor tendons |
| Metacarpal bones | Ulnar artery |
| Metacarpophalangeal (MCP) joints | Extensor tendons |
| Phalanges | Thenar and hypothenar eminences |

## BOX 3-4 Lower Limb

| Bony Landmarks | Soft Tissue Structures |
|---|---|
| Greater trochanter | Femoral triangle |
| Borders of the patella | Femoral nerve, artery, and vein |
| Adductor tubercle | Trochanteric bursa |
| Medial and lateral femoral condyles | Sciatic nerve |
| Medial and lateral femoral epicondyles | Sartorius muscle |
| Tibial plateaus and knee joint line | Quadriceps femoris muscle |
| Tibial tubercle/tuberosity | Infrapatellar tendon |
| Head and neck of the fibula | Hamstring muscles |
| Lateral malleolus | Tensor of the fascia lata |
| Anterior border of the tibia | Iliotibial tract (IT band) |
| Medial malleolus | Pes anserinus |
| Calcaneus | MCL and LCL of the knee |
| Fibular (peroneal) tubercle/trochlea | Common peroneal (fibular) nerve |
| Metatarsals | Popliteal artery |
| Styloid process (tuberosity) of 5th MT | Popliteal fossa |
| Cuboid | Gastrocnemius muscles |
| Navicular tubercle/ tuberosity | Posterior tibial artery |
| Sustentaculum tali | Anterior tendons (T, H, D) |
| Sesamoid bones in the foot | Dorsalis pedis pulse |
| | Fibularis (peroneal) tendons |
| | Medial collateral ligament (MCL-deltoid) |
| | Lateral collateral ligament (LCL) of the ankle lateral |
| | Ligament of the ankle |
| | Achilles (calcaneal) tendon |

guidance, anyone who conscientiously spends sufficient time in practice will eventually acquire good technique.

Hands that have cuts, open sores, warts, or other skin lesions are not suitable for massage treatments. It is important for therapists to take exceptional care of their hands if they are to be effective with the use of massage. Simple household, automotive, or garden work can be damaging to the hands. A few minutes spent raking leaves or sweeping a yard can easily cause a blister to appear. Adequate protection with suitable gloves is therefore essential. The use of a high-quality hand or skin conditioner helps to keep hands in good condition.

The hands must be thoroughly washed before and after treatment and should always be scrupulously clean. The use of a high-quality nailbrush is essential in order to remove dirt from under the edge of the nails. To be effective, hands should be washed for at least 30 seconds to a minute. Antibacterial soap may also be helpful. Careful drying with disposable paper towels is also highly recommended (see DVD Chapter 3-7).

Areas of hard, dry skin (callus) can be removed by gently rubbing a very mild abrasive, such as raw, granulated sugar, into the hands. A small amount of olive oil should be combined with the sugar to produce a paste that is then rubbed into rough areas of skin. This technique can be repeated several times each day until the areas of hard skin soften. Granulated sugar does not completely dissolve in olive oil and therefore retains its mildly abrasive texture when it is rubbed into the skin. The olive oil also helps to soften the skin. Care must be taken with clean-up following this technique because the sticky mixture of oil and sugar is difficult to remove if allowed to get onto the treatment linens or clothing. It is best to use paper towels to remove the oil and sugar from the hands before washing with soap and hot water (see DVD Chapter 3-8).

During massage treatments, the hands fulfill two main roles: they move the skin, subcutaneous tissues, muscles, and other structures, and at the same time they acquire information about the condition of those tissues. In this respect, the hands may be viewed as mobile sensors, relaying information to the therapist concerning the condition of the tissues being massaged. Moist, perspiring hands are a great disadvantage to the therapist and may be uncomfortable for the patient. Therapists may minimize this condition by frequently washing and drying their hands, possibly with some evaporating spirits.

It is important for the therapist to be relaxed during the application of massage, as most of the strokes are performed not with the hands alone but by using body weight and moving the body to different positions. Effective massage can be physically demanding, and the therapist who has strong, flexible hands and good upper body strength will likely find massage treatments much less tiring than those who are not as fit. Various exercises that strengthen and mobilize the hands and upper limbs in general will be of considerable benefit and should be seen as good preventive maintenance for the therapist.

In the great majority of both ancient and modern cultures, massage has been performed using one or both hands. Other body parts have been used, such as the feet and elbows, but they are not considered in the present text. Many different parts of the hand can be used for massage, including the palms, fingertips/pads, thumb tips/pads, ulnar border, knuckles, and all areas on the palmar surface of the hand. Figure 3-1 and Box 3-5 show several areas of the hand that can be used in massage. The same areas are shown on the accompanying DVD (see DVD Chapter 3-2).

## LUBRICANTS: POWDERS, CREAMS, AND OILS

If the therapist has warm, soft, dry hands, use of a lubricant may be unnecessary; however, most massage situations require the use of a lubricant to facilitate movement of the hands over the patient's body tissues. This is largely because perspiration on the skin surface (both on the therapist's hands and the patient's skin) produces a sticky situation that may well be uncomfortable for the patient. In addition, it will make it difficult for the therapist to perform the various strokes properly. Several types of lubricant are in common use. Although massage is generally regarded as a very safe treatment, minor problems can arise with the use of various types of lubricant. Some therapists develop an allergic reaction, as may the patient, and this will probably necessitate the use of a different medium (Bruze, 1999; Frosh, 1996; Sanchez-Perez & Garcia-Diez, 1999; Held, 2001; Lis-Balchin, 1999).

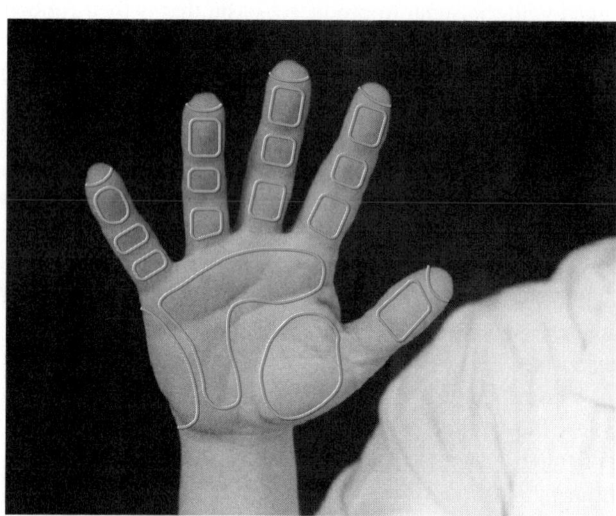

**Figure 3-1 Areas of the Hand Used in Massage**

Several areas of the hand can be used for massage. The circumscribed areas include the fingertips and finger pads, the thumb pad, the entire palmar surface, and the ulnar border of the hypothenar eminence. The "knuckle" region can also be used for massage, as can the back of the fingers.

**BOX 3-5 Areas of the Hands Used in Massage (DVD Chapter 3-2)**

The entire palmar surface of either or both hands
The ulnar border of the hypothenar eminence
One or more fingertips
One or more finger pads
Either or both thumb pads
The knuckle region

### Powder

Traditionally, the most common type of lubricant in this class is a finely powdered French chalk mixture or a mixture of starch, boracic, and chalk. In current practice, an unscented baby powder is probably the most suitable powder for massage. Heavily scented powders should be avoided, as many people find them offensive and a few are actually allergic to them. Powder has a great advantage over various oils and lotions as it allows the therapist to manipulate deep tissues without the risk of the hands slipping on an oily surface. Powder facilitates the movement of the hand over the skin surface, but when pressure is applied, the hand and skin move together on the deep structures. This effect may be impossible to achieve when oils are used as a lubricant. Although powder is an effective lubricant, it must be used with care. The powder will tend to get on the entire treatment area if the therapist shakes the container too vigorously. Apart from the obvious mess that requires clean-up, this can create a dangerous situation. Powder on the floor can produce a slippery surface that may cause the patient or the therapist to slip and fall. It is also important to avoid breathing the powder, as it is a serious contaminant if inhaled into the lungs (see DVD Chapter 3-3).

### Creams

Various kinds of cream may be used; for example, lanolin, vitamin E, or cold cream. For general use, a good-quality moisturizing cream may be preferable to liquid oils because of the convenience of application. A significant problem with the use of some creams concerns their absorption by the skin during the massage, leaving a sticky skin surface. This stickiness can make the massage difficult for the therapist to perform, and it may be uncomfortable for the patient.

Creams have similar problems to the oils with their use in massage. The cream should be a type that is absorbed slightly by the skin but is not so oily that a large amount remains on the skin surface during the massage. Only an amount sufficient to allow the hands to glide smoothly over the skin should be used, as too much lubricant prevents a firm grasp of the tissues and leaves an excessive amount on the patient's skin. The right amount depends on the dryness of the patient's skin and of the therapist's hands. Experience will enable the therapist to choose the correct amount. The proper amount of lubricant for one area should be put on both palms and applied to the area with the first stroking movement (see DVD Chapter 3-4).

### Oils

Many types of oils can be used for massage. They are particularly useful for treating the skin and subcutaneous tissues, especially scars, dry skin, and poorly nourished areas. However, many deep massage strokes cannot be effectively applied when oil is used as a lubricant. This is because the therapist's hand cannot grip the superficial tissues properly and move them on the deeper structures. Commonly used high-quality natural oils are olive, almond, and palm oil; however, many types of vegetable oil can also be used. Many types of baby oil are readily available and are a good alternative to the natural oils.

When applying the oil, it is best to pour a small amount into the hands and then apply it to the skin. This reduces the tendency for the oil to run over the patient's skin onto the linens. Oil of any type is difficult to remove from the patient's clothing or the treatment linens. For this reason, care should be exercised when applying any type of oil. Sufficient paper towels under the body part being massaged will help to eliminate problems related to oil spillage (see DVD Chapter 3-5).

### Soap and Hot Water

Soap and hot water may be used for the dirty or dry, scaly skin that is commonly encountered when a plaster cast has been removed from a limb/body part. Liquid soap, sufficient in quantity to produce large amounts of soapsuds, is required to make this technique effective. It is directed toward affecting the skin and subcutaneous tissues and is particularly suitable for removing dead, dry skin where the tissues are somewhat undernourished. A medicated or antibacterial soap may be helpful when using this technique. A modification of the basic technique of stroking is likely to be the most useful stroke. If possible, the therapist should immerse the limb in the hot water and soapsuds mixture. The temperature of the hot water must be carefully controlled and should be similar to that used for a comfortable hot bath.

Following massage treatment, any lubricant left on the skin surface should be removed, unless it is supposed to remain on the skin (e.g., lanolin or some other emollient). The lubricant should be applied sparingly to the therapist's hands rather than directly to the patient. If the patient is powdered or "flooded" with lubricants, the skin pores may become clogged, an effect that tends to defeat some of the aims of massage. When powder is used as the lubricant, in most cases it is not necessary to wash and dry the patient's skin following massage. However, if excessive powder remains on the skin, much of it can be removed by simply wiping the skin surface with a damp paper towel. The skin surface can then be dried with a paper towel. It is good practice to encourage patients to shower or wash the skin surface properly at their earliest convenience. When oils have been used as the lubricant, it is important to carefully remove them from the patient's skin with paper towels and then to wash and dry the skin.

## TREATMENT TABLES, CHAIRS, AND ACCESSORIES

The most important equipment for successful massage treatment is a pair of well-trained and experienced hands directed by an intelligent mind. Other equipment is important, however, as massage treatments should be practiced with the patient in well-supported and comfortable positions. In most cases, the patient lies or sits on some type of treatment table (plinth). Ideally, the table height should be adjustable to a position that is comfortable for the therapist. A proper position reduces the overall stress and strain to the therapist's back by minimizing the need to bend over the patient.

Adequate support for the patient's head, shoulders, and other body parts is extremely important, especially when a patient is lying facedown (prone lying). A wide variety of adjustable tables are available that greatly facilitate the practice of massage (Figure 3-2).

The adjustable features of these plinths help to ensure that the patient and the therapist are optimally positioned, and they significantly enhance the efficiency and overall comfort of the treatment for both patient and therapist. Other treatment table designs are available; Figure 3-3 presents one example.

These electrically powered types of tables are usually made of steel and are hydraulically operated. The retractable wheels allow them to be moved easily. In addition, they may have a variety of adjustable sections, which allow for the separate positioning of body parts; for example, when lying facedown, the patient's forearms can be supported on individually adjustable sections (Box 3-6).

Massage can also be given while the patient sits. Small, wooden massage tables traditionally have been used for this purpose, although in recent times a variety of seating devices have been designed for treatment. Figure 3-4 illustrates such a device. These chairs can be made of wood or metal and may be folded/collapsed for easy transportation. They can also be individually adjusted for the comfort of each patient. These chairs can be helpful for a patient who cannot lie facedown on a treatment table.

In addition to the equipment already described, two other devices are useful in massage treatments and are worthy of mention. The first is the so-called prone pillow. This device is laid flat on the treatment table and is designed to support the patient's head and shoulders when the patient lies facedown. It has the advantage of allowing a patient to be reasonably comfortable on a table that has no built-in face hole. Facial tissues should be used on the edges of the face hole to make the treatment more comfortable and hygienic for the patient. Some patients may find these pillows a little uncomfortable if their upper cervical joints are held in an extended position. Minor adjustments to the head position

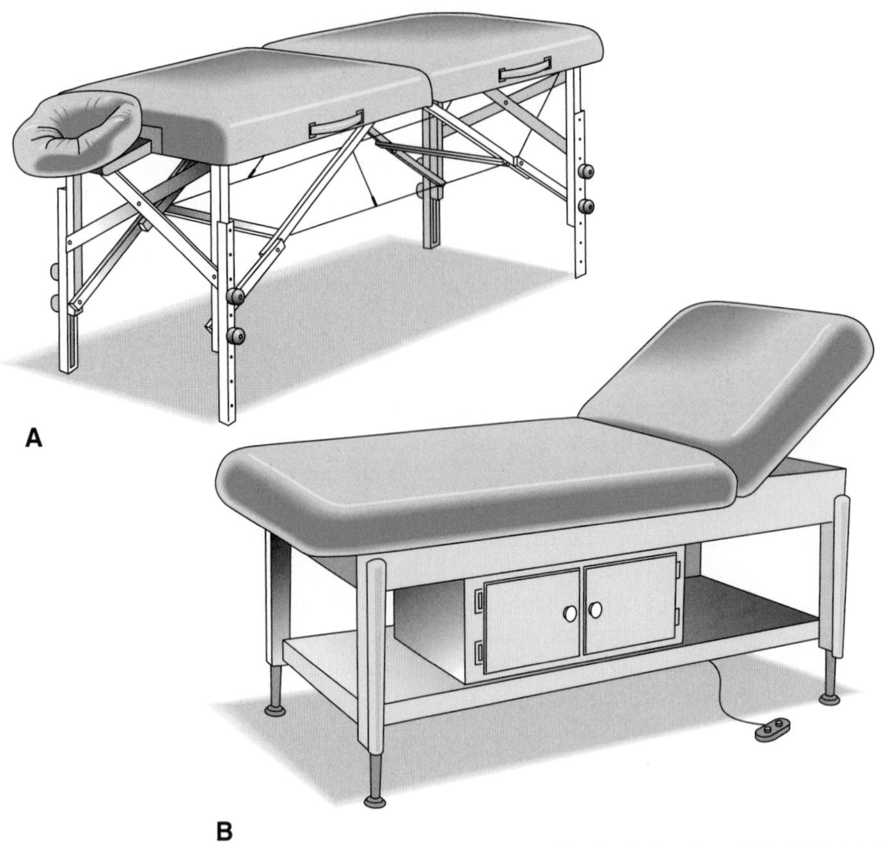


**Figure 3-2 Treatment Tables Suitable for Massage**

Treatment tables are generally constructed of wood or metal, with padded, vinyl-covered tops. The tabletop may have a face hole and several sections, which may be independently adjustable. Some tables are of fixed height, whereas others are electrically operated and hydraulically adjustable.

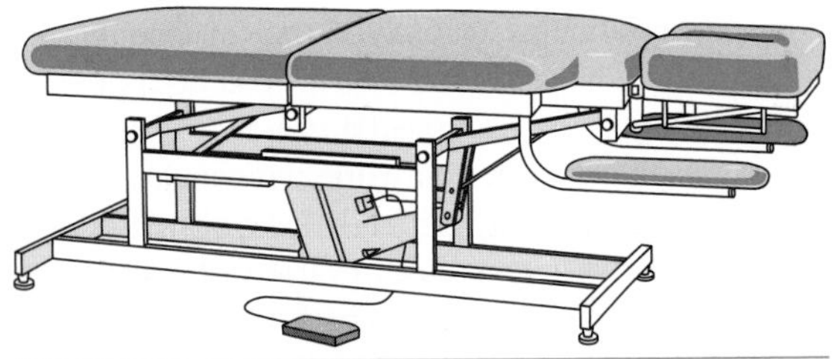

**Figure 3-3 An Electrically Operated, Hydraulic Treatment Table**

Note that the table is constructed of metal and operated hydraulically by an electric motor. It has adjustable forearm supports and a face hole in one end, and the other end can also be adjusted. Although the table is usually made of metal, similar features can be found on wooden plinths, although the height of these tables is not so easily adjustable (see Figure 3-2, *A*). The table should not be too wide, because having to lean over the patient places undue stress on the therapist.

**BOX 3-6 Components of an Ideal Treatment Table (i.e., One That Provides the Greatest Flexibility and Ease in Its Use)**

- Electrically operated and hydraulically adjustable in height
- Equipped with a face/nose hole
- Made in at least three sections, of which the two end portions can be adjusted to different angles
- Adjustable forearm rests
- Smooth rolling, retractable casters with a locking mechanism

using small folded towels placed under the shoulders can usually fix any such problems (Figure 3-5).

Another useful device is a wedge or bolster, a support usually placed so that the patient can lean against it. For this reason, the devices must be placed against a wall or other supporting structure. These devices can convert a nonadjustable flat treatment table into an effective plinth. The wedge can be turned around and laid flat on the plinth and used to support the patient's lower limbs. Figure 3-6 illustrates these uses.

Other simple devices can also help support the patient. For example, sandbags, sheets, towels, and small pillows can all be used to support specific areas of the patient's body when massage is part of a treatment plan. Certainly, it is

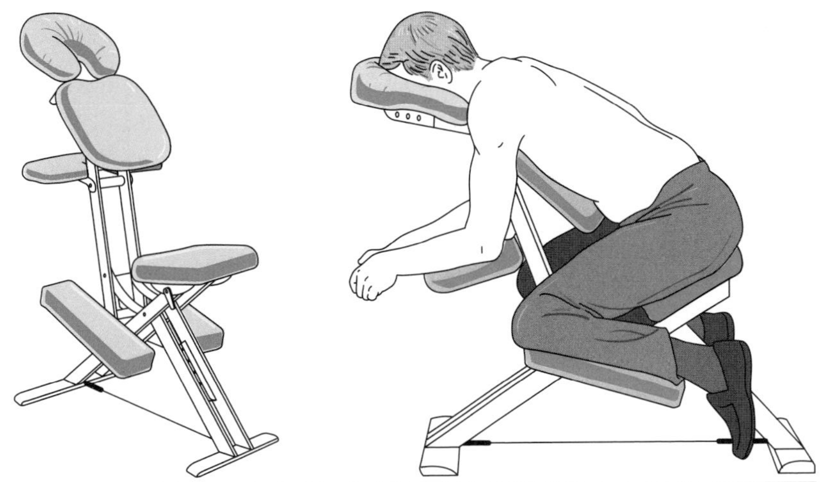

Figure **3-4** A Typical Massage Chair Useful for Treating the Upper Back and Posterior Neck and Shoulder Regions

The heights of the seat, headrest, and forearm rest are adjustable, making it easy to ensure the patient's comfort. These chairs are useful in the treatment of the head and posterior neck/shoulder region, both for massage and other rehabilitation techniques such as ultrasonic and electrical stimulation treatments.

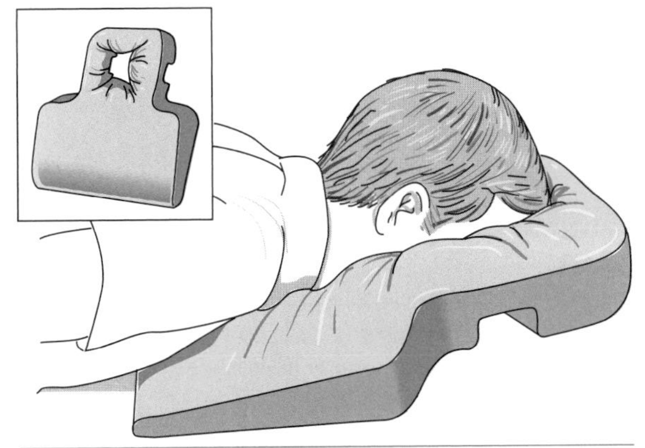

Figure **3-5** A Prone Pillow Used to Support the Head, Neck, and Shoulders

The pillow is placed under the patient's head and shoulders, allowing the face to be supported in the face hole. Most people find these pillows quite comfortable when lying facedown. The pillows can be very helpful when used with a treatment table that does not have a face hole. Paper towels should be used to cover the areas where the patient's face touches the edges of the hole.

important for patients to be supported comfortably during treatment; otherwise they may not be able to relax, and treatment may be less effective than it otherwise would be. Of course, between patient visits it is important to thoroughly clean all surfaces of the treatment table, chair, prone pillow, bolster, and other equipment. Several spray cleaners are readily available for this purpose; however, it is important to use one that will disinfect the equipment surfaces.

## DRAPING AND POSITIONING THE PATIENT

For massage treatments to be effective, it is critical that the patient be comfortably positioned and well supported. An uncomfortable patient will not be able to relax, and this will seriously interfere with the effect of the massage. Enough pillows are required to support all parts of the patient's body to maximize relaxation. The patient should be kept warm throughout the treatment, and any body parts that are not being massaged should be covered, when possible, with blankets, sheeting, or a similar drape. To relax the patient, the room should be warm and preferably quiet, and when possible the patient should be treated in private. It is very important to preserve the patient's modesty, and to that end the patient should be adequately covered at all times. At the same time, the body parts being massaged must be fully exposed and accessible. The actual position for massage will vary for each patient and each condition. The main criterion is that the patient be well supported and the part to be massaged readily accessible. The therapist should stand so that he or she can reach the patient comfortably without having to bend or stoop over the patient. For the therapist, most massage strokes consist of a combination of total body movements plus hand movements in contact with the patient's body. As much as possible, therapists should avoid flamboyant gestures, and the massage should be performed slowly and in a manner that is comfortable for the patient. Box 3-7 lists the basic patient positions for massage treatments.

The patient may be draped with any of a number of materials. The most versatile one is probably a clean, folded sheet. Sheets offer an effective method of draping a patient

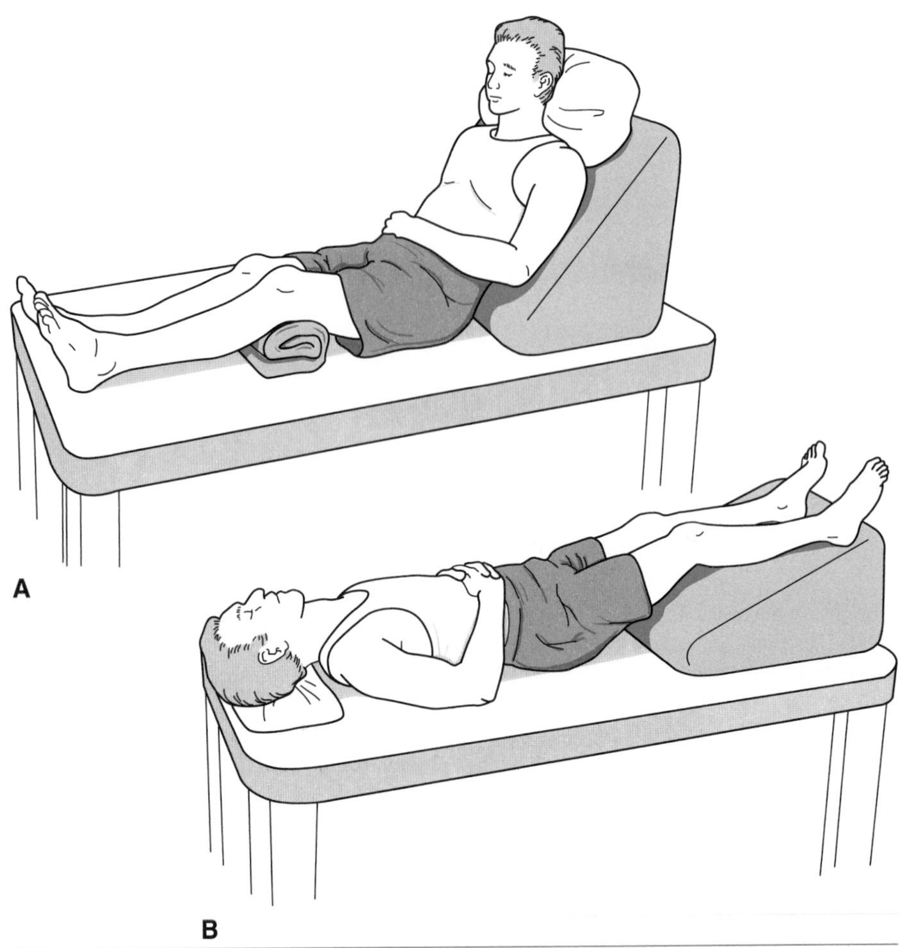


Figure 3-6 A Movable Wedge or Bolster to Support the Patient While Sitting or Lying

**A,** The wedge is used as a back support for a patient sitting upright on the treatment table. Note that for the wedge to be effective, some sort of support must be placed behind it. **B,** The wedge is used under the patient's lower limbs to elevate them (e.g., in cases of chronic edema in the legs). These devices are extremely useful with a basic flat treatment table (i.e., one where the ends cannot be lifted).

**BOX 3-7 Basic Patient Positions for Massage Treatment**

- Lying supine (facing the ceiling)
- Lying prone (facing the floor)
- Sitting upright on a plinth with both legs supported ("long sitting")
- Sitting upright on a stool or chair with the upper limb supported on a small table, the end of a plinth, or a pillow on the patient's lap
- Sitting upright on a stool facing a plinth, with the upper limbs and head supported on pillows
- Sitting in a forward-leaning position on a specialized massage chair

for treatment to any desired body parts. If possible, the patient's own clothing should not be used for draping, as it is very likely that some massage lubricant will end up on the clothing. In addition, the patient's clothing may impede the circulation; for example, if the trousers are rolled up to the knee in order to treat the calf. In therapeutic massage, the patient is always draped so that only the parts to be treated are exposed and the circulation is not impeded in any way. There is no situation that requires the patient to be completely naked and exposed. Indeed, sound ethical practice demands that the patient be adequately draped and not unnecessarily exposed.

Many techniques can be used to drape the patient. Consideration needs to be given ahead of time to the patient's final position and what draping will be required. For example, wrapping a folded sheet around a patient so that the loose end is in front is not a good idea if the patient will be lying facedown because the patient and the therapist will have to struggle to expose the back. A much more effective technique is to place a folded sheet around the front of the patient so that both of the loose ends are at the back of the patient. This may be called a "back opening" drape. When the patient then lies facedown on the treatment table, it will be a simple matter to open the sheets to expose the back.

Other typical drapes can be called "front opening" and "side opening." In each case, the drape must be performed in such a way as to cover the patient without risk of exposure during treatment. Additional sheets and towels can be used to cover those areas not receiving treatment. Figures 3-7 through 3-11 illustrate the basic patient positions and some typical draping techniques.

## BODY MECHANICS OF THE THERAPIST

Soft tissue manipulation can be strenuous work, especially if the patient is large or has muscular tissues. The therapist must use care and precision of movement, which are essential to reduce occupational stress, risks of back injury, and strain to other vulnerable regions, especially the wrists and hands.

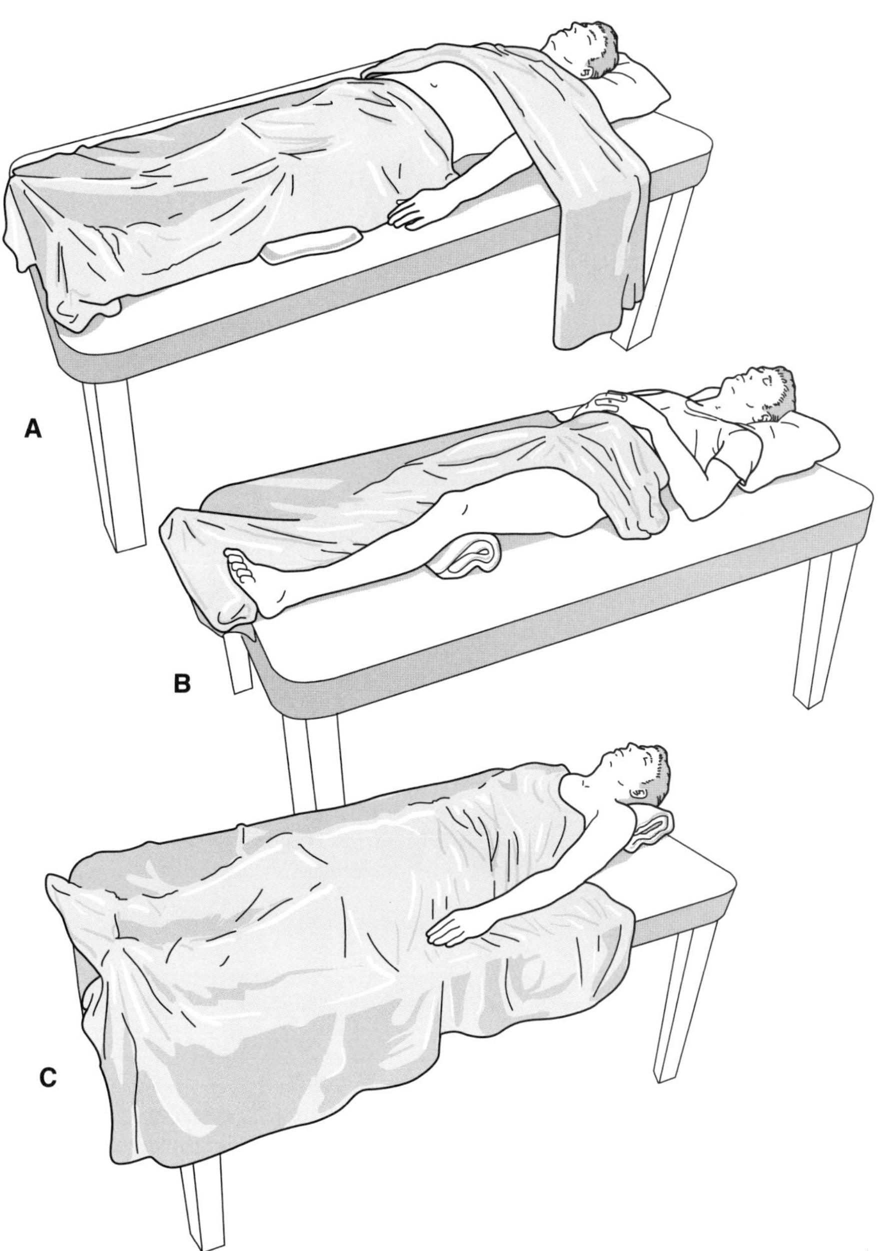


**Figure 3-7** Lying Supine (Facing the Ceiling)

**A,** The patient is draped for treatment to the abdomen. A rolled towel or small pillow can be used to support the neck, and a pillow or rolled towel should also be placed under both knees. **B,** The patient is draped for treatment to the lower limb. Rolled towels or small pillows can be used to support both the knee of the limb to be treated and the other knee. A larger pillow tends to get in the way of the treatment and is best avoided. **C,** The patient is draped for treatment to the upper limb. A small rolled towel placed under the neck affords easy access to the shoulder and neck region and may be preferable to a regular-sized pillow. Note that the upper limb can be treated with the patient in several different positions, depending on the available equipment and the range of motion present in the patient's shoulder region.

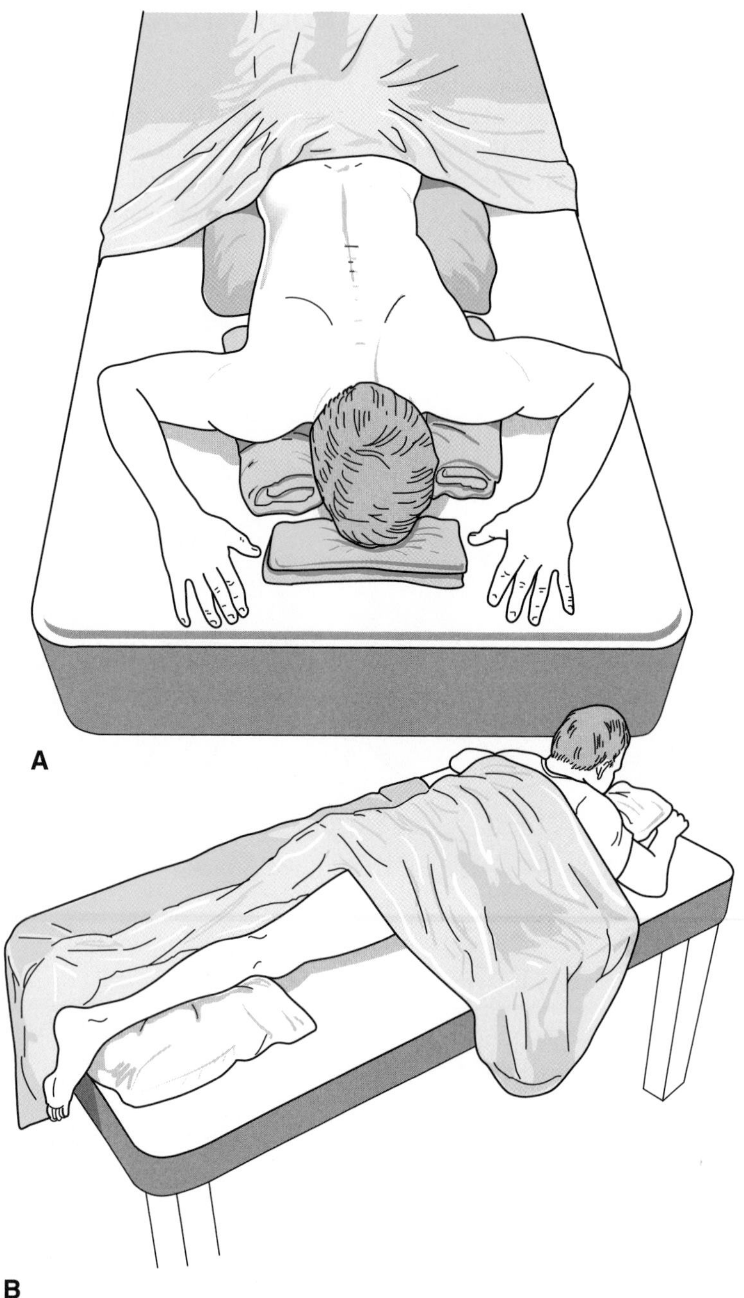


**Figure 3-8** Lying Prone (Facing the Floor)

**A,** The patient is draped and positioned for massage to the back region. Several methods can be used to support the patient in this position, but in all cases a pillow should be placed under the shin region of both legs. This allows some knee flexion, taking the stress off the sciatic nerve and its branches. In addition, a pillow should be placed under the abdomen so that the lower edge of the pillow is in line with both anterior superior iliac spines (ASISs). In this position, the lumbar spine remains flat and well supported. If the pillow is placed underneath the patient's hips, it causes too much hip flexion and related lumbar extension. The shoulders can be supported by a pillow or by two rolled towels placed at right angles to each clavicle. The patient can rest the head in a face hole in the treatment table or on a folded towel. Requiring the patient to turn his or her head to one side may be uncomfortable for some patients, depending on how much restriction to neck rotation is present. For this reason, it may be best to encourage the patient to rest his or her forehead on folded towels with the head and neck in the midline position. **B,** The patient is draped and positioned for treatment of the posterior aspect of the lower limb. The method of supporting the patient is similar to that shown in **A,** but the draping allows the lower limb to be fully exposed.

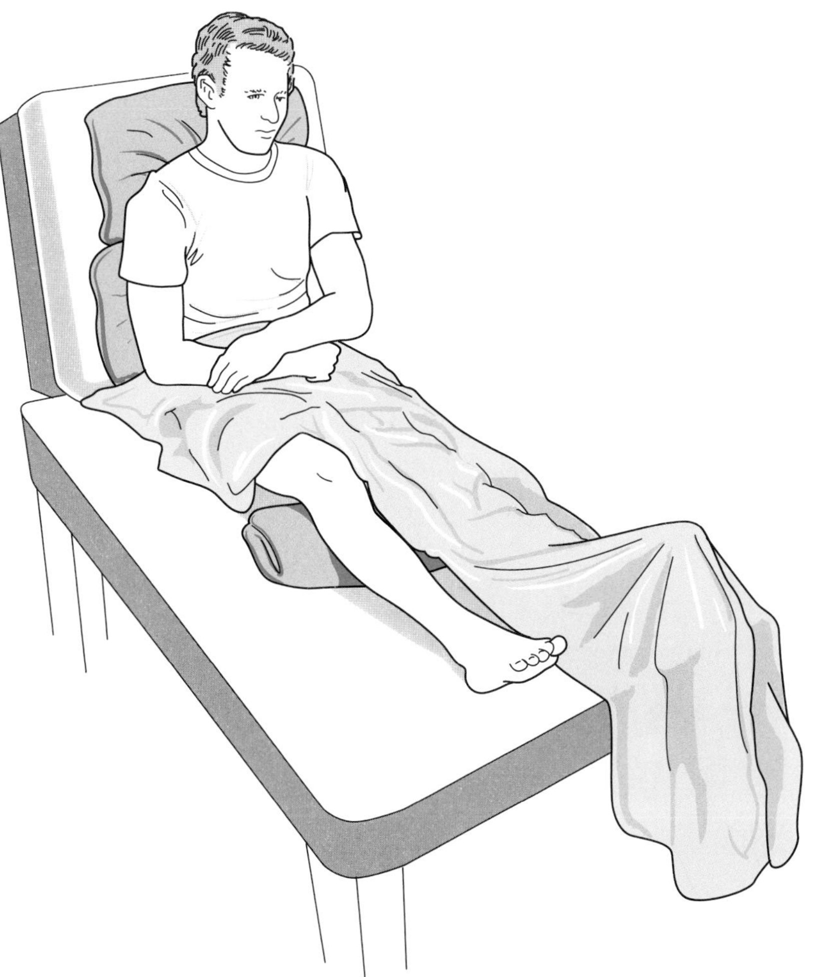

**Figure 3-9 Sitting Upright on a Plinth with Both Legs Extended (Long Sitting)**

This position is particularly suitable for treatment to the anterior aspect of the lower limb. The treated limb is best supported at the knee with a small rolled towel, as this allows the therapist's hands to work easily around the knee and calf region. A rolled towel or small pillow can also be used to support the other knee. It is important not to let the patient wear trousers or shorts where the legs are rolled up above the knee, if this constricts the blood flow to the leg. Because the lower limb is the part being treated, it is quite proper for the patient to wear his or her own clothing on the upper part of the body. If necessary, however, full draping is a simple procedure.

Controlled relaxation of the hands can be achieved only if the therapist's posture permits such relaxation. When the patient is lying on a treatment table, the so-called standing fall-out (walk standing) position is usually the most efficient stance. Backward and forward swaying with the knees and ankles bent then permits the therapist's arms and hands to be used over a large area with comparatively little movement at the hips and spine. Both feet should remain in contact with the floor at all times to maintain balance. This swaying motion makes it possible for the therapist to perform long, stroking movements rhythmically and smoothly, allows proper relaxation of arms and hands, and avoids the unnecessary fatigue associated with performing massage when standing in a strained, stooped position. It also uses the weight of the therapist's body to regulate the amount of pressure applied. This allows the therapist's body weight to be evenly distributed and makes it possible for him or her to move over a large area without bending the back. This is an important issue, especially because massage can be strenuous work. Figure 3-12 illustrates the basic concept of good body mechanics in moving along the lower limb of a patient while reducing the need for bending.

The therapist's right foot is aligned with the patient's feet and points toward them. The therapist's left foot points toward the patient's head and is aligned with the patient's knee. This wide stance allows the transfer of body weight between the two feet, thereby allowing the therapist's hands to move easily along the limb, without bending the knee or

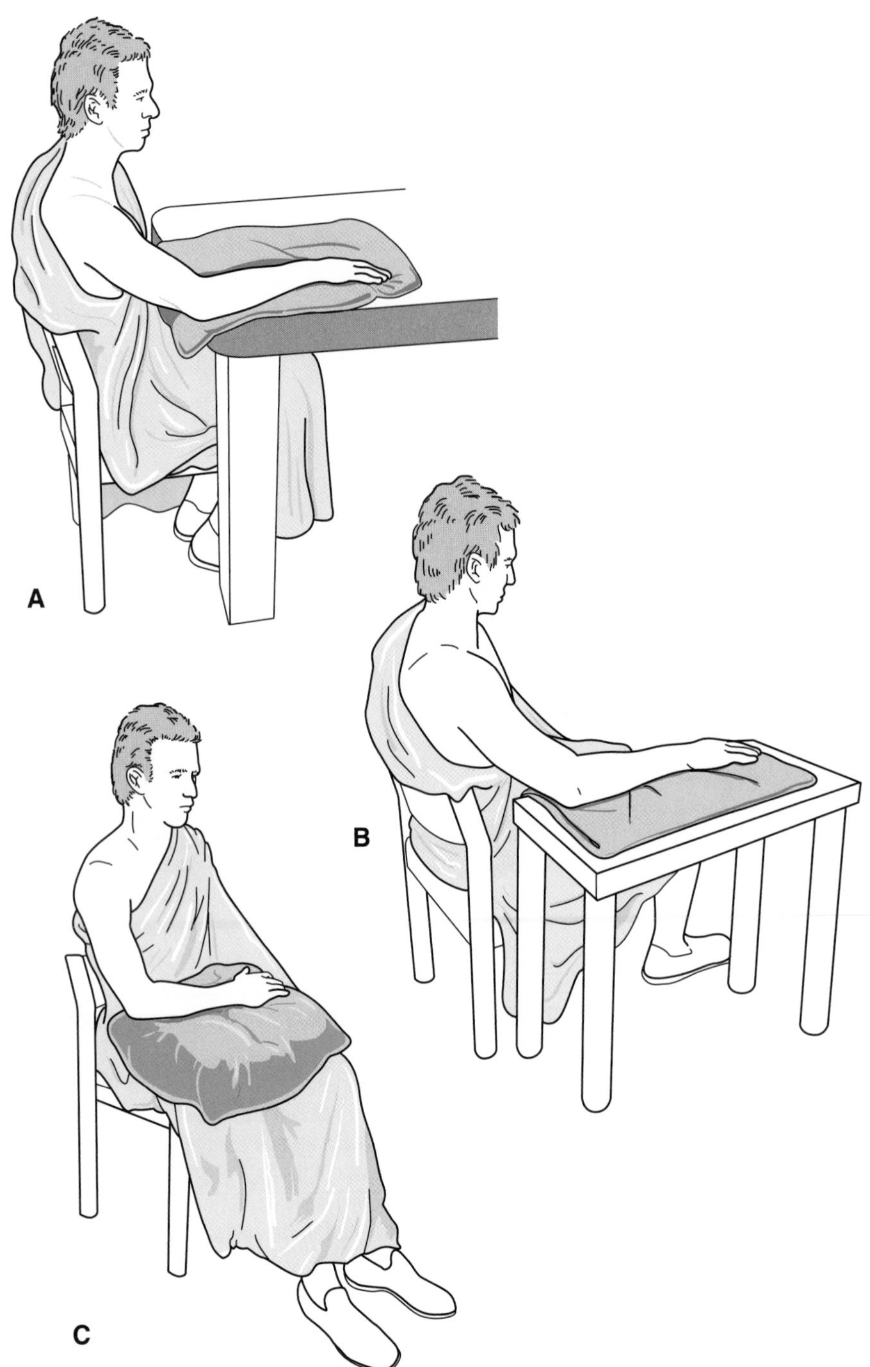


Figure **3-10** Sitting on a Stool or Chair with the Upper Limb Supported on a Small Table, the End of a Plinth, or a Pillow on the Patient's Lap

These positions are suitable for treatment of the upper limb or a part thereof. **A,** The patient sits at the end of a plinth with the arm supported on a pillow resting on the table. The draping allows easy access to the shoulder region while maintaining the patient's modesty. **B,** The patient is in a similar position, but the upper limb is supported on a small table. **C,** The patient's arm is supported on a pillow resting on the patient's lap. This is particularly useful for the patient who has a stiff or painful shoulder. In all three positions, the therapist may stand or sit to perform the massage.

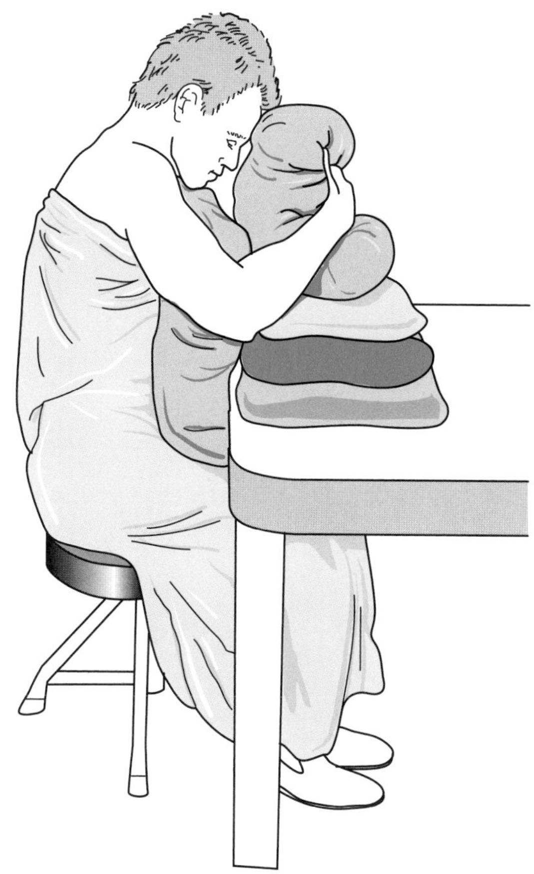

**Figure 3-11** Sitting Upright on a Stool, Facing a Plinth, with the Upper Limbs and Head Supported on Pillows

This position is especially well suited for treatment of the posterior neck and shoulder region. In this example, the patient holds a large pillow close to his chest so that his chin rests on the upper edge of the pillow. The patient then leans into the edge of the plinth and places his forearms on the pillows stacked in front of him. Note that the top pillow is folded in half and the patient rests his forehead on it. Even though the pillow supports the patient's head and face, there is plenty of room for him to breathe. Sufficient pillows should be used so that the patient sits upright and the head leans forward only slightly. This leaves the neck in a comfortable, well-supported position. The patient's chin is supported on the pillow wedged between the table and his chest. This pillow also keeps the draping sheet in its proper position when the arms are lifted up onto the plinth. A similar position can be achieved by the use of a specially designed massage chair (see Figure 3-4).

changing foot position. This facilitates a smooth and relaxed technique for the therapist and greatly contributes to the effectiveness of the treatment.

The height of the treatment table is important for reducing the risk of back strain for the therapist. The use of an adjustable-height treatment table is a significant asset in this regard. The height of the table should be such that the therapist can reach the body part in question while keeping his or her back upright. Fixed-height tables are a real problem for very tall therapists, as they have no option but to bend over the patient. Shorter therapists can remedy the situation by standing on a low platform. In any event, each individual therapist should make an effort to adjust the treatment table to a height that is most suitable for his or her body. In most cases, the treatment table will be at a suitable height when it is level with the greater trochanter of the therapist's femur. When the patient is seated on an ordinary chair, it is quite permissible for the therapist to sit on a chair facing the patient, especially if the therapist is particularly tall in stature. If the patient is seated in a special massage chair, a tall therapist may sit on a chair behind but facing the patient.

Because therapeutic massage is performed with the hands, the posture of the upper limbs is also important. If joint strain is to be minimized, excessive wrist flexion and hyperextension of the fingers must be avoided. Good body mechanics are essential for preventing injury to the therapist. Although the adjustable treatment tables are good for controlling the overall height of the patient, they often produce a significant problem for the therapist. This is seen during massage to the back region, especially on those treatment tables that have a face hole. In this case, the patient lies in the middle on the table with his or her face positioned in the hole. When the therapist stands by the side of the patient in order to massage the patient's back, the therapist has to twist his or her back into a most uncomfortable and stressful position. By positioning the patient at a slight angle *across* the plinth, the therapist is able to maintain good spinal posture, thereby significantly reducing mechanical stress on the spine. If necessary (when the patient is rather tall), the patient's feet can be supported on a pillow resting on the back of a chair placed alongside the plinth. Figure 3-13 illustrates this concept.

## ESSENTIAL COMPONENTS OF MASSAGE

All massage strokes have unique characteristics; however, there are several components of massage that are common to all techniques. Each of these is considered briefly here and elaborated on in the relevant description in Chapter 4. Careful attention to these components is necessary for the intelligent application of each massage stroke. Box 3-8 lists the essential components of good technique.

### Comfort and Support

The patient must be positioned comfortably with adequate support so that he or she can relax in the required position. Pillows are usually used to provide support, but they can sometimes get in the way of effective massage. A suitable alternative is rolled-up or folded toweling placed under the body part, perhaps the neck, shoulder, or knee. A patient who is in significant pain may not be able to keep still for long, and this makes a comfortable and well-supported position all the more important. Folded sheets or blankets can be used to drape the patient and also to keep the patient warm, especially if the patient is sensitive to cold. This can

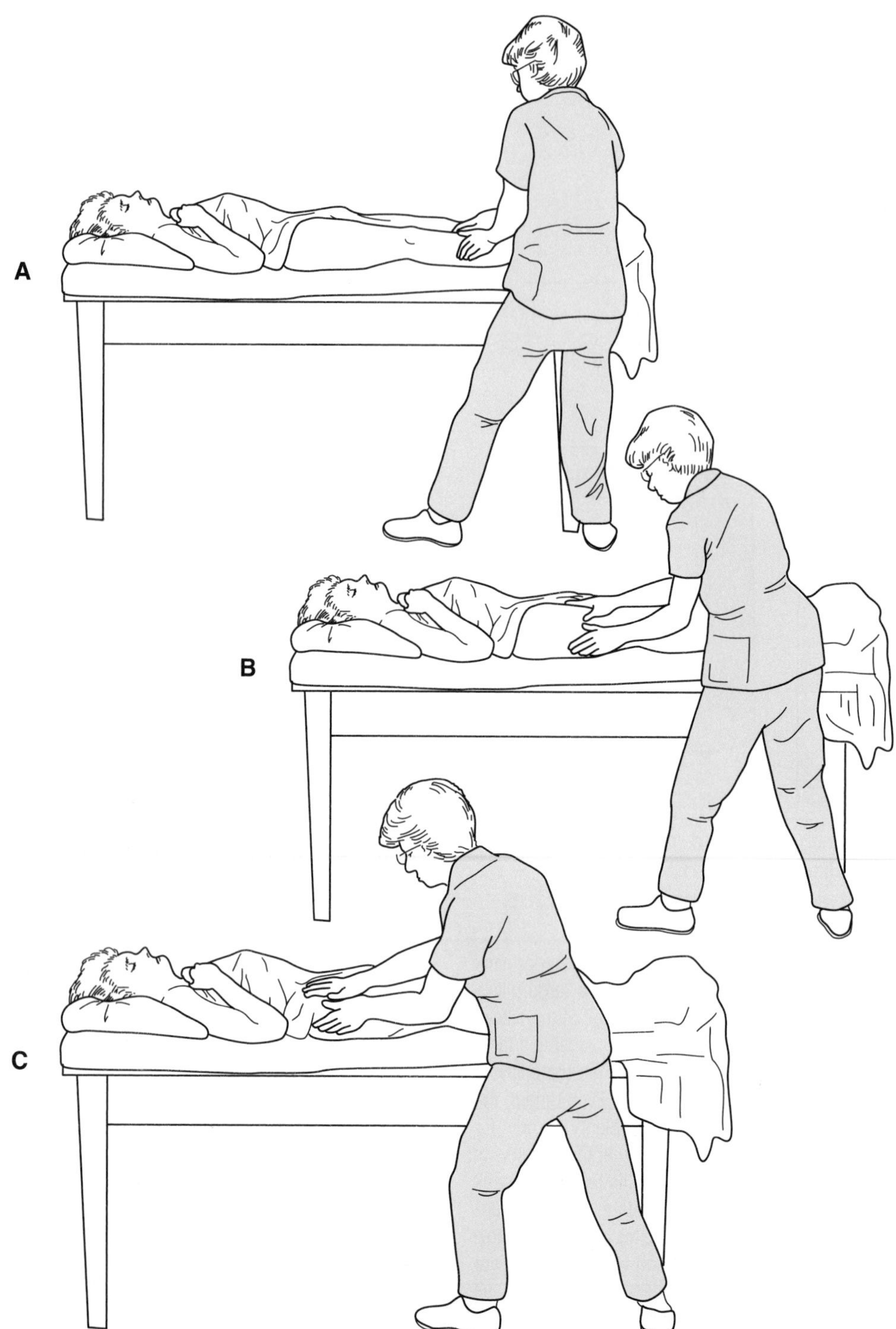


**Figure 3-12** Good Body Mechanics for a Therapist Treating the Lower Limbs

**A,** The therapist's back is held as straight as possible. **B, C,** Movement along the limb is achieved primarily by shifting the body weight forward. Such positions minimize the risk of back injury among therapists.

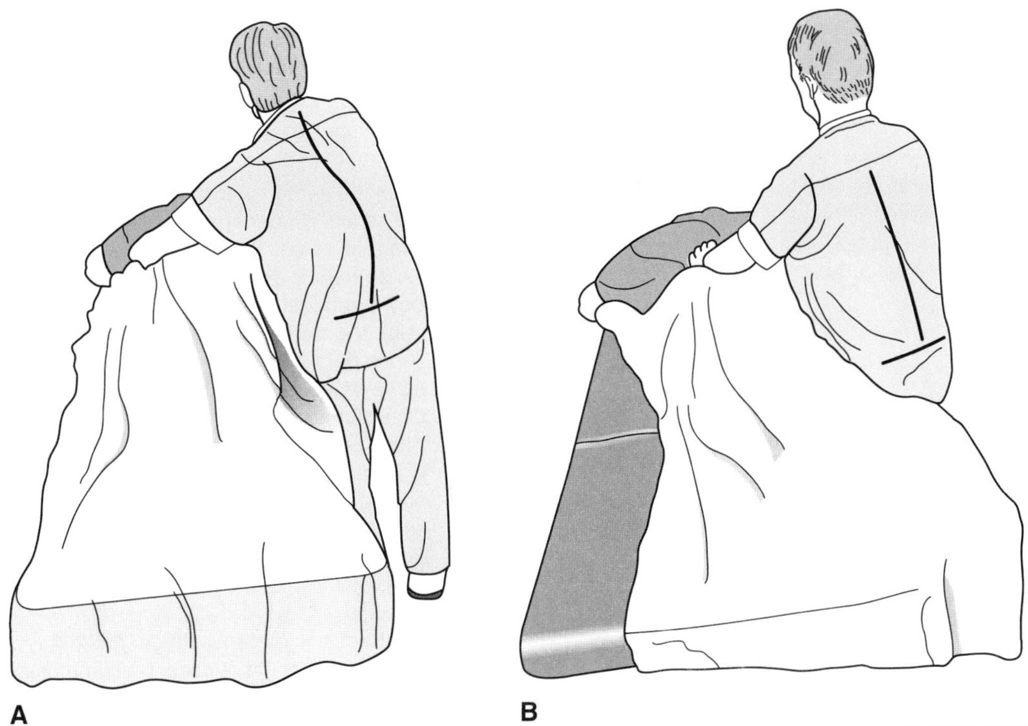


Figure 3-13 Good Body Mechanics for a Therapist Treating the Back Region

**A,** The therapist's spine has poor posture (scoliosis) during treatment of the patient's back region because the patient is positioned in the middle of the treatment table. **B,** By positioning the patient at a slight angle across the plinth, the therapist is able to maintain good spinal posture, thereby significantly reducing mechanical stress on the therapist's spine. If necessary, the pillow supporting the patient's feet can rest on the top of a chair placed alongside the plinth.

**BOX 3-8 Essential Components of Good Technique in All Massage Treatments**

- Comfortable and well-supported positioning of patients so they can be as relaxed as possible during treatment
- Flexibility of the therapist's hands so they fit the contours of the body part being massaged
- Using the correct rate of movement
- Maintaining the proper rhythm
- Regulating pressure and direction according to the stroke being performed, the type of tissues being treated, and the purpose of the stroke
- Maintaining proper postural stance and good body mechanics

be a surprising problem during summertime if an air-conditioning system is keeping the room temperature too low.

## Relaxation

An important component of all soft tissue manipulation relates to the level of relaxation present in the patient at the time of treatment. Massage is likely to be much more effective if the patient is as relaxed as possible, especially when techniques to treat muscle tissue are concerned. Relaxation may be thought of on two levels: general relaxation and local relaxation. *General relaxation* describes the overall state of the entire person; *local relaxation* refers to a specific body part. In each case, the therapist helps the patient to relax by eliminating as many of the factors that inhibit relaxation as possible. At the same time, the therapist encourages relaxation by paying special attention to factors that can promote it. Boxes 3-9 and 3-10, respectively, list the factors that tend to inhibit or promote relaxation.

**BOX 3-9 Factors That Tend to Inhibit Relaxation**

- Psychological factors such as a fear of hospitals or treatment clinics and the presence of domestic/personal problems
- Fear of unknown treatments
- Strange or new surroundings
- Untidy or dirty surroundings
- Unpleasant odors associated with hospitals/clinics
- Excessive noise
- Bright lights or total darkness
- Cold, drafty rooms
- Pain or fear of pain
- Breathing difficulty
- Fear of undressing
- Inadequate or uncomfortable support, draping, or positioning

**BOX 3-10 Environmental Factors That Promote Relaxation**

A quiet environment
Soft lighting
A pleasant-smelling treatment room
Moderate room temperature
A draft-free treatment area
A comfortable and well-supported position
A clean and tidy treatment area

Specific relaxation techniques may be used to help a tense patient to relax. Two common methods are the contrast and the induction techniques. In each case, the patient must be supported comfortably (i.e., with enough pillows to fully support the whole body or a part of it).

### *Contrast Method of Relaxation*

The principle of this technique is to facilitate relaxation by teaching the patient to become aware of the difference (the contrast) between strong muscle contraction and relaxation. The technique calls for the patient to contract groups of muscles as intensely as he or she can for about 3 to 5 seconds. The patient is then instructed to "relax" and "feel" the difference between the two states. As each body part is alternately tensed and relaxed in this manner, the patient gradually achieves a level of general relaxation. Although the contrast technique is often used to promote general relaxation, the principle can also be applied to facilitate local relaxation. The physiological rationale for the technique is that a muscle relaxes easily immediately after a strong contraction. A suitable sequence for the contrast method is explained in Box 3-11.

### *Induction Method of Relaxation*

As its name implies, with the induction method of relaxation the therapist *induces* the patient into a relaxed state, usually by talking to him or her. Careful attention to the patient's comfort and support is necessary, and suitable background music often helps. The patient closes his or her eyes and tries to imagine scenes described by the therapist or suggested by music (perhaps the sound of a flowing stream or falling rain). Mental imagery, an important part of this concept, distracts the patient's attention from his or her physical body. Muscle contraction is thus greatly reduced and relaxation promoted. It is important not to use music that has a recognizable tune or melody because this may distract the patient in an undesirable direction. In this regard, the sounds of nature can be especially helpful. It may also be helpful to ask the patient about his or her preference in terms of a particularly relaxing situation. For example, one patient may like the sounds of an ocean beach, whereas another may prefer those of the rain forest. In any case, it is important that the chosen sounds evoke pleasant memories or imaginary experiences for the patient.

**BOX 3-11 A Typical Sequence of Contractions Used in the Contrast Method of Relaxation**

1. Tense left foot and calf muscles (with toes pointing down and calf muscles contracting), then immediately relax the same muscles.
2. Tense left quadriceps, then immediately relax the same muscles.
3. Tense right foot and calf muscles (with toes pointing down and calf muscles contracting), then immediately relax the same muscles.
4. Tense right quadriceps, then immediately relax the same muscles.
5. Contract muscles of both buttocks and hamstring muscles, then immediately relax the same muscles.
6. Contract back extensors, pressing the head and shoulders into the plinth, then immediately relax the same muscles.
7. Contract abdominal muscles, tensing the anterior abdominal wall, then immediately relax the same muscles.
8. Contract pectoral muscles to roll the upper arms inward toward the midline, then immediately relax the same muscles.
9. Clench the left hand and tense the forearm and upper arm muscles, then immediately relax the same muscles.
10. Clench the right hand and tense the forearm and upper arm muscles, then immediately relax the same muscles.
11. Contract facial muscles (eyes shut tightly and teeth clenched), then immediately relax the same muscles.

As the therapist tries to talk the patient into relaxation, a basic strategy is to first concentrate on the general environmental factors. For example, when using the ocean beach theme, the therapist might say:

> *Imagine you are lying on the warm sand by the ocean. You are in Hawaii. It's warm but not too hot. The sun is baking the sand but, a cool breeze is blowing from the sea. You can hear the seagulls and the surf. You feel relaxed and tired, very tired.*

The aim of this phase of the technique is to set the stage and induce a level of general relaxation in the patient. In the next phase, the therapist focuses the patient's attention to specific body segments, usually beginning with the feet and working toward the head. In this case, the therapist might say:

> *Now think about your feet. Think about the warm sun shining on them. Think about how good the breeze feels as it blows through your toes. Now think about your legs. Imagine they feel heavy, very heavy, so heavy you can hardly move them, even if you wanted to. Now think about your hips. Again, they seem so heavy. All you want to do is relax into the warm sand.*

In a similar manner, the therapist directs the patient to think about the rest of his or her body, all the while encouraging him or her to relax. Obviously, the therapist speaks with a quiet, rather slow and unexpressive voice. If the patient falls asleep, he or she may be allowed to rest for a short while (10 minutes) and then is gently woken before continuing with treatment. Following such techniques, the patient will be very relaxed and his or her blood pressure is likely to be rather low. In this case, the patient should sit up slowly and sit with his or her legs over the edge of the table for 1 minute or more before standing. A patient who rises too quickly into the vertical position may faint, so great care is needed to prevent this occurring. In fact, all patients who are recumbent during massage treatments should take time and care in getting up off the table into the standing position, because their blood pressure is likely to be low after treatment (see Chapter 5, on the effects of massage, for more details).

## Direction of the Stroke

Massage strokes can be performed in many different directions, but the chosen position depends largely on the purpose of the individual stroke. The directions include centripetal (toward the heart, in the direction of venous and lymphatic flow), centrifugal (away from the heart, in the direction of the arterial flow), and in other specific anatomical directions.

In most cases, the direction of a massage stroke is related to some anatomical structure. For example, effleurage is given in a centripetal direction because it is designed to promote venous and lymphatic flow in the normal direction of the circulation. In contrast, deep frictions are performed at right angles to the target fibers (muscle, tendon, or ligament) in order to mobilize them. Therefore each stroke must be performed in the correct direction in order for the stroke to be effective. The specific direction for each stroke is described in Chapter 4.

## Pressure of the Stroke

The pressure exerted with each individual stroke varies, depending on the specific purpose of the stroke and the patient's physical problem. The pressure is sometimes constant but in other strokes variable. The choice of pressure depends largely on the function of the stroke. A good example is effleurage. In this technique, the pressure gradually increases throughout each individual stroke to be maximal at the end of the stroke. It always finishes in, or near, a group of superficial lymph nodes. The therapist might imagine pushing the venous blood and lymph in the superficial vessels in the direction of the circulation. As the volume of fluids increases, gradually increasing pressure is needed, and a definite pause is required at the end of the stroke to allow the valves in the vessels to close. In contrast, other strokes are extremely light, involving just the weight of the hand moving across the skin.

It is difficult to evaluate accurately the amount of pressure that is actually used, but the effect obtained depends to a great extent on the regulation of the pressure and the stimulation that it produces. Deep pressure may produce a strong stimulation and increase tension and pain, whereas lighter pressure may produce mild stimulation, induce relaxation, and diminish pain. The reaction to external stimulation varies among individuals and with the nature of the lesions under treatment. The therapist must be able to vary the pressure exerted with any stroke so that it is well within the patient's tolerance. There is a significant difference in the amount of pressure that needs to be exerted in order to be effective when treating a young man who is large (78 inches tall and 250 pounds) and muscular compared with an 80-year-old female who weighs 90 pounds and is very thin, possibly osteoporotic. The pressure used with any stroke always needs to be appropriate for the individual patient being treated. Specific descriptions of the pressure required for each stroke are given in Chapter 4.

## Rate and Rhythm of the Stroke

The rate (speed) at which each massage stroke is performed again depends on the particular function of the stroke. In most cases, massage strokes are performed relatively slowly, although some, such as hacking and clapping, are performed rapidly. As a general rule, most massage techniques (except percussion) should be slow, gentle, and rhythmic. A suitable rate occurs when the hand, or hands, move over the tissues at approximately 6 to 7 inches per second. At such a speed, the desired effects, both mechanical and reflex, can be obtained. Obviously, this rate is applicable to those strokes where the hands glide over the surface of the tissues. For strokes that move in a circular fashion, the rate will vary depending on which part of the hand is performing the stroke. For example, during thumb pad kneading, it would not be possible for the thumbs to cover 6 to 7 inches of tissue per second and at the same time perform the stroke properly.

Generally speaking, strokes that are performed slowly tend to be more relaxing, whereas rapid strokes are more stimulating. In all cases, it is important to perform the stroke with the correct rhythm, usually one that is as constant as possible. Continuity of treatment is important, and this is achieved by ensuring an appropriate rhythm to the particular massage technique. Chapter 4 indicates the appropriate rhythm and rate at which each stroke is to be performed. In addition, the massage strokes demonstrated on the accompanying DVD give a clear example of the relative speed at which the various strokes should be given.

## Duration and Frequency of Treatment

Massage treatment can be performed for many different purposes. It can be a general treatment for the whole body, using any number of combinations of strokes; alternatively, techniques can be chosen to achieve a specific effect in a specific structure. For example, the therapist might well use several massage techniques to treat an adherent scar on the hand. The *purpose* of the massage, therefore, determines how long the treatment is to be given and for how many sessions, depending on the specific goals of treatment.

Most commonly, therapeutic massage is performed as part of a total treatment plan. Thus, specific techniques might be integrated with other methods of treatment such as exercise therapy, electrophysical modalities, and home programs. When performed in these circumstances, each massage technique is practiced for several minutes at a time. Numerous repetitions of each stroke are given, depending on the desired result. For example, if the goal of treatment is to mobilize chronic swelling around the ankle region, appropriate massage strokes might be performed until the therapist observes a significant reduction in the swelling. This might take 10 to 15 minutes or possibly longer. In contrast, a full-body massage takes much longer to perform, around 45 minutes or longer in duration. Full-body massage is rarely used in modern rehabilitation but is popular in recreational massage.

Massage treatments can be given daily, if necessary, or even several times per day. This schedule may be impractical, however, and in practice many different treatment regimens are in common use. Massage, like many other rehabilitation procedures, should not be performed in a prescriptive manner. Unlike medications that require specific dose levels to be effective, massage treatment can be given in many different ways. It is not possible, or indeed desirable, to specify a particular number of treatments because in rehabilitation, massage should always be given as part of a total treatment program. It should not generally be used in isolation. The particular goals of a treatment plan determine the type and number of treatments needed to reach a successful outcome, and this may not be known at the beginning of treatment. It is important to remember that each patient is different and responds differently to treatment.

The duration of the treatment obviously varies according to the size of the area to be treated, the specific pathology, and the techniques chosen. Although the existing problem may be localized to a small area, there will undoubtedly be physiological disturbances in adjacent areas. Therefore, the treatment may not be limited to the diseased or injured area.

The size and age of the patient also affect the duration of treatment. At any given rate of massage, it takes less time to treat a comparatively small person because the amount of tissue being manipulated is less than that of a larger person. In addition, there are some cases in which treatment might proceed more slowly than usual; for example, if the patient was in significant pain.

In discussing the dosage of massage, various medical authorities recognize the variability of application and the difficulty of specifying doses. It would seem impossible to avoid either too little treatment or too much if the duration of each treatment is specified. Mennell emphasized the importance of intelligently observing the patient during treatment and the danger of over- or undertreating. He believed, however, that unless at some time there is evidence of an overdose, it is possible that the patient has been given too little treatment. This emphasizes the need for constant and intelligent observation of the patient and the response to the treatment. It also emphasizes the need to continually reevaluate the patient in light of the specific treatment goals.

### Changes in Signs and Symptoms

As the condition of the treated tissue changes, it may become necessary to alter the duration of treatment or the techniques being used. Keeping in mind that massage is a means to an end, the duration of the treatment may be shortened gradually as it accomplishes the desired results. If massage has not accomplished the desired results, the treatment duration may have been too brief or perhaps too long. The therapist should observe the patient closely if he or she is to appreciate the need to change the duration or mode of treatment. The duration of any massage treatment should therefore vary according to the lesion being treated and the size of the area, the rate of the movements, the age of the patient, and any change in signs and symptoms. To obtain maximal benefit from any massage treatment and to avoid inadequate treatment or overtreatment, it is essential that therapists have a solid scientific knowledge of massage and its physiological effects and that they apply the massage thoughtfully and intelligently, observing its effects carefully.

It is important to remember that each patient is unique. Even if two individuals have the same diagnosis, the problem will not affect them in the same manner. The same treatment given to each patient will not necessarily have the same effects. Therefore, all treatment needs to be customized to meet the specific goals determined for each individual patient. Careful reevaluation of the treatment and its effects will determine whether the treatment plan needs to be modified.

## INDICATIONS AND CONTRAINDICATIONS FOR THE USE OF MASSAGE

Treatment using any of the various soft tissue manipulation techniques is indicated when the demonstrated effects would be helpful to the patient. For example, if a particular technique has been shown to reduce edema, it may be appropriate for a patient who has an edematous limb. It is simply a question of matching the known effects of a treatment with the specific needs of the patient (as expressed in the treatment goals). All of the basic massage techniques covered in Chapter 4 are described individually, including specific indications and contraindications.

Contraindications to massage treatments are a little less obvious and require more explanation. A contraindication is a demonstrated circumstance in which the use of a particular treatment technique is highly likely to result in damage to the patient. The probability of damaging effects will vary significantly, both among treatments and for each individual patient. Nonetheless, it is possible to group a series of circumstances that are most likely to be problematic. Some are obvious and others are much more subtle. For example, a patient who has a large open wound cannot receive massage over the area of the wound. This is a common theme in the lists of contraindications given in Chapter 4, as are many other situations. In most cases, the problem that contraindicates treatment exists only in the area to be treated. For example, it would be perfectly acceptable to treat the right leg of a patient who had a large open wound on the left leg. However, in other circumstances, the patient may have a systemic illness that might contraindicate treatment with massage, although this is less likely. A patient with severe congestive cardiac failure might have swollen legs as a result of his or her condition. If enthusiastic attempts are made to massage the patient's legs and push the edema back into the circulation, this may put stress on the patient's heart. In this case, treatment with massage is probably best avoided.

To assist the reader in this area, three different designations are used to rate each of the situations that might contraindicate each of the techniques discussed in Chapter 4. The system used is as follows:

- The designation **A** means that the use of a particular technique is *always* contraindicated and should *never* be performed (e.g., the presence of a melanoma in the skin of the areas to be treated). This designation is also known as an *absolute contraindication.*
- The designation **U** means that the use of a particular technique is *usually* contraindicated and in most, but not all, cases *should not* be performed. The technique can be used under these circumstances, but it can only be given with *great care* (e.g., a person who has marked varicosity of the veins).
- The designation **R** means that the use of a particular technique is *rarely* contraindicated and *can,* in most cases, be performed safely and effectively. Very occasionally, however, an individual patient may not be able to receive treatment using the technique (e.g., a person who is hypersensitive when touched, perhaps because he or she is extremely hairy or ticklish). In such a case, an alternative technique (or treatment concept) may have to be used.

## SUMMARY

This chapter has considered the various components necessary for effective massage. These components included the background knowledge of surface anatomy, the various types of equipment used, draping and positioning of the patient, and the key factors concerned with the application of soft tissue massage. Ethical issues associated with the practice of massage were mentioned briefly, and readers were encouraged to investigate the various codes of ethics for those professions in which massage is practiced (see the list of web site references). It is clear from these topics that a great deal of background information is needed, in addition to detailed knowledge and skill related to the individual massage strokes. Chapter 4 discusses these techniques in detail.

## REFERENCES

Bruze M: Occupational allergic contact dermatitis from olive oil in a masseur, *J Am Acad Dermatology* 41:312-315, 1999.

Frosh R: Peanut and nut allergy: baby massage oils could be a hazard, *Br Med J* 313(7052):299, 1996.

Held E: Some moisturizers may cause trouble, *Intl J Dermatology* 40(1):12-13, 2001.

Lis-Balchin M: Possible health and safety problems in the use of novel plant essential oils and extracts in aromatherapy, *J Roy Soc Health* 119(4):240-243, 1999.

Mykietiuch A: Professional conduct and boundaries. *Massage Therapy J* (Winter):20-22, 1991.

Norton L: Complementary therapies in practice: the ethical issues, *J Clin Nurs* 4(6):343-348, 1995.

Sanchez-Perez J, Gracia-Diez A: Occupational allergic contact dermatitis from Eugenol, oil of cinnamon and oil of cloves in a physiotherapist, *Contact Dermatitis* 41(6):346-347, 1999.

### Web Site References

The American Physical Therapy Association (APTA)
http://www.apta.org

The American Massage Therapy Association (AMTA)
http://www.amtamassage.org

The American Nurses Association (ANA)
http://www.nursingworld.org

The American Occupational Therapy Association (AOTA)
http://www.aota.org

Australian Physiotherapy Association (APA)
http://apa.advsol.com.au

The Canadian Physiotherapy Association (CPA)
http://www.physiotherapy.ca

The Chartered Society of Physiotherapy (CSP)
http://www.csp.org.uk

Chapter 4

# Classification, Definitions, and Descriptions of the Basic Massage Strokes and Relaxed Passive Movements

As the brief history of massage presented in Chapter 1 revealed, there have been, and still are, many different ways of defining the various massage techniques. This chapter provides specific information about each of the traditional massage strokes that are based on the system known as *Swedish remedial massage*. The definitions and descriptions represent a current view of the various techniques. Of course, some of the descriptions of the strokes are at variance with earlier ones. This is not surprising, given the considerable disagreement over massage terminology used in the past. Indeed, it is hoped that the classification and descriptions detailed in this chapter are logical, accurate, and worthy of adoption. In most cases, photographic examples are given of each of the strokes to several body parts, and many of these strokes are also featured in Chapters 7 and 8, which address general and local massage techniques.

The DVD that accompanies this text demonstrates each of the basic strokes to all the main regions of the body in a way that cannot be replicated with still photographs. For each technique, the DVD section is identified, making it easy for the reader to view the technique in question. Of course, it is possible to pause and repeat the video section as needed. The video provides an opportunity for viewers to understand the finer points of each technique, such as the rate and rhythm. In addition, the surface anatomy sections of the DVD provide essential information to support the practical techniques demonstrated in the video.

A section on the techniques known as *relaxed passive movements* or simply *passive movements* follows the descriptions of the basic massage techniques. Although these techniques are not massage per se, they are important soft tissue manipulation techniques that need to be addressed. In general, these techniques should be used after massage and before active exercise. The basic techniques are demonstrated on the accompanying DVD, which features a section on relaxed passive movements for the neck, the upper limb, and the lower limb (see DVD Chapter 4).

Before defining the individual massage strokes, it is helpful to start with a definition of the general concept of soft tissue manipulation itself. Several terms are often used interchangeably, so it may be useful to mention these here as well. Soft tissue manipulation is described as follows:

> *A variety of manual techniques to the soft tissues of the body, designed to improve intertissue mobility and produce pain-free function.*

What then are the soft tissues of the body? Essentially, the soft tissue of the body comprises all structures that are not a direct part of the skeleton. Thus, the bones, and therefore the joints, can be considered as the hard tissues, together with articular and fibrous cartilage. In addition, the teeth, fingernails, and toenails can be classified as hard tissue. Although there is an entire discipline of manual therapy dedicated to mobilizing and manipulating the joints, one can argue strongly that even these techniques are directed at the soft tissues rather than the bones and joints themselves. The bones and joints do not bend and stretch during or in response to these techniques. Instead, it is the soft tissues surrounding the joints (skin, capsules, ligaments, tendons, etc.) that are affected, together with those muscles whose tendons span the joints being treated. A simple classification of soft and hard tissues is shown in Table 4-1.

Some of the structures/tissues listed in Table 4-1 are soft tissue in nature but cannot be massaged because of their

### Table 4-1 A Classification of Soft and Hard Tissues

| SOFT TISSUES | HARD TISSUES |
|---|---|
| Skin | Bones |
| Subcutaneous tissues | Teeth |
| Muscles | Finger and toenails |
| Tendons | Articular and fibrous cartilage |
| Ligaments | |
| Joint capsules | |
| Nerves | |
| Blood vessels | |
| Lymph vessels | |
| Heart and lungs* | |
| Abdominal organs* | |
| Pelvic organs* | |
| Brain* | |
| Eyes* | |

*These structures/tissues are soft tissue in nature but cannot be massaged because of their anatomical locations.

### BOX 4-1 Types of Soft Tissue Manipulation

All systems of massage and bodywork
Acupressure
Shiatsu
Rolfing
Reflexology
Point percussion techniques
Myofacial release techniques
Craniosacral techniques

anatomical locations (e.g., brain, heart, lungs). Although soft tissue manipulation can affect the abdominal viscera in a general way, it cannot be applied directly to a specific abdominal or pelvic organ. Clearly then, soft tissue manipulation can have an effect on almost all tissues of the body. Many of these effects are discussed in Chapter 5. There are a variety of techniques that can be considered as *types* of soft tissue manipulation, and these are listed in Box 4-1.

With regard to the various systems of massage and bodywork (another common term for a type of soft tissue massage), this text differentiates two basic groupings: recreational massage and therapeutic massage. Some of the specific massage strokes described in this text (or modifications of them) can be used for both recreational and therapeutic massage. In this regard, it is important to clearly differentiate between the two categories.

*Collins English Dictionary* defines the word *recreation* as "refreshment of health or spirits by relaxation and enjoyment." Other major English dictionaries use similar descriptions, and it is in this context that the term *recreational massage* is intended.

*Dorland's Medical Dictionary* defines *therapeutics* as "the branch of medical science concerned with the treatment of disease." Clearly intended in this definition is the assumption that a health problem exists that requires healing. For this reason, the term *therapeutic massage* is used to denote a massage treatment intended to facilitate healing when a specific health problem exists. This text deals only with various forms of therapeutic massage.

There are numerous variations of technique used in recreational massage. Although many of these techniques certainly feel good to the client, some may have little therapeutic value. Other techniques seem similar to the more therapeutic procedures. Of course, all of these techniques have considerable psychological value. For this reason, it is helpful to distinguish between recreational massage and therapeutic massage.

Recreational massage is defined as follows:

*The use of a variety of manual techniques designed to relieve stress and promote relaxation and general wellness in a person who has no definable health problem.*

Therapeutic massage is defined as follows:

*The use of a variety of manual techniques designed to promote stress relief and relaxation, mobilize various structures, relieve pain and swelling, prevent deformity, and promote functional independence in a person who has a specific health problem.*

In addition to these major distinctions, it may be helpful to define three basic ways in which therapeutic massage may be given to a patient. A specific chapter in the text is devoted to each of these concepts. In each case, various techniques are combined to form a massage sequence, and these may be given to the entire patient (Chapter 7), to one or more regions of the body (Chapter 8), or to a specific anatomical structure (Chapter 9).

General massage is defined as follows:

*A combination of different massage strokes applied to all the major regions of the body in a single treatment session in order to achieve particularly desired effects.*

Local massage is defined as follows:

*A combination of different massage strokes applied to an individual region of the body in order to achieve particularly desired effects.*

Focal massage is defined as follows:

*A combination of one or more different massage strokes applied to specific anatomical structures in order to achieve particularly desired effects.*

In addition to a detailed description of each massage stroke, the following sections discuss the specific effects of each technique and the common contraindications. This approach brings together all of the information pertinent to each stroke.

## CLASSIFICATION OF MASSAGE STROKES

Individual massage strokes can be classified in a number of ways. Here, they are grouped on the basis of the way in which each one is performed (e.g., a pressure stroke). Individual strokes are classified as described in Table 4-2.

Table 4-2 **A Classification of Massage Strokes**

| MANIPULATION (STROKE) | VARIATIONS |
|---|---|
| Stroking manipulations | Stroking<br>Effleurage |
| Pressure manipulations (pétrissage) | Kneading<br>Picking up<br>Wringing<br>Skin rolling |
| Percussion manipulations (tapotement) | Hacking<br>Clapping<br>Beating<br>Pounding |
| Vibration and shaking | |
| Deep frictions | Transverse<br>Circular |

## STROKING MANIPULATIONS

### Stroking

#### *Definition*

Stroking is a technique that a therapist performs with the palmar surface of either or both hands, thumbs, or fingers at variable pressure and speed, moving together or alternately in any direction on the surface of the body.

#### *Purpose*

Stroking can be useful to begin or finish a massage sequence. It allows the patient to become accustomed to the sensation of the therapist's hands and, likewise, gives the therapist an opportunity to get the feel of the patient's tissues. When performed slowly, it promotes relaxation, but when performed rapidly, it is very stimulating. It is also useful for joining sequences of other strokes.

#### *Basic Technique and Direction of Movement*

Stroking can be given in any direction; however, the direction should be one that is convenient for the therapist and comfortable for the patient. It usually moves in one direction at a time. Typically, the strokes move along a line parallel to the long axis of the body (lengthwise) or across (at right angles to) the long axis. Stroking can also be given at an angle to the long axis (diagonally). The movement should be continuous while the hand is in contact with the skin. It must be rhythmic; otherwise, the stimulus will be uneven. The beginning of each stroke must be definite but smooth. The manipulation may be performed with one or both hands. Both hands may be used, either alternately or simultaneously. When both hands are used alternately, one hand is lifted off the patient while the other makes contact. Stroking to small areas such as the face may be performed with the thumbs or fingertips instead of the whole hand.

#### *Rate of Movement*

Stroking may be performed slowly or rapidly, depending on the effects required. It may also be applied deeply or more superficially. Deep stroking is performed slowly and superficial stroking more rapidly. In most cases, however, stroking is performed at a moderate pace, the hands moving over the tissues at a speed of approximately 7 inches per second.

#### *Depth and Pressure*

The depth and pressure used for stroking techniques depend largely on the type of stroking being used. In general, superficial stroking requires much less pressure than does deep stroking, where greater force is applied, thereby affecting deeper structures.

#### *Variations*

Stroking is usually performed with the palmar surface of the entire hand, in which case it is called *palmar stroking.* It can also be performed with the thumb pads or fingertips, in which case it is called *thumb pad stroking* and *digital stroking,* respectively.

#### *Superficial Stroking*

Superficial stroking is usually slow and gentle, but it is firm enough for the patient to be conscious of the passage of the hands throughout the movement. When given in this manner, the stroke is extremely relaxing for the patient.

#### *Deep Stroking*

Deep stroking is given with much greater pressure and is usually performed slowly. Given in this manner, it tends to stimulate the circulation to the deeper muscle tissue. For this reason, it is generally given in the direction of the venous and lymphatic flow.

Figures 4-1, 4-2, and 4-3 show the different directions for the technique of stroking. In addition, the DVD demonstrates stroking on several body areas.

**STROKING**

| BODY PART | DVD CHAPTER |
|---|---|
| Back | 4-1 |
| Posterior neck and shoulders | 4-13 |
| Posterior aspects of the lower limb | 4-23 |
| Anterior aspects of the lower limb | 4-38 |
| Upper limb | 4-57 |

#### *Primary Effects of Stroking*

Therapeutic effects are produced mainly through direct mechanical impact on the tissues; however, there are reflex effects mediated through the sensory nervous system. The primary effects of stroking are as follows:

- Significant relaxation, producing a sedative effect, that may help relieve pain and muscle spasm (via a pain-gating mechanism)

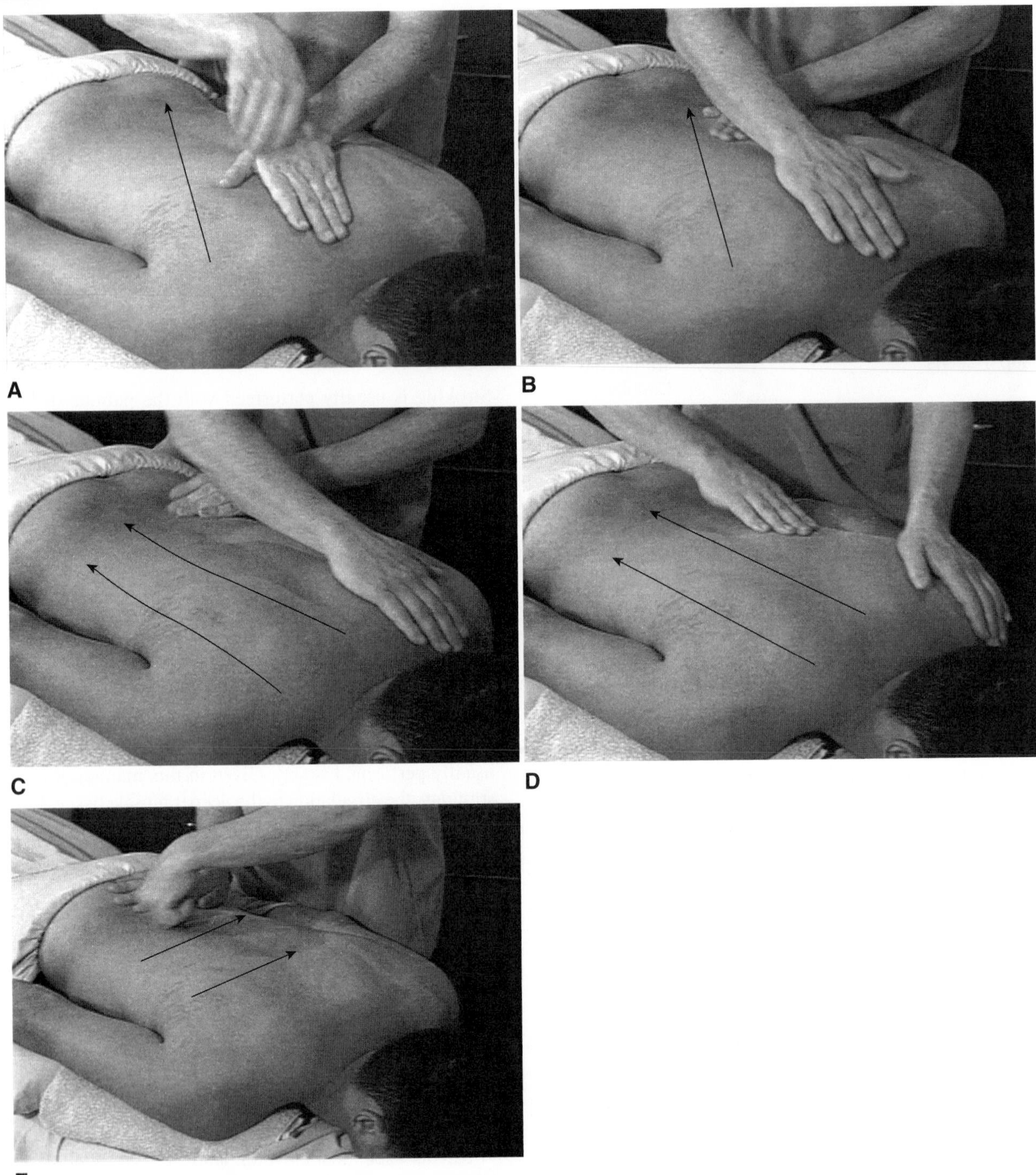


**Figure 4-1** Stroking to the Back

In this example **(A, B),** stroking is performed in a diagonal pattern to cover the patient's back region. Hands are used alternately, and the direction of the movement can be changed to cover the area in a different direction—that is, down the back **(C, D)** and across the low back region **(E).** See also DVD Chapter 4-2.

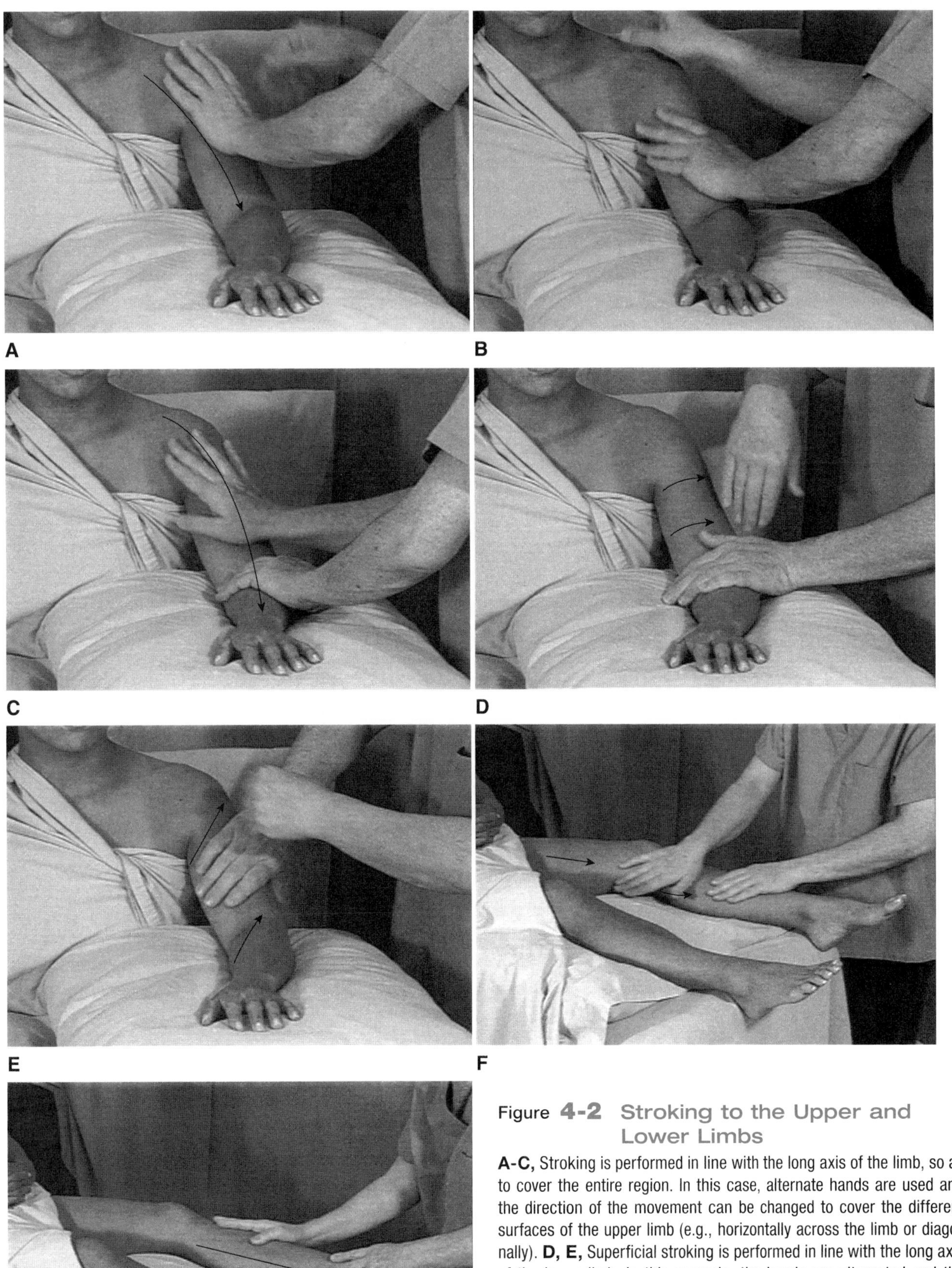


**Figure 4-2 Stroking to the Upper and Lower Limbs**

**A-C,** Stroking is performed in line with the long axis of the limb, so as to cover the entire region. In this case, alternate hands are used and the direction of the movement can be changed to cover the different surfaces of the upper limb (e.g., horizontally across the limb or diagonally). **D, E,** Superficial stroking is performed in line with the long axis of the lower limb. In this example, the hands are alternated and the direction of the movement can be changed to cover the different surfaces of the limb (e.g., horizontally across the limb or diagonally). The stroke is carried down to the knee **(F)** and may be extended all the way to the foot **(G),** if required. See also DVD Chapters 4-24, 4-39, and 4-58.

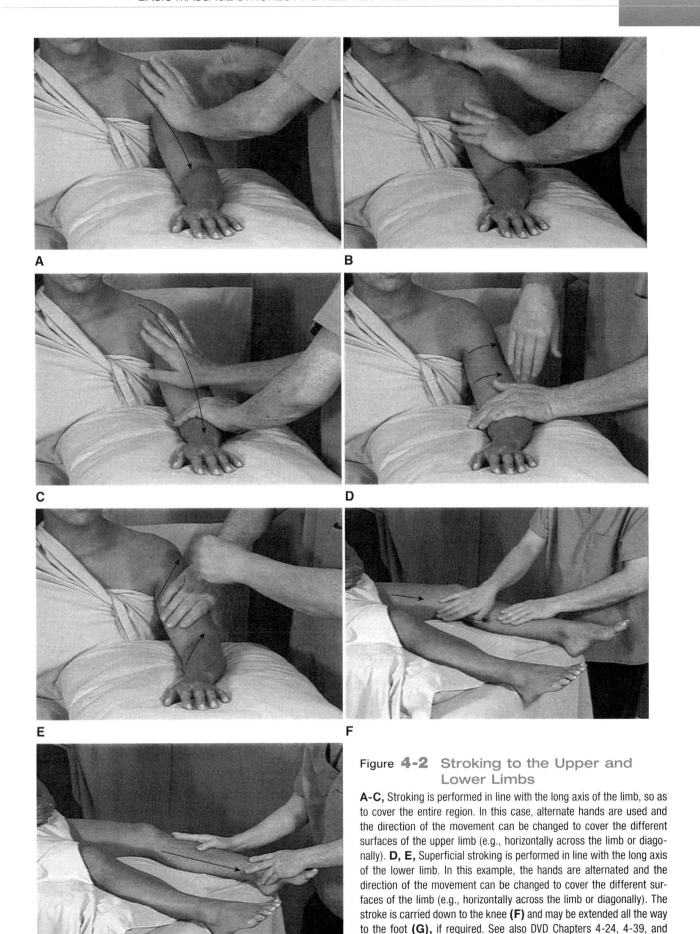

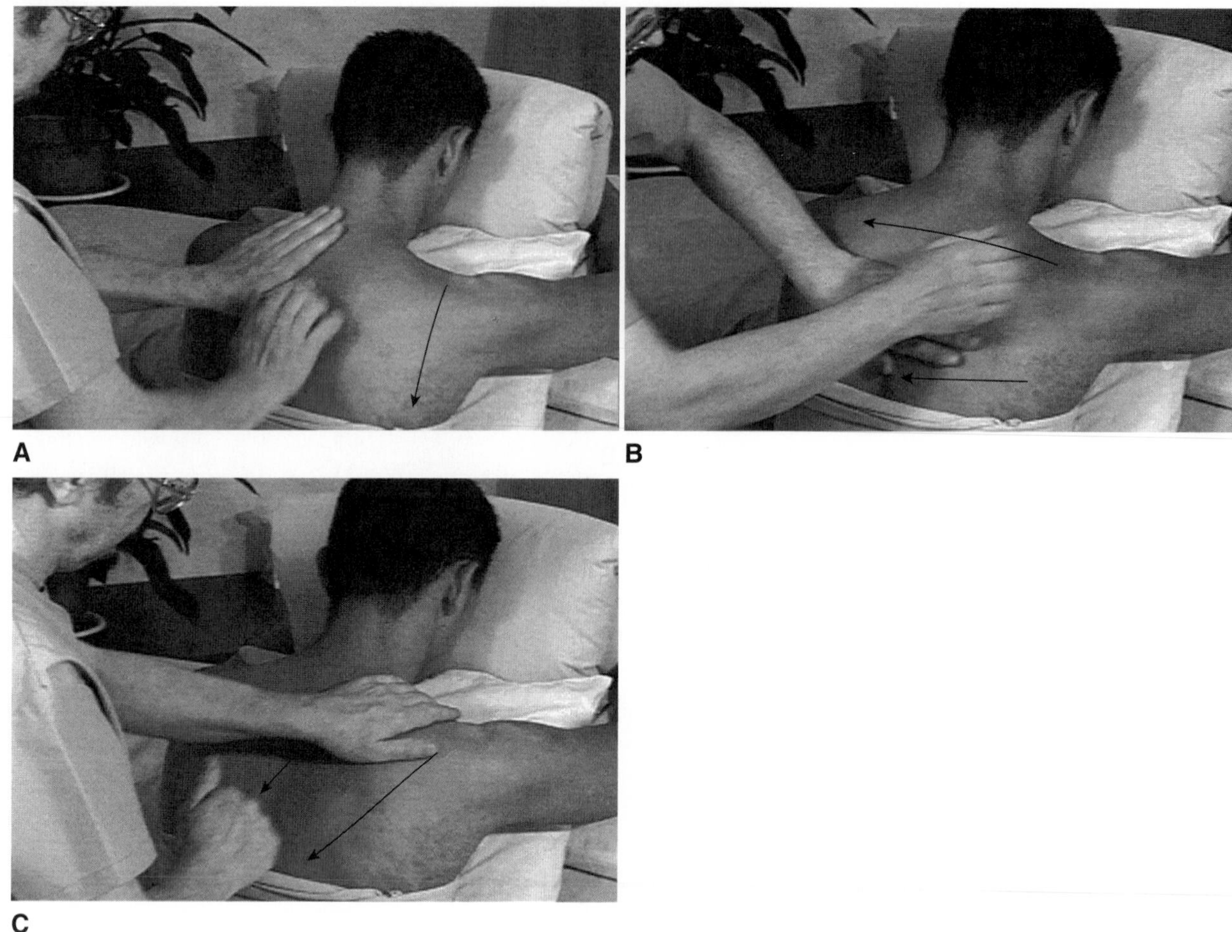


**Figure 4-3 Stroking to the Posterior Neck and Shoulder Region**

**A,** The stroking is performed in a vertical pattern to cover the patient's posterior neck and shoulder region. Hands are alternated, and the direction of the movement can be changed to cover the area in a horizontal **(B)** or diagonal **(C)** direction. See also DVD Chapter 4-14.

- A stimulating effect (when performed rapidly) on sensory nerve endings, resulting in a generalized, invigorating effect
- Dilation of the arterioles in the deeper tissues and in superficial structures when slow, deep stroking is applied

### *Therapeutic Uses of Stroking*

When included in a treatment sequence, stroking can be used to do the following:

- Increase blood and lymphatic flow in the superficial circulation.
- Relieve pain and muscle spasm, thereby promoting relaxation.
- Help both patient and therapist become accustomed to the feel of each other's tissues. For the patient, it is the sensation of the therapist's hands. For the therapist, it is the contours and quality of the patient's tissues.
- Join various massage manipulations (strokes) together into a smooth sequence and thus give continuity to the massage treatment.
- Relieve flatulence or other intestinal movement disorders by mechanical direct and reflex effects on the intestines.
- Promote relaxation and induce sleep in persons who have insomnia.

### *Indications for the Use of Stroking*

Stroking may be indicated as part of a treatment plan to help relieve, or reduce the effects of, the following conditions:

- Pain (acute or chronic)
- Muscle spasm (acute or chronic)
- Superficial scar tissue (in the skin)
- Flatulence, constipation, and general abdominal discomfort
- Insomnia

### Contraindications to the Use of Stroking

The general concept of contraindications is covered in Chapter 3. As a technique, stroking may be contraindicated when any of the situations listed in Table 4-3 are present.

## Effleurage

### Definition

Effleurage (from the French word *effleurer:* to skim) is a slow, stroking movement performed with increasing pressure in the direction of flow in the veins and lymph vessels (i.e., centripetal direction). The stroke finishes with a definite pause and, whenever possible, in a group of superficial lymph glands.

### Purpose

Effleurage is a stroke designed to move the fluid contents of the superficial veins and lymph vessels. It is particularly useful as a means of stimulating the circulation and as a stroke used between manipulations that tend to mobilize tissue fluids. For example, after a series of deep kneading strokes to a muscle, effleurage given to the area will help to move the fluids that have been mobilized by the kneading. It can also be a useful stroke to finish off a massage sequence.

**Table 4-3 Main Contraindications to the Use of Stroking**

| Contraindication | |
|---|---|
| Large open areas (e.g., burns or wounds) in the areas to be treated, especially if they are infected | A |
| Gross edema in the areas to be treated if there seems to be a possibility of splitting the skin | A |
| Cancer in the skin or any other tissue in the area to be treated | A |
| Serious infections in the tissues to be treated (tuberculosis, septic arthritis, etc.) | A |
| Lacerations, bruising, infections, or foreign bodies (e.g., glass, grit, metal) in the skin of the area to be treated | A |
| Acute or chronic skin conditions affecting the areas to be treated (e.g., psoriasis, eczema, or dermatitis) | U |
| Marked varicosities in the areas to be treated if damage to the vein wall might result (very light stroking may be possible) | U |
| Within 3 to 6 months following radiation therapy in the area to be treated (skin is usually hypersensitive) | U |
| Areas of hyperesthesia in the areas to be treated (i.e., those who are very sensitive/ticklish to touch) | R |
| Extremely hairy areas in the areas to be treated (if stroking causes pain) | R |

*A*, Always contraindicated; *U*, usually contraindicated; *R*, rarely contraindicated.

### Basic Technique and Direction of Movement

Effleurage is always given in the direction of the venous and lymphatic flow (i.e., toward the heart, in a centripetal direction). The manipulation is performed with the palmar surface of one or both hands, working either alternately or simultaneously. Small areas such as the face or foot can be treated with the fingers or the thumb of one or both hands.

The hand, or hands, must be relaxed and molded accurately to the shape of the part being treated. The stroke should be smooth and rhythmic and is directed toward a group of lymph glands, following the course of superficial veins and lymphatics, with the therapist always working from distal to proximal areas. At the end of each stroke, the therapist's hands may be allowed to gently stroke back to their starting position, or they may be lifted from the surface of the body and returned through the air to the starting position for the next stroke. Each method has advantages and disadvantages, so in practice, either technique is acceptable.

### Rate of Movement

Effleurage is performed quite slowly (about 7 inches per second) because the pressure exerted on the tissues is much greater than just the weight of the therapist's hands. Rhythm is extremely important with this stroke: as usual, it should be even so that each stroke is smoothly performed throughout the area being treated.

### Depth and Pressure

To affect the contents of the superficial veins and lymphatics, effleurage must be performed with significant pressure. Pressure should gradually increase throughout the stroke so that the venous blood and lymph are pushed through the veins and lymph channels. There should be a definite pause at the end of each stroke, at or near the appropriate group of superficial lymph glands. This allows the valves in the vessels to close, thus minimizing back flow. These changes in pressure during the stroke make it important to maintain firm but comfortable pressure on the tissues. The greatest pressure is exerted at the end of the stroke when the hands or hands are stationary.

Effleurage to a variety of body areas is depicted in Figures 4-4 through 4-6. In addition, on the DVD effleurage is demonstrated to several body areas, as noted in the following table.

**DVD EFFLEURAGE**

| BODY PART | DVD CHAPTER |
|---|---|
| Back | 4-3 |
| Posterior neck and shoulders | 4-15 |
| Posterior aspects of the lower limb | 4-25 |
| Anterior aspects of the lower limb | 4-40 |
| Upper limb | 4-59 |

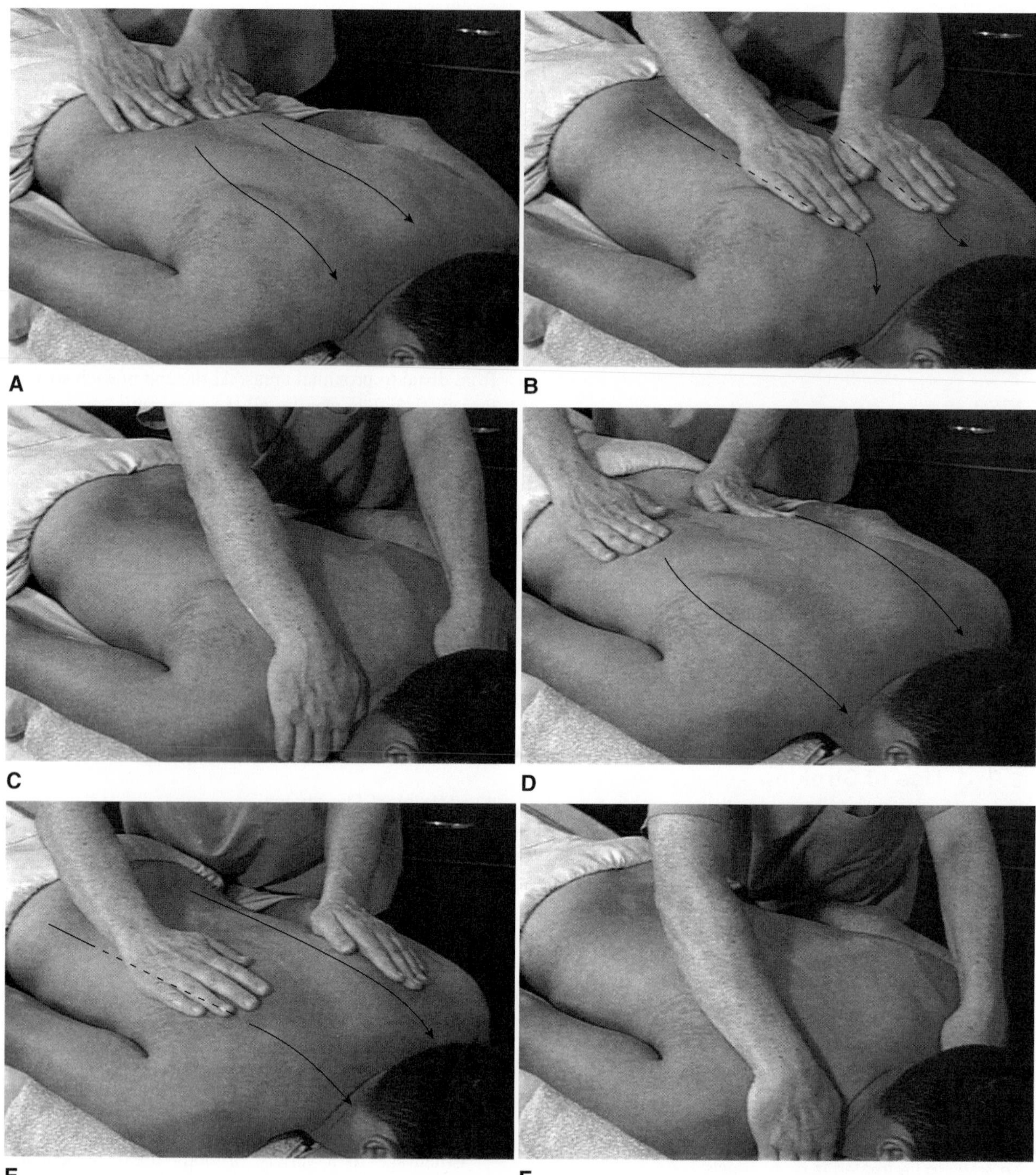


**Figure 4-4 Effleurage to the Back**

Effleurage is performed on the back, moving from the sacrum toward the head. Both hands are used so that the movements are mirror images of each other. The first stroke begins with the fingertips on the sacrum **(A)** and passes toward the head in a straight line **(B)**. At the upper fibers of the trapezius muscle, the hands turn outward to pass over the muscle belly to finish in the supraclavicular fossa, the fingers being allowed simply to fold over **(C)**. The second stroke begins just lateral to the first one on the sacrum **(D)** but passes more laterally up the back **(E)** in a similar fashion, once again to finish in the supraclavicular region **(F)**. Finally, the third stroke begins with the fingertips in a position similar to that for the previous stroke **(G)**. This time, however, the fingertips point outward and the hands pass up the sides of the chest wall **(H)** to finish with the ulnar border of each hand in the patient's respective axillary regions **(I)**. See also DVD Chapter 4-3.

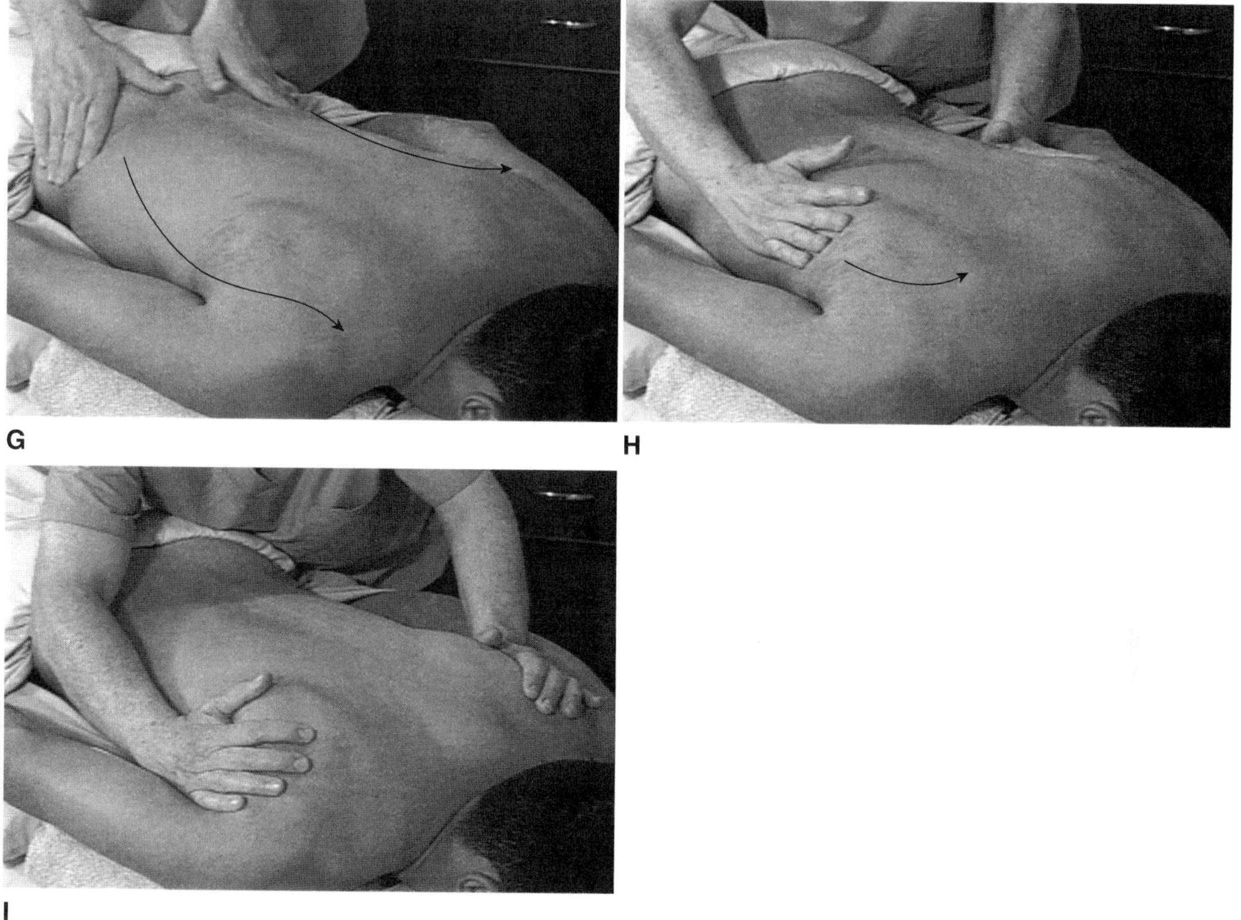


Figure **4-4**, cont'd

### *Primary Effects of Effleurage*

The therapeutic effects of effleurage are produced mainly through a direct mechanical impact on the tissues; however, there are reflex effects mediated through the sensory nervous system. When performed properly, effleurage has the following primary effects:

- An increase in the flow of venous blood in the superficial and deep veins toward the heart. When pressure is relaxed, the valves in the veins prevent backward flow.
- A stimulation of lymph flow, resulting in more rapid elimination of waste products.
- An increased flow in the veins and lymphatic vessels relieves the congestion in the capillaries, allowing vascular and lymphatic fluids to flow more readily into and out of the capillary beds, thereby stimulating the circulation and facilitating healing.
- An increase in the mobility of the skin and subcutaneous tissues, which in turn increases range of motion in joints and limb segments.
- Dilation of the superficial arterioles through the axon reflex, thereby stimulating the circulation.
- Stimulation of the large-diameter mechanoreceptors in the skin, thereby relieving pain (pain-gating mechanism), reducing muscle spasms, and promoting relaxation.

### *Therapeutic Uses of Effleurage*

When included in a treatment sequence, effleurage can be used to do the following:

- Increase blood and lymphatic flow in the superficial and deep circulation.
- Promote the absorption of inflammatory exudates in the subacute and chronic stages of soft tissue injuries (edema).
- Relieve pain and muscle spasm, thereby promoting relaxation.
- Follow other strokes (e.g., kneading, friction) that have deeper effects and thereby encourage the absorption of waste products into the lymphatic system.
- Help both patient and therapist become accustomed to the feel of each other's tissues. For the patient, it is the sensation of the therapist's hands. For the therapist, it is the contours and quality of the patient's tissues.
- Join various massage manipulations (strokes) together into a smooth sequence and thus give continuity to the massage treatment.

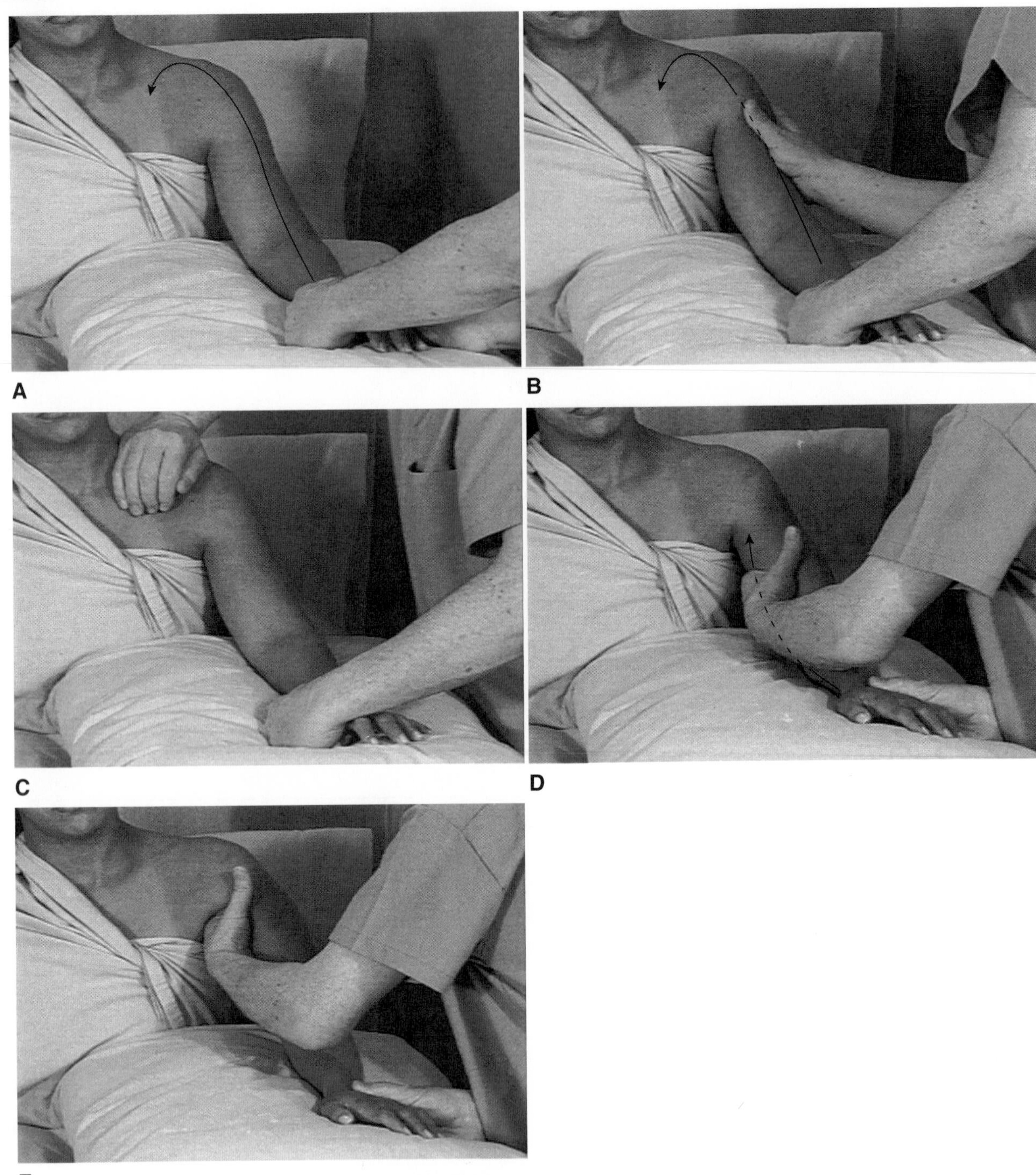


**Figure 4-5 Effleurage to the Upper Limb**

In this example, effleurage is performed with the patient in a seated position, with the forearm supported on a pillow. The stroke is performed in line with the long axis of the limb to cover the region. The therapist faces the patient and supports the patient's hand with one hand while using the other hand to perform the stroke. Movement begins at the hand or wrist **(A)** and passes up the lateral aspect of the forearm and arm **(B),** ending by curling over the posterior fibers of the deltoid muscle **(C)** to finish with the palm in the supraclavicular fossa. The therapist then changes hands and performs the stroke on the medial side of the limb, beginning at the wrist and passing up the medial aspect of the forearm **(D)** to finish in the axillary lymph glands **(E).** See also DVD Chapter 4-59.

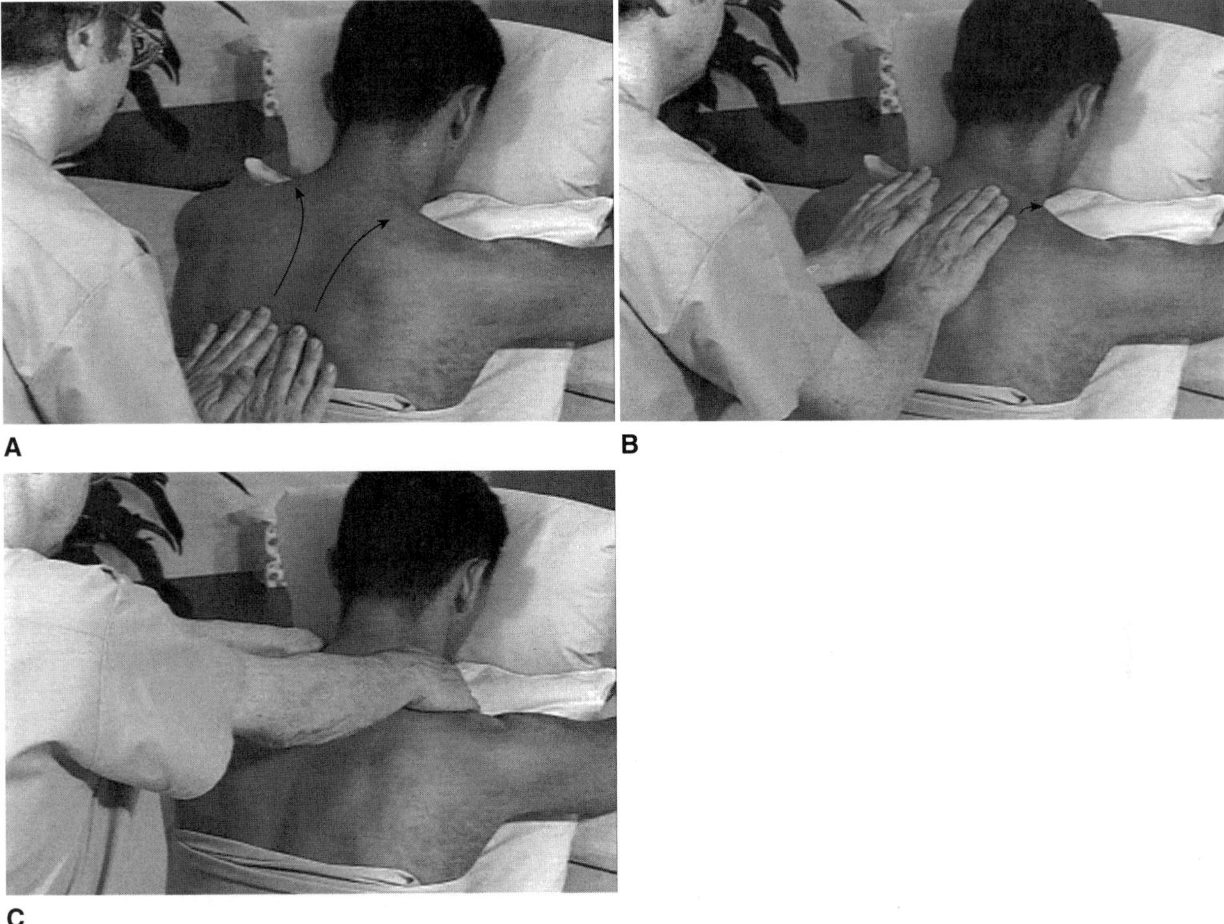


Figure **4-6** Effleurage to the Posterior Neck and Shoulder Region

The therapist stands behind the seated patient. The stroke begins with the fingertips together in the midline, approximately at the middle to the lower border of the scapulae **(A).** The stroke is performed in an upward direction **(B),** moving toward the base of the neck, finishing by allowing the hands to pass over the top of each trapezius muscle **(C),** to end with the palms in the supraclavicular lymph nodes. See also DVD Chapter 4-15.

### *Indications for Effleurage*

Effleurage may be indicated as part of a treatment plan to help relieve or reduce the effects of the following:

- Chronic edema, especially in the extremities
- Chronic pain, especially that associated with disturbances of the circulation
- Chronic muscle spasm
- Superficial scar tissue (in the skin) especially that associated with trauma to a limb

### *Contraindications to Effleurage*

The general concept of contraindications is covered in Chapter 3. As a technique, effleurage may be contraindicated when any of the situations listed in Table 4-4 are present.

## PRESSURE MANIPULATIONS

## Pétrissage

Pressure manipulations (*pétrissage,* from the French word *pétrir:* to knead), include several different massage strokes that are characterized by the application of firm pressure to the tissues. In the majority of cases, these strokes aim to mobilize deep muscle and tendon tissue, including the skin and subcutaneous tissues covering them. Four distinct types of stroke are discussed in this section: kneading, picking up, wringing, and skin rolling.

### *Kneading*

**Definition**

Kneading is a manipulation in which the muscles and subcutaneous tissues are alternately compressed and released.

**Table 4-4 Main Contraindications to the Use of Effleurage**

| Contraindication | |
|---|---|
| Large open areas (e.g., burns or wounds) in the areas to be treated, especially if they are infected | A |
| Cancer in the skin or any other tissue in the area to be treated | A |
| Serious infections in the tissues to be treated (tuberculosis, septic arthritis, etc.) | A |
| Gross edema in the areas to be treated if there seems to be a possibility of splitting the skin | A |
| Lacerations, bruising, infections, or foreign bodies (e.g., glass, grit, metal) in the skin of the area to be treated | A |
| Chronic swelling in the areas to be treated, in the lower limb associated with severe congestive cardiac failure or any other heart condition with which lower limb edema is associated | U |
| Acute or chronic skin conditions affecting the areas to be treated (e.g., psoriasis, eczema, or dermatitis) | U |
| Marked varicosities in the areas to be treated if damage to the vein wall might result (very light stroking may be possible) | U |
| Within 3 to 6 months following radiation therapy in the area to be treated (skin is usually hypersensitive) | U |
| Areas of hyperesthesia in the areas to be treated (i.e., those very sensitive/ticklish to touch) | R |
| Extremely hairy areas in the areas to be treated (if stroking causes pain) | R |

*A*, Always contraindicated; *U*, usually contraindicated; *R*, rarely contraindicated.

The technique produces movement in a *circular* direction. Each circular movement is divided into two roughly equal phases: compression and relaxation accompanied by a sliding movement of the hands, fingers, or thumbs. During the pressure phase of each stroke, the therapist's hands (or fingers or thumbs) and the skin move together on the deeper structures. During the release (relaxation) phase, the hands (or fingers or thumbs) glide smoothly to an adjacent area of tissue where the movement is repeated.

**Purpose**

Because of the compressive forces applied to the tissues, kneading strokes have a strong mechanical action and are designed to affect deep tissue. In particular, kneading aims to mobilize muscle and tendon fibers and other deep structures, thus promoting the normal function of muscles, which is not only to contract to produce movements but also to lengthen and allow movement in the opposite direction. To allow this, muscle fibers and other structures must be mobile. Kneading is also useful for mobilizing chronic swelling, especially where such swelling has become organized and is preventing normal joint and limb motion.

**Basic Technique and Direction of Movement**

Kneading is a stroke in which the therapist's hands and the patient's skin move together on the deeper structures whenever pressure is applied to the tissues. It can be performed with several parts of one or both hands, including the entire palmar surface and the pads/tips of the fingers or thumbs. In each case, the basic direction of the movement is circular. Pressure is applied during half of the circular motion and released with relaxation during the other half. Although kneading can be performed in a stationary manner (stationary kneading), it is more usual for the hands to move across the body surface during the technique. Movement of the hands is achieved during the relaxation phase of each circular motion. The hands usually move in parallel *lanes* to cover the entire area to be treated. The larger the area, the more lanes are needed. This type of kneading compresses the tissues and is therefore known as *palmar kneading.* Several variations of the technique can be used, and these will be considered in a later section. Figure 4-7 illustrates the concept of circular motion and movement in parallel lanes. It is common to most, but not all, types of kneading.

**Rate of Movement**

Kneading is performed slowly because of the pressure exerted on the tissues. If it is performed too quickly, it is likely to be ineffective or uncomfortable for the patient. The rate of movement is similar for both stationary kneading and the more common mobile versions. When using the whole hand(s), each circular movement should take about 3 to 4 seconds to complete. Obviously the rate is much lower if the finger pads or thumb pads are used to perform the massage, as they are so much smaller.

**Depth and Pressure**

As its name implies, kneading usually requires significant pressure on the tissues if it is to be effective. However, the pressure must be adapted to the tissues being treated, and it should be performed with much less pressure, especially on more delicate structures such as the backs of the hands or face. It is important for the pressure to be applied during only half of each circle. At such times, the hands are *not* moving on the skin; rather, the hands *and* the skin move over the deeper structures. It is not easy to quantify the actual pressure needed during kneading, but the experienced therapist will be able to apply the correct amount of pressure to treat the deep tissues effectively without harming the patient.

**Variations**

Several variations of the basic kneading stroke are used, and these are explained in the following sections.

***Palmar Kneading.*** When the entire palmar surface is used, the technique may be called *palmar kneading.* The basic palmar kneading stroke is also called *compression kneading, circular kneading, flat-handed,* and *whole-hand kneading.* In this manipulation the tissues are compressed upward and inward in a circular motion against the underlying tissues and then released. Overlapping lanes of circular strokes are used to cover a large area of the body, such as the back. If the tissues are flat, such as the back region,

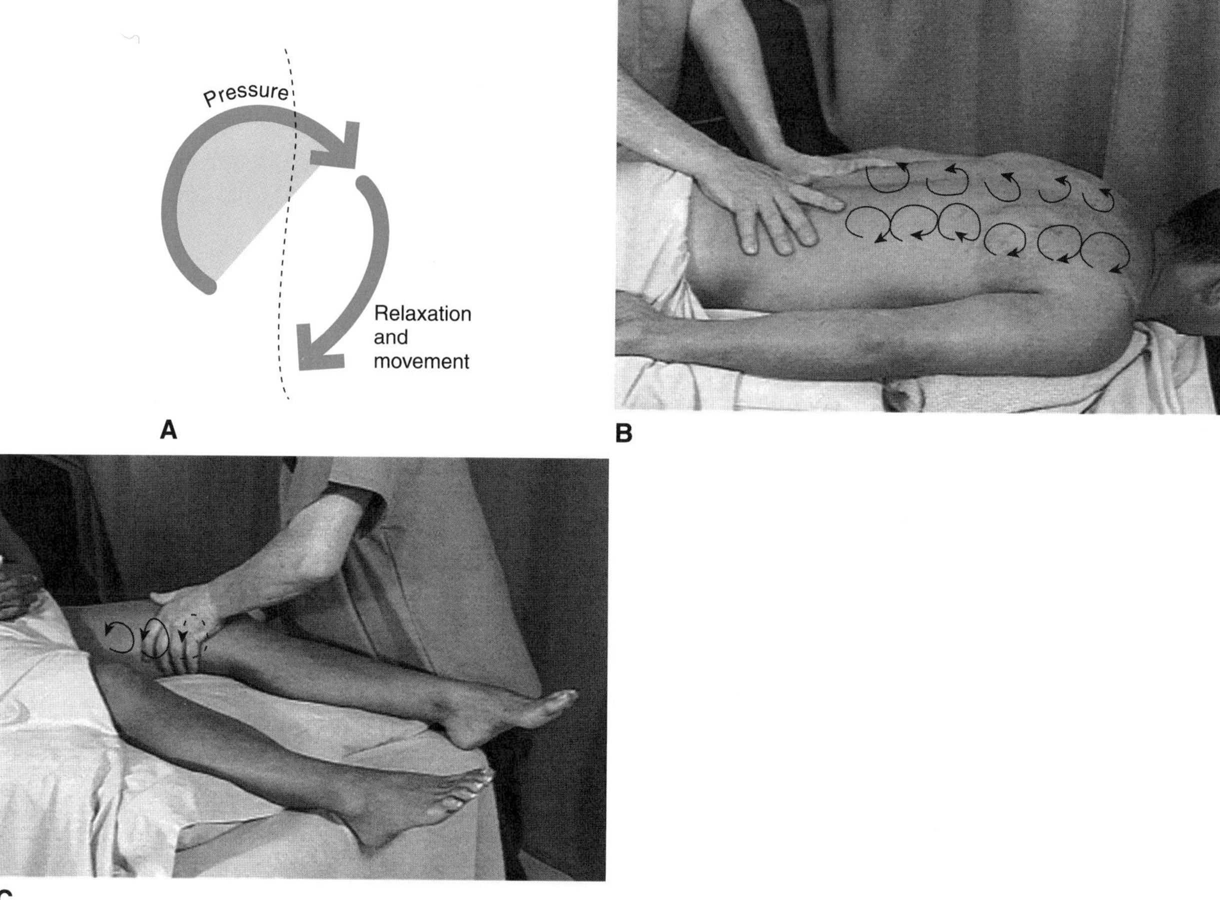


**Figure 4-7** Basic Technique and Direction of Movement for All Circular Kneading Strokes

The basic movement in all forms of kneading is circular. Pressure is applied during half of the circle, and relaxation with hand movement is allowed during the other half **(A)**. The hands usually progress along the body surface by moving in a series of parallel "lanes," as on the back **(B)**. The same concept is applied to the thigh **(C)**, except that the hands work on either side of the limb, usually beginning proximally. See also DVD Chapters 4-4, 4-26, and 4-41.

both hands can be used on the same plane of motion (side by side). In the limbs, however, the hands usually work opposite to each other (on either side of the limb). This produces more movement of the whole muscle masses involved.

Figures 4-8 and 4-9, *A,* illustrate the basic two-handed technique. The techniques shown in Figure 4-9 are good examples of the therapist's hands working opposite each other and out of phase. Palmar kneading, using one- and two-handed techniques, is also demonstrated on the DVD.

**DVD COMPRESSION KNEADING (WHOLE HAND)**

| BODY PART | DVD CHAPTER |
|---|---|
| Back | 4-4 |
| Posterior neck and shoulders | 4-16 |
| Posterior aspects of the lower limb | 4-26 |
| Anterior aspects of the lower limb | 4-41 |
| Deltoid, biceps, and triceps | 4-60 |

***Squeeze Kneading.*** Squeeze kneading is similar to the basic kneading technique; this time, however, the tissues are grasped and lifted upward and away from the underlying tissues, squeezed gently, and then allowed to relax. The squeezing is produced by a lumbrical action of the fingers, the tissues being squeezed between the palm and the fingers. It is usually performed on relatively large muscle masses, such as those in the thigh; however, it can be performed on small muscles by squeezing the tissues between the thumb and the finger pads. A variation of the technique lifts the tissues up and away from the underlying bone and then passes the tissues from one hand to the other while moving along the long axis of the muscle.

***Finger Pad Kneading.*** This technique is also called *digital kneading,* and it involves the basic palmar kneading stroke performed with one or more finger pads, using one or both hands. If the therapist's hands are placed opposite each

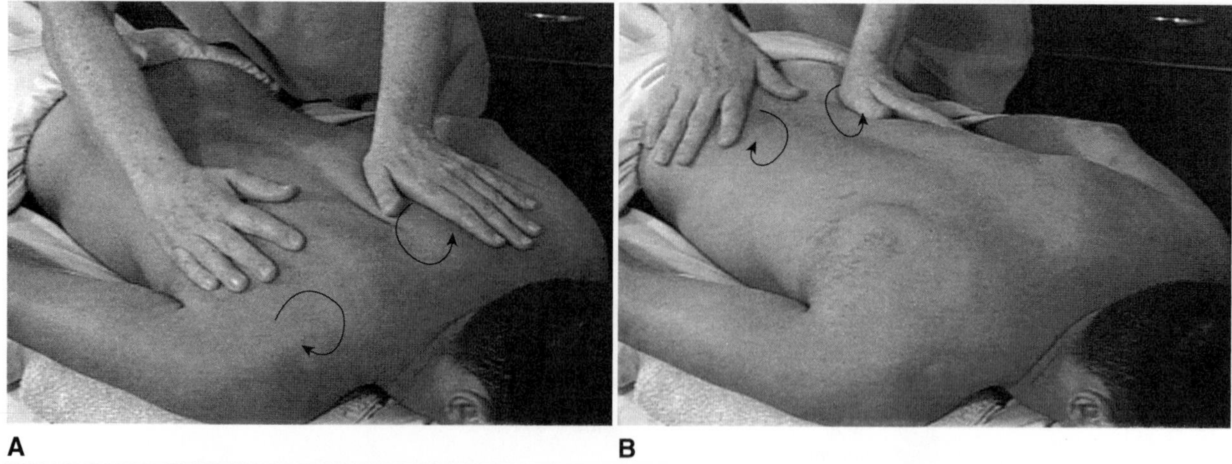

A B

Figure **4-8** Compression Kneading to the Back Extensor Muscles

The stroke usually starts at the upper fibers of the trapezius muscle and progresses along the back **(A)** toward the sacrum. If required, the fingers may turn outward slightly as the hands reach the lumbar region **(B).** This helps to avoid too much extension of the wrists at the sacral region. To avoid pinching the tissues, it is better to perform the technique with the two hands working out of phase (i.e., one hand compresses moving upward and inward, while the other relaxes moving downward and outward). See also DVD Chapter 4-4.

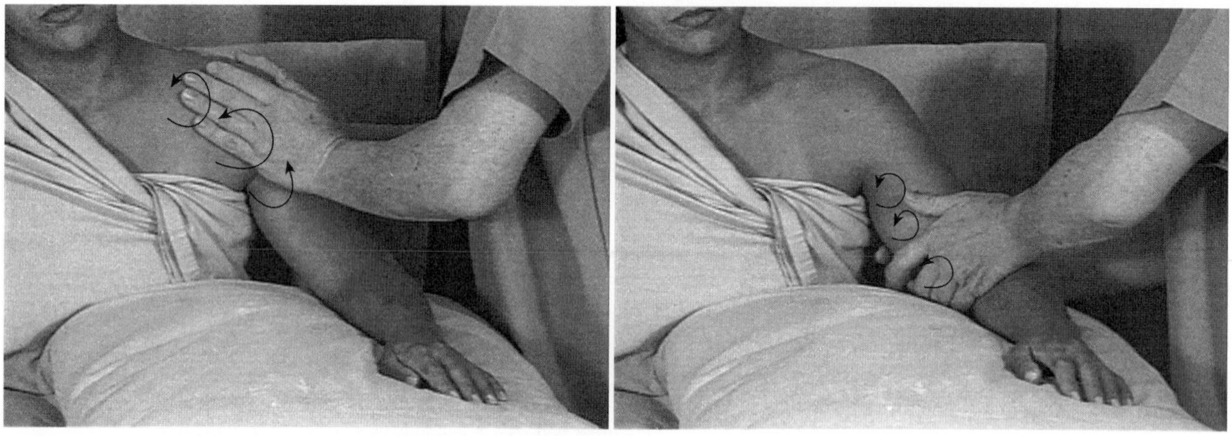

A B

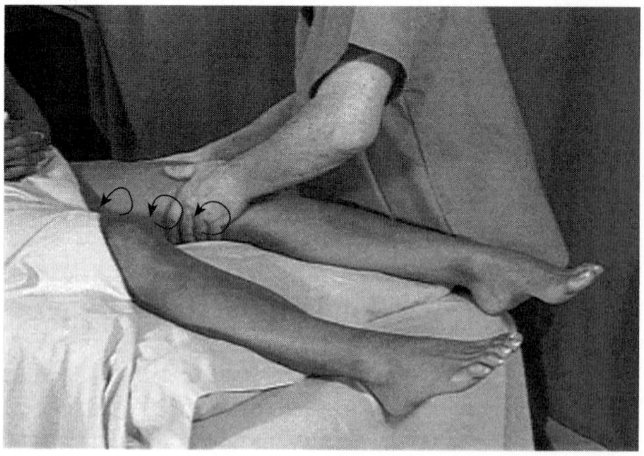

C

Figure **4-9** Compression Kneading to the Upper and Lower Limb Muscles

Two variations of the basic kneading techniques are illustrated. **A,** The hands are placed side by side on the deltoid muscle and work out of phase, beginning at the proximal end of the muscle and working toward its insertion. **B,** The hands now move down the limb, opposite to one another, to cover the biceps and triceps muscles. Palmar kneading is given along both muscles in a proximal (shoulder) to distal (elbow) direction. **C,** In the lower limb, the therapist's hands work opposite to each other. Compression is applied to the thigh muscles but, again, the hands work out of phase with each other. This technique works very well when it is possible to get both hands on either side of a muscle mass. It is easiest to start at the proximal part of the limb (hip) and work toward the distal part (knee). See also DVD Chapters 4-26, 4-41, and 4-60.

other, for example, around the knee region, then the finger pads usually work in *phase* with each other. It is quite possible, however, for the finger pads to work *out of phase,* and this is simply a matter of preference. The technique is useful for treating small- to medium-sized areas and areas of irregular shape (e.g., around the elbow, knee, or ankle). When both hands are used, they may work side by side in some situations, or opposite each other, as in Figures 4-10 and 4-11, which illustrate finger pad kneading around the elbow and knee regions, respectively. Finger pad kneading is also demonstrated on the DVD (see DVD Chapters 4-31, 4-48, 4-51, and 4-63).

DVD **FINGER PAD KNEADING**

| BODY PART | DVD CHAPTER |
|---|---|
| Elbow | 4-63 |
| Posterior aspects of the knee | 4-31 |
| Anterior aspects of the knee | 4-48 |
| Ankle | 4-51 |

***Thumb Pad Kneading.*** The basic palmar kneading stroke can also be performed with the pads of one or both thumbs, usually working side by side. This technique is especially useful along fusiform muscles (e.g., the flexors and extensors of the wrists and fingers or the anterior tibial muscles). It is also useful for the treatment of small areas in the hand, foot, and face. Figure 4-12 illustrates the stroke. Thumb pad kneading is also demonstrated to various body areas on the DVD (see DVD Chapters 4-35, 4-37, 4-50, 4-52, and 4-64 to 4-66).

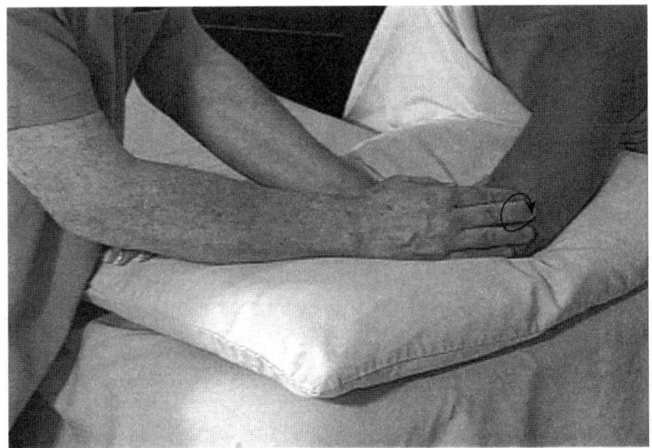

Figure **4-10** Finger Pad Kneading to the Elbow Region

In this example, the therapist's left hand supports the medial sides of the joint, while the finger pads of the right hand are used to perform the stroke. Alternatively, a two-handed technique can be used. In this case, the fingers may work either in phase or out of phase with each other, depending on the therapist's preference. The technique works well around irregular-shaped surfaces such as the face, elbow, knee, and ankle. See also DVD Chapter 4-63.

DVD **THUMB PAD KNEADING**

| BODY PART | DVD CHAPTER |
|---|---|
| Anterior tibial muscles | 4-50 |
| Calf muscles | 4-35 |
| Foot and toes | 4-37, 4-52 |
| Wrist and finger flexors | 4-65 |
| Wrist and finger extensors | 4-64 |
| Hand | 4-66 |

***Reinforced Kneading (Palmar Thumb Pad or Finger Pad).*** As its name might imply, reinforced kneading is a two-handed technique in which one hand *reinforces* the other. The basic palmar kneading technique is performed with one hand on top of the other, to reinforce the pressure of the stroke. It can be particularly useful for treating the lumbar region in large or very muscular patients, especially when extra effort would be required for effective treatment. This is especially true if the therapist is of relatively small stature and the patient is very large. The technique is illustrated in Figure 4-13 to the lumbar region. The technique can also be viewed at DVD Chapter 4-5.

Although reinforced kneading is usually performed using the whole palmar surface of the hand, it can also be given using the pad of just the thumb or using the finger pads. In these cases, reinforced thumb pad or finger pad kneading are useful techniques when extra pressure is needed in a small area. In the case of the thumb, one thumb is placed on the tissues and the other directly on top of it. The two thumbs move together to provide extra pressure when needed. Similarly, one set of finger pads can be placed on the skin and the finger pads of the other hand are simply placed on top of them, allowing much greater pressure to be exerted. These hand positions are useful for several techniques on deep muscles (see Chapters 8 and 9).

***Knuckle Kneading.*** *Knuckle kneading* is a technique for treating small areas where greater depth of pressure is required; for example, the sole of the foot. Pressure is applied with the dorsal surface of the middle or proximal phalanges, depending on the size of the area to be covered and the preference of the therapist. The stroke is performed with the closed fist, applying the same basic circular motions of palmar kneading. It is usually easier for the therapist to use a clockwise motion of the knuckles. Figure 4-14 illustrates the stroke, and it is also demonstrated at DVD Chapter 4-53.

## *Picking Up*

### Definition

*Picking up* is a technique in which the therapist grasps and squeezes muscles while simultaneously lifting them away from the underlying tissues and then releasing them. The grasping and releasing is performed in a circular motion, usually in the same direction as the muscle fibers (long axis).

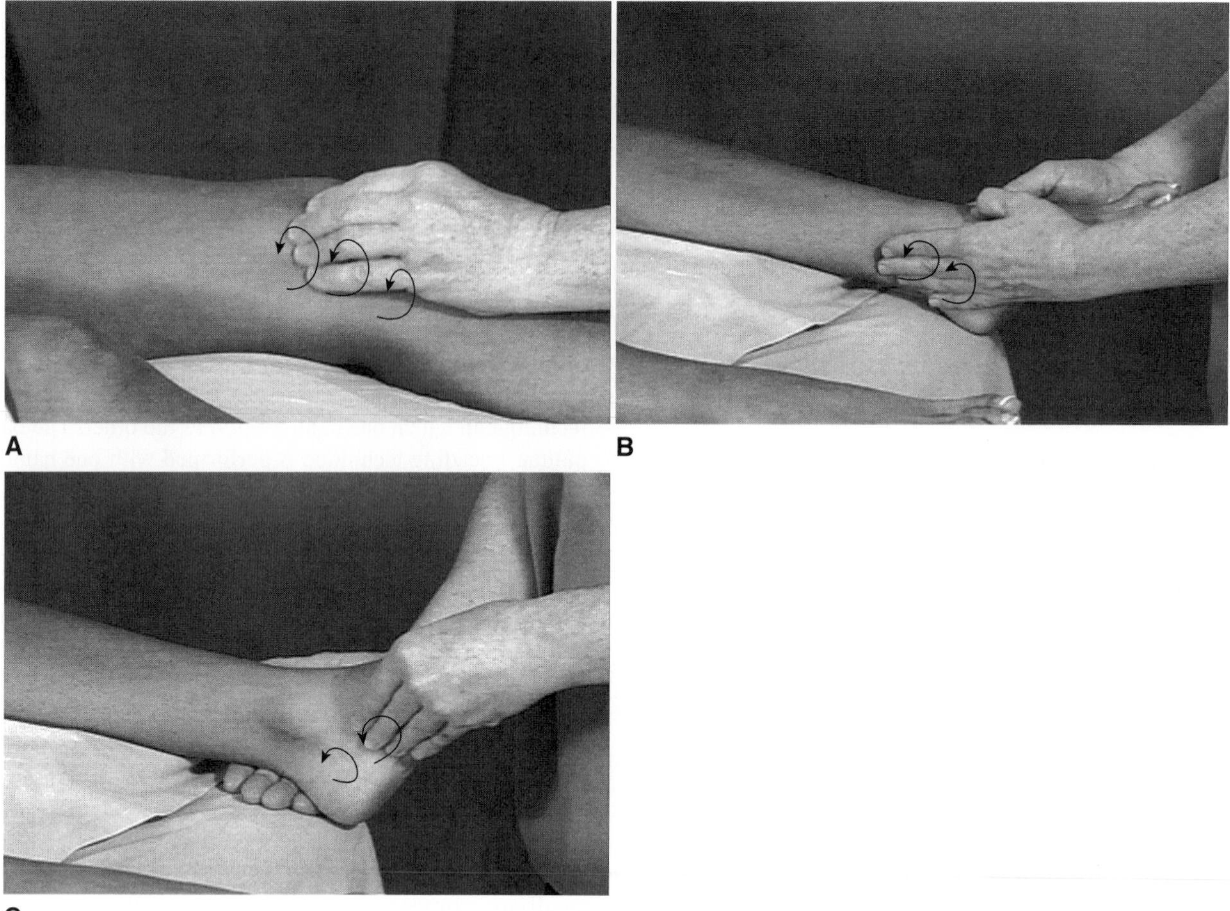

**Figure 4-11 Finger Pad Kneading around the Knee and Ankle**
In these examples, the therapist uses a two-handed technique with each hand working on opposite sides of the knee **(A)** and the ankle **(B).** The fingers may work either in phase or out of phase. In each case, the fingers cover all aspects of the joint structures, with particular attention to the ligaments, joint capsules, and tendons crossing the region. As an alternative, finger pad kneading may be given as a single-handed technique. In this example **(C),** the stroke is given to the medial aspect of the ankle region using the therapist's left hand. The other hand supports the lateral side of the ankle and heel. See also DVD Chapters 4-31, 4-36, 4-48, and 4-51.

**Purpose**

Picking up is performed largely on muscle tissue for the purpose of mobilizing individual or groups of muscles. It has a significant mechanical action on the muscle fibers and is designed to increase muscle mobility, thereby facilitating normal joint and limb function.

**Basic Technique and Direction of Movement**

The usual technique is a single-handed manipulation of a muscle or muscle group. The therapist grasps the tissue to be treated with his or her whole hand, the thumb being well abducted. On very wide muscle groups, the hands may be used together to give a wider grasp. The initial pressure is upward and inward in a circular motion toward the tissues. The therapist grasps the tissues between the palmar surfaces of all of the fingers and the palmar surface of the thumb. The intrinsic muscles of the fingers produce a lumbrical-like movement of the digits so that the tissues are lifted away from the underlying structures by a movement of wrist extension. The tissues are then released as the hand glides along the muscle belly to repeat the stroke.

A variation of the basic stroke is a two-handed technique in which the tissues are grasped and lifted away from underlying tissues by one hand and then *passed* to the other while still lifted away from deeper structures. The muscle is then released by the second hand. Progress is made along a muscle by passing the tissues from one hand to the other.

**Rate of Movement**

The movement should be slow, continuous, and rhythmic, and the whole muscle belly should be treated, generally from origin to insertion. Care should be taken to keep the grasp soft and supple, thereby avoiding pinching of the tissues.

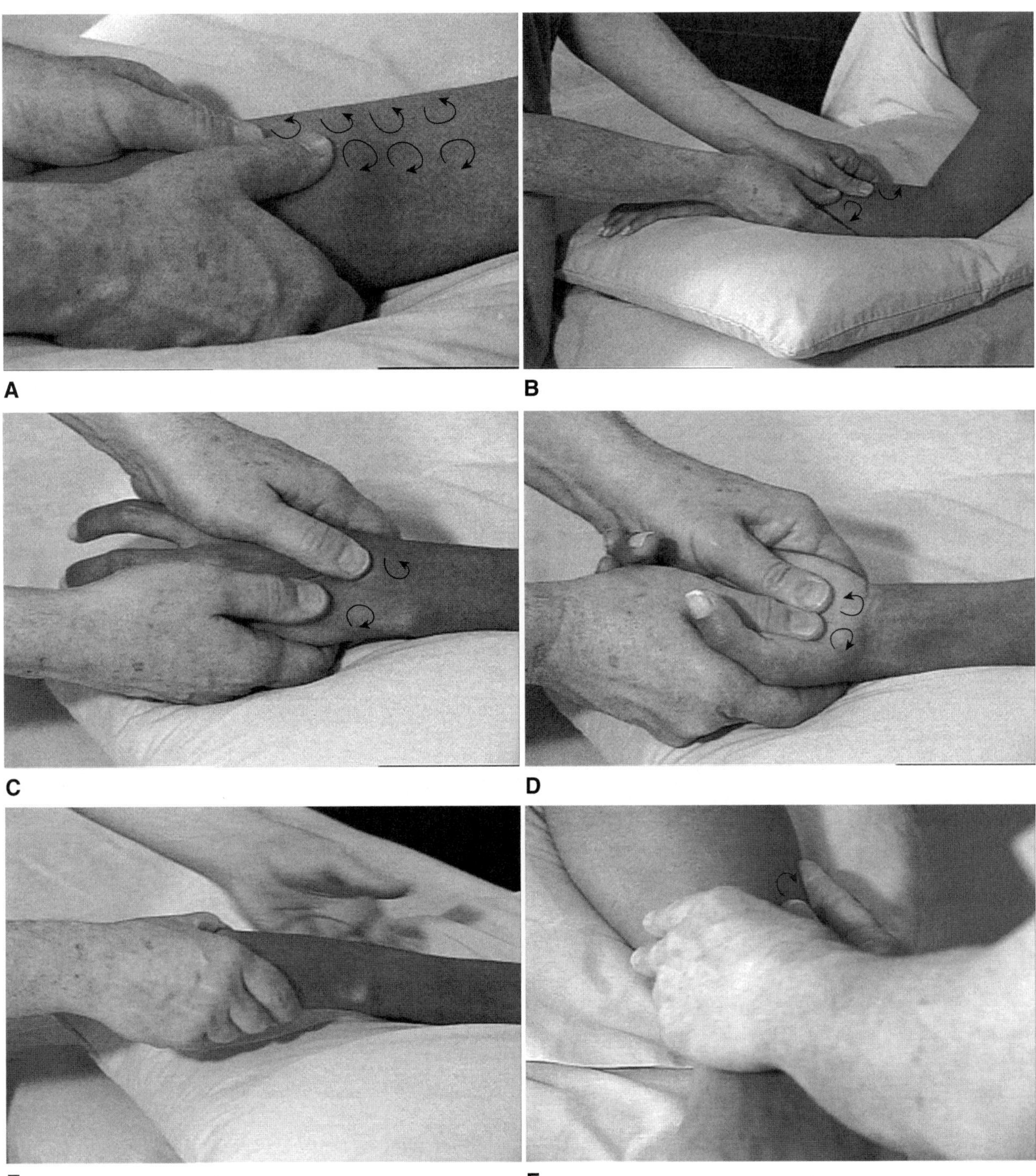


Figure **4-12** Thumb Pad Kneading to Muscles in the Forearm, Hand, Leg, and Foot

In this example, the therapist's thumbs work side by side **(A).** The thumb pads may work either in phase or out of phase with each other, depending on the therapist's preference, but the out-of-phase technique is usually more comfortable for the patient. The technique works well around small, irregular-shaped surfaces such as the face, hand, and foot and on long, fusiform muscle groups in the forearm **(B),** dorsum **(C),** palm **(D),** and fingers **(E)** of the hand. In the leg, thumb pad kneading is useful on the anterior tibial muscles **(F),** and the dorsum of the foot **(G).** Thumb pad kneading can also be given to the muscles on the sole of the foot, either as a single-handed (**H**) or double-handed **(I)** technique. The stroke can be given to the toes, either as a single-handed technique **(J)** or using two hands **(K),** in which case it is important to massage alternate toes to avoid discomfort for the patient. See also DVD Chapters 4-35, 4-37, 4-50, 4-52, and 4-64 to 4-66.

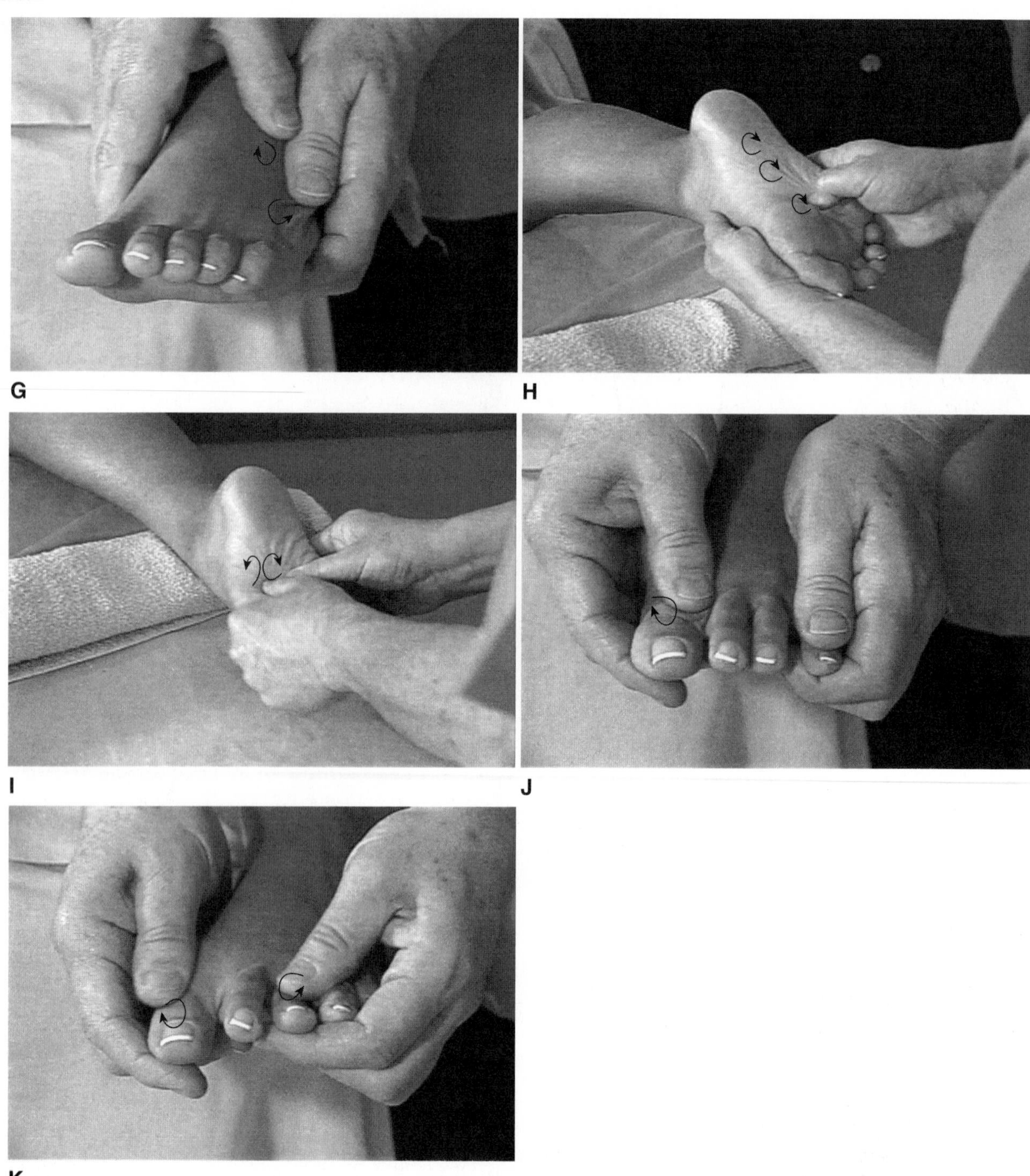


Figure 4-12, cont'd

**Depth and Pressure**

*Picking up* is a pressure manipulation (pétrissage) requiring a significant degree of pressure, especially over large muscles. Sufficient pressure must be exerted to grasp and lift the muscle tissue away from the underlying structures, moving them in a circular motion. The tissues are squeezed during the first half of the circular motion and released during the second half. In general, picking up is not as deep a technique as palmar kneading. Figure 4-15 illustrates standard picking up to the biceps, triceps, thigh, and calf, respectively. These techniques are demonstrated on the DVD as described in the following table:

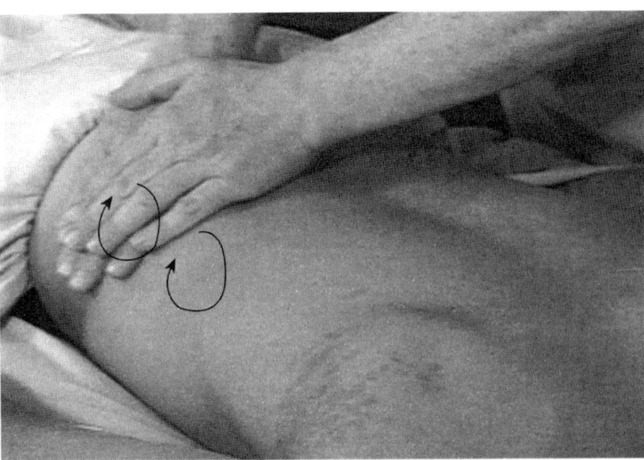

**Figure 4-13 Reinforced Kneading to the Lumbar Muscles**

One hand reinforces the other in this technique. The therapist follows the basic circular kneading technique, simply using one hand reinforced by the other. The technique provides extra pressure and is useful for deep muscle masses or large patients. See also DVD Chapter 4-5.

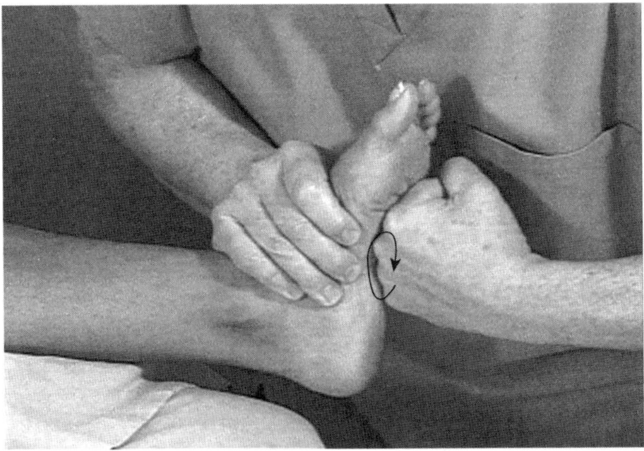

**Figure 4-14 Knuckle Kneading to the Muscles on the Sole of the Foot**

This is a modified kneading technique that is useful for applying extra pressure to the deep muscle layers on the sole of the foot. It can be used on other deep muscle masses where extra pressure is required. See also DVD Chapter 4-53.

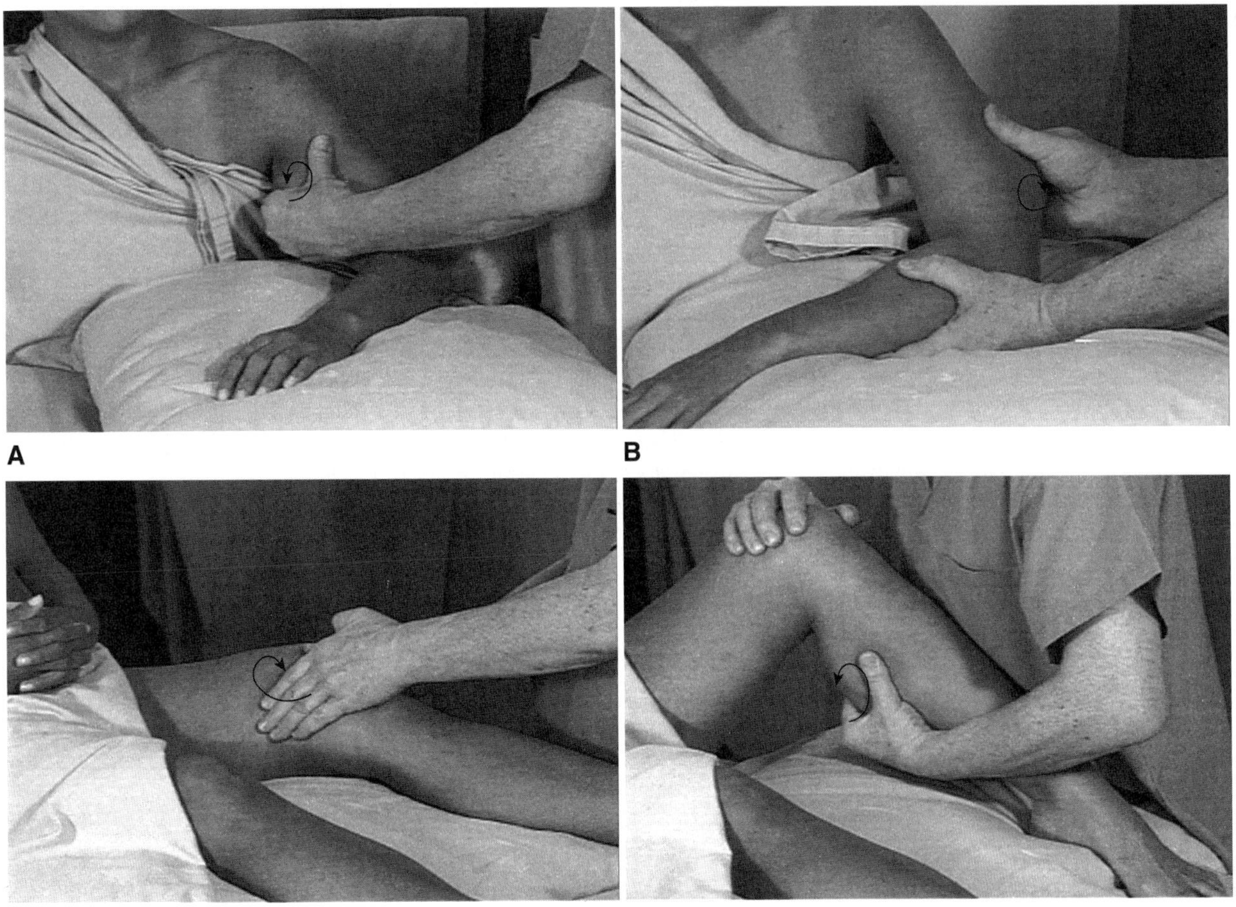

A

B

C

D

**Figure 4-15 Picking Up to Muscles in the Upper and Lower Limbs**

**A,** The biceps muscle is picked up using a single-handed technique. **B,** The triceps muscles are treated similarly. In these examples, the patient is seated comfortably at the end of a treatment table, with the upper limb supported on a pillow. In both examples, note that one of the therapist's hands provides counterpressure to support the arm while each muscle is being treated. **C,** The quadriceps muscle is usually quite large and is picked up using a two-handed technique. In this case, the thumbs are crossed, and the muscle is lifted away from the underlying bone with a circular motion. **D,** A single-handed technique is used to pick up the calf muscles. See also DVD Chapters 4-17, 4-27, 4-42, 4-49, and 4-61.

**PICKING UP**

| BODY PART | DVD CHAPTER |
|---|---|
| Posterior neck muscles | 4-19 |
| Upper fibers of the trapezius muscle | 4-17 |
| Thigh muscles | 4-27, 4-42 |
| Calf muscles | 4-33, 4-49 |
| Biceps and triceps | 4-61 |

### *Wringing*

**Definition**

Wringing is a pressure manipulation in which the tissues are lifted away from the underlying structures with both hands and then compressed alternately between the fingers and thumb of opposite hands, while progressing along the long axis of the muscles in question.

**Purpose**

Wringing is rather similar to picking up in terms of its purpose. It is also a technique performed largely on muscle tissue for the purpose of mobilizing individual muscles or groups of them. It has significant mechanical action on the muscle fibers because of the twisting motion that is imparted to the tissues. Like picking up, it is designed to increase muscle mobility, thereby facilitating normal joint and limb function.

**Basic Technique and Direction of Movement**

The hands are placed on the long axis of the muscle with the thumbs well abducted from the fingers. The tissues are grasped with both hands; lifted, using a lumbrical-like action; and then twisted between the fingers and thumb of opposite hands. Alternate radial and ulnar deviation of each wrist produces the classic twisting movement of the technique. The resulting motion is similar to that of wringing out a wet towel.

The hands move alternately down the long axis of the muscle, working across the muscle fibers and stretching the tissues. Wringing is used chiefly on large and loose groups of muscles. The techniques can be modified, however, to accommodate smaller muscles. In this case, wringing may need to be performed with the tips of the fingers and thumbs instead of the entire hands.

**Rate of Movement**

The stroke is performed at slow to medium speed—about 4 to 6 inches per second on a large muscle—and somewhat more slowly on smaller muscles. This stroke requires a particularly even rhythm if it is to feel comfortable to the patient. If the rhythm and pressure are erratic, it will be difficult for the patient to relax and for the technique to be effective. Wringing is one of the more difficult techniques to master because it requires considerable dexterity and coordination. However, when performed correctly, it is an extremely effective stroke to mobilize muscle tissue.

**Depth and Pressure**

Because the tissues are grasped and lifted from the deeper structures during wringing, it is obviously a stroke that demands reasonable pressure. It is a deep stroke designed to mobilize deep muscle tissue. As always, pressure must be regulated so that it does not pinch the patient and cause pain. This stroke requires the patient's muscle to be completely relaxed. If not, the technique cannot be performed properly. Figure 4-16 illustrates wringing to a variety of muscles, also demonstrated on the DVD as follows:

**WRINGING**

| BODY PART | DVD CHAPTER |
|---|---|
| Lateral chest wall | 4-6 |
| Upper fibers of the trapezius muscle | 4-18 |
| Posterior aspects of the lower limb | 4-28, 4-34 |
| Anterior aspects of the lower limb | 4-43 |
| Biceps and triceps | 4-62 |

### *Skin Rolling*

**Definition**

Skin rolling is a pressure manipulation in which the therapist lifts the skin and subcutaneous tissues away from the underlying structures and then *rolls* them over the deeper tissues.

**Purpose**

Skin rolling is primarily designed to mobilize the skin and subcutaneous structures. Because the skin is folded over on itself, it is also likely to move the contents of the superficial vessels and thus improve circulation to the area. Normal joint and limb movements require an adequate degree of extensibility in the skin and subcutaneous tissues. Skin rolling is a technique specifically designed to mobilize the skin and therefore improve joint and limb function that has been compromised by prolonged immobility.

**Basic Technique and Direction of Movement**

The therapist places both hands side by side, flat on the patient's skin surface, and with the thumbs stretched apart as far as possible. The extended fingers draw the tissues toward the thumbs, with a lumbrical-like action. This action lifts up a fold of skin between the fingers and thumbs. The thumbs then compress the tissues toward the fingers, rolling them around the body part in a wavelike motion, away from the therapist. The motion is repeated on the adjacent portion of skin until the entire area is covered.

**Rate of Movement**

Skin rolling is usually performed quite slowly (about 4 to 6 inches per second) while taking care not to pinch the tissues and cause pain.

**Depth and Pressure**

Skin rolling is performed to the skin and subcutaneous tissues and does not require significant pressure to be effective; however, if the skin and deeper structures are tight or the patient has a significant layer of body fat, it may be difficult to lift up a roll of skin without pinching the patient

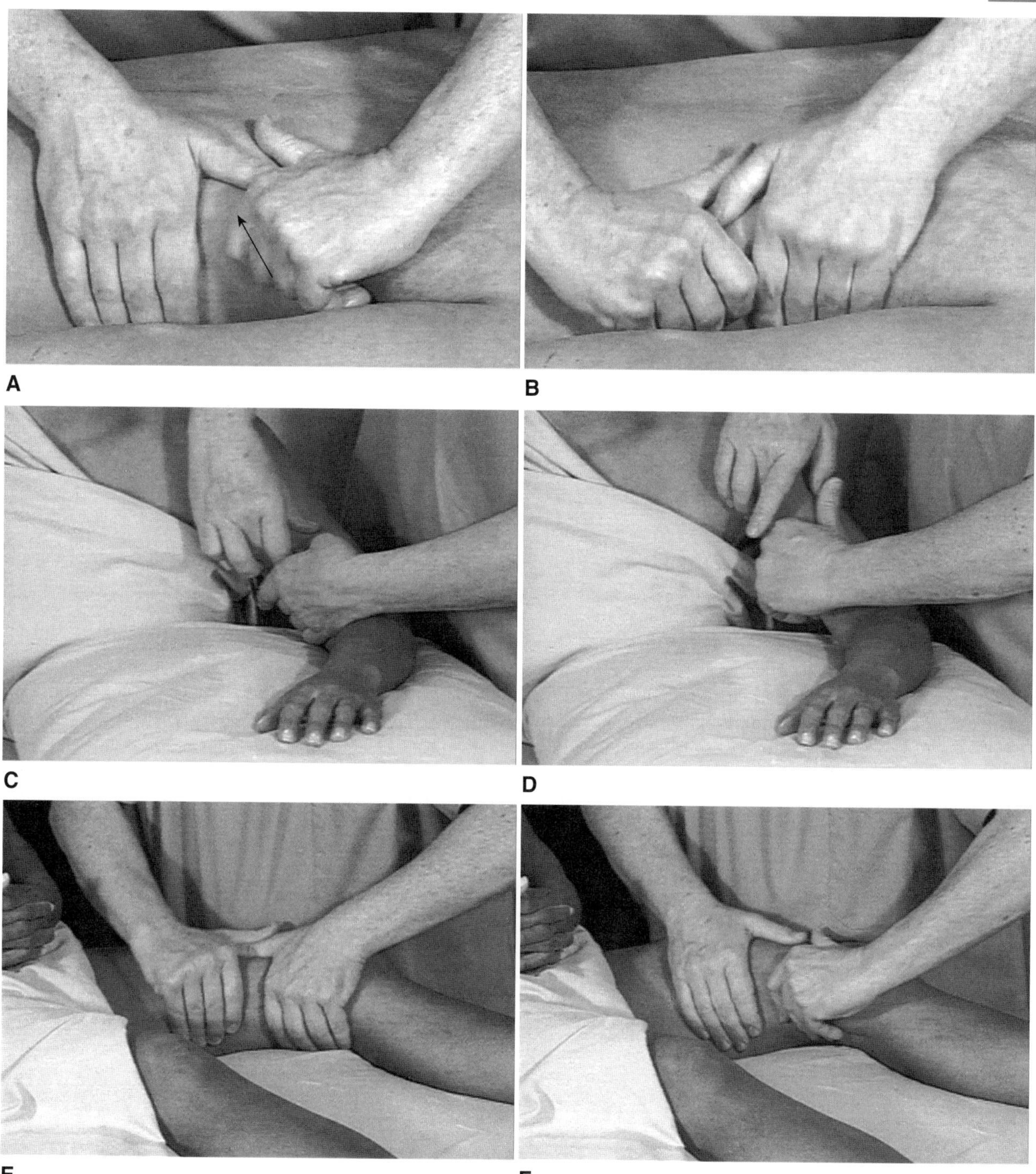

Figure 4-16 Wringing to Lateral Chest Muscles and Upper and Lower Limb Muscles

**A, B,** Wringing is performed to the lateral chest wall muscles. The twisting motion of the hands as they move across the long axis of the muscle group is illustrated. Pressure is applied between the fingers of one hand and the thumb of the other. **C, D,** With the patient seated and supported comfortably, wringing to the biceps can be performed. **E, F,** In a similar manner, wringing to the medial thigh muscles is depicted. See also DVD Chapters 4-6, 4-28, 4-34, 4-43, 4-62.

and causing pain. If the skin-fold thickness is more than 1 inch, the pressure may need to be reduced slightly to prevent pinching.

The skin and deeper structures are much more mobile in some parts of the body than in others. This means that it may be difficult if not impossible to perform the technique properly on some body parts. In any area that is naturally tight and relatively immobile (e.g., around the lower lumbar and sacral region), this technique cannot be performed well. In addition, it may not be possible to perform this technique on patients whose skin-fold thickness is greater than 2 to 3 inches, because it may be impossible to effectively produce a comfortable fold in the skin while lifting the tissues away from deeper structures. It is much easier to perform effective skin rolling if the skin is loose. Skin rolling can be given to small areas of the body, such as the dorsum of the hand or foot, in which case the thumb and fingertips are used to perform the technique. (NOTE: This technique is easy to practice on an animal that has very mobile skin, such as a cat or a dog.) Figure 4-17 illustrates skin rolling over the posterior thoracic region. See also DVD Chapter 4-7.

DVD

## Primary Effects of Pressure Manipulations (Pétrissage)

The therapeutic effects of the pressure manipulations (pétrissage) are produced mainly through a direct mechanical impact on the tissues. In addition, there are reflex effects mediated through the sensory nervous system, especially in the skin. These effects have been grouped into several categories, but, of course, they are all present to a greater or lesser extent. When performed properly, the pressure manipulations have the primary effects listed as follows.

### Effects on the Circulation

- Increased flow of venous blood in the superficial and deep veins toward the heart (when pressure is relaxed the valves in the veins prevent backward flow)
- Stimulation of lymph flow, resulting in more rapid elimination of waste products
- Increased flow in the veins and lymphatic vessels, which relieves the congestion in the capillaries, allowing vascular and lymphatic fluids to flow more readily into, and out of, the capillary beds, thereby stimulating the circulation and facilitating healing
- Dilation of the superficial arterioles through the axon reflex, thereby stimulating the circulation

### Effects on Muscles

- Increased blood supply to superficial and deep muscles
- Increased elimination of metabolic waste products in superficial and deep muscles
- Stretching of posttraumatic scar tissue in muscle
- Increased range of motion in muscle and a promotion of normal joint and limb function
- Reduction of muscle spasm as a result of the stimulation of the large diameter, mechanoreceptors in the skin, thereby relieving pain (pain-gating mechanism)
- Promotion of relaxation in superficial and deep muscle tissue

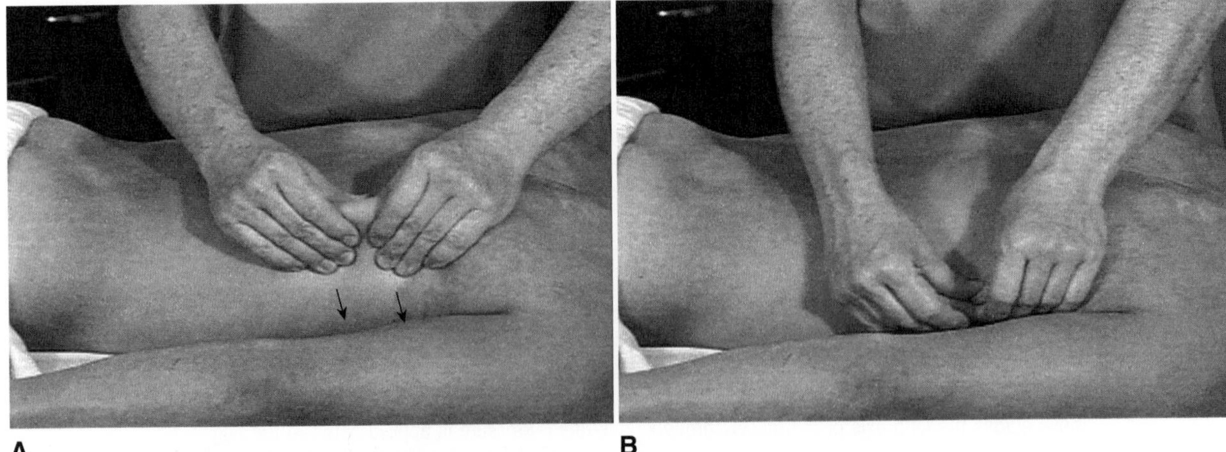


**Figure 4-17 Skin Rolling to the Lateral Chest Wall**

The hands are placed side by side, with the fingers and thumbs stretched apart. **A,** A large fold of skin is lifted up from the underlying tissues using a lumbrical action. **B,** This fold of skin is then pushed/rolled away from the therapist by moving the thumbs toward the fingers. In this fashion, the skin is rolled around the chest wall. The movement is then repeated on the adjacent tissues, with the hands moving down the back from the shoulder to the sacrum. See also DVD Chapter 4-7.

### Effects on the Skin and Subcutaneous Tissues

- Increased blood and lymph flow in the skin and subcutaneous tissues, which in turn produces a slight increase in skin temperature
- Stretching of posttraumatic scar tissue in muscle
- Increased extensibility and mobility of the skin and subcutaneous tissues, which in turn increases range of motion in joints and limb segments, thereby promoting normal function

### Therapeutic Uses of Pressure Manipulations (Pétrissage)

When included in a treatment sequence, pressure manipulations can be used to do the following:

- Increase blood and lymphatic flow in the skin and in superficial and deep muscles
- Promote the absorption of inflammatory exudates (edema) in the subacute and chronic stages of soft tissue injury
- Mobilize the skin and subcutaneous tissues
- Mobilize contractures in the superficial and deep muscles, tendons, ligaments, joint capsules, and neurovascular bundles
- Remove the accumulation of metabolic waste products in superficial and deep muscles
- Relieve pain and muscle spasm, thereby promoting relaxation

### Indications for Pressure Manipulations (Pétrissage)

Pressure manipulations may be indicated as part of a treatment plan to help relieve or reduce the effects of the following:

- Chronic edema, especially in the extremities
- Chronic pain (especially that associated with disturbances of the circulation)
- Superficial scar tissue in the skin and subcutaneous tissue, especially that associated with trauma
- Contractures in muscles, tendons, ligaments, joint capsules, and related structures

### Contraindications to the Use of Pressure Manipulations (Pétrissage)

The general concept of contraindications is covered in Chapter 3. As a technique, pressure manipulations may be contraindicated when any of the situations listed in Table 4-5 are present.

**Table 4-5 Main Contraindications to the Use of Pressure Manipulations**

| | |
|---|---|
| Large open areas (e.g., burns or wounds) in the areas to be treated, especially if they are infected | **A** |
| Cancer in the skin or any other tissue in the area to be treated | **A** |
| Serious infections in the tissues to be treated (tuberculosis, septic arthritis, etc.) | **A** |
| Gross edema in the areas to be treated if there seems to be a possibility of splitting the skin | **A** |
| Lacerations, bruising, infections, or foreign bodies (e.g., glass, grit, metal) in the skin or other tissues in the area to be treated | **A** |
| Arterial or venous pathology (especially thrombophlebitis and deep vein thrombosis) in the areas to be treated | **A** |
| Acute muscle tears in the areas to be treated (especially deep intramuscular hematomas) | **A** |
| Hypertonic or hypotonic limbs as the areas to be treated (very gentle massage only) | **U** |
| Chronic swelling in the areas to be treated, in the lower limb associated with severe congestive cardiac failure or any other heart condition with which lower limb edema is associated | **U** |
| Acute or chronic skin conditions affecting the areas to be treated (e.g., psoriasis, eczema, or dermatitis) | **U** |
| Marked varicosities in the areas to be treated if damage to the vein wall might result | **U** |
| Within 3 to 6 months following radiation therapy in the area to be treated (skin is usually hypersensitive) | **U** |
| Areas of hyperesthesia in the areas to be treated (i.e., those very sensitive/ticklish to touch) | **R** |
| Extremely hairy areas in the areas to be treated (if treatment causes pain) | **R** |

*A*, Always contraindicated; *U*, usually contraindicated; *R*, rarely contraindicated.

## PERCUSSIVE MANIPULATIONS (TAPOTEMENT)

### Classification

The percussive manipulations constitute a series of techniques characterized by various parts of the hand striking the tissues at a fairly rapid rate. Another name for this group of techniques is *tapotement* (from the French word *tapoter:* to tap). The hands usually work alternately, and the wrists are kept flexible so that the movements are light, springy, and stimulating. In the majority of cases these strokes aim to stimulate the tissues, either by direct mechanical means or by reflex actions. Four distinct types of percussive manipulation are discussed in this section: clapping, beating, hacking, and pounding.

### *Clapping*

#### Definition

Clapping is a one-handed or two-handed technique in which the cupped hands strike the skin surface rapidly, compressing the air and causing a vibration wave to penetrate into the tissues.

#### Purpose

Clapping is designed to stimulate the tissues by direct mechanical action. When performed over the ribs and lungs, the mechanical waves help to loosen secretions. Brisk, light clapping performed over muscle tissue stimulates muscle activity by direct mechanical activation of muscle spindle afferents, together with activation of the mechanoreceptors in the skin.

#### Basic Technique and Direction of Movement

Clapping is performed with alternate movements of the wrists, so that the palmar surfaces of the loosely cupped hands strike the tissues at a rapid rate. Figure 4-18 shows the position of the cupped hand. Movements of the cupped hands are produced by alternate flexion and extension of the wrists and *not* by flexion and extension of the elbows. It is important that both arms be held fairly straight but as relaxed as possible, as this position permits rapid wrist movements. The hands move back and forth over the muscle or area to be treated. Clapping may also be performed as a one-handed technique, and this is quite useful for small areas, perhaps on a child. A modification of the technique can even be performed on infants using rapid alternation of the finger pads of the index and middle finger (see Chapter 10).

#### Rate of Movement

Clapping is performed rapidly because the goal is to stimulate the tissues. The actual rate is determined by the therapist's ability to coordinate wrist movements, but it should be as fast as is comfortable for patient and therapist.

#### Depth and Pressure

Clapping is a stroke that is usually performed rapidly but lightly. This is why it is performed with wrist movements rather than elbow flexion and extension. Pressure can be increased, however, especially when treating large muscles or a patient with a large thorax.

#### Variations

***Finger Pad Clapping.*** A modified clapping technique can be performed on the neonate, using just the finger pads of the index and middle fingers. The two fingers are held straight, but fairly relaxed. The technique is one of rapid alternation of flexion and extension of the metacarpophalangeal joints, keeping the fingers straight. Only the pads of the two fingers touch the chest wall. The technique is rapid, with extremely light pressure to the chest wall (see Chapter 10). Figures 4-19 and 4-20 illustrate clapping to the thigh muscles and the posterior and lateral chest wall, respectively. These techniques are also demonstrated on the DVD (see DVD Chapters 4-9, 4-29, and 4-44).

D

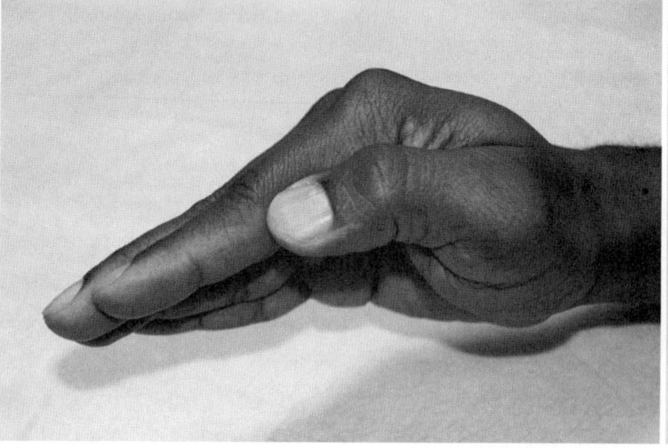

A

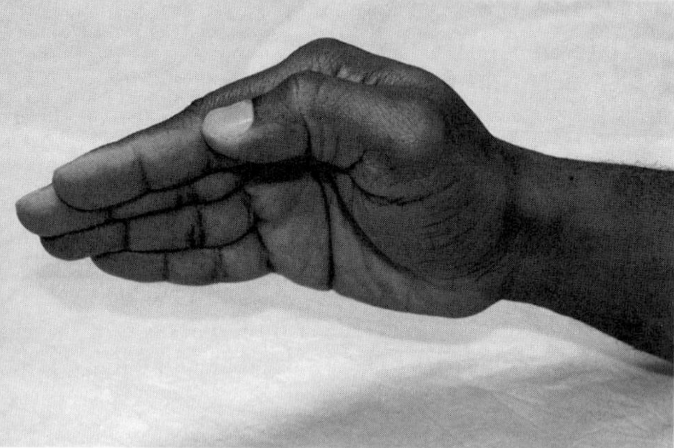

B

**Figure 4-18 The Cupped Hand Position Used to Perform Clapping**

**A, B,** Two views of the basic hand position for the clapping stroke. The hand is cupped by flexing the metacarpophalangeal joints (knuckles) and extending all the other joints in the fingers. The thumb is held close to the side to form part of the edge of the cup. As the hand strikes the tissues, the air trapped in the cup is compressed slightly, setting up a vibrating wave that travels into the tissues (i.e., the mechanical stimulus is transferred into the tissues). On no account should the fingers be held stiffly, as this produces a stinging or slapping effect. Instead, each hand is held closed but relaxed in the cupped position. See also DVD Chapters 4-7, 4-29, and 4-44.

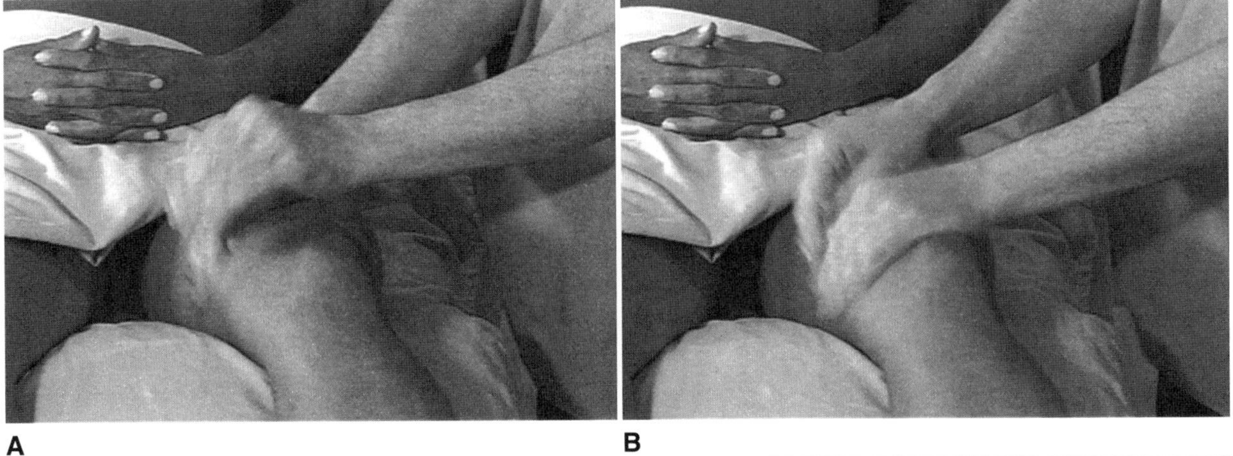


**Figure 4-19 Clapping to the Thigh Muscles**

The therapist stands at right angles to the long axis of the muscles to be treated. With the elbows held slightly flexed, the cupped hands alternately strike the skin surface, moving back and forth along the length of the muscle. Note that the flexion and extension occurs at the therapist's wrists rather than the elbow joints. See also DVD Chapters 4-29 and 4-44.

DVD **CLAPPING**

| BODY PART | DVD CHAPTER |
|---|---|
| Posterior thorax | 4-9 |
| Lateral thorax | 4-11 |
| Posterior aspects of the inner thigh | 4-29 |
| Anterior aspects of the inner thigh | 4-44 |

### *Beating*

**Definition**

Beating is a one-handed or two-handed technique in which the therapist's loosely flexed fingers and palm of each hand strike the part to be treated in rapid succession.

**Purpose**

Beating is similar to clapping and is designed to stimulate the tissues by direct mechanical action. Although it is similar to clapping, beating is more stimulating because the hand is closed. It can be particularly useful for stimulating the large muscles in the lower limbs.

**Basic Technique and Direction of Movement**

Beating is performed in such a way that the hand position is very similar to clapping, except that the fingers are flexed at the middle interphalangeal joints. In effect, the fingers of the cupped hands are simply closed. This means that the dorsal aspect of the middle and distal phalanges of the fingers and the heel of the hand make contact with the tissues. Beating is usually performed by alternately flexing and extending the wrists, not the elbows, while the rest of the arms are as relaxed as possible. The hands move along the body part being treated so as to cover the entire area involved.

**Rate of Movement**

Beating is performed rapidly because it aims to stimulate. The rate used should be comfortable for the patient and sustainable for the therapist.

**Depth and Pressure**

Beating is a stroke that is performed rapidly and with rather more pressure than clapping, because it is a more stimulating stroke. The pressure applied will vary according to the body part and the patient being treated. Figure 4-21 and the DVD illustrate beating to the inner thigh muscles (see DVD Chapter 4-45).

### *Hacking*

**Definition**

Hacking is a one-handed or two-handed stroke in which the lateral edges and dorsal surfaces of the fingers strike the skin surface in rapid succession to create a strong, stimulating effect.

**Purpose**

Hacking is used to stimulate the skin and subcutaneous tissue and both deep and superficial muscle tissue.

**Basic Technique and Direction of Movement**

The therapist, standing at right angles to the long axis of the muscles to be treated, flexes the elbows and abducts the shoulders so that the forearms are nearly horizontal, with the wrists near full extension (a praying position). The movement is a rapid alternation between pronation and supination of the forearms with the hands working out of phase with each other. It is the ulnar borders and dorsal surfaces of the third, fourth, and fifth fingers that actually strike the skin surface. The hands move back and forth along the muscles being treated.

The most common mistake in the performance of hacking is to flex and extend the elbows rather than to rotate the forearms. This can easily produce discomfort for the patient because the fingers strike the tissues too forcefully. During the movement, the hands almost touch each other. It is

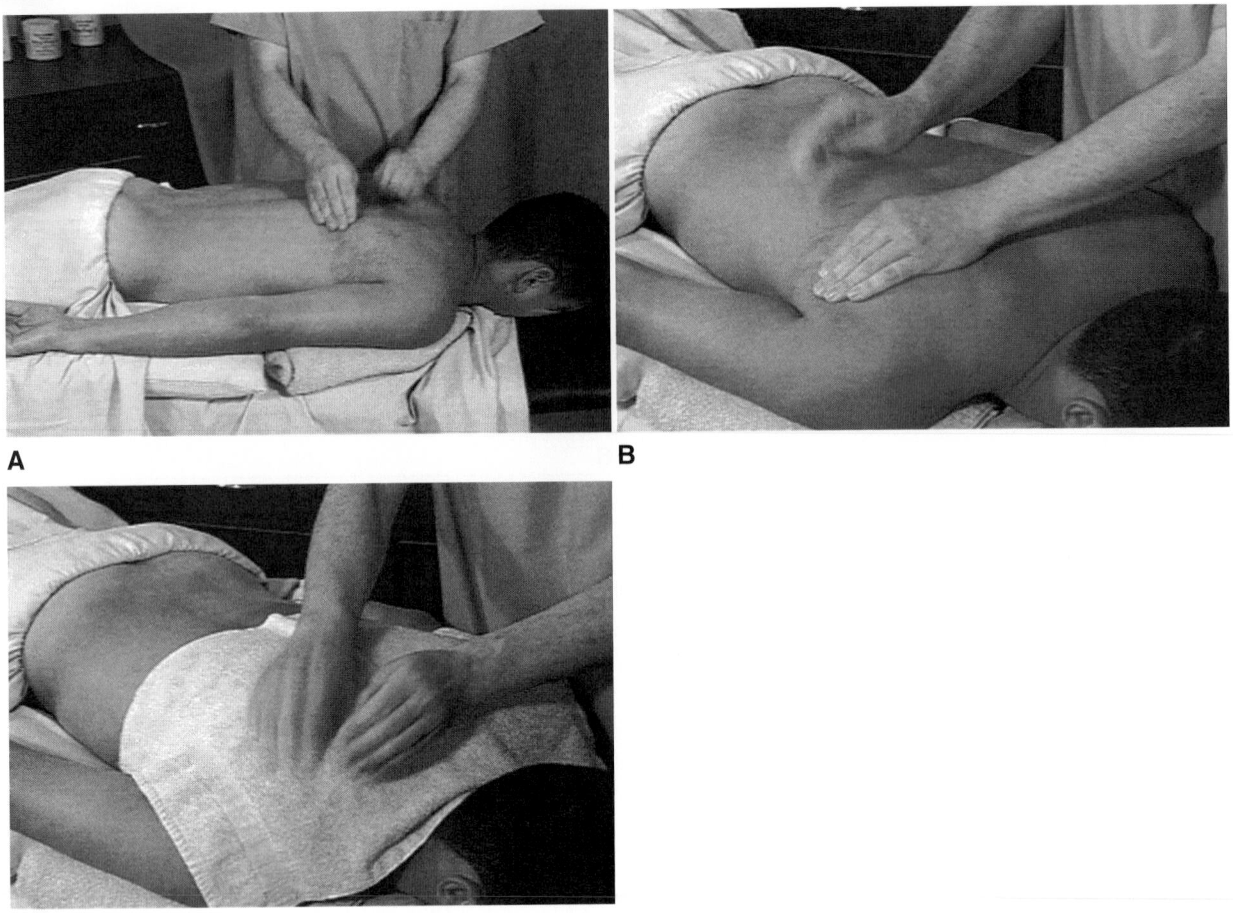

A

B

C

Figure **4-20** Clapping over the Posterior Chest Wall

The therapist stands at right angles to the long axis of the thorax. With the elbows held slightly flexed, the cupped hands alternately strike the skin surface **(A, B)** and move back and forth across the chest wall, over the lungs. Again, movement is produced by flexion and extension at the wrists rather than the elbow joints. This technique may also be performed over a folded towel **(C).** This dampens the effect of the stroke, allowing the therapist to exert greater pressure without causing a "slapping" sensation on the skin surface. The technique is used to help to loosen secretions in the lungs. See also Chapter 10 for more details and DVD Chapter 4-9. See also DVD Chapter 4-11 for a demonstration of the same technique to the lateral chest wall.

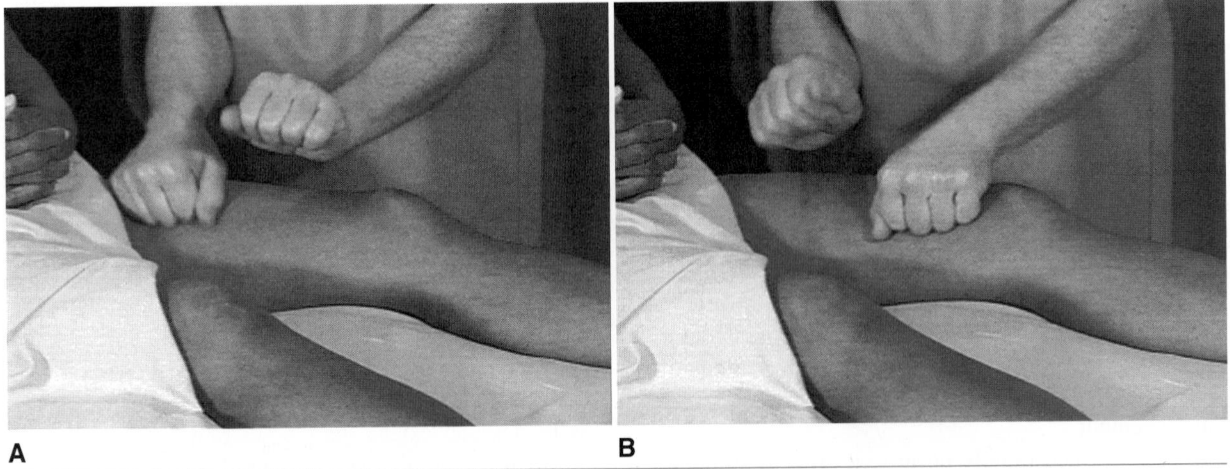

A

B

Figure **4-21** Beating to the Anterior Thigh Muscles

The basic alternating wrist action (flexion and extension) in beating is illustrated. The stroke is performed quite rapidly and with a little more pressure than that used with clapping. See also DVD Chapter 4-45.

important for the fingers and hand to be relaxed during the stroke; otherwise the fingers strike the skin surface with a degree of rigidity, causing an uncomfortable sensation for the patient. The manipulation is performed across the muscle fibers, and bony areas are carefully avoided.

Hacking is usually performed with two hands, but it can be done with only one. This variation might be useful in the treatment of small muscles, when it is difficult to fit two hands into the area. Figure 4-22 illustrates the basic hand positions for hacking to the anterior thigh muscles.

**Rate of Movement**

This is a difficult stroke to master because it has to be performed as rapidly as possible. It requires considerable coordination of effort, and it is better to perform it correctly at slower speeds than faster but incorrectly.

**Depth and Pressure**

Hacking must be performed rapidly but lightly. There is no pressure other than the weight of the relaxed fingers striking the skin surface in rapid succession. This produces a characteristic sound, as each finger is clearly audible as it strikes the surface.

Hacking is demonstrated on the DVD (see DVD Chapter 4-30), and viewers can hear the characteristic sound. The video is deliberately slowed down during part of the technique so that the hands are more visible as they strike the skin surface.

**DVD HACKING**

| BODY PART | DVD CHAPTER |
|---|---|
| Posterior aspects of the inner thigh | 4-30 |
| Anterior aspects of the inner thigh | 4-46 |

**Variations**

***Ulnar Border Hacking.*** This variation of hacking is performed in a similar way but uses the ulnar border of the hand and fifth digit on large fleshy areas for a deeper effect. This variation is similar to pounding, except that the fingers are held in extension, whereas in pounding they are flexed.

***Point Hacking.*** Only the fingertips are used to carry out this technique; typically the therapist uses only a single hand, but a two-handed technique can be performed. The very tips (points) of the slightly flexed fingers strike the skin surface when the wrist is alternately flexed and extended. It is used mainly on the face, but it could be used on any small area (perhaps on a child) where regular hacking was difficult to perform.

### *Pounding*

**Definition**

Pounding is a stimulating manipulation in which the ulnar borders of the loosely clenched and extended fists, alternately and in rapid succession, strike the part to be treated.

**Purpose**

Pounding is another of the stimulating strokes. It is somewhat deeper than hacking, as the hands are lightly clenched and the ulnar borders are used to strike the tissues. This pounding motion allows greater depth to the stroke.

**Basic Technique and Direction of Movement**

Pounding is a stroke that in many ways looks similar to hacking. The therapist stands at right angles to the long axis of the muscles to be treated, with elbows flexed and shoulders abducted so that the forearms are nearly horizontal. The wrists are comfortably held near full extension. The

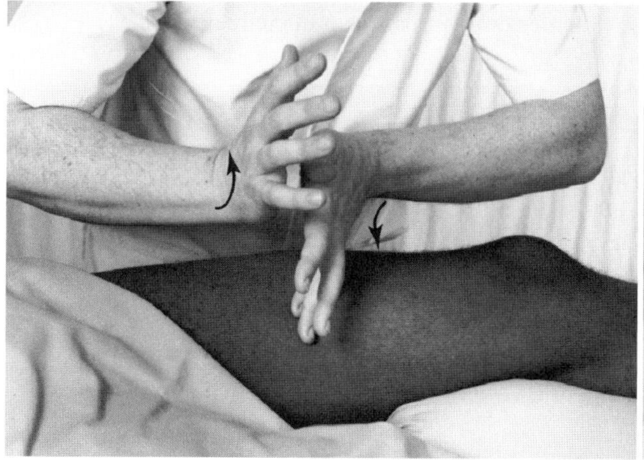

A

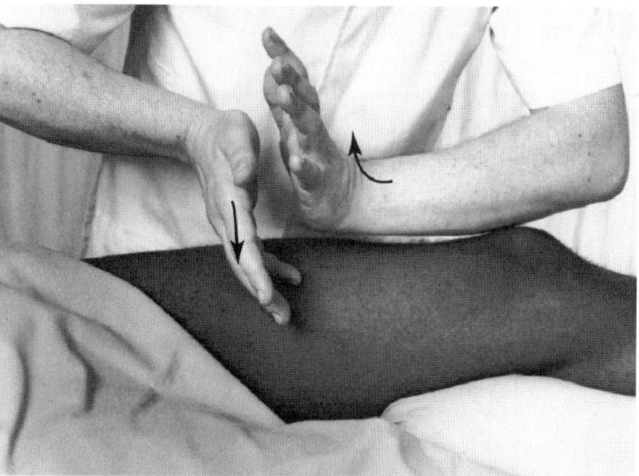

B

**Figure 4-22 Hacking to the Anterior Thigh Muscles**

The therapist stands at right angles to the long axis of the muscles to be treated. The forearms are nearly horizontal, and the wrists are almost fully extended. The movement is a rapid alternation between pronation and supination of the forearms with the hands working out of phase with each other. The lateral and dorsal surfaces of the third, fourth, and fifth fingers strike the skin surface one after the other, producing a characteristic sound. The hands move back and forth along the muscles to be treated. See also DVD Chapter 4-30.

movement consists of rapid alternation of pronation and supination of the forearms, with the hands working out of phase with each other. Unlike hacking, the fists are loosely clenched, and it is the ulnar borders of the hands and fifth digits that actually strike the skin surface. The hands move back and forth along the muscles to be treated. Figure 4-23 illustrates the hand positions for the technique of pounding.

**Rate of Movement**

The movement should be as rapid as the coordination of the therapist's hands allow; however, good technique should not be sacrificed for speed.

**Depth and Pressure**

Because the therapist uses the ulnar borders of his or her hands to strike the surface, this can be a much deeper stroke than hacking. It is therefore suitable for stimulating large, deep muscle masses. Pounding is also demonstrated in DVD Chapter 4-47.

DVD

## Primary Effects of Percussive Manipulations (Tapotement)

The therapeutic effects of the percussive manipulations (tapotement) are produced mainly through a direct mechanical impact on the tissues. In addition, important reflex effects are mediated through the sensory nervous system, especially in the skin and muscles. When performed properly, the percussion strokes have the following primary effects:

- Stimulation of mechanoreceptors in skin, muscle, and tendons, which facilitates muscle contraction
- Stimulation of the circulation of blood and lymph in superficial and deep muscle tissue
- Loosening of mucus in the lungs
- Pain relief as a result of stimulation of mechanoreceptors in the skin (pain gating)
- Dilation of the superficial arterioles through the axon reflex, thereby stimulating the superficial circulation
- Increased blood and lymph flow in the skin and subcutaneous tissues, which in turn produces a slight increase in skin temperature

## Therapeutic Uses of Percussive Manipulations (Tapotement)

When included in a treatment sequence, percussive manipulations can be used to do the following:

- Increase blood and lymphatic flow in the skin and subcutaneous tissues
- Stimulate the circulation of the superficial and deep muscle, thereby facilitating healing
- Relieve pain and muscle spasm, thereby promoting relaxation
- Loosen mucus in the lungs, thereby assisting with expectoration
- Facilitate muscle contraction and reeducation of function
- Relieve neuralgic pain following amputation, trauma, or another pathology
- Stimulate organ function

## Indications for the Use of Percussive Manipulations (Tapotement)

Percussive manipulations may be indicated as part of a treatment plan to help relieve or reduce the effects of the following conditions:

- Weak muscle contraction, or difficulty in initiating muscle activity associated with various neurological disorders
- Chronic pain (especially that associated with damage to nerves or disturbances of the circulation)

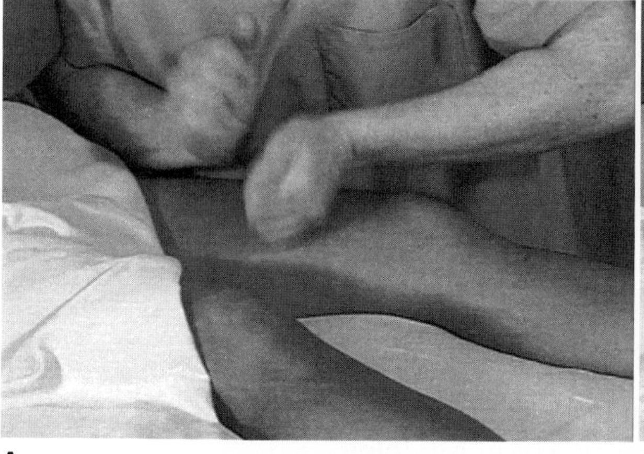

A

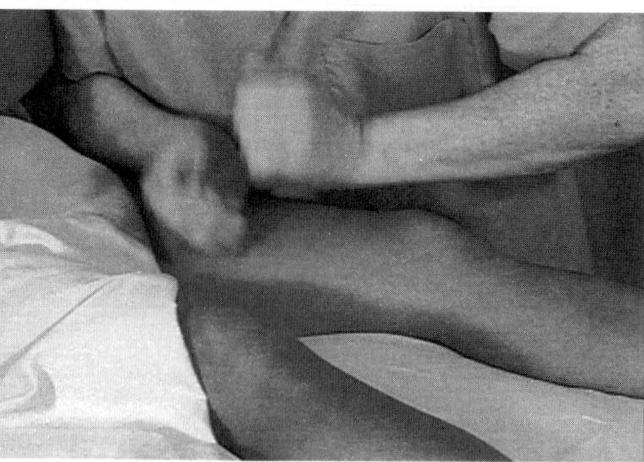

B

**Figure 4-23 Pounding to the Anterior Thigh Muscles**

The basic alternating wrist action in pounding is illustrated. The action is similar to hacking, except that the fingers are loosely flexed. The stroke is performed quite rapidly, moving back and forth along the muscles being treated, with a little more pressure than that used with clapping. See also DVD Chapter 4-47.

- Respiratory disorders associated with mucus retention, such as cystic fibrosis and bronchiectasis

### Contraindications to the Use of Percussive Manipulations (Tapotement)

The general concept of contraindications is covered in Chapter 3. As a technique, percussive manipulations may be contraindicated when any of the situations listed in Table 4-6 are present.

Table 4-6 **Main Contraindications to the Use of Percussive Manipulations**

| Contraindication | |
|---|---|
| Large open areas (e.g., burns or wounds) in the areas to be treated, especially if they are infected | A |
| Severe rib fractures (flail chest); only very fine, gentle vibrations may be used in the presence of a rib fracture | A |
| Over the thorax in cases of acute heart failure, especially if coronary thrombosis or embolism is involved | A |
| Over the thorax in cases of acute pulmonary embolism | A |
| Over the thorax in cases of severe hypertension | A |
| Cancer in the skin or any other tissue in the area to be treated | A |
| Serious infections in the tissues to be treated (tuberculosis, septic arthritis, etc.) | A |
| Gross edema in the areas to be treated if there seems to be a possibility of splitting the skin | A |
| Lacerations, bruising, infections, or foreign bodies (e.g., glass, grit, metal) in the skin or other tissues in the area to be treated | A |
| Arterial or venous pathology (especially thrombophlebitis and deep vein thrombosis) in the areas to be treated | A |
| Acute muscle tears in the areas to be treated (especially deep intramuscular hematomas) | A |
| Hyper- or hypotonic (spastic or flaccid) limbs in the areas to be treated (very gentle massage only) | U |
| Over newly formed scar tissue in the areas to be treated | U |
| Chronic swelling in the lower limb in the areas to be treated, associated with severe congestive cardiac failure or any other heart condition with which lower limb edema is associated | U |
| Acute or chronic skin conditions affecting the areas to be treated (e.g., psoriasis, eczema, or dermatitis) | U |
| Marked varicosities in the areas to be treated if damage to the vein wall might result | U |
| On bony regions in the areas to be treated, in very thin patients | U |
| Within 3 to 6 months following radiation therapy in the area to be treated (skin is usually hypersensitive) | U |
| Areas of hyperesthesia in the areas to be treated (i.e., those very sensitive/ticklish to touch) | R |
| Extremely hairy areas in the areas to be treated (if treatment causes pain) | R |

*A,* Always contraindicated; *U,* usually contraindicated; *R,* rarely contraindicated.

## VIBRATION AND SHAKING

### Vibration

#### *Definition*

Vibration is a one-handed or two-handed technique in which a fine shaking (tremor-like) movement is conveyed to the tissues by the hand or fingertips.

#### *Purpose*

Vibration is a stroke designed primarily to help loosen secretions in the lungs. It may also be used as a stimulating technique over muscle tissue, as it can stimulate muscle afferents.

#### *Basic Technique and Direction of Movement*

When given over the thorax to loosen and remove lung secretions, the hands may be placed successively over each of the various lung segments. In each case, the hands are placed lightly on the appropriate part of the thorax, with the elbows slightly flexed but relaxed. The patient is instructed to breathe in, during which time the therapist gives slight resistance to the inspiration. As the patient breathes out, the therapist vibrates both hands while simultaneously compressing the ribs to assist expiration. The technique may also be performed using a single hand if appropriate, in which case it is done in the same basic manner (see Chapter 10 for more details). Figure 4-24 illustrates the hand positions for the technique of vibrations applied to the thorax (see also DVD Chapters 4-10 and 4-12).

When vibration is used to stimulate muscle, each hand is placed as lightly as possible on the muscle with sufficient pressure to lightly grip the skin surface. The vibratory stimulus is delivered with the entire hand, but the fingertips focus much of the effort to the desired muscle. The technique can be performed with either or both hands, depending on the size of the muscle to be stimulated. When the technique is used to stimulate small muscles, the vibrations can be applied using just the fingertips.

#### *Rate of Movement*

The vibrations are performed as rapidly as possible, and the speed is limited by the therapist's ability to coordinate his or her hand movements.

#### *Depth and Pressure*

Vibrations are usually rather fine in quality. The hand pressure applied to the chest to resist inspiration and assist expiration will vary greatly, depending on the patient's tolerance and respiratory condition.

When stimulating muscles with vibration, the weight of the hand provides most of the pressure applied to the tissues.

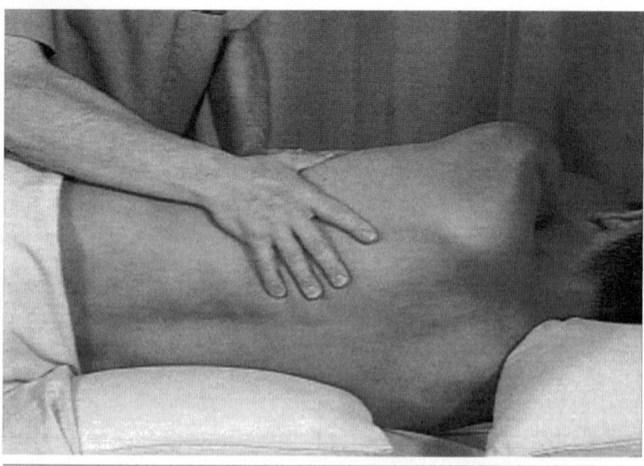

**Figure 4-24 Vibration to the Lateral Chest Wall**

In this example, the patient is in the side-lying position. The therapist's hands are placed on the lateral chest wall with the fingers spread widely so that the palms of the hands are about level with the eighth rib in the midaxillary line. Slight resistance is given as the patient breathes in, and a fine vibratory movement is imparted only as the patient breathes out. A similar technique to vibration is called *shaking*. It is performed in exactly the same way, except that the vibrations are somewhat coarser and therefore much slower in rate. See Chapter 10 for more details and DVD Chapters 4-10 and 4-12 for a demonstration of these techniques.

## Shaking

### *Definition*

Shaking is a one-handed or two-handed technique, similar to vibration but with much slower speed and greater amplitude of movement conveyed to the tissues by the hand(s).

### *Purpose*

Shaking is a vigorous stroke designed primarily to help loosen secretions from the lungs. It is similar to vibration but is usually performed more coarsely than vibrations. It may also be used as a stimulating technique over muscle tissue, as it can stimulate a stretch reflex.

### *Basic Technique and Direction of Movement*

Shaking is performed in the same basic manner as vibration, except that it is much slower with greater amplitude of chest movement. When performed over the thorax, the therapist places his or her hands over the appropriate lung segments. In each case, the hands are placed lightly on the thorax, with the elbows slightly flexed but relaxed. The patient is instructed to breathe in, during which time the therapist gives slight resistance to the inspiration. As the patient breathes out, the therapist shakes both hands several times while simultaneously compressing the ribs to assist expiration. The technique may also be performed using a single hand if appropriate, in which case it is done in the same basic manner (see Chapter 10 for more details).

When shaking is used to stimulate muscle, the hand is placed on the muscle with sufficient pressure to lightly grip the skin surface. A series of slow, fairly deep pushing strokes are delivered with the entire hand, with the fingertips held straight in order to focus the effort to the desired muscle. The technique can be performed with either or both hands, depending on the size of the muscle to be stimulated.

### *Rate of Movement*

Shaking is performed at a slow rate because the movement is coarse compared with the technique of vibration. About three to five shakes per second are typically delivered during each stoke.

### *Depth and Pressure*

Shaking is a more vigorous stroke than the vibration technique. Significantly more pressure is applied during the shaking of the chest, and therefore the amplitude of each movement is increased. The pressure applied is always within the patient's tolerance.

This basic technique for vibration and shaking is demonstrated on the DVD (see DVD Chapters 4-10 and 4-12).

**VIBRATIONS AND SHAKING**

| BODY PART | DVD CHAPTER |
|---|---|
| Posterior thorax | 4-10 |
| Lateral thorax | 4-12 |

## Primary Effects of Vibration and Shaking

The therapeutic effects of vibration and shaking are produced mainly through a direct mechanical impact on the tissues. In addition, important reflex effects are mediated through the sensory nervous system, especially in the skin and muscles. When performed properly, these strokes have the following primary effects:

- Stimulation of mechanoreceptors in skin, muscle, and tendons, which facilitates muscle contraction
- Loosening of mucus in the lungs
- Pain relief as a result of stimulation of mechanoreceptors in the skin (pain gating)
- Movement of gases when applied over the stomach and intestine

## Therapeutic Uses of Vibration and Shaking

When included in a treatment sequence, vibration and shaking can be used to do the following:

- Loosen mucus in the lungs, thereby assisting with expectoration
- Facilitate muscle contraction and reeducation of function
- Relieve neuralgic pain following amputation, trauma, or another pathology
- Reduce spasticity when applied longitudinally to a limb while simultaneously applying traction in the long axis
- Stimulate organ function

- Relieve flatulence
- Resolve chronic edema (a mechanical vibrator may be more useful in the relief of chronic edema)

### Indications for the Use of Vibration and Shaking

Percussive manipulations may be indicated as part of a treatment plan to help relieve or reduce the effects of the following conditions:

- Respiratory disorders associated with mucus retention, such as cystic fibrosis and bronchiectasis
- Weak muscle contraction, or difficulty in initiating muscle activity associated with various neurological disorders
- Chronic pain, especially that associated with damage to nerves or disturbances of the circulation
- Chronic problems with flatulence

### Contraindications to the Use of Vibration and Shaking

The general concept of contraindications is covered in Chapter 3. As a technique, vibration or shaking may be contraindicated when any of the situations listed in Table 4-7 are present.

Table 4-7 **Main Contraindications to the Use of Vibration and Shaking**

| Contraindication | |
|---|---|
| Large open areas (e.g., burns or wounds) in the areas to be treated, especially if they are infected | A |
| Severe rib fractures (flail chest): only very fine, gentle vibrations may be used in the presence of a rib fracture | A |
| Over the thorax in cases of acute heart failure, especially if coronary thrombosis or embolism is involved | A |
| Over the thorax in cases of acute pulmonary embolism | A |
| Over the thorax in cases of severe hypertension | A |
| Cancer in the skin or any other tissue in the area to be treated | A |
| Serious infections in the tissues to be treated (tuberculosis, septic arthritis, etc.) | A |
| Gross edema in the areas to be treated if there seems to be a possibility of splitting the skin | A |
| Lacerations, bruising, infections, or foreign bodies (e.g., glass, grit, metal) in the skin or other tissues in the area to be treated | A |
| Arterial or venous pathology (especially thrombophlebitis and deep vein thrombosis) in the areas to be treated | A |
| Acute muscle tears (especially deep intramuscular hematomas) in the areas to be treated | A |
| Chronic swelling in the lower limb in the areas to be treated, associated with severe congestive cardiac failure or any other heart condition with which lower limb edema is associated | U |
| Acute or chronic skin conditions affecting the areas to be treated (e.g., psoriasis, eczema, or dermatitis) | U |
| Marked varicosities in the areas to be treated if damage to the vein wall might result | U |
| On bony regions in the areas to be treated, in very thin patients | U |
| Within 3 to 6 months following radiation therapy in the area to be treated (skin is usually hypersensitive) | U |
| Areas of hyperesthesia (i.e., those very sensitive/ticklish to touch) in the areas to be treated | R |
| Extremely hairy areas (if treatment causes pain) in the areas to be treated | R |

*A*, Always contraindicated; *U*, usually contraindicated; *R*, rarely contraindicated.

## DEEP FRICTIONS (CYRIAX FRICTIONS)

Deep friction massage differs from the manipulations described previously. In effect, it is a massage system in itself, although it is designed principally to affect the connective tissues of tendons, tendon sheaths, ligaments, muscles, and other subcutaneous tissues. The most famous modern exponent of deep friction massage was James Cyriax, and his writings on the subject have become the established standards for the techniques (Chamberlain 1982; Cyriax, 1960; Cyriax & Coldham, 1984; Hammer, 1993).

Deep frictions are particularly useful for treating localized, chronic musculoskeletal lesions. The technique aims at mobilizing scar tissue secondary to fibrositis or trauma, as it is often painful and immobile. All of the soft tissues of the body have their own natural mobility and elasticity. This may be impaired by any local organization of fibrous tissue (scar tissue). The production and organization of fibrous tissue is the inevitable result of trauma or a rheumatic inflammatory process that does not heal properly. The result will likely be a painful loss of joint and limb function, which may eventually lead to deformity if untreated.

Deep frictions have a reputation for being painful for the patient, and this can certainly be the case. After several minutes of treatment, however, patients often feel very little discomfort or pain. Producing pain in the patient for therapeutic purposes is a time-honored concept (counterirritation) and can be a useful strategy. Painful stimulation is a well-known technique for the treatment of chronic pain (Quinn et al., 2002), particularly that associated with myofascial pain syndromes. It can be achieved using electrical stimulation or manual techniques. In fact, deep frictions are an excellent example of a manual treatment that produces an effective, if painful, response that triggers a resolution of chronic inflammation. If the patient cannot tolerate the initial discomfort of deep frictions, a few minutes of ice cube massage over the area can numb the skin and help the patient overcome the initial difficulty with the treatment.

## Classification and Definition

Deep frictions consist of small, accurately localized, deeply penetrating movements performed to specific structures. Therapists usually perform these deep strokes with their fingertips, though the thumb pad or palm can also be used. There are two basic types of deep friction stroke: transverse frictions and circular frictions. Transverse frictions consist of a series of short, deep strokes performed transversely across the fibers of the target tissue (see DVD Chapters 4-54 and 4-67). Circular frictions consist of a series or three or four deep circular movements performed on the same spot, gradually getting deeper into the tissues (see DVD Chapter 4-8).

## Purpose

Deep frictions are designed to mobilize tendons, tendon sheaths, ligaments, joint capsules, and muscle tissue, particularly when chronic adhesions or inflammation is present.

## Basic Technique and Direction of Movement

To obtain the firm contact with the skin that is necessary to apply deep friction movements, it is important that *no* lubricant be used. Deep friction movements over dry, scaly scar tissue should be applied without a lubricant, and when the treatment is completed, a small amount of lubricant should be applied to the area with stroking movements. The two types of friction strokes are quite different and will be described separately.

### *Transverse Frictions*

Transverse frictions are always performed at right angles to the long axis of the fibers in the target structures involved (i.e., across the fibers). Typically, the stroke is delivered by the index finger of one hand, reinforced by the tip of the middle finger placed on top. This allows the therapist to focus the necessary pressure to an exact spot during the stroke. Figure 4-25 illustrates the basic position of the fingers for the application of transverse frictions to a small area.

The following points of technique must be emphasized:

- Pressure must be applied to exactly the correct spot.
- Accurate localization of the lesion is essential if the technique is to be successful. A thorough knowledge of anatomy and excellent palpation skills are essential for the therapist.
- The structure to be treated must be placed on full stretch. The structure to be treated is usually a tendon, ligament, joint capsule, or muscle. Placing it on maximal stretch requires accurate anatomical knowledge and understanding of the applied biomechanics of the involved tissues.
- The fingers must move with the skin and subcutaneous tissues on the deeper ones. The fingertips and the skin surface must move together on the deeper tissues; otherwise the strokes are ineffective and it is easy to blister the skin. It may be helpful to wash and dry the skin and, if necessary, evaporating spirits may be applied to the part afterward to dry the skin surface even more.

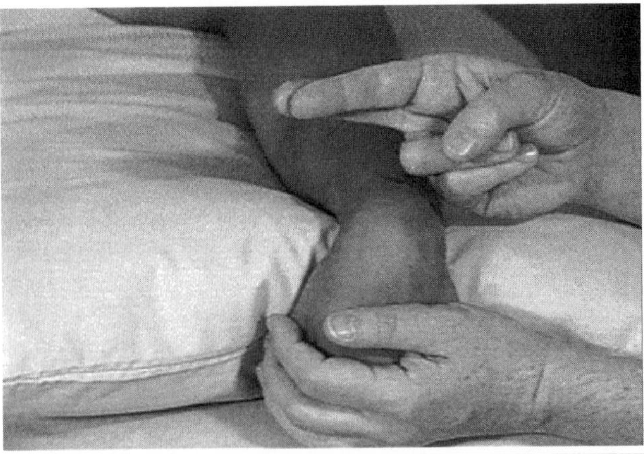

**Figure 4-25 Finger Positions for Transverse Frictions**

The tip of the index finger, reinforced by the pad of the middle finger, is usually used to apply pressure in this technique. Pressure is then exerted with these fingers in a series of pulling or pushing motions delivered at right angles to the fibers of the tissues involved. In most cases, the fingers will need to apply pressure with a curved motion to follow the contours of the limb. See also DVD Chapter 4-54.

- The movement is delivered with a transverse motion across the fibers. It is essential that the movement be performed at right angles to the direction of the fibers. This has been found to be the most effective method of mobilizing striated muscles. In addition, a slight arc of motion across the fibers is desirable, because most of the structures treated are not flat in cross section but curved. As the fingers move across the structure, pressure is usually applied in one direction only, either forward or backward. This produces a series of pulling or pushing strokes (see following figure).

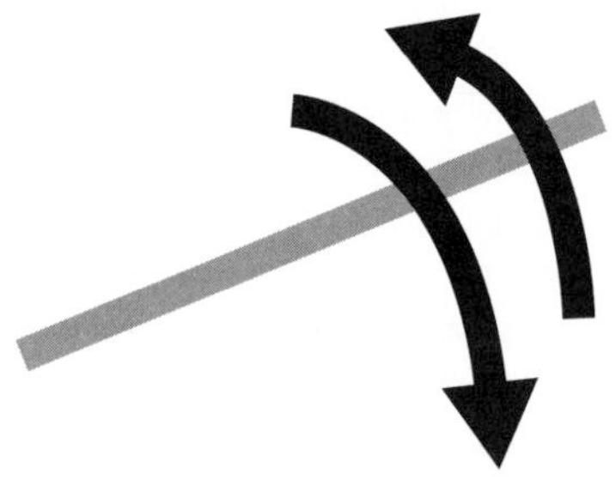


- The movements must have sufficient depth and sweep to reach the target tissue (lesion). This usually requires reinforcement by using two fingers or thumbs, especially when treating a large muscle such as the quadriceps. The strokes should begin lightly, and the pressure should be increased gradually until sufficient depth is reached. If the massage stroke is too localized, the manipulation will be ineffective and often painful. To be effective, it must cover a sufficient area surrounding the lesion as well.

Transverse frictions, properly administered, can be demanding on the terminal joints of the therapist's fingers. The use of a custom-made finger splint may help to prevent problems and to maintain effective treatment (Steward, Woodman, & Hurlburt, 1995). Figures 4-26 through 4-29 depict a variety of applications of transverse frictions. Although deep friction techniques are usually given using the pad of the index finger, reinforced by the middle finger, the stroke can also be given with one thumb alone or reinforced by the other thumb. Because the thumb pad is somewhat larger than the finger pad, it is useful for treating medium-sized muscles, for example, the muscles of the forearm or leg. Deep frictions can also be given with the finger pads of either or both hands. For the treatment of large, deep muscles, a reinforced finger pad technique can be helpful. The finger pads of one hand are placed on the skin overlying the target tissue, and the finger pads of the other hand are simply placed

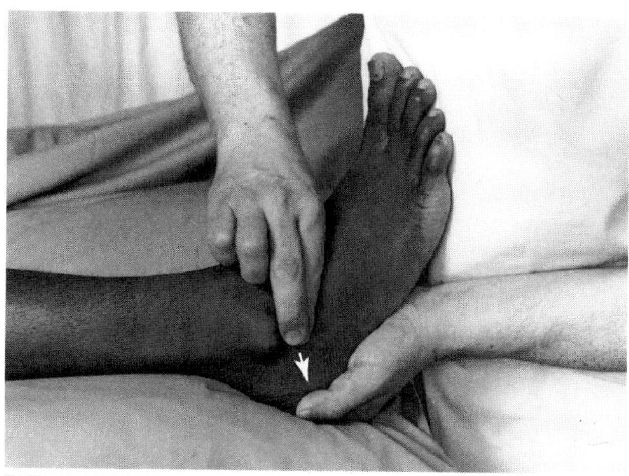

**Figure 4-26 Transverse Frictions to the Lateral Ligament of the Ankle**

The lateral ligament is first put on maximal stretch by inverting the forefoot and calcaneum. In this position, the exact point of tenderness is first determined, and the friction stroke is delivered at right angles to the fibers of the ligament. Pressure gradually increases during each pass across the ligament until significant pressure has been achieved. This gives the stroke its deep effects. In this case, the friction stroke is applied by the index finger and reinforced by the middle one.

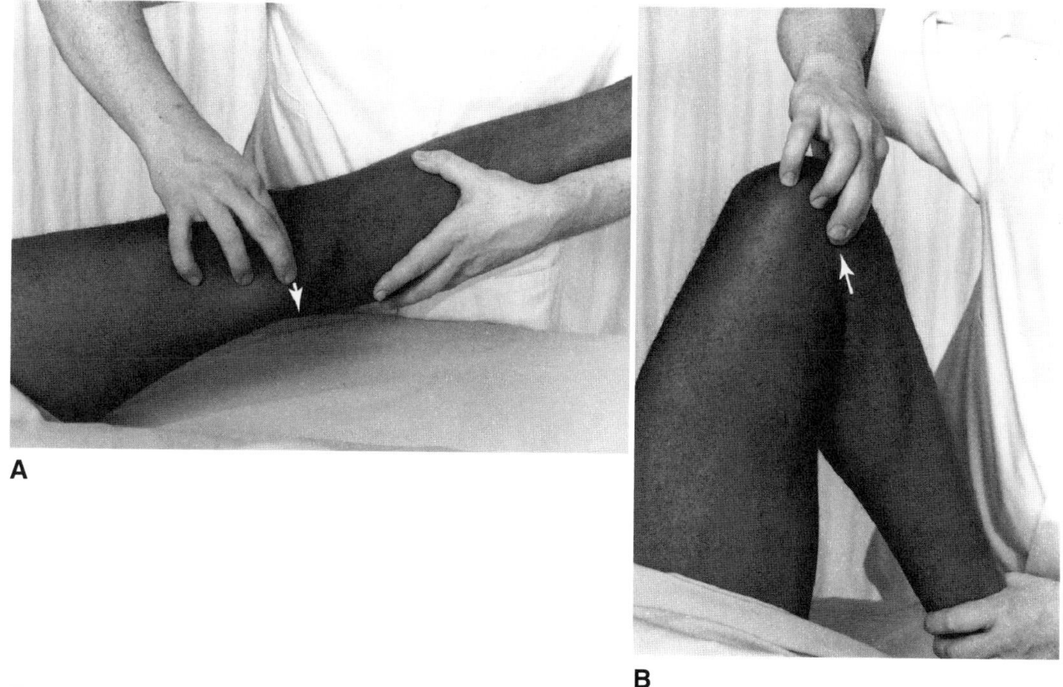


**Figure 4-27 Transverse Frictions to the Medial Ligament of the Knee**

The medial ligament is first put on maximal stretch. In the case of the medial (tibial collateral) ligament of the knee, this can be achieved with the knee in either full extension **(A)** or full flexion **(B)**. In this position, the exact point of tenderness is first determined, and the friction stroke is delivered across the fibers of the ligament. Pressure gradually increases during each pass across the ligament until a significant pressure has been achieved. The stroke is delivered with the index finger and reinforced by the middle one. See also DVD Chapter 4-54.

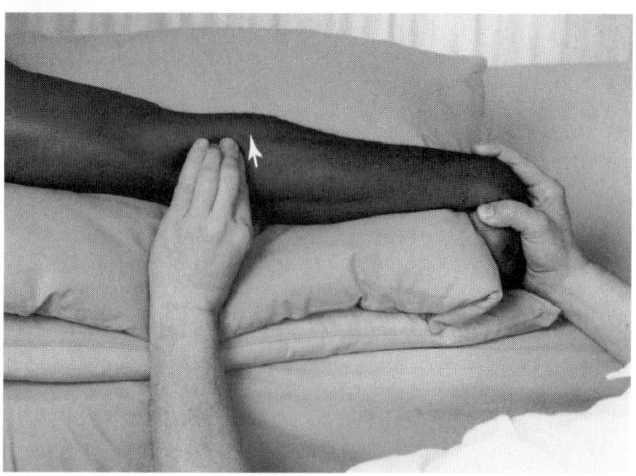

**Figure 4-28 Transverse Frictions to the Common Extensor Origin of the Forearm Muscles**

The common extensor origin is first put on maximal stretch by fully flexing the wrist and fingers with the elbow in extension and full pronation. In this position, the exact point of tenderness is first determined, and the friction stroke is delivered with a curved motion that follows the contours of the arm and is at right angles to the fibers of the tendon. Pressure gradually increases during each pass across the tissues until a significant pressure has been achieved. This gives the stroke its deep effects. In this case, the friction stroke is applied by the index finger and reinforced by the middle one.

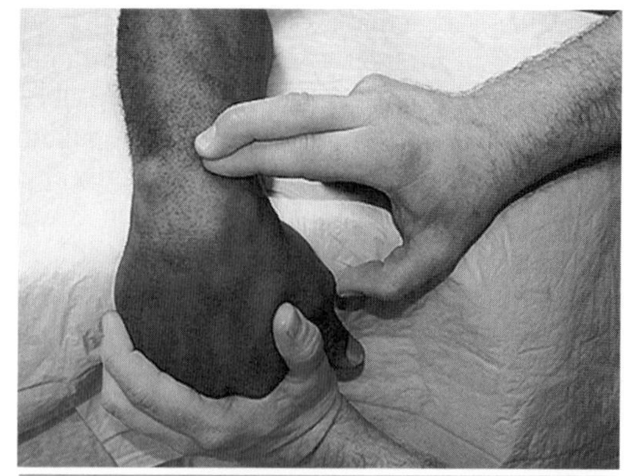

**Figure 4-29 Transverse Frictions to the Extensor Tendons of the Wrist**

The wrist and finger extensor muscles are first put on maximal stretch by fully flexing the wrist and fingers with the elbow in extension and full pronation. In this position, the exact point of tenderness is first determined, and the friction stroke is delivered with a curved motion that follows the contours of the wrist and is at right angles to the fibers of the tendons. Pressure gradually increases during each pass across the tissues until a significant pressure has been achieved. This gives the stroke its deep effects. In this case, the friction stroke is applied by the index finger and reinforced by the middle one. See also DVD Chapter 4-67.

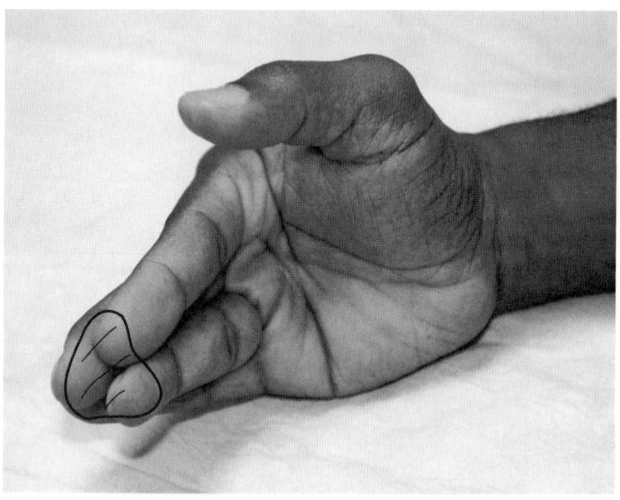

A

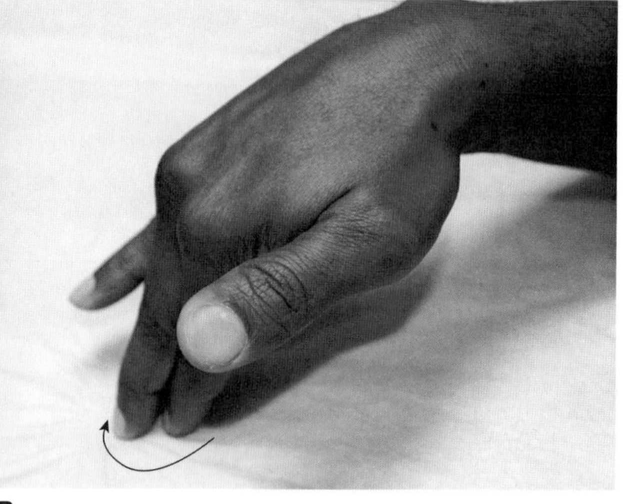

B

**Figure 4-30 Basic Finger Positions for Circular Frictions**

**A,** The tips of the index, middle, and ring fingers are used to form a small tripod-like arrangement. **B,** Pressure is then exerted with these fingers in a series of three or four small circles, each with gradually increasing pressure. See also DVD Chapter 4-8.

on top of them. This allows significant pressure to be exerted on deep muscle when needed (see Chapter 9).

### *Circular Frictions*

Circular frictions are usually performed along the long axis of the fibers in the target structures involved, typically the paraspinal muscles. The tips of the index, middle, and ring fingers form a small tripod, and this is used to perform the stroke. This tripod allows the therapist to exert the necessary pressure during the stroke. Figure 4-30 illustrates the basic position of the fingers for the application of circular frictions to a small area.

The following points of technique must be emphasized:

- Circular frictions may be performed with the tips of the second, third, and fourth digits or with the thumb. The corresponding digits of the other hand may reinforce the fingers if greater depth is required. When the fingertips are used, a small, tripod-like arrangement is made with the tips of the index, middle, and ring fingers, respectively. The index and ring fingertips touch each other, and the middle finger sits on top of them. An alternative technique is for the therapist to use the tip of the index finger reinforced by the middle one.
- The fingers should be pressed obliquely into the tissues before beginning the movement and then should move in very small circles, going slightly deeper with each successive circle of pressure. In this way, the superficial tissues are moved over the deeper ones. When the required depth has been obtained (usually after three or four circles), the pressure is released gradually and the fingers are lifted to an adjacent area so that the manipulation can be repeated.

Figure 4-31 illustrates the basic hand position for circular frictions to the paraspinal region.

## Rate of Movement

Both transverse and circular frictions are performed slowly with a steady rhythm.

## Depth and Pressure

Both transverse and circular frictions are very deep strokes. Significant pressure is applied to a small area of tissue, and it is important that the fingers do not move across the skin, lest a blister result because of the pressure. In both cases, pressure is gradually increased with the first few passes over the tissue being treated. This helps the patient to become accustomed to the sensation. It will be somewhat uncomfortable or even painful but should not be unbearable. An ice cube rubbed over the area for a few minutes may assist some patients if the technique is particularly painful for them. The temporary numbing often allows for the necessary pressure to be applied. Transverse and circular frictions are also demonstrated on the DVD.

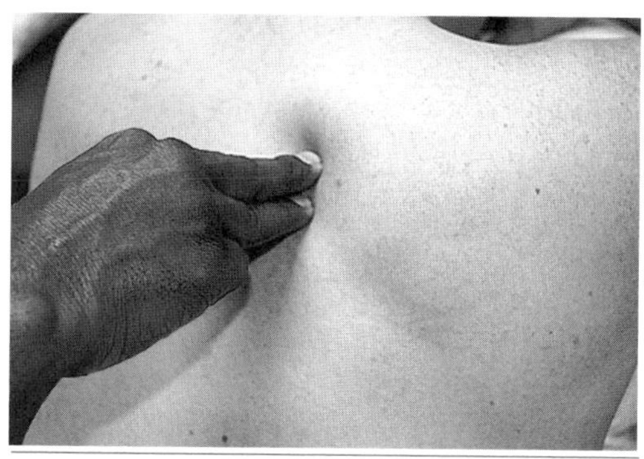

**Figure 4-31 Circular Frictions to the Paraspinal Region**

With the patient comfortably positioned in prone lying, the exact location of the problem area is first determined. The tips of the first three digits are used to form a small tripod-like arrangement. Pressure is applied through the fingertips in a small circular movement, gradually getting deeper. Three or four circles on each tender area are usually sufficient before pausing. The technique can then be repeated several times. The sensation for the patient is expected to be uncomfortable or painful, but not unbearable, at the beginning of treatment. After several minutes, however, the treated area should be somewhat desensitized. See also DVD Chapter 4-8.

**DVD DEEP FRICTIONS**

| BODY PART | DVD CHAPTER |
|---|---|
| Circular frictions to the back | 4-8 |
| Transverse frictions to the medial knee | 4-54 |
| Transverse frictions to the posterior wrist | 4-57 |

## Duration of Treatment

Treatment may last 5 to 20 minutes at each session; this may be repeated two or three times per week for as long as necessary.

## Primary Effects of Deep Frictions

The main effects of deep frictions are produced through a direct mechanical impact on the tissues. In addition, reflex effects are mediated through the sensory nervous system, especially in the skin. When performed properly, the deep frictions have the following primary effects:

- Stretching of posttraumatic scar tissue in muscles, tendons, tendon sheaths, ligaments, and joint capsules
- Local damage to the tissues, causing the liberation of a histamine-like substance (H substance) and other metabolites that act directly on the capillaries and arterioles in the area, causing localized vasodilation
- Vasodilatation producing an increase in the amount of tissue fluid in the local area, which distends the tissues (in effect, the stroke produces a controlled inflammation and at the same time mobilizes the structures that were not moving properly)

## Therapeutic Uses of Deep Frictions

When included in a treatment sequence, deep frictions can be used to do the following:

- Mobilize contractures (scar tissue) in the superficial and deep muscles, tendons, ligaments, joint capsules, and neurovascular bundles

- Increase blood and lymphatic flow in the skin and in superficial and deep muscles
- Promote the absorption of inflammatory exudates (edema) in the subacute and chronic stages of soft tissue injury
- Relieve pain and muscle spasm, thereby promoting relaxation and healing

### Indications for the Use of Deep Frictions

Deep frictions may be indicated as part of a treatment plan to help relieve or reduce the effects of the following conditions:

- Chronic lesions in the skin and subcutaneous tissues, muscles, tendons, tendon sheaths, ligaments, and joint capsules; for example, chronic muscle tears, tendinitis and partial tendon ruptures (tenoperiosteal tears), tenosynovitis, ligament sprains, induration of subcutaneous areas, and scar tissue
- Chronic pain associated with lesions in any of the musculoskeletal tissues
- Chronic superficial scar tissue in the skin and subcutaneous tissue, especially that associated with trauma

### Contraindications to the Use of Deep Frictions

The general concept of contraindications is covered in Chapter 3. As a technique, deep frictions may be contraindicated when any of the situations listed in Table 4-8 are present.

**Table 4-8 Main Contraindications to the Use of Deep Frictions**

| Contraindication | |
|---|---|
| Open areas (e.g., burns or wounds) in the areas to be treated, especially if they are infected | A |
| Cancer in the skin or any other tissue in the area to be treated | A |
| Serious infections in the tissues to be treated (tuberculosis, septic arthritis, etc.) | A |
| Gross edema in the areas to be treated if there seems to be a possibility of splitting the skin | A |
| Lacerations, bruising, infections, or foreign bodies (e.g., glass, grit, metal) in the skin or other tissues in the area to be treated | A |
| Arterial or venous pathology (especially thrombophlebitis and deep vein thrombosis) in the areas to be treated | A |
| Acute muscle tears in the areas to be treated (especially deep intramuscular hematomas) | A |
| Acutely inflamed joint tissues (joints, tendons, ligaments, tendon sheaths, joint capsules, etc.) in the area to be treated | U |
| Hyper- or hypotonic limbs as the areas to be treated (very gentle massage only) | U |
| Acute or chronic skin conditions affecting the areas to be treated (e.g., psoriasis, eczema, or dermatitis) | U |
| Marked varicosities in the areas to be treated if damage to the vein wall might result | U |
| Within 3 to 6 months following radiation therapy in the area to be treated (skin is usually hypersensitive) | U |
| Areas of hyperesthesia in the areas to be treated (i.e., those very sensitive/ticklish to touch) | R |
| Extremely hairy areas in the areas to be treated (if treatment causes pain) | R |

*A,* Always contraindicated; *U,* usually contraindicated; *R,* rarely contraindicated.

## RELAXED PASSIVE MOVEMENTS

### Terminology

Several terms are used interchangeably to describe these techniques. In all cases, the patient should be completely relaxed and play no part in the technique. This is why they are often called *relaxed passive movements.* Passive movements are those that can be performed without the patient being completely relaxed; indeed, it is often difficult for some patients to relax, perhaps because of pain. In this sense then, these patients may actually be helping the movement with a little active contraction of their own. This action could be described as an *assisted passive movement,* indicating that the therapist is producing the majority of the movement and the patient is assisting. Although this seems at first glance to be a reasonable concept, it is not the way passive movements are supposed to be performed.

These techniques are sometimes described as *passive physiological movements* to distinguish them from other types of passive movement, especially *passive accessory joint movements,* also known as *mobilizations.* They are called *passive physiological movements* because they are performed through the normal physiological range of motion present in the joint(s)—that is, the same range of motion that can be produced by active muscle contraction. Although these movements take place at various joint surfaces, they also involve stretching (movement) of the skin and subcutaneous tissues, tendons, ligaments and joint capsules, and neurovascular tissues. In contrast, passive accessory joint movements are performed through a range of motion that is present in a joint but is not under voluntary control, hence the term *accessory.* For example, the metacarpophalangeal joints of the fingers (knuckles) allow several ranges of active movement (i.e., flexion, extension, abduction, adduction, and circumduction). However, in addition to these ranges, the finger can be rotated to the left and right, on its long axis. Other ranges of accessory joint motion can be produced at these joints, but they can only be done passively. Accessory joint movements are also described as *joint play,* as they describe these important extra ranges of motion that are necessary for normal movement to occur in a joint. Of course, accessory ranges of motion in a joint are also physiological in the sense that they are a normal aspect of joint function. In this sense, they are part of the normal design features of the joint. It is just that these ranges are not under the independent control of voluntary muscle action.

Another technique, rightly classified as a specialized type of passive movement, is the so-called manipulation. These specialized techniques are usually performed through a few degrees of motion at the extremes of normal joint ranges. They are usually performed as a forceful, high-velocity thrust and must be carefully localized to be safe and effective. A distinguishing feature between a manipulation and other forms of passive movement relates to the degree of control that the patient has during the procedure. During a manipulation, the movement occurs in such a small range of motion and at such high speed that the patient cannot stop it even if he or she tried. In contrast, the patient is in complete control of all of the other types of passive movement techniques, assuming that the patient does not have paralysis of the appropriate muscles. For example, a patient with a complete brachial plexus lesion resulting in a totally paralyzed (flaccid) limb cannot stop passive movements performed on the arm, because this patient has no voluntary muscle control in the affected limb. Both mobilizations and manipulations form part of the general concept (along with soft tissue manipulations) of modern manual therapy (Grieve, 1994).

Another type of passive movement technique that deserves a brief mention is the so-called continuous passive motion (CPM) technique. In this case, a mechanical device is attached to the limb and moves selected joints through a controlled range of motion. The device can be set to produce the movements at certain speeds and desired ranges of motion, either continuously or intermittently. This treatment concept has been widely used in orthopedic practice, especially following joint replacement surgery. Because of their design characteristics, the relaxed passive movements produced by a CPM device are necessarily limited to restricted ranges of motion in certain joints (Morris, 1995; O'Driscoll & Giori, 2000; Sheppard et al., 1995).

In this text, the general term *relaxed passive movements* will be used to describe techniques with the following characteristics.

### Definition

Relaxed passive movements are slow, stretching movements performed throughout the normal or available physiological range of motion in a joint(s) or body region. Movements are repeated several times, with a gradually increasing degree of motion and sustained overpressure at the end of range.

### Purpose

Relaxed passive movements are designed to stretch out all of the soft tissues associated with a particular joint(s) or limb segment (e.g., the elbow joint, all of the joints in the hand, or the entire upper limb). Repeated stretching of tissues helps to restore lost ranges of motion and maintain normal tissue length and viability.

### Basic Technique and Direction of Movement

With the patient draped and properly supported in an appropriate position, the therapist holds the body parts to be moved in a firm but comfortable grasp. For the upper and lower limbs, movements will typically begin at the large, proximal joints (shoulder and hip) and progress down the limbs to the hands or feet. Three or four repetitions of each movement are performed, wherever possible going from the extreme of one movement to the limit of the opposite one (e.g., from the extreme of flexion to the limit of extension at the elbow). In this case, the elbow joint structures will be appropriately stretched, but the muscles normally affecting movement at both of the joints (biceps and triceps) will not be stretched. To stretch these two-joint muscles, the limb must be put through a combination of ranges (i.e., full flexion at both elbow and shoulder, followed by full extension at both joints). The moving limbs travel through a greater range of motion with each successive repetition, eventually finishing at the point of maximal movement with sustained overpressure. This point in the range must be reached on a consistent basis in order for an increase in the available range to be apparent. The position chosen for this technique will depend on the patient and therapist's preference because relaxed passive movements can be performed with the patient in a wide variety of positions.

### Rate of Movement

Relaxed passive movements should be slow and rhythmic so as to encourage the patient to relax during the procedure. If the patient experiences pain beginning at a certain point in the range, then the therapist should apply the movements up to the point of pain but not beyond. This means that movements are given for the most part in a pain-free range. As the patient relaxes into the movements, the range can be increased.

### Depth and Pressure

Relaxed passive movements should be applied with slight traction to the joints whenever possible but always with a sustained overpressure at the very end of the available range. The overpressure must be applied carefully, especially in those cases where the therapist has a significant mechanical leverage on the joint (e.g., when rotating the shoulder). In such cases, it might be possible to damage joint structures by overstretching or even dislocating them. Induced pain is always a major warning sign and limiting factor. Figures 4-32 to 4-35 show the different hand positions for relaxed passive movements to the neck, upper limb, and lower limb, respectively. The techniques are also demonstrated on the accompanying DVD (see DVD Chapters 4-21, 4-22, 4-55, 4-56, and 4-68).

*Text continued on p. 112.*

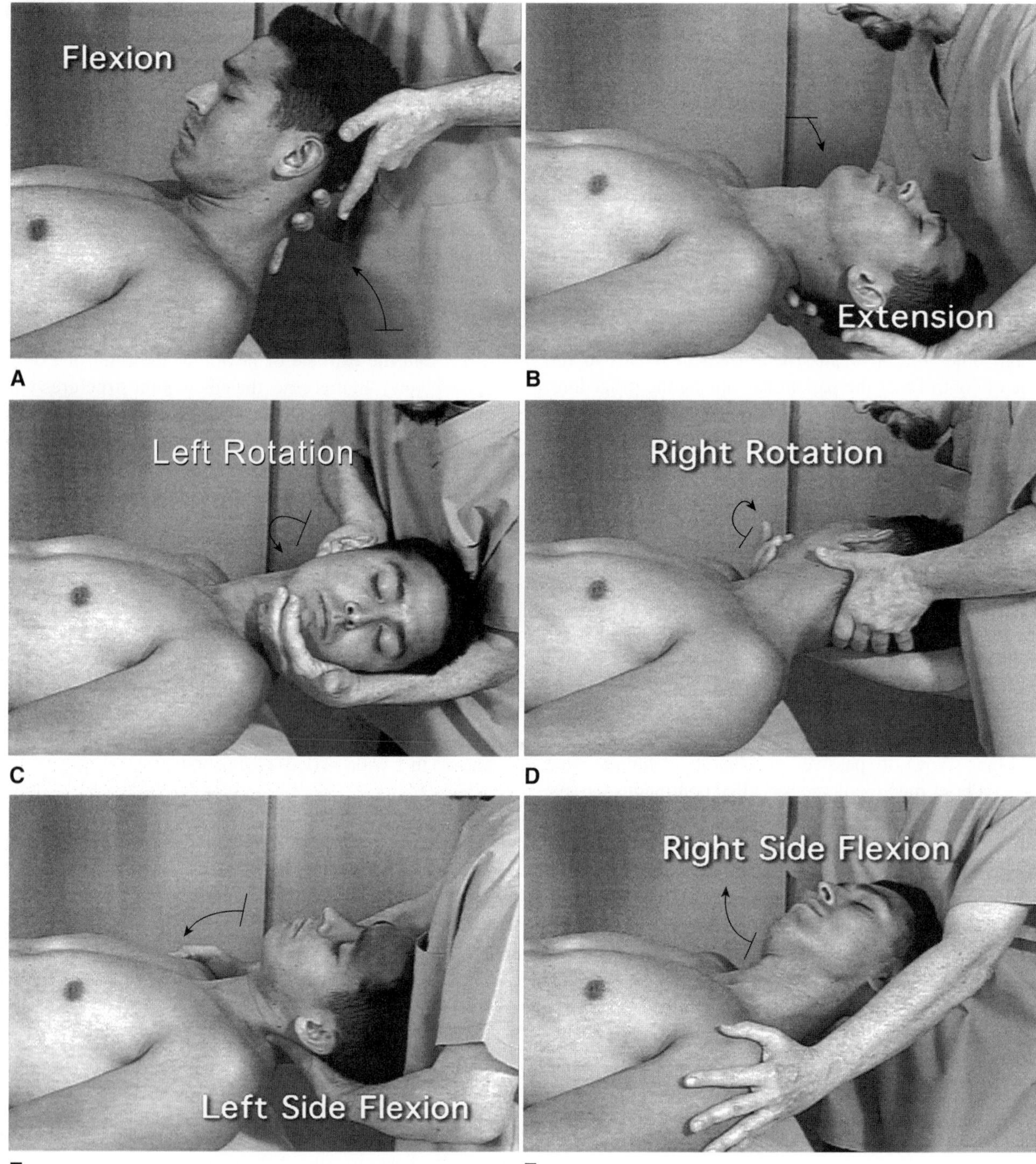


**Figure 4-32** Relaxed Passive Movements to the Neck

With the patient comfortably positioned in supine lying, the therapist moves the patient's head and neck into full flexion **(A),** and extension **(B).** The edge of the treatment table sometimes limits the range of extension in this position. The patient's face and chin are supported by the therapist's left forearm as his neck is moved into left rotation **(C).** In a similar manner, the neck is rotated to the right **(D).** The patient's neck is then moved into left **(E)** and then right **(F)** side flexion as the therapist applies counterpressure to the opposite shoulder. See also DVD Chapter 4-1. Relaxed passive movements can also be given with the patient's head supported on a pillow. This is helpful for the patient in extreme pain who finds it difficult to relax. Working well within the pain-free range, the head and neck are moved into flexion **(G),** extension **(H),** rotation to the left **(I)** and right **(J),** and then side flexion to the left **(K)** and right **(L).** See also DVD Chapters 4-21 and 4-22.

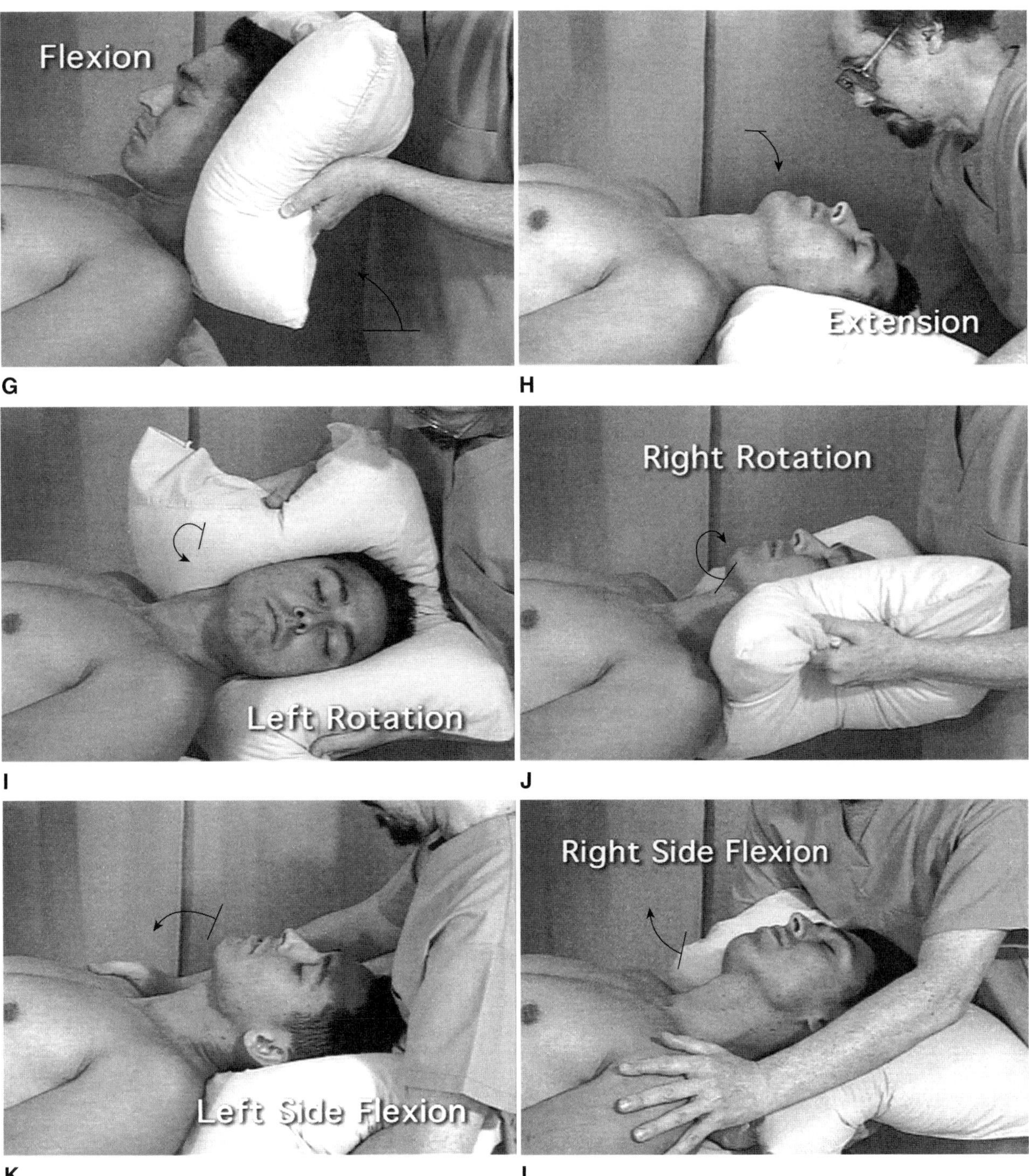


Figure 4-32, cont'd

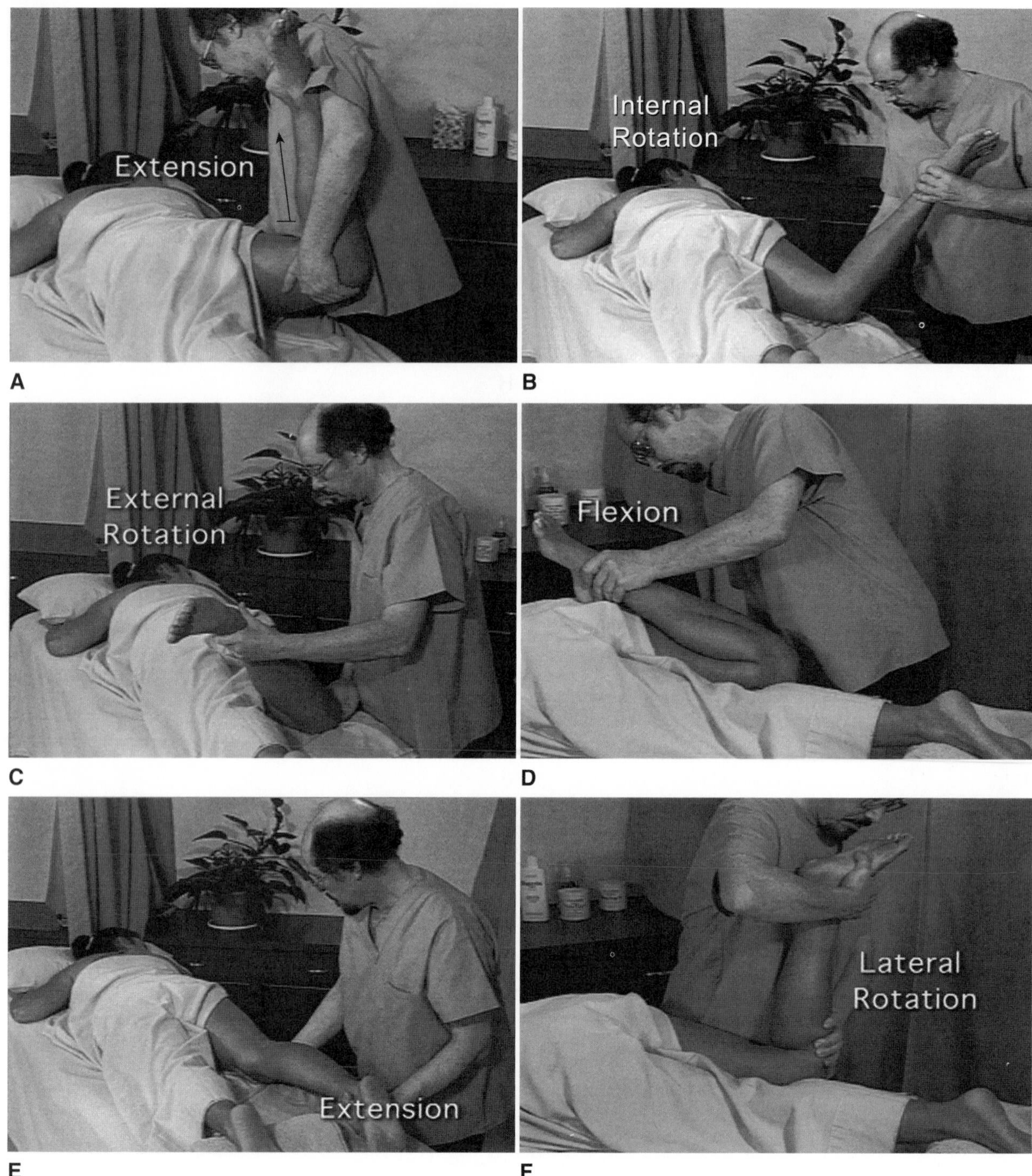


Figure **4-33** Relaxed Passive Movements to the Lower Limb with the Patient in Prone Lying

With the patient comfortably positioned in prone lying, many of the movements described in Figure 4-32 are possible. This position allows the therapist to move the patient's hip into full extension **(A)** with the knee held in midflexion. Internal **(B)** and external **(C)** rotation at the hip are also easily performed in this position. The knee can then be moved into full flexion **(D)** and then extension **(E).** The edge of the treatment table sometimes limits the range of extension in this position. This can be followed by lateral **(F)** and medial **(G)** rotation of the tibia on the femur. This is followed by dorsiflexion **(H)** and plantarflexion **(I)** of the ankle joint. Generalized circumduction **(J),** eversion **(K),** and inversion **(L)** are also possible. Relaxed passive movements can also be applied to the toes as a group, for example, flexion **(M)** and extension **(N)** and to each of the individual joints of the toes. See also DVD Chapter 4-56.

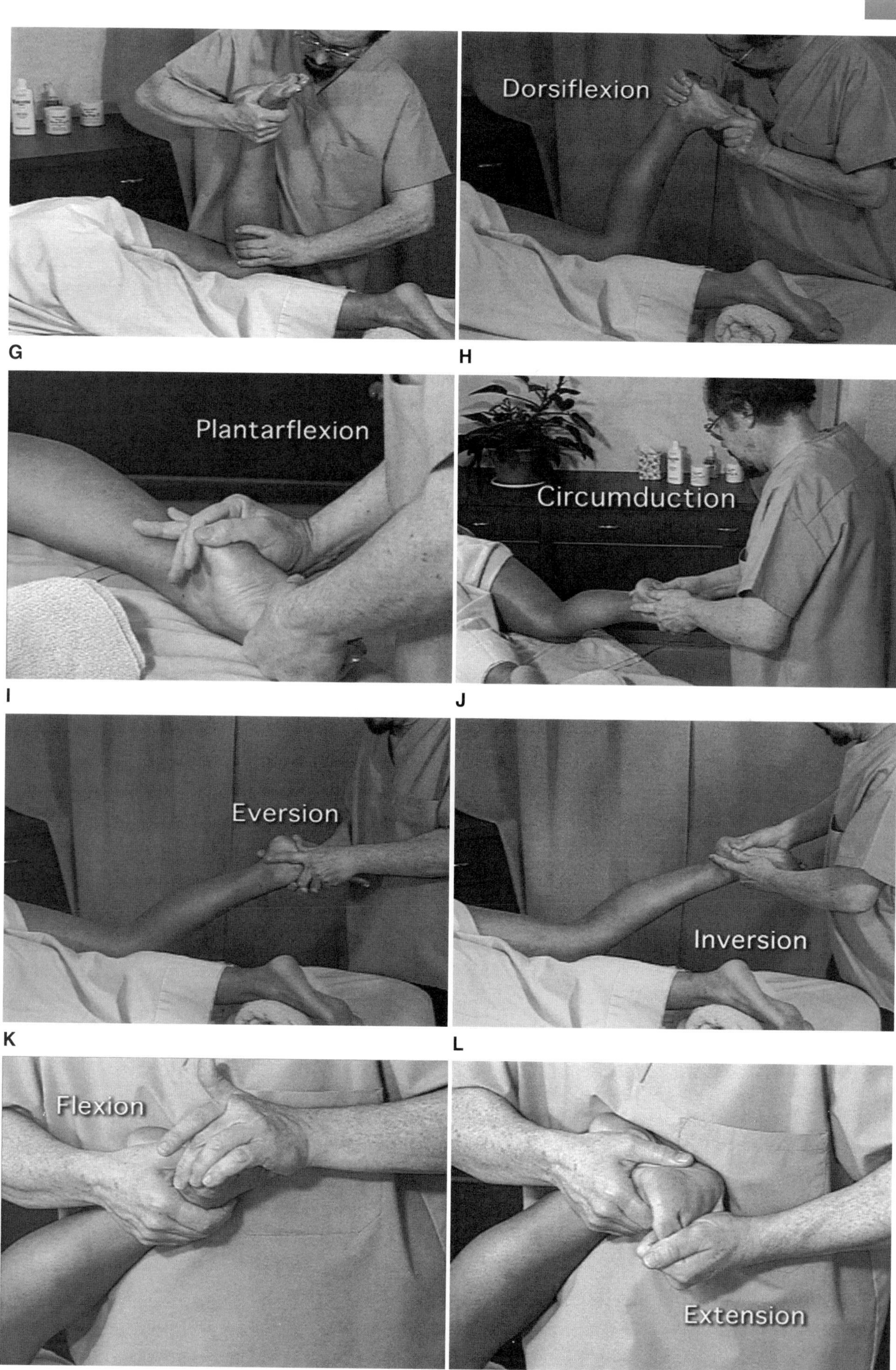
G
Dorsiflexion
H
Plantarflexion
I
Circumduction
J
Eversion
K
Inversion
L
Flexion
M
Extension
N

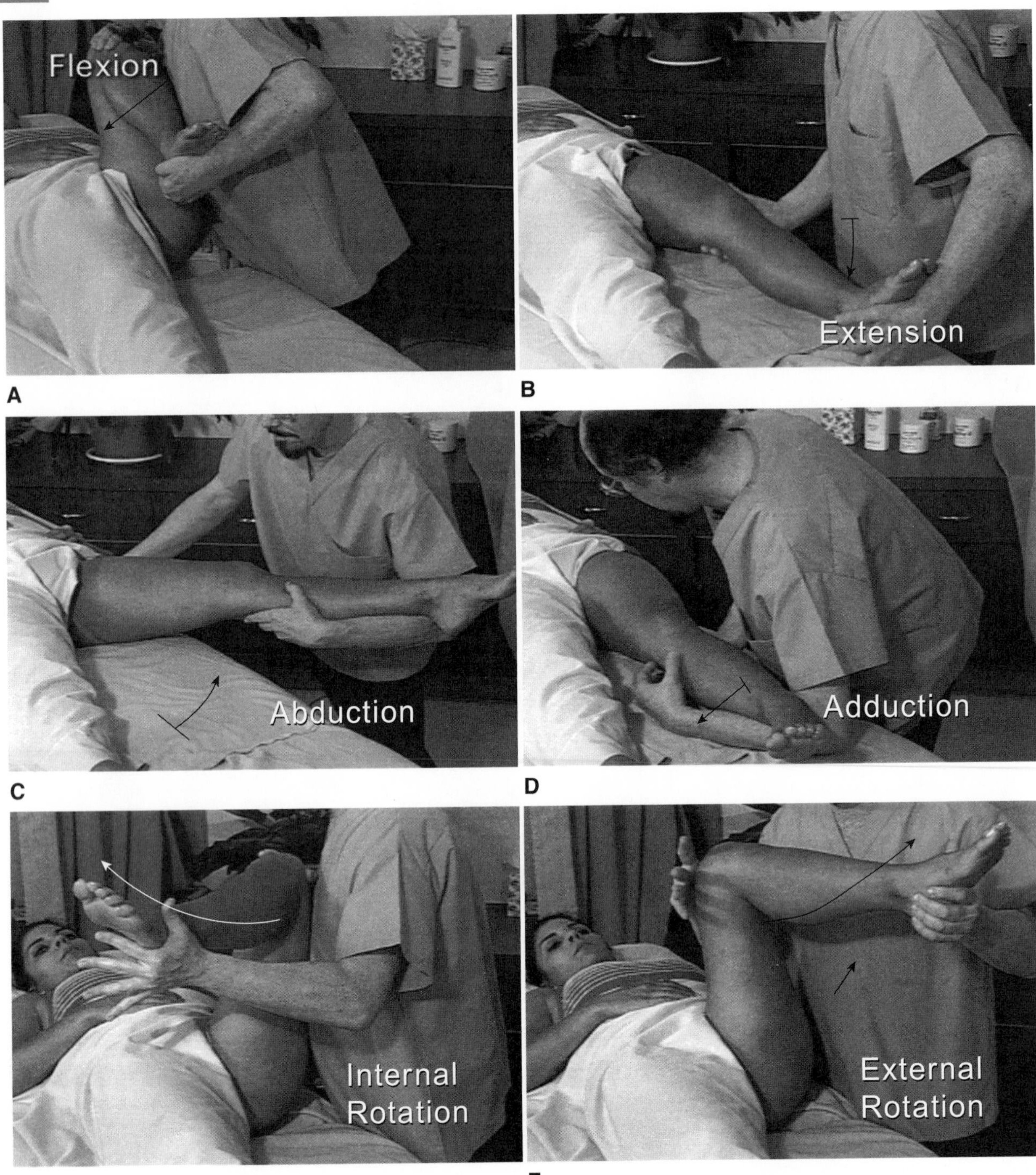


Figure **4-34** Relaxed Passive Movements to the Lower Limb with the Patient in Supine Lying

With the patient comfortably positioned in supine lying, the therapist moves the patient's hip and knee into full flexion **(A)** and then knee extension **(B).** The treatment table limits a full range of hip extension in this position. Passive movements to the hip in this position can also include hip abduction **(C),** adduction **(D),** and internal **(E)** and external rotation **(F).** Passive flexion **(G)** and extension **(H)** at the knee are also possible in this position. In the foot and ankle region, dorsiflexion **(I)** and plantarflexion **(J)** along with inversion **(K)** and eversion **(L)** are included in a basic routine for the lower limb. Relaxed passive movements can also be applied to the toes as a group; for example, extension **(M)** and flexion **(N),** and also to the individual joints of each toe, for example, abduction **(O)** and adduction **(P)** of the great toe. See also DVD Chapter 4-55.

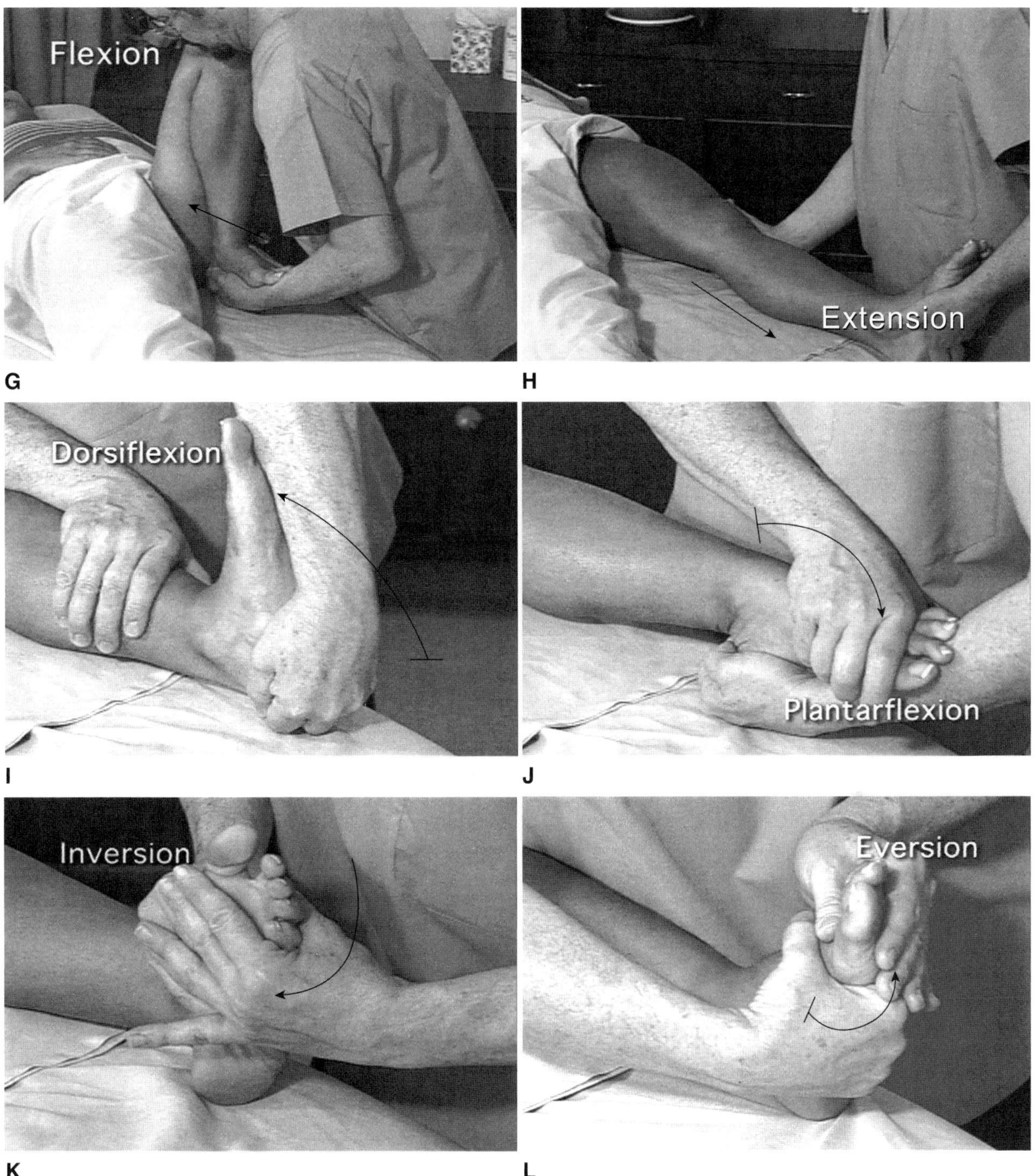


Figure **4-34**, cont'd

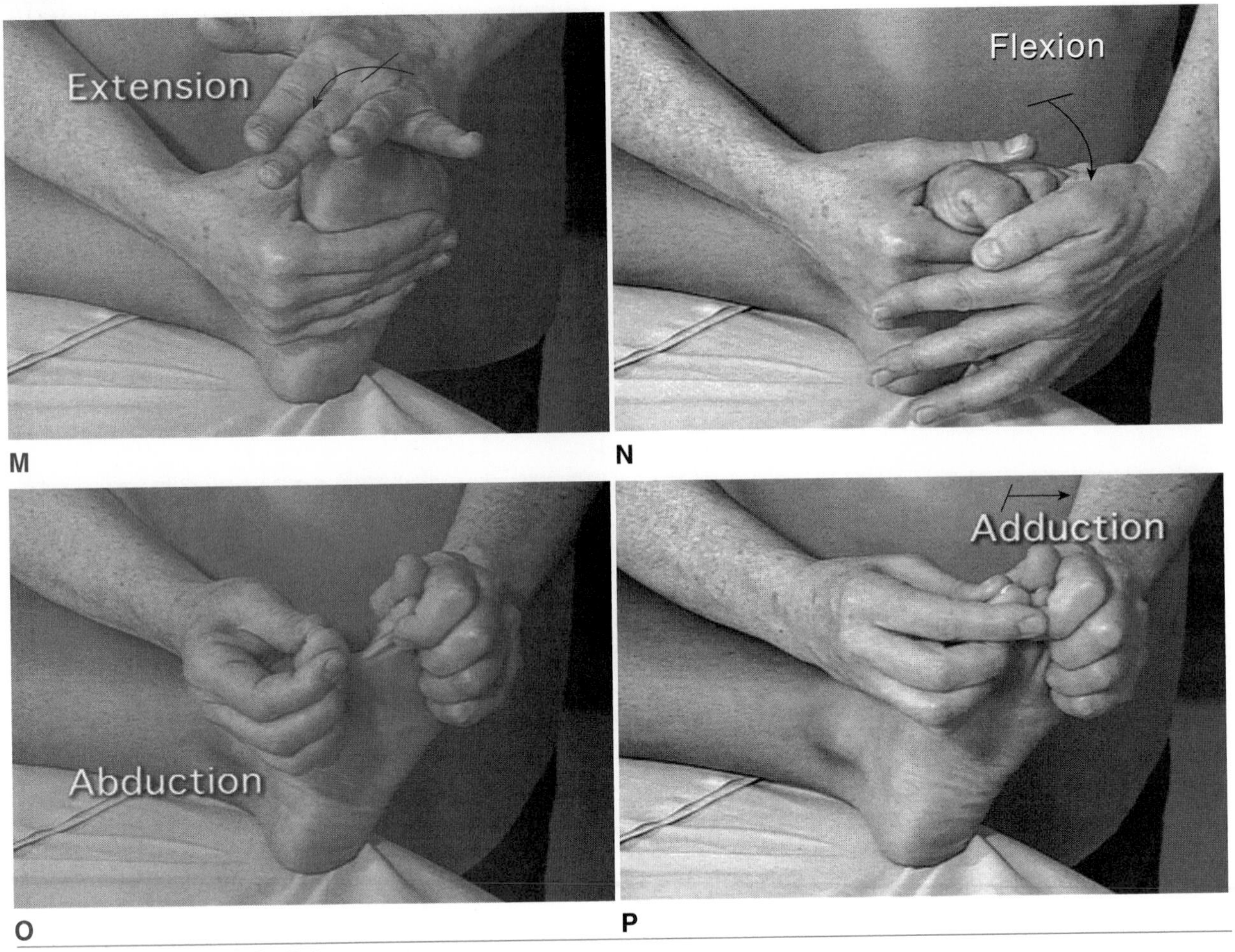

Figure **4-34**, cont'd

**RELAXED PASSIVE MOVEMENTS**

| BODY PART | DVD CHAPTER |
|---|---|
| Neck | 4-21, 4-22 |
| Posterior aspects of the lower limb | 4-56 |
| Anterior aspects of the lower limb | 4-55 |
| Upper limb | 4-68 |

## Primary Effects of Relaxed Passive Movements

Therapeutic effects are produced mainly through the direct mechanical impact of stretching the tissues and the *passive pumping* of blood and lymph during the movements. The primary effects of relaxed passive movements are as follows:

- A direct mechanical stretch on the connective tissues associated with all of the musculoskeletal and neurovascular structures, leading to increased range of motion in these tissues and an improvement in functional ability
- Pain and muscle spasm relief (via a pain-gating mechanism) leading to an increased range of motion and an improvement in functional ability
- Increased flow of blood and lymph in the limbs because of the mechanical pumping effect produced as the tissues are alternately squeezed and stretched (the increased circulation promotes healing and all levels of tissue viability)

## Therapeutic Uses of Relaxed Passive Movements

When included in a treatment regimen, relaxed passive movements can be used to do the following:

- Increase blood and lymphatic flow (passive pump) in the superficial and deep circulation in the limbs
- Relieve pain and muscle spasm, thereby promoting relaxation and improved range of motion
- Regain lost functional range of motion in skin, joint, muscle, tendon, and neurovascular tissue as a result of contractures and adhesions

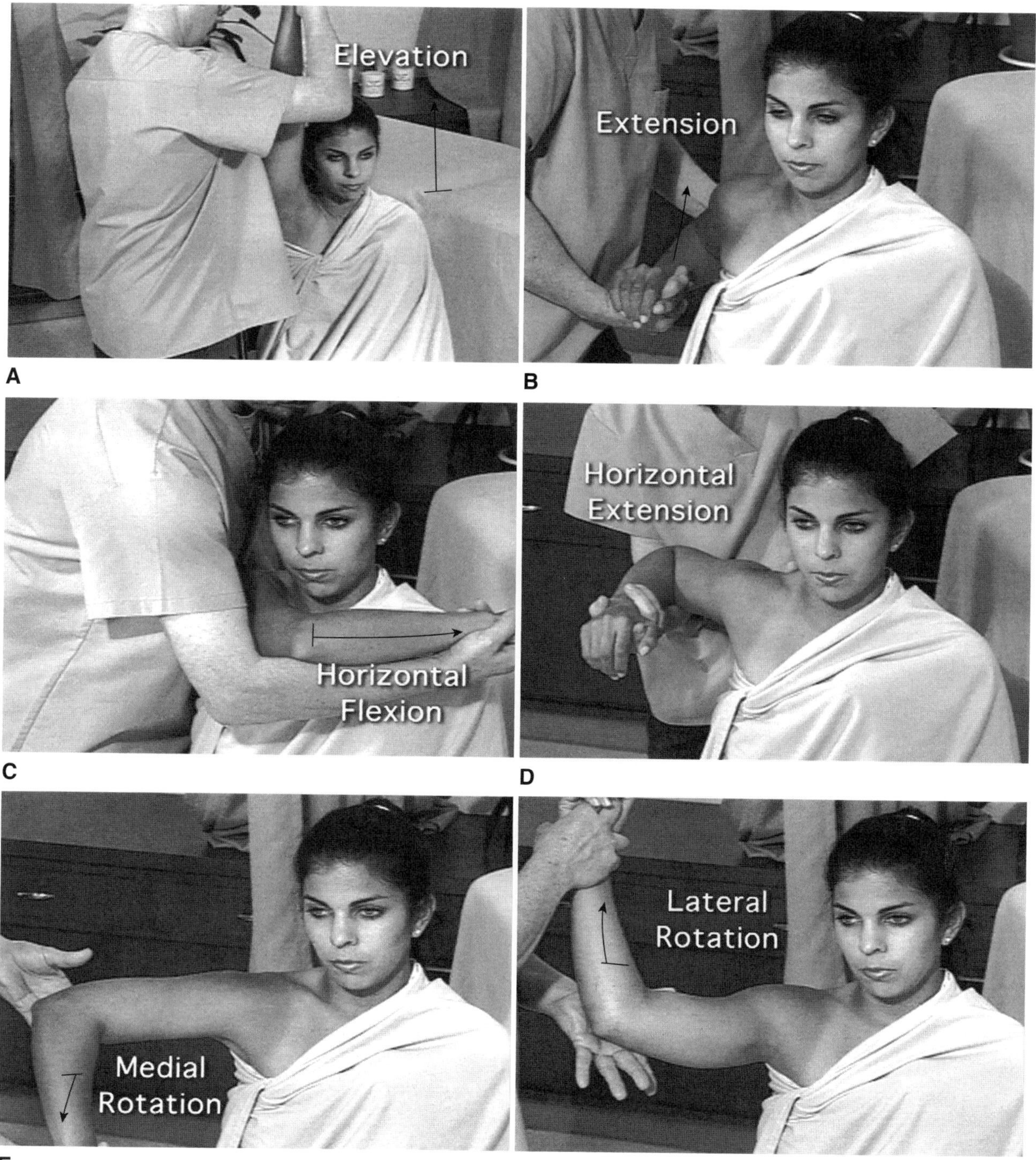


**Figure 4-35 Relaxed Passive Movements to the Upper Limb**

With the patient comfortably draped and seated, the therapist moves the patient's right shoulder into the fully elevated position, through flexion **(A)** and extension **(B).** Horizontal flexion and extension at the shoulder are shown in **(C)** and **(D),** respectively. With the patient's upper arm held horizontally and her elbow positioned at approximately 90 degrees of flexion, medial (internal) and lateral (external) rotation are performed in **(E)** and **(F),** respectively. Elbow flexion **(G)** and extension **(H)** are followed by flexion and extension of the wrist in **(I)** and **(J),** respectively. Relaxed passive movements can also be applied to the joints of the fingers as a group—that is, mass flexion and extension **(K, L)**—or to each of the individual joints in the hand and fingers. Two examples are shown here: abduction of the thumb **(M)** and extension of the thumb **(N).** See also DVD Chapter 4-68.

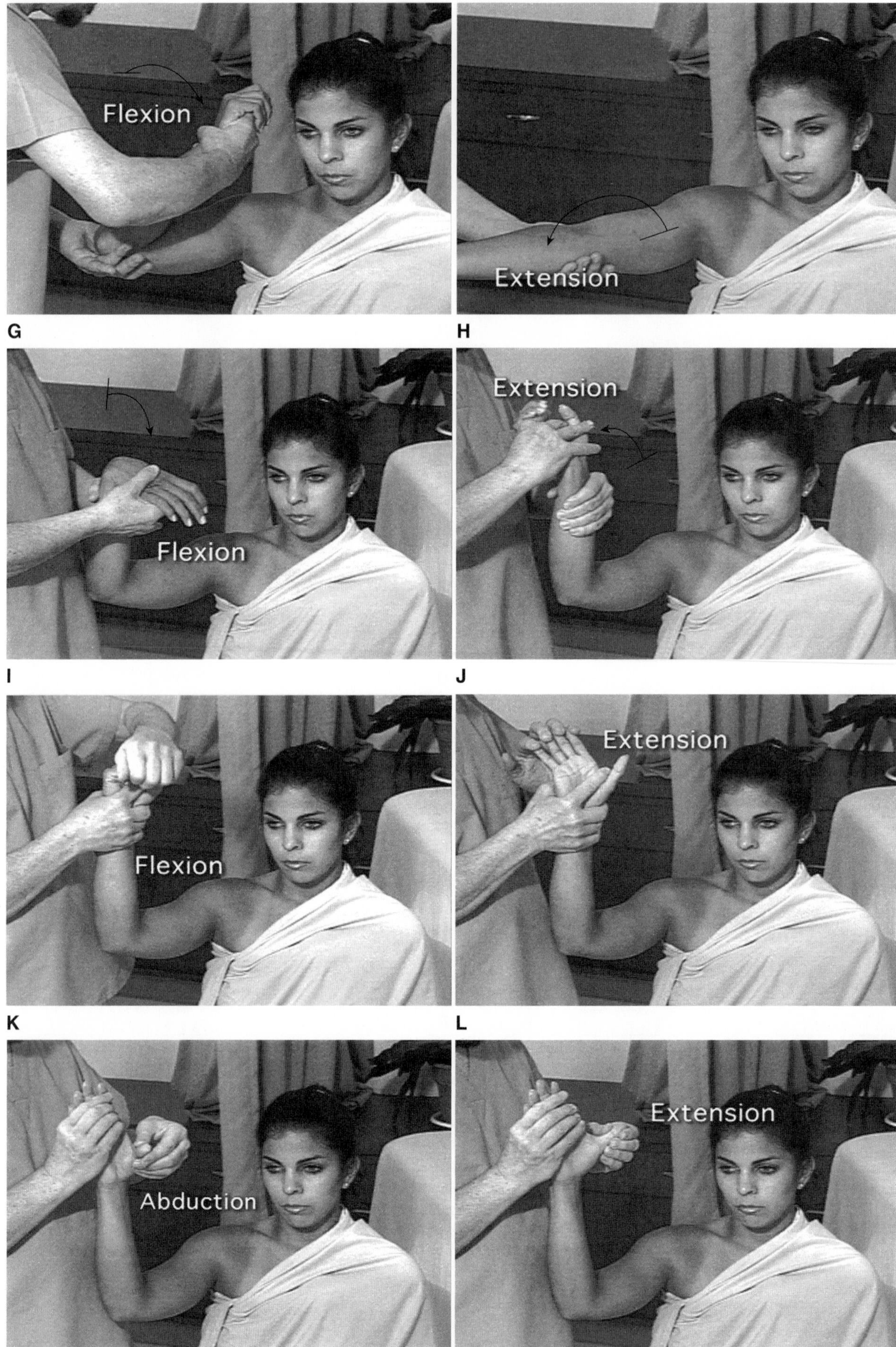
Flexion
Extension
Flexion
Extension
Flexion
Extension
Abduction
Extension

G H I J K L M N

### Table 4-9 Main Contraindications to the Use of Relaxed Passive Movements

| Contraindication | |
|---|---|
| Large open areas (e.g., burns or wounds) in the areas to be treated, especially if they are infected | A |
| Gross edema in the areas to be treated if there seems to be a possibility of splitting the skin | A |
| Deep vein thrombosis or other serious vascular pathology in the areas to be treated | A |
| Cancer in the skin or any other tissue in the area to be treated | A |
| Serious infections in the tissues to be treated (tuberculosis, septic arthritis, etc.) | A |
| Lacerations, bruising, infections or foreign bodies (e.g., glass, grit, metal) in the skin of the area to be treated | U |
| Marked varicosities in the areas to be treated if damage to the vein wall might result | U |
| Acute or chronic skin conditions affecting the areas to be treated (e.g., psoriasis, eczema, or dermatitis) | R |
| Within 3 to 6 months following radiation therapy in the area to be treated (skin is usually hypersensitive) | R |
| Areas of hyperesthesia in the areas to be treated (i.e., those who are very sensitive/ ticklish to touch) | R |

*A*, Always contraindicated; *U*, usually contraindicated; *R*, rarely contraindicated.

- Maintain the normal functional range of motion in body segments subjected to prolonged immobility or paralysis, thereby preventing contractures and adhesions

### Indications for the Use of Relaxed Passive Movements

Relaxed passive movements may be indicated as part of a treatment plan to help relieve or reduce the effects of the following:

- Pain (acute or chronic) preventing movement
- Muscle spasm (acute or chronic) preventing movement
- Superficial and deep scar tissue in the skin and subcutaneous tissue
- Prolonged immobility or paralysis
- Contractures/adhesions in joint capsules, ligaments, muscles, tendons, tendon sheaths, and neurovascular tissues

### Contraindications to the Use of Relaxed Passive Movements

The general concept of contraindications is covered in Chapter 3. The technique of relaxed passive movements may be contraindicated when any of the situations listed in Table 4-9 are present.

## SUMMARY

This chapter has reviewed the major elements of the techniques known as *Swedish remedial massage, deep frictions,* and *relaxed passive movements.* In each case, a detailed description was provided, together with illustrations and lists of therapeutic effects, uses, indications, and contraindications. The systematic organization of this material will hopefully allow the reader to choose appropriate techniques for a given patient. The accompanying DVD provides the viewer with the opportunity to see how each technique should be given, and easy access to each video clip can be found in the DVD menu.

## REFERENCES


Brosseau L, Casimiro L, Milne S et al: Deep transverse friction massage for treating tendonitis, *Cochrane Database Syst Rev* (4): CD003528, 2002.

Chamberlain G: Cyriax's friction massage: a review, *JOSPT* 4(1):16-22, 1982.

Cyriax J: Clinical applications of massage. In Licht S, editor: *Physical medicine library, vol 5: massage, manipulation and traction,* pp 122-139, Baltimore, 1960, Waverley Press.

Cyriax J, Coldham M: *Textbook of orthopaedic medicine, vol 2,* pp 9-21, London, 1984, Bailliere Tindall.

*Dorland's illustrated medical dictionary,* ed 30, Philadelphia, 2003, Saunders.

Grieve GP: *Modern manual therapy of the vertebral column,* London, 1994, Churchill Livingstone.

Hammer WI: The use of transverse friction massage in the management of chronic bursitis of the hip or shoulder, *J Manip Physiolog Therapeutics* 16(2):107-111, 1993.

Morris J: The value of continuous passive motion in rehabilitation following total knee replacement, *Physiotherapy JCSP* 81(9):557-562, 1995.

O'Driscoll SW, Giori NJ: Continuous passive motion (CPM): theory and principles of clinical application, *J Rehab Res Dev 37*(2):179-188, 2000.

Quinn C, Chandler C, Moraska A: Chronic tension headaches reduction with the use of cross friction massage techniques, *Am J Public Health* 92(10):1657-1661, 2002.

Sheppard MS, Westlake SM et al: Continuous passive motion: where are we now? *Physiotherapy Can* 47(1):36-39, 1995.

Steward B, Woodman R, Hurlburt D: Fabricating a splint for deep friction massage, *JOSPT* 221(3):172-175, 1995.

Chapter 5

# Mechanical, Physiological, Psychological, and Therapeutic Effects of Soft Tissue Manipulation

Soft tissue manipulation is an ancient art, practiced in many cultures and studied by both ancient and modern scholars. Despite its longevity and widespread use, however, comparatively few scientific studies were undertaken until the twentieth century. Before the early 1900s, the scientific literature on massage consisted largely of descriptive reports and observational records of the areas under study. The methods and standards used today did not exist 100 years ago. In fact, much of medical science was devoted to a description of anecdotal reports and deductive reasoning based on them. Also, the investigative methods available in the first half of the twentieth century were extremely crude by today's standards. It is easy to forget that electricity was only available as a public utility shortly after 1900 and that the modern electronic age only began in the 1930s. Suffice it to say that the electronic devices (especially computers) that are considered to be indispensable and taken for granted today did not exist in the early decades of the twentieth century. Indeed, much of the modern understanding of human physiology only began to take shape in the late 1890s and early 1900s. This was the era of Sir Charles Sherrington, who is known as the father of modern physiology. With these thoughts in mind, this chapter reviews both the historical understanding of how massage has its effects and some of the modern literature that continues to shed light on this ancient treatment.

The primary effect of manipulating the soft tissues of the body is mechanical in nature. The pressing, pulling, lifting, stretching, rubbing, and squeezing obviously impart a mechanical deformation on the tissues, and this occurs before most, but not all, of the other effects. These mechanical effects result in a wide variety of physiological and psychological responses. All three types of effect give rise to the therapeutic uses. It is worth noting at this stage that the anticipation of receiving a massage treatment is usually a positive experience for the patient. Therefore, a psychological effect might be produced even before the treatment begins.

According to the great Arabic philosopher and scholar Avicenna (980-1037), "The object of massage is to disperse the effete matters [metabolites] formed in the muscles and not expelled by exercise. It causes the effete matter to disperse and so removes fatigue" (Gruner, 1930). This statement from Avicenna clearly shows that classical scholars were very interested in understanding the mechanisms by which manipulation of the soft tissues (including massage) might have beneficial effects; however, the majority of writings have concentrated more on describing the techniques and the observed effects of treatment rather than on investigating these effects scientifically. The general effects of massage have been described and classified in several ways. Mennell (1945) referred to mechanical (pressure and tension), chemical, reflex, and psychological effects, but other authors described only general and local effects. This edition of the text continues to use the simple classification of mechanical, physiological, and psychological effects developed from the fourth edition.

The primary effects (mechanical, physiological, and psychological) are considered separately here, although they are interdependent. Each area has been subdivided into several sections, together with the appropriate research. In this way, relevant research findings have been classified according to the specific effects of massage—for example, the effect of massage on pain. Numerous studies have reported on the general effects of massage compared with other treatment techniques (e.g., Taylor et al., 2003); however, this text concentrates on the specific effects of massage. The reader interested in the more general effects and comparisons of massage with other treatments is referred to computer databases such as the Centre for Reviews and Dissemination (2005). A meta-analysis of massage therapy research can be found in the Database of Abstracts of Reviews of Effectiveness (Issue 2, DARE-20043309). The specific effects, indications, therapeutic uses, and contraindications for each of the basic massage strokes were presented in Chapter 4.

## MECHANICAL EFFECTS

The mechanical forces associated with squeezing, pulling, stretching, pressing, and rubbing strokes affect the tissues in a variety of ways. For example, the various techniques of kneading and wringing would be expected to have a considerable mobilizing effect (loosening or stretching) on the skin, subcutaneous tissue, and muscle tissue. In contrast, the gradually increasing pressure of effleurage would be expected to push the venous blood and lymph in the superficial vessels toward the heart, thus promoting good circulation and resolving chronic edema and hematoma. In a similar manner, the pressure and direction of stroking and effleurage techniques can promote movement of the intestinal contents.

The principal effects of each of the basic massage techniques were outlined in Chapter 4. Although the mechanical effects of massage are important to identify, it is the physiological effects that need to be considered in some detail, because these give rise to the therapeutic potential of soft tissue massage. The primary effect of massage, then, is to produce mechanical deformation of the tissues by means of rhythmically applied pressure and stretching. Applied mechanical pressure compresses and stretches the soft tissues and thereby distorts both the excitable and the nonexcitable tissues of the body. Excitable tissues are those structures that respond in some measurable and immediate way to an externally applied mechanical stimulus. Obvious examples are sensory nerves. The nonexcitable tissues are composed of structures such as bone, ligaments, and cartilage. Although these structures do not appear to respond immediately to the applied mechanical stimulus, they do in fact respond, but over a much longer period of time, sometimes taking several months. For example, a muscle that has undergone adaptive shortening (contracture) will obviously feel tight when stretched. If a mechanical stretch is applied to the muscle, especially on a continuous basis (serial casting), the body will re-engineer (lengthen) parallel and series elastic components, but this takes many weeks. Although the immediate effect of the stretching appears nonexistent, over time it becomes apparent. For example, Threlkeld (1992) investigated the mechanical effects of massage on connective tissues.

### Table 5-1 Examples of Excitable and Nonexcitable Tissues

| | |
|---|---|
| **Excitable Tissues** | Nerve cells of all types<br>Nerve fibers of all types<br>Voluntary motor fibers<br>Autonomic muscle fibers<br>Cardiac muscle fibers<br>Abdominal organ cells<br>Glands |
| **Nonexcitable Tissues** | Skin<br>Bone<br>Cartilage<br>Collagen tissues<br>Ligamentous tissue<br>Tendon tissue<br>Hair<br>Teeth<br>Nails |

Table 5-1 lists various tissues as excitable or nonexcitable based on their ability to respond immediately to an external mechanical stimulus. Note that the stimulus does not necessarily have to produce its effect directly. The effect can be produced by the activation of an appropriate reflex. For example, during the percussion strokes, the high-speed mechanical tapping of the skin and muscles activates the Ia sensory endings in the muscle spindles of the muscle being percussed, thereby activating the stretch reflex and thus facilitating the muscle.

Tissues labeled as excitable are capable of an immediate response to an external mechanical stimulus. The response can be mediated via an appropriate reflex or be the result of direct activation. Those tissues classified as nonexcitable show no immediate response to an externally applied stimulus; however, over time, with repeated stimulation, structural changes may become apparent.

The externally applied mechanical pressure can also affect the flow of blood and lymph and can therefore stimulate the circulation. This is a particularly important mechanical effect because the net result is an increased flow of blood and lymph in the target area, and this facilitates healing. A similar direct mechanical effect can occur in the lung tissue, where the percussion and vibration strokes can help to loosen mucus and promote drainage of excess fluids from the lungs (see Chapter 10).

Box 5-1 summarizes the mechanical effects of soft tissue manipulation using two primary categories: the effect that produces movement and the effect that mobilizes the tissues. In the case of the movement effect, the emphasis is on the movement of fluids in the circulatory system (blood and lymph). In the case of the mobilizing effect, the emphasis is on loosening and promoting intertissue mobility. These concepts are discussed in detail in the next section dealing with the physiological effects of massage.

**BOX 5-1 Primary Mechanical Effects of Soft Tissue Manipulation**

**Movement of**
Blood
Lymph
Lung secretions
Chronic edema
Intestinal contents
**Mobilization of**
Muscle fibers
Muscle masses
Tendons
Tendons in sheaths
Ligaments
Joint capsules
Skin and subcutaneous tissue
Fascia
Scar tissue
Adhesions
Chronic hematoma

**BOX 5-2 Physiological Effects of Soft Tissue Manipulation**

Increased blood and lymph flow
Increased flow of nutrients
Removal of waste products and metabolites
Stimulation of the healing process
Resolution of chronic edema and hematoma
Increased extensibility of connective tissue
Pain relief
Increased joint movement
Facilitation of muscle activity
Stimulation of autonomic functions
Stimulation of visceral functions
Removal of lung secretions
Promotion of local and general relaxation

The two primary effects of soft tissue manipulations are the movement of fluids and the mobilization of tissues. These effects have important physiological consequences, which give rise to the therapeutic uses for the various techniques.

It is important to remember that tissues that have adaptively shortened (contractures) cannot be suddenly made longer. The process of lengthening is one in which the natural mechanisms (collagen turnover) are stimulated by the mechanical stresses placed on the tissues. In effect, the tissues undergo an adaptive lengthening. Serial casting, where needed, can greatly facilitate this process as this places a continuous mechanical stretch on the tissues. Of course, soft tissue massage techniques can be used to prevent contractures from developing in the first place.

## PHYSIOLOGICAL EFFECTS

The mechanical stimulus given to the tissues during soft tissue massage causes the body to respond in different ways. It is appropriate to consider these responses as the physiological effects of massage, as they are the direct and indirect effects of the individual massage techniques (Goats, 1994a, 1994b). Some of the effects are immediate, whereas others are only apparent over time. This gives rise to the idea that massage can trigger a response in the tissues that begins a cascade of other effects, and some of these effects can be long lasting. This section considers the physiological effects under categories that relate to various tissues. The physiological effects of soft tissue manipulations are listed in Box 5-2 and discussed in the following sections.

### Effects on Blood Flow

Because all massage techniques involve some degree of manipulation of the skin and underlying tissues, it is reasonable to expect that they would have a considerable effect on the flow of blood and lymph in these tissues. In addition, swelling that has accumulated in such tissues would be expected to be similarly affected. However, Mennell (1945) believed that it is impossible to affect arterial circulation directly via the mechanical effects of massage. He theorized that applying massage pressure in the direction of the venous flow is comparable to the effect of squeezing any soft tube to empty it of fluid. If the muscles are relaxed, they constitute a soft mass containing tubes filled with fluid. Any pressure applied to the mass should push the fluid in these tubes in the direction in which the pressure is applied; therefore if sufficient pressure is applied to the entire mass, the deeper veins will also be emptied. Such pressure might at the same time retard arterial blood flow if it is forceful enough to compress the arteries and the veins.

Theoretically, if massage can increase the amount of venous blood brought to the heart, the heart rate or the stroke volume might increase and a greater amount of arterial blood would thus be carried to the periphery. In fact, there is little evidence of such a simple mechanical reaction of the arterial and arteriolar system to massage. Wakim (1949, 1955) found that following deep stroking and kneading massage, the average increase in total blood flow in normal, rheumatoid, arthritic joints was inconsistent. Moderate, consistent, and definite increases in circulation were observed after such massage to flaccid, paralyzed extremities. Vigorous, stimulating massage resulted in consistent and significant increases in average blood flow of the massaged extremity but produced no change in blood flow in the contralateral unmassaged extremity.

According to Pemberton (1932, 1939, 1950) the nervous system, probably through the sympathetic division, contributes to a reflex influence on the blood vessels of the parts concerned. He believed that it is probable, therefore, that vessels in the muscles or elsewhere are emptied during massage, not only by virtue of being squeezed but also through a reflex action. Pemberton stated that microscopic observation thus reveals that massage may cause almost all the smaller vessels to become visible because it promotes blood flow through them. Although there is little information on the type of massage that was used, several convincing experiments have been performed that show that massage increases circulation of the blood.

Wolfson (1931) studied the effect of deep kneading massage on venous blood flow in normal dog limbs and showed that massage greatly increased flow initially, followed by a fairly rapid decrease to a less than normal rate even before the end of stimulation. Immediately after cessation of the procedure, he noted that the flow rate slowly increased again to normal. He concluded that the actual volume of blood that passes through the limb during the period of stimulation and recovery is not greater than normal but that there is more complete emptying for a short time, so that a larger volume of fresh blood is brought to the part. He suggested that it would seem logical to use short but frequent massage treatments. Recently, Gregory and Mars (2005) have shown that massage (using controlled compressed air and an animal model) increases capillary dilation and therefore blood flow in skeletal muscle.

Carrier (1922) showed that light pressure produces almost instantaneous, though transient, dilatation of the capillary vessels, whereas heavier pressure may produce more enduring dilatation. Microscopic observation of fields in which only a few capillaries are open shows that pressure may cause nearly all the smaller vessels to become visible.

Pemberton (1945) described the work of Clark and Swanson, who made cinematographic studies of the capillary circulation in the ear of a rabbit utilizing a permanent window for observation. These studies demonstrated that following massage, more capillaries were opened and the rate of flow was faster. The *sticking* and emigration of leukocytes evidenced a change in the blood vessel wall. The increased blood flow as a result of massage was demonstrated as long ago as the mid-1890s (Brunton & Tunnicliffe, 1894-1895).

Many practitioners have claimed that the reflex effect of superficial stroking improves cutaneous circulation, especially blood flow in superficial veins and lymphatics; aids in the exchange of tissue fluids; increases tissue nutrition; and assists in the removal of the products of fatigue or inflammation. However, as long ago as 1939, Wright stated that such claims must be examined critically in the light of present-day knowledge of physiology. He maintained that it was difficult to make positive statements about reflex effects produced by massage. The situation today is in many ways similar.

Severini and Venerando (1967) reported that superficial massage produced no significant changes except in skin temperature. Deep massage did, however, increase blood flow and systolic stroke volume and decreased systolic and diastolic arterial pressure and pulse frequency. Interestingly, deep massage was also associated with increased blood flow in the untreated, contralateral limb. Bell (1964) demonstrated this effect using plethysmographic studies. He showed that blood volume—and thus the rate of blood flow—had doubled following deep stroking and kneading of the calf of one leg for 10 minutes. Moreover, Bell showed that the effect lasted 40 minutes, as compared with only 10 minutes following exercise. Bell recommended massage to treat edema of fractures because of its effects on venous and lymphatic flow.

Severini and Venerando (1967) also combined massage with a hyperemia-producing drug containing vanillyl and butoxyethyl nicotinate. The combined treatment led to a significant and prolonged rise in skin temperature. When the drug was used alone or with superficial massage, there was no change in circulation in muscles; but with deep massage, there was an appreciable and effective increase in blood flow in muscles. On a more central level, Barr and Taslitz (1970) showed that systolic and diastolic blood pressure tended to decrease after a 20-minute back massage. Delayed effects were an increase in systolic pressure and a small additional decrease in diastolic pressure. The heart rate increased. In addition, high blood pressure and associated symptoms were shown to reduce with massage therapy (Hernandez-Reif et al., 2000).

Massage has been studied for its effect on the circulation, as a means of preventing pressure sores (Dyson, 1978; Ek, Gustavsson, & Lewis, 1985; Olson, 1989). Massage for this purpose, however, does not follow traditional massage techniques. In most cases, it takes the form of a short period (30 to 60 seconds) of skin rubbing, the intention being to stimulate circulation to the areas of skin that are prone to develop pressure sores. Not surprisingly, the results of this kind of massage are difficult to interpret, let alone to use as a basis for making recommendations. In some studies, this type of massage seemed to increase local circulation; in others, it appeared to decrease it. It seems unlikely that a rapid skin friction massage would produce the kind of genuine increase in circulation that would prevent pressure sores. This is because this type of massage simply produces a small degree of mechanical friction on the skin surface. This would probably show up as a slight and short-lived change in surface temperature. On the other hand, a different kind of massage would be expected to produce a more profound effect on the circulation, especially if it involved deep kneading to muscles around the area, were that possible. A more efficient way of producing a rapid change in skin blood flow is massaging the area with an ice cube. In this case, it is the cold stimulus that produces profound vasodilation after the initial vasoconstriction (Michlovitz, 1996). Undoubtedly, a brief massage (1 to 3 minutes) with an ice cube is likely to be much more effective than a similar period of skin rubbing.

### Effects on the Lymphatic System

In the lymphatic capillaries and plexuses of the skin and subcutaneous tissue, lymph can move in any direction. Its movement depends on forces outside the lymphatic system. Its course is determined by factors such as gravity, muscle contraction, passive movement, and massage. If obstruction of the deeper lymphatics occurs in a part, it is still possible to keep the superficial lymphatics open, and if the part is massaged or given opportunity to drain by gravity, lymph moves through these other channels in the direction of the external force. These issues are considered in detail in Chapter 12.

Animal experiments show that there is little lymph flow when a muscle is at rest. Von Mesengeil's and Kellgren and Colombo's studies on the effects of massage on lymph flow observed increased lymph flow when the muscles were massaged. Cuthbertson (1933) noted that Von Mesengeil

*repeatedly injected China ink into corresponding articulations of rabbits. One joint was massaged and the corresponding one left as a control. In the legs without massage, the tendency of the colored material to pass toward the heart was very small, but in those legs subjected to massage, there was great absorption of the ink above the joint in the intermuscular connective tissues and in the lymphatic glands. The lymphatics passing up to the glands were deeply stained black.*

Kellgren and Colombo found that

*Massage always had a sure and effective influence in increasing the rapidity of the absorption of substances injected into animals in all the organs which can be subjected to manipulations— subcutaneous tissues, muscles, articulations, and serous cavities. The course which the injected substance followed during its absorption, was always that of the nearest lymphatic vessels and the glands into which they pass. Deep Effleurage was probably less effective than the squeezing and rolling of muscles and subcutaneous tissue.*

McMaster (1937) also showed that massage increased lymph flow by experiments in which the limbs of normal healthy subjects were massaged after intradermal dye injections.

Drinker and Yoffey (1941) cannulated the cervical lymph trunks in an anesthetized dog and were able to sustain lymph flow all day long by massaging the head and neck above the cannulas. When the massage was stopped, lymph flow either ceased or was negligible. The investigators stated that, in treating chronic inflammatory conditions in which fibrosis is sure to advance if tissue fluid and lymph remain stagnant in the part, massage in the direction of lymph flow is the preeminent artificial measure for moving extravascular fluid into lymphatics and for moving lymph onward toward the bloodstream. Drinker and Yoffey also found that the effects of posture were obvious and that lymph flow from a dependent, quiescent part was practically negligible. Therefore, to influence the flow of lymph most efficiently in any area, it seemed logical that the part should be elevated during the application of massage. Elevation means placing the part higher than the heart. In addition, the pathway for the fluids should be as straight as possible.

Ladd et al. (1952) compared the effects of massage, passive motion, and electrical stimulation on the rate of lymph flow in the forelegs of 15 dogs and found that massage was "significantly more effective than either passive motion or electrical stimulation in this series of animals." All three procedures were found to increase lymph flow much above that of the control period.

The idea of using mechanical forces to affect the circulation of blood and lymph is not limited to manual massage techniques. A variety of pneumatic devices have been developed that deliver a series of controlled (and often graduated) pressure changes along a limb surface. In effect, these devices perform a kind of mechanical massage. They have proved to be of considerable benefit in the treatment of many acute and chronic circulation disorders but especially in the treatment of lymphedema (Yamazaki et al., 1988). Of course, manual massage techniques also have an important role to play in the management of lymphedema (Andersen, 2000: Casley-Smith, 2000; Forchuk et al., 2004; Little & Porsche, 1998; Mason, 1993; Nickalls, 1996; Weinrich & Weinrich, 1990). See also Chapter 12 for an in-depth discussion on the concept of decongestive therapy for the management of lymphedema.

## Effects on the Blood

In 1904, Mitchell stated that in both healthy and anemic persons, the red cell count increased after massage. In anemic subjects the increase is greatest 1 hour after treatment. Schneider and Havens (1915) also showed that abdominal massage increases the hemoglobin and red cell count in blood taken from the finger at ordinary barometric pressures. Pemberton (1950) stated that massage unquestionably increases the hemoglobin and red cell values in the circulating blood and that there is a limited but definite increase in the oxygen capacity of the blood after massage. Lucia and Rickard (1933) found that massage consisting of gentle but firm stroking of a rabbit's ear at the rate of 25 strokes per minute for 5 minutes caused a local increase in the blood platelet count.

Bork, Karling, and Faust (1971), reporting the effects of whole-body massage on serum enzyme levels in normal persons, showed a significant rise in serum glutamic oxaloacetic transaminase, creatine phosphokinase, lactic dehydrogenase, and MK. These effects caused the authors to advocate that whole-body massage should be contraindicated for patients with dermatomyositis, especially serious cases.

Ernst et al. (1987) showed that a 20-minute whole-body muscle massage causes a dilution effect and changes blood fluidity. This effect was observed in both normal subjects and patients with ankylosing spondylitis. When these effects are coupled with the increased blood and lymph flow produced by massage, it is clear that this form of treatment has a significant role to play in maintaining and enhancing the overall nutrition of the tissues.

The changes described briefly here are not produced by a direct effect on the blood itself, but rather they reflect the overall effects of massage given to the person. Because the vascular system pervades every part of the anatomy, it is not surprising that the blood reflects the mechanical and physiological effects of massage. Increased or decreased levels of various substances carried in the blood are, in most cases, simply the result of the massage given to the soft tissues rather than a direct effect on the blood itself.

## Effects on Metabolism and the Healing Process

Very little recent experimentation has been reported on the effects of massage on metabolism, although several studies were performed more than 50 years ago. Cuthbertson (1933) reviewed the existing literature on this subject and conducted several experiments of his own. He arrived at the following findings:

- Urine output increases, especially after abdominal massage.
- Excretion of acid is not altered, and there is no change in the acid-base equilibrium.
- Excretion rates for nitrogen, inorganic phosphorus, and sodium chloride increase.
- In normal persons, there is no immediate effect on the basal consumption of oxygen or on pulse rate or blood pressure.

Pemberton (1939) believed, "In general the studies which have been made suggest broad and general influences may be exerted by massage and that it has no immediate or large effect on general metabolism per se." He agreed with the view that its cumulative effect on various metabolic processes lies in its effects on the circulation of the parts concerned.

The resolution of acute trauma or of chronic inflammation (healing) consists of a cascade of interrelated changes in the affected tissues. These changes depend entirely on the efficiency of the local circulation to the part, as all of the materials needed to resolve the inflammatory process must arrive at the scene via the bloodstream. In addition, all of the waste products must be removed from the area via the blood and lymph channels (Evans, 1980). Because massage has such profound effects on the blood and lymph systems, it seems obvious that it has the potential to be useful in stimulating the healing process, especially in the subacute and chronic phases of recovery.

It is important to remember the crucial importance of the lymphatic system in removing plasma proteins and other large molecules once they have been deposited in the interstitial fluid. These molecules are too large to reenter the capillaries and can only be eliminated via the lymphatic system. Facilitation of healing is therefore the by-product of the other (more direct) effects (e.g., increased blood and lymph flow) on the tissues.

## Effects on Muscle Tissue

More than 100 years ago, Maggiora (1891) described the physiological action of massage on muscle tissue. Many other writers have also described the effects of massage on muscle tissue. Much of the literature contains a relatively large number of positive statements and implications about the effects of massage on muscles, as compared with its effects on other systems and tissues of the body. Some of these statements cannot be substantiated by clinical observation or by scientific research. The present review considers separately the effects of massage on normal and abnormal muscle tissue.

### *Normal Muscles*

Kellogg (1919) observed that "Massage produces an actual increase in the size of the muscle structures. The muscle is also found to become firmer and more elastic under its influence." McMillan (1925) wrote, "The muscles are strengthened and made to grow by manipulation." According to Despard (1932), "Massage improves the nutrition of the muscles and consequently promotes their development." These observations are not supported by the contemporary literature, which generally agrees that massage alone does not increase muscle strength. Of course, if the massage is used as a method of preparing muscles for exercise (e.g., in sports massage, see Chapter 13), then strengthening would be expected to occur, providing a suitable regime of exercise was performed. Nonetheless, exercise, not the massage, is the reason why muscle strength would increase.

Mennell (1945) believed the theory that advocated kneading a muscle (working a muscle up) and thereby making it stronger was a complete delusion. He stated,

> *By one means alone can muscular strength be developed, and that is by muscular contraction, and no form of massage can do more than aid means indrectly.*

and again,

> *To use massage aright we must consider it entirely as a means to an end, that end being restoration of fuction.*

As a means to an end, massage may make it possible for a muscle to perform more exercise and thus develop its strength. This fact has been proven by experimental work done by Rosenthal, Mosso, and Maggiora (and by others cited in Cuthbertson [1933]), who have shown that a muscle fatigued by work or by electrical stimulation will be restored much more rapidly and thoroughly by massage than by rest alone of the same duration.

Nordschow and Bierman (1962) studied 25 normal, healthy, active subjects to determine whether massage manually applied could cause measurable muscle relaxation in normal human subjects, expressed as increased muscle length. A finger-to-floor test was used to measure tension in the posterior muscles of the back, thighs, and legs as each subject, standing with knees straight, bent forward and attempted to touch the floor with the fingertips. Following such an attempt, each subject then assumed a comfortable, well-supported prone position for 30 minutes of rest. The finger-to-floor test was then repeated. The subject then reassumed the prone position and was given 30 minutes of massage, 15 to the back and 15 to the posterior aspect of the lower extremity, allowing 7.5 minutes per limb. The authors concluded that manual massage causes relaxation, which is expressed as increased muscle length. Bell (1964) reported that muscle fatigue was relieved more quickly by massage and rest than by rest alone and suggested alternate bouts of exercise and massage in therapy (a method applied in some sports).

Smith and colleagues (1994) studied the effects of athletic massage on delayed-onset muscle soreness, creatine kinase, and neutrophil count. Their results indicate that massage reduces the negative effects of exercise on normal muscle. Presumably these effects are due to the increased circulation of blood and lymph, effectively washing out the metabolic by-products of exercise. The positive effects of massage on muscle recovery following intensive exercise are well known and have been studied in a variety of professional sports (Perkes et al., 2004; Robertson et al., 2004; Weerapong et al., 2005).

The term *muscle tone* is often used to describe the quality of a muscle that is firm and ready to contract; however, muscles at rest show no electromyographic activity (Goodgold & Erberstein, 1983). Therefore a muscle that exhibits tone cannot be at rest; it must be in a state of contraction. Although some statements in the literature imply that massage increases muscle tone, evidence to support this claim is inconclusive at best. Theoretically, however, several massage strokes would be expected to increase the fusimotor drive to a muscle. For example, any of the percussion (tapotement) strokes (hacking, clapping, beating, and pounding) would be expected to increase muscle spindle firing and, therefore, fusimotor output. Indeed, this is the mechanism by which massage strokes facilitate muscle contraction. It amounts to direct stimulation of stretch reflexes within the stimulated muscle.

Deep massage to normal muscle tissue will obviously have a strong mechanical mobilizing effect on the physical structure of the tissue itself. The mechanical effects (stretching, twisting, pressing, etc.) are likely to trigger physiological changes, especially in the series and parallel elastic components, effectively making it possible for the muscle to lengthen over time. The effect of stretching on human muscles is a complex issue, but the biophysics have important implications for soft tissue massage techniques and the use of passive stretching movements (De Deyne, 2001; Magnusson, 1998), especially in the sports sciences (Hemmings et al., 2000).

### Pathologic Conditions of Muscle

Fibrosis tends to occur in muscles that have been immobilized, injured, or lost their nerve supply. Significant shortening of the parallel and series elastic components (contracture) is often the end result. The muscle as a whole becomes shorter than its normal resting length, mainly because the fibrous tissue lacks elasticity and adhesions form between adjacent layers of connective tissue.

With the careful use of various massage techniques, it is possible to apply tension on this fibrous tissue, the objective being to prevent adhesions from forming and to break down small adhesions that have already formed. The techniques best suited to this purpose are various pressure manipulations (pétrissage) and the deep transverse friction technique (Iwatsuki et al., 2001). When supplemented by appropriate exercise and stretching regimens, massage techniques are an essential component in the restoration of muscle length and normal function.

A number of experimental studies have investigated the effects of massage on both injured and denervated muscle. These are considered separately here because the issues involved in each case differ significantly.

#### Injured Muscle

Lucas-Championnière (cited in Mennell [1945]) described some of the earliest experimental work in this area and summarized the results of Castex's work on the effects of massage on injured muscles. Animal muscles were subjected to crushing injury; then massage was given to one group and another group was used as a control. The researcher later microscopically examined the muscle tissue of both groups. The untreated parts showed the following characteristics: (1) dissociation into fibrils of the muscle fibers, as shown by well-marked longitudinal striation; (2) hyperplasia (often simple thickening) of the connective tissue; (3) an increased number of nuclei in the connective tissue; (4) interstitial hemorrhages; (5) an enlargement of blood vessels, with hyperplasia of their adventitious coats; and (6) usually intact sarcolemma (but, in one section, multiplication of nuclei gave an appearance that somewhat resembled interstitial myositis). In contrast, the massaged limbs had the following features: (1) normal-looking muscle, (2) no secondary fibrous bands separating the muscle fibers, (3) no fibrous thickening around the vessels, (4) greater general muscle bulk, and (5) no signs of hemorrhage.

#### Denervated Muscle

Although massage has been used quite extensively for the treatment of a muscle that has lost its nerve supply (denervated muscle), there is little information in the literature on its effectiveness. Some studies have been performed, however, mainly in an effort to determine its effect on the histopathological changes in the muscle itself, on atrophy, and on the strength of the muscle. No firm conclusions can yet be drawn from these results.

Chor et al. (1939) conducted an experiment to study the effects of massage on atrophy and the histopathological changes that occur in denervated muscle in primates. Two groups of rhesus monkeys were subjected to unilateral section of the sciatic nerve; the researchers then immediately sutured the nerves and immobilized the extremity in a plaster cast. After 4 weeks, they applied massage (stroking and kneading) and passive motion daily for 7 minutes to one group while keeping the control group at complete rest. After intervals from 2 months for some animals to 6 months for others, the researchers examined the muscles microscopically to determine the histopathological changes. The muscles kept at rest were pale and surrounded by thickened septa of fibrous tissue with whitish and yellowish streaks throughout. Microscopically, this fibrosis was clearly demonstrable, both surrounding muscle fibers and replacing atrophic ones. The massaged muscles were supple and elastic and showed considerably less fibrosis and adhesions. The extent to which muscle function is restored after reinnervation is determined largely by the ratio of functioning muscle fibers to fibrous tissue that has replaced degenerated muscle fibers. To some extent, by preventing the formation of inelastic fibrous tissue and adhesions, massage helped maintain a favorable ratio for greater recovery of function. This would be particularly important in terms of the overall length of a muscle, because this is a key factor in preserving the normal range of motion at any joint associated with the muscle.

In an earlier study, Chor and Dolkart (1936) compared muscle atrophy resulting from either disuse or denervation. They observed that disuse atrophy in a skeletal muscle develops slowly and is associated with simple structural changes. The loss of muscle bulk was attributed to a diminished quantity of sarcoplasm in the individual muscle fibers, the atrophic muscle fibers being narrower and packed closer together. The characteristic cross-striations persist, with no actual degeneration of the muscle fibers. The intramuscular blood vessels remain unaltered.

The muscle atrophy that follows nerve section or lesions of the anterior horn cells (e.g., poliomyelitis) is more than wasting from disuse. Its course is rapid, and characteristic changes occur. In addition to the shrinkage of the muscle fibers, degeneration of these cells follows. The cross-striations disappear, and the muscle cells begin to break down. In later stages, the disintegrated muscle cells are replaced by fibrous tissue and fat. Changes also occur in the intramuscular blood vessels. The number of capillaries increases, and the small intramuscular blood vessels show hypertrophy of the endothelium and an increase in their fibrous structure. Chor and coworkers believed that atrophy and degeneration of denervated skeletal muscle are inevitable and then showed that massage did not prevent atrophy up to a period of 6 weeks, but because of its effect on the amount of fibrous tissue formed, it did enable the muscles to return to normal more rapidly upon reinnervation.

In an early study, Langley and Hashimoto (1918) considered the effects of massage in denervated muscles from a single rabbit. Firm massage was begun on the third postoperative day. Treatment was discontinued on the seventh day because open lesions developed on the limb. Treatment was started again on the eleventh day with "gentler" massage, which was continued until 23 days after denervation. The researchers concluded that the effect of the treatment on atrophy was slight at best and that an increase in the growth of connective tissue is a possible result of massaging denervated muscle. Although interesting in itself, this study offers limited possible conclusions.

Hartman and colleagues (1919) tested both weight and work capacity of denervated muscles in 37 rabbits. One leg of the animals was given kneading and stroking massage. Both legs were given passive exercise. Treatment continued for periods of 7 to 190 days. The investigators noted no significant differences. They suggested that the weight of the muscle did not necessarily indicate the amount of contractile tissue present, because structural mass and function of the muscles differed considerably in 17 of the muscles tested.

Hartman and Blatz (1920) later tested the power of denervated gastrocnemius muscles of 60 rabbits. The muscles on one side were massaged for periods of 2 to 20 minutes daily, and both legs were given daily passive movement. The investigators tested the muscles at intervals of 10 to 14 days. They concluded (1) that "the treated limb on the whole did not appear to be any better off than the control"; (2) that massage was of no value; and (3) that there was invariably a decrease in power and no significant difference between treated muscles and controls.

Wright (1939) stated that more rigorous proof was required for the claims that muscle wasting can be prevented or muscle nutrition improved by providing massage but not movement. He believed that some local effects are undoubtedly produced in the muscle and that they may be due to chemical agents liberated into the blood to produce local or general effects. He also believed that massage might release some of the metabolites of muscle activity. He questioned whether direct mechanical stimulation could produce a direct muscle response in denervated muscle as reflex reactions are obviously excluded.

Suskind and colleagues (1946) studied the denervated gastrocnemius muscles of cats. Two 5-minute periods of effleurage and kneading were given daily to one limb; the other limb served as the control. The investigators measured the strength and weight of the muscles 28 days after sectioning. Results showed that the denervated muscles treated with massage were heavier and stronger than their untreated contralateral controls. The effect on muscle weight was slight but statistically significant. It seemed that massage had slowed down the gradual loss of contractile strength observed in skeletal muscle after denervation.

Wood and associates (1948) reported the effects of massage on weights and tensions of the anterior tibial muscles of 14 dogs. Bilateral section of sciatic nerves was performed, and one leg was given a daily period of massage (stroking and kneading) lasting for 10 minutes. The other leg was used as the control. The researchers tested the muscles at intervals from 13½ to 36 weeks following denervation. Results showed that all anterior tibial muscles in the treated animals appeared pale and small in size, compared with normal anterior tibial muscles. There was also a greater proportion of tendon to total bulk than in normal muscles, as well as a greater proportion of fatty tissue. It was impossible to distinguish treated tissue from untreated muscle on gross examination. Histological sections from anterior tibial muscles of treated animals (treated and untreated muscles) showed no significant histological differences. Wood concluded, "Massage was not effective in delaying denervation atrophy, as indicated by losses in strength and weight and by examination of histological sections in experimentally denervated anterior tibial muscles of the dog."

The primary effects of massage on muscle tissue can be summarized as follows:

- Massage does not directly increase the strength of normal muscle; however, as a means to an end it is more effective than rest in promoting recovery from fatigue produced by excessive exercise. Theoretically, then, massage makes it possible to do more exercise, which, in turn, increases muscular strength and endurance. This is an important factor in treatment. It would seem logical that massage should be given between periods of exercise when exercise is used to develop muscle strength and endurance. This is particularly relevant for sports medicine.
- Generally speaking, massage does not increase muscle tone, but certain strokes can be used to facilitate muscle activity (especially percussion techniques; see Chapter 9) that inevitably develops in immobilized, injured, or denervated muscle.
- Massage may reduce the amount of fibrosis.
- Massage does not prevent atrophy in denervated muscle. Even though a muscle may undergo considerable wasting, if fibrosis is minimal and circulation and nutrition are good, a small muscle may have greater power than a muscle with larger mass if the mass is the result of overgrowth of fibrous tissue that interferes with the function and recovery of the remaining innervated muscle fibers.
- The aims of massage in the treatment of denervated muscle should be to maintain the muscles in the best possible state of nutrition, flexibility, and vitality, so that after recovery (if this is possible) from trauma or disease, the muscle can function at its maximal potential.

## Effects on Bones and Joints

Key and colleagues (1934a, 1934b) conducted an experiment to determine the effects of heat, massage, or active exercise on local atrophy of the bone caused by immobilization of the part. Ten patients with normal lower extremities were used. Both extremities were placed in casts, which were bivalved and removed during treatment. One extremity was used as a control; the other was treated. The massage was given for 10 minutes, twice daily for 6 weeks. Roentgenograms were made before and at the end of the experiment. The investigators observed no significant differences between the treated and control limbs. They concluded that short periods of heat (five patients), massage (two patients), or active exercise (three patients) had little, if any, effect on local atrophy of bone secondary to immobilization in a plaster of Paris cast. These results are interesting; however, the experiment was performed on very small numbers of subjects and the results are certainly inconclusive.

In the past, massage was used widely in the treatment of fractures, and it was considered beneficial for aiding repair of the associated soft tissue injuries. It has not been established, however, whether massage actually helps to heal bone. It was the opinion of the Fracture Committee of the American College of Surgeons that, in the process of normal bone repair after fracture, "The effectiveness and rapidity of growth of tissue are dependent upon efficient circulation in the parts. . . . Therefore every effort must be made from the beginning to help the efficiency of the circulation."

Mock (1945) believed that because recent research had shown the tendency for callus to be formed along the lines of the new blood vessels formed at the site of fractures, any treatment that enhanced circulation in the area of the fracture without producing motion of the fragments should promote deposition of callus. Of course, this may be difficult with many of the deeper massage strokes, the objective of which is to deliberately squeeze and stretch the deeper muscle tissues. It is hard to see how these techniques can be given effectively without causing the bone fragments at a fracture site to move; however, if the fracture site is stable, massage techniques might be very useful.

Many of the structures that surround the various joints of the body, such as ligaments, bursas, capsules, and tendons, are often the site of chronic problems. In many instances of chronic dysfunction, the goal of treatment is to break down scar tissue in these structures and the adhesions between them. Traditionally, deep friction massage has been the technique of choice because its strong mechanical effect on scar tissue is useful in restoring a normal, painless range of motion to an affected joint (Cyriax, 1960, 1984; Hammer, 1993). (See also Chapter 9.)

Clearly, joints are designed to move under the influence of muscles and gravity, and there are many reasons why range of motion in a joint may be lost. Of course, continued loss of range in a joint contributes to chronic pain and adhesion, with the accompanying loss of function. Impaired range of motion can be restored to joints using a wide variety of treatments, including massage. This is particularly the case if the limited range is due to muscle spasm, pain, or contracture in the tissues surrounding the joint. Appropriate massage techniques can help to relieve pain and restore range of motion in these circumstances (Hernandez-Reif et al., 2001).

## Effects on the Nervous System

Although the literature offers little direct information on the actual effects of massage on the function of the human nervous system, the mechanical effects of massage clearly give rise to a number of important physiological effects. Indeed, massage techniques specifically directed at peripheral nerves were in common use in the early decades of the twentieth century. In her book *Massage and Medical Gymnastics,* Lace (1946) described so-called nerve manipulations—such as nerve stroking, nerve pressure with vibration, nerve friction, and nerve stretching—as a significant category of strokes. These techniques, though rarely used today, are still being given for specific nerve problems (Jabre, 1994).

Despite a paucity of information, it is possible to describe some likely effects based on what is known of the neurobiology of the nervous system. For example, whenever the skin is touched or the underlying tissues are manipulated, sensory receptors in a variety of tissues are activated. Afferent signals pass into the spinal cord, form synapses with various spinal neurons, and eventually find their way to the sensory cortex and other brain centers. At a spinal level, several spinal reflexes could be triggered, depending on the type and depth of massage technique and the part of the body being massaged. Similar reflex activation is likely at a variety of autonomic centers and brain nuclei. Some of these concepts are discussed in the next section on the effects of massage on pain. Clearly, there are many potential pathways by which soft tissue massage might have direct and indirect effects on the nervous system.

A number of studies have shown that many direct effects are indeed possible. Clear evidence from several well-controlled studies shows that massage (kneading) performed directly on a muscle causes significant depression of the amplitude of the H-reflex (Hoffman reflex) response, but only during the period of massage (Morelli et al., 1991; Sullivan et al., 1991). This effect was also recorded in patients with spinal cord injury (Goldberg et al., 1994). In contrast, Dishman and Bulbulian (2001) compared the effect of spinal manipulation and massage on motoneuron excitability and reported that the effects were transient, but the effects on the tibial H-reflex produced by spinal manipulation lasted longer than those of massage.

Goldberg and colleagues (1992) studied the effect of two intensities of massage on H-reflex amplitude and showed that a deeper massage technique produced a more pronounced reduction in H-reflex amplitude than did superficial massage. In each of the studies cited here, the inhibitory effect of the massage on H-reflex amplitude effectively lasted only during the time when massage was applied. Some subjects (especially those with spinal cord injury) did show a tendency for the inhibitory effect to continue when the massage had ceased, but it did not last long enough to be useful therapeutically. These results are also important because they indicate that massage of muscle tissue and its related structures (e.g., skin, subcutaneous tissues) can change the level of excitability of the spinal motor neurons. The effect is reflex in nature and is likely to be associated with increased firing of the pressure-sensitive receptors in muscle, especially the Golgi tendon organs, which are known to inhibit their relevant alpha motor nerve cells.

Despite promising early experimental studies on reflex control of circulation and neuromuscular responses to massage (Cuthbertson, 1933; McMaster, 1937; Pemberton, 1945) and strong support for hypotheses that massage has definite reflex effects, such effects seem to be hypothesized for want of any other rational explanation. The specific reflex mechanism responsible has not been clearly identified, nor has how simple or complex the reflex action(s) may be. Much work still must be done to clarify and verify these concepts by controlled clinical and laboratory studies, correlated with current physiological and neurophysiological concepts.

The work of Barr and Norman (1970) and Barr and Taslitz (1970) is an example of the kind of studies that need to be undertaken for a variety of massage treatments. In addition to the effects on blood pressure and heart rate of a 20-minute back massage, Barr and Taslitz reported (1) increased skin sweating and, thus, decreased resistance to galvanic current (galvanic skin response, or GSR); (2) after a slight decrease in body temperature (0 to 0.1° C) in the control period, an increase of 0° to 0.2° C at the end of the massage; and (3) increased pupil diameter, which, in their opinion, may or may not have been a result of massage. Their results indicate an increase in sympathetic activity in most indexes. More recently, massage therapy has been shown to be effective in treating problems associated with chronic neurological disorders, including Parkinson's disease (Hernandez-Reif et al., 2002) and spinal cord injury (Diego et al., 2002).

The idea of producing specific effects in the nervous system, or indeed in the neural control of many organs and systems, is not a new one. Traditional acupressure and many Eastern massage techniques are intended to affect a variety of nervous system functions (Chen et al., 1998). Examples of this principle can also be found in theories of reflexology, which hold that direct manual stimulation of various body areas (mainly, but not exclusively, the feet and hands) produces effects elsewhere in the body, and of the Japanese system of massage known as *shiatsu*. The more recent development of connective tissue massage (CTM) in the late 1930s is another good example of a technique that relies heavily on reflex effects in the nervous system. All of these treatment concepts use the important principle of *remote site stimulation* to achieve their effects. This principle simply means that stimulation in one part of the body can produce effects elsewhere. These concepts are discussed in more detail in Chapters 9, 11, 16, and 17.

### Effects on Pain

Since the very earliest of times, primitive humans probably knew that vigorously rubbing an injured area relieved pain. This behavior is clearly instinctive and is displayed by humans and many animals. Rubbing the skin stimulates cutaneous mechanoreceptors, and these afferent signals are able to temporarily block the transmission—and possibly the perception—of nociceptive (pain) signals. This effect is easy to demonstrate and is one that most people have experienced many times. Other modalities, such as mechanical vibration and electrical stimulation, can stimulate the same cutaneous receptors.

Since the mid-1960s, new theories and research on pain and its mechanisms of generation, transmission, perception, and treatment have had a significant bearing on the ancient art of massage (Wall, 1994). This new understanding has revived interest in the use of electrical stimulation (Belamger 2002; Mannheimer & Lampe, 1984; Robinson & Snyder-Mackler, 1995) and many forms of manual mobilizing technique (Grieve, 1994).

A complex picture has developed that provides a rationale for intervention in a variety of soft tissue problems, including various chronic pain syndromes. The specificity of nociceptors and mechanoreceptors and their relationship to the transmission and eventual perception of pain have been elucidated, together with the alteration of tonic levels of muscle activity. Because it is known that manual stimulation of afferent fibers carrying sensory information can have a significant effect on pain, this constitutes strong scientific support for the use of massage as a therapeutic measure to relieve pain. Beginning with the work of Melzack and Wall (1965), the concept of a neural *gate* in the region of the dorsal horn of the spinal cord gray matter has been central to intervention or research strategies involving pain. Although the original theory has undergone much review and revision, the central concepts remain intact.

A gate is designed to control movement from one place to another. When a gate is open, movement through it is permitted (possibly in both directions), and when it is closed, passage is denied. In this regard, the spinal gate is no different. Various cells are able to control the flow of nociceptive (pain information) from distal body parts to central sites in the nervous system. Nociceptive information is transmitted by small-diameter, slowly conducting fibers (A-delta and C fibers). The spinal gate may be closed by specific sensory impulses from mechanoreceptors (large-diameter fibers) in a variety of structures, but particularly in the skin of the affected area. When the gate is closed, nociceptive input is reduced, and this may significantly reduce the level of pain the patient perceives. Descending impulses are also able to affect the ability of the spinal gate to open or close. It should be remembered that the actual nociceptive signals are not in themselves painful. They are simply nerve impulses traveling in the peripheral and central nervous systems. Only when these signals reach the higher brain centers are they interpreted as painful.

The neurophysiological basis for gate control is a complex and developing model. It involves not only the neural pathways of the system but also complex interactions between various brain structures and neurotransmitters and hormones (enkephalins and endorphins). The area has been reviewed extensively in many texts that deal with different aspects of the physiology and management of pain. A detailed description is well beyond the scope of this text, and interested readers are referred to Wall (1994) for an excellent review of the subject.

Clearly, massage techniques have the capacity to produce significant afferent input by direct stimulation of large-diameter mechanoreceptors in many structures. Depending on the techniques in question, these structures will be mainly in the skin or in the skin and the deeper tissues. In either case, activation of the spinal gating mechanism, descending pain suppression influences, and release of endogenous opiates are reasonable explanations for pain relief produced by massage techniques.

Interaction of the somatic and the autonomic nervous systems and of the musculoskeletal and the visceral systems has always been assumed. In recent years, better understanding has shown that these interrelationships are more direct and predictable than was previously thought. An example of this better understanding can be found in the clinical approach to referred pain. It has long been assumed that referred pain is only the central interpretation of visceral or deep musculoskeletal pain through spinal connections to areas overlying the painful structures or related to them. In this view, permanent relief of this type of pain is achieved only by removing the original cause. Temporary relief usually involves a centrally acting drug that blocks the transmission or perception of pain. It has been demonstrated, however, that the peripheral pain site may contain reflexes that respond to direct peripheral intervention and that this intervention may even have a positive influence on the central cause of pain. This concept is illustrated particularly well in the trigger points of the myofascial pain syndrome (see Chapter 16). In this case, a variety of methods (some manual) can be used to desensitize the painful trigger points (Travell & Simons, 1983, 1992).

The effects of massage on the circulation of blood and lymph may also contribute to pain relief. Because certain massage techniques have a significant effect on the circulation, they may be expected to enhance removal from an affected area of pain metabolites (e.g., kinins). This washing-out effect could be a significant contribution to pain relief achieved with soft tissue massage.

Pain relief can also come from the relaxation effect produced by certain massage techniques (Meek, 1993). If muscle spasm is a significant cause of pain, then reducing the muscle spasm will help to relieve the pain. This effect was well known by Lucas-Championnière, whose technique of obtaining relaxation of muscles in spasm following a fracture by superficial stroking can be explained only as a reflex effect. The more generalized relaxation that can be achieved with massage may also contribute to pain relief, especially if such pain is of a central nature. It seems most likely then that the pain of neuromusculoskeletal origin is relieved by a number of mechanisms, depending on the specific pathology involved. For example, the common label of "low back pain" can refer to pain produced from a multitude of reasons. Massage therapy can be effective in an overall treatment plan and probably achieves its effects via a combination of the mechanisms previously described (Hernandez-Reif et al., 2001). Chronic pain of neuromusculoskeletal origin is clearly relieved by a number of mechanisms, depending on the specific pathology involved. For example, the common label of "low back pain" can refer to pain produced from a multitude of reasons. Nonetheless, massage has positive effects in relieving chronic pain (Walach et al., 2003), the serious dysfunction of fibromyalgia (Field et al., 2003; Lemstra & Olszynski, 2005), mechanical neck pain (Haraldsson, 2005), subacute low-back pain (Preyde 2000), and in reducing the many symptoms of migraine (Lemstra et al., 2002). Other studies have considered the effects of massage on experimental pain (Kessler et al., 2006) and the effectiveness, safety, and cost of massage therapy compared with acupuncture and spinal manipulation for back pain (Cherkin et al., 2003). Very recently, Lewis and Johnson (2006) undertook a systematic review of the effectiveness of therapeutic massage on musculoskeletal pain. The review reports equivocal findings that highlight the need for more rigorously controlled clinical trials.

## Effects on the Viscera

### *Abdominal Viscera*

Until quite recently, there was little published information on the effects of massage on the abdominal viscera. Mennell (1945) believed that the forceful abdominal massage once used primarily for its mechanical effects derived from a poor understanding of the gut. He pointed out that the slightest tap on the exposed intestine of a frog causes instant spasm of that portion plus cardiac inhibition, and that the effect of manipulation on involuntary muscle of the intestines can be observed during abdominal surgery. Excessive handling may result in overstimulation and temporary paralysis of the involuntary (smooth) muscle. This might produce the opposite effect, namely, inhibition of normal bowel function rather than stimulation.

Mennell believed that it was impossible to empty the small intestine mechanically. He believed that any action of massage on the intestines is almost, if not entirely, a reflexive response to the pressure of mechanical stimulation. This stimulation can increase peristalsis and thus hasten the emptying of the intestinal contents. He pointed out that some portions of the large intestine are quite constant in their relationship to the abdominal wall, and thus the direction of the passage of the contents in the duodenum, the ascending and descending colon, and the iliac portions of the colon can be followed.

Beard and Wood were convinced that massage of the abdomen with kneading and deep stroking (see Chapter 9) is effective in stimulating peristalsis to promote evacuation of flatus and feces from the large intestine. The patient can be taught these procedures, which may be performed while seated. The contents of the abdomen, with the exception of the duodenum and fixed portions of the colon, may easily be displaced or glide away from any pressure exerted on the abdominal wall, making it impossible to exert any mechanical effect of massage.

Klauser and coworkers (1992) conducted a well-controlled study of the effects of abdominal wall massage on colon function in both normal subjects and patients with chronic constipation. This study showed no significant differences in colon function in the two groups, and despite anecdotal reports from earlier writers, the results place in doubt the efficacy of such massage for the treatment of chronic constipation. Other authors (Emly, 1993) have drawn similar conclusions about the effects of abdominal wall massage.

Mennell believed that, though it may be possible to produce a mechanical effect with massage to some abdominal organs (e.g., prostate), the effects probably reflect a reflex reaction to mechanical stimulation. He said that it may be possible also to produce reflex contraction of smooth muscle of the spleen, but physiologically it is difficult to explain any beneficial effect. To expect any benefit from "shaking up the liver," as earlier writers had recommended, was quite wrong, according to Mennell, though abdominal massage may stimulate portal circulation and, thus, liver functions.

Some of the earlier writers have suggested massage treatment of the pancreas. Mennell thought it might be affected reflexly, but it seems likely that this is only an indirect effect of improved general vascular tone. Being a hollow organ, the gallbladder is, according to Mennell, amenable to the mechanical effects of massage. Because current knowledge of the effects of massage on the abdominal viscera is limited, it would seem unwise to perform any type of abdominal massage except to affect abdominal muscles—and possibly indirectly to influence the circulation and, through reflex response to pressure, to stimulate activity of the involuntary muscles of the intestines.

Special techniques are required to massage specific organs, and they should only be applied by those specially trained in these techniques. (Because of the harm that can result from abdominal massage, it should not be included in a general massage without prior medical consultation.)

Mennell questioned the use of massage for the kidneys. Although he noted that by kneading the kidneys during cystoscopy it is possible to see urine pass from the ureter into the bladder, he doubted that this is clinically practical. More recently, mechanical vibration massage has been shown to be helpful in assisting patients to pass stone fragments following extracorporeal shockwave lithotripsy (Kosar et al., 1999).

### *Effects on Other Viscera*

The heart and lungs are organs that can be affected by massage delivered to the thorax. Although massage is not applied directly to the heart except under special circumstances, massage can have an effect on cardiac function, especially to slow it down and promote relaxation (Diego et al., 2004). Direct massage of the heart is used as an emergency treatment in certain circumstances. When an abdominal incision has been made, the surgeon may massage the heart, either by compressing it between the diaphragm and the ribs or by incising the diaphragm and directly grasping the heart. Mennell knew of no direct action on the heart that could be achieved by externally applied massage movements other than the obvious mechanical compression. Indeed, Kouwenhoven and associates (1960) reported a 70% long-term survival rate for patients with cardiac arrest who were given closed-chest cardiac massage (see the appendix). The specific effects of massage on the lungs are considered in the next section.

Some forms of massage might be expected to affect various organs of the body by virtue of their reflex effects. Connective tissue massage is an obvious example: stimulation of specific areas on the posterior trunk region is expected to produce effects on a variety of organs and structures elsewhere in the body, especially the major organs. This concept relies on evoking an autonomic reflex by stimulating cutaneous afferents reflexly related to specific organs and structures (see Chapter 11).

Another example of the potential for massage techniques to reflexly affect the various organs of the body is expressed in the treatment concept of acupressure (see Chapter 17). In this case, finger or thumb pressure applied to specific points on the body is designed to produce reflex effects in various organs and systems. This is yet another excellent example of the principle of a remote site effect, in which stimulation at one part of the body produces an effect elsewhere, even in an apparently unrelated area.

## Effects on the Lungs

Percussive and vibratory massage techniques can be used in combination with other measures of chest physical therapy to prevent or treat acute and chronic lung conditions. The few controlled studies on the effects of chest physical therapy do not separate the effects of the various measures; however, many clinicians stress the importance of these types of massage techniques in the treatment of conditions such as emphysema, cystic fibrosis, bronchiectasis, asthma, atelectasis, and pneumonia.

Cyriax (1960, 1984) stated that percussive techniques, combined with postural drainage, can dislodge mucus and mucopurulent material from the bronchi and that gravity and vibration help to move the secretions from the insensitive periphery of the lungs to the area where the cough reflex is elicited. Such measures have been advocated in standard texts for many years. For example, Bendixen et al. (1965) recommended vibration and percussion with cupped hands (clapping) to shake loose secretions. Percussion is used in cases of "sticky, thick secretions that defy normal coughing efforts." Likewise, Cherniack, Cherniack, and Naimark (1972) believed that the role of physical therapy in the care of patients with acute respiratory failure could not be overemphasized. They advocated that while postural drainage is being performed to stimulate removal of secretions, "the chest should be pummeled with rapid repetitive strokes and vibrated" by the therapist, and that the patient should frequently cough and expectorate the loosened secretions. These techniques are also important in the prevention and treatment of recurrent respiratory tract infection in children (Zhu, 1998) and in other pulmonary issues in critical care and chronic lung disease (Jones & Rowe, 2000; McCarren et al., 2003, 2006).

Current texts on the topic (Frownfelter & Dean, 2006; Hillegass & Sadowsky, 1994; Irwin & Techlin, 1995; Watchie, 1995) continue to stress the importance of proper airway clearance and the need to teach the patient to use simple but effective home treatment techniques. For a more complete discussion of these issues, see Chapter 10.

## Effects on the Immune System

In addition to the direct mechanical effects described earlier, massage therapy can have powerful physiological and psychological effects, so it is not difficult to see that this might produce an effect on immune system function. In fact, the effect of massage on immune system function has been studied with varying results. Some studies, such as that conducted by Birk et al. (2000), show no significant effect on immune system function in patients with HIV, although Birk et al. did report that massage helped to minimize stress and improve overall function. In contrast, Diego et al. (2001) reported that adolescents with HIV responded well and showed improved immune function after massage therapy.

Massage therapy seems to be helpful in improving immune system function in patients undergoing treatment for various cancers, such as leukemia (Field et al., 2001) and breast cancer, where they show an increased immune and neuroendocrine function as a result of massage therapy (Hernandez-Reif et al., 2004). Massage also has a positive effect on immune system function following sport (Hemmings, 2000).

Positive effects on immune system function are also seen with massage given during academic stress (e.g., taking a test) (Zeitlin et al., 2000). Because massage is known to relieve anxiety, it is not surprising that it might have positive effects on immune system function as there is a clear link between its overall strength and the effects of stress. Not surprisingly then, massage can be an effective adjunct to the treatment of various psychiatric disorders where anxiety and stress are significant issues (Field et al., 1992), particularly when they lead to depression or compulsive behaviors such as bulimia (Field et al., 1998).

## Effects on the Skin

The direct effects of massage on the skin are difficult to evaluate because there are few studies in this area. Traditionally, however, the earlier writers proposed that massage had a direct effect on the superficial layers of the epidermis that freed the openings of the sebaceous and sweat glands. The mechanism was improved circulation, which directly improved the function of these glands (Krusen, 1941). Other early writers thought that sweating did not significantly increase but that sebaceous secretions might be expressed (Wright, 1939). According to Rosenthal (cited in Cuthbertson [1933]), massage increases the temperature of the skin by 2° to 3°C. He found that neurasthenic persons showed a greater increase in skin temperature than normal healthy persons in response to massage, and women showed a greater increase than men. He explained the differences by the fact that the entire nervous system, including the vasomotor nerves, is stimulated more easily in neurasthenic persons than in normal ones and in women more than in men. The increase in skin temperature may be caused by direct mechanical effects (friction) and indirect vasomotor action.

In contrast, Severini and Venerando (1967) reported that both superficial and deep massage led to a significant drop in skin temperature at the site of application. Barr and Taslitz (1970) observed increased sweating and decreased skin resistance to galvanic current in response to massage. They found much variation in skin temperature changes in both control and treatment periods and felt they could not infer that massage either increased or decreased skin temperature.

Clinical observation shows that, following massage to a part that has been in a cast for some weeks, definite improvements in the texture and appearance of the skin can be noted. If the skin has become adherent to underlying tissues and scar tissue has formed, friction movements and tension can be used to loosen the adherent tissues mechanically and to soften the scar. Massage techniques can also be helpful in the management of hypertrophic scars (Patino et al., 1999).

Bodian (1969) recommended massage to enhance the cosmetic results of eyelid surgery. The mechanism of the method he described "seems to be stretching and disruption of excess scar tissue." He found this massage useful in treating thick scars of the eyelid, keloids, overcorrected ptosis, overcorrected entropion, postoperative ectropion, and shallow fornices. As expected, the mechanical effects of massage tend to mobilize the skin and subcutaneous tissue, leaving it more pliable.

Because the skin is the organ that first comes into direct contact with the therapist's hands, it is not unreasonable to expect that massage would have at least some effects on skin. These effects can be helpful or harmful. For example, if too much powder or oil is used on the skin, it is likely that the skin surface will become clogged with the residue of the lubricant. This might easily lead to rashes and possible infections, especially in a patient with sensitive skin.

## Effects on Adipose (Fat) Tissue

Many have claimed over the years that massage removes deposits of adipose tissue (stored body fat). Krusen (1941) asserted that clinical observations did not support this theory and that attempts to reduce local fat deposits are futile.

Rosenthal (cited in Cuthbertson [1933]) investigated this problem experimentally. Vigorous massage was applied to certain areas of the abdominal wall of animals. Microscopic studies of the massaged and untreated areas showed no change in the fat in treated areas, even when the massage had been forceful enough to cause frequent small hemorrhages. Wright (1939) and Kalb (1944) came to similar conclusions.

At the present time, there is no credible evidence to support the contention that massage has any ability to reduce stored body fat. Subcutaneous body fat represents the body's attempt to store energy (metabolic fuel), and the only known way to reduce this fat is to use it. This means it is necessary to metabolize the stored energy, and the most reliable way to do this is with a program of active exercise. Because soft tissue massage is a passive treatment, it is intuitively unreasonable to expect that it can have any effect in reducing the total percentage of body fat.

The primary effects of massage depend on the individual stroke. Therefore the primary effects are listed separately for each of the major types of massage stroke (see Chapter 4 for details of each individual stroke).

## Effect on Cellulite

The concept of cellulite is a controversial issue, but it is one that deserves a degree of examination. *Cellulite* is not a medical term, but it is in widespread use and is the source of much confusion. Many people have the mistaken belief that cellulite is the same as normal adipose (fat) tissue. This is certainly not the case. Cellulite is the name given to describe the lumpy, irregular fatty deposits that appear as dimpled skin around the hips, buttocks, and thighs, giving rise to the characteristic orange-peel appearance. Cellulite is almost exclusively a female problem and is widespread. It is difficult to find a generally accepted scientific description of exactly what cellulite is. It seems to be the result of the collapse of the connective tissue *net* that supports the layer of subcutaneous fat cells in certain areas of the female anatomy. There may also be some local changes in the fat cells, although this is not substantiated. The situation is worsened if the individual is overweight, because there will be an extra accumulation of fat in the same areas that are prone to cellulite formation.

Beneath the skin is a layer of fat that varies in thickness, depending on many factors. Fat cells in the human are spherical in appearance and are held in position in an orderly arrangement, supported by a net of connective tissue. When the tissues are young, the skin usually appears smooth, supple, and elastic. For many reasons, the connective tissue net begins to degenerate and collapse in certain areas and is unable to support the fat cells in a smooth layer. These changes can occur in the teenage years, but the layer of fat is usually less visible then because the skin is still supple and elastic. However, the condition can become more problematic as one ages or if one is overweight, and this fat tends to accumulate around the hips, buttocks, and thighs.

The issue of whether massage can reduce the effects of cellulite has led to many claims, some reasonable, some fanciful, and others definitely misleading. Numerous treatments for cellulite have come on the market, most with many unsubstantiated claims. In recent years, a technique has emerged that seems to be effective for some cases, although only on a temporary basis. This treatment involves a mechanically induced, deep massage that resembles the manual stroke of skin rolling. These devices create a suction effect that pulls a roll of tissue up from the underlying structures, and then powered rollers enhance the lifting and rolling motion as the device is moved forward and backward across the skin and subcutaneous tissues. The concept is called *endermologie* (Figure 5-1). This technique does not break down the fat cells; rather, over time it might improve the connective tissue support system under the skin (net). The end result is a smoother-looking skin contour.

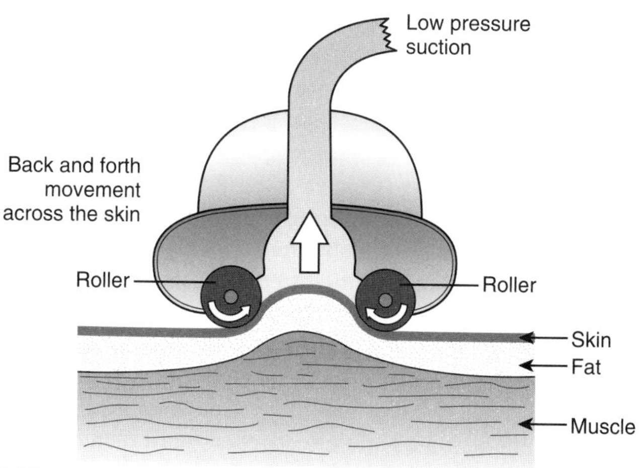


**Figure 5-1 Endermologie: A Mechanical Cellulite Treatment Concept**

The device imparts suction to the skin and subcutaneous tissues, lifting them up from their underlying support structures. The fold of tissues is then rolled through the machine, producing a strong mechanical stimulation to the tissues. The treatment is known as *endermologie.*

Several groups have studied the effects of the form of deep mechanical massage known as *endermologie,* in both animal models and human subjects, with varying results (Barel et al., 1997; Kinney et al., 1999; Lucassen et al., 1997; Pittet et al., 1999). Adcock et al. (2001), using a porcine model, showed that the treatment produced dense, longitudinal collagen bands in the middle dermal and deep subdermal regions, together with distortion and disruption of adipocytes. These changes progressively increased with the number of treatments. The authors also studied the effect of applying the device to the tissues in various ways and on the forces generated within the tissues. This led to the conclusion that "deep mechanical massage is highly dependent on the individual operator of the device." The demand for an effective treatment of cellulite is fueling tremendous interest in both the medical and cosmetic professions. The problem of cellulite is certainly a real one; however, the solutions at present are inconclusive and some are definitely controversial. Various forms of massage, both manual and mechanical, may prove to be effective treatments, but more research is needed in this interesting area.

## PSYCHOLOGICAL EFFECTS

Most people are familiar with the soothing effect of gentle massage, even when no lesion or physical disability is present (defined earlier as *recreational massage*). In therapeutic massage, the therapist's concentrated attention to the patient, combined with the pleasant physical sensations of the massage, often establishes a close and trusting bond. In these circumstances, patients may reveal to the therapist problems, worries, and facts about their health that they had thought too trivial to report to a physician. In this situation, of course, the therapist listens and holds any information in confidence. The therapist is careful to see that the patient does not become too dependent in the relationship and encourages him or her to report relevant information to a physician.

**BOX 5-3 Psychological Effects of Soft Tissue Manipulation**

- Physical relaxation
- Relief of anxiety and tension (stress)
- Stimulation of physical activity
- Pain relief
- General feeling of well-being (wellness)
- Sexual arousal
- General faith in the laying on of hands

Massage treatment can have negative psychological effects. The time and attention devoted to massage may exaggerate the seriousness of the disability in the patient's mind. Mennell (1945) warned, "It is easier to rub a disability into a patient's mind than it is to rub it out of his limb." Therapists must therefore take care to reassure the anxious patient and to correct any misunderstandings about the reasons for treatment.

Many of the physiological effects of massage described earlier have a significant psychological component. For example, pain relief has a dominant psychological component because it is strongly dependent on the patient's perception. In this way, pain relief is a legitimate psychological effect of massage. Each of the major psychological effects of massage is listed in Box 5-3 and discussed in the sections that follow.

### Relief of Anxiety and Tension (Stress) and the Promotion of Physical Relaxation

The relaxing and sedating effect of a general massage is well known and easily demonstrated. Mennell (1945) stated, "There is probably an effect on the central nervous system as well as a local effect on the sensory, and possibly the motor, nerves." Most people find that massage treatments are extremely relaxing. Certain strokes in particular promote physical relaxation; however, the concept of relaxation is not principally a physical one. It is just as much psychological as physiological. For muscles to relax, especially in an entire limb or the whole body, the person must be able to minimize the cortical drive passing to the relevant spinal motor neurons. This requires a conscious effort to let go. The reason some people find it difficult to relax their limbs might well be their inability to let everything go at the psychological level. Suitable massage techniques can contribute to this process, as they help the patient let his or her muscles and limbs relax.

Relief of anxiety and tension (stress) through massage is strongly linked to the promotion of relaxation identified previously. A patient who has significant anxiety and tension (stress) will find it hard, if not impossible, to relax. As massage promotes relaxation, it also helps to reduce anxiety and tension. This is because relaxation requires psychological release from anxiety and tension. This is one of the main reasons why recreational massage is so popular as part of a stress-reduction program. The relaxing and anxiety-reducing effects of massage have been investigated in many different types of study, especially for the anxiety suffered in terminal illness from cancer (Avakyan, 1990; Boone et al., 2001; Hernandez-Reif et al., 1999; Holland & Pokorny, 2001; Labyak & Metzger, 1997; Longworth, 1982; Meek, 1993; Rowe & Alfred, 1999; van der Riet, 1993).

Massage is also gaining popularity as an adjunctive treatment for the patient undergoing stressful medical procedures, such as those used in the critical care unit. In these cases, massage may be given to the foot or hand and is used to comfort the patient and to reduce the pain and anxiety concerning the procedure (Hayes & Cox, 1999; Hulme et al., 1999; Kim et al., 2001; Richards et al., 2000). Massage also helps to reduce the anxiety, stress, and pain associated with the treatment of burns, especially in children (Field et al., 1998, 2000; Hernandez-Reif et al., 2001). Massage treatments also seem to help relieve the pain and anxiety of premenstrual tension (Hernandez-Reif et al., 2000), and they promote sleep and relaxation in the critically ill (Richards, 1998). In addition, massage may be helpful in occupational situations as a means of relieving stress and anxiety in the workplace (Katz et al., 1999). The beneficial effects of massage in relieving stress and anxiety are perhaps the reason why recreational massage is so popular in the present day and why massage has endured the test of time as a worthy procedure.

### Stimulation of Physical Activity

Certain massage techniques can be stimulating and produce a strong sense of invigoration. These techniques have proved useful in the sporting world and have given rise to the concept of *sports massage,* which simply reflects the notion of using certain massage techniques to promote physical activity and optimal performance. A strong psychological impact often results from the application of suitable massage techniques (see Chapter 13).

### Relief of Pain

The physiological processes involved in pain relief through massage were discussed previously; however, the perception of pain is, of course, a psychological concept. It has important physiological substrates, but a conscious mind is required for the awareness of pain. Thus pain relief achieved with massage is as much a psychological effect as it is a mechanical and physiological one. It is quite possible that massage can have direct physiological effects, simply related to the fact that the patient is being touched by a caregiver. This is one reason why massage treatments can be so helpful for terminally ill patients who suffer significant pain.

In recent decades, nonpharmacological methods have become popular among nurses for the relief of pain in terminally ill patients (Degner & Barkwell, 1991; Mobily et al., 1994; Weinrich & Weinrich, 1990). A relatively new concept, known as *therapeutic touch,* has developed from this pursuit. The concept of therapeutic touch holds that pain relief can be achieved without actually touching the patient (Heidt, 1991; Ireland & Olson, 2000; Krieger, 1979, 1981; Owens & Ehrenreich, 1991). Technically, such techniques are not massage because they do not produce mechanical effects in the tissues. Their effectiveness must therefore be attributed to other (as yet undefined) mechanisms, but it cannot include activation of peripheral nerves if touching does not occur.

### Sexual Arousal

Massage techniques have been used for countless centuries as a means of stimulating sexual arousal. There is, in fact, little difference in the actual massage strokes involved. The major difference, however, lies in the specific areas of the body that are massaged. Stimulation of the skin of a number of body areas (the so-called erogenous zones) can produce sexual arousal. These include all genital areas, the buttocks, the insides of the upper thighs, the breasts, the neck, and many areas of the face. Stimulation of any of these areas has the potential to produce strong sexual arousal, especially if that is the intention of both parties.

Sexual arousal is not a simple reflex matter that requires only sufficient stimulation of certain body areas. It is as much a psychological process as it is physical: sexual arousal occurs in the mind as well as the body. Peripheral stimulation certainly helps, but the entire process is not a simple reflex action. Sexual arousal is not a treatment goal of traditional therapeutic massage, of the type used in rehabilitation, and for this reason the erogenous zones should be carefully avoided unless there is an overriding necessity to treat the area. Although the erogenous zones are particularly sensitive areas, massage to any part of the body can cause sexual arousal in a patient if that is the intention of the patient or the therapist. This is a delicate matter and highlights the importance of high ethical standards of practice for the therapist. If it seems that the patient is exhibiting unwanted responses, treatment should be terminated immediately.

### A General Feeling of Well-Being (Wellness)

There is little doubt that massage treatment is, by and large, a pleasant form of therapy. The general state of relaxation and stress relief, possibly coupled with pain reduction, induces a feeling of well-being in the patient. This feeling might also be linked to the liberation of endogenous opiates or some other substances as yet unidentified. At the very least, massage is a significant way of achieving a sense of wellness, and this may account, in part, for the popularity of recreational massage around the world.

### A General Faith in the "Laying on of Hands"

Many ancient cultures have a healing tradition in which a "healer" places his or her hands on, or close to, the affected area and a belief system that some kind of healing force is transferred to the tissues. This rather old idea has gained renewed interest, especially among nurses who call it *therapeutic touch*. It is used widely for chronic pain management (see the earlier discussion).

The idea that healing might be facilitated by the act of touching a person is, of course, very old and common to many ancient cultures. Indeed, this may be why it resonates to this day, even in more technologically advanced societies. If the act of touching a person makes that person believe (a psychological construct) that healing will take place, then it is not difficult to imagine that healing could, in fact, happen. If we adopt the premise that the human mind has the power to control bodily functions, it is conceivable that the mind could bring about positive physical changes in the body, including healing and pain control. This is the so-called mind-body connection. It is essentially a belief system that accepts the concept that the directives of the conscious mind can produce real physiological effects in the body. Because these effects can be produced by massage and related activities, they could be classified as psychological effects of the treatment that bring about real physiological changes for the patient.

In large areas of the world, many people, especially the elderly, have great faith in the religious healing tradition known as the *laying on of hands*. For the Christian community especially, this idea has great resonance because of the numerous biblical references, especially in the New Testament, to the healing works of Jesus Christ and his disciples. These convictions run deep in the psyche of many individuals, and these people are likely to be receptive to the positive effects of massage as a therapeutic tool, particularly because it involves direct touching by the therapist.

## PRIMARY THERAPEUTIC EFFECTS OF MASSAGE

The primary therapeutic effects of massage should now be obvious, as they are based on the mechanical, physiological, and psychological effects described earlier. Relaxation (local and general), pain relief, increased range of joint and limb motion, stimulation of blood and lymph circulation, and facilitation of healing are among the most prominent. Although some of these effects are common to all massage strokes, each technique has its own particular list of effects. The principal effects of each of the strokes described in Chapter 4 are combined into a single comprehensive list in Box 5-4. This list indicates the effects associated with all of the techniques described in Chapter 4, under the headings for each individual stroke.

## THERAPEUTIC USES OF MASSAGE

The therapeutic uses of massage are based on the primary effects (mechanical, physiological, and psychological) that were described earlier in the chapter. Although some of these uses are common to all massage strokes, each technique has its own particular list of therapeutic uses. The primary therapeutic uses for each of the strokes described in Chapter 4 are combined into a single comprehensive list in Box 5-5. This table indicates the therapeutic uses associated with all of the techniques described previously in Chapter 4, under the headings for each individual stroke.

The therapeutic uses of massage depend largely on the individual stroke. Therefore the therapeutic uses are listed separately for each of the major types of massage stroke (see Chapter 4 for details of each individual stroke).

## INDICATIONS FOR THERAPEUTIC MASSAGE

The mechanical, physiological, and psychological effects of massage give rise to the therapeutic effects. In turn, the therapeutic effects are the basis for the therapeutic uses. From these, it is possible to derive a list of indications for the use of therapeutic massage. Once more, many of these indications are common to all massage strokes, therefore each technique has its own particular list of indications. The primary indications for each of the strokes described in Chapter 4 are combined into a single comprehensive list in Box 5-6. This list cites the indications associated with all of the techniques described in Chapter 4 under the headings for each individual stroke.

## CONTRAINDICATIONS TO MASSAGE

Specific contraindications for each massage stroke were described in Chapter 4 and are summarized in Table 5-2. The presence of one of these conditions does not necessarily mean that treatment cannot be given; rather it indicates that careful consideration must be given before any treatment is performed. Each contraindication listed in Table 5-2 is followed by a letter (A, U, or R) to indicate how it should be interpreted. The designation *A* means that the use of a particular technique is *always* contraindicated and should *never*

## BOX 5-4 Primary Therapeutic Effects of the Various Massage Strokes

**Stroking**

Significant relaxation, producing a sedative effect, may be obtained and may help relieve pain and muscle spasm (via a pain-gating mechanism)

Stimulating effect (when performed rapidly) on sensory nerve endings, resulting in a generalized, invigorating effect

Dilation of the arterioles in the deeper tissues and in superficial structures when slow, deep stroking is applied

**Effleurage**

Increased flow of venous blood in the superficial and deep veins toward the heart; when pressure is relaxed, the valves in the veins prevent backward flow

Stimulation of lymph flow, resulting in more rapid elimination of waste products

Increased flow in the veins and lymphatic vessels relieves the congestion in the capillaries allowing vascular and lymphatic fluids to flow more readily into, and out of, the capillary beds, thereby stimulating the circulation and facilitating healing

Increased mobility of the skin and subcutaneous tissues, which in turn increases range of motion in joints and limb segments

Dilation of the superficial arterioles through the axon reflex, thereby stimulating the circulation

Stimulation of the large-diameter mechanoreceptors in the skin, relieving pain (pain-gating mechanism), reducing muscle spasms, and promoting relaxation

**Pressure Manipulations (Pétrissage)**

***Effects on the Circulation***

Increased flow of venous blood in the superficial and deep veins toward the heart; when pressure is relaxed, the valves in the veins prevent backward flow

Stimulation of lymph flow, resulting in more rapid elimination of waste products

Increased flow in the veins and lymphatic vessels relieves the congestion in the capillaries, allowing vascular and lymphatic fluids to flow more readily into, and out of, the capillary beds, thereby stimulating the circulation and facilitating healing

Dilation of the superficial arterioles through the axon reflex, thereby stimulating the circulation

***Effects on Muscles***

Increased blood supply to superficial and deep muscles

Increased elimination of metabolic waste products in superficial and deep muscles

Stretching of posttraumatic scar tissue in muscle

Increased range of motion in muscle and promotion of normal joint and limb function

Reduction of muscle spasm as a result of the stimulation of the large-diameter mechanoreceptors in the skin, thereby relieving pain (pain-gating mechanism)

Promotion of relaxation in superficial and deep muscle tissue

***Effects on the Skin and Subcutaneous Tissues***

Increased blood and lymph flow in the skin and subcutaneous tissues, which in turn produces a slight increase in skin temperature

Stretching of posttraumatic scar tissue in muscle

Increased extensibility and mobility of the skin and subcutaneous tissues, which in turn increases range of motion in joints and limb segments, thereby promoting normal function

**Percussive Manipulations (Tapotement)**

Stimulation of mechanoreceptors in skin, muscle, and tendons, which facilitates muscle contraction

Stimulation of the circulation of blood and lymph in superficial and deep muscle tissue

Loosening of mucus in the lungs

Pain relief as a result of stimulation of mechanoreceptors in the skin (pain gating)

Dilation of the superficial arterioles through the axon reflex, thereby stimulating the superficial circulation

Increased blood and lymph flow in the skin and subcutaneous tissues, which in turn produces a slight increase in skin temperature

**Vibration and Shaking**

Stimulation of mechanoreceptors in skin, muscle, and tendons, which facilitates muscle contraction

Loosening of mucus in the lungs

Pain relief as a result of stimulation of mechanoreceptors in the skin (pain gating)

Movement of gases when applied over the stomach and intestine

**Deep Frictions**

Stretching of posttraumatic scar tissue in muscles, tendons, tendon sheaths, ligaments, and joint capsules

Local damage to the tissues, causing the liberation of a histamine-like substance (H substance) and other metabolites that act directly on the capillaries and arterioles in the area, causing localized vasodilation

Vasodilatation produces an increase in the amount of tissue fluid in the local area, which distends the tissues; in effect, the stroke produces a controlled "inflammation" and at the same time mobilizes the structures that were not moving properly

**Relaxed Passive Movements**

A direct mechanical stretch on the connective tissues associated with all of the musculoskeletal and neurovascular structures, leading to increased range of motion in these tissues and an improvement in functional ability

Pain and muscle spasm relief (via a pain-gating mechanism) leading to an increased range of motion and an improvement in functional ability

Increased flow of blood and lymph in the limbs because of the mechanical pumping effect produced as the tissues are alternately squeezed and stretched; the increased circulation promotes healing and all levels of tissue viability

**BOX 5-5** Therapeutic Uses of Various Massage Strokes

**Stroking**
- Increase blood and lymphatic flow in the superficial circulation
- Relieve pain and muscle spasm, thereby promoting relaxation
- Help both patient and therapist to become accustomed to the feel of each other's tissues; for the patient, it is the sensation of the therapist's hands; for the therapist, it is the contours and quality of the patient's tissues
- Join of various massage manipulations (strokes) together into a smooth sequence to give continuity to the massage treatment
- Relieve flatulence or other intestinal movement disorders by mechanical direct and reflex effects on the intestines
- Promote relaxation and help to induce sleep in persons who have insomnia

**Effleurage**
- Increase blood and lymphatic flow in the superficial and deep circulation
- Promote the absorption of inflammatory exudates in the subacute and chronic stages of soft tissue injuries (edema)
- Relieve pain and muscle spasm, thereby promoting relaxation
- Follow other strokes (e.g., kneading, friction) that have deeper effects, thereby encouraging the absorption of waste products into the lymphatic system
- Help both patient and therapist to become accustomed to the feel of each other's tissues; for the patient, it is the sensation of the therapist's hands: for the therapist, it is the contours and quality of the patient's tissues
- Join various massage manipulations (strokes) together into a smooth sequence to give continuity to the massage treatment

**Pressure Manipulations (Pétrissage)**
- Increase blood and lymphatic flow in the skin and in superficial and deep muscles
- Promote the absorption of inflammatory exudates (edema) in the subacute and chronic stages of soft tissue injury
- Mobilize the skin and subcutaneous tissues
- Mobilize contractures in the superficial and deep muscles, tendons, ligaments, joint capsules, and neurovascular bundles
- Remove the accumulation of metabolic waste products in superficial and deep muscles
- Relieve pain and muscle spasm, thereby promoting relaxation

**Percussive Manipulations (Tapotement)**
- Increase blood and lymphatic flow in the skin and subcutaneous tissues
- Stimulate the circulation of the superficial and deep muscle, thereby facilitating healing
- Relieve pain and muscle spasm, thereby promoting relaxation
- Loosen mucus in the lungs, thereby assisting with expectoration
- Facilitation of muscle contraction and reeducation of function
- Relief of neuralgic pain following amputation, trauma, or another pathology
- Stimulation of organ function

**Vibration and Shaking**
- Loosen mucus in the lungs, thereby assisting with expectoration
- Facilitate muscle contraction and reeducation of function
- Relieve neuralgic pain following amputation, trauma, or another pathology
- Reduce spasticity when applied longitudinally to a limb while simultaneously applying traction in the long axis
- Stimulate organ function
- Relieve flatulence
- Resolve chronic edema (a mechanical vibrator may be more useful for relieving chronic edema)

**Deep Frictions**
- Mobilize contractures (scar tissue) in the superficial and deep muscles, tendons, ligaments, joint capsules, and neurovascular bundles
- Increase blood and lymphatic flow in the skin and in superficial and deep muscles
- Promote the absorption of inflammatory exudates (edema) in the subacute and chronic stages of soft tissue injury
- Relieve pain and muscle spasm, thereby promoting relaxation and healing

**Relaxed Passive Movements**
- Increase blood and lymphatic flow (passive pump) in the superficial and deep circulation in the limbs
- Relieve pain and muscle spasm, thereby promoting relaxation and improved range of motion
- Regain lost functional range of motion in skin, joint, muscle, tendon, and neurovascular tissue due to contractures and adhesions
- Maintain the normal functional range of motion in body segments subjected to prolonged immobility or paralysis, thereby preventing contractures and adhesions

be performed. The designation *U* means that the use of a particular technique is *usually* contraindicated and in most, but not all, cases should *not* be performed. The technique can be used under these circumstances, but it can *only* be given with great care. The designation *R* means that the use of a particular technique is *rarely* contraindicated and *can*, in most cases, be performed safely and effectively. Very occasionally, however, an individual patient may not be able to receive treatment using the technique. It is important to remember that contraindications generally apply to the area being treated. It is safe to treat areas that are not affected. For example, it would be safe to massage the neck and shoulders of a patient who had significant arterial disease in the lower limbs.

As always, the causes of the patient's current signs and symptoms are extremely important. For example, a patient

**BOX 5-6** Indications for the Use of the Various Massage Strokes

**Stroking**
Pain (acute or chronic)
Muscle spasm (acute or chronic)
Superficial scar tissue (in the skin)
Flatulence, constipation, and general abdominal discomfort
Insomnia

**Effleurage**
Chronic edema, especially in the extremities
Chronic pain, especially that associated with disturbances of the circulation
Chronic muscle spasm
Superficial scar tissue (in the skin), especially that associated with trauma to a limb

**Pressure Manipulations (Pétrissage)**
Chronic edema, especially in the extremities
Chronic pain, especially that associated with disturbances of the circulation
Superficial scar tissue in the skin and subcutaneous tissue, especially that associated with trauma
Contractures in muscles, tendons, ligaments, joint capsules, and related structures.

**Percussive Manipulations (Tapotement)**
Weak muscle contraction, or difficulty in initiating muscle activity associated with various neurological disorders
Chronic pain, especially that associated with damage to nerves or disturbances of the circulation
Respiratory disorders associated with mucus retention, such as cystic fibrosis and bronchiectasis

**Vibration and Shaking**
Respiratory disorders associated with mucus retention, such as cystic fibrosis and bronchiectasis
Weak muscle contraction, or difficulty in initiating muscle activity associated with various neurological disorders
Chronic pain, especially that associated with damage to nerves or disturbances of the circulation
Chronic problems with flatulence

**Deep Frictions**
Chronic lesions in the skin and subcutaneous tissues, muscles, tendons, tendon sheaths, ligaments, and joint capsules—for example, chronic muscle tears, tendinitis and partial tendon ruptures (tenoperiosteal tears), tenosynovitis, ligament sprains, induration of subcutaneous areas, and scar tissue
Chronic pain associated with lesions in any of the musculoskeletal tissues
Chronic superficial scar tissue in the skin and subcutaneous tissue, especially that associated with trauma

**Relaxed Passive Movements**
Pain (acute or chronic) preventing movement
Muscle spasm (acute or chronic) preventing movement
Superficial and deep scar tissue in the skin and subcutaneous tissue
Prolonged immobility and/or paralysis
Contractures/adhesions in joint capsules, ligaments, muscles, tendons, tendon sheaths, and neurovascular tissues

may present with chronic, gross swelling around the feet, ankles, and lower legs. On the surface, this seems an ideal indication for massage to mobilize the fluids and remove the swelling. However, if the swelling is the result of underlying congestive heart failure, the condition might contraindicate treatment unless the heart condition was well controlled. In this instance, swelling in the legs is probably a mechanism by which the patient's inadequate cardiovascular system has off-loaded fluid into the periphery as a means of reducing the pumping load on the heart. Mobilizing this fluid back into the cardiovascular system might overtax the patient's heart. This example highlights the importance of understanding the reasons for the patient's signs and symptoms.

## GENERAL PRECAUTIONS

Massage is a relatively safe treatment. However, patients can come to harm if given treatment in an inappropriate manner (Trotter, 1999). The therapist must carefully assess the patient's total situation. Box 5-7 lists many commonsense precautions that need to be observed before, during, and after treatment using massage. Observing these simple precautions reduces the risk of damage to a patient as a result of inappropriate or inadequate treatment. It is also important for therapists to protect themselves by taking precautions to avoid personal injury, particularly to the back or the hands (Green, 2000). Good posture and ergonomics are essential factors in reducing the risk of personal injury. These simple procedures minimize the risk of damage to the patient or to the therapist.

## SUMMARY

Therapeutic massage techniques have predictable mechanical effects on the tissues being manipulated, and these effects cause measurable physiological changes in the person being treated. These effects are therapeutically useful in the treatment of a variety of conditions. Researchers have investigated soft tissue massage for many decades, but many of the classic studies on the effects of massage briefly reviewed in this chapter have omitted any mention of the details of the massage techniques. Therefore conclusions drawn by the experimenters and clinicians had to be stated in quite general terms. Indeed, many references on the clinical use of massage state that "massage does (or does not) . . . ," "massage will (or will not) . . . ," "massage should (or should not) be used for . . . ," or "massage is indicated (or contra-

Table 5-2 **Summary of the Contraindications for the Use of Massage***

| Contraindication | |
|---|---|
| **Stroking** | |
| Large open areas (e.g., burns or wounds) in the areas to be treated, especially if they are infected | A |
| Gross edema in the areas to be treated if there seems to be a possibility of splitting the skin | A |
| Cancer in the skin or any other tissue in the area to be treated | A |
| Serious infections in the tissues to be treated (tuberculosis, septic arthritis, etc.) | A |
| Lacerations, bruising, infections, or foreign bodies (e.g., glass, grit, metal) in the skin of the area to be treated | A |
| Acute or chronic skin conditions affecting the areas to be treated (e.g., psoriasis, eczema, or dermatitis) | U |
| Marked varicosities in the areas to be treated if damage to the vein wall might result (very light stroking may be possible) | U |
| Within 3 to 6 months following radiation therapy in the area to be treated (skin is usually hypersensitive) | U |
| Areas of hyperesthesia in the areas to be treated (i.e., those who are very sensitive/ticklish to touch) | R |
| Extremely hairy areas in the areas to be treated (if stroking causes pain) | R |
| **Effleurage** | |
| Large open areas (e.g., burns or wounds) in the areas to be treated, especially if they are infected | A |
| Cancer in the skin or any other tissue in the area to be treated | A |
| Serious infections in the tissues to be treated (tuberculosis, septic arthritis, etc.) | A |
| Gross edema in the areas to be treated if there seems to be a possibility of splitting the skin | A |
| Lacerations, bruising, infections, or foreign bodies (e.g., glass, grit, metal) in the skin of the area to be treated | A |
| Chronic swelling in the areas to be treated, in the lower limb associated with severe congestive cardiac failure, or any other heart condition with which lower limb edema is associated | U |
| Acute or chronic skin conditions affecting the areas to be treated (e.g., psoriasis, eczema, or dermatitis) | U |
| Marked varicosities in the areas to be treated if damage to the vein wall might result (very light stroking may be possible) | U |
| Within 3 to 6 months following radiation therapy in the area to be treated (skin is usually hypersensitive) | U |
| Areas of hyperesthesia in the areas to be treated (i.e., those very sensitive/ticklish to touch) | R |
| Extremely hairy areas in the areas to be treated (if stroking causes pain) | R |
| **Pressure Manipulations (Pétrissage)** | |
| Large open areas (e.g., burns or wounds) in the areas to be treated, especially if they are infected | A |
| Cancer in the skin or any other tissue in the area to be treated | A |
| Serious infections in the tissues to be treated (tuberculosis, septic arthritis, etc.) | A |
| Gross edema in the areas to be treated if there seems to be a possibility of splitting the skin | A |
| Lacerations, bruising, infections, or foreign bodies (e.g., glass, grit, metal) in the skin or other tissues in the area to be treated | A |
| Arterial or venous pathology (especially thrombophlebitis and deep vein thrombosis) in the areas to be treated | A |
| Acute muscle tears in the areas to be treated (especially deep intramuscular hematomas) | A |
| Hyper- or hypotonic limbs as the areas to be treated (very gentle massage only) | U |
| Chronic swelling in the areas to be treated, in the lower limb associated with severe congestive cardiac failure or any other heart condition with which lower limb edema is associated | U |
| Acute or chronic skin conditions affecting the areas to be treated (e.g., psoriasis, eczema, dermatitis) | U |
| Marked varicosities in the areas to be treated if damage to the vein wall might result | U |
| Within 3 to 6 months following radiation therapy in the area to be treated (skin is usually hypersensitive) | U |
| Areas of hyperesthesia in the areas to be treated (i.e., those very sensitive/ticklish to touch) | R |
| Extremely hairy areas in the areas to be treated (if treatment causes pain) | R |
| **Percussive Manipulations (Tapotement)** | |
| Large open areas (e.g., burns or wounds) in the areas to be treated, especially if they are infected | A |
| Severe rib fractures (flail chest); only very fine, gentle vibrations may be used in the presence of a rib fracture | A |
| Over the thorax in cases of acute heart failure, especially if coronary thrombosis or embolism is involved | A |
| Over the thorax in cases of acute pulmonary embolism | A |
| Over the thorax in cases of severe hypertension | A |
| Cancer in the skin or any other tissue in the area to be treated | A |
| Serious infections in the tissues to be treated (tuberculosis, septic arthritis, etc.) | A |
| Gross edema in the areas to be treated if there seems to be a possibility of splitting the skin | A |
| Lacerations, bruising, infections, or foreign bodies (e.g., glass, grit, metal) in the skin or other tissues in the area to be treated | A |
| Arterial or venous pathology (especially thrombophlebitis and deep vein thrombosis) in the areas to be treated | A |
| Acute muscle tears in the areas to be treated (especially deep intramuscular hematomas) | A |
| Hyper- or hypotonic (spastic or flaccid) limbs in the areas to be treated (very gentle massage only) | U |
| Over newly formed scar tissue in the areas to be treated | U |
| Chronic swelling in the lower limb in the areas to be treated, associated with severe congestive cardiac failure or any other heart condition with which lower limb edema is associated | U |

*A,* Always contraindicated; *U,* usually contraindicated; *R,* rarely contraindicated.
*The contraindications to the use of massage depend largely on the individual stroke. Therefore the indications are listed separately for each of the major types of massage stroke (see Chapter 4 for details of each individual stroke).

Table 5-2 **Summary of the Contraindications for the Use of Massage—cont'd**

| | |
|---|---|
| Acute or chronic skin conditions affecting the areas to be treated (e.g., psoriasis, eczema, or dermatitis) | U |
| Marked varicosities in the areas to be treated if damage to the vein wall might result | U |
| On bony regions in the areas to be treated, in very thin patients | U |
| Within 3 to 6 months following radiation therapy in the area to be treated (skin is usually hypersensitive) | U |
| Areas of hyperesthesia in the areas to be treated (i.e., those very sensitive/ticklish to touch) | R |
| Extremely hairy areas in the areas to be treated (if treatment causes pain) | R |
| **Vibration and Shaking** | |
| Large open areas (e.g., burns or wounds) in the areas to be treated, especially if they are infected | A |
| Severe rib fractures (flail chest); only very fine, gentle vibrations may be used in the presence of a rib fracture | A |
| Over the thorax in cases of acute heart failure, especially if coronary thrombosis or embolism is involved | A |
| Over the thorax in cases of acute pulmonary embolism | A |
| Over the thorax in cases of severe hypertension | A |
| Cancer in the skin or any other tissue in the area to be treated | A |
| Serious infections in the tissues to be treated (tuberculosis, septic arthritis, etc.) | A |
| Gross edema in the areas to be treated if there seems to be a possibility of splitting the skin | A |
| Lacerations, bruising, infections, or foreign bodies (e.g., glass, grit, metal) in the skin or other tissues in the area to be treated | A |
| Arterial or venous pathology (especially thrombophlebitis and deep vein thrombosis) in the areas to be treated | A |
| Acute muscle tears (especially deep intramuscular hematomas) in the areas to be treated | A |
| Chronic swelling in the lower limb in the areas to be treated, associated with severe congestive cardiac failure or any other heart condition with which lower limb edema is associated | U |
| Acute or chronic skin conditions affecting the areas to be treated (e.g., psoriasis, eczema, or dermatitis) | U |
| Marked varicosities in the areas to be treated if damage to the vein wall might result | U |
| On bony regions in the areas to be treated, in very thin patients | U |
| Within 3 to 6 months following radiation therapy in the area to be treated (skin is usually hypersensitive) | U |
| Areas of hyperesthesia (i.e., those very sensitive/ticklish to touch) in the areas to be treated | R |
| Extremely hairy areas (if treatment causes pain) in the areas to be treated | R |
| **Deep Frictions** | |
| Open areas (e.g., burns or wounds) in the areas to be treated, especially if they are infected | A |
| Cancer in the skin or any other tissue in the area to be treated | A |
| Serious infections in the tissues to be treated (tuberculosis, septic arthritis, etc.) | A |
| Gross edema in the areas to be treated if there seems to be a possibility of splitting the skin | A |
| Lacerations, bruising, infections, or foreign bodies (e.g., glass, grit, metal) in the skin or other tissues in the area to be treated | A |
| Arterial or venous pathology (especially thrombophlebitis and deep vein thrombosis) in the areas to be treated | A |
| Acute muscle tears in the areas to be treated (especially deep intramuscular hematomas) | A |
| Acutely inflamed joint tissues (joints, tendons, ligaments, tendon sheaths, joint capsules, etc.) in the area to be treated | U |
| Hyper- or hypotonic limbs as the areas to be treated (very gentle massage only) | U |
| Acute or chronic skin conditions affecting the areas to be treated (e.g., psoriasis, eczema, or dermatitis) | U |
| Marked varicosities in the areas to be treated if damage to the vein wall might result | U |
| Within 3 to 6 months following radiation therapy in the area to be treated (skin is usually hypersensitive) | U |
| Areas of hyperesthesia in the areas to be treated (i.e., those very sensitive/ticklish to touch) | R |
| Extremely hairy areas in the areas to be treated (if treatment causes pain) | R |
| **Relaxed Passive Movements** | |
| Large open areas (e.g., burns or wounds) in the areas to be treated, especially if they are infected | A |
| Gross edema in the areas to be treated if there seems to be a possibility of splitting the skin | A |
| Deep vein thrombosis or other serious vascular pathology in the areas to be treated | A |
| Cancer in the skin or any other tissue in the area to be treated | A |
| Serious infections in the tissues to be treated (tuberculosis, septic arthritis, etc.) | A |
| Lacerations, bruising, infections, or foreign bodies (e.g., glass, grit, metal) in the skin of the area to be treated | U |
| Marked varicosities in the areas to be treated if damage to the vein wall might result | U |
| Acute or chronic skin conditions affecting the areas to be treated (e.g., psoriasis, eczema, or dermatitis) | R |
| Within 3 to 6 months following radiation therapy in the area to be treated (skin is usually hypersensitive) | R |
| Areas of hyperesthesia in the areas to be treated (i.e., those who are very sensitive/ticklish to touch) | R |

## BOX 5-7 Summary of the Basic Precautions for the Use of Massage

Obtain an accurate medical diagnosis.

Perform an appropriate physical (clinical) examination to determine how the medical condition is affecting the patient and develop a suitable treatment plan. Remember that massage techniques are best used in combination with other rehabilitation techniques rather than as the sole treatment.

Check carefully for possible contraindications to treatment.

Drape, position, and support the patient properly.

Ensure a high standard of cleanliness, especially for the therapist's hands.

Perform the massage properly while monitoring the patient's response.

Assess and document the patient's response to treatment so that modifications can be made if necessary.

Ensure good body mechanics, especially with patients who are large or obese.

Use appropriate devices to minimize work-related injury where appropriate.

indicated) in the treatment of . . . ." Such absolute statements are seldom based on knowledge or consideration of the effects of specific types, amounts, or sequences of massage techniques applied to specific tissues. There is still a great need to conduct controlled clinical and laboratory studies to evaluate the many possible combinations of the various components of massage.

There can be no doubt that massage has many beneficial mechanical, physiological, and psychological effects to offer, nor can there be any doubt that massage has many useful therapeutic applications. Despite ever more sophisticated medical technology, the ancient art of massage is still likely to reserve an important place in the twenty-first century and well beyond. It seems unlikely that any machine will be able to replace the sensitivity and power of trained human hands working in contact with another human being. The continuing popularity of various concepts of holistic health will also likely ensure that massage will continue to be a popular health care practice for the foreseeable future, especially as a nonpharmacological alternative.

## REFERENCES


Adcock DS, Paulsen S, Jabour K et al: Analysis of the effects of deep mechanical massage in the porcine model, *Plastic Reconstr Surg* 108(1):233-240, 2001.

Andersen L, Hojris I, Erlandsen M et al: Treatment of breast-cancer–related lymphedema with or without manual lymphatic drainage: a randomized study, *Acta Oncol* 39(3):399-405, 2000.

Avakyan GN: Pressure & massage therapy to relieve fatigue, *Adv Clin Care* 5(5):10-11, 1990.

Barr JS, Norman T: The influence of back massage on autonomic functions, *Phys Ther* 50(12):1679-1691, 1970.

Barr JS, Taslitz N: Influence of back massage on autonomic functions, *Phys Ther* 50:1679-1691, 1970.

Barel A, Lucassen G et al: The use of ultrasound imaging in the evaluation of cellulite treatment with a mechanical skin massage apparatus: 9, *Skin Res Technol* 3(3):188, 1997.

Belanger AY: *Evidence-based guide to physical agents,* Philadelphia, 2002, Lippincott Williams & Wilkins.

Bell AJ: Massage and the physiotherapist, physiotherapy, *JCSP* 50:406-408, 1964.

Bendixen H, Egbert L, Hedley-White J et al: *Respiratory Care,* St Louis, 1965, Mosby, pp 99-101.

Birk TJ, McGrady A, MacArthur RD et al: The effects of massage therapy alone and in combination with other complementary therapies on immune system measures and quality of life in human immunodeficiency virus, *J Alt Comp Med* 6(5):405-414, 2000.

Bodian M: Use of massage following lid surgery, *Eye Ear Nose Throat Mon* 48:542-547, 1969.

Boone T, Tanner M, Radosevich A: Effects of a 10-minute back rub on cardiovascular responses in healthy subjects, *Am J Chin Med* 29(1):47-52, 2001.

Bork K, Karling GW, Faust G: Serum enzyme levels after whole body massage, *Arch Dermatol Forsch* 240:342-348, 1971.

Braverman DL, Schulman RA: Massage techniques in rehabilitation medicine, *Phys Med Rehab Clinics of N America* 10(3):631-649, 1999.

Brunton TL, Tunnicliffe TW: On the effects of the kneading of muscles upon the circulation, local and general, *J Physiology* 17:364, 1894-1895.

Carrier EB: Studies on physiology of capillaries: reaction of human skin capillaries to drugs and other stimuli, *Am J Physiol* 61:528-547, 1922.

Casley-Smith JR: Changes in the microcirculation at the superficial and deeper levels in lymphoedema: the effects and results of massage, compression, exercise and benzopyrones on these levels during treatment, *Clin Hemorheology Microcirculation* 23(2-4):335-343, 2000.

Centre for Reviews and Dissemination: A meta-analysis of massage therapy research (provisional record), *Database of Abstracts of Reviews of Effectiveness,* Issue 2, DARE-20043309, 2005.

Centre for Reviews and Dissemination: A review of the evidence for the effectiveness, safety and cost of acupuncture, massage therapy and spinal manipulation for back pain (provisional record), *Database of Abstracts of Reviews of Effectiveness,* Issue 2, DARE-20038465, 2005.

Chen LC, Wang E et al: Exploration of the effect in improving bowel movement of using acupoint massage on post-cesarean section women [Chinese], *Nurs Res* 6(6):526-534, 1998.

Cherkin DC, Sherman KJ, Deyo RA et al: A review of the evidence for the effectiveness, safety and cost of acupuncture, massage therapy and spinal manipulation for back pain, *Ann Internal Med* 138(11):898-906, 2003.

Cherniack RM, Cherniack L, Naimark A: *Respiration in health and disease,* ed 2, Philadelphia, 1972, Saunders, p 452.

Chor H, Cleveland D, Davenport HA et al: Atrophy and regeneration of the gastrocnemius-soleus muscles: effects of physical therapy in monkey following section and suture of sciatic nerve, *JAMA* 113:1029-1033, 1939.

Chor H, Dolkart RE: A study of simple disuse atrophy in the monkey, *Am J Physiol* 117:4, 1936.

Crosman LJ, Chateauvert S, Weisberg J: The effects of massage to the hamstring muscle group on range of motion, *J Orthop Sports Phys Ther* 6(3):168-172, 1984.

Cuthbertson DP: Effect of massage on metabolism: a survey, *Glasgow Med J* (new 7th series) 2:200-213, 1933.

Cyriax J: In Licht S, editor: *Massage, manipulation and traction,* New Haven, Conn, 1960, Elizabeth Licht.

Cryiax J: *Textbook of orthopaedic medicine: treatment by manipulation, massage, and injection,* vol 2, ed 11, London, 1984, Bailliere-Tindall.

De Deyne PG: Application of passive stretch and its implications for muscle fibers, *Phy Ther* 81(2):819-827, 2001.

Degner L, Barkwell D: Nonanalgesic approaches to pain control, *Cancer Nurs* 14(2):105-111, 1991.

Despard LL: *Textbook of massage and remedial gymnastics,* ed 3, New York, 1932, Oxford University Press.
Diego MA, Field T, Hernandez-Reif M et al: HIV adolescents show improved immune function following massage therapy, *Int J Neurosci* 106(1-2):35-45, 2001.
Diego MA, Field T, Hernandez-Reif M et al: Spinal cord patients benefit from massage therapy, *Int J Neurosci* 112(2):133-142, 2002.
Diego MA, Field T, Sanders C et al: Massage therapy of moderate and light pressure and vibrator effects on EEG and heart rate, *Int J Neurosci* 114(1):31-44, 2004.
Dishman JD, Bulbulian R: Comparison of the effects of spinal manipulation and massage on motoneuron excitability, *Electromyog Clin Neurophysiol* 41(2):97-106, 2001.
Drinker CK, Yoffey JM: *Lymphatics, lymph, and lymphoid tissue: their physiological and clinical significance,* Cambridge, 1941, Harvard University Press, p 310.
Dyson R: Bed sores: the injuries hospital staff inflict on patients, *Nurs Mirror* 146:30-32, 1978.
Ek AC, Gustavsson G, Lewis DH: The local skin blood flow in areas at risk for pressure sores treated with massage, *Scand J Rehab Med* 17:81-86, 1985.
Emly M: Abdominal massage, *Nurs Times* 89(3):34-36, 1993.
Ernst E, Matrai A, Magyarosy I et al: Massage causes changes in blood fluidity, *Physiotherapy, JCSP* 73(1):43-45, 1987.
Evans P: The healing process at cellular level: a review, *Physiotherapy JCSP* 66(8):256-259, 1980.
Field TM: Massage therapy effects, *Am Psychol* 53(12):1270-1281, 1998.
Field T, Cullen C, Diego M et al: Leukemia immune changes following massage therapy, *J Bodywork Move Thera* 5(4):271-274, 2001.
Field T, Delage J, Hernandez-Reif M: Movement and massage therapy reduce fibromyalgia pain, *J Bodywork Move Thera* 7(1):49-52, 2003.
Field T, Ironson G, Scafidi F et al: Massage therapy reduces anxiety and enhances EEG pattern of alertness and math computations, *Int J Neurosci* 86(3-4):197-205, 1996.
Field T, Morrow C, Valdeon C et al: Massage reduces anxiety in child and adolescent psychiatric patients, *J Am Acad Child Adolesc Psychiatry* 31(1):125-131, 1992.
Field T, Peck M, Krugman S et al: Burn injuries benefit from massage therapy, *J Burn Care Rehabil* 19(3):241-244, 199.
Field T, Peck M, Hernandez-Reif M et al: Postburn itching, pain, and psychological symptoms are reduced with massage therapy, *J Burn Care Rehabil* 21(3):189-193, 2000.
Field T, Schanberg S, Kuhn C et al: Bulimic adolescents benefit from massage therapy, *Adolescence* 33(131):555-563, 1998.
Forchuk C, Baruth P, Prendergast M et al: Postoperative arm massage: a support for women with lymph node dissection, *Cancer Nurs* 27(1):25-33, 2004.
Frownfelter DL, Dean E: *Cardiovascular and pulmonary physical therapy,* ed 4, St Louis, 2006, Mosby-Elsevier.
Frulan AD, Brosseau L, Imamura M et al: Massage for low back pain, *Cochrane Database Syst Rev* [computer file](4):CD001929, 2002.
Giese S, Hentz VR: Posterior interosseous syndrome resulting from deep tissue massage, *Plastic Reconstructive Surgery* 102(5):1778-1779, 1998.
Goats GC: Massage: the scientific bases of an ancient art: part 1. The techniques, *Br J Sports Med* 28(3):149-152, 1994a.
Goats GC: Massage: the scientific basis of an ancient art: part 2. Physiological and therapeutic effects, *Br J Sports Med* 28(3):153-156, 1994b.
Goldberg J, Seaborne D, Sullivan S: The effect of two intensities of massage on H-reflex amplitude, *Phys Ther* 72(6):449-457, 1992.
Goldberg J, Seaborne D, Sullivan S et al: The effect of therapeutic massage on H-reflex amplitude in persons with a spinal cord injury, *Phys Ther* 74(8):728-737, 1994.
Goodgold J, Erberstein A: *Electrodiagnosis of neuromuscular disease,* Baltimore, 1983, Williams & Wilkins.
Green L: Injury prevention for massage practitioners, *Positive Health* 58:45-47, 2000.
Gregory M, Mars M: Compressed air massage causes capillary dilation in untraumatised skeletal muscle: a morphometric and ultrastructural study, *Physiotherapy JCSP* 91(3):132-137, 2005.
Grieve GP: *Modern manual therapy of the vertebral column,* London, 1994, Churchill Livingstone.
Gruner OC: *A treatise on the canon of medicine of Avicenna,* London, 1930, Lazac.
Haraldsson BG, Gross AR, Goldsmith CH et al: Massage for mechanical neck disorders, *Cochrane Database Syst* Rev 2, CD004871, 2005.
Hammer WI: The use of transverse friction massage in the management of chronic bursitis of the hip or shoulder, *J Manipulative Physiol Ther* 16(2):107-111, 1993.
Hartman FA, Blatz WE: Treatment of denervated muscle, *J Am Med Assoc* 74:878, 1920.
Hartman FA, Blatz WE, Kelborn LJ: Studies in regeneration of denervated mammalian muscle, *Am J Physiol* 53:109, 1919.
Hayes J, Cox C: Immediate effects of a five-minute foot massage on patients in critical care, *Intensive Crit Care Nurs* 15(2):77-82, 1999.
Heidt P: Helping patients to rest: clinical studies in therapeutic touch, *Holistic Nurs Pract* 5(4):57-66, 1991.
Hemmings B: Psychological and immunological effects of massage after sport, *Br J Ther Rehab* 7(12):516-519, 2000.
Hemmings B, Smith M, Graydon J et al: Effects of massage on physiological restoration, perceived recovery, and repeated sports performance, *Br J Sports Med* 34(2):109-114; discussion 115, 2000.
Hernandez-Reif M, Field T, Krasnegor J et al: Children with cystic fibrosis benefit from massage therapy, *J Pediatr Psychol* 24(2):175-181, 1999.
Hernandez-Reif M, Field T, Krasnegor J et al: High blood pressure and associated symptoms were reduced by massage therapy, *J Bodywork Move Ther* 4(1):31-38, 2000a.
Hernandez-Reif M, Field T, Krasnegor J et al: Lower back pain is reduced and range of motion increased after massage therapy, *Int J Neurosci* 106(3-4):131-133, 2001a.
Hernandez-Reif M, Field T, Largie S et al: Children's distress during burn treatment is reduced by massage therapy, *J Burn Care Rehabil* 22(2):191-195; discussion 190, 2001b.
Hernandez-Reif M, Field T, Largie S et al: Parkinson's disease symptoms are differentially affected by massage therapy vs. progressive muscle relaxation: a pilot study, *J Bodywork Move Thera* 6(3):177-182, 2002.
Hernandez-Reif M, Ironson G, Field T et al: Breast cancer patients have improved immune and neuroendocrine functions following massage therapy, *J Psychosomatic Res* 57(1):45-52, 2004.
Hernandez-Reif M, Martinez A, Field T et al: Premenstrual symptoms are relieved by massage therapy, *J Psychosom Obstet Gynaecol* 21(1):9-15, 2000b.
Hillegass EA, Sadowsky HS: *Essentials of cardiopulmonary physical therapy,* Philadelphia, 1994, Saunders.
Holland B, Pokorny ME: Slow stroke back massage: its effect on patients in a rehabilitation setting . . . including commentary by Heard L, *Rehab Nursing* 26(5):182-186, 2001.
Hulme J, Waterman H, Hillier VF: The effect of foot massage on patients' perception of care following laparoscopic sterilization as day case patients, *J Adv Nurs* 30(2):460-468, 1999.
Ireland M, Olson M: Massage therapy and therapeutic touch in children: state of the science, *Altern Ther Health Med* 6(5):54-63, 2000.
Irwin S, Techlin JS: *Cardiopulmonary physical therapy,* ed 4, St Louis, 2004, Mosby.
Iwatsuki H, Ikuta Y, Shinoda K: Deep friction massage on the masticatory muscles in stroke patients increases biting force, *J Physical Ther Sci* 13(1):17-20, 2001.
Jabre JF: Nerve rubbing in the symptomatic treatment of ulnar nerve paresthesiae, *Muscle and Nerve* 17:1237, 1994.
Jones A, Rowe BH: Bronchopulmonary hygiene physical therapy in bronchiectasis and chronic obstructive pulmonary disease: a systematic review, *Heart Lung* 29(2):125-135, 2000.
Kalb SW: The fallacy of massage in the treatment of obesity, *J Med Soc NJ* 41:406-407, 1944.
Katz J, Wowk A, Culp D et al: Pain and tension are reduced among hospital nurses after on-site massage treatments: a pilot study, *J Perianesth Nurs* 14(3):128-133, 1999.

Kellogg JH: *The art of massage,* ed 12 [rev], Battle Creek, Mich, 1919, Modern Medical.

Kessler J, Marchant P, Johnson M: A study to compare the effects of massage and static touch on experimentally induced pain in healthy volunteers, *Physiotherapy JCSP* 92(4):225-232, 2006.

Key JA, Elzinga E, Fischer F: Local atrophy of bone. I. Effect of immobilization and of operative procedures, *Arch Surgery* 28:935-942, 1934a.

Key JA, Elzinga E, Fischer F: Local atrophy of bone. II. Effects of local heat, massage, and therapeutic exercise, *Arch Surgery* 28:943-947, 1934b.

Kim MS, Cho KS, Woo H et al: Effects of hand massage on anxiety in cataract surgery using local anesthesia, *J Cataract Refract Surg* 27(6):884-890, 2001.

Kinney B et al: Cellulite treatment: a myth or reality: a prospective randomized, controlled trial of two therapies, endermologie and aminophylline cream, *Plast Reconstr Surg* 104(4):1115-1117, 1999.

Klauser AG, Flaschentrager J, Gehrke A et al: Abdominal wall massage: effect on colonic function in healthy volunteers and in patients with chronic constipation, *Z Gastroenterol* 30:247-251, 1992.

Kosar A, Ozturk A, Serel TA et al: Effect of vibration massage therapy after extracorporeal shockwave lithotripsy in patients with lower caliceal stones, *J Endourol* 13(10):705-707, 1999.

Kouwenhoven WD, Jude JR, Knickerbocker GG: Closed-chest cardiac massage, *JAMA* 173:1064-1067, 1960.

Krieger D: *Therapeutic touch: how to use your hands to help or to heal,* Englewood Cliffs, NJ, 1979, Prentice Hall.

Krieger D: *Foundations of holistic health nursing practices: the renaissance nurse,* Philadelphia, 1991, JB Lippincott.

Krusen FH: *Physical medicine,* Philadelphia, 1941, Saunders.

Labyak SE, Metzger BL: The effects of effleurage backrub on the physiological components of relaxation: a meta-analysis, *Nurs Res* 46(1):59-62, 1997.

Lace MV: *Massage and medical gymnastics,* London, 1946, J & A Churchill.

Ladd MP, Kottke FJ, Blanchard RS: Studies of the effect of massage on the flow of lymph from the foreleg of the dog, *Arch Phys Med* 33:611, 1952.

Langley JN, Hashimoto M: Denervated muscle atrophy, *Am J Physiol* 52:15, 1918.

Lemstra M, Olszynski WP: The effectiveness of multidisciplinary rehabilitation in the treatment of fibromyalgia: a randomized controlled trial, *Clin J Pain* 21(2):166-174, 2005.

Lemstra M, Stewart B, Olszynski WP: Effectiveness of multidisciplinary intervention in the treatment of migraine: a randomized clinical trial, *Headache* 42(9):845-854, 2002.

Lewis M, Johnson MI: The clinical effectiveness of therapeutic massage for musculoskeletal pain: a systematic review, *Physiotherapy JCSP* 92(3):146-158, 2006.

Licht S: *Massage, manipulation and traction,* New Haven, Conn, 1960, Elizabeth Licht.

Little L, Porsche DJ: Manual lymph drainage (MLD), *J Assoc Nurses Aids Care* 9(1):78-81, 1998.

Longworth JC: Psychophysiological effects of slow stroke back massage in normotensive females, *Adv Nurs Sci* 4:44-61, 1982.

Lucassen GW, van der Sluys W, van Herk JJ et al: The effectiveness of massage treatment on cellulite as monitored by ultrasound imaging, *Skin Res Technol* 3(3):154-160, 1997.

Lucia SP, Rickard JF: Effects of massage on blood platelet production, *Proc Soc Exper Biol Med* 31:87, 1933.

Maggiora A: De l'action physiologique du massage sur les muscles de l'homme, *Arch Italian Biol* 16:225-246, 1891.

Magnusson SP: Passive properties of human skeletal muscle during stretch maneuvers: a review [review with 83 refs], *Scand J Med Sci Sports* 8(2):65-77, 1998.

Mannheimer J, Lampe G: *Clinical transcutaneous electrical nerve stimulation,* Philadelphia, 1984, FA Davis.

Mason M: The treatment of lymphedema by complex physical therapy, *Aust J Physiother* 39(1):15, 1993.

McCarren B, Alison J, Herbert R: Manual vibration increases expiratory flow rate via increased intrapleural pressure in healthy adults: an experimental study, *Aus J Physiother* 52(4):267-271, 2006a.

McCarren B, Alison J, Herbert R: Vibration and its effect on the respiratory system, *Aus J Physiother* 52:39-43, 2006b.

McCarren B, Alison J, Lansbury G et al: The use of vibration in public hospitals in Australia, *Physiother Theo Prac* 19:87-98, 2003.

McMaster P: Changes in the cutaneous lymphatics of human beings and in the lymph flow under normal and pathological conditions *J Exp Med* 65:347, 1937.

McMillan M: *Massage and therapeutic exercise,* Philadelphia, 1925, Saunders.

Meek S: Effects of slow stroke back massage on relaxation in hospice clients, IMAGE, *J Nurs Scholarship* 25(1):17-21, 1993.

Melzack R, Wall PD: Pain mechanisms: a new theory, *Science* 150:971-979, 1965.

Mennell JB: *Physical treatment,* ed 5, Philadelphia, 1945, Blakiston.

Michlovitz SL: *Thermal agents in rehabilitation,* ed 3, Philadelphia, 1996, FA Davis.

Mitchell JK: *Massage and exercise in system of physiologic therapeutics,* Philadelphia, 1904, Blakiston.

Mobily P, Herr K, Nicholson A: Validation of cutaneous stimulation interventions for pain management, *Int J Nurs Studies* 31(6):533-544, 1994.

Mock HE: Massage in surgical cases. In *AMA handbook of physical medicine,* Chicago, 1945, Council of Physical Medicine.

Morelli M, Seaborne D, Sullivan S: H-reflex modulation during manual muscle massage of human triceps surae, *Arch Phys Med Rehab* 72:915-919, 1991.

Nickalls S: Fluid forces, *Nurs Times* 92(13):52-53, 1996.

Nordschow M, Bierman W: Influence of manual massage on muscle relaxation: effect on trunk flexion, *Phys Ther* 42:653-656, 1962.

Olson B: Effects of massage for prevention of pressure ulcers, *Decubitus* 2(4):32-37, 1989.

Owens M, Ehrenreich D: Application of nonpharmacologic methods of managing chronic pain, *Holistic Nurs Pract* 6(1):32-40, 1991.

Patino O, Novick C, Merlo A et al: Massage in hypertrophic scars, *J Burn Care Rehabil* 20(3):268-271; discussion 267, 1999.

Pemberton R: The physiologic influence of massage and the clinical application of heat and massage in internal medicine. In *Principles and practices of physical medicine,* vol 1, Hagerstown, Md, 1932, W. F. Prior.

Pemberton R: Physiology of massage. In *AMA handbook of physical therapy,* ed 3, Chicago, 1929, AMA Council of Physical Therapy.

Pemberton R: Physiology of massage. In *AMA handbook of physical medicine,* Chicago, 1945, AMA Council of Physical Medicine.

Pemberton R: Physiology of massage. In *AMA handbook of physical medicine and rehabilitation,* Philadelphia, 1950, Blakiston.

Perkes J, Dawson E, Ball D et al: Effects of massage on limb and skin blood flow after quadriceps exercise, *Med Sci Sports Exercise* 36(8):1308-1313, 2004.

Pittet JC, Cathaud M, Beau P et al: Evaluation of the anti-cellulite effect of a massage device by contact thermography and photography, *Skin Res Technol* 5(2):149, 1999.

Preyde M: Effectiveness of massage therapy for subacute low-back pain: a randomized controlled trial, *Can Med Assoc J* 162(13):1815-1820, 2000.

Richards KC: Effect of a back massage and relaxation intervention on sleep in critically ill patients, *Am J Crit Care* 7(4):288-299, 1998.

Richards KC, Gibson R, Overton-McCoy AL: Effects of massage in acute and critical care, *AACN Clinical Issues* 11(1):77-96, 2000.

Robertson A, Watt JM, Galloway SD: Effects of leg massage on recovery from high intensity cycling exercise, *Br J Sports Med* 38(2):173-176, 2004.

Robinson A, Snyder-Mackler L: *Clinical electro-physiology: electrotherapy and electrophysiological testing,* ed 2, Baltimore, 1995, Williams & Wilkins.

Rowe M, Alfred D: The effectiveness of slow-stroke massage in diffusing agitated behaviors in individuals with Alzheimer's disease, *J Gerontological Nurs* 25(6):22-34, 1999.

Schneider EC, Havens LC: Changes in the blood flow after muscular activity and during training, *Am J Physiol* 36:259, 1915.

Severini V, Venerando A: Effect on the peripheral circulation of substances producing hyperemia in combination with massage, *Eur Medicophys* 3:184-198, 1967a.

Severini V, Venerando A: The physiological effects of massage on the cardiovascular system, *Europa Medicophys* 3:165-183, 1967b.

Shoemaker J, Tiidus PM, Mader R: Failure of manual massage to alter limb blood flow: measures by Doppler ultrasound, *Med Sci Sports Exerc* 29(5):610-614, 1997.

Smith L, Keating M, Holbert D et al: The effects of athletic massage on delayed onset muscle soreness, creatine kinase, and neutrophil count: a preliminary report, *J Ortho Sports Phys Ther* 19(2):93-99, 1994.

Sullivan S, Williams L, Seaborne D et al: Effects of massage on alpha motoneuron excitability, *Phys Ther* 71(8):555-560, 1991.

Suskind MI, Hajek NA, Hines HM: Effects of massage on denervated skeletal muscle, *Arch Phys Med* 27:133-135, 1946.

Taylor AG, Galper DI, Taylor P et al: Effects of adjunctive Swedish massage and vibration therapy on short-term postoperative outcomes: a randomized, controlled trial, *J Alt Complementary Med* 9(1):77-89, 2003.

Threlkeld AJ: The effects of manual therapy on connective tissue, *Physi Ther* 72(12):893-902, 1992.

Travell JG, Simons DG: *Myofascial pain and dysfunction: the trigger point manual,* vol 1, Baltimore, 1983, Williams & Wilkins.

Travell JG, Simons DG: *Myofascial pain and dysfunction: the trigger point manual,* vol 2, Baltimore, 1992, Williams & Wilkins.

Trotter H: Hepatic hematoma after deep tissue massage, *New Eng J Med* 341(26):2019-2020, 1999.

van der Riet P: Effects of therapeutic massage on pre-operative anxiety in a rural hospital: part 2, *Australian J Rural Health* 1(4):17-21, 1993.

Wakim KG: The effects of massage on the circulation in normal and paralyzed extremities, *Arch Phys Med* 30:135, 1949.

Wakim KG: Influence of centripetal rhythmic compression on localized edema of an extremity, *Arch Phys Med* 36:98, 1995.

Walach H, Guthlin C, Konig M: Efficacy of massage therapy in chronic pain: a pragmatic randomized trial, *J Alt Complementary Med* 9(6):837-846, 2003.

Wall PD: *Textbook of pain,* New York, 1994, Churchill Livingstone.

Watchie J: *Cardiopulmonary physical therapy: a clinical manual,* Philadelphia, 1995, WB Saunders.

Weerapong P, Hume PA, Kolt GS: The mechanisms of massage and effects on performance, muscle recovery and injury prevention, *Sports Med* 35(3):235-256, 2005.

Weinrich S, Weinrich M: The effect of massage on pain in cancer patients, *Appl Nurs Res* 3(4):140-145, 1990.

Wiktorsson-Moller M, Oberg B, Ekstrand J et al: Effects of warming up, massage, and stretching on range of motion and muscle strength in the lower extremity, *Am J Sports Med* 11(4):249-252, 1983.

Wilkie DJ, Kampbell J, Cutshall S et al: Effects of massage on pain intensity, analgesics and quality of life in patients with cancer pain: a pilot study of a randomized clinical trial conducted within hospice care delivery, *Hosp J* 15(3):31-53, 2000.

Wolfson H: Studies on effect of physical therapeutic procedures on function and structure, *J Amer Med Assoc* 96:2020-2021 1931.

Wood EC, Kosman AJ, Osborne SL: Effects of massage upon denervated skeletal muscles of the dog, *Phys Ther Rev* 28:284-285, 1948.

Wright S: Physiological aspects of rheumatism, *Proc R Soc Med* 32:651-662, 1939.

Yamazaki Z, Idezuki Y, Nemoto T et al: Clinical experiences using pneumatic massage therapy of edematous limbs over the last 10 years, *Angiology* 2:154-163, 1988.

Zeitlin D, Keller SE, Shiflett SC et al: Immunological effects of massage therapy during academic stress, *Psychosom Med* 62(1):83-84, 2000.

Zhu X: A clinical investigation on massage for prevention and treatment of recurrent respiratory tract infection in children, *J Trad Chin Med* 18(4):2285-2291, 1998.

# Part Two
## Practice

# Chapter 6

# Soft Tissue Manipulation Techniques as an Evaluation Tool

The human hand is, without doubt, a bioengineering marvel. It can rightly be classified as one of the wonders of nature. It is capable of immense dexterity and sensitivity, yet it also possesses tremendous strength and functional ability. Indeed, there is no area of human ability or achievement that does not involve the hands as the center of the activity. Everything made by humans involves the hands. Every activity of daily living and every area of art, music, literature, and sporting ability involves the hands. Indeed, a person who loses both hands, or the use of them, is profoundly disabled and cannot survive without a great deal of assistance. Given the tremendously important role of the hand in all aspects of human existence, it is not surprising that the control of all aspects of hand function is vested in large areas of the sensory and motor cortex of the brain. Unlike any other species, humans have the enormous advantage of an advanced brain that is able to control an amazingly versatile hand.

Two major functions—sensory and motor—can be assigned to the hand. Sensory functions include the gathering of information received by the multitude of sensory receptors in the various parts of the hand. These sensory signals come from receptors in the skin and subcutaneous tissues, ligaments and capsules from each of the many joints in the hands, and a multitude of muscle and tendon afferents associated with every muscle capable of producing movement in the hand. Signals from these afferents are relayed to the brain, synthesized, and eventually interpreted as the experience of touching. A wide variety of functional information can be perceived in this manner, including object recognition, temperature, and texture. Together, they form the important evaluative ability that is known as *palpation,* and it is a major contributor to the information gathered from the patient concerning his or her movement dysfunction.

A more encompassing sensory experience is also associated with the hands. This may be loosely termed *psychic* sensitivity. Of course, all sensation is perceived at the cortical level; however, the special sensitivity of the hands may allow some individuals greatly increased awareness and integration of the sensory experience provided by touching. It would not be surprising to find that a person born completely blind would develop extremely sensitive hands. In fact, the history of massage makes it clear that people with serious visual loss were trained in massage, particularly because of their increased sensitivity and manual ability. There can be little doubt that the act of touching can produce significant responses in both parties. The act of touching can communicate many human emotions, and this may be one reason why soft tissue manipulation has proven such a potent therapeutic tool over the millennia and why so many people still have great faith in the "laying on of hands."

Although palpation is an important part of the examination of a patient, the value of soft tissue manipulation strokes as an evaluation tool has not been sufficiently appreciated. Palpation does play a major role in the examination of most body functions and certainly enjoys a prominent position in the evaluation and treatment of musculoskeletal disorders. The fact that such information gathered by palpation appears to be less objective than that gathered by instruments reflects more on the limitations of the instrumentation than on the powers of human observation. There is clearly great potential for soft tissue massage manipulations in the evaluation of all aspects of musculoskeletal function. This discussion examines the potential value of the sensory information received during the performance of the major groups of massage strokes.

## STROKING AND EFFLEURAGE

Superficial stroking gives initial information about the skin and superficial muscle groups. Contour, texture, tone, and temperature may reveal acute or chronic changes in these tissues. Tissues in one site can be compared with those of adjacent areas to determine whether the changes are local or generalized. In particular, the general *sensitivity* of the tissues can be determined. For example, if a patient flinches in pain as the hands move over the potential site of trigger points, this reaction clearly indicates a sensitive area of tissue. Apart from pain, areas of altered skin resistance, temperature, and compliance—factors secondary to local and regional autonomic changes—are the keys to locating these points. Information that the therapist gathers by superficial stroking can also be used as a reference point after specific therapeutic procedures have been applied. Changes noted later during superficial stroking provide important data on the effect of the procedures used.

Superficial stroking is helpful in measuring centrally induced, generalized muscle tension. It also provides time for the patient to adapt to the feel of the therapist's hands and to become accustomed to the increased sensory input. These strokes have traditionally been used to relax the patient, though some patients who are tactilely defensive may require a modified approach. It is important that the patient's entire body and the specific areas to be treated are relaxed; relaxation can be enhanced and evaluated by superficial stroking. All human beings are individually unique, as are their responses to treatment, including massage. There is no reliable way to predict with certainty which type of stimulation will have the greatest effect; however, experience indicates that sustained contact and rhythmic movement are soothing and relaxing for most people.

Deep stroking and effleurage can provide useful information about the degree and type of swelling in an area. Obviously, the more edema there is in an area, the tighter the tissues will feel as a reflection of the amount of interstitial swelling. It is quite possible to gauge this and then determine whether there is improvement (less tightness) following treatment. Because deep stroking and effleurage involve greater tissue pressure than superficial stroking, they can also provide useful information concerning the patient's overall sensitivity to pain in the treated areas.

## PRESSURE MANIPULATIONS (PÉTRISSAGE)

The nature of pressure manipulations, especially kneading and the various lifting strokes (wringing and picking up), gives them a unique role, particularly in muscle assessment. Local or generalized muscle tightness or atrophy of these structures can be identified as specific structures are isolated and mobilized. During treatment, the therapist can come back to an area that earlier resisted being mobilized or lifted, this time to judge the effectiveness of treatment. In this way, massage becomes a more dynamic part of treatment.

There is a characteristic feel of normal muscle tissue as it moves relative to its deep and superficial neighbors when massaged using the pressure manipulations. A significantly reduced degree of intermuscular mobility clearly indicates a problem; however, less obvious changes in intertissue mobility can be the cause of considerable pain and dysfunction. Information provided from feedback during these techniques can be extremely useful in helping the therapist to assess and monitor the patient's progress.

Other techniques, such as skin rolling, can be useful in identifying specific localized changes in the skin and subcutaneous tissues. These are similar to the evaluative techniques of connective tissue massage (CTM). A therapist can feel local connective tissue changes as his or her fingers and thumbs roll the skin and subcutaneous tissues. This may provide useful information concerning the mobility of the tissues and the appropriate areas that require treating (see Chapter 11 for more details).

## PERCUSSION AND VIBRATION MANIPULATIONS

Although percussion and vibration manipulations are techniques used primarily in the treatment of pulmonary disorders (see Chapter 10), a certain amount of information can be derived from their use, especially from vibrations. Although the strokes are generally performed over the chest wall, specifically over the ribs and intercostal muscles, these techniques can provide indirect evidence of inflation and compliance of the lungs and infiltration or adherence of the lungs and surrounding structures.

The classic percussive manipulations (clapping, beating, hacking, and pounding) involve the hands or fingers making only momentary contact with the tissue. In contrast, vibration and shaking techniques involve the hand(s) in direct contact throughout the technique. Obviously, a certain amount of time is needed for the hands to receive tactile information from the underlying tissue. This is difficult in a technique that is necessarily applied at high speed.

The therapist can use selective or precisely placed percussive techniques to test the reflex responsiveness of the patient's muscles and to stimulate specific muscles and tendinous structures. Rebound pain on percussion over a sensitive structure (ligaments, bone, nerves, etc.) often has specific meaning for certain orthopedic and neurological conditions (e.g., Tinel's sign).

## DEEP FRICTION TECHNIQUES

Deep friction strokes provide some of the most useful information about localized connective tissue structures. The compliance and adherence of connective tissue can be assessed. The compliance of fascia in various tissues and the overall mobility of ligaments, tendons muscle, joint capsules, tendon sheaths, and related structures can be identified and assessed.

Transverse friction can be used to assess joint capsule mobility, especially around superficial joints, and is generally more effective than longitudinal friction in producing plastic deformity of the target tissues. It may be necessary at times to combine the technique with passive movement or selected positioning to align specific structures and thereby provide appropriate presentation and tension of the tissue. As treatment is carried out over time, the patient's perception of pain is altered as the connective tissue lengthens. This does not happen quickly because the structure of the tissues is reengineered in response to repeated oscillatory stretching of adherent structures (plastic deformation).

## SUMMARY

All soft tissue manipulation techniques are designed primarily to move the tissues to some degree or other. Although the therapist's hands are primarily intended to move the tissues, at the same time, they are in the unique position of providing invaluable information to the therapist concerning the condition of the patient's tissues. This is the important evaluative function of all massage techniques. All of the strokes mentioned here have value, both as a part of the art of massage and as an assessment tool. If the therapist takes care to relate findings to specific anatomical structures, much of what normally passes as subjective information may prove to be more objective—and therefore more useful.

During treatment, the therapist can come back to an area that previously seemed very tight and resisted mobilization. The therapist might also return to an area where the effectiveness of treatment was difficult to judge. In this way massage becomes a more dynamic part of treatment. For example, a muscle might be unable to function effectively because of contracture of its tendon sheath as determined by palpation. When the problem is treated with the appropriate deep friction technique or some other stroke, the muscle complex may become more mobile and therefore capable of increased, pain-free range of motion. Thus, the therapist has both assessed and treated the problem.

# 7

# Chapter General Massage Sequences

Part Two of this text concerns the *practice* of the various soft tissue manipulations (massage strokes) described previously in Chapter 4. These techniques can be combined into a wide variety of massage sequences. Such a sequence is simply a collection of individual techniques put together with the intention of achieving a specific effect or series of effects. Of the many massage sequences that are possible, the selection of techniques should, to a large extent, be determined by the specific treatment goals. The massage sequences described in this text are by no means the only ones that could be practiced. Indeed, the possible sequences are practically endless. In this context, massage applied to the entire body is usually called *general massage,* which was defined in Chapter 3 as follows:

> *A combination of different massage strokes applied to all the major regions of the body in a single treatment session in order to achieve particularly desired effects.*

In contrast, massage applied to an individual body part is termed *local massage,* and massage given to a specific site, such as a ligament or tendon, is called *focal massage.* Local massage sequences are described in Chapter 8, and some examples of focal massage are discussed in Chapter 9.

Massage is never intended to be a substitute for therapeutic exercise in restoring a patient to full function. Because massage can improve the circulation of blood and lymph, mobilize soft tissues of all types, and promote healing, relaxation, and pain relief, it has many of the effects of exercise, with one important difference. Therapeutic exercise involves muscle contraction, usually with accompanying joint and soft tissue movement. In contrast, therapeutic massage is entirely passive in nature. In fact, relaxation of the patient is a necessary part of the treatment. This in no way implies that massage is inferior to exercise. It is simply different but complementary in every respect. In fact, it is appropriate to view soft tissue manipulation as an excellent way of preparing the tissues for active exercise. In this way it can be thought of as a passive warm-up. When followed by passive and active stretching, it can be an effective and indeed essential component of the routine of preparation for exercise. This is one of the major ways in which massage techniques can be used in sports (see Chapter 13 for more details).

In certain circumstances, therefore, when normal active physical exercise is not possible and if massage is not contraindicated, general massage can be extremely helpful. For conditions that require prolonged confinement to bed (e.g., terminal illness), daily massage of the entire body manually stimulates the general circulation and brings a sense of comfort, relaxation, and pain relief to the patient. For older people, general massage may substitute for some of their former muscular activity, but again, it cannot replace active exercise programs, nor is it intended as a replacement. It may not be possible to apply massage to older and terminally ill patients in exactly the same way as it is applied to younger and healthier individuals. For example, an older person will probably not be comfortable lying facedown on a treatment table or in bed. This means that the basic techniques will need to be modified to suit each patient. In many cases, massage to the entire body on a daily basis is not practical; however, massage only to the lower limbs is likely to be an effective means of stimulating the circulation of the lower limbs, and this is important in improving the general circulation.

## A SEQUENCE AND TECHNIQUE FOR GENERAL MASSAGE

A good general massage may produce fatigue in the patient. A feeling of mild lassitude and the desire to rest immediately after general massage are signs of a successful treatment, and for this reason the patient should rest for 60 to 90 minutes after treatment if possible. Significant fatigue should be avoided, and if the patient is not refreshed after a period of rest, the duration of the treatment has been too long or the massage technique too vigorous. As a general guide, about 45 minutes to 1 hour is adequate for most general massage treatments. In the general massage sequence described here, a recommended number of repetitions is given for each stroke so that the treatment can be completed within this time frame.

To accomplish the relaxation and sedation usually desired in general massage, the change from one type of movement to another must be smooth and uninterrupted, and a definite rhythm should be sustained through all movements. Certain adaptations of the Swedish remedial massage system seem to be well suited for this purpose. These movements are performed on an entire segment of each extremity without giving special attention to a particular muscle or muscle group. A type of massage sequence that follows specific muscle groups and muscles is more effective in the treatment of local injury or disease (see Chapters 8 and 9).

The sequence of strokes used in a general massage sequence should be such that the patient is not required to move or turn from side to side any more than is absolutely necessary. The therapist should change position as little as possible, and all movements should be efficient and quiet. The order of movements that facilitates this type of program is described next and can be followed from the general massage sequence presented in the following section.

The sequence begins with the patient in supine lying (facing the ceiling) with the therapist on the patient's right-hand side. A small pillow or rolled towel placed under the patient's head or neck allows the therapist's hands to move smoothly around to the back of the patient's neck and shoulders when treating the chest and neck. A similar pillow may be useful under the patient's knees, but it must be small or it will interfere with massage to the lower limb. The patient turns to the prone position (facing the floor), and the treatment concludes with massage to the back. (The therapist does not have to change position for this part of the treatment.) This entire sequence may be reversed if the therapist prefers to begin on the patient's left side. It is usually a matter of personal preference, although in some cases the layout of the room or treatment cubicle may determine on which side of the patient it is best to begin massage. The entire sequence is outlined here, together with the number of repetitions for each stroke.

## TECHNIQUES FOR A GENERAL MASSAGE SEQUENCE

Tables 7-1 to 7-5 describe general massage sequences for the lower limbs, upper limbs, anterior trunk, posterior trunk, and the head/neck area.

**Table 7-1 General Massage Sequence for Lower Limbs**

| LIMB | FIGURE | REPETITIONS |
|---|---|---|
| **Right Thigh** | | |
| Superficial stroking to the thigh | 7-1 | 4 |
| Palmar kneading to the quadriceps muscle | 7-2 | 3 |
| Palmar kneading to the posterior thigh | 7-3 | 3 |
| Palmar kneading to the medial and lateral thigh muscles | 7-4 | 3 |
| Deep stroking to the thigh | — | 3 |
| **Right Leg and Knee** | | |
| Superficial stroking to the leg | 7-5 | 3 |
| Thumb pad kneading to the anterior tibial muscles | 7-6 | 2 |
| Kneading to the calf muscles | 7-7 | 3 |
| Palmar kneading to the muscles of the leg | — | 3 |
| Stroking around the patella | 7-8 | 4 |
| Deep stroking to the popliteal space | — | 4 |
| Deep stroking with both hands to the entire leg | — | 3 |
| **Right Foot** | | |
| Superficial stroking to the dorsum of the foot | 7-9 | 2 |
| Thumb pad kneading to the dorsum of the foot | 7-10 | 2 |
| Deep thumb pad stroking to the plantar aspect of the foot | 7-11 | 2 |
| Deep palmar stroking to the plantar aspect of the foot | 7-12 | 4 |
| Deep digital stroking around the malleoli | 7-13 | 4 |
| Digital stroking to the Achilles tendon | 7-14 | 4 |
| Deep stroking to the leg and thigh | — | 3 |
| Superficial stroking to the right thigh, leg, and foot | — | 4 |
| **Left Thigh, Leg, and Foot** | | |
| All of the previous strokes are repeated on the left lower limb | — | |

### Table 7-2 General Massage Sequence for Upper Limbs

| LIMB | FIGURE | REPETITIONS |
|---|---|---|
| **Left Arm, Forearm, and Hand** | | |
| Superficial stroking to the upper limb | 7-15 | 4 |
| Deep palmar stroking to the deltoid muscle | 7-16 | 5 |
| Thumb pad kneading to the upper limb | 7-17 | 2 |
| Palmar kneading to the arm and forearm | 7-18 | 3 |
| Alternate palmar kneading to the upper limb | 7-19 | 3 |
| Thumb pad kneading to the dorsum of the hand | 7-20 | 2 |
| Thumb stroking to the palmar surface of the metacarpophalangeal joints | 7-21 | 4 |
| Thumb stroking to the thenar and hypothenar eminences | 7-22 | 4 |
| Thumb pad kneading to the thumb and fingers | 7-23 | 3 |
| Deep stroking to the upper limb | — | 3 |
| Superficial stroking to the upper limb | — | 4 |
| **Right Arm, Forearm, and Hand** | | |
| All of the previous strokes are repeated to the right upper limb | — | |

### Table 7-3 General Massage Sequence for the Anterior Trunk

| BODY AREA | FIGURE | REPETITIONS |
|---|---|---|
| **Upper Chest, Neck, and Shoulders** | | |
| Superficial stroking to the upper chest | 7-24 | 4 |
| Deep stroking to the shoulders and neck | 7-25 | 4 |
| Digital kneading from the sternum to the shoulder | 7-26 | 3 |
| Alternate deep stroking from the shoulder to the sternum | — | 4 |
| Digital stroking to the neck | 7-27 | 4 |
| Deep stroking to the areas of the jugular veins | 7-28 | 4 |
| Deep stroking to the neck | — | 4 |
| **Abdomen** | | |
| Superficial stroking to the abdomen | — | 4 |
| Deep stroking to the lower abdominal muscles | 7-29 | 4 |
| Deep stroking to the upper abdominal muscles | 7-30 | 4 |
| Palmar kneading over the colon | 7-31 | 3 |
| Deep stroking over the colon | 7-32 | 6 |
| Alternate squeeze kneading over the entire abdomen | 7-33 | 4 |
| Deep stroking to the lower abdomen | — | 4 |

### Table 7-4 General Massage Sequence for the Posterior Trunk and Pelvis

| BODY AREA | FIGURE | REPETITIONS |
|---|---|---|
| **Back and Hips** | | |
| Superficial stroking to the back | 7-34 | 4 |
| Deep palmar stroking to the back | 7-35 | 3 |
| Finger pad kneading over the upper fibers of the trapezius | 7-36 | 3 |
| Deep stroking over the upper fibers of the trapezius | 7-37 | 4 |
| Reinforced palmar kneading over the scapular region | 7-38 | 3 |
| Palmar kneading to the thoracic and lumbar regions | 7-39 | 4 |
| Palmar stroking to the lumbar region | 7-40 | 4 |
| Thumb pad kneading to the sacrum | 7-41 | 4 |
| Alternate palmar kneading to the gluteal muscles | 7-42 | 2 |
| Reinforced kneading to the gluteal muscles | 7-43 | 2 |
| Alternate palmar kneading over the entire back | — | 4 |
| Digital kneading to the erector spinae muscles | — | 1 |
| Deep stroking to the erector spinae muscles | 7-44 | 4 |
| Superficial stroking to the entire back | — | 4 |
| **Posterior Neck Region** | | |
| Superficial and deep stroking to the upper fibers of the trapezius muscle | — | 8 |
| Finger pad kneading to the upper fibers of the trapezius muscle | — | 3 |
| Deep stroking over the upper fibers of the trapezius muscle | — | 6 |

**Table 7-5 General Massage Sequence for the Head and Neck**

| BODY AREA | FIGURE | REPETITIONS |
|---|---|---|
| **Face and Anterior Neck** | | |
| Superficial stroking to the face | 7-45 | 2 |
| Thumb pad kneading to the forehead | 7-46 | 2 |
| Deep stroking to the forehead | 7-47 | 3 |
| Thumb pad kneading to the nose | 7-48 | 3 |
| Deep stroking to the supraorbital ridge | 7-49 | 4 |
| Deep stroking to the infraorbital ridge | 7-50 | 4 |
| Finger pad kneading from the temple to the cervical spine | 7-51 | 2 |
| Finger pad kneading from the temples to the shoulders | 7-52 | 2 |
| Deep stroking over the area of the jugular veins | — | 4 |
| Palmar kneading to the cheeks | 7-53 | 2 |
| Thumb pad kneading to the chin and lower jaw | 7-54 | 3 |
| Deep stroking to the chin and lower jaw | 7-55 | 3 |
| Deep stroking over the jugular veins | — | 4 |
| Superficial stroking of the face | — | 2 |
| **Scalp** | | |
| Finger pad kneading over the scalp | — | 2 |

## SPECIFIC TECHNIQUES FOR A GENERAL MASSAGE SEQUENCE

### Lower Limb

#### *Right Thigh*

The therapist stands at the side of the table on the patient's right side.

**Superficial Stroking to the Thigh**

Both hands reach around the thigh, covering it as much as possible, and stroke from the anterior superior iliac spine (ASIS) of the ilium to the knee. The stroke may be performed with the hands working alternately or simultaneously (Figure 7-1). The technique is repeated four times.

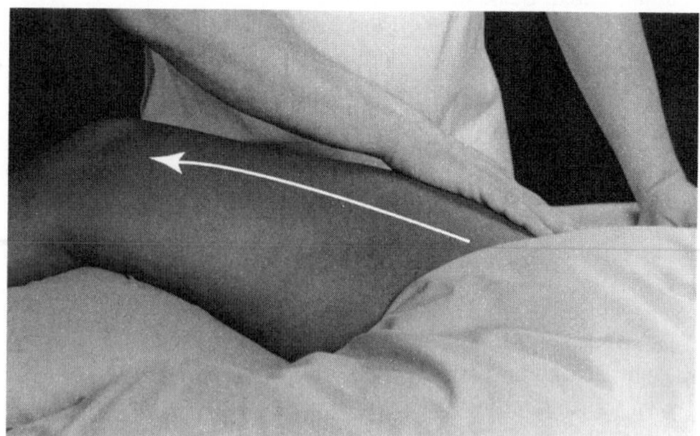

Figure **7-1**
Superficial stroking to the thigh.

**Palmar Kneading to the Quadriceps Muscle**

Palmar kneading is a modified squeeze kneading technique that begins with the ulnar border of the right hand placed below the patella and the thumb on its lateral border. The fingers are placed on the medial border of the patella. The left hand picks up the distal portion of the muscle above the patella (Figure 7-2, *A*). The right hand strokes over the patella toward the left hand as the ulnar border maintains firm contact during the upward pressure. The muscle is grasped between the thumb and the fingers using a lumbrical action to draw the tissues into the palms of the hands. The palmar surface of the fingers of the left hand pulls the muscles laterally as the surface of the abducted right thumb and palm simultaneously push the tissues medially (Figure 7-2, *B*). Then the surface of the palm and abducted thumb of the left hand push the muscles medially as the palmar surface of the fingers of the right hand pulls the tissues laterally (Figure 7-2, *C*). This push-pull movement is carried along the muscle, progressing from the distal part of the quadriceps to the proximal part. Movement is accomplished with gliding of the hands on the pull stroke of the kneading movement. This is not a pinching movement. The thumb and fingers of each hand sustain their relationship to each other during the entire movement. The push and pull are accomplished chiefly by flexion and extension of the arms at the shoulders and elbows as the movement progresses along the thigh. As the origin of the muscle is approached, the left hand is removed, and the right hand gently squeezes out at the origin of the muscle (Figure 7-2, *D*) and returns to the lower border of the patella with a superficial stroke. These movements are repeated three times.

**Palmar Kneading to the Posterior Thigh**

The hip and knee are flexed a little and the thigh rotated slightly externally. Both hands reach across the medial surface of the thigh, grasping the flexors at the knee (Figure 7-3, *A*), in a manner similar to the movement that was performed on the quadriceps muscle, except that the hands are held more transversely to the muscles as the hands progress along the muscle (Figure 7-3, *B*).

The movement is terminated a few inches below the hip joint. The left hand is removed; it crosses over the right hand

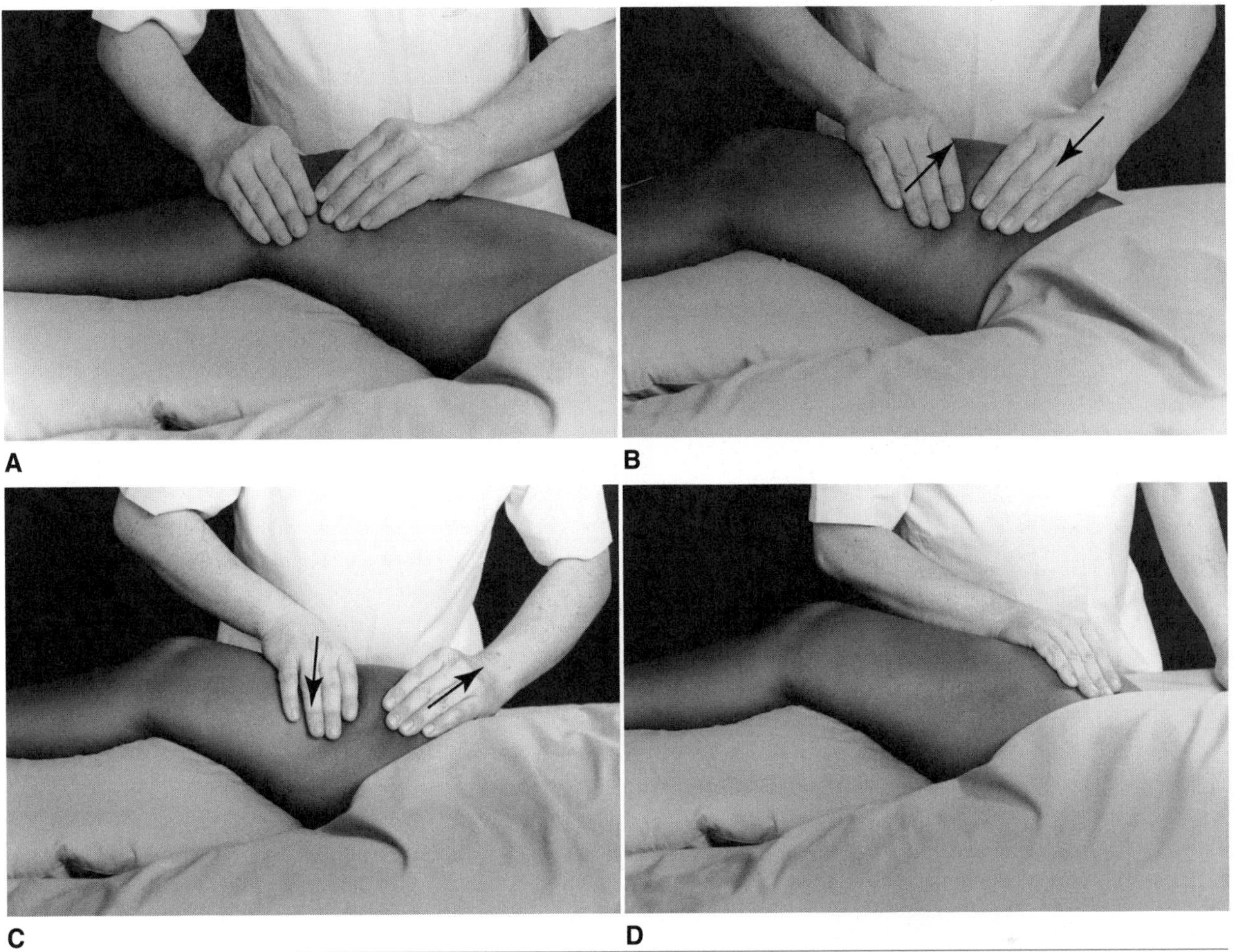

Figure 7-2
Palmar kneading to the quadriceps muscle.

to grasp the muscles above the knee (see Figure 7-3, *C*), and the right hand returns along the medial surface of the thigh with a superficial stroke. The movement is repeated three times.

**Palmar Kneading to the Medial and Lateral Thigh Muscles**

The hip may be slightly flexed and laterally rotated for this stroke, or it may be performed with the limb straight. Both hands grasp around the upper portion of the thigh (Figure 7-4, *A*); the hands perform the basic circular kneading technique, alternately rolling the muscles between the palms with firm pressure upward and relaxation while moving down the thigh toward the knee (Figure 7-4, *B*). Both hands return to the starting position with a deep stroke. The stroke is repeated three times.

**Deep Stroking to the Thigh**

Both hands grasp around the thigh just proximal to the knee joint, with the thumbs abducted and the fingers held together. The fingertips of opposing hands are in contact with each other on the posterior surface. With firm pressure of the entire palmar surface, the hands stroke upward to the upper portion of the thigh and then return to the knee with a superficial stroke. These movements are repeated three times.

### *Right Leg and Knee*

The therapist continues to stand on the patient's right side but is now positioned at the far end of the treatment table.

**Superficial Stroking to the Leg**

Both hands stroke from the knee to the ankle in the standard method for this technique, covering the entire surface of the leg (Figure 7-5). This movement is also repeated three times.

**Thumb Pad Kneading to the Anterior Tibial Muscles**

The thumb pad (distal phalanx) of each hand is placed in firm contact at the origin of the anterior tibial muscles; the remainder of the hand rests lightly on the surface of the leg (Figure 7-6, *A*). The thumbs move alternately in the basic manner for kneading, applying pressure in a circular manner. The hands glide to the more distal adjacent area as each circle is made. The movement progresses in this manner (Figure 7-6, *B*) to the ankle joint (Figure 7-6, *C*). The hands return to the starting position as the thumbs give deep stroking and the rest of the hand maintains light contact. The movements are repeated twice.

*Text continued on p. 156.*

A B

C

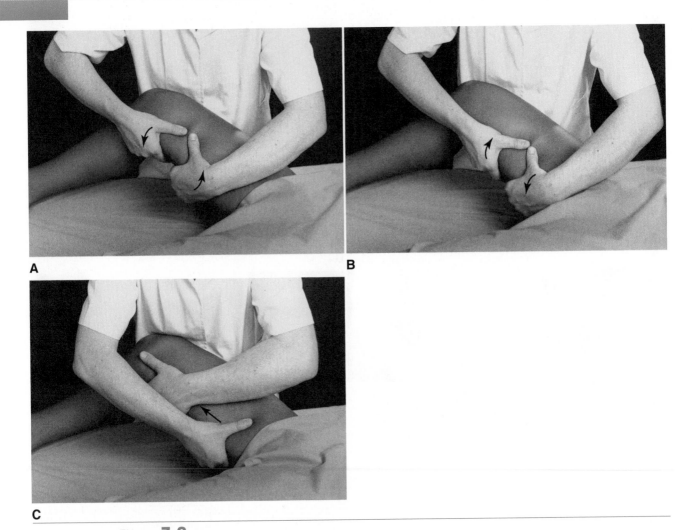

Figure 7-3
Palmar kneading to the posterior thigh muscles.

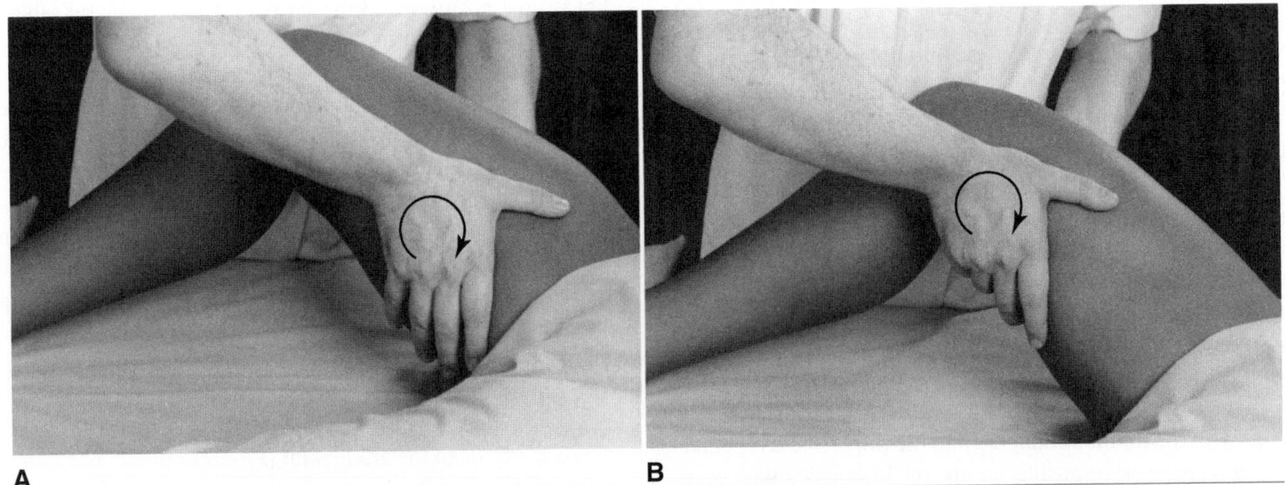

A B

Figure 7-4
Palmar kneading to the medial and lateral thigh muscles.

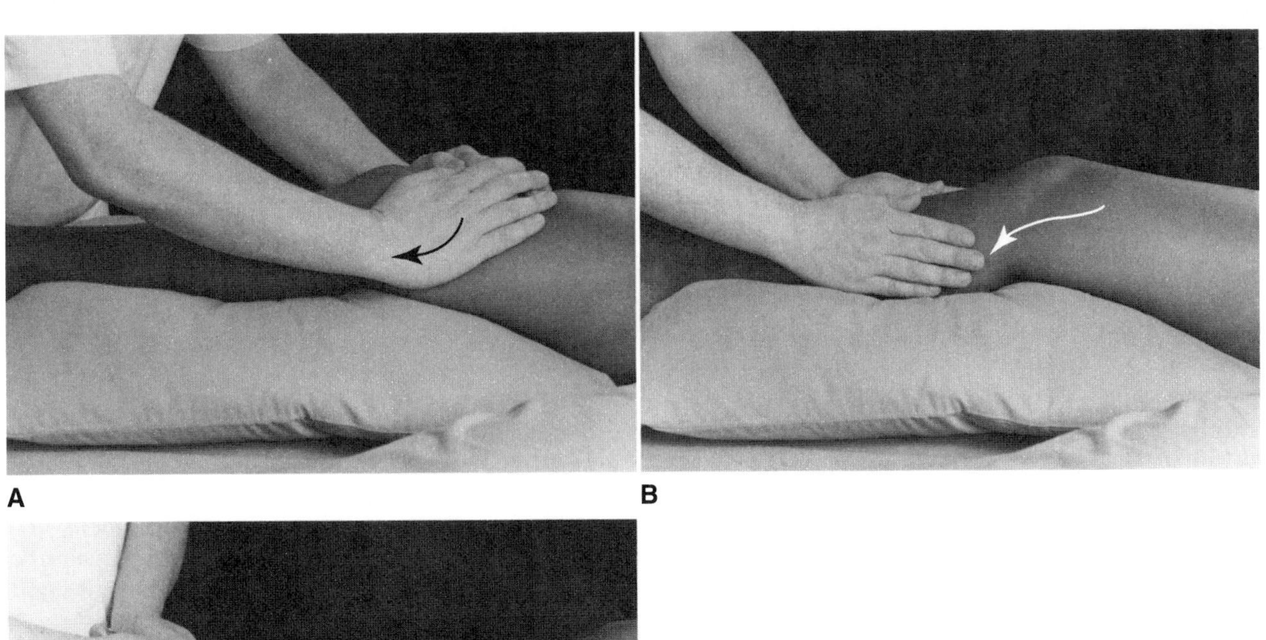

A

B

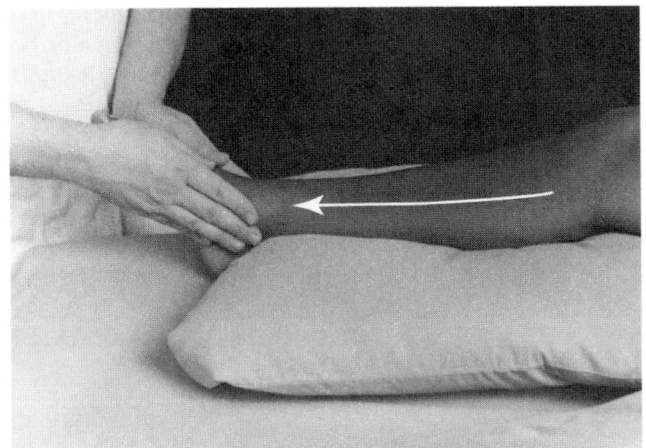

C

**Figure 7-5**
Superficial stroking to the leg.

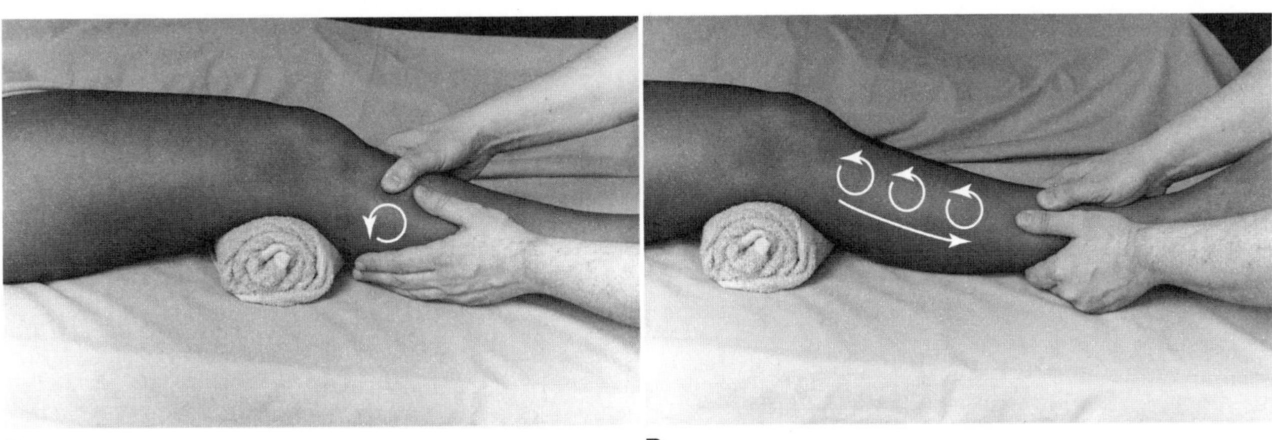

A

B

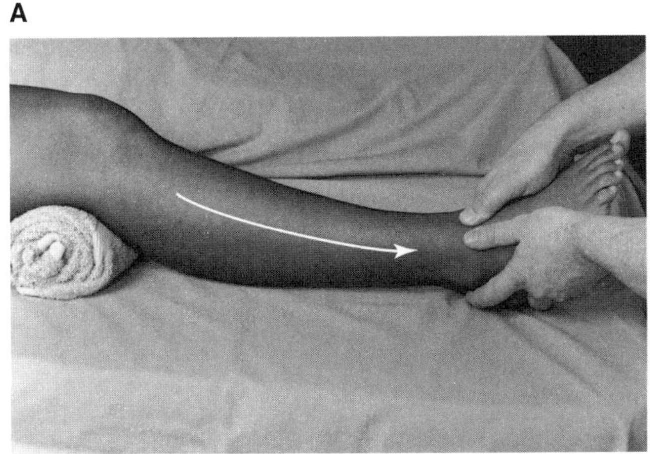

C

**Figure 7-6**
Thumb pad kneading to the anterior tibial muscles.

**Kneading to the Calf Muscles**

Kneading to the calf muscles is a modified squeeze kneading technique in which the right hand supports the slightly flexed knee joint at the medial border. The left hand grasps the lateral part of the muscle group just distal to the knee, and the muscles are pulled toward the lateral border of the leg with the palmar surface of the fingers exerting pressure (Figure 7-7, *A*). The palmar surface of the abducted thumb and thenar eminence push the muscles upward and toward the medial border of the leg (Figure 7-7, *B*). The fingers then glide distally, and these movements are repeated until the hand reaches the ankle (Figure 7-7, *C*). The hand returns to the knee with a deep stroke over the muscles. These movements are repeated three times.

The therapist then changes hands to massage the medial part of the muscle group. Supporting the knee with the left hand, the therapist repeats the procedure with the right hand three times.

**Palmar Kneading to the Muscles of the Leg**

The basic circular kneading stroke is performed as both hands grasp around the muscles at the knee and alternately roll the muscles between the palms with firm pressure upward, working toward the ankle. The hands are returned to the knee with a deep stroke over the muscles. (This is the same technique used in palmar kneading of the thigh; see Figure 7-4.) These movements are repeated three times.

**Stroking around the Patella**

The heels of both hands are placed at the lower border of the patella; the palmar surfaces of the distal phalanges of the fingers are in contact with the skin above the superior border of the patella (Figure 7-8, *A*). The thenar eminences of both hands stroke firmly around the patella in a circular movement by allowing the fingers to flex while the tips maintain light contact (Figure 7-8, *B*). The heels of the hands return to the beginning position with a superficial stroke distally, allowing the thumbs to glide lightly over the patella. These movements are repeated four times.

**Deep Stroking to the Popliteal Space**

The fingertips of both hands are placed together at the distal border of the popliteal space. Then they stroke firmly to the proximal border and return to the starting position with a superficial stroke. These movements are repeated four times.

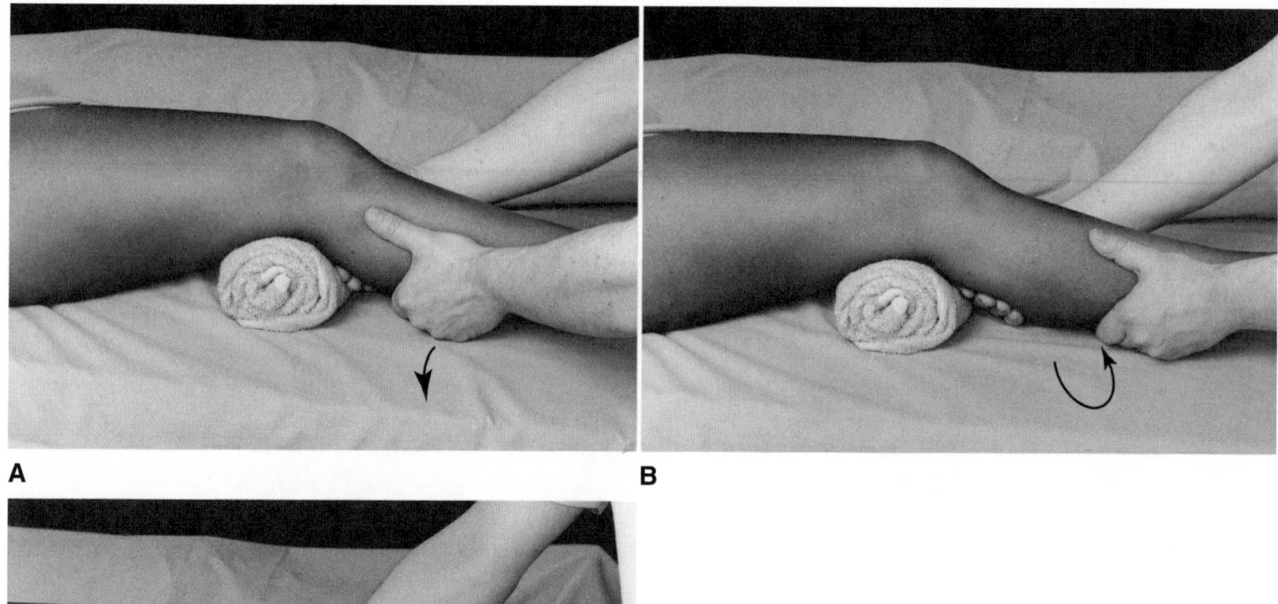

A B

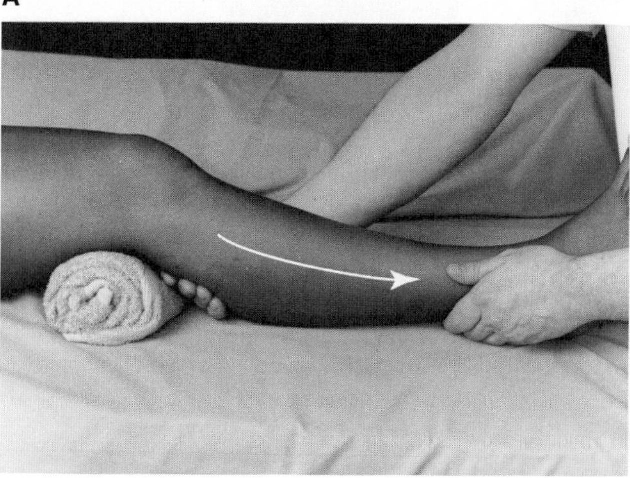

C

Figure 7-7
Kneading to the calf muscles.

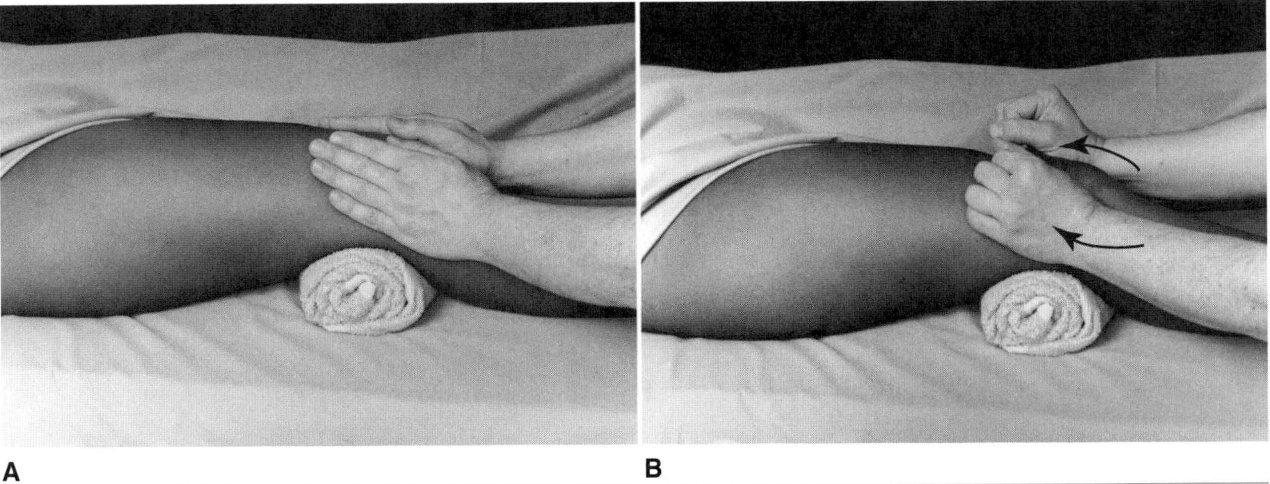

**Figure 7-8**
Stroking around the patella.

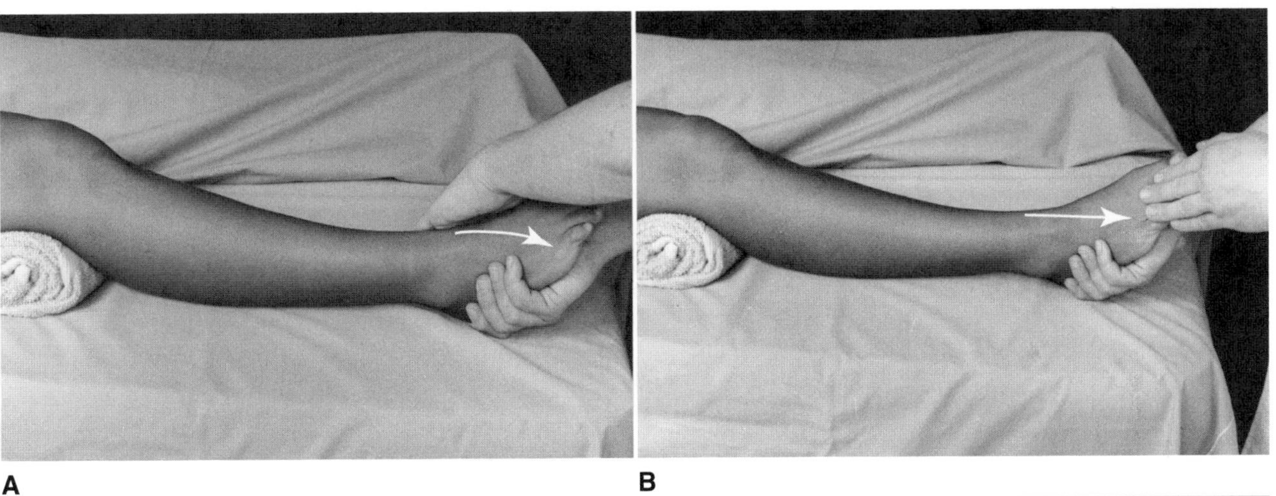

**Figure 7-9**
Superficial stroking to the dorsum of the foot.

**Deep Stroking with Both Hands to the Entire Leg**
Both hands begin the stroke at the ankle in a position similar to that shown in Figure 7-6, *C*. Both hands then stroke firmly toward the knee, returning to their starting position with a light, superficial stroke. These movements are repeated three times.

### *Right Foot*

The massage continues to the right leg and foot, with the therapist standing at the end of the treatment table facing the patient.

**Superficial Stroking to the Dorsum of the Foot**
The palmar surface of the right hand supports the sole of the foot while the left hand strokes from the ankle (Figure 7-9, *A*) to the end of the toes (Figure 7-9, *B*), alternating over the lateral and the medial dorsal surfaces. These movements are repeated twice.

**Thumb Pad Kneading to the Dorsum of the Foot**
Each thumb pad (distal phalanx) is placed in firm contact with the dorsal surface of the foot, the fingers resting on the foot's plantar surface (Figure 7-10, *A*). Standard thumb pad kneading, as described for the anterior tibial muscle groups, is performed progressing from the ankle to the metatarsophalangeal joints (Figure 7-10, *B*). The thumbs return to the ankle position while applying deep stroking over the same area. Thumb pad kneading is repeated in successive lanes until the medial, dorsal, and lateral surfaces (i.e., the entire dorsum) of the foot are covered. These movements are repeated twice.

**Deep Thumb Pad Stroking to the Plantar Aspect of the Foot**
The thumbs are placed at the base of the toes, the right one at the medial border of the plantar surface, and the left one at the lateral border. The fingers rest lightly on the dorsum

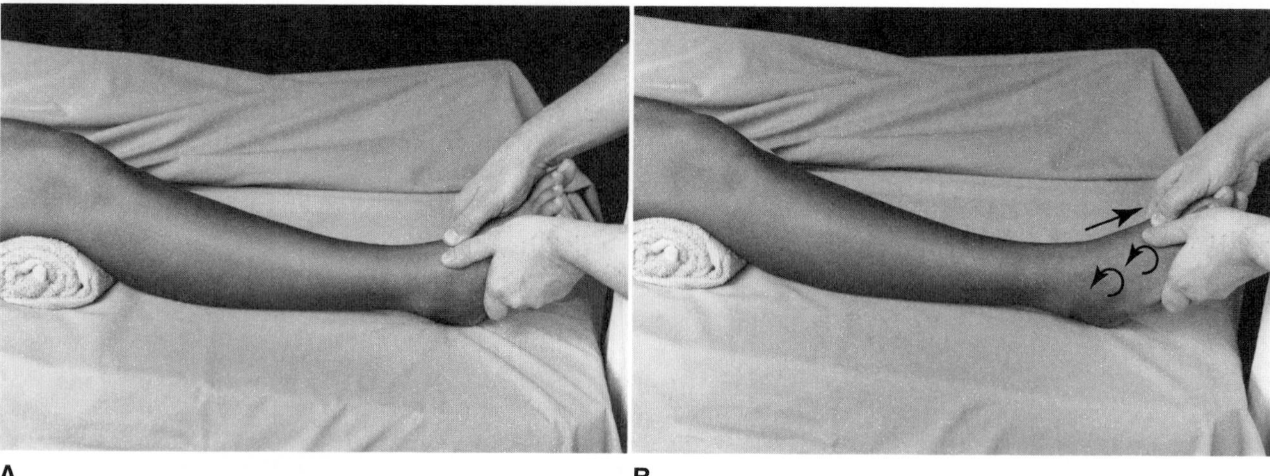
A B

Figure 7-10
Thumb pad kneading to the dorsum of the foot.

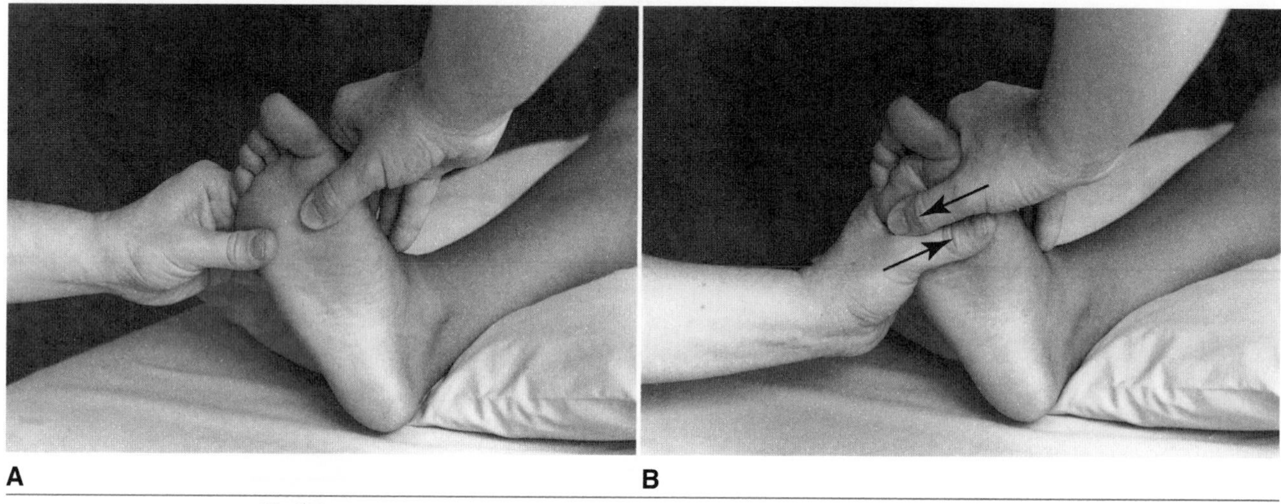
A B

Figure 7-11
Deep thumb pad stroking to the plantar aspect of the foot.

of the foot (Figure 7-11, *A*). The thumbs stroke firmly in opposite directions from the borders of the foot, passing in the center (Figure 7-11, *B*). The stroking progresses from the base of the toes to the heel. The thumbs are held relatively still so that movements of the hands can be produced by abduction and adduction of each arm at the shoulder. The thumbs are lifted from the skin, and the fingers maintain contact and return to the starting position with a superficial stroke. These movements are repeated twice.

**Deep Palmar Stroking to the Plantar Aspect of the Foot**

The therapist pivots to face across the end of the treatment table. The left hand on the dorsum of the foot provides support. The ulnar border of the right hand is placed firmly on the plantar surface at the base of the toes (the hand is supinated as in Figure 7-12, *A*). As the hand strokes firmly toward the heel with deep pressure, it is pronated and made to fit well into the arch (Figure 7-12, *B*), finishing with the palm flat on the table. These movements are repeated four times.

**Deep Digital Stroking around the Malleoli**

The therapist pivots back to face the head of the treatment table. Both hands are placed on the dorsum of the foot, with the tips of the fingers at the base of the toes and with the index fingers together and the thumbs crossed (Figure 7-13, *A*). The fingers perform deep stroking toward the ankle joint with firm pressure. At the ankle the hands separate, with the fingers of the left hand stroking around the lateral malleolus as the fingers of the right hand stroke around the medial malleolus (Figure 7-13, *B*). The palmar surfaces of the fingers keep firm contact, fitting into the contour of the foot as they circle back to the dorsum of the foot and return to the base with a superficial stroke. These movements are repeated four times.

**Digital Stroking to the Achilles Tendon**

The wrists are flexed, and the radial sides of the index fingers stroke firmly upward on each side of the tendon (Figure 7-14, *A*). Without losing contact, the hands turn so

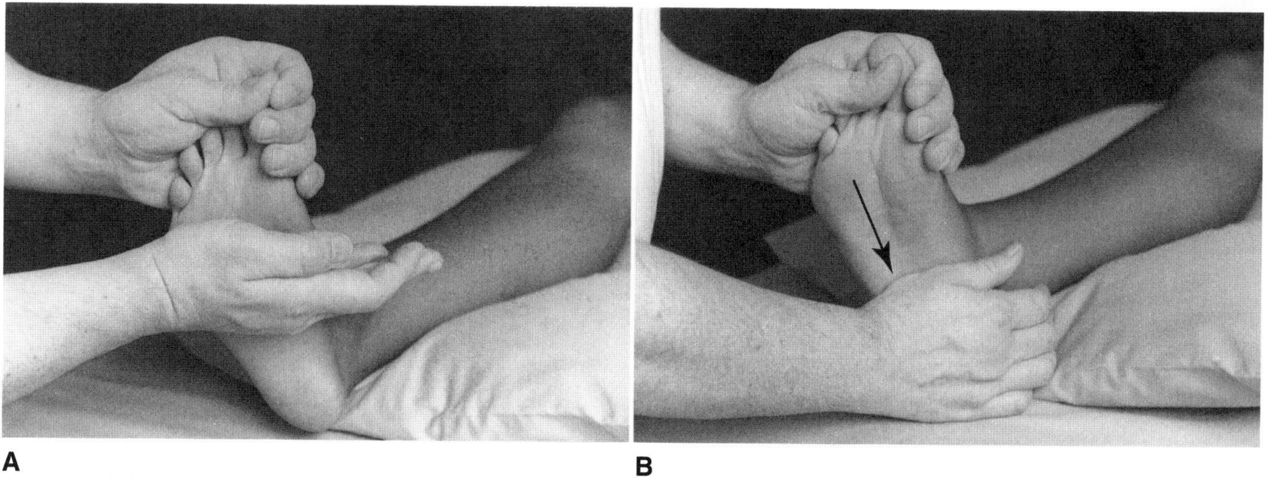


Figure 7-12
Deep palmar stroking to the plantar aspect of the foot.

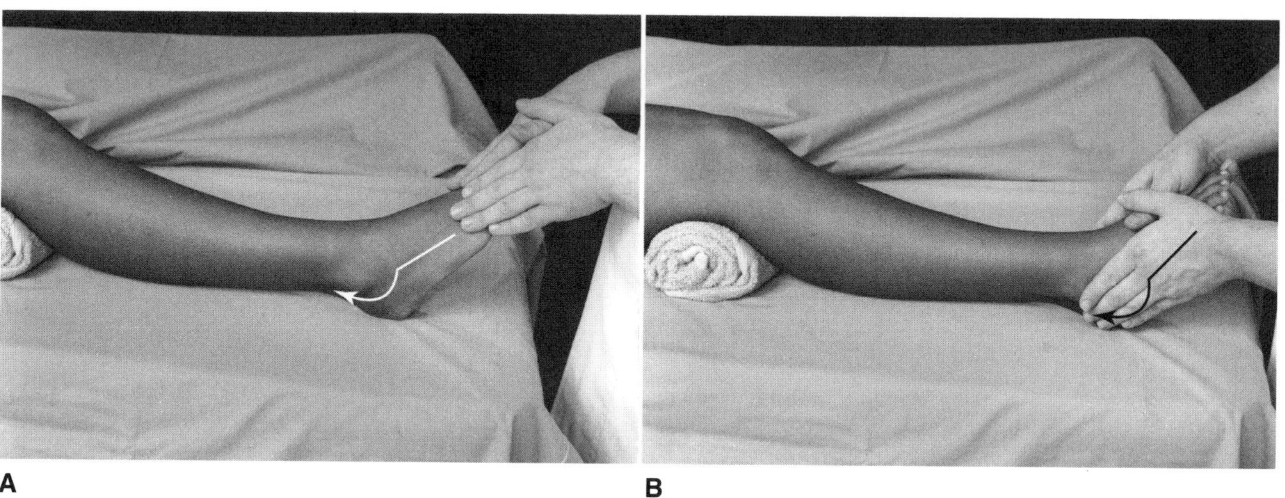


Figure 7-13
Deep digital stroking around the malleoli.

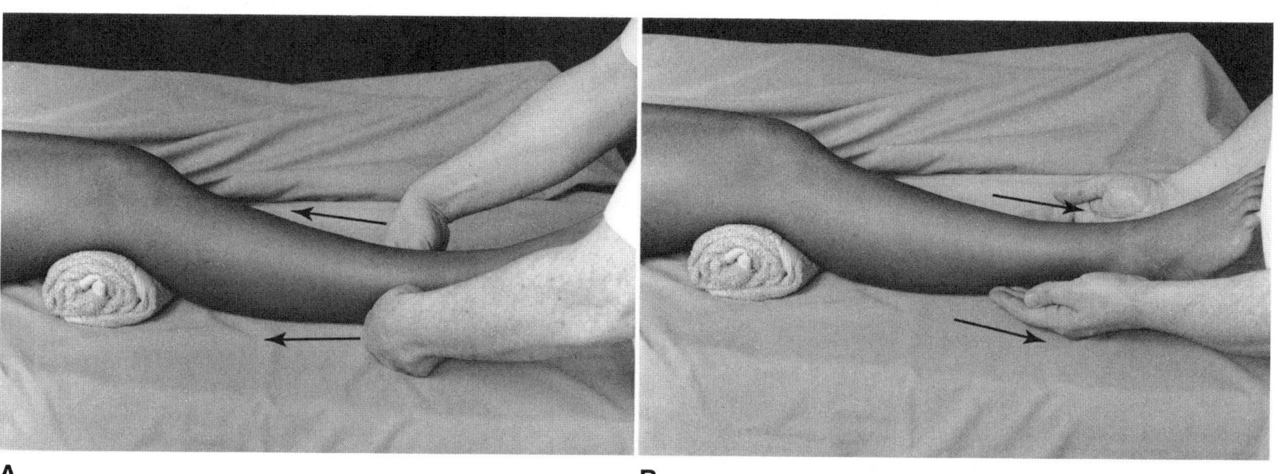


Figure 7-14
Digital stroking to the Achilles tendon.

that the ulnar side of the little fingers can stroke lightly downward to the heel (Figure 7-14, *B*). These movements are repeated four times.

**Deep Stroking to the Leg and Thigh**

The therapist returns from the foot to the side of the treatment table, and the hands glide into position for deep stroking of the leg and thigh. Both hands perform deep stroking beginning at the ankle region and covering all aspects of the limb, returning to the foot with a superficial stroke. These movements are repeated three times.

**Superficial Stroking to the Right Thigh, Leg, and Foot**

The therapist stands at the right side of the patient. Superficial stroking movements are performed on all aspects of the right lower extremity, working from the hip down to the foot. These movements are repeated four times.

### *Left Thigh, Leg, and Foot*

The therapist now moves around the end of the treatment table to stand at the left side of the patient. All of the movements described previously for the right lower limb are now repeated on the left side. All of the movements are the same, but the right- and left-hand positions are reversed.

## Upper Limb

### *Left Arm, Forearm, and Hand*

The therapist continues to stand at the left side of the treatment table, in a position that enables him or her to massage the upper extremity easily.

### *Superficial Stroking to the Upper Limb*

Both hands are placed on the deltoid muscle mass (Figure 7-15, *A*) and stroke together from the shoulder to the fingertips (Figure 7-15, *B*). This stroke may also be performed using an alternate hand technique if preferred. These movements are repeated four times.

**Deep Palmar Stroking to the Deltoid Muscle**

The hands are placed just distal to the borders of the deltoid muscle (Figure 7-16, *A*). With firm contact, the right hand

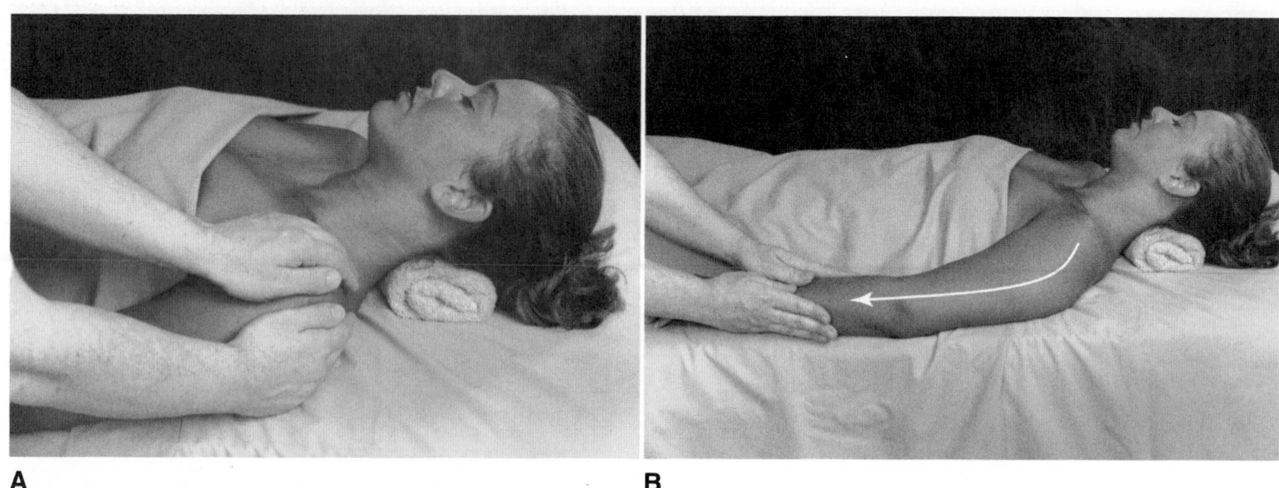

A B

Figure **7-15**
Superficial stroking to the upper extremity.

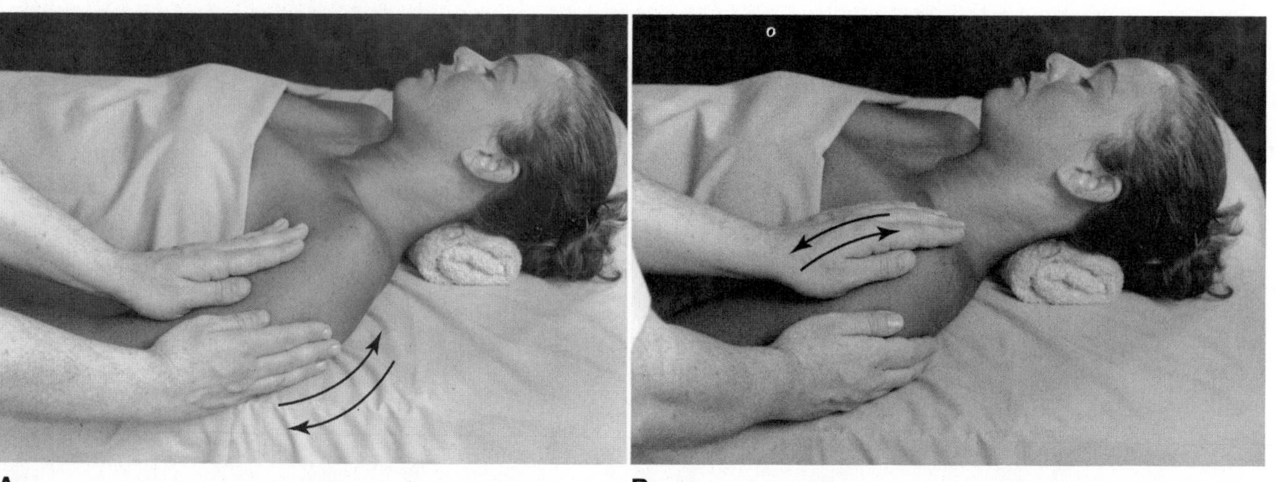

A B

Figure **7-16**
Deep palmar stroking to the deltoid muscle.

strokes upward over the posterior half of the deltoid toward the neck. As the right hand returns with a superficial stroke, the left hand strokes upward over the anterior half of the deltoid toward the neck (Figure 7-16, *B*). As it returns with a superficial stroke, the right hand starts its second stroke. These movements are repeated five times to each side of the deltoid.

**Thumb Pad Kneading to the Upper Limb**

Thumb pad kneading is performed to the entire surface of the upper limb in three sections: the anterior, lateral, and posterior surfaces (Figure 7-17). Kneading is performed from the shoulder to the wrist, the hands returning with a deep stroke from the wrist to the shoulder. These movements are repeated twice.

**Palmar Kneading to the Arm and Forearm**

With the right hand, the therapist performs palmar (compression) kneading as described for the leg while supporting the patient's arm with the left hand (Figure 7-18, *A*) and then allows the arm to rest on the table while the supporting hand passes to the wrist, giving support to the wrist while the forearm is kneaded (Figure 7-18, *B*). The therapist uses the right hand to knead tissues of the patient's lateral part of the arm and forearm. The right hand returns to the shoulder, and the left hand returns to the elbow with a superficial stroke, and kneading of the arm and forearm is repeated. At the end of the second lane of kneading, the left hand returns to the shoulder and the right hand returns to the elbow to support the arm in slight external rotation with the forearm in supination. Kneading to the medial tissues is then performed by the left hand as the right hand provides support. At the end of the second lane of left-hand kneading, both hands return to the shoulder with a deep stroke (similar to that performed on the leg and thigh). These movements are repeated three times with each hand, giving a total of six lanes of kneading for each aspect of the limb.

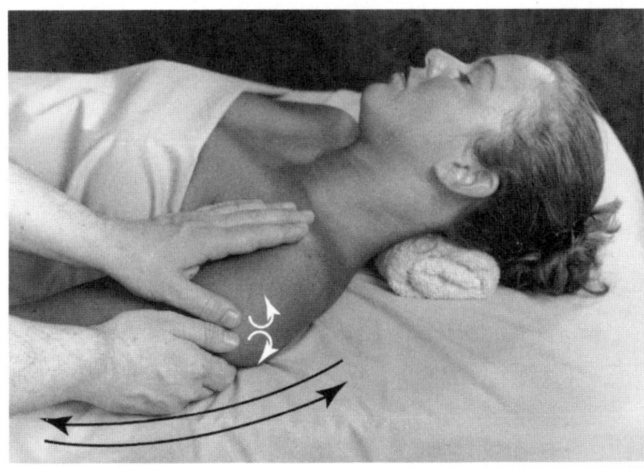

Figure **7-17**
Thumb pad kneading to the upper limb.

**Alternate Palmar Kneading to the Upper Limb**

Alternate palmar kneading, a two-handed movement, is performed on the upper extremity in the same manner described for the leg, this time working from the shoulder to the wrist (Figure 7-19). On the last repetition, the hands do not return to the shoulder with a deep stroke but remain at the wrist to begin thumb pad kneading to the dorsum of the hand. These movements are repeated three times.

**Thumb Pad Kneading to the Dorsum of the Hand**

Thumb pad kneading is performed to the spaces between the metacarpals. The stroke begins at the wrist and progresses toward the metacarpophalangeal (knuckles) joints (Figure 7-20). The movements finish with a deep stroking down the metacarpal spaces back to the wrist. The entire dorsum of the hand can be covered in this manner, working in the tissue spaces between the metacarpals. These movements are repeated twice.

**Thumb Stroking to the Palmar Surface of the Metacarpophalangeal Joints**

The patient's hand is held in supination and is supported on the fingers of both hands, with the left thumb at the medial border and the right thumb at the lateral border (Figure 7-21,

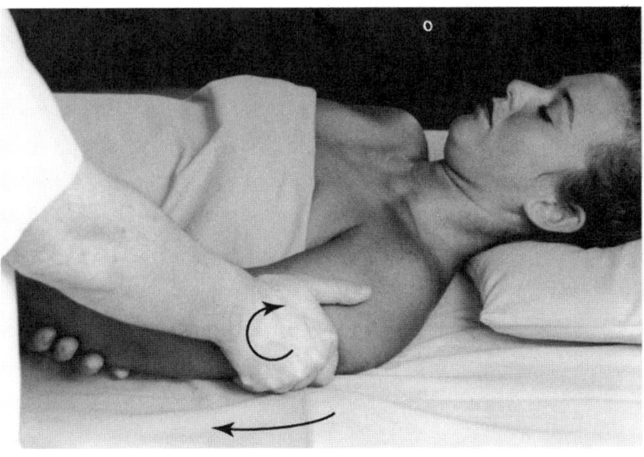

A

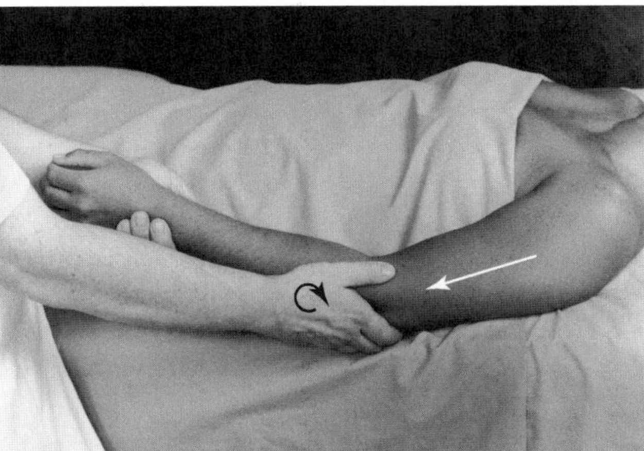

B

Figure **7-18**
Palmar kneading to the arm and forearm.

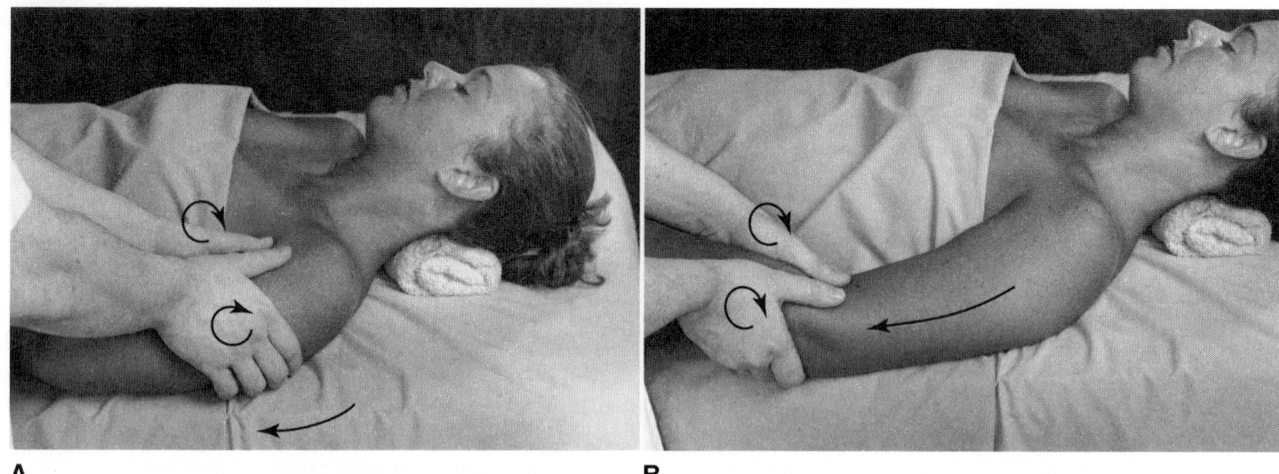


Figure 7-19
Alternate palmar kneading to the upper limb.

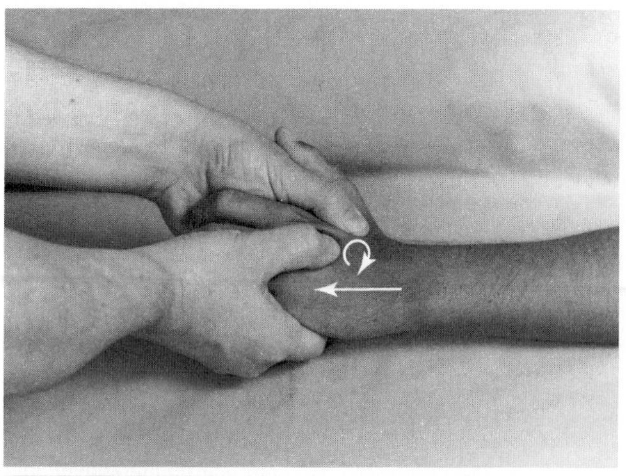

Figure 7-20
Thumb pad kneading to the dorsum of the hand.

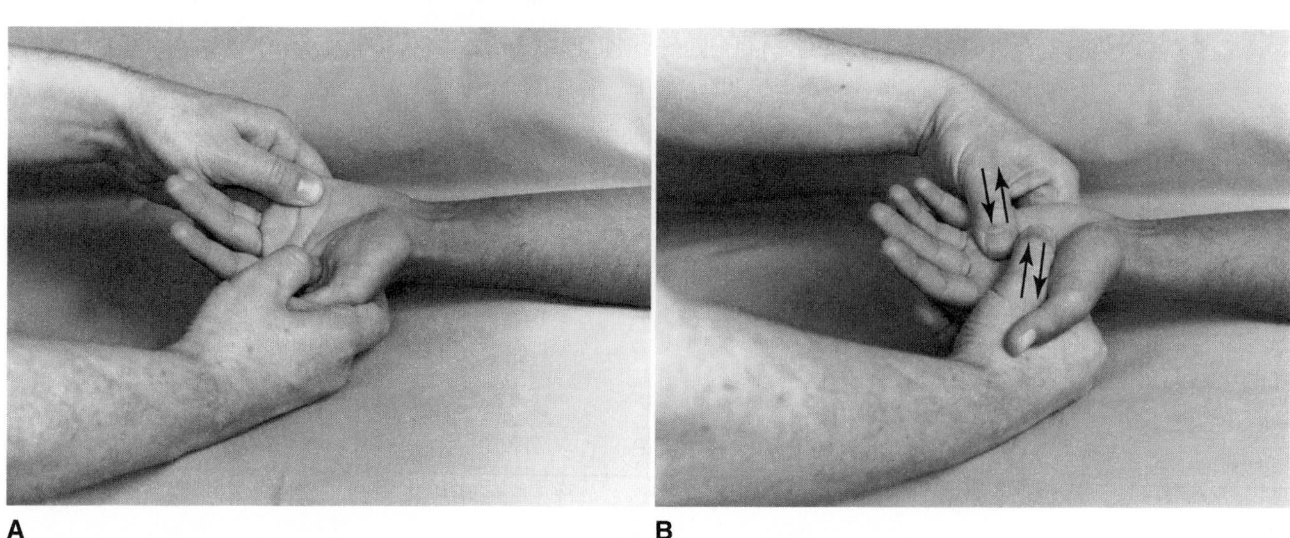


Figure 7-21
Thumb stroking to the palmar surface of the metacarpophalangeal joints.

*A*). The thumbs stroke toward and past each other (Figure 7-21, *B*) with firm pressure and return with light pressure, as described for the plantar surface of the foot. These movements are repeated four times.

**Thumb Stroking to the Thenar and Hypothenar Eminences**

The patient's hand is again held in supination, supported on the fingers of both hands, with the left thumb on the hypothenar eminence and the right thumb on the thenar eminence (Figure 7-22). The thumbs stroke alternately toward the wrist with firm pressure, returning with a light stroke. These movements are repeated four times.

**Thumb Pad Kneading to the Thumb and Fingers**

The hand is held in pronation and supported in the palm of the left hand. The right thumb, beginning at the metacarpophalangeal joint, kneads on a small area of the medial aspect of the little finger with firm pressure across the digit. The thumb passes lightly over the dorsum of the fingers and kneads on the lateral aspect. The thumb then strokes back lightly over the dorsum of the finger and repeats the movement in the area just distal. This procedure is continued to the tip of the finger (Figure 7-23, *A*). The thumb and the first finger then stroke firmly back to the base of the finger. The entire movement is performed twice on each finger. The thumb is massaged in the same manner, except that the right hand gives support while movements are performed with the left (Figure 7-23, *B*). These movements are repeated three times.

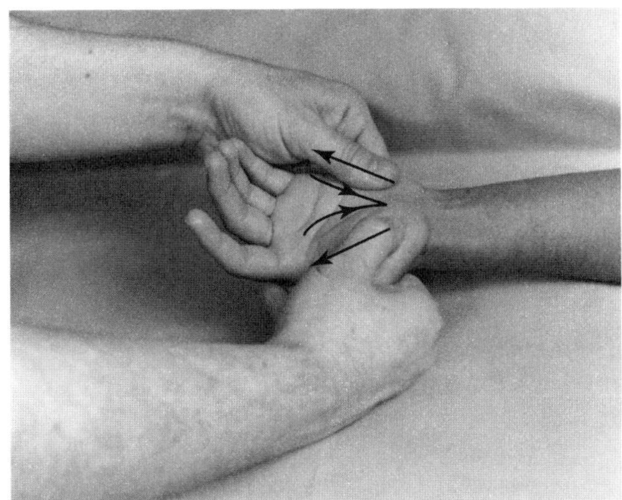

Figure 7-22
Thumb stroking to the thenar and hypothenar eminences.

**Deep Stroking to the Upper Limb**

Both hands stroke firmly upward from the wrist to the shoulder and return with a superficial movement. These movements are repeated three times. After the third deep stroke, the return stroke becomes the start of superficial stroking.

**Superficial Stroking to the Upper Limb**

Both hands stroke alternately from the shoulder to the fingertips. These movements are repeated four times.

### *Right Arm, Forearm, and Hand*

The therapist walks around the foot of the treatment table and stands at the patient's right side, near the right hand, and repeats all of the previous strokes, this time to the right upper limb. In each instance, the therapist's hand positions are now reversed.

## Anterior Trunk

### *Upper Chest, Neck, and Shoulders*

**Superficial Stroking to the Upper Chest**

The hands alternately stroke from the shoulders to the sternum. The relaxed hands stroke alternately from the left shoulder to the sternum, covering the area with a few overlapping strokes before moving to the right side without

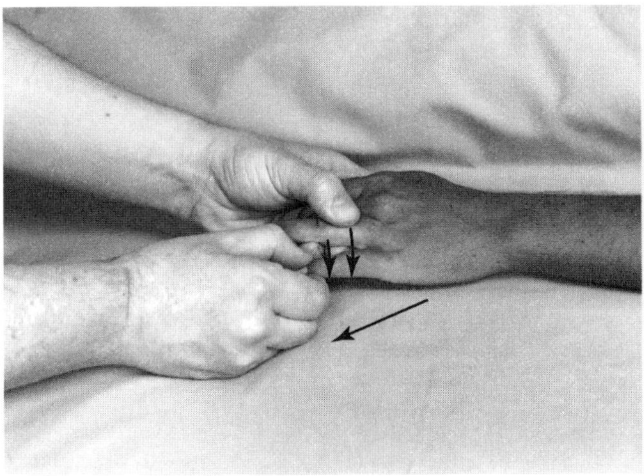

A

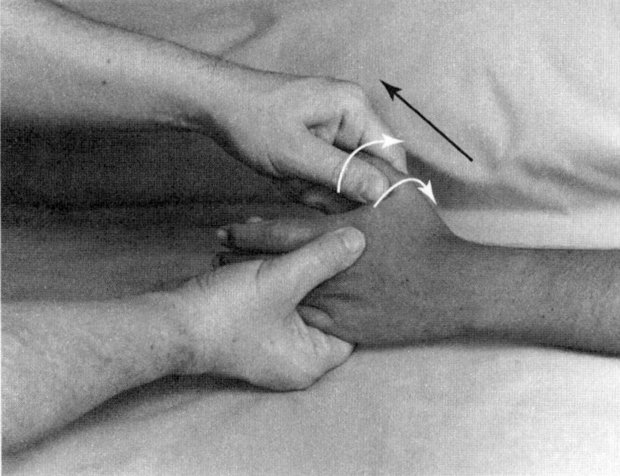

B

Figure 7-23
Thumb pad kneading to the thumb and fingers.

breaking contact (Figure 7-24). Alternatively, the right hand may start from the patient's right shoulder, and as it finishes the stroke at the sternum, the left hand starts the stroke from the left shoulder so that contact is not broken. These movements are repeated four times.

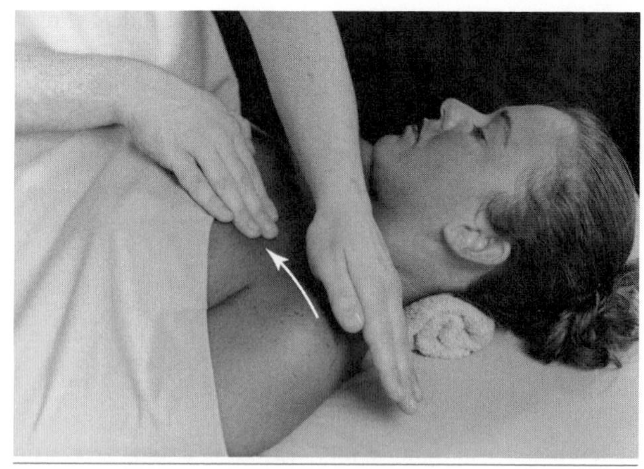

**Figure 7-24**
Superficial stroking to the upper chest.

### Deep Stroking to the Shoulders and Neck

Both hands, with the thumbs adducted, are placed with the fingertips at the mid to lower end of the sternum (Figure 7-25, *A*). The hands stroke simultaneously, the right hand passing lightly upward, then laterally and around the left shoulder joint, and the left hand passing lightly upward, then laterally and around the right shoulder joint (Figure 7-25, *B*). Both hands continue the movement, stroking toward the midline of the body along the upper fibers of the trapezius muscle (Figure 7-25, *C*).

After the fingertips meet at the lower cervical spine, the hands stroke around the neck, firmly drawing the muscles forward (Figure 7-25, *D*). Pressure is reduced as the hands stroke over the anterior surface of the neck and return to the starting position at the sternum. These movements are repeated four times.

A B C D

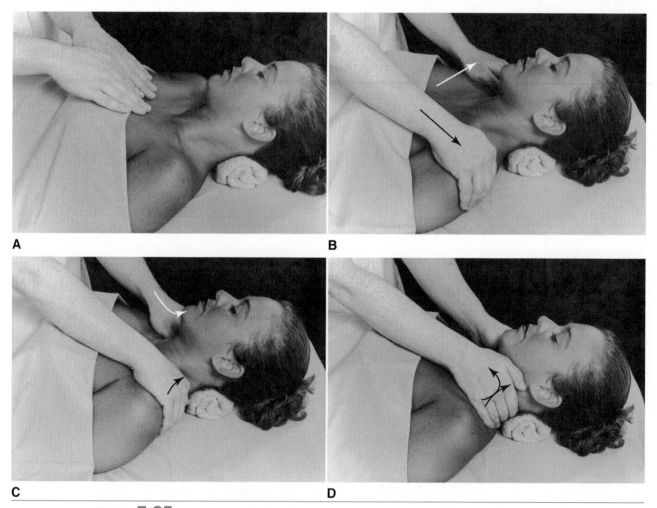

**Figure 7-25**
Deep stroking to the shoulder and neck.

### Digital Kneading from the Sternum to the Shoulder

The fingertips of the left hand are placed at the sternum over the upper fibers of the left pectoralis major muscle, and the right hand is placed over the left hand to reinforce it (Figure 7-26, *A*). The reverse hand position is equally acceptable. Kneading is then performed with the fingertips, moving in small clockwise circles with light pressure on the upward and outward part of the circle and firm pressure in the downward and inward part. Four circles are made, each succeeding one in an area nearer to the shoulder. As the fingertips reach the shoulder joint, the palm strokes around the joint (Figure 7-26, *B*), and the entire hand strokes deeply on its way to the sternum. These movements are repeated three times on the left side. With the hands in a reversed position (or the same position), the therapist performs the movement on the right side in counterclockwise circles (Figure 7-26, *C*). These movements are repeated three times on the right side.

### Alternate Deep Stroking from the Shoulder to the Sternum

The hands are in the same position as in Figure 7-25, *A*. With the entire palmar surface, the right hand strokes lightly to the left shoulder joint. The hands then stroke around the joint and return to the sternum with firm pressure (as in the previous movement). The movement is repeated on the right side. This alternate stroking is repeated four times.

### Digital Stroking to the Neck

The hands start in the position shown in Figure 7-26, *A*. The right hand strokes over the top of the left shoulder and in toward the midline of the body. When the fingertips reach the lower cervical spine, they stroke upward until the palm is in contact with the neck. The hand then draws the muscles forward with firm pressure (Figure 7-27, *A*), exerts light pressure over the anterior surface of the neck and the clavicle, and then returns to the starting position. The stroking is then performed in the same manner on the right side (Figure 7-27, *B*). The stroking is repeated four times.

### Deep Stroking to the Areas of the Jugular Veins

With the thumbs widely abducted, the fingers (palmar surface) of the right hand are placed on the left side of the neck and those of the left hand are placed on the right side of the patient's neck, with the borders of the index fingers at the lower tips of the ears (Figure 7-28, *A*). The hands stroke firmly downward to the base of the neck as the forearms are pronated and the arms abducted (Figure 7-28, *B*).

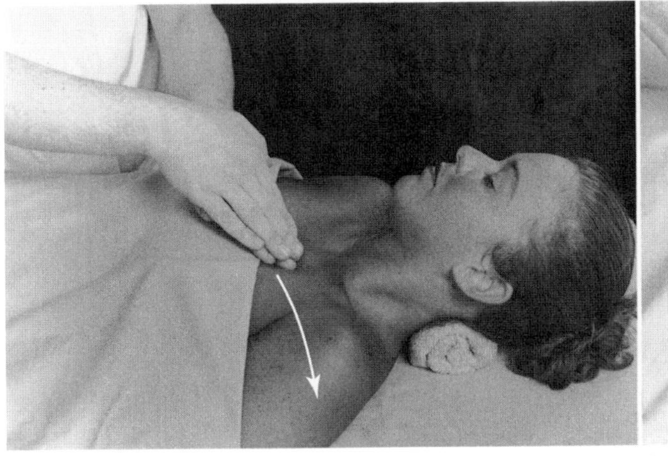

A

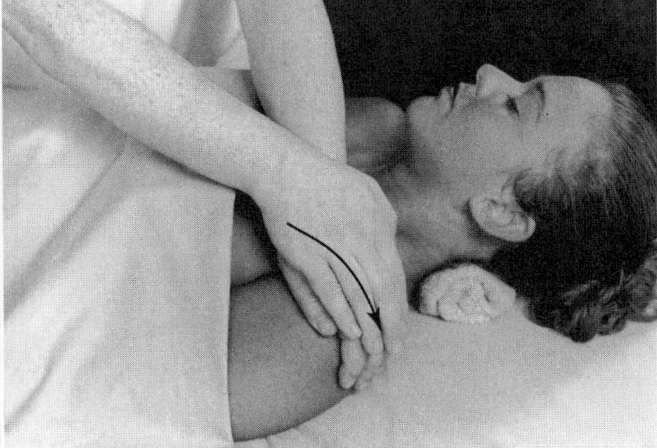

B

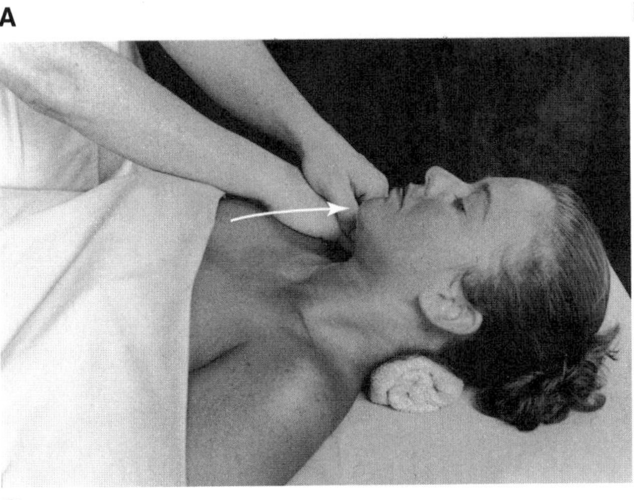

C

**Figure 7-26**
Digital kneading from the sternum to the shoulder.

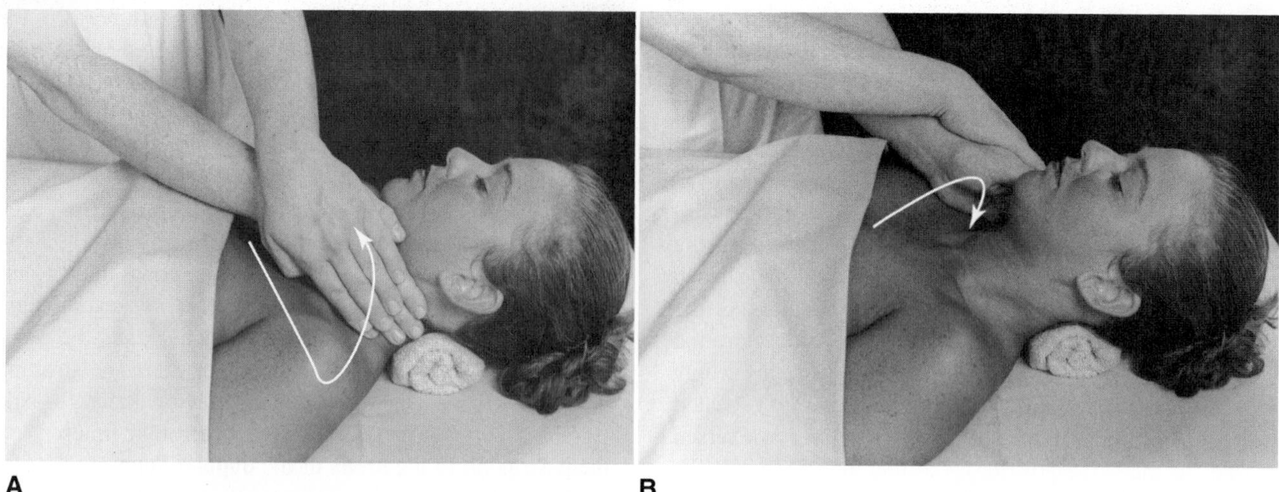


**Figure 7-27**
Digital stroking to the neck.

A

B

C

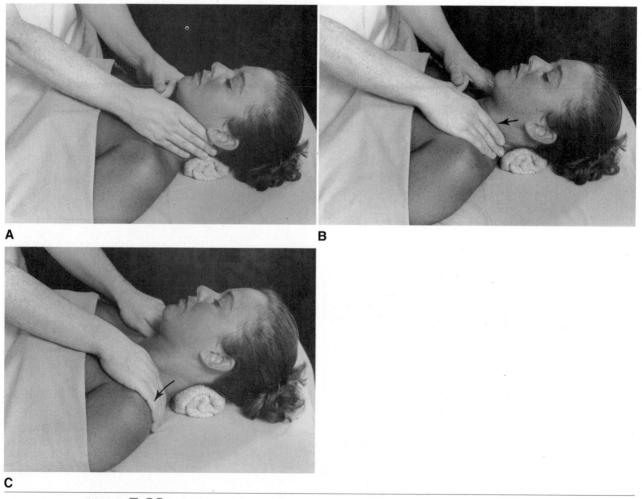

**Figure 7-28**
Deep stroking to the areas of the jugular veins.

The thumbs do not make any contact with the neck. With gradually lessening pressure, the hands continue the stroke to the tips of the shoulders (Figure 7-28, *C*). These movements are repeated four times.

**Deep Stroking to the Neck**

The therapist repeats the movements for deep stroking over the shoulder and around the neck (see Figure 7-25) but gradually reduces the pressure with each stroke until the last stroke is performed as superficial stroking.

### *Abdomen*

The therapist stands at the side of the treatment table to the right of the patient. The patient's knees are flexed and supported on a pillow so that there is no tension on the anterior and lateral abdominal muscles.

**Superficial Stroking to the Abdomen**

With the thumb widely abducted, the right hand is placed over the lower border of the left ribs; the left hand is similarly placed over the lower border of the right ribs. Both hands may stroke the tissues simultaneously or they can be used alternately. The stroke passes down over the abdomen and finishes at the upper margin of the symphysis pubis. Several lanes may be needed to cover the entire abdomen. The hands are lifted off at the end of the stroke and returned through the air to the starting position without contacting the skin. These movements are repeated four times.

**Deep Stroking to the Lower Abdominal Muscles**

The therapist places the fingertips of both hands side by side on the abdomen at the upper margin of the symphysis pubis (Figure 7-29, *A*). Both hands stroke lightly outward and upward, toward their respective left and right ASIS. Both hands continue following the crest of the ilium around toward the upper lumbar spine. The palms then turn and stroke forward with firm pressure around the waistline (Figure 7-29, *B*) and over the abdomen and back to the starting position. (The purpose of this movement is to manipulate the abdominal musculature, not to exert pressure on the abdominal viscera.) These movements are repeated four times.

**Deep Stroking to the Upper Abdominal Muscles**

One hand is placed so that the fingers lie over the costal margins of the lower left ribs while the palm is at the base of the sternum; the other hand is placed over the top for reinforcement (Figure 7-30, *A*). The hands stroke lightly in a lateral direction over the ribs, then down over the upper abdominal muscles (Figure 7-30, *B*), and then return to the starting position with firm pressure over the upper abdomen. These movements are repeated four times on the left side.

One hand is then placed with the fingertips at the base of the sternum and the palm over the lower anterior border of the right ribs (Figure 7-30, *C*). The therapist repeats the strokes described previously on the right side (Figure 7-30, *D*). To have the palm in good contact on this side of the abdomen, the wrist must be in full extension at the start of the stroke. These movements are repeated four times on the right side.

**Palmar Kneading over the Colon**

This stroke is designed to knead over the various sections of the colon. It is important therefore that the massage be given in the normal direction of flow in the colon. To begin the stroke, the therapist's right hand is placed over the lower right quadrant of the patient's abdomen (beginning of the ascending colon), so that the ulnar border of the hand lies alongside the pubic bone, just medial to the ASIS. The left hand reinforces the right hand directly or by gripping the right wrist. The ulnar border of the right hand lifts up the tissues in a scooping-like movement, performed by pressure with the ulnar border of the hand, rolling the hand over to the thenar border as the palm is pushed toward the fingertips, which are kept in contact with the skin during this scooping action. The fingertips are then moved to a more proximal point on the ascending colon as the hand rolls back onto its ulnar border and the movement is repeated. Using this movement, the massage progresses over the abdomen, covering the areas overlying the ascending, the transverse, and the descending colon (Figure 7-31, *A*). The movement is changed slightly over the descending colon so that the

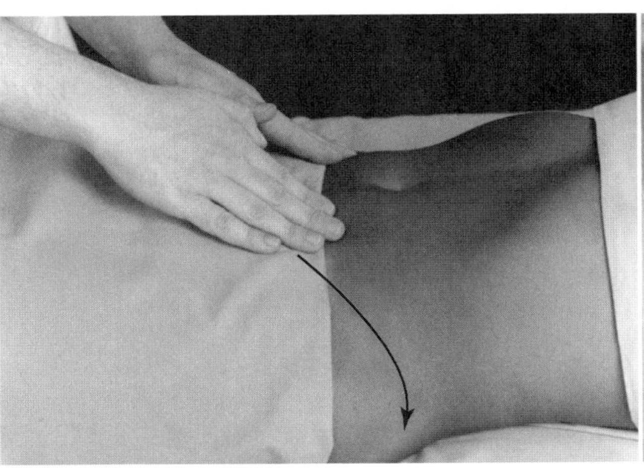

A

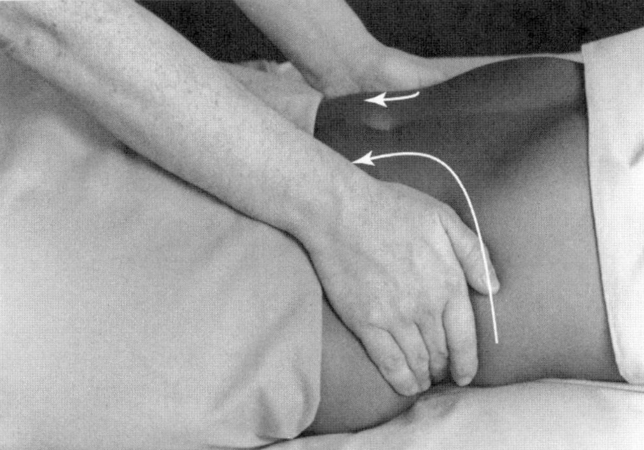

B

**Figure 7-29**
Deep stroking to the lower abdominal muscles.

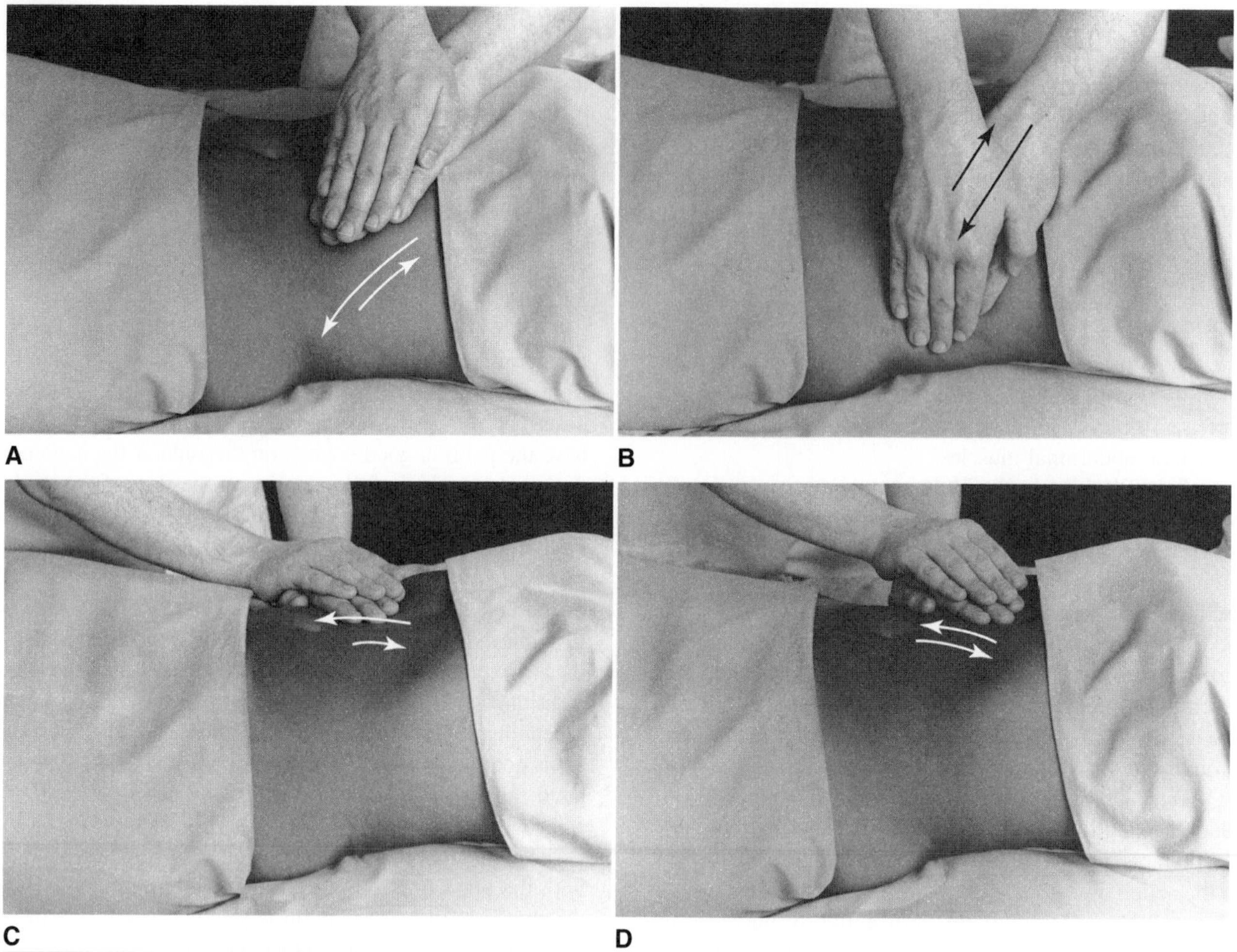

A B C D

Figure 7-30
Deep stroking to the upper abdominal muscles.

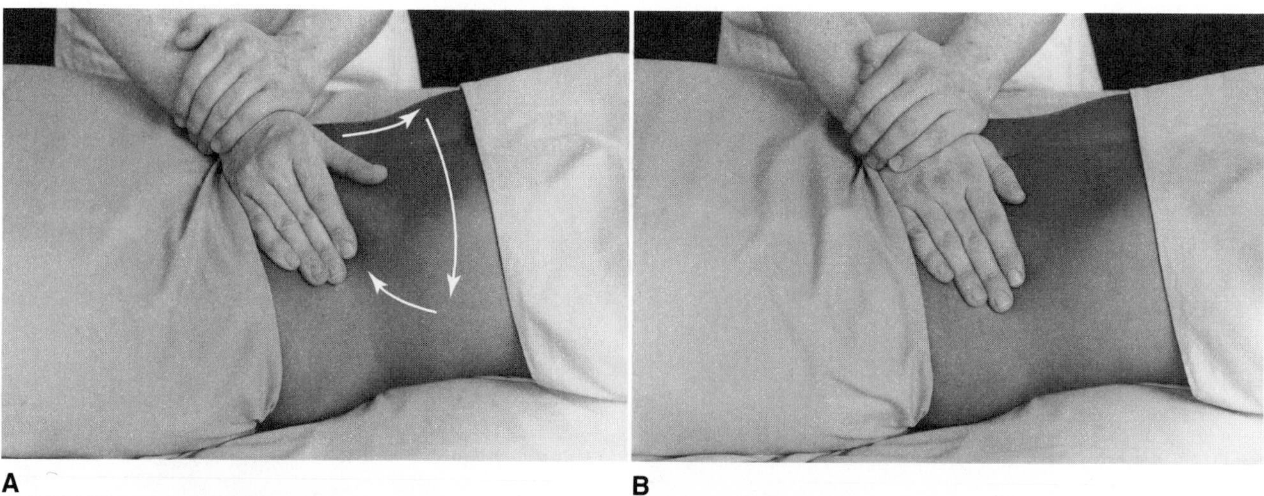
A B

Figure 7-31
Palmar kneading over the colon.

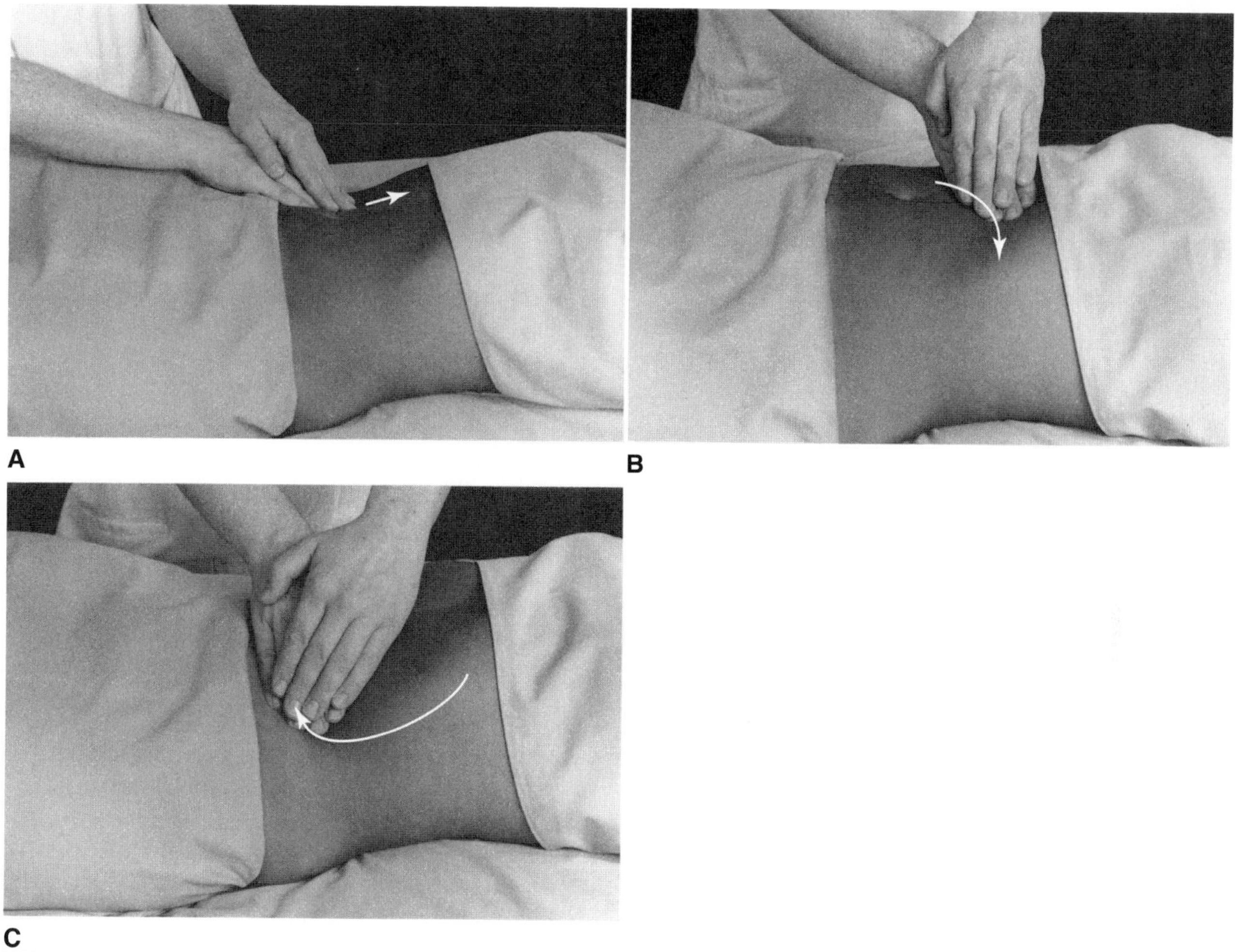

A

B

C

Figure 7-32
Deep stroking over the colon.

firm pressure is applied with the thenar eminence of the palm. The movement is completed with a firm stroke downward over the lower part of the area of the descending colon (Figure 7-31, *B*), with the hand passing lightly over the midline of the lower abdomen to the beginning of the ascending colon (starting position). These movements are repeated three times.

**Deep Stroking over the Colon**

The fingertips of the right hand are placed at the lower part (beginning) of the ascending colon, with the left hand reinforcing the right (Figure 7-32, *A*). The fingertips stroke firmly upward over the area of the ascending colon, across the area of the transverse colon (Figure 7-32, *B*), downward over the descending colon (Figure 7-32, *C*), and then lightly over the midline of the lower abdomen to the starting point. These movements are repeated six times.

**Alternate Squeeze Kneading over the Entire Abdomen**

At the right side of the abdomen, both hands, with the thumbs abducted, grasp the tissues and, by alternate flexion and extension at the elbows and the shoulders, progress across the abdomen with a kneading movement (Figure 7-33). Both hands return together to the right side with a

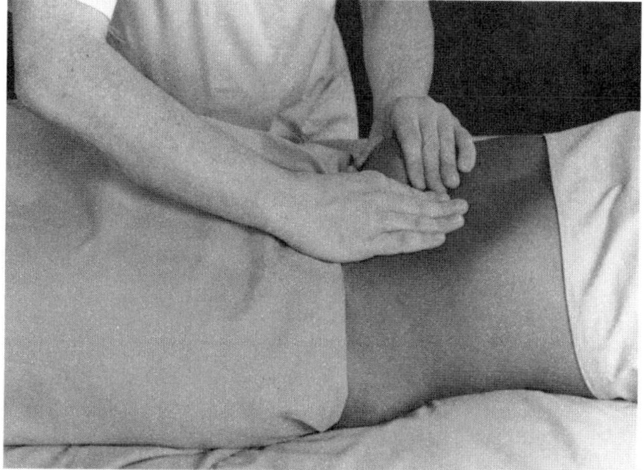

Figure 7-33
Alternate squeeze kneading over the entire abdomen.

superficial stroke. These movements are repeated four times.

**Deep Stroking to the Lower Abdomen**

Deep stroking to the lower abdomen is repeated (see Figure 7-32) with gradually reduced pressure to eventually become superficial stroking. These movements are repeated four times.

NOTE: If the patient suffers from chronic constipation, many of these strokes will need to be done in a depletive manner, beginning with the descending colon. See Colon Dysfunction in Chapter 9.

## Posterior Trunk and Pelvis

### *Back and Hips*

The therapist stands at the side of the treatment table on the patient's left. The patient is repositioned and comfortably supported in prone lying, with a pillow under the abdomen (lumbar spine region) and another under the ankles. The patient's head may be positioned in a number of ways, depending on what is comfortable (see Chapter 3; Figure 3-8).

**Superficial Stroking to the Back**

The therapist's right hand is placed over the right shoulder, and the left hand is placed over the left shoulder, with the thumbs just lateral to the spinous processes of the first cervical vertebra (Figure 7-34, *A*). Both hands, with thumbs abducted, stroke simultaneously to the sacrum, covering as much of the back as possible (Figure 7-34, *B*). The hands then return in the air to the starting position. These movements are repeated four times. The technique can also be performed using alternate hands, in the manner described in Chapter 4. At the end of the fourth stroke, the hands maintain contact so that they are in position to start deep palmar stroking.

**Deep Palmar Stroking to the Back**

For descriptive purposes, the technique is described in six steps, but in practice, each step blends in with the next as follows:

1. The fingers of both hands start the deep stroke at the lower border of the sacrum; the thumbs are crossed for reinforcement (Figure 7-35, *A*), and the hands stroke upward on each side of the spinous processes with firm pressure.
2. The hands separate at the neck and stroke over the top of the shoulder as the thumbs stroke up to the first cervical vertebra on both sides of the spinous processes (Figure 7-35, *B*). The hands then stroke back, drawing the muscles back also until the fingertips are at the top of the shoulder (Figure 7-35, *C*). At the same time, the thumbs stroke down on both sides of the cervical vertebrae. The hands, with thumbs adducted, then stroke laterally to the shoulder joint (Figure 7-35, *D*), down the sides of the back to the waistline, and then toward the midline (Figure 7-35, *E*) and down until the fingertips are at the lower border of the sacrum. (The thumbs cross to reinforce as the hands start the downward stroke to the sacrum.)
3. The hands stroke upward and over the shoulders as in step 2 (Figure 7-35, *A*) and return the stroke downward until the fingertips are even with the axilla (Figure 7-35, *F*), then pass laterally and stroke to the sacrum, again as in step 2.
4. The hands stroke upward and over the shoulder as in step 2, return the stroke downward until the wrists are at the waistline (Figure 7-35, *G*), then pass laterally and stroke to the sacrum, again as in step 2.
5. The hands stroke upward and over the shoulder as in step 2, return the stroke downward until the fingertips are at the waistline, then pass laterally and stroke to the sacrum (Figure 7-35, *H*), as in step 2.
6. The hands stroke upward, as in step 2, and return the stroke over the shoulder and then downward, with the hands spread to cover the entire back, and return to the sacrum (Figure 7-35, *I*).

These movements are repeated three times.

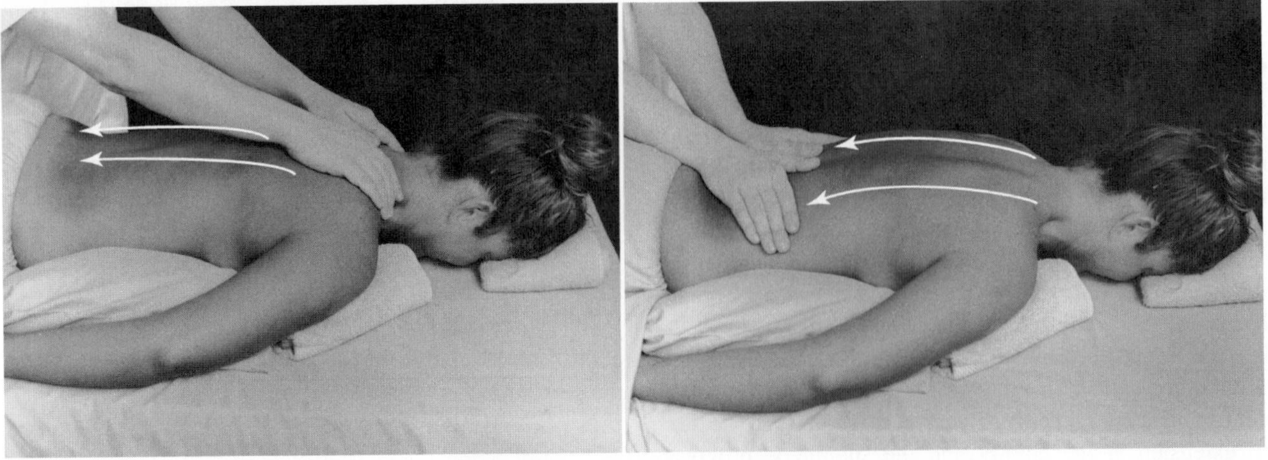


Figure 7-34
Superficial stroking to the back.

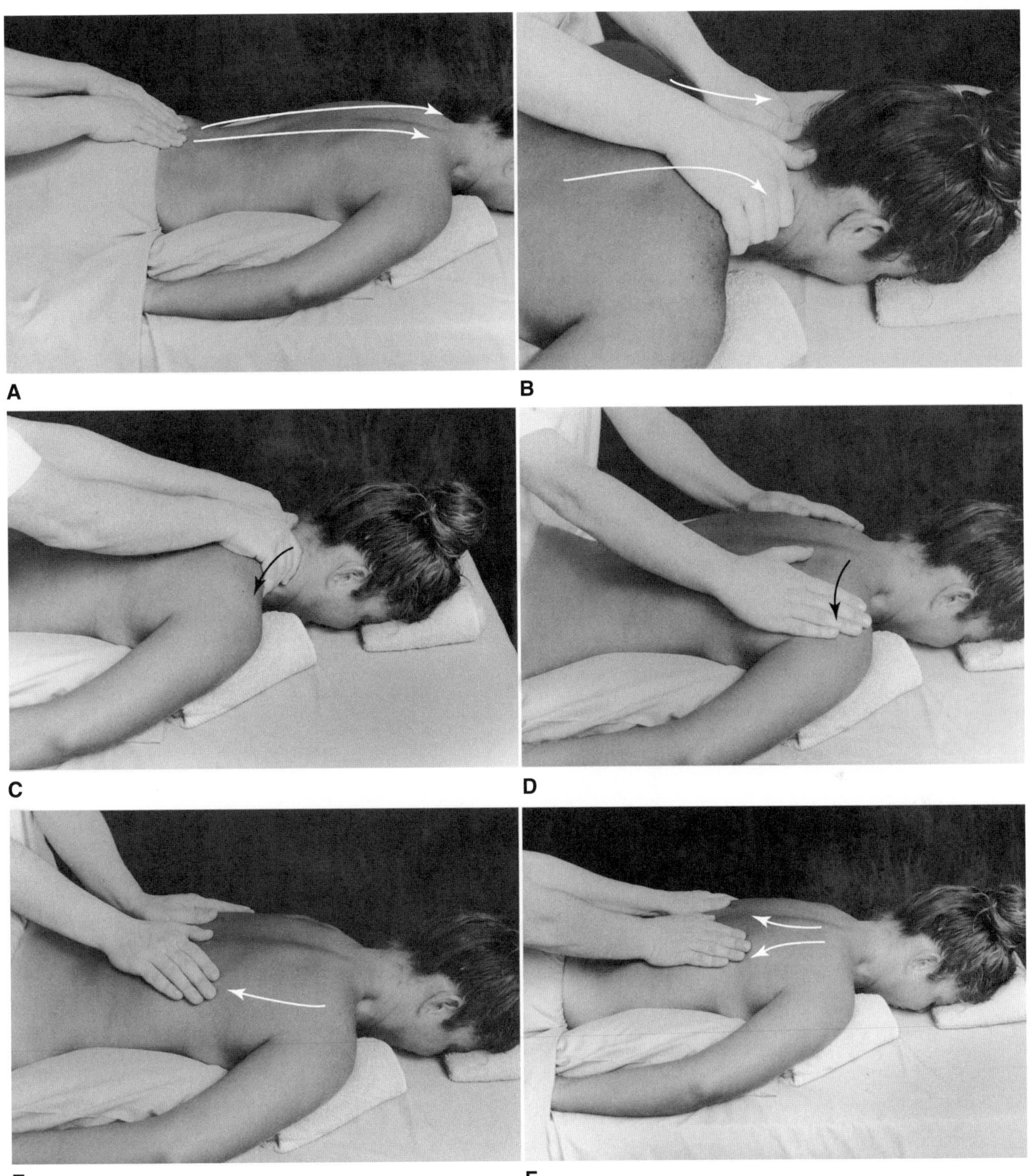


Figure 7-35
Deep palmar stroking to the back.

**Finger Pad Kneading to the Upper Fibers of the Trapezius**
The finger pads of the right hand, reinforced with the left hand, are placed at the upper cervical region of the upper fibers of the right trapezius muscle (Figure 7-36, *A*). They knead in small clockwise circles, progressing over to the acromion process (Figure 7-36, *B*). The fingers return to the starting position with a superficial stroke. These movements are repeated three times. The left side is kneaded in the same manner, except that circles are worked counterclockwise. Again, the movements are repeated three times.

**Deep Stroking to the Upper Fibers of the Trapezius**
The stroke begins with each thumb placed on the borders of the upper fibers of the trapezius muscle, lateral to the spinous processes of the upper cervical vertebrae. The palms of the hands rest on the belly of the upper fibers. Both hands stroke firmly along the muscle to the acromion process on each

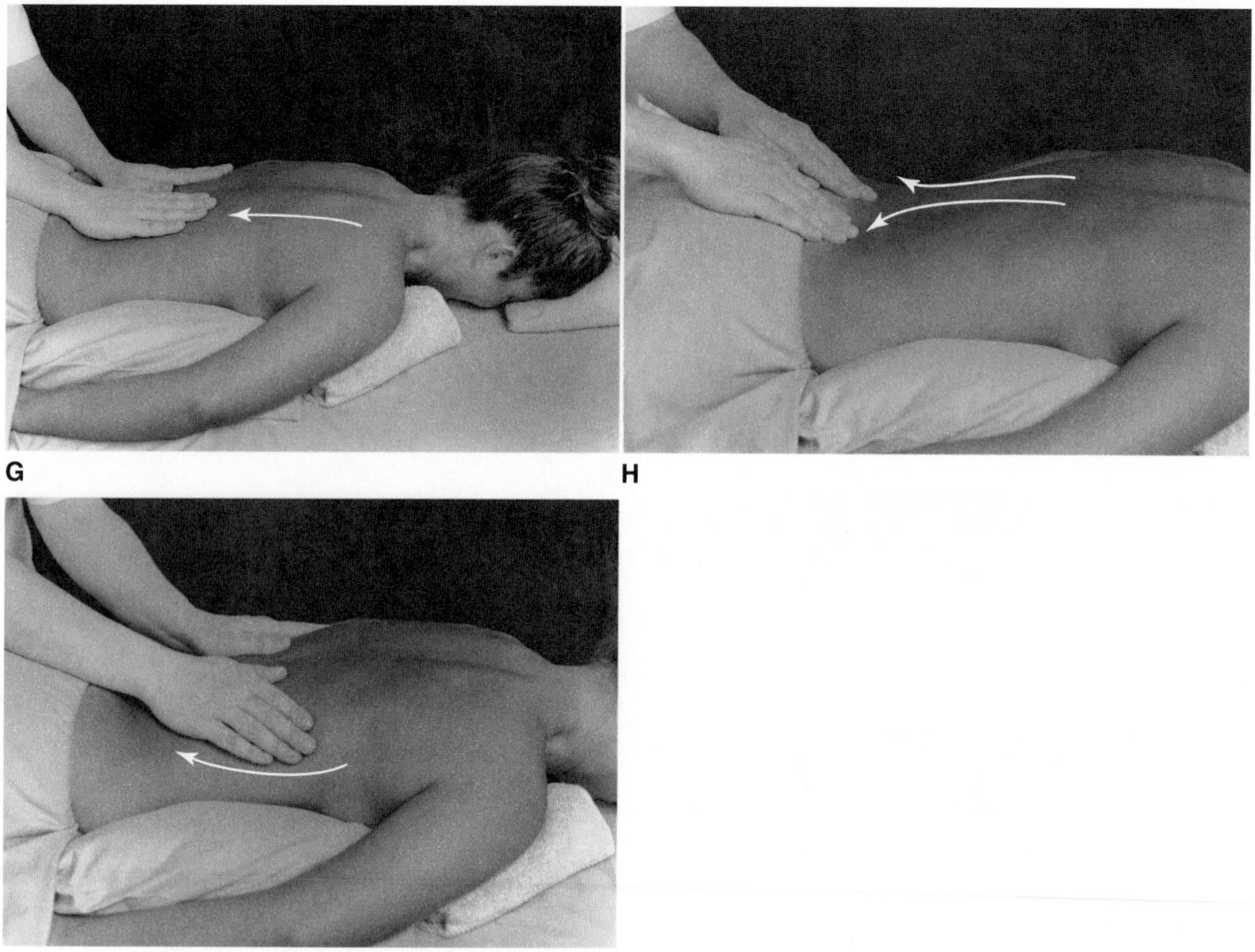

G

H

I

Figure **7-35**, cont'd

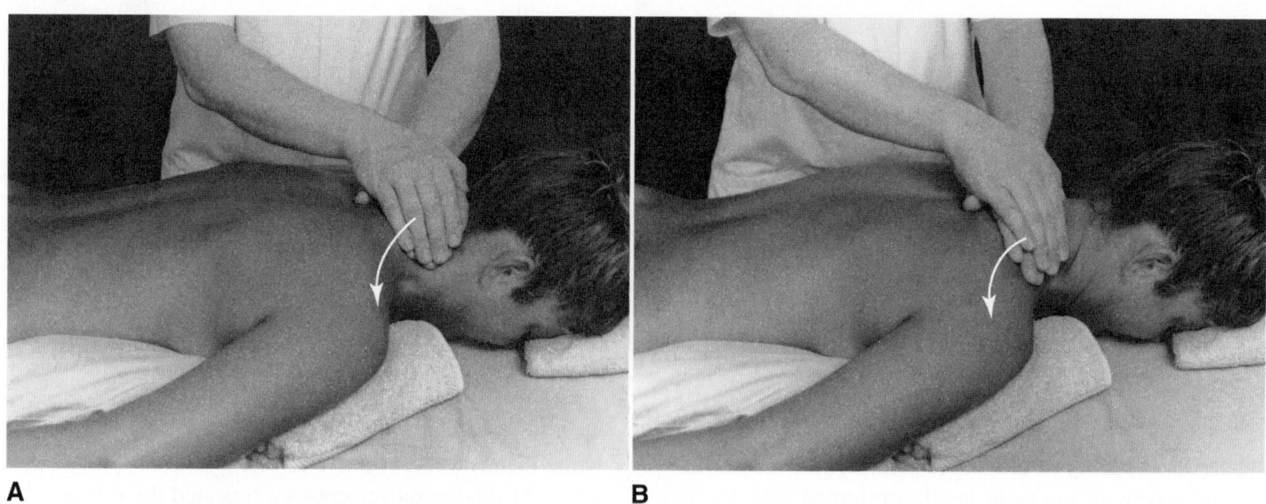

A

B

Figure **7-36**

Finger pad kneading to the upper fibers of the trapezius.

side, picking up the muscle as the thumbs reach the lower cervical region (Figure 7-37). The hands then relax and return with superficial strokes to begin again. These movements are repeated four times.

**Reinforced Palmar Kneading over the Scapular Region**

Reinforced by the left hand, the right hand is placed with the palm above the spine of the right scapula and the thumb just lateral to the spinous process of the upper thoracic vertebra. The palm kneads in a clockwise circle over the upper scapular region (Figure 7-38), then glides to make a second circle over the lateral border of the scapula, a third circle over the lower angle of the scapula, and a fourth circle over the medial border of the scapula. The movements are repeated three times.

Transition is made from one side to the other with no break in contact, the hand simply gliding across with a superficial stroke. To massage the left scapular region, the right hand is placed with the palm above the spine of the left scapula and the ulnar border of the hand just lateral to the spinous processes of the upper thoracic vertebrae. The kneading is performed in the same manner as for the right side, except that the circles are made counterclockwise. These movements are repeated three times.

**Palmar Kneading to the Thoracic and Lumbar Regions**

Palmar kneading to the thoracic and lumbar regions is a two-handed technique, but the hands work alternately on each side of the back. The therapist stands facing the patient's feet. Both hands are placed on the upper thoracic region with the thumbs together in the midline. The technique begins with the left hand stroking across to the lateral border of the right dorsal region with firm pressure (Figure 7-39, *A*). The left hand then kneads the tissues in the reverse direction back to the midline, where it remains stationary. At this point, the right hand strokes across to the left side of the thorax and kneads the tissues on its way back to the midline. As the right hand returns, it remains stationary in the midline, while the left hand again strokes laterally to the right side, this time a little lower on the thoracic wall. These strokes are repeated, the hands alternating in direction and progressing to the lower border of the lumbar region (Figure

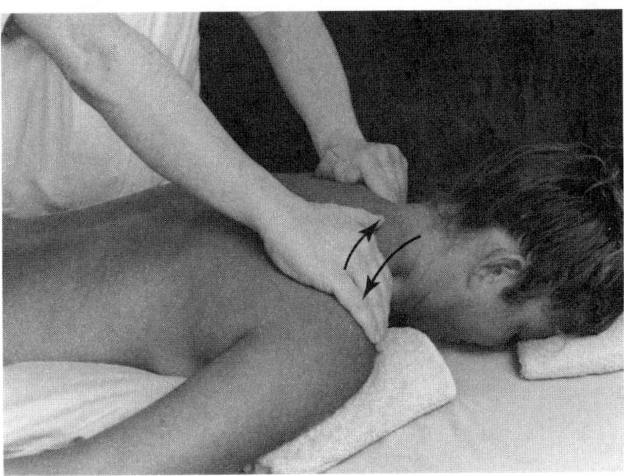

Figure 7-37
Deep stroking to the upper fibers of the trapezius.

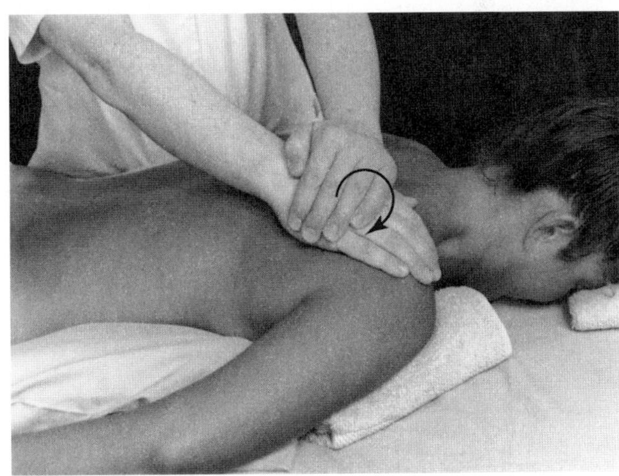

Figure 7-38
Reinforced palmar kneading over the scapular region.

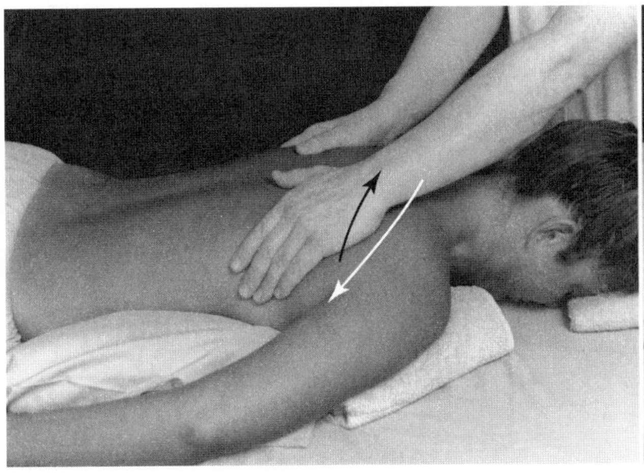

A

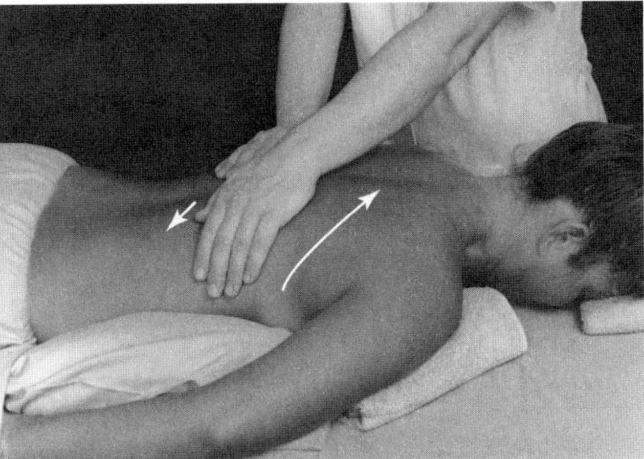

B

Figure 7-39
Palmar kneading to the thoracic and lumbar regions.

7-39, *B*). Before the left hand completes the stroke at the lower lumbar area, the right hand is removed and is placed on the upper dorsal region to start the entire kneading sequence again. The movements are repeated four times.

**Palmar Stroking to the Lumbar Region**

The right hand, reinforced by the left, is placed over the lower ribs on the right side, the fingers extending along the ribs (Figure 7-40, *A*). The hand strokes lightly from the spine to the lateral lumbar region of the right side and returns below the ribs, stroking toward the spine with firm pressure (Figure 7-40, *B*). These movements are repeated four times. The left side is massaged in the same manner as the right, except that the right hand is placed with the fingertips at the spine for the initial stroke. These movements are repeated four times.

**Thumb Pad Kneading to the Sacrum**

The therapist faces the patient's head and places the thumbs of both hands at the upper border of the sacrum, with the palms in contact with the back just above the iliac crest (Figure 7-41). The thumbs knead alternately in small circles with upward pressure, progressing to the lower border of the sacrum. At this point, both thumbs stroke along the sacrum with firm pressure to return to the upper border to begin the stroke again. The movements are repeated four times.

**Alternate Palmar Kneading to the Gluteal Muscles**

The ulnar border of the right hand is placed at the lower border of the gluteus maximus muscle (gluteal fold), and the ulnar border of the left hand is placed in the area of the origin of the gluteal muscles. The muscle mass is then grasped and kneaded in an alternating movement similar to that described for the quadriceps muscle. Several lanes of kneading may be required in order to cover the entire muscle group. Pressure is applied in such a manner as to avoid separating the buttocks (Figure 7-42). The left buttock is massaged in the same manner as the right. These movements are repeated twice on each side.

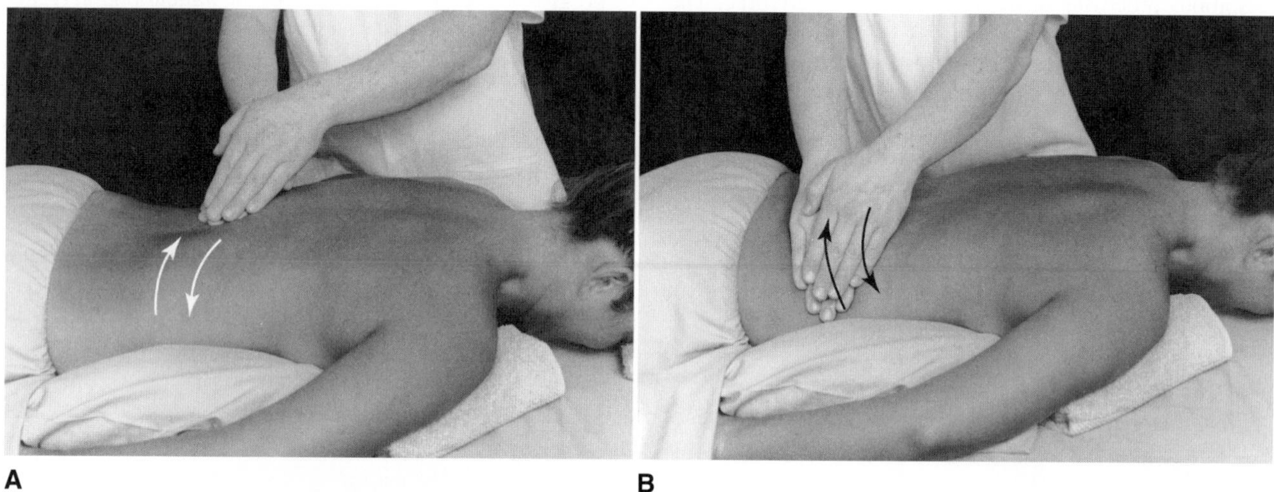


Figure 7-40
Palmar stroking to the lumbar region.

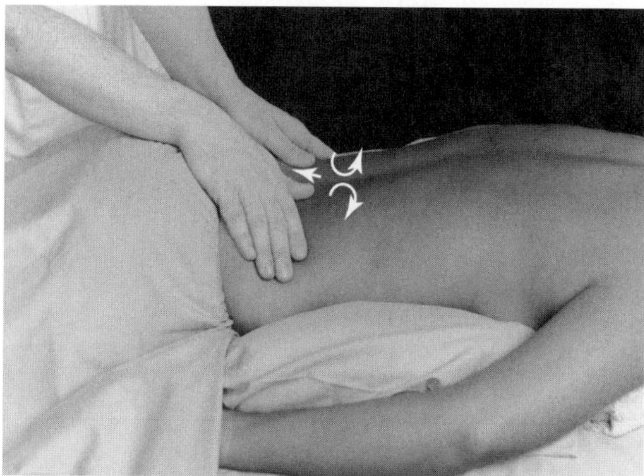

Figure 7-41
Thumb pad kneading to the sacrum.

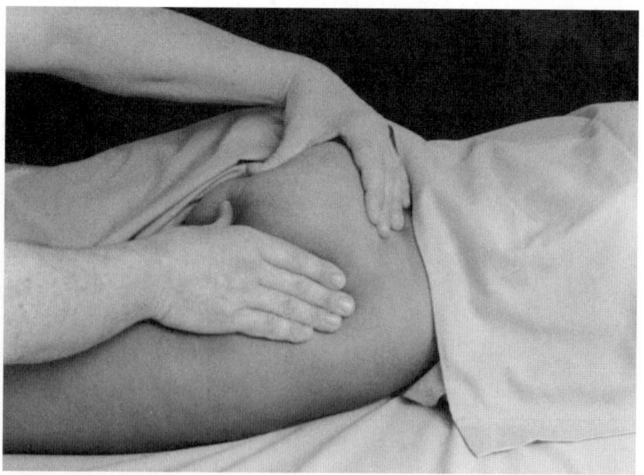

Figure 7-42
Alternate palmar kneading to the gluteal muscles.

### Reinforced Kneading to the Gluteal Muscles

One hand reinforces the other and performs deep kneading over the right gluteal muscle mass (Figure 7-43) in the same manner as for kneading over the colon, except that the heel of the hand exerts firm pressure toward the midline throughout the movement to avoid separating the buttocks. This movement is repeated twice. The left buttock is kneaded in the same manner as the right, with the same number of repetitions.

### Alternate Palmar Kneading over the Entire Back

This movement is the same as for alternate palmar kneading over the thoracic and lumbar regions (see Figure 7-39), beginning at the upper scapular region and continuing over the entire back. These movements are repeated four times.

### Digital Kneading to the Erector Spinae Muscles

For digital kneading to the erector spinae muscles, the therapist kneads the tissues between the thumb of one hand and the fingers of the other. This technique is similar to the wringing stroke described in Chapter 4. The finger pads (distal phalanges) of the first and second fingers of both hands are placed just lateral to the spinous processes at the lower cervical region, and the distal phalanx of each thumb is placed an inch or two below the fingertips. (This relative position of fingers and thumb is maintained for each hand throughout the movement.) Using a circular motion and firm pressure, the fingers of the right hand draw a portion of the muscle downward; simultaneously the left thumb, also with firm pressure, presses a portion of the muscle upward; then the right thumb presses a portion upward as the fingers of the left hand draw a portion of the muscle downward, again using a circular motion. The therapist progresses from one area to the next by gliding of the fingers during the period of firm pressure while the thumb of the same hand superficially strokes the area to be covered next. (This kneading of the tissues between the thumb of one hand and the fingers of the other is produced by alternate flexion and extension at the elbows and the shoulders.) The kneading is continued to the sacrum. This movement usually is not repeated.

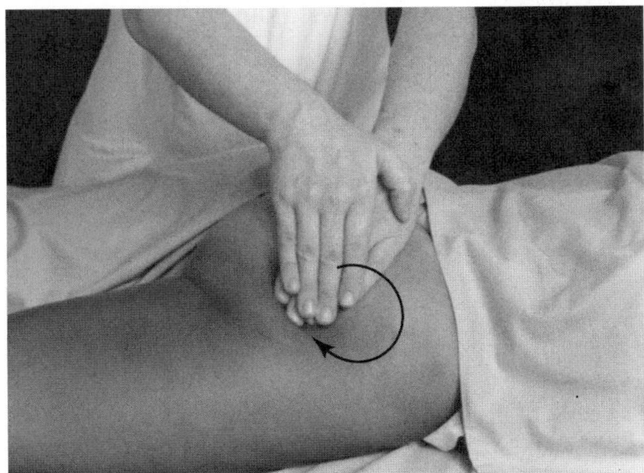

Figure 7-43
Reinforced kneading to the gluteal muscles.

### Deep Stroking to the Erector Spinae Muscles

The hands are used alternately in this classical deep stroking technique. The thumb pad of the therapist's right hand is placed over the center of the spine at the cervical region and moves with a deep stroke down the right side of the back to the sacrum. This allows the rest of the hand to cover the mass of the erector spinae muscles as it passes over the tissues. As the right hand approaches the end of the stroke (Figure 7-44, *A*), the left hand starts another deep stroke, this time over the left side of the back. The right hand returns in the air (Figure 7-44, *B*). These movements are repeated four times.

### Superficial Stroking to the Entire Back

Superficial stroking to the entire back is given to finish the general sequence to this region. The technique is identical to that described for the erector spinae muscles, except that the pressure used is significantly less and the entire back is covered with overlapping lanes of the stroke.

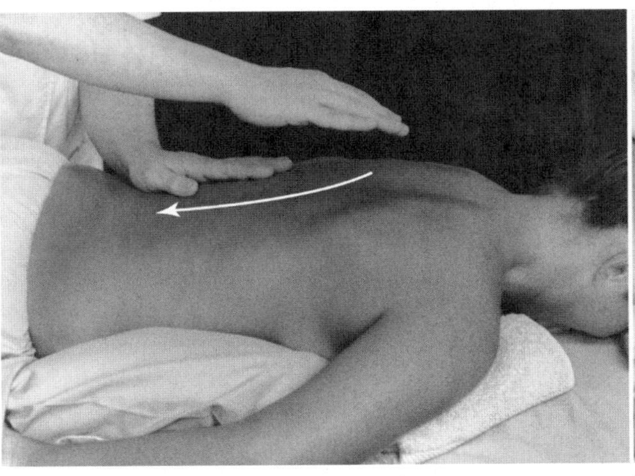

A

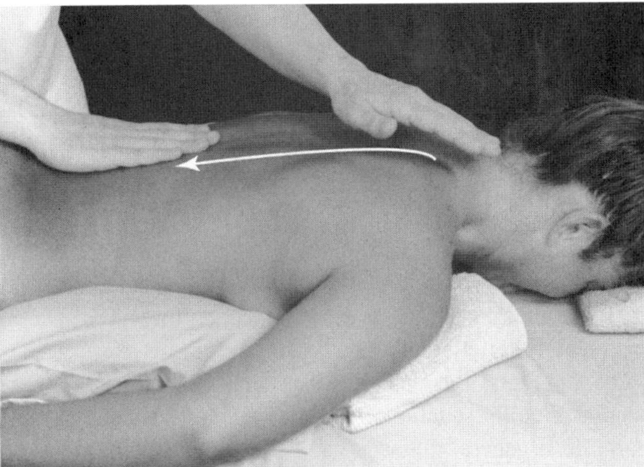

B

Figure 7-44
Deep stroking to the erector spinae muscles.

### *Posterior Neck Region*

#### Superficial and Deep Stroking to the Upper Fibers of the Trapezius Muscle

The thumbs are placed on the borders of the upper fibers of the trapezius muscle on both sides, just lateral to the spinous processes of the upper cervical vertebrae. The palms of the hands are in contact over the tops of the shoulders. Both hands stroke lightly to the acromion process on each side, picking up the muscle as the thumbs reach the lower cervical region. The hands return to the starting position with a superficial stroke. This movement is performed eight times, with increasing pressure, so that by the fifth stroke the therapist is applying deep stroking; the hands return to the starting position with superficial stroking.

#### Finger Pad Kneading over the Upper Fibers of the Trapezius Muscle

The fingertips of the right hand, reinforced by the left hand, are placed at the upper cervical region of the left trapezius muscle. As usual, the fingers knead in small clockwise circles, exerting heavier pressure over one half of each circle. Kneading progresses to the acromion process. The fingertips return to the starting position with a superficial stroke. These movements are repeated three times. The right side is kneaded in the same manner, except that the circles are made counterclockwise. These movements are repeated three times.

#### Deep Stroking over the Upper Fibers of the Trapezius Muscle

Deep stroking over the upper fibers of the trapezius muscle is performed in the same manner as that described for superficial and deep stroking over the upper fibers of the trapezius muscle (described earlier), except that the pressure starts deeply and is gradually lessened to superficial stroking. These movements are repeated six times.

## Head and Neck

### *Face and Anterior Neck*

Facial massage may be added to a general massage. Patients with insomnia frequently respond particularly well to facial massage, and it is a useful sedative in the treatment of headache. The movements are performed over a small area and should be gentle so that a lubricant is not usually necessary. As always, the therapist's hands should be washed and thoroughly dried before treatment. A small amount of fine unscented baby (talcum) powder may be used if the skin is moist from perspiration, but it should never be applied directly to the patient's face. Care is needed to ensure that the patient does not breathe the powder whenever it is used.

The technique for facial massage that follows is a type recommended for sedation in the treatment of headache and insomnia. If general massage has not been given, the treatment should include the chest and upper back movements described previously for general massage, and for the face, head, and neck (in the following section). The patient should be lying supine (recumbent) with the head supported on a small pillow or neck roll. The therapist stands facing the patient on either side of the table. All movements are performed with both hands in unison, with the exception of thumb pad kneading over the nose.

An alternative position is for the therapist to sit behind the patient's head (facing the patient's feet). In this case, the strokes are performed in a similar manner, but some of the directions will need to be reversed. It is important for the therapist to be comfortable during massage to the face because these tissues are so delicate compared to the rest of the body. It is therefore essential that the therapist has complete control of his or her hands, especially around delicate structures such as the eyes. Although the patient's eyes are usually closed during facial massage, they are still vulnerable to damage because the thin layer of skin that comprises the eyelids is their only protection.

#### Superficial Stroking to the Face

1. The therapist's palms are placed side by side on the forehead, with the thenar eminences on either side of the midline. The fingers are flexed slightly to fit over the head, with the fingertips resting lightly on the top of the head (Figure 7-45, *A*). The palms stroke to the lateral borders of the forehead (Figure 7-45, *B*) and return to the starting position by moving through the air while the hands pivot on the fingertips. These movements are repeated twice.
2. The movements are the same as in step 1, except that the fingertips rest at the hairline so that the palms are placed over the cheeks (Figure 7-45, *C, D*). They are repeated twice.
3. The fingertips glide lightly from the hairline to the temples. The thumb pads are placed together at the center of the chin (Figure 7-45, *E*). The thumb pads then stroke laterally along the border of the mandible to the tip of the ear (Figure 7-45, *F*) and return to the chin through the air. These movements are repeated twice.
4. The movements are the same as in step 3, except that the thumb pads start under the chin and stroke under the jaw to the tip of the ear. The movements are repeated twice.

#### Thumb Pad Kneading to the Forehead

The fingertips of each hand keep contact at the temple, and the thumb pads are placed together at the center of the lower border of the forehead (Figure 7-46, *A*). The thumb pads knead simultaneously, but out of phase with each other, in small circles (Figure 7-46, *B*), continuing up to the hairline. They return in the air to the lower border of the forehead at an adjacent lateral area. The strokes are repeated until the entire forehead is covered in a series of overlapping lanes. The movements are repeated twice.

#### Deep Stroking to the Forehead

The fingertips of each hand are kept in contact at the temples, and the palms are placed with the thumbs together in the midline of the forehead (Figure 7-47, *A*). The palms stroke laterally from the midline, with firm pressure (Figure 7-47,

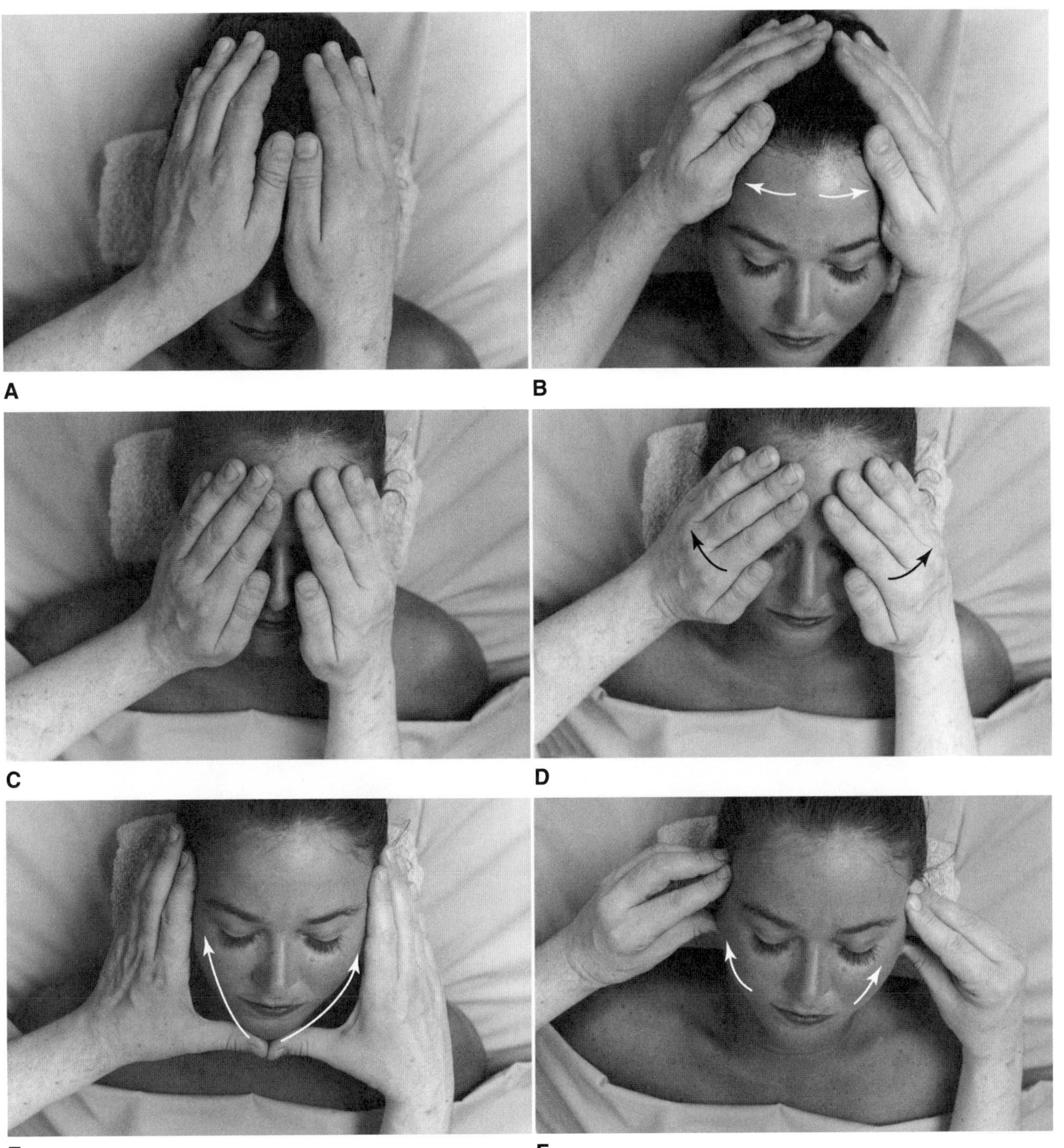


Figure 7-45
Superficial stroking to the face.

*B*), returning through the air. The movements are repeated three times.

**Thumb Pad Kneading to the Nose**

The fingertips are kept in contact at the temples, and the distal phalanges of the thumbs are placed at the tip of the nose (Figure 7-48, *A*). Alternate thumb pad kneading is performed on the sides of the nose, up to the bridge. The thumbs pause with firm pressure in the hollows formed by the bridge of the nose and the medial part of the supraorbital ridge (eyebrow) before returning through the air (Figure 7-48, *B*). These movements are repeated three times.

At the end of the third kneading stroke, the thumbs keep contact at the hollows, ready to start the next movement.

**Deep Stroking to the Supraorbital Ridge**

This movement flows from the previous one without breaking contact. The thumbs stroke outward with firm pressure over the supraorbital ridge (eyebrow) and return through the air (Figure 7-49). The movements are repeated four times.

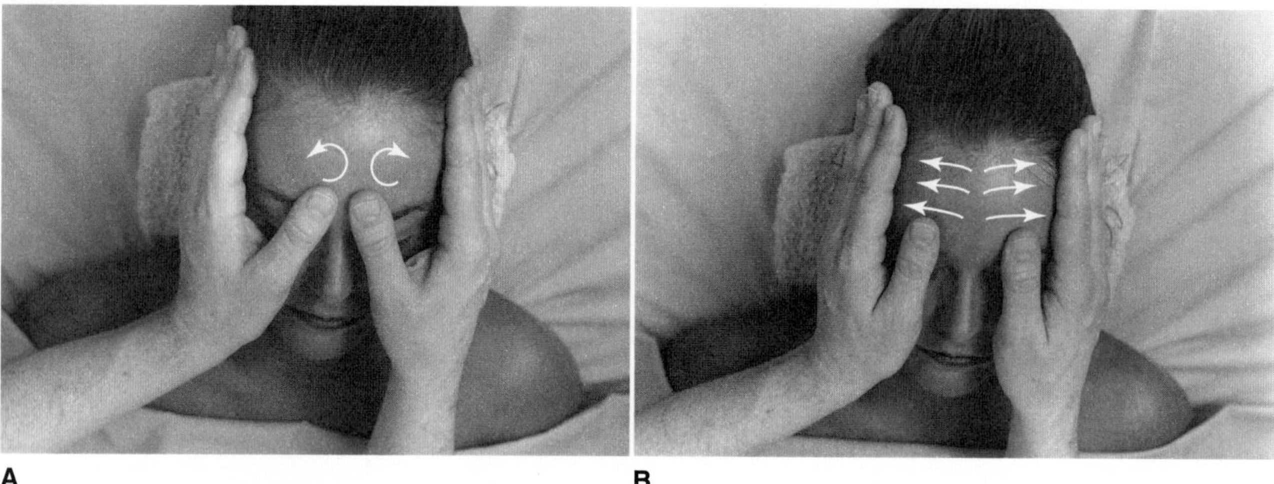

Figure 7-46
Thumb pad kneading to the forehead.

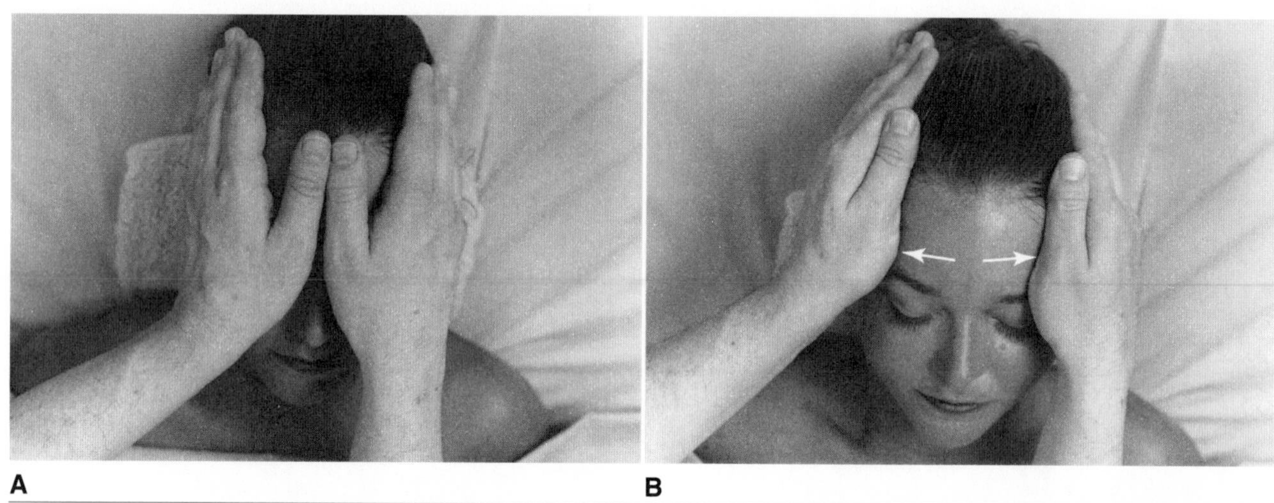

Figure 7-47
Deep stroking to the forehead.

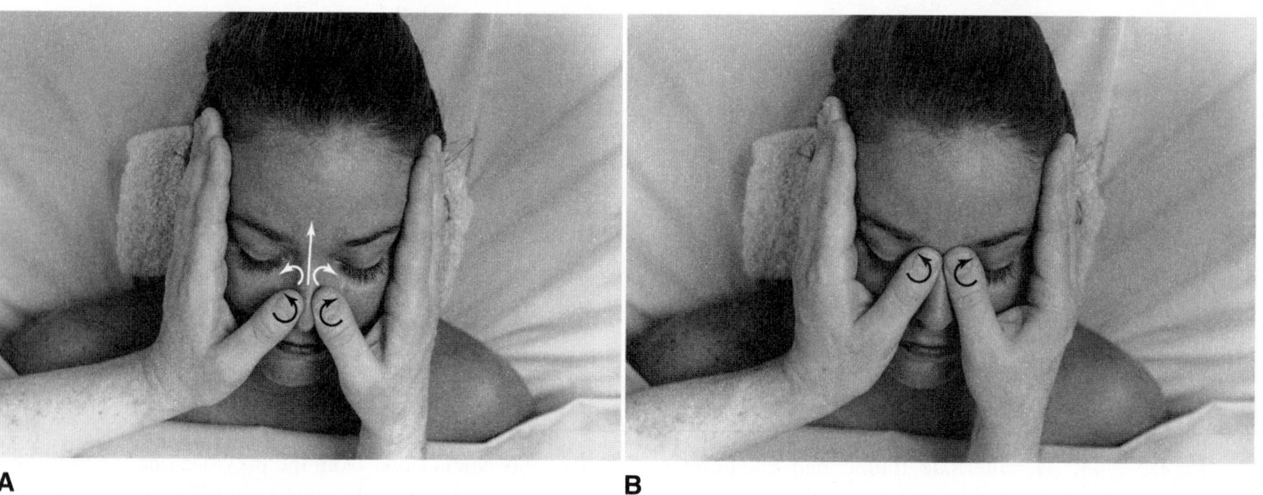

Figure 7-48
Thumb pad kneading to the nose.

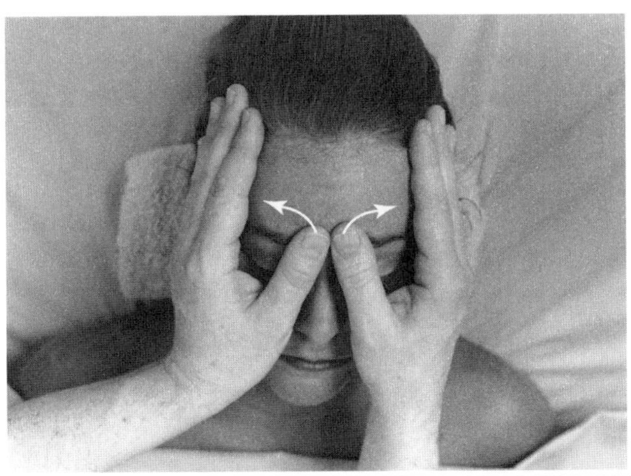

Figure 7-49
Deep stroking to the supraorbital ridge.

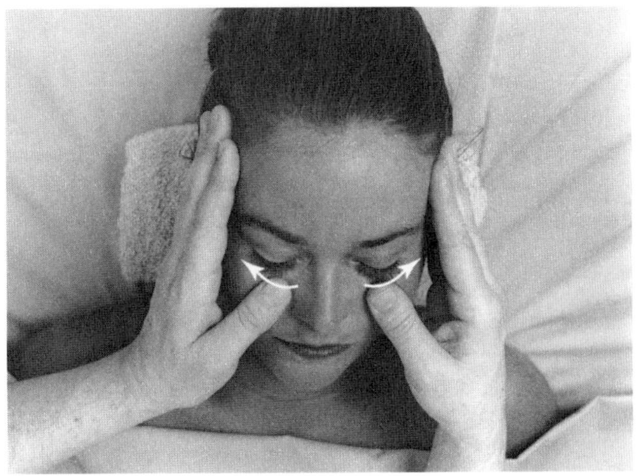

Figure 7-50
Deep stroking to the infraorbital ridge.

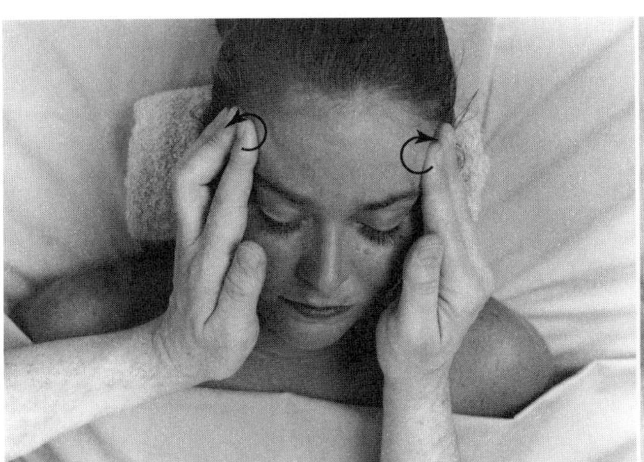

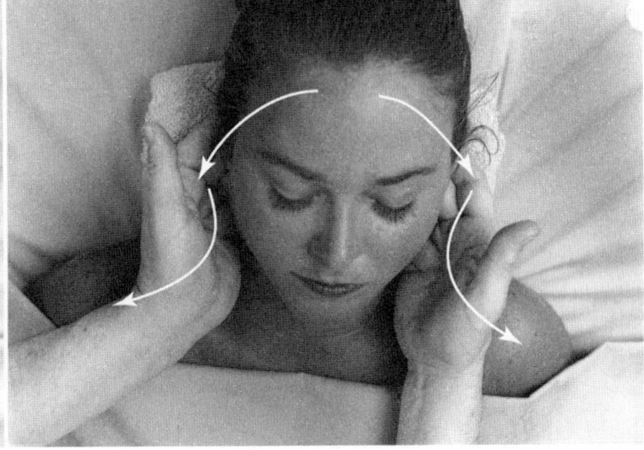

A B

Figure 7-51
Finger pad kneading from the temple to the cervical spine.

**Deep Stroking to the Infraorbital Ridge**

The hands remain in the same position as for stroking the supraorbital ridge, allowing the thumbs to stroke over the infraorbital ridge (Figure 7-50) and return through the air. The movements are repeated four times.

**Finger Pad Kneading from the Temple to the Cervical Spine**

Continuing on from the previous stroke, the thumbs remain in the air, and the fingertips (again without breaking the contact with the temples) simultaneously knead in small circles, starting at the midline of the temples and, following the hairline (Figure 7-51, *A*), continuing along the back of the ears until the fingers meet at the cervical spine (Figure 7-51, *B*).

Without breaking contact, the fingers stroke with firm pressure down the cervical spine to the seventh cervical vertebra. The thumbs then make contact with the anterior borders of the trapezius muscle, and the stroking is continued with the thumbs and fingers over the upper fibers of the trapezius, gradually reducing pressure to the tips of the shoulders. The hands again return to the temples through the air. These movements are repeated twice.

**Finger Pad Kneading from the Temples to the Shoulders**

The fingertips knead in small circles from the temples (Figure 7-52, *A*), passing in front of the ears to the mastoid processes. The strokes continue over both sternocleidomastoid muscles and the upper fibers of the trapezius muscles (Figure 7-52, *B*) to the tips of the shoulders. The hands then return through the air. The movements are repeated twice.

**Deep Stroking over the Area of the Jugular Veins**

This stroke is the same as that previously described for deep stroking over the areas of the jugular veins. With the thumbs widely abducted, the fingers (palmar surface) of the therapist's right hand are placed on the left side of the neck and those of the left hand are placed on the right side of the patient's neck, with the borders of the index fingers at the

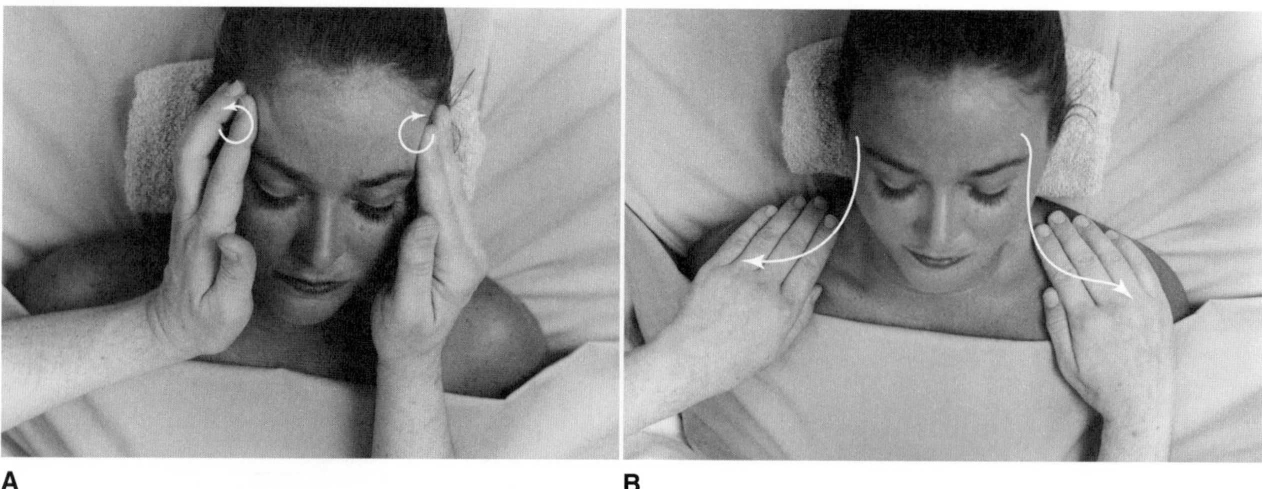


Figure 7-52
Finger pad kneading from the temples to the shoulders.

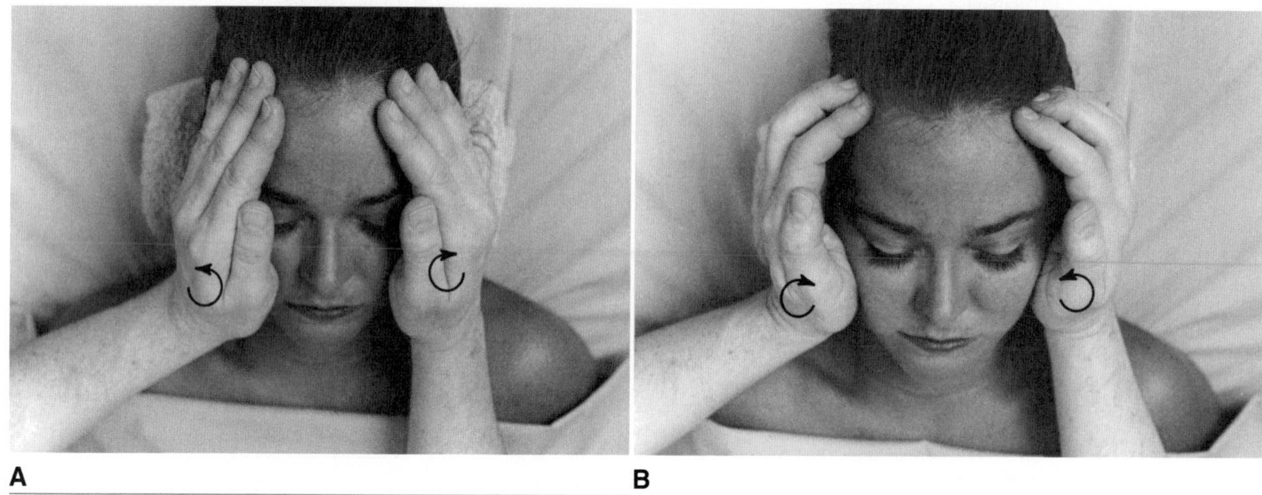


Figure 7-53
Palmar kneading to the cheeks.

lower tips of the ears (Figure 7-28, *A*). The hands stroke firmly downward to the base of the neck as the forearms are pronated and the arms abducted (Figure 7-28, *B*). The thumbs do not make any contact with the neck. With gradually lessening pressure, the hands continue the stroke to the tips of the shoulders (Figure 7-28, *C*). These movements are repeated four times.

**Palmar Kneading to the Cheeks**

The fingertips rest on the forehead while the palms rest lightly on the cheeks and knead in circles, three times in opposite directions (i.e., the right hand clockwise and the left counterclockwise) (Figure 7-53, *A*) and three times in the reversed directions (Figure 7-53, *B*). As with standard kneading, the palms do not move over the skin but with gentle pressure move the tissues over the bony surface underneath. The movements are repeated twice.

**Thumb Pad Kneading to the Chin and Lower Jaw**

The fingertips glide lightly to make contact below the ears. The thumbs are placed together at the center of the lower border of the chin (Figure 7-54, *A*) and knead simultaneously, but out of phase with each other, in small circles upward to the lower lip, returning with superficial stroking to knead over more lateral areas of the chin. They continue this kneading over the mandibles to the tips of the ears, covering the tissues in a series of overlapping lanes (Figure 7-54, *B*). These movements are repeated three times.

**Deep Stroking to the Chin and Lower Jaw**

Keeping the fingers in contact, the thumbs return to the midline of the chin as they were at the start of the previous movement. They then stroke with firm pressure from the chin to the tips of the ears (Figure 7-55) to return through the air. These movements are repeated three times.

A

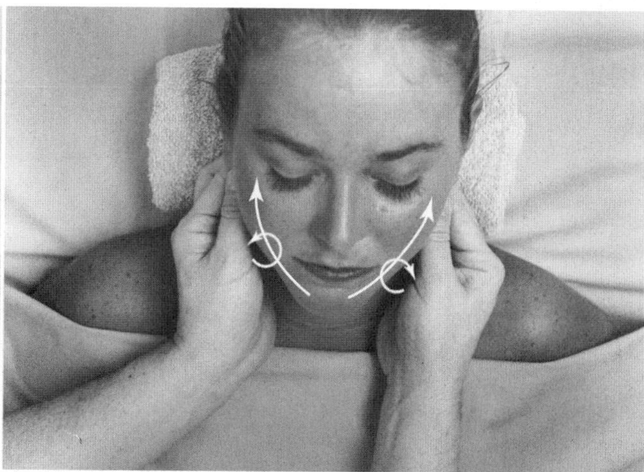
B

Figure 7-54
Thumb pad kneading to the chin and the lower jaw.

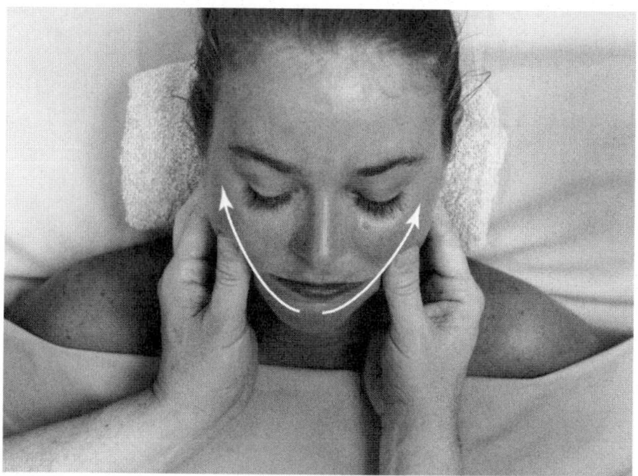

Figure 7-55
Deep stroking to the chin and the lower jaw.

**Deep Stroking over the Jugular Veins**
Without breaking contact after the preceding movement, the therapist repeats the procedures described for deep stroking over the area of the jugular veins (described earlier; see Figure 7-28). These movements are repeated four times.

**Superficial Stroking to the Face**
The movements are those described previously for superficial stroking to the face (see Figure 7-45).

### *Scalp*

**Finger Pad Kneading over the Scalp**
The therapist's thumbs are placed at the temples with the fingers spread apart and the fingertips placed on either side of the medial line of the scalp. A one-handed or two-handed technique may be used, depending on patient comfort and therapist preference. In either case, the finger pads knead with firm pressure in small circles, in sections, until the entire head is covered. In the one-handed technique, both hands are placed on the scalp, but one hand is stabilizing the head while the other hand kneads the scalp tissues. The hands are then reversed to massage the other half of the scalp. In the two-handed technique, the fingertips knead the tissues simultaneously but out of phase with each other. The fingertips keep contact with the skin and hair and move the scalp over the bony surface underneath. The pressure must be released before the fingertips are moved to each surrounding area, to avoid pulling the hair. The entire scalp can be covered twice with this technique.

## SUMMARY

The massage sequences described in this chapter are designed to cover the entire body in a single treatment session. The massage would take about 45 minutes to 1 hour to complete in the average patient. The actual sequence is, of course, made up of a series of individual massage strokes. As mentioned previously, there are many ways in which these basic massage strokes can be combined into a general massage sequence. This is simply one example of the possibilities. The number of repetitions indicated for each technique is the approximate number required to give a general massage within 1 hour at the usual rate of speed for each stroke (see Chapter 4). This must not be interpreted to mean that all general massage must be given for exactly 1 hour or that in all instances every movement must be performed in every area exactly the number of times suggested. The suggested massage sequence for each region of the body described in this chapter can also be used as a template for performing local massage. This concept is addressed in more detail in the next chapter.

# Chapter 8

# Local Massage Sequences

Local injury or disease can affect many different tissues, including skin, muscles, tendons, joints, nerves, blood, and lymph vessels. A therapist must have a thorough knowledge of the anatomy and physiology of the structures involved, together with an understanding of the pathological conditions in the tissues to be treated, if the treatment is to be as effective as possible. Muscles may be atrophied, decreased in tone, fibrotic, flaccid, or in spasm. Tissues may be edematous; joint effusion and inflammation may limit movement and produce pain. Adhesions and contractures may cause tendons to adhere to the surrounding structures, and the circulation may also be impaired. These problems are likely to prevent normal limb motion and therefore everyday functional abilities. Each of these potential problems must be evaluated and treated by techniques selected according to the changes present and the specific treatment goals.

A variety of massage strokes can be a useful part of a total treatment plan for managing an individual patient's condition, but massage techniques are simply one of many different options for the treatment of local trauma or disease. The best results are most likely to be achieved when the appropriate manual techniques, including massage, are combined with a suitable exercise program (or rest) and appropriate electrophysical agents (modalities). In this context, all soft tissue manipulation techniques, including massage, are simply adjunctive to the total treatment plan.

Each of the individual techniques described in Chapter 4 can be used separately or in combination with each other and with many other treatment approaches. The important point is for the therapist to gain a thorough understanding of how the patient's problems are affecting the tissues. Once this is properly understood, identifying appropriate treatment goals and choosing a suitable massage technique is relatively easy—it is simply a question of matching the needs of the tissues with the known effects of the massage technique. For example, if tendon and muscle contractures are limiting joint motion, then the mobilizing effects of kneading, wringing, picking up, and deep frictions might be helpful, especially when combined with other treatments such as exercise and appropriate electrophysical agents (EPAs). It is therefore proper for an experienced therapist to develop his or her own particular combination of massage techniques (a sequence) to be used as part of a specific treatment plan for local trauma or disease in a patient. Modern rehabilitation practice now encompasses a wide variety of treatment concepts, including many types of soft tissue manipulation. Although some of today's treatment concepts have been developed over the past 50 years, other techniques have been practiced for many centuries (see Chapter 1 on the history of massage). The combination of time-honored techniques and newer ideas has significantly increased the treatment options available to both patient and therapist.

It is important to recognize that there are many different ideas about massage strokes and how they can be combined into a *massage sequence,* sometimes called a *massage system.* Many of these systems of massage were popular in the early 1900s and were effective then, as indeed they are today; however, the development of modern rehabilitation methods has produced other procedures that are more effective than massage alone. For this reason, massage is rarely used as a sole treatment today; in fact, it can be argued that massage has its most beneficial effects when it is combined with other treatments to give a more rounded approach to the management of the patient's problem. In this regard, it is most appropriate to select suitable techniques from those detailed in Chapter 4 and combine them with any of a number of complementary techniques. This may well result in a mini-sequence of strokes, designed to achieve a particular effect, especially if it is directed to a specific anatomical structure such as a ligament or tendon. This may be termed *focal massage* to distinguish it from *local* or *general massage* (see Chapter 9 for examples).

The term *local massage* was defined in Chapter 4 as follows:

> *A combination of different massage strokes applied to an individual region of the body in order to achieve particularly desired effects.*

A combination of individual strokes represents a *local massage sequence,* and the specific strokes included in such a list can be many and varied. Based on the description and use of the individual strokes described in Chapter 4, the sequences listed in Tables 8-1 to 8-4 can be used for local massage treatments to the regions specified. The therapist can modify each list as desired and as needed to treat an individual patient. For example, a therapist could select a local sequence of techniques to treat the major muscles of a patient's upper arm (biceps and triceps). In this case, the therapist could use all of the techniques affecting these structures.

The rest of this chapter is devoted to a local massage sequence based on a concept of local massage developed by Albert Hoffa (1859-1907). Although this system can be used alone, it can also be combined with other suitable treatments. A modified version is presented here to suggest how this approach might be used. For purposes of completeness, all of the important areas of the body are discussed. Each area can be considered separately, and, when appropriate, they may be combined.

## THE HOFFA SYSTEM

Albert Hoffa's original work, *Technic der Massage,* was published in four editions, the last one in 1903 (see Chapter 1). The system developed by this eminent surgeon follows an anatomical pattern and is based on a knowledge of physi-

**Table 8-1 Local Massage Sequence for the Lower Limbs (I)**

| PROCEDURE | DVD CHAPTER | REPETITIONS |
|---|---|---|
| **Anterior Aspects (Patient in Long Sitting)** | **4-38** | |
| Superficial stroking to the whole limb | 4-39 | 3 |
| Effleurage to the whole limb | 4-40 | 3 |
| Compression kneading to the thigh muscles | 4-41 | 3 |
| Picking up to the quadriceps muscles | 4-42 | 3 |
| Wringing to the medial thigh muscles | 4-43 | 3 |
| Effleurage to the whole limb | 4-40 | 3 |
| Finger pad kneading around the patella | 4-48 | 2 |
| Picking up to the calf muscles | 4-49 | 3 |
| Thumb pad kneading to the anterior tibial muscles | 4-50 | 2 |
| Finger pad kneading to the ankle region | 4-51 | 2 |
| Thumb pad kneading to the dorsum of the foot and toes | 4-52 | 2 |
| Knuckle kneading to the plantar aspects of the foot | 4-53 | 3 |
| Effleurage to the whole limb | 4-40 | 3 |
| Relaxed passive movements to the lower limb | 4-55 | 3 |

**Table 8-2 Local Massage Sequence for the Lower Limbs (II)**

| PROCEDURE | DVD CHAPTER | REPETITIONS |
|---|---|---|
| **Posterior Aspects (Patient in Prone Lying)** | **4-23** | |
| Superficial stroking to the whole limb | 4-24 | 3 |
| Effleurage to the whole limb | 4-25 | 3 |
| Compression kneading to the thigh muscles | 4-26 | 3 |
| Picking up to the hamstring muscles | 4-27 | 3 |
| Wringing to the hamstring muscles | 4-28 | 3 |
| Effleurage to the whole limb | 4-25 | 3 |
| Finger pad kneading around the knee joint regions | 4-31 | 2 |
| Compression kneading to the calf muscles | 4-32 | 3 |
| Picking up to the calf muscles | 4-33 | 3 |
| Wringing to the calf muscles | 4-34 | 3 |
| Thumb pad kneading to the calf muscles | 4-35 | 2 |
| Finger pad kneading to the ankle region | 4-36 | 2 |
| Thumb pad kneading to the plantar aspects of the foot and toes | 4-37 | 2 |
| Effleurage to the whole limb | 4-25 | 3 |
| Relaxed passive movements to the lower limb | 4-56 | 3 |

Table 8-3 **Local Massage Sequence for the Upper Limbs**

| PROCEDURE | DVD CHAPTER | REPETITIONS |
|---|---|---|
| **All Aspects (Patient in Sitting)** | **4-57** | |
| Superficial stroking to the whole limb | 4-58 | 3 |
| Effleurage to the whole limb | 4-59 | 3 |
| Compression kneading to the deltoid, biceps, and triceps muscles | 4-60 | 3 |
| Picking up to the deltoid, biceps, and triceps muscles | 4-61 | 3 |
| Wringing to the biceps and triceps | 4-62 | 3 |
| Finger pad kneading around the elbow joint | 4-63 | 2 |
| Effleurage to the whole limb | 4-58 | 3 |
| Thumb pad kneading to the wrist and finger extensors | 4-64 | 2 |
| Thumb pad kneading to the wrist and finger flexors | 4-65 | 2 |
| Thumb pad kneading to the wrist and hand | 4-66 | 2 |
| Effleurage to the whole limb | 4-58 | 3 |
| Relaxed passive movements to the upper limb | 4-68 | 3 |

Table 8-4 **Local Massage Sequence for the Posterior Trunk and Pelvis**

| PROCEDURE | DVD CHAPTER | REPETITIONS |
|---|---|---|
| **Back (Patient in Prone Lying)** | **4-1** | |
| Superficial stroking to the entire back region | 4-2 | 3 |
| Effleurage to the entire back region | 4-3 | 3 |
| Compression kneading to the posterior trunk muscles | 4-4 | 3 |
| Reinforced kneading to the lumbar region | 4-5 | 3 |
| Effleurage to the entire back region | 4-2 | 3 |
| Wringing to the muscles of the lateral body wall | 4-6 | 3 |
| Skin rolling over the posteriolateral chest wall | 4-7 | 3 |
| Circular frictions to the paraspinal muscles | 4-8 | 2 |
| Effleurage to the entire back region | 4-2 | 3 |

ology. The movements are applied to certain muscles or muscle groups; this contrasts with some other systems that apply strokes either to an entire extremity or to a certain area of the body. Hoffa classified the essential massage strokes as effleurage (stroking), pétrissage (kneading), friction, vibration, and tapotement (percussion) and stated that these are only the framework on which an experienced therapist with good judgment may build up an effective treatment for a given patient's problem. He emphasized the value of massage for increasing venous and lymphatic circulation. One must keep in mind, however, the context in which he developed his system and, in particular, the range of treatment options available at the time and the state of medical knowledge. (The rehabilitation professions as we currently know them did not exist at that time.)

According to Hoffa, effleurage (stroking) is employed to stimulate circulation in the small veins in the muscles, particularly in the large veins or venous plexuses that lie in the grooves between the individual muscles. This is accomplished by making the hand conform closely to the contours of the part as the thumb and fingertips proceed along these interstices. Pétrissage (kneading) is used chiefly to increase the circulation in the muscles and to remove products in a manner analogous to that of friction. Friction movements are applied chiefly to break down pathologic exudates, deposits, and thickenings in tissue around joints and tendons and to help remove the waste products through the lymphatic system. Vibration and tapotement (percussion) are recommended to increase blood supply, reduce nerve irritability, and increase contraction of muscle fibers. These techniques are probably of little value in the treatment of local trauma, but they do have some specific uses for certain lesions; for example, the percussion and vibration techniques can be useful in treating some respiratory problems.

## Classification and Description of Local Massage Strokes Used in the Hoffa System

The following classification and description of massage strokes is a modification of the Hoffa system of massage as described by Gertrude Beard in the early editions of this text. In general, all of these descriptions match those defined in Chapter 4. The Hoffa system uses only a selected number of these techniques, and, of course, any appropriate combination of these techniques is possible.

### *Stroking (Superficial or Deep)*

Note that in the Hoffa system, deep stroking is similar to effleurage.

1. The direction of the deep stroke is always in the direction of venous blood and lymph flow.
2. The stroke is applied to the entire length of the muscle or muscle group, beginning at the insertion and continuing to the origin.
3. The hand returns over the same area with light pressure (superficial stroking).
4. The hand is made to conform to the shape of the muscle or muscle group, attempting to reach around and lift up the bulk of the muscle or group. The palmar surfaces of the entire hand or the distal phalanges of the fingers (finger pads) or of the thumb (thumb pad) are used, according to the size of the muscle.
5. The pressure is regulated according to the bulk of the muscles: light at the beginning of the deep stroke, increasing over the bulkiest part of the muscles, diminishing at the end of the stroke, and finishing with a squeeze-out movement. In performing the squeeze-out movement, the grasping surfaces of the hand are gradually approximated more closely as the muscle bulk decreases and the hand approaches the origin of the muscle. As the hand reaches the point of origin, it is pronated. The bulk of the tissue being massaged is thus squeezed out of the hand, and the hand is in position to start the return stroke.
6. The movements should be performed rhythmically.
7. The rate of movement should be relatively slow.

### *Kneading*

The kneading movements in the Hoffa system are performed with one or both hands (single-handed or two-handed kneading). The therapist can also perform these strokes with the distal phalanges of the thumb (thumb pad kneading) or the index and middle fingers (finger pad kneading) of one or both hands. Finger pad kneading is also called *digital kneading.*

Single-handed kneading is used on muscles that are not too large to be grasped in one hand. For very large muscles, two-handed kneading can be used. Digital kneading is used on narrow or flat muscles that cannot be grasped easily by the entire hand. As in stroking, the hand must conform to the size and shape of the muscles and make firm contact. The movement begins at the insertion of the muscle and is carried through to the origin.

#### Single-Handed Kneading

1. The hand is placed at the insertion of the muscle with the palmar surface of its ulnar border in firm contact (Figure 8-1, *A*).
2. The hand grasps around the bulk of the muscle and lifts it as much as possible from the underlying tissues (Figure 8-1, *B*).
3. The fingers and ulnar border of the hand follow along one border of the muscle or muscle group, and the thumb follows along the opposite border (see Figure 8-1, *B*).
4. The movement is one of grasping and releasing the tissues, and it is carried through to the origin of the muscle, finishing with a squeeze-out movement (Figure 8-1, *C*).
5. The thumb and fingers work simultaneously, but the pressure must be diminished as they approach each other, to prevent pinching.
6. Care must be used to keep the bulk of the muscle well back in the palm of the hand between the thenar eminence and the metacarpal pad of the palm (see Figure 8-1, *A*).
7. At the origin of the muscle, the hand is brought over into pronation and returned to the starting position with a superficial stroke over the area (Figure 8-1, *D, E*).

#### Two-Handed Kneading

1. One hand is placed at the insertion of the muscle, as in single-handed kneading; the other hand is placed just proximal to it (Figure 8-2, *A*).
2. Both hands grasp around as much of the muscle as possible. The palmar surface of the fingers of the left hand pulls the muscles laterally as the surface of the abducted right thumb and palm simultaneously pushes the tissues medially. Then the surface of the palm and abducted thumb of the left hand pushes the muscles medially as the palmar surface of the fingers of the right hand pulls the tissue laterally (Figure 8-2, *B*). Progression from the distal to the proximal part of the muscle is accomplished with a gliding of the hands on the pull stroke of the kneading movement. This procedure is similar to the technique of wringing described in Chapter 4, but it is not a pinching type of movement. The thumb and fingers of each hand should be kept in the same relation to each other during the entire movement. The push-and-pull movements are accomplished chiefly by flexion and extension of the arms at the shoulders and elbows. At the origin, the proximal hand is removed, and the distal hand finishes with the squeeze-out movement (see Figure 8-1, *D, E*) and returns to the starting position with a superficial stroke, as in single-handed kneading.

#### Two-Handed Digital Kneading

The therapist uses both hands (between the thumb and the index and middle fingers of each hand) to grasp the muscle at its insertion. The palmar surface of the left fingers pulls the tissues toward the therapist, while the right thumb pushes the adjacent tissues away. Then the right fingers pull the tissues while the left thumb pushes the adjacent tissues (Figure 8-3). Progression from origin to insertion is accomplished with a gliding of the fingers on the pull movement. Again, this should not be a pinching movement. The thumb and fingers of each hand are kept in the same relation to each other during the entire movement. The push and pull are accomplished chiefly by flexion and extension of the arms at the shoulders and elbows. The return stroke is performed with the fingers of the distal hand. This movement is used mainly for muscles of small to medium bulk. Care must be taken to ensure that the hands are held parallel to the length

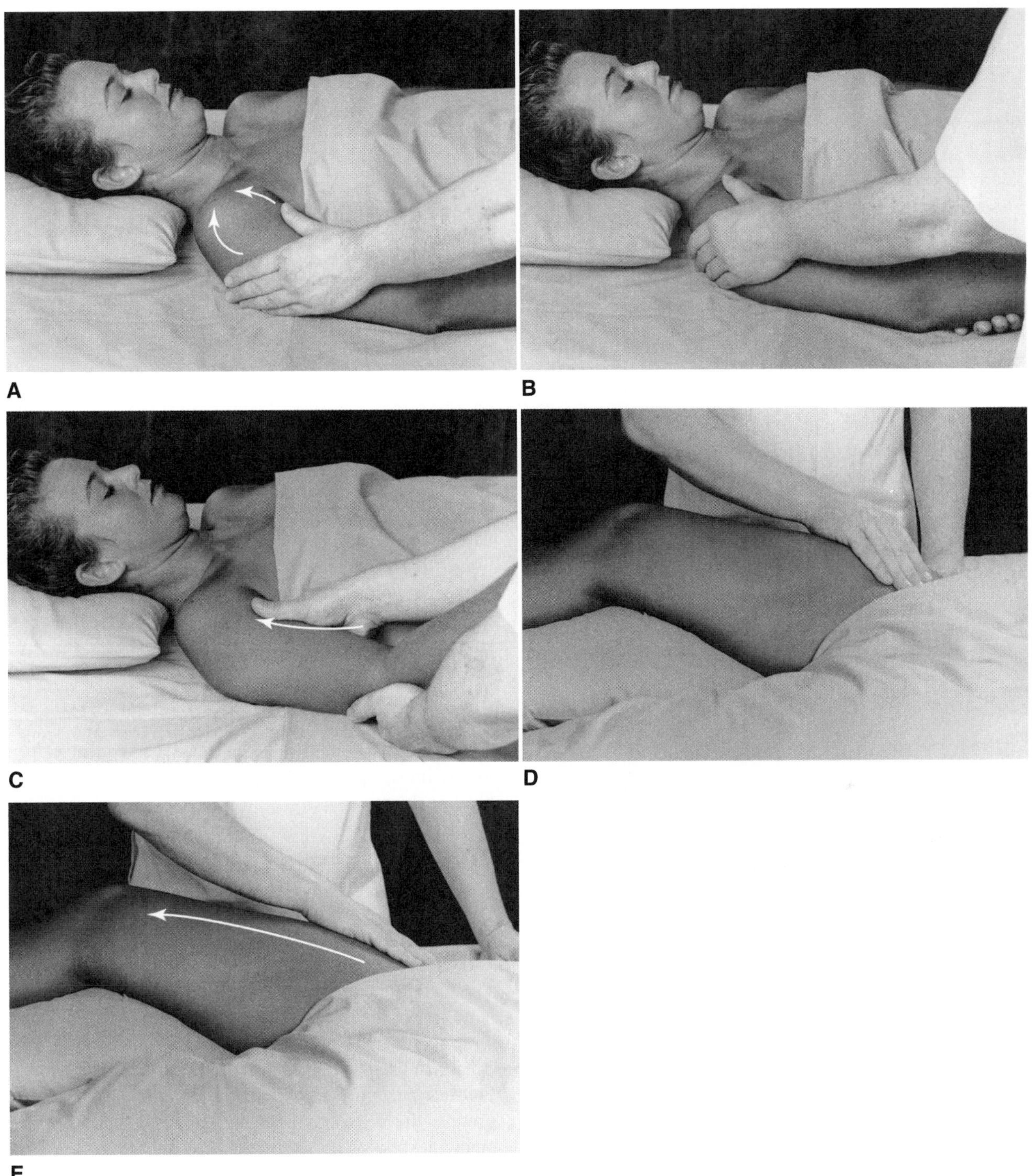


Figure 8-1
Single-handed kneading to the upper arm and thigh.

of the muscles, thereby allowing as much contact as possible. This technique produces a movement similar to the stroke called *wringing;* however, there is no twist in this stroke.

## Modified Hoffa Technique for Local Massage

The technique of local massage described next and its application to the anatomical sections of the body are modified from the classical Hoffa system. In the application of these massage strokes to an extremity, the proximal portion should be treated first, followed by the more distal segment or segments. Then special attention may be given to areas that require additional treatment. The stroking and kneading movements may be adapted to conform to the muscles of any body area. In the beginning of treatment, stroking precedes the kneading movement, and periods of stroking and

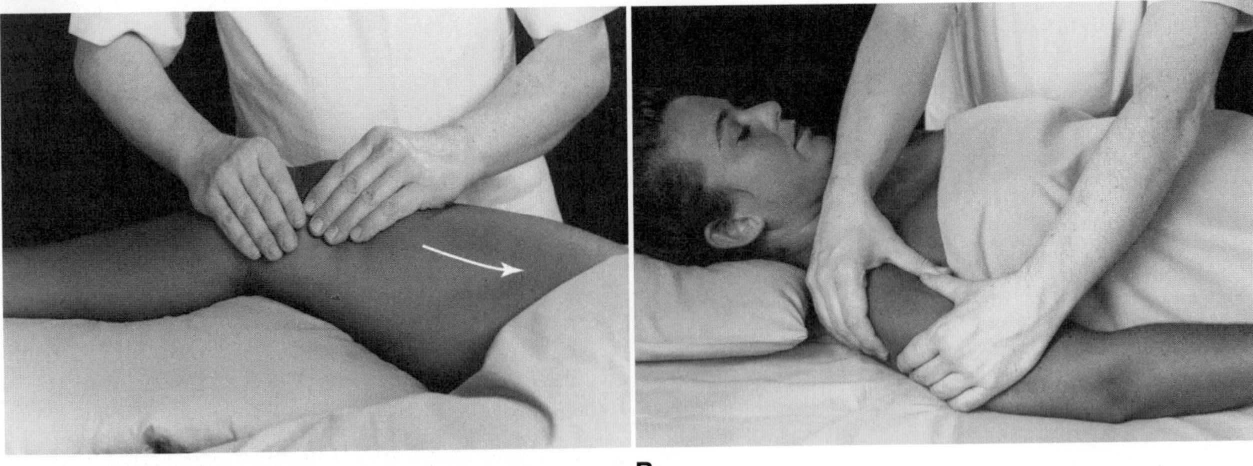


**Figure 8-2**
Two-handed kneading to the thigh and upper arm.

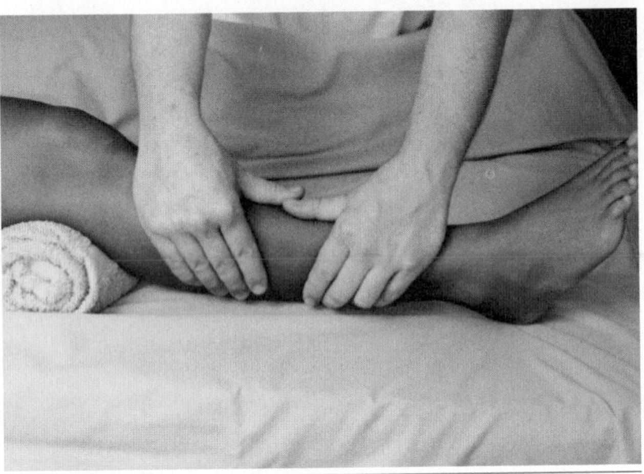

**Figure 8-3**
Two-handed digital kneading to the leg.

kneading should alternate according to the pathologic condition being treated, the desired effect, and the result being obtained from the massage. The final stroke should always be superficial stroking.

The order in which massage is given to the various muscle groups of each anatomical region depends on the condition being treated and the ability of the patient to be moved into the required positions. It may be necessary to alter the techniques slightly to avoid unnecessary changes of the patient's position. In general, the position of the patient should be changed as little as possible. The techniques, as described, are those that should be followed when it is possible to place the patient in the ideal position to perform each stroke. Under most circumstances, the patient should lie recumbent while receiving massage treatment.

All of the local sequences suggested for each body region are summarized at this point so that the reader can gain a clear understanding of their structure. Where possible, a detailed description follows with specific references to figures in the text that illustrate the various techniques. As a general guide, the therapist will repeat each technique three times. This modified Hoffa sequence is not demonstrated on the accompanying DVD.

### *Local Massage Sequence (Modified Hoffa System)*

Tables 8-5 to 8-8 describe local massage sequences for the lower limbs, upper limbs, posterior trunk and pelvis, and head/neck area.

## TECHNIQUE FOR A LOCAL MASSAGE SEQUENCE

### Upper Limb

#### *Right Arm*

The therapist stands next to the treatment table on the right-hand side of the patient. The patient is appropriately draped, lying supine in a comfortably supported position (see Figure 3-7, *C,* in Chapter 3), with the right arm slightly abducted. For treatment purposes, the arm is divided into three muscle groups: the deltoid muscle, the elbow extensors, and the elbow flexors.

**Deltoid Muscle Group**

***Stroking.*** The therapist's hands stroke alternately. Beginning at the insertion of the deltoid muscle (Figure 8-4, *A*), the thumb of each hand passes up the midline of the patient's muscle; the fingers of the left hand follow the posterior border of the muscle and curve around the origin to the center (Figure 8-4, *B*); the fingers of the right hand follow the anterior border in the same manner (Figure 8-4, *C*). Each hand returns to its starting position with a superficial stroke (Figure 8-4, *D*).

If the muscle is small, the entire muscle may be stroked with the left hand as the right hand supports the inner side of

### Table 8-5 Local Massage Sequence for the Upper Limbs

| LIMB | FIGURE | REPETITIONS |
|---|---|---|
| **Right Arm** | | |
| Deltoid muscle group | 8-4 | 3 |
| Elbow extensor muscle group (triceps and anconeus) | 8-5 | 3 |
| Elbow flexor muscle group (biceps, brachialis, and coracobrachialis) | 8-6 | 3 |
| **Right Forearm** | | |
| Medial muscle groups | 8-7 | 3 |
| Lateral muscle groups | 8-7 | 3 |
| **Right Hand** | | |
| Muscles of the radial section (thenar muscles, adductor pollicis, lumbricals, and interossei) | 8-9 | 3 |
| Muscles of the ulnar section (hypothenar muscles, lumbricals, and interossei) | 8-10 | 3 |
| Palmar surface | 8-11 | 3 |
| Dorsal surface | 8-12 | 3 |
| **Right Thumb and Fingers** | | |
| Dorsal surface | 8-13 | 3 |
| Palmar surface | 8-14 | 3 |
| **Left Arm, Forearm, and Hand** | | |
| All of the previous strokes are repeated to the left upper limb | | |

### Table 8-6 Local Massage Sequence for the Lower Limbs

| LIMB | FIGURE | REPETITIONS |
|---|---|---|
| **Right Buttock Region** | | |
| Gluteal muscles (gluteus maximus, medius, and minimus) | 8-15 | 3 |
| **Right Thigh** | | |
| Medial hamstring muscles (semimembranosus and semitendinosus) | 8-16 | 3 |
| Lateral hamstring muscle (biceps femoris) | 8-17 | 3 |
| Tensor of the fascia lata (including the iliotibial tract/band) | 8-18 | 3 |
| Anterior thigh group (rectus femoris, vastus medialis, vastus intermedius, vastus lateralis, and articularis genu sartorius) | 8-19 | 3 |
| Adductor muscle group (adductor, longus, adductor magnus, and gracilis) | 8-20 | 3 |
| **Right Leg** | | |
| Anterior tibial muscles (tibialis anterior, extensor digitorum longus, extensor hallucis longus, and fibularis/peroneus tertius) | 8-21 | 3 |
| Fibularis (peroneal) muscles (fibularis longus and fibularis brevis) | 8-22 | 3 |
| Calf muscles (gastrocnemius, soleus, and plantaris) | 8-23 | 3 |
| **Right Foot*** | | |
| Medial section | 8-24 | 3 |
| Lateral section | 8-25 | 3 |
| Dorsal section | 8-26 | 3 |
| Plantar section | 8-27 | 3 |
| **Right Toes** | — | 3 |
| **Left Buttock, Thigh, Leg, and Foot** | | |
| All of the previous strokes are repeated on the left lower limb | — | |

*Various structures in the foot, including skin, subcutaneous fat and connective tissues, muscles, tendons, tendon sheaths, ligaments, joint capsules, and neurovascular bundles.

### Table 8-7 Local Massage Sequence for the Trunk and Pelvis

| BODY AREA | FIGURE | REPETITIONS |
|---|---|---|
| **Back and Hips** | | |
| Paraspinal muscles | 8-28 | 3 |
| Trapezius and scapular muscles (trapezius, supraspinatus, infraspinatus, levator scapulae, rhomboid major, rhomboid minor, and teres major) | 8-29 | 3 |
| Latissimus dorsi muscle | 8-30 | 3 |
| **Abdomen** | | |
| Stroking over the entire abdomen | 8-31 | 3 |
| Stroking over the area of the colon | 8-32 | 3 |
| Kneading over the area of the colon | 8-33 | 3 |

## Table 8-8 Local Massage Sequence for the Head and Neck

| FACIAL MUSCLES | FIGURE | REPETITIONS |
|---|---|---|
| Frontalis | 8-34, *A* | 3 |
| Orbicularis oculi | 8-34, *B, C* | 3 |
| Nasalis | 8-34, *D* | 3 |
| Levator anguli oris | 8-34, *E* | 3 |
| Zygomaticus major and minor | 8-34, *E* | 3 |
| Orbicularis oris | 8-34, *F* | 3 |
| Depressor anguli oris | 8-34, *G* | 3 |
| Platysma | 8-34, *H* | 3 |

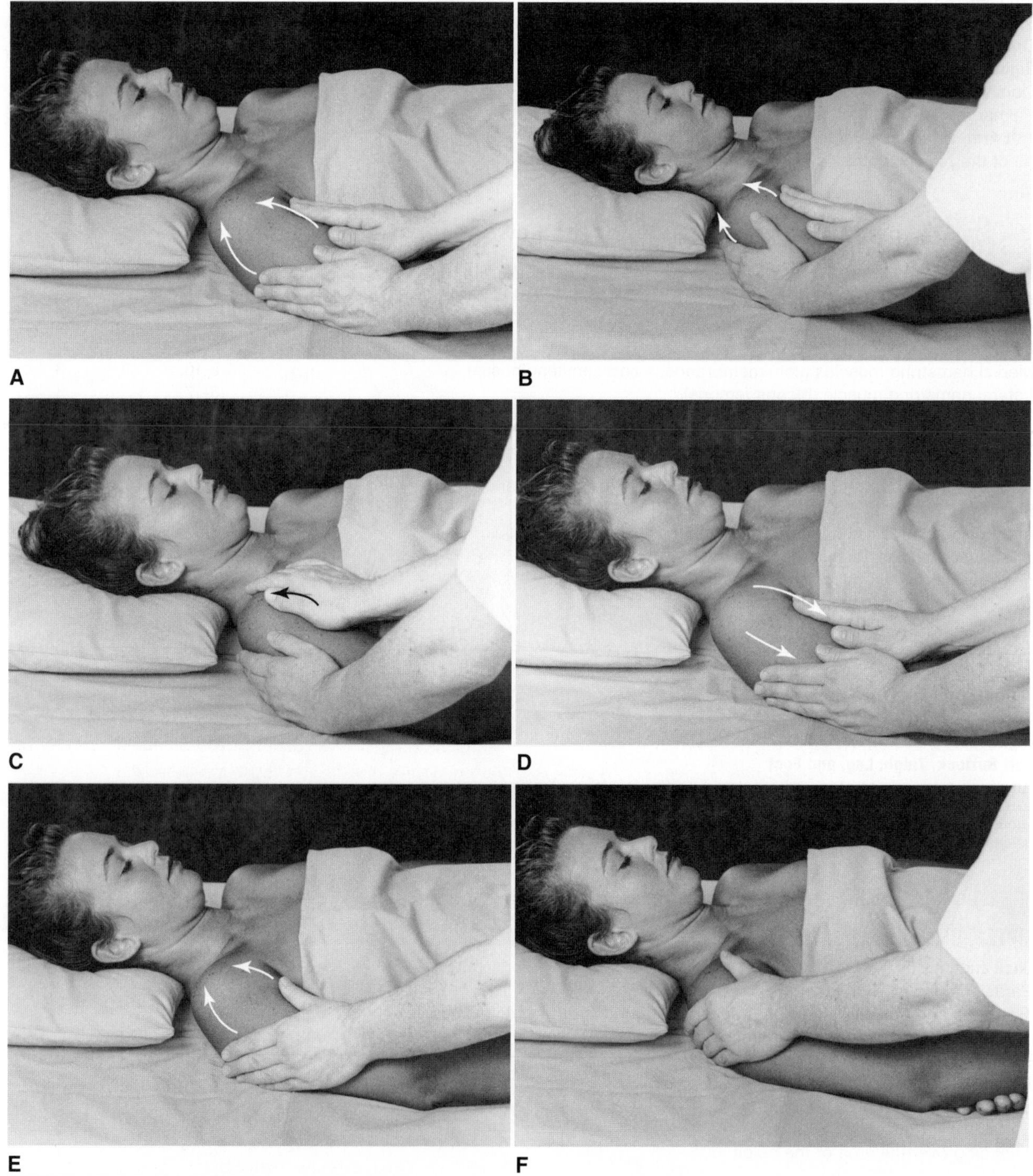


**Figure 8-4**
Local massage to the deltoid muscle group.

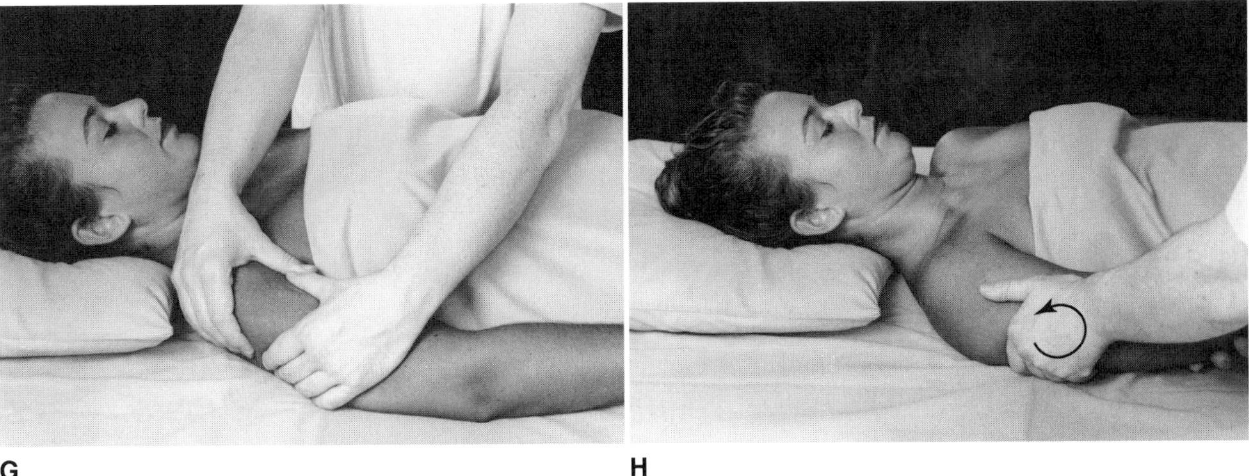

G H

Figure **8-4**, cont'd

the upper arm. The fingers of the left hand follow the posterior border of the muscle, and the thumb follows the anterior border (Figure 8-4, *E*); they meet at the acromion process in a squeeze-out movement (Figure 8-4, *F*). The left hand returns to its starting position with a superficial stroke.

***Kneading.*** Two-handed kneading is performed to the entire deltoid muscle, with the patient's arm partially abducted. Kneading progresses from the insertion to the origin of the muscle (Figure 8-4, *G*). The left hand performs a squeeze-out movement at the origin and returns to the starting position with a superficial stroke as the right hand returns through the air. Single-handed kneading may be performed with the left hand if the muscle is small, in which case the right hand would support the rest of the arm (Figure 8-4, *H*).

### Elbow Extensor Muscle Group

#### Triceps and Anconeus

***Stroking.*** The therapist's right hand supports the elbow; the left hand grasps around the muscle group at its insertion. The thumb follows the lateral border, and the fingers follow the medial border of the triceps as the hand strokes over the muscle (Figure 8-5, *A*). At the end of the stroke, the thumb passes around the posterior border of the deltoid, while the fingers move into the axilla and the hand performs a squeeze-out movement (Figure 8-5, *B*). The hand then returns to the starting position with a superficial stroke.

***Kneading.*** Single-handed kneading is performed over the same area that was stroked (Figure 8-5, *C, D*), and the hand returns with a superficial stroke. Two-handed kneading may be used if the muscle group is large. The patient's arm is partially abducted, and both of the therapist's hands grasp the triceps muscle, with the left hand at the insertion and the right hand just proximal to it (Figure 8-5, *E*).

### Elbow Flexor Muscle Group

#### Biceps, Brachialis, and Coracobrachialis

***Stroking.*** The left hand supports the elbow, and the right hand grasps the muscle group at its insertion below the elbow joint (Figure 8-6, *A*). The thumb follows the lateral border, and the fingers follow the medial border of the elbow flexor muscle group as the hand strokes over the muscles. At the end of the stroke, the thumb passes around the anterior border of the deltoid muscle, while the fingers move into the axilla and the hand performs a squeeze-out movement (Figure 8-6, *B*). The hand then returns to the starting position with a superficial stroke.

***Kneading.*** Single-handed kneading is performed over the same area that was stroked (Figure 8-6, *C, D*). Two-handed kneading may be used if the muscle group is large. Hand positions are the reverse of those described for two-handed kneading of the triceps muscle group (see Figure 8-5, *E*).

### Right Forearm

The therapist's forearm is divided longitudinally into two muscle groups: medial and lateral. Each group contains some of the wrist and finger flexors and extensors. Although this is not a strictly anatomical division, it greatly facilitates local massage to the forearm.

#### Medial Muscle Group

The patient's elbow is slightly flexed with the forearm in supination, while the arm rests on the table. A small pillow may be used to support the arm if necessary.

***Stroking.*** The left hand supports the forearm at the wrist. The right hand starts the stroking by grasping around the medial half of the forearm at the wrist (Figure 8-7, *A*). The thumb then passes up the midline of the forearm to the elbow and over the medial condyle of the humerus as the fingers pass up along the ulna and over the medial aspect to meet the thumb in a squeeze-out movement (Figure 8-7, *B*). The hand returns to the wrist with a superficial stroke.

***Kneading.*** Single-handed kneading is performed over the same area that was stroked (Figure 8-7, *C, D*), with the hand returning with a superficial stroke. Two-handed kneading is possible if the patient's forearm is particularly large.

#### Lateral Muscle Group

***Stroking.*** The therapist's right hand supports the wrist. The left hand starts the stroke by grasping around the lateral half of the forearm (Figure 8-8, *A*). The thumb then passes

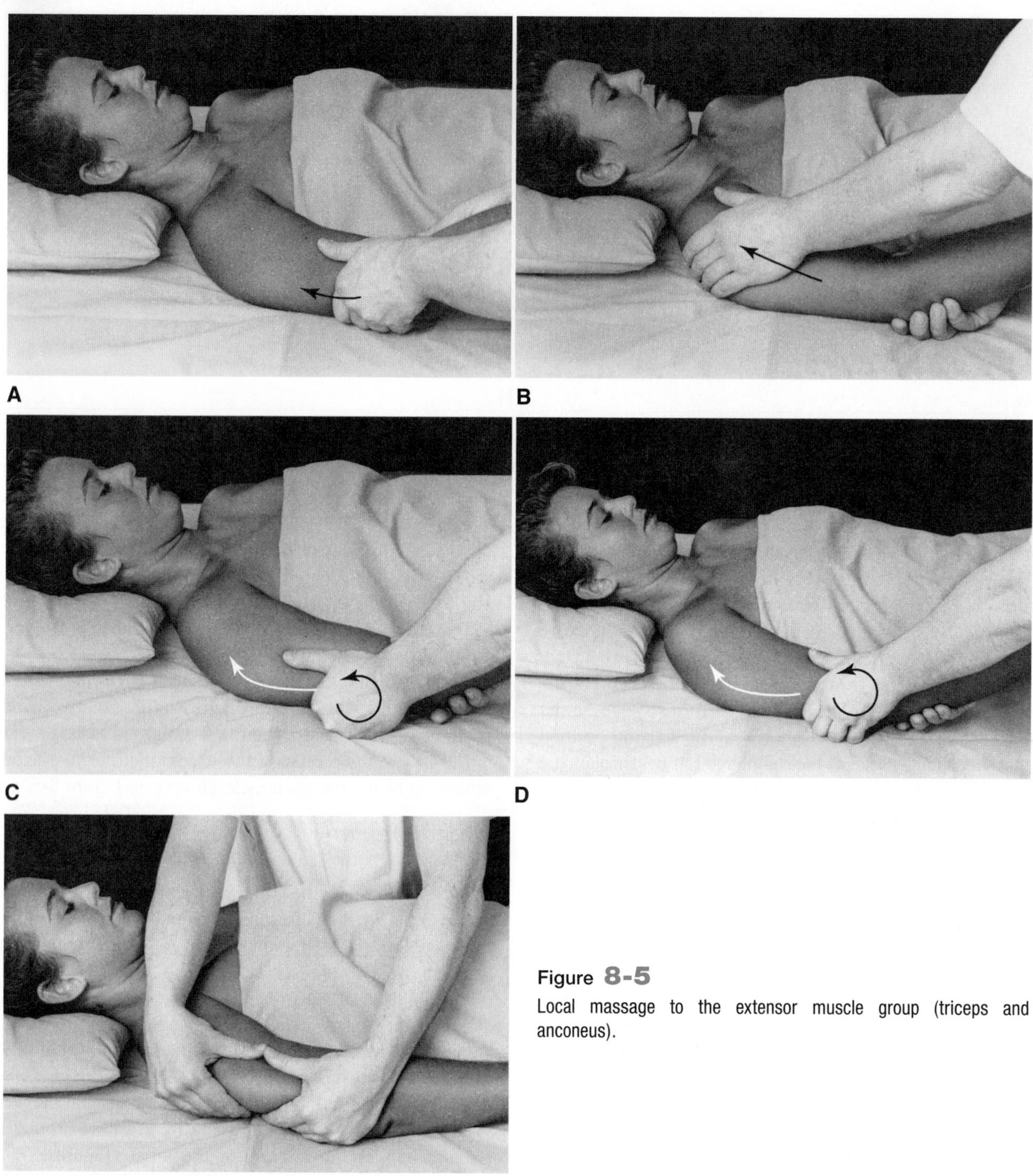


**Figure 8-5**
Local massage to the extensor muscle group (triceps and anconeus).

up the midline of the forearm to the elbow and over the lateral condyle of the humerus as the fingers pass along the radius and over the lateral condyle to meet the thumb in a squeeze-out movement (Figure 8-8, *B*). The hand returns to the wrist with a superficial stroke.

***Kneading.*** Single-handed kneading is performed over the same area that was stroked. The hand returns with a superficial stroke. Two-handed kneading is also possible if the patient's forearm is particularly large.

## Right Hand

### *Muscles of the Radial Section*

#### Thenar Muscles, Adductor Pollicis, Lumbricals, and Interossei

The patient's forearm and hand are in supination (facing the ceiling), with the thumb abducted and the forearm comfortably supported on the table. For treatment purposes, the various surfaces of the hand are divided in two different but overlapping ways. First, the hand is divided longitudinally

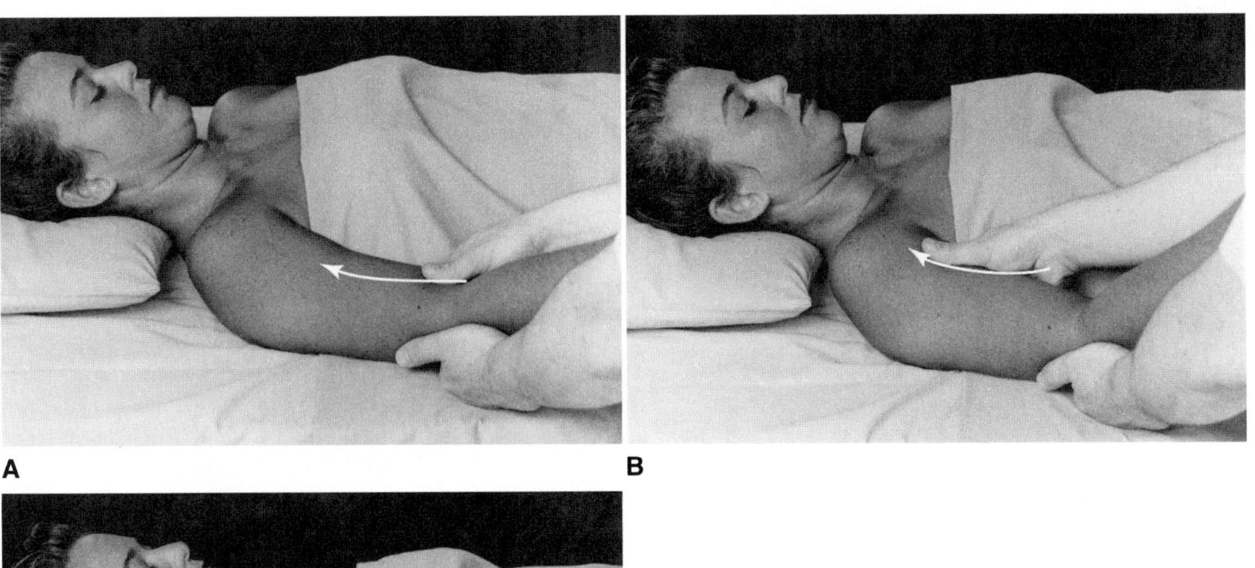

A B

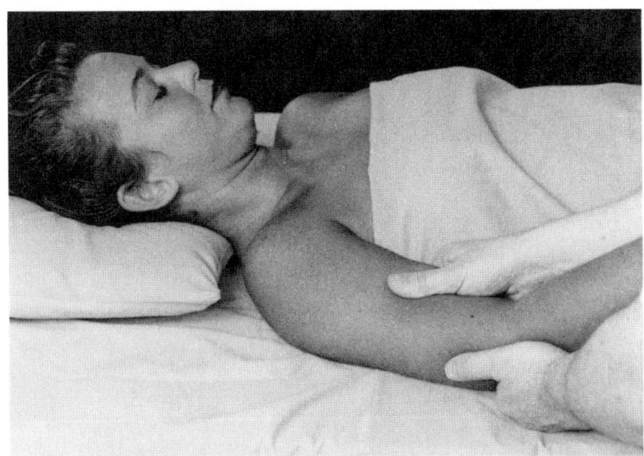

C

**Figure 8-6**

Local massage to the flexor muscle group (biceps, brachialis, and coracobrachialis).

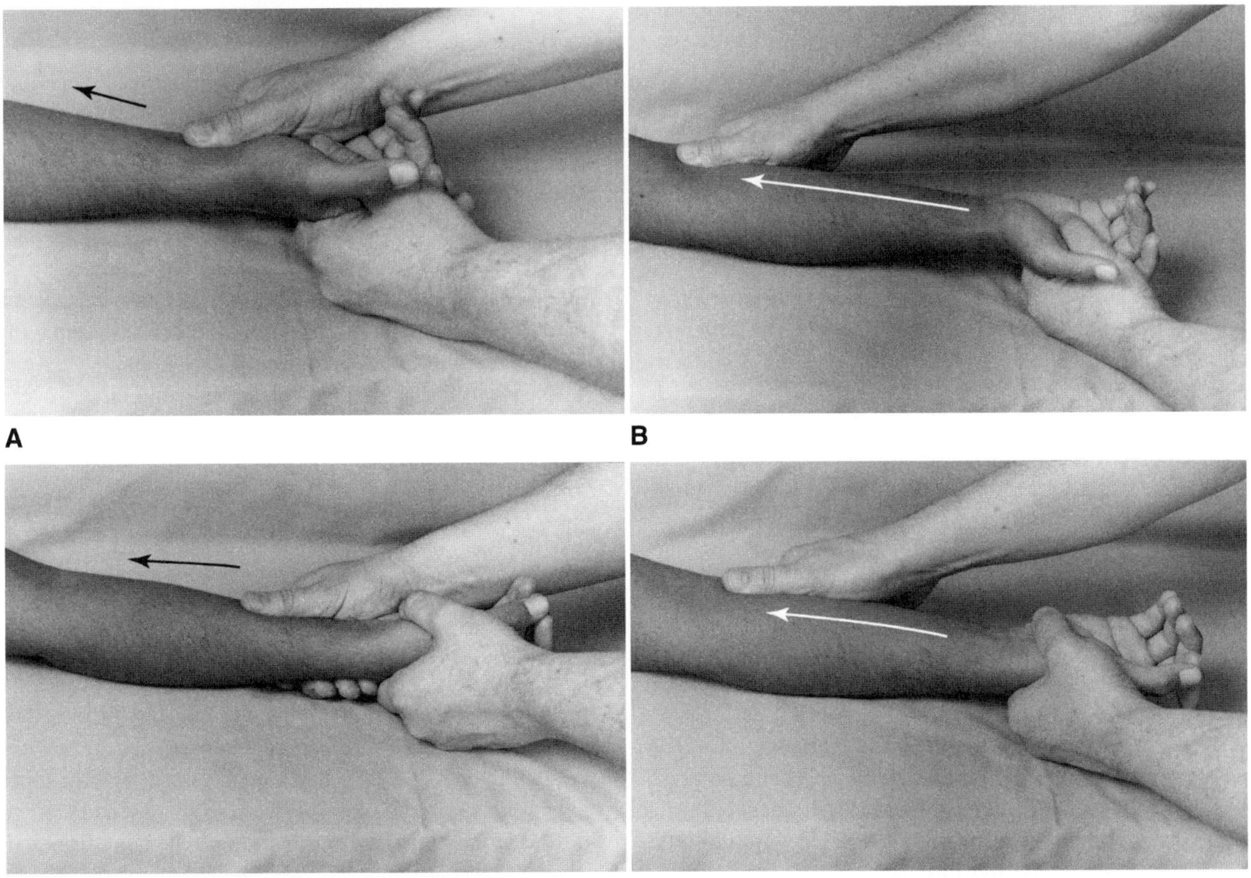

A B

C D

**Figure 8-7**

Local massage to the medial forearm muscle groups.

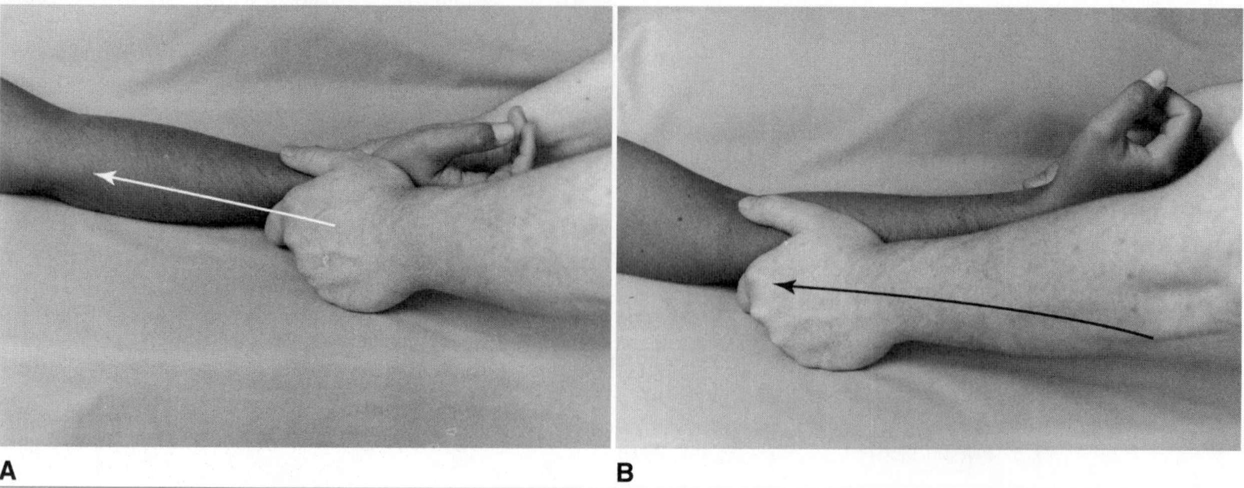


Figure 8-8
Local massage to the lateral forearm muscle groups.

into two halves—this time, a radial and an ulnar section. The hand is then divided into front (palmar) and back (dorsal) sections. All four sections are massaged. Once again, this division is not strictly anatomical, but it is suitable to use for local massage of the hand.

***Stroking.*** The therapist's right hand supports the patient's hand. The left hand grasps the radial half of the hand at the metacarpophalangeal joints. The thumb then passes up the midline of the palm (Figure 8-9) around the thenar eminence to the wrist. The fingers pass up the midline of the dorsal surface of the hand to join the thumb at the wrist with a squeeze-out movement. The hand returns with a superficial stroke.

***Kneading.*** Single-handed kneading is performed over the same area that was stroked (see Figure 8-9). The hand returns with a superficial stroke in the usual manner.

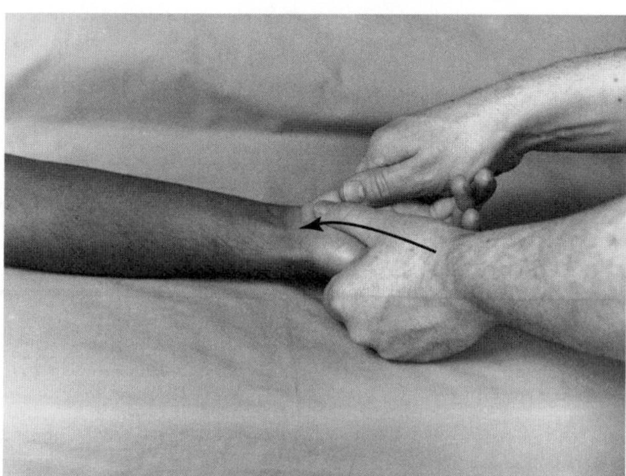

Figure 8-9
Local massage to the muscles of the radial border of the hand.

### *Muscles of the Ulnar Section*

#### Hypothenar Muscles, Lumbricles, and Interossei

***Stroking.*** The therapist's left hand supports the patient's hand. The right hand grasps the ulnar section of the patient's hand at the metacarpophalangeal joint line. The thumb then passes up the midline of the palm (Figure 8-10, *A*) around the hypothenar eminence to the wrist. The fingers pass up the midline of the dorsal surface of the hand to meet the thumb at the wrist with a squeeze-out movement. The hand returns with a superficial stroke.

***Kneading.*** Single-handed kneading is performed over the same area that was stroked (Figure 8-10, *B*), and the hand returns with a superficial stroke.

#### Palmar Surface

The patient's hand is supinated and supported by the therapist's hands.

***Stroking.*** The therapist's right hand supports the patient's hand while the thumb of the therapist's left hand strokes over each of the following areas: the thenar eminence, from the first metacarpophalangeal joint to the wrist (Figure 8-11, *A*); the interosseous and the lumbrical muscles, from the metacarpophalangeal joints to the wrist (Figure 8-11, *B*); and the hypothenar eminence, from the fifth metacarpophalangeal joint to the wrist (Figure 8-11, *C*). The thumb returns with a superficial stroke after each movement.

***Kneading.*** The thumb pad kneads in small circles over the same areas and in the same order as indicated for the stroking (see Figure 8-11), returning each time with superficial strokes.

#### Dorsal Surface

The patient's hand is in pronation. In effect, the therapist will be stroking in the interosseous spaces between the metacarpals, with pressure directed to each of the interosseous muscles.

***Stroking.*** The therapist's left hand supports the patient's hand. Using his or her right thumb, the therapist strokes over the ulnar side of the first metacarpal. The stroke is just proximal to the first interphalangeal joint, continuing to the wrist (Figure 8-12). The thumb pad returns with a superficial stroke along the radial side of the second metacarpal to its first interphalangeal joint; the thumb then strokes over this same area to the wrist. The thumb then slides over so that it can return along the ulnar border of the second meta-

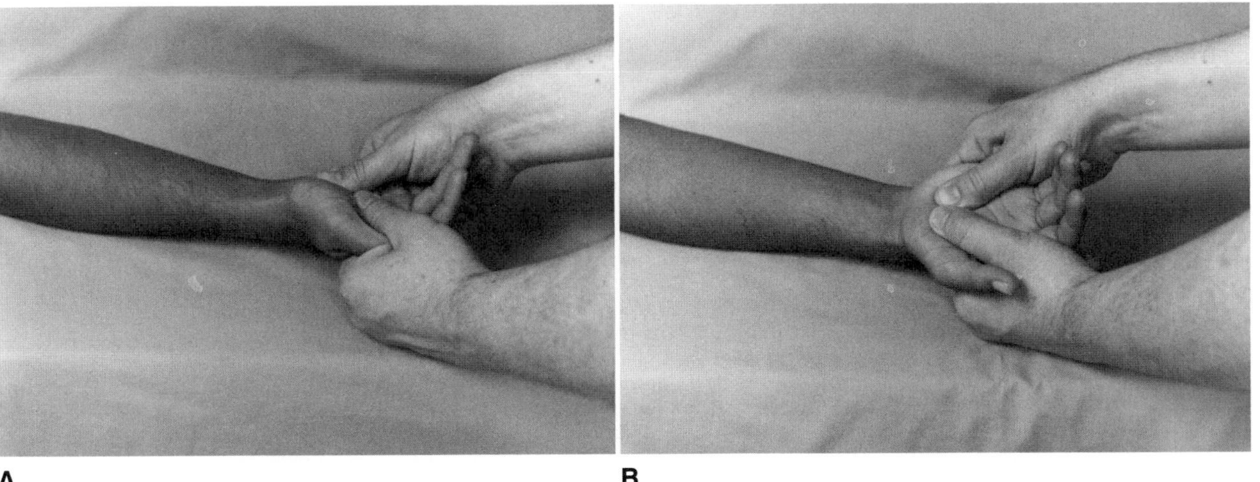
A B

**Figure 8-10**
Local massage to the muscles on the ulnar border of the hand.

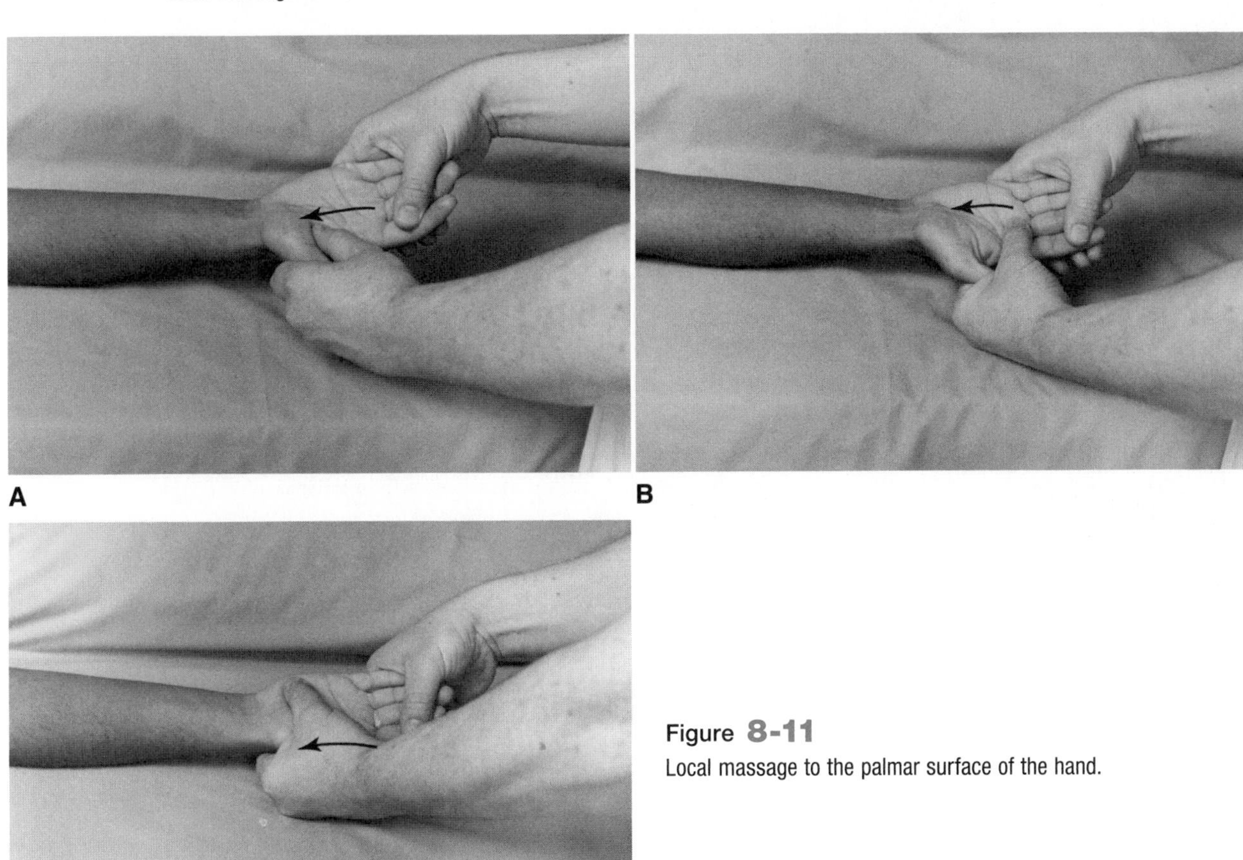
A B C

**Figure 8-11**
Local massage to the palmar surface of the hand.

carpal to the first interphalangeal joint and then strokes over the same area to the wrist. The same procedures are performed on the third and fourth metacarpal areas and the radial side of the fifth metacarpal.

***Kneading.*** The thumb pad kneads in small circles along each interosseous muscle from the insertion to the wrist, following the routine described for stroking.

### *Right Thumb and Fingers*

#### Dorsal Surface

The patient's hand is pronated and supported on the palmar surface by the fingertips of the therapist's left hand (Figure 8-13, *A*). These fingers also support the phalanges as needed to prevent flexion during the movements. The therapist's right thumb and index finger first stroke, then knead, the

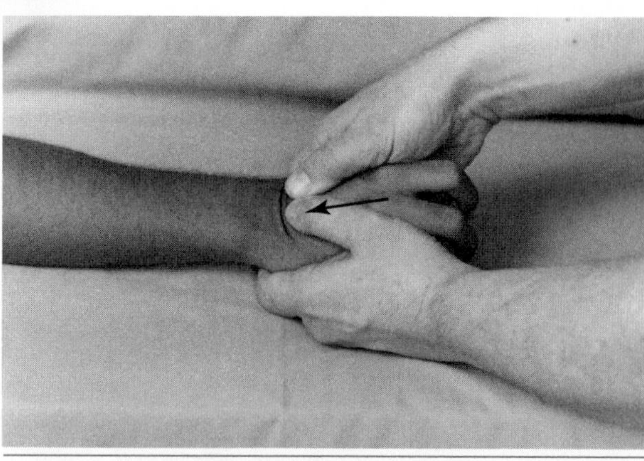

Figure **8-12**

Local massage to the dorsal aspect of the hand.

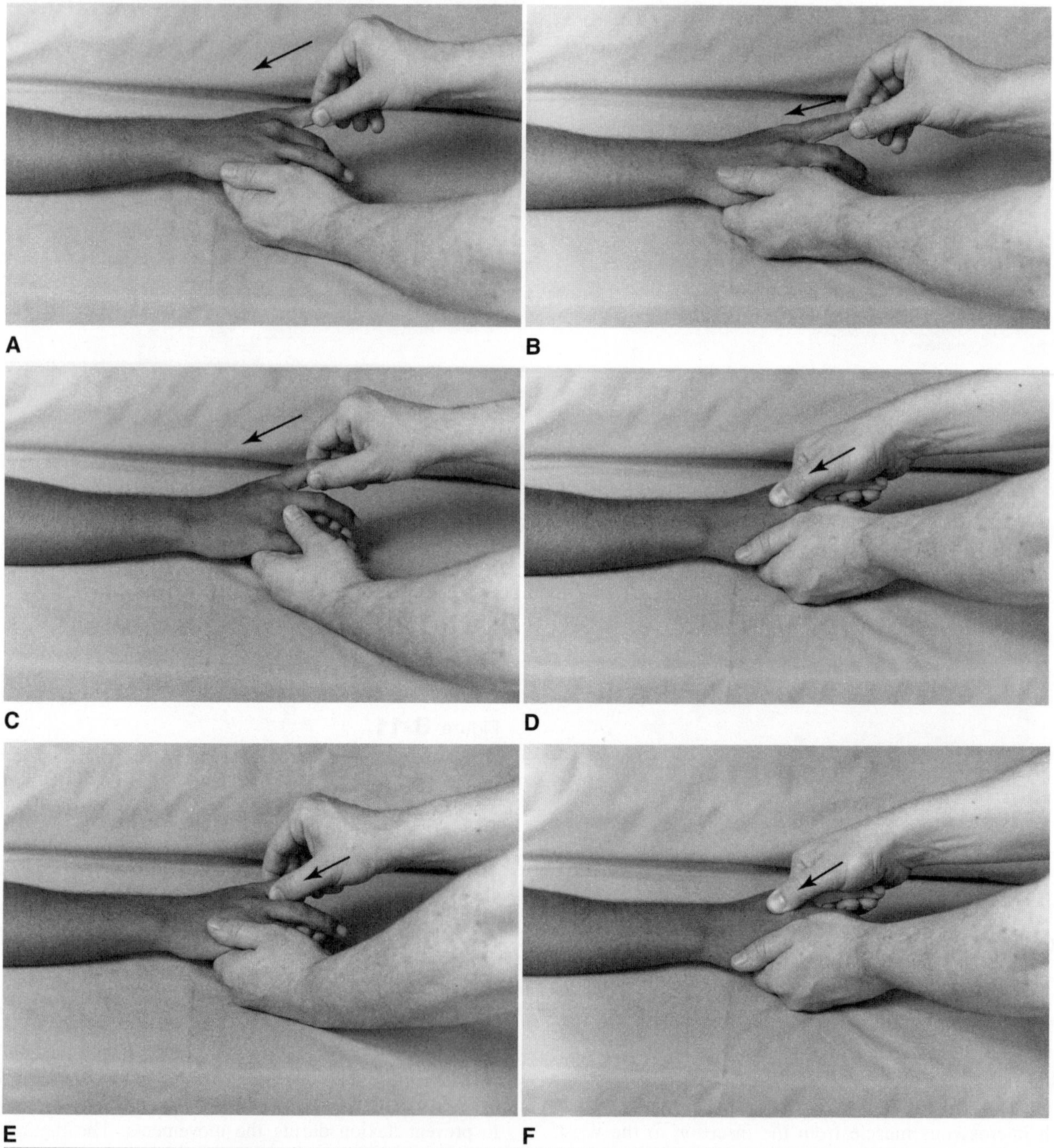

A

B

C

D

E

F

Figure **8-13**

Local massage to the dorsum of the thumb and fingers.

thumb and each succeeding finger in the following manner:

***Thumb Stroking.*** The thumb and the index finger grasp around the tip of the patient's digit (Figure 8-13, *A*). The index finger passes along the radial side of the digit to the metacarpophalangeal joint as the thumb passes along the ulnar side (Figure 8-13, *B, C*) and continues the stroke into the metacarpal-interosseous space (Figure 8-13, *D*). The thumb and the finger return to the tip of the digit with a superficial stroke.

***Thumb Pad Kneading.*** The finger supports, while the thumb pad kneads over the same areas that were previously stroked (Figure 8-13, *E, F*). The thumb and the finger return to the tip of the digit with a superficial stroke. The therapist's hand is then supinated so that the thumb can knead on the radial side of the patient's digit while the index finger supports the ulnar side. The thumb and the finger return to the tip of the digit with a superficial stroke.

**Palmar Surface**

The patient's hand is positioned in supination and supported by the therapist's left hand.

***Stroking and Kneading.*** The fingertips of the therapist's left hand support the patient's hand on the dorsal surface (Figure 8-14, *A*). The right thumb and index finger first stroke (Figure 8-14, *A, B*), then knead (Figure 8-14, *C, D*), the thumb and all the fingers in a manner similar to that performed on the dorsal surface, except that the massage begins with the little finger and progresses toward the thumb.

#### *Left Upper Limb*

The therapist stands by the treatment table on the left side of the patient. The movements described for the right upper limb can be used on the left side by simply reversing the hand positions described in the text and figures (see Figures 8-4 to 8-14).

### Lower Limb

#### *Right Buttock Region*

The therapist stands next to the treatment table on the patient's right side. The patient is lying prone, with pillows under the abdomen and the ankles; the head may be turned to either side for comfort, if required, or supported in the midline in a face hole or on folded towels (see Figure 3-8, *B*, in Chapter 3). Obviously, good draping is an important part of any massage technique to this part of the body. To massage the tissues properly, the entire posterior and lateral hip regions

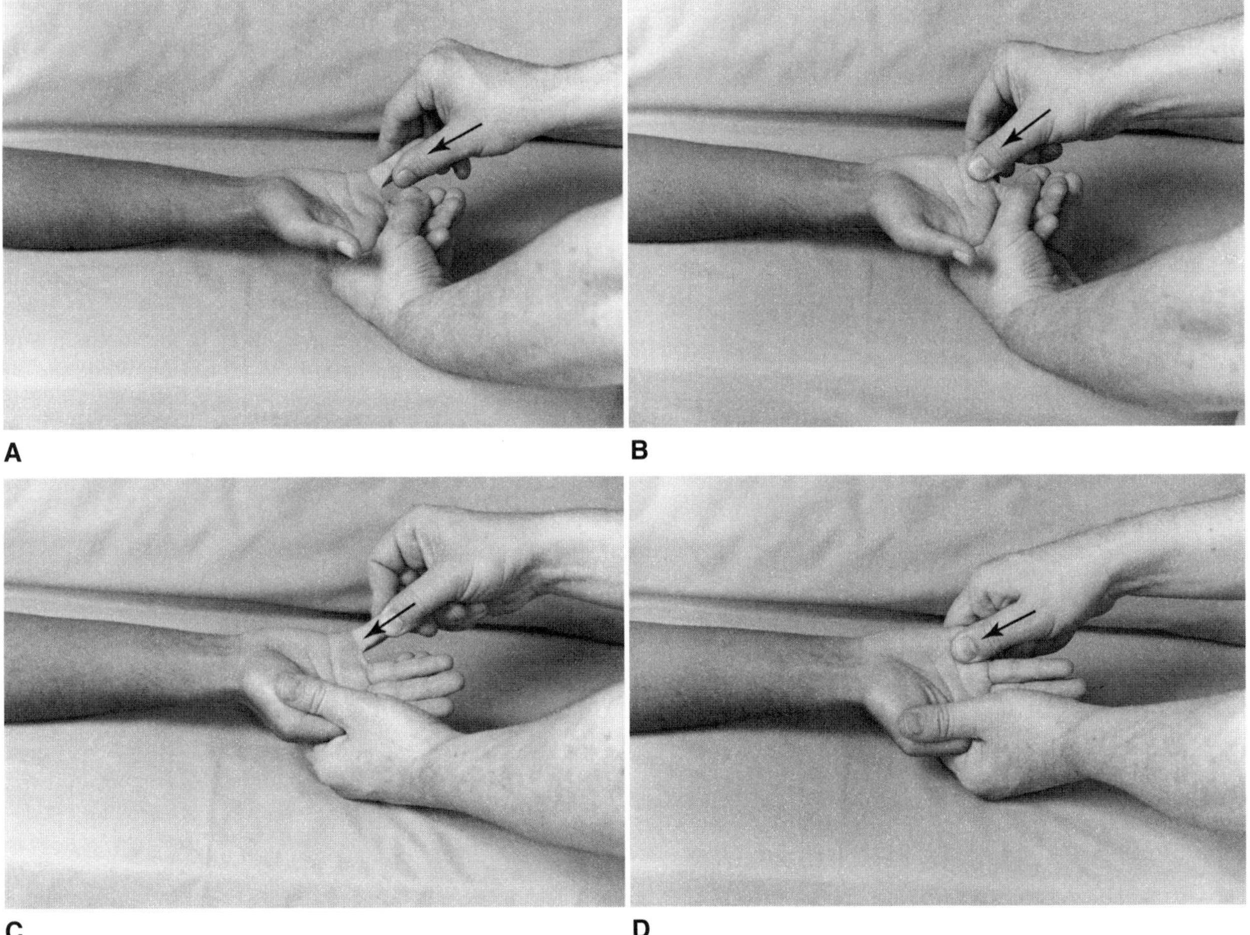


Figure 8-14
Local massage to the palmar surface of the fingers.

need to be fully accessible. If the patient is wearing loose-fitting underwear, he or she may be able to lift the back part of the right side up and over the entire right buttock so that the underwear rests around the patient's waist. Provided that the clothing remains loose and is not constrictive in any way, the procedure is perfectly acceptable. Alternatively, the patient will have to remove his or her underwear. A sheet, folded lengthways, can be placed along the entire left lower limb so that it covers the left buttock region, leaving the right buttock fully exposed. The rest of the folded sheet can be turned so that it covers the patient's waist and right lateral hip region (Figure 8-15, *B*).

### Gluteal Muscles

#### Gluteus Maximus, Medius, and Minimus

***Stroking.*** The left hand starts the stroke at the insertion of the gluteus maximus into the fascia lata (Figure 8-15, *A*) and follows the fibers of this muscle to its origin at the sacrum, coccyx, and ilium (along the gluteal fold in the midline). The right hand follows the fibers of the gluteus medius from its insertion at the greater trochanter of the femur to its origin on the crest of the ilium (see Figure 8-15, *A*). The hands stroke alternately and return with a superficial stroke. If the muscles are large, each one may be stroked separately. In this instance, the thumbs of the hands pass up the midline of the muscle being stroked.

***Kneading.*** Two-handed kneading is performed over the same area that was stroked (Figure 8-15, *B*). At the end of the stroke, the right hand performs a squeeze-out movement and returns with a superficial stroke, as the left hand returns through the air. If the patient is large, several lanes of kneading will be required in order to cover the muscle group.

### Right Thigh

The therapist stands at the side of the table on the patient's right. The therapist faces the patient, who lies prone and is comfortably supported. In most cases, a rolled towel or small pillow should be placed under the shin and ankle regions so that the knees are in slight flexion. This position reduces the stretching effect of the sciatic nerves and will be much more comfortable for the majority of patients (see Figure 3-8, *B*, in Chapter 3).

#### Medial Hamstring Muscles: Semimembranosus and Semitendinosus

***Stroking.*** While the therapist's right hand supports the patient's limb, the left hand begins at the insertion of the muscles, just below the medial condyle of the tibia, and grasps around the muscle group (Figure 8-16, *A*). The thumb strokes up the midline of the thigh as the fingers follow the medial border of the muscle group to meet the thumb at the gluteal fold. The stroke finishes with the usual squeeze-out movement (Figure 8-16, *B*). The hand returns with a superficial stroke.

***Kneading.*** Two-handed kneading is performed over the same area that was stroked.

#### Lateral Hamstring Muscle Biceps Femoris

***Stroking.*** The therapist's left hand supports the patient's limb at the medial aspect of the right knee. The therapist's right hand begins at the insertion of the muscle on the head of the fibula, grasping around the muscle. The thumb passes up the midline of the thigh (Figure 8-17, *A*), the fingers following the lateral border of the muscle to meet the thumb in a squeeze-out movement (Figure 8-17, *B*). The hand returns with a superficial stroke.

***Kneading.*** Two-handed kneading is performed over the same area that was stroked. Single-handed kneading may be used for both inner and outer hamstring groups if the muscles are small.

NOTE: The stroking and kneading movements to both inner and outer hamstring muscles may also be performed with the patient lying supine or on one side if he or she is unable to assume the prone position. In the supine position, one hand supports the knee in slight flexion, while the other hand performs the movement.

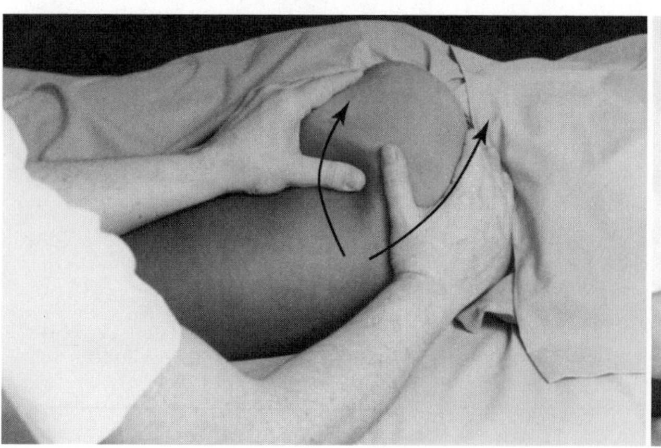

A

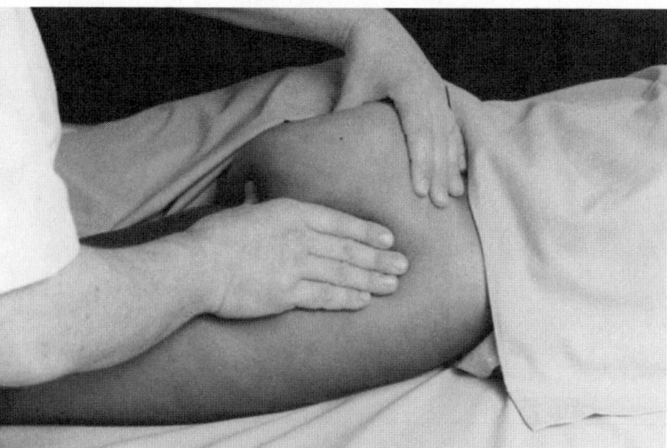

B

**Figure 8-15**
Local massage to the right buttock.

**Tensor of the Fascia Lata (Including the Iliotibial Tract/Band)**

The therapist stands next to the treatment table on the patient's right side. The patient is now comfortably repositioned in supine lying with appropriate draping (see Figure 3-7, *B*, in Chapter 3). A small rolled towel or pillow may be placed under the knee to support the knee in slight flexion, but it must not interfere with the massage.

***Stroking.*** The therapist's right hand supports the patient's thigh at the medial side of the knee, and the left hand starts the stroke at the insertion of the iliotibial tract (band) on the head of the fibula (Figure 8-18, *A*). The thumb follows the anterior border of the fascia and muscle, and the fingers follow the posterior border of the fascia and muscle as the hand strokes toward the origin. As the hand approaches the muscular portion, it spreads out to stroke over the muscle belly to its origin on the pelvis (Figure 8-18, *B*) and finishes with a squeeze-out movement. The hand returns with a superficial stroke.

***Kneading.*** Two-handed kneading is performed over the area that was stroked. Single-handed kneading may be used if the muscle is small.

### *Anterior Thigh Group*

**Rectus Femoris, Vastus Medialis, Vastus Intermedius, Vastus Lateralis, Articularis Genu, and Sartorius**

The therapist stands next to the treatment table on the patient's right side. The patient lies in the supine position, comfortably positioned and draped. A small pillow or rolled towel may be placed under the knee, and the limb can be allowed to roll out a little into external rotation if preferred.

***Stroking.*** The right hand supports the limb at the knee. The left hand is placed at the insertion of the patella tendon, with the thumb at the medial side and the fingers at the lateral border of the patella. The hand passes lightly over the patella, grasps around the muscle (Figure 8-19, *A*), and strokes to the origin of the rectus femoris at the anterior

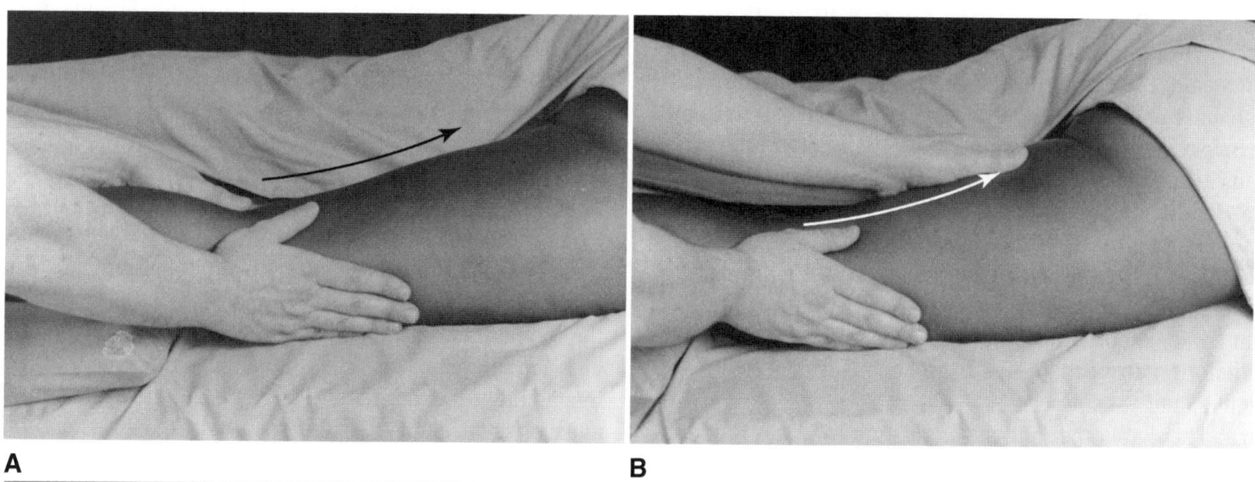

A B

Figure 8-16
Local massage to the medial hamstring muscle group (semimembranosus and semitendinosus).

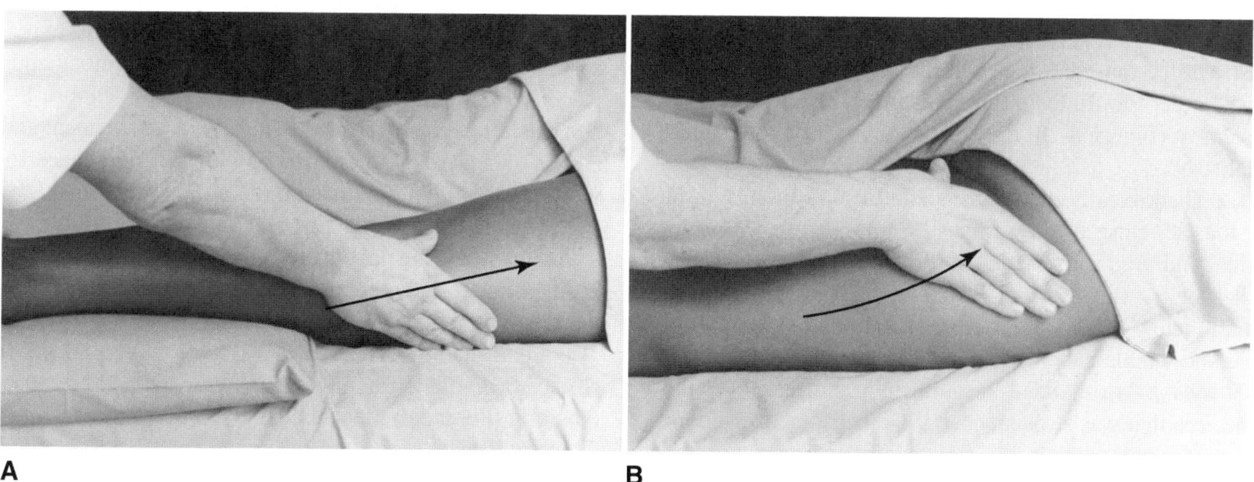

A B

Figure 8-17
Local massage to the lateral hamstring group (biceps femoris).

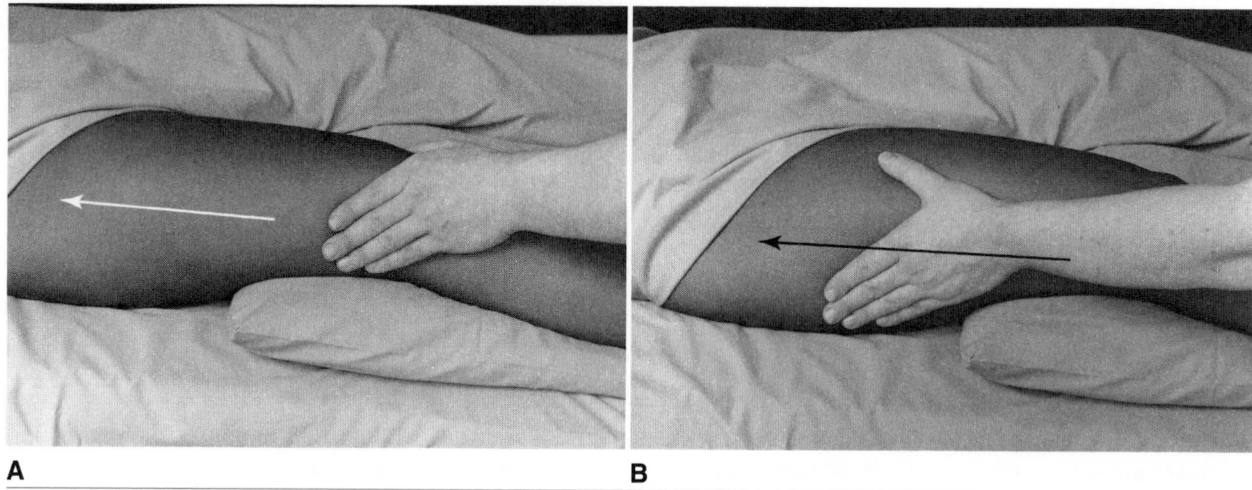


Figure 8-18
Local massage to the tensor fasciae latae muscle.

superior iliac spine (ASIS), where the thumb and fingers meet in a squeeze-out movement (Figure 8-19, *B*). The hand returns with a superficial stroke.

***Kneading.*** The right hand is placed at the lower border of the patella and passes lightly over it; the left hand picks up the muscle above the patella (Figure 8-19, *C*), and both hands knead the entire muscle to its origin (Figure 8-19, *D*). The right hand performs a squeeze-out movement (Figure 8-19, *E*) and returns with a superficial stroke (Figure 8-19, *F*). The left hand returns through the air. Single-handed kneading may be performed with the left hand while the right hand supports the extremity (Figure 8-19, *G*).

**Adductor Muscle Group: Adductor, Longus, Adductor Magnus, and Gracilis**

NOTE: There are other muscles in this group (e.g., obturator externus, pectineus), but these are probably too deep to be effectively massaged.

***Stroking.*** The right hand, reinforced by the left hand, starts the stroke at the insertion of the muscle group on the medial condyle of the tibia by grasping around the entire group (Figure 8-20, *A*). The thumb passes along the anterior border of the muscle group, and the fingers follow the posterior border toward the origin, finishing with a squeeze-out movement (Figure 8-20, *B*). The hand returns with a superficial stroke.

NOTE: Theoretically this stroke should end at the origin of the muscle, close to the symphysis pubis, but for obvious ethical and practical reasons, it should be completed a few inches below the inguinal ligament. In fact, it is best to remain below the midpoint of the femoral triangle in both male and female patients.

***Kneading.*** Two-handed kneading is performed over the same area that was stroked, observing the same restrictions over the femoral triangle. The right hand performs a squeeze-out movement at the end of the kneading and returns with a superficial stroke. The left hand returns through the air. Single-handed kneading may be used on a small adductor mass; the left hand can reinforce the right hand.

### *Right Leg*

The therapist stands at the foot of the treatment table, facing the patient. A small rolled towel is particularly useful to support the knee and still allow the therapist's hands to work around the knee. A small pillow can also be used for this purpose (see Figure 3-9 in Chapter 3).

**Anterior Tibial Muscles: Tibialis Anterior, Extensor Digitorum Longus, Extensor Hallucis Longus, and Fibularis/Peroneus Tertius**

***Stroking.*** The right hand is placed slightly distal to the ankle joint, and the right hand supports the ankle by grasping the foot at the medial arch. The left thumb passes along the anterior border of the tibia, and the index finger follows the lateral border of the muscle group (Figure 8-21, *A*) to the anterior surface of the head of the fibula, meeting the thumb in a squeeze-out movement. The other fingers maintain light contact with the skin throughout the movement. The hand returns to the starting position with a superficial stroke.

***Kneading.*** Two-handed digital kneading is performed over the same area that was stroked. The therapist may stand at the foot of the table and turn his or her body so as to reach across the tibia to knead the muscles. The right hand is placed proximally and the left hand distally (Figure 8-21, *B*). The left hand performs the squeeze-out movement at the end of the procedure, returning with a superficial stroke while the right hand returns in the air.

Alternatively, the therapist may move to the right side of the table (facing the patient) and perform two-handed kneading with the left hand placed proximally and the right hand distally. The right hand performs the squeeze-out movement at the end of the movement and returns with a superficial stroke while the left hand returns in the air.

**Fibularis (Peroneal) Muscles: Fibularis Longus, Fibularis Brevis**

NOTE: These muscles were formerly called *peroneus longus* and *brevis*.

***Stroking.*** The left hand is placed distal to the lateral malleolus while the right hand supports the ankle by grasping

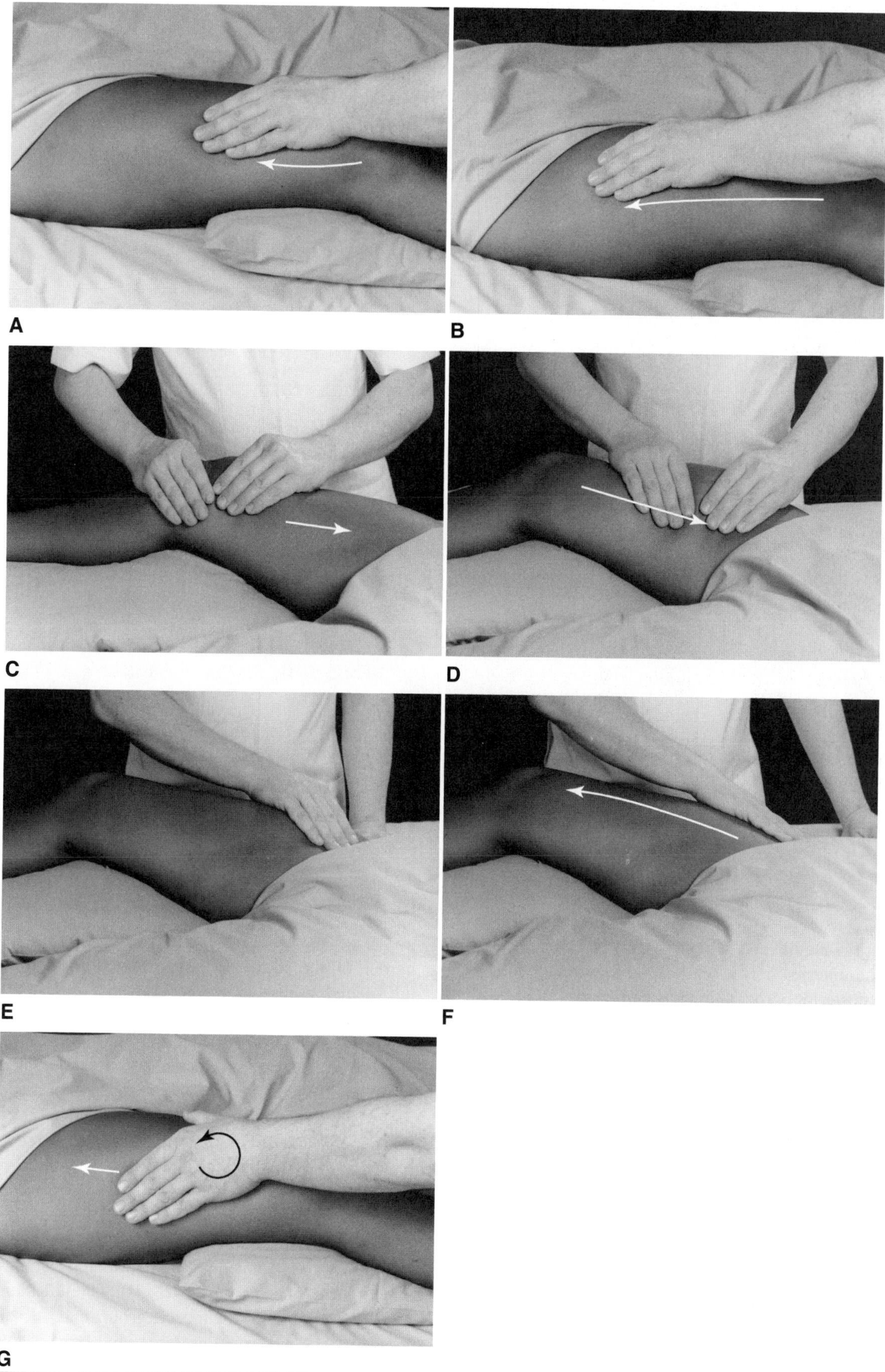


**Figure 8-19**
Local massage to the quadriceps muscle group.

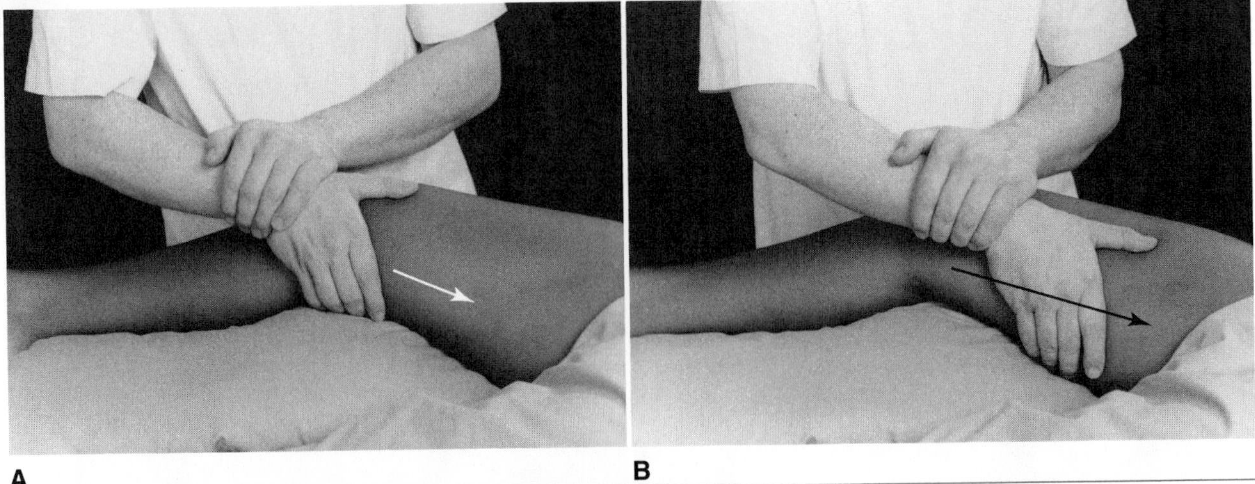

**Figure 8-20**
Local massage to the hip adductor muscle group.

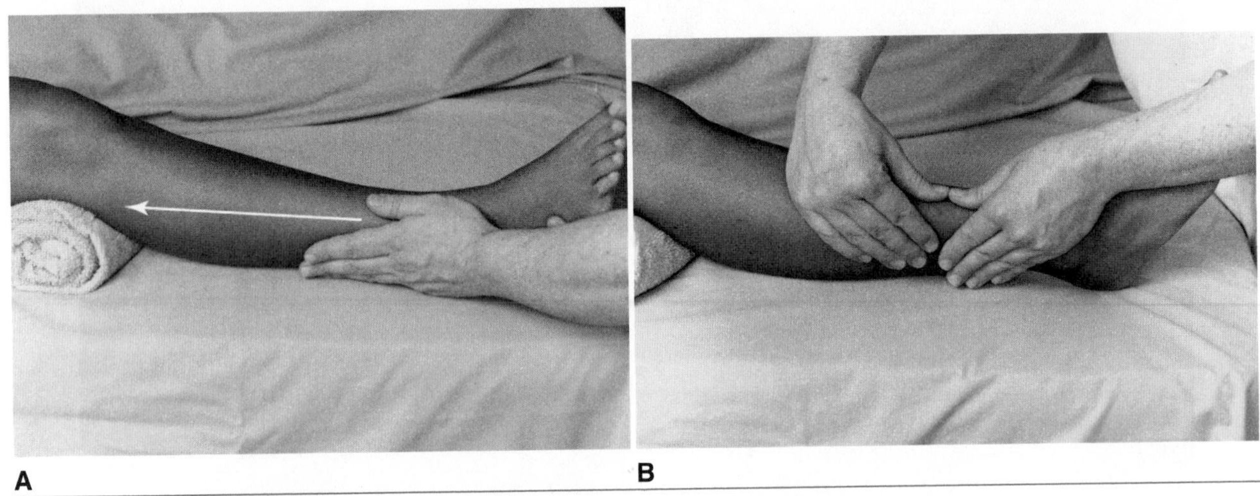

**Figure 8-21**
Local massage to the anterior tibial muscle group.

the foot at the medial arch (Figure 8-22, *A*). The left thumb follows the anterior border while the index finger follows along the posterior border of the muscle group (Figure 8-22, *B*) to the posterior surface of the head of the fibula, meeting the thumb in a squeeze-out movement. The hand returns to the starting position with a superficial stroke. The other fingers maintain light contact with the skin throughout the movement.

***Kneading.*** Two-handed digital kneading is given over the same area that was stroked. Procedures are similar to those described for two-handed digital kneading of the anterior tibial muscle group (Figure 8-22, *C*).

**Calf Muscles: Gastrocnemius, Soleus, and Plantaris**

The therapist stands next to the treatment table on the patient's right. The patient is comfortably supported and draped in prone lying (see Figure 3-8, *B*, in Chapter 3).

***Stroking.*** The therapist's left hand is placed on the heel, and the right hand stabilizes the patient's leg at the knee (Figure 8-23, *A*). The left thumb follows along the lateral border of the Achilles tendon and passes up the lateral border of the muscle group as the fingers follow along the medial border of the tendon and muscle group. The hand grasps around the muscle group and strokes toward the origins of the gastrocnemius muscle. The first stroke ends in a squeeze-out movement over the medial head (Figure 8-23, *B*); the second stroke ends in a squeeze-out movement over the lateral head (Figure 8-23, *C*). Additional strokes continue to alternate until the area is covered. The hand returns to the starting position with a superficial stroke.

If the muscle group is too large to be grasped in one hand, it may be massaged in two sections. The medial side of the muscle group is stroked with the left hand as the right hand supports the knee (Figure 8-23, *D*). The left thumb passes along the midline of the muscle group, and the squeeze-out movement is performed at the medial head of the gastrocnemius muscle. The lateral side of the muscle group is stroked with the right hand as the left hand supports the

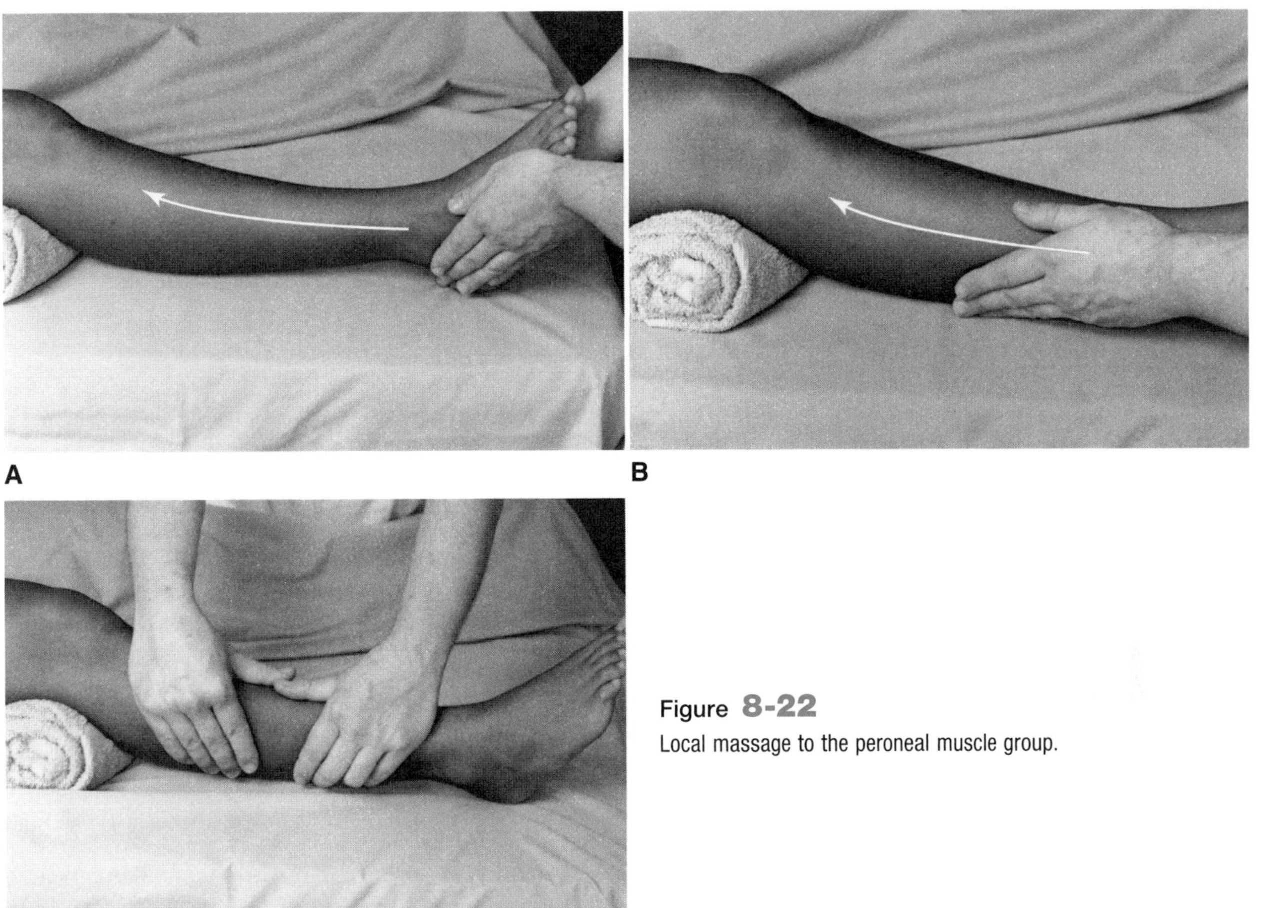


**Figure 8-22**
Local massage to the peroneal muscle group.

knee (Figure 8-23, *E*). The squeeze-out is done at the lateral head of the gastrocnemius muscle.

***Kneading.*** Two-handed kneading is performed to the same area that was stroked (Figure 8-23, *F*). The left hand returns to the starting position with a superficial stroke, and the right hand returns in the air. If the muscle group is very large, two-handed kneading is given over each half of the muscle group (Figure 8-23, *G*). Alternatively, if the muscle group is small, single-handed kneading may be used over the whole muscle group. In this case, the left hand kneads as the right hand supports the extremity.

If it is not possible for the patient to lie prone, this muscle group may be massaged with the patient supine. With the patient in this position, one hand supports the knee in slight flexion while the other performs the stroking movement (Figure 8-23, *H*).

Two-handed kneading is given with the therapist standing at the side of the table on the patient's right. The patient's thigh is rotated laterally so that both hands can grasp the muscle group easily (Figure 8-23, *I*). If the muscle group is small, single-handed kneading may be given with the left hand as the right hand supports the knee in slight flexion (Figure 8-23, *J*).

### *Right Foot*

The therapist stands at the end of the table, facing the patient. The patient lies in supine position, comfortably supported and appropriately draped, with a pillow supporting the knee. As an alternative, the patient may sit up on the treatment table (see Figure 3-9 in Chapter 3). For treatment purposes, the various surfaces of the foot are divided in two different but overlapping ways. First, the foot is divided longitudinally into two halves—this time, a medial and a lateral section. The foot is then divided into top (dorsal) and bottom (plantar) sections. All four sections are massaged. Once again, this division is not strictly anatomical, but it is suitable for use in local massage of the hand. The toes may be massaged separately from the rest of the foot.

#### Medial Section

***Stroking.*** The left hand supports the ankle on the lateral side, just proximal to the heel (Figure 8-24, *A*) while the right hand grasps the medial half of the foot at the toes. The thumb passes up the midline of the dorsum of the foot and below the medial malleolus as the fingers pass along the midline of the plantar surface and around the heel to meet the thumb in a squeeze-out movement (Figure 8-24, *B*). The hand returns to the starting position with a superficial stroke.

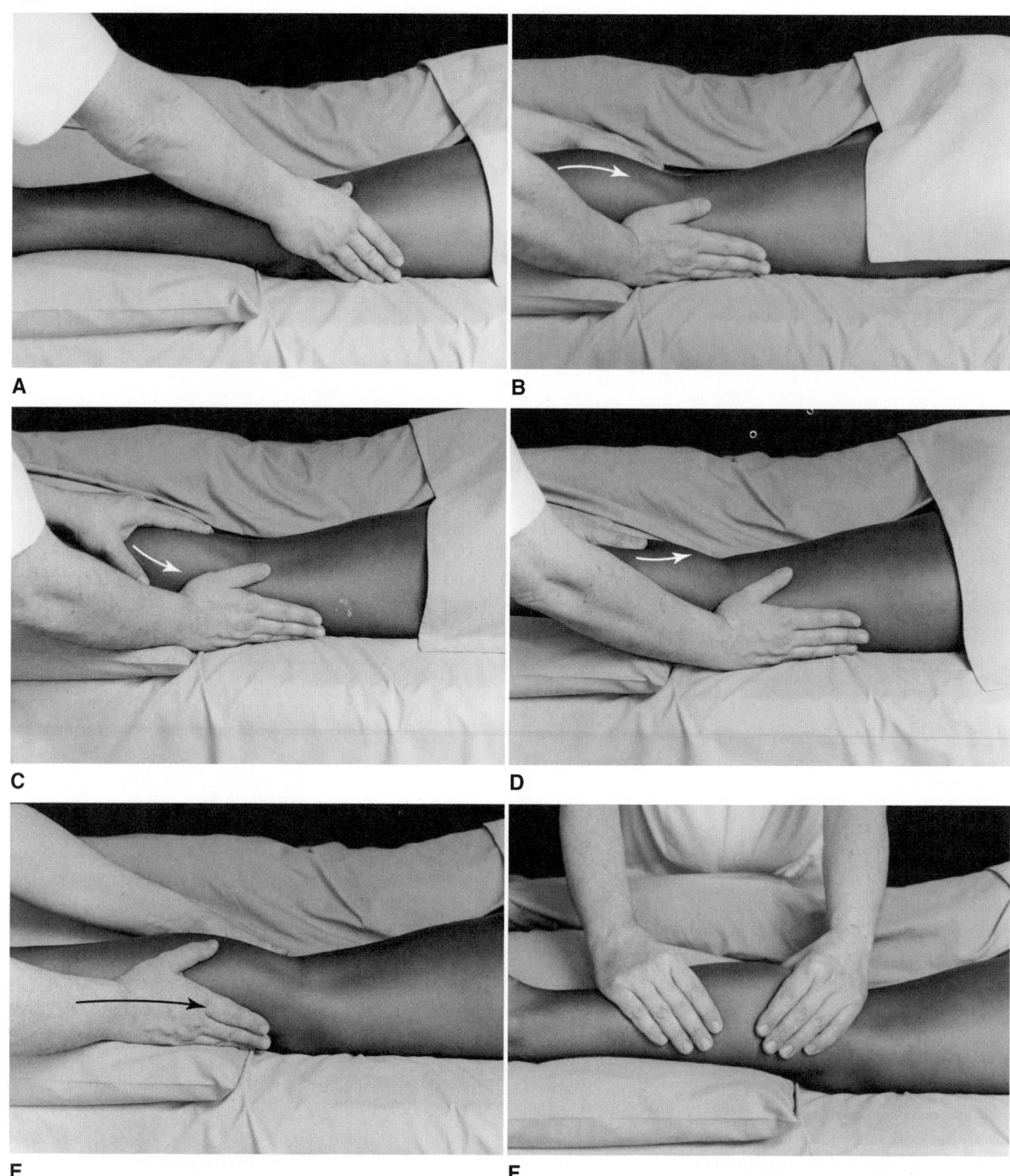


Figure 8-23
Local massage to the posterior muscle group of the leg (calf muscles).

***Kneading.*** Single-handed kneading is given over the same area that was stroked. The hand returns to the starting position with a superficial stroke.

**Lateral Section**

***Stroking.*** The right hand supports the ankle on the medial side, just proximal to the heel, while the left hand grasps the lateral half of the foot at the toes (Figure 8-25, *A*). The thumb passes along the midline of the dorsum of the foot and below the lateral malleolus. At the same time, the fingers pass up the midline of the plantar surface and around the heel to meet the thumb in a squeeze-out movement (Figure 8-25, *B*). The hand returns to the starting position with a superficial stroke.

***Kneading.*** Single-handed kneading is performed over the same area that was stroked. The hand returns to the starting position with a superficial stroke.

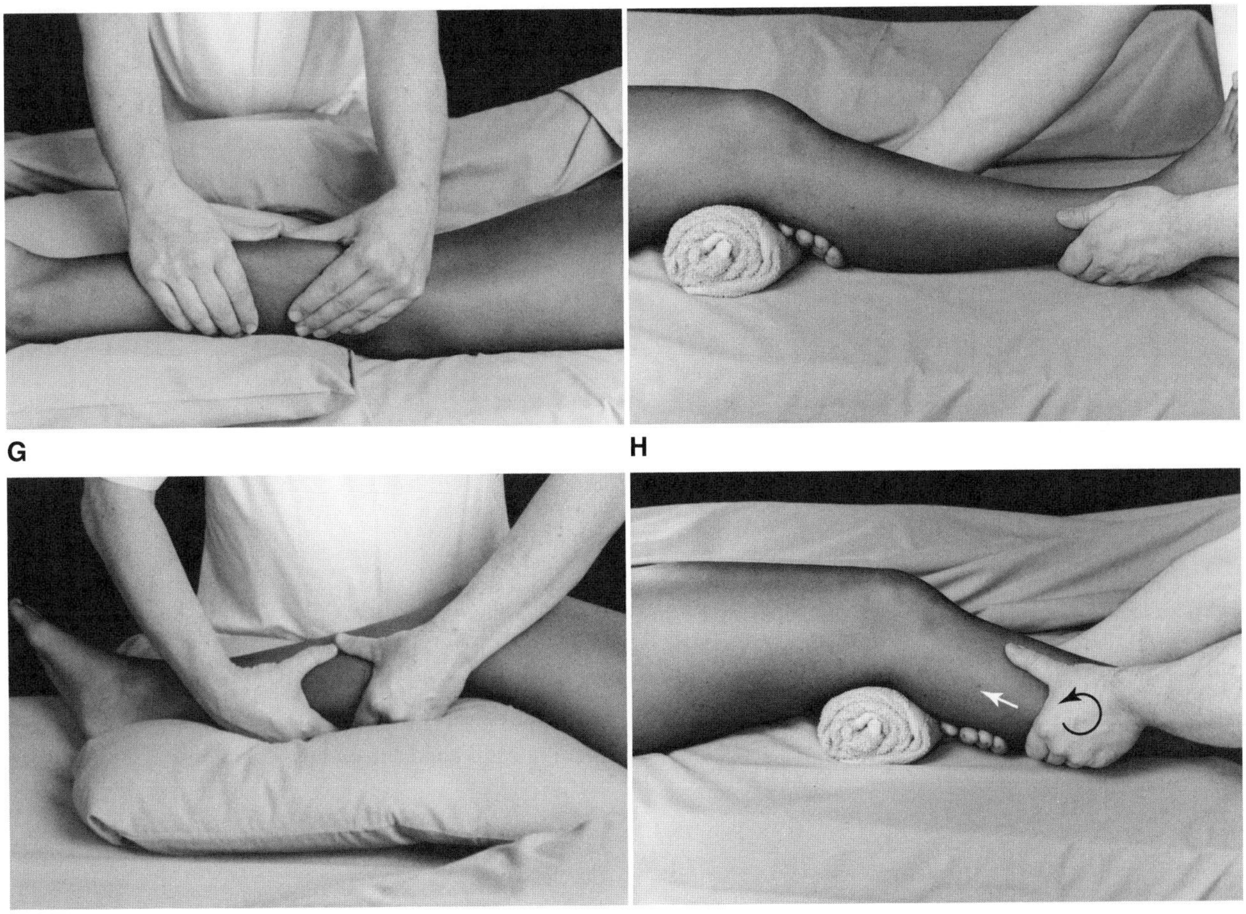

G H

I J

Figure **8-23**, cont'd

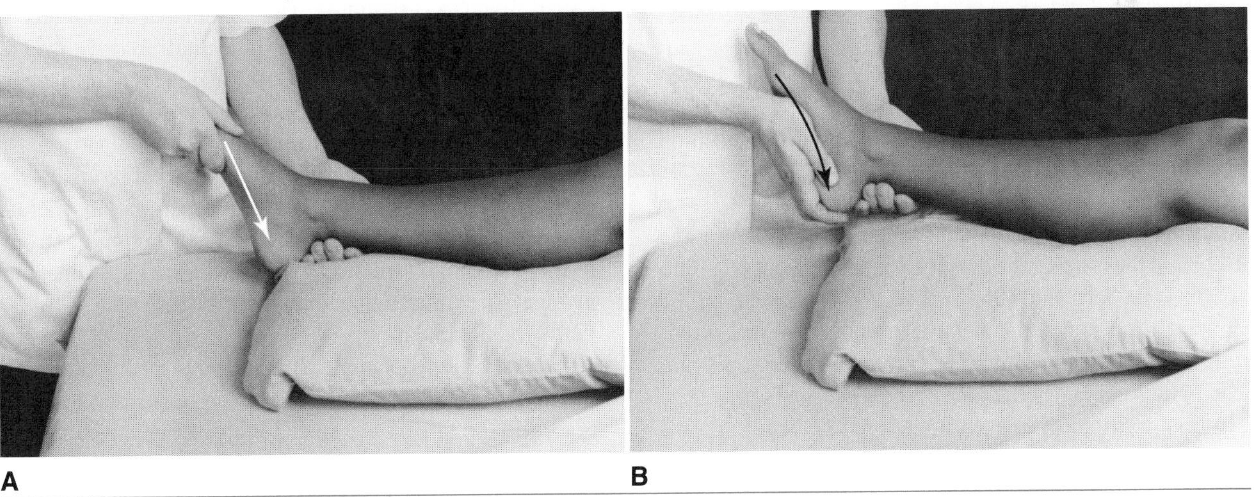

A B

Figure **8-24**
Local massage to the medial border of the foot.

**Dorsal Section**

***Stroking.*** The fingers of both hands are placed on the plantar surface of the foot to support it. The thumbs perform short, alternate strokes between the first and second metatarsal bones, progressing from the base of the toes to the ankle. Both thumbs together return to the starting position with a superficial stroke; they repeat the movements in each metatarsal space (Figure 8-26).

***Kneading.*** Kneading is given with one thumb moving in small circles over the same area that was stroked. The right thumb kneads over the first and second metatarsal spaces, and the left thumb kneads over the third and fourth

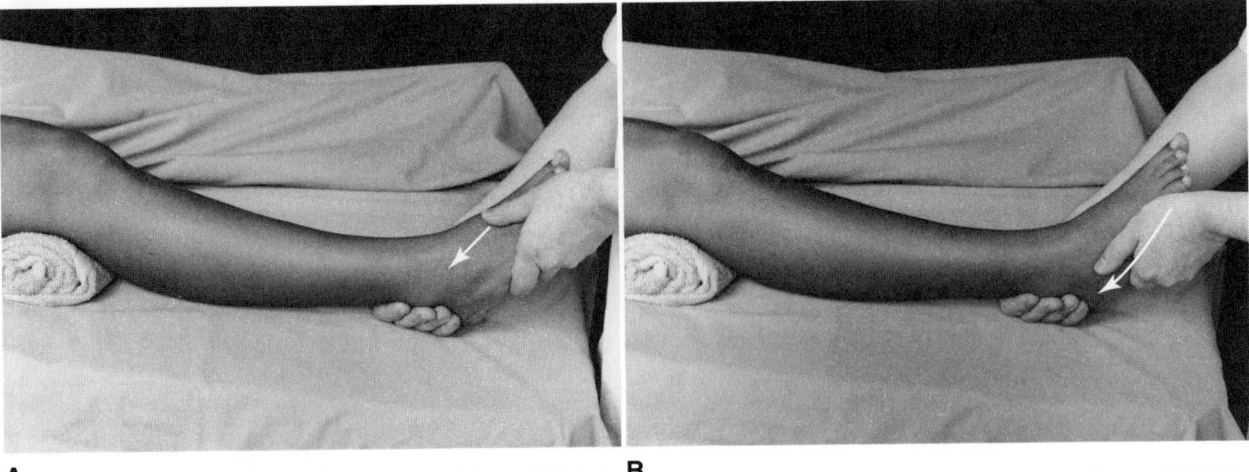


Figure 8-25
Local massage to the lateral border of the foot.

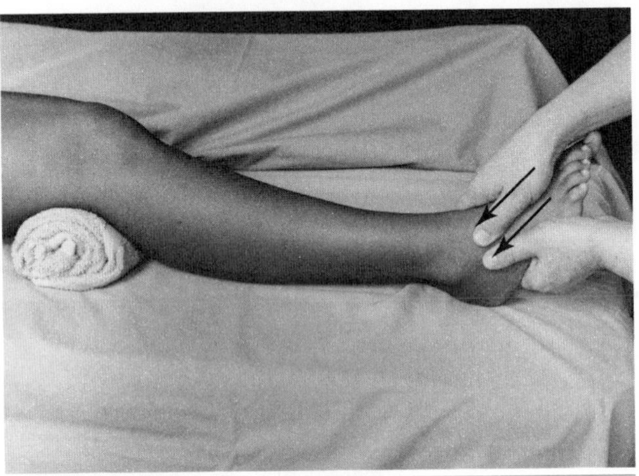

Figure 8-26
Local massage to the dorsum of the foot.

metatarsal spaces. The thumb returns to the starting position with a superficial stroke.

**Plantar Section**

***Stroking.*** The left hand supports the foot by grasping the forefoot and toes so that the dorsal surface of the foot fits into the palm of the left hand (Figure 8-27, *A*). The fingers of the right hand are flexed at the metacarpophalangeal and proximal interphalangeal joints. The proximal phalanges are placed in firm contact at the base of the toes (see Figure 8-27, *A*). In this position, the flexed fingers stroke firmly toward the heel (Figure 8-27, *B*). As the movement progresses, the right hand is rolled into pronation (Figure 8-27, *C*), and the fingers are extended to allow the heel of the hand to fit into the medial arch of the foot. The right hand is removed and returns through the air to the starting position.

### Right Toes

If there is reason to massage the toes, stroking and kneading techniques similar to those described for the thumb and fingers are appropriate (see Figure 8-13).

### Left Lower Limb

The therapist stands next to the treatment table at the patient's left side and facing the patient's head. The movements are performed as described for the right leg, except that the right hand substitutes for the left and the left hand for the right.

## Posterior Trunk and Pelvis

### Back

The therapist stands next to the treatment table on the patient's left side and facing the patient's head. The patient is appropriately draped and positioned comfortably, lying prone with pillows under the abdomen and ankles and rolled towels under the shoulders. The patient's head and face can be supported in a face hole or on a small folded towel (see Figure 3-8, *A*, in Chapter 3). Local massage to the back may be performed to three basic muscle groups—the paraspinal (erector spinae) group, the trapezius and scapular group, and the latissimus dorsi muscle—although, of course, some parts of these muscles overlap each other and are therefore massaged at the same time. With the exception of stroking to the paraspinal (erector spinae) group, all movements are given at one time to one side of the back.

**Paraspinal Muscles**

***Stroking.*** The therapist's thumbs are placed at the sides of the patient's spinous processes of the upper cervical vertebrae, and the fingers are placed in the supraclavicular fossae (Figure 8-28, *A*). Both thumbs stroke down firmly over the cervical region and, at the seventh cervical vertebra, are lifted and crossed. The fingers are then drawn backward lightly toward the seventh cervical vertebra (Figure 8-28, *B*), and the palms stroke firmly over the paraspinal (erector spinae) muscles from the seventh cervical vertebra to the sacrum.

The hands then separate and, with thumbs adducted, stroke with light pressure over the iliac crests (Figure 8-28, *C*) to the inguinal region and return to the sacrum (Figure 8-28, *D*). The hands then stroke back over the paraspinal muscles to the

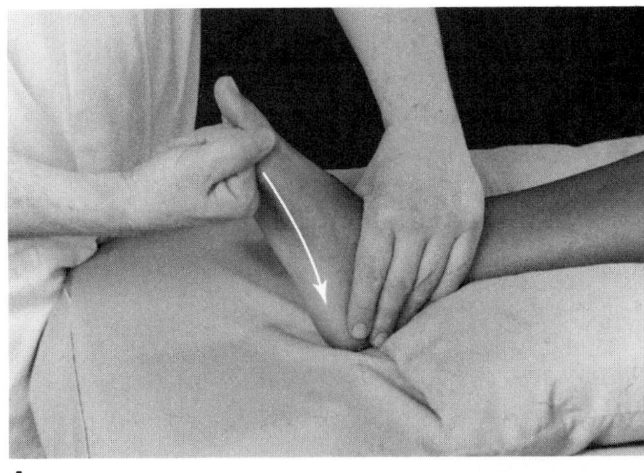
A

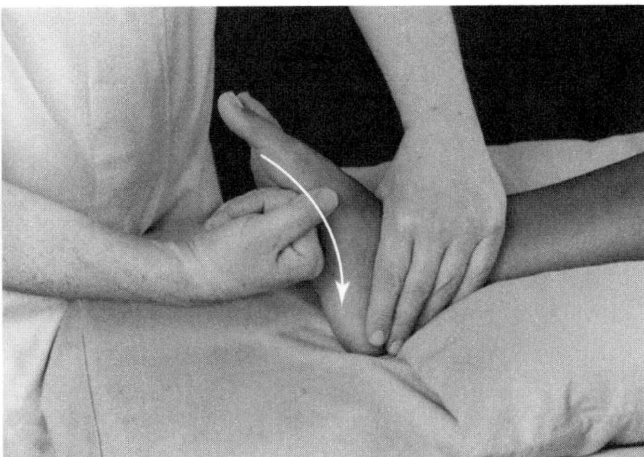
B

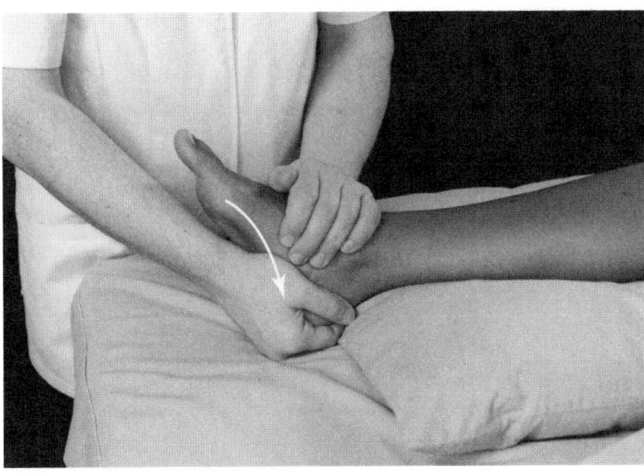
C

Figure 8-27
Local massage to the plantar surface of the foot.

seventh cervical vertebra, the thumbs again being lifted and crossed. Light pressure is used for the return stroke.

***Kneading.*** Two-handed digital kneading is performed, first to the right side and then to the left side, beginning at the cervical region and continuing to the sacrum (Figure 8-28, *E*). The right hand returns with a superficial stroke as the left hand returns through the air.

**Trapezius and Scapular Muscles: Trapezius, Supraspinatus, Infraspinatus, Levator Scapulae, Rhomboid Major, Rhomboid Minor, and Teres Major**

***Stroking.*** Starting on the right side, the therapist's right hand is placed over the patient's upper fibers of the trapezius muscle with the thumb at the lateral border of the spinous processes of the upper cervical vertebrae. The hand grasps around the upper fibers of the right half of the trapezius muscle and strokes laterally to the acromion process. As the right hand completes the movement, the left hand begins at the origin of the middle fibers of the trapezius muscle (Figure 8-29, *A*) and strokes across with the thumb abducted laterally toward the acromion process. Then the right hand, with the thumb abducted, is placed with the thumb beside the spinous processes and the ulnar border at the edge of the lower fibers of the trapezius (at the level of the twelfth thoracic vertebra). From this position, the hand strokes upward and laterally to the acromion process. As it reaches the acromion, the left hand starts the first stroking movement over the upper fibers of the trapezius. The right hand then strokes over the middle fibers (Figure 8-29, *B*), and the left hand strokes over the lower fibers. The movements are performed in the same manner on the left side, except that the left hand substitutes for the right and the right hand for the left.

***Kneading.*** The kneading movement starts on the right side.

*Upper fibers.* Two-handed digital kneading is given over the same area that was stroked. The right hand returns with a superficial stroke as the left hand returns through the air.

*Middle and lower fibers.* Two-handed kneading is performed over both areas (Figure 8-29, *C*). The right hand returns with a superficial stroke while the left hand returns through the air.

The movements are performed in the same manner on the left side, except that the left hand substitutes for the right and the right hand for the left.

**Latissimus Dorsi Muscle**

***Stroking.*** Starting on the right side, the therapist places his or her right hand (reinforced by the left hand) with the thumb at the lateral border of the spinous processes of

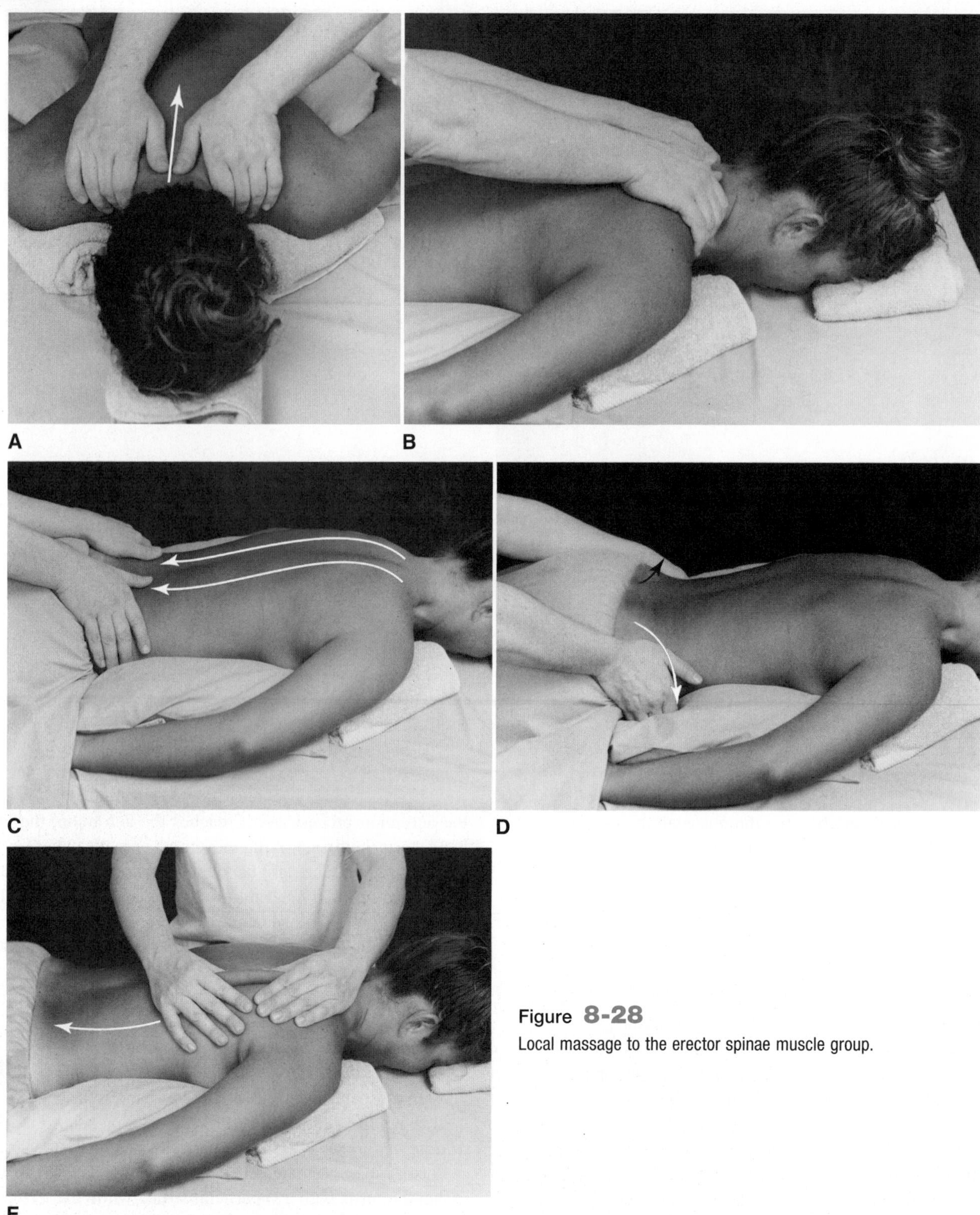

**Figure 8-28**
Local massage to the erector spinae muscle group.

the lumbar area and the ulnar border on the crest of the ilium (Figure 8-30, *A*). The thumb follows along the medial border of the muscle while the fingers follow along the lateral border. The hand turns into pronation as the fingers meet the thumb in the axilla in a squeeze-out movement (Figure 8-30, *B*). The hand returns with a superficial stroke.

***Kneading.*** Two-handed kneading is performed over the same area that was stroked (Figure 8-30, *C*). The right hand returns with a superficial stroke as the left hand returns through the air. If the muscle is too large to be covered with one hand, the stroking and kneading may be performed in two sections. The movements are given in the same manner

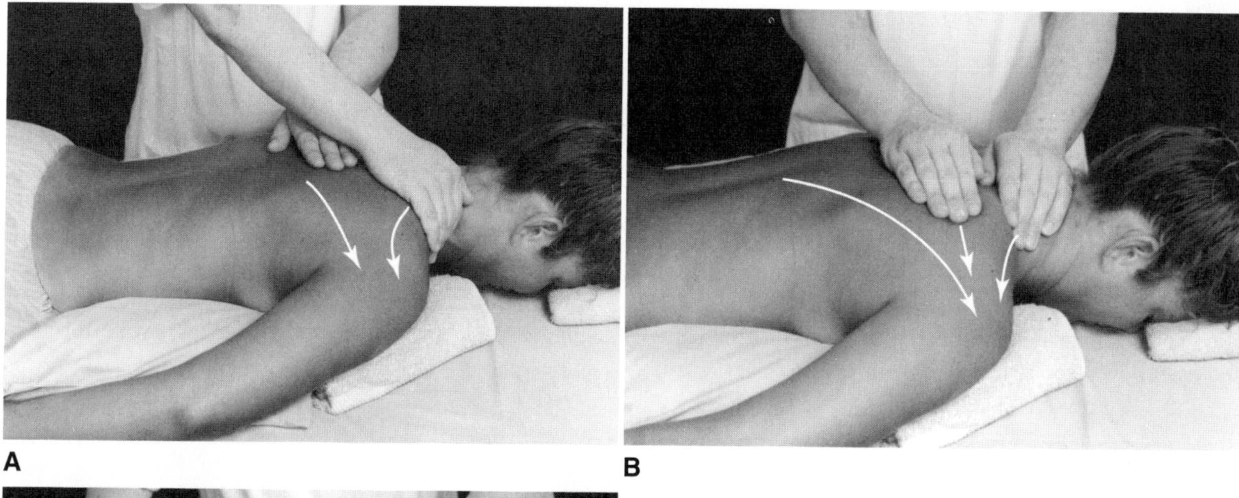


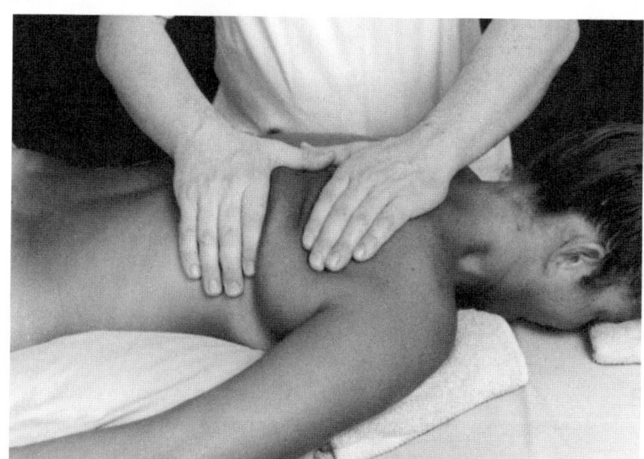


Figure 8-29
Local massage to the trapezius and scapular muscles.

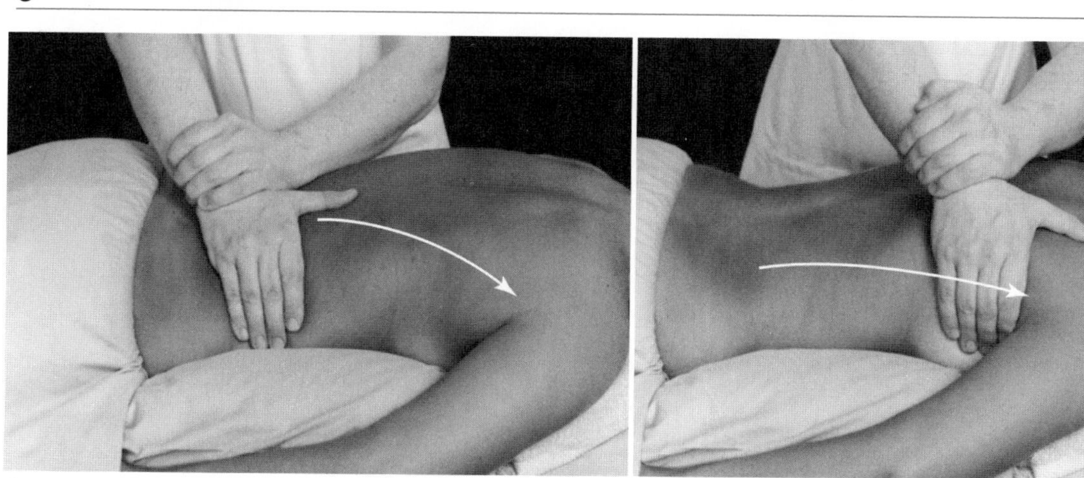


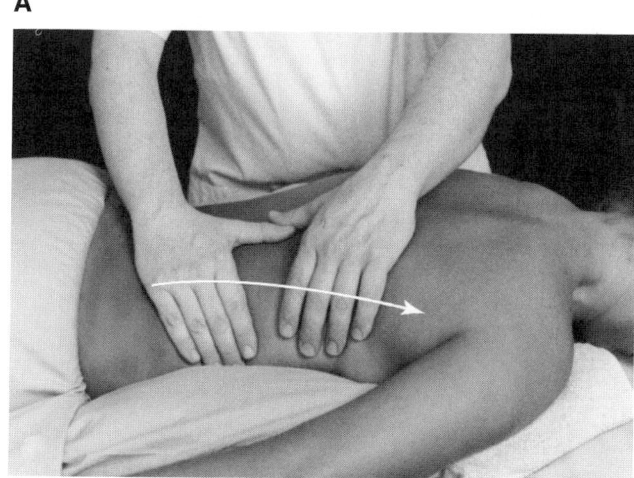


Figure 8-30
Local massage to the latissimus dorsi muscle.

on the left side, except that the left hand substitutes for the right and the right hand for the left.

## Anterior Trunk and Pelvis

### Abdomen

The therapist stands next to the treatment table on the right side of the patient. The patient is appropriately draped and positioned in supine lying, with the head and knees supported by pillows (see Figure 3-7, *A*, in Chapter 3).

***Stroking over the Entire Abdomen.*** Starting with the fingertips of both hands at the symphysis pubis (Figure 8-31, *A*), the hands stroke over the rectus abdominis muscle to its origin (Figure 8-31, *B*). The hands then stroke laterally with light pressure (Figure 8-31, *C*), with the fingers passing over the lower ribs. As the hands continue the lateral stroking over the dorsal part of the fibers, they turn (Figure 8-31, *D*) so that the fingertips stroke toward the spine.

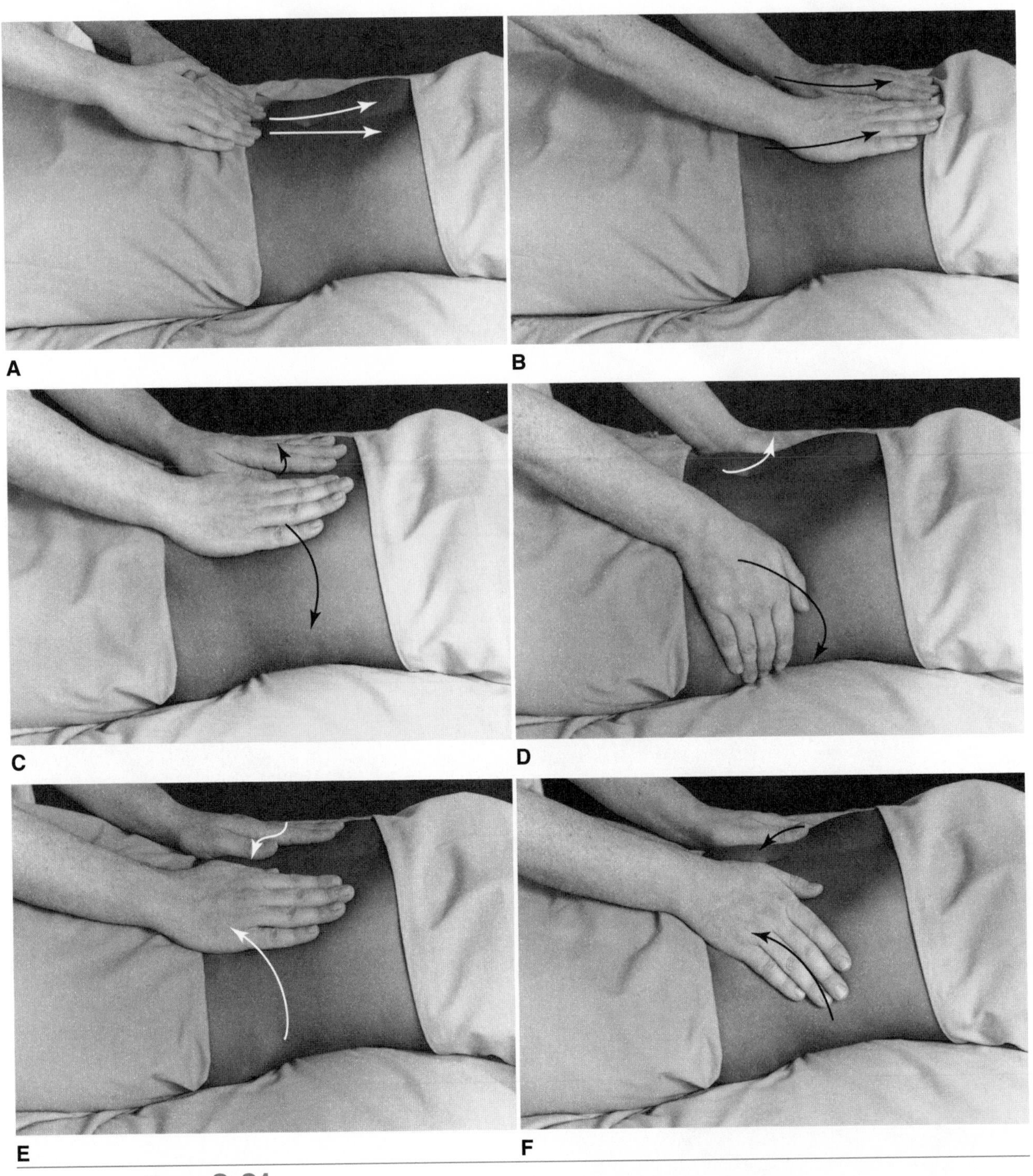


Figure **8-31**
Local stroking massage to the entire abdomen.

The hands then return over the same area with a firm stroke to the transverse abdominal muscles (Figure 8-31, *E*) and a light stroke down the rectus abdominis to the symphysis pubis. The stroking to the rectus abdominis and the lateral stroking are repeated, but the return stroke is given over the oblique abdominal muscles (Figure 8-31, *F*) toward the symphysis pubis.

***Stroking over the Area of the Colon.*** The fingertips of the right hand, reinforced by the left hand, are placed over the beginning of the ascending colon (cecum) in the right lower quadrant of the abdomen (Figure 8-32, *A*). They stroke upward with firm pressure over the area of the ascending colon (Figure 8-32, *B*), across the abdomen over the area of the transverse colon, and downward over the area of the descending colon. The hands return with a superficial stroke across the lower abdomen to the starting point (Figure 8-32, *C*).

***Kneading over the Area of the Colon.*** The fingertips of the reinforced right hand are placed about 2 inches (5 cm) above the area of the distal part of the descending colon (Figure 8-33, *A*). The fingertips are kept in contact with the skin, and together they move on the underlying tissue (as in standard palmar kneading movements). A circular movement with firm pressure is repeated several times in this one area and then followed by a firm stroke (Figure 8-33, *B*) over the area of the distal portion of the colon toward the rectum. With a light stroke, the therapist's hand returns to a point about 2 inches (5 cm) proximal to the starting point and repeats the movements. Progression is made in this manner over the rest of the areas of the descending colon, the transverse colon, and the ascending colon (Figure 8-33, *C*). It is important to perform this stroke in the direction specified, although this appears to be opposite to the normal direction of peristalsis. Performed in this manner, the kneading tends to clear the colon rather than cause congestion (see Chapter 9, Figure 9-7, for more details).

## Head and Neck

### *Face*

The therapist stands or sits at the head of the treatment table. The patient lies supine with a small pillow or neck roll to support the head. The following technique for massage of the face is based on the principles of the Hoffa method to the extent that the strokes are applied to individual muscles or muscle groups and the stroking movements follow the general longitudinal direction of the muscle fibers. It

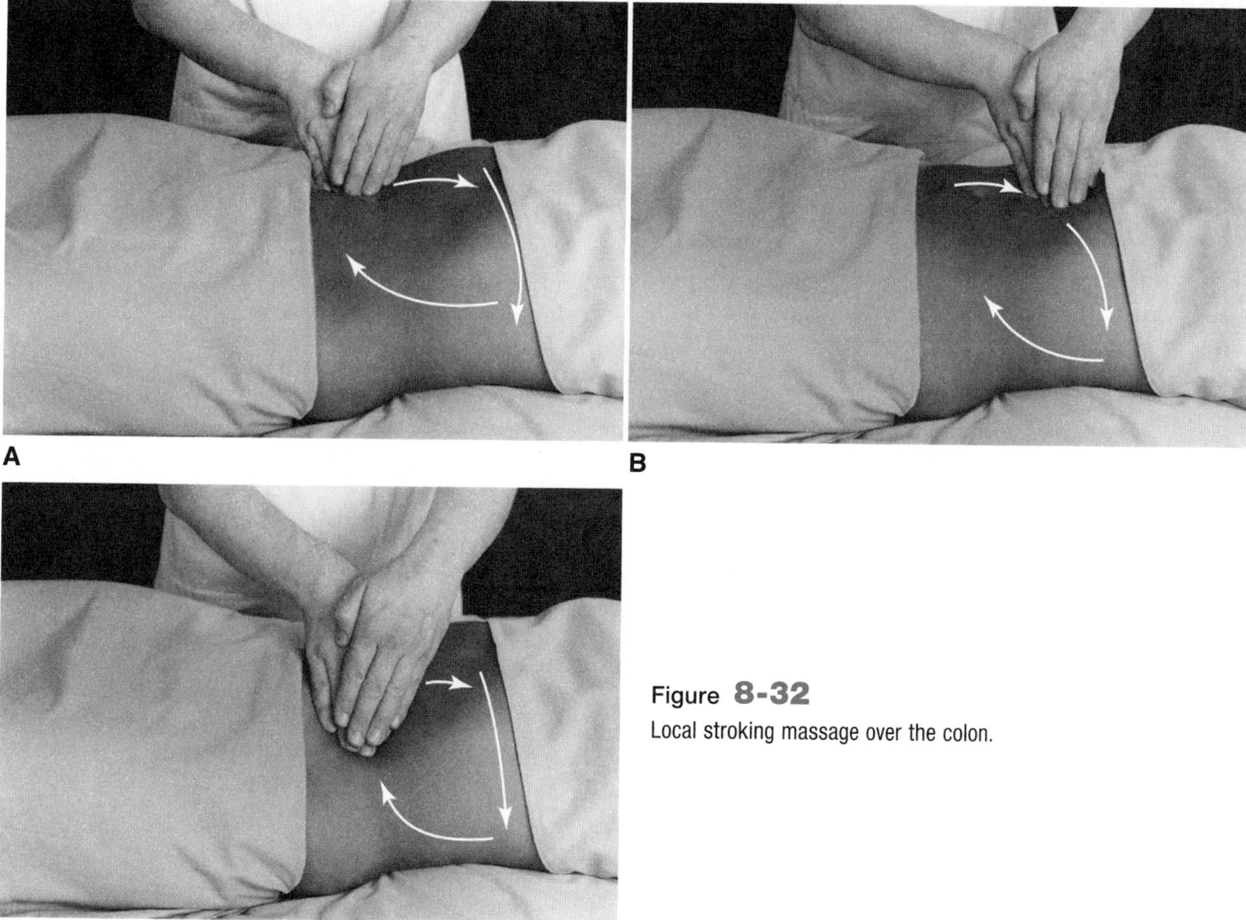


Figure **8-32**
Local stroking massage over the colon.

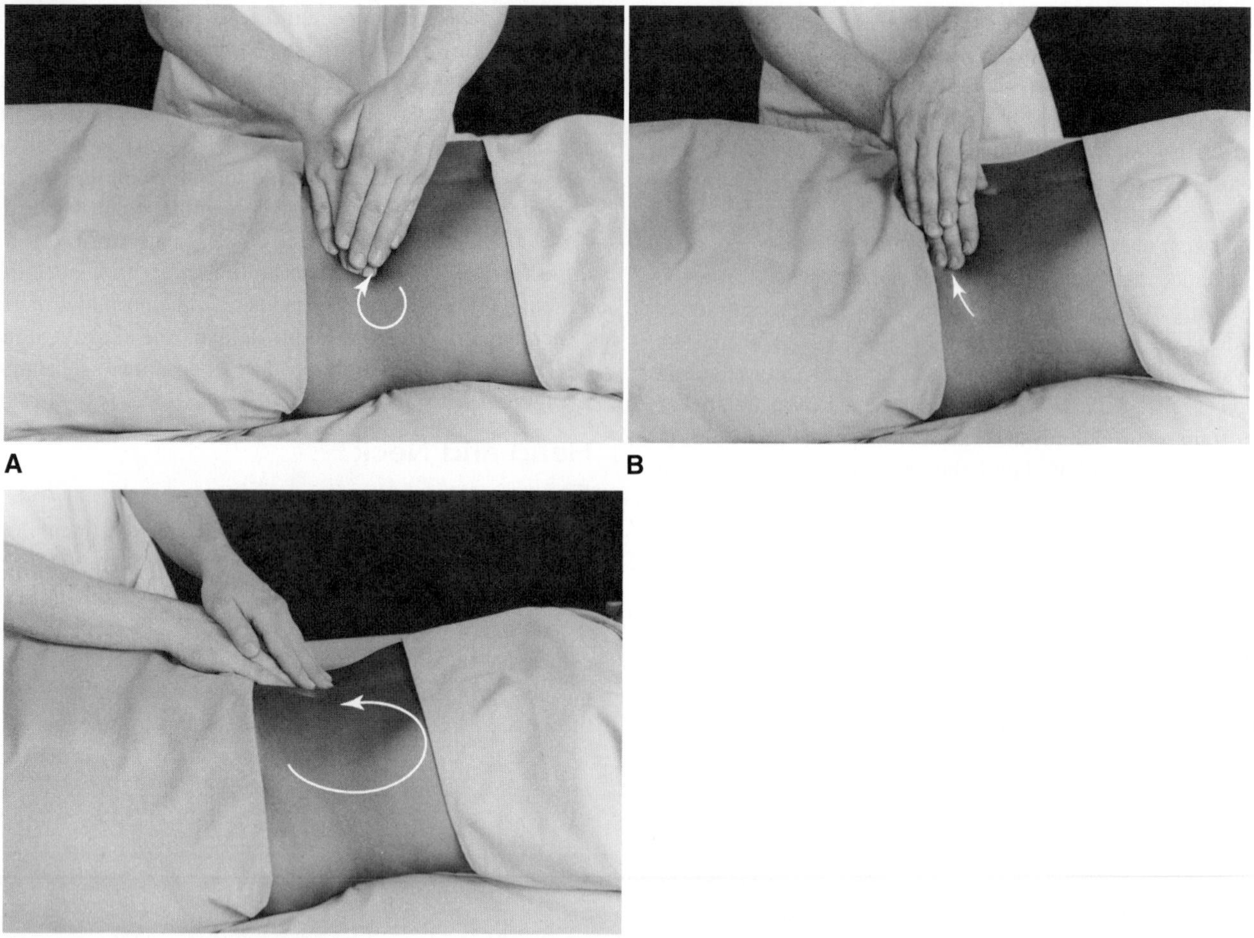

A

B

C

Figure **8-33**

Local kneading massage over the colon.

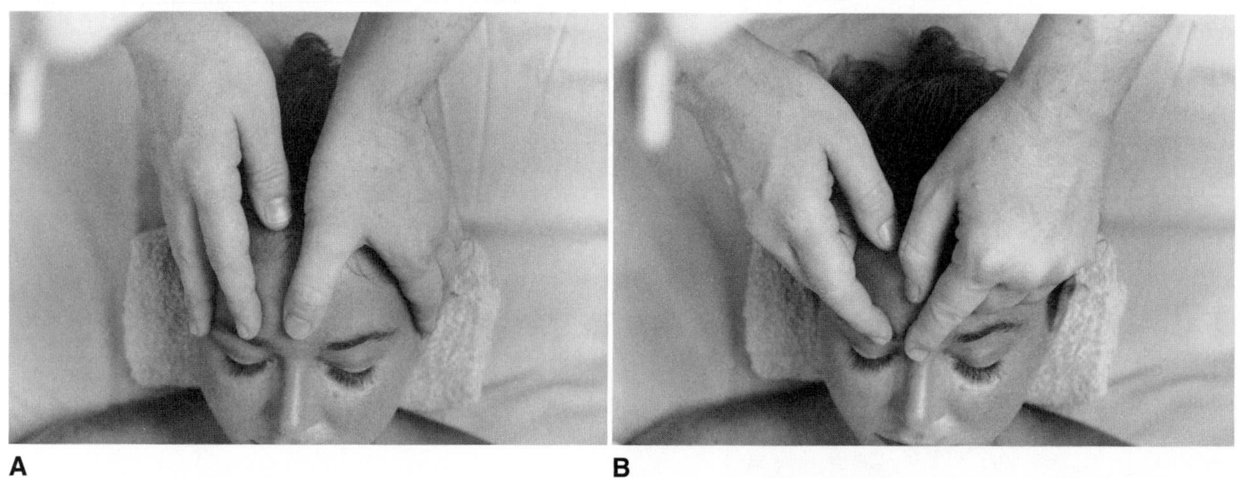


Figure **8-34**

Local massage to the muscles of the face.

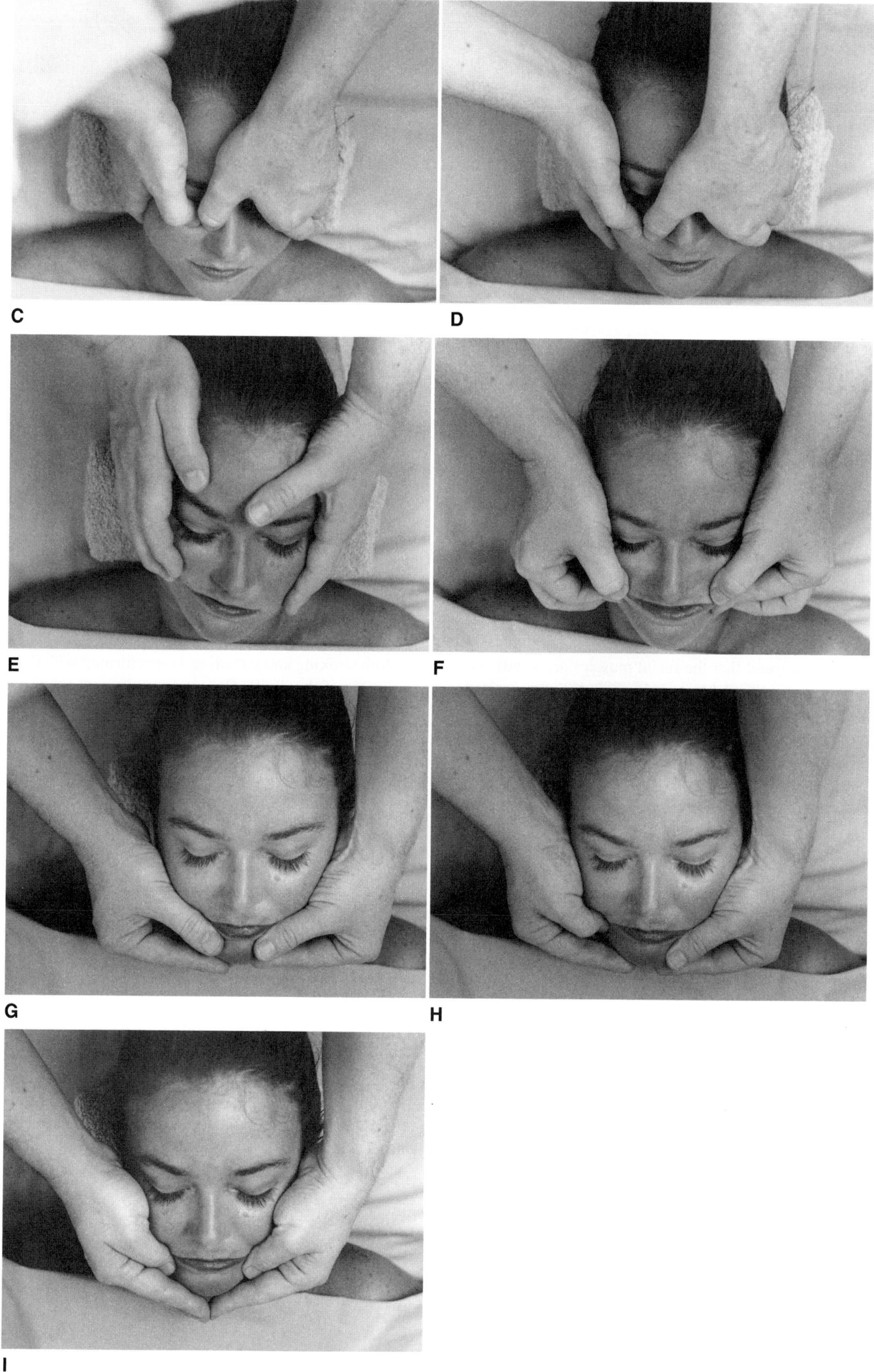

Figure 8-34, cont'd

### Table 8-9 Summary of the Actions of the Muscles of the Face

| MUSCLE | ACTION |
|---|---|
| Occipitofrontalis | Elevates eyebrow and root of the nose—wrinkles |
| Orbicularis oculi | Controls sphincter muscle of eyelids; reflex and voluntary control, fast or slow eyelid closure |
| Corrugator | Draws eyebrow medially and downward—frowning and in bright sunlight |
| Procerus | Draws down medial angle of eyebrow—transverse wrinkles on bridge of nose |
| Nasalis, two parts (transverse, alar dilator naris) | Elevates and widens nostrils as in deep breathing/sniff giving dilation of nose |
| Levator labii superiori, alaeque nasi | Lateral slip (long one) raises and everts upper lip; medial slip dilates nostril |
| Levator labii superioris | Raises and everts upper lip (sadness or serious look) |
| Zygomaticus minor | Elevates upper lip |
| Zygomaticus major | Draws angle of mouth upward and laterally as in laughing |
| Levator anguli oris | Raises angle of mouth NB: muscles 7, 8, 9, form naso-labial furrow |
| Orbicularis oris | Controls closure of lips; deep and oblique fibers compress lips against teeth; superficial parts—kiss |
| Risorius | Retracts angle of mouth—sardonic grin |
| Depressor anguli oris | Draws angle of mouth downward and laterally Opens mouth and sadness |
| Depressor labii inferioris | Draws lower lip down and slightly laterally (eating) |
| Mentalis | Raises and protrudes the lower lip (drinking) and expressing doubt |
| **Muscles of Mastication** | |
| Temporalis | Elevates jaw, close mouth, pulls jaw back |
| Buccinator (p) | Compresses cheeks against teeth |
| Masseter | Elevates jaw, clenches teeth |
| Medial and lateral pterygoids | Opens jaw, side-to-side grinding movements |

must be kept in mind that the facial muscles are small and delicate. They have little mass, are thin, and are located immediately over bony surfaces. A significant part of their structure is attached to the subcutaneous layers of the facial skin. For these reasons, the pressure of the massage strokes must be very light, particularly when the massage is being given to flaccid muscles. This type of massage is particularly applicable for facial paralysis and may help to prevent contractures and resolve fibrosis. Facial massage also provides significant sensory stimulation to the tissues, and this may assist in the recovery process if possible. This type of massage can also be readily taught to the patient. In this manner, treatment can be administered more frequently and at home.

In general, each stroke passes from insertion to origin, following the normal muscle action. Whenever possible, paralyzed muscles are supported in the position of normal function as the massage is being performed. In this regard, it is best for the patient to rest in supine lying, because gravity will have less effect on the facial muscles and structures than in the sitting position. Support may be given by one hand or by the fingers (Figure 8-34).

Both stroking and kneading are performed with the distal phalanges of the digits. One or more fingers, either or both thumbs, or the thumb and one or more fingers may be used to conform to the shape, size, and location of the muscles (see Figure 8-34). The muscles and muscle groups that are massaged are as follows:

| Muscle | Figure |
|---|---|
| Frontalis | Figure 8-34, *A* |
| Orbicularis oculi | Figure 8-34, *B, C* |
| Nasalis | Figure 8-34, *D* |
| Levator anguli oris | Figure 8-34, *E* |
| Zygomaticus major and minor | Figure 8-34, *E* |
| Orbicularis oris | Figure 8-34, *F* |
| Depressor anguli oris | Figure 8-34, *G* |
| Platysma | Figure 8-34, *H* |

At the completion of the local massage movements to the face, both hands perform superficial stroking from the chin to the temples (see Figure 8-34, *I*). Table 8-9 summarizes the main functions of the muscles of facial expression. Any of these muscles can be massaged in the manner described in this section.

Chapter 9

# Focal Massage Sequences

This chapter is designed to give a number of examples of how soft tissue manipulation (massage) techniques can be used as part of the treatment for specific pathologic situations. *Focal massage sequences* were defined in Chapter 4 as follows:

> *A combination of one or more different massage strokes applied to specific anatomical structures in order to achieve particularly desired effects.*

For example, a patient may have a large, chronic hematoma in the quadriceps muscle as a result of a severe blow to the thigh. When various massage techniques are directed to the treatment of the injured skin, subcutaneous tissues, and muscle tissues, it can rightly be called *focal massage.* In practice, however, massage techniques are given to more than just the affected tissues, so that the treatment is more like a combination of local and focal techniques. In the case of a hematoma in the thigh, some strokes will be given to the whole limb, whereas others will concentrate on the thigh and still others on the actual hematoma.

It is obviously not possible to describe focal massage techniques for all of the various structures in the body, nor is it necessary. Instead, the principles involved in the focal treatment of specific pathologies will be considered. It is important to emphasize that the focal massage techniques suggested here are meant to be used *in addition* to all of the other rehabilitation strategies that would be appropriate for a given situation. These can then be applied to any part of the anatomy affected by a similar problem. The following specific clinical problems are considered:

- Subacute or chronic edema
- Subacute or chronic hematoma
- Subacute or chronic cutaneous scar tissue
- Tendon or ligament adhesion
- Muscle contracture
- Colon dysfunction
- Muscle dysfunction

For each problem in the list, a specific massage sequence is suggested in a table format. The strokes that are given directly to the lesion/target tissue constitute the focal massage and have been italicized to mark their importance in the sequence. The other strokes have their own importance, in particular their effects on the surrounding circulation, thereby facilitating the entire healing process. All of the clinical problems discussed here are either subacute or chronic in nature. As a general rule, massage is not given to acutely inflamed tissues.

## DEPLETIVE MASSAGE

Before discussing each of the clinical situations listed, it is important to consider the concept of *depletive massage.* Because therapeutic massage is generally given to subacute or chronic conditions, there is commonly a significant problem with the local circulation. This may result in substantial interstitial swelling, more commonly called *edema.* Both subacute and chronic edema can be readily treated using a variety of massage techniques; however, the important adjunctive principle of depletive massage is needed for the treatment to be maximally effective.

Depletive massage is a concept used to describe the way in which certain strokes are applied to the tissues in the presence of subacute or chronic edema. Depletive massage can therefore be defined as:

> *The application of different massage strokes applied in a series of overlapping stages, beginning proximally and working distally in a subacute or chronically swollen limb.*

An important prerequisite for depletive massage techniques to be effective is the adjunctive use of elevation of the swollen limb. Because gravity tends to promote the collection of edema in the most distal parts of the affected limb, it makes sense that the swollen part should be elevated during treatment and afterward if possible. *Elevation* means that the swollen tissues must be higher than the patient's heart. In general, this means that the patient will lie supine on the treatment table and his or her limb will be supported on a bolster or several pillows (see Figure 3-6, *B,* for an example). It is important that the vessels draining blood and lymph from the swollen area have as straight a path as possible to the heart. Under these conditions, the various strokes are given to the tissues, beginning proximally and working distally to the end of the limb. This concept is depicted in Figure 9-1.

Depletive massage is therefore not a massage technique in itself, but rather a method of applying certain strokes. The techniques most often used in this way are stroking, effleurage, palmar kneading, finger pad kneading, and thumb pad kneading. A depletive method of application for each of these strokes simply involves massaging over proximal tissues first and then moving on to the more distal areas.

In Figure 9-1, *A,* the lower limb is divided into four sections, beginning at the thigh and finishing at the foot. The longer the limb, the more sections may be used. Typically, in the lower limb, section 1 would be the upper thigh and section 4 would be the forefoot and toes. Likewise, the upper limb is divided into four sections (Figure 9-1, *B*). Section 1 would be the upper arm, and section 4 would be the fingers and hand. The limbs are divided in this way to stress the importance of beginning the massage in the proximal sections. The rationale for this approach is that because the tissues are already congested, a pathway needs to be cleared before working on the swollen areas themselves. In this way, the venous and lymphatic channels will be opened to receive the fluids from the swollen areas.

Effleurage to the lower limb is a good example of this idea. Normally the stroke begins distally at the foot and ankle and finishes proximally in the femoral triangle (see Chapter 4). If this technique were applied to a very swollen foot, there would be no space to receive fluids, because the swelling causes collapse of the local capillaries, veins, and lymphatic vessels. The depletive massage concept aims to open up these vessels in the more proximal tissues first, thereby producing open channels that allow the fluids to move. Once the circulation is flowing in a more normal manner, the conventional direction and methods for the various strokes can be used.

At the end of treatment, there is the important issue of how to prevent the return of swelling in the limb when it becomes dependent again. The basic issue is one of pressure in the circulatory system. Essentially, there is a greater pressure (including gravity) forcing fluids into the tissue spaces than there is driving it back into the circulation. Over time, this pressure produces a net accumulation of fluids into the tissues (edema). The pressure tending to drive fluids back into the circulation can be increased with the use of elasticized stockings or socks. Many different types of stockings are available, but they all work in the same basic way. The better ones feature some kind of graduated pressure from distal to proximal in the garment. It is important that such a garment is applied at the end of treatment while the limb

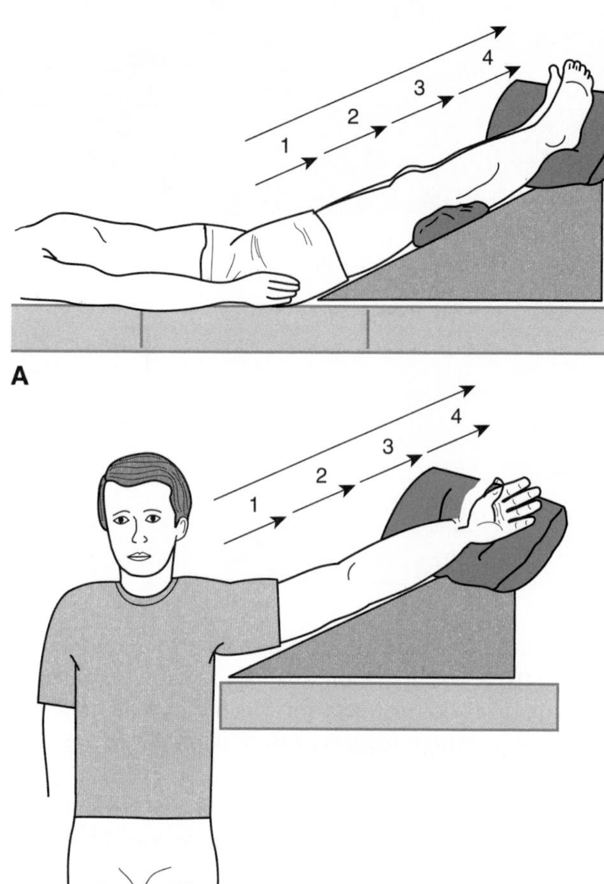


**Figure 9-1 The Concept of Depletive Massage for the Treatment of Chronic Edema**

**A,** The foot and lower leg region are chronically swollen. The patient is positioned so that the swollen limb is elevated higher than the heart, with the patient's legs comfortably supported and straight. The limb is divided into four sections: (1) the upper thigh, (2) the lower thigh and knee, (3) the calf and leg, and (4) the ankle and foot. Massage strokes begin at the thigh section and progress in several stages along the limb to eventually reach the toes. Stroking, effleurage, and the various forms of kneading can all be given in this manner. **B,** The forearm and hand are chronically swollen. The patient is positioned so that the swollen limb is elevated higher than the heart, with the entire limb comfortably supported and straight. The limb is divided into four sections: (1) the upper arm, (2) the elbow, (3) the forearm, and (4) the wrist and hand. Massage strokes begin at the upper arm section and progress in several stages along the limb to eventually reach the fingers. Stroking, effleurage, and the various forms of kneading can all be given in this manner.

is still in elevation. Of course, the patient is instructed to keep the limb elevated as much as possible during the day.

## CHRONIC EDEMA

Chronic interstitial swelling in the limbs (edema) is a potentially serious condition if it is allowed to persist, especially in older patients. It is typically produced by trauma to the tissues (such as a fall), or it is the result of an underlying problem with the circulation. In either case, long-term congestion of the tissues can lead to stiffness and pain, which can result in deformity and loss of function. In the lower limb, this may mean an inability to walk, resulting in the patient spending most of the day in a chair or bed. If the patient is older, this can lead to a serious health decline caused by inactivity. Removing edema and increasing functional range of motion in joints and soft tissues is therefore a top priority, especially in the elderly patient with a swollen lower limb. An exception to this case might occur if the swelling in the lower limbs is the end result of severe congestive heart failure. Fluids are then offloaded into the tissues to relieve the load on the heart (less fluid to pump). In this case, vigorous attempts to treat the swelling might result in cardiac complications. Obviously, close cooperation with the patient's medical team will be needed to manage the situation properly.

One of the reasons chronic edema is a potentially serious problem is that it tends to organize; it becomes thickened, thereby preventing normal movement and function. In addition, the stiffness is often painful, adding to the patient's unwillingness to move the affected parts. This lack of movement results in even more stiffness. Much of the stiffness is produced by a fibrosis that occurs in the interstitial spaces. Under normal circumstances, the plasma proteins are unable to escape from the capillaries into the interstitial fluid (tissue fluid) because their molecular size is too large to pass through the vessels. However, one of the consequences of local trauma to the tissues is that the capillary walls open up and allow these large molecules to pass into the tissues. Many of the plasma proteins are concerned with the ability of the blood to clot, and this process is triggered in the tissue spaces. The end result of the clotting process is the formation of fibrin threads, eventually leading to scar tissue. Such interstitial scarring causes adhesion of the various layers of the tissues and prevents the free movements of one tissue on another. A classic sign of this process is the presence of pitting edema. In this case, an indentation (pit) is left behind in the skin and subcutaneous tissues when the thumb is pushed into a chronically swollen area.

The importance of the lymphatic system in the resolution of chronic edema cannot be overstated. Once the acute inflammatory stage has passed and the capillary walls have closed up, the plasma proteins and other large molecules cannot get back into the capillary network. The only place for them to go is into the lymphatic vessels. In many ways, the lymphatic vessels act as the drainage system for the tissues. Because the lymphatic vessels are thinly walled, without a well-defined valve structure, any massage stroke that involves alternate squeezing and relaxation of pressure will have a powerful effect in promoting flow in this system. However, the normal architecture of the lymphatic system has to be in place for this to work efficiently. Where the lymphatic network has been disrupted, such as may be the case with significant lymph node resection, the swelling may be more widespread and treatment more challenging. This situation is considered at length in Chapter 12, which explores decongestive therapy for the treatment of lymphedema.

Localized, chronic edema can be mobilized using a variety of techniques, including massage. The basic sequence is listed in the tables that follow, and the specific focal massage techniques are italicized. Because the limb is elevated, the therapist may need to stand on a suitable platform, or the therapist may face the patient's foot and reverse the usual positioning (i.e., by working from knee to hip and from foot to knee). In each case, the massage is always performed from distal to proximal structures (Tables 9-1 and 9-2).

## HEMATOMA

A hematoma (bruise) is the consequence of bleeding in the tissues, usually as the result of direct trauma. In many cases, the trauma produces a compressive force on the tissues, such as in a kick, punch, or fall. The compressive force of the blow ruptures small capillaries and possibly the small arterioles and venules. The end result is bleeding into the tissue

**Table 9-1 Focal Massage Sequence for Chronic Edema in the Foot and Ankle Region**

| PROCEDURE* | REPETITIONS |
|---|---|
| Depletive stroking to the whole limb | 3 |
| Depletive effleurage to the thigh | 3 |
| Palmar kneading to the thigh | 3 |
| Wringing to the medial thigh | 3 |
| Picking up to the thigh | 2 |
| Depletive effleurage to the thigh | 3 |
| Finger pad kneading around the knee | 3 |
| *Palmar kneading to the calf and leg muscles* | 4 |
| *Thumb pad kneading to the anterior tibial muscles* | 4 |
| *Picking up to the calf* | 4 |
| Depletive effleurage to the thigh, calf, and leg | 3 |
| *Finger pad kneading around the ankle region* | 4 |
| *Thumb pad kneading to the foot* | 4 |
| Effleurage to the whole limb | 3 |

Italics indicate specific focal massage techniques.
*Performed with the patient supine and the lower limb elevated.

### Table 9-2 Focal Massage Sequence for Chronic Edema in the Forearm and Hand Region

| PROCEDURE* | REPETITIONS |
|---|---|
| Depletive stroking to the whole limb | 3 |
| Depletive effleurage to the upper arm | 3 |
| Palmar kneading to the biceps and triceps | 3 |
| Picking up to the biceps and triceps | 3 |
| Depletive effleurage to the upper arm | 3 |
| Finger pad kneading around the elbow region | 3 |
| *Palmar kneading to the forearm muscles* | 3 |
| *Thumb pad kneading to the forearm muscles* | 3 |
| Depletive effleurage to the upper arm and forearm | 3 |
| *Thumb pad kneading to the wrist, hand, and fingers* | 4 |
| Effleurage to the whole limb | 4 |

Italics indicate specific focal massage techniques.
*Performed with the patient sitting or supine and the upper limb elevated.

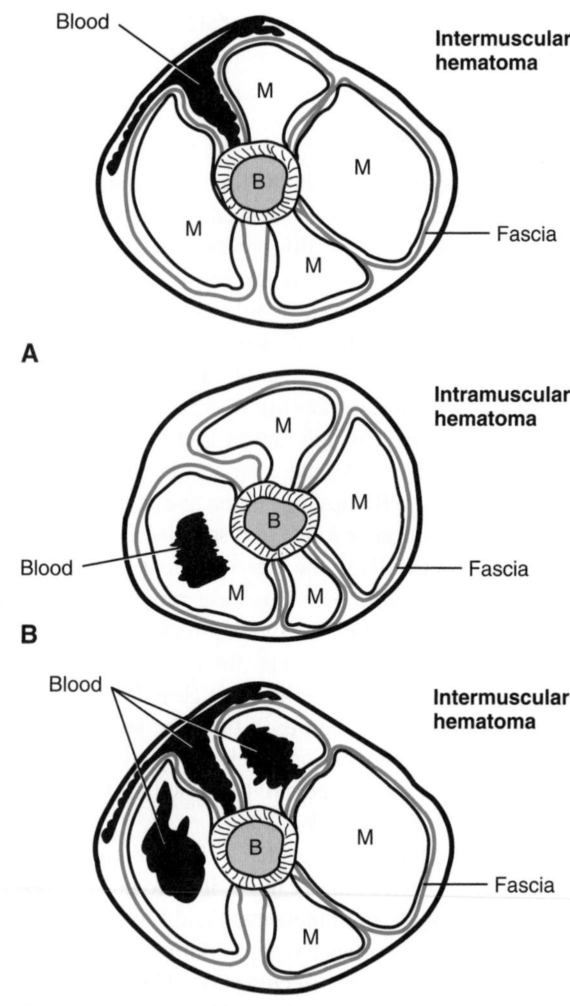


**Figure 9-2 Intermuscular and Intramuscular Hematoma**

These diagrams represent a cross-section through the mid-thigh region. Each muscle is contained within its own connective tissue bag. This bag is extremely thin, and a fine serous fluid is normally present in the potential space between the muscle bags. **A,** Trauma has caused bleeding into these potential spaces, between the muscles (hence the name), and into the subcutaneous tissues. The surface bruise may be widespread, affecting many different tissues in a wide area. **B,** Fibers have been ruptured deep within the muscle, and most of the bleeding is contained within the affected muscle. In this case, surface bruising may be much less than expected. **C,** A combination of both intermuscular and intramuscular bleeding is depicted—the result of severe trauma to a limb, perhaps in an automobile crash. There will be extensive surface bruising and bleeding deep with the muscles. *M,* Muscle; *B,* bone.

spaces. Alternatively, the bleeding can result from trauma associated with tearing of the tissues, perhaps by a broken bone or shattered glass fragments. In either case, the end result is bleeding into the tissue spaces as a result of a compressive force. Although the hope is that the bleeding will cease after a few minutes, especially with appropriate first-aid treatment, the trauma will initiate the body's reaction to injuries of all types, namely inflammation.

For minor trauma (a simple fall with no broken bones), the classic signs and symptoms of acute inflammation (pain, swelling, redness, and heat) will become maximal at about 24 hours after the injury. If all goes well, the healing process will take over and in about 7 to 10 days postinjury, most, if not all, of the original problems should be well on the way to full recovery. If healing is delayed for some reason (e.g., by poor circulation or infection), the condition may become subacute and eventually chronic if healing continues to be slow. During the acute stages of traumatic inflammation, massage is generally contraindicated because of the possibility of causing further disruption, and therefore possible bleeding, of the damaged capillaries. In the subacute and chronic stages, however, massage techniques can be particularly useful. These issues are addressed in much more detail in Chapter 5.

## Intermuscular Hematoma

A variety of massage techniques are useful as part of the treatment plan for a chronic hematoma. Of course, most bruises eventually heal, and the tissues return to normal color and texture. The colors of the bruise represent the different absorption rates of the bile pigments in the blood (bilirubin and biliverdin). The bruise confirms that capillaries have been broken and blood has leaked out into the interstitial spaces, especially between the fascial planes that separate one muscle from another (Figure 9-2, *A*). This kind of bruise is the so-called intermuscular hematoma. It is characterized by a widespread visible bruise, tenderness on palpation (especially at the site of the initial trauma), and pain on stretching of the tissues such as during related joint movements. In the limbs, gravity will usually cause the blood to track along the fascial planes between muscles and subcutaneous tissues toward the most distal areas. The best example of this effect is probably seen in the upper limb following a fracture of the head of the humerus. Although the fracture occurs at the shoulder region, the entire arm can appear purple in color as the blood tracks down the limb toward the hand. Interestingly, the discoloration spirals around the limb, clearly showing the pathway taken by the blood. In most cases, this type of hematoma will eventually heal, leaving minimal aftereffects. Occasionally, however, the bleeding between the muscles results in scar tissue formation, which causes muscle and skin stiffness because the muscles are not sliding properly on each other. The situation can be improved with a variety of treatments, especially massage and active movements where possible.

### Intramuscular Hematoma

A more potentially serious result of deep trauma is the formation of an intramuscular hematoma. As the name suggests, the bleeding has occurred from torn capillaries deep within the muscle tissue itself. There may be only a small surface bruise, but there is sizable internal swelling, which is often exquisitely tender in the acute stages of injury (Figure 9-2, *B*). It is likely that muscle fibers have been ruptured during an explosive muscle contraction, such as might occur during a sporting event. Alternatively, it can occur when the tissues are struck by an object traveling at high speed, such as a baseball or golf ball. The tremendous kinetic energy of the ball is absorbed in a small area of tissue, causing a huge compressive force. As a result, the tissue is destroyed, and the capillaries rupture and cause bleeding. Once triggered, the inflammatory process is implemented with all of the common signs of acute inflammation. The situation must be handled carefully because of the chance of causing further bleeding, especially within the next several days after the initial injury. In the acute and subacute situation, focal massage to this type of hematoma is usually contraindicated. If the hematoma becomes chronic, then focal massage can be an effective method of mobilizing the superficial and deep tissues. Great care is still needed, however, at this time because of the possibility of myositis ossificans, initiated by an overly vigorous treatment.

Although the two kinds of hematoma are obviously different, it is quite possible to have both types within the tissues at the same time. These hematomas might easily occur following severe trauma to a limb as a result of a motor vehicle crash. Figure 9-2, *C*, illustrates such a combination. In all cases, however, the basic approach to treatment using massage is similar. First, a series of depletive strokes is given to the region, followed by strokes that generally mobilize the tissues. These strokes are followed by focal massage using finger pad and thumb pad kneading around the center of the hematoma. The finger pad and thumb pad kneading is performed in a series of overlapping, concentric circles, beginning several inches from the center of the hematoma. Typically, this will be at the margins of the visible bruise. The overlapping circles of kneading gradually converge toward the center of the hematoma (Figure 9-3). If the tissues are tender and treatment elicits a painful response, it is a sign that the kneading should be given with only light pressure, especially to an intramuscular hematoma. These strokes are followed by effleurage to the entire limb. For best results, this type of massage sequence should be included with other treatment approaches, such as the use of appropriate electrophysical agents (modalities) and active exercise programs.

Suitable focal massage sequences to address an intermuscular and an intramuscular hematoma to the thigh are given in Tables 9-3 and 9-4.

## CUTANEOUS SCAR TISSUE

The treatment of cutaneous scar tissue has a long history in massage. Whenever the skin and subcutaneous tissues are cut, bleeding ensues, although it eventually ceases because of the clotting mechanisms of the blood. The clot is eventually converted to scar (fibrous) tissue, sealing the damage to the tissues. Depending on the size and depth of the original cut, the skin may be able to regenerate so that eventually

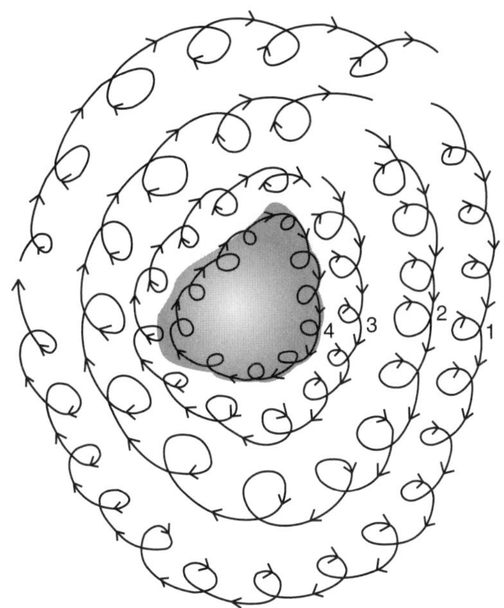


**Figure 9-3 The Concept of Concentric Kneading to Treat a Chronic Intermuscular or Intramuscular Hematoma**

Finger pad or thumb pad kneading is given in a series of overlapping concentric circles, beginning at the margins of the visible bruise and gradually working toward the center of the hematoma. The entire series of overlapping circles is repeated four times. Kneading pressure is light for the first series of strokes and gradually becomes deeper by the fourth repetition. If the tissues are tender and massage elicits pain, then only light pressure should be used.

### Table 9-3 Focal Massage Sequence for a Subacute/Chronic Intermuscular Hematoma in the Thigh Region

| PROCEDURE* | REPETITIONS |
|---|---|
| Depletive stroking to the whole limb | 3 |
| Depletive effleurage to the whole limb | 3 |
| Palmar kneading to the thigh | 3 |
| *Finger pad kneading in concentric circles around the margins of the hematoma* | 4 |
| Picking up to the thigh | 3 |
| Wringing to the thigh | 3 |
| Effleurage to the whole limb | 3 |

Italics indicate specific focal massage techniques.
*Performed with the patient supine and the lower limb elevated.

### Table 9-4 Focal Massage Sequence for a Chronic Intramuscular Hematoma in the Thigh Region

| PROCEDURE* | REPETITIONS |
|---|---|
| Depletive stroking to the whole limb | 3 |
| Depletive effleurage to the thigh | 3 |
| Palmar kneading to the thigh | 3 |
| *Finger pad kneading in concentric circles around the margins of the hematoma* | 4 |
| *Thumb pad kneading in concentric circles around the margins of the hematoma* | 4 |
| Wringing to the thigh | 3 |
| Picking up to the thigh | 3 |
| Effleurage to the whole limb | 3 |

Italics indicate specific focal massage techniques.
*Performed with the patient supine and the lower limb elevated.

the scar is difficult, if not impossible, to see. Obviously, the regenerative powers of the skin are closely related to the age of the individual. The older a person gets, the more time the skin takes to heal and the more obvious is the scarring that occurs following injury.

As the largest organ of the body, the skin is an important structure, and damage to the skin can have profound effects on the functional mobility of the patient. Human skin, and the subcutaneous tissues supporting it, is designed to be an elastic and mobile structure in most parts of the body. When it is cut surgically or lacerated by trauma, there is a strong tendency for the scar tissue to stick the various tissue layers together. When this happens, the skin loses its mobility, and functional movements are often impaired. For example, a deep laceration in the anterior thigh region can seriously restrict knee flexion. Without proper treatment, functional active range of motion in the knee can be seriously reduced, making it difficult for the patient to descend a flight of stairs or sit down in an armchair. Mobilization of the scar and surrounding tissue is therefore an important treatment goal

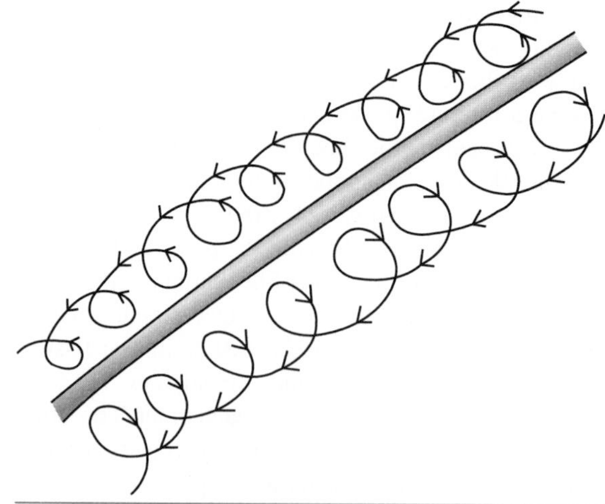

**Figure 9-4 Thumb Pad Kneading for a Linear Scar**

Several rows of thumb pad kneading are given to the skin adjacent to a linear scar, gradually working toward the scar. The direction of pressure in each circle of kneading is such that the tissues are pulled away from the scar. This means that the therapist applies pressure in a clockwise direction on the right side of the scar and counterclockwise on the left side. Alternatively, one side of the scar can be held down with one hand, while thumb pad kneading is given with the thumb pad of the other hand. As an alternative, thumb pad kneading can be given with both hands working simultaneously but out of phase with each other.

for such cases. Two different types of cutaneous scars will be considered here, although the basic massage treatment concepts are similar. These are linear and diffuse scars. Great care is needed when dealing with any fresh scar, especially one where the tissues are very thin. In these cases, focal massage techniques are probably best avoided until the scar has further healed.

## Linear Scars

This type of scar is typically the result of surgery or trauma with a very sharp object, such as a knife or glass. The focal massage techniques concentrate on mobilizing the scar by using thumb pad kneading. The concept of beginning the massage a short distance away from the target tissue and then working toward the lesion applies here. This technique mobilizes the surrounding tissues as well as the target tissues. The therapist may also find it helpful to hold down one side of the scar with the thumb and thenar muscles of one hand while the thumb pad of the other hand kneads the other side of the scar, pulling the tissues away from the scar. This means that the kneading will be given in a clockwise direction on the right side of the scar and a counterclockwise motion on the left side. Thumb pad kneading can also be given with both hands working simultaneously but out of phase. These concepts are depicted in Figure 9-4. Table 9-5 presents a suggested sequence for focal massage to a linear scar.

Table 9-5 **Focal Massage Sequence for Linear Scar Tissue in the Skin**

| PROCEDURE* | REPETITIONS |
|---|---|
| Stroking to the surrounding area | 3 |
| Effleurage to the area (or limb) | 3 |
| Palmar or finger pad kneading to the surrounding areas | 3 |
| *Thumb pad kneading along each side of the scar* | 4 |
| *Skin rolling across the scar in different directions* | 4 |
| Effleurage to the area (or limb) | 3 |

Italics indicate specific focal massage techniques.
*Performed with the patient comfortably supported and positioned so that the scar is readily available for treatment.

Table 9-6 **Focal Massage Sequence for Diffuse Scar Tissue in the Skin**

| PROCEDURE* | REPETITIONS |
|---|---|
| Stroking to the whole area | 3 |
| Palmar kneading to the whole area | 3 |
| *Finger pad kneading in concentric circles around the margins of the scar* | 4<br>4 |
| *Thumb pad kneading along the area of the scar* | 4 |
| *Skin rolling across the scar in different directions* | 3 |
| Effleurage to the whole limb | 3 |

Italics indicate specific focal massage techniques.
*Performed with the patient comfortably supported and positioned so that the scar is readily available for treatment.

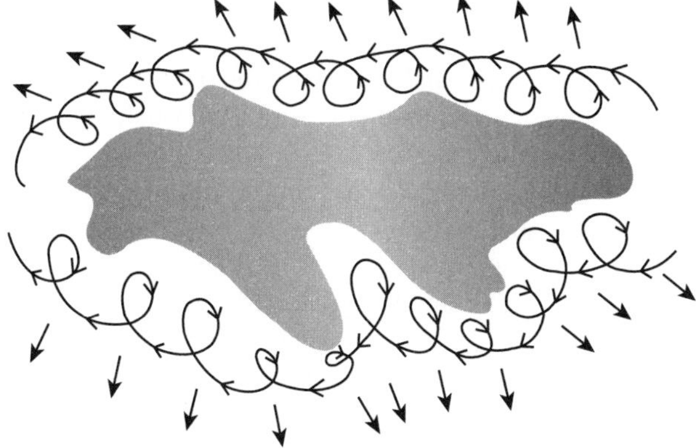

Figure **9-5** Thumb Pad Kneading for a Diffuse Scar

A series of overlapping, concentric circles of thumb pad kneading is given to the entire area. Kneading begins in the healthy tissues adjacent to the margins of the scar and then gradually works inwardly toward the center of the scar. The kneading is performed so that the tissues are pulled away from the center of the scar. Alternatively, the area of the scar can be halved and the same principles of kneading for a linear scar can then be applied (see Figure 9-4).

### Diffuse Scars

A diffuse scar is usually the result of major trauma or burning to the area; for example, extensive complicated fractures following a serious motor vehicle crash. A similar concept to the focal massage of a linear scar can be applied to the treatment of a diffuse scar. In this case, the total area of the scar can be divided in half and thumb pad kneading given to each side in a manner similar to that used for a linear scar (see Figure 9-4). Figure 9-5 and Table 9-6 presents a suggested sequence for focal massage to a diffuse scar.

## MUSCLE, TENDON, OR LIGAMENT ADHESION

Whenever there is unresolved (chronic) inflammation involving a muscle, tendon, tendon sheath, or ligament, there will be a certain amount of fibrous tissue forming a scar that tends to adhere to the surrounding tissues. Thus there will be a marked decrease in intertissue mobility, resulting in a greater or lesser degree of pain and dysfunction. Mobilizing these adherent tissues is an obvious priority in the treatment plan. A certain degree of improvement can be expected when tissues are stuck to their neighbor, but if this situation has existed for many weeks or months, adaptive shortening will have set in and it will be much more difficult to see improvements in range of motion in a short time frame. As mentioned previously in this chapter, the reengineering of collagen tissue does not occur overnight, and many weeks of treatment are often needed for patients to recover from serious contractures in muscles, tendons ligaments, and joint capsules. Some form of serial casting will probably be needed to produce long-term lengthening in contracted tissues, especially muscles and tendons.

In the case where there is a local binding of tissues, without serious adaptive shortening, focal massage techniques can be helpful for restoring pain-free range of motion. The general principle is that the techniques are given at right angles to the long axis of the affected, muscle, tendon, tendon sheath, or ligament. Here the technique aims at loosening the individual fibers in the structure by rolling them on their neighboring tissues. This is, in fact, the primary concept already described for the technique of deep friction (see Chapter 4). Although deep friction techniques are usually given using the pad of the index finger, reinforced by the middle finger, the stroke can also be given with one or two thumbs and with the finger pads of either or both hands. For example, the larger the muscle tissue to be treated, the more digits will be needed to cover the tissues. Deep frictions can also be given by the finger pads of one hand, reinforced by the other, when the structures to be treated are deep in the tissues. To be effective, deep frictions must be performed properly. The specific points of technique for transverse frictions were discussed in Chapter 4, and the reader is directed there for more details. Figure 9-6 illustrates the direction of the transverse friction strokes.

The general principles of mobilizing the areas surrounding the target tissue first and then working in to focus on the lesion itself are used in the sequence presented in Table 9-7. Finger pad and thumb pad kneading are given to the local area in order to promote the deep circulation and mobilize the tissues generally. Deep transverse frictions are then used to mobilize the exact areas of adhesion. Finally, effleurage is given over the area to promote the general circulation of blood and lymph throughout the treated area.

Generally speaking, the techniques used to treat an adherent tendon or ligament are the same ones used to treat a muscle contracture. Obviously, the majority of muscles are much larger than tendons and ligaments; therefore the techniques will need some adjustment to coincide with the larger physical size of most muscles, but the principles remain the same as those discussed previously. A suitable sequence of strokes is listed in Table 9-8. Note that there are more strokes directed toward mobilizing the whole muscle, especially if the muscle is large, such as the quadriceps femoris. If the muscle is small, such as one of the thenar muscles, it may not be possible to perform some of the techniques, so they will be omitted. Nonetheless, the aim of the treatment is to produce as much mobility as possible between the individual components of the muscle and its surrounding tissues. In this regard, a full range of relaxed passive movements will greatly help to maintain and increase muscle length (see Chapter 4 for examples).

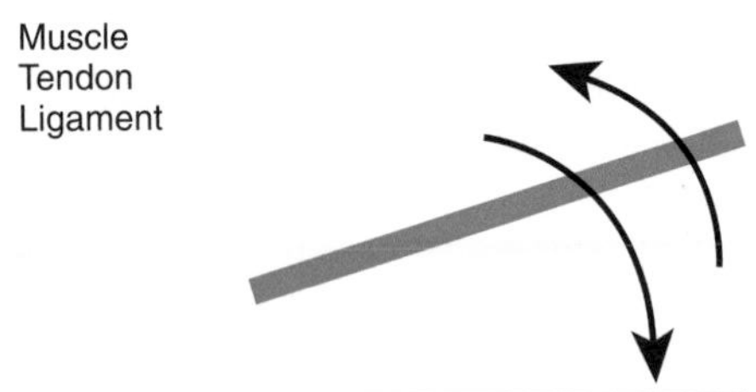


**Figure 9-6 Direction for Mobilizing Muscle, Tendon, or Ligament Adhesion**

Massage strokes are given at right angles to the long axis of the involved tissue. A curvilinear direction is used in most cases because the tissues are somewhat rounded in cross-section.

**Table 9-7 Focal Massage Sequence for Tendon or Ligament Adhesion**

| PROCEDURE* | REPETITIONS |
|---|---|
| Deep stroking to the whole limb | 3 |
| *Finger pad kneading in concentric circles around the margins of tendon or ligament* | 3 |
| *Thumb pad kneading around the tendon or ligament* | 4 |
| *Deep transverse frictions to the tendon or ligament* | 4 |
| Effleurage to the whole limb | 3 |

Italics indicate specific focal massage techniques.
*Performed with the patient comfortably supported and positioned so that the tendon or ligament is readily available for treatment; the tendon or ligament should be on full stretch for the treatment to be effective.

## COLON DYSFUNCTION

Various types of abdominal massage have been advocated for the treatment of disorders of colon (large intestine) function. Essentially, the goal of these forms of massage is to stimulate the normal flow of the contents of the large intestine. This technique can be taught to the patient and used at home, although in a modified way. As usual, the focal massage strokes are both preceded and followed by some general techniques to the abdominal wall. For treatment in a clinic, the patient is comfortably supported in the supine position, lying with pillows under both knees so that the hips and knees are in a small degree of flexion. This position removes stress on the anterior abdominal muscles, thereby helping the patient to relax (see Figure 3-7, *A*).

The two focal treatment techniques are deep stroking and reinforced kneading, and both are given using a modified,

**Table 9-8 Focal Massage Sequence for Muscle Contracture/Adhesion**

| PROCEDURE* | REPETITIONS |
|---|---|
| Depletive stroking to the whole limb | 3 |
| Depletive effleurage to the whole limb | 3 |
| Palmar kneading to the affected muscle(s) | 3 |
| *Finger pad kneading in concentric circles around the areas of the contracture* | 4 |
| *Thumb pad kneading to the contracture* | 4 |
| *Deep transverse frictions to the muscle at the contracture site* | 4 |
| Wringing to the affected muscle | 4 |
| Picking up to the affected muscle | 3 |
| Effleurage to the whole limb | 3 |

Italics indicate specific focal massage techniques.
*Performed with the patient comfortably supported and positioned so that the muscle is readily available for treatment; in most cases, the affected muscle should be on full stretch for the treatment to be effective. If the affected muscle is small, it may not be possible to perform palmar kneading, wringing, or picking up, in which case these strokes should be omitted.

depletive manner. The normal direction of flow in the large intestine is clockwise, and it is important not to use massage strokes in the reverse direction. However, to facilitate the normal emptying of the colon, a modified depletive technique is used. For the purposes of the massage strokes, the colon can be divided into four parts, beginning at the distal end: (1) the sigmoid colon and rectum, (2) the descending colon, (3) the transverse colon, and (4) the ascending colon. These segments of the colon are depicted in Figure 9-7. Assuming the colon is congested, it is important to clear the distal parts of the intestine before the proximal parts. If treatment began at the proximal end, it would clearly increase the already congested colon. Therefore, both stroking and kneading follow a course that begins at the distal end of the intestine and works backward to the beginning of the colon. Each segment (numbered 1 to 4) is treated in order, starting at the proximal end of the segment and working in the appropriate direction to the distal end. Although each segment is treated in the same direction as the normal flow in the colon, the progression of the segments is in the opposite direction (counterclockwise). In this manner, the contents of the colon are moved in a depletive manner. This concept is also illustrated in Figure 9-7.

A sequence of strokes, including focal techniques for the colon, is listed in Table 9-9. The sequence can be given to the patient by the therapist in a clinical setting, or the various strokes can be taught to the patient so that they may be performed at home several times per day. The patient is usually taught to use his or her right hand, reinforced by the left, while performing each stroke. Because the abdominal wall is mobile, these strokes can be given through a thin layer of material, such as a cotton T-shirt. This makes it easy for the patient to slide his or her hands over the abdominal tissues during the various stroking techniques. At the same time, when the deep kneading is performed, there is sufficient friction between the patient's hand, the T-shirt, and the skin of the abdomen for the stroke to be performed properly.

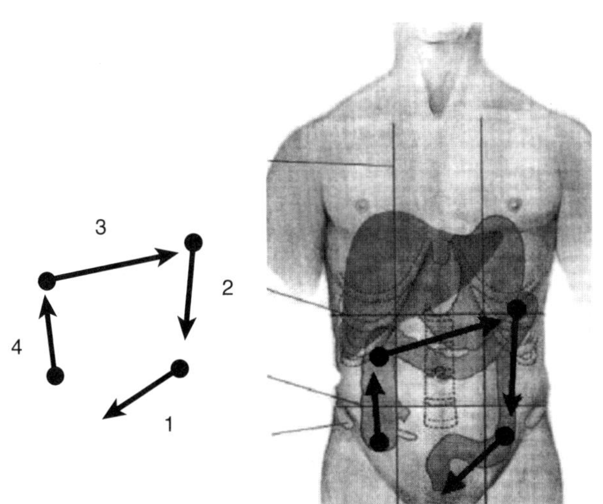


**Figure 9-7 Segments of the Colon and Direction of Treatment for the Depletive Strokes**

Each of the four segments of the colon is shown, together with an arrow to indicate the direction and order in which the depletive strokes are used. The four segments are *(1)* the sigmoid colon and rectum, *(2)* the descending colon, *(3)* the transverse colon, and *(4)* the ascending colon.

## MUSCLE DYSFUNCTION: FACILITATION OF MUSCLE CONTRACTION

Focal massage techniques can be used to facilitate a muscle contraction when the patient finds it difficult to initiate muscle activity. These techniques facilitate voluntary contraction of the muscle and do not strengthen it in any way. Several techniques are able to facilitate muscle contraction and therefore can be classified as legitimate focal massage strokes. The object is to stimulate afferent (sensory) nerve fibers in the muscle(s) concerned and the skin overlying the same muscle(s). In most, but not all, cases, the sensory nerve fibers innervating the skin that overlies a muscle(s) come from the same segments of the spinal cord that supply motor fibers to the same muscle(s). Therefore stimulating the skin over a muscle activates a wide range of mechanoreceptors that discharge a sensory barrage of impulses into the spinal cord at the same levels, which supply the motor nerves to the muscle beneath the skin. This barrage of sensory impulses raises the level of central excitability of the motor cells in the spinal cord, thereby making it easier for the patient to initiate a voluntary contraction.

In addition to stimulating sensory fibers in the skin, focal massage to a muscle has a much more powerful and direct effect on the muscle. The sensory fibers in the muscle spindles (especially the Ia afferents) are exquisitely sensitive to

**Table 9-9 Focal Massage Sequence for Colon Dysfunction**

| PROCEDURE* | REPETITIONS |
|---|---|
| Superficial stroking to the abdomen in a clockwise direction | 3 |
| *Deep, depletive stroking in a counterclockwise direction, beginning at the sigmoid colon* | 3 |
| *Reinforced palmar kneading in a counterclockwise direction, beginning at the sigmoid colon* | 4 |
| *Deep, depletive stroking in a counterclockwise direction to the whole abdomen, beginning at the sigmoid colon* | 4 |
| | 3 |
| Superficial stroking to the abdomen in a clockwise direction | 3 |

Italics indicate specific focal massage techniques.
*Performed with the patient supine, with knees supported in slight flexion.

changes in its overall length. Activating these fibers will stimulate the stretch reflex pathway, directly activating the muscle being massaged.

The type of manipulations that are most likely to be effective in facilitating muscle contraction are the percussive strokes, especially hacking, clapping, and vibrations. These techniques can be integrated into the rest of a treatment program as and where they seem most appropriate. They should be viewed as yet another option in the list of techniques available for muscle reeducation.

# Chapter 10

# Massage for the Patient with a Respiratory Condition

Massage techniques for patients suffering from respiratory disorders center around two basic concepts: (1) helping patients gain control of their breathing pattern by assisting them to relax, and (2) helping patients to loosen and clear mucus from their lungs. Although these are important issues for the patient, they are a relatively small part of the overall rehabilitation process for the management of pulmonary disorders. A wide variety of treatment techniques, including massage, have been used for this purpose over many decades in most parts of the world. This treatment is generally referred to as *chest physical therapy* (Frownfelter & Dean, 2006; Hillegass & Sadowsky, 1994; Irwin & Techlin, 2005; Watchie, 1995; Webber & Pryor, 1993).

Many patients who suffer from chronic respiratory distress could be significantly helped by some simple and cost-effective procedures. These techniques might be tried before more expensive equipment and medications are ordered, and, of course, much of the physical therapy involves teaching patients a variety of strategies to help themselves through distress plus techniques to prevent further episodes. These valuable and cost-effective treatments are lost if the patient receives only a machine and medication. Thus the typical goals of a chest physical therapy program are listed in Box 10-1.

Health statistics show a consistent increase in the incidence of chronic obstructive pulmonary disease (COPD). From 1950 to 1960, for example, deaths attributable to emphysema and chronic bronchitis increased more than fourfold (Carey, 1967). In an additional study (1950-1965), the mortality rate was shown to double every 5 years. Deaths increased almost eightfold, from 3157 patients in 1950 to 23,700 patients in 1965 (Weiss et al., 1969). By the late 1970s, data suggest that about 27% of adult males and 13% of females have symptoms of spirometric abnormalities indicative of COPD (Petty, 1978). To make matters worse, there has been a resurgence of serious diseases such as tuberculosis and the emergence of new and dangerous strains of flu viruses. It is clear from the statistics that the quality and duration of many lives are significantly affected by this disease. In effect, COPD is rapidly becoming one of the most important health problems of our time. It behooves health professions to upgrade their understanding and capacity to provide effective treatment. As with just about every facet of modern health care, a coordinated and consultative approach involving a variety of expert practitioners is likely to provide the best care for the patient.

Several important treatment concepts are involved in chest physical therapy, the most important of these being postural drainage, percussion, vibration and shaking, facilitation techniques, breathing exercise and retraining, relaxation techniques, posture correction and retraining, graded exercise, and endurance programs. In addition, patient and caregiver education are critical for patient compliance and long-term success. A detailed discussion of all these areas is well beyond the scope of this chapter. Instead, the intention here is to define and describe the contributions of massage techniques to the treatment of patients with a respiratory disorder; the part played by methods such as percussion and vibration is presented in detail, and other techniques are mentioned only briefly. The references cited earlier, together with other materials, provide excellent discussions of the specialty area of cardiopulmonary physical therapy, including details of treatment techniques (Frownfelter, 1987; Frownfelter & Dean, 2006; Hillegass & Sadowsky, 1994; Irwin & Techlin, 2005; Mackenzie, Imle, & Ciesla, 1989; Watchie, 1995; Webber & Pryor, 1993).

## RELAXATION

Relaxation is often an important issue for patients suffering from respiratory disease, especially one that is

## Box 10-1 Typical Goals of Chest Physical Therapy

Prevent the accumulation of secretions.
Improve mobilization and drainage of secretions.
Instruct patients in home bronchial hygiene programs.
Promote relaxation to avoid muscle splinting.
Maintain and improve chest wall mobility.
Restore the most efficient breathing pattern.
Instruct and retrain the use of respiratory muscles.
Develop respiratory muscle endurance and prevent venous stasis.
Improve and promote good posture.
Improve cardiopulmonary exercise tolerance.
Educate patients in every aspect of their condition so that they can take control of their own respiratory health.

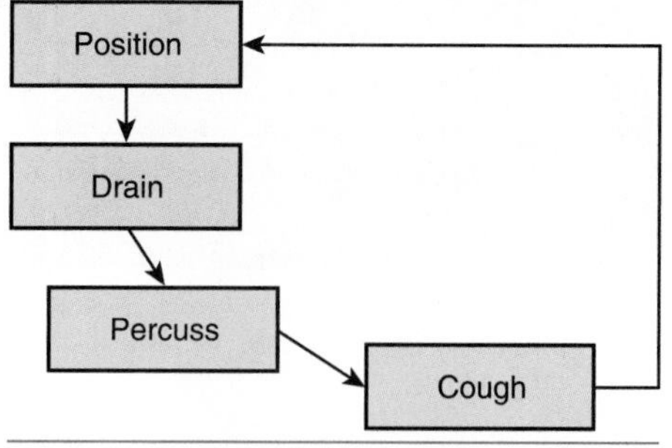


**Figure 10-1 Basic Steps in an Airway Clearance Technique**

The technique begins with the patient properly supported in the appropriate postural drainage position. The patient is allowed to rest and drain in this position for approximately 10 to 15 minutes. Percussion and vibration techniques are then applied, followed by deep breathing and an attempted cough. Deep breathing and coughing can be repeated a few times if the mucus is easily removed. The patient then rests in the postural drainage position, and the cycle is repeated until the chest is clear.

characterized by constricted airways or marked shortness of breath. Anxiety, fear, and outright panic are symptoms commonly associated with an inability to breathe. Not surprisingly then, people, especially children who suffer from chronic respiratory diseases such as asthma, find it difficult to relax and thus develop many postural problems related to their overactive muscles. Helping the patient to learn how to relax, breathe properly, and clear the airway of mucus is therefore an important goal of treatment. Because massage is especially effective in promoting relaxation and lowering anxiety and other techniques are effective in clearing the airway, it is not surprising that massage can be an effective treatment, especially for children with asthma (Fiels, 1998).

Various techniques are available to teach the patient how to relax. Two common strategies—the contrast and the induction methods—were discussed in some detail in Chapter 3 and will not be repeated here. Either of these methods are suitable; even a combination of the two approaches would also work well for some patients. An important modification, however, for both techniques relates to the position of the patient. Supine lying is a position in which most, if not all, patients with a respiratory disease will have difficulty breathing. A suitable alternative would be sitting upright in the bed or a comfortable armchair. Appropriate pillows should support the knees, lumbar spine neck, and perhaps the elbows and forearms. As patients learn to relax, they are better able to control their breathing. Being able to control breathing gives patients an important method to reduce their anxiety level and avoid panic. It also makes it possible for them to pay attention to their posture and to correct and prevent problems.

## AIRWAY CLEARANCE

The removal of mucus (sputum) from the airways and lungs is a major goal of treatment for any patient who has a pulmonary disorder characterized by significant mucus production. Clearing the airway paths is therefore a vital part of cardiopulmonary rehabilitation for both children and adults, and a variety of techniques have been developed to make this possible (Ciesla, 1996; Hugh, 1999; Jones & Rowe, 2000; Oberwaldner & Zach, 2000; Rivington-Law et al., 1984; Spotnitz, 1978; Williams et al., 2000; Zhu, 1998). Airway clearance requires the removal of adherent (and possibly infected) mucus with the application of three basic techniques:

1. Appropriate postural drainage
2. Appropriate manual techniques to help loosen mucus
3. Controlled breathing exercises and coughing to remove the mucus from the lungs

These three procedures are integrated into a total treatment process, in which there is an orderly progression from one part to another. Assuming the patient has been thoroughly screened and there are no contraindications to the procedure, treatment begins with the patient properly supported in the appropriate postural drainage position. The patient is allowed to rest in this position while the lung segments drain. Following a period of approximately 10 to 15 minutes, percussion and vibration techniques are administered to the appropriate parts of the patient's chest. Deep breathing and a cough then follow, several times if necessary. The patient is then allowed to rest in the drainage position, and the cycle is repeated until the chest is clear, unless the patient is fatigued, in which case treatment is discontinued. The basic concept is depicted in Figure 10-1.

## POSTURAL DRAINAGE

Postural drainage consists simply of allowing gravity to promote movement (drainage) of lung secretions toward the bronchial tree and the trachea, where the patient can expel them by coughing. Gravity both helps and hinders the normal movement of lung secretions. Essentially, gravity tends to drain the upper lobes and pool secretions in the lower lobes. The consistent movement of the cilia, which line the respiratory passages, together with the normal cough reflex usually ensure proper airway clearance of the respiratory passages. Under normal circumstances, the system is extremely efficient at keeping the airway clear; however, disease or the effects of surgery may render the patient unable to expel retained mucus from the lungs. Mucus retained in the lungs is a major focus for infection. The warm, dark, and damp environment deep within the lungs is the perfect incubation chamber for bacteria and viruses. If a serious infection occurs, it is costly to treat and can have serious, possibly fatal, consequences.

The technique of postural drainage requires a detailed understanding of the anatomy and physiology of the respiratory system. Placing the patient sequentially in a variety of positions makes it possible for gravity to promote the flow of secretions toward the mouth, where they can be expelled. Positioning depends on the specific part of the lung involved. Three basic positions are used:

1. Sitting upright
2. Lying flat on the back
3. Lying on one side

With the exception of the upright sitting position, the patient will need to be tipped; to do this, the therapist raises one end of the bed or treatment table to an appropriate angle. Two basic tipping heights are used:

Low tip = 12 to 14 inches (30 to 35 cm)
High tip = 18 to 20 inches (45 to 50 cm)

All measurements are made from the floor to the tip of the leg of the table or bed. The high tip is used mainly to drain various parts of the lower lobes. It is the combination of positioning and tipping the patient that makes postural drainage so effective. Because a detailed description of all of the postural drainage techniques is beyond the scope of this chapter, Figure 10-2 has been included to provide an easy-to-follow summary of the various positions. The reader is referred to other texts on the subject, including Frownfelter and Dean (2006) and Hillegass and Sadowsky (1994).

Certain diseases, such as cystic fibrosis, cause the production of large amounts of respiratory secretions. It is extremely important, especially in small children, that these secretions be removed daily; otherwise, the patient is likely to develop a serious, perhaps fatal, chest infection. Figure 10-3 illustrates a variety of postural drainage positions suitable for the treatment of small children. The positions illustrated in Figure 10-2 are not suitable for small children for many reasons, not the least of which is that the child will probably not keep still long enough for the drainage to be effective. As the child grows older, adult positioning techniques can be used. Watchie's book (1995) is another excellent source of information in this area.

### Primary Effects of Postural Drainage

The therapeutic effects of the postural drainage techniques are produced mainly through a direct mechanical impact on the tissues. Mucus that has pooled in the lower segments of the lungs is drained away using the effect of gravity to draw it out of the lungs. When performed properly, postural drainage has the following primary effects:

- Loosening and drainage of mucus from the lungs
- Increased blood and lymph flow in the skin and subcutaneous tissues, especially in the head
- A tendency for increased blood, intracranial, and intraocular pressure
- Unloading of the spine and abdominal viscera

### Therapeutic Uses of Postural Drainage

When included in a treatment sequence, postural drainage can be used to do the following:

- Loosen and drain mucus from one or more lung segments or lobes, thereby assisting with airway clearance and expectoration
- Encourage breathing if particular lung segments and lobes

### Indications for the Use of Postural Drainage

Postural drainage techniques may be indicated as part of a treatment plan to help relieve or reduce the effects of the following:

- Respiratory disorders associated with mucus retention, such as cystic fibrosis and bronchiectasis, in which the patient needs regular airway clearance for the rest of his or her life
- Respiratory infections associated with mucus/fluid buildup in specific lung segments or lobes

### Contraindications to the Use of Postural Drainage

The general concept of contraindications is covered in Chapter 3. As a technique, postural drainage may be contraindicated when any of the situations listed in Box 10-2 are present. The contraindications listed for the use of postural drainage techniques are all listed as *U,* meaning that the presence of the quoted conditions would normally contraindicate treatment. However, if it comes to a choice between airway clearance and the possible negative effects of postural drainage, then clearing the airway takes priority. Postural drainage techniques can be modified, especially in terms of the degree to which the therapist tips the patient's bed.

## PERCUSSION TECHNIQUES

Percussion techniques are discussed in more detail in Chapter 4 and encompass several techniques, but only clapping is used in the present context. The technique of clapping (or cupping) is used to help mobilize retained secretions adherent to the tracheobronchial tree. Percussion strokes send mechanical waves of vibration (pressure waves) through

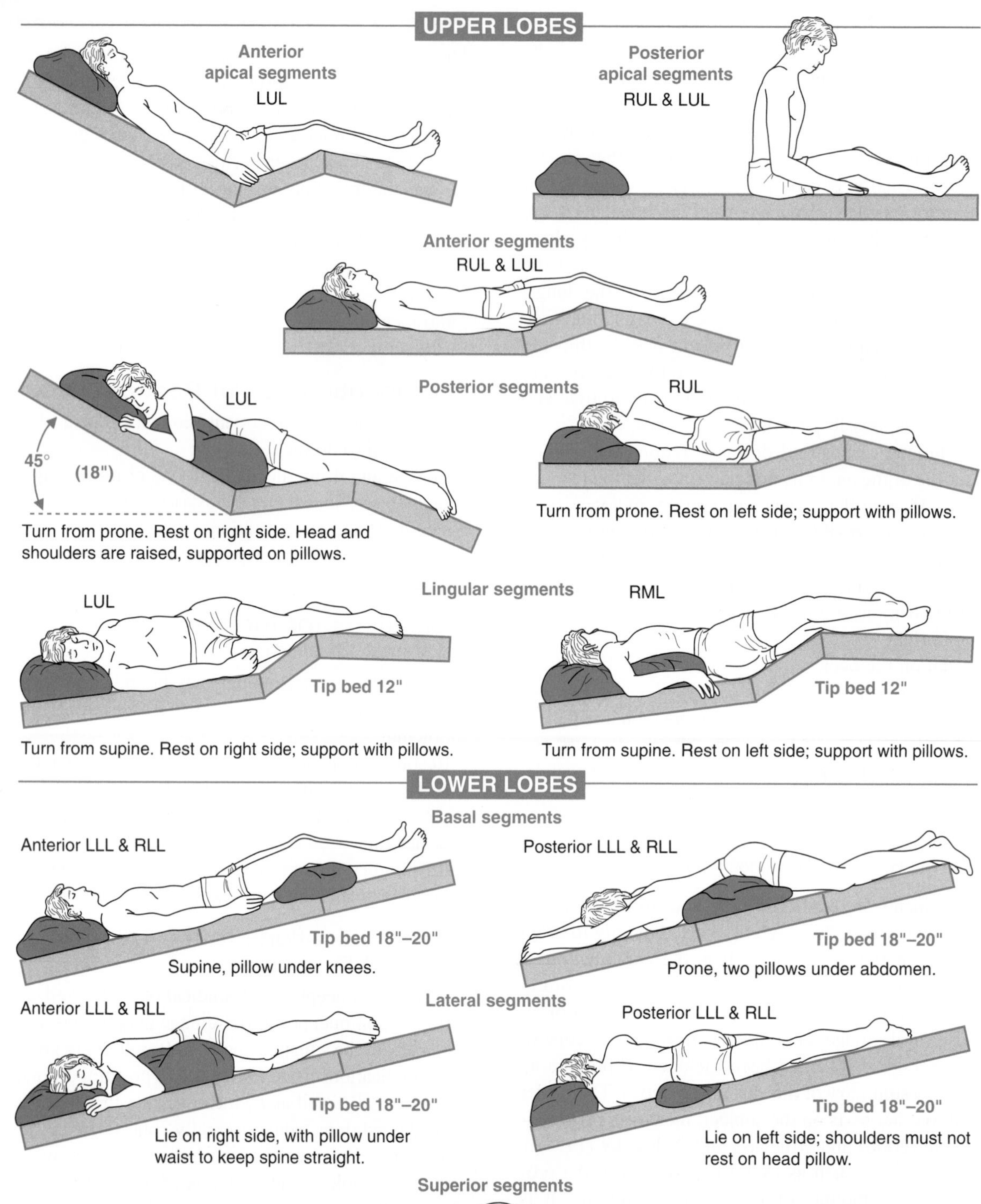
UPPER LOBES
Anterior apical segments
LUL
Posterior apical segments
RUL & LUL
Anterior segments
RUL & LUL
LUL
Posterior segments
RUL
45°
(18")
Turn from prone. Rest on right side. Head and shoulders are raised, supported on pillows.
Turn from prone. Rest on left side; support with pillows.
LUL
Lingular segments
RML
Tip bed 12"
Tip bed 12"
Turn from supine. Rest on right side; support with pillows.
Turn from supine. Rest on left side; support with pillows.
LOWER LOBES
Basal segments
Anterior LLL & RLL
Posterior LLL & RLL
Tip bed 18"–20"
Tip bed 18"–20"
Supine, pillow under knees.
Prone, two pillows under abdomen.
Anterior LLL & RLL
Lateral segments
Posterior LLL & RLL
Tip bed 18"–20"
Tip bed 18"–20"
Lie on right side, with pillow under waist to keep spine straight.
Lie on left side; shoulders must not rest on head pillow.
Superior segments
LLL & RLL
Prone, pillow under abdomen to flatten back.

**Figure 10-2 Basic Postural Drainage Positions**

Postural drainage positions to drain various lung segments in the adult patient. *LUL,* Left upper lobe; *RUL,* right upper lobe; *LLL,* left lower lobe; *RLL,* right lower lobe. *(From White GC:* Basic clinical competencies for respiratory care: an integrated approach, *Albany, NY, 1988, Delmar.)*

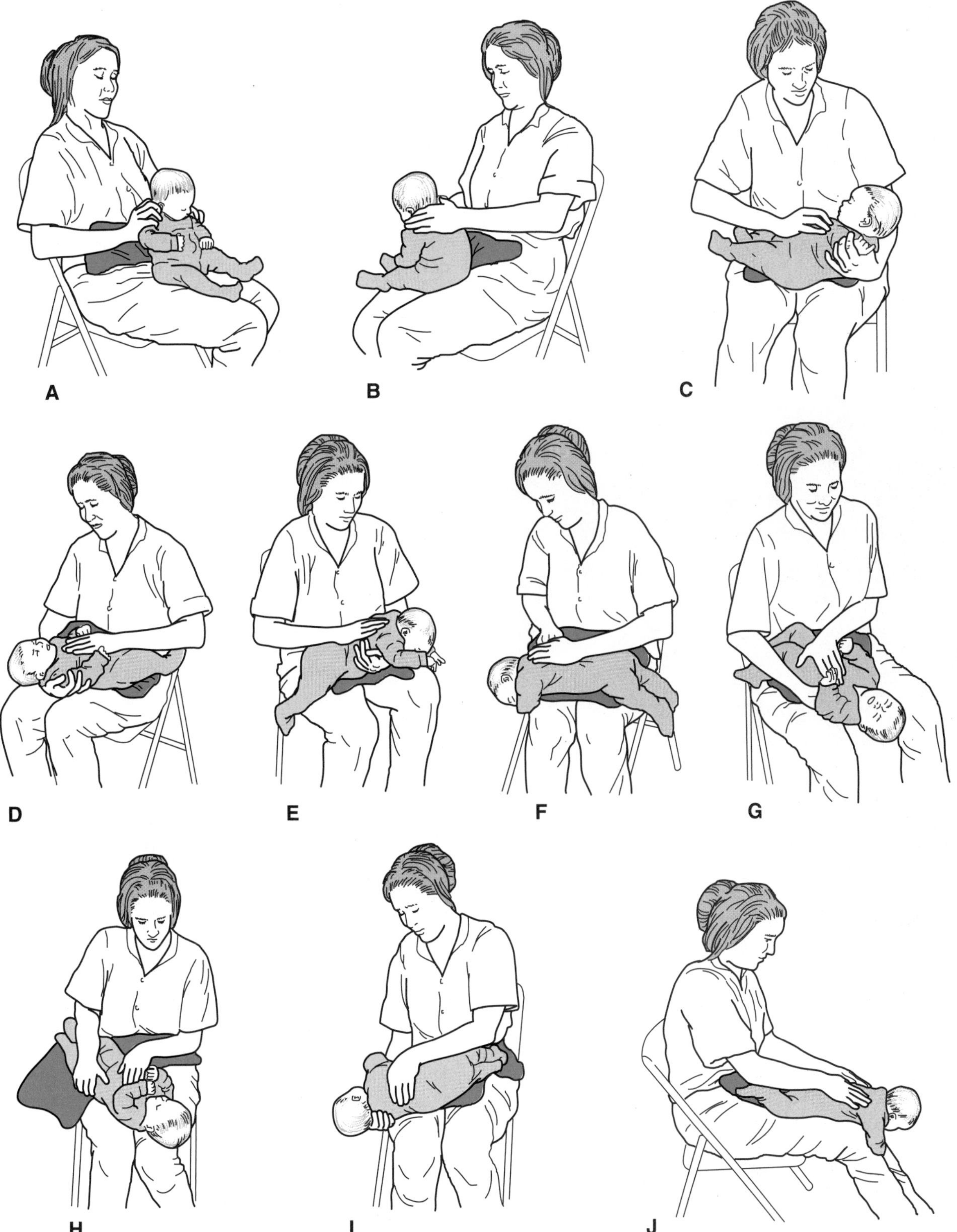


**Figure 10-3 Postural Drainage Positions Suitable for the Pediatric Patient**

Postural drainage positions to drain various parts of the lungs of small children. **A,** Apical segments of both upper lobes (BUL). **B,** Posterior segment of left upper lobe (LUL). **C,** Anterior segment of LUL. **D,** Anterior segment of right upper lobe (RUL). **E,** Posterior segment of RUL. **F,** Superior, or apical, segments of both lower lobes (BLL). **G,** Anterior segments of BLL. **H,** Right middle lobe (also done on other side for lingular segment of LUL). **I,** Lateral segment of right lower lobe (RLL); also done on other side for lateral segment of left lower lobe (LLL). **J,** Posterior segments of BLL. *(From Watchie J:* Cardiopulmonary physical therapy: a clinical manual, *Philadelphia, 1995, Saunders.)*

## Box 10-2 Main Contraindications to the Use of Postural Drainage

| Contraindication | |
|---|---|
| Severe rib fractures (flail chest). | U |
| Acute heart failure, especially when coronary thrombosis or embolism is involved | U |
| Acute pulmonary embolism | U |
| Severe hypertension | U |
| Arterial or venous pathology affecting the head and neck | U |
| Recent surgery to the brain or eye | U |
| Congestive cardiac failure or any other heart condition in which heart function may be affected by the pressure exerted on the heart by the postural drainage position | U |

*U*, Usually contraindicated.

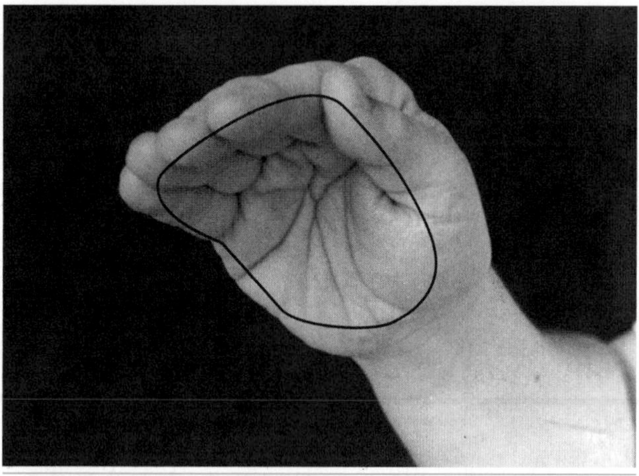

**Figure 10-4 The Hand in the Cupped Position Used to Perform the Technique of Clapping**

In this position, a layer of air is trapped and compressed as the hand strikes the skin surface. A vibrating wave is set up and travels into the tissues, producing the mechanical effects that help to loosen secretions. The line drawn on the hand represents the margins of the cup (see also Figure 8-18).

the rib cage and into the lungs to shake loose adherent mucus plugs in the bronchial tree. Because a mucous plug in a segmental bronchus could collapse a lung segment, it is extremely important that it be removed as soon as possible. Percussion and vibration techniques, together with the proper postural drainage positioning and deep breathing exercises, can help to dislodge a plug and to reexpand the lung segment or lobe. These techniques can also prevent mucus plugs from building up and closing off parts of the airway.

To perform clapping, the therapist keeps his or her hands cupped, fingers extended and held together, with wrists and arms relaxed and loose. The hands strike the chest wall rhythmically and alternately, focusing on the area of the lung being drained. Cupping the hands provides a cushion of slightly compressed air between the hands and the patient's chest wall, thereby mechanically delivering a vibration wave to the lungs (Figure 10-4; see Figure 8-18).

If necessary, the technique may be delivered through a folded towel placed over the patient's chest wall, as this dampens the force a little and helps to prevent unnecessary skin irritation or pain. Skin erythema (redness) can have several causes. If the therapist's hands are improperly cupped, a slapping or stinging effect may be produced, or too much force may be used over extremely sensitive tissues. The technique of clapping is discussed in detail in Chapter 4 and demonstrated on the accompanying DVD (see DVD Chapters 4-9 and 4-11). Figure 10-5 illustrates the technique of clapping to the right lower lobe, with the patient in a high tip position.

If the patient finds the technique uncomfortable, the therapist may place a thin towel, gown, or sheet over the area being treated. This does not significantly reduce the effectiveness of the technique, but it is usually much more comfortable for the patient. Figure 10-6 illustrates this concept, and it is also demonstrated on the accompanying DVD (see DVD Chapters 4-9 and 4-11).

Percussion is comfortable for patients when the technique is applied properly; the rhythm and consistency of force and the direction of movement can have a relaxing effect. Generally, little force is needed for percussion; it is the cupping, not the force, that is effective. The force of the percussion must be determined for each patient. For example, different amounts of force would be needed for a child, a large adult, or a frail, elderly patient who has recently had surgery. Conditions such as cystic fibrosis, atelectasis, and bronchiectasis are characterized by the presence of thick, tenacious secretions and may need more vigorous chest physical therapy and more percussive force to mobilize and remove secretions. At the other extreme, a modified clapping technique can be performed on the neonate, using just the finger pads of the index and middle fingers. The two fingers are held straight but fairly relaxed. The technique is one of rapid alternation of flexion and extension of the metacarpophalangeal joints, keeping the fingers straight. Only the pads of the two fingers touch the chest wall. The force of the percussion is easily modified to suit the patient's condition. The technique is simple to practice on the edge of a table, but it is difficult to maintain a rapid tapping for any length of time. This is not an issue for the neonatal chest because prolonged tapping is probably not helpful. Short bursts of *finger clapping,* each lasting 15 to 30 seconds, are easy for the therapist to perform and for the patient to tolerate. In most cases, the pressure will be extremely light.

The therapist should have a plan for hand movements during percussion so that the hands do not wander aimlessly on the patient's thorax. The therapist's hands can work in a circular pattern or along the chest, but the pattern should be consistent throughout the treatment. Percussion should not be applied in one spot for any length of time because it becomes irritating. Once skin contact is made, the percussion should continue consistently for approximately 1 to 3 minutes, although the time varies according to the tolerance and needs of the patient.

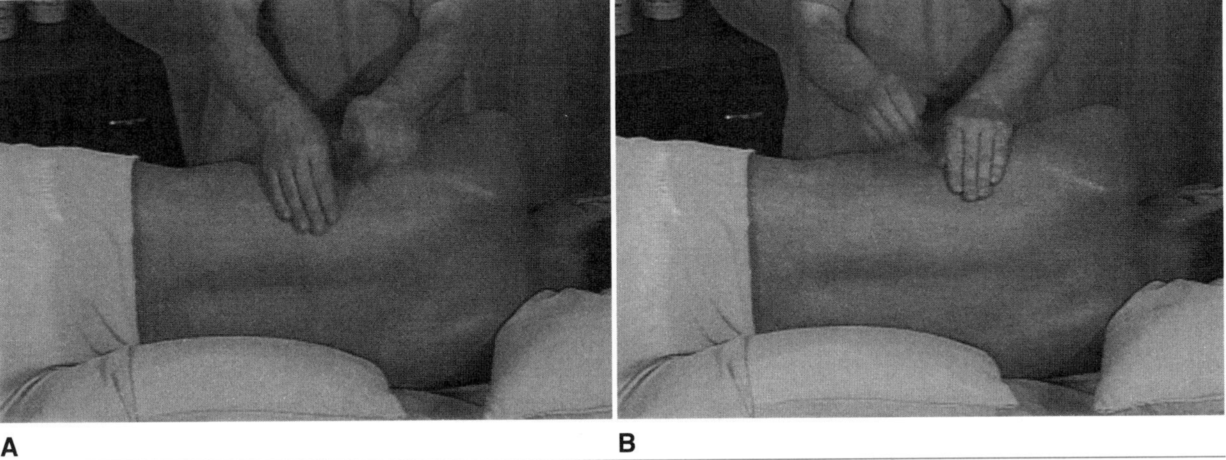


**Figure 10-5 Clapping to the Right Lower Lobe**

**A,** The patient is in the left side-lying position with the foot of the bed elevated 18 to 20 inches (high tip).
**B,** The wrist movements alternate during the performance of clapping to the right lower lobe.

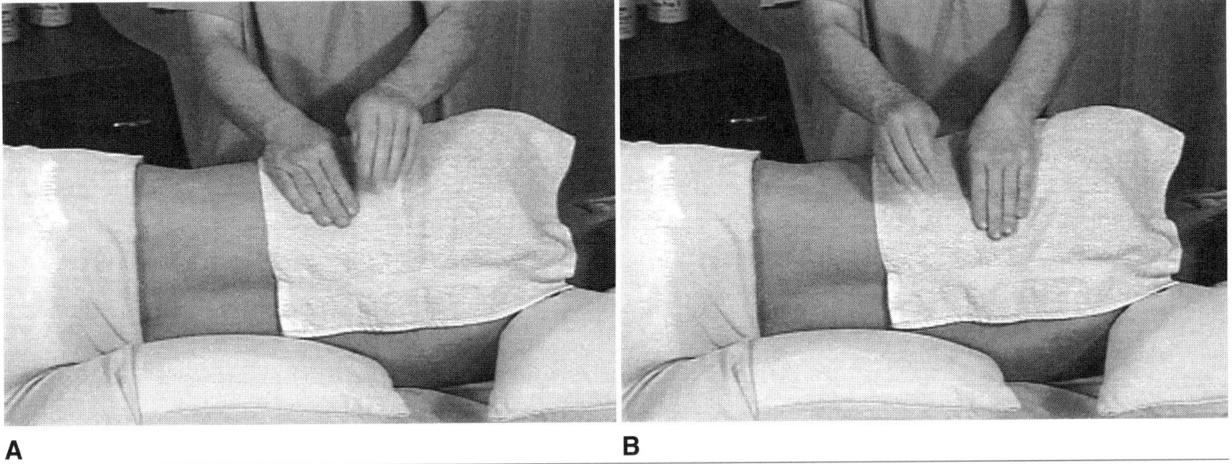


**Figure 10-6 Use of a Towel during the Technique of Clapping to the Chest**

The patient is in the left side-lying position with the foot of the bed elevated 18 to 20 inches (high tip). A towel covers the anterolateral and posterolateral aspects of the chest during the performance of clapping.

Percussion should be applied only over the bony thorax. Although the vibration wave spreads out into the tissues in all directions, it must be remembered that the lower margin of the lungs is adjacent to the eighth rib in the midaxillary line. When the patient is lying in the high tipped position, the pressure of the abdominal organs may push the lungs toward the neck. In short, if the objective of percussion is to affect the lungs, it is essential that the therapist perform the technique over lung tissue rather than the abdominal viscera. Care should be taken when applying percussion to the anterior aspects of the chest and at the lateral basilar rib areas because the rib ends are attached loosely and sometimes not attached at all (i.e., floating ribs). The heel of the therapist's hand should not make contact with bony prominences such as the spine of the scapula, clavicles, or vertebral column, especially if the patient is thin and elderly.

For obvious reasons, percussion must not be given over the breast tissue in a female patient. If necessary, when treating the anterior aspects of the middle lobes, the whole chest should be covered with a towel and the patient instructed to gently push the breast tissue toward her neck, away from the area to be percussed. This is usually easier to do with the opposite hand, but either hand can be used, depending on which is more comfortable for the patient. The therapist can then mold the towel around the patient's hand so as to make it clear which area is to be treated. The patient keeps her hand on the breast tissue at all times during the percussion. In the case of an obese patient, it will also help if the patient raises the same arm above her head during the percussion. For example, if percussion is given to the anterior aspect of the right middle lobe, the right forearm would be flexed upward toward the patient's head. The patient's left hand would then be free to lift the right breast tissue away from the area to be treated. The right arm should be supported on pillows as needed for patient comfort.

The primary effects, therapeutic uses, indications, and contraindications of the percussive manipulations are listed in Chapter 4. Special attention should be paid to the list of contraindications with regard to the use of clapping. If the thorax is damaged (e.g., multiple rib fracture) or there is serious cardiac disease, clapping may be contraindicated, in which case a less vigorous technique such as fine vibrations may be needed.

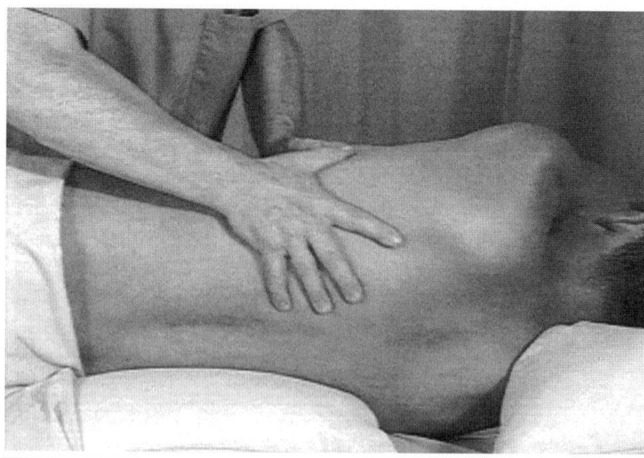

**Figure 10-7 Vibration to the Right Lower Lobes**

The patient is in the left side-lying position with the foot of the bed elevated 18 to 20 inches (high tip). The therapist applies the vibration technique only during the expiratory phase of the patient's breathing cycle.

## VIBRATION AND SHAKING

Vibration and shaking techniques are also used routinely with postural drainage, although they can be used with the patient in many positions. They are generally performed after percussion, or they alternate with it. Percussion is given to loosen adherent mucus plugs and to aid in their movement toward the bronchi and trachea, where the secretions can be coughed up or removed by suction.

Vibration and shaking are both performed during the patient's *expiratory phase* of breathing, at which time the patient's chest is compressed simultaneously with the vibratory movement. Chest compression is extremely important in making vibration effective. The amount of chest compression is determined by several factors such as chest wall mobility, age of the patient, chest deformities, new postoperative incisions, chest trauma, or fractured ribs. In some cases, the therapist may actually perform a *rib-springing* technique with the vibration, using a good deal of force in mobilizing the chest wall. This technique is possible only in a patient with a mobile thorax.

To accomplish the vibration or shaking stroke, the patient is asked to take a deep breath in through the nose, pause for a moment, and then blow all the air out through the mouth. As the patient begins to inhale, the therapist applies slight resistance to the movement of the chest wall. This encourages localized expansion of the lungs in the areas beneath the therapist's hands. The resistance offered to inspiration is gradually reduced as the peak of inhalation is reached. After a momentary pause, chest compression and vibration are performed as the patient exhales. To obtain maximal benefit, the patient is encouraged to breathe out for as long as he or she can, always within tolerance. Figure 10-7 illustrates the vibration technique, and a demonstration can be viewed on the accompanying DVD (see DVD Chapters 4-10 and 4-12).

To perform the vibration or shaking stroke, the therapist tenses all of the muscles in both shoulders and arms. This cocontraction allows the therapist to transfer a vibration wave to the patient's chest wall and lung tissue. The vibration continues throughout exhalation. The shaking maneuver is identical to vibrations, except that it is performed with a lower frequency and higher amplitude of movement. In effect, the vibrations are much slower and deeper than they are with the standard vibration technique. If a more aggressive form of chest compression and vibration (or shaking) is needed, the patient takes a deep breath and the therapist springs the ribs in compression three or four times during exhalation. If the patient is unable to take a deep breath on his or her own, intermittent positive-pressure breathing (IPPB) devices or a self-inflating bag technique may be used to promote deep breathing. The vibration technique is the same in both procedures. The patient is mechanically given a large breath, and vibration is performed from the peak of inhalation through the expiratory phase. Experience has demonstrated that atelectasis and pneumonia can be cleared more quickly when an ultrasonic nebulizer or heated aerosol is used half an hour before the chest physical therapy treatment, whether or not the IPPB or self-inflating bag technique is used.

For some patients, vibration may be indicated even when percussion techniques would not be applicable. These include patients who have recently undergone surgery (including open heart surgery and thoracotomy, in which pain and splinting would be increased) and those who have hemorrhaged or fractured ribs. It must be emphasized that the contraindications to postural drainage, percussion, vibration, and shaking are relative. Priorities must always be considered. For example, if a patient has a poor cardiovascular function that is exacerbated by atelectasis, the atelectasis must be cleared. This situation calls for proper decision making from the various members of the team caring for the patient.

## DEEP BREATHING AND COUGHING

The basic procedure illustrated in Figures 10-4 to 10-7 can be repeated several times. However, it is helpful for patients to breathe normally between each percussive session; otherwise they may become dizzy from too many deep inspirations. As the mucus loosens, the patient may wish to cough and clear the secretions. A suitable covered receptacle or facial tissues should always be within the patient's reach. If the patient wishes to pause and attempt to cough to expel the mucus, it is often best to try this at the end of an expiration. Certainly the patient needs to inhale and get some air behind the mucus, but the cough is likely to be more productive if given at the end of the expiration, especially if the patient is unable to develop sufficient pressure behind the cough. It is as if the mucus is already on its way out of the airway and the cough at the end of expiration gives it the final push. This is important with sticky mucus, because the patient can become exhausted quickly from wasted efforts to clear mucus using an ineffective coughing technique.

The normal cough requires the patient to take a deep breath and to hold it briefly (closing the glottis and vocal cords). As the breath is held, the intrathoracic pressure is increased mainly because of the contraction of the abdominal muscles. The pressure is suddenly released (opening the glottis and vocal cords) in an explosive exhalation. The patient with an endotracheal tube cannot cough because the tube passes through the glottis and between the cords, preventing them from closing. Similarly, a tracheostomized patient has a tube below the cords and is unable to build up intrathoracic pressure by closing the glottis and cords. In either case, coughing, the major mechanism for clearing secretions from the lungs, is not functioning. A cough may be simulated by using the self-inflating bag (with tracheostomy or endotracheal cuff inflated to seal off the airway), giving a large inspiratory volume and holding the bag for 2 or 3 seconds, then popping the bag open quickly. The therapist begins chest compression and vibration during the hold period of bag inflation and continues throughout the exhalation phase.

A variety of devices, such as the ultrasonic nebulizer, can be of tremendous benefit, especially if given just before postural drainage. This form of therapy helps liquefy secretions, making them easier to loosen and expectorate. IPPB treatments can also be administered in conjunction with postural drainage, percussion, vibration, and shaking to distribute air peripherally in the lungs. This air distribution increases the chances of getting air beyond the secretions and making the cough more productive. A variety of mechanical vibrating devices have also been used to loosen lung secretions. Because these are not manual techniques, they are not considered further here. The interested reader is referred to Doering et al. (1999). In addition, reference to their use can be found in many of the standard texts mentioned previously in this chapter.

## PASSIVE MOVEMENTS OF THE LOWER LIMBS

There seems to be a potential use for relaxed passive movements of the lower limbs to significantly modify alveolar ventilation during sleep in patients with congenital central hypoventilation syndrome (CCHS). Gozal and Simakajornboon (2000) showed that moving the lower limbs passively has an effect on ventilation during sleep, possibly via activation of mechanoreceptor-afferent pathways rather than by respiratory entrainment. This interesting finding has important implications for the use of passive movement procedures.

## SUMMARY

The clinical effectiveness of chest physical therapy has been demonstrated on patients with a wide spectrum of respiratory problems that are either the direct result of respiratory disease or secondary to some other medical or surgical condition—for example, spinal cord injury, cerebrovascular accident, myocardial infarction, or neuromuscular disorders. These patients have many common respiratory problems—poor ventilation and ineffective cough—and, as a result, they have retained and often infected lung secretions. Factors that contribute to these problems are muscle weakness or paralysis, poor coordination, lack of endurance, and abnormal breathing patterns.

Debilitated and dependent patients exhibit a marked decrease in general activity level, often including an inability to change basic body positions. In a bedridden patient, turning from side to side affects general postural drainage of each lung. Gravity becomes both a positive and a negative factor in lung drainage: positive in that the uppermost part of the lung is drained, and negative in that secretions accumulate in the dependent lobes. Thus patients paralyzed on the right side are more likely to turn to the right because they have use of the left extremities. They find it difficult to turn to the left side and may develop pneumonia in the right lung. Quadriplegic patients lying on their backs are likely to develop bilateral posterior basal pneumonia or pneumonia in the superior segments of the lower lobes. The importance of frequent position changes for postural drainage cannot be overemphasized. These frequent changes for paralyzed patients require a total team effort from the staff caring for the patient.

Patients with neuromuscular disorders such as myasthenia gravis or Guillain-Barré syndrome require help in achieving or maintaining clear lungs so that they can maximize their rehabilitation. Shortness of breath is often caused by the accumulation of secretions in the airways; this frightens many patients and greatly limits their activity and progress. A program of bronchial hygiene—consisting of postural drainage, percussion, vibration, and breathing retraining—should be given before exercise. This will allow the patient to tolerate more activity because the airway is clear. The patient should rest after bronchial hygiene procedures, as they are often tiring.

To gain expertise in chest physical therapy, therapists must be skilled in giving percussion and vibration, postural drainage, breathing exercises, exercise programs geared to the patient with respiratory problems, and other modalities of respiratory therapy. Although the trend is toward ever more expensive high-tech equipment and medications, the intelligent use of basic chest physical therapy concepts can prevent problems from arising in the first place and is a more cost-effective approach in the long term. This is especially the case for patients who have chronic lung disease and wish to spend as much time as possible in their own homes. It is worth remembering that the need to breathe is paramount. No human being can survive for more than a few minutes without being able to breathe, yet breathing is a vital function that most people completely take for granted until they are unable to do so. Teaching a patient to maintain a clear airway can have a profound impact on the patient's ability to live a normal life.

## REFERENCES


Carey FE: Emphysema: the battle to breathe, *US Department of Health, Education and Welfare Public Health Service Publication No. 1715,* 1967.

Ciesla ND: Chest physical therapy for patients in the intensive care unit, *Phys Ther* 76(6):609-625, 1996.

Doering T, Fieguth HG, Steuernagel B et al: External stimuli in the form of vibratory massage after heart or lung transplantation, *Am J Phys Med Rehabil* 78(2):108-110, 1999.

Fiels TP: Children with asthma have improved pulmonary functions after massage therapy, *J Pediatrics* 132(5):854-858, 1998.

Frownfelter DL: *Chest physical therapy and pulmonary rehabilitation: an interdisciplinary approach,* Chicago, 1987, Year Book.

Frownfelter DL, Dean E: *Cardiovascular and pulmonary physical therapy,* ed 4, St Louis, 2006, Elsevier.

Gozal D, Simakajornboon N: Passive motion of the extremities modifies alveolar ventilation during sleep in patients with congenital central hypoventilation syndrome, *Am J Resp Crit Care Med* 162(5):1747-1751, 2000.

Hillegass EA, Sadowsky HS: *Essentials of cardiopulmonary physical therapy,* Philadelphia, 1994, Saunders.

Hugh: The child with a chronic condition: children with cystic fibrosis benefit from massage therapy, *J Child Fam Nurs* 2(5):366-367, 1999.

Irwin S, Techlin JS: *Cardiopulmonary physical therapy,* ed 4, St Louis, 2004, Mosby.

Jones A, Rowe BH: Issues in pulmonary nursing. Bronchopulmonary hygiene physical therapy in bronchiectasis and chronic obstructive pulmonary disease: a systematic review, *Heart Lung: J Acute Critical Care* 29(2):125-135, 2000.

Mackenzie CF, Imle PC, Ciesla N: *Chest physiotherapy in the intensive care unit,* ed 2, Baltimore, 1989, Williams & Wilkins.

Oberwaldner B, Zach MS: Mucous clearing respiratory-physiotherapy in pediatric pneumology [in German], *Schweiz Med Wochenschr* 130(19):711-719, 2000.

Petty TL: *Chronic obstructive pulmonary disease,* New York, 1978, Marcel Dekker.

Rivington-Law BA, Epstein SW, Thompson GL et al: Effect of chest wall vibrations on pulmonary function in chronic bronchitis, *Chest* 85(3):78-381, 1984.

Spotnitz B: A system for self-administration of vibration in respiratory physiotherapy, *Respir Care* 23(10):960-961, 1978.

Watchie J: *Cardiopulmonary physical therapy: a clinical manual,* Philadelphia, 1995, Saunders.

Webber BA, Pryor JA: *Physiotherapy for respiratory and cardiac problems,* Edinburgh, 1993, Churchill Livingstone.

Weiss EB et al: Acute respiratory failure in chronic obstructive lung disease, I. Pathophysiology, *Disease-a-Month,* October 1969.

Williams MT et al: Energy expenditure during physiotherapist-assisted and self-treatment in cystic fibrosis, *Physiother Theory Pract* 16(2):57-67, 2000.

Zhu S: A clinical investigation on massage for prevention and treatment of recurrent respiratory tract infection in children, *J Trad Chinese Med* 18(4):2285-2291, 1998.

# Chapter 11

# Connective Tissue Massage

Unlike previous chapters, which have considered the various strokes that make up the method known as *Swedish remedial massage,* this chapter is the first to focus on a different but parallel system of soft tissue manipulation. Connective tissue massage (CTM)—or in German, *bindegewebsmassage*—is a total system of specialized soft tissue manipulation techniques originally developed in Europe between the two world wars. It is a good example of a treatment that produces a remote site effect. This concept is well known in many Eastern systems of massage and traditional methods of treatment. Essentially, stimulation given to one part of the body has a profound effect on tissues apparently unrelated to the treatment site. Acupuncture, reflexology, and the more modern concept of trigger point stimulation share this conceptual foundation.

As modern understanding of physiology increases, it is becoming clearer that there is a sound rationale for the use of these concepts, even though they may seem at first glance unlikely. CTM is a significant area of practice, deserving of a book in its own right. As with the other systems of massage described briefly in this text, the intention in this chapter is only to introduce the reader to the basic concepts involved. Many massage textbooks address this topic, but the most comprehensive and authentic materials on the subject in English are still probably the works of Elizabeth Dicke (1978) and Maria Ebner (1985). Other important sources of information in this area can be found in Bischoff and Elminger (1963), Holey (1995b), and Luedecke (1969).

## BRIEF HISTORY AND THEORETICAL FOUNDATIONS

Connective tissue massage, as its name suggests, is a system of manual techniques specifically aimed at affecting the connective tissues in the body, especially the skin. Elizabeth Dicke, a German physiotherapist, was the first to describe the technique in the late 1920s and early 1930s. Dicke was suffering from a serious circulatory impairment in her right leg that resulted in the development of endarteritis obliterans of the limb. This painful condition was so severe that surgeons recommended amputation. In an attempt to relieve the accompanying low-back pain, Dicke discovered an unexpected effect in her leg when she rubbed certain areas on the posterior pelvic region. While she applied pulling strokes to the skin of her posterior pelvic region, she was aware of a sensation of warmth rushing into her affected leg. After 3 months of this massage (performed by a colleague), the severe symptoms began to subside. Within a year, she was back at work as a physiotherapist. A great deal of clinical study and evaluation followed this initial experience. Dicke, along with her colleagues, refined her original stroking technique to treat many pathologically involved tissues and organs. She went on to develop the method of *bindegewebsmassage* now widely used in Europe, especially in Germany, and well known in most parts of the world. Broadly speaking, Dicke and others claimed that this massage affects the autonomic nervous system and, by reflex action, corrects imbalances in the vegetative functions of the body. CTM is not just another massage stroke but rather a complete system of treatment that happens to use soft tissue massage as a means of inducing reflex activity in various tissues.

## REFLEX ZONES (HEAD'S ZONES)

Since the late 1890s, it has been known that visceral disease can be associated with visible and palpable changes in the skin in well-defined areas of the body. These areas are known as *Head's zones,* after Head (1889), who first described them.

As the primitive embryo develops, three layers of tissue begin to differentiate into an outer layer (ectoderm), a middle layer (mesoderm), and an inner layer (endoderm). The ectoderm develops into the skin and nervous system, while the endoderm forms the various internal organs of the body. The middle layer (mesoderm) gives rise to the various structures of the musculoskeletal system. By the end of the fourth week of gestation, a series of approximately 39 to 44 distinct cube-shaped bulges develop bilaterally within the mesodermal layer. These bulges are known as the *mesodermal somites,* and they divide the mesoderm into 44 segments (cranial to caudal).

As the nervous system develops further (from the ectoderm), a pair of nerve roots (spinal nerves) form adjacent to most of the original mesodermal somites. These nerve roots will eventually contain sensory, motor, and autonomic nerve fibers that will innervate skin, muscle, bone, and viscera. These connections give rise to the important concepts of *dermatomes, myotomes,* and *sclerotomes* (areas, respectively, of skin, muscle, and bone that are supplied by a single spinal nerve root). The skin of the posterior trunk retains most of the orderly innervation, originally derived in company with the 38 to 44 primitive segments. This gives rise to the notion that areas of skin on the posterior trunk have an embryonic link to various musculoskeletal and internal organs of the body (Head's zones). Figure 11-1 illustrates this concept.

A key concept underpinning CTM and other systems involving manipulation of the soft tissues is that pathologic changes affecting any of the structures derived from a mesodermal somite eventually give rise to signs and symptoms in any related structures, especially in the skin and connective tissues. The fact that visceral lesions may give rise to changes in other areas is well known; for example, liver and gallbladder problems can be reflected in the right mid- to lower posterior costal segments (T6 to 10) and in the right

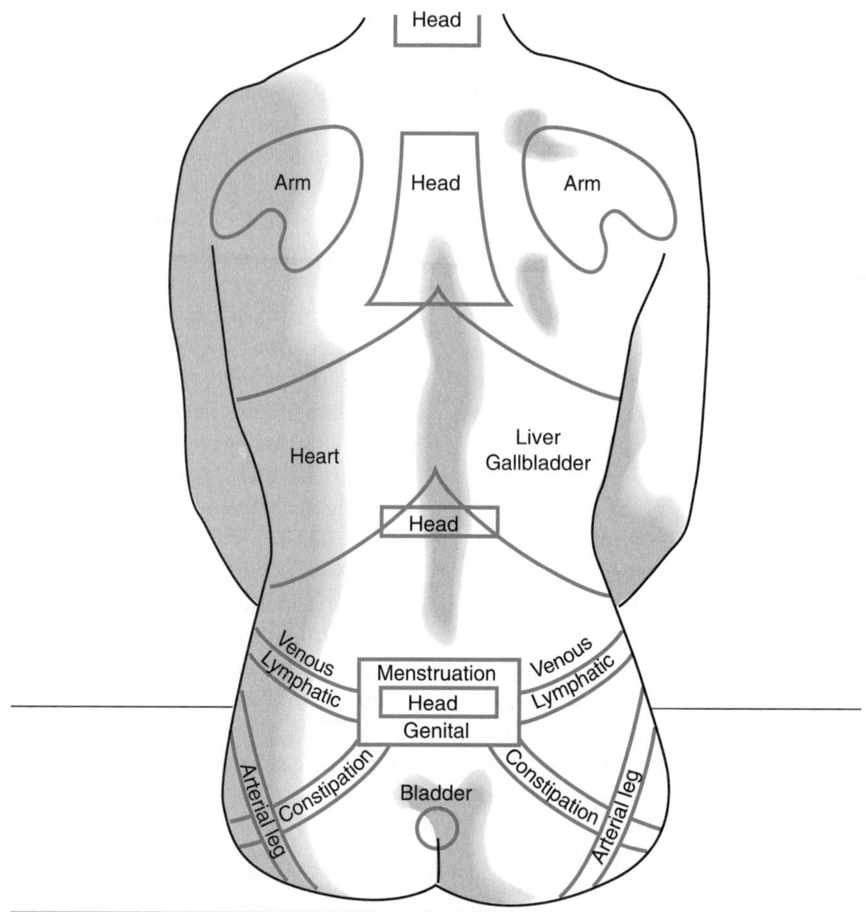


**Figure 11-1 Body Areas (Head's Zones) Represented on the Posterior Trunk**

The number of zones depicted is not exhaustive. The intent is to show considerable overlap of zones and the functions they represent. There are zones for many parts of the body, including one for the head and zones for menstrual, genital, and colonic function, all overlying or radiating from the sacrum. These narrow zonal bands are generally described as being 5 to 8 cm wide. A stomach zone lies within the heart zone and may also be represented above the left scapula. *(Modified from Ebner M:* Connective tissue massage: theory and therapeutic application, *ed 2, Huntington, NY, 1985, Robert E Krieger.)*

upper rectus region. The changes that take place in a related zone are detectable by palpation of the skin and subcutaneous tissues of the same area. The connective tissues have characteristic areas of local tension. There is a certain tightness of the different layers against each other where normally there would be a limited amount of movement between them (Hirschberg, Fatt, & Brown, 1986). Within each zone of influence of a spinal segment or segments, there is often a circumscribed area that is related to a particular organ; these areas are known as *maximal points*. These changes can be detected by palpation of the area. Holey (1995a) and Holey and Watson (1995) described the basic concepts of zone recognition and inter-rater reliability in the detection of these zones.

A key treatment concept in CTM is the following:

*Since visceral pathology is known to produce changes in the connective tissues of the skin in well-defined zones, treatment to the connective tissues of the skin in a defined zone can produce effects on other structures that are derived from the same mesodermal segment.*

This concept forms an important part of the rationale for the effects of CTM. There is no direct mechanical effect in many cases because the areas of skin treated are some distance away from the point of effect. This is more obvious with treatments such as acupressure and reflexology. Because there is often no direct mechanical effect from the manipulation, the most likely explanation for the treatment effect is that it is the result of a reflex, in this case an autonomic reflex. An autonomic reflex has all of the usual characteristics of a reflex—namely, it has receptors at one end, effectors at the other, and a pathway in between. The receptor side of the reflex is part of the somatic nervous system, whereas the effector part belongs to the autonomic nervous system. The pathway in between is formed by nervous connections from both systems.

The receptors are a wide variety of afferent endings in the skin, subcutaneous tissues, blood vessels, muscles, and the viscera. The effectors are largely smooth muscle fibers in a variety of tissues, such as blood vessels, viscera, glands, and the skin. The pathway is formed by the various interconnections between the afferent fibers of the somatic nervous system and the efferent fibers of the autonomic nervous system, especially through the sympathetic chain of the sympathetic division and the sacral outflow of the parasympathetic system. Figure 11-2 illustrates this concept.

The autonomic reflex described previously connects the stimulation (including massage) of afferent receptors in the skin and subcutaneous tissue with potential responses in many different types of tissue. It is an important concept to help explain the mechanisms involved with the remote-site effects seen with CTM and other soft tissue manipulations. It is important to remember that the lumen of the small arterioles is largely under the control of sympathetic nerve fibers. When these fibers are active, they cause the smooth muscle in the arteriolar walls to contract, thereby producing vasoconstriction. When sympathetic fiber activity decreases, however, the smooth muscle relaxes and vasodilation occurs. This brings more blood, and therefore oxygen and nutrients, to the tissues. It also allows waste products from the tissue to be removed more efficiently. These effects are likely to facilitate healing in the tissues. It is also possible that a similar effect could be produced by a chemical rather than neural activation of autonomic reflex activity. Soft tissue manipulation could cause the local or general liberation of chemical substances that activate such a reflex. For example, vasoactive intestinal polypeptide (VIP) has a profound effect on the circulation and on systemic pain relief and has been associated with CTM (Kaada & Torsteinbo, 1987, 1989). It is also possible that afferent signals reaching the sensory cortex might also trigger the release of various brain chemicals, thereby stimulating reflex autonomic activity. For more detailed descriptions of the theory and practice of CTM, the reader is referred to Dicke (1978), Ebner (1962, 1965, 1968, 1978, 1985), Goats and Keir (1991), Haase (1968), Helmrich (1969), Michalsen and Buhring (1993), Schliack (1965, 1978), and Tophoj (1970).

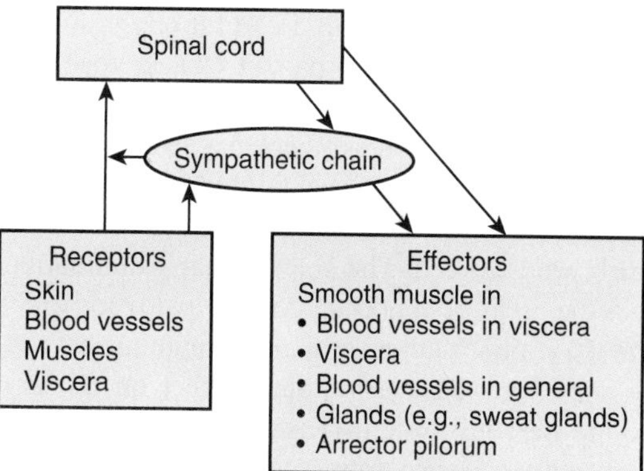


**Figure 11-2 Principles of an Autonomic Reflex**

An autonomic reflex consists of a response in the effectors, produced by stimulation of the receptors. The receptors are part of the somatic nervous system, whereas the effectors consist of largely smooth muscle tissue in the autonomic nervous system. Interconnections at the spinal cord, the sympathetic chain, and the sacral outflow provide the pathway for the reflex.

## BASIC DIAGNOSTIC TECHNIQUE FOR CONNECTIVE TISSUE MASSAGE

The patient sits on a firm surface with the hips and knees at right angles and the feet supported on a stool. The whole of the back must be exposed, but the patient's anterior aspect should be covered during evaluation and treatment. The therapist may sit or stand behind the patient, whichever is most comfortable or suitable. No lubricant should be used.

The evaluation begins with a careful observation of the posture and muscles of the patient's back, together with careful palpation of the cutaneous structures. Some zones may appear swollen, whereas others may seem drawn inward. Diagnostic palpation may reveal tightness and tissue tension in certain areas of the back. These areas are often unilateral and fairly well defined. The object of the examination is to map out the areas of abnormal contour/palpation and relate these to the patient's other signs and symptoms, but the evaluation itself may have a profound effect on the patient's autonomic nervous system (Kisner & Taslitz, 1968). The therapist makes an accurate record of the findings of the examination for future reference and comparison.

There are two distinct types of technique in CTM. One is a diagnostic stroke and the other a treatment technique, although many times these two strokes are identical. During the examination phase, the therapist uses manual techniques to identify changes in the surface connective tissue that may not be visible. These diagnostic techniques are used in a bilateral, symmetrical fashion to compare the two sides of the body. Lifting of skin folds is performed with a fold of tissue large enough to distract the skin from the fascial layer underneath (Figure 11-3).

In another technique, the fingertips are used to move the skin over the underlying structures (Figure 11-4). The force of the fingertips is sufficient only to maintain contact with the skin and is directed in line with the reflex zones. These

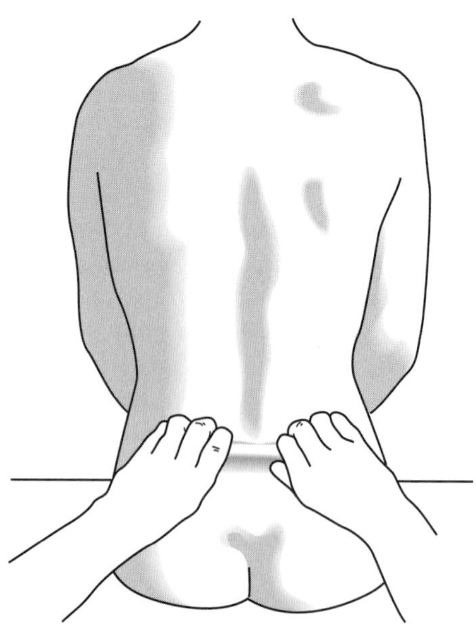

**Figure 11-3** A Diagnostic Stroke Using a Skin Fold

The tissues are grasped to pull a roll of tissue into the hands. Lifting of skin folds is done to compare the two sides of the body. The fold of tissue must be large enough to distract the skin from the fascial layer underneath.

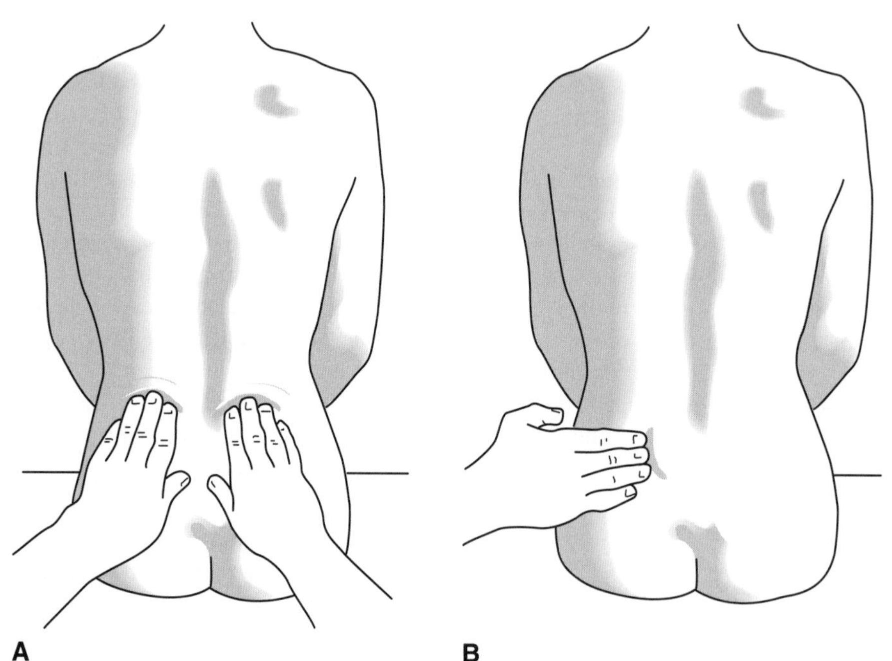


**Figure 11-4** Diagnostic Techniques Using the Fingers to Move the Tissues

**A,** Both hands are used to push a fold of tissue over the areas of interest. **B,** The fingertips of one hand are used for the same purpose. Pressure may be exerted with one or more of the fingertips, the objective being to feel the underlying tissue contours and tensions.

reflex zones have definite boundaries and locations (see Figure 11-2).

Another diagnostic stroke pulls a fold of tissue under the third finger, followed by and reinforced by the fourth finger (Figure 11-5). Individual preference for a particular diagnostic technique determines which procedure is most effective for a given patient and therapist. All are equally acceptable. Resistance encountered during any of these manual techniques usually corresponds with a cutting or scratching sensation felt by the patient. The therapist may feel a tearing sensation if the movement is carried too far.

Anecdotally, this method of massage seems to have a profound influence on autonomic function and has been successful in treating fibromyalgia (Brattberg, 1999), cervical syndromes (Heipertz, 1965), reflex sympathetic dystrophy (Solheim & Weber, 1980), pain (Teirich-Leube, 1968), anxiety states (McKechnie et al., 1983), subacute asthma (Robertson et al., 1984), and decubitus ulcers (Zandonini et al., 1980). Applied skillfully, CTM can be directed to specific pathologic conditions with predictable results (Frazer, 1978). In contrast, Reed and Held (1988) were not able to demonstrate changes in autonomic function in a range of healthy middle-aged and elderly patients. Of course, there is likely to be considerable difference between the responses detected in patients who have a demonstrated problem and in those who are healthy.

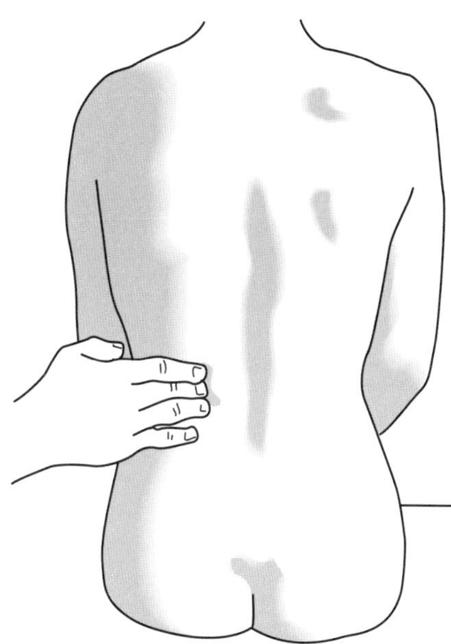

**Figure 11-5 Diagnostic Techniques Using the Fingers of One Hand to Move the Tissues**

The fingertips of one hand are used to pull a fold of tissue under the third finger, followed by and reinforced by the fourth finger, the objective being to feel the underlying tissue contours and tensions for diagnostic purposes. (NOTE: This technique is also used as a treatment technique in connective tissue massage, although some clinicians prefer to use the index finger reinforced by the middle one in a similar manner to the deep friction technique.)

All massage techniques require skill and experience on the part of the practitioner if they are to be maximally effective. This skill must be developed under the supervision of an experienced therapist; it cannot be learned from a textbook. The basic concepts, however, can be learned from reliable sources. In this regard, Ebner's descriptions of the techniques are excellent. Bischoff and Elminger (1963), Teirich-Leube (1976), and Tappen (1988) also offer excellent descriptions and illustrations.

## BASIC TREATMENT TECHNIQUE

Following the initial examination, the treatment proper may begin. Two types of strokes are usually performed: short and long. These strokes always start in the sacral, gluteal, or lumbar region, in that order. The strokes are produced by a tangential pull of the middle finger supported by either the ring or the index finger. Some practitioners prefer to use the index finger supported by the middle one. In effect, it makes no difference to the technique; however, it is important for the individual therapist to use a technique that works well for his or her own hand and yet is effective in treating the patient. The issue largely relates to the relative lengths of the individual fingers and the manual dexterity of the therapist. Figure 11-6 shows a suitable finger position that is effective for most people, particularly because it is easier to deliver controlled pressure with the index finger than with any of the other digits, especially when it is reinforced by the middle finger.

Strokes progress upward and outward to the affected zones as soon as possible. Ebner suggested that "the interrelation of all autonomically supplied structures makes it advisable to start every treatment in the sacral area, to make certain of a normal vascular reaction at the root of the autonomic supply tree. It is, however, important to progress as soon as possible into the affected segments." This concept gives rise to the notion of the *basic back section* as the beginning of a treatment session with CTM (Ebner, 1962). Because the lowest part of the autonomic nervous system is the sacral outflow of the parasympathetic division, the skin overlying the sacral areas is the place where the back section begins. Long and short CTM strokes are used around the borders of the sacrum and lower back regions, progressing upward. Figure 11-7 illustrates the length (short or long) and direction of these strokes.

CTM techniques can be applied to most areas of the body, not only the back; however, it is common for therapists to treat the back first (the basic back section) and a more peripheral body part. A detailed discussion of this technique for all body parts is beyond the scope of this text, but several excellent works describe the basic concepts of CTM and its use in most parts of the body. Although last published in the mid-1980s, Maria Ebner's book (1985) on CTM remains arguably the most authoritative source on this topic in the

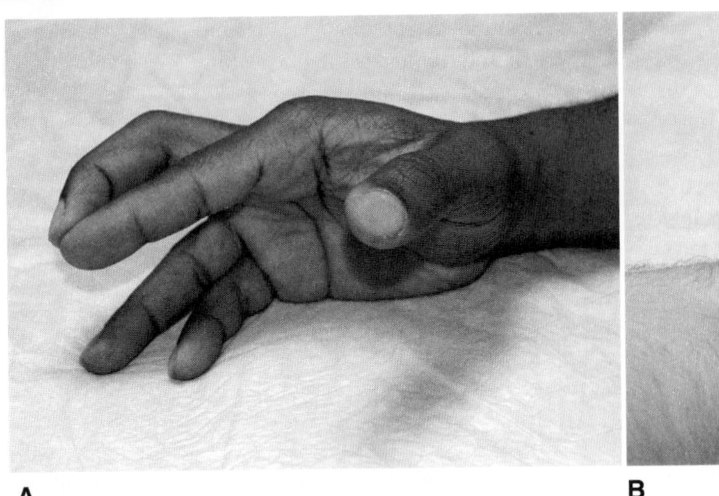

A

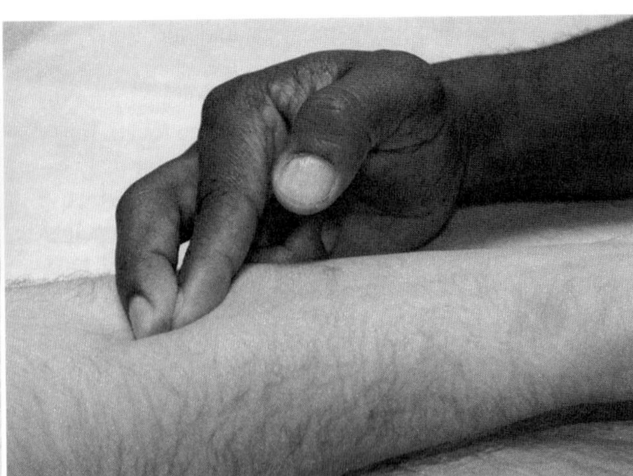

B

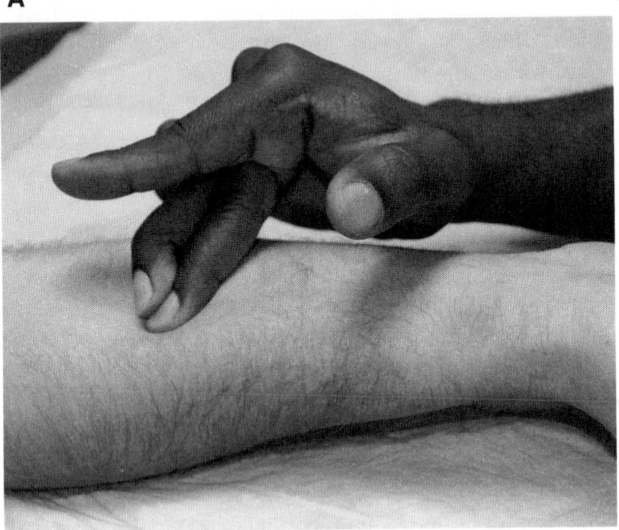

C

**Figure 11-6 Finger Positions Suitable for the Treatment Phase of CTM**

The pad of the index finger, reinforced by the middle finger **(A** and **B),** can be used to deliver both the short and long connective tissue massage (CTM) strokes. Alternatively, the pad of the middle finger, reinforced by either the index or ring finger, can be used **(C).** The individual preference of the therapist determines which hand position is most effective.

English language. Figure 11-8, *A,* illustrates CTM strokes for a variety of areas in the upper limb, and part *B* of the figure illustrates those strokes when applied to areas of the lower limb.

## EFFECTS OF CONECTIVE TISSUE MASSAGE

The patient usually feels either a cutting or a scratching sensation, or possibly dull pressure. These responses gradually fade as the patient recovers from the condition. Local and general responses are produced.

### Local Responses

The most obvious response to CTM is the local response visible over the treated areas. After several minutes, bright-red stripes appear on the skin, tracing the areas where the therapist has applied pressure. This local erythema (redness) is the result of a triple response produced in the tissues. The pressure of the fingers on the tissues produces minor trauma to the area, and this releases various substances that trigger the reflex. Release of histamine, together with other substances, produces the marked vasodilatation of the area. The local sensations are not usually painful for the patient, but if the skin is very hairy, the patient may experience some uncomfortable sensations when the hair is pulled.

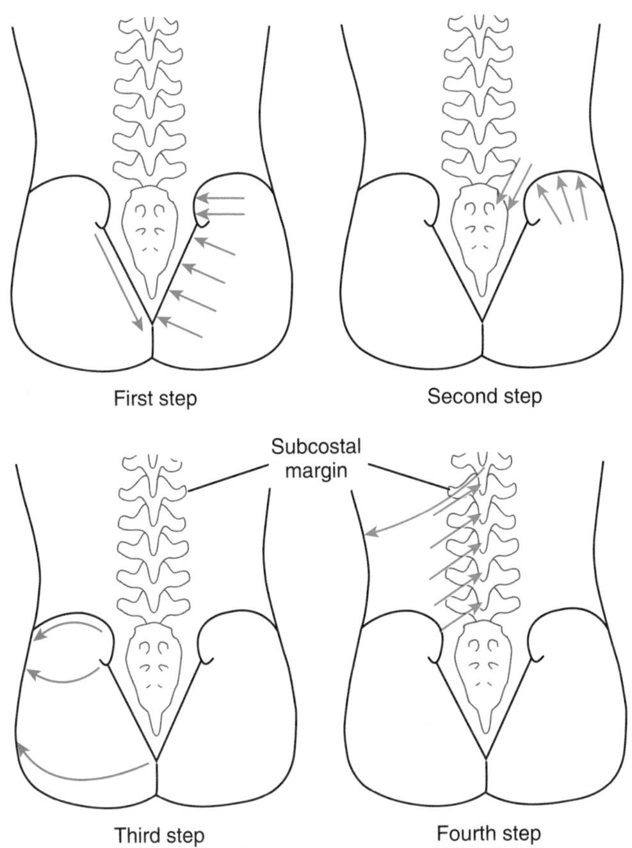


**Figure 11-7** Short and Long CTM Strokes to the Posterior Trunk

The arrows indicate the length (short or long) and the direction of the connective tissue massage (CTM) strokes in the basic back section. *(Adapted from Ebner M:* Connective tissue massage: theory and therapeutic application, *ed 2, Huntington, NY, 1985, Robert E Krieger.)*

### General Responses

The general response to CTM varies greatly, particularly depending on which areas are treated. General responses consistent with an effect on the autonomic nervous system can last several hours after treatment. These effects include stimulation of the circulation, reduced blood pressure (with extensive treatment), shortness of breath, heart palpitations, headache, dizziness, perspiration, increased glandular activity, increased visceral organ function, and rebalancing of autonomic activity by stimulation of parasympathetic activity.

## TREATMENT INDICATIONS

Connective tissue massage has diagnostic and therapeutic implications and has been used clinically to treat the signs and symptoms of circulation disorders, rheumatic diseases, malfunctions of internal organs, autonomic and central nervous system disorders, respiratory conditions (Robertson et al., 1984), connective tissue disorders, and decubitus ulcers (Zandonini et al., 1980). CTM has also been widely used in the treatment of autonomic disturbances of the cardiovascular system. Reflex sympathetic dystrophy (RSD) is an excellent example of such a condition, although the present understanding of this syndrome is far from complete (Brattberg, 1999; Fialka, Sadil, & Ernst, 1991; Solheim & Weber, 1980). CTM techniques may be helpful for the treatment of various pain syndromes (Heipertz, 1965; Teirich-Leube, 1968), especially those associated with vascular disorders. CTM has also been used to treat various psychosomatic and anxiety disorders (Helmrich, 1969; McKechnie et al., 1983).

## TREATMENT FREQUENCY AND DURATION

Following the initial examination at each treatment session, the treatment proper may begin. Each session usually consists of a general back treatment (a back section) followed by specific treatment to various zones or parts of the back or other body areas. A total treatment (including back examination) may take 30 to 40 minutes to complete and may be repeated daily for up to 10 to 12 treatments. Some patients occasionally require longer courses of treatment (several weeks); alternatively, others may show significant improvement within a few days of commencing treatment.

## CONTRAINDICATIONS

There are relatively few contraindications to CTM; however, the patient must be carefully monitored throughout treatment for signs of an abnormal autonomic response. If the patient complains of dizziness, heart palpitations, or other unusual sensations, treatment should be stopped and the patient allowed to rest. Treatment with CTM may not be possible when the patient has certain cardiac conditions, cancer or tuberculosis, certain generalized skin conditions (e.g., psoriasis) affecting the skin to be treated, and open wounds, sores, or other skin lesions over the areas where CTM would be given.

Note that hairy skin on the back or other body areas may be too painful for the patient to receive treatment. With the patient's permission, the hair may be removed so that treatment can be given.

## SUMMARY

Connective tissue massage is a relatively new treatment concept but one that continues to grow in popularity. The use of CTM undoubtedly requires specialized knowledge and experience to be maximally effective. As with most, if not all, modern rehabilitation practices, CTM is likely to achieve the best results when used in combination with other techniques in a total treatment plan tailored to meet the needs of the individual patient. The therapist wishing to incorporate CTM in his or her daily practice will need specialized training to develop skill and competence in its use. As a treatment option, CTM provides an important addition to the repertoire of rehabilitation techniques.

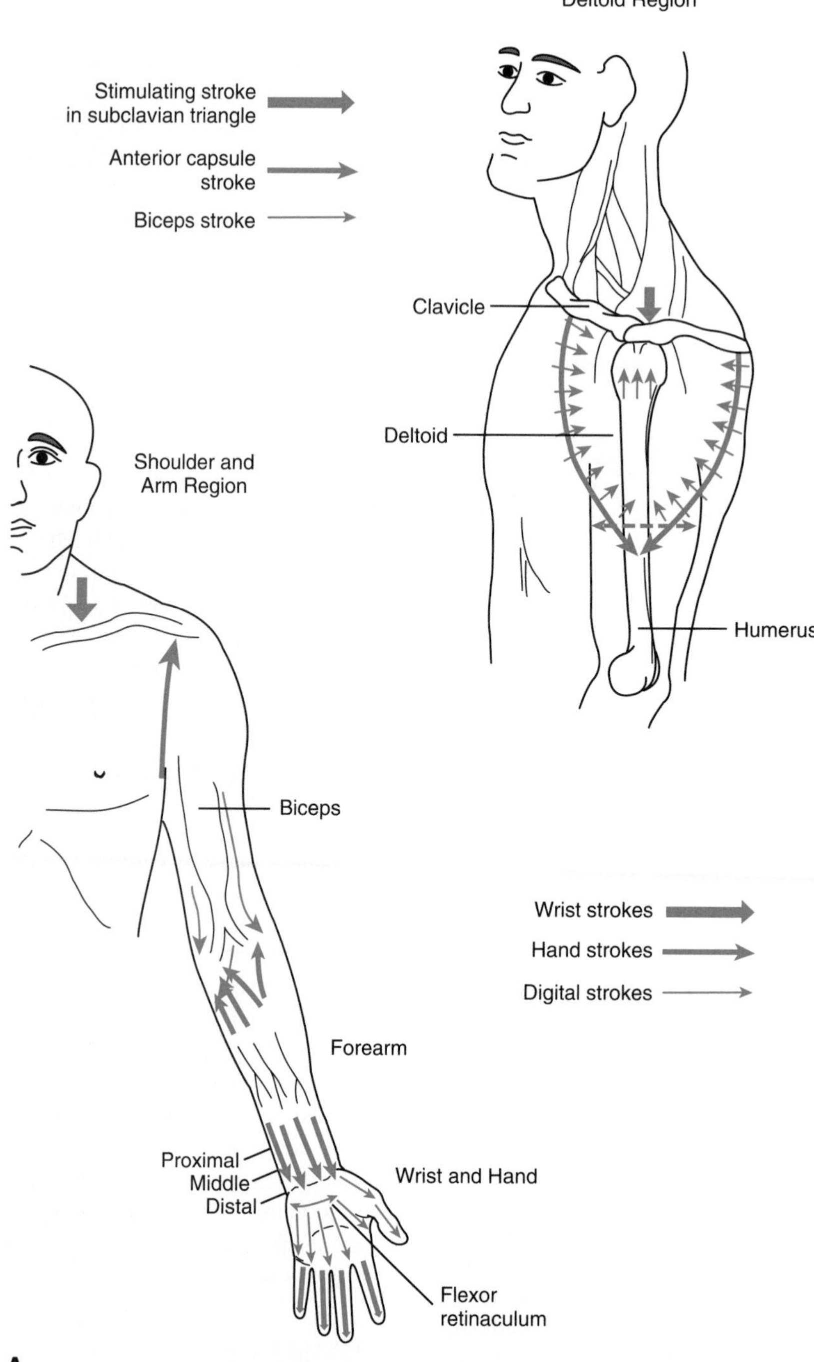


**Figure 11-8 Short and Long CTM Strokes to the Upper and Lower Limbs**

**A,** The arrows indicate the length (short or long) and the direction of the connective tissue massage (CTM) strokes for a variety of areas in the upper limb. *(Adapted from Ebner M:* Connective tissue massage: theory and therapeutic application, *ed 2, Huntington, NY, 1985, Robert E Krieger.)*

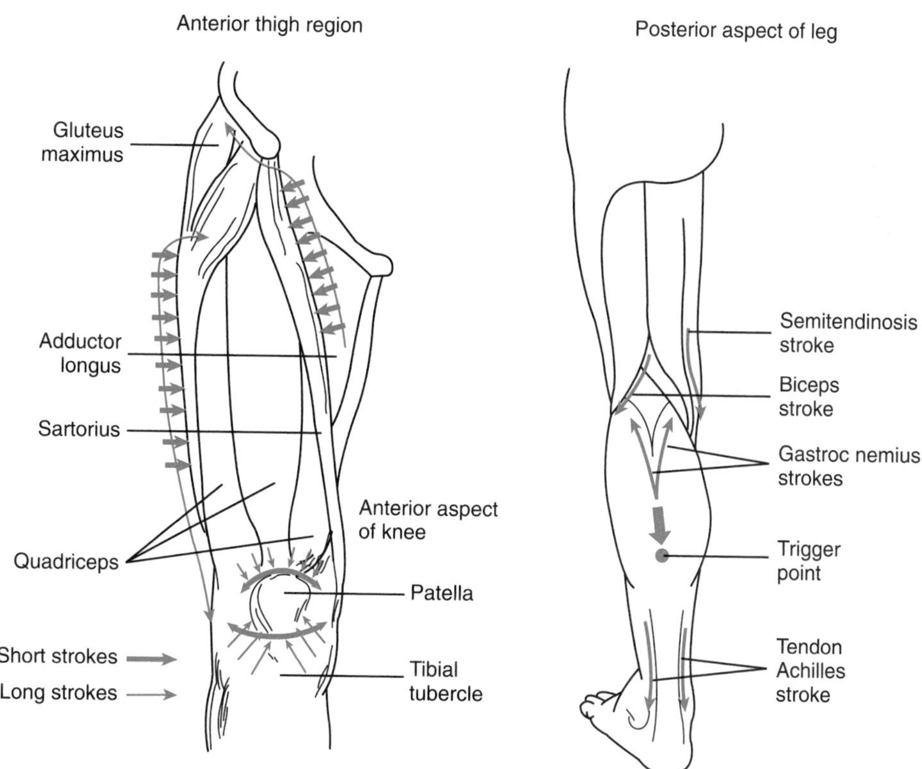


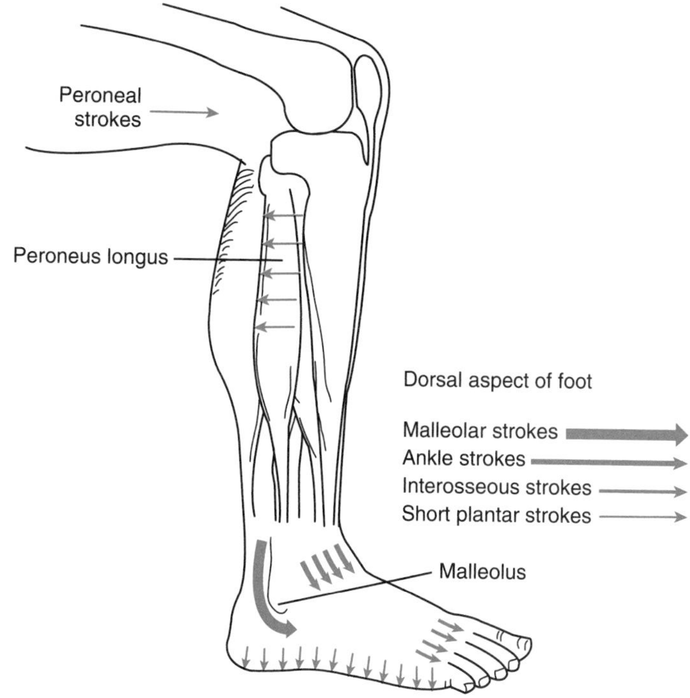


Figure **11-8, cont'd**

**B,** The arrows indicate the length (short or long) and the direction of the CTM strokes for a variety of areas in the lower limb.

## REFERENCES


Bischoff I, Elminger G: Connective tissue massage. In Licht S, editor: *Massage, manipulation and traction,* Baltimore, 1963, Waverley Press.

Brattberg G: Connective tissue massage in the treatment of fibromyalgia, *Euro J Pain* 3(3):235-244, 1999.

Dicke E: Origin and development of the method. In Dicke E, editor: *A manual of reflexive therapy of the connective tissues,* Scarsdale, NY, 1978, Sidney S Simon.

Ebner M: *Connective tissue massage: theory and therapeutic application,* Edinburgh, 1962, E & S Livingstone.

Ebner M: Connective tissue massage, *South Afr J Physiother* 21(3):4-7, 1965.

Ebner M: Connective tissue massage: therapeutic application, *N Z J Physiother* 3(14):18-22, 1968.

Ebner M: Connective tissue massage, *Physiotherapy JCSP* 64:208-210, 1978.

Ebner M: *Connective tissue massage: theory and therapeutic application,* ed 2, Huntington, NY, 1985, Robert E Krieger.

Fialka V, Sadil V, Ernst E: Reflex sympathetic dystrophy (RSD): a century of investigation and still a mystery, *Eur J Phys Med Rehab* 2(2):26-28, 1991.

Frazer F: Persistent postsympathetic pain treated by connective tissue massage, *Physiotherapy JCSP* 64:211-212, 1978.

Goats GC, Keir KA: Connective tissue massage, *Brit J Sports Med* 25(3):131-133, 1991.

Haase H: Connective tissue massage: physiological effectiveness fundamentals and technics [in German], *Z Arztl Fortbild (Jena)* 62(13):734-736, 1968.

Head H: *Die Sensibilitatsstorungen der Haut bei viszeral Erkrankungen,* Berlin, 1889.

Heipertz W: Significance of new studies on connective tissue massage in the treatment of the cervical syndrome [in German], *Beitr Orthop Traumatol* 12(6):332-334, 1965.

Helmrich HE: Psychosomatic aspect of connective tissue massage [in German], *Z Psychosom Med Psychoanal* 15(1):56-62, 1969.

Hirschberg G, Fatt I, Brown RD: Measurement of skin mobility in the upper back, *Scand J Rehab Med* 18(4):173-175, 1986.

Holey EA: Connective tissue manipulation: towards a scientific rationale, *Physiotherapy JCSP* 81(12):730-739, 1995a.

Holey EA: Connective tissue zones: an introduction, *Physiotherapy JCSP* 8(7):366-368, 1995b.

Holey EA, Watson M: Inter-rater reliability of connective tissue zones recognition, *Physiotherapy JCSP* 81(7):369-372, 1995.

Kaada B, Torsteinbo O: Vasoactive intestinal polypeptides in connective tissue massage: with a note on VIP in heat pack treatment, *Gen Pharmacol* 18(4):379-384, 1987.

Kaada B, Torsteinbo O: Increase of plasma beta-endorphines in connective tissue massage, *Gen Pharmacol* 20(4):487-489, 1989.

Kisner C, Taslitz N: Connective tissue massage: influence of the introductory treatment on autonomic functions, *Phys Ther* 48(2): 107-119, 1968.

Luedecke U: History, basis, and techniques of connective tissue massage, *Aust J Physiotherapy* 15(4):141-148, 1969.

McKechnie AA, Wilson F, Watson N et al: Anxiety states: a preliminary report on the value of connective tissue massage, *J Psychosomatic Res* 27(2):125-129, 1983.

Michalsen A, Buhring M: Connective tissue massage [in German], *Wien Klin Wochenschr* 105(8):220-227, 1993.

Reed B, Held J: Effects of sequential connective tissue massage on autonomic nervous system of middle-aged and elderly adults, *Phys Ther* 68(8):1231-1234, 1988.

Robertson A, Gilmore K, Frith PA et al: Effects of connective tissue massage in subacute asthma [letter], *Med J Aust* 140(1):52-53, 1984.

Schliack H: Scientific bases of the connective tissue massage according to Dicke (reflex massage of the connective tissue), *Scalpel* 118(23):467-477, 1965.

Schliack H: Theoretical bases of the working mechanism of connective tissue massage. In Dicke E, editor: *A manual of reflexive therapy of the connective tissues,* Scarsdale, NY, 1978, Sidney S Simon.

Solheim LF, Weber L: Post-traumatic reflex dystrophy: conservative treatment with connective tissue massage and exercise [in Norwegian], *Tidsskr Nor Laegeforen* 100(25):1497-1499, 1980.

Tappen FM: *Healing massage techniques: holistic, classic, and emerging methods,* ed 2, Norwalk, Conn, 1988, Appleton & Lange.

Teirich-Leube H: Connective tissue massage in pain syndromes, *Hippokrates* 39(15):577-579, 1968.

Teirich-Leube H: *Grondbeginselen van de Bindweefselmassage,* Uitgeversmaatchappij Lochem, 1976, De Tijdstroon, B.V.

Tophoj EA: The hypothetical basis for connective tissue massage [in Danish], *Nord Med* 83(44):1403-1404, 1970.

Zandonini G, Leoni V, Marcato MG: Connective tissue massage in the treatment of decubitus ulcer [in Italian], *Arch Maragliano Patol Clin* 36:71-75, 1980.

# Chapter 12

# Decongestive Therapy for the Treatment of Lymphedema

Rachel Fey-Larsen

Lymphedema, a disorder characterized by chronic swelling, affects approximately 140 million to 250 million people worldwide. This chapter explores a treatment technique for lymphedema known as *complete decongestive therapy* (CDT). The components consist of skin and wound care, lymphatic massage, compression, exercise, and patient education. Because of the possible complications associated with lymphedema, this technique should only be performed by or under the direction of a licensed medical professional after a thorough evaluation and plan of care have been established.

Lymphedema is an excessive accumulation of protein-rich fluid in the tissues caused by a transport failure of the lymphatic system and may be acquired through primary or secondary causes. Primary lymphedema is usually caused by a developmental disorder of the lymphatic system. It may manifest in infancy, adolescence, or late adulthood. Primary lymphedema occurs predominantly in females and typically affects either of the lower extremities. It is estimated that approximately 1 in 6000 individuals will acquire primary lymphedema (Dale, 1985).

Secondary lymphedema is most commonly caused throughout the world by filariasis, a parasitic infection that is carried by mosquitoes and settles in the lymphatic vessels. According to the Centers for Disease Control, filarial lymphedema is thought to affect as many as 120 million people in more than 80 countries.

In developed countries, cancer or its treatment is the most common cause of secondary lymphedema—the result of blockage by the tumor itself, excision of lymph nodes, or radiation therapy. Kissin et al. reported a 25% incidence of lymphedema after mastectomy, rising to 38% in patients treated with axillary lymph node dissection and radiation (Kissin et al., 1986). A comprehensive literature review concluded that the overall incidence of arm edema after mastectomy was 26% with a range from 0% to 56% within 2 years (Erickson et al., 2001). Patients who undergo treatment for cervical, vulvar, and prostate cancer have similar incidences for lymphedema of the lower extremities. The risk increases with an increase in the number of lymph node dissections and radiation therapy (Petereit et al., 1993).

Refer to DVD Chapter 12 for video demonstrations of the techniques described in this chapter.

## THE LYMPHATIC SYSTEM

The lymphatic system is a one-way drainage system that functions in concert with the circulatory system. It is primarily responsible for the uptake of plasma proteins that leak from the vascular system, as well as uptake of antigens and bacteria from the interstitium. It also transports fat from the gastrointestinal system, filters body fluids, and fights diseases with the production of white blood cells. Uptake of these molecules from the tissue spaces occurs via diffusion and osmosis across the lymph capillary membranes. Once in the lymph capillaries, the lymph fluid moves through a system of vessels and lymph nodes, where it is filtered and eventually returned to the circulatory system.

### Lymphotomes

Tissue fluid drainage occurs in distinct regions of the body called *lymphotomes*. These lymphotomes contain lymph vessels (collectors) that carry lymph fluid along their routes to a common chain of lymph nodes. Lymphotomes are divided by *watersheds*, narrow anatomical zones where the direction of lymphatic flow changes. There are four lymphotomes of the trunk, which are separated by watersheds in the midsagittal and transverse planes. These are designated *right and left thoracic lymphotomes* and *right and left abdominal lymphotomes*. Each of the extremities contains

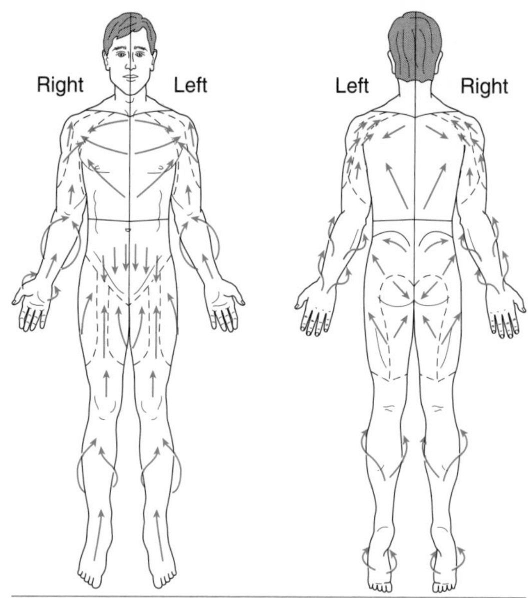


**Figure 12-1**
Drawing of body designating lymphotomes, watersheds, and direction of flow.

numerous lymphotomes as well. If a particular lymphotome becomes overwhelmed with excess fluid, superficial tissue fluids may cross the watersheds by way of collateral vessels called *anastomoses* that offer alternate routes of drainage. In this way, excess fluid can be drained into a normally functioning area and decrease the lymphatic load on the involved lymphotome (Figure 12-1).

## Lymph Capillaries

The lymphatic circulation originates with microscopic vessels called *lymph capillaries.* They are located in most tissues of the body except for the central nervous system, splenic pulp, and bone marrow. The endothelial cells walls of these vessels open and close at the cell junctions to allow the passage of fluids in response to pulse pressure, relaxation and expansion of adjacent arterioles, external compression, and muscle activity. The lymph capillaries contain two sets of valves; the interendothelial junctions prevent the backflow into the interstitium during contraction, and the intralymphatic valves prevent backflow within the lumen during expansion (Figure 12-2).

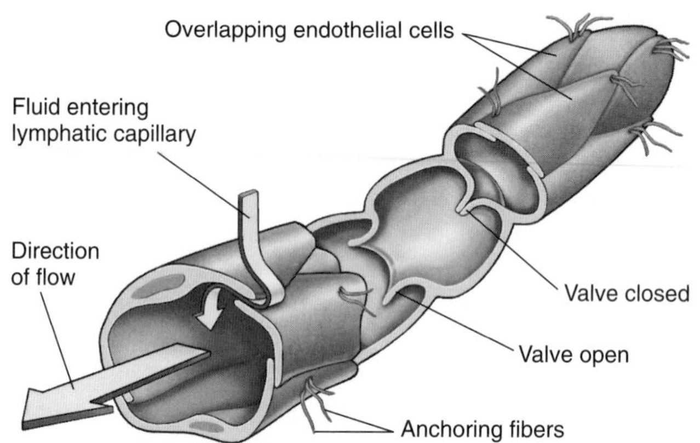


**Figure 12-2**
Schematic of lymph capillary. *(From Thibodeau G, Patton K:* Anthony's textbook of anatomy and physiology, *ed 17, St. Louis, 2003, Mosby.)*

## Collectors

The lymph capillaries combine to form larger afferent *collectors* located in the subdermal channels. The cell walls of the collectors are muscular and also contain valves to prevent backflow of the lymphatic fluid. The sections between these valves, called *lymphangions,* contract in response to autonomic sensory input and lymph volume. The afferent collectors eventually lead to lymph nodes where the lymphatic fluid is filtered. The filtered lymphatic fluid then exits the nodes through the efferent collectors. These collectors eventually unite to form larger lymphatic trunks, which finally lead to the main ducts: the *thoracic duct* or the *right lymphatic duct* (Figure 12-3).

## Trunks

The right lymphatic duct terminates at the juncture of the right internal jugular and right subclavian vein, where the fluid is returned to the vascular system. It is primarily responsible for draining the right thoracic lymphotome and arm and the right side of the face and neck. The thoracic duct originates in the pelvic region at about the level of the second lumbar vertebrae and begins with a large expanse of lymphatic tissue called the *cisterna chyli.* The thoracic duct receives lymph from the trunks of the lower extremities and

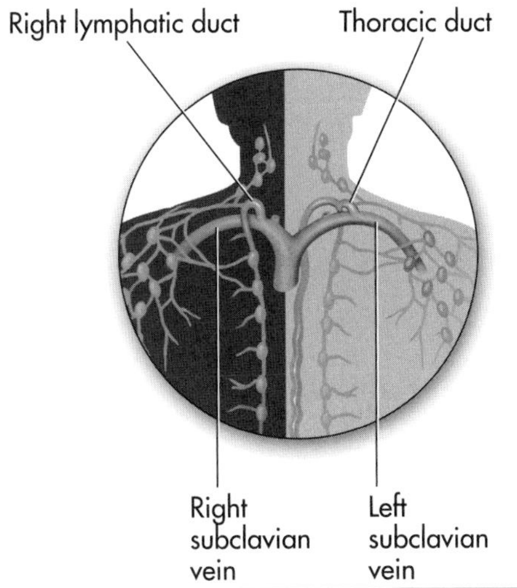


**Figure 12-3**
The right lymphatic duct drains into the right subclavian vein, and the thoracic duct drains into the left subclavian vein. (*From Thibodiau GA, Patton KT:* The human body in health and disease, *St. Louis, 2005, Mosby.*)

the intestinal trunk, and it eventually empties into the juncture of the left internal jugular and subclavian vein. It is responsible for drainage of the gut, the abdominal lymphotomes, the lower extremities, the left thoracic lymphotome, the left arm, and the left side of the face and neck (Figures 12-4 and 12-5).

## PATHOPHYSIOLOGY

Lymphedema may occur under several conditions:

- When a high load is placed on the lymph system that exceeds its working capacity. The lymph system is intact; however, it is unable to handle the increased load, and the excess fluid builds up in the tissues. This condition is sometimes known as *high-flow edema, high-volume insufficiency,* or *dynamic insufficiency.*
- When there is a breakdown in the transport capacity of the lymphatic system, either because of dysplasia of the lymphatic structures (primary lymphedema) or mechanical interruption of the system as a result of surgery or injury (secondary lymphedema). This condition may be referred to as *low-flow edema, low-volume insufficiency,* or *mechanical insufficiency.*
- Finally, a combination of the two conditions is called *safety-valve insufficiency.* Insufficiency or blockage of the lymphatic system can cause an increase in the hydrostatic pressure within the vessels. This causes their walls to weaken, which leads to leaking of the proteins and fluids into the interstitium. This in turn causes an increase in the colloid osmotic pressure in the tissue spaces, leading to even more fluid leakage (Davis, 1998; Humble, 1995). As a consequence, an increased accumulation of inflammatory agents occurs in the tissues, triggering a chronic inflammatory response. Ultimately, these processes may lead to fibrosis of the subcutaneous tissues and other skin changes such as hyperkeratosis and papillomatosis.

In addition to the subcutaneous skin changes that occur in chronic lymphedema, the risk of infection increases as a result of the decreased ability to fight infection and the increased concentration of tissue proteins. Multiple bouts of cellulitis can lead to even further degradation of the subcutaneous tissues. The individual's normal activities may decrease as well, resulting in decreased pumping action of the muscles. This contributes even more to the insufficiency of the lymphatic system. Without treatment to minimize the edema, the patient may begin to experience other complications associated with chronic swelling, such as loss of mobility, joint stiffness, weakness, pain, and poor psychological adjustment (Figure 12-6).

## PRINCIPLES OF TREATMENT

Because of the complexity of the disorder, it is often best to adopt a team approach to management. Members of the team may include a physician, nurse, physical or occupational therapist, the patient, family members, certified garment fitter, nutritionist, and psychologist. Always use sound clinical judgment when initiating treatment, and consult the referring physician when in doubt. Also, be mindful of absolute and relative contraindications and precautions before initiating treatment (Table 12-1). Absolute contraindications indicate that treatment is not appropriate

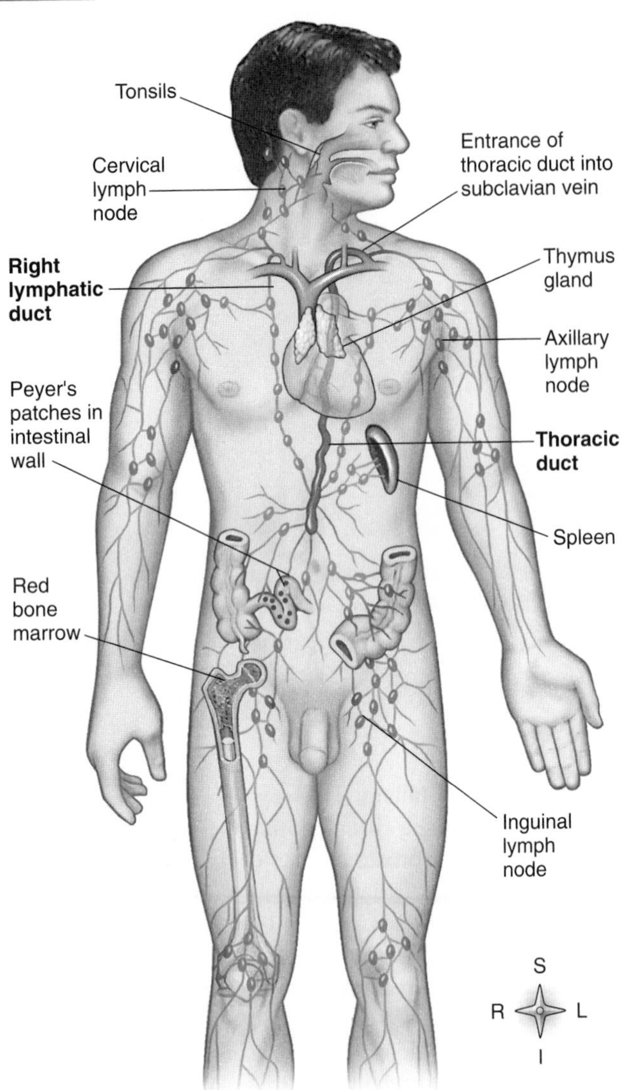


**Figure 12-4**
Schematic of lymphatic system. *(From Thibodeau G, Patton K:* Anthony's textbook of anatomy and physiology, *ed 17, St. Louis, 2003, Mosby.)*

in the presence of certain conditions. Relative contraindications and precautions indicate that treatment may be appropriate in the presence of certain conditions only with proper monitoring and good clinical reasoning. When in doubt, consult the prescribing physician.

Treatment for lymphedema begins with a thorough assessment of the patient and includes a comprehensive history and physical examination. Once the evaluation has been completed, treatment may be initiated. Although severity of the disease process, physical limitations, and lifestyle will ultimately determine the frequency and duration of treatment, in general the best results are achieved with daily treatments over a period of 2 to 3 weeks. If there are complications such as fibrosis, scar tissue, or wounds, the treatment may need to be extended beyond this time frame.

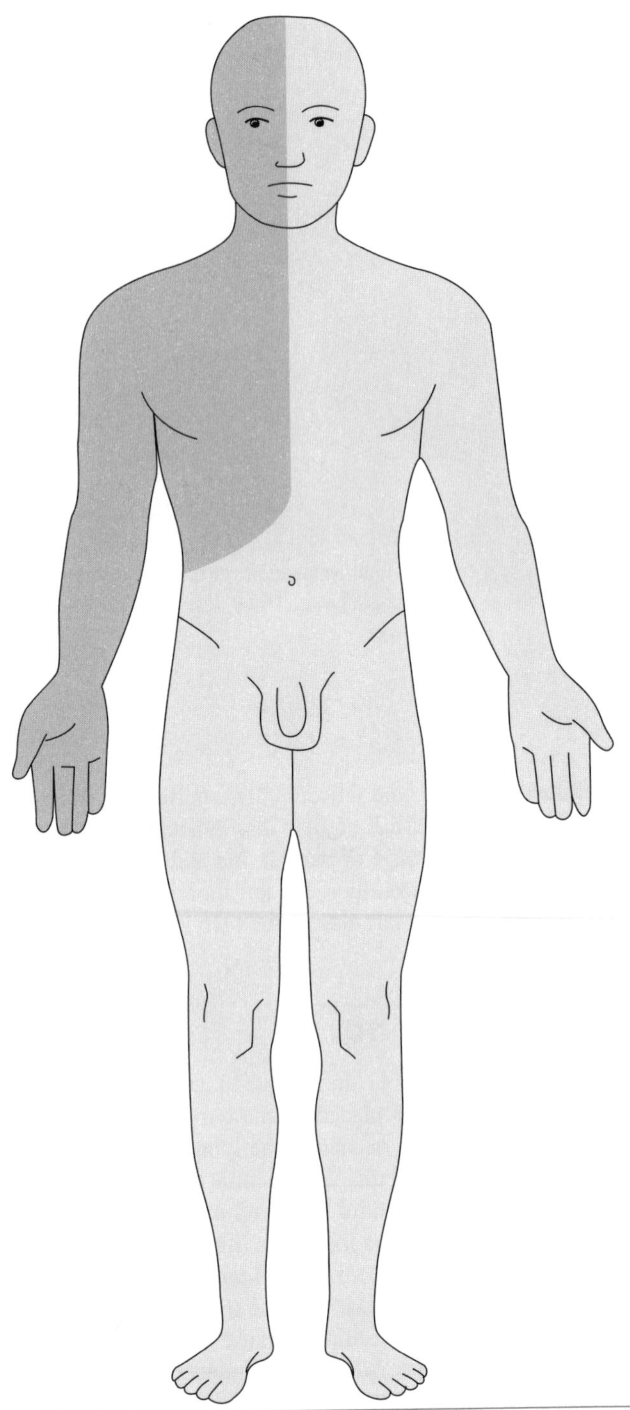

**Figure 12-5**
The *dark-shaded area* is drained by the right lymphatic duct. The *light-shaded area* is drained by the thoracic duct. *(From Thibodeau G, Patton K:* Anthony's textbook of anatomy and physiology, *ed 17, St. Louis, 2003, Mosby.)*

After the initial treatment phase is completed, the patient will begin the second phase of the treatment with a self-management program. Follow-up may or may not be necessary afterward, depending on the patient's response to treatment.

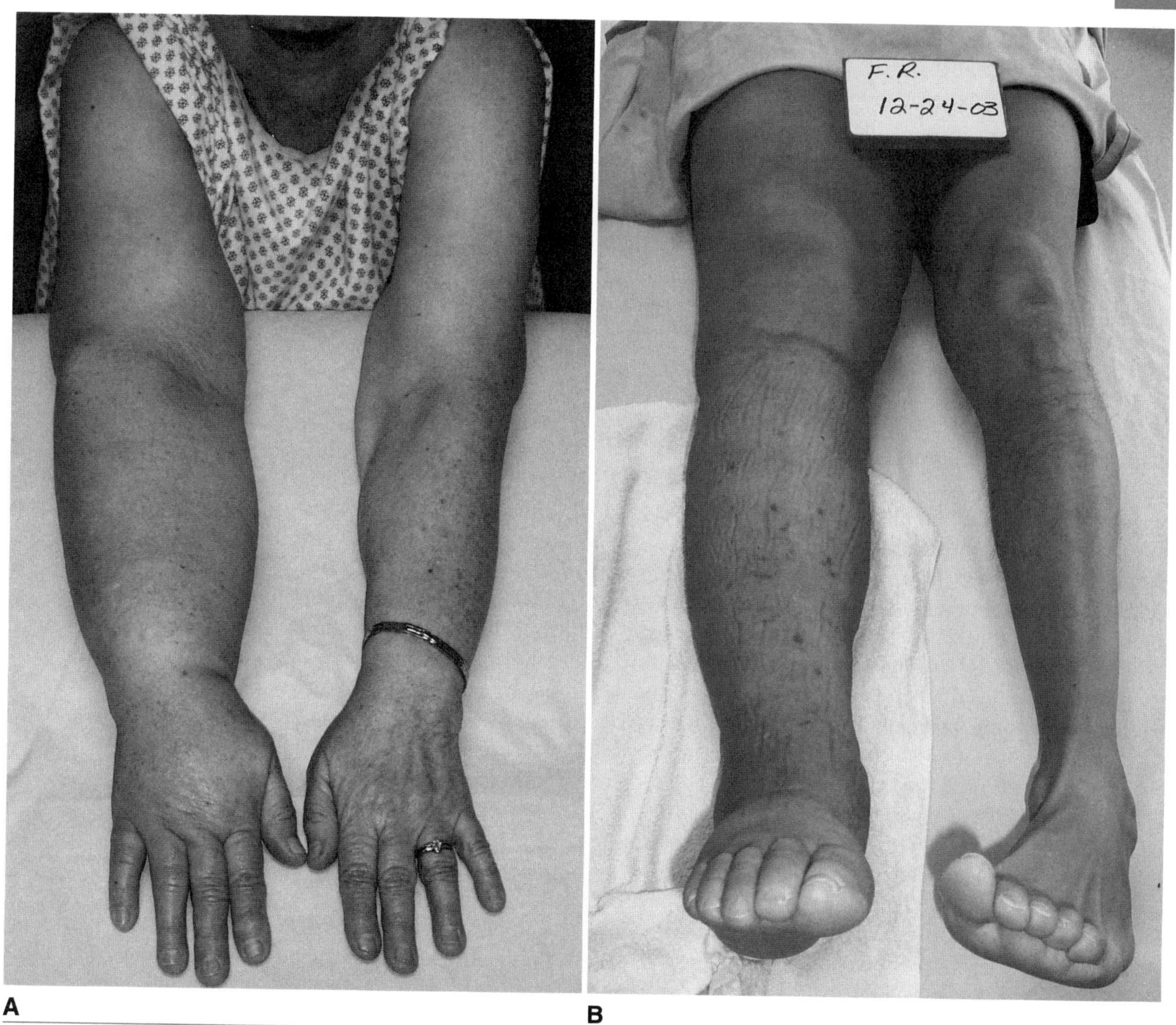


**Figure 12-6**
Examples of upper extremity **(A)** and lower extremity **(B)** lymphedema.

**Table 12-1 General Contraindications and Precautions for Therapy**

| | LYMPH FLUID MOBILIZATION | COMPRESSION | EXERCISE |
|---|---|---|---|
| Acute bacterial infection | Absolute | Absolute | Precaution |
| Malignancy | Relative | Relative | Precaution |
| Acute congestive heart failure | Absolute | Absolute | Absolute |
| Diabetes or arterial disease | | Precaution | |
| Insensate limb | | Precaution | Precaution |
| Acute deep vein thrombosis | Absolute | Absolute | Absolute |
| Low blood counts | | | Precaution |

## EVALUATION

### History

The initial evaluation is the first step in the management of lymphedema, and a good evaluation begins with a detailed medical history. First, identify the causative factor, or the event that predisposed the individual to a compromised lymphatic function. This may include lymph node excision, radiation therapy, neoplasm, or paralysis. Note whether a precipitating event such as an injury, infection, air travel, or punctures to the skin may have triggered the onset of noticeable swelling. Also, rule out the possibility of heart failure, unidentified neoplasms, deep vein thrombosis, or other vascular disorders that may present similarly. Next, identify any other treatments for lymphedema that the patient may have had and whether they were successful. Also determine the patient's lifestyle. Is he or she working, retired, or disabled? How has the swelling affected his or her daily life and function? Has the patient had to give up hobbies or has participation become more difficult? Finally, determine the patient's goals for treatment. Perhaps his or her goals are to improve mobility, to restore a healthy body image, or simply to be able to lift a gallon of milk out of the refrigerator.

### Physical Exam

After taking the medical history, it is time to move on to the physical exam. Observe the patient's posture and alignment, and note any abnormalities. Observe the skin in the entire affected quadrant. Look for excessive skin folds, lack of bony prominences, scarring or adhesions, and skin changes such as thickening of the skin (hyperkeratosis), rough areas (papillomatosis), orange peel consistency (peau d'orange), or wounds (Figure 12-7). It may be necessary to perform a full musculoskeletal examination of adjacent joints including palpation, strength, range of motion, and special tests to address any concomitant problems that may have arisen as a consequence of the lymphedema.

The next step in the physical exam is to quantify the amount of edema in the extremity. This can be done using water displacement methods or calculated volume derived from girth measurements. It has been shown that geometric formulas correlate strongly with water displacement methods (Karges et al., 2003; Sander et al., 2002), and because girth measurement is quicker and easier to perform, it is the preferred method for many clinicians. It is also a good idea to take pictures initially and periodically during the course of treatment to help support the data.

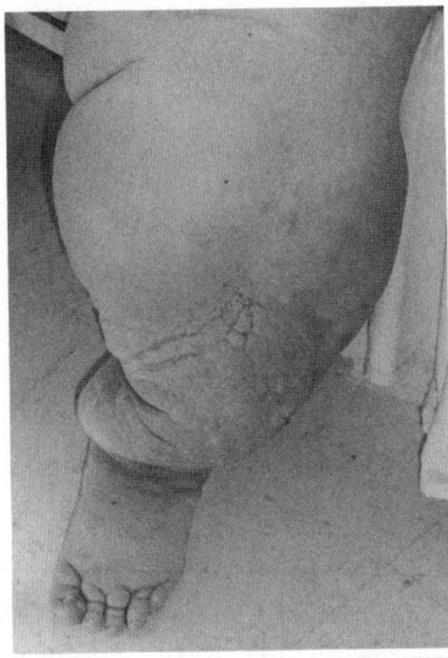

**Figure 12-7**
Hyperkeratosis.

The volumetric method is a water displacement method using a tool called a *volumeter.* Water is filled into a special vessel just to the overflow spout. The extremity is placed in the vessel, and the displaced water flows out of the spout and into a beaker where the volume can be measured.

Girth measurements can be performed by taking circumferential measurements at 10-cm intervals and applying the following formula for volume of a truncated cone at each segment:

$$V=(h)(C^2+Cc+c^2)/12(\pi)$$

where $V$ is the volume, $h$ is the height between intervals, $C$ is the circumference at one end of the segment, and $c$ is the circumference at the other end of the segment. The total volume is the sum of all segments. In unilateral involvement, the normal limb can be used to determine the amount of edema present. Progress should be tracked on a weekly basis to determine the efficacy of treatment (Casley-Smith, 1998; Karges et al., 2003; Sander et al., 2002).

After the examination has been completed, take some time to discuss your findings and explain the treatment rationale. Patients tend to be more compliant when they have clear goals and a basic understanding of the treatment rationale. This is especially important for this type of therapy because so much of the success is directly related to the patient's ability to follow through with the program at home.

## SKIN AND WOUND CARE

Before beginning treatment, the skin needs to be cleansed thoroughly and moisturized using a pH-balanced, alcohol-free, and fragrance-free lotion. The presence of a wound necessitates an evaluation performed by a medical professional licensed to perform wound care. Ideally, the wound care can be performed in the clinic before each session, but if not, the patient will need to have this addressed elsewhere before initiating treatment.

## LYMPH FLUID MOBILIZATION

Lymph fluid mobilization is the massage component of the five-part treatment regimen known as *decongestive therapy.* The goals of the technique are fourfold: increase peristalsis of the lymphangion, break down fibrotic tissue, increase lymph volume in collateral and primary vessels, and decrease congestion in the interstitium.

There are several basic principles to keep in mind when performing lymph fluid mobilization:

- Treatment begins at the termination of the lymphatic system, clearing proximal lymphotomes before moving into more distal, affected lymphotomes.
- The direction of the massage is in the direction of a cleared lymphotome.
- An affected area is treated long enough to elicit a tissue response.

- Gentle pressure is applied, just enough to stimulate the lymphatic system but not the circulatory system.

Some schools teach highly specific stroke techniques to accomplish this technique, whereas others maintain that the specific manner in which the actual strokes are performed is not critical to the outcome. The following strokes are commonly applied in lymph fluid mobilization, but may be adapted depending on the body area being treated.

## STROKES

*Standing circles.* Applied mainly over lymph nodes and large areas such as the abdomen. Using the palmar surface of the hand or fingers, a stretch is applied to the skin in a circular pattern. Gentle pressure is applied in the direction of lymph flow. The pressure is then released while maintaining skin contact through the remainder of the arc (Figure 12-8).

*Pump stroke.* Applied mainly to the extremities. Place the hand on the extremity with the thumb and fingers facing proximally along the long axis. Begin with the hand cupped and thumb and distal fingers in contact with the skin. Slowly lower the hand and flatten the palm. Gradually return to the cupped position as you progress proximally along the extremity (Figure 12-9).

*Turn stroke.* Applied mainly on large surfaces, such as the abdomen, chest, back, or thigh. Begin this stroke with the hand slightly cupped and the ulnar aspect of the hand in contact with the skin and facing the direction

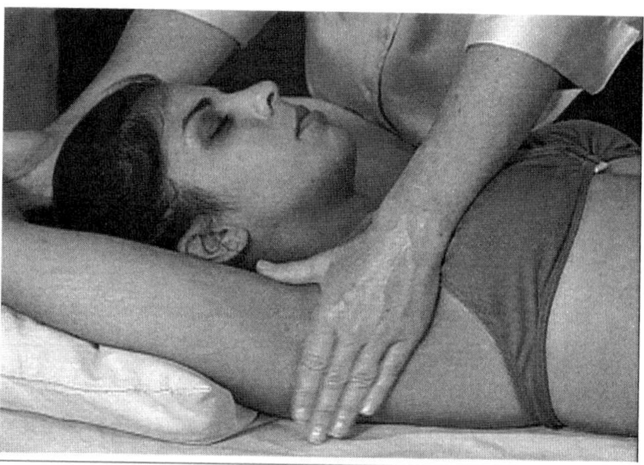

Figure 12-8
Standing circles at the axilla.

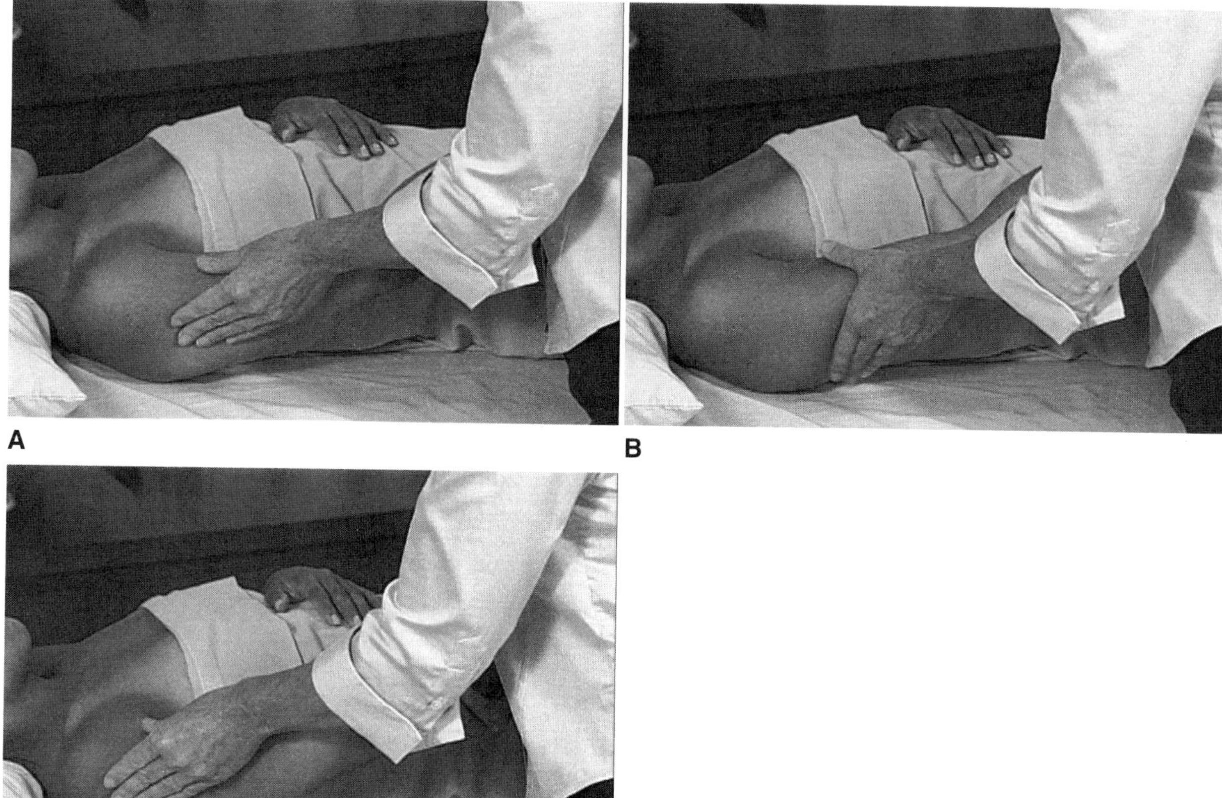

Figure 12-9
Start **(A)**, middle **(B)**, and end **(C)** of the stroke along the arm.

of intended lymph movement. Gradually transfer skin contact across the palm as the hand is brought into ulnar deviation and the palm flattens. Then lift the ulnar side of the palm slightly, and finish the stroke with the tips of the thumb, index, and middle fingers adducted slightly and in contact with the patient's skin (Figure 12-10).

*Thumb circles.* Used in very small or fibrotic areas. Apply a half-arc with the distal end of the left thumb. Apply a half-arc with the other thumb in the opposite direction. Alternate this movement as you progress in the desired direction of lymph flow (Figure 12-11).

These strokes may be combined in a variety of ways as you progress through the massage sequence.

## SEQUENCES AND PATHWAYS

The instructions in this section are meant to provide a general plan for mobilizing stagnant tissue fluid through the lymphatic system and should be considered guidelines only, as each unique case will determine the best course of action. *Common sequences* in this section are combined to form larger *treatment pathways.*

### Common Sequences

#### *Brief Cervical Sequence* (Figure 12-12)

**Patient Is Supine** (Figure 12-13)

- Standing circles to bilateral supraclavicular fossae and cephalic chains, alternating five times each, for a minimum of 25 revolutions

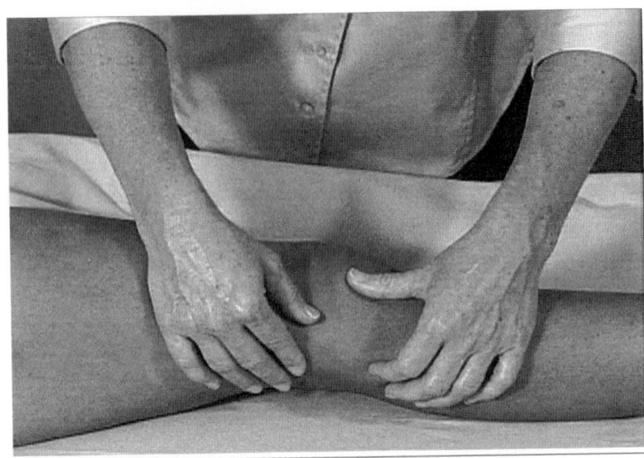

Figure 12-11
Thumb circles at the lateral knee.

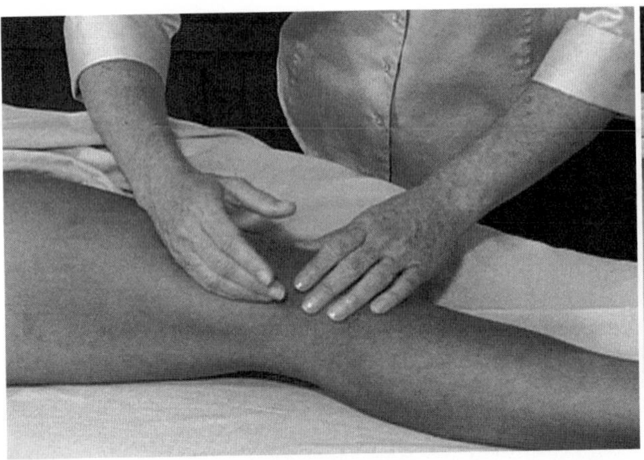

A

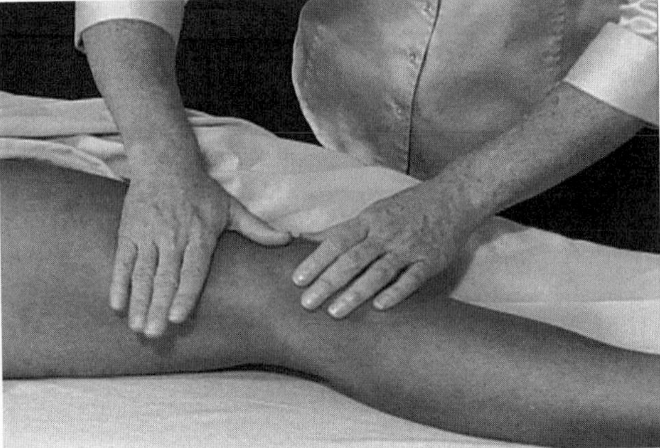

B

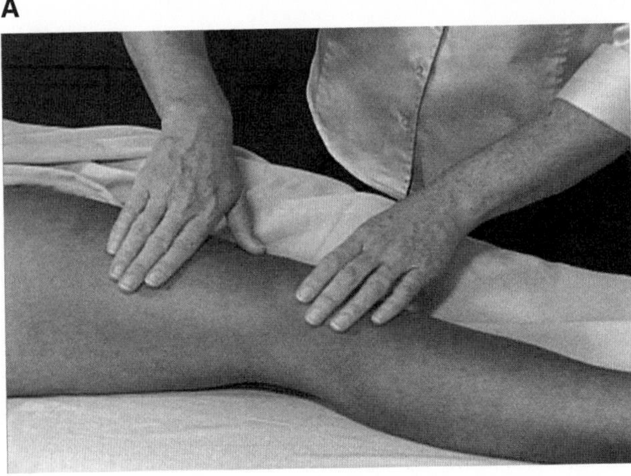

C

Figure 12-10
Start **(A),** middle **(B),** and end **(C)** of the stroke.

### *Brief Abdominal Sequence* (Figure 12-14)

**Patient Is Supine** (Figure 12-15)

- Turn strokes × 5 to each quadrant of abdomen, with the pumping direction toward the cisterna chyle. Repeat the entire abdominal sequence five times.
- Patient should perform diaphragmatic breathing consisting of a deep breath followed by forced exhalation and simultaneous compression of the abdominal muscles using the palms of the hands. Repeat five times.

### *Secondary Arm Sequence* (Figure 12-16)

**Patient Is Supine**

- Pump stroke from shoulder to neck
- Pump stroke along lateral aspect of upper arm to deltoid region
- Pump stroke along posterior aspect of upper arm to deltoid region
- Pump stroke along medial aspect of upper arm in a spiral pattern toward lateral or posterior aspect and on to deltoid region (Figure 12-17)
- Standing circles to the anticubital area, pumping in an upward direction
- Standing circles around the olecranon process in a doughnut pattern (Figure 12-18)
- Pump or turn strokes along the medial forearm, then the lateral forearm, spiraling medially and laterally from the midline to the anterior side
- Thumb circles to the dorsum of the hand, from the base of the fingers to the wrist, then massage each finger separately if involved (Figure 12-19)

### *Secondary Leg Sequence* (Figure 12-20)

**Patient Is Supine**

- Standing circles to the inguinal nodes of the involved side
- Pump or turn strokes along the thigh

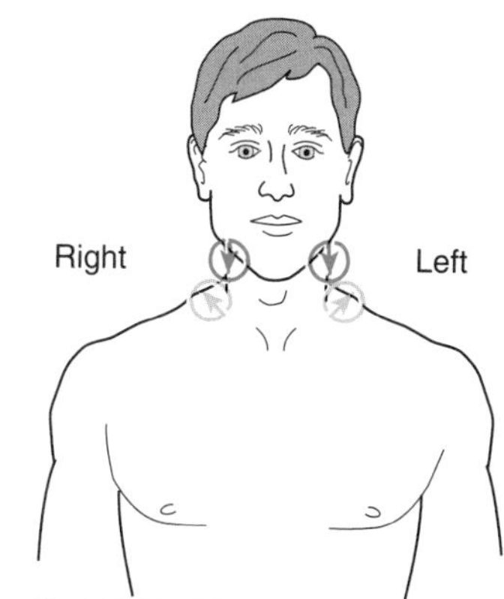


Figure **12-12**
Schematic of the brief cervical sequence.

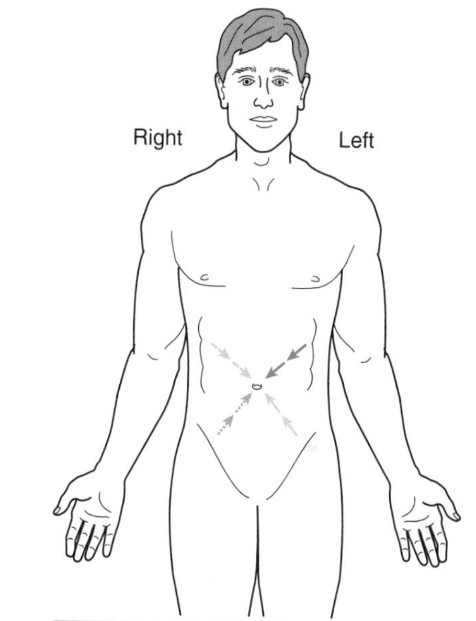


Figure **12-14**
Schematic of the brief abdominal sequence.

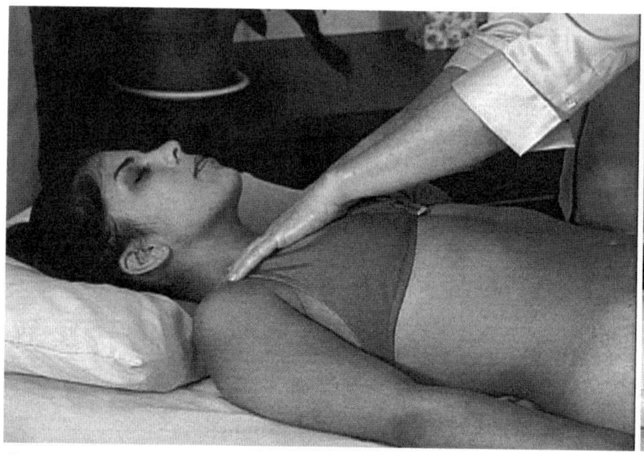
A

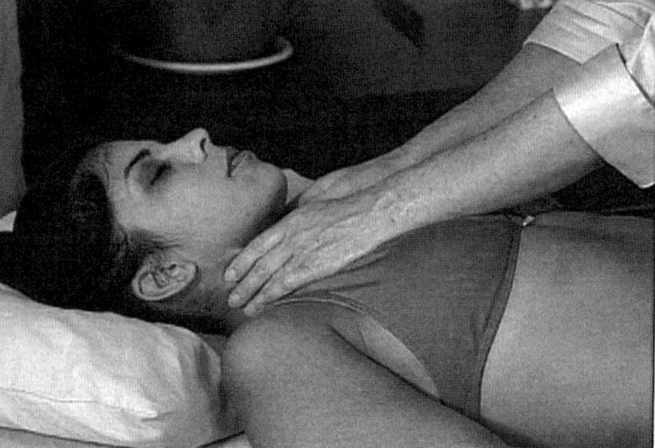
B

Figure **12-13**
Both hand positions for the brief cervical sequence.

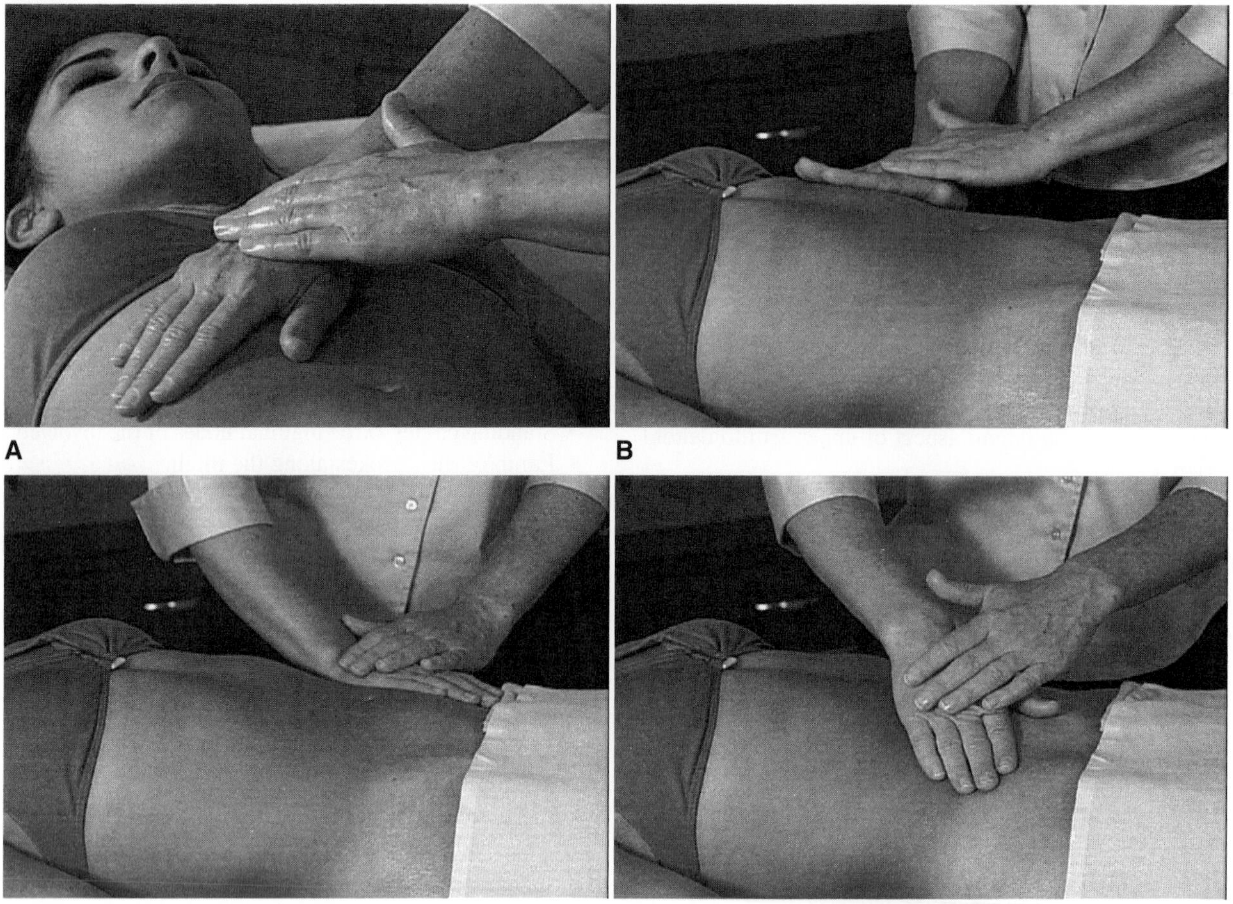

A

B

C

D

Figure **12-15**

Each hand position for the brief abdominal sequence.

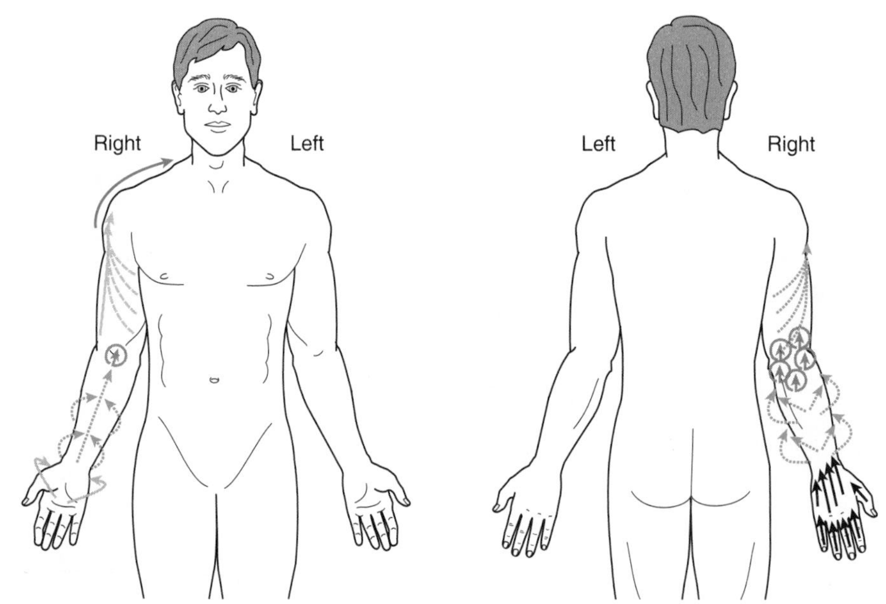


Figure **12-16**

Schematic of the secondary arm sequence.

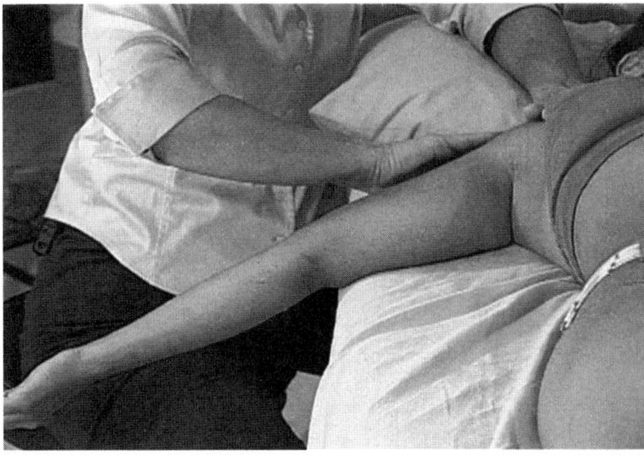

Figure **12-17**
Spiral motion from the elbow to the deltoid.

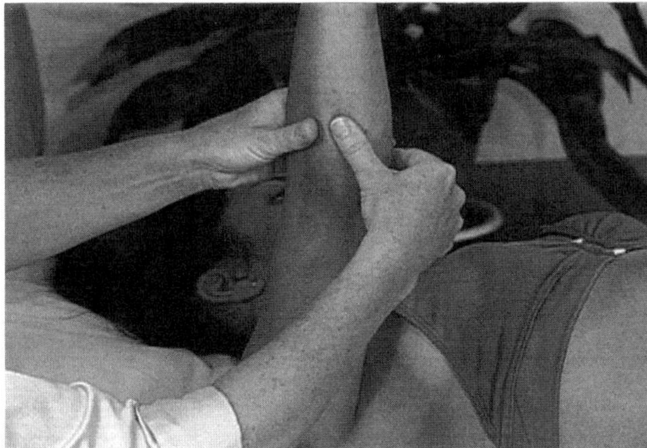

Figure **12-18**
Doughnut pattern around the olecranon.

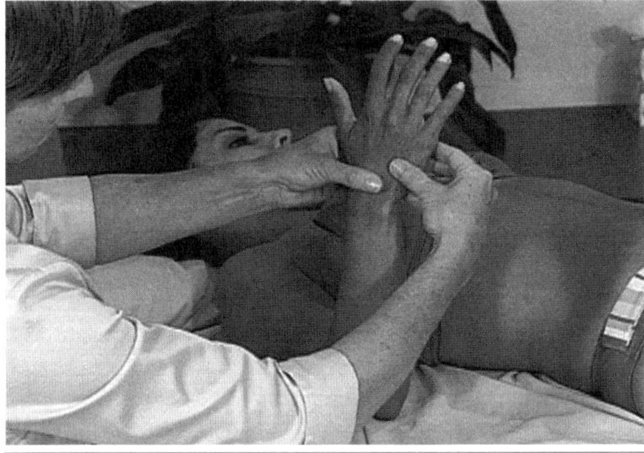

Figure **12-19**
Thumb circles to the dorsum of the hand.

  - From the lateral knee to the iliac crest
  - From the anterior knee to the iliac crest
  - From the medial knee to the lateral iliac crest
- Standing circles with both hands in the popliteal fossa (Figure 12-21)
- Alternating thumb circles toward the popliteal fossa along lateral knee from the posterior to the anterior aspect (Figure 12-22)
- Alternating thumb circles along the medial knee from the posterior to anterior aspect
- Pump strokes along the anterior lower leg from the ankle to the knee
- Pump strokes along the posterior lower leg from the ankle to the popliteal fossa
- Standing circles around the lateral and medial malleoli
- Alternating thumb circles along the dorsum of the foot from the base of the toes to the ankle
- Effleurage of the entire leg

## Treatment Pathways

### *Secondary Unilateral Upper Extremity Involvement* (Figure 12-23)

**Patient Is Supine**

- Brief cervical sequence
- Standing circles progressing along the supraclavicular nodes from both shoulders to the supraclavicular fossa
- Brief abdominal sequence
- Standing circles to the contralateral axilla
- Standing circles to the ipsilateral groin
- Standing circles to the ipsilateral axilla
- Turn strokes across the chest
  - From the anterior superior midsagittal watershed to the contralateral axilla
  - Across the watershed
  - From the ipsilateral axilla to the watershed and across to the other side
  - Pumping direction toward the contralateral side
- Pump or turn strokes along the anterior ipsilateral trunk
  - From the ipsilateral transverse watershed to the inguinal area
  - Across the watershed
  - From the axilla to the watershed and across

**Patient Is Prone or Sidelying**

- Turn strokes across the back
  - From the posterior superior midsagittal watershed to the contralateral axilla
  - Across the watershed
  - From the ipsilateral axilla to the watershed and across
- Turn strokes along the side of the trunk
  - From the posterior ipsilateral transverse watershed to the ipsilateral iliac nodes
  - Across the watershed
  - From the ipsilateral axilla to the watershed and across

**Patient is Supine**

See Figure 12-16 for the secondary arm sequence.

NOTE: Be sure to repeat clearance of the proximal areas of lymphatic flow occasionally.

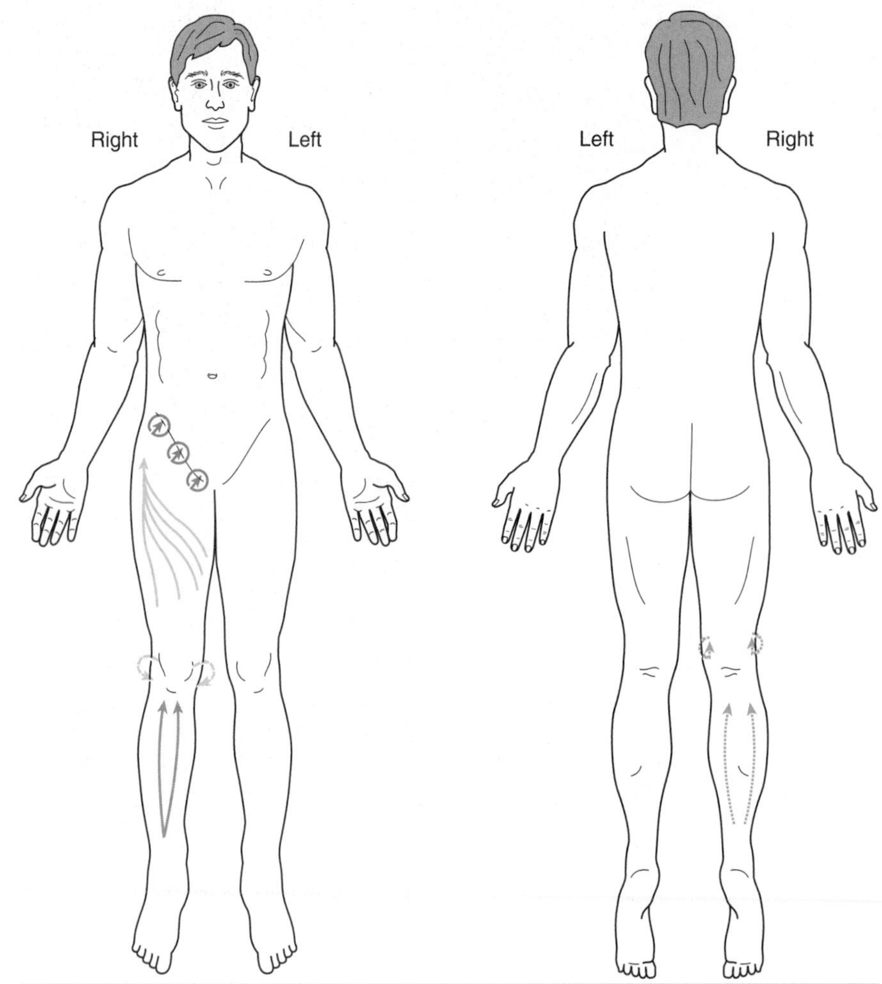


Figure 12-20
Schematic of the secondary leg sequence.

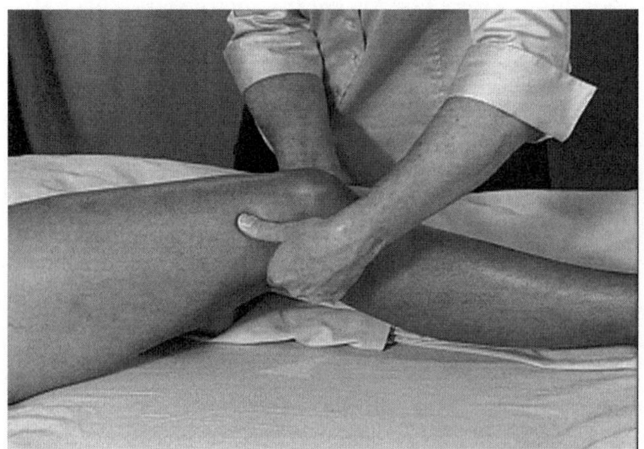

Figure 12-21
Stationary circles in the popliteal fossa.

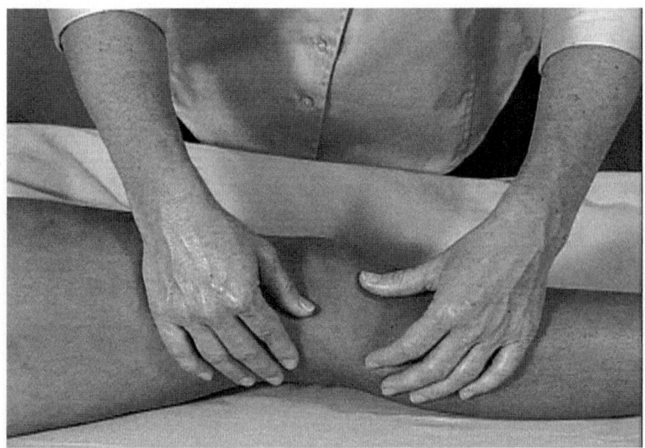

Figure 12-22
Alternating thumb circles to the lateral knee.

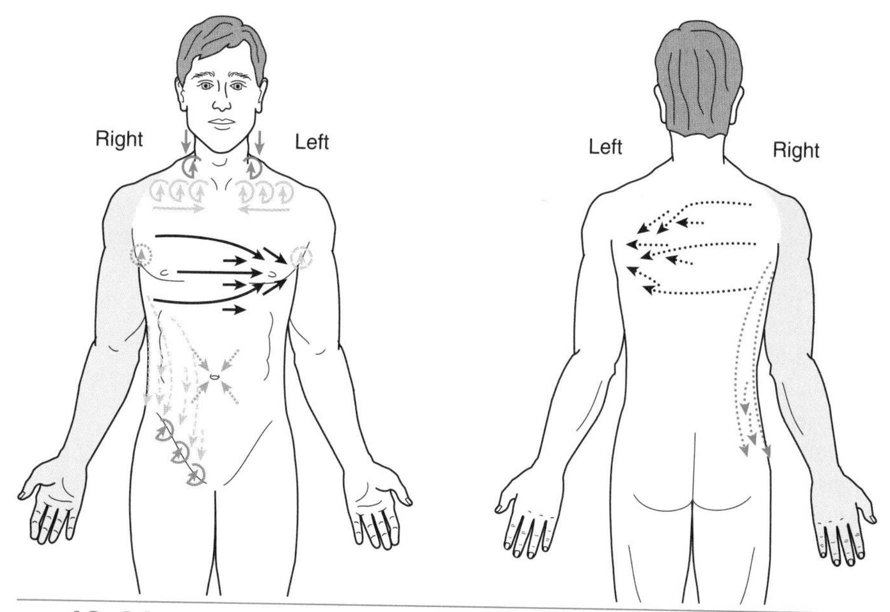


Figure **12-23**

Schematic of trunk clearance for secondary unilateral involvement.

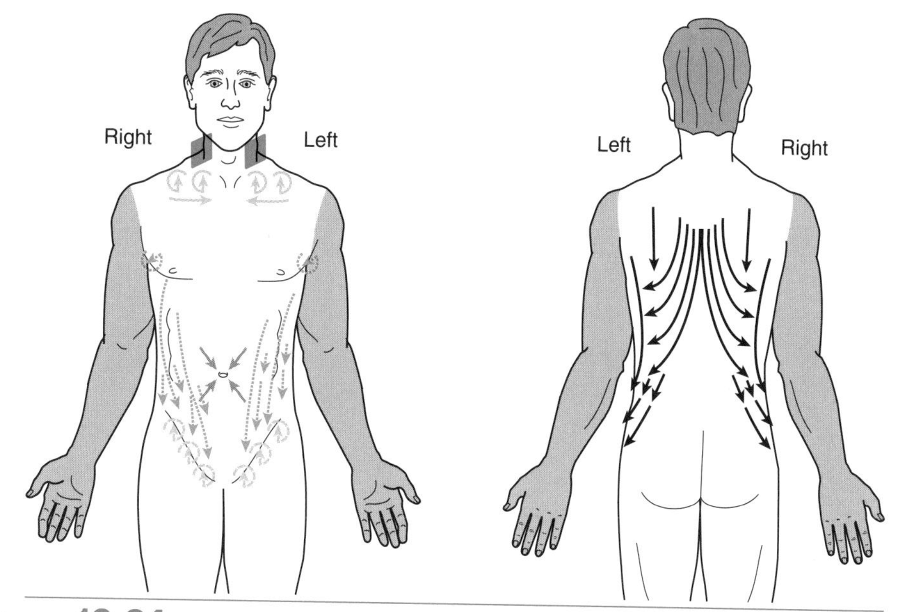


Figure **12-24**

Schematic of trunk clearance for secondary bilateral upper extremity involvement.

### *Secondary Bilateral Upper Extremity Involvement* (Figure 12-24)

**Patient Is Supine**

- Brief cervical sequence
- Standing circles progressing along the supraclavicular nodes from both shoulders to the supraclavicular fossa 5 times
- Standing circles to right axilla 25 times
- Standing circles to right groin 25 times
- Brief abdominal sequence
- Pump or turn strokes along the right side of the trunk
    - From the transverse watershed to the inguinal area
    - Across the watershed
    - From the axilla to the watershed and across

**Patient Is Prone or Sidelying**

- Turn strokes along the right side of the trunk
    - From the posterior transverse watershed to the iliac nodes
    - Across the watershed
- From the right axilla to the watershed and across
- Secondary arm sequence to the right side

**Patient Is Supine**

- Repeat pathway on the left side

NOTE: Be sure to repeat clearance of the proximal areas of lymphatic flow occasionally.

### *Secondary Unilateral Lower Extremity Involvement* (Figure 12-25)

**Patient Is Supine**

- Brief cervical sequence
- Brief abdominal sequence
- Standing circles to ipsilateral axilla
- Standing circles to contralateral groin
- Standing circles to ipsilateral groin
- Turn or pump strokes along ipsilateral side of trunk
  - From transverse watershed to axilla
  - Across transverse watershed
  - From ipsilateral groin and iliac crest to watershed and across
- Turn strokes along lower abdomen
  - From midsagittal watershed to contralateral groin and iliac crest
  - Across midsaggital watershed
  - From ipsilateral groin and iliac crest to midsaggital watershed and across
- Turn or pump strokes along ipsilateral buttocks
  - Along side of hip to iliac crest
  - From gluteal fold to iliac crest
  - From iliac crest to transverse watershed and across
- Secondary leg sequence

### *Secondary Bilateral Lower Extremity Involvement* (Figure 12-26)

**Patient Is Supine**

- Brief cervical sequence
- Brief abdominal sequence
- Standing circles to right axilla
- Standing circles to right groin
- Turn or pump strokes along right side of trunk
  - From transverse watersheds to ipsilateral axilla
  - Across transverse watersheds
  - From bilateral groin and iliac crest to ipsilateral watershed and across

**Patient Is Prone or Sidelying**

- Turn strokes along right side of the back
  - From posterior transverse watershed to ipsilateral axilla

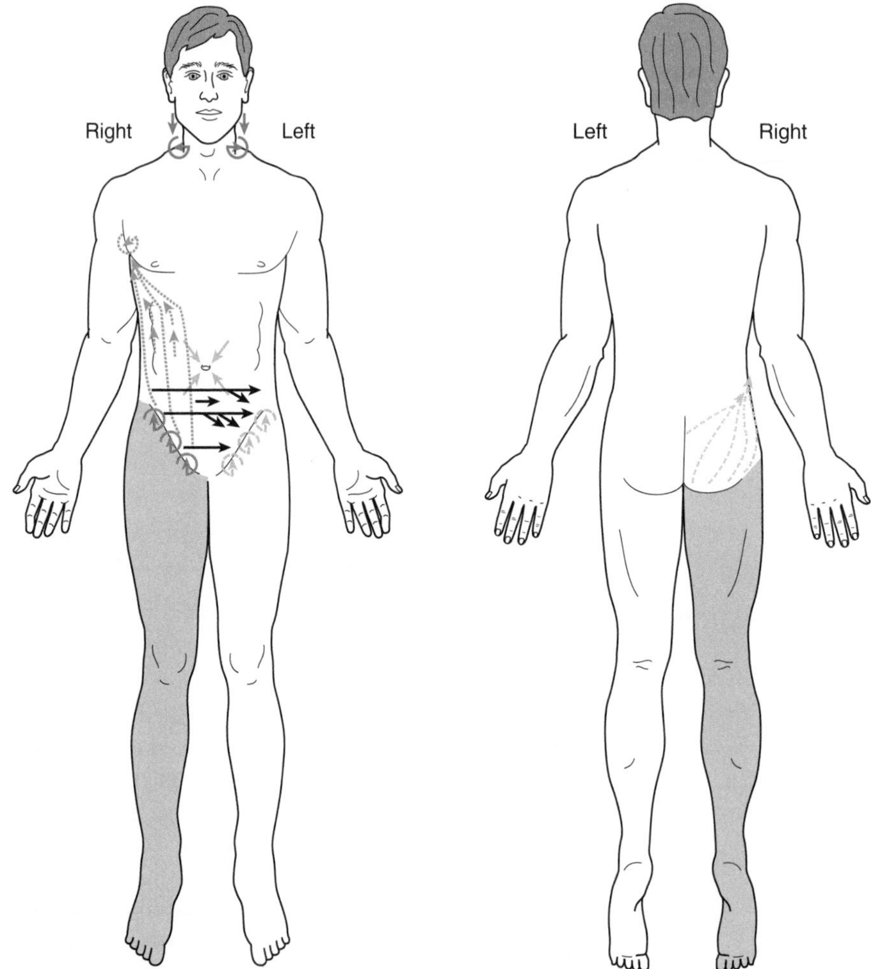


Figure **12-25**
Schematic of trunk clearance for unilateral lower extremity involvement.

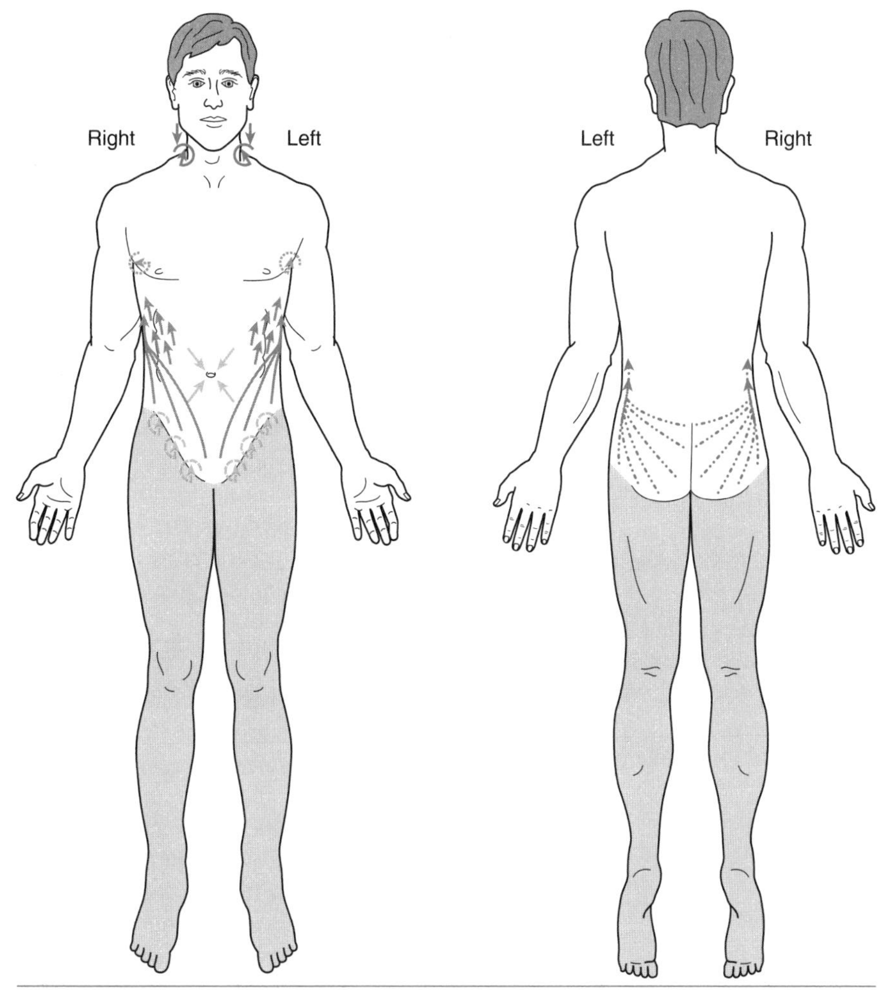


**Figure 12-26**
Schematic of trunk clearance for bilateral lower extremity involvement.

  - Across watershed
  - From iliac crest and buttocks to ipsilateral watershed and across
- Turn or pump strokes along right buttocks
  - Along side of hip to iliac crest
  - From gluteal fold to iliac crest
- From iliac crest to transverse watershed and across
- Secondary leg sequence to the right side
- Repeat the entire pathway on the left side.

### Other Lymphedema of the Extremities

Follow the appropriate pathways used for secondary lymphedema with these exceptions:

- Primary UE lymphedema is usually associated with lymphedema in other areas as well. Use the normal routes of drainage through the nodes, but do not direct fluid into another lymphotome that may be involved.
- Primary LE lymphedema is often unilateral, so tissue fluid may be directed into adjacent, uninvolved lymphotomes. You may use the normal pathway through the lymph nodes, and be sure to clear proximal areas often.
- Filarial lymphedema can be treated through the normal lymphatic pathways.
- Chronic venous insufficiency is usually associated with lymphostasis. It can be treated similarly to primary LE lymphedema.

## COMPRESSION THERAPY

Immediately following lymph fluid mobilization, compression must be applied. During the clinical phase of treatment, this usually involves a multilayer system of bandages consisting of a stockinette, padding, and layered compression bandages. The purpose of the compression is to prevent reaccumulation of evacuated tissue fluid, augment the external compression achieved through the skin and atmospheric pressure, break up fibrosis, and reshape the limb. It should be worn at all times during the day and night but may be taken off for showering, provided it is reapplied immediately afterward.

### Bandaging Components

- Stockinette
  - The initial layer used to keep the bandages clean and absorb moisture from the skin
  - No compression component to this layer
  - Tubular dressing sold in large rolls can be cut to fit the length of the arm
  - Softer, nonelastic products are best
- Padding
  - The second layer is used to provide protection to bony prominences and to facilitate more even compression and shape the limb
  - No compression component to this layer
  - Sold in individual rolls in varying widths
- Foam
  - Used in conjunction with the padding layer to help shape the limb and break up fibrotic areas
  - Varying densities of foam sold in precut shapes or in sheets for custom shaping
  - Commonly used around malleoli, knees and elbows, dorsum of hand and foot, and areas of high fibrosis
  - Foam chips also available for very fibrous areas
- Short stretch bandages
  - Final layer of bandages used to provide compression
  - All-cotton fibers sold in individual rolls of varying widths
  - Short stretch achieved via the weave of the fibers; no elastic in these bandages
  - Short stretch provides high working pressure and low resting pressure
  - Because a change in tissue pressure helps drive tissue fluid into the lymphatic vessels, short stretch bandages are desired over long stretch bandages because they provide higher pressure with muscle activity and lower pressure at rest
  - Applying more layers distally and decreasing the amount and width of layers, while progressing proximally, helps to achieve a proper compression gradient.

*Application of compression bandages to the arm (Box 12-1):*

**Supplies**

1-yard stockinette
One to two rolls elastic gauze wrap, 1- to 2-cm width
Foam padding in various shapes
Two rolls cotton padding, 10-cm width
One short stretch bandage, 6-cm width
One to two short stretch bandages, 8-cm width
1 short stretch bandage, 10-cm width
Paper tape, 2-inch width

*Application of compression bandages to the leg (Box 12-2):*

**Supplies**

1 to 2 yards stockinette
One to two elastic gauze bandages, 1- to 2-cm width
Various foam pieces as indicated
Two to three rolls of cotton padding, 10- to 15-cm width
Short stretch bandages (depending on the size and shape of the leg)

- One 6-cm width
- One to two, 8-cm width
- One to two, 10-cm width
- One to two, 12-cm width

### Compression Garments

Once the patient has achieved maximal reduction of the limb, he or she can be fitted into a compression garment. There are many different options for patients, including various styles, colors, fabrics, and compression ratings. Unless you have been certified, your best bet is to establish a relationship with a certified fitter and collaborate on the best options for your patient. These garments can be costly, so there is little room for mistakes. It is suggested that each patient is issued two garments, one to wash and one to wear. Make sure they are replaced according to the manufacturer's instructions in order to maintain the optimal compression.

## THERAPEUTIC EXERCISES

These exercises facilitate the action of the muscle pump, which helps drive the tissue fluid through the lymphatic system. These and other appropriate exercises also increase the strength and range of motion of the affected limb and should improve function and mobility, which is often the ultimate goal of therapy.

Remember the following key points when prescribing an exercise program for your patients (Table 12-2):

- Normal movements cause desirable changes in total tissue pressure. Encourage patients to use the limb as normally as possible.
- All exercises should be performed with compression on the limb.
- The exercises should progress proximally to distally to empty central lymphatics first.
- The exercises prescribed for lymphedema should be performed without weights or with very low weight, and they should be performed with few repetitions and plenty of rest between sets.
- These exercises may need to be modified according to the individual abilities of the patient.
- Remember that only licensed medical professionals are qualified to prescribe an exercise program to individuals with chronic or acute medical conditions.

## PATIENT EDUCATION

Patient education regarding management of lymphedema should begin with the first day that the patient walks into the clinic and continue with every visit. The educational goals for therapy are as follows:

- Understanding and compliance of all precautions related to lymphedema
- Independence with self-bandaging

*Text continued on p. 263.*

## BOX 12-1 Application of Compression Bandages to the Arm

1. Apply stockinette to the arm from the hand to the shoulder; make a cutout for the thumb.

2. Anchor the finger bandage at the wrist, then cross over the dorsum of the hand to the fifth digit, spiraling distal to proximal.

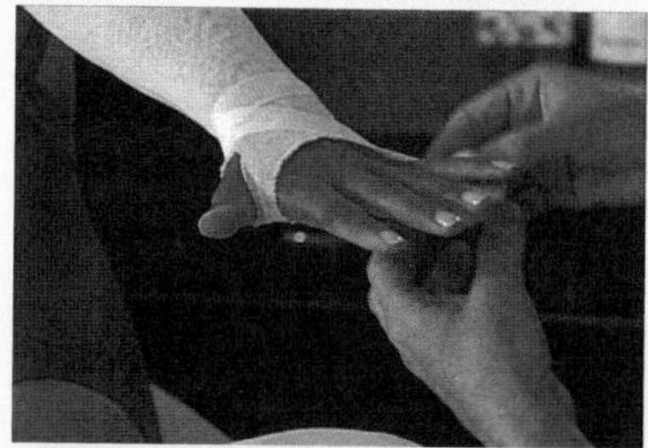

3. Bring the bandage around the wrist, over the dorsum of the hand to the fourth digit, and spiral distal to proximal; continue in this manner until all fingers and the thumb are covered.

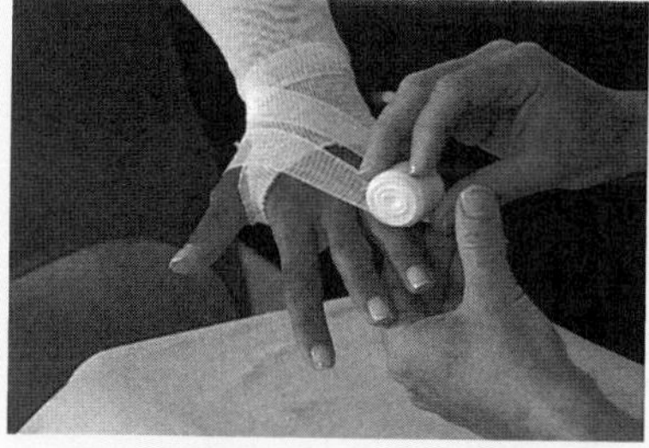

4. Apply foam over any areas of fibrosis or where reshaping is desired.

5. Anchor padding layer at the wrist, then bring across dorsum of hand, through the web space of thumb, and repeat.

6. Continue spiraling up the arm, folding extra padding into the anticubital area; it may require two rolls to cover the entire arm.

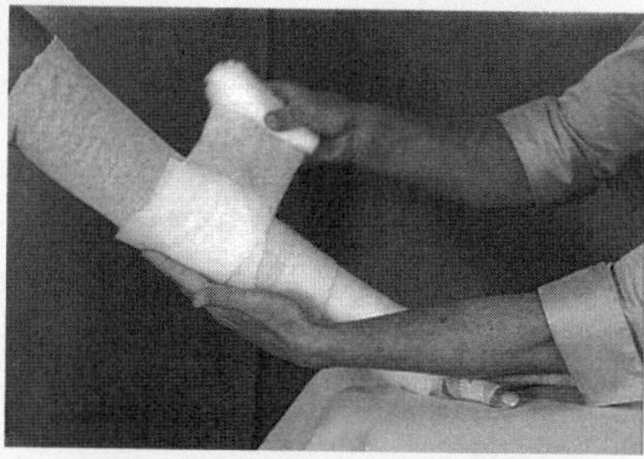

7. Lightly anchor the 6-cm compression bandage at the wrist, then cross over the dorsum of the hand, through the web space of the thumb, and repeat (be sure to get compression across all metacarpophalangeal joints).

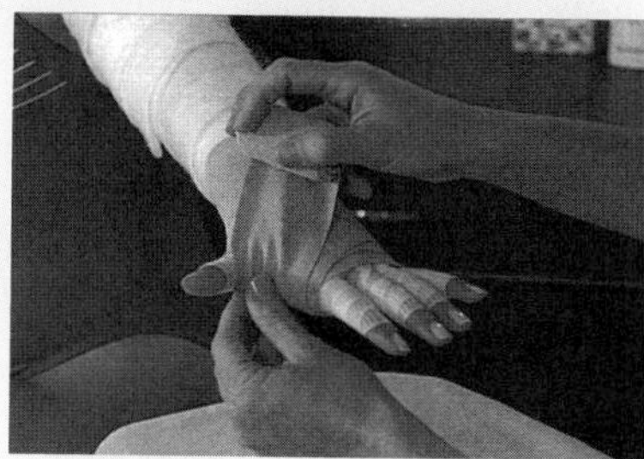

8. Continue by spiraling up the arm with a ¼-inch overlap; you should end about midway up the forearm; secure with tape.

9. Next, secure the 8-cm bandage just above the wrist, over the previous layer, and spiral up the arm with a ¾-inch to 1-inch overlap.

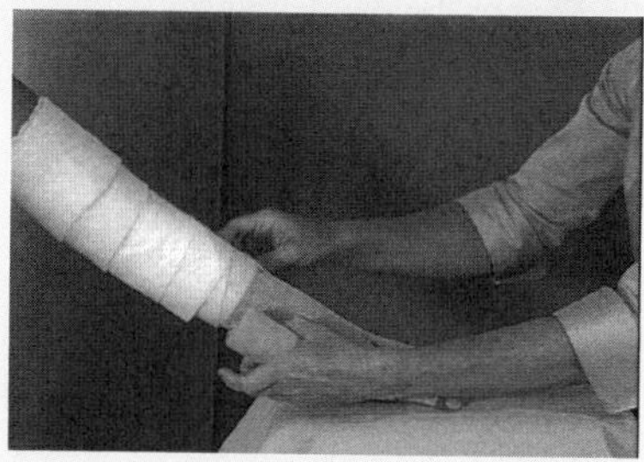

10. When you reach the elbow, use a figure-8 (spica) pattern to prevent binding in the anticubital space; you should end just above the elbow.

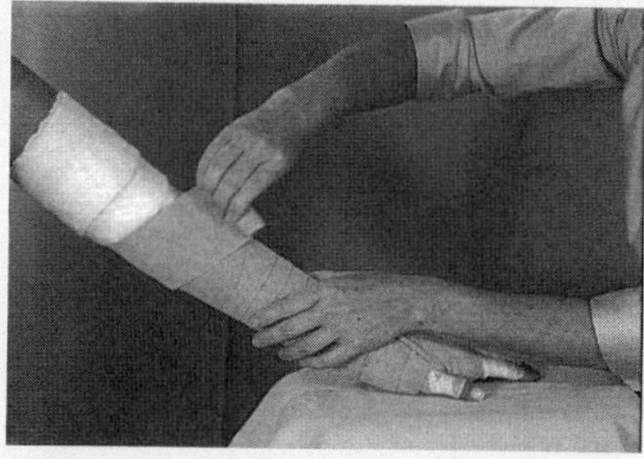

11. Begin spiraling with the 10-cm bandage at the point where you left off with the 6-cm bandage (approx. midway up the forearm); with a 1.5 to 2-cm overlap.

12. Use a figure-8 pattern at the elbow; you may continue with this pattern up the arm; widen your use of layers as you progress up the arm.

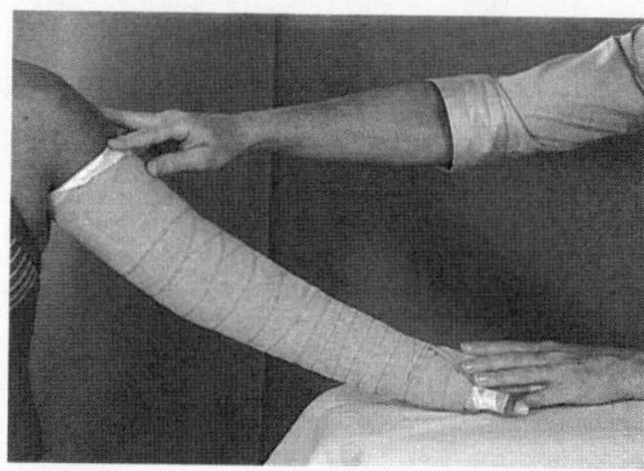

## BOX 12-2 Application of Compression Bandages to the Leg

1. Apply stockinette along the entire length of the leg and foot.

2. Anchor the elastic gauze bandage at the forefoot and over the dorsum to the tip of the great toe; spiral up distally to proximally, then around the forefoot and across the dorsum.

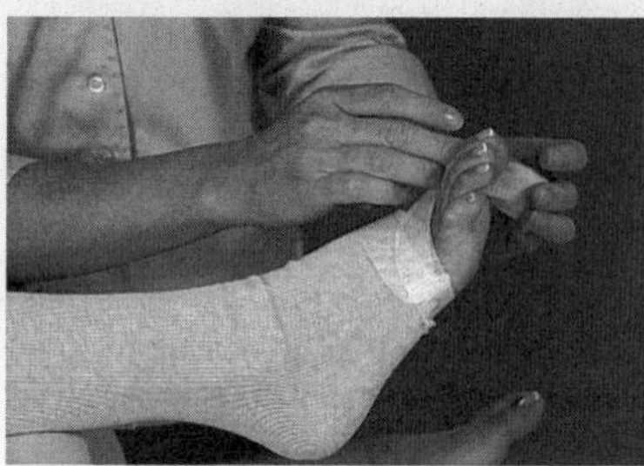

3. Bring the bandage to the distal end of the second digit and spiral distally to proximally, then around the forefoot to the third digit; continue in this pattern until all toes are covered, wrapping the fourth and fifth digits together.

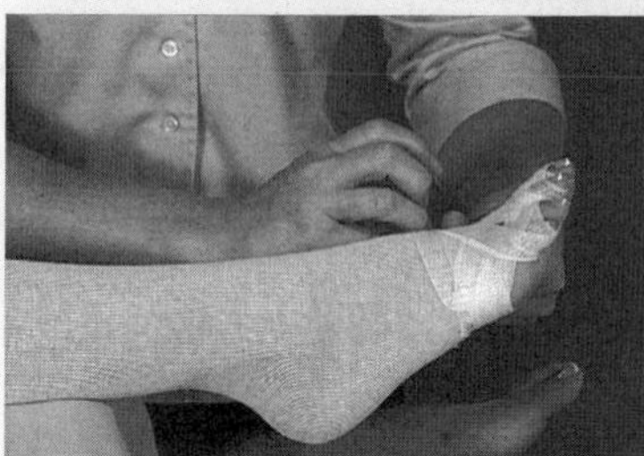

4. Apply foam over fibrous areas or where reshaping is desired.

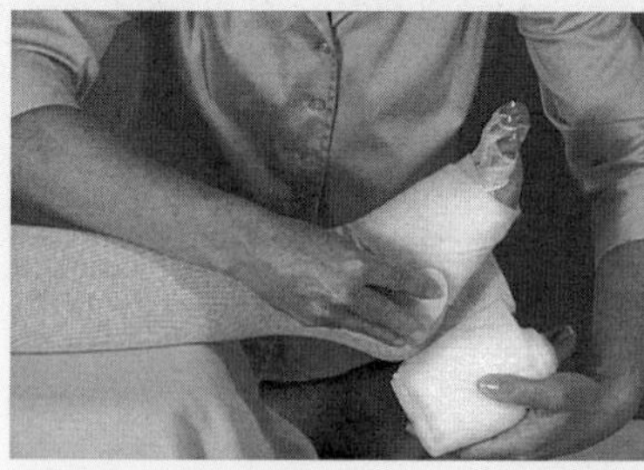

5. Begin spiraling the padding layer up the leg from the foot to the knee.

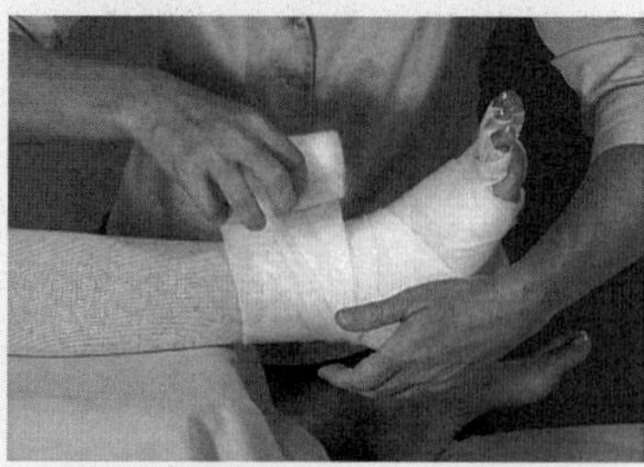

6. Begin with the 6-cm compression bandage at the metatarsophalengeal joints and spiral up to the heel; make figure-8 patterns crossing over the ankle and heel until the heel is entirely covered; use a ¼-inch to ½-inch overlap.

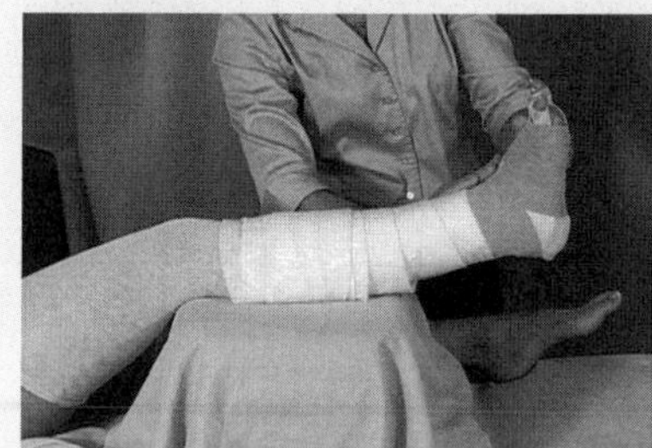

7. Continue up the leg with the 8-cm bandage; use a ½-inch to 1-inch overlap.

8. Continue with the 10-cm bandage to just below the knee; the layers should be wider as you continue up the leg; secure with tape.

9. Apply padding from the knee to the hip; add any foam as needed; the remainder of the bandaging may be done in the standing position.

10. Begin with the second 10-cm compression bandage using a spica wrap at the knee; spiral up the thigh with a 1-to 2-inch overlap.

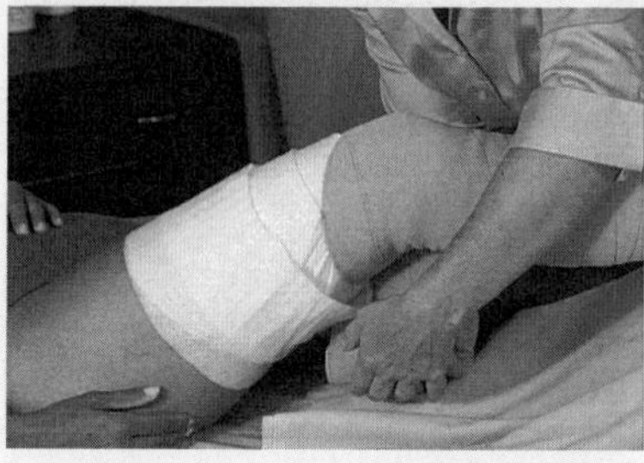

11. Continue with the 12-cm bandage with increasing width of overlapping; can be continued around the waist for extra security.

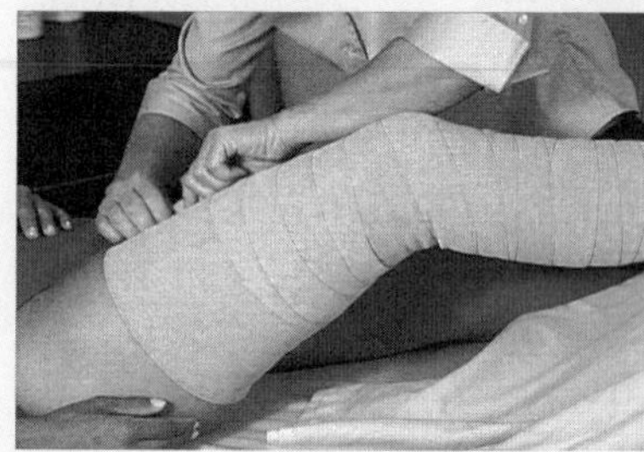

12. Apply wide tape to the bottom and back of the heel, forming a stirrup to lock the bandages in place; it may also be necessary to tape around the knee and vertically up the thigh to secure bandages well.

### Table 12-2 Suggestions for Exercises

| ALL LYMPHEDEMA | UPPER EXTREMITY LYMPHEDEMA | LOWER EXTREMITY LYMPHEDEMA |
|---|---|---|
| Deep abdominal breathing | Shoulder circles | Trunk rotation |
| Cervical rotation | Shoulder flexion | Marches |
| Cervical flexion/extension | Shoulder abduction | Heel slides |
| Cervical sidebending | Shoulder ER/IR | Hip abduction |
| | Elbow flexion/extension | Straight leg raises |
| | Forearm pronation/supination | Long arc quads |
| | Wrist extension/flexion | Ankle pumps |
| | Finger extension/flexion | Ankle circles |

### BOX 12-3 Lymphedema Risk Reduction Practices

**Skin Care: Avoid Trauma/Injury and Reduce Infection Risk**
- Keep extremity clean and dry.
- Apply moisturizer daily to prevent chapping/chaffing of skin.
- Pay attention to nail care; do not cut cuticles.
- Protect exposed skin with sunscreen and insect repellent.
- Use care with razors to avoid nicks and skin irritation.
- If possible, avoid punctures such as injections and blood draws.
- Wear gloves while doing activities that may cause skin injury (e.g., gardening, working with tools, using chemicals such as detergent).
- If scratches/punctures to skin occur, wash with soap and water, apply antibiotics, and observe for signs of infection (i.e., redness).
- If a rash, itching, redness, pain, increased skin temperature, fever, or flulike symptoms occur, contact your physician immediately.

**Activity/Lifestyle**
- Gradually build up the duration and intensity of any activity or exercise.
- Take frequent rest periods during activity to allow for limb recovery.
- Monitor the extremity during and after activity for any change in size, shape, tissue, texture, soreness, heaviness, or firmness.
- Maintain optimal weight.

**Avoidance of Limb Constriction**
- If possible, avoid having blood pressure taken on the at-risk arm.
- Wear loose-fitting jewelry and clothing.

**Compression Garments**
- Garments should be well-fitting.
- Support the at risk-limb with a compression garment for strenuous activity (e.g., weight lifting, prolonged standing, running).
- Wear a well-fitting compression garment for air travel.

**Extremes of Temperature**
- Avoid exposure to extreme cold, which can be associated with rebound swelling or chapping of skin.
- Avoid prolonged (>15 minutes) exposure to heat, particularly hot tubs and saunas.
- Avoid immersing limb in water temperatures above 120° F.

**Additional Practices Specific to Lower-Extremity Lymphedema**
- Avoid prolonged standing or sitting.
- When possible, avoid crossing legs.
- Wear proper, well-fitting footwear.

From National Lymphedema Network, Inc., 2007.

- Independence with self-massage
- Independence with home exercise program

On the first visit, the therapist gives the patient a thorough lesson in the basic anatomy and physiology of the lymphatic system and explains the rationale for treatment. Precautions are discussed, and the patient is given a written handout. On the second visit, the patient is taught the home exercise program, which he or she performs daily in the clinic after bandages have been applied. The patient learns self-bandaging on the third visit and should be independent before the weekend because bandages will need to be reapplied during that time. The patient learns self-massage at the start of the second week and reviews it until independence is achieved (Box 12-3).

After the patient is discharged from therapy, he or she should continue with phase 2, consisting of daily self-massage and exercises, adherence to precautions, and compression. Remember that each patient's goals are different, and varying lifestyles may play a role in the ability of the patient to be compliant with a rigorous home program. The therapist will help the patient to set reasonable goals and a home management program that fits his or her lifestyle, personality, and individual goals. Occasional follow-up sessions will allow the therapist to monitor progress and adapt the home program if necessary.

## REFERENCES


Araujo JA, Curbelo JG, Mayol AL et al: Effective management of marked lymphedema of the leg, *Intl J Dermatol* 36:389-392, 1997.

Avrahami R, Haddad M, Zelikovski A: Combined surgical correction of bilateral congenital lower limb lymphedema with associated anomalies, *Lymphology* 31:65-67, 1988.

Augustine E: Physical therapists play an important role in treating lymphedema, *Oncol Nurs Forum* 23:421-422, 1996.

Bernas MJ, Witte CL, Witte MH: The diagnosis and treatment of peripheral lymphedema, *Lymphology* 34:84-91, 2001.

Box R, Reul-Hirche H, Bullock-Saxton J et al: Physiotherapy after breast cancer surgery: results of a randomized controlled study to minimize lymphoedema, *Breast Cancer Res Treat* 75:51-64, 2002.

Brennan M, Miller L: Overview of treatment options and review of the current role and use of compression garments, intermittent pumps, and exercise in the management of lymphedema, *Cancer* 83(suppl):2821-2827, 1998.

Casley-Smith JR, Boris M, Weindorf S et al: Treatment for lymphedema of the arm-the-casley-smith method, *Cancer* 83(suppl):2843-2859, 1998.

Cohen SR, Payne DK, Tunkel RS: Lymphedema strategies for management, *Cancer* 92(suppl):980-987, 2001.

Coward DD: Lymphedema prevention and management knowledge in women treated for breast cancer, *Oncol Nurs Forum* 26:1047-1053, 1999.

Dale RF: The inheritance of primary lymphedema, *J Med Genet* 22:274-278, 1985.

Daroczy J: Pathology of lymphedema, *Clin Dermatol* 13:433-444, 1995.

Davis S: Lymphedema following breast cancer treatment, *Radiol Technol* 70:42-56, 1998.

Dini D, Del Mastro L, Gozza A et al: The role of pneumatic compression in the treatment of postmastectomy lymphedema: a randomized phase III study, *Ann Oncol* 9:187-190, 1998.

Erickson VS, Pearson ML, Ganz PA et al: Arm edema in breast cancer patients, *J Natl Cancer Inst* 93:96-111, 2001.

Foldi E: Treatment of lymphedema, *Cancer* 83(suppl):2833-2834, 1998.

Foldi E: Treatment of lymphedema and patient rehabilitation, *Anticancer Res* 18:2211-2212, 1998.

Foldi E, Foldi M, Clodius L: The lymphedema chaos: a lancet, *Ann Plast Surg* 22:505-515, 1989.

Foldi E, Foldi M, Weissleder H: Conservative treatment of lymphoedema of the limbs, *Angiology* 36:171-180, 1985.

Franzeck UK, Spiegel I, Fischer M et al: Combined physical therapy for lymphedema evaluated by fluorescence microlymphography and lymph capillary pressure measurements, *J Vascular Res* 34:306-311, 1997.

Harris SR, Hugi MR, Olivotto IA et al: Steering Committee for Clinical Practice Guidelines for the Care and Treatment of Breast Cancer: clinical practice guidelines for the care and treatment of breast cancer, *CMAJ* 164:191-199, 2001.

Hock K: Lymphedema and exercise, *Oncol Nur Forum* 25:1310, 1998.

Horan D, McMullen M: Assessment and management of the woman with lymphedema after breast cancer, *J Am Acad Nurse Pract* 10:155-159, 1998.

Huang JH, Kwon JY, Lee KW et al: Changes in lymphatic function after complex physical therapy for lymphedema, *Lymphology* 32:15-21, 1999.

Humble CA: Lymphedema: incidence, pathophysiology, management and nursing care, *Oncol Nurs Forum* 22:1503-1509, 1995.

Humble CA: Author discusses role of physical therapy in lymphedema care, *Oncol Nurs Forum* 23:422, 1996.

Ikomi F, Schmid-Schonbein GW: Lymph transport in the skin, *Clin Dermatol* 13:419-427, 1995.

Johansson K, Albertsson M, Ingvar C et al: Effects of compression bandaging with or without manual lymph drainage treatment in patients with postoperative arm lymphedema, *Lymphology* 32:103-110, 1999.

Karges JR, Mark BE, Stikeleather SJ et al: Concurrent validity of upper-extremity volume estimates: comparison of calculated volume derived from girth measurements and water displacement volume, *Phys Ther* 83:134-145, 2003.

Kasseroller RG: The vodder school: the vodder method, *Cancer* 83(suppl):2840-2842, 1998.

Kim DI, Huh S, Lee SJ et al: Excision of subcutaneous tissue and deep muscle fascia for advanced lymphedema, *Lymphology* 31:190-194, 1991.

Kissin MW, Querci della Rovere G, Easton D et al: Risk of lymphoedema following treatment of breast cancer, *Br J Surg* 73:580-584, 1896.

Ko DSC, Lerner R, Klose G et al: Effective treatment of lymphedema of the extremities, *Arch Surg* 133:452-458, 1998.

Leduc O, Leduc A, Bourgeois P et al: The treatment of upper limb edema, *Cancer* 83(suppl):2835-2839, 1998.

Lockhart JS: Case study: management of lymphedema, *Oncol Nurs Forum* 26:507-509, 1999.

Martin KP, Foldi E: Are hemodynamic factors important in arm lymphedema after treatment of breast cancer? *Lymphology* 29:155-157, 1996.

McElrath TJ, Runowicz CD: Preventing and managing lymphedema, *Contemporary Ob Gyn* 45:115-129, 2002.

McKenzie DC, Kalda, AL: Effect of upper extremity exercise on secondary lymphedema in breast cancer patients: a pilot study, *J Clin Oncol* 3:463-466, 2003.

McNeely M, Magee DJ, Lees AW et al: The addition of manual lymphatic drainage to compression therapy for breast cancer related lymphedema: a randomized controlled trial, *Breast Cancer Res Treat* 00:1-12, 2004.

Meek AG: Breast radiotherapy and lymphedema, *Cancer* 83(suppl):2788-2797, 1998.

Megens A, Harris SR: Physical therapist management of lymphedema following treatment for breast cancer: a critical review of its effectiveness, *Phys Ther* 78:1302-1311, 1998.

Miller AJ, Bruna J, Beninson J: A universally applicable clinical classification of lymphedema, *Angiology* 50:189-192, 1999.

Mirolo BR, Bunce IH, Chapman M et al: Psychosocial benefits of postmastsectomy lymphedema therapy, *Cancer Nurs* 18:197-205, 1995.

Morgan RG, Casley-Smith JR, Mason MR et al: Complex physical therapy for the lymphoedematous arm, *J Hand Surg* 17B:437-441, 1992.

Mortimer PS: Managing lymphedema, *Clin Dermatol* 13:499-505, 1995.

Mortimer PS: The pathophysiology of lymphedema, *Cancer* 83(suppl):2798-2801, 1998.

Mortimer PS: Implications of the lymphatic system in CVI-associated edema, *Angiology* 51:3-7, 2000.

Newman ML, Brennan M, Passik S: Lymphedema complicated by pain and psychological distress: a case with complex treatment needs, *J Pain Sympt Manage* 12:376-379, 1996.

Norman SA, Miller LT, Erikson HB et al: Development and validation of a telephone questionnaire to characterize lymphedema in women treated for breast cancer, *Phys Ther* 81:1192-1205, 2001.

Petereit DG, Mehta MP, Buchler DA et al: A retrospective review of nodal treatment for vulvar cancer, *Am J Clin Oncol* 16:38-42, 1993.

Pressman PI: Surgical treatment and lymphedema, *Cancer* 83(suppl):2782-2786, 1998.

Ramos SM, O'Donnell LS, Knight G: Edema volume, not timing, is the key to success in lymphedema treatment, *Am J Surgery* 178:311-315, 1999.

Rhinehart-Ayres M: Lymphedema references, *Rehabil Oncol* 20:20-23, 2002.

Rockson SG: Lymphedema, *Am J Med* 110:288-295, 2001.

Ryan TJ: Landmarks in the understanding of lymphatic function and the management of edema, *Clin Dermatol* 13:417-418, 1995.

Ryan TJ: Mechanical resilience of skin: a function for blood supply and lymphatic drainage, *Clin Dermatol* 13:429-432, 1995.

Sander AP, Hajer NM, Hemenway K et al: Upper-extremity volume measurements in women with lymphedema: a comparison of measurements obtained via water displacement with geometrically determined volume, *Phys Ther* 82:1201-1211, 2002.

Schunemann H, Willich N: Lymphoedema of the arm after primary treatment of breast cancer, *Anticancer Res* 18:2235-2236, 1998.

Skobe M, Detmar M: Structure, function, and molecular control of the skin lymphatic system, *J Invest Dermato Symp Proc* 5:14-19, 2000.

Szuba A, Cooke JP, Yousuf S et al: Decongestive lymphatic therapy for patients with cancer—related or primary lymphedema, *Am J Med* 9:296-300, 2000.

Tengrup I, Tennvall-Nittby L, Christiansson I et al: Arm morbidity after breast conserving therapy for breast cancer, *Acta Oncologica* 39:393-397, 2000.

Tiwari A, Cheng KS, Button M et al: Differential diagnosis, investigation, and current treatment of lower limb lymphedema, *Arch Surg* 138:152-159, 2003.

Tobin MB, Lacey HJ, Meyer L et al: The psychological morbidity of breast cancer-related arm swelling, *Cancer* 72:3248-3252, 1993.

Todd JE: A study of lymphoedema patients over their first six months of treatment, *Physiotherapy* 85:65-76, 1999.

Tribe K: Treatment of lymphoedema: the central importance of manual lymph drainage, *Physiotherapy* 81:154-156, 1995.

Williams AF, Vadgama A, Franks PJ et al: A randomized controlled crossover study of manual lymphatic drainage therapy in women with breast cancer-related lymphedema, *Eur J Cancer Care* 11:254-261, 2002.

Williams C: Compression therapy for lymphoedema from vernon-carus, *Br J Nurs* 7:339-343, 1998.

Woods M, Tobin M, Mortimer P: The psychosocial morbidity of breast cancer patients with lymphoedema, *Cancer Nurs* 6:467-461, 1995.

Wozniewski M, Jasinski R, Pilch U et al: Complex physical therapy for lymphedema of the limbs, *Physiotherapy* 87:252-256, 2001.

# Chapter 13

# Massage in Sport

Catherine Ortega

Sports massage has gained popularity since the 1980s with the increased participation of all ages in aerobics and the worldwide visibility of sport. However, it is insufficient to define sports massage simply as massage applied to athletes. Often the term *sports massage* is used synonymously with the term *deep tissue massage* to justify the use of painful pressures on athletes. This usage is often based on the misconception that the muscular bulk of an athlete necessitates abuse to the connective tissues to deliver an effective intervention. This generalization is also an inaccurate description of sports massage. Sports massage is the use of soft tissue mobilization to enhance performance among individuals who are placed in physical achievement situations. An achievement situation is one in which (1) there is public verifiability of performance (an audience), (2) there is a known criteria of success, (3) an individual is responsible for the outcome, and (4) there is a challenging task. Athletes spend most of their time in physical achievement situations during training or competition.

The idea that sports massage differs from therapeutic massage applied to nonathletes may be misleading. It is not that the techniques used with sports massage are so radically different; rather, the difference lies in the ability of the practitioner to vary the dosage, timing, and amount of pressure based on the needs of the athlete to best enhance performance outcomes. This requires an understanding of periodization for a sport (Mayhew, 1995); specifically, the therapist must know the repetitive cycle that an athlete will undertake several times during a year in order to prepare for peak performance during competition. The knowledgeable practitioner is aware of what point in this cycle an athlete or team is in order to apply the appropriate skills and, thereby, assist the athlete with preparation and recovery.

The additional value that sports massage provides to athletes when compared with other populations is in the psychological effects that can be attained to enhance performance. A positive adjustment in mood, an acquired sense of well-being, a decrease in anxiety, and a decrease in fatigue—all of these are reported and demonstrated psychological responses associated with massage intervention (Hernandez-Reif et al., 2001; Robertson et al., 2004; Stock et al., 1996). The athlete can benefit from these effects before competition or between bouts of training to manage the associated stressors of sport (Loehr, 1994).

Sports massage based on the timing of performance or in response to injury is applied to attain different goals, such as to promote relaxation, increase circulation, diminish adhesion formation, or decrease pain (Farr et al., 2002). It is adjustment based on the demands of the sport and to best enhance performance that distinguishes sports massage from another clinical therapeutic intervention. It is the skilled ability on the part of the therapist that adds the psychological and anxiety management effects for performance that contribute to positive functional outcomes.

Sports massage, as with any therapeutic treatment, must begin with a comprehensive evaluation to ascertain the source of the problem and construct a treatment plan. For any population requiring therapeutic intervention, one treatment modality is insufficient to fully restore full function or treat disability. Similarly, with an athletic population, massage is but part of a regimen of treatment that also includes resistance or flexibility exercises; physical agents such as ice, ultrasound, or electrical stimulation; and other manual therapy interventions such as joint manipulation. It is this combination of applied therapeutic intervention to address imbalances that will promote healing and performance, thus enhancing functional movement for the elite athlete. Although the body of knowledge regarding the mechanisms through which these effects occur continues to expand with scientific investigations, it is important to remember that sports massage is not a new intervention and has been in existence since early civilizations (Callaghan, 1993; Hemmings, 2000).

## HISTORY OF SPORTS MASSAGE

Massage as a form of treatment for athletes has existed for thousands of years. The Greeks may have been the first to use massage for athletes as a precompetition and postcompetition intervention. In truth, the original writings regarding massage are from the works of Hippocrates dated around 400 BC (De Domenico & Wood, 1997; Schoitz, 1958). Wrestling was a popular sport in ancient Greece, as were track and field events. Early manuscripts describe manual therapy intervention to treat trauma as well as promote recovery. Historical accounts describe the treatment for a wrestler who has finished a wrestling match and sustained a dislocated shoulder by stating that, "The physician must be experienced in many things, but assuredly also in rubbing; for things that have the same name have not the same effect. For rubbing can bind a joint that is too loose and loosen a joint that is too hard" (De Domenico & Wood, 1997). Also, Hippocrates describes that "it is necessary to rub the shoulder gently and smoothly; but the joint should be moved about, not violently but so far as it can be done without producing pain" (Paris & Loubert, 1990). This account describes the intervention for shoulder realignment by different manual maneuvers and the use of massage to coax the tissues to respond to realignment. Thus, sports massage—that is, massage applied to enhance performance for athletes—has existed as one of the early applications of soft tissue mobilization intervention.

The different professionals who use massage techniques were described in Chapter 1. As these practitioners continue to apply and advocate the value of massage therapy, sports massage continues to gain validity among athletes and administrators. Athletic trainers are constantly bombarded with participants in aquatic and athletic events clamoring for massage techniques to manage musculoskeletal concerns (Bell, 1999). In present-day competition, the medical teams as part of the United States delegations to the Atlanta (1996) and Sydney (2000) Olympic Games were responsible for administering daily comprehensive massage and specific soft tissue mobilization to the more than 100 athletes of the United States Olympic team. The delegation for Great Britain administered more than 1000 soft tissue treatments during the Atlanta Olympic Games in 1996. An investigation performed in the United Kingdom to quantify the use of massage by physiotherapists at athletic events revealed important findings. Specifically, the study found that the percentage of time devoted to providing massage therapy treatment to athletes ranged from 24% to 52.2%, and the overall median percentage of total treatments for massage was 45.2% (Galloway & Watt, 2004). More and more athletes seek this treatment from qualified professionals with positive results. These statistics demonstrate that it is becoming common for elite competitors to require soft tissue massage as part of their training and competition regimen. Why are massage techniques in such high demand? Why do therapists apply them so frequently? This may be due both to the perceived and validated effects of massage.

## THERAPEUTIC EFFECTS OF MASSAGE FOR AN ATHLETE

The effects of massage for athletes are similar to those for nonathletes as listed in Box 13-1 and discussed in Chapter 5. Although limited conclusive investigations have been performed regarding the mechanisms of action to date, specific massage techniques continue to be used to induce specific change within athletic populations.

### Delayed Onset Muscular Soreness

Athletes are at high risk for delayed onset muscular soreness (DOMS). DOMS is the soreness and stiffness in the exercised joints and muscles that occurs with a new physical activity or with strenuous activity undertaken after an extended rest period. Although often associated with eccentric exercise because of the hypothesized microtearing of fibers associated with these activities (Connolly et al., 2003), DOMS occurs after other forms of training activities as well. Temporary soreness can last for several hours after any unaccustomed exercise; however, a distinguishing characteristic with DOMS is that pain appears later and can last from 24 to 96 hours after activity (MacArdle et al., 2001). DOMS can vary from muscle tenderness to debilitating pain and affects athletic performance by causing reduced joint motion, shock attenuation, and reduction in peak torque (Cheung et al., 2003). Compensatory mechanisms can place an athlete at increased risk of further injury. To date, there is not one definitive documented cause of DOMS; however, various hypotheses exist as to the manifestation of DOMS. These are listed in Box 13-2. It is most probable that the cause of DOMS is a combination of these factors rather than any one factor.

**BOX 13-1** Positive Effects of Sports Massage

1. Improve circulation.
2. Decrease edema/inflammation.
3. Promote relaxation and decrease arousal.
4. Decrease stress and competitive anxiety.
5. Enhance mental recovery/invigoration.
6. Decrease/manage pain.
7. Decrease delayed onset muscular soreness (DOMS).
8. Increase range of motion (ROM).
9. Decrease adhesions.
10. Increase tissue extensibility.
11. Decrease spasm.
12. Enhance sense of well-being.
13. Promote neurological excitability.

**BOX 13-2 Potential Causes of Delayed Onset Muscular Soreness (DOMS)**

1. Exercise can result in the local accumulation of metabolic waste, which sensitizes A-delta and C fibers causing pain (McArdle et al., 2001).
2. Acute inflammation may result in DOMS.
3. According to DeVries (1966), exercise induces muscular edema resulting in pain substance production, producing a reflex spasm and thereby prolonging ischemia.
4. Eccentric exercise leads to minute tears or damage of the connective tissues of the muscle-releasing creatine kinase (CK), myoblobin (Mb), and troponin I, all contributing to the manifestation of pain.
5. DOMS may also arise from calcium regulation alterations of the cell.
6. Any combination of the above factors may lead to DOMS.

Adapted from McArdle WD, Katch FI, Katch VL: *Exercise physiology: energy, nutrition, and human performance,* ed 5, Philadelphia, 2001, Lippincott Williams & Wilkins.

Researchers have hypothesized that massage intervention can decrease soreness and promote recovery to facilitate continued training and competition for an athlete. The mechanical pressure applied with massage techniques can increase muscle compliance, decrease passive and active stiffness, and thereby increase joint and muscular range of motion (Weerapong et al., 2005). The mechanical pressure can also help to increase blood flow and promote increased tissue temperature through rubbing (Hinds et al., 2004).

Investigative results have varied because of differences in investigative rigor and methodologies. However, in a randomized clinical trial with a control group (N=7) and an experimental group (N=7), Smith et al. (1994) demonstrated positive results. This group found that 30 minutes of soft tissue massage administered 2 hours after isokinetic eccentric exercise of the upper extremity resulted in decreased reported levels of DOMS and decreased measures of serum creatine kinase levels within the massage group. An investigation was conducted with 8 male subjects performing downhill walking to induce DOMS followed by a 30-minute massage therapy intervention on one leg of each subject (Farr et al., 2002). Significantly higher levels of pain and tenderness were measured in the nonmassaged limb 24 hours after activity with a significant difference between limbs. There was also a demonstrated decrease in isometric strength compared with baseline 1 hour after the walk. These findings support the hypothesis that sports massage following activity can promote recovery and thereby facilitate continued training and competition at peak performance.

DOMS has been incorrectly attributed to an accumulation of lactic acid or elevated serum lactate levels (MacArdle et al., 2001). Some argue that massage can mechanically promote lactate removal. Hemmings et al. (2000) found no significant difference in blood lactate levels between two groups of boxers that performed two bouts, of upper-body ergometry. The groups were measured between bouts, with the control group (N=8) performing passive rest and the experimental group (N=8) receiving massage therapy. The blood lactate level was higher in both groups following the second bout of exercise performance without massage intervention; therefore, there was no significant difference in blood lactate levels after maximal activity. A significant difference was found with a higher perception of recovery level reported by the massage intervention group, suggesting that DOMS can manifest without elevated lactate levels and can be relieved with massage treatment.

Conclusive evidence regarding the effectiveness of massage on DOMS is lacking (Jonhagen et al., 2004). It appears that for each investigation that demonstrates positive physiological effects of massage on DOMS recovery, there is another with findings to the contrary. Robertson et al. (2004) demonstrated no significant difference in the physiological effects of massage when compared with passive recovery in a group (N=9) performing high-intensity cycling. A systematic review by Ernst (1998) failed to generate a meta-analysis because of variations in methodologies of included investigations. Investigations with larger samples, greater methodological rigor, and a comparison of standard treatment protocols are needed to arrive at a definitive conclusion. Results of this systematic review emphasized the potential systemic effects of massage therapy with emphasis on the fact that massage intervention need not be an extended full-body session but that benefits are attained by the direct and local mechanical pressure effects on the muscles treated.

Therefore comprehensive or *full-body massage* as well as *spot work,* as the abbreviated specific tissue treatment has been called, continue to be used on athletes regularly (Galloway & Watt, 2004). These techniques, which are used to promote recovery for DOMS, allow continued intensive training with lower levels of pain and fatigue reported by elite and novice athletes (Hinds et al., 2004; Hemmings et al., 2000; Robertson et al., 2004; Smith et al., 1994).

### Technique and Dosage for DOMS

When treating DOMS, the primary goal is to decrease pain. Treatment can vary from an extended full-body massage that can be 1 hour in length to an abbreviated 15- to 20-minute session for the extremities or a specific body part. To begin a treatment session, effleurage such as stroking with light pressure should be used to promote circulation, stimulate superficial blood flow, and facilitate local and general relaxation. This gentle introduction of the therapist's hands to the athlete's tissues will begin to allow relaxation of the mind and body and thereby decrease any protective spasm that might be present as a result of pain. The pressure should be light to accommodate the tissue tenderness that is the hallmark of DOMS. The therapist should pay particular attention to signals denoting relaxation by the athlete. These signs could include deep, rhythmic breathing; decreased tension within the superficial tissue being stroked; or closed eyes with relaxation of facial muscles. If any of these signs do not begin to occur within 5 minutes, the pressure may be too deep and an adjustment must be made to decrease the force applied.

Following initial relaxation, which can begin to occur within 4 to 5 minutes, the therapist can then progress to moderate compression with pétrissage such as gentle kneading and wringing. This is a deeper application of massage but should not cause the athlete to perform sustained muscle contractions or increase tension in the tissues. If this begins to occur, the pressure is too deep and should either be modified or the technique adjusted. Pétrissage could be discontinued and only effleurage used for the entire treatment dose. To avoid inducing pain and causing further tissue damage, pétrissage techniques should not be applied with deep pressure or long duration when treating DOMS. No more than half of the entire duration of the massage intervention should be used for pétrissage. This is then followed by moderate-pressure effleurage. Active range of motion exercise without resistance has been demonstrated to facilitate recovery from DOMS in combination with massage (Lane & Wenger, 2004). Therefore, active assisted range of motion (AAROM) can be incorporated within a treatment session before the final transition to light pressure effleurage to conclude the treatment. One can envision the treatment session as one-third initial light effleurage, one-third moderate pétrissage, and a final one-third with moderate effleurage to include AAROM concluding with light effleurage.

DOMS can last for 96 hours (4 days), so that repetitive treatments can be applied over a period of days to alleviate symptoms. Multiple treatments with massage appear to be more effective than a single dose of treatment (Tidus & Shoemaker, 1995). Also, just as DOMS is most likely caused by a combination of factors, it appears that the ideal treatment is a combined approach that includes massage therapy, active recovery, and even cryotherapy (Cheung et al., 2003).

## Massage for Acute Injury

### *Initial Inflammation*

Acute injuries frequently occur during sport competitions, or so it may appear. Most of us can remember seeing an athlete sustain a strained hamstring while running a 400-meter sprint, a cyclist take a tumble when racing in a pack, or a quarterback receive a blow to the trunk and double over to the ground in pain. This initial acute stage of an injury results in obvious pain and short-term dysfunction; however, this initial stage also results in physiological changes beyond the dysfunction. These include electrolyte imbalance and fluid imbalance as well as local and general circulation alterations (Cailliet, 1996).

The acute phase of an injury with the initial inflammatory reaction lasts from onset of the injury to 4 to 6 days later and is characterized by tissue sensitivity. Pain results from vascular and cellular responses with the altered chemical state irritating nerve endings (Cailliet, 1996). There can be increased edema, muscle guarding, and increased tissue tension. The initial inflammatory reaction occurs with the signs of inflammation including heat, redness, and loss of function. Pain at rest is also present and can be can be exacerbated with movement. Some argue that massage should not be undertaken during this stage because of the potential for greater harm. This greater harm can occur if the therapist is not skilled with the application of massage and is not attuned to tissue response and tissue texture changes. The view that massage is absolutely contraindicated with acute injury is negated with findings by Stearns (1940). In a classic work regarding the effect of movement on fibroblastic activity, the researcher concluded that fibrils form almost immediately during the healing process and external forces are responsible for the physical arrangement of these fibers. Therefore, skilled massage with passive movement of the traumatized tissues can enhance the healing process.

Although it is not reasonable to apply great pressure to a bruised or painful region, moderate to light pressure in the application of massage to an acute injury can facilitate formation of fibroblasts and also manage pain through the stimulation of mechanoreceptors. Light to moderate effleurage (as recommended with the treatment of DOMS) can promote circulation to manage fluid imbalance and prevent excessive edema. Specific and deep pressures should not be applied directly to muscles with palpable tears, to inflamed tendons, or to ligaments with laxity caused by strain. Rather, effleurage to promote circulation, manage pain, and promote the formation of fiber should be applied to adjacent structures rather than directly on these newly injured tissues.

Rhythmic effleurage strokes with light to moderate pressure can convey calm in the midst of an injury situation that may appear out of control to an athlete. There is an invaluable sense of confidence that the therapist can help instill in the athlete (Moritz et al., 2000) through this therapeutic touch. The repetitive movement can contribute to relaxation and diminish the anxiety or sense of threat felt by an athlete when confronted with an injury (Brewer, 1994). Massage can also be a helpful means to convey support. The athlete who receives manual massage treatment may also acquire a sense of support and empathy from the therapist providing care. Adherence to rehabilitation has been associated with social support (Duda et al., 1989; Prochaska & Marcus, 2001). The athlete who perceives support through the massaging hands of a therapist will be better able to commit to a treatment regimen and begin the road to a successful recovery.

### *Repair and Healing*

Repair and healing follow the inflammatory reaction of an injury and can continue for approximately 14 to 21 days after the onset of injury (Enwemeka, 1991). Inflammation continues to decease with removal of noxious stimuli. There is new growth of capillary beds, and granulation and collagen tissues begin to form. The newly formed tissues are fragile at this time. Morphological changes in rat tendons demonstrate increased fibroblast proliferation in tendonitis-induced rats that were treated with soft tissue mobilization (Davidson et al., 1997). Although this may not directly translate to humans, these findings suggest that healing may be promoted through increased fibroblast recruitment resulting from massage treatment.

Newly formed connective tissue fibers are fragile because they are unorganized. Massage therapy techniques can be applied more specifically to the affected tissues to facilitate alignment of connective tissue fibers. As pain continues to subside, massage techniques can increase in pressure. Treatment should once again begin with light effleurage to promote relaxation and prepare the tissue for deeper pressures to follow with pétrissage. Deep friction massage (DFM), initially described by Cyriax and Russell (1990) and as described in Chapter 4, can be applied without excessively painful pressures. Care should still be taken when applying pressure to healing muscle fibers and tendons because of the fragility of the newly formed tissues.

## Massage for the Chronic Injury

Injuries have been classified as chronic based on time from initial onset as well as according to the events occurring within the healing process. Some authors would argue that chronic is anything that is not acute and therefore would include injuries that are in the subacute phase. Within this discussion, a chronic injury is one in which the events of healing have progressed through the acute and subacute phases. Therefore the tissues have completed the initial inflammatory process of the acute phase with reduction in inflammation, followed by the beginning of repair and healing of the injured site that occurs in the subacute phase (Kisner & Colby, 2002). Maturation and remodeling of tissue are the events within the chronic stage of tissue healing.

### *Maturation and Remodeling*

The maturation process overlaps with the end of the subacute phase and, depending on the severity of the injury, can continue for months. During this stage of maturation, the collagen fibers increase in tensile strength, they begin to align into a more organized orientation (Enwemeka, 1991; Noyes et al., 1984), and the size of the wound and scar decreases. Remodeling of tissue is affected by factors such as vascular supply and stressors placed on the tissue. It is during this stage of healing that deep cross-friction massage can be most beneficial to facilitate organized alignment of the connective tissue fibers (Brosseau et al., 2007). Effleurage to promote circulation with stronger pressure to reach the full thickness of the involved structure should be used. Massage with pétrissage to penetrate deeper tissues, DFM to realign fibers, and, again, exercise to include gentle stretching can be applied until the tenth to fourteenth week of recovery. Beyond this period of time, the scar formed will resist elongation and remodeling, so that lengthening will have to occur at tissues away from the injury site.

This stage of healing demands deeper pressures to affect healing. However, the therapist should continue to monitor the athlete during the treatment session to ascertain the appropriate depth needed to reach the tissue lesion area while not causing excessive pain. If the pressure is too great, the muscle will tense to prevent trauma to the tissue. If the therapist insists on using deep pressures while the muscle is in a protective spasm or contraction mode, bruising can occur. Some athletes believe that this is a good outcome and a necessary indicator of an effective massage treatment. Sometimes therapists mistakenly encourage these beliefs.

There is an analogy used within the discipline of Chinese medicine when discussing massage therapy for tissues that are resistant to pressure because of protective spasm. The therapist should think about wanting to visit a friend at home. One would go to the friend's house and politely knock on the door. It may be necessary to knock a couple of times if the person inside did not hear the first knock. If there is no answer, it would not be appropriate to "charge through" or crash into the front door without being invited. One might go to a side window and tap there in case the friend is in the back of the house and did not hear the front door. Your friend may let you in by the side door (Figure 13-1).

Similarly, the tissue that you are treating may be too sensitive for the pressure used or the tissue tension may be unresponsive to the specific technique. Instead of adding

**Figure 13-1**
When trying to produce changes upon deep tissues, alternate techniques may need to be applied for superficial tissues to relax.

more pressure with the same technique on the same tissue, a different pressure with a different technique may be needed to coax the tissue to relax and allow the application of an effective treatment.

Deeper pressure may be merited to relieve a protective spasm; however, if there is no relief of tissue tension within a short period of time (approximately 60 seconds maximum), pressure should be changed and another approach used. This is similar to tapping at the front door; the therapist should then try the side window. The session should not continue with painful pressure applied that, because of charging through the tissue, can result in bruising. If you knock on the door and your friend is not home, and if you knock on the side window and no one is home, you would come back another day. This is true for massage intervention as well. If the tissue is not ready for that depth of pressure and particular technique, the therapist should use patience by varying technique and pressure to decrease tissue tension and return to that tissue during another session. When injuries are in the chronic stage, the athlete can become frustrated with the time needed to heal and the therapist must encourage the athlete and display patience to continue to progress with recovery. If the tissue is resistant to relaxation, the therapist should not rush or force tissue to relax because this impatience may further frustrate or worry the athlete. It is never a positive outcome to have bruising or hematoma formation after massage therapy. This can slow healing and impair performance as a result of pain (Figure 13-2).

### *Chronic Inflammatory Conditions*

Athletes will commonly train or compete with a *chronic injury*. This term can be misleading because it is used to refer to the healing phase of injury and also to an injury that is of a chronic inflammatory nature. The choice of massage intervention should vary with these manifestations of tissue insult. Chronic injuries as described in the previous section necessitate deeper pressures and transverse fiber techniques to promote remodeling with exercise to return to full sport participation.

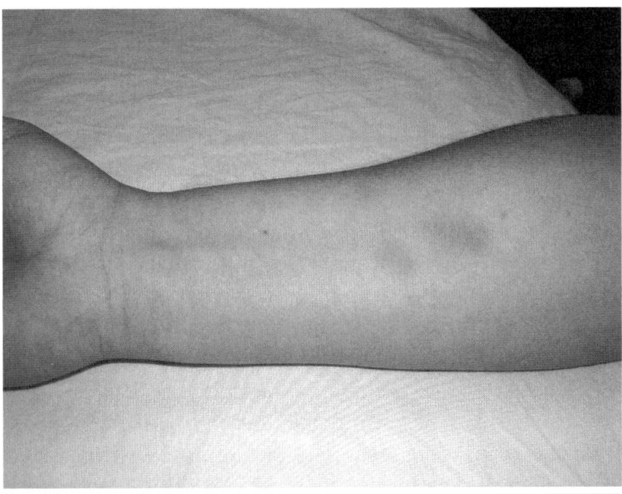

**Figure 13-2**
Bruising of superficial tissue is an outcome of inappropriate excessive pressure with massage therapy techniques.

Chronic inflammatory conditions are the result of repetitive stress with insufficient time for recovery and repair. Muscular imbalances can contribute to the manifestation and lack of healing with chronic inflammatory conditions. There exists a continual state of inflammation with increased collagen production resulting in immature, fragile tissue. The continually formed young structure, whether it be tendon, ligament, or fascia, is constructed of weaker and inflamed tissue. As the microtrauma or stretch continues to be placed on the tissue, myofibroblasts can remain overactive, limiting motion. The constant inflammation can be of a low grade with periods of exacerbation, and this inflammation contributes to pain and limited function.

The initial massage therapy treatment is the same as for an acute injury in the inflammatory stage. The treatment sequence should include adjunct therapy such as ice and AAROM (Goats, 1994a, 1994b; Meeusen & Lievens, 1986; Swenson et al., 1996). The imbalance should be identified in the surrounding musculature and targeted to intervention. Deep tissue work, positional release, and myofascial release techniques (described in Chapter 4) can be beneficial to reestablish normal tissue extensibility in conjunction with flexibility exercises. When the inflammatory phase can be controlled, progressive exercise should be introduced following soft tissue massage to further establish normal movement patterns and muscular balance.

Athletes will train and compete with chronic inflammatory conditions such as tendonitis and fascitis. Most competitive athletes with a competitive season longer than 6 months will receive treatment for tendonitis or fascitis of some affected body part during the competitive or training season. It has been found that fascial components lose their pliability as the ground substance solidifies, elastin loses its resiliency, and collagen can develop aberrant cross-links. Thus, tissue injuries that have not completed the full cycle of rehabilitation to correct imbalance will cycle through the inflammatory process repetitively. The tissue will progressively tighten as it is subjected to microtrauma and misguided, nonsystematic attempts to return to full activity.

If a chronic condition has resulted in scar tissue formation, deeper tissue intervention may be needed. One such technique, called *augmented soft tissue mobilization* (ASTM), is based on the principles of cross-friction massage. It is a soft tissue technique that "uses ergonomically designed instruments that assist therapists in rapid localization and effective treatment of areas exhibiting excessive soft tissue fibrosis" (Melham et al., 1998). The purpose is to introduce microvascular trauma and capillary hemorrhage that results in a localized inflammatory response. This intervention is similar to the deep tissue technique performed with a massage T-bar (Figure 13-3) to treat chronic tendinopathy.

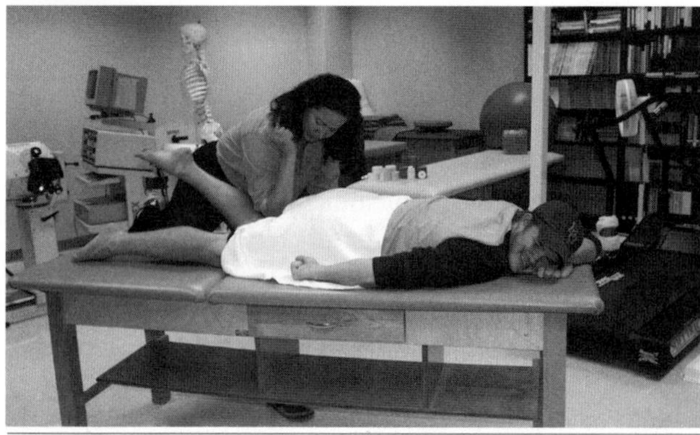

Figure **13-3**

Excessive pressure will deter relaxation and also cause the athlete to contract muscles, thus hindering an effective massage intervention.

Figure **13-4**

Athlete education regarding the timing for massage is critical.

These techniques attempt to increase cellular activity and promote circulation to a tissue that has excessive scarring from prolonged inflammation (National Athletic Trainers' Association, 2004). The acute injury phase is induced to then progress the tissue through the subacute and chronic healing phases of recovery. Initial findings demonstrate improved healing on fibrous tissues, such that comparison groups with varying pressure of ASTM demonstrated a significantly higher number of fibroblasts in the groups that received ASTM with heavy pressure when compared with groups that received lighter or moderate pressure (Gehlsen et al., 1999). These treatment techniques show promise in early stages of investigation and should be monitored for outcomes with larger samples to validate inclusion in future therapy protocols.

Chronic inflammatory conditions can impair an athlete's ability to train and compete at full potential. As training proceeds, the inflammation can be exacerbated and the athlete must alter the practice regimen. The use of massage techniques can facilitate the healing process. In the case of chronic inflammatory conditions, skilled massage is essential for healing to occur (National Athletic Trainers' Association, 2004).

## Massage Dosage

### *Massage before Competition*

The seasoned athletic competitor is more likely to use massage therapy before competition than is the novice competitor. This is the result of more frequent exposure to professionals who implement therapeutic massage and also greater knowledge regarding the athlete's own to this modality. Elite athletes have greater experience with competition and have had more opportunity to experiment with interventions to promote recovery.

All athletes can have misconceptions regarding massage, such as massage therapy will make them too relaxed and, therefore, decrease the arousal needed for competition. Another misconception espoused by athletes is that massage before competition will make their muscles weak. In a review, Weerapong et al. (2005) concluded that although massage therapy produced positive effects such as to reduce muscular soreness, there was no evidence to support the claim of muscle functional loss. Although the beliefs that athletes possess may be unfounded, perception is critical to performance. The knowledgeable professional will not only educate the athlete about the positive impact of massage but will also use techniques within the massage therapy repertoire to diminish the feeling and perception of fatigue or excessive relaxation before competition (Figure 13-4).

The specific timing of the massage intervention is related to the goal of treatment. The athlete with a chronic injury may need assistance to prepare the tissues for activity. This treatment would be *spot work,* or specific techniques applied to a particular body part. This *pre-event warm-up* can be done within 30 minutes of the preparatory activity for competition. For example, in the treatment of patellar tendonitis, effleurage is initially used upon the anterior thigh and peripatellar region to promote circulation and prepare the tissue for further intervention. Specific acupressure and muscular release techniques can be applied to the rectus femoris proximal insertion to release tension at the attachment. Deep friction massage with moderate pressure can be applied at the insertion points of the patellar tendon and along the midsubstance area of the tendon. Pétrissage such as kneading followed by tapotement should be used before AAROM and stretching. This pre-event warm-up should take approximately 20 minutes so that the athlete can then continue with active warm-up before activity. Therefore precompetition massage techniques are limited effleurage and pétrissage followed by specific muscular release techniques and moderate pressure transverse friction to promote specific tissue circulation, ending with tapotement and elongation activities (Figure 13-5).

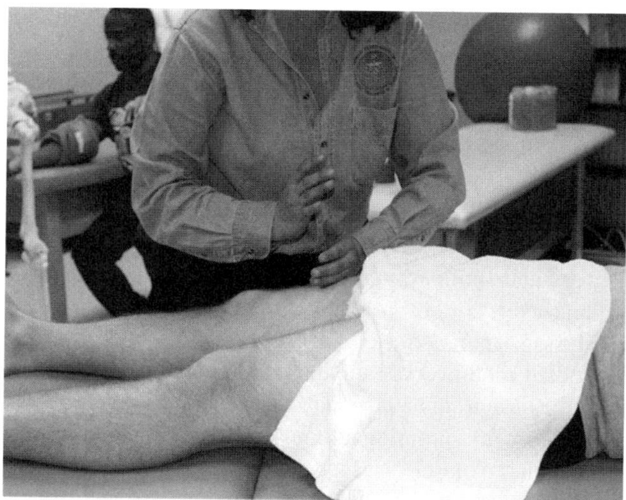

Figure **13-5**
Specific techniques to enhance alertness, improve circulation, and decrease stress can be used before competition.

The athlete who is reporting worry, tension, fatigue, muscular soreness, or heaviness in the legs (which can be a symptom of fatigue and dehydration) would benefit from a comprehensive massage intervention before competition. The treatment should be completed with a minimum of 1 hour before competition. Massage has been demonstrated to decrease pain in orthopedic conditions as well as alter electroencephalography (EEG) patterns and increase serotonin levels indicative of relaxation and diminished arousal. It is recommended that athletes not receive a full-body massage immediately before competition because they may not have sufficient time to attain the needed arousal to perform; however, the timing before performance can vary with personal preference. The athlete should experiment with massage before a practice bout outside of competition to ascertain his or her response to this type of treatment.

The comprehensive precompetition massage treatment should provide relaxation with effleurage stroking followed by pétrissage with specific muscular release techniques on tight insertions and acupressure release performed on specific trigger point areas found (see Chapter 4 regarding Travell's trigger point therapy). Tapotement with tapping, cupping, and shaking of the extremities and spine should be used to counter excessive relaxation and potential malaise that may occur with too much effleurage. The use of chopping can create an invigorating sensation for competition later in the day. Gentle AAROM activity can be done with effleurage to complete the treatment. The therapist must be sure to check the athlete's specific response later in the day for future use of massage before competition.

### Massage Between Competitions

Many athletes have more than one competition within the same day. Some sports necessitate performance for several consecutive days. Recovery for subsequent athletic performance is imperative in sport, particularly with events that have multiple rounds or bouts of activity. Events such as a cricket test match, a baseball road trip, the Olympic Games, or a tennis grand slam event can last for days and require efficient recovery and replenishment to maintain peak performance.

Massage has been demonstrated, although inconclusively, to promote lactate mobilization from the bloodstream, but massage has not been definitively linked to performance. An investigation by Mondero and Donne (2000) performed with 18 trained cyclists tested four recovery interventions to include passive recovery, active recovery at 50% maximal oxygen update, massage, and a combined regimen of massage and active recovery. Participants performed two simulated 5-kilometer maximal effort cycling bouts separated by 20 minutes of recovery time. Measurements of blood lactate, performance time, and heart rate were taken at 3-minute intervals during recovery. Results demonstrated that combined recovery of massage with active motion was the most efficient intervention for maintaining performance time during the second bout of cycling. Massage therapy allows the athlete to maintain peak performance for each competition.

When treating an athlete between exercise bouts, it is important to note that sports massage, similar to any therapeutic massage intervention, necessitates attention to principles of hygiene. An athlete should never be massaged without having cleansed the area to be treated. The only exception to this practice would be a medical emergency such as muscle cramping as a result of heat illness. In this instance, immediate intervention is needed, and sustained massage pressure can alleviate this painful symptom.

Every athlete should be required to bathe before therapeutic massage to decrease the spread of bacteria. This practice contributes to a comfortable environment for the practitioner and the athlete and helps ensure a more effective treatment session. Although there are no contraindications to performing massage immediately after competition, it is in the athlete's best interest to consume some form of carbohydrate and begin fluid replenishment after competition and before massage therapy intervention. This replenishment of nutrients and fluids promotes ideal recovery, decreases the potential for muscular cramping, and begins preparation for the next bout of competition or training.

The structure of the massage session will be determined by the timing of the next bout of competition or training. If the athlete is to continue to compete on the same day, massage can be beneficial and will necessitate a shortened intervention rather than a thorough, full-body massage. Long strokes—with moderate pressure on the extremities to decrease soreness and enhance circulation—are commonly referred to as a *quick flush* of the extremities. This movement can take approximately 30 minutes and may be all that is needed with gentle stretching to prepare for the next competition.

### Massage after Competition

A postcompetition intervention is usually associated with preparation for another competition on a subsequent day. However, this intervention can be used for recovery or preparation on the same day between bouts of competition. The effleurage described previously can be applied with moderate pressure followed by deeper pressure, continuing with deep kneading and tapotement of the trunk and extremities. Release techniques specific to the muscles used in the sport can be applied. For example, the pitcher in baseball should have deeper pressure applied to the subscapularis insertion points or the midsubstance of the teres minor. Cross-friction can be applied along these muscles to promote tissue relaxation. The tennis player and football player will need specific release techniques performed to the piriformis muscle and other deep rotators of the hip. The cyclist should have the iliopsoas at the lower abdominal region released with deep tissue pressure and cross-fiber massage bilaterally. Familiarization with the movements and demands of the athlete's sport will direct the therapist to the treatment needed for specific muscles.

Tapotement used toward the end of the massage promotes an invigorating feeling for the athlete. Finishing with effleurage and gentle stretching enhances relaxation and tissue elongation. A full-body comprehensive treatment between matches (postcompetition) can take an hour or longer depending on the tissue tensions encountered and the readiness of the athlete to release tension (Figure 13-6).

## Massage as Maintenance

The fascial system has been demonstrated to tighten as a protective response to repetitive microtrauma. Competing and training for sport is nothing if not trauma. Comprehensive massage and massage techniques used for a specific part of the body is often part of an informed athlete's training and competition routine. Because of the repetitive nature of training and the continuous demands placed on the connective tissues while executing the repetitive movements of sport, tissues can develop excessive tension. If not addressed with flexibility and range of motion movements, this excessive tissue tension can result in a tightened myofascial system. Elite athletes demonstrate tissue imbalances, such as baseball players with external rotation beyond 100 degrees and limited internal rotation less than 90 degrees (Ellenbecker, 2001).

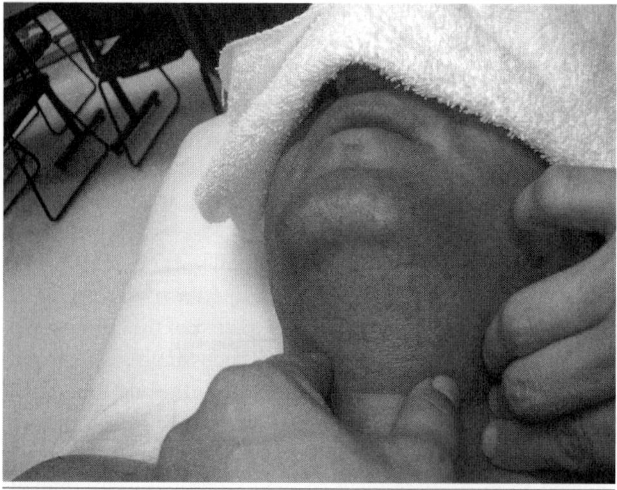

**Figure 13-6**
Postcompetition massage entails more comprehensive treatment.

Massage therapy restores imbalances that cause limited functional mobility. In a randomized clinical trial, pretest/posttest design of 20 subjects, soft tissue mobilization combined with proprioneuromuscular facilitation on the subscapularis muscle was been demonstrated to increase shoulder external rotation and overhead reach after just one session (Godges et al., 2003). This is another example of the benefits massage can provide the elite athlete to restore balance of the musculoskeletal system during training and competition.

### Periodization Training

In 1972, Leonid Mateyeev first introduced periodized training as a resistance training concept. It has developed into a training structure for informed athletes desiring to peak and compete systematically. The theory is that training should occur in cycles to enhance performance. A large training cycle is called a *macrocycle* and is divided into smaller cycles known as *mesocycles*. There are four mesocycles: the preparation phase, the first transition phase (precompetition), the competition phase, and the second transition phase (active recovery). Each mesocycle has specific training components, and this regimen is used to prevent staleness and injuries that can occur with overtraining.

Training was initially phased within cycles to attain one period of peak performance during the macrocycle of a year. This concept has been adjusted in sports that require peak performance several times throughout a year. Sports such as cycling, tennis, football, and golf require the creation of several macrocycles. The informed practitioner will ascertain within which mesocycle the athlete is competing and adjust the massage therapy treatment dose (Figure 13-7).

The *preparation phase* emphasizes high-volume and low-intensity strengthening with aerobic conditioning and flexibility. This is the beginning of a training macrocycle, and the athlete who has not been active will experience significant DOMS. Techniques described in the DOMS section presented earlier in the chapter are critical to keep this athlete injury-free and motivated to continue with training. Weekly full-body therapy intervention is beneficial at this time. The *first transition phase (precompetition)* is characterized by strength training of moderate intensity and

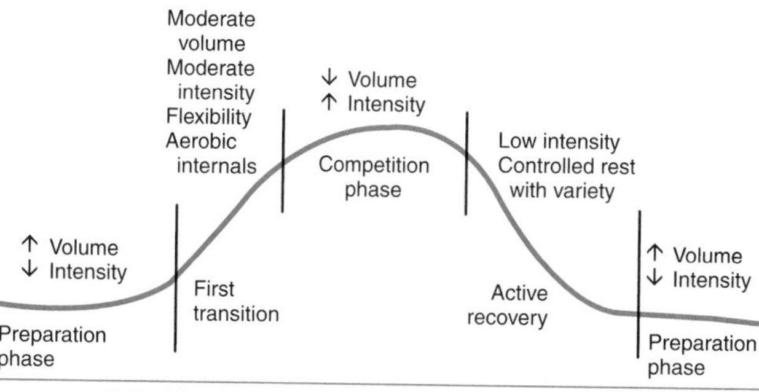


**Figure 13-7**

The periodization cycle optimizes athletic performance throughout the year. *(Adapted from McArdle WD, Katch FI, Katch VL:* Exercise physiology: energy, nutrition, and human performance, *ed 5, Philadelphia Lippincott Williams & Wilkins.)*

moderate resistance, as well as aerobic interval training with sprint activities interspersed by recovery. Sport-specific drills are performed to prepare for competition. The massage dosage remains similar to the first phase of this cycle with flexibility being an important adjunct to treatment. The *competition phase* follows with emphasis on low-volume, high-intensity strengthening one to two times in the week of competition and interval training with sport-specific activities. The athlete should receive daily massage therapy intervention if possible while in competition. The *second transition phase (active recovery)* includes low-intensity conditioning with recreational activities. Massage intervention can be done three to four times per week, and if there is an injury, it should be performed daily to promote healing. Sport-specific activities are avoided until the beginning of the next first transition phase.

Applying massage therapy techniques and varying the dosage specific to the training cycle of an athlete is the distinguishing feature of sports massage. This is the science applied to the art of the healing touch that constitutes excellence among practitioners and enhances performance for the athlete.

## Psychological Effects That Enhance Performance

Everyone experiences stress. Elite athletes are no exception to this fact (Anshel, 2000). One of the powerful effects of therapeutic massage for an athlete in competition is relaxation and mental stress relief. Competitive state anxiety, which is a sense of threat induced by a competitive situation, has been shown to be detrimental to performance (Anshel, 2000; Martens et al., 1990). Massage intervention has the potential to affect anxiety levels among elite athletes. In an investigation by Hernandez-Reif et al. (2001), two randomly assigned groups of adults who received massage were compared with a group that received progressive muscle relaxation. The treatment dosage was 20-minute sessions two times per week for 5 weeks. The massage therapy group demonstrated statistically higher levels of serotonin and dopamine. This may explain in part the improved mood reported by individuals who received massage therapy. Subjects within this group were also measured to have lower levels of anxiety. In a pretest/posttest design, adults (N=26) were given chair massage and a control group of adults (N=24) were asked to relax in a chair (Field et al., 1996). Findings demonstrated that the massage group had de-creased levels of anxiety. Although this was not applied to athletes, the result does suggest that single does massage intervention can affect anxiety levels. Changes in hormonal levels as measured by cortisol levels following massage induce a relaxation response and reduce anxiety, and the adjustment of the mood state also causes relaxation through psychological mechanisms (Weerapong et al., 2005).

Cailliet (1997) maintained that pain is a sensory experience that is no longer considered to be proportional to the degree of tissue damage. Furthermore, pain is influenced by expectancy, anxiety, fear, attention, learning, and, of course, injury. Massage has been directly demonstrated to decrease pain, and this has been hypothesized to be part of the healing process. However, a soft tissue intervention that can diminish anxiety and promote alertness though invigorating techniques could diminish the perception of pain through the psychological pathways in addition to the physical pathways.

## Evidence Regarding Massage

The current evidence regarding massage therapy intervention is limited with a dearth of available data regarding the transfer to performance of the hypothesized effects. The available evidence is even more scant with regard to elite athletes. For example, there has been a reduction in systolic and diastolic blood pressure in individuals who received a 15-minute massage therapy intervention in the workplace (Cady & Jones, 1997). This has yet to be demonstrated among elite athletes. Systematic reviews have attempted to provide recommendations based on the current body of knowledge.

Deep friction massage, also known as *cross-friction massage to promote healing,* initially proposed by Cyriax (1990), presents with varied reports regarding effectiveness. The systematic review by Brosseau et al. (2007) was unable to validate the use or nonuse of DFM to enhance functional outcomes with tendonitis because of the small sample size of the randomized clinical trials. At this point in time, therapists can choose to use DFM based on the varied success rate, clinical experience of success, and immediate, short-term pain-relief characteristics reported by athletes.

More investigations with rigorous methods are needed for conclusive evidence.

A randomized clinical trial design by Preyde (2000) included subjects with a mean age of 46 years with subacute back pain. These subjects reported less intensity of pain and a decrease in the quality of pain when compared with groups that received soft tissue manipulation alone, remedial exercise with postural education, or sham comprehensive massage (control group). Similar findings have been demonstrated with chronic low back pain. The conclusion drawn by the systematic review by Dryden et al. (2004) is that the current evidence supports the use of massage therapy for orthopedic patients with low back pain. Other patients may experience pain that can be relieved with massage as an adjunct to a full, comprehensive program.

These pain-reduction effects of massage therapy have been long lasting. All of the systematic reviews regarding the physiological and psychological effects of massage emphasize the need to identify the mechanisms of action with massage and randomized controlled trials with rigor to capture the definitive effect of massage therapy. It should be noted that elite athletes provide an excellent population on which to investigate the effects of massage on healing tissue but are an underinvestigated population because of lack of access. This group requires the attention of the evidence-based practitioner.

## Caveats Specific to Elite Athletes

All sports massage should begin with a quick interview of the athlete to determine his or her schedule for the day, any existing injuries, the athlete's current training regimen, and his or her next bout of activity. With this knowledge the therapist will be able to select the appropriate massage treatment dose and technique to best enhance performance.

Certain caveats come to mind when dealing with elite and recreational athletes based on the fact that these individuals are used to pushing through pain. Many cyclists train to "feel the burn" that comes with high-intensity training and revel in the ability to remain in that painful zone for long periods of time. This is not uncommon for athletes who are truly passionate about their sport and their training. This is why we watch and appreciate sport—because we see individuals reach deeply within to move beyond the physical fatigue and pain to accomplish unbelievable feats. The therapist must remember this when applying treatment. An athlete may have a greater ability to ignore or overcome physical pain that is being applied to the tissues by the therapist. In applying massage techniques, the focus should be on the response of the athlete but also on the response of the tissue beneath the therapist's fingers. This response should be gauged throughout the treatment. Inattention to signals of pain or changes can prolong recovery because of inadvertently induced trauma.

Understanding the phases of tissue healing, the cycles of training, and the anatomy of the body is critical when applying sports massage. Using deep friction massage on a newly injured hamstring muscle that is in the inflammatory phase of healing can cause localized edema, which adds days to healing. The application of ASTM to athletes who are in the competition phase of the periodization cycle could decrease their ability to change direction during their event later in the day. The knowledge that the pectoralis minor inserts at the coracoid process directs the therapist to release tension

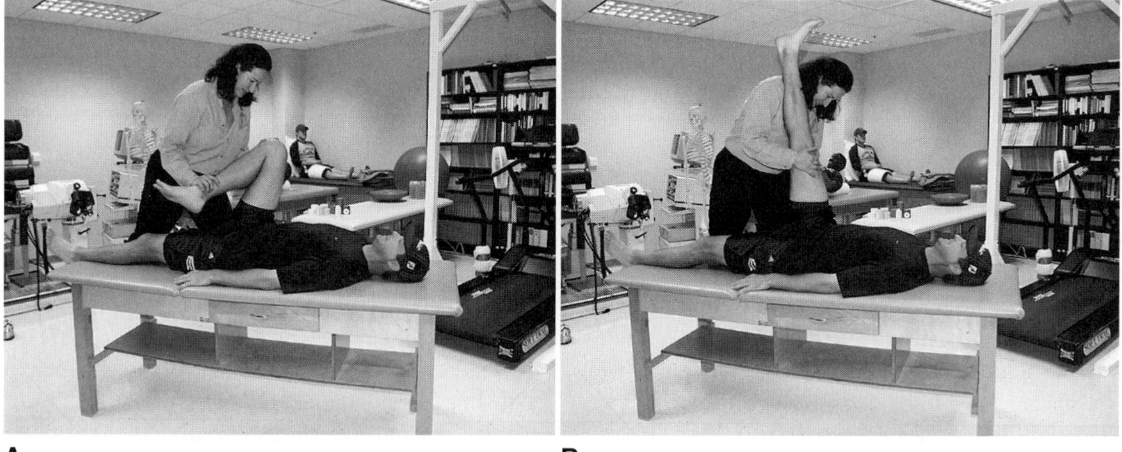

A B

**Figure 13-8**

**A,** Effective sports massage can include active range-of-motion techniques. **B,** Effective sports massage can also include stretching techniques.

on this tendon when massage along the midsubstance of the pectoralis musculature is painful or does not decrease tissue tension. Application of science combined with the art of manual techniques makes for effective sports massage therapy (see Figures 13-7 and 13-8).

## REFERENCES


Anshel M: Sources of acute stress and coping styles in competitive sport, *Anxiety Stress Coping* 13:1-26, 2000.

Bell GW: Aquatic sports massage therapy, *Clin Sports Med* 18(2):427-435, 1999.

Brewer BW: Review and critique of psychological adjustment to athletic injury, *J Appl Sport Psychol* 6:87-100, 1994.

Brosseau L, Casimiro L, Milne S et al: Deep transverse friction massage for treating tendinitis, *Cochrane Database Syst Rev,* 1:2007.

Cady SH, Jones GE: Massage therapy as a workplace intervention for reduction of stress, *Percept Mot Skills* 84(1):157-158, 1997.

Cailliet R: *Soft tissue pain and disability,* ed 3, Philadelphia, 1996, FA Davis.

Callaghan MJ: The role of massage in the management of the athlete: a review, *Br J Sports Med* 27(1):28-33, 1993.

Cantu RI, Grodin AJ: *Myofascial manipulation: theory and clinical application,* ed 2, Gaithensburg, Md, 2001, Aspen.

Cheung K, Hume P, Maxwell L: Delayed onset muscle soreness: treatment strategies and performance factors, *Sports Med* 33(2):145-164, 2003.

Connolly DA, Sayers SP, McHugh MP: Treatment and prevention of delayed onset muscle soreness, *J Strength Cond Res* 17(1):197-208, 2003.

Cottingham JT, Maitland J: A three-paradigm treatment model using soft tissue mobilization and guided movement-awareness techniques for a patient with chronic low back pain: a case study, *J Orthop Sports Phys Ther* 36(3):155-167, 1997.

Cyriax J, Russell G: *Textbook of orthopedic medicine,* vol 2, London, 1990, Tindall & Cassall.

D'Ambrogio KJ, Roth GB: *Positional relief therapy: assessment and treatment of musculoskeletal dysfunction,* New York, 1997, Mosby.

Davidson CJ, Ganion LR, Gehlsen GM et al: Rat tendon morphologic and functional changes resulting from soft tissue mobilization, *Med Sci Sports Exerc* 29(3):313-319, 1997.

De Domenico G, Wood E: *Beard's massage,* ed 4, Philadelphia, 1997, Saunders.

Dryden T, Baskwill A, Preyde M: Massage therapy for the orthopedic patient: a review, *Orthop Nurse* 23(5):327-332, 2004.

Duda JL, Smart AE, Tappe MK: Predictors of adherence in the rehabilitation of athletic injuries: an application of personal investment theory, *J Sport Exerc Psychol* 11:367-318, 1989.

Enwemeka CS: Connective tissue plasticity: ultrastructural, biomechanical and morphometric effects of physical factors on intact and regenerating tendons, *J Orthop Sports Phys Ther* 14(5):198, 1991.

Ernst E: Does post-exercise massage treatment reduce delayed onset muscle soreness? A systematic review, *Br J Sports Med* 32:212-214, 1998.

Farr T, Nottle C, Nosaka K et al: The effects of therapeutic massage on delayed onset muscle soreness and muscle function following downhill walking, *J Sci Med Sport* 5(4):297-306, 2002.

Field, T, Ironson G, Scafidi F et al: Massage therapy reduces anxiety and enhances EEG pattern of alertness and math computations, *Intl J Neurosci* 86(3-4):197-205, 1996.

Frulan AD, Brosseau L, Imamura M et al: Massage for low-back pain, *Cochrane Database Syst Rev* 4:CD001929, 2002.

Galloway SD, Watt JM: Massage provision by physiotherapists at major athletics events between 1987 and 1998, *Br J Sports Med* 38(2):235-236, 2004.

Gehlsen GM, Ganion LR, Helfst R: Fibroblast responses to variation in soft tissue mobilization pressure, *Med Sci Sports Exerc* 31(4):531-535, 1999.

Goats GC: Massage—The scientific bases of an ancient art: part 1. The techniques, *Br J Sports Med* 28(3):149-152, 1994a.

Goats GC: Massage—The scientific basis of an ancient art: part 2. Physiological and therapeutic effects, *Br J Sports Med* 28(3):153-156, 1994b.

Gogdes JJ, Mattson-Bell M, Thorpe D: The immediate effects of soft tissue mobilization with proprioceptive neuromuscular facilitation on glenohumeral external rotation and overhead reach, *J Orthop Sports Phys Ther* 33:713-718, 2003.

Hemmings B: Psychological and immunological effects of massage after sport, *Br J Sport Rehabil* 7(12):516-519, 2000.

Hemmings B, Smith M, Graydon J et al: Effects of massage on physiological restoration, perceived recovery, and repeated sports performance, *Br J Sports Med* 34(2):109-114; discussion 115, 2000.

Hernandez-Reif M, Field T, Krasnegor J et al: Lower back pain is reduced and range of motion increased after massage therapy, *Intl J Neurosci* 106, (304):131-145, 2001.

Hinds T, McEwan I, Perkes J et al: Effects of massage on limb and skin blood flow after quadriceps exercise, *Med Sci Sports Exerc* 36(8):1308-1313, 2004.

Jonhagen S, Ackermann P, Eriksson T et al: Sports massage after eccentric exercise, *Am J Sports Med* 32(6):1499-1503, 2004.

Kisner C, Colby LA: *Therapeutic exercise: foundation and techniques,* ed 4, Philadelphia, 2002, FA Davis.

Lane KN, Wenger HA: Effect of selected recovery conditions on performance of repeated bouts of intermittent cycling separated by 24 hours, *J Strength Cond Res* 18(4):855-860, 2004.

Loehr JE: *The new toughness training for sports,* New York, 1994, Penguin.

Martens R, Burton D, Vealey RS et al: Development and validation of the Competitive State Anxiety Inventory-2. In Martens R, Vealeyn RS, Burton D, editors: *Competitive anxiety in sport,* Champaigne, Ill, 1990, Human Kinetics.

Mayhew TP, Rothstein JM, Finucane SD et al: Muscular adaptation to concentric and eccentric exercise at equal power levels, *Med Sci Sports Exerc* 27:868-873, 1995.

McArdle WD, Katch FI, Katch VL: *Exercise physiology: energy, nutrition, and human performance,* ed 5, Philadelphia, 2001, Lippincott Williams & Wilkins.

Meeusen R, Lievens P: The use of cryotherapy in sports injuries, *Sports Med* 3(60):398-414, 1986.

Melham TJ, Sevier TL, Malnofski MJ et al: Chronic ankle pain and fibrosis successfully treated with a new noninvasive augmented soft tissue mobilization technique (ASTM): a case report, *Med Sci Sports Exerc* 30(6):801-804, 1998.

Mondero J, Donne B: Effect of recovery interventions on lactate removal and subsequent performance, *Intl J Sports Med* 21(8): 593-597, 2000.

Moritz SE, Feltz DL, Fahrback KR et al: The relation of self-efficacy measures to sport performance: a meta-analytic review, *Res Q Exerc Sport* 71(3):280-294, 2000.

National Athletic Trainers' Association: *Proceedings of the NATA Annual Symposium,* Baltimore, 2004, NATA.

Noyes FR, Keller CS, Grood ES et al: Advances in understanding of knee ligament injury repair and rehabilitation, *Med Sci Sports Exerc* 16:427, 1984.

Paris S, Loubert P: *Foundation of clinical orthopaedics,* St Augustine, Fla, 1999, Institute Press.

Pope A, Silverberg R, Johnson J et al: The effects of soft tissue mobilization on the immature burn scar: results of a pilot study, *J Burn Care Rehabil* 17(3):252-259, 1996.

Preyde M: Effectiveness of massage therapy for subacute low-back pain: a randomized controlled trial, *CMAJ* 162:1815-1820, 2000.

Prochaska JO, Marcus BH: The transtheoretical model: application ot exercise. In RK Dishman, editor: *Advances in exercise adherence,* Champaign, Ill, 2001, Human Kinetics.

Quinn C, Chandler C, Moraska A: Chronic tension headaches reduction with the use of cross friction massage techniques, *Am J Public Health* 92(10):1657-1661, 2002.

Robertson A, Watt JM, Galloway SD: Effects of leg massage on recovery from high intensity cycling exercise, *Br J Sports Med* 38(2):173-176, 2004.

Schoitz EH: Manipulation treatment of the spinal column from the medical-historical standpoint, *J Norwegian Med Assoc* 78:359-372, 1958.

Smith LL, Keating MN, Holbert D et al: The effects of athletic massage on delayed onset muscle soreness, creatine kinase, and neutrophil count: a preliminary report, *J Orthop Sports Phys Ther* 19(2):93-99, 1994.

Stearns ML: Studies of the development of connective tissue in transparent chambers in the rabbit ear, *Am J Anat* 67:55-97, 1940.

Stock D, Baum M, Rosskopf P et al: Electroencephalogram activity, catechyolamines, and lymphocyte subpopulations after resistance exercise and during regeneration, *Eur J Appl Physiol Occup Physiol,* 72(3):235-242, 1996.

Swenson C, Sward L, Karlsson J: Cryotherapy in sports medicine, *Scand J Med Sci Sports* 6(4):193-200, 1996.

Tidus PM, Shoemaker JK: Effleurage massage, muscle blood flow and long-term post-exercise strength recovery, *Int J Sports Med* 16:478-483, 1995.

Weerapong P, Hume PA, Kolt GS: The mechanisms of massage and effects on performance, muscle recovery and injury prevention, *Sports Med* 35(3):235-256, 2005.

Chapter 14

# Massage for the Baby and Infant

The use of various forms of soft tissue manipulation (massage) for babies and infants has been described and promoted for many centuries and in some Eastern cultures (India and China) for millennia. The use of various forms of tactile stimulation is therefore a time-honored method of promoting relaxation, contentment and normal development in babies and infants. Rocking the baby, gently rubbing the head, stroking the hands and feet, and simply touching the baby's skin are examples common to many cultures.

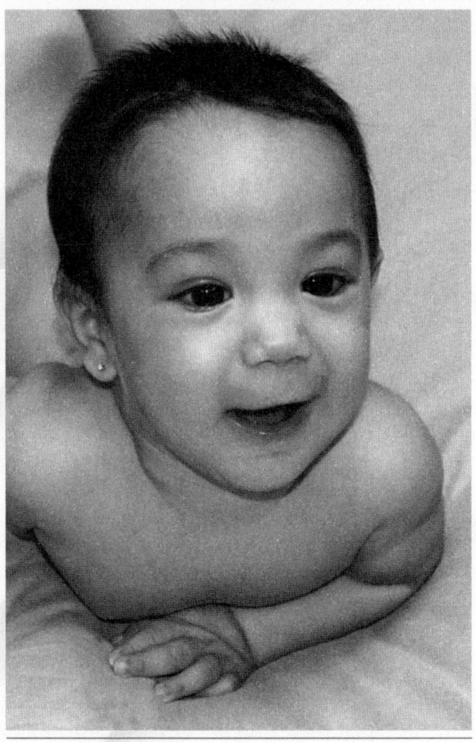

As an extension of this common practice, the use of specific massage techniques for babies and infants is a well-recognized method to promote bonding between the child and the parent or caregiver. Massage has a beneficial effect on the development, alertness, and emotional status of the baby and can continue to any age. It strengthens the bonding process and helps establish a warm, positive parent-child relationship.

Massage is beneficial for all babies and infants, regardless of whether they have problems. In terms of an age differential between babies and infants for massage, a *baby* is usually considered to be a child less than 3 months old and an *infant* is 3 to 12 months of age. Obviously, the major difference between the use of massage in these two groups is that the younger the baby, the greater the care required (especially much less pressure). Benefits to both parents and baby include pleasure, confidence, communication, relaxation, reassurance through skin contact, development of body awareness, and calmness (Adamson, 1996; Agarwal et al., 2000; Booth et al., 1985; Debelle, 1981; Field, 1995, 1999; Ireland, 2000; Lindrea & Stainton, 2000; Mainous, 2002; McClure, 1989, 2000; Ottenbacher et al., 1987; Reid, 2000; Wall, 1998; Watson, 1999). In addition, infant massage may also be of value in improving the mother-infant interaction for mothers with postnatal depression, thereby avoiding the many problems that can result for both mother and child (Onozawa, 2001) (Box 14-1).

Infants who undergo surgery can be included in this category, as can the preterm baby. These babies need to learn that touch can be pleasurable because some of their early experiences (such as monitoring devices, various life support, and other invasive procedures) have been painful or uncomfortable. A variety of studies provide evidence of the benefits of massage for the preterm infant, such as improved weight gain, fewer facial grimaces, less fist clenching, and enhanced

**BOX 14-1 Situations That Suggest the Benefits of Massage for a Baby or Infant**

- For a colicky baby who cries when being fed. Often the baby continues to be tense and irritable long after the cause of the colic has been identified and treated.
- For an anxious baby who dislikes rapid changes of position, does not need much sleep, and is hypersensitive to external stimuli.
- For an irritable baby who exhibits abnormal neurological signs, hyperactivity, and persistent primitive reflexes.

development of the sympathetic nervous system (Browne, 2000; Dieter et al., 2003; Feldman, 1998; Field et al., 1986, 1987; Kuhn et al., 1991; Ottenbacher et al., 1987; Rice, 1975; Scafidi et al., 1993; Solkoff et al., 1975; White-Traut & Goldman, 1988; White-Traut & Pate, 1987). Although many studies report beneficial effects of massage in the preterm infant, there are significant methodological issues that still need to be resolved (Vickers et al., 2000). In contrast, babies who are not particularly active can be stimulated, rather than relaxed, with massage techniques that alternate light tickling with gentle, firm pressure.

Massage has effects on babies and infants similar to those on adults, and it is not surprising that it can be helpful for a number of conditions, such as asthma (Field, 1998), colic (Huhtala et al., 2000; Larson, 1990), and infantile congenital myogenic torticollis (Xu, 1992). Although massage is beneficial, it is not without risk, and a few studies have explored issues that might be a problem, especially for the baby or infant (Joyce, 1996; White-Traut & Goldman, 1988).

Further reading can be found in a number of texts that address various aspects of the many benefits and techniques of baby or infant massage (Auckett, 1982; Drehobl, 2000; Fan, 1999; Gordon & Adderly, 1999; Heinl, 1991; Leboyer, 1976a, 1976b; McClure, 1989; Prudence, 1984; Schneider, 1982; Tiquia, 1986; Walker, 1996).

## TECHNIQUE FOR BABY OR INFANT MASSAGE

Preparations for massage of a baby or infant include attention to all of the factors listed previously (see Chapter 3), with special attention paid to creating a peaceful atmosphere (no phones or loud noises, etc.). Soothing music may be beneficial, as well as subdued lighting, appropriate room temperature (no drafts), and the use of a natural massage oil (e.g., almond, olive, or apricot). A small amount of baby powder can be used as an alternative, being careful not to pepper the baby with powder as this may create a problem if the powder is inhaled. Although massage may be given at almost any time of the day or night, it will probably be most effective when both parent and baby are relaxed and the baby is not hungry. A suitable time might be immediately following a warm bath. Parts of the baby or infant not being massaged may be covered with a light blanket or towel if necessary to maintain body temperature. Maintaining a proper body temperature is important because the baby's entire skin surface may be exposed during massage.

For a very young baby, massage should begin with the baby positioned in supine lying on a soft pillow supported on the lap of the parent, caregiver, or therapist. In this position, eye contact with the baby can be maintained while massage to the front of the body is completed. It is also important for the parent or therapist to talk in soothing tones to the baby during the procedure. An older baby or infant can be positioned on a soft pillow on a table, bed, sofa, or some other suitable surface in such a way as to allow the person performing the massage to be comfortable and maintain good posture. The baby or infant can be positioned in prone lying, although the head will obviously need to be turned to one side. Again, this is probably most easily accomplished with the child lying on a soft but thick pillow.

Because the baby or infant will most likely want to move around during the massage, it is important that each technique be adapted to suit the individual circumstance. As such, the various massage techniques cannot be rigidly prescribed or applied to the baby, and this is especially the case with the timing of each stroke and the parts of the hand used for these techniques. If the baby or infant is very small, the person performing the massage may only need to use his or her fingertips, whereas the anterior surface of the fingers and palm may be used on a larger child. Quite obviously then, the size of the therapist's hand and the child's body will affect the specific modification needed. Frequent pauses may be needed and will interrupt the usual flow of individual massage strokes. In general, massage flows from head to toe, covering all of the body, back and front. The technique applied consists of a gentle modified stroking, and the position is adapted to wherever the baby is most comfortable at any given time. If the baby or infant begins to cry or becomes distressed or agitated, massage should obviously cease.

## GENERAL WHOLE-BODY STROKING

The baby or infant is comfortably positioned in supine lying. Gentle stroking begins at the side of the head and passes down each upper limb to the hands. A second stroke begins again at the side of the head, this time passing down the chest and abdomen and along each lower limb to the feet. Each stroke is slow and gentle, and the entire sequence of movements can be repeated at least six times. The posterior aspect of the baby or infant can also be massaged in a similar manner. This time, the baby or infant is positioned in prone lying with the head comfortably turned to one side. The first stroke begins at each shoulder girdle region, and the therapist's hands pass out and along the arms to the hands. The therapist then lifts his or her hands off the baby, and the second stroke begins again at the shoulder girdle. This time, the therapist's hands move down the baby's back, over the buttocks, and along the lower limbs to the foot. The entire sequence of strokes is then repeated at least six times. A single- or two-handed technique can be used, as seems appropriate. When a two-handed technique is used, the therapist's hands may be used in a simultaneous or alternate fashion. Figure 14-1 illustrates these techniques.

## HEAD AND FACE

The therapist strokes the crown of the baby's head with his or her thumbs using gentle, circular movements. Then, with the fingertips, the therapist strokes from the head down along the side of the face, including the forehead, eyebrow, temple, eye, ear, nose, cheek, and lower jaw. A single- or two-handed technique may be used. Figure 14-2 illustrates stroking to the head and face.

## UPPER LIMBS

With the child supported in the supine position, massage can begin with the therapist's hands placed on the shoulder girdle of each upper limb, with the fingertips resting on each scapula region. The therapist then passes the hands across the baby's shoulders, rounding them forward, moving down the arms to the hands. The therapist's hands should encircle the baby's arms and gently squeeze each arm from shoulder to wrist, then massage the baby's hands and fingers using gentle pressure applied between the tips of the therapist's thumb and forefinger. Stroking the back of the hand with the thumb tends to encourage the fingers to open. Each stroke should finish by taking the hands off the body to begin again at the shoulders. It is usual to massage both upper limbs at the same time, although a single limb can be

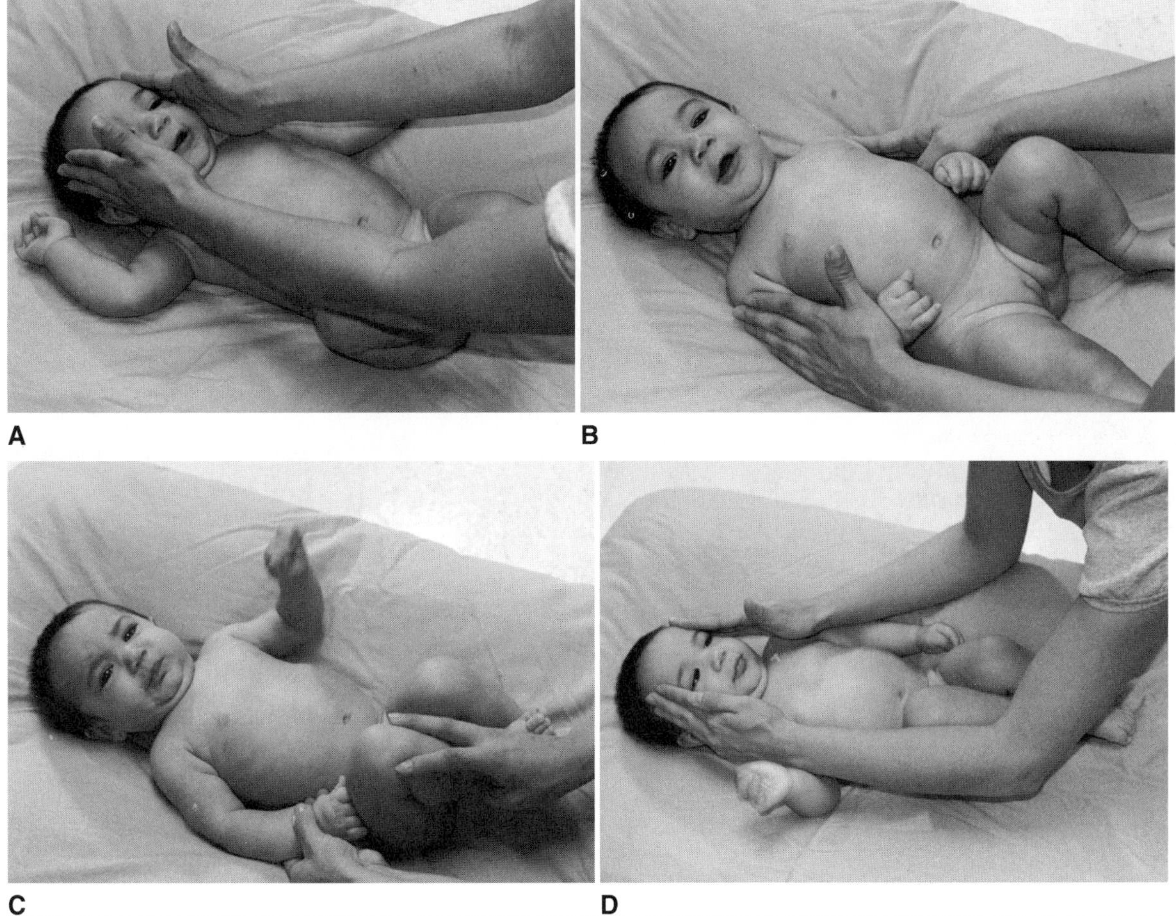


**Figure 14-1 Stroking to the Whole Body**

The baby (or infant) is comfortably positioned in supine lying. Gentle stroking begins at the side of the head and passes down each upper limb to the hands **(A, B, and C).** The next stroke begins at the side of the head **(D),** this time passing down the chest, abdomen **(E),** and along each lower limb to the feet **(F, G, H, and I).** The sequence of movements is then repeated at least six times. The entire sequence of strokes is then performed to the posterior aspect, with the baby or infant repositioned into prone lying **(J, K, L, and M).** A single- or two-handed technique can be used, as seems appropriate. Movements are slow, with only light pressure.

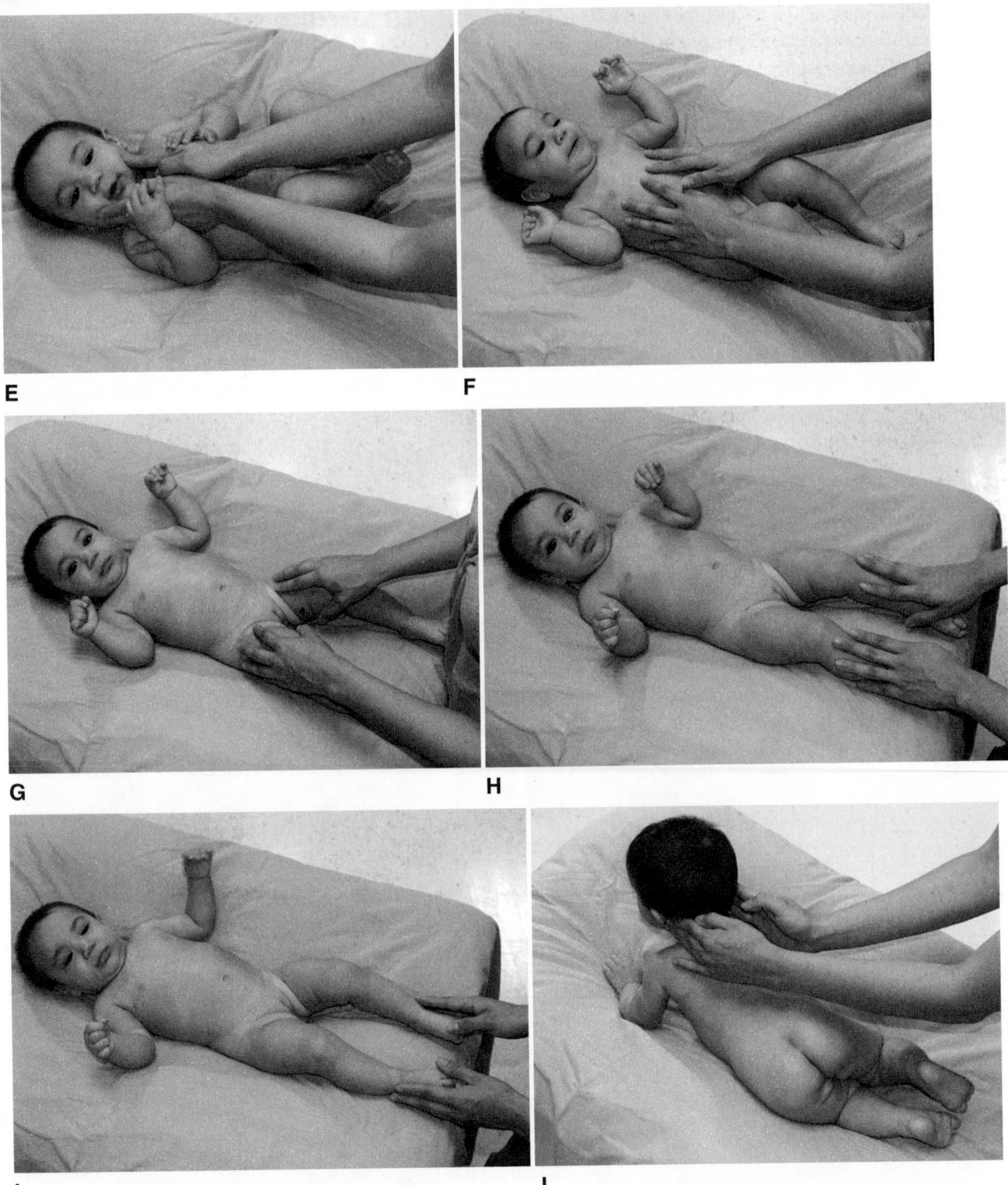

Figure 14-1, cont'd

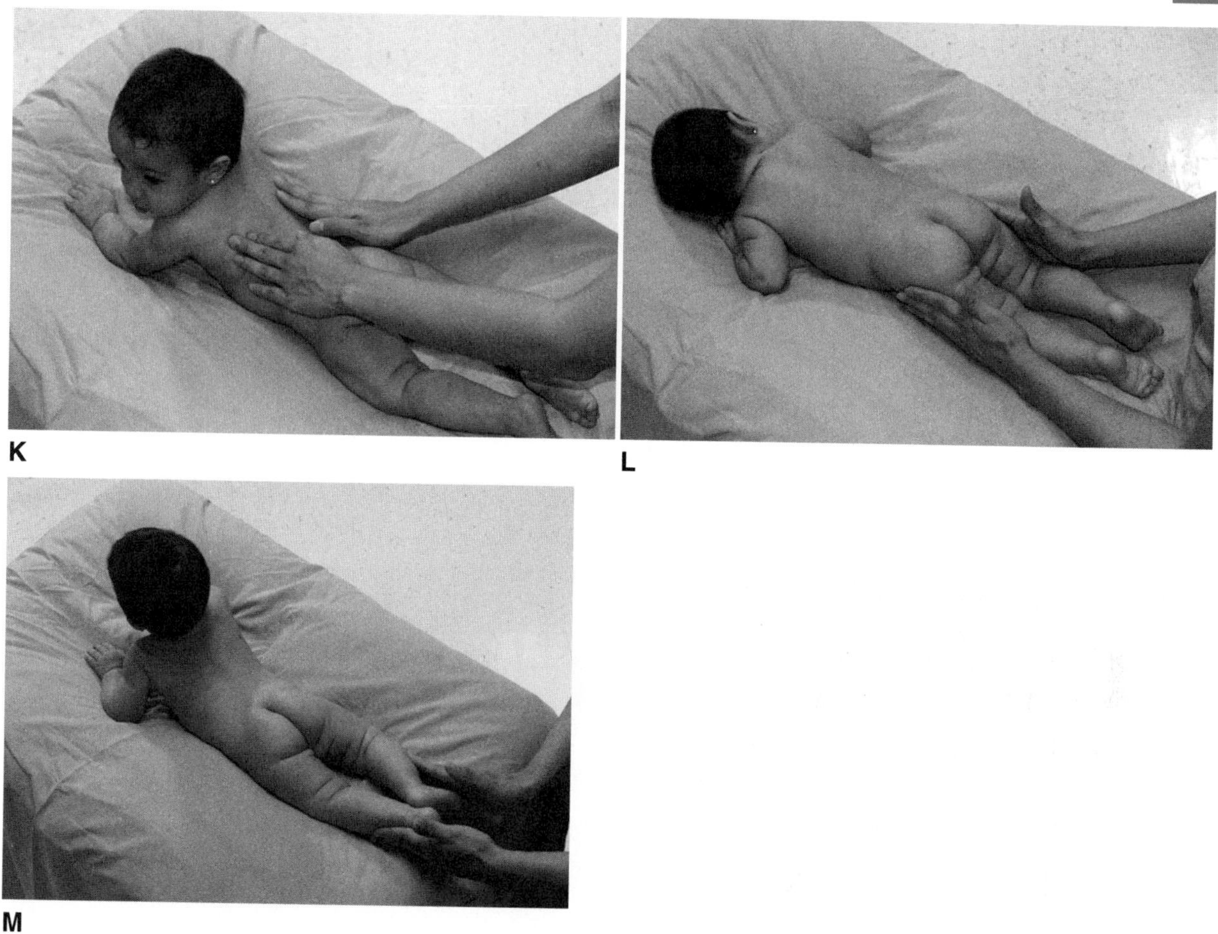


Figure **14-1**, cont'd

massaged at a time if desired. Figure 14-3 illustrates stroking to the upper limbs and hands.

## CHEST AND ABDOMEN

The anterior and lateral chest walls can be stroked using a two-handed technique, in which the finger pads stroke outward from the chest from the sternum, following the line of the ribs to the side of the body. The strokes can be given alternately or simultaneously (Figure 14-4, *A*). Abdominal discomfort may be helped by the use of circular, clockwise stroking, beginning around the umbilicus (Figure 14-4, *B*) and then following the course of the large intestine. The movements must be performed in a clockwise manner to follow the normal direction of intestinal flow. Pressure should be applied with the finger pads and may increase slightly as they move over the right side of the lower abdomen (iliac region). Figure 14-4, *C* illustrates this technique.

## LOWER LIMBS

With the child supported on a soft pillow in supine lying, massage begins with the therapist's hands placed on the sides of the hip (hip adductor muscles) of each lower limb (Figure 14-5, *A*). The hands then pass down the limb to the feet, finishing at the toes (Figure 14-5, *B*). The therapist's hands should be removed at the toes and begin again at the hips. This stroke can be performed with one or two hands and should be repeated several times.

Beginning at the upper thigh, massage continues as the therapist's hands encircle the baby's legs and gently squeeze each area from hips to feet (Figure 14-5, *C*). The ankles, feet, and toes can be massaged using gentle pressure applied between the tips of the therapist's thumbs and fingers. In this case, the thumb pads should be used to massage the muscle on the soles of the feet (Figure 14-5, *D*). Massage may be given simultaneously to each leg, or they can be

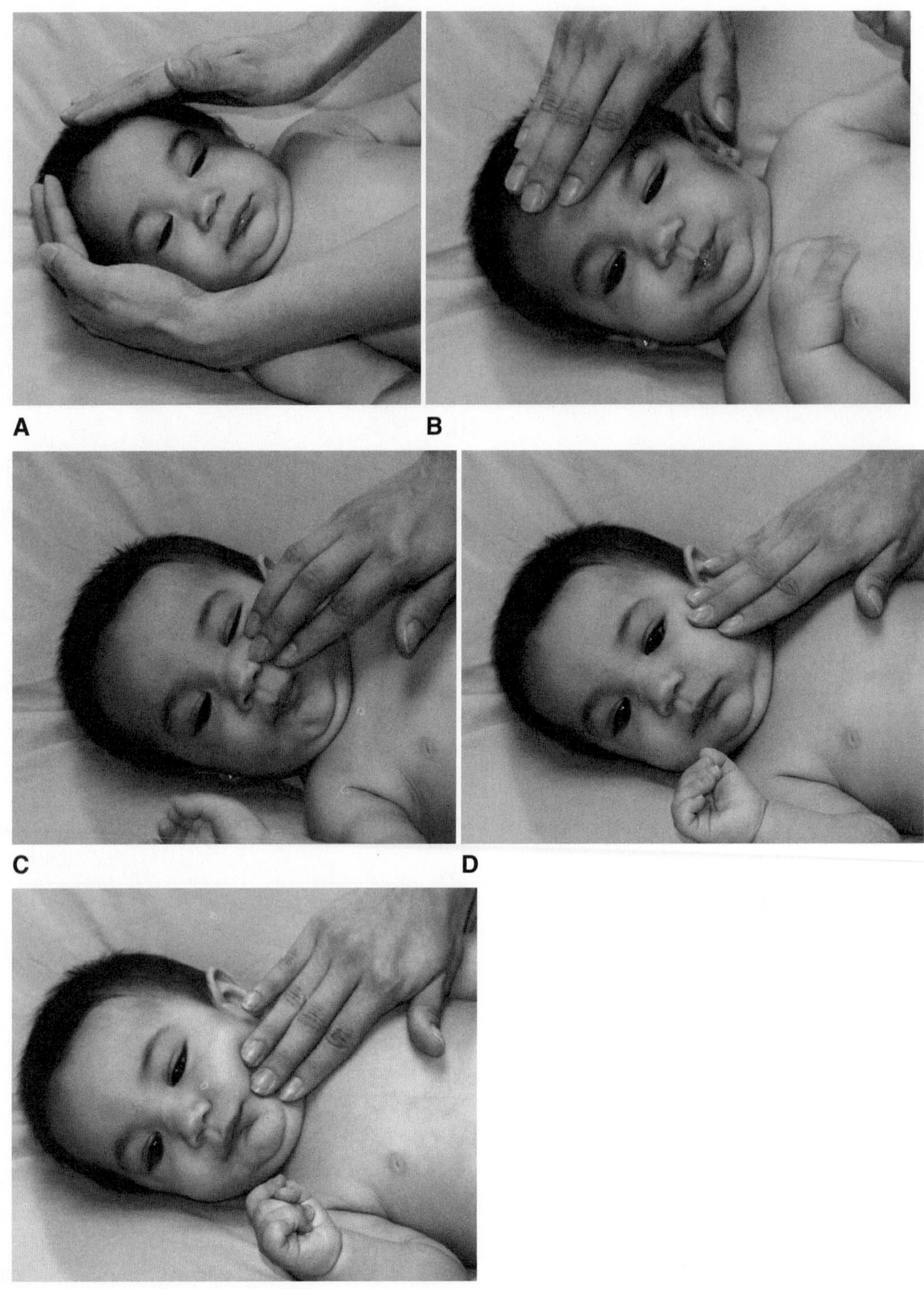

**Figure 14-2 Stroking to the Head and Face**

The baby (or infant) is comfortably positioned in supine. Gentle stroking is given to the skin on the crown of the head **(A)** and the forehead **(B)** using only gentle strokes, especially to the very young baby. Stroking then continues down the face, including around the eye and ear **(C),** the cheek and nose region **(D),** and then the lower jaw **(E).** A single- or two-handed technique can be used, as seems appropriate. Movements are slow, with only minimal pressure.

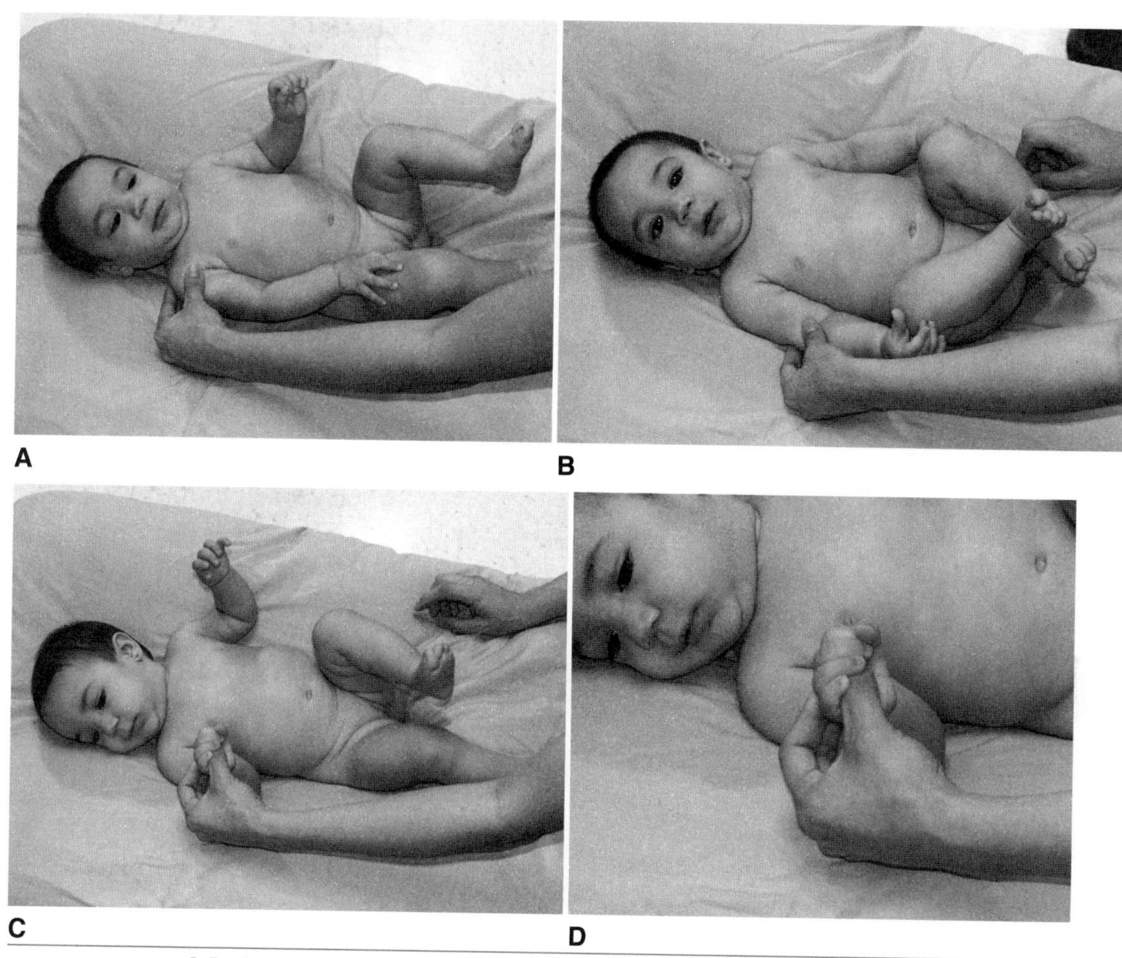


**Figure 14-3 Massage to the Upper Limbs**

The child is supported on a pillow in the supine position. Massage can begin with the therapist's hand placed on the shoulder girdle of either upper limb or both, with the fingertips resting on the scapular region **(A).** The hand then passes from the shoulder and moves down the arm to the elbow **(B),** forearm, and hand **(C).** The therapist's hands should encircle the baby's arms, gently squeeze each arm from shoulder to wrist, and then massage the baby's hands and fingers using gentle pressure applied between the tips of the therapist's thumb and forefinger **(D).** It is common to massage both upper limbs at the same time, although the limbs can be massaged separately, especially if the child is restless.

treated individually. Each stroke should finish by taking the hands off the body to begin again at the upper thigh. Rubbing the soles of the feet together is usually pleasant and calming for the baby. Depending on the size of the baby or infant's limbs and the therapist's hands, it may be necessary to reposition the baby into prone lying so that the therapist can properly reach the posterior aspects of the lower limb. In most cases, however, the hands of the person massaging the baby will be able to reach all the way around the limbs, and it should not be necessary to change positions.

## BACK

The baby or infant can be positioned in either prone or side lying. In either position, the child's head will need careful support. Using flat hands, gentle stroking begins from the base of the neck, the hands moving down the back, finishing at the buttocks (Figure 14-6, *A*). Once again, it may be possible for a therapist to use a single hand on a very small baby or infant. The technique can be given using one or two hands as seems most appropriate.

A second stroke, resembling a gentle finger-pad kneading technique, can be applied in a circular motion down either side of the baby's spine, from the neck to the buttocks (Figure 14-6, *B*). As in whole-hand kneading to the back of an adult, care is required in order to avoid pinching the tissues together in the midline when using a two-handed technique. Because the tissues in a baby or infant are relatively small in area, it may be best to perform the stroke with only one hand at a time.

## BUTTOCKS

The mass of muscles that together form the buttock region can be massaged with a gentle jiggling of the area. The open

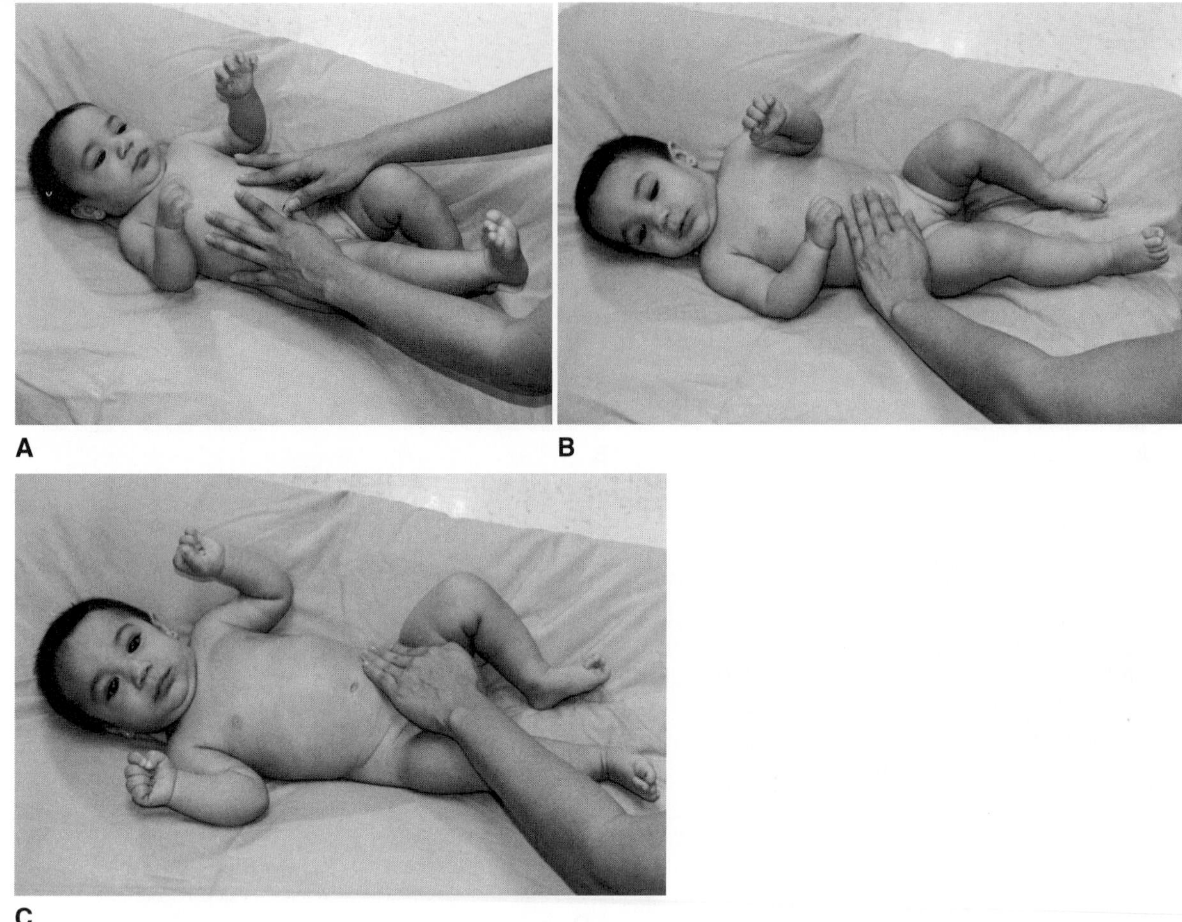

**Figure 14-4** Massage to the Chest and Abdomen

The baby (or infant) is comfortably positioned on a soft pillow in supine lying. Gentle stroking is given to the anterior and lateral chest walls, using only gentle strokes, especially to the very young baby. **A,** Stroking begins with the fingertips together in the center of the sternum, moving down and outward, following the line of the ribs to the lateral chest wall. A single- or two-handed technique can be used, as seems appropriate. Movements are slow, using only light pressure. **B,** The fingertips stroke over the abdomen with a clockwise motion beginning at the umbilicus. Pressure is light but may increase slightly over the right illiac region **(C).**

fingers are simply placed on the buttock, and a jiggling (coarse vibration) is imparted to the tissues. The buttocks can also be massaged using a modified squeeze kneading technique, using the fingers and thumb pads. Care must be used to avoid pinching the buttocks. Figure 14-7 illustrates these techniques.

## SUCKLING

Stimulating the rooting reflex causes the baby to open the mouth and nuzzle, searching for the nipple. This may be achieved by gently stroking from the cheek to the mouth. Such gentle touch may help a baby who is having difficulty suckling.

## SUMMARY

Close body contact can be provided through activities other than massage, such as breast-feeding, bottle-feeding with the baby cuddled against the bare chest, a cuddle in bed with parent(s), carrying in a front pack, and having a bath with parent(s). All of these activities will help to foster close bonding between the baby and parent(s) and provide a strong basis for the emotional and physical development of the child. Obviously, these activities are necessarily limited to certain individuals, whereas massage can be given by a variety of people, including parents, siblings, relatives, caregivers, and many types of health care professionals. Apart from the desirable emotional (psychological) benefits

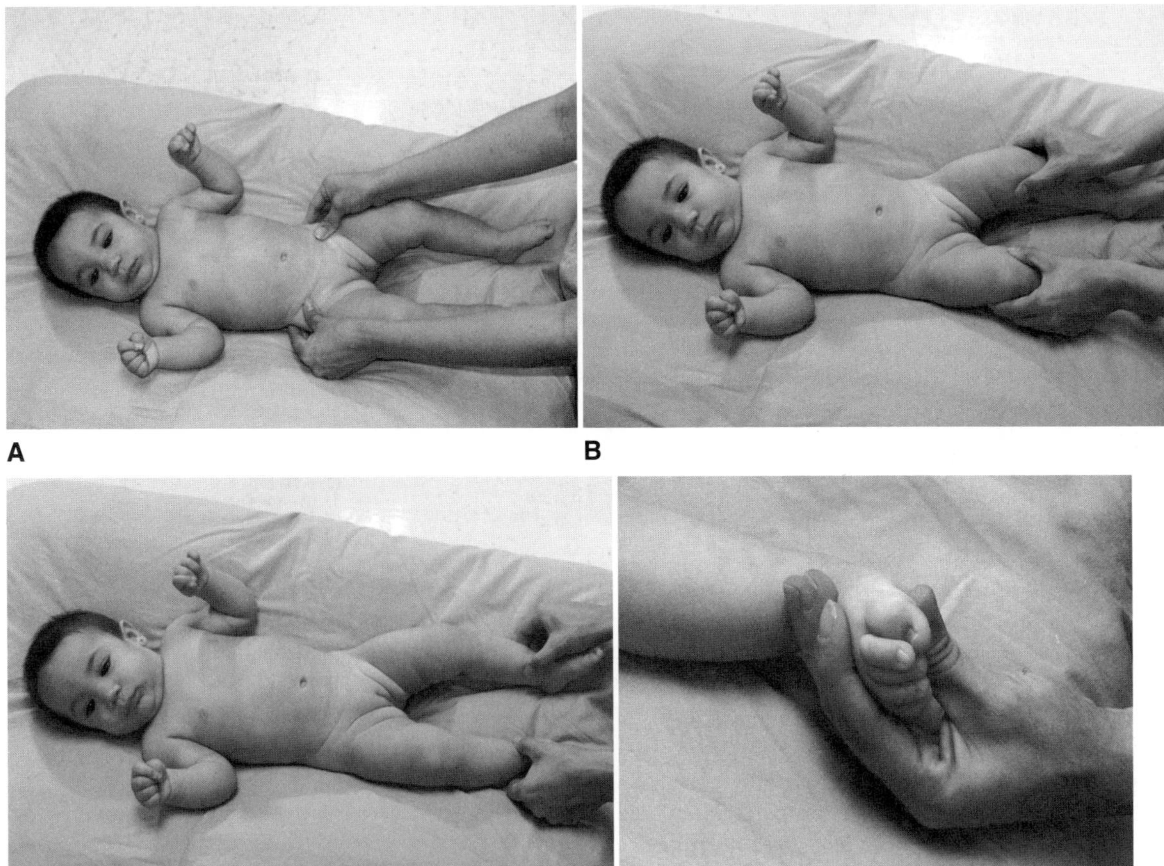


Figure **14-5** Massage to the Lower Limbs

**A,** Massage to the lower limbs begins with the therapist's hands at the sides of each hip with the thumbs placed medially. The hands then stroke down the limb **(B)** to the feet, finishing at the toes with gentle pressure. During the stroke, the hands reach around the entire surface of each limb, but the hands should be removed at the toes to begin again at the hips. This stroke can be performed with one or two hands and should be repeated several times. Beginning again at the upper thigh, massage continues as the therapist's hands encircle the baby's legs **(C),** gently squeezing each area from hips to feet. The ankles, feet, and toes are massaged using gentle pressure applied between the tips of the therapist's thumbs and fingers. **D,** The thumb pads are also used to massage the muscle on the soles of the feet.

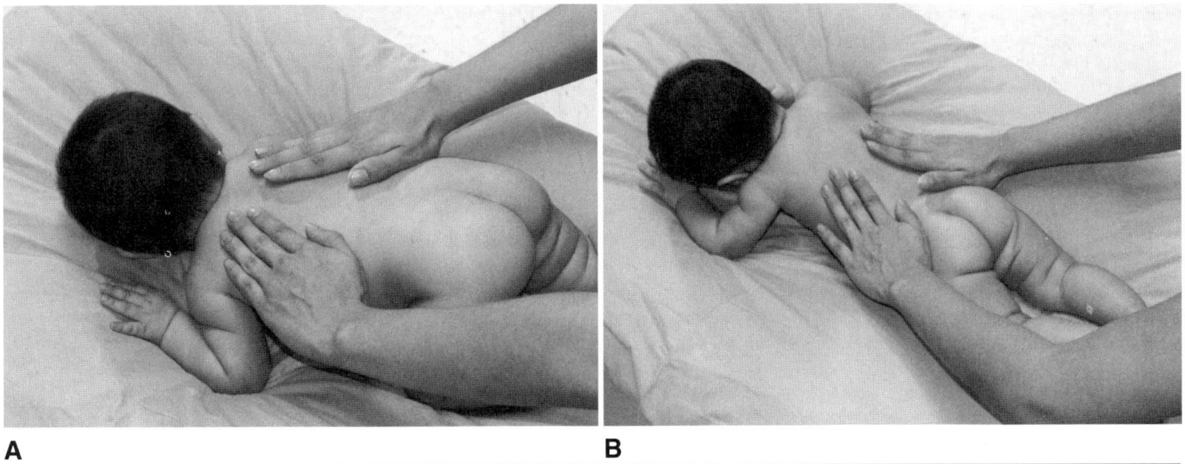

A

B

Figure **14-6** Massage to the Back

The baby (or infant) is comfortably positioned in prone or side lying. **A,** Gentle stroking is given to either side of the spine with flat hands or the palmar surfaces of the fingers, using only gentle strokes, especially to the very young baby. The strokes proceed from the base of the neck to the buttocks. A modified type of finger-pad kneading is performed to the tissues on either side of the spine, again beginning at the neck and moving to the buttocks. **B,** Gentle circular movements are performed with the fingertips, using either a single- or two-handed technique as seems appropriate.

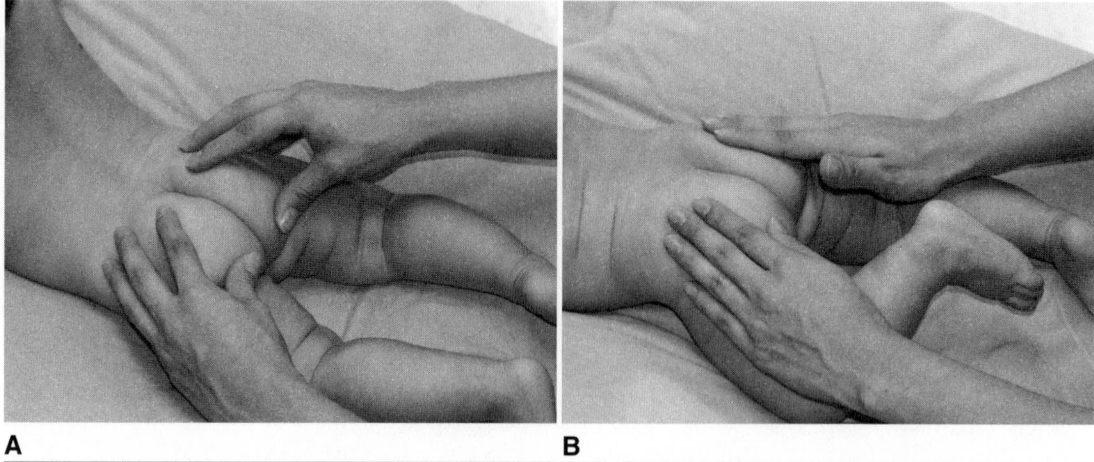

A B

**Figure 14-7 Massage to the Buttock Region**

**A,** The baby (or infant) is comfortably positioned in prone lying on a soft pillow. The open finger pads are placed on the buttock region, and a gentle jiggling (vibration) is imparted to the muscles. This can be a single- or two-handed technique. **B,** Modified squeeze kneading can also be performed to each buttock. The thumb and finger pads gently squeeze the skin and underlying tissues, slowly covering each buttock area.

of massage to both the child and the person performing the strokes, it is important to remember that these techniques have all of the other direct mechanical and physiological benefits described previously (see Chapter 5). All aspects of so-called normal child development will be facilitated by effective massage, and the sensitive parent, caregiver, or therapist will be able to identify, at an early stage, any abnormality in the child's anticipated motor abilities. For these reasons, massage to the baby and infant is an excellent way to promote the physical and psychological development of the child.

## REFERENCES


Adamson S: Teaching baby massage to new parents, *Complement Ther Nurs Midwifery* 2(6):151-159, 1996.

Agarwal K, Gupta A, Pushkarna R et al: Effects of massage and use of oil on growth, blood flow and sleep pattern in infants, *Indian J Med Res* 112:212-217, 2000.

Auckett A: *Baby massage: Parent-child bonding through touching,* New York, 1982, Newmarket Press.

Booth CL, Johnson-Crowley N, Barnard KE: *Infant massage and exercise: worth the effort? Am J Maternal Child Nursing* 10(3):184-189, 1985.

Browne JV: Developmental care-considerations for touch and massage in the neonatal intensive care unit, *Neonatal Netw* 19(1):1-7, 2000.

Cline K: *Chinese massage for infants and children: traditional techniques for alleviating colic, teething pain, earache, and other common childhood conditions,* Rochester, Vt, 1999, Inner Traditions International.

Debelle B: Relaxation and baby massage, *Aust Nurs J* 10(5):16-17, 1981.

Dieter J, Field T, Hernandez-Reif M et al: Stable preterm infants gain more weight and sleep less after five days of massage therapy, *J Pediatr Psychol* 28(6):403-411, 2003.

Drehobl K: *Pediatric massage: for the child with special needs,* Orlando, Fla, 2000, Academic Press.

Fan Ya-Li: *Chinese pediatric massage therapy: traditional techniques for alleviating colic, colds, earaches, and other common childhood conditions,* Boulder, Colo, 1999, Blue Poppy Enterprises.

Feldman A: Intervention programs for premature infants: how and do they affect development? *Clin Perinatol* 25(3):613-626, 1998.

Field T: Massage therapy for infants and children, *J Dev Behav Pediatr* 16(2):105-111, 1995.

Field T: Children with asthma have improved pulmonary functions after massage therapy, *J Pediatr* 132(5):854-858, 1998.

Field T: Massage therapy: more than a laying on of hands, *Contemp Pediatr* 16(5):77-78, 1999.

Field T, Scafidi S, Scafidi F et al: Tactile/kinesthetic stimulation effects on preterm neonates, *Pediatrics* 77:654-658, 1986.

Field T, Scafidi F, Schanberg S: Massage of preterm newborns to improve growth and development, *Pediatr Nurs* 13(6):385-387, 1987.

Gordon J, Adderly B: *Brighter baby: boosting your child's intelligence, health and happiness through infant therapeutic massage,* New York, 1999, Regnery.

Heinl T: *The baby massage book: shared growth through the hands,* Boston, 1991, Sigo Press.

Huhtala V, Lehtonen D, Heinonen R et al: Infant massage compared with crib vibrator in the treatment of colicky infants, *Pediatrics* 105(6):1328, 2000.

Ireland A: Massage therapy and therapeutic touch in children: state of the science, *Altern Ther Health Med* 6(5):54-63, 2000.

Joyce B: Peanut and nut allergy: baby massage oils could be a hazard, *BMJ* 313(7052):299, 1996.

Kuhn C, Schanberg S, Field T et al: Tactile/kinesthetic stimulation effects on sympathetic and adrenocortical function in preterm infants, *J Pediatr* 119:434-440, 1991.

Larson C: Infant's colic and belly massage, *Practitioner* 234(1487):3396-3397, 1990.

Leboyer F: *Birth without violence,* New York, 1976a, Knopf.

Leboyer F: *Loving hands: the traditional Indian art of baby massage,* New York, 1976b, Knopf.

Lindrea K, Stainton J: A case study of infant massage outcomes, *Am J Matern Child Nurs* 25(2):95-99, 2000.

Longhua X: Massage treatment of infantile congenital myogenic torticollis, *J Trad Chinese Med* 12(3):202-203, 1992.

Mainous R: Infant massage as a component of developmental care: past, present, and future, *Holist Nurs Pract* 17(1):1-7, 2002.

McClure V: *Infant massage: a handbook for loving parents,* New York, 1989, Bantam.

McClure V: Infant massage, *Am J Matern Child Nurs* 25(5):276, 2000.

Onozawa D: Infant massage improves mother-infant interaction for mothers with postnatal depression, *J Affect Disord* 63(1-3):201-207, 2001.

Ottenbacher K, Muller L, Brandt D et al: The effectiveness of tactile stimulation as a form of early intervention: a quantitative evaluation, *Develop Behav Pediatr* 8:68-76, 1987.

Prudence B: *Pain erasure,* New York, 1984, Evans.

Reid T: Baby massage classes, *Practicing Midwife* 3(4):30-31, 2000.

Rice R: Premature infants respond to sensory stimulation, *Am Psychologic Assoc Monitor* 6(II):8, 1975.

Scafidi F, Field T, Schanberg S: Factors that predict which preterm infants benefit most from massage therapy, *Dev Behav Pediatr* 14(3):176-180, 1993.

Schneider V: *Infant massage,* New York, 1982, Bantam.

Solkoff N, Yaffe S, Weintraub D et al: Effects of handling on the subsequent development of premature infants, *Develop Psychol* 1:765-768, 1975.

Tiquia R: *Chinese infant massage,* Melbourne, 1986, Greenhouse.

Vickers E: Massage for promoting growth and development of preterm and/or low birth-weight infants, *Cochrane Database Syst Rev* Computer file(2): CD000390, 2000.

Vickers A, Ohlsson A, Lacy JB et al: Massage for promoting growth and development of preterm and/or low birth-weight infants, *Cochrane Database Syst Rev* [computer file](2):CD000390, 2000.

Walker P: *Baby massage: a practical guide to massage and movement for babies and infants,* New York, 1996, St. Martin's Press.

Wall F: Baby massage: probably of benefit, *Prof Care Mother Child* 8(4):86, 1998.

Watson G: Using massage in the care of children, *Pediatr Nurs* 10(10):27-29, 1999.

White-Traut R, Goldman M: Premature infant massage: is it safe? *Pediatr Nurs* 14(4):285-289, 1988.

White-Traut R, Pate C: Modulating infant state in premature infants, *J Pediatr Nurs* 2(2):96-101, 1987.

Xu S: Massage treatment of infantile congenital myogenic torticollis, *J Trad Chinese Med* 12(3):202-203, 1992.

## SUGGESTED READINGS

Massage for mother and baby, *Mod Midwife* 4(12):s1-s4, 1994.

# Chapter 15

# Massage in Palliative Care

The term *palliative care* is usually described as the use of various procedures designed to relieve anxiety and suffering, without treating the direct cause of the problem, on a person who is terminally ill. In many cases, the person who is terminally ill will also be elderly, but of course, terminal illness can and does affect individuals of all ages. This chapter will consider the contribution that massage can make as a palliative treatment, especially to the quality of life for the elderly person who is terminally ill.

## ANCIENT VERSUS MODERN CARE OF THE DYING

It seems obvious that health care in the developed world is radically different in the twenty-first compared to the first century. In ancient times, the patient was certainly the center of attention, and there was little technology and few invasive procedures. Health care of the day relied on natural remedies of all kinds, especially on medicines derived from plant and animal sources, and massage, in all its ancient forms, was a widely used and well-respected treatment. In contrast, modern health care has become high tech and in many cases depersonalizing for the patient and his or her family members. It is often conducted in noisy, busy, and confusing circumstances, and this has special importance for those patients who are terminally ill and approaching the end of life.

A century ago, whether as the result of trauma, disease, or old age, it was common for a person to die at home surrounded by family and loved ones. Typically the atmosphere was quiet, calm, and respectful. Family members themselves cared for the dying relative directly. Physicians of the day attended patients in their home for those able to afford their services, and often pro bono for those who could not. When required, physicians had powerful narcotics at their disposal to relieve patient suffering. Compared to the present day, the available medical options for treatment were greatly limited; however, it can be argued that the simple care of the dying patient was much more personal. This is partly because so few medical options were available and when nothing further could be done, there was little choice for the patient and his or her relatives. In addition, the common practice was for elderly relatives to live with their own family members. Indeed, today it is still the custom in many parts of the world for the eldest son in a family to have the first responsibility for taking care of his elderly parents. In this way, several generations of family members live in the same household. Because life-threatening childhood and adult diseases were rampant, it was not uncommon for a child to experience the death of one or more siblings or parents. In these circumstances, children grew up with direct personal experience of caring for a relative who was dying.

In many parts of the industrialized world, there is a growing tendency for elderly relatives to live alone or with their spouse until they are at the stage where they can no longer take care of themselves, at which point they are admitted to various levels of nursing home care. As the end of a normal life span approaches, illnesses of various kinds are unfortunately very common. At this time, modern medical and surgical procedures can be highly invasive, painful, uncomfortable, and a source of great anxiety for the patient and his or her relatives. In these situations, massage treatment can be especially helpful in easing the suffering of the dying patient and in promoting a caring communication between health care providers, relatives, and the patient. Thus, the caring bond that develops has effects similar to the massage given to a baby or infant (see Chapter 14). In this way, massage has a special role to play at both the beginning and end of life, and, of course, at all times in between.

Increasing medical mechanization and pharmacological advances can contribute to a dehumanizing patient experience. The isolation and lack of physical contact perceived by many patients has encouraged a search for ways to provide closer human contact, such as therapeutic touch and a renewed interest in massage. A wide variety of health care practitioners, with varying levels of training, use massage in providing care for their patients. For patients of all ages, the judicious use of massage can ameliorate the discomfort of invasive techniques and provide a sense of reassurance and caring.

A variety of studies have shown massage to be an effective treatment in the palliative care of the dying (Billhult & Dahlberg, 2001; Birk et al., 2000; Burke et al., 1994; Evans, 1995; MacDonald, 1997; Simpson, 1991; Stevensen, 1995; White, 1988; Wilkinson, 1996). In particular, massage has been shown to be an effective adjunct for the management of the anxiety and pain of terminal illness, especially that caused by cancer (Ahles et al., 1999; Grealish et al., 2000; McCaffery & Wolff, 1992; Pan et al., 2000; Simpson, 1991; Weinrich, 1990; Wilkie et al., 2000; Wolff, 1992).

Another technique that appears to be helpful in palliative care is the so-called therapeutic touch. As mentioned in Chapter 1, this concept is somewhat controversial. Although the name implies a touching technique, the original concept of therapeutic touch does not require the therapist to physically touch the patient. The therapist's hands move over the part to be treated without making physical contact. Obviously then, the technique cannot have any direct mechanical effect on the tissues. This does not mean that the technique has no benefit: it simply means that it cannot be explained by the accepted mechanical and physiological mechanisms. In fact, the original technique claimed to balance energy fields around the affected parts (Feltham, 1991; Krieger, 1973, 1979, 1981). Obviously, any technique for which the therapist does not have to physically touch the patient is potentially useful, especially for the patient who is hypersensitive. However, it would be incorrect to describe this technique as a form of massage.

## MASSAGE TECHNIQUES FOR THE ELDERLY PATIENT WHO IS TERMINALLY ILL

Massage can be particularly useful for reducing anxiety, promoting relaxation, and relieving pain, not only for patients suffering from a wide range of musculoskeletal and neurological problems (Doehring, 1989; Furlan et al., 2000; Hayes, 1999; Kim et al., 2001) but also for the elderly person who is terminally ill. Of course, not all terminally ill patients are elderly. Regardless of age, however, the constantly changing needs of the patient must be considered at all times. An individual's tolerance, age, and skin condition (dryness, tightness, fragility) must be taken into account when massage is performed. For the elderly person who is otherwise healthy, these are the only reservations to be considered; otherwise, any of the techniques previously described are suitable. However, some modifications of these techniques will be needed for the elderly patient who is terminally ill.

The importance of touch as a means of communication, to impart a sense of well-being and confidence, should not be ignored or underestimated. The average person has approximately 18,000 $cm^2$ of skin, a sensitive area for touch, and, of course, the skin is the largest organ of the body. It has millions of nerve endings, and stimulating them can be a potent way of accessing the wider nervous system. This might induce autonomic reflexes, which in turn can account for many of the observed physiological effects of massage (Labyak & Metzger, 1997; Skull, 1945; see also Chapter 5). Massage creates pleasant sensations (in most cases) that can have a soothing or stimulating effect, promotes increased flexibility and elasticity in the skin and underlying tissues, and improves interactions between patient and therapist (Montague, 1978; Pratt & Mason, 1981). Hippocrates (ca. 460-375 BC) wrote of mobilizing the body's natural recuperative powers (White, 1988).

Touching another person can have powerful effects on both parties. Touch can communicate an intention—in the case of therapeutic touch and massage—to heal, recruit, balance, or share inherent energy or promote relaxation (Krieger, 1979; Regan & Shapiro, 1988). An increase in hemoglobin has been reported (Krieger, 1973, 1976; Pemberton, 1945), as has the release of acetylcholine and histamine (as well as histamine-like substances; Skull, 1945). Furthermore, Siegel (1986) believed that it is possible to activate the body's immune system through loving, healing touch and self-healing.

## TECHNIQUES

The massage techniques that can be used for the frail-elderly and terminally ill person include effleurage, stroking, and light kneading. The patient may not be able to be comfortably positioned in the more usual positions adopted for massage treatments (see Chapters 4, 7, and 8). Therefore the therapist must be able to adapt his or her technique to the particular needs of the patient. This also applies to individual techniques, as these may have to be modified if the patient cannot tolerate the more usual techniques. Often the most valuable technique may be one that involves pressure, as in stationary kneading or squeeze kneading. In some cases, a modified shiatsu or acupressure technique (see Chapter 17) might effectively relieve symptoms (Stevensen, 1995). The usual rate, rhythm, pressure, timing, and other features of each stroke may need to be modified to suit the particular patient. For example, stroking performed at the usual speed may be uncomfortable, but it may be quite effective when performed at a slow rate and slightly deeper pressure. The therapist will need to experiment to determine the most effective techniques for an individual patient.

Effleurage, stroking, and light kneading can be applied, as needed, to body parts where symptoms are present. For example, if the patient has significant leg pain, massage can be directed to the affected areas. If, however, the patient cannot tolerate the sensation of the therapist's hand moving on his or her skin, an alternative technique will be needed. Attention to the feet, hands, and face may be all that is acceptable or needed. Indeed, those who are hypersensitive and cannot tolerate even the lightest brush of a bed sheet on their skin may often be physically and emotionally comforted by gentle pressure to the face and scalp. Reflexology (see Chapter 16) techniques may be particularly well suited for this purpose because they can be performed on the palm of the hand, the sole of the foot, and the ear. These techniques have been used to good effect for patients who have terminal cancer (Stephenson et al., 2000).

Terminally ill patients have specific needs:

1. *Pain control.* Pain may be preventing sleep, restricting eating, or interfering with communication.
2. *Material comfort.* Comfort can be provided by a bed or chair, privacy, and physical attention from caregivers.
3. *Psychological comfort.* This need includes the respect for personal dignity that comes from attentive caregivers who provide appropriate information, the presence of loved ones, physical contact, and the opportunity to express feelings.

Principles of reflexology have the potential to address these needs. A practitioner—a family member, friend, or caregiver—can provide physical contact in a private place, with the patient in a preferred position in bed or in a chair. As the section on reflexology explains (see Chapter 16), the relaxing and pain-relieving effects are achieved through stimulation of autonomic reflexes and improved circulation, both physiologically and functionally, as in the flow of energy (Dobbs, 1985). Further reading on the topic of massage in palliative care can be found in Graham (1913), Krieger (1979), Levine (1982), Montague (1978), Pemberton (1945), Pratt and Mason (1981), Regan and Shapiro (1988), and Siegel (1986).

## SUMMARY

The willingness, tolerance, and needs of frail-elderly and dying persons should always guide the application of massage. The use of massage in palliative care is growing rapidly and can be performed by many different health care professionals, as well as by the patient's relatives and friends. The basic techniques can easily be adapted and taught to family members and caregivers. No less important than the technical skill of the hands is the caring intention of the person performing the massage. Although modern medical science has much to commend it, there is no real substitute for the loving touch of a human being who genuinely cares about the suffering of a dying person.

## REFERENCES


Ahles TA, Tope DM, Pinkson B et al: Massage therapy for patients undergoing autologous bone marrow transplantation, *J Pain Symptom Manage* 18(3):157-163, 1999.

Billhult A, Dahlberg K: A meaningful relief from suffering: experiences of massage in cancer care, *Cancer Nurs* 24(3):180-184, 2001.

Birk TJ, McGrady A, MacArthur RD et al: The effects of massage therapy alone and in combination with other complementary therapies on immune system measures and quality of life in human immunodeficiency virus, *J Altern Complement Medicine* 6(5):405-414, 2000.

Burke C, Macnish S, Saunders J et al: The development of a massage service for cancer patients, *Clin Oncol* 6:381-385, 1994.

Dobbs BZ: Alternative health approaches, *Nurs Mirror* 160(9):41-42, 1985.

Doehring K: Relieving pain through touch, *Advanc Clin Care* 4(5): 32-33, 1989.

Evans B: Nursing: an audit into the effects of aromatherapy massage and the cancer patient in palliative and terminal care, *Complement Ther Med* 3(4):239-241, 1995.

Feltham E: Therapeutic touch and massage, *Nurs Standard* 5(45):26-28, 1991.

Furlan AD, Brosseau L, Welch V et al: Massage for low back pain, *Cochrane Database Syst Rev* [computer file](4): CD001929, 2000.

Graham D: *Massage, manual treatment, remedial movements: history, mode of application and effects, indications and contraindications,* Philadelphia, 1913, JB Lippincott.

Grealish L, Lomasney A, Whiteman B: Foot massage: a nursing intervention to modify the distressing symptoms of pain and nausea in patients hospitalized with cancer, *Cancer Nurs* 23(3):237-243, 2000.

Hayes J: Immediate effects of a five-minute massage on patients in critical care, *Intensive Crit Care Nursing* 15(2):77-82, 1999.

Kim MS, Cho KS, Woo H et al: Effects of hand massage on anxiety in cataract surgery using local anesthesia, *J Cataract Refract Surg* 27(6):884-890, 2001.

Krieger D: *The relationship of touch with intent to help or heal, studies of in-vivo haemoglobin values,* In Proceedings of the American Nurses Association Ninth Nursing Research Conference, Kansas City, 1973, American Nurses Association.

Krieger D: Nursing research for a new age, *Nurs Times* 72:1-7, 1976.

Krieger D: *Therapeutic touch: how to use your hands to help or to heal,* Englewood Cliffs, NJ, 1979, Prentice Hall.

Labyak SE, Metzger BL: The effects of effleurage backrub on the physiological components of relaxation: a meta-analysis, *Nurs Res* 46(1):59-62, 1997.

Levine S: *Who dies?* Garden City, NY, 1982, Anchor/Doubleday.

MacDonald G: Massage as an alternative respite intervention for primary caregivers of the terminally ill, *Altern Ther Clini Pract* 4(3):86-89, 1997.

McCaffery M, Wolff M: Pain relief using cutaneous modalities, positioning, and movement, *Hosp J* 8(1/2):121-153, 1992.

Montague A: *Touching,* Toronto, 1978, Harper & Row.

Pan CX, Morrison RS, Ness J et al: Complementary and alternative medicine in the management of pain, dyspnea, and nausea and vomiting near the end of life: a systematic review, *J Pain Symptom Manage* 20(5):374-387, 2000.

Pemberton R: Physiology of massage. In *AMA Handbook of physical medicine,* ed 3, Chicago, 1939, American Medical Association.

Pratt JW, Mason A: *The caring touch,* London, 1981, Heyden.

Regan G, Shapiro D: The power of touch. In *The healer's handbook,* New York, 1988, Element Books.

Siegel BS: *Love, medicine & miracles,* New York, 1986, Harper & Row.

Simpson J: Massage: positive strokes in palliative care, *NZ Nurs J* 84(6):15-17, 1991.

Skull CW: Massage: physiologic basis, *Arch Phys Med* 261:159-167, 1945.

Stephenson NL, Weinrich SP, Tavakoli AS: The effects of foot reflexology on anxiety and pain patients with breast and lung cancer, *Oncol Nurs Forum* 27(1):67-72, 2000.

Stevensen C: The role of shiatsu in palliative care, *Complement Ther Nurs Midwifery* 1(2):51-58, 1995.
Weinrich MW: The effect of massage on pain in cancer patients, *Appl Nurs Res* 3(4):140-145, 1990.
White JA: Touching with intent: therapeutic massage, *Holistic Nurs Pract* 2(3):63-67, 1988.
Wilkie DJ, Kampbell J, Cutshall S et al: Effects of massage on pain intensity, analgesics and quality of life in patients with cancer pain: a pilot study of a randomized clinical trial conducted within hospice care delivery, *Hosp J* 15(3):31-53, 2000.
Wilkinson S: Palliative care: "get the massage," *Nurs Times* 92(34): 61-64, 1996.
Wolff M: Pain relief using cutaneous modalities, positioning, and movement, *Hosp J: Physical* 8(1/2):121-153, 1992.

# Chapter 16

# Soft Tissue Manipulation in Complementary/Alternative Medicine

Modern health care practice has begun to embrace the concept of *complementary/alternative medicine* (CAM) as an important approach for treating illness and promoting health and wellness. Other terms that encompass similar ideas are *holistic medicine* and *integrative medicine.* Since the 1980s, there has been a growing acceptance of the efficacy of CAM as an alternative to orthodox medical practice. Many of the treatment concepts that fall into the category of CAM have their origins in traditional Eastern medicine. Systems of care such as acupuncture and acupressure are good examples. In contrast, some more modern concepts also fit into this category. These techniques include myofascial release and rolfing structural integration. This chapter briefly considers several treatment concepts that are good examples of both ancient and modern specialized systems of soft tissue manipulation. They are sometimes referred to as *bodywork systems* (McPartland & Miller, 1999; Oschman, 1997).

Further evidence of the growing interest in CAM can be seen in the increasing support from many national research granting agencies. Many of these organizations have been promoting vigorous research into the efficacy and use of techniques such as acupuncture, acupressure, shiatsu, reflexology, herbal medicine, moxibustion, and homeopathy (Vickers, 1995). Surveys of Western medical practitioners in the Netherlands, Great Britain, New Zealand, the United States, and Canada have highlighted a growing interest in and willingness to accept CAM (Carpenter & Neal, 2005; Eisenberg et al., 1993; Hadley, 1988; Lynoe & Svensson, 1992; Micozzi, 1996; Verhoef & Sutherland, 1995; Wharton & Lewith, 1986). This is particularly the case in the management of chronic pain and musculoskeletal dysfunction (Sarac & Gur, 2006). The most widely used techniques are those that appear to be more efficacious, such as acupuncture, the deep pressure and stretching employed in acupressure, shiatsu, myofascial release, and rolfing structural integration.

The *body therapies,* as many of the complementary techniques are called, encompass a wide range of both ancient and modern treatment concepts, including, but not limited to, the following:

- Acupressure
- Acupuncture
- Alexander techniques
- Applied kinesiology
- Biodynamic massage
- Chiropractic
- Craniosacral therapy
- Deep muscle therapy
- Feldenkrais
- Hellerwork
- Huna techniques
- Integrated psychophysical balancing
- Integrative neuromuscular therapy (NMT)
- Internal organ chi massage (Chi Nei Tsang)
- Lomi massage (various systems)
- Muscle energy techniques
- Myofascial release
- Neuromuscular release or technique
- Orthobionamy
- Osteopathy
- Pilates method
- Point percussion therapy
- Polarity therapy
- Postural integration
- Reflexology
- Reiki
- Rolfing structural integration
- Shiatsu
- Therapeutic touch

- Tragerwork
- Trigger point techniques
- Zone therapy

Although a detailed discussion of all of these methods is well beyond the scope of this book, a number of these techniques are briefly explored here, especially those in which soft tissue manipulation is an important part of the treatment concept. These techniques include myofascial release, reflexology, trigger point massage, rolfing structural integration, and a brief discussion of the lesser-known techniques of point percussion therapy and craniosacral therapy. Chapter 17 reviews some more ancient systems of massage, especially those with an Eastern heritage. These include acupressure, shiatsu, traditional Oriental massage, and Huna (Hawaiian) massage.

The proliferation of complementary/alternative practitioners, both within and outside of the established health care systems, is evidence of dissatisfaction with the orthodox medical approach. In general, modern (orthodox) medicine has focused on treating illness rather than promoting wellness and preventing disease. In contrast, much of the focus of CAM is directed toward promoting wellness and preventing disease, without the use of drugs or surgery (Fritz, 2004; Jahnke, 1985) and detoxification (Cassar, 1999). Although these techniques are popular, they are not without risk. Many of the complementary/alternative techniques produce their beneficial outcomes by invoking a reflex autonomic effect. It is important to note that when autonomic responses are elicited—for example, with connective tissue massage (CTM), acupressure, shiatsu, reflexology, trigger point, and myofascial techniques—problems can arise. Although most techniques are perfectly safe, contraindications need to be taken seriously. These may include pregnancy, serious cardiopulmonary conditions, and psychological problems such as panic disorder. The safe and effective practice of any of the complementary/alternative therapies requires proper training and certification where appropriate.

A large and varied group of individuals practices the *bodywork* therapies. Many of them are established health care professionals, such as physicians, nurses, physical and occupational therapists, and many others. These professionals have incorporated complementary/alternative techniques into their daily practice in an effort to broaden the treatment options available for their patients. In other cases, the practitioner may simply specialize in one type of treatment (e.g., reflexology). In all situations, it is in the patient's best interest to carefully research and discuss all of the potential treatment options available. Once a particular treatment option has been determined, choosing a well-qualified and appropriately certified therapist becomes extremely important. One need only search the Internet for a short time to realize the enormous number of complementary/alternative therapies being advertised. More importantly, there are very few regulations governing the content or claims made on some of these web sites. Misleading claims and incorrect information are unfortunately quite common.

A key principle in many of the treatment concepts listed earlier is the idea of balancing various body systems. Although this notion has its roots in ancient Chinese philosophy, it has an important modern-day equivalent. Here the emphasis is placed on the proper integration of body systems, both within a system and from one system to another. For example, this concept has well-known parallels in the proper regulation of autonomic functions. In this case, the proper balance of sympathetic and parasympathetic activity results in the efficient functioning of the digestive system (balancing within the system). This in turn contributes to the proper functioning of the whole body, leading to wellness, and a well body is less prone to disease and dysfunction.

Many of the complementary/alternative therapies incorporate soft tissue manipulation techniques (massage) as a major part of their practice (Westland, 1996), especially to counterbalance the negative effects of gravity on the body. The ever-present force of gravity coupled with aging and a stressful modern lifestyle place a significant burden on the musculoskeletal system in just about everyone. Muscles, tendons, fascia, joint capsules, and ligaments often become tight (shortened), resulting in postural malalignment and movement dysfunction. The net result is often chronic pain and a host of other physical and psychological symptoms. In contrast, many of these issues can be significantly reduced, if not eliminated, by restoring the correct structural integrity (valance) to the affected body system(s). This concept will be a familiar theme in many of the treatment systems described in this chapter and Chapter 17.

## MYOFASCIAL RELEASE TECHNIQUES

Myofascial release is a relatively new concept in the larger picture of Western medical thought; however, techniques similar to it can be found in classical Eastern health and medical writings. As its name suggests, the techniques of myofascial release refer to a specialized system of prolonged manual stretching of the fascial tissues of the body, to the point where there is a release of tension. This release of tension is felt by the therapist and implies a slight lengthening of the fascial tissues (J.F. Barnes, 1997; M.F. Barnes, 1997a; M.F. Barnes, 1997b). It should be emphasized that the stretching technique is a subtle one. Tension is applied slowly and gently and is released in a similar manner. There is some evidence to suggest that fascia may have an ability to contract in a way similar to smooth muscle, and, if so, it may have the ability to relax and thereby lengthen (Schleip et al., 2005).

Fascia is a much-neglected tissue of the body, often being thought of as simply a connective tissue scaffolding associated with muscles and tendons. In fact, it is an extremely important whole-body network, on a par with the vascular or nervous system. Fascial tissue does indeed provide a scaffold-like net to every type of tissue in the body, even down to the extracellular level. As such, the fascial system connects all parts of the body together with a continuous web of tissue. There is a tradition of describing different body systems in a particular order. For example, there is a tendency to think of the bony skeleton as the foundation of the body, with all the other structures attached to it or contained by it. Alternatively, bones can be rightly considered as rigid spacers entrapped in a fascial net. One might imagine a classic circus tent, where the canvas material and rigging are held up by the giant wooden masts. Without the tent poles, the material of the tent has no defined shape and will not function properly on its own.

Fascia is a type of connective tissue that has three layers: superficial, potential space, and deep. It has important biomechanical properties and greatly assists in maintaining muscle force. The interconnectedness of the fascial system throughout the body is extremely important, because many acute and chronic musculoskeletal problems have their origins in this tissue. Excessive strain, poor ergonomic environments, trauma, and abnormal postural alignment are among the common causes of strain of the fascial system. This strain leads to a type of contracture (tightness), which in turn causes pain and restricted movements. In fact, a host of symptoms can be caused in many different body parts as the long-term result of restricted fascial movement. Whereas a fasciotomy to release tight fascia can result in a 15% loss of muscle strength, myofascial release techniques reduce constriction and pain without compromising muscle strength (Manheim, 2001). Symptomatic relief of the pain produced by this situation obviously will not cure the underlying tightness somewhere in the fascia. A treatment technique that is directly applied to the fascia is likely to be more effective at producing a long-term solution. For example, myofascial release techniques, in conjunction with trigger point stimulation, can be extremely important to the long-term success of therapy because the fascia tightens and shortens with inflammation (as the potential space swells), heals slowly (because of a poor blood supply), and is a pain focus (because of its abundant nerve supply).

## Assessment

Myofascial release techniques cannot be effective unless they are applied following a detailed assessment of the patient. In addition to the more usual multisystem examination of the patient, a detailed assessment of the myofascial system is required. Visual assessment of the patient's posture is essential in order to identify the areas where the fascial system is tight. This can be seen as postural asymmetry, sometimes obvious and at other times subtle. This cannot be done properly unless the patient is suitably undressed so that the surface features are clearly visible. These findings can be confirmed by palpation later in the procedure. Although a certain degree of postural asymmetry is normal, it is important to recognize when it is associated with the patient's symptoms and when it is not.

## Technique

The patient is comfortably positioned and well supported so that he or she is able to relax as much as possible. Typically, the patient will be in prone or supine lying on a treatment table. Once the therapist has identified the areas to be treated (from the assessment), his or her hands are gently but firmly placed on the skin surface. Once the hands are in the proper position, no movement occurs between the therapist's hands and the underlying skin. For this reason, it is important for both the patient's skin and the therapist's skin to be clean and dry. No lubricant should be used.

A wide variety of specific techniques can be used, depending on the body part to be treated. For example, on the posterior trunk, the therapist's hands can be placed flat on the patient's back, whereas on the limbs, the therapist's hands may lightly grasp around the patient's tissues. Figure 16-1 illustrates these two different types of hand positions. There are, of course, many variations, depending on the areas to be treated.

In Figure 16-1, *A,* the therapist gradually applies pressure to the patient's skin and underlying tissues while simultaneously stretching them apart. The therapist achieves this result by pushing his or her hands apart in opposite directions. The therapist's right hand pushes toward the patient's right hip while the therapist's left hand applies pressure toward the patient's left shoulder. Good body mechanics are essential during this technique, especially because it can take several minutes to complete. Wherever possible, the therapist should use his or her own body weight to provide the pressure needed during the technique. As the tissues are stretched, some movement (lengthening) will occur, but eventually, a block to further stretching will be felt. At this point, pressure is maintained for as long as it takes for the tissues to release the tension. The therapist will feel this release of tension as the resistance to the stretching gives. This can typically take anywhere from 90 to 120 seconds to happen, although sometimes it will occur sooner. As the tissue tension is released, the therapist's hands remain in the same position but continue to apply a stretching tension at the new tissue length. In this manner, the tissues are stretched out as the therapist follows the releasing of the tissues. It may take several applications of tension to chase the tight areas of fascia in the tissues. Once again, it must be emphasized that the technique is a subtle one. Pressure is gentle but firm. The therapist's hands are feeling their way into the tight areas.

Figure 16-1, *B,* illustrates a different technique. In this case, a gentle traction force is applied to the entire upper limb. As the limb elongates in a telescopic-like manner, a block to further movement is felt, at which point the tension is maintained until the tissues release. Further tension is applied at the new length. Once again, this process is repeated several times until a more normal tissue length has been achieved.

Myofascial release is a specialized technique, requiring proper training and experience. As with many other forms of soft tissue manipulation, it does not replace other reha-

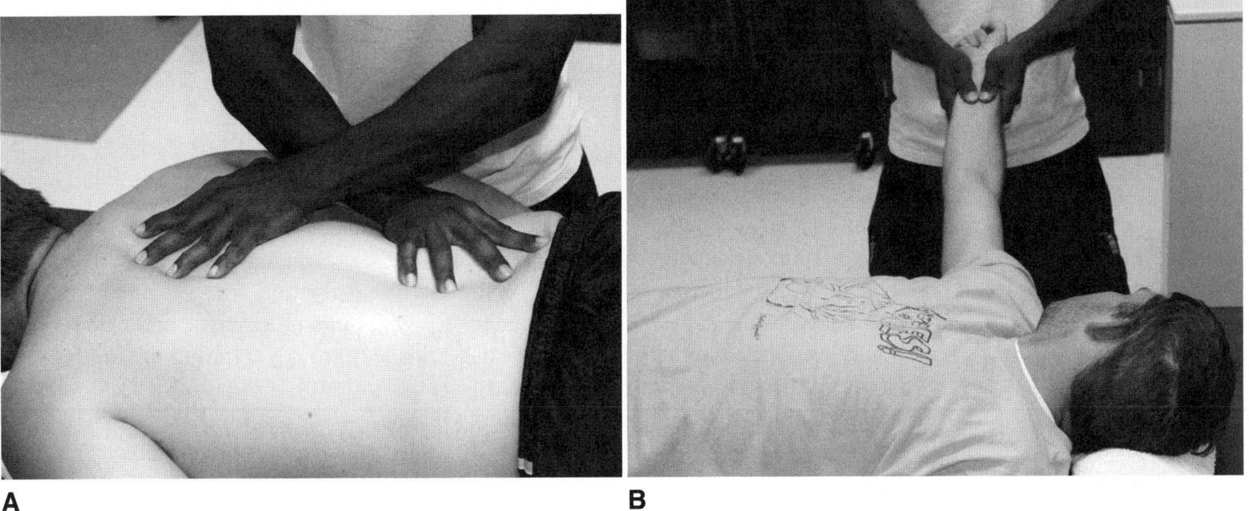

**Figure 16-1** Two Different Myofascial Release Techniques

**A,** The therapist's hands are placed flat on the patient's lower back. The therapist's arms are crossed so that a stretching effect can be given to the underlying tissues. **B,** The patient's wrist is lightly grasped with the upper limb in external rotation and elbow in full extension. Gentle traction is applied to the whole limb to produce a sustained lengthening effect.

bilitation procedures, but rather it compliments them in an important way. Myofascial release allows the tissues to return to their normal physiological state (or close to it) so that other techniques, such as therapeutic exercise and manual mobilization, can be maximally effective. Manheim (2001) has provided postural assessment methods and a detailed description of techniques of myofascial release. Other authors have provided a wide range of descriptions of the technique and its use (Mock, 1997a, 1997b, 1998; Morris, 1999: Shea & Keyworth, 1997; Stone, 2000; Whalen, 1999).

Although the exact mechanisms responsible for the effectiveness of myofascial release techniques have not been clearly identified, there are several possibilities. Although connective tissue has a certain degree of extensibility, it does not behave like an elastic band. The tensions placed on the fascia during myofascial release techniques are often relatively small and subtle. Once a significant degree of intertissue adhesion (contracture) has occurred, it is unlikely that these techniques can effectively restore a normal range of motion to the tissues. In this case, especially if significant deformity has occurred, a different approach is required. Stretching techniques are important; however, the tension needs to be continuous so as to provide a triggering mechanism for the connective tissue to increase in physiological length. Serial casting is an example of a technique that uses the concept of continuous tension to increase the range of tissue motion.

The role of myoglobin in myofascial pain and its dispersion (and associated pain relief) by massage techniques has been studied (Brendstrup et al., 1957; Danneskiold-Samsøe et al., 1982, 1986; Krusen et al., 1965; Simons, 1990). Ronald Melzack (1981) has reported on the similarity of the neural mechanisms involved in the relief of pain produced by acupuncture, acupressure, ice massage, and trigger point stimulation. This hyperstimulation analgesia is one of the oldest recorded remedies and should become a useful technique for relieving pain of musculoskeletal lesions, especially when chronic conditions have affected posture, gait, and other activities (Ehrett, 1988; Friction et al., 1985; Friedmann, 1989; Ingber, 1989; Kine & Warfield, 1986). The presence of type C nociceptors and adaptive shortening in the muscles and fascia contribute to the pain of chronic disorders (Reynolds, 1981; Rubin, 1981). Mobilization of peripheral nerves and manipulation (stretching and releasing) of the fascia that is continuous with nerve roots relieve pain and help to restore function (Cantu & Grodin, 2001).

## TRIGGER POINT THERAPY

A trigger point—also called a *myofascial trigger point* (MTrP)—is a sensitive spot on the body surface that, when stimulated, causes local and referred pain elsewhere in the body. The stimulated spot literally triggers a painful response somewhere else in the body—hence its name. Depending on the location of the trigger point, it may also cause a local, painful muscle twitch. Myofascial trigger points are commonly found in taut bands, which are often felt as contraction knots within a muscle. Both local twitch responses and the referred pain are mediated through a spinal cord reflex. Many of these sensitive spots occur in the myofascial structures of the body and are often the focal points of the concept of a myofascial pain syndrome. This syndrome is often confused with fibromyalgia and is characterized by musculoskeletal pain that originates from a hyperirritable spot (Brendstrup et al., 1957; Danneskiold-Samsøe et al., 1982, 1986; Friction et al., 1985; Hey & Helewa, 1994; Kine & Warfield, 1986; Kostopoulos & Rizopoulos, 2001;

Reynolds, 1981; Rubin, 1981; Simons, 1990; Waylonis et al., 1988; Yunus et al., 1988).

These *trigger points*—called *myofascial triggers* by Janet Travell and *myodysneuric points* by R. Gutstein—are sensitive points or areas that produce pain some distance away (Travell, 1981; Travell & Simons, 1983, 1992).

An *active trigger point* may be found in tight or taut fascial or muscular bands. It may be in the skin (scar tissue), a ligament, a tendon, or even deeper at the joint capsule or periosteal level. Knowledge of the location of acupuncture points associated with pain may help to locate an active trigger point, as about 70% of both points are located at the same site (Hong, 2000; Melzak, 1981). Active trigger points often produce a localized sharp pain that may radiate to the referred, or target, area some distance away. Any or all of the signs or phenomena in the following list may be associated with manual or electrical stimulation of an active trigger point:

- Sharp, localized pain
- Sharp, referred pain
- Movement restriction
- Muscle weakness
- Protective muscle spasm
- Lowered skin resistance
- Fibrositic nodules
- The "jump" sign on palpation
- Secondary trigger points in agonistic and antagonistic muscles (overloaded through splinting the injured muscle in compensation)
- Autonomic responses

Figure 16-2 illustrates the sites of common trigger points and associated muscle groups. The referred pain and any

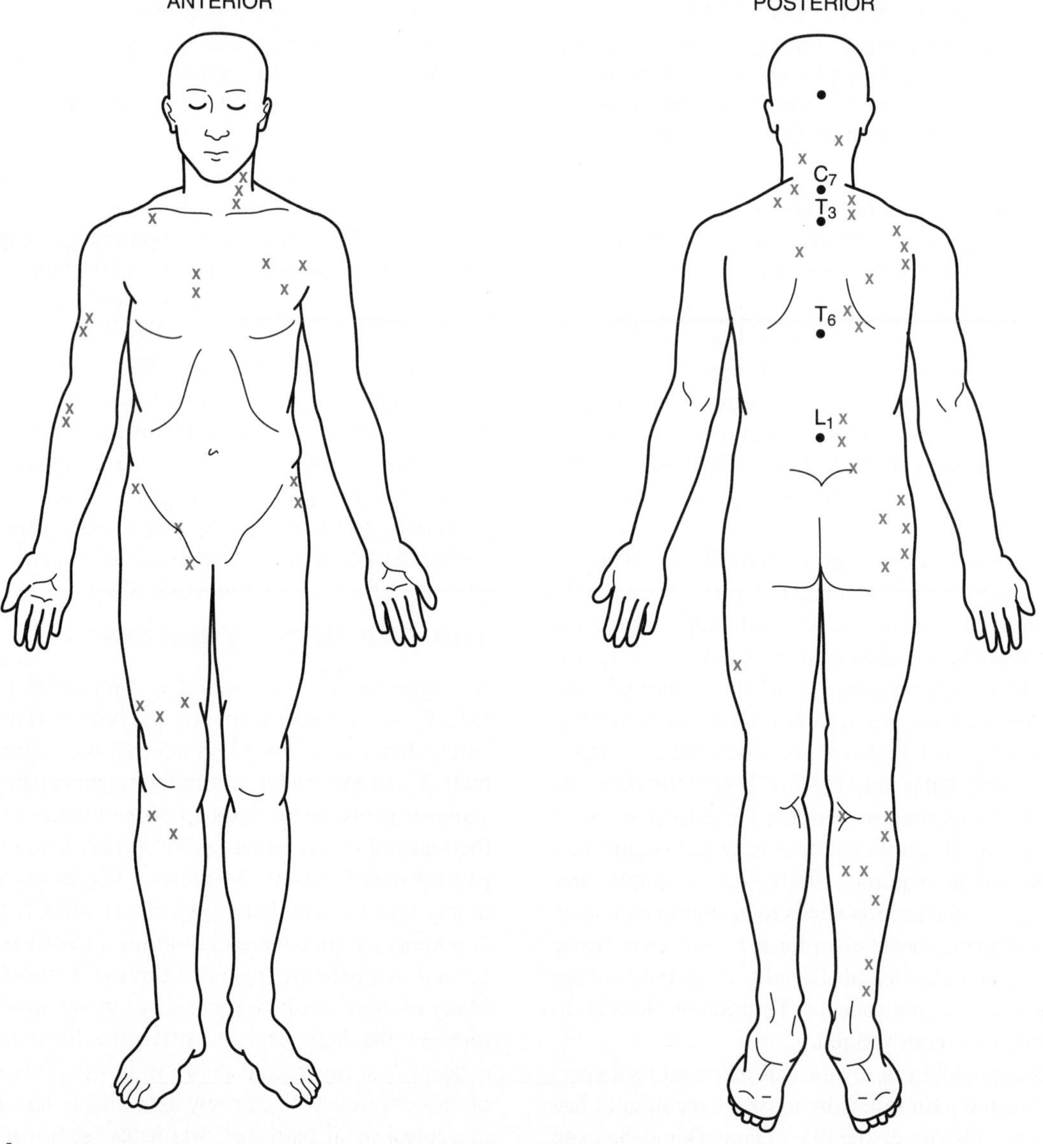


**Figure 16-2 Common Trigger Points**

**A,** The common sites of trigger points in the body. **B,** The muscles associated with these points.

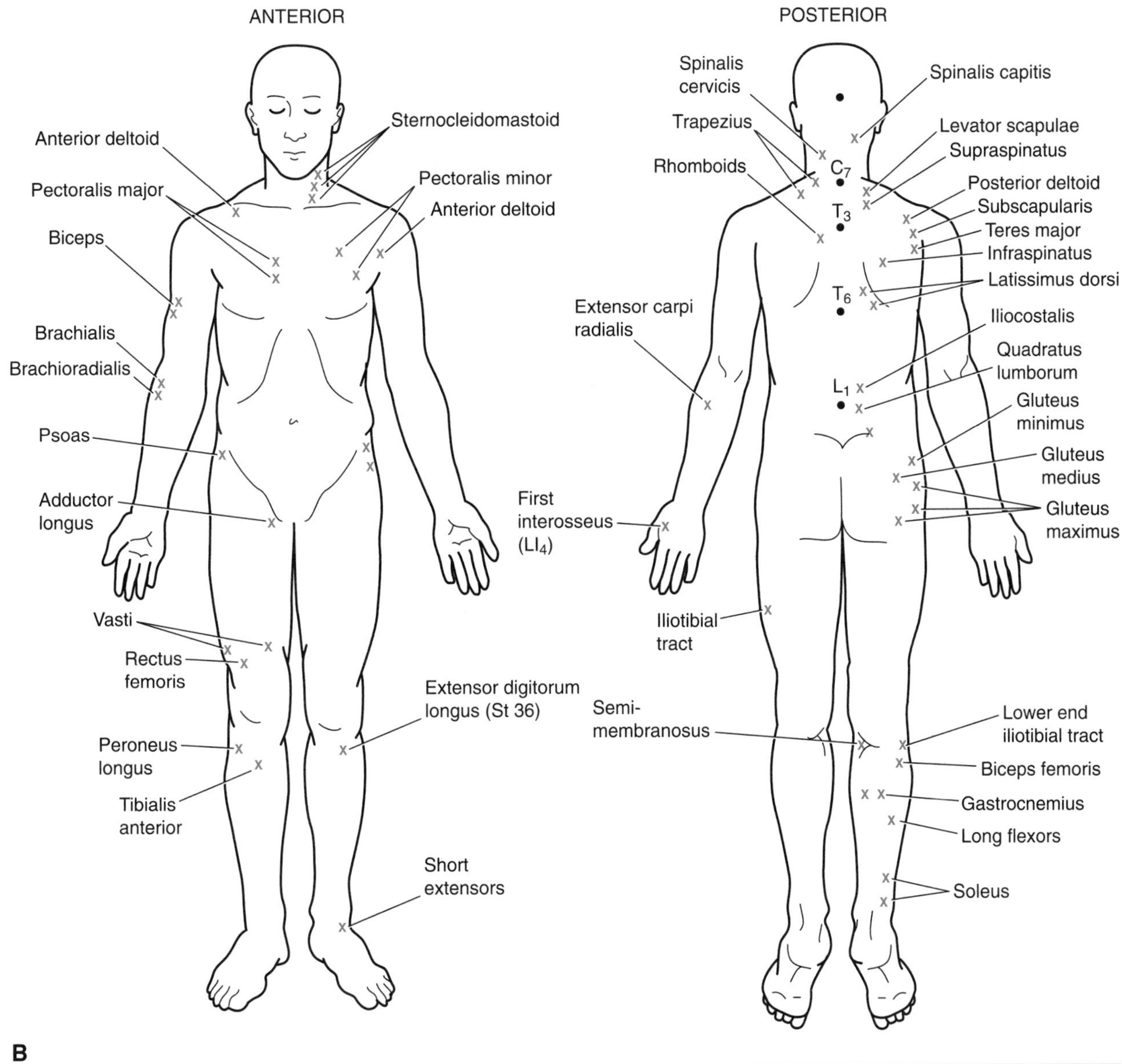


Figure **16-2**, cont'd

motor, sensory, or autonomic responses are ameliorated by desensitizing (releasing) the active primary point(s). Together with appropriate myofascial release techniques (discussed earlier), the treatment of active trigger points is an important adjunct to the management of chronic musculoskeletal conditions (Laing et al., 1973; Lundberg et al., 1984). In addition, careful palpation and awareness of any associated acupuncture points can assist in the assessment of related soft tissues (Fischer, 1988; Goldenberg, 1989).

An active trigger point can be desensitized using a sustained pressure. There are several ways in which mechanical pressure may be given, including the use of one finger, two or more fingers, a knuckle, an elbow, or by strumming (as in applying connective tissue massage) with the fingers extended (Kostopoulos & Rizopoulos, 2001; Kovacs et al., 2000; Manheim, 2001; Peppard, 1983; Travell & Simons, 1983).

## Stimulation Technique

Active trigger points can be located in a number of ways, including direct digital palpation by the therapist (or patient, where appropriate) or with the use of trigger point location devices. These devices are usually small, handheld instruments that are used to apply a small voltage to the skin and tissues. The device emits a low continuous tone when applied to the skin a short distance (6 to 8 inches) away from an active point. The probe is then moved toward the trigger point. When located directly over the point, the tone changes to a high-pitched note and an indicator light may also illuminate. In effect, the device has located the area of lowered skin resistance associated with an active trigger point. Ohm's law predicts that when the same voltage is applied to a lowered resistance, a greater current will flow, and this is the operating principle for these devices. Although these devices can be useful, they do have limitations, not the least of which is the fact that they are usually removed in order for direct digital pressure to be applied. A much more useful device is a ball-headed hand probe. These devices allow pressure to be concentrated into a small area without puncturing the skin. They are ideal for manual trigger/acupuncture point stimulation and may allow the patient to self-administer treatment at home. These probes are also ideal for electrical stimulation of trigger points. Figure 16-3 illustrates such a device.

Once located, pressure is gradually applied to the point for a brief period of time (5 to 10 seconds). During this time the patient should experience significant discomfort/pain at the trigger point site and, importantly, in the referred areas. The patient may often exclaim loudly, confirming that the pressure is on the right spot. This is important because the technique does not work well if pressure is applied to the wrong area. Following the initial, brief, 5- to 10-second period of stimulation, the patient should be asked to report his or her sensations. One of three possible reactions is likely:

1. The local and referred pain *decrease* (positive response).
2. The local and referred pain are *unchanged* (positive response).
3. The local and referred pain *increase* (negative response).

The preferred response is that the local and referred pain should begin to decrease with this brief period of stimulation. If the local and referred pain are unchanged, then this may also be regarded as a positive response because it may mean that a longer period of pressure is needed for the patient to experience a decrease in symptoms. If the patient's local and referred pain increase with the brief application of pressure, it is a negative response and indicates that continued application of pressure will probably be unsuccessful. Because the point is extremely sensitive, a different strategy is indicated. It is often the case with chronic musculoskeletal lesions that more than one active trigger point is present and, in some way, there is a complicated interaction between the points. In effect, they may be triggering each other. If local and referred pain increase significantly with the initial, brief application of pressure, treatment should cease and the therapist should look for other active points in the area. These should be treated, and then the therapist can return to the point that was initially made worse by stimulation, as it may now be responsive to treatment. If it continues to be exacerbated by direct pressure, an alternative treatment should be tried (for example, electrical stimulation or perhaps ice cube massage using the corner of a standard rectangular ice cube). Assuming that the patient's pain symptoms decrease with the initial 5 to 10 seconds of pressure, then treatment can continue for about 1 to 5 total minutes of stimulation.

An alternative protocol consists of rapid icing with the edge of an ice block or parallel sweeps of vapocoolant spray

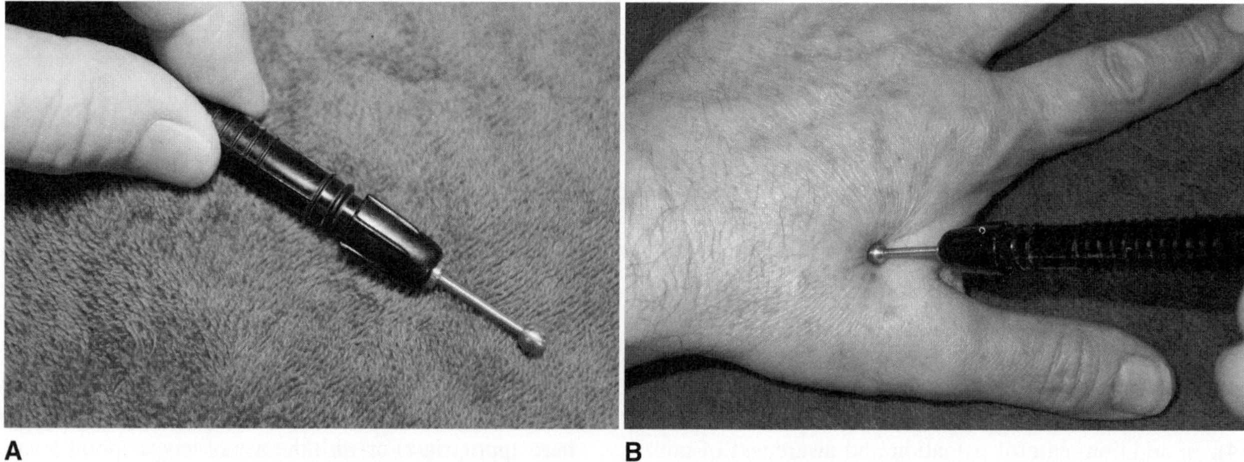


**Figure 16-3 Ball-Headed Hand Probe for Trigger/Acupuncture Point Stimulation**

**A,** A ball-headed hand probe used to apply manual pressure to an active trigger/acupuncture point. The ball has a diameter of approximately 5 mm and is made of chrome-plated steel. Other sizes of probe-tip are available and can be interchanged with the handle. **B,** A ball-headed probe is used to apply pressure to a sensitive acupuncture point (large intestine 4) in the hand. The probe can also be used to apply electrical stimulation to the same point.

given at the rate of 4 cm per second, holding the bottle/can 50 cm away from the skin (Mance et al., 1986; Simons, 1985; Wolfe, 1988). Simons (1985) claimed that fluorimethane sprays are safe. Immediately following the icing (cube or spray), a gentle sustained stretch is applied. As the muscle relaxes, it lengthens slightly. This is the so-called spray-and-stretch technique. Next, the therapist applies pressure for about 1 minute (as for acupressure) over the trigger point. The depth of pressure can be gradually increased, or it can be applied intermittently, alternating with slight release. Ice or spray and stretch can be repeated as required.

It must be emphasized once again that the various techniques used to desensitize active trigger points are just one part of the total treatment program, customized for each individual patient. In addition, a suitable home program incorporating postisometric relaxation (contact–relax) techniques can be used to maintain gains after trigger point treatment. Depending on the location of the active trigger points, it may be possible for the patient to apply a self-treatment at home. The home program should also involve stretching gently to resistance, contracting against gentle pressure for 10 seconds, maintaining this range and relaxing, and then gently and passively taking up the slack to gain greater range. The cycle should be repeated three to five times and may be used with self-administered trigger point stimulation (Chaitow, 1981).

Active trigger points may also be desensitized using other treatment techniques, including dry needling, ultrasound, low level laser therapy (LLLT), acupuncture, acupressure, and various forms of electrical stimulation (Alon & De Domenico, 1987; Gam et al., 1998; Lein et al., 1989; Offenbacher, 2000; Travell & Simons, 1983, 1992).

## REFLEXOLOGY

*Reflexology* is an ancient concept of health promotion and treatment based on the principle of activating reflex responses to the manual stimulation of various areas of the skin on the feet, hands, and ear, corresponding to the internal organs and other structures. Reflexology, also known as *reflex zone therapy,* dates back to folklore in China and India around 5000 years ago (Crane, 1997). Having not been used actively over many centuries, the Rwo-Shr method reemerged in Taiwan during the twentieth century (Adamson, 1994). There is evidence of its use in Egypt before 2000 BC, and in Europe a book on the topic was written in 1582 (Sahai, 1993). Two of the most influential contemporary contributors to the revival of interest in reflexology were Americans: an ear, nose, and throat specialist, William Fitzgerald, in the early 1900s, and a physical therapist, Eunice Ingham, in the 1930s. They undertook research into the therapeutic use of pressure and found that it relieved pain in areas of the body that corresponded to zones identified on the feet (Ingham, 1984). Crystalline deposits were found at nerve ending sites in the feet and hands, and they were thought to reflect disease in the corresponding organ or area of the body. It is interesting to note that Fitzgerald claimed that the body could be divided into 10 longitudinal zones. This concept relates to the 10 main lines in traditional Thai massage (see Chapter 17). Furthermore, some authors suggest that the energy channels, or meridians, of acupuncture and the zones of reflexology correspond (Dougans & Ellis, 1991). One of Eunice Ingham's students, Doreen Bayly, introduced reflexology into the United Kingdom in the 1960s (Bayly, 1982). In 1973 the International Institute of Reflexology was founded in the United States, and there are other associations in various countries (Adamson, 1994).

Proponents of reflexology claim that applying pressure systematically to reflex areas on the feet clears congested energy channels and returns the body to homeostasis. That is, the natural healing powers of the body are recruited, toxins are cleared in the circulation of blood and lymph, and flow in the indefinable energy channels (Booth, 1994) is restored.

Although some of these claims may seem unreasonable, there is, in fact, a rational physiological explanation for how reflexology might work. The explanation is based on the activation of the well-known concept of an autonomic reflex. This is the same reflex activated during connective tissue massage techniques and previously described in Chapter 11 (see Figure 11-2). Stimulation of various mechanoreceptors, especially in the skin, activates the sensory (input) side of an autonomic reflex. The effector (output) side of the reflex involves the various glands and smooth muscles of the internal organs and small arterioles in the affected areas. The small arterioles are extremely important because they provide a blood supply to the vast majority of the tissues of the body and are absolutely essential to the normal healing process.

The anatomy of the nervous system, both central and autonomic, provides the framework to explain these pathways. For example, the skin on the soles of the feet receives innervation from the upper sacral nerve roots (S1 and S2), relaying impulses to the same levels of the sacral parts of the spinal cord. This is the same part of the spinal cord where the motor nuclei of the sacral portion of the craniosacral division of the parasympathetic nervous system are located. Interconnections between these two systems could provide the reflex pathway needed for an autonomic reflex that could affect organs and structures supplied by this division. Furthermore, sensory information from the soles of the feet travels in the posterior columns of the spinal cord (fasciculus gracilis) to eventually synapse in the nucleus gracilis. The nucleus gracilis is physically located in the region of the junction between the spinal cord and the medulla oblongata of the brain stem. This is the same area in which efferent (motor) fibers from the vagus and other cranial nerves are located. Because the vagus nerve (tenth cranial) supplies the major organs, activation of the motor fibers can potentially affect the function of these organs and, through them, the rest of the body. In a similar way, connections are also possible between the sensory input from the skin of the sole of the foot and the sympathetic side of the autonomic nervous system. In this case, neurons in the fasciculus gracilis traveling in the thoracic portions of the posterior columns are in close proximity and, through branching collateral axons, may synapse with cells in the lateral horns of the spinal cord. The lateral horns contain the cells of origin of the sympathetic nervous system, innervating not only the major organs of the body but also the smooth muscles of the small arterioles of the entire vascular system. Thus, a number of potential pathways exist to explain how stimulation of the sole of the foot might affect internal organs and other parts of the body.

In a similar manner, sensory input from the skin and tissues from the palm of the hand is relayed to the nucleus cuneatus (via the fasciculus cuneatus), located adjacent to the nucleus gracilis. Presumably, interconnections exist between these systems, thereby allowing stimulation of sensory afferents in the hand to activate an autonomic reflex mediated by efferent fibers in the vagus and other cranial nerves in the vicinity. Interestingly, the skin overlying the external ears is supplied primarily by sensory neurons from the third cervical nerve roots and can theoretically use the same pathways. Of course, it is also possible that sensory input from the feet, hands, or ear reaching the sensory cortex is relayed to the various motor components of the autonomic nervous system, thereby activating an autonomic reflex with multiple segments (peripheral, spinal, brain stem, and cortical) in the pathway.

Because the two sides of the autonomic nervous system tend to work in harmony with each other (e.g., sympathetic activity causes the heart rate to increase, whereas parasympathetic activity slows it down), it may indeed be possible to rebalance internal organ activity. In contrast to a reflex effect on the internal body organs, other Oriental massage systems are designed to affect the organs by direct mechanical stimulation through the overlying tissues (Chia & Chia, 1997).

The same relaxing benefits of a full body massage are attributed to reflexology techniques. Indeed, Thomas (1989) reported reduced anxiety levels in elderly patients, whereas Lockett (1992) reported a calm feeling with a desire to sleep, In a randomized controlled study of 35 women with premenstrual syndrome, Oleson and Flocco (1993) found that reflexology techniques decreased symptoms significantly ($P<0.01$) when compared to a placebo. The women reported that the principal benefit was relaxation; many fell asleep during a 30-minute treatment session. Subjects reported that they had greater energy on the following day and continued to feel more relaxed 2 months after the study.

The soles of the feet and the palms of the hand are the primary areas of skin used in reflexology. These areas are then divided into zones representing various internal organs. This concept is also applied to the skin over the outer ear (pinna) where the various body structures are also represented. Of course, the ear is rather small, making it more problematic to treat with a manual technique that uses the fingers and thumbs. A more usual approach is to use acupuncture, because it is much easier to localize the stimulation using a fine needle. This kind of therapy is usually called *auriculotherapy.* The points on the ear can also be stimulated using electrical stimulation (electrotherapy).

In most cases then, pressure is applied to the skin of the hands and feet; for example, the skin of the posterior medial heel corresponds to the prostate, whereas the skin on the posterior lateral heel relates to the ovary. Centrally, farther forward but still over the calcaneum is the sciatic nerve zone. The medial border of the foot represents the spinal column: the cervical spine is at the base of the great toe, and the coccyx is at the upper part of the calcaneum. The great toe is related to the head, the pineal and pituitary glands, and the sinuses; the throat area lies over the metatarsophalangeal joint. On the medial two toes are the eye zones; the fourth and fifth toes correspond to the ear. Over the metatarsal heads, from medial to lateral, are the thyroid and parathyroid glands, the bronchial tree, the chest, and the lungs. Beneath the thyroid and parathyroid are the stomach and then the pancreas zone. The heart, spleen, kidney, and central nervous system are in zones in the center of the foot, the liver along the lateral border below the metatarsal heads, and the ascending (right foot) and descending (left foot) colon down the remainder of the lateral border to the calcaneum. The bladder is represented in the medial arch, and the sigmoid colon is represented along the anterior border of the calcaneum.

On the palms of the hands, the spinal column runs from the outer border of the proximal phalanx of the thumb (the cervical spine) to the wrist. Again, the representation of various organs mirrors that found on the feet, from the tips of the fingers to the proximal aspect of the wrist, where the ovary or prostate zone is situated. The various body parts represented on the sole of the foot and the palm of the hand are subjects of considerable research. Omura (1994), in a lengthy review of the topic, describes this concept in detail and offers an excellent source of information. There are a number of different maps of the areas representing different body parts, and two of these are illustrated in Figure 16-4. Illustrations of the zones can be found in many texts and articles (Booth, 1994; Downing, 1974; Hillman, 1986; Lidell, 1984; Omura, 1994; Tappan & Benjamin, 1998).

Reflexology involves an initial assessment of the feet to palpate for tender areas and signs of thickening or tension. The therapist also checks for calluses, corns, hard skin, and signs of skin disruption secondary to peripheral vascular disease or diabetes. Individual reflex zones are given more attention if they are tender, but typically an overall reflexology session lasts between 30 and 40 minutes. The client should be seated in a reclining chair or with the feet elevated on a stool. The therapist sits in a comfortable, well-supported position facing the soles of the client's feet. The therapist's thumb and index finger are most often used to move in the manner of a caterpillar across the client's reflex zones.

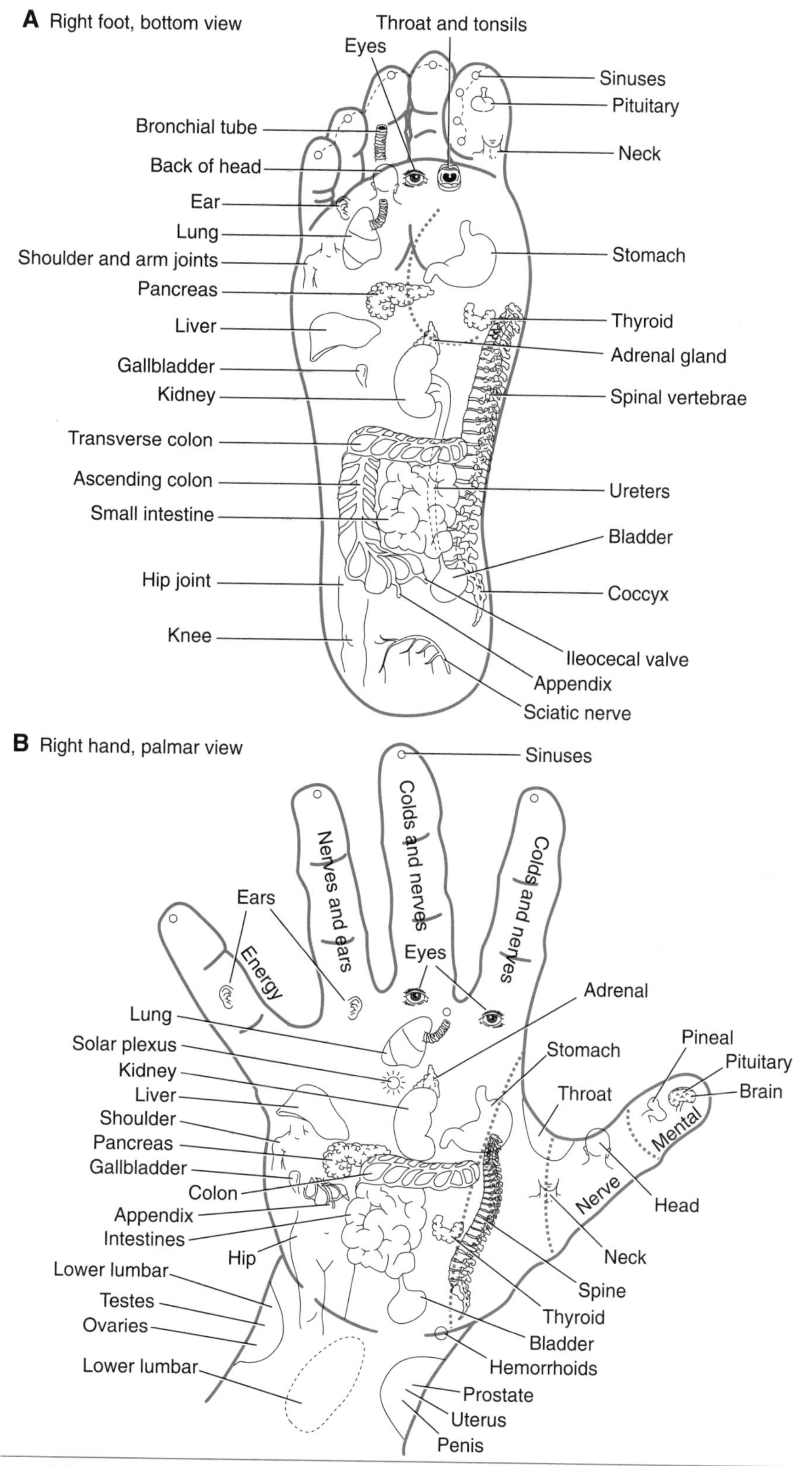


**Figure 16-4 Areas on the Hand and Foot Used in Reflexology**

A map of various organs and body parts on the sole of the foot **(A)** and the palm of the hand **(B),** used in reflexology. *(From Tappan FM, Benjamin P:* Tappan's healing massage techniques: holistic, classic and emerging methods, *ed 3, Norwalk, Conn, 1998, Appleton & Lange.)*

A typical treatment might begin with relaxation, using three techniques on each foot. First, the palms and fingers of each of the therapist's hands cradle both borders of the client's foot. Pressure is applied to push forward with the palm of one hand while pulling backward with the fingers of the other; then the pushing and pulling are reversed to rotate the foot alternately into inversion and eversion. Contact should be maintained at all times. Next, the therapist holds the metatarsals firmly with one hand, ensuring that the ball of the thumb is placed in the transverse arch. The other hand grasps the toes and flexes them over the thumb, working it sequentially along the base of the metatarsophalangeal joints from medial to lateral. The third technique is rotation of the ankle and is used to accustom the client to having his or her feet handled and to promote relaxation. Supporting the heel in the contralateral hand, the therapist holds around the outside of the lateral malleolus with the thumb to stabilize the leg, grasps the medial side of the toes and foot, and rotates it in alternate directions a few times, moving through dorsiflexion, pronation, plantar flexion, and supination. These three introductory techniques are repeated on the other foot.

The treatment involves alternately holding with one hand and manipulating with the other. The thumbs are used on the soles to press into the reflex zones, while the other hand and fingers work the foot over the thumb. Bending the joints of the thumb allows it to walk forward and backward over a point, much like the movement of a caterpillar. A hooking stroke with the thumb, akin to a short stroke in CTM, is used on tougher areas on the heel. In the forefoot, the phalanges and metatarsals can be rotated over the thumb. The index fingers can be used to walk along the toes and to flex and extend them.

Beginning with the toes, the therapist works systematically through the zones to the heel. In the hand, he or she works from the fingertips to the wrist. Specific techniques for each zone are suggested in texts on reflexology, especially Ingham's revised work. It is not within the scope of this book to provide prescriptive details for reflexology; rather, the intention is only to introduce the concepts and basic techniques. Specialized training is necessary for anyone interested in using reflexology in a clinical setting. Further reading can be found in Bayly (1982), Dougans and Ellis (1991), Downing (1974), Holey and Cook (1998), Inghan (1984), Kunz and Kunz (1987), Lidell (1984), and Tappan and Benjamin (1998).

## ROLFING STRUCTURAL INTEGRATION

*Rolfing structural integration* is a treatment concept in which the proper alignment and functioning of various body structures (e.g., muscles, tendons, joints, nerves, fascia, skin) is promoted. *Rolfing* is the popular name for the original concept developed in the United States by Ida P. Rolf and now known around the world. It is a treatment concept based on the notion of whole-body alignment through soft tissue manipulation and movement education. From a technique point of view, it has many similarities to a number of massage traditions, especially myofascial release techniques, and yet it has many characteristics all of its own.

Rolfing aims at a whole-body effect, produced by the proper alignment and movement of many structures, such as muscles, tendons, joints, fascia, and skin. For this reason, Rolfing was named as *structural integration,* meaning that the treatment is designed to achieve the proper integration of various body structures so that they are able to function in the most efficient way possible. Rolf claimed that when the body tissues are properly aligned and functioning, they produce the optimal conditions for the health of the mind and body as a fully integrated system. Of course, these concepts are not unique to Rolfing. In fact, they are the basis of many different treatment methods, both ancient and modern. Rolf died in 1979 at the age of 83, but her work continues through the Rolf Institute of Structural Integration, which certifies practitioners in her methods.

A significant part of the traditional Rolfing approach is devoted to a careful analysis of the client's postural and movement patterns. Treatment intervention may then combine deep pressure to trigger points in muscles and other structures, with myofascial stretches along the muscles to achieve structural integration. Some Rolfing techniques can involve very deep strokes akin to those used in CTM. They can be applied to trigger points using the thumbs, the elbows, the heels of the hands, and even the knees. Deep strokes and intense pulling on the soft tissues can provoke acute and intense erythema—and even local bruising. The use of very deep strokes can produce severe discomfort for the client and is an unfavorable side effect; indeed, some clients may experience a cathartic response with intense negative psychological effects such as depression and anxiety. Fortunately, less intense techniques can be used to avoid significant problems.

Any technique that produces serious discomfort or pain should be chosen advisedly, because less vigorous techniques claim a similar neurophysiological effect and achieve the desired pain relief and soft tissue mobilization to integrate relationships among structures and return them to their normal alignment. In addition to the various manual techniques used in Rolfing, client education in the use of more effective and less stressful movement patterns now forms a significant part of the treatment session. Further reading on Rolfing can be found in Oschman (1997).

## POINT PERCUSSION THERAPY

As its name implies, point percussion therapy is a type of massage in which various parts of the therapist's hand are used to percuss (strike) the patient's tissues. To apply point percussion therapy, familiarity with both Western and Eastern techniques is required. In particular, a knowledge of traditional Chinese medicine facilitates one's understanding of the rationale and mechanisms involved.

## Principles of Therapy

### *Positioning of the Muscles and Soft Tissues*

- Sustained stretch (for inhibition)
- Placement of postural muscles in middle to inner range, of phasic muscles in outer range or on stretch (both for facilitation)

### *Techniques*

- To achieve inhibition, slow, deep, and penetrating massage is used in a regular and soothing manner.
- To achieve facilitation, fast, light, changing, and stimulating massage is used.

In each case, it is important to concentrate on the rhythm.

## General Techniques

General massage using effleurage:

- Picking up (with one hand or both)
- Circular kneading (using the web space, four fingers or the whole palm, one hand, or both hands)
- Clapping using a slightly cupped, relaxed palm
- Shaking (for each muscle bulk)
- Squeezing (for each muscle bulk)

## Specific Techniques

For localized sites such as trigger points or acupuncture points, the following specific treatment techniques can be applied to the points or areas of tightness:

- Cross-fibers techniques (transverse deep friction using a thumb or index finger).
- Pressure techniques (using a thumb or index or middle finger reinforced with other fingers) by any of the following methods: press in and release, press in and rotate, press in and vibrate (upward and downward to each side of the point).
- Percussion using a tapping movement:
  - One finger (the index or middle finger reinforced with other fingers) is used. The movement comes mainly from the wrist.
  - Three fingers held together (thumb, index and middle fingers). This is a medium to strong tapping, and the movement comes from the elbow.
  - Five fingers held together. With all the fingers held together, the tapping is very strong, with the movement coming from the shoulder and elbow.
  - It is recommended that therapists begin more gently and progress to the stronger technique.
- Knocking achieved by using the fingers held loosely in a line. The movement is carried out in the line of the meridians or channels.
- Pinching with the thumb and index finger, either involving a pinch and release or a pinch and rotational or vibrating movement.
- Flicking, a specific technique for the fingers and toes from the sides of the fingers and toes to the tips on the anterior and posterior aspects of the nail roots to the tips.

## GENERAL SEQUENCE

An application of point percussion therapy for a child with cerebral palsy, aimed to inhibit muscle spasticity, could be undertaken using the following sequence:

1. The therapist assesses the child thoroughly, analyzes the findings in relation to spasticity, and plans a treatment program based on priorities.
2. If there is limited range of motion in a joint, the therapist assesses the focus of the restriction or tightness of muscles.
3. The spastic muscle is slowly positioned in a sustained stretch posture.
4. The therapist prepares the muscle by using a general massage technique. Effleurage, gentle picking up, and kneading may be used, depending on the body part.
5. The therapist selects and locates the acupuncture points according to the priorities in relation to spasticity (for example, points at or near the joint, muscle, tendon, or other soft tissue structures; points for analgesic effect; or stimulation of energy flow [chi] along the channels or meridians).
6. Using specific techniques to press the acupuncture points, the therapist performs deep frictions to any trigger points or area of tightness, concentrating on rhythm.
7. Percussion (using three fingers) is performed, moving downward along the meridians and including all those relevant to the area to be treated. Concentrating on the acupuncture points or area of tightness, the therapist applies percussion a few more times.
8. More stretching is applied as soon as the muscle relaxes.
9. Massage is applied to clear the channels and disperse tension.
10. Stimulation massage or percussion is directed to the antagonistic muscle group.
11. The sequence is repeated three to five times, depending on the condition.
12. The child is asked to contract the antagonistic muscle group or is positioned so as to facilitate contraction of the muscle.

Point percussion therapy has also been suggested for intellectual stimulation (when applied to the head), for epilepsy and other systemic disorders, around specific joints, and on the trunk (Jia, 1984; Wang, 1991).

## CRANIOSACRAL THERAPY

Craniosacral therapy (CST) is a treatment concept that claims to be able to promote self-healing and wellness by detecting and releasing restrictions in the flow of cerebrospinal fluid in the craniosacral system. Other terms used to describe these concepts include the following:

- Cranial osteopathy
- Cranial therapy

- Biocranial therapy
- Craniopathy
- Sacro-occipital technique (SOT)

The modern understanding of the concept of craniosacral therapy has developed from the original work of Andrew Taylor Still (1828-1917). Still's study of anatomy and physiology and their interrelationship to form and function eventually led to the foundation of the osteopathic profession. By the late 1880s, the fundamental principles of osteopathy included the notion that the healthy body is an integrated, self-regulating, and self-healing system. In 1892, Still was instrumental in starting the American School of Osteopathy along with William Smith. Interestingly, in 1893, Daniel D. Palmer visited the school for consultation with Still, and by 1897, he began his own school of manipulative therapy, which launched the chiropractic profession.

William G. Sutherland (1873-1954), a student at the osteopathic school under the leadership of Still, is credited as the originator of the techniques known as *cranial osteopathy,* more commonly called *craniosacral therapy.* Sutherland developed the concept that small degrees of motion might be possible between the individual cranial bones and that such movement might be able to be felt by palpation of the skull. His ideas included the notion that when the flow of brain and spinal fluids are inhibited, there would be an effect on the central nervous system and therefore on many other body systems. By the mid-1940s, Sutherland's ideas had grown in popularity in the field of osteopathy.

A number of Sutherland's students went on to make significant contributions to the refinement of cranial osteopathy (craniosacral therapy), especially Harold I. Magoun. In turn, one of Magoun's best-known students is John E. Upledger. In fact, the more recent development of craniosacral therapy is usually credited to Upledger because of the work he did from 1975 to 1983 at Michigan State University in the United States. Bertrand DeJarnett introduced similar evaluation and treatment concepts to the chiropractic profession, now known as *craniopathy* and *sacro-occipital techniques.*

Significant controversy has surrounded CST since the technique began to be popular in the mid-1980s. Numerous authors have challenged the fundamental concepts involved and the assumptions made concerning the functioning of the supposed craniosacral system, such as Gilliam (1998), Green et al. (1999a), Hartman and Norton (2002a), Green et al. (1999b), Kostopoulos and Keramidas (1992), McPartland and Mein (1997), Quaid (1995), and Rogers and Witt (1997). Proponents of CST claim to be able to detect a craniosacral rhythm or pulse that has a frequency of approximately 10 to 14 Hz and is independent of the cardiovascular pulse. CST advocates claim that the so-called pulse or rhythm can be felt in the cranium, sacrum, cerebrospinal fluid, and membranes (meninges) that contain the craniosacral system. The various characteristics of this pulse are considered essential to a well-balanced and healthy body.

The so-called craniosacral rhythm is detected by the therapist's fingertips, and an interpretation is then made. Because there is no instrument available to detect or measure this rhythm or its normal fluctuations in a noninvasive manner, there are no objective data of healthy versus unhealthy rhythms. Indeed, the evaluation and the entire treatment process are subjectively based and are likely due to a strong placebo effect.

Practitioners of CST claim to be able to not only detect the craniosacral rhythm but also to use gentle pressure (about 5 grams) to release restrictions in the craniosacral system. They further claim that this will balance the system and lead to an improvement in the functioning of the central nervous system and thereby the body as a whole. CST is claimed to stimulate the natural healing processes and to increase resistance to disease; see Elsdale (1996), Greenman and McPartland (1995), Gillespie (1985), Upledger (1995, 1997), and Upledger and Karni (1979). Practitioners of CST also claim to be able to evaluate and free movements in the bones of the sacrum and skull. Because the cranial bones eventually fuse, it is impossible to see how they could move one on another.

Craniosacral therapy is, then, an evaluation and treatment system with a dubious scientific foundation. Nonetheless, advocates of the therapy have developed and made numerous claims for many techniques, including but not limited to the following:

- Cranial base release
- Fourth ventricle technique
- Sphenoid release technique
- Ear-pull decompression
- Palming-decompression technique
- The parietal hold and lift
- Frontal decompression
- Balancing the glabella and bregma
- Zygoma palpitation
- Mandible compression/decompression
- Sacral release technique
- Sacroiliac decompression
- Core link technique

Practitioners claim that CST can be effective in a wide range of conditions, listed in Box 16-1. Practitioners also claim that the benefits of CST include the following:

- Increased sense of relaxation
- Pain relief
- Change in behavior patterns, leading to an improvement in relationships with friends, family, colleagues, and so on
- Greater capacity to manage life in general
- Better management of specific disease symptoms
- Reduced stress
- Improvement of psychological issues
- Reduction of effects of past trauma
- Improved sense of well-being

Despite the development of an outwardly complex system of evaluation and treatment, CST continues to have serious

**BOX 16-1** Indications Claimed for the Use of Craniosacral Therapy

Arthritis
Asthma
Autism
Back pain
Birth trauma
Bronchitis
Cerebral palsy
Colic
Depression
Digestive problems
Drug withdrawal
Dyslexia
Exhaustion
Fall or injury
Frozen shoulder
Hormonal imbalances
Hyperactivity
Immune system disorders
Insomnia
Lethargy
Menstrual pain, premenstrual syndrome
Migraine
Postoperative conditions
Problems during and after pregnancy
Reintegration after accidents
Sciatica
Sinusitis
Spinal curvatures
Sports injuries
Stress-related illnesses
Tinnitus and middle ear problems
Temporomandibular joint (jaw) disorders
Visual disturbances
Whiplash injuries

scientific accusations leveled at its fundamental concepts. Numerous authors have addressed the validity and reliability issues surrounding CST, and, in general, their findings report marginal validity and little, if any, reliability (Green et al., 1999a; Hartman & Norton, 2002b; Moran & Gibbons, 2001; Rogers et al., 1998; Upledger, 1977; Wirth-Pattullo & Hayes, 1994). For example, in 1999 an extensive review of the scientific evidence for CST by the British Columbia Office of Health Technology Assessment (BCOHTA) stated that although there is some evidence to support a craniosacral rhythm, impulse, or primary respiration independent of other measurable body rhythms (heart rate, or respiration), there is no valid evidence that this rhythm "can be reliably perceived by an examiner or that it has any influence on health or disease states." Furthermore, the researchers concluded, "there is insufficient scientific evidence to recommend craniosacral therapy to patients, practitioners or third party payers for any clinical condition" (Green et al., 1999b).

Hartman and Norton (2002b), two faculty members at the University of New England College of Osteopathic Medicine, concluded:

> *Our own and previously published findings suggest that the proposed mechanism for cranial osteopathy is invalid and that interexaminer (and, therefore, diagnostic) reliability is approximately zero. Since no properly randomized, blinded, and placebo-controlled outcome studies have been published, we conclude that cranial osteopathy should be removed from curricula of colleges of osteopathic medicine and from osteopathic licensing examinations.*

In conclusion, CST is a treatment concept surrounded by serious controversy. Although there is not a great deal of evidence to support the claims of its advocates, there is little doubt that satisfied clients and patients can be identified. One need only search the Internet to find dozens of web sites touting the many benefits of CST. To the uninformed, CST seems plausible and credible; however, the most important claims of CST cannot be scientifically justified. Therefore, the technique cannot be recommended as a legitimate form of soft tissue manipulation. The issue of whether CST and similar techniques should be taught at all in modern rehabilitation practice is an important question (Ehrett, 1988). In general, CST is not taught because the evidence to support its use is sparse and dubious at best.

## REFERENCES

### Introduction

Carpenter JS, Neal JG: Other complementary and alternative medicine modalities: acupuncture, magnets, reflexology, and homeopathy, *Am J Med* 118(12 suppl 2):109-117, 2005.

Cassar M: Massage for detoxification, *Positive Health* 39:45-49, 1999.

Eisenberg DM, Kessler RC, Foster C et al: Unconventional medicine in the United States: prevalence, costs and patterns of use, *N Engl J Med* 328:246, 1993.

Fritz S: *Fundamentals of therapeutic massage,* ed 3, St Louis, 2004, Mosby.

Hadley CM: Complementary medicine and the general practitioner: a survey of general practitioners in the Wellington area, *NZ Med J* 101:766, 1988.

Jahnke R: The body therapies, *J Holistic Nurs* 3(1):7-14, 1985.

Lynoe N, Svensson T: Physicians and alternative medicine, an investigation of attitudes and practice, *Scand J Social Med* 20:55, 1992.

McPartland J, Miller B: Bodywork therapy systems, *Phys Med Rehabil Clin N Am* 10(3):583-602, 1999.

Micozzi M: *Fundamentals of complementary and alternative medicine,* New York, 1996, Churchill Livingstone.

Oschman JL: Structural integration (Rolfing), osteopathic, chiropractic, Feldenkrais, Alexander, myofascial release and related methods, *J Bodywork Movement Ther* 1(5):305-309, 1997.

Sarac AJ, Gur A: Complementary and alternative medical therapies in fibromyalgia, *Curr Pharm Des* 12(1):47-57, 2006.

Verhoef MJ, Sutherland LR: General practitioners' interest in alternative medicine in Canada, *Social Sci Med* 41(4):511-515, 1995.

Vickers A: Research in complementary medicine and the work of the RCCM, *Midwives,* January:14-16, 1995.

Westland G: Specialist report: biodynamic massage, *Complement Ther Nurs Midwifery* 2(2):47-51, 1996.

Wharton R, Lewith G: Complementary medicine and the general practitioner, *Br Med J* 292:1498, 1986.

### Myofascial Release Techniques

Barnes JF: Why myofascial release is unique, *Clin Bull Myofascial Ther* 2(1):43-46, 1997.

Barnes MF: The basic science of myofascial release: morphologic change in connective tissue, *J Bodywork Movement Ther* 1(4):231-238, 1997a.

Barnes MF: Efficacy study of the effect of a myofascial release treatment technique on obtaining pelvic symmetry, *J Bodywork Movement Ther* 1(5):289-296, 1997b.

Brendstrup P, Jespersen K, Asboe-Hansen G: Morphological and chemical connective tissue changes in fibrositic muscles, 16:438-440, 1957.

Cantu RI, Grodin AJ: *Myofascial manipulation: theory and clinical application,* ed 2, Gaithensburg, Md, 2001, Aspen.

Danneskiold-Samsøe B, Christiansen E, Anderson RB: Myofascial pain and the role of myoglobin, *Scand J Rheumatol* 15:175-178, 1986.

Danneskiold-Samsøe B, Christiansen E, Lund B et al: Regional muscle tension and pain ("fibrositis"), *Scand J Rehab Med* 15:17-20, 1982.

Ehrett SL: Craniosacral therapy and myofascial release in entry-level physical therapy curricula, *Phys Ther* 68(4):534-540, 1988.

Friction JR, Kroening R, Haley D et al: Myofascial pain syndrome of the head and neck: a review of clinical characteristics of 164 patients, *Oral Surg* 60(6):615-623, 1985.

Friedmann LW: [Letter to the editor.] *Am J Phys Med Rehab* 68(5):257-258, 1989.

Ingber RS: Iliopsoas myofascial dysfunction: a treatable cause of "failed" low back syndrome, *Arch Phys Med Rehab* 70:382-385, 1989.

Kine GD, Warfield CA: Myofascial pain syndrome, *Hosp Pract* 21(9):194-196, 1986.

Krusen FH, Kottke FJ, Ellwood PM: *Handbook of physical medicine and rehabilitation,* Philadelphia, 1965, Saunders.

Manheim CJ: *The myofascial release manual,* ed 3, Thorofare, NJ, 2001, Slack.

Melzack R: Myofascial trigger points: relation to acupuncture and mechanisms of pain, *Arch Phys Med Rehab* 62:114-117, 1981.

Mock LE: Myofascial release treatment of specific muscles of the upper extremity (levels 3 and 4): part 1, *Clin Bull Myofascial Ther* 2(1):5-23, 1997a.

Mock LE: Myofascial release treatment of specific muscles of the upper extremity (levels 3 and 4): part 3, *Clin Bull Myofascial Ther* 2(4):51-69, 1997b.

Mock LE: Myofascial release treatment of specific muscles of the upper extremity (levels 3 and 4): part 4, *Clin Bull Myofascial Ther* 3(1):71-93, 1998.

Morris CE: Healthy practice. Myofascial release: an overview, *Calif Chiropract Assoc J* 24(11):27-29, 1999.

Reynolds MD: Myofascial trigger point syndromes in the practice of rheumatology, *Arch Phys Med Rehab* 62:111-114, 1981.

Rubin D: Myofascial trigger point syndromes: an approach to management, *Arch Phys Med Rehab* 62:107-110, 1981.

Schleip R, Klingler W, Lehmann-Horn F: Active fascial contractility: fascia may be able to contract in a smooth muscle-like manner and thereby influence musculoskeletal dynamics, *Med Hypotheses* 65(2):273-277, 2005.

Shea MJ, Keyworth D: Myofascial release: blending the somatic and orthopedic models, *Clin Bull Myofascial Ther* 2(1):65-75, 1997.

Simons DG: Familial fibromyalgia and/or myofascial pain syndrome? *Arch Phys Med Rehab* 71:258-259, 1990.

Stone JA: Prevention and rehabilitation: myofascial release, *Athletic Therapy Today* 5(4):34-35, 2000.

Travell J: Identification of myofascial trigger point syndromes: a case of atypical facial neuralgia, *Arch Phys Med Rehab* 62:100-106, 1981.

Waylonis GW, Wilke S, O'Toole D et al: Chronic myofascial pain: management by low-output helium-neon laser therapy, *Arch Phys Med Rehab* 69:1017-1020, 1988.

Whalen W: Healthy practice: myofascial release in workers' compensation, *Calif Chiropract Assoc J* 24(7), 1999.

Yunus MB, Kalyan-Raman UP, Kalyan-Raman K: Primary fibromyalgia syndrome and myofascial pain syndrome: clinical features and muscle pathology, *Arch Phys Med Rehab* 69(6):451-454, 1988.

## Trigger Point Therapy

Alon G, De Domenico G: *High voltage stimulation: an integrated approach to clinical practice,* Chattanooga, Tenn, 1987, Chattanooga Corp.

Brendstrup P, Jespersen K, Asboe-Hansen G: Morphological and chemical connective tissue changes in fibrositic muscles, *Ann Rheum Dis* 16:438-440, 1957.

Chaitow L: *Instant pain control,* Northamptonshire, United Kingdom, 1981, Thorsons.

Danneskiold-Samsøe B, Christiansen E, Anderson RB: Myofascial pain and the role of myoglobin, *Scand J Rheumatol* 15:175-178, 1986.

Danneskiold-Samsøe B, Christiansen E, Lund B et al: Regional muscle tension and pain ("fibrositis"), *Scand J Rehab Med* 15:17-20, 1982.

Fischer AA: Documentation of myofascial trigger points, *Arch Phys Med Rehab* 69:286-291, 1988.

Friction JR, Kroening R, Haley D et al: Myofascial pain syndrome of the head and neck: a review of clinical characteristics of 164 patients, *Oral Surg* 60(6):615-623, 1985.

Gam AN, Klarming S, Larsen LH et al: Treatment of myofascial trigger points with ultrasound combined with massage and exercise: a randomized controlled trial, *Pain* 77(1):73-79, 1998.

Goldenberg DL: Treatment of fibromyalgia syndrome, *Rheum Dis Clin North Am* 15(1):61-71, 1989.

Hey LR, Helewa A: Myofascial pain syndrome: a critical review of the literature, *Physiother Can* 46(1):28-36, 1994.

Hong C: Myofascial trigger points: pathophysiology and correlation with acupuncture points. *Acupunct Med* 18(1):41-47, 2000.

Kine GD, Warfield CA: Myofascial pain syndrome, *Hosp Pract* 21(9):194-196, 1986.

Kostopoulos D, Rizopoulos K: *The manual of trigger point and myofascial therapy,* Thorofare, NJ, 2001, Slack.

Kovacs FM, Abraira V, Pozo F et al: Local and remote sustained trigger point therapy for exacerbations of chronic low back pain: a randomized, double-blind, controlled, multicenter trail, *Spine* 22(7):786-797, 2000.

Laing DR, Dalley DR, Kirk JA: Ice therapy in soft tissue injuries, *NZ Med J* 78(8):155-158, 1973.

Lundberg T, Nordemar R, Ottoson D: Pain alleviation by vibratory stimulation, *Pain* 20:25-44, 1984.

Lane P: Neuromuscular therapy: history and uses, *Positive Health* 47:48-51, 1999.

Lein DH Jr, Clelland JA, Knowles CJ et al: Comparison of effects of transcutaneous electrical nerve stimulation of auricular, somatic, and the combination of auricular and somatic acupuncture points on experimental pain threshold, *Phys Ther* 69(8):671-678, 1989.

Mance D, McConnell B, Ryan PA et al: Myofascial pain syndrome, *J Am Podiatr Med Assoc* 76(6):328-331, 1986.

Manheim CJ, Lavett DK: The myofascial release manual, Thorofare, NJ, 1989, Slack.

Melzack R: Myofascial trigger points: relation to acupuncture and mechanisms of pain, *Arch Phys Med Rehab* 62:114-117, 1981.

Offenbacher S: Physical therapy in the treatment of fibromyalgia, *Scand J Rheumatol* 113(suppl):78-85, 2000.

Peppard A: Trigger-point massage therapy, *Phys Sports Med* 1(5):59-162, 1983.

Reynolds MD: Myofascial trigger point syndromes in the practice of rheumatology, *Arch Phys Med Rehab* 62:111-114, 1981.

Rubin D: Myofascial trigger point syndromes: an approach to management, *Arch Phys Med Rehab* 62:107-110, 1981.

Simons DG: Myofascial pain syndromes due to trigger points: treatment and single-muscle syndromes, *Manual Med* 1:72-77, 1985.

Simons DG: Familial fibromyalgia and/or myofascial pain syndrome? *Arch Phys Med Rehab* 71:258-259, 1990.

Travell J: Identification of myofascial trigger point syndromes: a case of atypical facial neuralgia, *Arch Phys Med Rehab* 62:100-106, 1981.

Travell JG, Simons DG: *Myofascial pain and dysfunction: the trigger point manual,* vol I, Baltimore, 1983, Williams & Wilkins.

Travell JG, Simons DG: *Myofascial pain and dysfunction: the trigger point manual,* vol II, Baltimore, 1992, Williams & Wilkins.

Waylonis GW, Wilke S, O'Toole D et al: Chronic myofascial pain: management by low-output helium-neon laser therapy, *Arch Phys Med Rehab* 69:1017-1020, 1988.

Wolfe F: Fibrositis, fibromyalgia and musculo-skeletal disease: the current status of fibrositis syndrome, *Arch Phys Med Rehab* 69:527-531, 1988.

Yunus MB, Kalyan-Raman UP, Kalyan-Raman K: Primary fibromyalgia syndrome and myofascial pain syndrome: clinical features and muscle pathology, *Arch Phys Med Rehab* 69(6):451-454, 1988.

## Reflexology

Adamson S: Best feet foremost, *Health Visitor* 67(2):61, 1994.

Bayly DE: *Reflexology today,* Wellingborough, United Kingdom, 1982, Thorsons.

Booth B: Reflexology, *Nurs Times* 90(1):38-40, 1994.

Chia M, Chia M: *Chi Nei Tsang: internal organ chi massage,* New York, 1997, Healing Tao Books.

Crane B: Chinese origins. In *Reflexology: the definitive practitioner's manual,* Rockport, Mass, 1997, Element.

Dougans I, Ellis S: *Reflexology: foot massage for total health,* Shaftesbury, United Kingdom, 1991, Element Books.

Downing G: *The massage book,* New York, 1974, Random House.

Hillman A: Zone therapy, *Nursing* 3(6):225-227, 1986.

Holey E, Cook E: *Therapeutic massage,* Philadelphia, 1988, Saunders.

Ingham ED: *Stories the feet can tell* [revised as *Stories the feet have told thru reflexology*], St Petersburg, Fla, 1984, Ingham.

Kunz K, Kunz B: *The complete guide to foot reflexology,* New York, 1987, Prentice Hall Press.

Lidell L: *The book of massage: the complete step-by-step guide to Eastern and Western techniques,* London, 1984, Ebury Press.

Lockett J: Reflexology: a nursing tool? *Aust Nurses J* 22(1):14-15, 1992.

Oleson T, Flocco W: Randomised controlled study of premenstrual symptoms treated with ear, hand, and foot reflexology, *Obstet Gynecol* 82(6):906-911, 1993.

Omura Y: Accurate localization of organ representation areas on the feet & hands using the bi-digital O-ring test resonance phenomenon: its clinical implication in diagnosis & treatment: part 1, *Acupuncture Electro Ther Res Int J* 19:153-190, 1994.

Sahai ICM: Reflexology: its place in modern healthcare, *Prof Nurse* 8(11):722-725, 1993.

Tappan FM, Benjamin P: *Tappen's handbook of healing massage techniques: classic, holistic, and emerging methods,* ed 3, Norwalk, Conn, 1998, Appleton & Lange.

Thomas M: Fancy footwork, *Nurs Times* 85(41):42-44, 1989.

## Rolfing Structural Integration

Oschman JL: Structural integration (Rolfing), osteopathic, chiropractic, Feldenkrais, Alexander, myofascial release and related methods, *J Bodywork Movement Ther* 1(5):305-309, 1997.

## Point Percussion Therapy

Jia LH: *Pointing therapy.* Shandong, China, 1984, Shandong Science & Technology Press.

Wang ZP: *Acupressure therapy: point percussion treatment of cerebral palsy birth injury, brain injury and stroke,* Melbourne, 1991, Churchill Livingstone.

## Craniosacral Therapy

Ehrett SL: Craniosacral therapy and myofascial release in entry-level physical therapy curricula, *Phys Ther* 68(4):534-540, 1988.

Elsdale B: Craniosacral therapy, *Nurs Times* 92(28):173, 1996.

Gillespie BR: Dental considerations of the craniosacral mechanism, *Cranio* 3(4):380-384, 1985.

Gilliam J: Science or fiction, *Phys Ther* 78(8):904-905, 1998.

Green C, Martin CW, Bassett K et al: A systematic review of craniosacral therapy: biological plausibility, assessment reliability and clinical effectiveness, *Complement Ther Med* 7(4):201-207, 1999a.

Green C, Martin CW, Bassett K et al: *A systematic review and critical appraisal of the scientific evidence on craniosacral therapy,* Vancouver, BC, 1999b, British Columbia Office of Health Technology Assessment.

Greenman PE, McPartland JM: Cranial findings and iatrogenesis from craniosacral manipulation in patients with traumatic brain syndrome, *J Am Osteopath Assoc* 95(3):182-8; 191-192, 1995.

Hartman SE, Norton JM: Craniosacral therapy is not medicine, *Phys Ther* 82(11):1146-1147, 2002a.

Hartman SE, Norton JM: Interexaminer reliability and cranial osteopathy, *Scientific Rev Altern Med* 6(1):23-34, 2002b.

Kostopoulos DC, Keramidas G: Changes in elongation of falx cerebri during craniosacral therapy techniques applied on the skull of an embalmed cadaver, *Cranio* 10(1):9-12, 1992.

McPartland JM, Mein EA: Entrainment and the cranial rhythmic impulse, *Altern Ther Health Med* 3(1):40-45, 1997.

Moran RW, Gibbons P: Intraexaminer and interexaminer reliability for palpation of the cranial rhythmic impulse at the head and sacrum, *J Manipulative Physiol Ther* 24(3):183-190, 2001.

Quaid A: Craniosacral controversy, *Phys Ther* 75(3):240, 1995.

Rogers JS, Witt PL: The controversy of cranial bone motion, *J Orthop Sports Phys Ther* 26(2):95-103, 1997.

Rogers JS, Witt PL, Gross MT et al: Simultaneous palpation of the craniosacral rate at the head and feet: intrarater and interrater reliability and rate comparisons, *Phys Ther* 78(11):1175-1185, 1998.

Upledger JE: The reproducibility of craniosacral examination findings: a statistical analysis, *J Am Osteopath Assoc* 76(12):890-899, 1977.

Upledger JE: Craniosacral therapy, *Phys Ther* 75(4):328-330, 1995.

Upledger JE: *Your inner physician and you,* Berkeley, Calif, 1997, North Atlantic Books and UI Enterprises.

Upledger JE, Karni Z: Mechano-electric patterns during craniosacral osteopathic diagnosis and treatment, *J Am Osteopath Assoc* 78(11):782-791, 1979.

Wirth-Pattullo V, Hayes KW: Interrater reliability of craniosacral rate measurements and their relationship with subjects' and examiners' heart and respiratory rate measurements, *Phys Ther* 74(10):908-916; discussion, 917-920, 1994.

# Chapter 17

# Eastern Systems of Soft Tissue Manipulation

Various forms of massage have been practiced in Eastern cultures for millennia. Indeed, some of the world's oldest medical writings come from ancient Eastern cultures and describe various forms of soft tissue manipulation (massage) as an important medical healing art (see Chapter 1). Several of these systems are closely linked and have since been adapted by different cultures in many parts of the modern world. This chapter explores some of these systems and the interrelationships among them. Many of these systems are related to ancient Chinese culture, specifically to Taoism. This philosophy recognizes health as a state of balance or harmony within the individual and between the individual and nature. A state of ill health is seen primarily as an imbalance within the various internal and external forces that affect overall health. Intervention is therefore directed to restoration of the natural balance and harmony within the individual.

In traditional Chinese medicine, the human bodily functions are controlled by a vital force or energy, called *qi* (often written as *chi* but pronounced as *chee*), which circulates between the organs and throughout the body along channels called *meridians*. There are 12 main meridians, corresponding to 12 major organ functions of the body. The organ systems have the same names as those used today (i.e., stomach, kidney, heart, liver, etc.), but they represent a functional aspect of the organ, rather than an anatomical/physiological description. According to traditional Chinese medical thinking, good health results when the vital energy (qi) flows in sufficient quantity and quality through each of the 12 meridians and organ systems. Each of the 12 systems can be affected by appropriate stimulation of acupuncture points located along each meridian. In this way, the flow of the vital energy (qi) of the body can be regulated.

Traditional Chinese medical theory is grounded largely in the Taoist concept of *yin*—the positive, active male force—and *yang*—the negative, passive female force—in which ill health is seen as an excess or deficiency in the flow of the vital energy. Treatment is therefore aimed at rebalancing the system by using various methods (including acupuncture and acupressure) to restore the correct energy flow (Maciocia, 1989). A detailed and exhaustive treatment of each of these systems is well beyond the scope of this book. The intention here is simply to introduce the reader to a selected number of Eastern systems of massage and explore some of their interrelationships.

## ACUPRESSURE

As its name suggests, the concept of acupressure is closely related to acupuncture. In both cases, the skin and underlying structures are stimulated at specific sites, known as *acupuncture points*. Stimulation at such sites should be seen as a method of accessing internal body systems, primarily by means of the peripheral nervous system. As its name implies, acupressure can be simply described as *the application of pressure to specific acupuncture points,* and in order to understand the principles of acupressure, one must first address the basic elements of acupuncture.

In classical acupuncture, stimulation is usually performed using several very fine but solid needles (acupuncture needles). Figure 17-1 illustrates an acupuncture treatment to the lower limb in a child with hemiplegia affecting the right side of the body. Multiple needles have been inserted at specific points along the lower limb. In addition, needles are also inserted into the upper limb and head of the patient (not shown).

As an alternative, stimulation can also be given using electricity, and this is known as *electroacupuncture*. Two basic techniques are used: electrical stimulation (from a specially designed unit) is applied directly to the needles

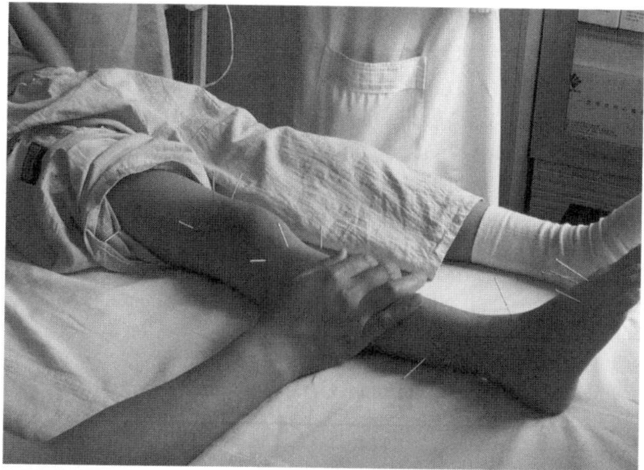

Figure **17-1** Acupuncture Treatment to a Child with a Hemiparetic Lower Limb

A series of acupuncture needles have been inserted into a variety of points along the lower limb in a child with hemiplegia affecting the right side of the body. The affected right upper limb and the child's head (not shown) were also treated with acupuncture during this procedure.

that have already been inserted into the tissues; alternatively, electrical stimulation can be applied directly to each acupuncture point, using various surface electrodes. In this case, needles are not used and the skin is not penetrated. This technique can only be used safely with certain types of stimulation, such as high-voltage pulsed direct current (HVPDC). In the case of acupressure, stimulation is usually provided by direct digital pressure (finger or thumb), or with a handheld probe, to each appropriate acupuncture point.

There is a wealth of information on the topic of acupuncture, both on its place as a foundational concept in traditional Chinese medicine and regarding its emergence into contemporary health care (Filshie & White, 1997; Hopwood, 1997; Lewis, 1999; Linde et al., 2001; Sorgen, 1998; Vickers & Zollman, 1999). In fact, acupuncture is rapidly becoming an integral part of modern rehabilitation practice (Kerr et al., 2001) and a useful tool in primary care settings (Rega, 1999; Ross, 2001). The effect of acupuncture on various internal organ functions is another area in which there is a growing body of knowledge that in many, but not all, cases supports this ancient practice (Beal, 1999; Hu 2000; Takeuchi et al., 1999; Vickers, 1966; Vilholm et al., 1998; Wan 2000; Zhou et al.1999). However, acupuncture is not a treatment without some risk to the patient (Odsberg et al., 2001; White et al., 2001). Of particular concern is the possibility of introducing serious infection by the use of "dirty" needles. There has, therefore, always been an important need to sterilize the needles used in acupuncture treatments. With the advent of disposable needles, the risk of cross-contamination has been greatly reduced. Other adverse effects consist largely of unwanted reactions to the treatment.

From an historical perspective, there have been three main schools of thought concerning the preferred method for selecting acupuncture points for treatment, namely, select points:

- According to syndromes
- According to affected channels
- According to time-related points

The selection of acupuncture points for treatment within the scope of traditional Chinese medicine is usually made according to syndromes, whereas the Japanese-based Meridian Therapy School emphasizes the selection of points according to the *channels* involved. Other historical methods of selecting points for treatment include those determined according to *point category, symptoms, seasons,* and *five elements*. Modern acupuncture practice uses a combination of historical and contemporary methods to locate and select points for treatment (McDonald, 1999).

Acupuncture/acupressure points may be situated in an isolated location on the skin surface, or they may be found along a specific line of distribution—the so-called meridians. The meridians represent pathways (lines) on the body that run from various internal organ systems to the skin surface. Although the history of acupuncture and herbal medicine can be traced back to northern and southern China more than 4000 years ago, it was not until around 300 BC that the first text on traditional Chinese medicine (TCM) appeared and the concept of acupuncture was fully described. This famous text was the *Huangdi Nei Ching Su Wen* (usually referred to as the *Nei Ching*) or *The Yellow Emperor's Classic of Internal Medicine.* The text is said to have been written by Huang Ti (Huangdi), the Yellow Emperor himself, and in it, the meridians along which the life force, or energy, of the body (qi) flows and their acupuncture points are presented in diagrams. In total there are about 1000 acupuncture points, and in TCM, stimulating them is said to affect the flow of yin and yang (the opposing and complementary negative and positive energy sources) so that the body systems are maintained in proper balance (Beal, 1992). Figure 17-2 illustrates the location of some of the classical acupuncture points and the meridians associated with them.

The effects of acupuncture on pain have been studied for many years, both from a neurophysiological viewpoint and from its clinical application in both acute and chronic pain (David et al., 1998; Lao et al., 1999; Romoli et al., 2000; Vickers et al., 2004; Wedenberg et al., 2000). Of course, pain relief using hyperstimulation techniques can also be achieved through acupuncture and acupressure, as well as through techniques already presented such as trigger point stimulation, reflexology, point percussion therapy, and connective tissue massage. These techniques are effective because, histologically, the points and their immediate surrounding areas are associated with the same nerves, pressure, and stretch receptors (Weaver, 1985). Associated modalities—for example, *cupping* and the use of *transcutaneous electrical nerve stimulation* (TENS)—can have similar effects (Anderson et al., 1974; Baldry, 1989; Fox & Melzack, 1976; Han, 1987; Lewit, 1979; Melzack, 1981, 1985; Travell & Simons, 1983, 1992).

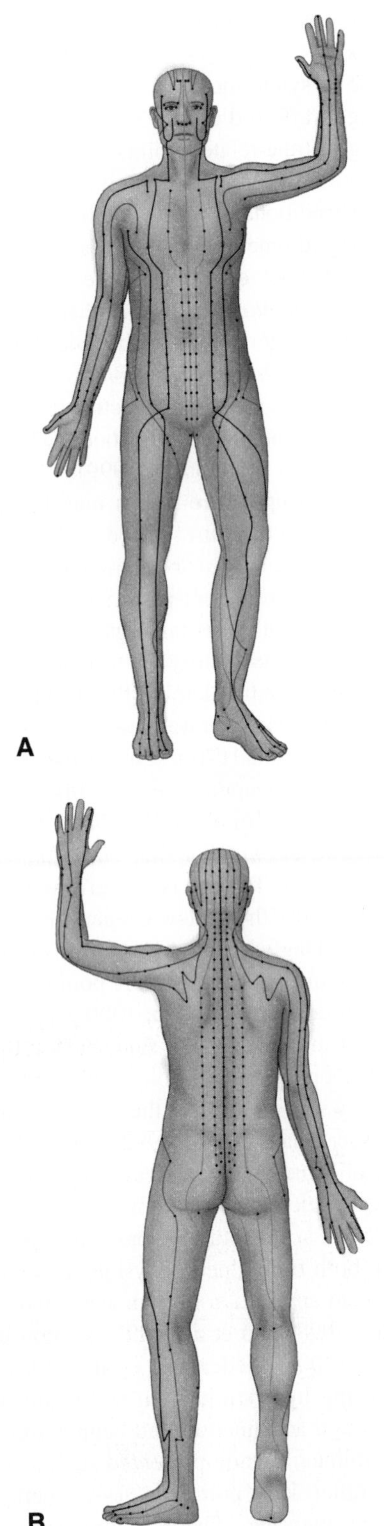


**Figure 17-2 Location of Selected Classical Chinese Acupuncture Points and Meridians**

**A,** The location of a variety of classical Chinese acupuncture points. Some of the points are used to invoke pain relief, whereas others are used to produce stimulation or inhibition of various body organ systems. **B,** The location of the 10 classical meridians is illustrated. The meridians represent lines of association between a number of acupuncture points and an internal organ system (e.g., the liver organ system). Stimulation of points along the meridians is a way of affecting the function of the organ system they represent. Thus, each of the acupuncture points is named after a specific system (e.g., St-36 is the stomach 36 point and has a specific location on the skin, just below the knee).

Although it is beyond the scope of this book to provide detailed information concerning the neurophysiological basis of acupuncture and associated techniques in pain relief, there is abundant evidence of their effectiveness. The therapeutic effects of acupuncture, especially on pain, can be explained in part by the conventional understanding of neurophysiological concepts. The insertion of an acupuncture needle stimulates A delta nociceptor fibers, entering the spinal cord in the region of the dorsal horn. The A delta fibers are activated in response to the needle insertion/removal and to the twisting of the needles during the treatment. These fibers are rapidly adapting and responsible for the sharp, stabbing quality of pain. Activation of these fibers can produce a segmental inhibition of impulses traveling in the unmyelinated C fibers. Pain relief is also mediated by activation of the descending pain suppression mechanism and stimulation of endogenous opioid peptide release in the periaqueductal gray matter, spinal cord, and elsewhere. Various other substances, including serotonin, catecholamines, glutamate, and gamma-aminobutyric acid (GABA), may also mediate cardiovascular and analgesic effects. In addition, evidence that nitric oxide may play a role in mediating cardiovascular responses through the gracile nucleus–thalamic pathway has recently become available. Activation of these mechanisms helps to explain how the insertion of needles in one part of the body can have a long-lasting effect on pain felt elsewhere (He, 1987; Kerr et al., 1978; Sheng-Xing, 2004). These mechanisms also explain how acupressure and electroacupuncture can relieve pain.

Originally, acupuncture was one of a range of external therapies that included moxibustion (burning of the herb *Artemisia vulgaris,* a type of chrysanthemum) and traditional Chinese (amma) massage (Armstrong, 1972; Cheng, 1987). Before the invention of material capable of being honed fine enough to actually puncture the skin, pieces of stone and bone were used to press points on the skin. The response to stimulation of some points corresponds to that associated with the Head's zones mentioned previously in association with reflexology and connective tissue massage (see Chapters 11 and 16). It is widely accepted that some acupuncture points correspond to sites in specific Head's zones and some with trigger or motor points. At least 50% of acupuncture points are located directly over nerve trunks, the other half are within 0.5 cm of the trunks, and more than 70% coincide with trigger points (Chaitow, 1979, 1981; Melzack, 1981).

In modern rehabilitation practice, acupressure is growing rapidly in popularity (Romanchok, 1997), particularly as a technique that may be taught to the patient for self-treatment purposes. It is effective for relieving pain of musculoskeletal origin and for relieving muscle fatigue (Avakyan, 1990; Heinke, 1998; Hsieh et al., 2006; Li & Peng, 2000; Yip & Tse, 2006). Acupressure also appears to be effective for treating a number of problems in the area of women's health and reproductive medicine (Beal, 1999; Hoo, 1997). Acupressure seems to be particularly effective for reducing the problems of nausea and vomiting in a wide variety of situations (Bowie, 1999; Chen et al., 2005: Cummings, 2001; Dibble et al., 2000; Harmon et al., 2000; Klein & Griffiths, 2004; Shenkman et al. 1999; Steele et al., 2001; Stern et al., 2001; Youngs, 2000). Acupressure can also promote relaxation, reduce anxiety, and encourage restful sleep (Agarwal, 2005; Chen et al., 1999; Tsay et al., 2005). In contrast, acupressure does not seem to promote weight loss (Ernst, 1997).

Although acupressure is typically applied to the acupuncture points by means of pressure applied through the thumbs or fingers, it can also be given with the heel of the hand or, in some cases, with the elbow. Finger pressure to acupuncture points can be administered with the tip of one finger (the index or the middle digit), or pressure can be applied with the thumb tip. Limited circular frictions progressing more deeply to static pressure over the point are given for 1 to 5 minutes. Numerous texts are available that prescriptively give information about point location and indications for applying acupressure, particularly for orthopedic conditions and pain relief. A plan for selecting points should take into account not only the symptoms but also the relative deficiency or excess in the meridian on which the point is situated. Further reading would elucidate both the underlying philosophy and the two frameworks, or diagnostic models, of the five elements and eight principal patterns.

Acupressure should not be given over contusions, scar tissue, vascular problems such as varicose veins, or an irregularity in the skin (e.g., moles, warts, acne lesions). An adverse autonomic or psychophysiological response may occur in children younger than 7 years, whose autonomic nervous system is immature, and in those with severe cardiac conditions.

The many hundreds of acupuncture points can be divided into two main groups, those associated with pain relief and those concerned with the stimulation of various organ systems. In fact, both acupuncture and acupressure are good examples of treatment concepts that produce a remote site effect, largely mediated by an autonomic reflex (see Chapters 5, 11, and 16). Points are named by their meridians, which are linked to their sources in the internal organ systems. Two examples are the powerful acupuncture points used in anesthesia and in the treatment of pain: the large intestine (LI-) 4 and the stomach (St-) 36. LI-4 is found in the middle of the web space between the metacarpals of the thumb and index finger. In Chinese it is called *Ho-Ku,* which means "meeting valley." The St-36 point is located slightly lateral and distal to the insertion of the patella tendon onto the tibial tuberosity (Figure 17-3).

Stimulation of the St-36 point is illustrated in Figure 17-3, *B.* The point lies slightly lateral and distal to the insertion of the patella tendon on the tibial tuberosity and, once again, is a location in which self-treatment is possible.

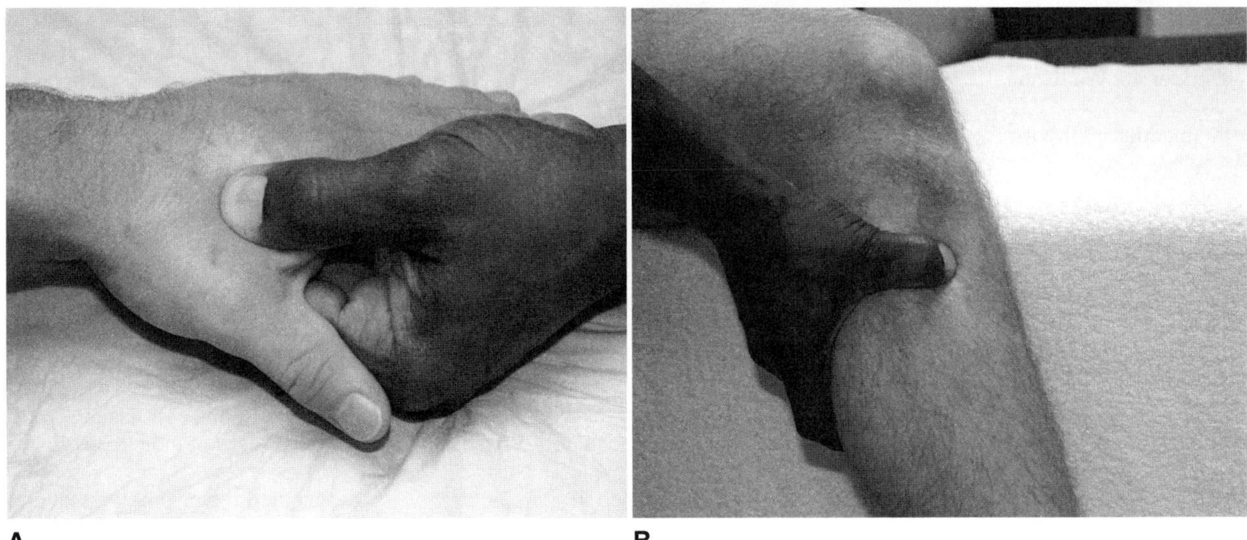


Figure **17-3** Acupressure Technique to the LI-4 and St-36 Points

**A,** Stimulation of the LI-4 point. In many cases, the patient can be taught to self-administer treatment to this point, as it lies in an easily accessible area, midway in the web space between the thumb (first) and second metacarpal bones. **B,** Stimulation of the St-36 point. The point lies slightly lateral and distal to the insertion of the patella tendon on the tibial tuberosity and, once again, is a location in which self-treatment is possible.

The classic method of locating each specific point is by the use of directions given in body inches *(cun)*. Each person's *cun* is slightly different in length and should be used to locate each point on the body. The length of the middle phalanx of the middle finger, or the distal phalanx of the thumb, can be used as the unit of length for the body inch, or *cun*. For the LI-4 point, the interphalangeal joint of the thumb is placed in the middle of the outstretched web of the other hand. By rolling up onto the tip of the thumb, the meeting valley point is found. It is hypersensitive and is readily detected by palpation and other methods.

A point finder can be used, or the simple method of identifying the sore spot by digital palpation can be used. A point finder is a small, handheld device that is moved slowly over the skin surface in the target area. A small voltage is applied to the skin, and when the probe is placed over an acupuncture point (a point of much lower resistance), a light or a buzzer is activated. Stimulation of LI-4 may be indicated in the classic hemicranial and frontal headache, toothache, pain and paralysis of the upper limb, asthma, hemiplegia, facial paralysis, temporomandibular joint pain, and for anesthesia and analgesia in general. St-36, *Tsu-san-li* ("walk 3 more miles"), is one *cun* lateral and distal to the tibial tuberosity. It is highly sensitive and is also favored for anesthesia and analgesia. It can be useful for nausea and vomiting; lumbar pain; headache; edema; or aching of the hips, knees, or legs in general.

Table 17-1 has been adapted from a number of the texts (Academy of Traditional Chinese Medicine, 1975; Chaitow, 1971; Tappan & Benjamin, 1998). It provides examples of useful points for a range of symptoms, injuries, and related problems that are common. A number of other points may be of use for the conditions and symptoms referred to in Table 17-1. Those interested in using acupressure as part of a comprehensive treatment plan should look for them in the texts listed in conjunction with this section. If acupressure techniques prove to be useful, it may be possible to teach the patient how to self-administer the treatment, thereby enabling the patient to manage his or her own problem when needed.

## SHIATSU

The modern practice of shiatsu has enjoyed a great deal of popularity, especially because of the growing interest in complementary/alternative medicine (CAM). Shiatsu means "finger pressure" and is a form of bodywork that originated in Japan around the turn of the twentieth century. Although the name is relatively new, the basic concepts of shiatsu have come from the ancient Chinese practice of Amma (meaning to press and rub), which is still practiced throughout China. Shiatsu includes stimulation of specific points and rotation and stretching of joints (Nolan, 1989). In classical shiatsu, the hands, thumbs, elbows, forearms,

**Table 17-1 Some Acupuncture Points, Their Positions, and Related Indications**

| POINT | LOCATION | INDICATIONS |
|---|---|---|
| B-40 (bladder 40, Wei-Chung) | Center of popliteal fossa | Leg cramp, low back pain, sciatica, knee joint pain, heat stroke |
| B-60 (bladder 60, Kunlun) | Midpoint between posterior margin of lateral malleolus and Achilles tendon | Low back pain, sciatica, ankle joint disorders, soft tissue sprains |
| GB-20 (gallbladder 20, Feng-chih) | Midpoint of line from tip of mastoid to posterior midline groove between trapezius and sternocleidomastoid | Tension headache, migraine, stiff neck, vertigo |
| GB-21 (gallbladder 21, Chieng-ching) | Midpoint between the C7 and the acromion process | Shoulder pain, neck pain with rigidity, upper extremity motor problems |
| GB 30 (gallbladder 30, Huan-tiao) | Point at outer one-third of a line from greater trochanter to base of coccyx | Hip joint pain, soft tissue disorders of the hip, low back pain |
| LI-15 (large intestine 15, Chien-yu) | Acromial depression in mid-deltoid with arm abducted to 90 degrees | Pain and motor problems of arm and elbow, shoulder joint, and soft tissue disorders |
| SI-3 (small intestine 3, Hou-chi) | Apex of the distal palmar crease on ulnar side of a clenched fist | Low back pain, neck pain and rigidity, upper extremity weakness |
| GB-34 (gallbladder 34, Yangling Chuan) | Anterior to the neck of the fibula | Knee and lower extremity pain |
| LI-11 (large intestine 11, Chu-chih) | At radial end of flexed elbow fold | Shoulder pain, elbow pain, soft tissue disorders of the elbow |

knees, soles of the feet, or toes can be used to administer treatment. There is also strong evidence of the influence of ancient Chinese medical culture on the practice of shiatsu; for example, some proponents include moxibustion in treatment regimens and, of course, the use of manual pressure on specific acupuncture points. Furthermore, the belief that human beings are dependent on the flow of energy or life force (*ki* in Japanese) is the basis for the stimulation of specific points.

Shiatsu, like most of the Oriental systems, approaches health from a holistic viewpoint. The overriding concept is that there are dynamic relationships between the individual and the environment. Essentially, the ascending, male, active principle, *yang,* should be in harmonious balance with the descending, passive, female principle, *yin,* as this determines the proper flow of the life force energy, *ki.* Disruptions in this flow are said to result in imbalance, disharmony, and illness, which can be detected through the *hara,* or lower abdomen. The *hara* is also the point from which the pressure of the body's weight comes from the person applying shiatsu. This simple and effective holistic approach has been acknowledged worldwide and has gained significantly in popularity.

Because shiatsu has much in common with acupressure techniques, it is not surprising that it can be used for similar purposes. It can be effective in treating pain and many musculoskeletal problems. Shiatsu treatments have also been used to manage postoperative issues involving intestinal obstruction (H 2000). In addition, shiatsu techniques have been used in pregnancy and childbirth (Hunter, 1999; Yates, 1999). In contrast to its usefulness during pragnancy and childbrith, shiatsu also has a place in palliative care (Stevensen, 1995). In company with many other deep pressure techniques, shiatsu treatments are not without problems. Damage to nerves and blood vessels is possible if the therapist is careless in applying pressure over sensitive areas (Herskovitz, 1992; K., Tsuboi & Tsuboi, 2001).

There are several different emphases, or types, of shiatsu. These include *namikoshi,* which reflects a Western approach with a physiological basis; *tsubo* therapy, which aligns closely with acupuncture; and *Zen* shiatsu, which incorporates the complexities of the meridians. All varieties have a common theme, and that is to rebalance and therefore revitalize both the body and the mind.

There are three main shiatsu techniques:

- *Sustained pressure* on a *tsubo,* or pressure point, at right angles to the body, used to tone the body by increasing the flow of blood and energy in the area. This is similar to the basic acupressure technique.
- *Passive and active stretching and squeezing* for the muscles and joints, used to disperse blocked blood or energy flow.
- *Holding and gently rocking* the body part, using little or no pressure, used to calm and counteract overactive, or agitated, energy.

The basic shiatsu pressure technique can be applied to the body through any of the parts mentioned previously. With the therapist's body well balanced, the body weight is applied through the hands, the ball (hypothenar eminence) of the thumb (the part used most often), or another part of the arm or leg. Figure 17-4 illustrates these techniques.

A systematic procedure for shiatsu treatment is described in Box 17-1. The box gives the order and type of technique using a variety of body areas. The procedure described in the box is only one of many possibilities, and the selection of techniques to be used in a particular treatment is determined by the therapist each time he or she treats the patient.

Some shiatsu techniques are similar to those of traditional Thai massage and have much in common with the

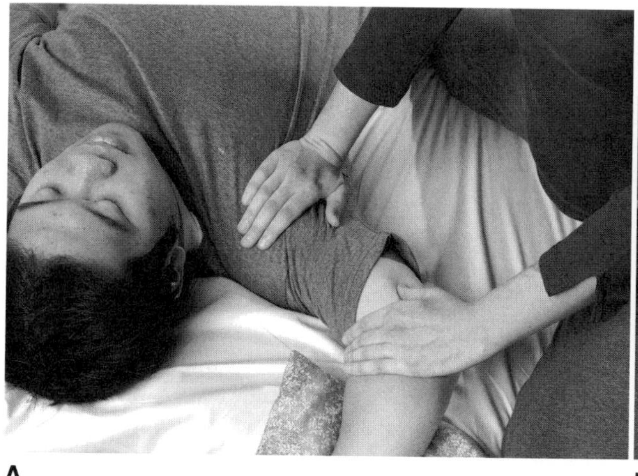
A

B

**Figure 17-4**
Examples of shiatsu techniques.

**BOX 17-1** An Example of a Sequence of Techniques for a Shiatsu Treatment

With the client lying prone on a mat on the floor or a broad, wide, low plinth, begin on the back, stretching to loosen it and to establish a rhythm. Apply pressure down both sides of the spine with the palms and thumbs. Points on the sacrum and iliosacral joints are pressed; then the buttocks are squeezed and pressure is applied through the elbow to their upper curve. Press down the center of the back of each leg, first with the palms, then with the knees. Press on the ankle points; stretch the leg in each direction; then crook the knee in and the foot out to press down the lateral border. Walk the hands along the soles of the feet. Press along the top of each shoulder; rotate the shoulder blades; press the area between the shoulder blades; then loosen the shoulder muscles using the feet. Turn the client to the supine position, and open the chest by leaning the body weight through the hands onto the client's shoulders. Press along the spaces between the ribs, then press underneath on the back and sides of the neck, ending with a stretch to the neck achieved by gently elongating it by lifting the head upward and forward. Beginning at the top of the head, run the fingers through the hair, gently pull it, then finger-massage the ears. Work with the fingertips on the face, including the temples, around the eyes, the nostrils, the mouth, and across the jaw, concluding behind the midline of the base of the skull.

The arms should be managed one at a time. Press down the inside with the palm facing up using a flat hand, then with the palm facing down, along the back of the forearm to the tip of the shoulder. Pull the fingers, concentrating on the point between the thumb and the forefinger (LI-4). End by shaking the arm to relax it. Work with both hands flat using a circular kneading technique on the *hara* in the lower abdomen, then press up gently under the lower borders of the ribs and thence down the midline, ending at the navel. Use a rocking motion to calm the hara. Massage the legs one at a time, working from the groin to the feet. Press down the inside of the leg to the knee, then return to the groin and work down the front of the thigh. Manipulate the patella to loosen it; then press down the inside with one thumb and down the outside of the calf with the other. Dorsiflex and plantarflex the foot, pull the toes, and conclude by shaking the leg to relax it.

Huna massage tradition of Hawaii. Detailed information can be gained from specific texts and in particular from a general massage book that includes both Eastern and Western methods. Further reading on shiatsu can also be found in Beresford-Cooke (1998), Booth (1993), Box (1984), Dahong (1984), Finger (1998), Formby (1997), Greim (1999), Hare (1988), Harris and Pooley (1998), Lidell (1984), Nolan (1989), Pooley (1998), Tappan and Benjamin (1998), and Woodhouse (1998).

## TRADITIONAL ORIENTAL MASSAGE

Various massage techniques have enjoyed a prominent place in the history and practice of TCM (see Chapter 1). In the Oriental medical tradition, various pressure and rubbing strokes are known as *Amma* massage. Amma massage has an ancient history and has been associated with blind practitioners. It is used to normalize body functions and to encourage relaxation of the tired soft tissues of the body. It has a calming influence on the nervous system (Serizawa, 1973). There are three types of Amma massage:

- *Rubbing and pressure,* much like kneading and frictions but applied with the knuckles of the lightly clenched hand
- *Finger and palm work,* as in picking up and wringing
- *Passive stretches* for the joints, similar to relaxed passive movements

Amma massage was used only to reinvigorate tired muscles and joints. Similar Western-based techniques, the so-called Swedish remedial massage techniques, were introduced in 1868 during the Meiji restoration in Japan. The Japanese recognized the similarities of the two and combined them to develop their own system of six basic massage techniques that incorporated the rubbing, pressure, and finger work of Amma massage and some Swedish techniques, especially vibration and percussion (tapotement). The six basic techniques include the following:

- *Rubbing and stroking,* using flat hands or the ball (thenar eminence) of the thumb or the palmar surface of the metacarpophalangeal joints of the fingers. A constant but light pressure is applied.
- *Circular motion massage,* using the relaxed palm or the tips of the fingers but with the motion originating at the wrist and light to moderate pressure.
- *Kneading massage,* using the thumb, index and middle finger alone, or all four fingers together for tendons crossing joints.
- *Pressure massage,* using the palms, the thumbs, or four fingers to apply 3 to 5 kg of pressure for 3 to 5 seconds. The body weight, not the fingers alone, is used to apply the pressure. Pressure should always be directed toward the center of the client's body and should be increased gradually. It is similar to the pressure techniques applied in shiatsu.
- *Vibration massage,* in which the fingers or palms are placed firmly on the skin and vibrated rhythmically and gently.
- *Tapping massage,* alternating hands to tap the client's body rhythmically with the palms, fingertips, and backs of the fingers or with the lateral border of the hand. The

tapping is light and rapid. The pressure should be around 1 kg. These techniques are closely related to those used in point percussion therapy (Jia, 1984).

The massage techniques practiced as part of TCM are effective in the management of musculoskeletal pain and dysfunction (Cheng, 2001; Hong, 1997; Li & Zhong, 1998; Puustjarvi & Pontinen, 1990; Zumo, 1984). Further reading on the topic of massage in the general concept of TCM can be found in Ehling (2001), Hao (1997), James (1996), Serizawa (1973), and Wright (1995).

## TRADITIONAL THAI MASSAGE

As its name suggests, traditional Thai massage is a form of bodywork integral to the historical medical culture of Thailand. The true origins of Thai massage are unknown, but given its similarities to other Oriental systems, it is possible to speculate that massage was more than likely introduced from India with the expansion of the Indian culture and Buddhism into Thailand.

Recommendations for healing massage are recorded in the *Ayur Veda,* the classic Indian text of around 1800 BC (see Chapter 1). At *Wat Pho,* a famous temple in Bangkok where traditional Thai massage is taught, Ajahn Chivakakomarapad, a Buddhist medical doctor, claimed in a stone inscription on the wall (Silajarug) that he knew the origins of all the lines of linkage in the human body. He presented around 72,000 lines, but 10 main lines (Sen Pratarn) were the most important. Today, knowledge of these 10 lines is the basis of traditional Thai massage (Tapanya, 1993).

The imaginary lines in Thai massage closely match the meridians of traditional Chinese medicine along which the life force energy called *chi* flows and on which the acupuncture points lie. Similarly, the 10 Thai main lines function as energy pathways or are described as the functional circulation in the body. These nonspecific systems function as balancing mechanisms for the body, linking a series of specific points on the surface with the deeper organs. In this way, the body's mental, digestive, nervous, circulatory, and reproductive processes, and, thus, nutrition, consciousness, and energy, are harmonized.

Illness and functional disorders are claimed to be the result of disruption of 1 or more of the 10 main lines. It is suggested that pressure applied to a specific point (similar to acupressure techniques) along the relevant line may produce a physiological effect in the periosteum, fascia, muscles, blood vessels, or nerves that is perceived as a moving impulse. As a result, pain may be relieved, circulation improved, muscles relaxed, and organ function improved. The 10 main lines of traditional Thai massage originate at the level of the umbilicus and are listed in order as follows:

1. *Itha* runs down the front of the left leg, up the back of the left leg, across the left buttock, up the left side of the back, up the back of the left side of the head, and over the top of the left side of the head, ending at the left nostril.
2. *Pingkala* runs the same route as *Itha* but on the right side. Both *Itha* and *Pingkala* should be attended to for headache or neck or back pain.
3. *Smana* runs up the middle of the thorax, through the neck and chin, and along the upper surface of the tongue. Chest, heart, jaw, and oral symptoms may arise from disruption along *Smana.*
4. *Kalathale* runs down both arms, through the fingers, through both legs, and through the phalanges. Symptoms in the arms or legs are related to *Kalathale.*
5. *Sahutsarungsi* runs down the inside of the left leg, across the base of the toes, up the outside of the left leg, across the left tibial crest, through the left nipple, and diagonally up to the left eye. The left leg and eye are governed by the functional circulation along *Sahutsarungsi.*
6. *Thavare* runs the same route as *Sahutsarungsi* but on the right side of the body. Symptoms in the right leg and eye are related to *Thavare.*
7. *Chunthapusang* runs up to the left nipple and up the left side of the neck, and it ends on the left ear lobe. The left ear relies on uninterrupted flow along *Chunthapusang.*
8. *Ruchum* runs the same route as *Chunthapusang* but on the right side. *Ruchum* is the line for the right ear.
9. *Sukhamung* runs to the stomach, internal organs, anus, and urethra. The health of the internal organs depends on *Sukhamung.*
10. *Sikkhine* runs to the genital organs, and their functioning depends on *Sikkhine.*

There are two main types of traditional Thai massage. Thai massage in the *grand palace* is given using the hand, arm, or elbow. There is no stretching, and it is used only for therapeutic purposes. Thai massage for the people is undertaken to maintain the functional circulation and for general health and well-being. The therapist's hand, arm, elbow, leg, and foot are used, and stretching is included, much as in shiatsu (Box 17-2).

Thai massage has much in common with other Oriental and Western massage traditions. This is not surprising, as Per Henrik Ling developed much of the Western concepts

**BOX 17-2** Major Elements of Thai Massage

Pressing and releasing, the degree of pressure being judged in relation to the tolerance of the recipient. Pressure is applied along the main lines in a regular and rhythmic fashion at points around 5 cm apart, beginning at the origin near the umbilicus and proceeding to the end point. Picking up, where muscle is lifted away from the bone and squeezed hacking, particularly to the calf muscles stretching for joints manipulation of joints, especially those of the fingers and toes.

of Swedish remedial massage (see Chapter 1) from traditional Chinese massage techniques. Further reading on traditional Thai massage can be found in Lidell (1984), Nolan (1989), and Gold (2006).

## HUNA MASSAGE

The ancient cultures from the Hawaii islands are famous for a unique combination of massage techniques and healing traditions known as *Huna massage.* It is based on the life principles in the millennia-old Polynesian philosophy of Huna, which has been described as "Kahuna magic" (Steiger, 1982). This body and mind work was formerly reserved for the shamans (healers) of Polynesia who mastered the wisdom. The fundamental concepts of the Huna tradition are described in Biegler (1999), Feinberg (1990), Hoffman (1982), A. Lawrence (1994), L. Lawrence (1994), and Paltin (1986).

*Huna* is a Hawaiian word that, when split up and put together in different ways, has several meanings: *huna* is "the secret or hidden knowledge"; *hu* is *yang,* the male principle, the giving and active part; *na* is yin, the female principle, the receiving and passive part; *una* is telepathy, a way to communicate; and *hua* is seeds or fruit.

Huna tradition, with the bodywork to balance the male and female principles, aims to cleanse away old patterns and old habits and prepare the soil for new crops. A philosophy that teaches how to "sow in proportion to what is harvested" is a tradition to which many cultural and social groups relate. The seven principles of Huna philosophy are simple, dynamic, proactive, optimistic, and of great current interest. This philosophy clearly illustrates how we create our own experiences and circumstances in life, via our thought patterns and belief systems. It also teaches the concept of changing undesirable patterns of thought and action, so as to inspire an individual's intentions and goals in life. In this way, Huna can be an effective tool to create an increased level of consciousness and personal growth.

Characteristics of the form of massage practiced in the Huna tradition are beauty and rhythm, as it is performed as a dance. The simple dance steps provide the basis for rhythmic movements of the arms, which are meant to feel like waves moving lovingly across the body. The arms being used at full length ensures very good contact. The dance gives a deep feeling of joy and is a formidable grounding whereby the giver and the recipient together have the opportunity to recharge their energy.

The music accompanying the massage is mainly Polynesian—beautiful, cheerful, and stirring. By means of dance, music, and touch, all levels of consciousness are activated: physical, emotional, mental, and spiritual. The massage itself incorporates deep effleurage and kneading along the trunk and limbs, together with passive stretching of the joints, in a manner similar to the application in shiatsu.

Courses teaching Huna massage are designed for people who seek self-development and self-healing and those who want to do professional body and mind work. In Scandinavia, the training is built up in seven modules, each a complete unit. This makes it possible for anyone to take the modules at his or her own pace and as required. In New Zealand and Australia, a module is presented twice a year that has been adjusted to the needs of these countries. Apart from basic instruction in Huna massage and the principles of Huna philosophy, special techniques such as pregnancy massage, joint massage, draining, astral dancing, and body reading are included.

The old Hawaiian traditional method of massage, using the hands and emphasizing special breathing techniques, is combined with release techniques, which include the Eastern philosophies of polarity, energy points, and energy flows (or chakras). The links between the Chinese traditions of maintaining balance in the energy level for optimal health are an integral part of the Huna philosophy. Like many of the techniques described in Chapters 16 and 17, Huna massage aims to enhance energy and teach intuitive guidance in order to train the senses to transform and direct energy.

## REFERENCES

### Acupuncture


Anderson DG, Jamieson JL, Man SC: Analgesic effects of acupuncture on the pain of ice water: a double-blind study, *Can J Psychol* 28:239-244, 1974.

Armstrong ME: Acupuncture, *Am J Nurs* 72(9):1582, 1972.

Baldry PE: *Acupuncture trigger points & musculo-skeletal pain,* New York, 1989, Churchill Livingstone.

Beal MW: Acupuncture and related modalities, part 1: theoretical background, *J Nurse Midwifery* 37(4):254-259, 1992.

Beal MW: Acupuncture and acupressure: applications to women's reproductive health care, *J Nurse Midwifery* 44(3):217-230, 1999.

Calmels P: A scientific perspective on developing acupuncture as a complementary medicine, *Disabil Rehabil* 21(3):129-130; discussion 137-138, 1999.

Chaitow L: *The acupuncture treatment of pain,* Northamptonshire, United Kingdon, 1979, Thorsons.

Chaitow L: *Instant pain control,* Northamptonshire, United Kingdom, 1981, Thorsons.

Cheng X: *Chinese acupuncture and moxibustion,* Beijing, 1987, Foreign Language Press.

David J, Modi S, Aluko AA et al: Chronic neck pain: a comparison of acupuncture treatment and physiotherapy, *Br J Rheumatol* 37(10):1118-1122, 1998.

Filshie J, White A: *Medical acupuncture*, Edinburgh, 1997, Churchill Livingstone,

Fox EJ, Melzack R: Transcutaneous electrical stimulation and acupuncture: comparison of treatment for low back pain, *Pain* 2:141-148, 1976.

Han JS: *The neurochemical basis of pain relief by acupuncture: a collection of papers 1973-1987,* Beijing, 1987, Chinese Medical Science & Technology Press.

He L: Involvement of endogenous opioid peptides in acupuncture analgesia, *Pain* 31(1):91-121, 1987.

Hopwood V: *Acupuncture and related techniques in physical therapy,* New York, 1997, Churchill Livingstone.

Hu J: Acupuncture treatment of common cold, *J Trad Chinese Med* 20(3):227-230, 2000.

Kerr DP, Walsh DM, Baxter GD: A study of the use of acupuncture in physiotherapy, *Complement Ther Med* 9(1):21-27, 2001.

Kerr FW, Wilson PR, Nijensohn DE: Acupuncture reduces the trigeminal evoked response in decerebrate cats, *Exp Neurol* 61:84-95, 1978.

Lao L, Bergman S, Hamilton GR et al: Evaluation of acupuncture for pain control after oral surgery: a placebo-controlled trial, *Arch Otolaryngol Head Neck Surg* 125(5):567-572, 1999.

Lewis L: Acupuncture: another therapeutic choice? *Patient Care* 33(11):149-152, 1999.

Lewit K: The needle effect in the relief of myofascial pain, *Pain* 6:83-90, 1979.

Linde K, Vickers A, Hondras M et al: Systematic reviews of complementary therapies: an annotated bibliography, part 1: acupuncture, *BMC Complement Altern Med* 1:3, 2001.

McDonald J: Missing the point: a discussion of strategies for acupuncture point selection, *Pacific J Oriental Med* 15:26-38, 1999.

Maciocia G: *The foundations of Chinese medicine,* Edinburgh, 1989, Churchill Livingstone.

Melzack R: Myofascial trigger points: relation to acupuncture and mechanisms of pain, *Arch Phys Med Rehab* 62:114-117, 1981.

Melzack R: Hyperstimulation analgesia, *Clin Anaesthesiol* 3(1):81-92, 1985.

Odsberg A, Schill U, Haker E: Acupuncture treatment: side effects and complications reported by Swedish physiotherapists, *Complement Ther Med* 9(1):17-20, 2001.

Rega P: Acupuncture in disaster medicine, *Ann Emerg Med* 34(4, pt 1), 1999.

Romoli M, van der Windt D, Giovanzana P: International research project to devise a protocol to test the effectiveness of acupuncture on painful shoulder, *J Altern Complement Med* 6(3):281-287, 2000.

Ross J: An audit of the impact of introducing microacupuncture into primary care, *Acupunct Med* 19(1):43-45, 2001.

Sheng-Xing M: Neurobiology of acupuncture: toward CAM, *Evid Based Complement Alternat Med* 1(1):41-47, 2004.

Sorgen C: Nontraditional medical treatments grow in popularity as patients and healthcare organizations find new arrangements, *Hosp Top* 76(1):9-14, 1998.

Takeuchi H, Jawad M, Eccles R et al: The effects of nasal massage of the "yingxiang" acupuncture point on nasal airway resistance and sensation of nasal airflow in patients with nasal congestion associated with acute upper respiratory tract infection, *Am J Rhinol* 13(2):77-79, 1999.

Tappan FM, Benjamin P: *Tappen's handbook of healing massage techniques: classic, holistic, and emerging methods,* ed 3, Norwalk, Conn, 1998, Appleton & Lange.

Travell JG, Simons DG: *Myofascial pain and dysfunction: the trigger point manual,* vol I, Baltimore, 1983, Williams & Wilkins.

Travell JG, Simons DG: *Myofascial pain and dysfunction: the trigger point manual,* vol II, Baltimore, 1992, Williams & Wilkins.

Vickers AJ: Can acupuncture have specific effects on health? A systematic review of acupuncture antiemesis trials, *J Royal Soc Med* 89(6):303-311, 1966.

Vickers AJ, Rees RW, Zollman CE et al: Acupuncture for chronic headache in primary care: large, pragmatic, randomised trial, *Br Med J* 328(7442):744, 2004.

Vickers A, Zollman C: ABC of complementary medicine: acupuncture, *Br Med J* 319(7215):973-976, 1999.

Vilholm OJ, Moller K, Jorgensen K et al: Effect of traditional Chinese acupuncture on severe tinnitus: a double-blind, placebo-controlled, clinical investigation with open therapeutic control, *Br J Audiol* 32(3):197-204, 1998.

Wan Q: Auricular-plaster therapy plus acupuncture at zusanli for postoperative recovery of intestinal function, *J Trad Chinese Med* 20(2):134-135n, 2000.

Wedenberg K, Moen B, Norling A et al: A prospective randomized study comparing acupuncture with physiotherapy for low-back and pelvic pain in pregnancy, *Acta Obstet et Gynecol Scand* 79(5):331-335, 2000.

White A, Hayhoe S, Hart A et al: Adverse events following acupuncture: prospective survey of 32 000 consultations with doctors and physiotherapists, *Br Med J* 323(7311):485-486, 2001.

Zhou J, Li Z, Jin P: A clinical study on acupuncture for prevention and treatment of toxic side-effects during radiotherapy and chemotherapy, *J Trad Chinese Med* 19(1)16-21, 1999.

## Acupressure

Agarwal A, Ranjan R, Dhiraaj S et al: Acupressure for prevention of pre-operative anxiety: a prospective, randomised, placebo controlled study, *Anaesthesia* 60(10):978-981, 2005.

Avakyan GN: Pressure and massage therapy to relieve fatigue, *Adv Clin Care* 5(5):10-11, 1990.

Beal MW: Acupuncture and acupressure. Applications to women's reproductive health care, *J Nurse Midwif* 44(3):217-230, 1999.

Bowie RA: Acupressure and prevention of nausea and vomiting, *Br J Anaesthesia* 83(3):542, 1999.

Chen HM, Chang FY, Hsu CT: Effect of acupressure on nausea, vomiting, anxiety and pain among post-cesarean section women in Taiwan, Kaohsiung, *J Med Sci* 21(8):341-350, 2005.

Chen ML, Lin LC, Klu SC et al: The effectiveness of acupressure in improving the quality of sleep of institutionalized residents, *J Gerontol Series A—Biolog Sci Med Sci* 54(8):M389-M394, 1999.

Cummings M: Hand acupressure reduces postoperative vomiting after strabismus surgery (n=50), *Acupunct Med* 19(1):53-54, 2001.

Dibble SL, Chapman L, Mack KA et al: Acupressure for nausea: results of a pilot study, *Oncol Nurs Forum* 27(1):41-47, 2000.

Ernst E: Acupuncture/acupressure for weight reduction? A systematic review, *Wien Klin Wochenschr* 109(2):60-72, 1997.

Harmon D, Ryan M, Kelly A et al: Acupressure and prevention of nausea and vomiting during and after spinal anaesthesia for caesarean section, *Br J Anaesthesia* 84(4):463-467, 2000.

Heinke DP: *Relieving pain with acupressure,* New York, 1998, Sterling.

Hsieh LL, Kuo CH, Lee LH et al: Treatment of low back pain by acupressure and physical therapy: randomised controlled trial, *Br Med J* 25;332(7543):696-700, 2006.

Hoo JJ: Acupressure for hyperemesis gravidarum, *Am J Obstet Gynecol* 176(6):1395-1396, 1997.

Klein J, Griffiths P: Acupressure for nausea and vomiting in cancer patients receiving chemotherapy, *Br J Community Nurs* 9(9):383-388, 2004.

Li YC, Peng C: Treatment of 86 cases of facial spasm by acupuncture and pressure on otopoints, *J Trad Chinese Med* 20(1):33-35, 2000.

Romanchok D: Process acupressure: alternative therapy for the holistic patient, *PT OT Today* 5(32):10-14, 1997.

Shenkman Z, Holzman RS, Kim C et al: Acupressure-acupuncture antiemetic prophylaxis in children undergoing tonsillectomy, *Anesthesiology* 90(5):1311-136, 1999.

Steele NM, French F, Gatherer-Boyles CJ et al: Effect of acupressure by Sea-Bands on nausea and vomiting of pregnancy, *J Obstetr Gynecol Neonatal Nurs* 30(1):61-70, 2001.

Stern RM, Jokerst MD, Muth ER et al: Acupressure relieves the symptoms of motion sickness and reduces abnormal gastric activity, *Altern Ther Health Med* 7(4):91-94, 2001.

Tsay SL, Wang JC, Lin KC et al: Effects of acupressure therapy for patients having prolonged mechanical ventilation support, *J Adv Nurs* 52(2):142-150, 2005.

Weaver MT: Acupressure: an overview of theory and application, *Nurse Pract* 10(8):38-42, 1985.

Yip YB, Tse SH: An experimental study on the effectiveness of acupressure with aromatic lavender essential oil for sub-acute, non-specific neck pain in Hong Kong, *Complement Ther Clin Pract* 12(1):18-26, 2006.

Youngs PJ: Acupressure and prevention of nausea and vomiting, *Br J Anaesthesia* 85(5):807-808, 2000.

## Shiatsu

Beresford-Cooke C: *Shiatsu theory and practice: a comprehensive text for the student and professional,* New York, 1998, Churchill Livingstone.

Booth B: Shiatsu, *Nurs Times* 89(46):38-40, 1993.

Box D: Made in Japan, *Nurs Times,* 80(17)39-40, 1984.

Dahong Z: Skillful hands bring relief, *World Health* 15, May 1984.

Finger G: Shiatsu, *Alterna Health Practit* 4(2):147-148, 1998.

Formby J: Shiatsu massage for careers, *Complement Ther Med* 5(1):47-48, 1997.

Greim R: Shiatsu and Jin Shindo: the balance of yin and yang, *DNA Reporter* 24(2):1999.

Saito H: Preventing and resolving post-laparotomy intestinal obstruction: an effective shiatsu method, *Am J Chinese Med* 28(1):1441-145, 2000.
Hare ML: Shiatsu acupressure in nursing practice, *Holistic Nurs Pract* 2(3):68-74, 1988.
Harris PE, Pooley N: What do shiatsu practitioners treat? A nationwide survey, *Complement Ther Med* 6(1):30-35, 1998.
Herskovitz SM: Shiatsu massage-induced injury of the median recurrent motor branch, *Muscle Nerve* 15(10):1215, 1992.
Hunter C: Shiatsu therapy in labour, *Australian Nurs* J 6(8):36, 1999.
Lidell L: *The book of massage: the complete step-by-step guide to Eastern and Western techniques,* London, 1984, Ebury Press.
Nolan B: Sorting out your yin and yang, *Nurs Times* 85(35):58-60, 1989.
Pooley N: The pinning down of Shiatsu, or what I learned from my research experience, *Complement Ther Med* 6(1):45-46, 1998.
Stevensen C: The role of Shiatsu in palliative care, *Complement Ther Nurs Midwif* 1(2):51-58, 1995.
Tappan FM, Benjamin P: *Tappen's handbook of healing massage techniques: classic, holistic, and emerging methods,* ed 3, Norwalk, Conn, 1998, Appleton & Lange.
Tsuboi K, Tsuboi: Retinal and cerebral artery embolism after "shiatsu" on the neck, *Stroke* 32(10):2441, 2001.
Woodhouse D: On-site seated acupressure massage, *Posit Health* 32:55-56, 1998.
Yates S: Shiatsu and massage in pregnancy and childbirth, *Posit Health* 41:39-41, 1999.

## Traditional Oriental/Chinese Massage

Cheng B: Treatment of protrusion of the lumbar intervertebral disc by massotherapy, *J Trad Chinese Med* 21(2):110, 2001.
Ehling D: Oriental medicine: an introduction, *Altern Ther Health Med* 7(4):71-82, 2001.
Hao Z: Introduction to the Eastern comprehension of massage, *J Aust Traditional Med Soc* 3(1), 1997.
Hong Z: Curative effects of Chinese massage on 50 muscular torticollis children, *Shanxi Nurs J* 11(3), 1997.
James W: A Chinese massage adventure, *J Aust Trad Med Soc* 2(4):127-129, 1996.
Jia LH: *Pointing therapy,* Shandong, 1984, Shandong Science & Technology Press.
Li Y, Zhong S: Spinal manipulation in China, *J Manipulative Physiol Ther* 21(6):399-401, 1998.
Puustjarvi A, Pontinen G: The effects of massage in patients with chronic tension headache, *Acupunct Electro-Thera Res* 15(2):159-162, 1990.
Raclariu A, Alecu S, Loghin M et al: A consultation system integrating Chinese medical practice in herbal therapy, acupuncture and acupressure, *Stud Health Technol Inform* 43(pt A):285-289, 1997.
Serizawa K: *Massage,* Tokyo, 1973, Japan Publications.
Wright CK: Massage by nurses in the United States and the People's Republic of China: a comparison, *J Transcult Nurs* 7(1):24-27, 1995.
Zumo L: Cases of frozen shoulder treated by manipulation and massage, *J Traditional Chin Med* 235(4):213-215, 1984.

## Traditional Thai Massage

Gold R: *Thai massage: a traditional medical technique,* ed 2, St Louis, 2006, Elsevier.
Lidell L: *The book of massage: the complete step-by-step guide to Eastern and Western techniques,* London, 1984, Ebury Press.
Nolan B: Sorting out your yin and yang, *Nurs Times* 85(35):58-60, 1989.
Tapanya S: *Traditional Thai massage,* Bangkok, 1993, Duang Kamol.

## Huna Massage

Biegler C: Kahi loa: traditional Hawaiian healing massage, *Posit Health* 45:43-49, 1999.
Feinberg R: Spiritual and natural etiologies on a Polynesian outlier in Papua New Guinea, *Soc Sci Med* 30(3):311-323, 1990.
Hoffman E: *Huna: a beginner's guide,* Atglen, Penn, 1982, Shiffer.
Lawrence A: *Healing with Huna,* 1994, ALLME.
Lawrence L: *Huna: ancient miracle healing practices and the future of medicine,* 1994, Zinn.
Paltin S: Huna of Hawaii: a system of psychological therapy and practice, *Hawaii Med J* 45(6):213-218, 1986.
Steiger B: *Kahuna magic,* Rockport, Mass, 1982, Para Research.

# Appendix

## Closed-Chest (External) Cardiac Massage

External cardiac massage (also known as closed-chest cardiac massage) is included here because it is a technique that all persons involved in direct patient care of any type should know for emergency treatment of cardiac arrest. The external cardiac compression is part of the concept of cardiopulmonary resuscitation (CPR). The technique somewhat resembles the shaking and vibration procedures described in Chapters 4 and 10; however, it is performed only over the sternum and much more slowly.

If a quick check for the presence of the pulse at the carotid arteries on both sides of the trachea confirms that a patient's heart has stopped, the patient should be placed supine on a solid support such as the floor or a firm plinth or stretcher (whichever is quickest). The patient's head should then be tilted backward to ensure an open airway. This can usually be achieved by placing one hand under the neck and lifting the cervical spine upward (Figure A-1), allowing the head and neck to fall into the extended position (head tilt, chin lift). If the airway is obstructed internally (perhaps by the tongue), it must be cleared before any other procedures are performed. The reader is referred to national or local Heart Association guidelines for currently recommended procedures for clearing an obstructed airway.

Before compression and ventilation can begin, the CPR provider must determine where to place his or her hands on the patient's chest. One of several ways to do this is to place the index finger of one hand on the patient's xiphoid process (see Chapter 2). Two fingers of the other hand are then placed next to this finger (Figure A-2). The first finger is removed and the flat hand placed on the chest next to the two fingers, on the same side as the patient's head. It is important that *no pressure* be applied to the ribs or abdominal contents. Pressure is applied directly to the lower third of the sternum.

Because the sternum is a relatively narrow structure, the heel of the palm of only one hand is positioned in direct contact with the skin while the other hand is used to reinforce it (Figure A-3). The rescuer's fingers are spread and raised so that pressure is applied *only to the sternum and not to the ribs or abdomen.* Vertical pressure sufficient to depress the sternum 1 inch (2.5 cm) or a little more is applied and quickly released. If the patient is a child, one hand may be used with less pressure. If an infant (less than 1 year old) is being resuscitated, the fingertips may be used, and much less pressure, at a rate of at least 100 times per minute.

It is assumed in CPR training that respiratory suppport will be required with all cardiac arrests. Therefore a single provider of CPR must perform a basic cycle of both circulatory support and artificial ventilation. The provider applies a basic cycle of chest compression at approximately 100 strokes per minute, giving two quick breaths to the patient after each set of 30 compressions. After approximately five complete cycles (30 compressions and two breaths per cycle), the patient should be reassessed to determine whether a pulse is present, in which case the CPR ceases immediately. When two providers are available, one performs the compression and the other delivers ventilation. This regimen of CPR can be applied to children and adults. During the ventilation phase, the patient's nostrils may be lightly squeezed to seal off the nasal passages during the inflation cycle of the ventilation (see Figure A-I).

In all situations, an advanced life support or emergency medical team must be summoned at the earliest moment, and CPR efforts should be continued until the team arrives or until effective circulation and ventilation have been

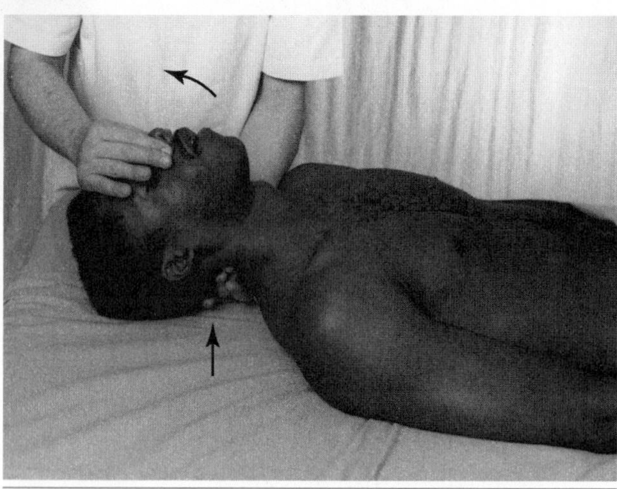

**Figure A-1 Hand Positions to Ensure An Open Airway for Artificial Respiration**

An open airway is ensured by lifting the cervical spine upward while the patient is lying supine. This causes the head to fall into extension (head tilt, chin lift) and prevents blockage of the airway, provided there is no internal blockage. The nostrils may be squeezed together lightly to close them off when blowing into the patient's lungs.

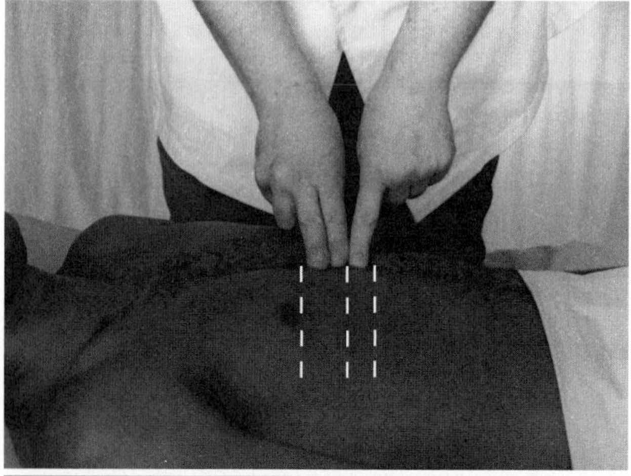

**Figure A-2 Locating the Area over the Sternum Where Pressure Is Applied during External Cardiac Compression**

The index finger of the hand farthest from the patient's head locates the xiphoid process as the other hand is placed on the sternum, two finger breadths from the xiphoid.

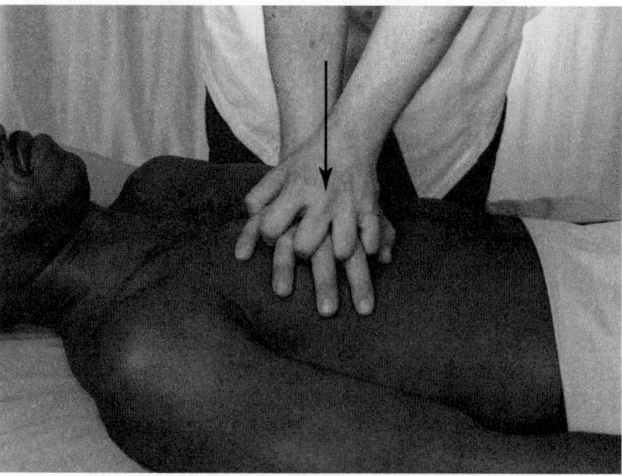

**Figure A-3 Hand Positions for External Cardiac Compression**

In an adult, pressure is applied using the heel of the palm of one hand reinforced by the other. Sufficient pressure is applied to displace the sternum by approximately 1 inch (2.5 cm). Pressure must be applied *only* to the sternum to avoid damaging the ribs or abdominal organs. A single-handed technique may be used to deliver cardiac compression to a child.

restored. When the patient is a child or when cardiac arrest is associated with hypothermia, prolonged resuscitation efforts may be justified and should be continued even after long periods of unconsciousness.

Unless much care is taken to perform these procedures properly, fractures of the ribs and sternum, as well as laceration and rupture of soft tissues, such as liver, spleen, pancreas, lungs, and blood vessels, can easily occur. Although there are, of course, individual variations, most medical standards for CPR and emergency cardiac care recommend that all health care workers involved in any capacity in direct patient care be certified in basic life support techniques and be well-informed about the CPR plan of the facility in which they work. It is usual, nowadays, for a basic CPR certificate to be valid for 1 year. For certification, a qualified CPR instructor must verify that the person has demonstrated knowledge of when to perform CPR. Sufficient psychomotor skills for correct timing and technique for both one- and two-person rescues must also be demonstrated. The practice necessary to develop these skills and the repeated demonstration of them should be performed on a training manikin under the supervision of a certified CPR instructor.

# Index

Page numbers followed by *b* indicate boxes; *f*, figures; *t*, tables.


**A**

Abdomen
  alternate squeeze kneading over, 169-170, 169f
  in baby and infant massage, 283, 286f
  deep stroking to, 167, 167f, 168f, 170
  local massage to, 210, 210f
  superficial stroking to, 167
  viscera, 128-129
Achilles tendon, digital stroking to, 158, 159f
Acromion process, 38, 39f
Active trigger points, 298-301
Activity, physical, effects of massage on, 132
Acupressure, 310-314, 311f, 312f, 313f, 314t
Adipose (fat) tissue, effects of massage on, 130
Airway clearance, in respiratory condition, 226, 226f
Amma massage, 316-317
Anatomical position, 37
Anconeus, massage of, 191, 192f
Ankle
  anterior structures of, 44-46, 45f
  in baby and infant massage, 283, 287f
  chronic edema in, focal massage sequence for, 217t
  finger pad kneading around, 84f
  transverse frictions to, 101f
Anxiety, effects of massage on, 131-132
Arm
  anatomical landmarks of, 39, 39f
  in baby and infant massage, 281, 285f
  effleurage to, 78f
  left, 151t, 160-161, 160f
  palmar kneading to, 82f, 161, 161f
  relaxed passive movements to, 113-114f
  right, 151t, 188, 191, 193-194f, 194
  stroking to, 73f
  wringing to the muscles of, 89f
Assisted passive movement, 104
Auriculotherapy, 302
Autonomic reflex, 237, 237f

**B**

Babies, massage for, 279-288
Back
  alternate palmar kneading over, 175
  anatomical landmarks of, 41-42, 41f, 42f
  in baby and infant massage, 285, 287f
  deep palmar stroking to, 170, 171-172f
  effleurage to, 76-77f
  general massage sequence for, 151t
  local massage sequence for, 185t
  palmar kenading to, 82f
  stroking to, 72f, 206-210, 208f
  superficial stroking to, 170, 170f, 175
Beating strokes, 93, 94f
Biceps, massage of, 191, 193f
Bicipital aponeurosis, 39, 39f
Blood, effects of massage on, 119-120, 121-122
Body therapies, 294-295
Bolster, in massage, 54, 56f
Bone, effects of massage on, 125
Boric acid powder, in massage, 21
Brachialis, massage of, 191, 193f
Breathing, deep, in respiratory conditions, 233
Buttocks
  in baby and infant massage, 285-286, 288f
  kneading to, 175

**C**

Calf muscles, kneading to, 156, 156f
Cellulite, effects of massage on, 130-131, 131f
Cheeks, palmar kneading to, 180, 180f
Chest. *See also* Chest wall
  in baby and infant massage, 283, 286f
  clapping technique to, 231f
  massage sequence for, 163-164, 164f
Chest *(Continued)*
  physical therapy for, 225, 226b
  superficial stroking to, 163-164, 164f
Chest wall
  lateral
    vibration to, 98f
    wringing to, 89f
  posterior
    clapping over, 94f
    skin rolling to, 90f
Chin
  deep stroking to, 180, 181f
  thumb pad kneading to, 180, 181f
Chinese massage, 316-317
Circular frictions, 102-103, 102f, 103f
Circular kneading, 80-81, 81f
Circulation, effects of pétrissage on, 90
Clapping (cupping), 92, 92f, 227, 230, 230f, 231f
Colon
  deep stroking over, 169, 169f
  dysfunction, focal massage sequence for, 222-223, 223f, 223t
  kneading massage over, 169, 169f, 211, 212f
  palmar kneading over, 167, 168f, 169
  stroking over, 211, 211f
Comfort, patient positioning for, 61, 63
Complementary/alternative medicine (CAM), 294-307
Complete decongestive therapy (CDT), 245
Compression kneading, 80-81, 82f
Compression therapy, 259-260, 261b, 262b
Connective tissue massage (CTM), 7, 235-243
Continuous passive motion (CPM), 105
Contrast relaxation method, 64, 64b
Coracobrachialis, massage of, 191, 193f
Coughing, in respiratory conditions, 233
Craniosacral therapy (CST), 305-307, 307b
Creams, in hand preparation, 52-53
Cutaneous scar tissue, 219-221
Cyriax friction massage, 99-104

**D**

Decongestive therapy, 250
Deep frictions, 99-104, 104t, 146-147
Delayed onset muscular soreness (DOMS), 267-269, 268b
Deltoid muscle group, massage of, 188, 190-191f, 191
Denervated muscle, 123-125
Depletive massage, 215-217, 216f
Diagnostic stroke, 238, 238f
Diffuse scars, 221, 221t
Digital kneading, 81, 83
Direction, of massage, 18-19, 65
Dorsum
  of foot, 157, 157f, 158f
  of hand, 161, 162f, 195-196, 196f
Draping, of patients, 55-57, 57-61f
Dry massage, 21
Duration, of massage, 22-23, 65-66
Dying, ancient versus modern care of, 290-291

**E**

Eastern massage systems. *See* Massage, Eastern systems of
Edema, chronic, 216, 216f, 217t, 218t
Effleurage, 146. *See also* Stroking
  contraindications to use of, 80t
  description of, 14-15, 17-18t, 75
  history of, 14-15
  in massage, 75, 76-77f, 77, 78-79f
Elbow, finger pad kneading to, 83f
Elderly, massage for, 291-292
Electroacupuncture, 310
Equipment, for massage, 53-55, 54b, 54f, 55f, 56f
Erector spinae muscles
  deep stroking to, 175, 175f
  digital kneading to, 175
  local massage to, 206-207, 208f
Ethical issues, in soft tissue manipulation, 49-50
Evaluation, of lymphedema, 249-250
External occipital protuberance, 37, 38f
Extremities. *See under* specific body parts

**F**

Face
  in baby and infant massage, 281, 284f
  local massage to, 211, 212-213f, 214
  superficial stroking to, 151, 176 , 177f, 181
Fatty tissue, effects of massage on, 130
Femoral condyle, lateral and medial, 44f
Femoral triangle, 43, 43f
Finger pad clapping, 92, 93f, 94f
Finger pad kneading, 81, 83, 83f, 84f
Finger
  clapping technique to, 230
  in connective tissue massage, 239-240, 239f, 240f
  local massage to dorsum of, 195, 196f, 197
  local massage to palmar surface of, 197f
  thumb pad kneading to, 163, 163f
Fingertips technique, in connective tissue massage, 238-239, 238f, 240f
Flat-handed kneading, 80-81, 82f
Focal massage, 149
Focal massage sequences, 70, 215
Foot
  anatomical landmarks of, 44-46, 45f
  areas used in reflexology, 302, 303f, 304
  in baby and infant massage, 283, 285, 287f
  chronic edema in, focal massage sequence for, 217t
  knuckle kneading to, 87f
  left, 160
  right, 157-158, 157f, 158f, 159f, 160, 203-206, 205f, 206f
  thumb pad kneading to, 85-86f
Forearm
  anatomical landmarks of, 39-40, 39f
  chronic edema in, focal massage sequence for, 218t
  general massage sequence for, 151t
  palmar kneading to, 161, 161f, 162f
  thumb pad kneading to, 85f
  transverse frictions to, 102f
Forehead
  deep stroking to, 176-177, 178f
  thumb pad kneading to, 176, 178f
Frequency, of massage, 23, 65-66
Friction, 7, 14
  circular, 102-103, 102f, 103f
  deep, 99-104, 104t, 146-147
  description of, 14, 16-17t
  transverse, 100-102, 100f, 101f, 102f, 147

**G**

General massage, definition of, 149
General sequence, in complementary/alternative medicine, 305
Gluteal muscles
  alternate palmar kneading to, 174, 174f
  massage to, 198, 198f
  reinforced kneading to, 175, 175f

**H**

Hacking strokes, 93, 95, 95f
Hair powder, in massage, 21
Hamstring muscle group, local massage to, 198, 199f
Hand
  anatomical landmarks of, 40-41
  areas of hands used in, 52b
  areas used in reflexology, 302, 303f
  in baby and infant massage, 281, 283, 285f
  chronic edema in, focal massage sequence for, 218f
  local massage to the dorsal aspect of, 196f
  massage to palmar surface of, 195f
  preparation of, 50-52, 52f
  thumb pad kneading to, 85f, 161, 162f

Hard tissue, classification of, 70t
Head
  anatomical structures of, 37, 38f, 50b
  in baby and infant massage, 281, 284f
  general massage sequence for, 152t
  local massage sequence for, 190t
Head's zones, in connective tissue massage, 235-237, 238f
Healing, effects of massage on, 122
Hematoma, 217-219
  intermuscluar, 218-219, 218f, 219f
  intramuscular, 218f, 219, 219f
Hips
  anatomical landmarks of, 42
  general massage sequence for, 151t
Hoffa system, of local massage, 184-188
Huna massage, 318
Hyperkeratosis, 250, 250f
Hypothenar eminence, 163, 163f, 194, 195f

I

Immune system, effects of massage on, 129
Infants, massage for, 279-288
Infraorbital ridge, deep stroking to, 179, 179f
Injury
  to muscle, 123
  sports, 269-275
Intermittent positive pressure breathing (IPPB) devices, 232, 233
Interossei, massage to, 194, 195f

J

Jaw
  deep stroking to, 180, 181f
  thumb pad kneading to, 180, 181f
Joint play, 104
Joints, effects of massage on, 125
Jungular veins, deep stroking over, 165, 166f, 167, 179-180, 181

K

Kneading. *See also* Massage; Stroking
  characteristics of, 79-81, 81-83f, 83
  compression, 80-81, 82f
  description and definition of, 15t, 79-81, 83
  digital, 81, 83
  finger pad, 81, 83, 83f, 84f
  flat-handed, 80-81, 82f
  history of, 14
  knuckle, 83, 87f
  palmar, 80-81, 82f
  reinforced, 83, 87f
  single-handed, 186, 187f
  squeeze, 81
  thumb pad, 83, 85-86f, 153, 155f
  two-handed, 186, 188f
  two-handed digital, 186-187, 188f
Knee
  anatomical landmarks of, 43-44, 44f
  finger pad kneading around, 84f
  transverse frictions to, 101f
Knuckle kneading, 83, 87f

L

Latissimus dorsi muscle, 42, 42f
  local massage to, 207-208, 209f, 210
Laying on of hands, 133
Leg. *See also* Thigh
  anterior structures of, 44, 45f
  in baby and infant massage, 283, 285, 287f
  deep stroking to, 155f, 157, 160
  palmar kneading to, 82f, 156, 156f
  pick up to muscles in, 87f
  posterior structures of, 46-47, 47f, 48f
  relaxed passive movements to, 108-112f
  right, 200, 202-203, 202f, 204-205f
  stroking to, 73f
  superficial stroking to, 153, 155f, 160
  thumb pad kneading to, 85f, 153, 155f
  two-handed digital kneading to, 188f
  wringing to the muscles of, 89f
LI-4, acupressure technique to, 313, 313f
Ligament adhesion, focal massage sequence for, 221-222, 222f, 222t
Linear scars
  in skin, focal massage sequence for, 221t
  thumb pad kneading for, 220f, 221f
Local massage, 70, 149, 184
Local massage sequence
  Hoffa system of, 184-188

Local massage sequence *(Continued)*
  for lower limbs, 184t
  for posterior trunk and pelvis, 185t
  for upper limbs, 185t
Lower limbs. *See also under* specific body parts
  anatomical structures of, 51b
  in baby and infant massage, 283, 285, 287f
  general massage sequence for, 150t
  local massage sequence for, 184t, 189t
  muscles, wringing to, 89f
  passive movements of, 233
  relaxed passive movements to, 108-112f
  short and long CTM strokes to, 242-243f
Lubricants
  in hand preparation, 52-53
  in massage, 20-21
Lumbar region
  palmar kneading over, 173-174, 173f
  palmar stroking to, 174, 174f
  reinforced kneading to, 87f
Lumbricles, massage to, 194, 195f
Lungs, effects of massage on, 129
Lymphedema, 245-263
Lymph fluid mobilization, in lymphedema, 240-251
Lymph system
  effects of massage on, 120-121
  function of, 246-247, 246f, 247f, 248f
  mobilizing stagnant tissue fluid through, 252-253, 253f, 254f, 255, 255f, 256f, 257-259, 257f, 258f, 259f

M

Malleoli, deep digital stroking around, 158, 159f
Manipulations
  pressure, 146
  in specialized passive movement, 105
Massage. *See also* Connective tissue massage; Kneading; Stroking
  complementary/alternative medicine in, 294-307, 305
    craniosacral therapy as, 305-307
    general sequence as, 305
    myofascial release as, 295-297, 297f
    point percussion therapy as, 304-305
    reflexology as, 301-302, 303f, 304
    rolfing structural integration as, 304
    trigger point stimulation as, 297-301, 298-299f, 300f
  component of, 15, 18-21, 24-34t, 63b
    comfort and support as, 61, 63
    direction as, 18-19, 65
    duration as, 22-23, 65-66
    frequency as, 23, 65-66
    patient position as, 21-23
    pressure as, 19-20, 65
    relaxation as, 63-65, 63b, 64b
    signs and symptoms changes as, 66
    therapist position as, 21-23
  contraindications to, 66-67, 133, 135-136, 137-138t
  definitions of, 6
  description of techniques (strokes), 7, 11-12, 12-13t, 14-15, 15t, 16-18t
  dry, 21
  Eastern systems of
    acupressure as, 310-314, 311f, 312f, 313f, 314t
    Chinese, 316-317
    Huna, 318
    shiatsu as, 314-316, 315f, 316b, 316t
    Thai, 317-318, 317b
  effects of
    mechanical, 117, 118-119, 119b
    physiological, 119-131, 119b
    psychological, 131-133, 131b
    therapeutic, 133, 134-135b
  focal, 149
  general, 149
  hacking in, 93, 95, 95f
  history of, 3-6
  local, 70, 149, 184
  local sequences
    Hoffa system, 184-188
  media (lubricant) as, 20-21
  movement in
    friction as, 14, 16-17t
    kneading as, 14, 15t
    prétissage as, 7, 11, 12-13t
    stroking and effleurage as, 14-15, 17-18t
  in palliative care, 290-292
  precautions in, 136, 139b
  rate and rhythm as, 20, 65

Massage *(Continued)*
  recreational, 5, 70
  requirements for
    equipment as, 53-55, 54b, 54f, 55f, 56f
    ethics as, 49-49
    hand preparation as, 50-52, 52b, 52f
    lubricants as, 52-53
    surface anatomy knowledge as, 50
  sequence for, 183
  signs and symptoms changes, 66
  sports, 132, 266-277, 267b
  terminology of, 6-7
    chronology of, 8-11t
  therapeutic, 5, 70, 149
  therapist position as, 21-22
  wedge, 54, 56f
Mechanical effects, of massage, 117, 118-119, 119b
Mesodermal somites, 236
Metabolism, effects of massage on, 122
Metacarpophalangeal (MCP) joints, 41, 161, 162f, 163
Muscle
  denervated, 123-125
  dysfunction, focal massage sequence for, 223-224
  effects of massage on tissue, 122-125
  effects of pétrissage on, 90
  focal massage sequence of, 221-222, 222f
  injured, 123
  normal, 123
  pathologic conditions of, 123
  tibial, anterior, thumb pad kneading over, 153, 155f
  tissues of, effects of massage on, 122-125
  tone, 123
Myofascial release techniques, 295-297, 297f
Myofascial trigger point (MTrP), 297-299

N

Neck
  anatomical structures of, 37-38, 38f, 50b
  deep stroking to, 164, 164f, 167
  digital kneading from sternum to, 165, 165f
  digital stroking to, 165, 166f
  effleurage to, 79f
  general massage sequence for, 151t, 152t
  local massage sequence for, 190t
  relaxed passive movements to, 106-107f
  stroking to, 74f
Nervous system, effects of massage on, 125-126
Nose, thumb pad kneading to, 177, 178f

O

Oils, in hand preparation, 53

P

Pain, effects of massage on, 126-128, 132
Palliative care, massage in, 290-292
Palmar kneading, 80-81, 82f. *See also under* body regions
Palpation, 145
Paraspinal muscles
  circular frictions to, 103f
  massage to, 206, 208f
Passive accessory joint movements, 104
Passive physiological movements, 104
Patella, stroking around, 156, 157f
Patient
  draping and positioning of, 55-57, 56b, 57-61f
  lymphedema and education of, 260, 263, 263b
  position of, 21-23
  relaxation of, 63-65, 63b, 64b
  with terminal cancer, massage techniques for, 292
Pediatric patients, postural drainage positions for, 229f
Pelvis
  anatomical structures of, 50b
  general massage sequence for, 151t
  local massage sequence for, 185t, 189t
Percussion
  classification of, 91-93, 95-97
  contraindications to, 97t
  manipulations in, 91-93, 95-97
  techniques, 227, 230-232
  vibration manipulations in, 146
Peroneal muscles, 44
Pétrissage. *See also* Stroke; Stroking
  contraindications to, 91, 91t
  description of, 7, 11-12, 12-13t
  effects of, 90-91
  evaluation of, 146

Pétrissage *(Continued)*
history of, 7, 11-12
indications for, 91
kneading as, 79-81, 83-84, 86, 146
picking up as, 83-84, 86, 87f, 88
primary effects of, 90-91
skin rolling as, 88, 90, 90f
therapeutic uses of, 91
wringing as, 88, 89f
Physical activity, effects of massage on, 132
Physiological effects of massage
on blood, 119-120, 121-122
on cellulite, 130-131, 131f
on immune system, 129
on lungs, 129
on lymphatic system, 120-121
on metabolism and healing, 122
on nervous system, 125-126
on pain, 126-128
on skin, 129-130
on soft tissue manipulation, 119b
on tissues
adipose (fat), 130
muscles, 122-125
Picking up, 83-84, 86, 87f, 88
Pillow, prone, in massage, 53-54, 55f
Point hacking, 95-96, 96f
Point percussion therapy, in massage, 304-305
Popliteal fossa, 46, 46f
Popliteal space, deep stroking to, 156
Position
of patient, 21-22, 55-57, 56b, 57- 61f
of therapist, 21-22
Postural drainage, 226-227, 228f, 229f, 230t
Pounding, 95-97, 96f
Powder
in hand preparation, 52
use in massage, 21
Precautions, in massage, 136, 139b
Pressure
in massage, 19-20, 65
in stroking, 19-20, 65
Prone pillow, in massage, 53-54, 55f
Psychological effects, of massage, 131-133, 131b, 275
Pump stroke, in lymphedema, 251, 251f

Q

Quadriceps muscle group, local massage to, 201f

R

Rate, of massage, 20, 65
Recreational massage, 5, 70
Reflexology, in massage, 301-302, 303f, 304
Reflex stroking, 21
Reflex zones, in connective tissue massage, 235-237
Reinforced kneading, 83, 87f
Relaxation
as component of massage, 63-65
environmental factors promoting, 64b
factors inhibiting, 63b
for patients with respiratory condition, 225-226
physical, promoting, 131-132
Relaxed passive movements, 69, 104-105, 106-114f, 112, 115, 115t
Rhythm, of massage, 20, 65
Rib-springing technique, 232
Right lower lobe, clapping to, 231f
Risk reduction practices, for lymphedema, 263b
Rolfing, in massage, 304
Rolling, skin, 88, 90, 90f, 146

S

Sacro-occipital technique (SOT), 306
Sacrum, thumb pad kneading over, 174, 174f
Safety valve insufficiency, 247
Scalp, finger pad kneading over, 181
Scapular muscles, local massage to, 207, 209f
Scapular region, kneading over, 173, 173f
Scarpa's triangle, 43
Sexual arousal, effects of massage on, 132
Shaking, in massage, 98-99, 99t, 232
Shiatsu, 314-316, 315f, 316b, 316t
Shoulder
anatomical landmarks of, 38-39, 38f
deep stroking to, 164, 164f, 165, 165f
digital kneading from sternum to, 165, 165f
effleurage to, 79f
finger pad kneading from temples to, 179180f
Skin, massage of
effects on, 129-130
focal sequence, 221t
for lymphedema, 250
rolling of, 88, 90, 90f, 146
Soap, in hand preparation, 53
Soft tissue
classification of, 70t
classifications of hard tissues and, 70t
in complementary/alternative medicine, 294-307
manipulation, description and types of, 69, 70b
massage of, 5
Spine, cervical, finger pad kneading from temple to, 179, 179f
Sports massage, 132, 266-277, 267b
Spray-and-stretch technique, 301
Squeeze kneading, 81
Standing circles strokes, 251, 251f
Sternocleidomastoid muscle, 37, 38f
Stimulation techniques, 299-3--301, 300f
Stroke
clapping, 92, 92f
classification of, 70, 71t
direction of, 65
effleurage as, 75, 76f, 77, 78-79f
hacking, 93, 95, 95f
kneading as, 79-81, 81-83f, 83
long, 239-240, 241f
for lymphedema patients, 251-252, 251f, 252f
percussion manipulations as, 91-93, 95-97
pétrissage as, 7, 11-12, 79-81, 81-87f, 91
picking up as, 83-84, 86, 87f, 88
pounding, 95-97, 96f
pressure of, 65
shaking as, 98-99
short, 239-240, 241f
skin rolling as, 88, 90, 90f
stroking as, 71, 72-74f, 74-75
tapotement as, 91-93, 95-97
vibration as, 97-99, 98f
wringing as, 88, 89f
Stroking. *See also* Kneading; Massage
contraindications to use of, 75t
deep, 71, 72-74f, 146
in Hoffa system, 185-186
definition of, 71
description of, 14-15, 17-18t
history of, 14-15
manipulations in, 71, 72-74f, 74-75, 76-79f, 77, 79
rate of movement in, 71
reflex, 21
superficial, 71, 146
in Hoffa system, 185-186
whole-body, in baby and infant, 280-281, 281-283f
St-36, acupressure technique to, 313, 313f
Subcutaneous tissues, effects of pétrissage on, 91
Suckling massage, 286
Support, patient positioning for, 61, 63
Supraorbital ridge, deep stroking to, 177, 179f
Surface anatomy, knowledge of, 50
Swan feathers, in massage, 21
Symptoms, changes in, 66

T

Tapotement, in massage, 91-93, 95-97
Tendon
Achilles, digital stroking to, 158, 159f
focal massage sequence for, 221-222, 222f, 222t
Tension, effects of massage on, 131-132
Tensor fasciae latae muscle, massage to, 200f
Thai massage, 317-318, 317b
Therapeutic effects, of massage, 133
Therapeutic exercises, for lymphedema, 260, 263t
Therapeutic massage, 5, 70, 149
Therapeutic touch, 5, 132, 133, 291
Therapist
body mechanics of, 57, 59, 61, 62f, 63f
position of, 21-23
Thigh
anterior muscles, 199-200, 201f, 202f
beating to, 94f
hacking to, 95f
pounding to, 96f
structures of, 42-43, 43f
deep stroking to, 153, 160
finger pad clapping to, 93f
left, 150t, 160
palmar kneading to, 152-153, 153f 154f
posterior structures of, 46-47, 46f, 47f
right
local massage to, 58f, 198-199
massage sequence for, 150t, 152-153
superficial stroking to, 152, 152f
two-handed kneading to, 188f
Thoracic region, palmar kneading over, 173-174, 173f
Thumb circles stroke, for lymphedema, 252, 252f
Thumb pad kneading. *See* Kneading, thumb pad
Thumb, local massage to dorsum of, 195, 196f, 197
Tibial muscles, anterior, thumb pad kneading over, 153, 155f
Tibial tuberosity, 44, 44f
Tissues
excitable and nonexcitable, 118t
soft and hard, classification of, 70t
Toes, 196f, 206
Transverse frictions, 100-102, 100f, 101f, 102f, 147
Trapezius
deep stroking to, 171, 173, 173f, 176
finger pad kneading to, 170-171, 172f
local massage to, 207, 209f
superficial stroking to, 176
Treatment tables, for massage, 53-54, 54b, 54f
Treatment technique, in connective tissue massage, 238
Triceps, massage for, 191, 192f
Trigger point stimulation, 297-301, 298-299f, 300f
Trunk
anatomical structures of, 50b
general massage sequence for, 151t
local massage sequence for, 185t, 189t
Tsubo therapy, 315
Turn stroke, for lymphedema, 251-252, 252f

U

Ulna, styloid process of the, 39f
Ulnar border
hacking to, 95
of right hand, massage to, 194-195, 195f
Unction, 20
Upper limbs. *See also under* specific body parts
anatomical structures of, 51b
in baby and infant massage, 281, 283, 285f
general massage sequence for, 151t
general massage sequences for, 160-161, 160f, 161f, 162f, 163, 163f
local massage sequence for, 185t, 189t
muscles, wringing to, 89f
relaxed passive movements to, 113-114f
short and long CTM strokes to, 242-243f

V

Vertebra prominens, 40, 41f
Vibration
contraindications to, 99t
in respiratory conditions, 232, 232f
technique of, 97-99, 98f, 146
Viscera, effects of massage on, 128-129
Volumetric method, for lymphedema, 240

W

Water, hot, in hand preparation, 53
Wedge, in massage, 54, 56f
Wellness, effects of massage on, 132-133
Whole-hand kneading, 80-81, 82f
Wound care, for lymphedema, 250
Wringing, in massage, 88, 89f
Wrist
anatomical landmarks of, 40, 40f
transverse frictions to, 102f

# TRY IT NOW!

**Perfect your timing and technique with the companion DVD**

Use the enclosed DVD to see how to perform techniques, including all the elements of massage you can't learn from a book!

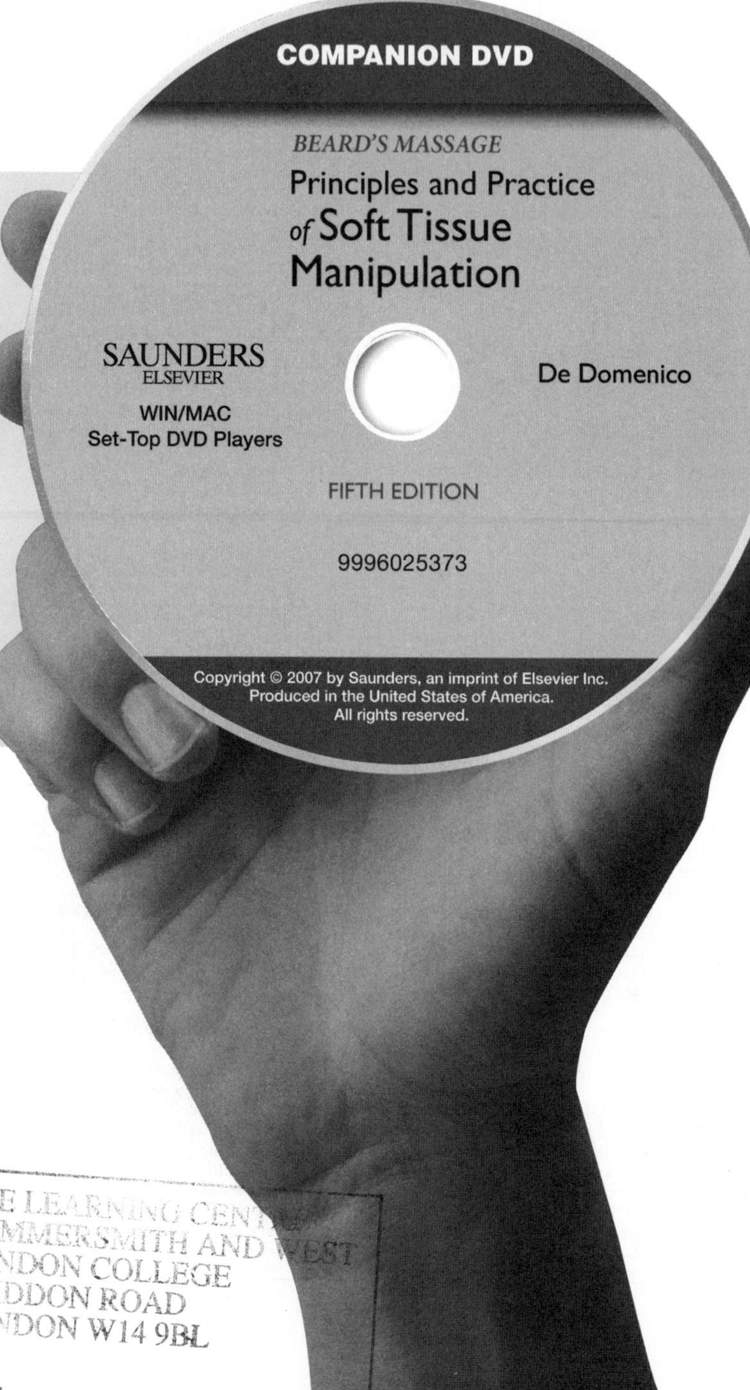


## With the DVD, you can...

- Watch **visual demonstrations** of massage being performed.
- Learn how to execute every stroke of **techniques described in the book.**
- Solidify your understanding of concepts and procedures with **nearly two hours of engaging video footage.**

**Take advantage of the complete book/DVD package!**

Look for the **icons** in the text that direct you to specific video clips on the DVD, developed to enhance textbook discussions with fully integrated audiovisual demonstrations.

## Simply insert the DVD into your computer or DVD player to get started!